C000221003

QUEEN'S PARK RANGERS

A COMPLETE RECORD

Gordon Macey

The Breedon Books
Publishing Company
Derby

First published in Great Britain by
The Breedon Books Publishing Company Limited
44 Friar Gate, Derby, DE1 1DA
1993

ISBN 1 873626 40 1

Printed and bound by Hillmans Printers, Frome, Somerset.
Covers printed by BDC Printing Services Limited of Derby.

Contents

This book is dedicated to
Sandra, Karen, Andrew & Neil

Acknowledgements

I WOULD like to acknowledge the help given to me in the preparation and research associated with this book. First, to Tony Williamson for pointing me in the right direction of achieving my aspirations in having a complete history book on Queen's Park Rangers published, and also for his help in producing the basis for the players' and managers' biographies and for providing several of the older photographs. I would also like to record my thanks to the various members of my family who have given their time: my parents, Phyllis and Cyril, for the hours spent at Colindale Newspaper Library looking for missing line-ups; my daughter, Karen, for helping in researching the Southern League days; and my wife, Sandra, for her audio-typing skills.

Thanks are also due to Ray Spiller for permission to use data from various AFS publications, Dave Twydell for allowing me to use his book *Grounds for a Change* to trace the club's early nomadic life. Finally I wish to record my thanks to Adam Spencer, Pauline and other members of staff at the Grange Museum in Neasden and the Archives at Cricklewood Library for accommodating my numerous requests for copies from the early 1900s local newspapers. To anyone else who has assisted, please accept my thanks for your efforts and apologies for not naming you individually.

Photographs have also been supplied by Action Images, Cricklewood Community History Library & Archive, Colorsport, Hulton-Deutsch Library and EMPICS of Nottingham.

Gordon Macey
July 1993

Queen's Park Rangers' Honours

Division One Runners-up 1975-76

•

Division Two Champions 1982-83
Runners-up 1967-68, 1972-73

•

Division Three Champions 1966-67

•

Division Three South Champions 1947-48
Runners-up 1946-47

•

FA Cup Finalists 1981-82

•

League Cup Winners 1966-67
Finalists 1985-86

•

Southern League Champions 1907-08, 1911-12

•

Western League Champions 1905-06

•

London League Champions 1905-06

•

Football Combination Champions 1981-82, 1982-83

•

London Midweek League Champions 1949-50, 1953-54

•

London Challenge Cup Winners 1932-33, 1938-39, 1955-56, 1965-66

•

Southeast Counties League Champions 1963-64, 1965-66, 1967-68, 1977-78, 1981-82

•

Southern Junior Floodlight Cup Winners 1964-65 (Joint), 1987-88

•

Southern Charity Cup Winners 1912-13

The Queen's Park Rangers Story

ALTHOUGH the club was officially formed in 1886, the story of Queen's Park Rangers FC really begins four years earlier, in a newly-built residential estate of West London, where two local youth club teams, St Jude's Institute and Christchurch Rangers, were founded in 1882.

St Jude's was formed by Jack McDonald and Fred Weller for the boys of Droop Street Board School, the venture being supported by the Revd Gordon Young. The Christchurch boys' team, meanwhile, was formed by George Wodehouse senior and, indeed, the Wodehouse family maintained their connection with Queen's Park Rangers for over 60 years, with both George Wodehouse senior and his son being players and directors of the club.

It was these two teams that joined together to form Queen's Park Rangers. The amalgamation was initiated after a match between the two sides in 1886. George Wodehouse senior played in the match watched by a friend, who suggested a merger between the clubs would be a good idea.

That idea became a reality a few weeks later, when some of the Christchurch Rangers members joined St Jude's. The name of Queen's Park Rangers, suggested by E.D.Robertson, was chosen because the members were based in the Queen's Park district of West London. The surviving members of the Christchurch club continued playing under the name of Paddington.

A gymnasium was fitted up and members of the new club were enrolled at a subscription of 7s 6d (37p) for the season. They were fortunate in enlisting the support of Mr Walter Cross, whose unflagging zeal and not inconsiderable monetary support, steered the club through many of its early difficulties. Mr Cross later became a director of the club.

Much useful assistance was also rendered by the brothers Harry and Joe Spurr, Harry Creber and Tom Handford. Mr C.Lynch was the first secretary and the fixture list was confined to friendly matches against Stanley, Tottenham Hotspur, Brentford, Fulham, Old St Stephen's and Clapton.

The colours adopted were Oxford and Cambridge Blue halved shirts and matches were played on a piece of ground owned by Welford's Dairy, known as Welford's Fields, which was behind the 'Case is Altered' public house to the south of Kensal Rise Station. The rent for the ground was only £8 per annum. The club's assets were few: only the four upright posts and the two lengths of tape to form the crossbar. These had to be carried to and from the club's headquarters whenever matches were played. The question of shorts was also acute, but one supporter who owned riding stables in Maida Vale came to the rescue by giving each of the players a pair of riding pants in which to play their first match.

The QPR club grew fast and in 1888 it was deemed advisable to move to better, enclosed accommodation. The London Scottish ground at Brondesbury was secured for the annual rent of £20. It was anticipated that the rent would be met by being able to charge gate money for the home matches. However, this did not work out as the officials of the club had hoped, for on many occasions the takings did not amount to more than 1s 6d (7p).

Money was not the only problem in regard to the London Scottish ground. By the middle of the second season at Brondesbury, 1889-90, the pitch became so waterlogged that football was impossible. The remaining matches had to be staged on opponents' grounds.

High-scoring games were common in those days and in three successive games, Rangers netted a total of 26 goals with only two conceded.

Through the demands of the landlord, the club were unable to obtain a fixed tenure of the ground in Brondesbury, so they moved to the Home Farm at Kensal Green. Rangers did not stay long at Home Farm, however, probably less than a full season. The next move was to Kensal Rise Green, shortly followed by another move, this time to the Gun Club ground at Wormwood Scrubs.

By the start of the 1892-93 season, Rangers were yet again moving home, this time to the Kilburn CC ground in Harvest Road. Whilst at the Harvest Road ground, the club's colours were changed to green and white hoops and Rangers won their first trophy, the West London Observer Cup.

The first season at the Kilburn CC ground saw Rangers enter their first league competition, the West London League which consisted of ten clubs, including Rangers' arch rivals, Paddington.

The home match against Paddington was when the colours of green and white were worn for the first time. The match was a very tempestuous game, in which Rangers went down 2-0. Due to the bad feeling between the two sides and lack of fit players, Rangers refused to play the return game. They finished their first League season in sixth place with 16 points.

The highlight of the season was undoubtably beating Fulham in the West London Observer Cup Final. The trophy was competed for by clubs in West London and had generally been won by Stanley and Fulham. After defeating Stanley in the semi-final, Rangers went on to meet the newly-crowned league champions, Fulham, in the Final at the Kensal Rise Athletic ground, where they won 3-2 after extra-time.

The triumphant team was: Harry Creber (goalkeeper); Robert Rushbrook and Herbert Teagle (backs); James McKenzie, Thomas Harvey and Alan Maund (half-backs); Edward Wallington, William Ward, Charles Davies, Albert Morris and Frank Collins (forwards). Two of the goals were scored by Wallington.

Rangers went on to successfully defend the Cup in seasons 1893-94 and 1894-95. The trophy was then handed over to the London League for competition by that body.

In the 1894-95 season, Rangers also won the London Cup for the first time. They beat Minerva in the first round, Electric Athletic in the second and then drew with Polytechnic in the Final at Harvest Road.

The replay took place the following week at the Polytechnic's ground at Merton Hall, Wimbledon, where Rangers held their own, despite injuries to McKenzie, Knight, Smith and goalkeeper Hiscocks. Fifteen minutes before the end, Polytechnic scored what seemed to be the winning goal. However, Smith returned to the field, against medical advice, and kicked-off. He took a return pass and ran straight through the defence to score the equaliser. In the last minute, Handford scored the winner for Rangers.

With an improved team for the 1895-96 season, the club entered the FA Cup — then also known as the English Cup — for the first time. Rangers were drawn against their fierce league rivals Old St Stephen's at home. The match, on Saturday, 12 October 1895, was played in front of the largest crowd in the club's history. It was estimated that 3,000 people packed into the Harvest Road ground for the game. The match ended in a 1-1 draw and on the following Tuesday, Rangers lost the replay 1-0 at the Old St Stephen's ground of Wormholt Farm.

The following season, 1896-97, Rangers did not fare any better in the FA Cup. They were beaten 3-1 at home by Marlow, one of the original entrants back in 1872.

By now, Rangers had moved grounds again, this time to the Kensal Rise Athletic Ground. They took out a ten-year lease at an initial cost of £100 per annum, rising to £150 per annum. The services of Jock Campbell, who had previously trained Third Lanark, Woolwich Arsenal and Tottenham Hotspur, were secured and under his supervision great times were expected of the team. Brentford attracted a record attendance to the Kensal Rise ground and Rangers officials were kept very busy collecting sixpences from the impatient crowd, some of whom scaled the fences in their haste to see the game.

Season 1897-98 saw Rangers win their first FA Cup tie. Their first victims were Windsor & Eton, beaten 3-0 in the preliminary qualifying round at Kensal Rise. In the first qualifying round, they beat Wolverton 2-1 at home, having switched the tie from Wolverton. The next victims were Chesham Generals, beaten 4-0 at Kensal Rise. Alas, Rangers' good run came to an end in the third qualifying round at Clapton, where they went down 3-0.

The name of Queen's Park Rangers was now becoming a recognised force in metropolitan football. In those days, visits from provincial Football League sides to the capital were limited to the FA Cup Final. Therefore, it was considered to be a rare stroke of business enterprise to get the famous West Bromwich Albion to play Rangers at West Kilburn. The terms agreed were for West Brom to receive £40 minimum, or half the gate money. As over £140 was taken, the venture was deemed to be a financial success. The Throstles included such famous names as Billy Bassett, Alf Flewitt, Roddy McLeod, 'Baldy' Reynolds, Billy Williams and Joe Reader. The only downside was the result, Rangers losing 4-1.

The next season, 1898-99, saw the introduction of professionalism at Queen's Park Rangers. The change came largely because of events surrounding the London Cup tie against Richmond Association in September. During the game, Sammy Brooks was sent off. The club were fined £4 by the London FA and had their ground closed for 14 days. Rangers resented the punishment and withdrew from all London FA competitions.

This move robbed the club of their principal fixtures and caused unrest amongst the better players. Rangers had difficulty in preventing those players accepting inducements to sign for other teams. Given this, and the fact that the demand for first-class football had become apparent in London, the move to become a professional club was raised.

After many lengthy committee discussions, it was decided to hold a meeting at St Jude's Institute to form a professional organization. A committee was elected and, in due course, the Queen's Park Rangers Football & Athletic Club became a limited company with a nominal capital of £5,000 on shares of 10s (50p) each. The company was registered in December 1898, with A.Lythaby, Leo Hawkes, A.Devenish, W.Cross, A.Teagle, Jess Saxby, H.E.Cleverly, W.Hiscox, J.Taylor and W.L.Wood as directors and G.H.Mousell as secretary.

On the playing front, Rangers lost 3-0 at Richmond Association in the first qualifying round of the FA Cup, but in preparation for the following season, they made a successful application to join the Southern League. The Reserves applied, also successfully, to become members of the London League. So, Queen's Park Rangers finished their amateur career on top with the Reserves winning the West London League's First Division title. They were unbeaten in that competition and conceeded only two goals in the season.

In previewing the new season, the local newspaper had a special interview with Mr G.H.Mousell, the club's secretary. It read, in part:

The startling development and rapid advancement of the Queen's Park Rangers during the past few months has caused the eyes of the whole football world in the south to be turned in this direction. The vitality of this local club is to a very great extent due to the enthusiasm of their hard-working secretary. It was therefore with distinct expectations of a pleasant half-hour that I called on Mr Mousell at 89 Lancefield Street, Queen's Park, the office of the club. Mr Mousell has a great objection to anything in the nature of an interview, but was very willing to give the fullest information with regard to the club and their intentions for the future.

He stated: "Your readers already know that we have been successful in our application to join the Southern League. We have also joined the new Southern Counties League for midweek matches, although our home matches are arranged for Mondays, that being the day upon which we expect to see decent gates. In this League we meet Woolwich Arsenal, Southampton, Millwall, Bristol City, Reading, Tottenham Hotspur, Chatham and the new professional team at Portsmouth. These, in addition to the matches in the Southern League — to say nothing about the visits for a few First Leaguers to play a few friendlies — will provide a good programme for the coming season."

"I presume that you have entered for the English Cup?" I hazarded.

"Rather," said Mr Mousell.

"Shall you take on the Kutlies who are to visit England next season?"

"I don't know yet, we may."

"How about your team?"

"Well, I think that we have a good lot, and if they play up to their reputations I shall be much disappointed if we are not among the first three."

"Whom do you consider to be your best catch?"

"Personally, I think Bedingfield, our centre-forward from Aston Villa."

"I hear that you have a good trainer for the teams?"

"Yes, we have secured Jock Campbell, the best-known football trainer in the world. He was the only official trainer ever appointed to train men for the Scotch Internationals, which he did for two seasons. Since then he has trained Sunderland, Tottenham Hotspur, Woolwich Arsenal, etc."

"Are there any improvements at Kensal Rise to be made in the arrangements for the accommodation of the public?"

"Yes, we are about to erect an uncovered stand on the opposite side of the ground to the pavilion, for which we shall charge an extra threepence. According to the support we receive, we shall add further improvements, and thus hope to make the accommodation equal to any in London. We mean to extend special privileges to ladies. It is suggested that ladies should be charged half-price for their season tickets, which would admit to ground and pavilion, and we hope to have a tea-room set apart for their use."

"Of course, you will charge the sixpence now you offer such good fare?"

"Yes, and we shall get it without any complaint. We also get between 7,000 and 8,000 who paid sixpence when we received a friendly visit for the First Leaguers, and I am sure we shall have a much larger attendance next season, although the sixpence will be charged. Season tickets will be made ready in a few days, which will admit to all matches on the ground only."

"When will your first match at home take place?"

"On Saturday, 2 September, against Brighton United, although we shall have a practice match between the two teams on Friday evening the 1st September."

"Is there anything you would like me to convey to our readers?"

"Only I should like to say what a fine body of men the directors are. Since starting, they have worked day and night and travelled thousands of miles in search of good men, and if success comes to Queen's Park Rangers, no one knows better than I that it is solely the work of our directors, most of whom are sound business men, and men who have served the Rangers well for years. I only hope that the public will appreciate their labours. We had hoped to purchase the ground, and although

Queen's Park Rangers pictured in 1900-01. Back row (left to right): J.Campbell, D.Christie, J.Bellingham, H.Clutterbuck, A.McConnell, W.Goldie. Middle row: T.Gray, W.Keech, A.Hitch, H.Skinner, A.Foxall. Front row: T.Downing, P.Turnbull, P.Humphreys.

the shares have been well taken up, they have not gone off sufficiently well to enable the directors to do this."

Mr Mousell concluded by saying that a first-class football club seemed to be a necessity in any and every district now, and should be supported by those able to do so.

Prior to the start of the following season, the board held a public meeting to appeal for support on the new venture into professionalism and on 2 September 1899, Queen's Park Rangers began their professional life in grand style by beating Brighton United 6-0 in a Southern League match at home in front of an attendance of 6,000. Unfortunately, as Brighton United, along with Cowes, withdrew from the league before the end of the season, the result was expunged.

The following week, then, Rangers played what later became their first recognised match in the Southern League. They were beaten 1-0 by Tottenham Hotspur, watched by a crowd of 16,000. Rangers did not have to wait long, however, for their first professional victory. It came in their next match, at home to New Brompton, whom they beat 2-0 with goals by Peter Turnbull and Fred Bedingfield.

Rangers had mixed success in their first league season, finishing mid-table by winning 12 and losing 14 of their 28 matches. Their leading goalscorer was Fred Bedingfield with 21 goals (17 League and four FA Cup).

The club made a heavy financial loss during the season, despite taking over £1,067 in gate money at two Cup ties, and it was only monetary assistance from the directors which saved Rangers from extinction.

Rangers had considerable success in the FA Cup in 1899-1900, reaching the second round proper after starting their campaign in the preliminary qualifying round. Having disposed of London Welsh, Fulham, West Hampstead, Wandsworth and Civil Service in convincing style — and on the way scoring 22 goals with only three against in five games — in the fifth qualifying round they beat Luton Town 4-1 after a 1-1 draw to go on to meet mighty Wolves at home in the first round proper.

A big crowd was expected for the game at Kensal Rise. In order to accommodate the numbers, the gates were opened three hours prior to the kick-off. The match was played on a very heavy pitch, which was certainly to Rangers' advantage. Haywood put Rangers one up at half-time. In the second half, Wolves had the wind behind them and were favourites. But they scored only once, through Miller, and the tie went to a replay the following Wednesday at Molineux.

The First Division side were expected to overcome the Southerners easily on their own immaculate playing surface, but Rangers pulled off one of the biggest Cup surprises by winning 1-0. Fred Bedingfield was their hero, scoring the only goal late in the second half. Due to an injury sustained in the first half, he missed most of the second period but came on near the end and hit the winner.

Rangers were now drawn at home to fellow Southern League side Millwall Athletic and their 2-0 defeat was a disappointment after the heady success at Wolverhampton. The preparation for the match was not helped by the fact that some of the players were involved in a brawl the night before the game. Turnbull and Cowie were detained overnight in police custody

There were a large number of changes for the start of 1900-01 and amongst the departures were Bedingfield, Cowie, Crawford, Hannah, Haywood, Knowles, Smith and White, all of whom had played over 20 games the previous season. Arrivals included James Bellingham, David Christie and William Goldie (all from Scotland), Jack Cole (Wales), William Pointing (Southampton), Tom Gray (New Brompton), A.Foxall (Liverpool) and Percy Humphreys and William Manning, both from Cambridge.

Performances matched those of the previous season with Rangers finishing eighth again after a good start with the first home game resulting in a 7-1 victory over Swindon Town, including the first-ever hat-trick for Rangers in a Southern League game, scored by Downing.

Rangers had a hand in the destination of the title when, in their last home game, they beat Bristol City, who needed the two points to pip Southampton. The leading scorer was Percy Humphreys with 12 League and Cup goals, including a run of five in seven games.

Due to reaching the second round proper of the FA Cup the previous season, Rangers joined the competition in the third qualifying round in 1900-01. Here they beat Fulham by 7-0 with five different players hitting the target. In the next round, Watford were the opponents and after a 1-1 draw at Cassio Road, Rangers won the replay 4-1 with Percy Humphries scoring a hat-trick, although the crowd was a disappointing 2,000. In the final qualifying round, Rangers were drawn away to Luton Town, whom they had beaten at the same stage in the previous year's competition. This time, though, Rangers crashed out 3-0.

At the end of the season, the club's landlord took advantage of a new point of law, decided in the Appeals Court, and terminated Rangers' lease on the ground. The club were in dire financial straits yet again, due to lack of income through the gates and, with the exception of Keech and Newlands, all the players left.

For the start of 1901-02, thanks to the efforts of a director, Mr T.R.Eagle, a ground was obtained at the rear of St Quintin's Avenue, near Latimer Road, Notting Hill. The players had to change in the nearby Latimer Arms public house and run down the road to the pitch, much to the delight of the local boys who could not afford the penny admission.

The pitch, though, was poor and during Rangers' time there it was used for an open air party to celebrate the coronation of King Edward VII. All very jolly, but it did not help the condition of the playing surface.

Among the incoming players were Charles Aston (from Aston Villa), John Bowman (from Stoke, later Rangers' manager), Harry Collins (Burnley), Ben Freeman (Grays United), Hugh McQueen (Derby County), Harry Millar (Sheffield Wednesday), John Stewart (Hibernian) and Jabez White (Grays United).

Due to this significant change in playing personnel, success was not forthcoming and 11 of the 15 away games ended in defeat, including a 7-1 reverse at Reading and a 6-1 defeat at Millwall. Yet the week before the Millwall game, Rangers had beaten Northampton 5-1 at home.

Attendances, though, were not significantly down on the previous season and a record crowd of 12,000 paid to see the Christmas home game against Tottenham Hotspur. The total gate receipts for the season were £3,320 and Rangers finished 12th with only nine wins from 30. Leading scorer was Harry Millar with 12 goals (seven League and five Cup).

As an established Southern League side, Rangers were again given byes to the third qualifying round and after beating Crouch End Vampires and West Norwood (against whom Harry Millar scored all four, the first four-goal tally in one game for any Rangers player), Rangers were drawn against Luton Town yet again, and the outcome was the same as the last encounter, Luton winning 2-0.

There were big problems off the pitch, too. Local residents were not happy with a professional football club in their midst and successfully petitioned the estate owner. He served notice on the Rangers to leave at the end of the season. Thus, the directors faced yet another gloomy outlook to a new season. They had no ground, scarcely any money and at the end of 1901-02, most of the players left, as had players the previous season.

One of the best players, John Bowman, wanted to return to the amateur game, but was persuaded to stay with the club and he became the new secretary. Bowman was instrumental in obtaining the move back to one of the club's former grounds at Kensal Rise. The landlords, All Saints' College, charged a rent of £420 per annum for a two-year lease, but due to increased gate receipts of £4,500, a profit of £600 resulted at the end of the season.

Amongst the players who signed for the season were two Queen's Park Rangers returnees, Alfred Hitch from Nottingham Forest and Harry Skinner from Grimsby. Among the other arrivals were Harry Abbott (Blackburn Rovers), John Hamilton (Millwall Athletic) and Tom Wilson (London Caledonian).

Rangers won one and drew two of their first three games but their next eight games bought seven defeats. And due to bad weather and an anomaly in the fixture list, they finished the season with six successive home games followed by five successive away games.

But their performances improved after the New Year, with only one defeat in the last eight home matches, and the most exciting game at home was the 4-3 victory over reigning champions, Portsmouth. The heaviest defeat was the 6-0 thrashing by Millwall, the second successive season they had scored six at home against Rangers.

Rangers finished ninth and their leading scorer was John Blackwood, who scored ten goals despite playing in only 15 matches. Seven of his goals came in four consecutive matches.

Remarkably, for the fourth successive season Rangers were drawn against Luton Town in the FA Cup. The difference this time was that it was a third qualifying round tie and at home. But the outcome was the same with Luton winning 3-0 in front of 8,000 spectators, the second highest crowd of the season at Kensal Rise.

Due to the club's increased stability there was not a mass exodus of players at the end of 1902-03 — and there were some new faces, amongst them Arthur Archer (New Brompton), William Cross (Third Lanark), George Milward (Chesterfield), Albert Bull (Reading) and Neil Murphy (Sheffield United).

The season proved to be Rangers' most successful in the Southern League to date and they finished fifth, only two points behind second-placed Spurs. The defence was the key to the improvement with only 37 goals conceded in 34 League games. From the middle of October to the middle of February, Rangers lost only two games out of 14. Included in that run was a 6-1 victory over Portsmouth, who finished ahead of Rangers. In October, the ground attendance record was broken for the visit of Southampton, the eventual champions, when 15,000 spectators witnessed the season's only home defeat.

Rangers' chance of an even better final position was not helped by the fact that in the last ten matches they had five wins and five draws. If only two of the draws had been victories, then Rangers would have finished runners-up.

Six players — Archer, Collins, Hitch, Milward, Newlands and Wilson — each appeared in at least 30 of the 34 League games. The leading goalscorer for the season was again John Blackwood with 20 goals, all scored in the League, from only 24 appearances. Helped by the improved performance, the season's gate receipts rose to £6,000.

The FA Cup, though, brought no joy and Rangers lost 3-1 to Fulham in a replay at Craven Cottage in front of 18,000 spectators, the biggest crowd to watch QPR that season.

Rangers' two-year lease on the ground had expired and due to their success, the landlord demanded £2,000 for a new five-year lease. This represented a 100 per cent increase on the existing agreement. As this was beyond their financial capabilities, Rangers offered to increase the rent to £300 per annum or to buy the lease for £1,500. The landlord refused to negotiate, so yet again Rangers were on the move, this time to the Agricultural Showground in Park Royal. It was Rangers' tenth ground in less than 20 years existence. The Agricultural Showground was a 100-plus acre site which had been purchased by the Royal Agricultural Society for £26,146 in 1902. A vast sum of money was required to develop it and in a few months the Society had spent £42,000 before any permanent structures were erected.

The Royal Agricultural Society formed a private company, Park Royal Limited, and one of their fund-raising ideas was to sub-let parts of the area. Queen's Park Rangers became one of the principal tenants, with their use of the Horse Ring, an oval-shaped enclosure. There were two levels of banking all round, with a seated grandstand on the north side and a smaller reserved grandstand opposite. The large arena had a capacity of 40,000 spectators, 5,000 of whom were under cover.

A crowd of 12,000 came to the first home game in 1904-05 and, despite the remoteness of the ground, attendances over

Battle for the ball during a Southern League game between QPR and Plymouth Argyle at Park Royal in 1904.

Queen's Park Rangers' ground at Park Royal from behind the western goal, taken during a Southern League game in 1905.

the season were slightly increased over the previous year. As most fans lived in the Kensal Rise area, they had to now take public transport instead of the short walk they had previously enjoyed. Special trains were laid on for home games from Paddington (return fare 5d) and Westbourne Park (4d), also from Southall and Hounslow (6d).

New players included the Scottish international John Cross (Third Lanark), Fred Bevan (Reading), Harry Singleton (New Brompton) and Arthur Howes (Brighton). Despite the new players and the new ground, success was not forthcoming and Rangers finished back in seventh place, 12 points behind the champions, Bristol Rovers. Ironically, Rangers' biggest victory of the season was 5-0 at home to Bristol Rovers in January. The leading scorer for the season was Fred Bevan with 20 goals.

In February 1905, Neil Murphy became the first player to gain a full international cap whilst with Queen's Park Rangers. He was chosen to play for Ireland against England at Middlesbrough. He also gained two more caps that season, against Scotland in Glasgow and Wales in Cliftonville. He scored one of the goals in the 2-2 draw against the Welsh.

Due to their higher league position the season before, Rangers had a bye to the sixth and final qualifying round of the FA

A public practice match at Park Royal in August 1905, as Queen's Park Rangers prepare for the coming season.

Cup. They were drawn at home to fellow Southern League rivals Brentford, who won 2-1.

Before the start of the 1905-06 season, John Bowman, the club's long-serving player-secretary, moved to Norwich City. His replacement at right-half was William Yenson, signed from Bolton Wanderers. A number of other players joined Rangers for the new season. They included Matt Kingsley (West Ham), Sid Sugden (Nottingham Forest) and James Cowan (Aston Villa).

Rangers got off to a good start in with two wins in the first three matches. Then they hit a bad patch, losing six of the next seven. Performances improved, though, and the season ended with two of the last three home matches resulting in a 6-0 win over Watford and then QPR's record Southern League victory, 7-0 over Bristol Rovers.

They finished in a disappointing 13th place with Fred Ryder leading scorer on 15 goals. Financially the season was a bad one for the club, who reported a loss of £400.

Despite their poor Southern League performances, Rangers did win their first trophy as a professional club, lifting the midweek Western League championship. This competition consisted of Rangers, Southampton, Plymouth Argyle, Tottenham Hotspur, Bristol Rovers, Millwall, Portsmouth, West Ham United, Reading, Fulham and Brentford.

The previous season, Rangers had finished bottom of this league with only 15 points. This season they finished top with 26 points, one ahead of Southampton, from their 20 matches. The title was not decided until the final match, admission for which was raised to 3d, when Plymouth visited Park Royal on Easter Tuesday, If Rangers lost, they would finish third, behind Southampton and Plymouth. But they won 1-0 to clinch the championship.

Towards the end of the season, George Newlands, who had joined Rangers in September 1900, was awarded a testimonial against Bristol Rovers, which raised £116 14s 7d.

In 1905-06, the FA doubled the number of clubs in the first round proper of the FA Cup to 64. This gave Rangers a bye to the first round, where they were drawn to play the eventual Southern League champions, Fulham, at Craven Cottage. In what was only their second appearance in the Cup proper, Rangers lost 1-0 before a crowd of 7,000.

Before the 1906-07 season started, leading goalscorer Fred Bevan, who was on the transfer list at his own request, was sold to Bury for £340. The campaign turned out to be Rangers' worst in the Southern League as they finished 18th out of 20 clubs. Yet they began confidently enough following the usual pre-season signings. Newcomers included John McLean (Millwall), Tom Green (Middlesbrough), Dennis O'Donnell (Sunderland), Edward Anderson (Sheffield United), Sid Blake (Newcastle United) and Joseph Fidler (Fulham).

Admission charges for the season were set at 3d for adults and 1d for children. Overall, Rangers' Southern League performances were disappointing and attempts to find a successful team failed. Only two away victories were gained, one at bottom-place Northampton Town and the other at Southampton. At home there were three isolated highlights: there was a 5-0 win over luckless Northampton; a 6-1 defeat of Swindon; and a 3-1 win over Tottenham in front of the second successive attendance of 15,000. Sid Sugden was top scorer with nine goals.

In the FA Cup, Rangers lost to Bristol Rovers in an Eastville replay and it was now five years since they had won an FA Cup game.

At the end of the season, Rangers learnt that their landlords, the Royal Agricultural Society, were suffering a financial crisis and were selling the Show Ground to raise money. Thus QPR were forced into yet another move.

In the search for a new home, Rangers considered many options, including grounds in the Notting Hill, Shepherd's Bush and Kilburn areas. Finally, they agreed to move to the brand-new Park Royal stadium, built by the Great Western Railway Company.

The stadium was only half a mile from the Royal Agricultural Showground and had its own railway station, thus making it easily accessible for the supporters. Of the 60,000 capacity, 9,000 were under cover, of whom 4,000 were seated. The two-and-a-half acre site was situated between Coronation Road and the Great Western Railway. Season tickets were available at £1 10s (£1.50p) and 15s (75p) for men, and 15s and 10s 6d (52p) for women.

Before the start of the 1907-08 season, Rangers appointed their first team manager. He was James Cowan, a Scotsman from Aston Villa. Whilst at Villa, Cowan had won five League Championship and three FA Cup medals. Among the new players he signed were Archie Mitchell from Aston Villa and Charlie Shaw from Port Glasgow.

Mitchell was one of the finest players ever to play for the club and was a regular member of the team for 14 seasons. He later returned in the early 1930s as manager. Shaw, a goalkeeper, only missed two League matches in his six years at the club.

Among the players signed were Fred Pentland (Brentford), Alfred Gittens (Luton Town), William Barnes (Luton Town), Evelyn Lintott (Plymouth Argyle), John McDonald (Grimsby Town) and Alfred Walker (Nottingham Forest).

Queen's Park Rangers, 1907-08. Back row (left to right): H.Laurie, E.Handford, J.White, S.Downing, J.Webb, C.Shaw, J.McLean, A.Mitchell, A.Nicholas, J.Macdonald, A.Gittens. Middle row: F.Pentland, S.Sugden, A.Rodgers, E.Hitchcock, W.Yenson (captain), A.Walker, P.Skilton, J.Fidler, Anderson. Front row: S.Morris, W.Barnes, Ainsworth, E.H.Lintott.

With his signings, Cowan had completely reshaped the team, especially the forward line, and great things were expected of the new side in their new home with a new manager. By the end of the season, no one was disappointed as Rangers finished as Southern League champions, two points in front of Plymouth Argyle.

As the Park Royal Stadium was not complete for the start of the season, Rangers had to play their early home games at the Show Ground. The first match was against Tottenham Hotspur and ended in a 3-3 draw in front of only 8,000 spectators. This was followed by another home draw against New Brompton and an away defeat in the return with Tottenham, hardly championship-winning form.

At this point Rangers' form turned for the better and they had a run of 15 games in which they won 11 and lost only once, at home to Millwall on 2 November, the day Rangers played at their new Park Royal ground for the first time. A crowd of 16,000 witnessed the 3-2 defeat.

By Christmas Day, Rangers and Plymouth topped the table, both on 27 points from 19 games, followed by Bristol Rovers who were three points behind. Such was the interest in the battle between the leaders that a crowd of 29,768 (a Southern League record) watched the goalless draw between QPR and Plymouth at Park Royal.

On Good Friday, the sides met in what was billed as the championship decider. The match ended in a 1-1 draw, putting Rangers in pole position as Plymouth had to win in an attempt to close the gap at the top. Rangers could have secured the title the following week, against Northampton, but suffered a rare home defeat.

The championship was clinched, two days later, on 20 April with a 4-0 home victory over West Ham. Fred Cannon became the hero of the afternoon by scoring a hat-trick but the celebrations must have taken their toll as the remaining two matches both ended in heavy defeats, 5-2 at Southampton and 8-3 at Swindon. Leading goalscorers for the season were Alf Walker and Alf Gittens, both with 16.

During the season, Evelyn Lintott became the first man to play for the full England team whilst with QPR (there was a gap of 64 years before Rangers had their second full England cap — Rodney Marsh in November 1971). Lintott had already made two appearances for the England amateur side prior to his inclusion in the England team that won 3-0 against Ireland at Cliftonville. He went on to win two more full caps, against Wales and Scotland, and three more amateur caps before the end of the season. Alas, his football career was tragically short as Lintott was killed in action on the first day of the Battle of the Somme during World War One. He was then a Leeds City player.

For the first time in six seasons, Rangers managed to win an FA Cup tie in 1907-08. They beat Reading at home in the first round, 1-0 with the goal being scored by William Barnes before a massive 28,000 crowd. In the second round, though, they went out 2-1 to fellow Southern Leaguers, Swindon Town.

By winning the Southern League championship, Rangers faced Manchester United, the Football League champions, in the first-ever FA Charity Shield match. The game was played at Stamford Bridge in front of a crowd of 12,000 and was the Rangers' biggest occasion, so far, in the club's history.

The United team included many household names of the day, including Billy Meredith, the 'Welsh Wizard'. Rangers took the lead through Fred Cannon and held their advantage until a superb solo goal by Meredith drew United level. At the end of the 90 minutes, Lord Kinnaird, the FA secretary, suggested that the match be replayed in August as a curtain-raiser for the new season.

Following their success the previous season, Rangers resigned from the Southern League and applied to join the Football League for 1908-09. Stoke had resigned from Division Two, so a ballot was proposed for all interested clubs. Much to Rangers' surprise and annoyance, Tottenham Hotspur, who had finished ten points and seven places below QPR, were elected. This left Rangers in a crisis as they were not members of the Southern League any more.

Faced with the prospect of playing in the South-Eastern League, whose standard was below reserve level, Rangers feared a players exodus and the real prospect of the club folding. However, after lengthy negotiations the Southern League Management Committee relented and by increasing the number of teams in their First Division to 21, they readmitted Rangers.

As the season's fixtures had already been published, Rangers had to arrange their matches for midweek dates. Credit for the club's survival went to the secretary, Mr Wood. Having got Rangers reinstated, he had to arrange the fixtures so that the adverse impact on finances was as little as possible.

All the upheaval surrounding the failed Football League election bid left the players unsettled and Fred Pentland, who was on the verge of the England team, decided to move to Middlesbrough, for a club record fee of £350, despite being offered wages of £4 per week to stay.

Shortly after the season started, Evelyn Lintott also left, having been captured by Bradford City for a reported fee of £1,000. The incoming players included J.MacDonald (Lincoln City), Alonzo Drake (Birmingham) and Harry Duff (Manchester City). The biggest signing was made midway through the season when Walter Greer was signed, despite strong competition from Preston North End. Greer became the club's second full Irish international when he played against England at Bradford in February 1908. He went on to win two more caps, against Scotland and Wales in March.

The Charity Shield replay before the start of the new

Queen's Park Rangers in 1908-09, pictured with the Southern League shield. Back row (left to right): T.C.Foster, H.G.Saltwell, J.Saxby, Shaw, Nicholls, F.J.Watton, E.Hart, W.L.Wood (honorary secretary). Second row: Duff, Nugent, Gillespie, Macdonald, Lintott, McLean, Downing, Fidler, McEwen, Drake. Seated: McDonald, McNaught, Turner, Snelgrove, Cannon, P.G.Skilton, Gittins, Barnes, Mitchell, McKenzie. Front row: Beaumont, Rogers, Morris, Law.

campaign was a great opportunity for Rangers to put the traumas of the summer behind them and get back to playing football. The match against Manchester United, again played at Stamford Bridge, was used as a curtain-raiser for the new season. The team was the usual line-up with the exception of Pentland, who was replaced by J.McNaught, an amateur from Hounslow, on the right wing.

The match ended in a 4-0 win for United, who proved to be too strong for a gallant Rangers team. After the match, both sides went to the Alhambra Theatre in Leicester Square, where they watched a Bioscope replay of the game. Rangers' share of the gate receipts was £100 which they donated to the following charities: St Mary's Hospital (£50), Willesden College Hospital (£25), Acton College Hospital (£15) and Willesden Children's Aid (£10).

Not surprisingly, Rangers' League performances in 1908-09 were nowhere near the previous season's standard. They finished in 15th place, only three points ahead of the bottom club, and scored only three goals in their first eight games. But the defence was as good as the forwards were bad and conceded only four goals in those eight matches. There then followed a run of five wins in six games, which was followed by a spell of five matches without a win. The biggest win was 5-1 at home to Swindon at the end of March. Leading scorer for the season was William Barnes with ten goals.

Due to the smaller attendances caused by poor performances and the fact that most matches were midweek, a loss of £866 was reported for the season. This loss would have undoubtedly been greater, had it not been for the fees received for the sale of Pentland and Lintott and the money raised by supporters in response to the club's appeals.

In the FA Cup first round, Rangers were drawn at home to West Ham United. That the match at Park Royal ended in a goalless draw was due mainly to the performance of the West Ham goalkeeper, Kitchen. The Hammers scored the only goal of the replay, so yet again, Rangers fell at the first hurdle.

For the 1909-10 season, Rangers were back to normal, not having to play in midweek all the time, and the change worked wonders as they had one of their more successful seasons, both on and off the pitch. New recruits included William Wake (Exeter City), William Steer (Kingston Town), James Travers (Aston Villa) and A.Whyman (New Brompton).

Team stability was a vital part of the improvement. Only 20 different players were used and of those, ten each played in over 35 of the 42 matches. The season started with an unbeaten run of eight games and the first defeat was at home to Millwall. This was followed by another good run of only one defeat in 11 matches. Again the defeat was, surprisingly, at home.

The first away defeat did not arrive until the 21st game of the season, when Rangers lost 4-0 to Coventry at Christmas. At the turn of the year, QPR were top of the table, on goal-average from Swindon.

The second half of the season belonged to Brighton, who gained 32 points from their 21 games. Rangers eventually finished third, eight points behind the champions. One of the deciding factors was the 2-0 defeat at Brighton in April. Rangers would have been closer to the top, had they not lost three of their last four matches, including a 1-0 defeat at Swindon which robbed them of second place. Leading scorer was William Steer with 27 goals (22 League and five Cup).

The improvement in the first team's performance was reflected by the Reserves, who reached the semi-finals of both the London Cup and the Southern Charity Cup. At the end of the season the club announced a profit of £253 compared to the loss of £866 the previous season.

But the most exciting part of the 1909-10 season was the FA Cup run which took Rangers into the last eight for the first time in their history. They beat Norwich City in a home replay, knocked out Southend United, also in a home replay, and then had to travel for the third time to fellow Southern League opposition, on this occasion to West Ham. Also for the third time, the first match ended in a draw.

After 90 minutes of the Park Royal replay there were still no goals but with only three minutes of extra-time remaining, Steer scored his fifth Cup goal in three rounds to send Rangers further into previously unchartered territory.

The draw for the fourth round was not kind, however, and gave Rangers a long trip to Football League side, Barnsley, who won 1-0, their goal being a fluke according to QPR fans!

Such was the fervour of the Rangers supporters that by the time the team's train reached Paddington Station, several thousand people had assembled to meet it. As the train steamed in, its engine decked in the club colours of green and white, there was a rush for the team's compartment. But the older

Queen's Park Rangers in 1910-11. Back row (left to right): W.Wake, E.Hart (director), W.Cross (director), J.H.Fielding (director), James Cowan (manager), W.L.Wood (honorary secretary), A.Nicholls. Second row: A.Hartwell, J.Macdonald, R.Browning, C.Shaw, H.Butterworth, H.Pullen, T.Leigh, E.Handford, W.J.Brown. Seated: H.Brindley, J.Bradshaw, J.Fidler, A.Whyman, A.Mitchell, W.H.O.Steer, W.Barnes, S.Morris, D.McKie, J.J.Riddings. Front row: J.McNaught, G.Smith, T.Wilson, A.G.Wyatt.

hands amongst the players avoided the crush by getting out of the train on the wrong side and running back to Royal Oak Station.

Following their FA Cup exploits of the previous season, Rangers were looking forward to another long and profitable run in the competition in 1910-11, but in the first round they were drawn against Bradford City, one of the better sides. Rangers managed to force a goalless draw at home but the replay went to form with Bradford winning 4-0.

The 1910-11 League season had also opened full of optimism as most of the players decided to stay at the club. New signings were made to bolster the forwards, including Horace Brindley (Norwich City), D.McKie (Chorley), Robert Browning and Herbert Butterworth (Oldham Athletic).

Rangers' first match was a 5-0 thrashing of Coventry at home, but only two wins were achieved in the next 13 games before things began to pick up after the New Year with only one defeat in the last 17 matches. The defence was very economical and conceded only 12 goals from Janaury. In the last away game of the season, at Watford, Rangers had to play the whole 90 minutes with only ten men because William Brown missed the train.

At the end of the season, Rangers were in sixth place, 13 points behind the champions, Northampton Town. Leading goalscorer was Browning with 18.

At the start of 1911-12 there were the usual changes of playing personnel for a new season. James Cowan strengthened the side with the signings of Arthur Smith (Brierley Athletic), E.Revill (Chesterfield), Gilbert Ovens (Bristol Rovers) and H.Thornton.

Rangers started the season in championship form by winning the first four matches, scoring a total of ten goals and conceding none. After ten matches they were unbeaten and had dropped only two points.

By setting such a pace at the top of the table, QPR became the team everyone wanted to beat and the first team to do so were Swindon Town, who won 3-1 at Park Royal in front of a crowd of 25,000, who paid receipts of £700. The defeat was immediately followed by another, this time 5-1 at Northampton, but by the turn of the year Rangers topped the Southern League with 31 points from 21 games, followed by Northampton Town with 28 points..

By the beginning of April, Rangers still led the table, now with 45 points to Plymouth's 42 and Northampton's 40 (although Northampton had two games in hand). But QPR then won only two of their next seven games. With Plymouth winning four on the trot, Rangers had to avoid defeat in the last match, at Norwich, to clinch the title. They managed a 1-1 draw and so lifted the championship one point ahead of Plymouth, who won again, 2-0 at New Brompton.

At Easter, due to the coal-miners' strike, Rangers played two matches at the White City Stadium instead of their Park Royal home. The first of these, on Good Friday, was against Southampton and a crowd of 62,000 is reported to have attended. The newspapers of the day confirm the figure, but it is certainly an oddity as the next day only 20,000 turned up and the normal attendance for the season was under 10,000. In the author's opinion there was probably a typographical error in the papers and the most likely attendance was 26,000 as the White City Stadium had a capacity of around 60,000.

Joint leading scorers for the season were McKie and Rangers' record-signing Revill, both with 16 goals.

Rangers' championship aspirations had not been hindered by a long Cup run as they went out in the first round. After a goalless home draw against Bradford City, they travelled to Bradford for the second successive year and were beaten 4-0.

As Southern League champions, Rangers were invited to play in their second FA Charity Shield match. This time they met the Football League champions Blackburn Rovers at White Hart Lane. Due to bad weather, only 7,111 people, who paid a total of £262, watched a poor game played in torrential rain. Blackburn won 2-1 and the proceeds were sent to the Titanic Disaster appeal.

Immediately after the FA Charity Shield match, Rangers travelled overnight to Paris where they were to play Fulham, the next day, in an exhibition match. Having left London on Saturday evening, Rangers did not arrive at their hotel until 7am on Sunday.

The match, kicking-off at midday, was for the Dubonnet Trophy and, not surprisingly, Fulham won quite easily by 4-1, McKie scoring for Rangers, who then played one more game in France before moving on to Germany for another six games.

The French and German opposition were not up to the English standard and Rangers overcame them by an aggregate score of 40 goals to seven. The teams they beat were Paris

Red Star 9-2 (Tosswill 3, McKie 3, Birch 3); Saarbrücken 12-1 (Revill 6, Birch 3, Whyman, Sangster, Tosswill); Kaiserslauten 1-0 (Browning); Mannheim 3-0 (Wake, Tosswill, McKie); Pforzheim 7-3 (Browning 4, Radnage, Revill, McKie); Nuremburg 5-1 (Browning 2, Marchant, McKie, Tosswill); and Stuttgart 2-0 (Wake, Revill).

Rangers were determined to retain the Southern League title in 1912-13 and signed two strong players before the season, Jimmy Birch (Aston Villa) and William Thompson (Plymouth Argyle). Birch was to become one of Rangers' longest-serving heroes, remaining at the club for 14 seasons.

QPR began the defence of their title in fine form by winning six and drawing four of their first 11 matches, the only defeat coming at Bristol Rovers. They then had a run of six games without conceding a goal, the run being ended by Norwich City.

But their form deserted them in the New Year and they went nine matches without winning, a run which certainly cost them the championship. The title was lost in the last but one game of the season when Rangers travelled to Plymouth, where they lost 2-0, Plymouth going on to take the title with 50 points with Rangers in fourth place.

The main problem was scoring goals and in 38 League games, only 46 were netted. Leading scorer was Jimmy Birch with 18 goals (15 League and three Cup).

In the 1912-13 FA Cup, Rangers were drawn against a Yorkshire club for the fourth successive season, this time Halifax Town. The match, played at Park Royal, was a good one for the 11,000 crowd with Rangers winning 4-2. In the next round they travelled to Ayresome Park and were unlucky not to take Middlesbrough to a replay, eventually losing 3-2. The crowd of 25,000 was the largest that Rangers had played in front of during the season. QPR did have some success during the season, though, when they won the Southern Charity Cup.

In an attempt to regain the Southern League championship in 1913-14, Rangers signed J.Miller (Glasgow), James Fortune (Leeds City), H.Strugnell (Aston Villa) and H.Jefferies (Aberdeen). Jefferies was signed as cover for Nicholls, who had taken over in goal following the transfer of Charlie Shaw to Glasgow Celtic.

The season did not start very well, with three successive defeats and only one win in the first eight games. By the end of the year, Rangers had a fairly even record of seven wins, seven draws and six defeats with 24 goals for and 23 goals against. After a poor spell early in the New Year, they picked up and won four games on the trot in March. Had there been football pools in those days, they would not have been a team to follow as they drew none of their final 14 games of the season.

Rangers finished just above midway, eighth with 41 points, nine behind champions Swindon Town. Despite their fluctuating fortunes, though, Rangers were relatively consistent with their team selection and eight players made over 30 League appearances each during the season. Leading scorer was Jimmy Birch with 20 (16 League and four Cup).

In the 1913-14 FA Cup, Rangers had a good run and reached the last eight for only the second time. They beat Bristol City (in extra-time of a replay), Swansea Town, who were in the Second Division of the Southern League, and Birmingham, whom they beat 2-1 at St Andrew's. Alas, for the third time they were drawn away, this time travelling to Anfield to meet First Division Liverpool. A 36,500 crowd saw Liverpool take a 2-0 lead. Then Rangers were awarded a penalty which Birch, unusually for him, missed. When they were awarded a second penalty, skipper Richie Mitchell took the responsibility and scored. This meant a rousing finish but Liverpool held on to gain a semi-final place.

Before the start of the 1914-15 season, James Cowan resigned as manager and was replaced by James Howie, a former Scottish international. Howie recognised the good players that Cowan had assembled and he did not make many signings for the new season. The incoming players included a new goalkeeper R.McLeod (Newport County), T.Millington (Bury) and David Donald (Watford).

The season again started badly with only one win in the first nine matches and it was not until the middle of December that Rangers won a home game, although from the beginning of December they began a climb up the table with a run of 12 games in which they lost only once.

Due to the war, which broke out in August 1914, attendances were down and Rangers, along with all the other clubs, had to struggle to keep going and see the season out.

In February 1915, the Army commandeered the Park Royal ground and Rangers had to move out. They played the remaining home fixtures at their old Kensal Rise ground in Harvest Road. The rest of the season was played out with mixed success, the last 13 games producing six wins, two draws and five defeats. The heaviest of those losses was 5-2 at home to Watford.

At the end of a disappointing season, Rangers were in 12th place. Leading scorer was again Jimmy Birch with 17 goals.

Hoping for a Cup run as good as the year before, Rangers had been disappointed to be drawn against Second Division Glossop in the first round. But at least it was at home for a change and they managed a 2-1 win. They faced another Second Division side, this time Leeds City, at home in a tie which was settled in Rangers' favour when Simons, a recent acquisition from Fulham, scored the only goal to put QPR into the third round for the second successive year.

As they were drawn at home again, and the fact that Rangers had never lost a third-round match, hopes were high on repeating the previous season's last-eight place. The visitors this time were Everton, currently lying in fourth place in the First Division.

As the Park Royal ground was now unavailable and the National Athletic Stadium was considered to be too small, the tie was played at Stamford Bridge, where some 33,000 people saw an exciting game. Everton were leading 2-1 a few minutes before end, when following a corner a mêlée erupted in the Everton area which resulted in players from both sides being sent off and a penalty to Rangers. Unfortunately, history repeated itself with the penalty being missed and Rangers going out to a team from Merseyside.

Football continued throughout World War One as best it could and there were no national leagues, only regional ones. The Football League ran two regional competitions for its clubs in the Midlands and North of England. As no competition had been organised for the five London clubs, it was suggested that they and the Southern League clubs in the London area formed their own league. So Rangers, along with fellow Southern League clubs Brentford, Croydon Common, Crystal Palace, Millwall, Watford and West Ham United, joined Football League clubs Arsenal, Chelsea, Clapton Orient, Fulham and Tottenham Hotspur in the London Combination competition.

The first season of wartime football in 1915-16 consisted of two main competitions under the aegis of the London Combination. From September to January was the Primary League and from February to April was the Secondary League. There were no cup competitions organised to replace the suspended FA Cup. As was the case for all teams during this period, team selection was a matter of finding 11 available players. Now and again, guests from other clubs were called upon to make up the numbers.

Rangers did not fare too well in the initial Primary League and finished in eighth out of 12 with only eight wins out of their 22 games. They did not do much better in the Secondary Competition, winning only two of their 14 games. QPR were able to call on very few established players and subsequently had six goals put past them in each of three games. Although there were 14 teams in the league, each club played home and away against only seven of them. When the league was drawn to a close, Rangers were in 13th place, one point above bottom-placed Reading.

Leading scorer over all the season was Humphries with nine goals from 22 appearances. The only regular players were the left-winger G.Fox, Captain Archie Mitchell and left-half William Wake.

For the second season of wartime football, the London Combination ran only one league with 14 clubs in it. Each team played the others home and away at least once and, like the previous season, they then played half of the sides again. The difference being that all the results counted in the same league table.

Rangers did not start off too well with only one win in

their first eight games and overall won only ten and lost 20 of their scheduled 40 matches. Their home match against Watford in December was postponed due to bad weather and when the league could not find a mutually agreeable free date, as the result would not affect the main positions, it was left unplayed.

Leading scorers for the season were G.Dale, V.Hassan and W.Lawrence, all with ten goals. They were certainly the main forward force of the season as the next highest scorer was own-goals with three! Archie Mitchell, the club's centre-half, played in all 39 games, including one as an emergency centre-forward.

For the third season of wartime football, the London Combination was reduced to ten clubs, with each team playing the others home and away twice. The season started a little better than the previous one for Rangers with four wins in the first nine games. They then lost three on the trot, followed by three straight wins. Overall they won only 14 of their 36 matches and those victories included all four matches against Clapton Orient, who finished bottom, 20 points behind the next club.

At the end of the season, the Football League gave permission for a War Fund tournament, the only stipulation being that all admission monies were passed on to war charities. Rangers played Crystal Palace and Millwall, winning both home games and losing both away games.

Leading goalscorers for the season, all with eight, were W.Draper, G.Fox and Walters. More players were available throughout the season and J.Denoon, G.Fox and F.Grendon, each played in at least 35 of the 40 matches.

The war ended too late for the football authorities to get the Football League and FA Cup back to normal, so a fourth season of 'wartime' competitions was organised. Due to the economic situation, players had been paid only minimal expenses and no wages during the war. When the war was over, the FA allowed a maximum of 15s (75p) per week to be paid. Despite several pleas, led by Arsenal, for a £2 per week wage to be paid, the authorities refused to budge.

The London Combination was played under the same format as the previous season with each club having four matches against each of the others. After the end of hostilities, crowds came back to football in an attempt to return to normality. The away game at Chelsea over Christmas had an attendance of 15,000, the largest crowd to watch Rangers for over three years.

By the end of the season, attendances had risen again and 20,000 watched the second away league game at Chelsea. Once Rangers were able to call on a settled side, results improved with a run of five successive victories during February and March, during which Rangers scored 22 goals. The run included their biggest 'wartime' victory, 7-1 over Tottenham Hotspur.

Rangers finished the final war league competition in fifth place, ten points behind Brentford, the champions. To add a little more interest to the end of the season, the London FA ran a London Victory Cup competition. Rangers had a bye in the first round and were drawn away to Chelsea in the second round. They did not progress any further, losing 2-0. Chelsea went on to win the trophy, 3-0 against Fulham.

Leading scorers for the season were G.Dale and J.Smith with 18 and 16 goals respectively. J.Denoon, G.Fox and Archie Mitchell were the mainstays of the team, missing only eight matches between them all season.

During the war, Rangers suffered the tragedy of some of their players being killed in action on the battlefield. Amongst them were Lieutenant H.Thornton, J.Butler and J.Pennifer. D.Higgins suffered bad injuries and was never able to play again.

In 1917, the Rangers' ground had been turned into allotments to help the war effort. This meant that Rangers had to move to a new ground to continue their wartime games. They tried the ground of the disbanded Shepherd's Bush FC in Ellerslie Road, but it was little more than an open field on the edge of the White City exhibition area and could not offer much in the way of facilities. All it had was a pavilion located along its southern side.

The stand from the abandoned Park Royal ground was re-erected at Ellerslie Road, with offices and dressing-rooms underneath. The ground was later to become known as Loftus Road, after the street running along its eastern edge.

The 1919-20 season turned out to be Rangers' last Southern League campaign. Following the war, they had to re-establish themselves in the Southern League at their new home. Amongst the new signings were J.Merrick (Aston Villa) and Fred Blackman (Leeds City). Players like G.Fox and J.Smith made their debuts but had played for the club in wartime competitions.

The season started well with no goals conceded in the first four games and after a defeat at Southampton, QPR then had a run of eight games before losing again. In those eight games their opponents scored in only one match. So, in the first 13 games, Merrick, Rangers' new goalkeeper, had kept 11 clean sheets. Alas, they then went on to concede 13 in the next four games, including five at Swindon Town.

Halfway through the season, Rangers had 11 victories and four draws from their 21 games. The New Year started in fine style with a 7-1 home win over Bristol Rovers, with J.Smith scoring four. There was a complete change-around from the start of the season, when the defence did not let any goals through, as now it was the forwards who were not scoring.

There was a run of four games when Rangers scored no goals. The season ended with moderate success with more losses than wins and Rangers settled into sixth place, four points below the next club. Leading scorers for the season were, yet again, Jimmy Birch with 17 goals and J.Smith with 15 goals. Smith and J.Baldock were ever-presents in the League.

Rangers' last FA Cup run as a non-League side was short-lived. They were drawn away to the strong Aston Villa side in the first round. Despite a good fight, they lost 2-1 in front of a crowd of 33,000. Rangers' last goal as a Southern League team was scored, not surprisingly, by Jimmy Birch.

At the end of the season, a proposed move to create a regionalised Third Division of the Football League became a reality. Without exception, all the First Division clubs left the Southern League to form the Third Division. As the northern non-League clubs did not follow suit until a year later, the first season of the Third Division did not have the Southern Section suffix attached.

For their new beginning in the Third Division of the Football League, Rangers appointed a new manager, former Southend manager Ned Liddell. During the summer, Liddell was busy acquiring new players and amongst his pre-season signings were G.Grant (Millwall), R.Faulkner (Blackburn Rovers), Herbert Middlemiss (Tottenham Hotspur), E.Grimsdell (Guildford United) and goalkeeper Len Hill (Southend United).

Another notable signing was that of Mick O'Brien, a left-half from South Shields. He was signed as a replacement for Archie Mitchell, who left to become manager at Brentford. Whilst at Rangers, O'Brien won the first two of his Irish international caps. He was also selected for the Football League team in an Inter-League match in November 1921. O'Brien became Rangers' manager in 1933, when his playing days were over.

During the season, another important signing was made, that of Arthur Chandler from the Hampstead club. Yet due to the poor financial situation of QPR, the total outlay on all new players was only £25!

Rangers' life in the Football League began with two home defeats, at the hands of Watford and Northampton Town, the Watford game being watched by a crowd of 20,000. Thereafter, things improved and with half the season gone, Rangers had 26 points from their 21 games.

The second half of the season was mixed but at the end of this initial League campaign, QPR finished third, six points behind the champions, Crystal Palace. With a little more consistency in the early games they would have made a strong challenge for the title. Leading scorers were Smith with 19 goals and Jimmy Birch (16).

At the end of the season, Rangers awarded a testimonial to two of their long-serving players, Archie Mitchell and Jimmy Birch. Mitchell had been at the club since 1907 and Birch since 1912, and had both been first-team regulars. Mitchell retired before the following season but Birch played on for another five seasons before joining Brentford in 1926.

The highlight of the 1920-21 season was undoubtedly the FA Cup victory over Arsenal. In the first round, Rangers were

Chatting before a training session in August 1922. From left to right are manager Ned Liddell, players Leach, Dawes, Gregory and Butler, and directors messrs Hargreaves, Wood and Elliott.

drawn at home to the Gunners and were full of confidence as they had not conceded a goal in their previous five matches. Their hopes were well-founded and on a mud-bath of a pitch, in front of a crowd of 20,000, QPR won 2-0 with goals from Chandler and O'Brien, his only strike of the season.

In the second round, though, Rangers put in a gritty performance in front of a 41,000 crowd at Turf Moor but lost 4-2 to Burnley, the eventual First Division champions.

The Football League had another change of format for the 1921-22 season when northern clubs formed another division, thus bringing in the Third Divisions South and North. The champions of each regional section were to be promoted into the Second Division and the bottom two clubs in each region had to apply for re-election.

Rangers had a busy close season and amongst their new recruits were the amateur international Arthur Reed (Tufnell Park), Harold Edgely (Aston Villa), Alex Ramsey (Newcastle United) and J.Bradshaw (Aberdare Athletic). None of the new players cost Rangers a penny. Incidentally, at this time a season ticket for the centre stand at Loftus Road cost £4 4s 0d (£4.20).

Rangers had a good start to the season with only one defeat in their first nine matches but they were not prolific scorers, having netted only eight goals in those nine games. The next four games included two heavy defeats but then there was a run of 16 matches with only one defeat. Unfortunately this form was not maintained and Rangers won only two of their last eight matches to finish fifth, 12 points behind the leaders, Southampton. The leading goalscorers were again Jimmy Birch, with 17 goals, and J.Smith (11).

For the second successive season, Rangers were drawn against Arsenal in the first round of the FA Cup. This time they had to travel to Highbury where they earned a goalless draw but, in the replay, Arsenal gained revenge for their previous season's Cup exit with a 2-1 win at Loftus Road.

Before the start of the 1922-23 season, Rangers reduced the cost of season tickets for the centre stand to £3 7s 6d (£3.37). Ground admission was 1s 6d (7p) and seats were 2s (10p) or 3s (15p).

The main departure was goalscorer J.Smith to Swansea Town. On the incoming side were players such as R.Parker (South Shields), C.Gregory (Yeovil Town), A.Davis (Aston Villa), Charles Rance (Tottenham Hotspur) and E.Butler (Ebbw Vale).

The season started well. After a defeat and a draw in their

Knees up! Rangers' players John, Pournham, Bain, Watson and Hill limber up under the watchful eye of trainer W.Draper before the start of the 1922-23 season. Draper had appeared for the club as a player during World War One.

first two matches, QPR then had a run of five successive wins, scoring ten goals and conceding only two. Unfortunately this was followed by seven matches without a win. The run was halted with a 4-1 win at home against Aberdare, but it was another six matches before Rangers won again.

They then went another seven games before winning another match and although they enjoyed a good finish with six wins in eight games, Rangers finished in their lowest position to date, 11th with 42 points from 42 games. Leading scorers were Parker with 20 (16 League and four Cup) and Davis with 13 goals (all League).

In 1923, the FA Cup Final was due to be played at the new Wembley Stadium for the first time, so there was an extra incentive and in the first round Rangers beat London rivals Crystal Palace, from the Second Division, 1-0. In the second round they disposed of Third Division North club Wigan Borough 4-2. The crowd of 23,454 at Wigan was the highest that Rangers played in front of that season.

In the third round, Rangers were drawn at home against South Shields, then a mid-table Second Division side who had just knocked out mighty Blackburn Rovers. But the Tynesiders did not prove much of a hurdle and Rangers reached the last eight with a comfortable 3-0 victory to move into the quarter-finals for only the third time in their history. But their hopes were dashed when Sheffield United scored the only goal of a tight game. The crowd of 20,000 was Rangers' best home attendance of the season.

Due to their poor financial position, Rangers were unable to compete with the wealthier clubs when it came to buying or retaining players. And during the summer of 1923, two of the more experienced players did not accept the new terms and moved on: John Gregory, who had been at Rangers for 11 seasons, went to Yeovil as player-manager; and Harold Edgely joined Stockport County. The other major departure was Arthur Chandler, who was sold to Leicester City for a club record fee of £3,000.

In replacing these experienced players, Rangers spent only £150 in acquiring J.Cameron (Heart of Midlothian), James Keen (Newcastle United), G.Benson (Stalybridge Celtic), Richard Oxley (Southport), William Pierce (Bedlington Colliery) and Shirley Abbott (Portsmouth).

Rangers began the season with two wins in their first three games — both victories being over Brentford — but this was followed by a run of nine matches which produced only two further wins. To add to the financial problems, attendances had dropped to below 10,000 due to the poor performance of the team, and although results improved towards the end of October, up to the end of the year, however, things got worse again with only one win and one draw in eight matches. Amongst the defeats was a 7-0 thrashing by the eventual champions, Portsmouth at Fratton Park. In the New Year, Rangers suffered a run of eight successive defeats, in which they only scored twice and conceded 22 goals, Reading beating them 4-1 and 4-0 in one week.

QPR were now in the re-election zone and their cause was not helped by two heavy defeats around Easter. Thus, despite winning three of their last four home games, they ended the season bottom of the table, two points behind Bournemouth, the other team applying for re-election. Leading goalscorer was Parker with 14 goals.

The Reserves did not fare much better, finishing one place off the bottom in the London Combination.

Fortunately for Rangers and Bournemouth — and Hartlepool and Barrow from the Northern Section — all the clubs were re-elected.

Following their long run in the Cup the previous season, Rangers were hoping for similar success in 1923-24. But, drawn at home against First Division Notts County in the first round, and despite giving one of their better performances of the season, the Londoners went down 2-1 in front of crowd of 15,000.

Rangers' poor performances of the previous season meant the normal summer clear-out and the introduction of new faces

Queen's Park Rangers in 1925-26, when they finished rock bottom of the Third Division South.

for 1924-25. Amongst the recruits were William Ogley (Newport County), Charles Brown (Southampton), James Moore (Halifax Town), E.Ford (Hinckley United) and George Harris (Notts County).

The overall season's performances were not much better than the campaign before — and the start was much worse, with only one win in the first ten games. At the end of November, performances improved with a run of three straight wins, including the first home win, against Brighton.

Christmas saw the extremes of Rangers that season with a 5-0 defeat at Norwich followed the next day by a 4-3 home win over Newport. The next game was another heavy defeat, 4-1 at home to Exeter City. So in only three games, Rangers had conceded 12 goals. There then followed a disastrous run of nine games in which they scored in only one of them before the final four games produced three wins and a draw, which pulled Rangers two places above the re-election zone.

The team's inconsistent performances were reflected by the number of players tried: 29 appeared and only four — Birch, Brown, Ford and Ogley — made 30 or more appearances. Leading goalscorers were Johnson and Myers, both with ten goals, although seven of Myers' were in the FA Cup.

Due to their poor League position the season before, Rangers had to enter the FA Cup in the fifth qualifying round in 1924-25 and they drew 4-4 with Clapton at home, in a memorable match in which Myers scored all four Rangers' goals. In the replay, Birch helped QPR to a 2-0 win.

In the sixth and final qualifying round, Rangers were drawn at home again, this time to fellow Third Division South side Charlton Athletic, and following a 1-1 draw they went to The Valley and won a tight game 2-1. In the first round proper Rangers were yet again first out of the hat. Their opponents were Stockport County of the Second Division, but this time Rangers did not earn a replay, losing 3-1 in front of 19,640 fans, their biggest crowd of the season, home or away.

Before the start of the 1925-26 season, the Rangers board decided that, after two poor years, a change of leadership was required and manager Ned Liddell was replaced by Bob Hewison, the former Northampton Town boss. Along with the departure of Liddell, several of the more experienced players also left.

Len Hill, who had been the regular goalkeeper for the past five seasons, signed for Southampton. Ben Marsden, another five-seasons man, went to Reading. Colin Myers, despite topping the goal charts, left after only one season, for Exeter City.

Hewison did not have much money to spend in replacing the departing players but his signings included goalkeeper George Hebden (Leicester City), John Middleton (Leicester City), Dick Burgess (Aberdare Athletic), Joe Spottiswood (Swansea Town) and Henry Hirst (Preston North End). A significant law change came into force at the start of the season. There now had to be two opponents between the attacker and the goal to be onside; previously it was three.

The mass change of playing staff was evident in the first game, when no less than seven of the team were making their debuts for Rangers. Not surprisingly, it took time for the side to settle down and only one win was achieved in the opening seven matches. The main problem seemed to be the defence, as 15 goals were conceded, although the forwards failed to score in only two games.

But if the first half of the season was poor, the second half was nothing short of a disaster. Rangers gained only one win in 20 matches. Ironically, they won their last game of the season, 3-2 at home to Northampton Town.

But by then it was far too late and they finished bottom, a massive 14 points behind Charlton Athletic, the team immediately above them. So, for the second time in three years, QPR had to apply for re-election. Again, a large number of players had been tried in an attempt to find a winning combination, and only three — Burgess, Hebden and Pierce — played in over 30 games. The leading goalscorer, with only eight goals, was Burgess; and the average attendance had now dropped to only 8,000 from over 14,000 on Rangers' entry to the Football League.

In the 1925-26 FA Cup, Rangers were drawn at non-League Gravesend & Northfleet in the first round. A restructuring of the competition affected the round titles, as the last 64 clubs now played in the third round, not the first. The match at Gravesend ended in a 2-2 draw, with both Rangers' goals coming from the veteran Jimmy Birch. In the replay Rangers overcame the Southern League side 2-0, Birch again scoring twice.

The draw for the next round pitted Rangers at home against Charlton Athletic, the same opponents as in the same stage in the previous season's competition. Again the match ended

Queen's Park Rangers in 1928-29. Back row (left to right): Deanus, Pearce, Sweetman, Woodward, McNab, Cunningham, Nixon, Young, Mayson. Second row: Mr Todd, Mr Cohen, Mr Boyer, Crompton, Armstrong, Eggleton, Neil, Thompson, Cockburn, Mr Wodehouse, Mr Bowman, Mr Hewison. Seated: Mr Elliott, Mustard, Kellard, Vallance, Whatmore, Price, Johnson, Smith, Mr Fielding. Front row: Foster, Coward, Goddard, Rounce, Arrowsmith.

in a 1-1 draw at Loftus Road. Unfortunately for Rangers, history did not repeat itself in the replay as they lost 1-0 at The Valley, only 7,246 turning up for the game.

Following Rangers' successful re-election campaign, many changes were made during the summer of 1926. The main non-playing departure was that of the secretary, Mr W.L.Wood, who had been associated with club since he first saw them play at the Welford Fields in 1887. Later in 1898, when the club turned professional, he became a director, and four years later was appointed honorary secretary. When Rangers joined the Football League and the workload increased, Wood became the club's first salaried secretary.

Only seven of the previous season's players were retained: Dick Burgess, Tommy Cable, George Hebden, Jack Middleton, Jock Patterson, William Pierce and Sidney Sweetman. Players signed during the summer included Howard Hooper (Leicester City), John Young (West Ham United), John Collier (Hull City), Fred Hawley (Brighton), C.Gough (Clapton Orient), Percy Varco (Aston Villa), James Lofthouse (Bristol Rovers) and George Charlesworth (Bristol Rovers).

And that was not the end of the new arrivals. During the season, Rangers made two further significant signings. First was a busman from Redhill by the name of George Goddard, who, in his eight seasons at Rangers, went on to become the club's most prolific goalscorer. The other mid-season signing was Jimmy Eggleton from Lincoln City. Eggleton played for five seasons before joining the training staff. He remained at the club during World War Two, when he took the responsibilities of trainer, assistant secretary, groundsman, boilerman and general maintenance man.

For all the comings and goings for the new season, the most important and longest-lasting change was the decision to alter the club's colours to blue and white, whilst retaining the distinctive hooped shirts.

The first game saw no less than nine players making their debuts. However, the change of colours did not bring Rangers a change of luck at the beginning of the season, as they did not record their first win until the sixth game. Following the acquisition of Goddard in September, results improved as more goals were scored, Goddard scoring ten goals in his first 12 matches.

With the slight increase in success, the crowds were starting to come back to Loftus Road, with the average up to nearly 10,000. In the second half of the season, away form improved and Rangers ended with four successive away wins, all without a goal being conceded. They finished 14th, seven points above the clubs applying for re-election, and despite a more settled season, only three players appeared in 30 or more of the 42 games. John Lofthouse was ever-present at outside-left and the leading scorers were George Goddard with 23 goals and Lofthouse with 14.

Due to the club secretary forgetting to submit an entry form to the Football Association by the closing date, Rangers did not take part in the FA Cup in 1926-27, but following the improvement in their League form there was no mass exodus of players during the close season. Only five men left the club — E.Ford (to Merthyr Town) and George Charlesworth (Crystal Palace), whilst William Young, Jonah Wilcox and George Hebden all went to Gillingham. The players signed as their replacements were J.Stephenson (Watford), W.Turner (Bury), Andy Neil (Brighton) and John Duthie (Norwich City).

Following the departure of Hebden, the first-choice goalkeeper was Joseph Cunningham, signed from Newport County the previous season. And midway through the season, two very capable amateur inside-forwards were signed, George Rounce (Uxbridge) and J.C.Burns (Crypto).

Rangers began the season with five wins and a draw in their first eight games, scoring 17 goals in the process. Indeed, it was not until the eighth game that they failed to find the net, but, alas, the goals dried up in October and November with only two in eight matches. By mid-season, Rangers had slipped to halfway with 22 points from 21 games. In the New Year, their scoring touch returned with three being scored in each of four successive matches, followed by a four, Goddard scoring seven of those 16 goals.

There were some strange results over Easter, when a 6-1 away win at Newport on Good Friday being followed by a 7-0 defeat at Southend the following day. Rangers must have had travel fatigue!

The ups and downs continued and within three days of each other, a 5-1 defeat was followed by a 5-0 win, both at home. Rangers finished tenth, their goals tallies for and against at home and away being very even, 37-35 and 35-36. With the exception of the champions Millwall, no team scored more away from home than Rangers.

Five players missed six or less games each, which helped the consistency. The leading goalscorers were, again, George Goddard, this time with 26 goals from 33 games, and James Lofthouse with 13.

After their non-appearance in the FA Cup in 1926-27, Rangers were eager for a good run in the competition and they seemed to have an excellent opportunity after being drawn at home to Southern League side Aldershot in the first round. However, Rangers became another League scalp for the non-Leaguers when they lost 2-1 in front of crowd of only 4,000, Rangers' lowest attendance of the season.

Rangers now had the foundations of a successful side. The middle trio of the forward line consisting of Burns, Goddard and Rounce were probably the best acquired by one club from the amateur ranks. The defence also had a stable look with Cunningham in goal and defenders Sweetman and Young.

Signed to add even more resilience to the centre of the defence were Jock McNab, a Scottish international, and William Cockburn, both signed from Liverpool. The other signings included Ernest Whatmore (Bristol Rovers), Oliver Thompson (Chesterfield) and Stephen Smith (Clapton Orient). For around £1,000, Rangers had managed to put together their strongest team for many seasons.

The season started with a Goddard hat-trick in the 4-3 home win over Torquay United and Rangers remained unbeaten in their first nine matches, winning five and drawing four. Their first defeat was 3-1 at Walsall. The crowds were now returning to Loftus Road with 22,000 attending the home game against newly-relegated neighbours Fulham.

Rangers went another six matches before losing again and by this time, Goddard had found a rich scoring vein, with 14 goals in 11 games. At the mid-point of the season, QPR had 27 points and were looking good for the title.

Alas, their fortunes turned in the New Year with only one win in seven matches, including a 5-0 defeat at Fulham and a 4-1 reverse at Watford. But March saw Rangers come back to form with five straight wins, including the club's record winning margin of 8-0 over Merthyr Town. Goddard scored four and Jock Burns three in that game — and in that run, Rangers scored 19 goals and conceded only three.

Following the New Year slip, Rangers were now back in contention for the title, but with only two wins in their last eight matches, they finished sixth, only two points behind the champions Charlton Athletic. Although they lost only once at home, it was the number of draws — 14 in all — that cost Rangers top spot.

George Goddard scored a club record 37 League goals in the season, plus one in the FA Cup. The next highest scorer was Jack Burns with 13.

The improved performance on the field was reflected in the financial situation of the club, whose accounts showed a record profit of £1,400 for the season. Some of the money was spent on repairing parts of the ground and improving the playing surface.

As they were having a good run in the League at the time of the first round of the Cup in 1928-29, Rangers were confident of doing well in the competition, especially when they drew Southern League side, Guildford City. Rangers were not daunted by the trip to Surrey, but for the second successive year they were beaten by a non-League side, this time 4-2 in front of a crowd of 10,000, Guildford's highest attendance for some years.

Before the start of the 1929-30 season, Rangers received a bid from Millwall for full-back Sidney Sweetman, who could not hide his bitter disappointment at being released, for he was a 100 per cent Rangers man. Only because the fee received from Millwall would help strengthen the club, did he reluctantly agree to go.

Amongst the other departures were H.Vallence to Brighton and J.Woodward to Merthyr. The replacements signed included Bernard Harris (Luton Town), H.Moffatt (Walsall), Herbert Young (Newport County), John Yates (Aston Villa) and brothers Harry and George Wiles, amateurs from Sittingbourne.

Rangers began the new season full of optimism after their close run to the title, but with two draws, two defeats, and only one win in the first five matches, they were soon disappointed. One problem was that the normally reliable Goddard scored only three goals in the first 11 games.

Even at this stage, Plymouth and Brentford were pulling away from the rest. Rangers continued to hold their own, but made no impression on the top two. And by the middle of the season, they had only 22 points from 21 games.

Things slightly improved from mid-February after which they won four successive games, scoring 14 goals, but following crowd trouble at one of Rangers' home games, the FA closed Loftus Road for a fortnight and prohibited QPR from playing within a six-mile radius of the ground. The 'home' match against Coventry, another one of the chasing pack, was played at Highbury, where receipts from the attendance of 25,000 more than compensated for the closure of Loftus Road — and as Rangers picked up two valuable points with a 3-1 win, things could not have worked out better.

The punishment must have inspired Rangers, as then won nine out of their last 11 games, the only reverses being 4-0 at Plymouth, the eventual champions, and 3-0 away to second-placed Brentford. Following the Plymouth defeat, Rangers took revenge in their next game by beating Swindon Town 8-3 at home, with Goddard scoring his third hat-trick of the season. He was to add another at Brighton a week later.

Rangers finished third, 17 points behind Plymouth and ten behind Brentford. Goddard, who was the Third Division South's leading scorer, equalled his record of 37 League goals in a season, but this time managed two in the FA Cup, taking his tally to a record 39 for the season. The next highest scorer was George Rounce with 16 goals.

In the Cup, Rangers had been relieved to be drawn against fellow League opposition, having been knocked out by non-League sides in the two previous seasons. They met Luton at home in the first round and won an exciting game 3-2, the winner coming from a Pierce penalty.

In the second round, Rangers were again at home, this time to Lincoln City of the Northern Section. The Londoners won 2-1 at the first attempt, both goals from Jack Burns. QPR were now in the third round for the first time in seven years and they went across London to Second Division Charlton Athletic. Having managed to draw 1-1 at The Valley, in a game watched by over 22,000 people, Rangers were confident of moving into the fourth round. It was not to be, for they lost 3-0 in front of 22,000, the largest crowd of the season at Loftus Road.

During the summer of 1930, Rangers lost the services of Andy Neil and John McNab, both of whom retired from football. They also released William Cockburn, who signed for Swindon Town. New players included Norman Smith (Sheffield Wednesday) as a replacement for Neil, Albert Legge (Charlton Athletic), Ralph Hoten (Northampton Town), Arthur Sales (Chelsea), Arthur Daniels (Watford) and William Shepherd (Watford). Archie Mitchell, the former Rangers player, rejoined the club as coach to the juniors.

As Rangers had enjoyed such a good season the year before, and with the nucleus of the side still at the club, there were high hopes of a better League position for 1930-31. Yet despite winning their opening game, 3-0 at home to the League's new boys Thames FC, Rangers then lost two out of the next three.

In the fourth match, at Watford, George Goddard was injured and had to miss four matches. He reappeared for only one game before aggravating the injury and having to miss another eight.

At first it looked as though Goddard would not be missed too much, as Rangers scored three goals and won their first match without him. But they then had a run of six consecutive defeats, including 4-1 at Swindon followed the next week by 6-2 at Torquay. Goddard returned to League action in December, at home to Newport County, and Rangers won 7-1 with Goddard scoring a hat-trick. Including Cup games after his return, his goal tally was 13 in six games, with two hat-tricks. And with him back in the side, results improved and Rangers had their second seven-goal victory before Christmas. They had scored a total of 20 goals in four games alone.

After the New Year, though, results were not as good as expected and included two heavy defeats, at Northampton Town (6-0) and at Luton Town (5-1). Their home form was better with five wins out of the last six matches and the end of the season included a run of five successive wins, but it was too late to get Rangers up the table and they finished eighth.

One interesting point was that every home game finished with a winner, there were no draws (15 wins and six defeats). With 57 goals, Rangers also recorded their highest home goals total since joining the Football League. Due to a number of injuries throughout the season, only three players appeared in more than

30 League games. Inevitably, and despite his injury, the leading goalscorer for the season was once again George Goddard with 29 goals. His 25 in the League came from only 28 appearances. The next highest scorer was George Rounce with 18.

In the FA Cup, Rangers were drawn at home to Thames, the side elected to the Third Division in place of Merthyr Town at the end of the previous season. Rangers were hopeful of progress as they had already beaten Thames 3-0 on the opening day of the season and Goddard returned to the first team for the Cup tie and scored twice in a 5-0 win.

In the next round, Rangers faced a long trip north to play Crewe Alexandra, who were struggling near the foot of the Northern Section. Rangers won again, this time 4-2 with two more goals from Goddard. Unfortunately, they had to take to the road again for the third round, this time to Bristol Rovers, where they lost 3-1 before a crowd of 24,000, the largest attendance for any of their matches that season.

During the summer of 1931, manager Bob Hewison left Rangers to manage Bristol City. He was replaced by John Bowman, who had been player and secretary at QPR in the early 1900s. Unfortunately, ill health forced Bowman to resign after a couple of months and he was succeeded by Archie Mitchell.

Encouraged by the increase in attendances and success of the club, the directors negotiated to play their home games just up the road from the Loftus Road ground at the spacious White City Stadium for 1931-32. The stadium had accommodation for 60,000, including 6,000 under cover, whilst Loftus Road was used for reserve matches only.

Rangers were, as usual, active on the pre-season transfer market. One of the outgoing players was Jack Burns, who went to neighbours Brentford. His replacement was the England amateur international player Jim Lewis, who was signed from Walthamstow Avenue. Other signings included Thomas Wyper (Charlton Athletic), Stanley Cribb (West Ham United), William Haley (Fulham) and Ernest Hall (Bedworth Town).

The first game at the White City Stadium on 5 September attracted an attendance of 18,907, who witnessed a 3-0 defeat at the hands of Bournemouth. The season continued badly with only one win, at Swindon, in the first 13 games. By this time, Rangers were bottom and Mitchell made three major signings. He secured the services of Leslie Adlam and Ted Goodier from Oldham Athletic and Chelsea's Scottish international Andy Wilson, who had overcome suffering a shattered hand in World War One. The effect on the performances was dramatic as Rangers then won eight League games on the trot. The outstanding performance was from the winger Stanley Cribb, who managed 16 goals in a run of 12 League and Cup games.

On 2 January, in the game that ended the run of eight consecutive League wins, away to Brentford, Rangers suffered a heavy blow when Goddard received an injury which kept him out of the side until the end of the season. Following Goddard's injury, Rangers form fell away despite good performances from Jack Blackman as replacement centre-forward. They won only two of the next 13 matches, although one of those victories was a resounding 7-0 thrashing of Gillingham, when Harry Wiles scored four in his first game of the season.

Rangers were sliding down the table and suffered another set-back when they lost 6-1 at Northampton the week after Easter. By the end of the season, Rangers were down in 13th place with 42 points from their 42 games. Centre-half Jimmy Armstrong was the mainstay of the defence and he missed only two games all season. The leading goalscorers were Goddard with 19 and Cribb with 18.

In 1931-32, Rangers had opened their FA Cup campaign with a home game against amateurs Barnet. The first FA Cup tie to be played at the White City attracted a crowd of only 6,853, although those who turned up certainly got their money's worth as the game produced ten goals, Rangers winning 7-3. Stanley Cribb scored a hat-trick with Goddard and Coward both scoring two.

In the next round Rangers were again at home to a non-League side, this time against Scunthorpe United and George Rounce scored a hat-trick in QPR's 4-1 win, although the attendance was again disappointing at just under 8,000.

The draw for the third round gave Rangers a home tie against the team at the top of the Second Division, Leeds United. Goddard had been injured the week before the Leeds game and hopes now rested on his replacement, 19-year-old Jack Blackman. The game ended in a 3-1 win for Rangers, with Cribb scoring twice. His goals were the result of well-timed passes from Andy Wilson, who although marked by England international Willis Edwards, was Rangers' match-winner. The attendance was 41,097, which still stands as Rangers' record home 'gate'.

The Londoners had now reached the fourth round for the first time in ten years and it was too much to hope for a fourth successive home draw. They were paired away to Huddersfield Town, who were near the top of the First Division. The gulf showed as Rangers were outclassed, losing 5-0 at Leeds Road. Thus their four cup ties had produced 24 goals, an astonishing average of six per game!

Despite not attracting the bigger attendances they had hoped by moving to the White City, Rangers remained there for 1932-33. The two goalkeepers used in the previous season were both released, Thomas Pickett going to Bristol Rovers and Joseph Cunningham to Walsall. Ernie Beecham, from Fulham, was the replacement 'keeper and other arrivals included Edward Marcroft (Middlesbrough), Albert Brown (Blyth Spartans) and Walter Barrie (West Ham United).

QPR opened the season with a home match against local rivals Brentford and the attendance was an encouraging 24,347, nearly double the previous season's average. Unfortunately Rangers lost 3-2 and it was not until their fifth game that they took both points from a match.

Results improved with four wins, three draws and two defeats in nine matches and the biggest win was 5-2 at home to Cardiff City, when Marcroft scored a hat-trick. Better performances, however, did not bring in the crowds and, indeed, by the end of November, attendances were down to around 6,000. The White City echoed on match days with the sparse crowd spread out in the large stadium.

By early New Year, Rangers were sliding down the table and there were two particularly bad defeats — 7-0 at Coventry City and 5-1 at Newport County.

It also became obvious that Rangers were struggling financially and it was going to be difficult for them to see the season out. The directors had no option but to ask the players to forego some of their wages, promising to pay the balance at the end of the season. The job of telling the staff fell to the youngest director, Albert Hittinger. He asked the players to accept £4 a week until the full amount could be paid. Both sides honoured the agreement.

Attendances were now so poor that only 2,800 watched the last home game of the season, Rangers' lowest-ever home 'gate' as a Football League side. They finished 16th, eight points above the re-election clubs.

The only ever-present was new goalkeeper Ernie Beecham, although Ted Goodier missed only one game. Goals were shared fairly evenly by four players — George Goddard (15), George Rounce (14), Richard Brown (13) and Jack Blackman (11).

There was one glimmer of success when the Reserves won the London Challenge Cup. Another highlight of the season was on 4 January, when the White City stadium was selected to host what was advertised as 'the first ever public experimental floodlight match'.

Given those poor attendances in 1932-33, Rangers were hoping that a good FA Cup run with attractive home ties might bring the crowds (and their money) back to the White City. In the first round Rangers drew 1-1 at the former Football League side Merthyr Town, who were now playing in the Southern League. The non-Leaguers were easily overcome in the replay, QPR winning 5-1 with Goddard scoring a hat-trick.

In the second round, Rangers went through after another home replay, this time winning 3-1 against Torquay with George Rounce hitting a hat-trick. In the third round, though, the Londoners went down 2-0 at Darlington, who finished the season bottom of the Third Division North.

By now the club's overdraft at the bank had increased to £34,549, so the directors decided to move back to Loftus Road for 1933-34. Most of the debt was owed to the former chairman,

QPR's Tom Pickett punches clear from a Leeds United attack during the FA Cup game at the White City in January 1932, a match which attracted a record crowd of 41,097.

Queen's Park Rangers players meet an Austrian government minister before the friendly game against First Vienna FC.

the late Mr J.H.Fielding. Subsequently, his son, Charles Fielding, showed great generosity and cancelled the whole outstanding debt of £20,000. The club's other saving grace was that they had kept the old ground on and not sold it as they at first intended doing after moving to White City.

In order to have a fresh start back 'home', the directors appointed former player Mick O'Brien as manager. He signed a number of new players including Albert Blake (Watford), George Emmerson (Cardiff City), Frank Eaton (Reading), George Clarke (Crystal Palace), James Allen (Huddersfield Town), Joe Devine (Sunderland) and Bill Mason from Fulham, as cover for Beecham.

Another signing made during the season was that of Alex Farmer from Nottingham Forest. Farmer was to be connected with the Rangers club for over 40 years as player, trainer and director.

One of the manager's more awkward tasks was to bring a youngster called Hurley into line. He was often late for training and was sacked three times by O'Brien. The trouble was that Hurley came to the ground on a second-hand motor bike, which was not very reliable. The matter went to the board, who decided to raise Hurley's salary so that he could afford the train fare and not use his bike for getting to work. It was hardly worth it, for Hurley never appeared in Rangers' first team!

The move back to Loftus Road proved successful in that Rangers won their first seven home games, scoring 18 goals with only four against. But their away form was the opposite with only one win and two draws in the same period. And at the beginning of September, the club reluctantly agreed to sell top scorer George Goddard in order to raise some much needed cash.

During November and December, Rangers remained unbeaten in the League and at Christmas they enjoyed a 4-1 win at Gillingham, where Blackman, Goddard's replacement, scoring a hat-trick.

Good home form continued to keep Rangers near the top of the table but although they suffered only one defeat in seven away games between November and the beginning of February, for the final quarter of the season, they failed to improve on their travels and defeats of 5-0 at Reading, 4-1 at Bristol Rovers and 4-1 at Crystal Palace, saw them finish in fourth place, seven points behind champions Norwich City, but equal on points with runners-up Coventry City. One interesting fact occurred during the away game at Luton Town. Rangers lost 4-2, but both their goals were scored by the Luton defender Kingdom. It is the only time an opponent has scored two own-goals in the same game against Rangers.

Leading goalscorer for the season was Jack Blackman with 31 goals (24 League and seven Cup). The next highest was George Emmerson with 12.

In the FA Cup, Rangers beat non-League Kettering 6-0 and the crowd of 14,000 was well up on the corresponding Cup attendance at the White City in the previous season. In the second round, they beat Third Division North side New Brighton 4-0 in a replay, Jack Blackman scoring all four.

In the third round, Rangers were drawn away to Nottingham Forest. The result went with the form book as Forest ran out 4-0 winners. Yet again Rangers' Cup ties had produced a large number of goals with 16 in only four matches.

Rangers did not move into the pre-season transfer market in such a big way as normal and the three main signings for 1934-35 were international Jimmy Crawford from Chelsea, Tom Dutton (Leicester City) and Sam Abel (Fulham). As the club were still recovering financially from the move to the White City, O'Brien was unable to add further talent and during the season the directors let it be known that they would listen to offers for any of the players. In the New Year, Joe Devine signed for Birmingham.

In the first four matches of the season, Rangers scored nine goals which produced two wins and a draw, Gordon Reed scoring four of the goals. But then QPR hit a poor patch with only two wins in the next 13 games. The goals dried up and in a sequence of five games, Rangers scored in only one. New signing Abel was tried at centre-forward, but moved to the right wing when Jack Blackman returned after injury.

Christmas saw the biggest win of the season, a 6-3 victory over Clapton Orient, and the forwards now rediscovered their touch, two of the next three home games ending in 4-1 victories.

The away form in the New Year was disappointing and due to the lack of success, attendances began to drop again. The erratic form was evident over Easter when the three games produced 19 goals: a 5-1 home win over Torquay United on Good Friday was followed the next day by a 5-1 defeat at Bristol City; and on Easter Monday, Torquay gained revenge with a 7-0 win.

Rangers finished 13th but if their away form had been anywhere near as good as their home form, then they would have finished much closer to the champions Charlton Athletic. Indeed, they had won only twice away from home, including a victory on the last day of the season, and had scored only 14 goals in their 21 away games. The mainstays of the team for the season were Jack Blackman (38 games), Albert Blake (37) and Ted Goodier (40). The leading goalscorer was again Blackman with 19.

Rangers had started their 1934-35 Cup trail at home with a 2-0 win over amateurs Walthamstow Avenue. In the second round they were drawn at home again, to fellow Third Division South rivals Brighton & Hove Albion, who won 2-1.

For 1935-36, the Rangers directors decided on a change at the helm and appointed Billy Birrell as manager. Birrell, a former Middlesbrough star, had been manager at Bournemouth for the previous four years. And as with most new managers, there was plenty of activity on the transfer market.

Only Abel, Allen, Barrie, Bartlett, Blackman, Blake, Crawford, Farmer, Hammond, March, Mason and Russell were retained. On the incoming side were Billy Carr (Derby County), Jonty Rowe (Reading), Ernie Vincent (Manchester United), Harry Lowe (Watford), David Samuel (Reading), Reg Banks (West Bromwich Albion) and Jack Fletcher (Bournemouth). During the season other signings were made, including Frank Lumsden (Huddersfield Town), David Ovenstone (Raith Rovers) and Johnny Ballentyne (Partick Thistle). However, the most significant arrival was that of Tommy Cheetham from the Army in India.

The season began with two defeats and a draw and for the fourth match, Cheetham was introduced. It was a move that no one ever regretted, for in his first two games he scored six goals: two came on his debut, in a 3-2 home win over Brighton, and four in the 5-0 win against Aldershot. It seemed that Cheetham was the person who decided if Rangers won or not. If he did not score, they did not win — and if he did score, they won. This was true for all but five games to the end of the season.

Cheetham scored his second hat-trick in a 4-3 win at Newport and in seven games from the end of October he scored 12 goals altogether, a club record. He also set a record by scoring in nine successive home games.

By the halfway point of the season, Rangers had 25 points from their 21 games, but as in the previous season it was their away form which was letting them down.

The New Year began with four straight wins, including a 5-1 home victory over Swindon, but the sequence ended with their biggest defeat of the season, a 6-1 hammering at Coventry. Their form to the end of the season was mixed with Cheetham scoring only once in the last eight games as Rangers settled for fourth place, four points behind champions Coventry City.

Not surprisingly, despite his barren patch, the leading scorer was Tommy Cheetham, whose total for the season was 37 goals from 36 games. The next highest was Harry Lowe with 15.

In December 1935, the Queen's Park Rangers Supporters' Club was formed with the motto, 'To Help Not Hinder'. During the first season of operation, the Supporters' Club handed over a cheque for £100 to the parent club to help towards the cost of crush barriers for the terracing and the trainer's equipment.

At the end of the season, a testimonial match for Jimmy Eggleton took place between teams representing Rangers present and Rangers past. Despite poor weather, a large crowd turned out to see old favourites such as Arthur Chandler, Sid Sweetman, Joseph Cunningham, Joe Devine and Jack Burns.

Rangers' involvement in the FA Cup had been short-lived in 1935-36. Drawn away to Kent non-League side Margate, QPR lost 3-1. Their goal was scored by — who else? — Tommy Cheetham.

For the start of the 1936-37 season, Billy Birrell made further

Queen's Park Rangers in 1934-35. Back row (left to right): Jones, Barrie, March, Hammond, Crawford, Watson, Ridley, Dutton, Blake, Blackman. Middle row: D.Richards (tariner), Bartlett, Russell, Abel, Beecham, Langford, Allen, Mason, Reid, Ashman, Farmer, J.Eggleton (assistant trainer). Front row: Emmerson, McCarthy, Devine, C.H.Bates (director), C.W.Fielding (chairman), T.O'Brien (secretary-manager), A.E.Pearsall (vice-chairman), Goodier.

signings. One of the most important newcomers was Arthur Jefferson, who was on the books of non-League Peterborough United when he was offered a trial at the end of the previous season. Jefferson impressed and was given a contract.

It was the beginning of a long partnership as Jefferson played first-team football at Rangers until 1950, making an immediate impact despite missing the last two months at his first season following a cartilage operation.

Other arrivals were Wilf Bott (Newcastle United), Hugh McMahon (Reading) and Arthur Fitzgerald (Reading).

The highlight of the first half of the season was a 7-2 home win over Southend United, with five different players finding the net. Christmas bought three good wins — 4-0 at home to Exeter City, 5-0 at home against Bristol City and 3-0 in the return match at Exeter. So, at the halfway stage, Rangers had 24 points from their 21 games.

The New Year started with a run of four games without a win, followed by four successive victories. During that latter run, Rangers had another big win, this time 6-0 against Cardiff City, when Charlton and Fitzgerald both scored hat-tricks.

The good run continued until the week before Easter when Rangers lost for the first time in nine matches. By now, they were fourth in the table, but they did not win for another seven matches and at the end of the season were ninth with 45 points, 13 behind the champions, Luton Town. Leading goalscorers were Fitzgerald with 21 (17 League and four Cup) and Lowe with 17 (all League).

In the 1936-37 FA Cup, Rangers' tie against Brighton attracted 16,000 fans, one of the larger crowds of the season at Loftus Road. QPR won comfortably, 5-1 with Fitzgerald scoring a hat-trick.

The second round took Rangers to non-League South Liverpool and following their recent results against non-League opposition, they must have been apprehensive about the trip. They managed to scrape through 1-0 with Fitzgerald again being the match-winner, but in the third round, Rangers were on the road again to the North-West, this time to Second Division Bury, who were high in the table. Rangers lost a close game by the only goal.

Having been close to the top the previous season, Rangers made some good signings in an attempt to reach the elusive promotion place in 1937-38. Players who arrived included Norman Smith (Charlton Athletic), Jack Cape (Manchester United), John Gilfillan (Portsmouth) and Joe Mallett (Charlton Athletic). Mallett came initially to Rangers on loan from Charlton, but when he gave a good performance, he was immediately recalled by Jimmy Seed, the Charlton manager. However, Mallett could not settle at The Valley and in February 1939 rejoined Rangers on a permanent basis.

The season started full of promise with two wins and a draw, but the second home game, against Millwall, ended in a 2-0 defeat, a result that had a significant bearing on the ultimate destination of the championship. With overall better results, attendances began to increase again, much to the delight of the directors who had endured several financially lean years, and the year ended with four straight wins, so after 21 games, Rangers had 28 points and only four defeats.

After they suffered their second home defeat, 2-1 against Bournemouth, Rangers had a good run which took them back to the top of the table, nine points ahead of Millwall. But then they hit a bad patch, winning only once in five games. And despite winning five of the last seven matches, they finished third, three points behind promoted Millwall. So, had Rangers won their home game against the Lions, they might have been champions instead.

Overall, though, it had been a successful season with Rangers in top place for 12 weeks and in second place for 13 weeks. Leading goalscorers were Arthur Fitzgerald (20), Wilfred Bott (19) and Tommy Cheetham (17).

In March 1938, two signings were made that were to play a significant part in the future success of the club. The first was Reg Allen, a goalkeeper playing for Corona FC, an amateur club in the Hanwell & District League. He was given a trial and signed directly after giving an excellent performance in the annual Brentford Hospital Cup match.

The other arrival was centre-half Alf Ridyard, who signed from West Bromwich Albion on 16 March, the transfer deadline day.

In the first round of the Cup in 1937-38, Rangers were drawn away to fellow Third Division South side Bristol Rovers. And when the game kicked-off, none of the 7,000 crowd would have predicted that QPR would achieve their biggest ever FA Cup victory.

However, that is exactly what happened as Rovers succumbed to a rampant Rangers side, who won 8-1. Arthur Fitzgerald and Tommy Cheetham both scored hat-tricks with Wilfred Bott getting the other two. The second-round draw again took Rangers westwards, this time not quite so far, to Swindon Town, who won 2-1.

As usual, new players joined during the close season of 1938.

One of those new signings was to return to the club in the 1960s and become the most successful manager in Rangers' history. He was, of course, Alec Stock, who was signed from Southern League side, Yeovil Town.

The other newcomers were John Devine (Aberdeen), Arthur Warburton (Fulham) and Harry Pearson (Coventry City).

Before the start of the season, the Supporters' Club gave the parent club some £1,500 to pay for the roof over the new terracing at the Loftus Road end of the ground. The new standing area cost a total of £7,000 and could accommodate 6,000 people. It was officially opened by the Rt Hon Herbert Morrison at the home game against Crystal Palace on 29 October.

The season began in fine style with a 4-2 win at Reading followed by a 5-0 home victory against Exeter City. As the team was virtually the same that had done so well the season before, great things were expected of Rangers. And after two successive defeats in early September, they were back on the winning trail with a spell of four wins and two draws. The main change was that Cheetham had regained his scoring touch.

Rangers suffered their first home defeat at the end of October, when they lost 2-1 to Crystal Palace. They made up for it in the next game when they thrashed Aldershot 7-0, with Cheetham scoring four. At this point he had netted ten goals in the last five games. Christmas saw another big win, this time 5-0 at home to Cardiff City.

At the turn of the year, Rangers had 23 points from their 21 games, a record of eight wins, seven draws and six defeats. January saw two wins and two defeats and Cheetham scored another hat-trick.

In February, the club were still £20,000 in debt and up to now, they had resisted several offers for Cheetham. But the directors decided to accept Brentford's offer of £5,000 in order to alleviate some of the bank overdraft. Following his departure, Rangers lost their way and slid down the table. The goals completely dried up in mid-March with a run of six games and no goals scored.

The season ended with three successive 1-1 draws, which earned QPR final position of sixth, with 44 points. In fact, Rangers, Ipswich Town, Bristol City, Swindon Town and Aldershot all finished with the same number of points.

The leading goalscorer was Cheetham with 27 goals (22 League and five Cup), the next highest were Arthur Fitzgerald and Wilfred Bott, both with nine.

The Reserves had a successful season by finishing as runners-up in the London Combination and winning the London Challenge Cup for the second time. During the season they had a run of only one defeat in 28 games.

In 1938-39, Rangers' FA Cup campaign had started with an away tie against Crystal Palace. A week before the game, Bill Mason, the first-choice goalkeeper, was injured. This meant an early call-up for the young Reg Allen. He played with maturity above his age and enabled Rangers to earn a replay with a 1-1 draw. From that game he hardly missed a match before his record-breaking transfer to Manchester United in 1950.

The replay took place at Loftus Road two days later and Rangers won 3-0, with two goals from Cheetham and a Bott penalty. The next round saw Rangers away to Hartlepools United, who were near the bottom of the Northern Section, and Rangers ran out 2-0 winners. Their reward was a third-round home tie against Second Division West Ham United, a match which attracted Rangers' biggest home crowd of the season, some 22,408, but West Ham just had the edge and won 2-1.

Two months after Tommy Cheetham's departure, Billy Birrell resigned as manager. He was replaced by Ted Vizard, who had been manager at Swindon Town for the past six seasons.

Before the start of the ill-fated 1939-40 season, Ted Vizard managed to persuade the old Millwall favourite Dave Mangnall out of retirement to join Rangers. Vizard wanted him to pass on his experience to the younger players. Other new arrivals were Arthur Bonass (Chesterfield), John Barr (Third Lanark) and John McColgan (Plymouth Argyle). But the Football League lasted for only three games, in which Rangers drew two and lost one, before war was declared and the Football League was suspended.

When war was declared on 3 September 1939, football found itself in a very different position from that of August 1914, when the Football League and the FA Cup were allowed to continue for one more season. This time, with the threat of air raids, the Government at first prohibited large public gatherings and the game went into cold storage.

After a few days, however, the law was relaxed a little and eventually some form of regionalised competition was allowed, the Government again seeing that to continue with sport in some form would be good for public morale. Of course, wartime football — with its high-scoring games, often scratch teams and guest player system — was not always ideal, but most clubs kept going and Rangers did as well as most.

The League organised regional competitions for those clubs who wished to continue playing. Rangers were placed in the South (B) League along with Aldershot, Bournemouth, Brentford, Brighton, Chelsea, Fulham, Portsmouth, Reading and Southampton.

Queen's Park Rangers manager Billy Birrell, the club's most successful manager since James Cowan. During his four years in charge up to the outbreak of World War Two, Birrell was unlucky not to take QPR into the Second Division.

QPR goalkeeper Reg Allen, on his debut for the club, grabs the ball during the FA Cup first-round game against Crystal Palace at Selhurst Park in November 1938.

As in World War One, clubs were allowed to use guest players when, due to Services commitments, they were unable to field a full side of their own players.

Rangers started their wartime football with a friendly against an Army XI, which the League side won 10-0. The Army line-up was never made public, the official reason being for security!

The regionalised league started with an away game at Reading, which ended in a 2-0 win for the home side. Rangers were slow starters but certainly found improvement with nine straight wins. Some of the scores were impressive — 8-3 at Fulham, 5-2 against Portsmouth, 7-0 at Brentford. The main goalscorer was Dave Mangnall, who netted 14 in seven games. As each team had to play the others only twice, the league was over by January. Rangers were unbeaten at home and finished top with 26 points, two ahead of Bournemouth.

The regional leagues were then shuffled slightly and a second competition started. Rangers lost Brentford, Chelsea, Fulham, Portsmouth and Southampton from their league and gained Clapton Orient, Crystal Palace, Norwich City, Southend United and Watford.

But they could not quite regain the form they had shown in the first half of the season. They started with two wins, two draws and two defeats in the first six games, one of each at home and away. Results improved towards the end of the season, which did not finish until the beginning of June. The best results at home were 5-4 against Brighton, 4-0 against Clapton Orient and 5-0 against Bournemouth. Rangers finished the second half in second place, four points behind the winners, Crystal Palace. Their leading goalscorer overall was Mangnall with 40 from 35 games.

In order to generate a little more competitiveness, a League War Cup was organised for those clubs interested. The first and second rounds were to be two-legged with all the other rounds being one game, and a replay if necessary. The Final was played at Wembley Stadium. Due to the number of entrants, a one-legged preliminary round had to be played. Rangers were drawn away to Southend United and their interest in the trophy was short-lived as they lost 1-0.

For the second season of wartime football, the competition was split into two regional sections, North and South. The idea was for teams to play as many games as possible against the other teams in their region, but because clubs would not all be able to play the same number of games, it was decided to run the competition on a goal-average basis and therefore not award points for a win or draw. Rangers played 23 games: ten teams home and away, two teams away only and a second home game against Fulham.

Rangers' start in the South Regional League was at Fulham and ended in a 3-1 defeat. The next five matches were all at home, resulting in three wins, a draw and a defeat. But more importantly for this season was the goal tally of 13 for and 15 against. The goal-average was not improved in the next few games with 17 being conceded in five games. The league games continued until the new year. By this time Rangers had played 17 matches and had a goal-average of below even, at 0.825.

The league resumed after the cup competitions in May and continued for another month. In this time, Rangers played six games, scoring 14 goals and conceding 20. When the league was brought to a close, Rangers' goal-average was down to 0.783 (47-60) and put them 26th out of the 34 clubs.

For 1940-41 there was also a London Cup, comprising two leagues of six teams, with each team playing the others home and away. Following that, the top two sides of each league would go into a knock-out to decide the overall winners. Rangers' league included Aldershot, Brentford, Chelsea, Crystal Palace and Fulham. The matches were played in two groups of five, split by the League War Cup competition (see below). Rangers started the London Cup with two defeats by Fulham, 4-1 away and 7-5 at home. They did, however, manage to win two games in the first half of the competition. By the interval, Rangers' five games had produced 32 goals. When the Cup resumed in April, Rangers won three and drew one of their remaining games. The final table saw Rangers in third place with 11 points, only one off a semi-final place.

The League War Cup, meanwhile, was played under the more traditional knock-out format, although each round was over two legs. In the first round Rangers were drawn against Crystal Palace, winning the tie by an aggregate of 4-2. The next round saw Aldershot as their opponents. The Recreation Ground club were an unpredictable force, due to the number and quality of their guest players, many of whom were servicemen stationed in the Hampshire garrison town. Rangers lost the away tie 2-1 but managed to win 4-2 in the home leg to go through 5-4 on aggregate.

In the third round they were paired with neighbours Chelsea, who had beaten Brentford in the previous round. For a change, the first leg was at home. Rangers won 2-0 and, by winning the away leg 4-2, they progressed into the last eight of the competition.

In the fourth round they were drawn against Leicester City, whom they beat 2-1 in the home leg with goals from Dave Mangnall. It was the third consecutive game in which Mangnall had scored twice. Rangers were now optimistic about reaching the semi-final but Leicester won the second leg 6-1 to go through to the last four by a margin of 7-3.

Due to service calls on some of their players, Rangers had to use a number of guests in order to fulfil their matches in each of the competitions. The leading goalscorer for the season in all competitions was Dave Mangnall with 33 (14 League, 10 London War Cup and nine League War Cup). The next highest Rangers scorer was Harry Lowe with nine.

For 1941-42 there was a normal league for the clubs in and around London. The 16 teams in the London League played each other once at home and once away and 12 London clubs were joined by Aldershot, Brighton, Portsmouth and Reading. Rangers started with a fine 5-2 win on the south coast at Brighton, but this was followed by five successive defeats and the next nine matches only produced two wins.

The main problem was in defence. On six occasions in the first 13 games, Rangers conceded three or more goals. Their best win in this time was 4-1 at home to Millwall. The forwards, mainly Mangnall, were scoring goals, but they were usually ending up losers in a high-scoring game. From Christmas, Rangers won only two out of their next nine matches but they ended the season with three straight wins, the biggest being 5-0 in the final game, at Watford. Rangers finished in tenth place with 25 points, nine points above bottom club, Watford.

Also for 1941-42, the London War Cup took in the 16 teams who played in the London League, split into four groups of four. Each club played the others home and away with the group winners going into a knock-out to decide who would meet in the Final to be played at Wembley.

Rangers' group consisted of Aldershot, Brentford and Millwall. They started with a draw against Millwall, followed by a win against Aldershot. Unfortunately, they then lost the next three games, including two 2-1 defeats by Brentford, the eventual Cup winners. Although Rangers won the last game of the round robin stage, they finished in third place out of the four teams.

The only real regular players for the season were Alf Ridyard, at centre-half, with 32 appearances and Dave Mangnall with 28. Mangnall was again the leading Rangers scorer, this time with 12 goals. The main scorers were the guest players, who scored 24 between them.

Still wartime football was ever-changing and for 1942-43, the South Regional League came into being when the previous season's London League was taken over by the Football League with Southampton and Luton Town added to the 16 clubs. Each team was due to play the others home and away. However, due to various reasons each team played only 28 of the scheduled 34 games. For instance, Rangers never met Aldershot, Portsmouth or Watford.

The season started with a draw and defeat. This was followed by a good run of nine games, eight wins and a draw. After 11 games, Rangers had scored 28 goals and conceded 16. There was then a slight loss of form which resulted in three defeats, including a 6-0 reverse at Tottenham Hotspur. Six out of the next eight were won, so Rangers were up towards the top of the table but, despite finishing with three straight wins, they were unable to catch Arsenal at the top. Rangers finished the season with 18 wins in 28 games and were in third place, five points behind the champions.

Apart from guests, the leading players were Harry Brown, who did not miss a game all season, B.Burley, Joe Mallett and Alf Ridyard. The leading goalscorer was Reg Swinfen with 16 from 22 games.

The 1942-43 League War Cup was played in two regional stages. Clubs from the south were split into three groups of four and a group of six. The group winners were to play in the semi-final and Final (South), with the winners meeting the North winners in the Cup winners' match to decide the overall holders. Rangers' group consisted of Brentford, Clapton Orient and Southampton.

They began with a 2-1 win at the holders Brentford and followed it with another 2-1 win, this time at home to Southampton. With a draw and a win from the next two games, Rangers were looking good for the semi-final stage. Their last away game in the qualifying competition was at Southampton, the only team who could stop Rangers winning the group.

If Rangers won, then they could not be caught but the result was a disappointing 4-1 defeat. So, Rangers had to win their last game to go through, or hope that Southampton lost at home to Brentford on the same day. Brentford did not help Rangers, going down 2-1 at The Dell, but the Loftus Road club ensured their semi-final place with an emphatic 8-1 over Clapton Orient, with Heathcote scoring four.

The four teams through to the semi-finals were Rangers, Arsenal, Reading and Charlton Athletic. Charlton beat Reading at White Hart Lane, whilst a week later, Rangers met Arsenal at Stamford Bridge, where a crowd of over 54,000 saw Arsenal outclass Rangers by 4-1. Rangers' goal was scored by Johnny Pattison. The Gunners went on to win the Cup, beating Charlton 7-1 in the Final.

In 1943-44, the season was played along the same format as the previous year. The South Regional League consisted of 18 teams, each playing each other home and away. As in the previous season, Rangers did not meet two of the sides, this time Crystal Palace and Luton Town.

Following their good performances towards the end of the previous season, Rangers started the new campaign full of confidence. Their first four games were all won, with Heathcote scoring seven of the ten goals. Rangers remained unbeaten until the ninth game, when they lost 3-1 at Brighton, but recovered immediately to beat Southampton 7-0 at home the following week, Heathcote scoring a hat-trick.

Rangers then lost three on the trot, including a remarkable game at home to Chelsea. Due to several injuries and non-availabilities, the Loftus Road club had to field a young and inexperienced side and went down 11-2. Amazingly, though, they remained unbeaten for the remaining 16 matches in the league. That run included a sequence of five straight wins, followed by five successive draws.

The better results were achieved as Rangers were able to be consistent with their team selection. Seven players missed only up to five games each throughout the league season and Rangers finished in third place in the league, only six points behind the champions, Tottenham Hotspur. Their final record was 14 wins, 12 draws and only four defeats. The leading goalscorer was Bill Heathcote with 36 (29 League and seven Cup). The next highest was Reg Swinfen with 14 (six League and eight Cup).

Towards the end of the season, Ted Vizard resigned as manager in order to take a similar position at Wolverhampton Wanderers. He had been at Loftus Road for five years and had run the club under very difficult circumstances. He was replaced by Dave Mangnall, Rangers' prolific goalscorer. Mangnall was a police officer by profession and had no pretensions towards football management. He was persuaded by a friend to apply and his station superintendent typed out his application letter.

Once again the League War Cup was split into four groups of either four or five teams. Having progressed to the knock-out stage last time, Rangers were hoping for more of the same this year. They were grouped with Arsenal, Clapton Orient, Fulham, Luton Town and Reading. Although there were six sides in the group, each team still played only three teams home and away. Rangers, for instance, did not meet Fulham and Reading.

They started with a 5-2 win at Clapton Orient and a home draw against the previous year's Cup winners, Arsenal. Rangers then won all four of their remaining games, including a 4-1 victory at Arsenal. So, after their six games, they were unbeaten and had scored 25 goals. Because Reading had won all six they finished top of the group and pushed Rangers into second place. It was a little unfair on Rangers, for Reading had played only the three weakest teams.

The 1944-45 South Regional League remained in its established wartime format of 18 clubs and this time Rangers were not scheduled to meet Chelsea or Watford.

Now 38 years old, Dave Mangnall decided to end his playing days and concentrate on the management side. The season started strangely with Rangers scoring four in each of the first two games, but losing both. They lost 7-4 at Crystal Palace and 5-4 at home to Southampton. Things did not improve dramatically, with only two draws in the next four games and Rangers' first victory of the season was at home to Millwall, whom they beat 4-1.

Despite losing only twice in the next 13 games, Rangers never produced the form of the previous two seasons and their best performance before Christmas was the 7-0 home win against Crystal Palace, with Heathcote netting another hat-trick. In December and January, Rangers were involved in some high-scoring games with seven out of nine games producing six or more goals. Unfortunately for Rangers supporters, they were evenly spread with 27 goals for and 25 against.

Things settled down after the break for the Cup competition, Rangers resuming with two 1-1 draws and two home victories, 1-0 and 3-0. But their season finished with two defeats and by this time Rangers had slipped to ninth in the table with 30 points from their 30 games. The champions were again Tottenham Hotspur, who lost only one match all season.

Over one-third of Rangers' appearances for the season were made by guests, with only Joe Mallett being an ever-present. The other Rangers regulars were Sam Abel (28 games), William Heathcote (31), Alf Ridyard (33) and Jack Rose (31). The leading goalscorer was, once again, Heathcote with 23 goals (20 League and three Cup).

For the League War Cup in 1944-45, Rangers found themselves back in a normal four-team qualifying group along with Aldershot, Tottenham Hotspur and West Ham United. They had a good spell and with three wins and two draws from their first five games went into the final match needing a draw to qualify for the knock-out stage.

Their opponents for that last game were West Ham, who could pip Rangers for the top if they won. The match was played before a large crowd of 20,000, who saw the Hammers win quite easily by 5-0. The group finished very close with West Ham on nine points, Rangers on eight and Tottenham on seven. Aldershot finished with no points, having lost all six matches.

Before what was to be the final wartime season, Dave Mangnall gave an interview to a local newspaper in which he assessed the club's prospects for the forthcoming year. He expressed his desire to continue with the philosophy of fielding younger players when the regulars were unavailable and using guests only as a last resort.

He was looking forward to having Reg Allen and Johnny Barr back at the club, following their release from prisoner-of-war camps in Germany. They had both been held for four years. Allen had been captured in Norway, Barr in the Western Desert. Harry Brown, the current first-choice goalkeeper, was stationed nearby and was expected to be available for most matches. Twenty-three of the club's professionals were still in the Forces, but as many had been called up at the beginning of the war, they would be amongst the first to be released.

With the war in Europe won, and the Japanese war entering its final stages, more clubs entered competitive football for the season. First and Second Division sides were split into two 42-match leagues, north and south, whilst the Third Division sides were split even further and Rangers, along with the other teams, found themselves in something bewilderingly called the Third Division South (North).

They began with five successive victories, including a 6-2 win at Mansfield Town. The main reason for the good start was that it was not only Heathcote who was scoring goals and six different players netted in those five wins. The next five games produced three more wins and two draws, so after ten games Rangers topped the table with 18 points and a goal tally of 28 for and six against.

Their first defeat came at Ipswich Town, where they lost 2-1, but this did not affect Rangers too much as they scored five more straight wins before drawing the next game. Their first home defeat, by 2-1, was on Boxing Day against Norwich City, but by now Rangers had assured themselves of the title, finishing six points ahead of Norwich City. The mainstays of the side were ever-present Jack Rose and Reg Allen, and Harry Daniels, Joe Mallett and Alf Ridyard, all of whom missed only one game each. Leading scorer, for the third successive season, was Bill Heathcote, this time with 22 goals.

For 1945-46 the qualifying competition of the League War Cup was divided into two leagues of nine teams, with the top two going on to the knock-out stage. Following their league success, Rangers were confident of progressing through the qualifying stages of the competition and they began with a 4-1 home win over Ipswich Town, but then lost the next two away games.

Rangers then regained their form and remained unbeaten for the remaining 13 matches. Although they scored in only three of their eight away games, their 100 per cent home record saw them finish on top of the group. Walsall were second, one point behind.

Rangers and Walsall were joined in the last four by Bournemouth and Bristol Rovers. The semi-finals were to be one match only with a replay if necessary. So when Rangers were drawn at Bournemouth, they were a little disappointed at not having a home game in search of a place in the Final. The match at Dean Court attracted a crowd of 13,000, who saw a very competitive match end in a 1-1 draw, Rangers' goal being scored by Heathcote.

Having got Bournemouth back home, Rangers were hopeful of winning a place in the Final against Walsall, who had won 3-1 at Eastville. The match at Loftus Road drew a crowd of 15,000, but they saw Rangers go down 1-0.

The most significant feature of the 1945-46 season was, of course, the reintroduction of the FA Cup, although in order to give it wider appeal and also taking into account the vagaries of the transient nature of football at this time, every tie up to and including the quarter-finals was to be played over two legs.

Rangers' first-round opponents were the amateurs Barnet, from the Athenian League. The first leg was played at Barnet's Underhill and attracted 6,800 spectators, to set a ground record at the time. Rangers went 6-0 ahead before Barnet scored two late goals, so the final result was a convincing 6-2 win, the goals coming from Neary (3), Mallett (2) and Heathcote. In the second leg, Barnet scored in the first minute to reduce the gap to three but, despite a strong performance, the amateurs were unable to add to their tally. Rangers scored two late goals, through Swinfen (85 minutes) and Neary (87), to go through on aggregate by 8-3.

In the second round they were drawn against Ipswich Town, the first leg being at home where, in an entertaining match, Rangers took the lead after eight minutes with a goal by Neary. Stock then added a second before half-time and Rangers scored twice more after the break to win 4-0. In the second leg, a week later at Portman Road, Ipswich made a valiant effort to claw themselves back into the tie, but after Daniels had scored in the 15th minute and Addinall had netted with a back-heel after half an hour, the game fizzled out and Rangers progressed to the third round with a 6-0 aggregate.

The third round draw paired Rangers with Crystal Palace, who, like Rangers, were top of their section of the league. The first leg at Loftus Road proved to be a typically hectic Cup tie with the 20,080 crowd getting their money's worth, despite not seeing a goal. The following Wednesday saw the second leg at Selhurst Park. The match was played in a steady downpour of rain accompanied by a gale force wind. After 90 minutes there were still no goals, so extra-time was played but, due to the condition of the pitch, the referee abandoned the game after 27 minutes of the extra period.

Both sides agreed the score should stand, so a replay on a neutral ground was required. That was staged at Fulham's Craven Cottage a week later. One interesting rule explained in the programme for that game was:

'Should the game remain a draw after 90 minutes, an extra ten minutes each-way will be played. If the position remains the same at the end of extra-time, the game must be continued and the first goal scored will determine the winners.'

Again the game was very close, but Rangers managed a goal by Addinall to go through in normal time.

The next round saw Rangers up against Southampton, the first leg at The Dell. In the third minute Southampton were awarded a penalty for handling the ball against Jefferson. Reg Allen saved the shot from Roper, which gave Rangers and their travelling fans hope. In the 32nd minute Mallett sent a pass to Addinall, who took the ball in his stride to put it past Stansbridge in the Saints' goal. Then Rangers held out in the second half to come back to the Bush with a precious one-goal lead.

The second leg was a close and competitive game with Rangers holding out to win 4-3, with a hat-trick by Addinall. This put the Londoners into the next round with an aggregate win of 5-3.

In the fifth round, Rangers met near-neighbours Brentford. The first leg was played at Loftus Road in front of a crowd of nearly 20,000 and Brentford's higher League status soon showed as they scored three goals. Rangers managed one goal, through Pattison, but it meant an uphill task in the second leg at Griffin Park. In the second game Rangers put up a good fight but were unable to break down the Brentford defence and the match ended goalless. So, by virtue of their home defeat, Rangers went out of the FA Cup by a 3-1 aggregate.

Rangers had played 11 games in the competition that season and had been watched by over 186,000 people.

For the return season of peacetime football, Rangers relied mostly on players who had joined the club during the war, although there were some notable signings made at the beginning of the season. One of them was a familiar face to the wartime supporters — Cyril Hatton from Notts County, who had guested for the club during the war when he was in London. His transfer fee of £1,000 was the first four-figure sum that Rangers had ever paid for a player. Dave Mangnall then paid another four-figure sum for the services of Fred Durrant, the Brentford centre-forward. Other newcomers included Don Mills, a miner from Rotherham, Reg Saphin (Ipswich Town) and Ivor Powell's brother, George, who came from Fulham. On the outgoing side were reserve goalkeeper Harry Brown, who went to Notts County as part of the Hatton deal, and Alec Stock, who joined Yeovil Town as manager.

Following a good final season of wartime football, Rangers were confident of a successful 1946-47 campaign and they started with an unbeaten run of nine games. After conceding one goal in each of their first two matches, they then went seven games without letting their opponents score. This run, which consisted of six wins and three draws, took Rangers to the top of the table and their first defeat came in the tenth game, at home to Bristol Rovers.

By now, QPR and Cardiff City were the teams to beat and Rangers' visit to Ninian Park drew a crowd of 50,000, the largest attendance ever to see a Rangers' Third Division game. An exciting match ended in a 2-2 draw which put QPR down into third place, their lowest position all season. Good results continued, though, with a run of six straight wins, including a 7-0 home defeat of Swindon Town, which put Rangers back on top of the table, although the Christmas period was mixed with a win, a draw and a defeat.

The New Year started with two more signings: Reg Dudley (Millwall) and Johnny Hartburn (Yeovil Town), who was recommended to the club by the Yeovil manager and former QPR player, Alec Stock.

Then results began to go badly when a number of key players were missing through injury. Rangers lost four of their next seven games and dropped to second place before the forwards rediscovered their goalscoring touch and netted four in each of the next three games.

By now, Cardiff were beginning to pull away from Rangers and although QPR lost only once in a run of 13 matches, they drew too many games and could not catch the Welshmen. Ironically, the last game of the season was at home to the

AAA sprint champion Macdonald Bailey puts Rangers players Fred Ramscar, Billy McEwan, Fred Durrant and George Smith through their paces at Loftus Road in January 1948.

champions, Cardiff City, who were now seven points clear. The match attracted Rangers' biggest attendance of the season, some 25,000, who saw Cardiff win another memorable game, 3-2.

So, despite never being out of the top three all season, Rangers finished second, nine points behind Cardiff and six in front of third-placed Bristol City. Ivor Powell and Reg Allen both missed only one game each, both through injury. The leading goalscorers were Johnny Pattison with 17 (12 League and five Cup), Cyril Hatton with 15 (12 League and three Cup) and Fred Durrant with 14, all scored in the League.

After the FA Cup had reverted to its regular format, the two-legged affair of the transitional season now abandoned, Rangers' Cup trail in 1946-47 began at home to non-League Poole Town. The Southern League side put up a good fight and earned a 2-2 draw, but in the replay Rangers' experience showed through and they won 6-0. In the second round, Rangers had to travel to fellow Third Division South club, Norwich City. The match, unusually played on a Thursday, ended 4-4. The replay, six days later at Loftus Road, finished in a 2-0 win for Rangers.

The third round paired them with First Division Middlesbrough, although Rangers did have home advantage, and the tie, played in front of a 22,000 crowd, ended in a 1-1 draw, Rangers thus having to replay for the third successive round. This time, though, QPR went out 3-1.

Although Rangers were financially solvent, it was difficult for them to ignore repeated offers for goalkeeper Reg Allen, especially when one club had offered £10,000, at that time a record for a 'keeper. Allen was looking to further his career and asked for a move, to which QPR reluctantly agreed. Then, as details of his transfer were being agreed, Allen changed his mind and, much to everybody's relief, decided to stay at the club.

In order to improve their squad for an assault on the Third Division South championship in 1947-48, Rangers made two costly signings. They paid their record fee of £2,000 for George Smith, the Brentford centre-half, and the same figure to Wolves for Fred Ramscar, who had first appeared for the club as a guest during the latter part of the war.

Rangers started the season with five straight wins, scoring 13 goals and conceding only one. Not surprisingly, they were top of the table and looked determined to stay there. In their next game, however, they dropped their first point of the season and slipped to second place behind Bournemouth, who had played more games.

Rangers returned to the top with four more successive wins, including a 4-1 victory at Aldershot, followed by another 4-1 win at home to Notts County. Their first defeat was a 2-0 reverse at home to Swindon Town and it was quickly followed by a 3-1 defeat at Swansea. By now, attendances were well over the 20,000 mark, bringing much welcome cash into the club. The first half of the season finished with five wins and a draw and at the halfway stage, Rangers had 35 points from 23 games.

At the turn of the year, QPR had enjoyed five-goal home victories, against Watford and Bristol Rovers. Then they made three successive draws and dropped to second place in the table, soon regaining top spot, however, with a run of eight games in which they lost only once.

By now, Rangers and Bournemouth had pulled away from the other clubs and when the sides met at Dean Court on 14 April, Bournemouth had to win to stand any chance of catching QPR. The match attracted a crowd of 25,495 with over 10,000 more locked out. The only goal of the game, scored 16 minutes from the end by Reg Durrant, meant that Rangers now needed only two points from their remaining five games to take the

Reg Allen saves from a Tottenham attack at White Hart Lane in October 1948. The other QPR player is George Powell.

title and the coveted promotion place. The following week, alas, nerves must have told on Rangers as they lost 5-2 at Norwich. But a goalless draw at home to Swansea ensured that the title belonged to Queen's Park Rangers, who thus won promotion for the first time in their history.

Attendances had increased dramatically during the season with over 450,000 people watching the home League games and a total attendance of over one million seeing Rangers in all games that season. This increased revenue enabled them to make a very important purchase, that of the freehold of the ground, together with the 39 houses adjoining in Ellerslie and Loftus Roads. The cost of £26,250 was met by the issue of shares which, due to the club's success, were fully taken up.

The mainstays of the team for the season were Ivor Powell (41 games) and George Smith (38 games). Leading scorers were Cyril Hatton (25), Danny Boxshall (13) and Fred Durrant (12). Various injuries were suffered during the season, the most severe being the double fracture of the leg and a broken nose sustained by Reg Dudley in the match against Bristol City in November. He missed the remainder of the season.

Due to their high League position the year before, Rangers received a bye into the third round of the FA Cup in 1947-48. They were drawn at non-League Gillingham, where the match, which ended in a 1-1 draw, attracted a record gate of 23,002 to Priestfield Stadium. The replay drew another large crowd, 28,000, to Loftus Road, where Rangers overcame the Southern League side 3-1.

Their reward was an attractive home tie against First Division Stoke City and so, for the third successive Saturday, Rangers were in Cup action. It must have been to their liking, for they outplayed the Potters to win 3-0, Cyril Hatton proving the match-winner with two goals.

The draw for the next round paired Rangers with Second Division Luton Town and in front of 30,000 at Loftus Road, QPR again showed their ability and won 3-1. They were now in the last eight and thoughts were on them reaching the semi-finals for the first time.

What they really wanted was a home draw and their prayers were answered when they came first out of the bag against First Division Derby County. A hard-fought match ended in a 1-1 draw, Rangers' goal being scored by Johnny Hartburn. The replay at the Baseball Ground was watched by a crowd of 31,588, who saw Derby score after only four minutes. Just as Rangers were playing themselves back into the game, Bill McEwan tore ligaments and limped badly for the rest of the game. Rangers then had more bad luck when Reg Allen, in saving a shot, broke a finger and had to leave the field. George Powell went in goal and was beaten within a minute for Derby's second goal.

As Rangers now had only nine men, Allen reappeared for the second half, playing on the right wing. Derby took full advantage of the weakened Rangers team and scored three more goals to win 5-0 and progress to the semi-finals, where they lost to Manchester United.

Before the start of the 1948-49 season, Rangers became the first British club to make an official trip to Turkey. The team left Northolt Airport on 19 May and arrived in Istanbul, following refuelling stops in Geneva and Athens. Rangers played four matches, all at the 22,000-capacity Istanbul Stadium. The first match on 22 May was against Fenerbahçe and ended in a 1-1 draw. The next game was won 1-0 against Galatasaray, the only goal coming from a Cyril Hatton penalty. On 29th May the third game of the trip was staged and this time the opponents were Beşiktaş. Rangers won comfortably, 5-2, but lost George Stewart with a broken leg. The final game, on the following day, was against the Turkish Olympic side and ended in Rangers' only defeat of the trip, the score being 2-1.

Dave Mangnall kept faith with the squad of players who had gained promotion and did not make any pre-season signings. This was compared to Lincoln City, the team promoted from the Northern Section, who spent around £40,000 on new players and were relegated at the end of the season.

The season started with three wins and a draw in the first four games, which meant that Rangers were soon on top of the Second Division. But they then had a poor run in which they went five games without a win, suffering two heavy, consecutive defeats, 4-1 at Grimsby and 5-0 at Fulham. In the match at Craven Cottage, Albert Smith was injured and did not play again that season. The next away game, at Tottenham, drew a massive crowd of 69,718, who saw Rangers lose by the only goal of the game and slip to 14th in the table. Up to Christmas they had mixed success with four wins, a draw and six defeats.

After the New Year, results did not improve and following a run of three straight defeats, Rangers dropped to 19th and looked likely candidates for relegation. Another blow was the loss of Cyril Hatton, who was injured at the beginning of January and missed the rest of the season. The defence then managed to go four games without conceding a goal and a run of five games unbeaten took Rangers up to 12th place and away from the relegation battle before the season finished with a 2-0 home win over Leeds United. QPR were 13th, although only four points above the relegation zone.

The tightness of the situation was evident when, having lost at home to Sheffield Wednesday after Easter, Rangers dropped five places. Due to the number of injuries they suffered QPR used 33 different players during the season. The only regulars were Reg Allen (40 games), Arthur Jefferson and George Powell (both 39). Leading goalscorer for the season was Bert Addinall, with only nine goals.

Now that they were in the Second Division, Rangers had entered the FA Cup in the third round for 1947-48. They were drawn at home to Huddersfield Town, who were near the bottom of the First Division, and in a poor match both defences had the upper hand. The closest thing to a goal was when Huddersfield's Glazzard saw his shot cleared off the line by George Powell. In the replay, Rangers' forwards were again well marked, but the home side were better organised up front and won 5-0, the score being kept down only by a sterling performance from Reg Allen.

Before the start of the 1949-50 season, George Smith left to join Ipswich Town and was replaced by Horace Woodward of Tottenham Hotspur, who cost a club record fee of £10,500. Other newcomers included Johnny McKay (Irvine) and Stan Gullan (Clyde). On the outgoing side were Johnny Hartburn (to Watford) and Doug Campbell (to Crewe Alexandra).

Rangers started with the first League goal of the new campaign, when Bill Pointon scored after only 25 seconds at Elland Road. Again Rangers had a good start to the season, with three wins and four draws in the first seven games, which put them into second place. The defence was playing well and they went five games without conceding a goal.

But then they hit a bad patch, going ten games without a win, a run which included four successive home defeats. By now Rangers were down to 20th in the table, dangerously close to the relegation places. Their winning touch returned against Bury at home, but a further four games before the next victory dropped them to bottom of the Second Division. The main problem seemed to be scoring goals, and from October to Christmas, in only three games did they find the net more than once.

The New Year saw another win, this time at Luton, but the next game ended in Rangers' biggest defeat of the season, 5-0 at home to Barnsley. Another poor run followed which again put Rangers bottom. Two successive wins at Plymouth and at home against Chesterfield lifted them back out of the bottom two and the win at Plymouth was to be hugely significant by the end of the season.

These two victories were followed by four straight defeats putting Rangers back in the relegation zone but they managed to finish third from bottom by virtue of two wins and a draw in their final four games, finishing only two points ahead of relegated Plymouth Argyle. With the exception of Reg Allen, Horace Woodward and Cyril Hatton, no players appeared in more than two-thirds of the 42 League games. Leading scorer was yet again Bert Addinall with 11 goals.

In the third round of the FA Cup, Rangers had been drawn at home to First Division Everton. They had the better of the opening quarter and might have scored, but for two goal-line clearances by the Everton full-backs. In the second half, Everton's stamina told and they went ahead after 51 minutes. Rangers pressed hard but with only 15 minutes to go, Reg Allen dropped a spinning cross into his own net.

A major change in the playing personnel took place during the 1950 close season when Reg Allen joined Manchester United for £11,000, then a record fee for a goalkeeper. Frank Neary also moved, to Millwall, and another departure was Arthur Jefferson, who had been at the club since 1936. He went to Aldershot on a free transfer. On the incoming side were Bill Waugh (Luton Town), Ernie Shepherd (Hull City), Lewis Clayton (Barnsley), Johnny Poppitt (Derby County), Robert Cameron (Port Glasgow) and Tony Ingham from Leeds United.

Tony Ingham, of course, went on to become the club's record appearance holder and over 40 years later is still associated with the club. Another change in 1950 was the appointment of former player Alex Farmer as head trainer.

The season started with a win and a draw in the first two home games before Rangers went down 6-2 at Leicester. They then held their own with two wins, two draws and two defeats in the next six games, and the following game, at home to Grimsby, resulted in Rangers' biggest Second Division victory, 7-1. Ernie Shepherd scored a hat-trick, with Bert Addinall and Cyril Hatton both netting twice.

Due to the poor performances of recent times, attendances had fallen to below 20,000, which was putting a strain on the club's finances. Rangers' away form was decidedly different to their home form: they lost eight successive away games between October and January, but lost only twice at home during the same period. There were two heavy consecutive away reverses, 7-0 at Barnsley and 5-1 at Hull City, but in four home wins, Rangers scored three goals, the majority by Cyril Hatton and Bert Addinall.

Tony Ingham's QPR career began on 25 November with a home game against Doncaster Rovers. It was not a good start as Rangers lost for only the second time at home that season and at the end of the first half of the season, they were 16th.

After Christmas, results averaged themselves out as QPR won, drew and lost the same number of games. The best period was a run of five unbeaten games, but otherwise there was no real consistency, although their League position remained constant at 17th from 20 January to 7 April.

In order to add punch up front, Rangers signed Conway Smith from Huddersfield just before the transfer deadline and he went on to score seven goals from nine games. QPR's home form had improved from the previous season and they recorded 13 wins and five draws from their 21 games at Loftus Road. Unfortunately, away results were nearly an exact mirror image with 14 defeats and five draws. Rangers finished 16th with 40 points. The only regulars were Des Farrow, with 39 appearances, and Bert Addinall with 38. Leading scorers were Bert Addinall with 19 goals and Cyril Hatton 16.

Rangers' third-round FA Cup opponents in 1950-51 were fellow Londoners, Millwall. Team selection was a problem for Dave Mangnall with several players being injured or not fit enough to play on the heavy ground. Amongst the missing players were Des Farrow, David Nelson and Tony Ingham and Millwall adapted better to the conditions before winning a close game 4-3. Rangers had tried too many short passes and wasted a number of good chances. Their only consolation was the revenue from a crowd of 25,777.

During the 1951 close season, Rangers were not heavily involved with the transfer market. Indeed, their only dealings were the signing of Harry Gilberg from Tottenham Hotspur and the selling of Reg Saphin to Watford and George Wardle to Darlington.

The season started with a 2-0 home win over West Ham United in front of a crowd of nearly 20,000. This was followed by three draws and a defeat in the next four games before another two home wins helped Rangers into eighth place, which as it turned out was to be their highest point of the season. The first-ever home League game with Everton, who had been relegated, provided the most exciting game of the season with

Queen's Park Rangers in September 1949. Back row (left to right): Dave Mangnall (manager), Woodward, Saphin, Allen, Sherwood, Reay. Second row: Parkinson, Dudley, A.Smith, Rose, Heath, G.Powell, M.Powell, Eggleton. Seated: McEwan, Duggan, Addinall, Ramscar, Pattison, Wardle, Hudson. Front row: Nicholas, Twiss, Pointon, Mackay, Woods.

a 4-4 draw, but the remainder of the first half of the campaign was disappointing with only one win in 13 games. Rangers slumped to 19th and were heading for the relegation zone. In order to boost the team, they signed Mike Tompkys from Fulham and Joe Spence from Portsmouth.

During December, Rangers were the team to watch if you wanted to see goals because 26 were scored in only five games. But only eight went in at the right end as far as QPR fans were concerned.

The New Year saw Rangers down in the relegation zone with only 17 points from 24 games. Indeed, they were so far adrift that three wins in their next four games moved them up only one place. Then, following only one point out of the next eight, they dropped to the bottom of the table, a position they never managed to improve on for the remainder of the season.

A rare success step a 4-2 home win over Sheffield United and a 2-1 win at Bramall Lane to complete the double over the Blades and it was ironic that once Rangers' relegation was confirmed, they won three of their last four games, ending the season with 34 points, level with the other relegated club, Coventry City, and only two points behind Barnsley and Swansea Town.

So, after four years in Division Two, Rangers were back in their more familiar surroundings of the Third Division South. In order to arrest the fall of the side, various players were tried throughout the season, which resulted in only Harry Gilberg and Conway Smith being regulars. Leading scorers were Smith with 13 and Bert Addinall with 12.

In the FA Cup, they were drawn away to Brentford, a tie that attracted a crowd of 35,000 to Griffin Park. They saw injury-hit Rangers lose 3-1 as many players were used out of position in an attempt to cover the missing men. Gilberg had moved back into the half-back line, Waugh changed from the left to the right wing and Smith moved from inside-left to right. Rangers' only goal came from one of the deputies, Ernie Shepherd, and this early exit meant that Rangers had never won an FA Cup tie whilst they were a Second Division side.

In an attempt to regain their higher status, Rangers appointed Jack Taylor to replace Dave Mangnall as manager. Taylor, aged 38, had previously played for Wolves, Hull City and Norwich City and had been a successful manager with the Dorset non-League side, Weymouth. Following relegation, Rangers did not have the finances to go into the transfer market in an attempt to get back into the Second Division, their only signing being Gordon Quinn, from local amateur side Eastcote.

Nobody left the club pre-season but just after the start, Bill Muir joined Torquay United and halfway through the season, Harry Gilberg signed for Brighton.

Life back in the Third Division did not start well for Rangers, who managed only three points, all draws, from their first five games. Initially, attendances were better than for the previous season, with over 23,000 at the first home match, but that level of support was not maintained and as attendances dropped to around the 10,000-mark, it all added to the club's financial problems.

Rangers' first win came in the home game against Walsall and was followed by another in the next match before two successive away defeats, 4-1 at Aldershot and 5-0 at Leyton Orient, saw them slide to 18th. In a bid to strengthen the side, Taylor signed George Mountford, a right winger from Stoke City, and after his arrival, Rangers had a run of six games without defeat and managed to get back to mid-table. But Bristol Rovers won both the Christmas games to halt the revival.

The New Year saw two defeats, a win and three successive draws, but the next game, at Swindon, gave Rangers only their second away win of the season. It was then another 11 games before they won again but in this period they had two high-scoring draws, 3-3 at home to Brighton and 4-4 at Bristol City. By now, Rangers were in 21st place, just above the re-election places, and if it had not been for three successive 1-0 victories towards the end of the season, they would have gone straight

Queen's Park Rangers centre-forward Bert Addinall appears to be putting a restraining hand on Everton's Harry Leyland at Loftus Road in October 1951, when the sides drew 4-4 in a Second Division match.

through from Second Division to re-election in one year. As it was, they finished 20th, equal on points with Gillingham and only three points above re-elected Shrewsbury Town. Again, a large number of players were used during the season, with only Harold Brown and Tony Ingham appearing in more than three-quarters of the League games. The leading scorer was again Conway Smith with 15 goals (13 League and two Cup).

After being relegated, Rangers had found themselves back in the first round of the FA Cup in 1952-53, where they were drawn at home to Shrewsbury Town who were then third from bottom of the Third Division South. As Rangers' only away win to date had been at Gay Meadow, they were confident of progressing and, indeed, were 2-0 up at half-time. But Shrewsbury fought back to score twice early in the second half to take the tie to a replay. The match the following Thursday also ended in a 2-2 draw, so Chesterfield still did not know who would be their opponents in the second round. The second replay at neutral Villa Park saw Rangers outplayed to lose 4-1. This meant that they had gone eight FA Cup games without a victory.

QPR were busy in the transfer market in the summer of 1953, signing Jim Taylor (Fulham), Bert Hawkins (West Ham), George Petchey (West Ham), Derek Barley (Arsenal), Willie Hurrell (Millwall) and Peter Fallon (Exeter City). Another signing who was to remain with the club for a long time was

Head tennis for this Rangers' training session in July 1953.

Peter Angell from Slough Town. The outgoing players included Horace Woodward (to Walsall), William Waugh (Bournemouth), Oscar Hold (March Town) and Bill Heath (Dover).

As in the 1920s, a change of kit — this time to white shirts and blue shorts — was made in an attempt to change the club's fortunes. Another innovation at Loftus Road was the installation of floodlights. The first in West London, they were officially turned on for a friendly against Arsenal on 5 October.

The season did not start as well as supporters had hoped. The first game, at home to Brighton, ended in a 2-1 defeat. The next, at Bristol City, was won 2-1, but Rangers did not have much success at home and lost the next three matches at Loftus Road and did not even manage a goal in any of them. A second away win, at Swindon Town, helped to keep Rangers off the bottom of the table. The first home win, 2-0 over Walsall, came in the eighth game of the season. This was followed by three successive draws, which pulled Rangers up to 15th place. Another win, again away, at Crystal Palace, followed. By now Rangers had only four wins, three of them away from home. In the remainder of the first of the season they managed only one more victory in a run of 11 games. The heaviest defeat of 5-0 coming on Christmas Day at Colchester United.

The New Year saw another away win, 4-1 at Aldershot with Petchey scoring a hat-trick. Rangers then went five games without scoring and dropped to 22nd in the table, only two points off the re-election places. In order to arrest the decline, two significant signings were made in February. They were Willie Clark, from Petershill, and Albert Pounder, from Charlton Athletic. Their arrival had a dramatic effect on results with the next two home games each resulting in 5-1 victories over Newport County and Torquay United. Rangers went on to win all their remaining home games for the season.

Their away form, though, was not so good with only two wins out of nine games. By the end of the season Rangers had crept up to 18th place with 42 points. The four clubs below them all finished on 40 points and Bournemouth and Swindon could not even be split by goal-average. The regular players for the season were Tony Ingham and Jim Taylor. The leading scorers were Conway Smith (12 goals) and Ròbert Cameron (10).

In order to raise some extra finance and get the players and spectators accustomed to floodlit football, Rangers played several friendlies under lights during the season. The visitors were Fenerbahçe from Turkey, neighbours Brentford, West Ham United, Chelsea, Charlton Athletic and a team from Amsterdam. Another bonus for the supporters was a friendly against Manchester United, which was part of the Reg Allen transfer deal.

In the first round of the FA Cup in 1953-54, Rangers had been drawn against Shrewsbury Town for the second successive season. Again they had home advantage and managed to break their Cup jinx with a 2-0 victory. The second-round draw paired them with Birmingham League side Nuneaton Borough, who had produced the shock of the first round by knocking out Watford, 3-0 at home.

It seemed that another shock was on the cards when Nuneaton scored first at Loftus Road and it was not until the last minute that Rangers equalised through a Tompkys goal. But in the replay at Nuneaton's Manor Park ground, Rangers won a close-fought match 2-1.

Rangers' luck held when they were drawn at home to Port Vale in the third round. Vale were top of the Third Division North, so QPR faced a difficult hurdle in their attempt to get to the fourth round for the first time since 1948. The match was played on a fast-thawing pitch which had been frozen solid for the previous three days. Rangers had the better of the first half, but Vale scored early in the second. With five minutes remaining, QPR missed a good opportunity to equalise and thus went out of the competition for another year.

In the close season of 1954, manager Jack Taylor made only a couple signings, both from non-League football when Tom Fidler came from Hounslow and Keith Rutter from Methley United. The players who left were Derek Barley (to Aldershot), Jim Taylor (Tunbridge Wells), Bert Hawkins (Cheltenham Town) and Johnny Poppitt (Chelmsford). Peter Fallon had to retire on medical advice due to an injury.

Rangers had one of their better starts for some time, winning three and drawing four of their first seven games, which took them to third place. By the halfway point, they were still in the top six with 26 points from 23 games.

The New Year brought mixed success but after winning only one of their last nine games, Rangers slid down the table to finish a disappointing 15th with 44 points. The main scorers were Conway Smith (18 goals), Willie Clark (15) and Bob Cameron (13).

Rangers' FA Cup trail in 1954-55 had ended almost before it had begun — and in sensational fashion, too. The first-round visitors to Loftus Road were Walthamstow Avenue of the Isthmian League. Rangers were mindful of the Avenue's exploits two years earlier, when they reached the fourth round, only going out to Manchester United after a 1-1 draw at Old Trafford.

Rangers had the better of the first half and went in leading 2-0 with goals from Fidler and Smith. But Walthamstow soon pulled a goal back and, thus inspired, they equalised through Len Julian's low shot. Only the efforts of both 'keepers prevented more goals.

The replay the following Thursday at Green Pond Road followed the pattern of the first game as Rangers again went in at half-time leading 2-0. Walthamstow scored midway through the second half and levelled the tie with three minutes remaining. There were no goals in extra-time and another replay was needed to see who would meet Darlington in the next round.

The third game was at neutral Highbury, kicking-off at 2 o'clock on a Monday afternoon. With injuries to both recognised 'keepers, Rangers had to field an untried lad in Alan Silver. There were no goals by half-time, but in the second half the amateurs adapted better to the heavy pitch, playing long balls in the air and not along the ground. The revised tactic paid handsome dividends and Walthamstow scored four times without reply to record Rangers' biggest defeat by a non-League side in the FA Cup.

Again many friendlies were played under lights, the visitors including Tottenham Hotspur, Stoke City, Hull City, Fulham and the Austrian sides, LASK of Linz, 1st Simmering Sportklub, and Columbia. Also at the end of the season there was a testimonial match for four of the club's long serving players, Tony Ingham, Ernie Shepherd, Stan Gullan and Lewis Clayton.

During the 1955 close season, Rangers signed Bill McKay (from Deal Town), Bill Nelson (West Ham), Mike Hellawell (Salts) and George Dawson (Motherwell). Outgoing players included Brian Nicholas (to Chelsea), Lewis Clayton (Bournemouth) and Joe Spence, who retired on medical advice.

Rangers started the season with two draws and a win but had to wait another eight games before they collected both points again. The next two home games both ended in victories to confirm Rangers' mid-table position but the main problem was their away form, with many of the defeats being heavy ones — 5-2 at Northampton, 4-1 to Colchester and 4-0 at Southampton. Together with worsening home performances, Rangers had a run of eight successive defeats, which took them to next-to-bottom of the table.

The first glimmer of hope came on Boxing Day at Aldershot, when QPR managed their first away win for a year, but they saw the New Year in on only 19 points from their 26 games and were in 21st place. The forwards were still finding the net, but the defence was hardly watertight and January and February saw only two wins and two draws from eight games. Again Rangers met heavy defeats — 4-1 at Ipswich and 5-1 at Southend.

QPR began March with a 7-1 hammering at Leyton Orient, although the next home game saw a temporary halt to the decline with a 6-2 win over Colchester United. By now Rangers were perilously close to the danger zone and three more successive defeats saw them fall to 20th, only three points off the re-election zone.

To compound the problem, Rangers had played more games than the teams around them. The next match, at home to Millwall, was going to be a key affair as the Lions were currently one of the teams in the re-election places, but Rangers pulled off a good 4-0 win to keep Millwall below them. One of their goals was scored by Tony Ingham, his first for the club.

By winning their last three games, Rangers managed to pull clear and finish in 18th place with 39 points, five above the re-elected clubs. Leading scorers were Conway Smith again (19 goals), Bob Cameron (13) and Willie Clark (11).

In the first round of the FA Cup, Rangers lost 2-0 at Southend, not an entirely unexpected result as Southend had won at Loftus Road earlier in the season.

Among the visitors for the floodlit friendlies were Fulham, Portsmouth and Rampla Juniors from Montevideo. A more unusual activity at Loftus Road in 1955-56 had been the staging of Rugby League matches. Three games were played with the idea of introducing Londoners to the northern-based game.

One success story of the season was the Reserves, who won the London Challenge Cup, beating Barnet, Millwall, and then Arsenal in the semi-final at Highbury. The Final was against Brentford at Griffin Park and despite having lost the toss for venue, Rangers triumphed to take the trophy for the third time.

Rangers were fairly active in the transfer market before the 1956-57 season began. Players signed included Cecil Andrews (Crystal Palace), Tommy Quigley (Portsmouth), Terry Peacock (Hull City) and Peter Lay (Nottingham Forest). The departures were Conway Smith, who joined Halifax Town, Harry Brown (to Plymouth Argyle), Willie Clark (Berwick Rangers) and Ernie Shepherd, who became player-manager of Hastings United.

The fixtures at the beginning of the season were unusual in that Rangers had to play two home and then two away for the first 14 games. They began with two away games — a defeat and a win — and then a win and a draw from their first two home games which put them sixth place in the first published table.

But having sold their main goalscorers, QPR struggled to find the net and in order to boost the forwards, Jesilimi Balogun, a Nigerian, was signed from non-League Skegness Town. He immediately made an impact by scoring on his debut against Watford.

Results were inconsistent, though, and by December, Rangers were halfway down the table with 23 points from 23 games. Due to some heavy defeats — like 5-1 at Coventry and 4-2 at Aldershot — they had a poor goal-average.

Better performances were achieved from Christmas with only one defeat in ten games. Included in that run were convincing wins of 5-3 at home to Exeter City and 4-2 at Watford. Rangers moved into fifth place but they could not sustain this form and won only one of the next eight games, sliding back to tenth. The season ended on a high note, though, with a 5-0 home win against lowly Gillingham, Arthur Longbottom scoring a hat-trick. Rangers eventually finished tenth with 47 points. Leading scorers were Arthur Longbottom with 15 goals and Mike Hellawell with eight.

In the 1956-57 FA Cup, Rangers faced Western League Dorchester at Loftus Road, where Mike Hellawell gave the home side a half-time lead. Les Locke added a second after the interval and late in the game, when the part-timers began to tire, Rangers scored twice more through Jesilimi Balogun and Robert Cameron.

In the second round they faced another non-League side, Tooting & Mitcham United of the Isthmian League, and nearly 11,500 fans crammed into their Sandy Lane Ground to see a spirited display from the amateurs. Balogun scored after 15 minutes to ease the pressure on Rangers and when Longbottom added a second after half-time, the outcome was decided. The draw for the third round did not do Rangers any favours as they faced a long trek to First Division Sunderland. The match, played in front of 30,500 people, went to form with the Wearsiders scoring four goals without reply.

League success in 1957-58 was of paramount importance to all clubs in the Third Division's Northern and Southern sections because the top 12 in each would form a non-regionalised Third Division with the bottom 12 making up a new Fourth Division. In an attempt to secure a top-half place, Rangers were busy in the transfer market. They signed Bill Finney (Birmingham City), Eddie Smith (Colchester United), Bert Allum (Brentford), Doug Orr (Hendon) and Bob Fry (Bath City). Mike Hellawell went to Birmingham as part of the Finney deal and also released were Tom Quigley (to Worcester City), Jesilimi Balogun

(Holbeach United) and Albert Pounder (Sittingbourne).

Rangers started with two 1-0 home wins, over Brentford and Colchester, but then lost the next two games, one 6-0 at Southend United. Another heavy defeat, 5-0 at Southampton, soon followed and QPR were in 21st place, a long way from their target position of 12th. Three wins on the trot helped, but that run was ended by defeat at Shrewsbury. The next two games were won, the first a tremendous 5-0 victory at Northampton, and by the end of November, Rangers had clawed their way to ninth place. Around Christmas there was a remarkable run of six successive 1-1 draws, three at home and three away.

The New Year saw Rangers just in the wrong half of the table, in 13th place with 28 points from 26 games, and so far their home form had been the only saving grace, for QPR had won eight and drawn one of their ten matches at Loftus Road. Their away form, in contrast, was causing concern with seven defeats in ten games away from The Bush.

January and February saw only two wins and Rangers slipped to 15th. Another spell of one win in six was not sufficent to get them up to the halfway mark but eventually they broke back into the top half with two successive home wins at the end of March. With four matches remaining they were 12th, two points above Crystal Palace, who they had to play twice.

The first meeting was at Selhurst Park, where Rangers won 3-2 to give themselves some breathing space. Three days later, when Rangers also won the return, 4-2, the pressure was off and all they had to do was to avoid heavy defeats in their last two games. They drew at Aldershot and beat Shrewsbury at home to ensure their Third Division place, finishing tenth, six points away from the Fourth Division cut-off line. The competition was very close that season and Rangers were in fact only eight points off second place.

Their defence was a model of consistency with Pat Woods, Tony Ingham, George Petchey, Keith Rutter and Peter Angell missing only three games between them. The leading scorers were Arthur Longbottom with 18 goals and Leslie Locke with 14.

Just before the transfer deadline day in March, Rangers had sold their promising goalkeeper Ron Springett to Sheffield Wednesday. His replacement was Ray Drinkwater, signed from Portsmouth.

In 1957-58, the first round of the FA Cup had pitted Rangers against non-League opposition in Clapton of East London. Due to the Isthmian side's small ground, the tie was played at Ilford FC, where a crowd of 8,000 witnessed a good cup tie with Rangers having the upper hand in the first half and taking the lead through Alec Dawson. Clapton played with much more confidence after the interval and equalised after 55 minutes with a goal from Ken Barnett. Despite being under pressure, Rangers held on for a replay.

That match was played two days later under lights at Loftus Road, where Rangers' experience told and they ran out 3-1 winners. Their next opponents were another non-League side, the fourth they had met in five ties. This time Rangers had to travel to meet Hereford United in a match which was decided by an injury to goalkeeper Ron Springett, who had to leave the field. He would normally have been replaced by Peter Angell, but he was not playing due to injury. So Pat Kerrins took over the green jersey. In an attempt to keep the ball away from him, Rangers tried an all-out attacking game with their ten men. It was a plan that failed miserably as Hereford equalled the biggest victory for a non-League side over a League side, of 6-1. Two years earlier, Midland League Boston United had inflicted a similar scoreline on Derby County at the Baseball Ground.

For the start of their new era in the non-regionalised Third Division, Queen's Park Rangers made a couple of new signings before the start of 1958-59. John Pearson came from Brentford and Clive Clark from Leeds United. Those to leave the club included Bill Finney (Crewe Alexandra), Ted Smith (Chelmsford), Terry Peacock (Sittingbourne) and Cecil Andrews (Sittingbourne).

The new structure meant that the bottom four clubs in the Third Division would be relegated to the Fourth and two would be promoted to the Second Division, as opposed to one from each of the Northern and Southern regional sections. With the onset of the 'national' Third Division, Rangers were now looking forward to meeting new opposition. However, as most clubs found out, the extra expense of long away trips did not help their financial position, due mainly to the loss of a number of local derby games which always brought in extra revenue.

The season started well with two draws and a win to put Rangers in sixth place, but then on their travels they did not fare well with three successive 2-0 defeats, at Tranmere, Bournemouth and Doncaster. Down to 19th place, they halted the run with two home wins and then a spell of ten matches, in which they only lost once, took them to fifth.

In those ten games, QPR scored two or more goals in eight of them with Arthur Longbottom netting hat-tricks at Stockport and at home to Halifax. But this good spell came to an end when Rangers lost three games on the trot and dropped back into the lower half of the table. In an attempt to halt the decline, Tommy Anderson, a winger from Bournemouth, was signed, but he left at the end of the season. Over Christmas, Rangers won two and lost two to end the year in 13th place.

The New Year started badly with five successive defeats in which QPR conceded 18 goals. They were now 20th and another signing, that of George Whitelaw, a centre-forward from Sunderland, was made to boost the forward line. This time the deal was successful and Rangers enjoyed seven wins in nine games, their biggest victory being 5-0 at home to Wrexham.

QPR were now just back in the top half of the table, in 11th place, but Wrexham gained revenge in the next game, beating Rangers 1-0. This was followed by another away defeat, at Brentford, and the season ended with two wins and a draw in the last four matches putting Rangers in 13th place with 46 points from 46 games. Leading scorer was Arthur Longbottom with 20 goals, followed by Mike Tompkys with eight.

In the FA Cup, Rangers had won a hard-fought match at Fourth Division Walsall, the only goal coming from Alec Dawson. The second round paired them with fellow Third Division rivals, Southampton, who although seven places above Rangers in the table, were only two points ahead. Rangers had two good early chances and were denied by Southampton's young goalkeeper Tony Godfrey. Rangers had more of the play but the Saints defended resolutely and scored the only goal late in the game, leaving Rangers to rue their missed chances.

Loftus Road was selected for an England v Scotland international match towards the end of the 1958-59 season — between English and Scottish taxi drivers!

Before the new season, Jack Taylor left to become manager of Leeds United and was replaced by a former Rangers player, Alec Stock. Since leaving Loftus Road just after the war, Stock had taken non-League Yeovil to the fifth round of the FA Cup, a run which included the famous win over Sunderland. Leyton Orient had gained promotion in Stock's first season in charge and he had most recently been assistant manager at AS Roma and Arsenal. Rangers, of course, were hoping for a successful period with Stock at the helm. They were not to be disappointed.

Stock's signings for the season were Bournemouth's Brian Bedford for a bargain at £750, Jimmy Andrews (from Leyton Orient), Jimmy Golding (Tonbridge) and Ken Whitfield (Brighton). He also signed two promising youngsters, Mike Keen and John Collins, on professional forms. Yet another new player was Joe Cini, a Maltese international from Floriana. Mike Pinner, the England amateur international goalkeeper joined Rangers, although he remained an amateur, and Stock released Tommy Anderson to Torquay, Stuart Richardson (Oldham Athletic), George Whitelaw (Halifax Town), Mike Powell (Yiewsley), Alec Dawson (Sittingbourne) and Robert Cameron, who followed Jack Taylor to Leeds.

The season started promisingly with three wins, a draw and a defeat and the defence was as stable as in the previous season, conceding goals in only one game out of the first five. After an away defeat at York, Rangers went seven matches before losing again, and in those seven games the defence was still the key to success, letting in only three goals. QPR had now climbed to the top of the table with 20 points from 14 games and their goal-average was impressive — 28 for and only eight against. Jimmy Golding made an impact by scoring five goals in his first four matches.

Rangers' tenure at the top was short-lived, however, and in

Brian Bedford, who cost £750 from Bournemouth in July 1959 and top-scored with 27 goals that season. In 1961-62, Bedford equalled George Goddard's record of 39 League and Cup goals. Bedford's tally included six hat-tricks.

only three weeks they dropped to ninth, a slide which continued with only two points from seven games. And following three more defeats around Christmas, they were down in 12th place by New Year.

The year 1959 began with two impressive wins, 3-2 at Newport County where Brian Bedford scored a hat-trick, and 5-1 at home to Accrington Stanley. Over the next six weeks, their home form continued to be good but away from Loftus Road, Rangers continued to struggle. Nevertheless, they were still sixth, nine points behind the leaders, before a home game against table-topping Southampton ended in QPR's second home defeat of the season. Their last nine games saw only two wins, the best being 5-0 at home to Bradford City, and by the end of the season Rangers were in eighth place with 49 points. Their home record had been good with 14 wins and seven draws. Alas, the away form did not come anywhere near to that with only four wins and 13 defeats. Leading scorer was Brian Bedford with 27 goals (25 League and two Cup).

Rangers' opponents in the first round of the FA Cup were fellow Third Division side Colchester United at Layer Road. They looked to have the match won after taking a three-goal lead, although Colchester hit back with two goals in the second half. In the second round, QPR had home advantage over Port Vale, a team they had played in the League the previous Saturday.

Rangers took a grip on the game with three good goals but Vale fought back in the second half — Rangers appeared to relax — and drew level. This meant a replay two days later at Vale Park. Once again Rangers took the lead and held their advantage up to half-time, but in the second half Vale came out in much more determined mood and scored twice to go through to the third round.

As Alec Stock was trying to build up his squad for the new season, Rangers were involved with the usual transfer activity during the summer of 1960. The new players included Peter Carey (Leyton Orient), Mike Bottoms (Harrow Town) and David Cockell (Hounslow). Leaving were George Petchey and Pat Kerrins, both of whom were transferred to Crystal Palace, and others not retained included Les Locke (to Guildford City), Walter Colgan, and Joe Cini.

For the new season Rangers reverted back to their more familiar colours of royal blue and white hoops with white shorts. The change did not bring immediate success, however, as Rangers lost their first two games, both away. Eventually, though, they moved from the bottom of the table to second place with three successive wins and also made another signing, that of Mark Lazarus from Leyton Orient for £3,000. Lazarus went on to become the only player to be bought and sold three times by the club, all in the space of seven years. He made an impact straight away by scoring the only goal of the game in his debut, at Colchester.

The side dropped to eighth place, then climbed back to third when another signing was made in order to boost the forwards. Bernard Evans was signed from Wrexham for £2,000 and his arrival could not have been made more dramatic. In his second game, on 3 December against Tranmere, Rangers recorded their highest-ever score of 9-2. Four players — Bedford, Clark, Lazarus and Evans — each scored twice. Two three-goal victories followed and Rangers were on the move at the halfway point of the season.

The good results continued into the New Year with their unbeaten run being extended to 11 games, in the last four of which they scored a total of 13 goals.

This well of success had taken Rangers to the top of the League, four points clear of second-placed Bury, who had a game in hand. And with this upturn in form, attendances increased with 14,500 watching the home win over Bury. Their unbeaten run ended with a 3-1 defeat at Grimsby before Rangers recovered to win their next three games to remain at the top.

A goalless draw at Southend United ended Rangers' hold on first place, but as the next home game was against bottom club Chesterfield, and Rangers had not lost at home all season, they were confident of regaining the lead. However, not for the first time and certainly not the last, QPR lost a game they should have won easily. Not only did they lose their unbeaten home record, they also allowed the teams below them to close the gap.

Rangers now had ten matches to go but in the next game they lost 1-0 at Bury, who were now top. The next two home games were won, but the following two away were lost and Rangers were out of the promotion places. They had two big wins in the run-in — 5-1 at home to Halifax and 6-1 at Torquay — but a 3-1 defeat at Reading meant that Rangers had lost the chance to gain promotion as Walsall were now three points ahead with only one game to go. That shock home defeat by Chesterfield had certainly cost Rangers vital points. Four players were ever-present: Peter Angell, Ray Drinkwater, Keith Rutter, and, for the fifth sucessive season, Tony Ingham. QPR's leading scorers for the season were Bedford with 37 (33 League and four Cup) and Evans with 16 (all League).

The 1960-61 season saw the introduction of a new cup competition for Football League clubs, due to be played in midweek under floodlights, although as some clubs still did not have floodlights they had to kick-off in the afternoon. Rangers' first opponents were Port Vale, the side who had knocked them out of the FA Cup the previous season. Another coincidence was that the two sides had again met in a League game immediately before the Cup tie. This time Port Vale went through with two goals in extra-time of a replay at Vale Park.

The draw for the first round of the FA Cup again paired Rangers with Walthamstow Avenue, then top of the Isthmian League. Rangers held on to win 3-2, all their goals coming from prolific scorer Brian Bedford. The next opponents were Coventry City, again at Loftus Road. In the League, QPR had already beaten Coventry at home and drawn at Highfield Road, so they were expecting to progress but Coventry won a disappointing game 2-1.

In an attempt to go one better in 1961-62, Rangers made some important signings. Players to arrive included Roy Bentley (from Fulham), Jim Towers (Brentford), George Francis (Brentford), Bill Williams (Portsmouth) and John McCelland (Lincoln City). The out going players included Arthur Longbottom to Port Vale and Clive Clark to West Brom for £17,500. During the season Mark Lazarus was sold to Wolves for £26,000 and re-signed five months later for £16,000.

Goals started flowing at both ends right from the start, Rangers' first seven games yielding 32. After ten matches they were in eighth place and the game against Bournemouth saw the end of Tony Ingham's remarkable sequence of 250 consecutive appearances. The goals kept coming with a 6-2 home win over Halifax Town, a 4-2 away win at Newport County and a 5-3 home victory against Southend. Brian Bedford was the main scorer with hat-tricks against Halifax and Southend. Two more draws and a two wins saw Rangers go up to fourth place. An away defeat at Bristol City ended the run but the goals soon returned as Rangers won three of their next four games, including a 6-0 hammering of Torquay.

At the turn of the year Rangers were fifth with 31 points from 24 games, having scored 62 goals. But the goals dried up in January and February, with only one being scored in each of the next six games and all but one match ending in defeat. Then Rangers scored three or more in each of their next eight games, the only point dropped being in a 3-3 draw at home to Peterborough. Bedford scored in every one of those games.

The result of this excellent run was that Rangers were back up to fourth in the table, only two points off a promotion spot — and they had two games in hand. But it was very close at the top and QPR dropped to sixth following a home defeat and an away draw at Bradford. Despite remaining unbeaten for the last seven games of the season, they were unable to close the gap on the leaders and finished fourth, three points behind promoted Grimsby. The goal scored by John McCelland in the 2-0 home win against Notts County was Rangers' 100th League goal of the season, the first time that they had passed the century mark. Leading scorers were Bedford with 39 (34 League and five Cup), Evans with 22 (18 League and four Cup) and Towers with 16 (15 League and one Cup).

In the first round of the League Cup, Rangers adapted well to the heavy conditions in a home tie with Crystal Palace, a game played in torrential rain. Once again they had met cup opponents in the previous League game and this time Rangers used the knowledge of their opponents, gained four days earlier, to good advantage. Brian Bedford opened the scoring and Peter Angell added a penalty to give Rangers a 2-0 lead at half-time. The second half saw more goals with George Francis scoring on his debut and Bedford getting another before Palace pulled two goals back. Francis ended a memorable debut by scoring the fifth in the last minute. The crowd of 10,565, was only bettered by three other ties.

The second round brought First Division Nottingham Forest to Loftus Road. John Collins made his debut as a replacement for the cup-tied McClelland but Nottingham Forest's extra experience showed through and they won an entertaining game by 2-1.

Rangers had started their 1961-62 FA Cup campaign in South Wales at Barry Town's Jenner Park, from where they were pleased to escape with a 1-1 draw, thanks to an own-goal ten seconds from time. The replay was a different affair when Rangers hammered in seven goals without reply. Bedford scored a hat-trick with Collins and Evans each getting two. Barry's only consolation was the £850 they received from their share of the gate money. The second round saw Rangers again on the road to a non-League side, this time to Ashford Town, where they won 3-0 in front of a capacity 5,000 crowd. In the third round Rangers had to travel again, to First Division Burnley. The Londoners held Burnley to one goal in the first half, but immediately from the restart, Collins was adjudged to have fouled Jimmy McIlroy and QPR went 2-0 down from the penalty-spot. Burnley stepped up a gear and scored four more, Rangers replying with a Bernard Evans goal late in the game.

The early season transfer activity in 1962-63 saw the signings of Frank Large (from Halifax Town), Frank Smith (Tottenham Hotspur), Andy Malcolm (Chelsea) and Jimmy Dugdale (Aston Villa). On the outgoing side were Jim Towers (Millwall), Michael Bottoms (Oxford United) and Rodney Slack (Cambridge United).

The previous season's success led the board to decide on a move back to the White City stadium for first-team matches, with the reserves and junior teams remaining at Loftus Road. The decision was supported by Alec Stock, who saw the fine

Action from the game against Bournemouth at the White City in March 1963.

stadium as an ideal stage for his team. The move was planned for the beginning of October, once the ground was fully prepared.

Rangers began the season full of confidence and opened with an unbeaten run of seven games consisting of five wins and two draws. Again the goals were flowing, with 14 being scored in only three games. Not surprisingly, Rangers were soon top of the table and looked to be the team to beat. That first defeat came at Selhurst Park, 1-0, and it was the first time in 34 League games that QPR had failed to score. This was followed two games later by the first home reverse, in what was the last match at Loftus Road before the move, and these set-backs put Rangers down to third in the table.

The first home game scheduled for the White City Stadium on 1 October was postponed due to heavy rain, so Rangers fans had to wait until the following Saturday to see their team in new surroundings. The return to the bigger stadium did not draw the larger crowds as expected and, as before, the ground looked empty even with around 10,000 people inside. Rangers' form did not improve either and they lost three games in succession. Performances improved with four victories in succession, Rangers scoring 14 goals in the process, and having been down to 11th place they were now back up to fifth. During December, they signed Stuart Leary from Charlton Athletic. Leary was an all-round sportsman and also played first-class cricket for Kent. Despite his presence, though, QPR ended the year with four consecutive draws.

The New Year started badly with three successive defeats, the worst being 5-0 at Swindon, but due to bad weather, Rangers played only one League game in January and two in February. An improvement in the climate was not matched by Rangers' performance and they lost twice more and dropped to 12th. Two good wins followed but this form was not maintained and Rangers saw out the remainder of the season in mid table, winning only one of their last ten games.

The main problem had been the defence, who were conceding at least two goals per game as Rangers finished 13th, only five points above relegated Bradford. Leading scorers were Bedford with 26 (23 League and three Cup) and Lazarus 19 goals (18 League and one Cup).

In the first round of the League Cup, Rangers met Second Division Preston North End at Loftus Road. Preston scored in the first half and held on to their advantage by getting a second after the break. Rangers pulled one back through Collins, but they could not get the equaliser.

The first round of the FA Cup had paired Rangers with a Welsh side for the second successive season. This time Newport County were their opponents at the White City, the first QPR game watched by the author of this book, incidentally. Rangers recovered from a 2-0 interval deficit to win 3-2 and in the second round they knocked out Southern League Hinckley Athletic 7-2, with Brian Bedford getting a hat-trick and three Rangers goals coming in the closing stages.

The third-round tie at Second Division Swansea was postponed several times because of heavy snow and the game was not played until three weeks after the original date. Rangers held the Swans in the first half, but conceded two goals early in the second and were unable to get through a well-organised defence.

After only ten months at the White City, QPR moved back to Loftus Road for the start of the 1963-64 season and before the campaign began, Tony Ingham announced his retirement after a record 548 senior appearances for the club. Other departures were Michael Barber to Notts County, Bill Williams (West Bromwich Albion), John McCelland (Portsmouth) and Frank Large (Northampton Town). Stock signed a number of players as replacements, including Dick Whittaker (Peterborough), brothers Ray and Pat Brady and Terry McQuade (Millwall), Derek Gibbs and Malcolm Graham (Leyton Orient). Goalkeeper Peter Springett, a promising apprentice and brother of Ron, signed professional forms.

Off the field, there was an attempt by businessman John Bloom to take control of the club. At the annual meeting in November, he lost a vote to unseat Bert Farmer from the board and, as it transpired, Rangers were right to reject him as shortly afterwards Bloom's washing machine company, Rolls, went into receivership.

The season started with a defeat followed by three wins but Rangers' form thereafter was mixed and after 14 games they were 11th. Results took a turn for the worse with four defeats taking them down to 18th before the bad run was checked with a 4-4 draw at Luton. The next home game, with leaders

Queen's Park Rangers line-up in 1961-62. Back row (left to right): Large, Drinkwater, Williams, F.Smith, Ingham. Middle row: Baker, Anderton, Keen, Rutter, Barber, Collins. Front row: McClelland, Bedford, Bentley, Evans, Towers, Lazarus.

Coventry, produced nine goals but Rangers scored only three of them. Then a home win over Oldham was followed by four defeats and at the halfway stage, QPR were 17th with only 22 points. The New Year started with yet another home game producing nine goals — and again Rangers lost, this time 5-4 to Southend. QPR then won only two games in a run of 12 and were stuck in 18th place.

In January, George McLeod was signed from Brentford with Mark Lazarus going in the opposite direction.

Three successive wins over Easter lifted Rangers up a couple of places, but with only three more wins before the end of the season they did not improve their position much. The forwards regained a bit of form and by the end of the season, Rangers had crept up to 15th place, still their worst position for eight years. Yet despite that they had a fairly settled side and used only 19 players all season. Leading scorers were Brian Bedford (25 goals) and Stuart Leary (14).

Rangers had to make a short trip to Aldershot for the first round of the League Cup in 1963-64. With several regular players out injured they gave a debut to Frank Sibley, who at the age of 15 years 274 days became the youngest player to represent the club in a first-team match. The weakened side were unable to hold the Fourth Division club and lost 3-1.

Visitors to Loftus Road for the first round of the FA Cup were Gillingham, who were setting the pace at the top of the Fourth Division. The first half was a close affair with each side scoring once. In the second, Rangers underlined their higher status to score three more goals without reply. A hard-fought second-round tie at Colchester ended with Stuart Leary scoring the only goal late in the second half.

In the third round Rangers faced the longest trip possible, at Carlisle United who were second in Division Four. Their chances were hampered when they lost Bedford with a heavy cold just before the game and they played below par, allowing Carlisle to score a goal in each half without reply.

Poor finances did not allow Alec Stock to sign any expensive players for 1964-65. The only incoming player was Billy McAdams from Brentford. Malcolm Graham, who joined Barnsley, was the only outgoing player. And before the season began, Rangers offered professional terms to several products of the excellent youth scheme including Bobby Nash, twins Ian and Roger Morgan, Tony Hazell, Ron Hunt, Mick Leach and George Jacks.

Another newcomer was a certain Jim Gregory, who joined the board in November 1964 after turning down an approach by First Division Fulham. Five months later Gregory was elected chairman of the club and the rest is, as they say, history.

Rangers started with two wins and two draws to go top of the table, but it was very tight and they dropped eight places when they lost the next game, 4-1 at Walsall, and another four places after losing 1-0 at home to Reading. Two draws and a heavy defeat in the return at Reading did not halt Rangers' slide down the table but they held their own with two wins, two defeats and a draw in their next five matches. Four wins in the next five moved them up only two places, the best victory being 7-1 at home to Luton, when Brian Bedford and Mike Keen both scored hat-tricks. But the next away game, at Peterborough, ended in a 6-1 defeat. The first half of the year finished with two defeats and two wins.

After Christmas, Rangers won three successive games to move up to 12th place and, as in previous years, they were the team to watch for goals — in a run of five games three of them contained five or more goals, the biggest score being an 8-1 defeat at Mansfield. With three successive defeats, Rangers were back to 16th place and again the end of the season was played out without any hope of promotion and, barring disasters, no chance of relegation. The final ten games produced only three wins. By the end of the season Rangers were in 14th place with 46 points. Leading goalscorers were, once again, Brian Bedford with 26 (23 League and three Cup) and Stuart Leary with 14 (13 League and one Cup).

In the first round of the League Cup, Rangers had the opportunity to gain revenge for the previous season's defeat by Aldershot. This time they had home advantage and won 5-2, Bedford and Collins each scoring twice. The next round saw Rangers travel to Third Division rivals, Reading, who had scored a League double over them within the previous fortnight. The game went to form, Reading winning 4-0.

Rangers' opponents in the first round of the FA Cup in 1964-65 were Bath City, the Southern League side managed by former QPR favourite Ivor Powell. Stuart Leary headed the first goal and when John Collins added a second, the tie was won. The second round paired Rangers with Peterborough United and although the match was at home, QPR must have been apprehensive as the week before they had lost 6-1 at London Road. The Posh soon established themselves and with 15 minutes to go they led 3-1 before Ray Brady and Brian Bedford scored in the last 12 minutes to earn a replay. The replay was another close affair. Rangers took the lead through Billy McAdams and held it until 20 seconds before the end when Peterborough equalised. QPR conceded another goal early in extra-time and went out of the Cup by two goals to one.

With chairman Jim Gregory's backing, Rangers were able to make some significant signings for 1965-66. The main arrivals were Les Allen (from Spurs for a club record fee of £20,000), Ian Watson (from Chelsea for £10,000), Keith Sanderson (from Plymouth Argyle for £5,000), Jim Langley (from Fulham for £2,000) and Alan Wilks (from Chelsea on a free transfer). Sanderson was still an amateur and had a full-time job at NCR in Marylebone Road. Nobody left for another club before the season kicked-off, although Peter Angell announced his retirement and in early September, prolific scorer Brian Bedford was transferred to Scunthorpe United for £3,750.

Following the big signings, hopes were high of a successful season but the first game, when all the new arrivals made their debuts, was a disaster with Rangers losing 6-1 at Griffin Park. Things did not get much better and in the first published tables, Rangers were in 18th place. Eventually they inched their way up to 12th place, but this was followed by two successive defeats. The end of October saw a turn for the better, though, and Rangers remained unbeaten for the rest of the year, winning six out of seven League games. Les Allen was the main scorer with nine in five games and in November, Mark Lazarus joined Rangers for the third time in his career.

Due to bad weather, both the Christmas games against Oldham Athletic were postponed but the New Year began in style with a 7-2 home win over York. The next home game also produced a big win, 6-2 against Swansea, and Rangers were now third behind Millwall and Hull City. They suffered their first defeat for 12 games at Mansfield, but recovered and were still in third place, although ten points adrift of the two clubs above them.

In March, Alec Stock made what was undoubtedly his best purchase for Queen's Park Rangers when he signed Rodney Marsh from Fulham for £15,000. Marsh's first home game was against Millwall, a match which Rangers had to win if they wanted to close up on the leaders. In less than four minutes, Marsh had scored his first goal for QPR who went on to win 6-1.

The next two matches were both won by 4-1 and Rangers were now seven points behind Hull with two games in hand. But then they hit a bad patch and won only two of their next ten games to rule themselves out of a chance of promotion. Eventually they recovered some pride with three successive wins to maintain third place, but they were still 12 points behind Millwall.

After 80 minutes of the game at Millwall on 2 October 1965, Frank Sibley became the first Rangers substitute, when he came on for John Collins. Leading scorer for the season was Les Allen with 33 (30 League and three Cup).

Rangers' first game in the 1965-66 League Cup was at home to fellow Third Division side Walsall. A dour match ended 1-1, Rangers' goal being scored by Walsall half-back Sissons, who turned the ball past his own 'keeper. The replay was more entertaining. Rangers took the lead through Roger Morgan and John Collins and then Walsall hit back to level the scores. Extra-time looked certain but Walsall scored with the last kick of the game to take the tie 3-2.

The 1965-66 FA Cup trail started at Colchester where Rangers had a goal disallowed in the first minute and then found themselves 3-1 down after half an hour, their goal coming from Collins. They fought back and pulled level midway through the second half with goals from Roger Morgan and Sanderson. Indeed, near the end Rangers thought that they had scored the winner but it was disallowed. The replay was much easier, though, and Rangers ran out 4-0 winners.

In the second round Southern League Guildford City were the visitors and were kept in the game by their goalkeeper Vasper before Rangers' experience told in the second half when they scored three goals without reply. Fortune favoured Rangers again in the third round when they were paired at home with Shrewsbury Town. With a home game against Third Division opposition, QPR were hoping to progress to the fourth round for the first time since 1948 but the game ended in a goalless draw. In the replay Rangers were to regret missed chances as Meredith scored the only goal of the game for Shrewsbury.

As Alec Stock had established a strong squad during the previous season, he did not enter the transfer market in the summer of 1966. The only departures were Bobby Nash, who moved to Exeter City, and Billy McAdams, who went to Barrow.

Interest in football was at its highest for many years following England's victory in the World Cup Final and Rangers fans were looking forward to another successful season. They were not to be disappointed, although the League campaign started badly with a home draw and an away defeat to put QPR into 20th place. The next two games, both at home, ended in victories with Marsh scoring his first Rangers hat-trick in the 4-0 win against Middlesbrough. An away draw was followed by two impressive wins, 6-0 at home to Doncaster Rovers and 7-1 at Mansfield, with another three goals from Marsh at Field Mill. The pattern was repeated with an away point and a 5-1 win, followed by a 4-2 victory over Grimsby Town and Swansea Town respectively. Rangers were now second and had scored 35 goals in only ten matches.

The unbeaten run was extended to 15 matches with three more wins and two draws, the 2-1 home win over Torquay United on 15 November taking Rangers to the top of the table. They were never displaced for the rest of the season, a run of 30 games, although having reached first place they lost the next game, 1-0 to Oldham Athletic at home. They remained unbeaten for the rest of the year, with four wins and two draws, and by the halfway point they had 35 points from 23 games and had scored 64 goals.

In the New Year, QPR consolidated their hold on the top by extending their unbeaten run to 20 matches — 13 wins and seven draws— and during February and March they played 11 games and conceded a goal in only two of them. Their biggest victories in that time were 4-0 at home to Bournemouth and Darlington and a 5-1 win at home to Scunthorpe United. After the Scunthorpe game, Rangers needed only two points from their remaining eight matches to clinch the title and so hopes were high of a celebratory drink or two on the way back from the game at Walsall, but the champagne had to be kept on ice as the Saddlers inflicted upon QPR only their third defeat of the season.

However, the next game, at Oldham Athletic, ended in a 1-0 win and the championship was Rangers'. The title-winning goal was scored by Alan Wilks, who had come in for Rodney Marsh after he was injured in the previous game. The Third Division trophy was presented by Len Shipman, president of the Football League, before the home game against Oxford United on 22 April, after which Rangers rewarded their fans with another win, this time 3-1.

Having lifted the title, QPR seemed to relax and won only one of their last five matches. They lost twice, at Bristol Rovers and at Oxford United in their last match as a Third Division side, and by the end of the season were a record 12 points ahead of second-placed Middlesbrough. For the second time in their history, Rangers had scored more than 100 goals in a League season, the century coming with Wilks' goal in a 1-1 draw at Swindon.

Not surprisingly, the team was a very settled side with ten players appearing in 40 or more of the 46 games. Leading goalscorers were Rodney Marsh with a club record 44 goals (30 League and 14 Cup), Mark Lazarus with 21 (16 League and five Cup) and Les Allen with 20 (16 League and four Cup).

For the 1966-67 League Cup, the two-legged Final was to be replaced by one match at Wembley, in order to heighten the status of the competition, and the clubs responded with only Liverpool and Everton refusing to enter.

Rangers' League Cup campaign started on 23 August 1966 with Sir Stanley Rous, president of FIFA, switching on the new floodlights at Loftus Road. He said that he hoped that this was the beginning of a bright new future for the club. Little did he know how prophetic those words were to become.

The lights must have been to Marsh's liking as he scored

Queen's Park Rangers line-up in 1966-67. Back row (left to right): Moughton, Hunt, Allen, I.Morgan. Sibley, Leach, Hazell, P.Springett, Sanderson, Langley, Collins. Front row: Watson, Marsh, Keen, R.Morgan, Lazarus.

four goals in the 5-0 first-round win over Colchester United, the other goal coming from Mark Lazarus. The draw for the second round took Rangers to the Recreation Ground to meet Aldershot of the Fourth Division and in a close match, Aldershot opened the scoring in the first half. Les Allen equalised before half-time and the 1-1 draw meant a replay at Loftus Road the following week. The winners of the tie had been drawn at home to the winners of the Bristol Rovers-Swansea Town match.

In the replay, Rangers took the lead through a Jim Langley penalty after 75 minutes and consolidated their position with a second goal from Rodney Marsh in the 81st minute. Rangers had now reached the third round for the first time in their history and their next opponents were Swansea, who by coincidence had visited Loftus Road four days earlier for a League game which Rangers won 4-2. Interest in the League Cup was increasing and a crowd of nearly 13,000 saw the Swansea tie.

The Welshman took the lead in the 32nd minute when Ivor Allchurch went around two defenders before firing the ball past Peter Springett. Rangers equalised in the 59th minute when a Tony Hazell shot was deflected past his own 'keeper by the Swansea centre-half Brian Purcell. A replay was looking likely but in the 89th minute, Rangers won a corner. Les Allen took it and Mike Keen headed the winner.

The draw for the fourth round gave Rangers a home tie over First Division Leicester City and the match attracted a crowd of 20,735, who saw an electrifying game. Leicester's side contained a number of current internationals like Gordon Banks, Derek Dougan and Peter Rodrigues. The opening goal was scored by Roger Morgan in the 21st minute. Dougan equalised within a minute and scored a second after 41 minutes, but Rangers came out fighting in the second half and equalised after 56 minutes when Les Allen's chipped shot hit the crossbar, came down and went in off Gordon Banks.

Rangers regained the lead a minute later when Sanderson released Lazarus down the wing and Les Allen scored from his cross. Three minutes later, Lazarus scored the fourth and Rangers held on to win 4-2 to progress to the last eight.

Their next opponents were Carlisle United, who were at the top of the Second Division, and again Rangers were favoured with a home draw. Another good crowd — 19,146 — saw Rangers again prove themselves capable in higher company. Rodney Marsh scored twice and Carlisle could manage only one goal, so QPR were through to the last four.

The draw for the two-legged semi-finals paired Rangers with Birmingham City whilst West Bromwich Albion met West Ham United, thus opening up the possibility of an all-West Midlands or an all-London Cup Final.

Rangers' first-leg game was at St Andrew's where a crowd of 34,295 saw First Division Birmingham take the lead through Barry Bridges after only four minutes. But Rangers were not overawed by their opponents and Rodney Marsh brought Rangers level in the second half. This was followed shortly afterwards by another goal, this time from Roger Morgan before Lazarus added a third to give Rangers a comfortable cushion. Even then they were not finished and Les Allen scored a fourth.

With a three-goal lead, Rangers were confident of becoming the first side from the Third Division to appear in a Wembley Final. The crowd of 24,604 for the second leg was Rangers' biggest home gate of the season and at half-time the match was still goalless, although of course, Rangers were still leading the tie by three goals. After 53 minutes, Marsh made it 5-1 on aggregate and then scored another before Birmingham got one back. But Mike Keen ended it with another goal to give Rangers a 3-1 win on the night and a 7-2 aggregate win. In the other semi-final, West Brom beat West Ham 6-2 on aggregate to reach the Final for the second year in succession.

The 1967 League Cup Final attracted a then competition

Above: **Rodney Marsh's famous equaliser in the 1967 League Cup Final against West Brom.** ***Below:*** **Marsh is congratulated by Mark Lazarus, Roger Morgan and Les Allen.**

record crowd of 97,952 to Wembley Stadium. Both sides had similar records in getting to the Final: West Brom had a goal tally of 21-6 and Rangers' was 23-7.

QPR started nervously and conceded a goal after only seven minutes. The scorer was the former Rangers player Clive Clark, who took a pass from Doug Fraser and shot from the left past Peter Springett.

Rangers fought back and thought that they had scored with a spectacular overhead kick from Rodney Marsh, but the referee disallowed it for offside. Then Rangers hearts sank still further when Albion increased their lead in the 36th minute after Clark beat the offside trap and ran in to fire the ball past a stranded Springett.

The First Division side exerted still more pressure and would have scored again through Jeff Astle, had it not been for a splendid save from Springett. So at half-time Rangers went in two goals down.

After the interval Albion still controlled play and as the game entered its last half-hour, Rangers were still two goals adrift. Then, after 63 minutes, Lazarus was fouled on the right-hand edge of the penalty area. Les Allen took the free-kick and Roger Morgan was able to get a header on target and past goalkeeper Shepherd to give QPR some hope. The crowd urged the Third Division side on and it must have inspired Marsh. With 75 minutes gone he collected the ball just inside the Albion half and managed to dribble his way through the defence to place a right-foot shot into the far corner of the goal for Rangers' equaliser. It was one of the best goals ever seen at Wembley and the Stadium resounded to the famous chant of 'Rodnee — Rodnee'.

Tony Brown then had a good chance to restore West Brom's lead but missed his shot and with only nine minutes remaining, Ron Hunt started a run with the ball from just inside his own half. He played a one-two with Lazarus and continued into the Albion penalty area. Shepherd, the West Bromwich goalkeeper, came out to smother the ball and collided with

Queen's Park Rangers parade the League Cup around Wembley Stadium after their sensational victory over West Brom.

Hunt. The ball ran loose to Lazarus who knocked it into the unguarded net. The Albion players were claiming a foul on the 'keeper but referee Walter Crossley adjudged that it had been a 50-50 challenge and awarded the goal to Rangers, who held on for those final nail-biting nine minutes to lift the trophy.

The unique three-handled cup was presented to Mike Keen by the The Lord Mayor of London, Sir Robert Bellinger. The only disappointment for Rangers was that as they were a Third Division side, they were not allowed to take their place in the following season's Fairs Cup competition. Their place was given to the losing Finalists West Bromwich Albion, as only First Division sides were nominated by the Football League.

In the first round of the 1966-67 FA Cup, Rangers were drawn at home to non-League Poole Town and opened the scoring through Marsh after 41 minutes. A nasty head injury caused debutant goalkeeper Mike Kelly to miss the second half and he was replaced between the posts by veteran defender Jim Langley. The loss of the 'keeper gave the Southern League side some hope but eventually Rangers went through 3-2 with Marsh completing his hat-trick.

The second round saw Rangers at home again, this time to fellow Third Division side, Bournemouth. After 23 minutes, Keith Sanderson was fouled in the penalty area and Jim Langley put Rangers ahead from the spot. Bournemouth fought hard and it was not until the 87th minute that Mark Lazarus scored to make the tie safe. In the third round Rangers travelled to Sheffield Wednesday for an intriguing match in which the goalkeepers were brothers — Peter Springett for Rangers and Ron Springett for Sheffield Wednesday. First Division class showed and the Owls won by 3-0. It was Rangers' first Cup defeat in ten games, not bad for a Third Division side.

Before the 1967-68 season started, Rangers were invited to play in the four-team Olive Tournament based in the town of Jaen, which boasted a Spanish Second Division club. The other sides were Malaga and AS Roma, Alec Stock's old side. QPR lost the first match 1-0 to the hosts Jaen and in the third-place play-off they met Malaga. Rodney Marsh scored first, but tiredness caught up with Rangers who eventually lost 5-1.

Alec Stock relied on practically the same squad for the club's return to the Second Division. The only player movements were the retirement of Jim Langley (who at the age of 38 years and 96 days was the oldest man to have appeared in the first team) and the arrival of Chelsea's Allan Harris as Langley's replacement. The other transfer was unique when goalkeeping brothers Ron and Peter Springett exchanged clubs, QPR and Sheffield Wednesday.

The other player missing at the start of the campaign was Rodney Marsh, who had broken a bone in his foot during pre-season training.

The season began with a draw at Portsmouth — Rangers' goal coming from Roger Morgan — and was followed by five successive wins which, not unnaturally, put QPR top of the Second Division. They lost the next game, 1-0 at home to Derby County, who were in their first season under Brian Clough,

Les Allen looks in need of some repair. He scored Queen's Park Rangers first-ever goal in Division One.

but recovered with two more wins before losing a derby at Crystal Palace by the only goal in a game which attracted 38,006 fans, the largest crowd to see Rangers that season.

With a sequence of two wins and two defeats, Rangers fell to fifth in the table, but the visit of Middlesbrough in November saw the comeback of Rodney Marsh, who scored QPR's goal in a 1-1 draw.

At the end of that month, Mark Lazarus left Loftus Road for the third time when he signed for Crystal Palace for £12,000, and at the halfway point of the season, Rangers were in second place with 28 points from 21 games. An unbeaten run took them back to the top, ahead of Portsmouth and Blackpool, but the good spell ended with a 4-0 defeat at Derby.

In order to boost their goalscoring and hold on to a promotion place, Rangers signed Frank Clarke from Shrewsbury Town for £34,000 and the next three games all ended in 1-1 draws, which allowed Ipswich and Blackpool to close the gap. When Blackpool visited Loftus Road, Rangers knew that they could not afford to lose as the Seasiders were now only a point behind in third place. As it was, Rangers won 2-0 with goals from Ian Morgan and Clarke to begin a run of four successive victories in which they did not concede a goal.

With six games remaining, Rangers had 49 points whilst Ipswich and Blackpool each had 46 points, although Ipswich had a game in hand. Rangers then began to wobble and when they lost 3-1 at Middlesbrough it allowed Ipswich to go to the top. Another away defeat the following week, at Cardiff, meant that Rangers were still in second place but now only one point ahead of Blackpool. Then a win and a draw — at top-placed Ipswich — meant that if Rangers won their last two games, then they would be promoted, probably on goal-average providing Blackpool did not win both of theirs by big margins.

The penultimate weekend of the season saw Rangers at home to Birmingham City, whilst Blackpool were at Derby. Both promotion-chasing sides won by two-goal margins, so the decision went to the last game of the season with Rangers now only 0.2381 of a goal ahead of Blackpool in the race for the First Division. QPR were away at Aston Villa, with Blackpool away at Huddersfield.

At half-time at Villa Park, Rangers were losing 1-0 and then learned that Blackpool were ahead at Huddersfield. Mick Leach equalised for QPR early in the second half, with a goal that was hotly disputed by the Villa players who claimed that the ball had not gone over the line after rebounding off the crossbar. As news came through that Blackpool were now 3-1 ahead, Rangers travelling fans were getting worried, but with eight minutes remaining, Rangers attacked again and in attempting to clear the ball, Villa full-back Keith Bradley turned it past his own goalkeeper to give QPR the lead. That was how the results stayed and Rangers were in the First Division for the first time in their history. The final table saw Ipswich Town on 59 points and Rangers and Blackpool on 58 points each, Rangers being promoted by 0.21 of a goal. They also became only the second side ever to go from the Third to First Division in successive seasons.

The main feature of the season for Rangers was their home form. They won 18, drew twice and lost only one, conceding only nine goals all season at Loftus Road. Four players, Allan Harris, Tony Hazell, Mike Keen and Ian Morgan, were ever-presents and the leading goalscorers were Rodney Marsh, with 14 goals, despite missing nearly half the season, and Ian Morgan and Mick Leach, both with ten. Leach had scored a goal in each of the last three games, which, of course, proved so vital.

Earlier in the season, Rangers, now a Second Division club and holders of the trophy, received a bye in the first round of the League Cup before beginning their defence at home to Second Division Hull City, whom they beat 2-1. In the third round at home to Oxford United, Rangers looked for revenge as Oxford had been the last Third Division side to beat them. They got off to a good start, Alan Wilks scoring in the first minute, and he went on to set a club record by netting all five in QPR's 5-1 win.

In the next round, against First Division Burnley, Rangers again had home advantage but although never really outclassed, they could not match Burnley's experience and went down 2-1, although Bobby Keetch was unlucky when his header in the final minutes went just over the bar.

Promotion to Division Two had also meant that Rangers entered the FA Cup in the third round in 1967-68 and after being drawn at home to Preston North End they were hopeful of reaching the fourth round for the first time in 20 years, having beaten Preston the previous week in the League. But Preston had learnt some lessons from that and won the Cup game 3-1, Rangers' goal coming from Mike Keen.

Before the start of the 1968-69 season, in his desire for Rangers to have a stadium worthy of their new First Division status, chairman Jim Gregory had discussions with Brentford with a view to merging the clubs. The new organization would use Brentford's Griffin Park as it had a capacity of 40,000, but fans of both clubs were against the move and after a few preliminary meetings, the idea was dropped. Gregory then put his efforts into turning Loftus Road into a stadium fit for top-level football and soon after the start of the season, a new stand, costing £210,000, was opened on the South Africa Road side of the ground. It was built on top of where the old earth bank and terracing used to stand.

Before the season started, however, manager Alec Stock resigned and was replaced, in a caretaker capacity, by Bill Dodgin. So despite having guided Rangers to the First Division, Stock never picked a side to play at the top level.

For their first campaign in the top flight, Rangers did not sign any players in the pre-season period, but soon after the start, former Chelsea centre-forward Barry Bridges was transferred from Birmingham City. The only departing player was Colin Moughton, who joined Colchester United.

Rangers' first game in Division One was at home to Leicester City, one of the sides they had beaten on the way to winning the League Cup some 18 months earlier, and a crowd of 21,494 packed into Loftus Road for the historic occasion. Again Marsh was missing through injury, his place being taken by Alan Wilks. Leicester went ahead and despite several chances, most of them falling to Wilks, Rangers had to wait until Les Allen came on as substitute before they drew level, Allen scoring the club's first goal in Division One.

QPR soon found life difficult in the top flight and their next two games both ended in defeats, 4-1 at Leeds and 3-1 at Wolverhampton. Two home draws followed and Rangers were already only one place off the bottom. Four straight defeats were followed by two draws before Rangers recorded their first victory in Division One, beating Ipswich Town, who had been promoted with them, 2-1 at Loftus Road. Another win followed and Rangers were 19th in the table. But they did not stay there for long as their next five games all ended in defeat.

Although the forwards were scoring goals — seven in three games at one stage — the defence was breached too often and at the beginning of November, Tommy Docherty was appointed manager in place of Dodgin, who had joined Fulham. Docherty, though, lasted only 28 days before being replaced by Les Allen, who became player-manager.

November also saw the return of Rodney Marsh, but his presence did not really improve results although another home win, 2-1 over Nottingham Forest quickly followed his reappearance. By the halfway point of the season, Rangers were bottom of the table with only 11 points from 21 games. The remaining four games of the year yielded only one point and on Boxing Day, Rangers went down 4-0 at home to West Brom.

The New Year did not bring any improvement. In January, Rangers sold Mike Keen to Luton Town and after two draws and three successive defeats they looked certainties for relegation. The other worrying factor was that the best players were being sold and at the beginning of February, Roger Morgan was sold to Tottenham Hotspur for £110,000. Ironically, Morgan's first game for Spurs was against Rangers at Loftus Road, when he lined up against his twin brother, Ian, for the first time. A competitive match ended 1-1, Tottenham's goal, scored by Greaves, being hotly disputed as Rangers claimed he handled the ball.

But if Rangers thought that their luck was out, they had further shocks to follows. The next nine matches were all lost and QPR's relegation was confirmed. The disastrous run included a 5-0 defeat at Coventry and Rangers' record defeat, 8-1 against Manchester United in QPR's first-ever visit to Old Trafford. During the home game against Liverpool at the end of March, a 16-year-old called Gerry Francis came on as substitute to make his debut.

After they were doomed, Rangers avoided defeat in their last three games but still finished the season with only 18 points, an all-time low for the First Division. In their 42 League matches they scored only 39 goals and conceded 95. And they gained only three points away from home all season. Ian Watson was ever-present in a side that was constantly being changed in an attempt to find a winning formula. The leading goalscorers were Mick Leach and Barry Bridges, both with a miserly eight goals.

As a First Division side, Rangers had been given a bye in the first round of the League Cup before being drawn at Fourth Division Peterborough United. QPR were now in the unaccustomed position of the giants for a cup tie and were hoping to put their poor League form behind them and gain some confidence from a cup run. But Peterborough completely outplayed them to win 4-2.

In the FA Cup, Rangers fared little better. Drawn at Aston Villa in the third round, they were forced to make six changes from the previous week's team, due to injuries. Goalkeeper Alan Spratley and youth player Alan Glover made their debuts and Rangers scored first through Ian Morgan, but then Villa, urged on by a crowd of nearly 40,000, took control and scored twice to put Rangers out of another cup.

Following relegation, Rangers went into the transfer market in the 1969 close season in an attempt to regain their First Division place. They signed Terry Venables for £70,000, a club record fee, from Tottenham Hotspur, and Clive Clark was re-signed from West Brom. Clark came as part-payment for the transfer of Alan Glover to The Hawthorns. Bobby Keetch had left the club to play for the South African side, Durban City, and Les Allen gave up playing to concentrate on managing the club. Despite several offers for Rodney Marsh, Rangers managed to hold on to their star player to underline their determination to win promotion.

Indeed, their season started promisingly with four wins and a draw in the first five games, the best victory being a 6-1

Queen's Park Rangers in 1969-70. Back row (left to right): Turpie, Collman, Lane, Finch, Busby, Evans, Sibley, Wilkes, Gillard. Middle row: T.Nixon, Hazell, R.Springett, Kelly, Spratley, Leach, McGovern, Francis, Clark. Front row: Clement, Bridges, Harris, Hunt, Metchick, Venables, Clarke, Marsh, Watson.

hammering of Blackpool, with Marsh scoring a hat-trick. Rangers lost the top spot following a 3-0 defeat at Birmingham City but four more consecutive wins put them back in first place. In order to strengthen the defence, Vic Mobley was signed from Sheffield Wednesday for £55,000, but Rangers slipped to third with a run of only two wins and three draws in seven games. They remained in second place after two successive victories, but then failed to win any of the next four and dropped to fifth place. At the end of November, Rangers scored four goals at Bolton Wanderers, but still lost when the Trotters hit six.

Mike Ferguson was signed from Aston Villa to add width to the forward line and at the midpoint of the season, Rangers had 27 points from 21 games. The year ended with two wins and two draws.

January did not see an improvement in Rangers' League position and they won only once in four games. They were briefly back to second place following two successive wins, 2-1 at Hull City and 4-0 at home to Norwich City, but their form then deserted them at a crucial time, coinciding with the sale of Frank Clarke to Ipswich Town.

With ten games to go, Rangers were only one point behind second-placed Cardiff City, but they won only once in those final games, 4-2 at home to Aston Villa, although the run-in did contain five consecutive draws. They dropped to ninth place by the end of the season, eight points behind promoted Blackpool. The only regular players during the season were Barry Bridges, Rodney Marsh and ever-present Tony Hazell. Leading goalscorers were Bridges with 24 (21 League and three Cup) and Marsh with 21 (12 League and nine Cup).

In the 1969-70 League Cup, Rangers were drawn away at Third Division Mansfield Town in the second round. Bridges scored after three minutes, only for Mansfield to equalise after 21 minutes. Early in the second half, Ian Watson scored with a long-range shot but Mansfield did not give up and deserved their 65th-minute equaliser. In the replay Rangers completely outplayed Mansfield and took the lead with a Venables penalty after 17 minutes, adding two more through Clement and Marsh before half-time. Clarke scored a fourth after the interval to clinch an easy win. In the third round, Rangers were home to another Third Division side, Tranmere Rovers. Mick Leach and Frank Clarke scored within 90 seconds of each other to give Rangers a half-time lead but the second half belonged to Rodney Marsh, who scored four times to give Rangers a 6-0 win. They had another home draw in the fourth round, this time against First Division Wolves. But it was Rangers who looked the First Division side and went in at half-time leading 3-0, the goals coming from Barry Bridges and Frank Clarke (two). Wolves fought back in the second half and pulled a goal back through Wilson, but it was not enough.

Rangers were now in the last eight for the first time since their victorious season of 1966-67 and in the fifth round the Rangers travelled to Maine Road where they were outclassed by Manchester City's international trio of Lee, Bell and Summerbee. At half-time City had scored three without reply and when they relaxed in the second half, the game died and Rangers' good cup run came to an end.

The third round of the FA Cup had seen Rangers at home to Northern Premier League side South Shields, a game which saw Marsh return to the side following a four-match suspension. The non-Leaguers were no match for Rangers and went on to lose 4-1 with Marsh marking his return by scoring twice.

QPR had now ended their FA Cup jinx by reaching the fourth round for the first time in 22 years and now they travelled across London to meet Charlton Athletic. The game did not start well for Rangers, who were two goals down after 23

Aston Villa goalkeeper John Dunn dives bravely at the feet of Queen's Park Rangers' Frank Clarke during the game at Loftus Road in February 1970.

minutes, but within 12 minutes they fought back to equalise through Marsh. After the interval, Marsh worked his way through the Charlton defence and looked like completing his hat-trick, but instead passed to Clarke, who side-footed the ball into the empty net for the winner.

In the fifth round, Rangers were at home to Derby County. They dominated the game but had to wait until the second half to take the lead with a Dave Mackay own-goal and move into the last eight of the competition, equalling their best-ever progress in the FA Cup. The sixth-round draw gave them another home tie, against neighbours Chelsea. The match attracted a ground record of 33,572 people and was one of the best seen at Loftus Road for many seasons. Chelsea proved too strong for QPR, the main destroyer being Peter Osgood, who scored a hat-trick. Rangers netted through a Venables penalty and a Bridges header, but Chelsea eventually went into the semi-finals with a 4-2 win.

There were many changes on the playing side for 1970-71 and by early season the following had left the club: Barry Bridges (to Millwall) for £40,000; Mike Kelly (Birmingham City); Keith Sanderson (Goole Town); Clive Clark (Preston North End); Dave Metchick (Arsenal); and Bobby Turpie (Peterborough United). Vic Mobley had to retire early in the season due to injury. Replacements were Frank Saul (from Southampton), Phil Parkes (from Walsall for a bargain £15,000) and Andy McCulloch (Walton & Hersham).

The season began badly for QPR with two defeats before things improved slightly with a draw and a win away from home. But Rangers were down in 18th place and not looking likely to go much higher. Indeed, the next five games produced only one win and the heaviest defeat was 6-2 at Middlesbrough, which dropped Rangers to 20th before they regained some form and won four out of their next five matches. The best scores were both achieved at home, 5-1 against Orient and 5-2 against Birmingham City. The Birmingham game saw Marsh score a hat-trick against his former teammate Mike Kelly.

By now, Rangers had climbed into ninth place, but just as quickly as that better form arrived, it evaporated and QPR went another nine games before winning again. After half the season they were 15th with only 17 points.

The New Year brought a change in the manager's office with coach Gordon Jago replacing Les Allen, who had joined Swindon Town. Jago's promotion coincided with a slight improvement in results as the defence went four games without conceding a goal and two home wins helped pull Rangers away from the teams below them. Early in the year, Allan Harris went to Plymouth Argyle for £5,000 and Barry Savage joined from Millwall.

But results did not improve with Rangers winning only one of their next seven games to drop to 17th place, only six points from a relegation spot. However, victory at Watford and two successive home wins lifted them back to 12th and away from immediate danger. Rangers had probably their best spell through to the end of the season when they lost only once in their last ten games to finish 11th with 43 points. Leading goalscorer was Rodney Marsh, whose 23 goals helped to save the season for Rangers. The next highest scorer was Terry Venables with 11, five of which were penalties.

Rangers' first opponents in the 1969-70 League Cup were top-of-the-table Cardiff City at Loftus Road. The match turned out to be an exhibition of all that was good about Rangers' style of football. They scored after seven minutes, through a Bridges header, and that was followed three minutes later by another from Saul. Marsh was beginning to dazzle the Cardiff defence and added a third goal. The fourth was a Venables penalty after Francis had been felled in the box after 30 minutes and that was how the score remained.

Their third-round opponents were neighbours Fulham with Rangers making the short journey to Craven Cottage. The return of Marsh to his former club attracted a crowd of 31,729, Fulham's biggest attendance for several years. The Cottagers had a half-time lead through Barrett whilst Rangers' best chance was a Venables free-kick after 63 minutes which Seymour in the Fulham goal just got a hand to. A minute later, Fulham scored again when a Barrett shot was deflected past Parkes by Halom.

In the third round of the FA Cup, Rangers were drawn at home to fellow Second Division side Swindon Town. The match was played on a cold, foggy day and on a frozen pitch, conditions which did not help to make for an entertaining game. There was no score at half-time, but after the interval, Swindon scored twice before Rangers pulled one back through a Marsh penalty. It was not enough and, yet again, QPR exited the competition at the first attempt.

During the 1971 close season, Jim Gregory let it be known that he was looking for buyers for the club, but no offers were forthcoming so Gregory remained in control. Gordon Jago made a couple of early-season signings in Terry Mancini from Orient for £25,000 and John O'Rourke from Coventry City for £60,000. He released Alan Wilks to Gillingham for £3,000.

Jago was trying to get the fans more involved with the club, he instigated an open day. It was a chance for the fans to meet the players, have their photographs taken with them and to get their autographs. The idea was something that Jago had seen when he was working in the United States.

QPR started the season with a fine three-goal victory over Sheffield Wednesday, which was followed by an even spell of two wins, two draws and two defeats in the next six games. A 3-0 win over Watford lifted them to third place. Another win, defeat and draw followed but the defence was playing well and Rangers then went four games without conceding a goal, a sequence ended by three successive 1-1 draws. Another 3-0 home win, this time over Bristol City took them back to third, where they stayed until the end of January.

On 10 November, Rodney Marsh became the second Rangers player to be capped at full England level whilst with the club. Marsh came on as substitute for the last ten minutes of the game against Switzerland at Wembley.

For Rangers the year ended with a run of five wins in six games, enabling them to hold on to third place, three points behind second-placed Millwall.

A sixth successive home win saw them climb to second, above Millwall on goal-average, but just as Rangers were in a good position to challenge for a promotion place, their form deserted them and they lost three games on the trot to drop out to sixth place and out of the race. At this point, Manchester City approached Rangers with a bid of £200,000 for Rodney Marsh. Although Marsh was financially secure at Loftus Road, he wanted to further his career with a move to a First Division club, so Rangers reluctantly agreed to sell him. His last game was the match at Bristol City on 4 March, exactly five years after Marsh shared in Rangers' Wembley triumph.

Frank Saul was another departure in March when he joined Millwall for £3,000. Rangers had 12 matches left and, ironically, having let Marsh go they remained unbeaten in that time, winning six and drawing six. The defence only conceded two goals in the run. By the end of the season, Rangers were fourth, two points behind promoted Birmingham City and three behind champions Norwich City. They were left to reflect on those three games prior to the departure of Marsh, who still finished as the club's leading scorer for the season with 20 goals. The next highest was John O'Rourke with nine.

In February, at short notice, Rangers had arranged a friendly match with West Brom as both sides were out of the FA Cup and did not have a match. In order to let people know about the game, Rangers became the first club to advertise on television. They used a photograph of Rodney Marsh with a voice-over giving details of the game. It must have worked as a larger than expected crowd of 7,087 turned up for the Friday night game.

In the second round of the 1971-72 League Cup, Rangers were drawn at home to Birmingham City in a rematch of the 1967 semi-final. QPR had the upper hand in the first half but were kept out by the Birmingham goalkeeper Dave Latchford. In the second half, 18-year-old Gerry Francis upstaged his 17-year-old namesake, Trevor, to score the first goal of the game with a diving header. After an hour, Marsh headed in a Saul corner to seal Rangers' victory. The next round saw Fourth Division Lincoln City visit Loftus Road and the match went with form with Ian Morgan scoring after 21 minutes. Although Lincoln equalised, Andy McCulloch added a second to give Rangers a half-time lead. Marsh made it 3-1 with a penalty before Lincoln scored again to bring the gap back to one goal. There was to be no cup shock, however, and the game was decided late on when Saul scored Rangers' fourth.

The fourth round draw also gave Rangers a home game against a side from a lower division, Bristol Rovers from the Third. Jarman gave the Eastville club a half-time lead which they held on to until five minutes before the end. Then Shepherd, the Bristol goalkeeper, was adjudged to have carried the ball outside the area and Marsh scored direct from the free-kick. In the replay at Eastville, however, Rangers lost to the only goal of the game, scored 12 minutes before the end by Allan.

Rangers met Fulham at Loftus Road in the third round of the FA Cup. In the first half, Phil Parkes was the busier of the two goalkeepers and was beaten by a dipping 25-yard shot from Conway. Rangers forced their way back into the game with a Mancini goal after 76 minutes and the tie went to a replay at Craven Cottage the following Tuesday evening. By not losing, Rangers had set a new club record of 21 home games — League and Cup — without defeat.

The replay was even more exciting than the first match. Again Fulham took the lead, this time through Cross after 20 minutes. Dave Clement equalised one minute into the second half to set up a thrilling climax to the game. But after 75 minutes, Cross scored his second to put Rangers out at the third-round stage for the sixth time in seven years.

As Rangers had gone so close to promotion the previous season manager Gordon Jago went into the transfer market in the summer of 1972 to buy the extra resources needed to go up. Jago made three significant signings: before the start of the season he signed the Republic of Ireland international Don Givens from Luton Town; in September, Stan Bowles arrived from Carlisle United for a record fee of £110,000 and was seen as the ideal replacement for Rodney Marsh; and in October, Dave Thomas, the Burnley winger, joined Rangers.

Another new feature was the building of the new Ellerslie Road Stand, which replaced the old tin-roofed structure, and with the development of that side of the ground, the club moved their administration offices and dressing-rooms to the South Africa Road Stand.

The season started a little disappointingly with only one win in the first five matches. However, Rangers were still unbeaten as all their other games had ended in draws, their only victory being a 4-2 home win over Sheffield Wednesday. The next game, at home to Nottingham Forest, saw the debut of Stan Bowles. He inspired Rangers to a 3-0 win, scoring the second goal. Two draws followed before Rangers lost for the first time that season when they were beaten 4-1 at Hull.

They were now tenth in the table and returned to their winning ways with five successive wins, with Givens and Bowles scoring the majority of their goals. This run took them to second in the table, one point behind leaders Burnley, but two defeats in the next four games, including their first home defeat of the season, saw them drop to third. The year ended with four wins, a draw and another defeat. In December, Manchester City visited Loftus Road for a testimonial match for Frank Sibley who had retired from football through injury.

The New Year saw Rangers back in second place, a position they maintained until the end of the season. January and February saw a run of six unbeaten games in which only one goal was conceded and the biggest victory was 5-0 at home to Swindon Town, when Bowles scored his first hat-trick for the club. Rangers extended their unbeaten run to 11 games with four more victories and a draw.

In four days they had two big home wins, 4-0 against Blackpool and 5-0 over Portsmouth and although the next game ended in a 2-0 defeat at Oxford, those goals were the only two conceded in the final ten games of the season.

With five games to go, Rangers assured themselves of promotion with a goalless draw at Cardiff. They now wanted to overtake leaders Burnley for the title but, despite winning their last four games, they were unable to catch the Turf Moor club, who finished one point ahead of QPR.

Rangers' last game of the season was at Sunderland, who had beaten Leeds United the previous Saturday to win the FA Cup. With promotion assured for Rangers, and Sunderland's FA Cup on display, the 43,265 crowd were expecting to see a friendly encounter. It was not to be as the referee had to take both sides off the pitch for ten minutes, for tempers to cool down. The Rokerites' tempers were not helped by Rangers winning 3-0 and Tony Hazell knocking the Cup off its table with one of his clearances.

The settled nature of the Rangers team towards the end of the season was shown by the fact that the same team played in all but two of the last 14 games, Delve replacing Bowles in these instances. Gerry Francis was the only ever-present, but four others only missed five games between them. The leading goalscorers were Don Givens with 26 (23 League and three Cup) and Bowles with 18 (17 League and one Cup).

The second-round draw of the 1972-73 League Cup paired Rangers with the side that they had beaten at Wembley five years earlier. QPR had to travel to The Hawthorns to meet West Brom, who were bottom of the First Division. Tony Brown scored a 27th-minute penalty to give Albion the lead but two minutes before half-time, Rangers equalised with a Don Givens shot. After 62 minutes, Albion scored again with an unfortunate own-goal. Dave Clement headed a Brown cross away, but it struck Ian Evans on the back of the head and looped back past Phil Parkes for what turned out to be the winner.

In the third round of the FA Cup, Rangers were drawn at home to non-League Barnet from North London. The Southern League side were outplayed in the first half, but a fine performance from their goalkeeper McCelland and some poor finishing by the Rangers forwards ensured that the match was still goalless at half-time. In the second half, Barnet became a little more adventurous and with ten minutes to go they nearly scored when Powell hit a post with a left-foot shot. With neither side managing a goal, the tie went to a replay at Underhill, where a crowd of 10,919 squeezed in to see if Barnet could go one better than the previous Saturday. But Rangers' experience eventually told and they scored three second-half goals without reply, through Leach after 68 minutes, Bowles five minutes later and a Mancini header near the end.

In the next round at Oxford. Rangers gave a very professional performance with two first-half goals, through Clement and Givens, and then defended resolutely in the second half when Oxford committed themselves to all-out attack.

QPR had to travel again in the fifth round, this time to First Division Derby County. Rangers soon found out what life in the First Division would be like when Kevin Hector scored a hat-trick within 13 first-half minutes. Derby went in at half-time with a four-goal lead and although in the second half Rangers were more organised, pulling a goal back through Leach after 53 minutes and making it 4-2 after 65 minutes through Givens, Derby ran out easy winners.

For their return to Division One in 1973-74, Rangers made only one signing, albeit a hugely experienced one in Frank McLintock, who had captained Arsenal to the League and FA Cup double in 1971. Certainly, Gordon Jago had a more experienced set of players than had Alec Stock in 1968 and he was confident of making an impact on the First Division. Of the players to leave Loftus Road, Ian Morgan joined Watford, Mike Ferguson went to Cambridge United and Alan Spratley signed for Swindon Town.

This season saw a change to the relegation and promotion between the First and Second Divisions. It was now three up and three down. Rangers' return to the top flight began with four draws and a defeat in their first five games, but the crowds were returning to Loftus Road and over 28,000 saw the game against West Ham. QPR's first win of the season came in the return at Upton Park, where Rangers won 3-2, with the winner coming from debutant Ron Abbott.

That victory put Rangers ninth, the highest they had ever been in the First Division, but they lost two out of their next five games. After winning 3-2 at Newcastle they later had a run of four successive wins, including their first home victory, 2-0 against Arsenal. It was the first time Rangers had beaten the Gunners for over 50 years. The 3-0 home win over Coventry in the 15th game gave Rangers 18 points, the sum total of the number they had gathered all season in their previous First Division campaign. The first half of the season ended with three draws followed by a defeat and a win. After 21 games, Rangers were sixth with 23 points.

New Year's Day saw a 3-0 home win over Manchester United in front of a crowd of 32,339 people. A game which was to be the last appearance by George Best for United. Rangers won their next game and followed it with two draws, which took them back to sixth before they suffered their first home defeat of the season when Norwich City won 2-1 at Loftus Road. The match was one of many played on a midweek afternoon due to the three-day week imposed by the Government during a strike by power workers which ruled out the use of floodlights. With a run of three wins and three draws, Rangers were up to fourth in the table but four defeats in the last six matches ended their hopes of a UEFA Cup place.

On 3 April, in Lisbon, Phil Parkes and Stan Bowles made their international debuts for England in the goalless draw against Portugal. Bowles kept his place for the next game, against Wales in Cardiff, where he scored one of the goals in a 2-0 win, thus becoming the first player to score for England whilst with Rangers.

Another ground record was set for the visit of champions Leeds United when 35,353 people watched Rangers lose a close game 1-0. QPR ended the season with a 1-1 draw at Arsenal to finish eighth with 43 points, their highest position ever in the Football League. Only 18 different players appeared during the season and the ever-presents were Stan Bowles, Don Givens and Phil Parkes. Leading goalscorers were again Bowles (with 23) and Givens (15). The average home attendance of nearly 23,000 was the best-ever for Rangers.

After the last League game of the season, Rangers played Crystal Palace in aid of the Ron Hunt Testimonial Fund. Ron was another player who had to retire from the game through a knee injury.

In the 1973-74 League Cup, QPR started with a home game against Tottenham Hotspur. Spurs had won the trophy for the past two seasons and were looking for a hat-trick of wins, but Don Givens put Rangers ahead in the 31st minute, from a pass from Terry Venables, and in the second half QPR played the better football and although unable to add to their tally they went through.

The third round brought Sheffield Wednesday to Loftus Road. The Owls' goalkeeper was the former Rangers player Peter Springett, who kept goal in the 1967 League Cup winning side, and neither he nor anyone else could have envisaged the result of this cup game. Cameron, the Wednesday full-back, scored an own-goal after only three minutes, trying to clear a Bowles cross. Ten minutes later, Francis scored a second for QPR but then Wednesday drew level with goals from Knighton and Prendergast. Mick Leach immediately restored Rangers' lead and at half-time they led 3-2.

The second half turned into a rout as Givens, Bowles, Leach and another own-goal increased Rangers' tally to seven. Givens scored his second and Rangers' eighth near the end to record the club's biggest-ever League Cup score of 8-2.

Giantkillers Plymouth Argyle of the Third Division were the visitors to Loftus Road for the next round. Plymouth had won at First Division Burnley in the previous round but Rangers were confident following their resounding win in round three. Plymouth attacked from the start, though, and Rangers managed to hold them until half-time, but the second half was a different story as the West Country side scored three goals without reply. The defeat ended Rangers' unbeaten home record of 24 matches.

Phil Parkes became the most expensive goalkeeper in the world when he moved from Queen's Park Rangers to West Ham for £565,000 in February 1979.

In the FA Cup, Rangers had been drawn away to neighbours Chelsea in the third round and a robust game was typified by the duel between Ron Harris and Stan Bowles. The match ended goalless and heavy rain saw the replay postponed at the last minute and rearranged for a week later. Chelsea were weakened by injuries and Rangers took full advantage with a non-stop attacking game. It was a surprise, then, that they scored only once, through Stan Bowles just after the hour mark.

The next round saw Rangers at home to Birmingham City. Mick Leach scored before half-time and when Don Givens netted a second after the break, Rangers were on their way to the fifth round where they met Coventry City in a typical cup tie. Both sides played attacking football, yet the only thing the game lacked was a goal. The replay the following Tuesday was just as exciting. Cross opened the scoring for Coventry in the first half, but before half-time Givens had equalised. The second half followed the same pattern with Cross giving Coventry the lead again, only for Thomas to level a couple of minutes later. The game looked certain for extra-time when, well into injury-time, QPR were awarded a free-kick just outside the area. Bowles ran up to take it and bent the ball around the wall and inside the post for the winning goal. There was not even time to restart the match.

Having reached the last eight, QPR were hoping for a home tie in their quest for their first ever semi-final place. The draw was kind to Rangers, giving them yet another home tie, this time against Leicester City, a match which attracted 34,078 to Loftus Road. Leicester's cause was not helped when Alan Birchenall had to cry off and was replaced by debutant Joe Waters. At half-time neither side had managed a goal, although Rangers came close when Bowles headed against the bar. But the second half belonged to Waters. He scored twice to kill off any hopes Rangers had of reaching the last four and it was Leicester who progressed to the semi-final.

Following their good form the previous season Rangers made only one new signing in the summer of 1974, when David Webb joined them from Chelsea. In September, Don Rogers was signed from Crystal Palace, in a deal which saw Terry Venables and Ian Evans go in the opposite direction.

The goals did not exactly rush in at the start of season as neither Rangers nor their opponents scored more than once in any of the first six games. QPR won only once — at Leeds — and drew three in that run. They had to wait until 5 October before winning their second match, 1-0 at home to Ipswich, by which time they were bottom of the table.

Also, at the beginning of October, Gordon Jago resigned as manager in order to join Tampa Bay Rowdies in the North American Soccer League. His replacement at Loftus Road was Dave Sexton, who had led Chelsea to victories in the FA and European Cup-winners' Cup. Jago's last act as manager was to sell one of the fans' favourite players, Terry Mancini, to Arsenal. The same month also saw the England debut of two more Rangers players. Gerry Francis started the match against Czechoslovakia at Wembley and Dave Thomas came on as a substitute.

Sexton's first home game in charge was against Liverpool on 19 October. Although Rangers lost, the new manager's influence was soon at work as they won four of the next five matches, to move up to 14th.

Having assessed his squad, Sexton moved into the transfer market, signing Don Shanks from Luton Town and Don Masson from Notts County for £300,000. The only player released was long-serving Tony Hazell who joined Millwall.

Rangers' good run came to an end with three straight defeats and after 21 games they were in 17th place with 17 points, having won only six of their games and being beaten ten times.

The year ended with four successive wins, including 2-1 victories at White Hart Lane and 3-0 at Stamford Bridge, but the next game, at home to Burnley, ended in yet another home defeat, the sixth so far. Rangers then remained unbeaten for six games, winning three and drawing three, which took them up to tenth, the highest they had been all season. Their best result was the 4-1 home win over the future champions Derby County and their hero that day was Don Givens with a hat-trick.

QPR's unbeaten run came to an end at Goodison Park when Everton won 2-1, but with two home wins at Easter, Rangers moved up to seventh before only one win in their final seven games dropped them back to 11th by the end of the season. Leading goalscorers were Don Givens 21 (17 League and four Cup) and Stan Bowles with 12 (ten League and two Cup).

In the 1974-75 League Cup second round, they had been drawn at home to Orient, who were near the bottom of the Second Division. The O's made most of the running and took the lead early in the second half with a goal from Phil Hoadley. It looked as though Rangers would be going out to their London rivals, but ten minutes before the end Francis scored the equaliser from a Busby cross. Orient claimed that he was offside but the referee ignored their protests and the goal stood.

The replay at Brisbane Road a week later was a much more comfortable affair for Rangers. Although there were no goals by half-time, they held the upper hand and after 55 minutes Gillard sent over a cross which Francis headed in. Two minutes later, Givens added a second from a Bowles pass and on the hour Bowles himself scored to make it 3-0.

In the third round they met Newcastle United at home. Rangers were wary as the Geordies had already won in the League at Loftus Road that season and, indeed, straight from the kick-off they went ahead through Malcolm Macdonald. John Tudor added a second in the eighth minute and when Macdonald scored a third before half-time, Rangers looked a beaten side. Macdonald completed his hat-trick three minutes into the second half and Rangers had suffered their biggest League Cup home defeat.

In the third round of the FA Cup, Rangers travelled to meet Third Division Southend United. Ian Gillard gave QPR a half-time lead with a 30-yard shot from a Bowles free-kick. They added to this soon after the break when Gerry Francis scored a second and then Rangers relaxed and a mistake by Leach let in Guthrie to score for Southend. A minute later, Cunningham scored the equaliser and Rangers were fighting to stay in the competition. The replay at Loftus Road saw Southend defending bravely and they kept Rangers out until the 70th minute when Don Givens scored with a header from Thomas's corner. Six minutes later Givens scored with another header, after the 'keeper had saved his initial shot, and Rangers went through 2-0.

In the fourth round QPR were at home to Notts County and due to Chelsea and Fulham also being at home, they switched to Friday night. The move seemed to suit Rangers, who totally outplayed Notts in a very one-sided match. They scored three times in the first half — through Thomas, a Bowles penalty after he had been brought down by the 'keeper, and Givens. The second half was an anticlimax as Rangers easily progressed into the last 16.

In the fifth round Dave Clement gave Rangers the lead at Upton Park, only for Holland to equalise before half-time. The second half saw West Ham step up a gear and they scored again through Robson. Despite their efforts, Rangers could not force a replay, so West Ham went into the sixth-round draw.

Towards the end of the season, Rangers played a cricket match at Loftus Road against a John Edrich XI in aid of the Mick Leach Testimonial Fund. Rangers had more representation in the England team in the Home International series. The game against Wales saw three Rangers players in the same England side for the first time as Ian Gillard joined Francis and Thomas in the starting line up. The next game against Scotland saw Francis score twice in England's 5-1 win.

Hopes were high for the 1975-76 season following the establishment of a strong squad of players. The only addition before the start was that of John Hollins from Chelsea. During their pre-season games, Rangers beat the West German champions Borussia Mönchengladbach 4-1 and the Portuguese champions Benfica 4-2.

The season could not have got off to a better start as Rangers won their opening game 2-0 against Liverpool in front of a crowd of 27,113. It was the first time that the Merseysiders had lost to QPR and the match saw Gerry Francis score what turned out to be BBC TV's 'Goal of the Season'. The first away game was just as spectacular when Rangers won 5-1 at champions Derby, with Bowles getting a hat-trick. The Rams were the third national champions that Rangers had beaten within a month.

In September, England manager Don Revie appointed Gerry Francis as the nation's captain, a great honour not only for Francis but also for the club. Three draws followed before a home win over Manchester United took Rangers up to third in the table. A 2-0 win over Leicester City in the next home game put them on top of the First Division for the first time in their history. After another win, at home to Newcastle United, Rangers lost their first match, 2-1 at Leeds United. They bounced straight back, though, with a 5-0 hammering of Everton, to complete a Merseyside double. Rangers were eventually knocked off the top by a 2-0 defeat at Burnley, but returned to pole position the following week with a 1-0 win over Sheffield United.

Three successive draws saw Rangers drop down to fourth place, but two home wins and two draws saw them back on top at the half point of the season. They had 28 points from their 21 games and had lost only twice.

The year ended badly with three away defeats in four games, the only success being on Boxing Day against Norwich City. Another away defeat, followed by a home win, kept Rangers in fifth place and their next game saw the start of one of the best periods in the club's history, for they gained 23 out of the next 24 points. They won 11 and drew once between 31 January and 10 April.

The run started with a 2-0 win at Villa Park and was followed by a 4-2 home win over Wolverhampton Wanderers. A 3-0 win at Tottenham Hotspur moved Rangers up to third and a week later they were second after a 2-0 home victory over Ipswich Town. The next two games, both away, saw a 1-0 win at Leicester City and the only point dropped with a 0-0 draw at Sheffield United.

At the end of March, Rangers transferred Don Rogers to Swindon Town in exchange for Peter Eastoe, but because they were in the championship race, Eastoe had to wait until the following season for his debut. Rangers reached the top of the table again with a resounding 4-1 win at home against Coventry City and two more away wins followed, 2-0 at Everton and 1-0 at Stoke City. QPR were now a point clear of Manchester United and two clear of Liverpool, but had played a game more. After the 1-0 home win over Manchester City, they had a 2-1 away win at Newcastle United and were still on top but could be caught if Manchester United and Liverpool won their games in hand.

By now, though, Rangers had guaranteed themselves a place in Europe. On 10 April, they won 4-2 at home to Middlesbrough, Liverpool drew at Aston Villa and Manchester United lost at Ipswich Town. This meant that Rangers were a point clear of Liverpool and had played the same number of games. So if Rangers won their three remaining games, they would be League champions, even if Liverpool won all theirs.

Rangers had one away game and two home games to come. On Easter Saturday they were at Norwich City and a large number of fans made the trip to East Anglia. The match was a very tense affair. Both sides scored once before half-time but disaster struck in the second half when Morris put Norwich ahead. Boyer scored a third and Don Givens got one for Rangers, but despite all the efforts, Rangers could not equalise. Their players and fans were even more disheartened when the news came through from Anfield that Liverpool had beaten Stoke City 5-2.

Rangers now had to win their two remaining home games and hope that Liverpool lost one of their two remaining away

Gerry Francis and delighted QPR fans after he opened the scoring against Liverpool at Loftus Road in August 1975. It turned out to be BBC TV's 'Goal of the Season'.

games. QPR beat Arsenal on Easter Monday, but Liverpool also won 3-0 at Manchester City. On the last Saturday of the season, Rangers were at home to Leeds United, but Liverpool were not playing due to international commitments. Rangers beat Leeds 2-0 in front of their largest attendance of the season, 31,002, and this meant that they had finished their games and were top of the First Division. Now they had to wait for ten days until Liverpool played at Wolves. The situation was if Liverpool won they would be champions and, if they lost, Rangers would be champions. As the goal-average was so close (Liverpool 63-30, Rangers 67-33) a 1-1 or 2-2 draw would also give the title to Liverpool, but a higher scoring draw would keep Rangers on top. The Wolves had their own incentive for winning as they needed two points to avoid being relegated if Birmingham City lost their match, on the same night.

At half-time, Wolves led through a John Richards goal. They held on until 13 minutes before for the end when Kevin Keegan equalised. When news came through that Birmingham had won so Wolves could not stay up, the fight went out of them and Liverpool scored twice more, through Toshack and Kennedy, to win 3-1 and take the title. Rangers were only 13 minutes away from the League title. A new club record of remaining unbeaten at home was set as QPR won 17 and drew four of the 21 games.

The goals were shared around evenly between Givens (13), Bowles and Francis (both 12) and Thomas (11).

With their increased success and recognition, Rangers had been able to play two prestigious friendlies early in the new year. In February, Red Star Belgrade were the visitors for Mick Leach's testimonial game. A month later, Dinamo Moscow also played at Loftus Road in a friendly. Rangers had two more internationals in the end-of-season Home International Championship when Dave Clement was selected for England and Don Masson for Scotland.

David Webb celebrates with a big cigar and a bottle of champagne at the end of QPR's magnificent 1975-76 season.

In the second round of the League Cup in 1975-76, Rangers were drawn away to Third Division Shrewsbury Town. Bates gave Shrewsbury the lead after eight minutes and they then had an appeal for a penalty turned down. At half-time Rangers were looking likely victims of a giantkilling, but they improved dramatically after the break and scored after 50 minutes through a Webb header from a Thomas corner. Masson added a second, from another Thomas corner and after 82 minutes, Thomas scored from a Masson pass. Three minutes from the end, Leach completed the scoring.

The next opponents were Charlton Athletic at Loftus Road. Powell scored in the first half to give Charlton a half-time lead and midway through the second half, Bowles equalised. In the replay the following week at The Valley, Charlton again caused problems for Rangers but in the second half, QPR went ahead through Thomas after 70 minutes. Masson and Bowles added further goals to give Rangers a 3-0 win.

The draw for the fourth round paired QPR with Newcastle United, the side that had knocked them out of the previous season's competition. Rangers scored first after eight minutes when Leach chipped the advancing 'keeper, but within a minute Burns had equalised. Six minutes later, Malcolm Macdonald gave Newcastle the lead and Nulty made the game safe for the Magpies with a third goal right on time.

In 1975-76, the FA Cup third-round draw brought Rangers up against Newcastle United yet again, the third cup tie between the sides in just over a year. Newcastle packed their defence with nine men for most of the game and although Bowles managed to hit the crossbar just before half-time, that was as close Rangers could get. They became more frustrated in the second half, as Newcastle were not prepared to attack and the game petered out into a goalless draw. The replay at St James' Park followed the same pattern with Rangers having most of the chances. They could have been three up in the first 17 minutes, but Francis and Masson both hit the woodwork before Newcastle scored the opening goal through Gowling before the break. Masson equalised early in the second half and when Rangers were awarded a penalty it looked as though they would take the lead, but Bowles missed with his spot-kick. This inspired Newcastle, who were also awarded a penalty. Craig converted it to give the Tynesiders a 2-1 win and a third successive cup victory over Rangers.

As the 1976-77 season dawned, Dave Sexton was happy with his squad and the only transfer activity concerned players who could not command a regular first-team place. John Beck went to Coventry City, Keith Pritchett to Brentford and Richard Teale to Fulham. And just after the season got under way, Martyn Busby joined Notts County. The only addition to the squad was Eddie Kelly from Arsenal.

This season there was a change in the League rules concerning the splitting of teams on equal points in the table and it was now decided to use goal-difference instead of goal-average to determine the highest placed side. Rangers did not start very well, with a 4-0 home defeat by Everton followed by another loss, 1-0 at West Ham United. Results then improved and QPR pulled away from the bottom of the table with a run of three wins and two draws. They were now ninth in the League but two defeats dropped them back to 14th. Their performances did not come anywhere near the quality of those at the end of the previous season and Rangers continued with mixed success.

Their next nine matches produced only six points, with two wins and two draws. The defeats were not particularly heavy but Rangers seemed to be unable to defend as well as before. The year ended with them in 18th place with 14 points, only one point off the relegation zone.

The New Year saw three wins and a draw lift QPR up two places, but a poor run of only one goal in five games dropped

Gerry Francis' second penalty in the UEFA Cup quarter-final first leg match against AEK Athens at Loftus Road in March 1977.

them back towards the 'drop zone'. Their next three games produced five points to put them in 15th place, but still far too close to the relegation positions for comfort. Four defeats in the next five games sent them down to 20th place and back into a relegation place. The table was very close with the bottom 11 clubs covered by only five points. Rangers' last four games were all against teams in the top half of the table but luckily for QPR their form returned and they won three and drew one in those final games. This meant that they ended the season in 14th place with 38 points, four away from the three relegation places.

Despite the inconsistent performances there were five players who missed a maximum of two games only. They were Ian Gillard, Don Givens, John Hollins, Don Masson and Phil Parkes. The joint leading goalscorers, with 19 goals each, were Stan Bowles (five League, three Cup and a British record of 11 in the UEFA Cup), and Don Givens (ten League, two Cup and seven in European games).

Of course, the real highlight of Rangers' season was the UEFA Cup and their first-ever European match was at home to the Norwegian side, SK Brann of Bergen. The game provided a good exhibition of European football with Rangers always looking the better side, although the first goal did not come until the 29th minute when Bowles got on the end of a Webb flick. Four minutes later, Bowles scored again and he completed his hat-trick in the 64th minute. Masson finished the evening off with a fourth with five minutes remaining. The second leg was a formality with Rangers scoring another seven goals, including a second European hat-trick for Bowles. The other scorers were Givens (two), Thomas and Webb.

The second round paired Rangers with Slovan Bratislava of Czechoslovakia, QPR having to travel first this time. They produced one of the best displays by an English team in Europe, mainly due to the skilful planning of Dave Sexton, and Bowles took his European tally to eight with two first-half goals. Slovan scored once before for the break to leave Rangers just in front at the interval, but the second half was the reverse of the first with Bratislava scoring twice to Rangers' once, the third Rangers goal being scored by Givens.

An entertaining match ended all-square at 3-3 and meant that the Czechs had to win the second leg because of Rangers' big tally of away goals. They came in attacking mood, but were no match for Rangers, who were certainly enjoying their first European season. Givens, with two goals in the 18th and 32nd minutes, and Bowles, with a goal before the break, gave Rangers a three-goal lead at half-time. Givens completed his hat-trick with a penalty and Clement scored a fifth. Slovan did manage two goals, but Rangers went through by an aggregate of 8-5.

The third-round saw Rangers facing the West German side 1.FC Cologne. The first leg was at Loftus Road, where Rangers scored twice in the first half through Givens and Webb. Their superb performance was capped with a fine goal from Bowles to give QPR a three-goal cushion for the return game. The main factor, though, was that they had not conceded an away goal. The second leg was played in front of a fanatical 41,000 crowd and when Masson scored a very important early goal, it meant that the Germans had to score five to go through. They managed three before half-time and Rangers were not helped by having Dave Clement sent off for punching a rival. Soon after the interval, Cologne scored again to make the scores level. Parkes then made three excellent saves to deny the Germans a winning goal and as the tie finished level at 4-4, Rangers went through on the away-goals rule.

They had now reached the last eight but had to wait nearly three months for the fourth round to be played. Their opponents were AEK Athens, who had to visit London first. Such was the interest in the game, and due to the fact that the Loftus

Road pitch was suffering from the poor weather, that Rangers wanted to play their home leg at Wembley Stadium on the Thursday, a day later than scheduled. As it was, they ended up at Loftus Road as the Greeks did not wish to delay the game for a day and insisted on playing on the Wednesday.

The AEK tactics were soon evident and it was not surprising that Rangers were awarded two penalties before half-time. Francis scored them both and with another Bowles goal, Rangers had a three-goal lead at half-time. They were unable to add to their tally in the second half, though.

QPR went to Athens, missing three key players — Thomas and Francis, who were injured in the previous League game and Clement, who was suspended. The Greeks attacked right from the start and soon scored. Two more goals followed and Rangers had to defend strongly to survive. They were unable to score a valuable away goal and the tie went to extra-time and then penalties. With the scores level after the first mandatory five kicks, the competition moved into the sudden-death phase. The Greeks went first and scored. The next Rangers kicker was David Webb, who missed and sent AEK through to the semi-final.

In the 1976-77 League Cup, Rangers met Second Division Cardiff City in the second round and, although they were away, QPR soon exerted their superiority with two first-half goals. The scorers were Bowles (32 minutes) and Thomas (37 minutes). Rangers extended their lead in the 63rd minute, with a goal from Clement, and Cardiff scored a consolation in the 87th minute.

The third-round draw paired Rangers with Third Division Bury at Loftus Road, where McLintock scored with a header in the first minute from a Masson free-kick. Seventeen minutes later, another Masson kick was headed in by Givens. Bury fought hard in the second half but could not manage a goal until the 89th minute.

The fourth round took Rangers across London to Upton Park in a match that did not start well for QPR, who lost Dave Thomas, having been fouled by Lampard in the first minute. Rangers did not let the loss affect them too much, though, and managed to score a goal in each half against a rugged West Ham defence. Their goals came from Bowles, after 37 minutes, and Clement, three minutes before the end.

The fifth round gave Rangers another London derby, this time at home to Arsenal. Both sides scored before half-time — Masson for Rangers and Stapleton for Arsenal — but the second half saw Rangers grab the initiative when Webb scored what proved to be the winner.

Rangers had now reached the last four of the League Cup for the second time in their history and now met Aston Villa in a two-legged semi-final, the first leg to be played at Loftus Road. The match was very even, with neither side getting a real opening, and finished goalless, which made Villa favourites to go through to the Final.

The second leg was one of the games of the season. Again, neither side could score in the first half but after the break Villa took the lead through Deehan. With only eight minutes remaining, Rangers were awarded a penalty. But Burridge saved Francis' spot-kick and it looked like the end for Rangers. Two minutes later, however, Francis atoned for the miss by scoring the equaliser and the game went to extra-time. Deehan put Villa back in front, only for substitute Eastoe to equalise again.

As away goals did not count double in the competition, a third game was required. Rangers won the toss for venue and chose Highbury. The replay attracted a crowd of 40,438, which took the total attendance for this semi-final tie to over 117,616. Rangers looked the more likely to score in the early stages but could not convert their chances and Villa fought back, Brian Little scoring twice before half-time. After the break he completed his hat-trick to kill off Rangers' hopes of reaching a second League Cup Final.

The third round FA Cup draw brought Shrewsbury Town to Loftus Road. The Shrews played well above their Third Division status and were holding Rangers at half-time. Indeed, they had four clear chances to take the lead but were foiled by excellent goalkeeping from Parkes.

After 51 minutes, Eastoe crossed to Bowles, who fired the ball into the net and QPR made the game safe 15 minutes later when Givens converted another Eastoe pass.

In the fourth round Rangers went to Manchester United, where a massive crowd of 57,422 packed Old Trafford on a very cold day. The pitch was frozen and was surprisingly passed fit by referee Ken Burns. The players struggled to keep their feet and the only goal of the game was scored by Lou Macari after Parkes had slipped and let go of the ball.

Before the 1977-78 season started, Rangers' manager Dave Sexton resigned and joined Manchester United. Sexton felt that he had achieved all he could with the resources available at Loftus Road. He was replaced by Frank Sibley, a former Rangers player, who now had to try to find a cohesion between the experienced players who had done so well over the previous two seasons and the inexperienced youth players who were breaking into the first-team squad. Sibley brought in Dave Needham (Notts County) and Brian Williams (Bury), and offered professional terms to Barry Wallace, Steve Perkins and Paul Goddard. Martyn Busby rejoined the club from Notts County, but players to leave included Tony Tagg (to Millwall), Eddie Kelly (to Leicester City) and Dave Thomas (to Everton).

The close-season changes had their unsettling effect on the side and Rangers began with two defeats — at home to Aston Villa and at Wolverhampton Wanderers — and a draw. Their first victory, by 3-0, came in the home game with Leicester City. Four successive draws followed, which put Rangers in 13th position in the table, and then they lost the next four matches, including a 5-1 home defeat by Everton.

In an attempt to improve results Sibley re-entered the transfer market and signed Leighton James (from Derby County), Paul McGee (from Toronto Blizzard) and Ernie Howe (from Fulham). Before the end of the year, other players had left including David Webb (to Leicester City), Don Masson (to Derby County) and, after only six months at the club, Dave Needham to (Nottingham Forest).

The additional changes to the personnel had some impact as Rangers managed two wins and a draw in their next three games. The second victory was a 2-0 home win over Liverpool, in front of a crowd of 25,625. Rangers had now pulled up from 19th place to 17th, still too close to the relegation places. They did not win again before the year end and had a sequence of three draws and six defeats, which dropped them into a relegation place with only 15 points from 24 games.

January saw only the fourth win of the season, a 2-1 victory at home against Norwich City, but with one defeat in the next five games they pulled out of the bottom three into 19th place before another two defeats and a draw put them back in the danger zone. Fortunately, their home form returned and three successive wins at Loftus Road, against Middlesbrough, Arsenal and Coventry City, again lifted Rangers up to 19th place. With the bottom two clubs, Newcastle United and Leicester City, now adrift of the rest of the League there was now just one relegation place to be avoided.

With five games to go, Rangers were one point behind West Ham United and Wolverhampton Wanderers, but did have matches in hand. A 3-0 win at Newcastle lifted them up to 17th place and one point now covered the four teams trying to avoid the drop. Two goalless draws at home kept Rangers ahead of the others and although they lost their last game, 3-1 at Chelsea, they managed to avoid relegation by one point.

Towards the end of the season, one of the club's longest serving players, Mick Leach, left to join the North American side Detroit Express. Leading goalscorer was Stan Bowles with only nine, followed by Eastoe and Givens with seven each.

In the 1977-78 League Cup, Rangers started with a second-round home tie against Fourth Division Bournemouth. Rangers scored in each half, through Givens and Eastoe, to meet Aston Villa, the side that had beaten them in the semi-finals in the previous season. Despite their poor League form, Rangers put up a good performance at Villa Park before losing to a hotly-disputed penalty, given in the 40th minute for a tackle by Givens on Villa centre-half Ken McNaught. Andy Gray scored from the spot and Villa held on to win 1-0.

In the FA Cup, Rangers' third-round opponents were non-League Wealdstone. Givens scored after seven minutes when Lightfoot, the Wealdstone goalkeeper, was slow in coming for a Hollins free-kick. The 'keeper made amends with several good saves before half-time, but after 50 minutes Bowles set up James for the second; and when Bowles himself scored with a penalty

QPR's Ron Abbott rises high above West Ham's Derek Hales during the 6-1 hammering of the Upton Park club in an FA Cup fourth-round replay at Loftus Road in January 1978.

after 63 minutes, the fight went out of the Southern Leaguers. The scoring was completed in the 70th minute when Ernie Howe netted his first goal for the club.

QPR's fourth-round match at Upton Park, a typical Cup tie, ended in a 1-1 draw. In the replay at Loftus Road the following Tuesday, Robson put the Hammers ahead after only four minutes. Givens levelled the scores before half-time, but no one could have foreseen what the second 45 minutes would bring. After 49 minutes, Shanks hit the post with a header and Hollins netted the rebound. Four minutes later, Abbott touched on a Hollins free-kick to Busby, who made it 3-1. Busby scored again with a header from James' cross and Bowles netted the fifth from the spot after Taylor had handled Gillard's cross. In the 82nd minute, James completed the scoring with a free-kick which bent around the five-man defensive wall. The 6-1 win for Rangers was West Ham's heaviest ever FA Cup defeat.

The fifth-round draw gave Rangers a home tie against

Nottingham Forest. QPR scored in the 19th minute, with a Busby header from a James corner, and it was not until the last minute that Martin O'Neill scored to earn Forest a replay. The game at the City Ground was just as close as the first one. Robertson gave Forest the lead, but Rangers scored before half-time through Shanks and the tie went to extra-time. In the first minute of the additional 30, Dave Clement was sent off for a second bookable offence, but again Rangers refused to give in and a second replay was required.

Rangers lost the toss for venue and had to return to Nottingham three days later, when O'Neill put Forest ahead in the third minute. He collided with Parkes, who needed four minutes' attention before he could recover. Again, Rangers had to defend strongly and their efforts paid off in the 64th minute when Bowles equalised after a mistake by Clark, the Forest full-back. Forest responded and regained the lead a minute later and sealed the match with a third goal ten minutes before the end.

During the 1978 close season, Frank Sibley resigned as manager and was replaced on a temporary basis by Alec Stock before, in August, a permanent appointment was made when Steve Burtenshaw became the new Rangers boss. Burtenshaw had been at the club previously as coach during Gordon Jago's days. His entry into the transfer market saw the arrival of Glenn Roeder (from Orient), Rachid Harkouk (from Crystal Palace) and Billy Hamilton (from Linfield). Clive Allen signed full-time professional forms after finishing his apprenticeship. The departures were Don Givens (to Birmingham City), Brian Williams (to Swindon Town) and Leighton James (to Burnley).

The season started disastrously with three defeats and a draw, and the 5-1 reverse at Arsenal put Rangers on the bottom of the table, an omen for the rest of the season. Their first win came at Middlesbrough and was followed the next Saturday by their first home win. The next four games produced one win, one draw and two defeats to move Rangers up into 13th place, which turned out to be their highest spot all season. With only two points from the next seven games, they looked precarious and athough not in a relegation place they were fast heading that way.

Due to bad weather Rangers saw the year out with three successive home games, in which they were hoping for a change of fortune. The first one ended in a 2-1 victory against Manchester City, with both goals coming from Billy Hamilton. An entertaining 2-2 draw on Boxing Day against Tottenham was followed by a bad 4-1 defeat at the hands of Leeds United. So at the halfway point of the season QPR were in 19th place with only 15 points from their 21 games.

The New Year started with three successive draws, followed by five straight defeats. The fixtures were not helping Rangers as they had seven home games, with only one away game, then eight away games with just one at home.

This poor showing meant that Rangers now had several approaches from other clubs regarding the availability of their better players. In February, West Ham offered a world record fee for a goalkeeper of £550,000 for Phil Parkes, which Rangers accepted. Also allowed to leave was Peter Eastoe who joined Everton.

The poor run ended at Stamford Bridge, where Rangers recorded only their second away win of the season. Chelsea's predicament was worse than Rangers as they were one of the two teams below them. The victory sequence was very short-lived, however, and with only one point from the next possible ten, Rangers were now in the relegation zone and falling away from the teams above them. They were four points behind Wolverhampton Wanderers and had played two games more. With their position looking ominous, Rangers gave a full debut to Clive Allen in the home game against Coventry City. He responded with a hat-trick in the 5-1 win.

Yet despite this fine win, Rangers could now not avoid the drop and chairman Jim Gregory sacked Burtenshaw and looked for a replacement who would return Rangers back to the First Division in the shortest possible time. His choice was a surprising one, he appointed Tommy Docherty again. Docherty's previous spell at Rangers was not a success and had lasted only 28 days. His reappointment was announced before the final home League game against Ipswich Town. And his arrival did not inspire his new team, who were beaten 4-0. Leading goalscorers were Busby, Eastoe and Goddard each with only six goals.

Rangers' opponents for the second round of the League Cup that season were Second Division Preston North End at Deepdale. Rangers scored first, thanks to an own-goal by Preston defender Baxter. However, Preston were level within seven minutes. Two minutes before half-time, Eastoe restored Rangers' lead with a 20-yard shot and they took control after the break and scored again through Eastoe.

The fourth round saw Swansea City, top of Division Three, visit Loftus Road. Rangers scored twice in the opening four minutes, through McGee and Eastoe, and Swansea, who were without Curtis and Charles, the heroes of their second-round win over Tottenham Hotspur, could not pull back from that position. The fifth-round draw again saw Rangers at home, this time to Leeds United. The first half was goalless but Rangers very nearly had a penalty. Referee Clive Thomas awarded a spot-kick to Rangers, three minutes before the break, when Currie appeared to handle an Eastoe cross. But following Leeds protests, he spoke to a linesman and changed his mind, giving a free-kick a foot outside the box instead. Leeds scored with Hawley's mishit shot two minutes after the interval and the fight went out of Rangers. Hankin scored a decisive second before the end to leave Rangers rueing their bad luck.

The third-round FA Cup draw gave Rangers a short trip across the borough to Craven Cottage to meet Fulham. The match was postponed on the scheduled Saturday and played the following Tuesday. Rangers' attitude highlighted their lack of confidence, whilst Fulham, who were fifth in the Second Division, had the more determined approach and it was not surprising when they scored first through Margerrison to take a half-time lead. A second goal from Davies killed off any Rangers' attempt at a revival and they went out at the first hurdle of the FA Cup for only the second time in seven years.

Due to Docherty's influence there was no exodus of players following relegation. In fact, his presence enabled Rangers to sign three key players for 1979-80: Chris Woods (from Nottingham Forest), Tony Currie (from Leeds United) and David McCreery (from Manchester United). Also signed were apprentices Dean Neal and Gary Waddock, along with Peter Davidson (from Berwick Rangers), Gary Micklewhite (from Manchester United) and Martyn Rogers (also from Manchester United). The departures saw the transfer of Gerry Francis to Crystal Palace and John Hollins to Arsenal.

Rangers' first game in the Second Division for six seasons ended in a 2-0 home win over Bristol Rovers, the goals coming from Goddard and Allen, a partnership that was to serve Rangers well in the coming seasons. The good start was not maintained, however, and QPR lost their next three games, including a 4-1 reverse at home to Leicester City. After four games, Rangers were in the Second Division relegation zone at 20th place.

Docherty re-entered the transfer market and signed Bob Hazell from Wolverhampton Wanderers, Steve Wicks (from Derby County) and Steve Burke (from Nottingham Forest). Paul McGee left the club and went to Preston North End.

Rangers' form now returned and they went seven games without defeat. The run included five wins and two draws, and the best results were 3-0 victories over Fulham, West Ham United and Cardiff City, all at home. Astonishingly, Rangers had moved up 18 places to second, although their unbeaten sequence ended at Roker Park with a 3-0 defeat by Sunderland. Rangers response was immediate with a 7-0 thrashing of Burnley at home the following week. The long-serving Burnley goalkeeper Alan Stephenson was injured and Billy O'Rourke made his debut. Although beaten seven times, he made some tremendous saves to keep the score to single-figures.

Four more unbeaten games followed and Rangers were on top of the table at the end of November. Docherty was not finished with the transfer market and before the year was out he had signed Gordon Hill (from Derby County) and sold Derek Richardson to Sheffield United, Peter Davidson back to Berwick Rangers, Billy Hamilton (to Burnley) and — the greatest surprise of all — the transfer of the fans' favourite Stan Bowles to Brian Clough's Nottingham Forest. The effect of all the ins and outs on the club was felt as Rangers never won a game in December.

Left: Stan Bowles, QPR's controversial but brilliant forward. _Right:_ The young Clive Allen was given his full debut and soon established himself as a consistent goalscorer.

At the halfway point of the season QPR had dropped back to seventh place with 25 points. The New Year started in the same way as the old one finished, with two more defeats to put Rangers in ninth place. Form improved with a run of ten matches in which Rangers only lost once and the best results were 3-0 wins at Preston North End and Burnley. One unusual feature of the three goals against Burnley was that both full-backs, Shanks and Gillard, scored. This good spell had Rangers back up to fourth place, only four points behind the leaders, Chelsea.

After an away defeat and a win, Rangers lost ground with a run of four successive draws which left them in sixth place with only two games remaining, still four points away from a promotion place. Despite getting those four points with two wins, Rangers still missed promotion by one place. The leading goalscorers were Clive Allen, with a remarkable 30, and Paul Goddard with 16. Allen showed his consistency in scoring as his haul did not include any hat-tricks.

The League Cup had changed its format in 1979-80 with the second round now a two-legged affair. The theory was that as the round was already seeded, the lower grade teams would be assured of a money-spinning home tie against a better side. The change made it very difficult for a giantkilling act as the 'giants' had a second opportunity in the event of a defeat in the first game.

Rangers' first opponents were Bradford City, who were second in Division Four at the time. The first leg at Loftus Road ended in a narrow 2-1 win for Rangers. McCreery had given them a half-time lead, only for Stainforth to equalise midway through the second half. But two minutes later, Neal restored Rangers' lead. The second leg saw Bradford attacking in an attempt to wipe out Rangers' one-goal advantage. With away goals counting double in the event of an aggregate draw, the Yorkshiremen knew that a 1-0 win would take them through. But Rangers' experience showed and they triumphed on the night with goals from Gillard and Roeder to win 4-1 on aggregate.

The third round gave Rangers a trip to Third Division Mansfield Town. The Stags held out for the first hour but two goals in a minute, from Bowles and Allen, ended their hopes. Currie added a third to give Rangers a comfortable 3-0 win. In the next round, Rangers were drawn at home to Wolverhampton Wanderers, who were just two places below QPR in the League. Rangers scored in the 39th minute when the Wolves 'keeper, Bradshaw, let Clive Allen's 25-yard free-kick go through his legs. The second half was evenly fought and it looked as though Rangers would progress into the next round as they still led after 90 minutes. But Hibbitt scored an injury-time equaliser to take the tie to a replay at Molineux. In the replay, Wolves scored after only eight minutes, through Carr, and held on to their lead until half-time. The second half saw an all-out assault on the Wolves goal by Rangers and they were very close to scoring on many occasions. The best chance fell to substitute Burke, whose shot was parried by Bradshaw for a corner. But it was Wolves who went through to the quarter-final by the only goal.

In the 1980 FA Cup, the third-round draw gave Rangers a home tie against long-time rivals, Watford. The game started well for QPR when Hazell scored his first goal for the club in the fifth minute. But he turned from hero to villain eight minutes later when he handled the ball in the area to give Watford a penalty, which Bolton converted. Watford took the lead after 29 minutes with a Rostron header, which Rangers claimed Hazell had headed clear before it crossed the line. The second half was disappointing for Rangers as they never seriously troubled the Watford defence.

During the 1980 close season, Rangers sold top scorer Clive Allen to Arsenal for a club record fee of £1,250,000. It was a strange move on Arsenal's part as Allen went on to Crystal Palace before he played a competitive match for the Gunners. Also to leave was Allen's striking partner Paul Goddard, who joined West Ham United. The other players to move away were Karl Elsey (to Newport County) and Mick Walsh (to FC Opporto). Docherty signed Tommy Langley (from Chelsea), Andy King (from Everton) and Barry Silkman (from Brentford). He also gave full-time professional terms to apprentices Wayne Fereday, Warren Neill, Mark O'Connor, Andy Pape, Dean Wilkins and Ian Stewart. The fans, though, were concerned that no reputable replacements had been signed for Goddard and Allen.

The 1980-81 season started with an away defeat at Oldham Athletic. For the first home game, Docherty gave Fereday his debut and he responded by scoring twice in the 4-0 win over Bristol Rovers. The glory was short-lived, though, as Rangers failed to win any of their next five games. The run was ended with another 4-0 victory over a Bristol team, this time City. But another defeat and a draw followed which put Rangers down to 18th place. Results did not improve and after 14 games QPR were in the Second Division relegation zone.

Without the fans' support and with such poor results, Tommy Docherty's reign as manager ended in November. He was replaced by former player Terry Venables, who had enjoyed managerial success at Crystal Palace. Venables immediately bought Simon Stainrod from Oldham Athletic and the new manager's arrival had a good effect on the side as they won three games in succession. After two defeats and a draw, Venables returned to his old club, Crystal Palace, to sign Terry Fenwick, Mike Flanagan, and John Burridge. He also gave professional forms to Ian Dawes. The year ended with two wins and a draw to put Rangers in 12th place after 24 games. The best win was the 3-0 home victory over top-of-the-table West Ham United on Boxing Day.

The New Year began with three wins and a draw to move Rangers up into eighth place. Results were then even with two wins, three draws and two defeats in the next seven games. In February, Venables again went into the transfer market and re-signed Gerry Francis from Crystal Palace, along with Tony Sealy, with Tommy Langley going in the opposite direction. Before the transfer deadline day in March, Chris Woods joined Norwich City. Rangers then suffered a bad reverse, losing 4-0 at Orient. Although this was followed by a 1-0 home win over Grimsby Town, QPR had a run of five games in which they scored only one goal. The last home game of the season, on 25 April 1981, was the last to be played on grass at Loftus Road for some time, as the club announced its intention to lay the first artificial surface in the Football League. The game, against Cambridge United, ended in a resounding 5-0 win, with two goals coming from debutant Ian Muir. At the end of the game, the fans were invited on to the pitch to take away lumps of grass as souvenirs. The season ended with an entertaining 3-3 draw at Shrewsbury Town, which left Rangers in eighth place in the table. The change in managership and the different styles of play was evident in the fact that 30 different players appeared during the season. The stalwarts were defenders Ian Gillard, Steve Wicks, Don Shanks and Glenn Roeder. The leading goalscorers were Tommy Langley with nine goals and Dean Neal with eight.

Rangers' opponents in the second round of the 1980-81 League Cup were Derby County. The first leg was at Loftus Road and Derby held the home side to a goalless draw in an uninspiring game. The second leg was a complete opposite and provided the fans with an exciting Cup tie. Despite both sides hitting the woodwork, neither could score before the 90 minutes were up and extra-time had to be played. Again no goals were forthcoming and the tie went to penalties. Wicks scored for Rangers and Steve Powell missed for Derby. Shanks, Roeder and Gillard all scored with theirs and Derby scored each time as well. So when Gordon Hill came up to take Rangers' fifth kick, he knew that if he scored, Rangers were through. He made no mistake and QPR became the first side to win a League Cup tie without scoring a goal in normal time.

The third-round draw gave Rangers another trip to the Midlands, this time to Meadow Lane to meet Notts County. The Magpies were third in the table at the time and their better form showed. Rangers managed to keep the score down to one goal, a penalty, before half-time. Ten minutes into the second half, Langley equalised to give Rangers some hope, but it simply inspired Notts County, who went on to score three more goals and run out easy winners by 4-1.

In the third round of the FA Cup that season, Rangers met London rivals Tottenham Hotspur at Loftus Road. The match was played at a hectic pace in a gale-force wind. The Tottenham defence seemed interested only in kicking the ball as far as they could and when Rangers were unable to break through, the match ended in goalless draw. The replay at White Hart Lane four days later was played in conditions more suitable for football. Rangers lost Flanagan after only six minutes with an injury and conceded two first-half goals to Crooks and Galvin. Immediately after the interval, Stainrod reduced the arrears with a header, but Glenn Hoddle added a third to make the game safe for Tottenham.

Rangers decision to install a plastic pitch for 1981-82, at a cost of £350,000, was not to the liking of the rest of the Football League. As QPR had pointed out, they had not broken any rules as the League regulations did not stipulate the surface a match had to be played on. The main factor behind the decision was that the ground could be hired out on non-match days to earn the club extra revenue. The main complaint from the players and fans was the high bounce the ball got when hitting the surface. Also, that it did not stop as on a grass pitch. This meant that different skills were required to play on the surface. During the season, more sand was put into the pitch which, although it helped, it did not reduce the bounce by much. Rangers had to allow each of their opponents a day's practice before each League game so that they could become acquainted with the new surface. Another innovation for the forthcoming season was the introduction of three points for a League win.

On the transfer front, Venables bought back Clive Allen from Crystal Palace, John Gregory (from Brighton) and Gary Bannister (from Sheffield Wednesday). He also gave professional forms to apprentices Graham Benstead and Alan McDonald. On the out-going side were David McCreery and Dean Neal, to North American side Tulsa Roughnecks, Don Shanks to Brighton and Steve Wicks to Crystal Palace.

The season started with a fine 3-1 away at Wrexham, but the main focus of attention was the first home game the following Tuesday against Luton Town. This was the first-ever Football League match on an artificial surface. Andy King scored the first 'artificial' goal for Rangers. But Luton spoiled the party with two goals to inflict a home defeat on QPR. Their first home win came in the next game when Newcastle United were beaten 3-0 nil. Rangers had difficulty in adapting to a different surface each week as they won their home games and lost the away ones for the next seven matches. They were now in seventh place and hoping to improve their away form to make a challenge for promotion.

They gained only their third away point of the season so far, with a 1-1 draw at Orient, and the next two games, one at home and one away, both ended in wins to move Rangers up to third place. The next home game ended in 1-1 draw against Rotherham United, the first goal conceded at home by Rangers for six matches.

In September, Rangers sold Andy King to West Bromwich Albion and Barry Silkman to Orient. The remainder of the year was fairly even with three wins, two draws and three defeats in the eight games. The New Year saw Rangers in fourth place with 34 points from their 21 games.

Poor weather and their involvement in Cup ties restricted Rangers to only two League games in January, both of which ended in draws. February saw three wins and two defeats. At the end of February, Gerry Francis left to join Crystal Palace and Steve Wicks came in the opposite direction. Two more away reverses dropped Rangers down to ninth place and they were starting to lose touch with the leading clubs. Three successive home wins resulted in a move two places up the table, the best win being 4-0 over Charlton Athletic.

Due to the fixture congestion, Rangers had to play twice a week and although they initially had some good wins, including a 7-1 home victory against Bolton Wanderers, the effects began to tell and they ended the season with two away defeats. In the last away game, at Luton Town, Glenn Roeder was sent off, a decision that was to have a sorry outcome at the end of May.

Rangers finished the season in fifth place, two points behind promoted Norwich City. The leading goalscorer was Simon Stainrod with 24 goals (17 League and seven Cup) and Mike Flanagan with 12 (ten League and two Cup).

Amongst the events staged on the artificial surface during the year were a Rugby sevens tournament, an international hockey tournament and the Woman's FA Cup Final. During the bad weather in January, two non-League sides, Barnet and Hendon, both used the ground, on the same day, to play their games.

Rangers were drawn at home, against Portsmouth, in the first leg of the second round of the 1981-82 League Cup, which was eventually sponsored for the first time this season as the Milk Cup. Complaints were made from other teams that Rangers had an unfair advantage in playing one-off Cup ties on their surface, but the League refused to order them to play their games away from home. The match against Portsmouth showed the opposition's fear of the pitch and Rangers won easily by 5-0. The return leg at Fratton Park was put out of Pompey's reach immediately with a second-minute goal from Flanagan. Portsmouth replied with goals from Rafferty and a Doyle penalty. Waddock was sent off in the 53rd minute for a bad tackle, but Micklewhite equalised again for Rangers to take them through by seven goals to two.

The third-round draw brought Third Division Bristol City to Loftus Road. Rangers scored through Flanagan and Stainrod before half-time. Allen added a third three minutes into the second half to complete the scoring. The fourth round saw Rangers travelling to Watford, with the sceptics looking forward to Rangers failing away from their plastic pitch. They held the Watford front-line to just one goal before half-time, but an injury to Hazell, who had marked Blisset out of the game, swung the tie in favour of the home side. They took advantage and scored three more goals through Armstrong, Blissett and Taylor. Stainrod did get one back, with a penalty, but Rangers crashed out 4-1.

It was the FA Cup, however, which brought Queen's Park Rangers most joy in 1981-82. Their third-round opponents were Middlesbrough and as Rangers were at home they were confident of the game going ahead as scheduled, despite the countrywide freeze at the time. The Loftus Road pitch was in perfect condition and led to an entertaining game. Rangers

Left: **Simon Stainrod, signed from Oldham Athletic in November 1980 for £270,000.** ***Right:*** **John Gregory, joined Rangers from Brighton in June 1981, for £275,000.**

bought in Peter Hucker, for Burridge, in goal, a position young Hucker never gave up for the remainder of the historic season.

Thompson gave 'Boro the lead in the first half and, try as they could, Rangers did not score before the break. The second half was all Rangers, though, with Jim Platt in the 'Boro goal being outstanding. He was finally beaten in the 70th minute by a Stainrod shot after the QPR player had weaved his way around a static defence. With no further scoring, the tie went to a replay at Ayresome Park.

After numerous attempts to play the game, it finally took place the Monday before the next round was due to be played. Rangers played good football and scored twice, both from Stainrod, before the break. After the interval, Middlesbrough pulled one back through Otto and equalised two minutes later with a twice-taken Thompson penalty. No more goals came before the 90 minutes were up and extra-time was needed. The match was taking its toll on the older players and Warren Neill came on for Tony Currie after ten minutes of extra-time. With the minutes running out and no goals forthcoming, it looked as though the tie was heading for a second replay. But three minutes before the end, Neill headed the winning goal to take Rangers to the Lancashire coast the following Saturday to meet Blackpool in the fourth round.

The match at Bloomfield Road was a hard fought Cup tie with the Fourth Division side giving a good account of themselves and earning a replay with a goalless draw. The game at Loftus Road was a different matter. Allen scored after 25 minutes and Stainrod added a second from the spot before half-time. Allen scored his second early in the second half, after a Flanagan shot had rebounded off the bar, and completed his hat-trick in the 60th minute with an unstoppable header. Entwistle scored for Blackpool, but Allen was not finished and he scored his fourth and Rangers' fifth five minutes later.

Rangers' fifth-round opponents were Grimsby Town, who coincidently visited Loftus Road the week before in a League game and therefore had recent experience of the pitch. The scoring was opened by Stainrod in the 27th minute and was followed ten minutes later by a goal from Allen. After the break, Howe extended Rangers lead in the 65th minute. Although Moore pulled one back for Grimsby in the 72nd minute, Rangers went through to the quarter-finals by three goals to one.

Rangers had reached the last eight of the FA Cup for only the fourth time in their history and were hoping for a home draw to help them to gain a semi-final place for the first time. The draw was kind with Crystal Palace coming to Loftus Road, although with such a lot at stake, the game was not an entertaining one to watch for the uncommitted. Both sets of supporters had their moments of hope, but with the game heading for a replay both sides seemed content to play out time. However, in the 88th minute Clive Allen turned in the box and shot past Barron in the Palace goal to put Rangers in the semi-finals.

The other sides in the semi-final draw were Tottenham Hotspur and West Bromwich Albion from the First Division, and Second Division Leicester City. The draw kept the two London sides apart with Rangers getting West Bromwich Albion, the tie to be played at Highbury. A crowd of over 45,000 packed Arsenal Stadium, many of them to see if Queen's Park Rangers could reach their first FA Cup Final. It was ironic that their opponents were the team they had beaten on their only other visit to Wembley Stadium back in March 1967.

The main threat for Rangers was the front running and aerial power of Cyrille Regis. Terry Venables played a master stroke and deputed Hazell to follow Regis wherever he went. It was a ploy that worked out exactly as planned. The first half was a dour encounter with neither side creating a clear opportunity. In fact, there were no corners at all in the first 45 minutes. Albion had to substitute former Rangers player King after he had broken his nose.

Again neither side had a clear scoring chance and it looked as though the tie was heading for extra-time. But in the 72nd minute when Ally Robertson, the Albion defender, tried to clear the ball from his six-yard box, Clive Allen stuck out a leg in an attempt to block the clearance and the ball hit him and rebounded into the net. Albion now had to go on all-out attack and the final ten minutes were nerve-racking. But thanks mainly to Hazell's dominance over Regis, Albion were unable to score and Rangers were on their way to Wembley.

The 1982 FA Cup Final was an all-London affair as Tottenham Hotspur had beaten Leicester City 2-0 at Villa Park. Venables had done his homework on the Tottenham team but his plans were upset early on with an injury to Clive Allen after only ten minutes. Although he carried on, he was not at his most dangerous and was eventually replaced by substitute Gary Micklewhite, who immediately crossed for John Gregory to get in a header that was well saved by Clemence.

With no real scoring chances and little excitement, the match petered out and went into extra-time. The main chances in normal time had fallen to Steve Archibald, who missed them all.

After 109 minutes, Tottenham took the lead through a Hoddle shot that was deflected past Peter Hucker by Tony Currie. Rangers did not give up and with just five minutes remaining, they won a throw-in on the left. Stainrod took a long throw which was nodded on by Hazell and Terry Fenwick headed the flick-on in to the net. The Final ended in a 1-1 draw and meant a replay the following Thursday again at Wembley Stadium.

The second match was a much better one. Rangers had to make a change in defence as captain Glenn Roeder was suspended after being sent off at Luton two weeks earlier. His place was taken by the third-round hero, Warren Neill. Clive Allen did not recover from his injury and Gary Micklewhite continued in his place. Roeder's absence meant that Tony Currie was captain for the game.

After six minutes, Currie tackled Roberts in the penalty area and referee Clive White awarded a penalty. Hoddle scored from the spot to give Tottenham an early lead. Rangers attacked well and thought that they had scored when Micklewhite had the ball in the net, but the effort was disallowed due to Stainrod being in an offside position, although whether he was interferring with play was extremely doubtful as he was out on the left wing. In the second half, it was all Rangers with Gregory having a chipped shot headed off the line by Hoddle with Clemence beaten. Fenwick was then fouled in the penalty area and the linesman waved for a penalty but was overruled by the referee. Despite all their valiant efforts Rangers were unable to equalise and the FA Cup went to North London.

During the summer of 1982, Rangers faced another attempt by the Football League to get them to replace the artificial surface. The League's annual meeting eventually decided to request any other clubs thinking of switching surfaces to get permission from the League first. The concession to Rangers was that they could keep their surface as they had not broken any rules.

Due to the optimism within the club, Venables did not feel it necessary to strengthen the squad in his quest for promotion. The only players to leave were long-serving Ian Gillard who joined Aldershot, Ernie Howe (to Portsmouth) and John Burridge (to Wolverhampton Wanderers).

Rangers' first game of the season was away to Newcastle United, who had just signed Kevin Keegan. His presence produced a crowd of 36,185 to St James' Park, the largest attendance for a Rangers' game all season. Inspired by Keegan, Newcastle won by the only goal of the game. Rangers then won three of the next four matches, the other being a draw, to confirm themselves as the bookies' favourites for promotion. Sheffield Wednesday then became only the third team to beat Rangers on plastic.

Following another away win and a home draw, Rangers won three successive games to go top of the table in the middle of October. Their stay at the top was short-lived, though, as they lost 2-1 at Middlesbrough the following week. A seven-match unbeaten run had them back on top. The best results in that run were a 4-1 away win at Cambridge United and a 4-0 home win over Grimsby Town. Two consecutive defeats, including Chelsea's second 'artificial win' in two seasons, dropped Rangers down to second. This was the lowest they went for the rest of the season.

At the halfway point of the season, Rangers were four points behind leaders Wolverhampton Wanderers. An away reverse at Derby County was followed by a run of five wins and a draw, in which Rangers conceded only one goal. The best wins were 3-0 at Crystal Palace and 6-1 at home to Middlesbrough, which included a Clive Allen hat-trick. An away defeat at Bolton

Glenn Hoddle's penalty settles the 1982 FA Cup Final replay for Spurs against Queen's Park Rangers.

Wanderers was followed by a 4-0 home win against Rotherham United, which took Rangers back to the top of the table, where they stayed for the remainder of the season.

QPR had now found a rich vein of scoring as they went one better with a 5-1 win against Charlton Athletic in the next game. These games were the start of another seven-match unbeaten run. The only points dropped were in the home match with Leicester City which ended in a 2-2 draw. By now, Rangers were eight points clear of second-placed Wolves and had a game in hand. Third-placed Fulham were a further four points behind. The 1-0 home win over Leeds United on 23 April assured Rangers of promotion and they now had their sights firmly on the Second Division championship, a title they had not won when gaining promotion before.

The next game, at Carlisle United, was lost by the only goal, which now meant that Rangers would clinch the title if they won the next match against third-placed Fulham, and if Wolverhampton did not win their game. Fulham gave Rangers a hard time as they were still in the promotion race, but goals from Gregory, Sealy and Stainrod completed a 3-1 win for QPR. The news then came through from The Valley that Charlton had pulled back from 3-0 down to draw 3-3 with Wolves, thus giving the Second Division title to Rangers. The trophy was presented before the next home game, which was ironically against Wolves, Rangers confirming their superiority with a 2-1 win.

Despite gaining only one point from their last two away games, Rangers finished ten points ahead of Wolves and a further five ahead of the other promoted side, Leicester City. A lot of critics claimed that Rangers had only won promotion because of the unfair advantage they had with their pitch. What they failed to point out was the tremendous away record, of ten wins and four draws, Rangers had enjoyed. Due to the consistency of the side, only 21 players were used during the League season, the ever-presents being Ian Dawes, John Gregory and Peter Hucker. The leading goalscorers were Tony Sealy and John Gregory, both with 16, followed by Clive Allen with 13.

The second round draw for the 1982-83 Milk Cup paired Rangers with Rotherham United, with the first leg to be played at Millmoor. The game was played on a slippery pitch following rain earlier in the day. Rotherham took the lead after 41 minutes but Rangers equalised through Gregory with 13 minutes remaining. As QPR now seemed to have the upper hand it looked as though it would be enough to give them a draw, and leave all to play for in the second leg. However, Seasman scored a second for the home side only two minutes later, thus giving Rotherham a one-goal advantage for the return game. The Millers came to Loftus Road with only one intention, that of stopping Rangers scoring and their player-manager, Emlyn Hughes, used all his experience in marshalling the defence and, despite many efforts, Rangers were unable to get through and went out of the Cup at the first hurdle. This is the only time that Rangers have been eliminated from the League Cup — in any of its forms — at the two-legged second-round stage.

Having been knocked out of the Milk Cup early on, Rangers were hoping for more success in the FA Cup. Their third-round opponents were West Bromwich Albion, the side that they had beaten in the previous years semi-final. This time Albion had home advantage and were looking for revenge. Rangers were suffering from a number of injuries, including one to 'keeper Peter Hucker which meant that junior Graham Benstead had to make his debut in goal. The match was more entertaining than the previous encounter between the two sides. At half-time the score was 1-1, with both goals coming from the penalty spot, Fenwick being the successful scorer for Rangers. The second half saw Albion take the lead through

Owen and increase it with a goal from Eastoe. Micklewhite pulled one back for Rangers but it was not enough and Rangers had now lost at the first tie in both Cup competitions.

Towards the end of the 1982-83 season, Rangers chairman Jim Gregory had announced his intention of relinquishing control of the club. With no outside interest shown, he made an offer to manager Terry Venables, who Gregory considered would be the ideal man to run the club. The deal was that Gregory would retain financial control and Venables would be able to buy-in and move towards taking a controlling interest. Venables was interested and spent a long time talking to various backers. After a while he was unable to raise enough capital to make the deal viable and Jim Gregory decided to stay on at the club.

During the summer, John Gregory joined the growing list of Rangers England internationals when he played on the tour to Australia.

Before the 1983-84 season started, the Football League decided to allow shirt sponsorship for the first time. It was a practise that was already in existence in many European countries and it was felt that the sponsorship would give much-needed income to the clubs. Rangers were approached and agreed a deal, with the brewery firm, Guinness. As their brewery was at Park Royal there was certainly a connection, if somewhat historic, with the club.

Venables made his first sortee into the transfer market for over a year when he signed Mike Fillery from Chelsea. He also signed on professional terms two promising apprentices, David Kerslake and Martin Allen. Kerslake was, at the time, the most capped England Youth international and therefore was a good signing for the club. On the out-going side were Tony Currie, who joined Vancouver Whitecaps and two of the fringe first-team players Dean Wilkins (to Brighton) and Ian Muir (to Birmingham City).

Rangers' return to the First Division started with an away game at Old Trafford, which they lost 3-1 in front of 48,742 people, the largest crowd to see QPR that season. A goalless draw on Bank Holiday Monday at Southampton was followed by the first win of the season, 2-1 at home to Aston Villa. Another draw and a defeat had Rangers down in 16th place. Form improved with a run of four successive wins, to move them up to third in the table. A total of 11 goals were scored in those four games and none were conceded, but the good run was ended by Liverpool, who won 1-0 at Loftus Road in front of the biggest home crowd of the season, 27,140. By now, Rangers had sold Bob Hazell to Leicester City. Hazell, in fact, ended his Rangers career unconscious on a stretcher having been knocked out in the home game with Sunderland.

An away win at Norwich City put Rangers back to third, but they then lost their second successive home game to drop back down the table. The remainder of the year saw Rangers holding their own with four wins and four defeats. This put them in ninth place at the halfway stage. Towards the end of the year, Rangers signed Jeremy Charles from Swansea City and let Glenn Roeder go to Newcastle United.

The New Year started with a flourish including a resounding 6-0 home win over Stoke City, this being Rangers first 'six' in the First Division. This was followed by a 2-0 win at Highbury to give Rangers the double over Arsenal, something undreamed of a few years earlier. A poor spell of only one win in six matches followed, though, and the most worrying aspect was the lack of goals, Rangers managed to score in only one match in a sequence of five.

A 2-1 home win over Coventry City ended the lean spell and after losing the next match at Watford, QPR came into form. They moved into contention for a European place with an unbeaten run of nine games, including a sequence of six successive wins. The forwards had rediscovered their scoring ability and Rangers failed to score two or more only twice in this time. Despite losing the last game of the season, 3-1 at Everton, they had done enough to finish fifth in the League and clinch a place in the following season's UEFA Cup competition.

Again the consistency of the side meant that only 20 players were used during the season, nine of those appearing in 30 or more games. The leading goalscorers were Simon Stainrod with 16 (13 League and three Cup) and Clive Allen with 15.

Rangers' opponents in the second round of the Milk Cup were Crewe Alexandra from the Fourth Division. The first leg was at Loftus Road, where QPR opened the scoring after only 13 seconds, when Simon Stainrod shot past the Crewe 'keeper. Six minutes later, King equalised and a real Cup tie looked on the cards. After 19 minutes, however, Stainrod scored his second to restore Rangers' advantage and when Gary Waddock added a third one minute before the break, they were looking on course for a comfortable win. The second-half display was certainly not mirrored in the scoreline. Crewe played well above their mid-table Fourth Division status and caused Rangers a lot of problems. But they were unable to score; Rangers, on the other hand, did, and five more times at that, through Stewart (57), Allen (58), Micklewhite (65), McDonald (82) and Stainrod (88) to complete his hat-trick. The opinion of all present was that the 8-1 score was one of the biggest injustices for some time.

With a seven-goal advantage Rangers relaxed in the second leg. This allowed Crewe to show what could have been in the first leg as the Cheshire side won by three goals to nil. The third-round draw took Rangers to East Anglia to meet Ipswich Town in a match that produced a very entertaining Cup tie. At half-time, the game was evenly poised at 1-1, the goals coming from Stewart for Rangers and Wark for Ipswich. The second half, though, saw the home side take the initiative and Wark and Mariner scored for them. Gregory managed to pull one back for Rangers, but it was not enough and they went out by the odd goal in five.

In the third round of the 1983-84 FA Cup, Rangers had a long trip to Yorkshire to meet Huddersfield Town. The Second Division side looked more at home in the wintery conditions and it was not surprising that they took a half-time lead through Lillis. Rangers tried to get back into the game after the break and Gregory managed to equalise, only for Stonehouse to score the winner minutes later.

During the summer of 1984, Barcelona approached Rangers with a view to offering Terry Venables and his assistant Allan Harris similar positions at the Spanish club. Chairman Jim Gregory did not stand in their way and wished them all success in the future. Gregory again tried to find a buyer for the club, but as before was unsuccessful and decided to remain in control. His main concern was the empty position in the manager's office and his search ended when Alan Mullery was appointed in time for the start of the new season.

Again Rangers were well represented during the England close-season tour to South America. The party included Terry Fenwick, Clive Allen and Simon Stainrod. Fenwick and Allen made appearances, but Stainrod was unlucky and never came off the bench in any of the three games.

Mullery's only purchase on the transfer market was the signing of Gary Bannister from Sheffield Wednesday. His arrival meant the departure of Clive Allen, this time to Tottenham Hotspur. The only other player to leave was Mark O'Connor who joined Bristol Rovers.

The season started with a 3-1 home win over West Bromwich Albion, two away draws and a 3-0 home win. A disastrous 5-0 defeat at Tottenham Hotspur followed, and a week later Rangers conceded five again, but this time they did not lose as they also scored five. This remarkable result came in the home game against Newcastle United. Rangers were four goals down at half-time, due to an outstanding display by the Newcastle winger Chris Waddle who had scored three and made the other.

What Mullery said at half-time must have had an effect as Rangers pulled back to 4-3 with goals from Bannister, an own-goal and one from Gregory. Wharton made 5-3 to Newcastle in the 84th minute and Rangers' fightback seemed over. But Wicks made it 5-4 a minute later and as the clock moved to 90 minutes, Micklewhite scored the equaliser. What manager Jack Charlton said to his side after giving away a four-goal lead is not printed anywhere!

Sanity was restored with a 1-1 draw at Southampton, but the next home game saw Luton Town win for the third successive time on the artificial pitch. No wonder they installed one themselves!

Rangers had now slipped to 14th in the table and only one win in the next six matches dropped them further into trouble, down to 18th place. Mullery signed John Byrne, who had

Action from QPR's visit to the Victoria Ground, Stoke, in December 1984. Rangers won 2-0.

impressed him in the recent Cup tie against York City. He also added Robbie James from Stoke City to the squad.

Alas, things were not as harmonious at the club as they had been in recent times and following the home win over bottom-of-the-table Stoke City, Mullery was sacked as manager. His replacement in a caretaker capacity was, yet again, Frank Sibley. Sibley's first action was to buy the experienced Michael Robinson from Liverpool. Results did not improve, though, with two wins and two draws before the end of the year. At the halfway point Rangers were in 16th place with 23 points, only four points off a relegation place.

The New Year bought new hope of a climb away from the foot of the table with two successive away wins. First at doomed Stoke City and then at London rivals, West Ham United. The good run did not continue, though, with the next four games producing only two points. The losses included a heavy 4-0 defeat at home to Southampton.

By now teams were not afraid of the surface and were prepared to play their normal game on it. Sibley was reassessing the playing squad and allowed several players to leave. They were Tony Sealy (to Fulham), Gary Micklewhite (to Derby County), Simon Stainrod (to Sheffield Wednesday), Jeremy Charles (to Oxford United) and Graham Benstead (to Norwich City).

Rangers managed to remain in mid table as they won all their home games but lost all their away games in a run of 12 matches. The matches were still producing goals with three resulting in six or more. The best wins were 3-0 against Ipswich Town, 4-2 over West Ham United, to give Rangers a League double over the East Enders, and 4-3 against Leicester City. The home successes kept Rangers just above the fight for the relegation places. The alternating sequence ended with the last game of the season when Manchester United won 3-1 at Loftus Road. Rangers finished the season in 19th place, just one point above relegated Norwich City. It was very close at the bottom as Rangers would have been five places higher up the League with only two more points. Despite the poor performances from the team, three players played in every game: Gary Bannister, Ian Dawes and Peter Hucker. The leading goalscorers were Bannister with 28 (17 League and 11 Cup) and Wayne Fereday with ten (seven League and three Cup).

After the end of the season, Loftus Road was the venue for the Barry McGuigan v Eusebio Pedroza WBA featherweight world championship fight.

Rangers started on the Milk Cup trail with a second-round tie against York City, the first leg being at York's Bootham Crescent ground. Bannister opening the scoring, only for Houchen to equalise. Fenwick gave Rangers a half-time lead with a penalty two minutes before the break, but Walwyn equalised again five minutes into the second half. Rangers' experience then came through and they scored twice more, through Fereday and Bannister again, to take a two-goal lead into the second leg.

QPR increased their advantage to five with three early goals in the home leg, Bannister (twice) and Fereday scoring inside the first 30 minutes. Chippendale got one back before half-time for York, but a Micklewhite goal midway through the second half gave Rangers a comfortable 8-3 aggregate win.

The third-round saw Aston Villa as the visitors to Loftus Road. The match was a hard-fought one, with Hucker keeping Rangers in the game with some good saves. The only goal came after 65 minutes when Gregory scored with a 25-yard shot.

In the next round, Rangers had to travel to Southampton, where they took the lead through a Fenwick penalty after Bannister had been fouled in the area. Southampton fought back and equalised in the 65th minute, through Curtis, to take the tie to a replay.

The match at Loftus Road was played in windy conditions and a wet and slippery pitch, making it difficult for the players. With the wind blowing straight down the pitch it was a distinct advantage to play with it and QPR were unable to capitalise on this extra help in the first half, which ended goalless. Southampton did not fare any better in the second half, although they should have scored in the 85th minute, but Moran's penalty kick was very weak and easily saved by Hucker.

Even with an extra 30 minutes, neither side could score and

a second replay was necessary. Rangers called correctly in the toss for venues and the sides returned to Loftus Road a fortnight later to try again. This time the game was more open with both sides creating chances. Waddock opened the scoring in the 17th minute, when he half-volleyed a poor punch from Shilton back past him. Neill added a second after 40 minutes and a minute into the second half, Fenwick sealed the game with Rangers' third. Southampton tried to get back into the game but could not score and Fenwick added a fourth from the spot to take QPR through to a fifth-round tie with Ipswich Town. The match was played on a frozen Portman Road pitch, which became more slippery as the game went on. The conditions did not lend themselves to a good game and, not surprisingly, the game finished goalless.

The replay was the following Monday at Loftus Road. Stainrod, who was playing in place of the Cup-tied Byrne, was sent off in the 24th minute for an off-the-ball incident, and this did not help Rangers and Ipswich took the lead through D'Avery three minutes later. They increased their advantage with a Zondervan goal four minutes after that and Bannister managed to score five minutes before half-time to give Rangers some hope. The second half was a close affair but the extra man helped Ipswich as they coped with Rangers' attacks and kept their goal intact. With no goals after the break, Ipswich became the first side to beat Rangers in a Cup tie on the plastic pitch.

Rangers' third-round opponents in the FA Cup this season were Doncaster Rovers, who were managed by Billy Bremner. Rangers had been drawn away for the third successive year and the result was also the same as the previous two, with QPR again going out to a lower division side. The only goal of the game was scored by Harle in the second half.

Due to UEFA not sanctioning their matches to be played on artificial surfaces, Rangers had to play their home ties in the 1984-85 UEFA Cup at Arsenal's Highbury ground. This was not the first time that Rangers had played home games at Highbury. They had staged a Division Three South game there in March 1930 when the Loftus Road ground was closed following crowd trouble.

Rangers' first-round opponents were Icelandic side, KR Reykjavik, with the first leg away. Stainrod scored after 23 minutes and Rangers led the part-timers at half-time. In the 64th minute, Stainrod's shot was parried by the goalkeeper and Bannister scored from the rebound. Stainrod added a third after 75 minutes to give Rangers a three-goal cushion for the second leg. The match at Highbury was a formality, especially after Bannister (twice) and Charles had given Rangers a three-goal lead at half-time. Bannister completed his hat-trick in the 60th minute to give QPR a 7-0 aggregate win. The only disappointing thing about the evening was the low attendance of only 6,196, who looked lost in the spacious Arsenal Stadium.

The second round paired Rangers with Partizan Belgrade of Yugoslavia. Rangers were expecting a much harder contest than the previous round as Partizan were experienced European campaigners. The first half was all action with Gregory scoring after 12 minutes, only for Klincarski to equalise a minute later. Partizan took the lead in the 24th minute through Mance, but this time Rangers equalised a minute later with a Fereday goal. A minute before the break, Stainrod scored to give Rangers the lead again. The second half saw one of the best Rangers performances of recent years when they completely mastered their more experienced opponents, scoring three more goals without reply, through Neill, after 55 minutes, and Bannister with two, in the 59th and 83rd minutes.

Rangers were confident of progressing as they were taking a four-goal lead into the second leg. The return match in Belgrade was played in front of a very intimidating crowd. Partizan attacked from the start and scored an early goal through Zlvkovic. Rangers nearly held on to half-time but just before the break, Wicks fouled Zlvkovic in the area and Kalicanin scored from the spot. QPR were still two goals ahead over the tie, but disaster struck a minute into the second half when Hucker failed to hold on to a cross and gifted a third goal to Jezic. After 65 minutes the tie was back on level terms when Zlvkovic scored his second and Partizan's fourth.

Rangers now had to score to stay in the competition but went out on the away goals rule. They also made history, for the wrong reason, as this was the first time a British side had gone out of an European competition having held a four-goal lead from the first leg.

During the summer of 1985, Frank Sibley was replaced as caretaker manager by Jim Smith, the successful Oxford United boss. Smith's initial entry into the transfer market was to bring Leroy Rosenior to the club from Fulham and to let Ian Stewart go to Newcastle United.

Great things were anticipated with the arrival of Smith, who had taken Oxford United into the First Division for the first time in their history. His first match in charge ended in a 1-0 home win over Ipswich Town. An away defeat at West Ham United was followed by two successive 2-1 wins to put Rangers third in the table. With four defeats in the next five matches, Rangers dropped down to 12th place and Smith's honeymoon was over, although two home wins followed, including a memorable 2-1 victory over Liverpool. Rangers' success was dependant on the partnership which was developing between Bannister and Byrne, but the next three games failed to see a Rangers goal and they slid back down to 13th place.

Two wins and two draws in November revived their fortunes slightly, but the performances were not as consistent as Smith and the fans would have liked. In December, Smith let John Gregory go to Derby County and signed Clive Walker from Sunderland. The transfer dealings did not herald a success, for Rangers lost all five League games in December, managing to score only one goal in the month.

The New Year saw QPR in 14th place with 30 points from their 24 games. Although not as high up the table as they would have liked, there seemed no real danger from relegation as the bottom two teams, West Bromwich Albion and Ipswich Town, were beginning to lose contact with the rest of the table. New Year's Day saw the visit of Smith's old side, Oxford United. The match proved to be one of the more entertaining games of the season with Rangers winning 3-1. Their goalscoring touch seemed to have returned as they scored three in each of three successive games. Unfortunately it did not continue as Rangers won only one point from the next six games to drop down to 16th in the table, but a safe nine points above a relegation place.

Rangers form then took a turn for the better with an unbeaten run of eight games, five wins and three draws. The most satisfying win was the 6-0 thrashing of local rivals Chelsea on Easter Monday. The previous game at Oxford had produced another entertaining game, which finished in a 3-3 draw. Despite losing the last two games of the season, Rangers finished in a mid-table position of 13th with 50 points. The regular players for the season were Ian Dawes, yet again an ever-present, Alan McDonald and Terry Fenwick. The leading goalscorers were Bannister with 18 and Byrne with 15.

Rangers' Milk Cup trail in 1985-86 began with a home tie against Hull City, from the Second Division. Smith had made three changes to the previous League side in an effort to improve results. He brought in Barron, Wicks and Kerslake for Hucker, McDonald and Allen. The changes had the desired effect as Kerslake scored his first goal for Rangers after 13 minutes. Barron made two good saves to keep the score to 1-0 at half-time.

After the break, Rangers scored twice more, through Dawes (52 minutes) and Bannister (63 minutes) to take a three-goal advantage to the second leg at Boothferry Park. The match was a very one-sided affair with Rangers winning by 5-1 and easily going through to the third round with an aggregate of eight goals to one. The scorers for the Rangers in the second leg were Kerslake and Rosenior, both with two, and Fillery.

The third-round draw paired Rangers with near neighbours Watford, with Rangers having to travel the short distance to Vicarage Road. Again Smith made three changes from the previous week's team. This time he left out Kerslake, James and Rosenior, and brought in Allen, Fillery and Byrne. Watford were awarded a penalty in the 24th minute when Barron pulled down a Watford forward in the area. However, he made amends by saving Jackett's spot-kick.

The match remained scoreless at the interval. Rangers had already lost the services of Fenwick, who had to go off after 20 minutes with a hamstring injury. They battled on in the second half and their efforts were rewarded when Byrne scored after 54 minutes following a good move between Fillery and

Fereday. Watford were unable to get back into the game and Rangers recorded their first win at Watford for 16 years.

The fourth-round draw brought Nottingham Forest to Loftus Road. With both sides out on the pitch for their pre-match warm up the floodlights failed. Despite the efforts of the electricity board and club officials, the referee decided to call the game off after waiting an hour for the power to return. The match was re-scheduled for the following Monday.

The evening was very cold and damp and the pitch had to have extra sand put on it to stop the players slipping. Despite the conditions, both sides played their part in an extremely exciting Cup tie. Rangers were awarded a dubious penalty after six minutes, from which Fenwick scored. Forest then set out on attack and were unlucky not to score on several occasions. With no further goals before the interval, Rangers were happy with their half-time lead. The second half was much the same as the first. Forest's efforts were rewarded after 80 minutes with a Clough equaliser. But with 90 minutes approaching, Bannister reacted quickest to a parried save from the 'keeper and scored Rangers' second. Davenport was sent off in the arguments that followed and then Birtles made a hash of a clearance and Byrne lobbed the ball over Sutton in the Forest goal for Rangers' third.

The fifth-round draw brought Rangers' nearest neighbours, Chelsea, to Loftus Road. The match attracted a capacity 27,000 crowd who paid a club record receipts of £132,572. Rangers took the lead after 12 minutes when Byrne scored after Rougvie failed to cut out a Fereday cross. Chelsea were back level after 24 minutes, though, when Nevin nipped in after a Murphy corner had been flicked on by Rougvie and Lee. McDonald had an opportunity to give Rangers the lead again in the 27th minute, but he just missed with an acrobatic scissor kick. However, the best chance fell to Bannister in the 42nd when he had only the 'keeper to beat, but missed the target.

The second half was just as entertaining with both sides having the chances to score the winner. Chelsea came closest when Dixon's 'goal' was ruled out for offside.

The replay at Stamford Bridge was another stirring Cup tie. Again both sides had chances to score but neither could manage it. McDonald was marshalling the Rangers defence well and not letting the Chelsea strikers have much room, whilst at the other end Niedzwiecki, in the Chelsea goal, was stopping everything shot at him by Byrne and Bannister. After 90 minutes there were still no goals and extra-time was required. Both sides were suffering from tiredness and players were needing constant treatment for cramp. Midway through the first period of extra-time, Rangers won a corner which James took. His cross was met firmly by McDonald who headed into the net to give Rangers the lead. With time running out Chelsea were trying all sorts of ideas to break through the resolute Rangers defence. A minute from time Niedzwiecki tried to dribble the ball upfield but he lost it to Bannister on the halfway line. He passed it to Robinson, who scored with a 50-yard shot to give Rangers a two-goal victory.

Their reward for beating Chelsea was a two-legged semi-final against Liverpool. The first leg was played at Loftus Road and televised live by ITV. Having already beaten Liverpool in the League at home earlier in the season, Rangers were hopeful of a good result to take to the second leg at Anfield. QPR got a good start and won early corners while Liverpool were still adapting to the pitch. In the 24th minute, Martin Allen crossed from the right and Fenwick scored at the far post. Rangers continued to have the upper hand, but despite two good efforts they could not add to their tally before half-time. The second half saw Liverpool change their tactics as they tried to squeeze Rangers away from their goal by playing the offside game just inside their own half. This was successful in thwarting Rangers attacks.

Liverpool should have scored after 62 minutes when Rush was unmarked in the area but his shot was weak and Barron saved. With no goals being scored in the second half, Rangers took a narrow one-goal lead to the second leg three weeks later at Anfield. Again the match was televised live by ITV, much to the pleasure of the Rangers fans unable to get to Liverpool.

Liverpool attacked from the start and McMahon scored midway through the first half. Just before half-time the referee adjudged that Dawes had handled a cross in the area and awarded Liverpool a penalty. Robinson, who had joined Rangers from Liverpool, spoke to 'keeper Barron whilst Molby was waiting to take the kick. The advice must have been good as Molby's spot-kick was saved by Barron by the foot of the right hand post. With just the one goal before the break, the sides were level on aggregate and an exciting second half was in prospect.

Terry Fenwick, signed for Rangers shortly after Terry Venables became manager and went on to win almost all his England caps as a QPR player.

In the 58th minute, Bannister won the ball from Lawrenson and passed to Allen, who crossed hard into the box. In attempting to clear, Beglin hit the ball against Whelan and it ended up behind Grobbelaar in the Liverpool net. Rangers were now back in front on aggregate. However, the lead did not last long as 12 minutes later, Johnston scored with a lob from a flick on by Rush. With extra-time approaching, Rangers attacked again. This time Fereday crossed from the right, looking for Robinson in the box. In trying to beat Robinson in the air Gillespie only managed to head the ball into his own net for Rangers second goal. Rangers held out for the last five minutes and went through to the Final courtesy of two own-goals.

In the Final, Rangers met Jim Smith's old team, Oxford United. Following two very entertaining League encounters between the two sides, everybody was looking forward to a good Wembley Final, which attracted a crowd of 90,396 who paid £897,646.

Alas, the game did not live up to expectations and the first half an hour was a fairly dour affair. The Oxford midfield trio of Hebberd, Phillips and Houghton then started to exert their authority on the game and five minutes before half-time, Hebberd took a pass from Aldridge and shot past Barron. The second half was dominated by Oxford as Rangers seemed to lose their way against a hard-running side. Six minutes after the break, Houghton finished off a move he began on the halfway line, to score Oxford's second.

Gary Bannister causes the Oxford United defence some problems during the 1986 Milk Cup Final.

Rangers replaced Allen with Rosenior, which added a bit of life to the Rangers attack. The first shot on target for Rangers came in the 72nd minute when Dawes had a long-range effort turned over the bar by Judge. Aldridge then missed a couple of good chances before Charles completed the scoring in the 86th minute. This was one of Rangers worst performances for some time and had a numbing effect and the players and supporters alike.

In the FA Cup, yet again Rangers faced a long trip in the third round. This time they had to travel to Cumbria to meet Carlisle United. Due to the bad weather the game was postponed on the original date and was eventually played nine days later. The match was played on a bitter cold and frosty evening which suited the Second Division side. Carlisle scored in the first half through Cooke and, despite trying to raise their game, Rangers never managed to look threatening and went out at the first attempt for the fourth successive season.

During the summer of 1986, the World Cup in Mexico took place and Rangers were represented by Terry Fenwick in the England squad and Alan McDonald in the Northern Ireland team. On the transfer front, manager Jim Smith was making a few changes to his line-up. In came David Seaman (from Birmingham City), Alan Brazil (from Coventry City), Sammy Lee (from Liverpool) and apprentice Justin Channing. Out went Steve Wicks to Chelsea and Steve Burke to Doncaster Rovers.

Guinness did not renew their shirt sponsorship contract, which had run for three years. Their place was taken by the local Blue Star Garages company.

The season did not start too well as Southampton beat Rangers 5-1 at The Dell in the opening game. Two debutants had differing fortunes that day. David Seaman in the Rangers goal letting five and Colin Clarke netted a hat-trick for the Saints. Rangers then won the next three games to raise their confidence. The third win, 2-0 away at Newcastle United, took them to second in the table, but two goalless draws and three defeats followed and Rangers slipped back down the table to 15th. The poor run was ended with two successive home wins, over Wimbledon and Tottenham Hotspur. It was then another nine matches before Rangers won again. The first success in ten games came in the Christmas home fixture against Coventry City, when Rangers won 3-1, with goals from Byrne, Bannister and Allen. At the halfway point of the season Rangers were in 15th place with 24 points, just one point off the relegation places.

At the beginning of January, Michael Robinson left Rangers and joined the Spanish side, Osasuna. A month later, Peter Hucker joined Oxford United. Rangers started the New Year with two defeats, at Chelsea and at home to Everton, before a string of four straight wins pulled them away from the danger zone and up in to the middle of the table at 11th place. In March, Smith made another signing when he brought Les Ferdinand from non-League side Hayes.

Although only one of the next six games was won, Rangers remained in a safe mid-table position. The next win came at Watford on Easter Monday but QPR ended the season with seven games without a win and had a run of six consecutive matches when they scored one goal. This poor finish meant that Rangers had won only one out of their last 12 matches. Some of the defeats were heavy: 4-1 at Coventry and at home to Arsenal and a massive 7-1 reverse at Sheffield Wednesday. Rangers finished the season in 16th place, six points above Charlton Atheltic, who had to go through the new play-off matches to retain their First Division status. David Seaman was the only really regular player during the season, although five others played 34 or more League games. The leading goalscorers were Gary Bannister with 16 (15 League and one Cup) and John Byrne 14 (11 League and three Cup).

The biggest event concerning Rangers during the second half of the season was the news, in February, that Jim Gregory had finally found a buyer for his controlling stake in the club. He sold out to Marler Estates, who were run by David Bulstrode, and who already owned Fulham. As Marler were a property company, there was a lot of speculation as to the real reason they had bought into two football clubs. It was then announced that Rangers and Fulham would merge into one club and would play at Loftus Road. This would enable Marler to develop the Craven Cottage site into a housing estate. The people involved under estimated the fans reaction to the proposed 'Fulham Park Rangers' team and the idea was reduced to a ground sharing arrangement. Following a pitch invasion by fans during the home game against Manchester City, David

Bannister tries a somewhat unorthodox tackle on Nottingham Forest's Johnny Metgod at the City Ground in October 1986.

Bulstrode changed the plans and personally acquired Rangers from Marler to quash all talk of mergers and ground sharing. Thus both sides were able to keep their identities and grounds.

Rangers' opponents in the two-legged second round of the 1986-87 Milk Cup were Blackburn Rovers. The first match was played at Loftus Road, where Blackburn took the lead in the 19th minute with a goal from Garner. Byrne managed an equaliser six minutes later to send the sides in level at half-time. The second half saw both sides going for goal, but due to good defending on both sides, no goals were forthcoming and it looked as though the 1-1 score would be carried forward to Ewood Park. Then in injury time, Alan Brazil scored the all-important goal for Rangers to give them a slender lead for the second leg.

Blackburn scored first, in the second game, after 12 minutes through Simon Barker to tie the aggregate score. But Bannister restored Rangers advantage in the 40th minute with a glancing header. A minute later, Blackburn were awarded a penalty which Seaman managed to push round the post. Four minutes after the break, Walker put Rangers ahead on the night and two up overall but in the 67th minute Quinn scored from the spot to close the gap to one goal. Rangers then showed their First Division experience and kept Rovers out for the rest of the game.

The third-round draw took QPR across London to Selhurst Park to meet Charlton Athletic. The match was played in stormy conditions and the pitch was very much different to what Rangers were used to. Charlton adapted better to the conditions and it was no surprise when Thompson gave them the lead. It looked as QPR might get a second chance when the floodlights failed after 69 minutes, but electricians managed to repair the fuse and the game restarted. No further goals were scored in the remaining 20 minutes and Rangers exited the Cup that they had got to the Final of the year before.

Their visitors for the third round of the FA Cup that season were Leicester City. Leicester had already won in the League at Rangers earlier in the season and were not worried about the pitch. Smith gave them the lead after only five minutes, which they held until the interval. The second half was one of Rangers best for several years. Fenwick equalised after 48 minutes with a long-range free-kick, then Leicester regained the lead through a McAllister penalty after James had fouled Smith in the box.

QPR were then awarded a penalty which Fenwick converted to bring the scores level again. Two minutes later, Lee put Rangers in front for the first time with a 25-yard volley. After 65 minutes, James scored a fourth with another tremendous free-kick and Byrne added a fifth 13 minutes later. Leicester were unable to get back into the game and Rangers had triumphed 5-2.

In the fourth round Rangers went to Luton Town, who had knocked out Liverpool in the third round. As Luton also had an artificial pitch by now, Rangers were on equal terms with their opponents. Both sides fought hard and had no goals to show for their efforts by the break. The second half started in the same way and looked as though the tie would end goalless. But after 83 minutes, Johnson felled Byrne in the penalty area and Fenwick scored from the spot. Five minutes later, Bannister fouled Newell in the Rangers box and Harford equalised from the resultant penalty. The two sides met again at Loftus Road the following Wednesday. Rangers had not beaten Luton on an artificial pitch and so were looking to break their duck.

Fenwick headed Rangers into the lead after 17 minutes. Byrne added a second five minutes after the break and Rangers looked comfortable for a fifth-round place. Luton fought back and scored through Harford six minutes later, but despite their attempts, Rangers held on and went through to meet Leeds United at Elland Road.

Rangers went behind early on to a Baird goal and although they drew level, centre-back Ormsby scored with a header from a corner midway through the second half to restore Leeds' lead. Rangers were unable to find a second equaliser and went out of the competition.

During the summer of 1987 there were a large number of changes to the playing personnel at Loftus Road as Jim Smith was very active on the transfer market. He bought in Mark Dennis (from Southampton), Paul Parker (from Fulham), Dean Coney (from Fulham), Kevin Brock (from Oxford United), David Pizanti (from FC Cologne), John O'Neill (from Leicester City) and Danny Maddix (from Tottenham Hotspur). He also signed apprentices Tony Roberts and Brian Law on professional forms. He released Mike Fillery (to Portsmouth), Robbie James (to Leicester City), Sammy Lee (to Osasuna), Leroy Rosenior (to Fulham), Gary Chivers (to Watford) and Clive Walker (to Fulham). When Blue Star did not renew their sponsorship deal, they were replaced as shirt sponsors by the Dutch Tourist Board.

The transfer activity seemed to have paid dividends as Rangers got off to a flying start. Their first game, at West Ham United, saw four of the signings — Dennis, Parker, Coney and Brock — make their debuts as QPR won 3-0, with new boy Brock getting the third with a long-range free-kick. The first home

Martin Allen scores for QPR in their 1-1 draw at Carrow Road in October 1987.

Bannister hammers the ball past Forest's Steve Sutton at the City Ground in December 1987.

game ended in a disappointing 1-1 draw with Derby County. but the next five games were all won, with only one goal being conceded. The best result was the 3-1 home win over Chelsea, when Bannister scored a hat-trick. At this time Rangers were top of the table five points clear of second-placed Tottenham Hotspur.

Their first defeat came at Oxford United, but was followed by two more wins and Rangers were still top, although now only three points clear of Liverpool, who had two games in hand. Rangers next match was at Anfield, and with John Barnes in tremendous form, the Merseysiders knocked QPR off the top with a 4-0 win. A home win against Portsmouth was followed by four successive draws and Rangers were now in third place with the sides immediately below them closing the gap.

Their early-season form had deserted them and they lost the next four games, to slip to sixth in the table. After a lot of speculation about his future, Terry Fenwick joined Tottenham Hotspur in December. Also leaving were John O'Neill who, could not get a regular place and joined Norwich City, and Gavin Peacock, who joined his father, Keith, at Gillingham.

Jim Smith made two signings at this time. Mark Falco joined from Glasgow Rangers and Nicky Johns was signed as cover for David Seaman from Charlton Athletic. Over the Christmas and New Year holiday games, Rangers were unbeaten with two wins and two draws, the home win over Oxford United avenging their first defeat of the season.

At the halfway point of the season Rangers were in sixth place with 33 points and although they won only two of their next five games, Rangers held on to that position. In March, Smith made another significant signing when Trevor Francis joined on a free transfer from Glasgow Rangers. And just before the transfer deadline day, Gary Bannister signed for Coventry City.

The arrival of Francis had an uplifting effect on the club and they won their next five matches. A draw and another win followed and Rangers were up into third place, four points behind second-placed Manchester United, but a massive 15 points away from the leaders, Liverpool. If it had not been for the ban on English clubs in European competitions, Rangers would have had something to play for in their four remaining matches. As it was they drew two and lost two of those final games to finish in fifth place with 67 points.

The home game on 23 April, against Sheffield Wednesday, was the last match to be played on the artificial pitch, as the club had decided to revert back to grass for the new season. The decision was welcomed by players and supporters alike, who had not really taken to the surface. Also, after six years the plastic was showing its age and needed a considerable amount of maintenance. With the various chopping and changing that went on with team selection, only Paul Parker, Alan McDonald and Martin Allen played in more than 35 games. The leading goalscorers were Gary Bannister, with ten before his departure, and Dean Coney and Mark Falco, both with seven.

Rangers second-round opponents in the 1987-88 Milk Cup were Millwall from the Second Division. The first leg at Loftus Road was not a good one to watch. Millwall hit the woodwork twice in the opening 15 minutes, but Rangers took the lead after 38 minutes with a goal from Gary Bannister. McDonald added a second in the 64th minute, after Sheridan had miskicked in front of an open goal, before Millwall pulled one back after 78 minutes to give themselves some hope for the second leg.

Rangers played the sweeper system — which had taken them to the top of the First Division — to great effect and totally contained the Millwall forwards. The match was a tedious game, with Rangers only intent on preserving their one-goal lead, and not surprisingly the match was goalless, Rangers having done their job to go through to the next round.

The third-round draw took them to meet Third Division Bury at a muddy Gigg Lane in a game played in heavy rain. Robinson gave Bury the lead after 26 minutes, as they adapted better to the conditions. Rangers nearly scored in the 34th minute, when Fereday was cynically tackled from behind when he was just outside the area with only the goalkeeper to beat. QPR increased their tempo after the break and were unlucky when a McDonald header hit the bar. Bury managed to keep their goal intact and pulled off a giant-killing act by one goal to nil.

The Simod Cup had been going for two years — initially as the Full Members' Cup — prior to Rangers entering it for the first time in 1987-88. The competition was for First and Second Division sides and the draw was split into north and south with the two area winners meeting in a Wembley Final. All ties were to be settled on the night with extra-time and then, if necessary, penalties. There were to be no replays.

QPR were drawn at home to Reading and when the draw was made, the gap between the two sides could not have been greater, for Rangers were top of the First Division and Reading were bottom of the Second. Due to an injury to David Seaman, Nicky Johns made his debut in goal for Rangers.

The match started as expected with Rangers eventually taking the lead after 31 minutes through Allen. But they seemed to relax in the second half and were caught by a Reading side who had nothing to lose. James equalised in the 69th minute and when Tait scored four minutes later, Rangers were facing an embarrassing defeat. Their misery was completed when James scored his second and Reading's third in the 79th minute. At least, Rangers could say that they went out to the eventual winners as Reading won at Wembley, but were relegated to the Third Division, thus preventing them from defending their first-ever trophy.

Rangers faced an interesting trip to non-League Yeovil Town in the third round of the 1987-88 FA Cup. Yeovil were famous as Cup giantkillers, especially on their notorious sloping pitch. They gave a good account of themselves and went close to scoring on a couple of occasions in the first half. A minute before the break, though, Falco scored to give Rangers the lead. Again after the break, Yeovil put pressure on the Rangers defence, but further goals from Falco, in the 78th minute, and Brock, two minutes before the end, saw Rangers through a difficult game.

The fourth-round saw QPR entertain West Ham United. Rangers knew what to expect as their previous League game had been a 1-0 home defeat by the Hammers. A crowd of 23,631 crammed into the ground, but some 2,000 more people gained admission with forged tickets, which caused one section of the West Ham fans to spill on to the pitch. The game was held up for an hour whilst the police and stewards cleared the pitch.

There were no goals before half-time, but two minutes into the second half Pizanti, who was playing instead of the injured Dennis, scored with a tremendous 25-yard shot. Cottee equalised two minutes later, but Rangers regained the lead in the 63rd minute with a Bannister shot from the edge of the area. Allen confirmed Rangers' fifth-round place with a third goal with seven minutes remaining.

Their next opponents for Rangers were Luton Town, and as Rangers had home advantage they were looking for the same outcome as in the fourth round the previous season. QPR had the upper hand in the first half, but could not convert their possession into goals and the sides went in level at the break. Then Rangers took the lead after 59 minutes, when Neill squeezed a shot passed Sealey in the Luton goal.

But they were pulled back level after another seven minutes when Harford's header bounced up higher than expected off the artificial surface. Neither side were able to score again and the tie went to a replay at Kenilworth Road.

Again Rangers had more of the play but could not score. After 60 minutes Harford and Neill were chasing a Stein pass when Neill, in attempting to clear the ball for a corner, only succeeded in volleying it passed Seaman as it bounced up and hit his shin. Rangers continued to attack without success and went out of the FA Cup by that unlucky own-goal.

Before the 1988-89 season got underway, activity in the transfer market saw the arrival of Ossie Ardiles (from Tottenham Hotspur), Simon Barker (from Blackburn Rovers), Mark Stein (from Luton Town). The players to leave were John Byrne (to Le Harve), Ian Dawes (to Millwall) and Warren Neill (to Portsmouth). Smith also signed, on professional forms, the apprentices Robert Herrera and Bradley Allen.

Rangers' first home match on the new grass pitch was a friendly against the Egyptian champions, Al-Ahly, which ended in a 1-1 draw. Such was the interest in the game that it was televised live to most of North Africa.

In order to mark its centenary, the Football League held a knock-out competition for the top eight teams from the previous season. Rangers were drawn at home to Arsenal in the first round in a match which was the first competitive one on the new grass pitch. Rangers were obviously still getting used to it, as Arsenal won 2-0, their goals coming from Adams, in the third minute, and Marwood in the 76th.

The League season started with an away match at Old Trafford, where Rangers gave a solid performance to earn a goalless draw. That was their only point from the first nine available as they lost their next two games.

Everyone at the club was then shocked by the unexpected death of chairman David Bulstrode, who died two days before the Southampton home game. Although not popular with the fans on his arrival at the club because of the talk of merger, he had won their respect and support following his personal involvement with the club. His replacement was Richard Thompson, who at the age of 24 was the youngest chairman in the League.

Rangers' on-the-field fortunes were revived by a Trevor Francis inspired 2-0 home win over Sheffield Wednesday, and the first away win followed a week later at Derby County. Rangers were now in 11th place, having been down to 17th at one time. The good run did not continue, though, with only one win in the next five matches. A good 3-0 home win over Newcastle United was followed by two 1-0 defeats. Rangers had now won only four of their first 14 matches and were in 13th place.

The next match, a 2-1 home win over Coventry, was Jim

Mark Stein celebrates his goal against Derby at the Baseball Ground in September 1988.

Smith's last as manager. He resigned during the week to take over at bottom-of-the-table Newcastle United and his first activity at St James' Park was to sign Kevin Brock from Rangers.

Jim Smith's replacement, in a temporary capacity, was Peter Shreeves, who had been Smith's assistant. Gavin Maguire left to join Portsmouth in December, and chairman Thompson told Shreeves that he had a month to prove himself whilst a permanent appointment was being sought. Two weeks later, Trevor Francis was made player-manager and Shreeves left the club.

Under Francis' control, things did not improve overnight and they did not win under him until the away game at Southampton. The year ended with Rangers in 12th place with 23 points.

January and February were not good months for Rangers as they drew four and lost the other three matches played. This was mainly due to the number of injuries to key players, especially to player-manager Francis and leading scorer Mark Falco.

In the last six of those games, QPR scored only one goal, which was a penalty, and were down to 16th in the table, only one point away from the relegation places. Francis then made his first entry into the transfer market when he bought in Nigel Spackman (from Liverpool), Andy Gray (from Aston Villa) and the experienced Peter Reid (from Everton). A month later he also bought Colin Clarke (from Southampton) and Andy Sinton (from Brentford). The only player to leave in this time was Dean Coney, who joined Norwich City.

With the arrival of the new players, results began to improve and Rangers won three of their next four games — two of them away from home — to pull away from the bottom of the table. The run was ended by a 4-1 reverse at Everton, but Rangers then had another good sequence of five wins from six games. This had moved them up to seventh place, but a 2-0 defeat at Liverpool in the final game of the season dropped them back to ninth place with 53 points. Again the changes of management were reflected in the teams selected with only Paul Parker and David Seaman appearing in more than 30 League games. The leading goalscorers were Mark Falco with 15 (12 League and three Cup) and Trevor Francis with ten (seven League and three Cup).

In the Milk Cup in 1988-89, Rangers' second-round opponents were Cardiff City, who were one off the bottom of the Third Division. The first leg at Loftus Road looked as though it would be easy for Rangers, as they went two goals up in the first 26 minutes, the scorers being Francis and Fereday. However, the Welshmen raised their game and were unlucky not to score, being denied by Johns in the Rangers goal. And when it looked as if QPR would have to settle for a two-goal lead, Allen scored a third in the final minute.

The second leg at Ninian Park saw Rangers give one of their better performances. Cardiff scored first through Curtis after seven minutes, but Stein equalised only three minutes later and the second half belonged to Rangers, who added further goals from Falco (56 minutes), Maddix (60) and Falco again (81). So Rangers had won 4-1 to go through to the third round by an aggregate of 7-1.

Their next opponents, at home, were fellow First Division side Charlton Athletic, who took the lead in the first half with a goal from Williams when there was a misunderstanding between Maddix and Seaman. It looked as though they would hold on, but in the 57th minute they had Shirtliff sent off for retaliation. Two minutes later, Francis equalised for Rangers and in the 82nd minutes scored the winner with a spectacular overhead kick.

In the fifth round, Rangers were home again to a First Division London side, this time Wimbledon. The game was a good one with two contrasting styles on display — Rangers' passing game against Wimbledon's ploy of aiming all high balls at Fashanu. Gibson missed a chance after 26 minutes, when he miscued in front of Seaman. And in the 76th minute, Coney thought he had scored for Rangers but the referee disallowed the goal for a foul on the Wimbledon 'keeper. With neither side scoring, the tie went to a replay at Plough Lane.

This match was very similar to the first with not much to show between the sides. Eventually, though, QPR triumphed with the only goal, from Falco in the second half.

It was after this game that Trevor Francis was appointed

Left: Ossie Ardiles chases Steve Hodge and Nigel Clough of Nottingham Forest in the Milk Cup in January 1989. *Right:* Now Peter Reid takes the ball away from Forest's Pearce and Hodge in a First Division game in February 1989.

David Kerslake scores against Forest in the First Division match at the City Ground in 1988-89.

manager, replacing caretaker Peter Shreeves. The quarter-final draw took Rangers to the City Ground to meet Nottingham Forest. With Francis, Falco and McDonald missing through injury, Rangers met a Forest team in top form and they killed the tie with four goals before half-time, Chapman completing a hat-trick. Stein did get one for Rangers before the break, but having lost Ardiles with a cracked fibula, they had no hope of recovery in the second half. After the interval, Chapman scored his fourth and Forest's fifth before Kerslake got a late consolation for Rangers.

The third round draw of the FA Cup gave Rangers an awkward trip to Old Trafford to meet Manchester United. But Francis had done his homework and QPR managed to contain the United attack. However, bad injuries to Francis and Falco in the first half-hour limited Rangers' scoring opportunities and the match ended in a 0-0 draw and necessitated a replay.

At Loftus Road, there were still no goals before the break, and although Stein broke the deadlock in the 57th minute, this was was cancelled out in the 75th minute by a Gill equaliser for United. After 90 minutes, with the score at 1-1, extra-time was needed. Graham, who had come on as a substitute for United at the start of the extra 30 minutes, put them ahead just before the end of the first 15 minutes of the extra period. It looked as though it would be enough to see United through, but McDonald scored with a header in the 120th minute to force a second replay.

Rangers lost the toss for the venue and the sides met again at Old Trafford the following Monday, when QPR found United back to their best form. The Londoners never looked like causing an upset, especially after Alan McDonald was sent off following a challenge on Hughes. United scored three second-half goals without Rangers replying, so despite some entertaining matches, they were out at the first hurdle of the FA Cup yet again.

This season the Simod Cup was not split into two regional sections as in previous years. Having received a bye in the early rounds, Rangers entered the competition in the third round with an away tie at Sheffield Wednesday. The games did not attract good crowds and only 3,957 people were at Hillsborough to see QPR triumph in extra-time by 1-0.

Rangers were now in the last eight and travelled to Watford in their quest for a semi-final place. They had to field three young players — McCarthy, Herrera and Kerslake — due to the non-availability, through injury and suspension, of first-choice players, and their reshuffled side did well to hold Watford to a 1-1 draw after extra-time. Rangers' goal came in the second half of normal time through Coney. The match was decided by penalties, which Rangers won 2-1, following three saves from David Seaman.

The semi-final against Everton at Goodison Park was played in heavy rain, which made the pitch slippery, and even with a place at Wembley awaiting the winners, only 7,472 people attended the match. Given the conditions they saw an entertaining game. Rangers had several good opportunities to score before Pat Nevin headed the only goal of the game after 68 minutes.

Before the 1989-90 season began, Trevor Francis bought Kenny Sansom (from Newcastle United) and Paul Wright (from Aberdeen) and released Wayne Fereday (to Newcastle United), Mark Fleming (to Brentford), Mark Dennis and Andy Gray (to Crystal Palace), and Ossie Ardiles, who became manager of Swindon Town.

The main arrival at Loftus Road during the summer was Don Howe, who joined the coaching staff. Howe had a good reputation as a coach and currently held that position with the England team. Before the season started, Francis reintroduced the Supporters' Club's open day. This time the afternoon consisted of a cricket match between Rangers and their hosts Shepherd's Bush CC. One or two of the cricketing performances took the eye, particularly David Seaman's bowling and Alan McDonald's exploits behind the stumps.

The Football League season began with a 2-1 home win over promoted Crystal Palace and was followed by a 1-1 draw at Chelsea. Rangers then went four games without scoring a goal. They were still missing Francis, who had not fully recovered from his injury at Old Trafford at the beginning of the year. Martin Allen, who had had his disagreements with Francis, especially when his daughter was born, joined West Ham United in September. At the same time Francis signed David Bardsley from Oxford United, with Mark Stein going in the opposite direction.

Francis came back into the side for the away game at Aston Villa and his return could not have been more telling. He scored all three of Rangers' goals in their 3-1 win. The magic did not last long, though, as the next three games were all lost and Rangers were down in 17th place in the table with only nine points. Despite drawing their next two games, they slipped further down the table into a relegation place of 19th, only two points off the bottom.

Before the next game, at home to Liverpool, Nigel Spackman the club's PFA representative, expressed publicly the players' disapproval of Francis' management style. He was promptly dropped from the team to face his old side, but despite all the off-the-pitch issues, Rangers put up a good team performance to beat Liverpool 3-1 in a rousing game. After the next two games, which yielded only one point, chairman Richard Thompson sacked Francis and installed coach Don Howe as manager.

In order for Howe to concentrate on the footballing side of the job, Clive Berlin was appointed to handle all the financial affairs of the club. Howe's first signing was to complete the transfer of Ray Wilkins from Glasgow Rangers, which Francis had negotiated. Later in the month, he paid Rangers' first £1 million fee, for Roy Wegerle from Luton Town. At this time, David Kerslake joined Swindon Town, Nigel Spackman went to Glasgow Rangers and Peter Reid became player-manager at Manchester City.

Howe's first two games in charge both resulted in wins, 3-0 at Crystal Palace and 4-2 at home to Chelsea. These two games were the only time that Wilkins and Reid played together for Rangers, before Reid's departure. Their experience in midfield would certainly have been to Rangers advantage if they had stayed together. The year ended with two draws to put Rangers in 13th place, still only two points away from the drop zone.

January saw the departure of Trevor Francis, the player, to Sheffield Wednesday, although still registered, he never appeared for Rangers after he left the manager's position. Also, Paul Wright returned to Scotland to join Hibernian, as he could not settle in London.

Rangers' League form picked up in the New Year and they went nine matches in which they only lost once. Their best victory in this run was the 3-1 home win over Tottenham Hotspur.

On the transfer deadline day, Don Howe had reluctantly agreed a deal with Arsenal for the transfer of David Seaman, who had stated that he wanted to join a bigger club to further his England career when his contract expired in the summer. The deal involved John Lukic coming to Rangers on loan for the remainder of the season. But after everything had been agreed, Lukic changed his mind and Seaman was still at Rangers, although it was obvious that his heart was not with QPR any more. One newcomer was Dominic Iorfa, a Nigerian international, from Standard Liege.

Rangers managed to remain in mid-table until the end of the season, but their results were not impressive as they won only twice in the final nine games. They were still scoring goals in each game, but the defence was not as solid as it had been earlier in the year. The final League table saw Rangers in 11th place with 50 points, seven clear of the relegated sides. The three regular players in another changing season were Alan McDonald, Andy Sinton and Kenny Sansom. The leading goalscorers were Colin Clarke and Andy Sinton, both with only eight each.

The second round of the 1989-90 Milk Cup bought Fourth Division Stockport County to Loftus Road for the first leg. Rangers got off to a flying start with two goals, from Spackman and Clarke, in the opening five minutes. Stockport then got themselves organised and held Rangers until the break. And

Don Howe looks pensive as his team battle away for First Division points.

after 75 minutes, McInerney scored for County to give them something to play for in the second leg.

At Edgeley Park, Stockport gained an early upper hand and Rangers had Seaman to thank for keeping them in the game. Angell hit a post before half-time to give County inspiration for the second half and it needed all the experience of Parker and Reid to keep the Fourth Division side out. When they started to tire, Rangers came into the game more, but still could not score. But with the game ending goalless, Rangers went through by the narrowest of margins.

The third-round draw gave QPR a home tie with Coventry City. The Midlanders started the better side and scored first in the 30th minute when Seaman allowed a speculative shot from Downs go through his hands and into the net. Drinkell increased Coventry's lead in the 62nd minute to give Rangers a lot to do in order to get at least a replay. Wright pulled one back from the penalty spot in the 81st minute, but it was not enough and Rangers went out of the competition.

The third-round draw of the FA Cup paired QPR with Cardiff City, the side they had beaten in the Milk Cup in the previous season. This time Rangers had to travel to South Wales and they dominated the game but, thanks to Hansbury in the Cardiff goal, the match remained goalless and meant a replay the following Wednesday. The first half of the replay followed the same pattern as the original match, and again Rangers were unable to turn the supremacy into goals. After the break, however, Wilkins finally broke the deadlock with a headed goal after 78 minutes, and Wegerle added a second two minutes later to take Rangers through.

In the fourth round they were away again, this time at Arsenal, and interest in the game was high as Don Howe was returning to the club where he had considerable success as a coach. He had done his preparation well as Rangers managed a creditable goalless draw after restricting the Arsenal forwards to long-range shots.

The replay was a tremendous Cup tie with Rangers outplaying Arsenal in all departments, although with no score at half-time, it looked as though it would take the extra 30 minutes to separate the sides. Then, as if it had been scripted, the opening goal arrived via Kenny Sansom, his first for Rangers, against one of his previous clubs. He played a one-two with Wegerle before shooting past Lukic. The match was in the balance until the final minute when Sinton scored Rangers' second.

Their reward was a trip to the Lancashire coast to meet Third Division Blackpool in the fifth round. Groves gave Blackpool the lead after only three minutes, when Seaman hesitated in coming for a cross, but Rangers equalised right on half-time when Clarke side-footed a Sinton pass into the net. Clarke gave Rangers the lead eight minutes into the second half, when he turned in the box and shot into the goal at the far post. But the lead lasted only four minutes as Eyres equalised for the Seasiders and the Third Division side then held on for a replay, Rangers' third in as many rounds.

The game at Loftus Road saw Rangers outplay the opposition but they could not convert any of the many clear-cut chances they created. Although they did have the ball in the net twice, the goals were disallowed. Blackpool battled all through the 90 minutes and in the extra-time that followed.

A second replay was needed and the toss for venues gave Rangers home advantage and the following Monday the two sides returned to Loftus Road. Again Blackpool held their ground and stopped Rangers from scoring in the first half, but a minute after the break, Wright, the Blackpool defender, inadvertently trod on the ball when attempting a clearance and Sinton took adantage and scored the opening goal.

The Third Division side now had to attack and in doing so left gaps for Rangers. Sansom scored the second after 70 minutes — a replica of his goal against Arsenal in the previous round — and the scoring was completed in the 84th minute when Barker scored from the penalty spot, after he himself had been fouled.

The draw for the sixth round gave Rangers their first home draw of the competition. Unfortunately, though, the visitors were Liverpool. The tie was put back a day so that it could be televised and what a great match the nation's armchair viewers enjoyed. Rangers had already beaten Liverpool at home in the League and were confident of doing so again to reach the semi-finals for only the second time.

Indeed, things looked good when Wilkins gave Rangers the lead after 29 minutes with a spectacular shot. Liverpool, though, equalised after 55 minutes with a typical Barnes free-kick which bent around Rangers' defensive wall. Then Rush put Liverpool in front in the 79th minute with a shot from the edge of the area. It now looked all over for Rangers, but they were not finished and Barker grabbed an equaliser two minutes before the end. This meant Rangers had to replay again for the fourth successive time.

They now faced their ninth Cup match, having progressed through only three rounds. In the game at Anfield, Peter Beardsley scored an early goal for Liverpool and although Rangers fought back well, they could not score before the break. The second half continued in the same manner and with time running out, Wilkins thought he had scored when he lobbed the ball over Grobbelaar, only to see Hysen clear it off the line. As Rangers were unable to turn their extra possession into goals, it was Liverpool who progressed in to the semi-finals.

At the end of the 1989-90 season, David Seaman finally joined Arsenal for a record fee of £1,300,000. During the summer of 1990, the World Cup was held in Italy and Rangers were represented in the England camp by Paul Parker, who was outstanding in the games he played, and Don Howe, who as coach was so close to seeing his efforts rewarded with a place in the Final. Whilst in Italy, Howe lined up Jan Stéjskal as Seaman's replacement. Stéjskal was the current Czechoslovakian goalkeeper. However he would not be able to join Rangers until his club, Sparta Prague, had been knocked out of the European Cup.

On his return from Italy, the only signings Howe made were those of Clive Wilson (from Chelsea) and Andrew Impey (from Yeading, who had won the FA Vase the previous May). Colin Clarke was the only other player to leave, when he joined Portsmouth. KLM did not renew their three-year shirt sponsorship deal and Rangers looked for a new sponsor. The sportswear firm Influence took a one-year contract. Influence was owned by the Kumar Brothers, who were already the manufacturers of the Rangers kit under the Influence brand name.

The season did not start too well with only one win, home to Chelsea, in the first four games. The next home game saw Luton Town as the visitors and they met Rangers in devastating mood, running in six goals, with Wegerle getting two against his old club. With two draws and a defeat in their next three games, Rangers were down to 12th in table and not playing as well as they could.

The next game, away to Leeds United, saw the debut of Stéjskal. He joined Rangers after an earlier-than-expected exit from the European Cup for Sparta Prague. Stéjskal had a nervous start and conceded two early goals, but Rangers then fought back to win 3-2. Wegerle's goal, which involved a run from wide on the right and took him past six defenders, was named as the goal of the season on ITV.

Following the away win, Rangers had one of their worst-ever runs. They lost the next eight League games, the main problem being the number of goals conceded. And the number of injuries to players did not help stabilise the team. Key players missing were Parker, McDonald and Maddix.

In November, Bobby Gould joined Don Howe as assistant manager and it was his knowledge of the lower divisions that triggered Rangers into buying defenders Darren Peacock from Hereford United and Andy Tilson from Grimsby Town. They made their debuts in the game at Derby and had it not been for a last-minute equaliser, Rangers would have recorded their second away win of the season. But at least they had avoided defeat for the first time in two months.

This poor run saw Rangers in 19th place and three points away from the safe position of 17th. The only team below Rangers were Sheffield United, who had gained only four points from their 16 matches. The Boxing Day game against Liverpool ended in a 1-1 draw, to be followed by a 3-2 win over Sunderland. This was QPR's first home win since beating Luton back in September.

Their first game of 1991 was at bottom-placed Sheffield

QPR striker Les Ferdinand battles past Aston Villa's Paul McGrath.

United, who having started their revival at Christmas beat Rangers 1-0 to leave the Londoners entering the New Year in a dire position at the wrong end of the table. The next two games produced only one point and in February, Rangers bought Rufus Brevett from Doncaster Rovers, another Gould recommendation. This eventually allowed Kenny Sansom to join Coventry City, just prior to the transfer deadline.

Although Bobby Gould moved on to West Bromwich Albion in February, to replace Brian Talbot as manager following the Albion boss' sacking after a 4-2 home defeat by Woking in the FA Cup, his influence had been felt at the club and Rangers embarked on an unbeaten run of 11 games. The main area of improvement was in the defence, particularly with the return of Maddix to the side after his injury.

During the run, Rangers had five clean sheets and conceded only one goal in each of the others. Les Ferdinand had emerged as the main goalscorer with seven in seven games. These results lifted Rangers away from the relegation zone up to ninth place and easily the best result was QPR's first-ever win at Anfield, when they beat Liverpool by 3-1. They could not maintain their good spell and only won one of the final five games. At the end of the season, Rangers were in 12th place with 46 points, some 12 points away from the bottom three.

Despite the changing fortunes, three players were ever-presents Andy Sinton, David Bardsley and Ray Wilkins, who used his experience as a steadying effect on the players around him. The leading goalscorers were Roy Wegerle with 19 and Les Ferdinand with ten.

Rangers' second-round opponents in the Littlewoods Cup — as the League Cup was now called — were Peterborough United, the first leg being at Loftus Road. Peterborough, under the management of Mark Lawrenson, gave QPR a hard fight in the first half, but they had a half-time lead thanks to a Ferdinand goal in injury time. After an hour, Maddix scored and when Wegerle added a third after 73 minutes, the tie was looking safe for Rangers.

The second leg at London Road was not a particularly good game as Rangers' three-goal cushion meant that the Posh had to score early to have any chance of going through. Indeed, Sansom netted an own-goal but this was cancelled out by Ferdinand before half-time. The second half saw Rangers protecting their lead and they went through 4-2 on aggregate.

In the third round they had a home tie against Blackburn Rovers, who were third from bottom of the Second Division. Falco gave Rangers the lead in the seventh minute, only for Hill to level the scores nine minutes later. But Barker scored against his old club in the 31st minute to restore Rangers' lead and there were no further goals, despite several good efforts from both sides.

Rangers' next opponents were Leeds United, again Rangers being fortunate with a home draw. With Leeds in fifth place and Rangers having lost their previous six games, their confidence was not very high. It showed early on as Leeds scored after only two minutes, through McAllister. Fairclough added a second after 11 minutes and Chapman made it 3-0 six minutes later to virtually end the contest. In the second half, Leeds defended strongly against a poor Rangers attack and denied their forwards any real scoring opportunities.

For the second time in three years, Rangers were drawn away to Manchester United in the third round of the FA Cup. This time the tie was put back two days to accommodate the new Sky TV, who televised the game live on their satelite system. Hughes gave United the lead but it was short-lived as Maddix equalised. Rangers were not at full strength due to the long-term injuries and as Tilson and Peacock were Cup-tied.

Channing made his first appearance after recovering from a fracture of the fibula. However his luck was out as he suffered a reoccurance of the injury and had to be substituted before half-time. In the second half, the reorganised Rangers defence subdued the lively United attack and it looked as though history would repeat itself and Rangers would get a second chance in the replay. However, Brian McClair scored a goal near the end to snuff out Rangers' FA Cup dreams for another season.

Rangers entered the Zenith Data Systems Cup — the old Full Members' Cup under yet another new name — in the second round, having received a bye in the first. They were drawn at Southampton, the scene of their previous League game which they had lost 3-1. Rangers were without several first-choice players and had to include youngsters Law, McCarthy, Allen and Meaker. The Saints scored twice in the opening 17 minutes, with goals from Shearer and Horne. A minute before half-time, Shearer scored his second and Southampton's third.

Due to injury, Sinton did not appear for the second half and Rangers' attacking options were curtailed. Then a serious injury to Paul Parker saw them down to ten men as Wegerle had also gone off injured after an hour. The fourth Southampton goal came courtesy of an own-goal from Law to complete a very miserable and costly evening for Rangers.

During the summer of 1991, chairman Richard Thompson sacked Don Howe, saying that he wanted a younger man to run the team. It was perhaps a little unfair on Howe, who had done a good job under extreme difficulties during the previous season. Indeed, the good results in the last quarter of the season had renewed confidence for the forthcoming campaign.

Howe's replacement was Gerry Francis, who had proved his managerial ability with Bristol Rovers, the club he had taken into the Second Division with limited resources. Francis was a popular choice for the fans as they remembered his part in the excellent Rangers team of the mid-1970s. In his first excursion into the transfer market, Francis bought two players who had played under him at Bristol Rovers. They were Dennis Bailey (from Birmingham City) and Ian Holloway (from Bristol Rovers).

He also bought Gary Thompson and Tony Witter from Crystal Palace before the season started. The players to leave included Mark Falco (to Millwall) and a fit again Paul Parker, who joined Manchester United for a record fee of around £2 million. Yet another new shirt sponsor was signed for the season. This time it was Brooks, another sportswear manufacturer, who signed a three-year deal. They also re-designed the club's kit and took over the running of the club shop.

The season started with an away game at champions Arsenal. Despite the disappointment at the manner of Don Howe's departure, there was a good feeling around the club following Gerry Francis' arrival and his first match in charge so very nearly ended in an upset. Rangers led Arsenal by 1-0, Bailey scoring on his debut, into the last minute. Merson then equalised in the dying seconds of the game to rob Rangers, and Francis, of a famous victory. Alas, the game saw a serious injury to Wilkins, which kept him out until the end of November.

The first home game ended in a 2-0 defeat by Norwich City

Gerry Francis, a great Rangers star as a player who returned to the club as manager.

and was followed by another six games before Rangers recorded their first win. Rangers were now bottom of the table with only four points from their eight games. Their first success came at Luton Town, when Barker scored the only goal of the game.

Rangers were now helped by the arrival of Paul Walsh on loan from Tottenham Hotspur and after another good performance in the following game, a 2-2 draw against Chelsea, Francis tried to sign Walsh on a permanent basis. But despite having had his differences with the Spurs management, the player decided to return to White Hart Lane.

Rangers' second win of the season was also away, 1-0 at Wimbledon. This was followed, a week later, by their first home win, 3-1 over Everton, with Barker scoring twice. This moved QPR out of the relegation zone for the only time before December. Francis then bought Gary Penrice from Aston Villa in an attempt to increase his forward options.

The next three games, though, were all lost to drop Rangers back to 21st place. But the away game at Notts County, which ended in a 1-0 win, marked the start of an unbeaten run of 11 games and the year ended with three wins and three draws to move Rangers up to 15th place with 27 points.

The year 1992 began with a trip to Manchester United, who were top of the First Division and with games in hand. The match kicked-off later than usual as it was televised live by ITV and viewers saw Rangers get off to a flying start with two goals in the first five minutes, Dennis Bailey and Andy Sinton being the scorers.

Bailey's pace was causing numerous problems for the United defence. He had another good chance — which was cleared of the line — before he scored Rangers' third goal before half-time. QPR were giving one of their best performances for many years and in front of a nationwide television audience, too. McClair pulled one back for United midway through the second half, but Bailey completed his hat-trick soon afterwards to restore Rangers three-goal lead. Wegerle missed an open goal

David Bardsley is challenged by John Harkes of Sheffield Wednesday at Hillsborough in December 1992.

five minutes before the end, but it did not matter as Rangers had recorded their first-ever win at Old Trafford — and by the resounding margin of 4-1.

QPR's next four games all ended in draws before their unbeaten run came to an end in the middle of February at Boundary Park when Oldham Athletic won 2-1. Oldham were the last side to have beaten Rangers back in November.

QPR then had another good run with three wins and four draws in the next seven games. The two home wins in that time both four-goal victories, 4-0 over Manchester City and 4-1 against Leeds United, the eventual champions. The main scorer was again Ferdinand with five goals in five matches. Before the transfer deadline, Roy Wegerle became the latest £1 million player to join Kenny Dalglish at Blackburn Rovers.

These wins had now moved Rangers up into eighth place and they had lost only once in 19 League games, a complete contrast to the first part of the season. All good things have to come to an end, though, and Rangers then lost three successive games by 2-1. They won their last two games, against relegated Luton Town, and against Crystal Palace thanks to an own-goal from Humphreys, and ended the season in 11th place with 54 points.

The backbone of the side during the season was David Bardsley, Darren Peacock, Andy Sinton, Jan Stéjskal and Clive Wilson, all of whom missed only a maximum of four games. Leading goalscorers were Dennis Bailey with 11 (nine League and two Cup) and Les Ferdinand with ten (all League).

Rangers' second-round opponents in the 1991-92 Rumbelows Cup were Third Division Hull City, and for the first time in seven years Rangers were away in the first leg. In front of a disappointingly low crowd of only 4,979, Rangers took a first-half lead through Thompson. They increased it after the break with two goals from Simon Barker to give themselves a comfortable three-goal advantage for the home leg.

At Loftus Road, Rangers had the upper hand for most of the game and scored through Bardsley after 28 minutes. Within the next three minutes, Thompson had added two more before Young scored Hull's first goal of the tie in the 38th minute. Bailey added two more for Rangers in the 56th and 79th minutes to give them an aggregate 8-1 win.

The third round took Rangers to Maine Road to meet Manchester City. Despite their poor League form, QPR gave a good performance and restricted the City front line to a handful of chances, which were saved by Stéjskal. Rangers did not create any clear-cut chances themselves but managed to take the tie to a replay at Loftus Road, where they got off to the best possible start with a goal after only seven minutes. It was scored by Gary Penrice, his first for Rangers.

Alas, that lead lasted only for three minutes before Heath scored for City. After 62 minutes, Wilkins deflected the ball passed Stéjskal to give City the lead and when Quinn added a third 12 minutes later, Rangers were on their way out of the competition.

Again Rangers received a bye in the first round of the Zenith Data Systems Cup and were drawn away to Norwich City in the second round. With the fans not taking to this competition in the early rounds, only 4,492 people turned up at Carrow Road for the tie. Beckford opened the scoring for Norwich and Sinton equalised before the break. Then, with the game heading for extra-time, substitute Impey scored with seconds of normal time remaining to give Rangers a 2-1 win.

The third-round draw saw Rangers at home for only the second time ever in the competition. It was also their third home game within six days, the previous two both ending in 3-1 defeats. With the game being televised live by Sky, Rangers were hoping for a change in fortune. It was not to be as Palace scored twice before the interval, through Thomas and Gabbiandi. QPR were looking a very dispirited side and it was not surprising when Young scored a third for Palace after 56 minutes.

Rangers then seemed to wake up when it was too late and Bardsley pulled one back two minutes after Young's goal. Wilkins closed the gap to one goal when he scored after 77 minutes and the last 13 minutes saw an all-out assault on the Palace goal, but Martyn and the defenders in front of him held firm and Rangers could not get the goal to take the tie to extra-time.

Rangers' third-round opponents in the 1991-92 FA Cup were Southampton at The Dell. The Saints were bottom of the First Division and as Rangers had just beaten top-of-the-table

Darren Peacock and Ray Wilkins in action at Highfield Road in August 1992.

Manchester United, 4-1 at Old Trafford, they were probably expecting to win the Cup tie. But not for the first time QPR looked a completely different team to the one that played three days earlier. Southampton scored twice in the first half, with goals from Wood and Le Tissier, and Rangers were unable to get into any rhythm and went out.

The 1992-93 season saw one of the biggest changes ever to League football in England. The Football Association formed the Premier League and the Football League was reduced to three divisions. The Premier League was in fact the old First Division. The Second, Third and Fourth Divisions all moved up one to become the new First, Second and Third Divisions respectively.

During the close season Rangers were the only Premier League side not to participate the transfer market, for Francis was happy with his squad, particularly after the good finish to the previous season. Once again Rangers had a new shirt sponsor. Brooks had not renewed their deal and were replaced by the first national independent radio station, Classic FM.

Rangers' FA Premier League career started in front of the Sky cameras on Monday, 17 August at Maine Road, where Andy Sinton gave Rangers a 1-1 draw with a goal early in the second half. QPR's first home game was only two days later, against Southampton. Despite Francis' reservations about playing two games so close together, Rangers gave a good performance and won 3-1, with two goals from Ferdinand.

The next two games also ended in victory and Rangers were now on top of the Premier League. They had gone top with a 1-0 away win at Coventry City, with Impey scoring the only goal. Rangers' first defeat of the season followed — unfortunately at close rivals Chelsea — and then there were two home goalless draws and Rangers had not scored in the three games since going top of the table.

In September, David Bardsley joined the ever-growing number of Rangers' England internationals when he appeared as a substitute against Spain in Santander. A good win at Southampton was followed by two more draws and a superb team performance in beating Tottenham Hotspur 4-1 at home. Rangers were now in fourth place, four points behind leaders Blackburn Rovers.

In October, Gary Waddock and Andy Tilson joined Francis' old club, Bristol Rovers. Justin Channing also went to Rovers, but on loan. His transfer was made permanent in January.

With four defeats in the next six games, Rangers started to lose touch with leaders, their only win in this time being a 2-0 success at Wimbledon. Rangers were back to their winning ways in the home game against Oldham, but with two more defeats they went into the last game of the year in ninth place, ten points off the top. The final game of 1992 was at home to Everton and Rangers were three goals up against Everton's nine men, Southall and Rideout having been sent off, when substitute Barlow scored twice. Then Sinton completed his first-ever hat-trick to give Rangers a 4-2 win.

The New Year started with a 1-0 win at Middlesbrough. The result was all the more impressive as Rangers were without Holloway and Wilkins, who had cracked a bone in training, and then they lost Penrice with a broken leg during the game. For the next home game, Rangers had Holloway back but had lost Ferdinand with a groin strain. Manchester United won a bruising game 3-1 which left Rangers in sixth place.

QPR then remained unbeaten for the next five matches — two wins and three draws — and Francis made only his second excursion, for the season, into the transfer market when he signed Devon White from Cambridge United. The win over Coventry City was best remembered for the sliced own-goal by Pearce, who managed to find the net with his back to the goal and aiming forwards.

In February, Rangers had two more additions to their list of current internationals when Les Ferdinand made a scoring debut for England against San Marino at Wembley and Tony Roberts made a well-deserved substitute appearance in goal for Wales against the Republic of Ireland in Dublin.

Left: **Andrew Impey.** *Centre:* **Clive Wilson.** *Right:* **Dennis Bailey.**

Rangers were now up in fourth place although the following group were closing the gap and a poor run of five defeats in the next seven games dropped them to seventh. The middle of the table was very congested with 13 teams covered by only seven points and QPR's only win in this period was at home to Norwich City, who had led the table at one stage. The performances was all the more impressive when one considered the weakened sides that Rangers had to field due to injuries.

The remainder of the season was very promising with four wins and three draws from the last seven games. The two wins over Easter produced a total of 15 goals and two hat-tricks within three days for England new boy Les Ferdinand. Rangers finished the season in fifth place in the inaugural Premier League and as London's top side. Their improved performances increased the average League attendance at Loftus Road to over 14,600, the highest figure since the 1985-86 season.

The regular players during the season, all with at least 37 League appearances were David Bardsley, Les Ferdinand, Andrew Impey, Alan McDonald, Darren Peacock, Andy Sinton and Clive Wilson. The leading goalscorers were Les Ferdinand with 24 (20 League and four Cup) and Bradley Allen with 11 (ten League and one Cup).

Rangers' second-round opponents in what was now the Coca-Cola Cup — the League Cup in reality — were Grimsby Town of the new First Division. The first leg at Loftus Road was a close game with Ferdinand giving Rangers a half-time lead with a goal in the 45th minute. Watson scored a deserved equaliser six minutes into the second half before Ferdinand netted his and Rangers' second after 69 minutes to give them a slender lead for the second leg.

With a big crowd at Blundell Park, the kick-off was delayed for ten minutes. The first half saw Grimsby go close but with no goals before the break, Rangers were still ahead. Then Sinton scored an own-goal and Mendonca added a second to leave Rangers trailing on aggregate before Bailey netted near the end to take the game to extra-time. No more goals were scored and the tie was to be decided on penalties. Grimsby went first and the sequence was: 0-1, 1-1 (Wilkins), Grimsby miss, 2-1 (Sinton), 2-2, 2-2 (Wilson missed), 2-3, 3-3 (Holloway), 3-4, 4-4 (Bardsley), Grimsby miss. This meant that if Alan McDonald scored, Rangers would be through. He made no mistake and Rangers were into the third round by the narrowest of margins, the match finally being settled at 10.27pm.

The third-round draw took Rangers to Bury, scene of a giantkilling act back in October 1987. Heavy rain before the game made the pitch difficult and with both sides trying to master the conditions, the first half was scoreless. The only notable event was a crude two-footed tackle that resulted in Andy Sinton being carried off. With both sides still unable to score, it looked as though extra-time would be needed, but five minutes before the end, Peacock headed Rangers in front from a corner. With Bury now committed to attack, Allen scored with practically the last kick of the game to give Rangers a flattering 2-0 win.

The next round saw QPR visiting Hillsborough to meet Sheffield Wednesday. Despite heavy rain for the previous three days, the pitch was in perfect condition which suited Wednesday. Bright scored after 30 minutes and when Hirst made it 2-0 three minutes later, Rangers were already looking a beaten side. It was not unexpected when Wednesday scored again after 66 minutes, through Palmer, and again in the 85th minute with a Nilsson goal. The team performance was so bad that Francis publicly apologised to the travelling fans.

Rangers' third-round opponents in the FA Cup, were Swindon Town who were near the top of the First Division. They were managed by Glenn Hoddle and the match was billed as a duel between Wilkins and Hoddle. With Sky Television selecting the game for live transmission, the match was played on a Monday night. Swindon should have scored twice in the opening 15 minutes, but Rangers then took hold on the game with three goals in five minutes.

The first, in the 21st minute, and the second, two minutes later, were identical, a Holloway cross and a downward Ferdinand header. The third, after 26 minutes, was scored by Penrice, who turned in the box and shot past Hammond in the Swindon goal.

The second half saw Swindon enjoy the majority of the possession, but Roberts was in exceptional form in goal and made several good saves, including a great double save. Swindon were unable to turn their possession into goals and Rangers went through by three goals to nil.

The next round saw Manchester City as the visitors to Loftus Road and produced a very entertaining match. Rangers should have scored early on when Wilson lost his footing in front of the goal, and when Ferdinand nearly beat Coton to a poor back-pass from McMahon. Right at the end of the first half, Ferdinand should have given Rangers the lead but was inches short of a ball across the goal.

After the break, City's defence seemed more organised, although Rangers had one further opportunity to take the lead. When Allen crossed from the right, the ball was left by both

Andy Sinton bursts past Manchester United's Paul Ince at Loftus Road in January 1993.

Left: Jan Sťejskal. _Centre:_ Tony Roberts. _Right:_ Ian Holloway.

the defender and goalkeeper and Ferdinand again was just short of sliding it into the net. QPR paid for their missed chances in the 71st minute, when White scored with a powerful shot, and four minutes later, Vonk added a second following a scramble in the goalmouth after a Holden corner. Although Rangers scored in injury-time with a goal from Holloway, they went out of the competition.

Yet, despite exits from the Cups, Rangers, of course, ended the 1992-93 season as London's most successful FA Premier League club and the fans felt that Gerry Francis' exciting young team could, indeed, bring glory to Loftus Road in the months ahead.

Rangers Managers

James Cowan (1907-1914)

Former Scottish international half-back James Cowan, who was born near Dumbarton in October 1868, became the first manager of Queen's Park Rangers when he joined the club for the start of the 1907-08 season. He came from Football League giants, Aston Villa, with whom he had gained five League championship medals and two FA Cup winners' medals as well as playing in another Final which Villa lost. In all he was the veteran of 354 games for Villa.

Cowan brought about Rangers' first period of sustained success, beginning in his initial season when they won the Southern League title and held a fine Manchester United side to a 1-1 draw in the FA Charity Shield. Off-the-field problems prevented him from taking the club into the Football League, where his team would surely have competed strongly. Under Cowan, Rangers won the Southern League for a second time in 1912. He resigned before the start of the 1914-15 season and returned to Scotland, where he died in December 1918.

Jimmy Howie (1914-1920)

Jimmy Howie, who succeeded James Cowan as Queen's Park Rangers' manager, was another former Scottish international, although he had little chance to build on his predecessor's good work, for the game was about to be interrupted by World War One. Indeed, he had only one 'peacetime' season and that was played out with the war already gathering momentum across the Channel.

From Ayrshire, Howie played for Kettering and Bristol Rovers in the Southern League before signing for Newcastle United in May 1903. In the early years of this century, he became known as the finest inside-right in the game when he won three caps for Scotland and helped Newcastle into four FA Cup Finals, three of which they won, and to three League Championships. Altogether he scored 83 goals in 235 games for the Magpies before being transferred to Huddersfield Town in December 1910, at the age of 32.

Highlights of his spell in charge of QPR were a third-round FA Cup tie against Everton at Stamford Bridge in 1915 and, four years later, the club's first game at Loftus Road. He left Rangers in the spring of 1920, during the first post-war season, and then had a four-year spell as manager of Middlesbrough. He later returned to London, where he ran a tobacconist's business. Howie died in January 1963.

Ned Liddell (1920-1925)

Ned Liddell was a native of Sunderland, where he was born in 1878. After working in a Wearside shipyard and playing amateur football, he carved out a useful career for himself as a centre-half with Southampton, Gainsborough Trinity, Clapton Orient (for whom he made over 200 appearances), Southend United and Woolwich Arsenal. His career with the Gunners was restricted to two League appearances because shortly after he signed, the competition was suspended due to the war. He returned to Southend as manager in November 1920 before QPR saw him as the man to take over from Jimmy Howie.

The following season was Rangers' first in the Football League, so Liddell had the distinction of selecting the team for the club's first League game, when the Southern League's First Division effectively became the new Third Division.

His first season in charge saw Rangers knock his old club, Arsenal, out of FA Cup and finish third in table. However, this proved to be the best of his five seasons in charge, although Rangers reached the quarter-finals of the FA Cup in 1923. The following year, they had to seek re-election, although it has to be said that Liddell had no money available to strengthen the side, and he left in 1925.

Liddell later managed Fulham and Luton Town, guiding the Hatters to the Third Division South title in 1937, and scouted for West Ham, Chelsea, Brentford, Portsmouth and Spurs. He was still actively involved in the game at the time of his death in 1968, when he was 90.

Bob Hewison (1925-1931)

Bob Hewison was another North-Easterner, born at Beckworth, Newcastle, in 1899. He joined Newcastle United as a wing-half in July 1908 and remained at St James' Park until the outbreak of World War One, during which he played regularly for Leeds City.

In 1919-20, Hewison, who was recovering from a broken leg sustained the previous season, was asked to act as secretary during the period that the Leeds club were being wound up after being found guilty of making illegal payments to players. He then returned to St James' Park and played a few more games for Newcastle before taking over as player-manager of Northampton Town, who signed him for a fee of £250.

He joined Queen's Park Rangers from

the Cobblers in the summer of 1925, but suffered a poor first season as Rangers finished bottom of the Third Division South and again had to apply for re-election in those financially difficult days.

The following season, Hewison managed the first Rangers side to play in the now famous blue and white hoops. Their best League finish during his six years in charge was the third place they attained in 1929-30, although they were 17 points adrift of being promoted. However, Hewison is most noteworthy in Rangers' history for the signing of George Goddard, the club's most prolific goalscorer of all time.

In 1930-31, Rangers slipped back to eighth place and that summer Hewison left the club and in March 1932 joined Bristol City, who had just been relegated to the Third Division South. He spent 18 years at Ashton Gate, although from October 1938 to May 1939 he was suspended after a joint FA-League enquiry found several members of the club guilty of making illegal payments.

Hewison resigned in March 1949 and then managed Guildford City and Bath City and scouted for Bristol Rovers. He died in Bristol in the spring of 1964.

Archie Mitchell (1931-1933)

John Bowman was the original choice to take over from Bob Hewison. Bowman was a QPR director at the time when the move to the White City was being prepared and was appointed manager in the summer of 1931, but was forced to step down through illness before the new season began.

The man to eventually take over from Hewison was already well-known to Queen's Park Rangers supporters, for he had played over 300 games for the club from 1907 to 1921 (see also *A-Z of Rangers Stars)*.

Archie Mitchell had been signed by James Cowan, who had played alongside him at Aston Villa, and he proved a great servant at centre-half, helping Rangers to win two Southern League titles. In August 1921 he became player-manager of Brentford but they were heading for re-election when, in December 1924, he resigned to concentrate on looking for new players. He left Griffin Park altogether in April 1925 and then coached abroad and managed non-League Dartford before rejoining QPR to coach the reserve team.

As the club moved to the White City, they had intended that former player and secretary John Bowman should take over as manager, but after a couple of months he fell ill and Mitchell, already on the staff, was very much a last-minute appointment.

Initially he was allowed to buy to build a side around George Goddard, but the move to a new ground was a disaster and attendances dropped alarmingly. There was only one real highlight — a memorable 3-1 win over the Second Division leaders, Leeds United, in the FA Cup — and the club moved back to Loftus Road. Within 18 months of taking over, Mitchell was gone too. He never managed in the League again and died in April 1949.

Mick O'Brien (1933-1935)

Mick O'Brien, an Irish international centre-half who was born in Kilcock in August 1893, won his caps whilst playing for seven English clubs, although his nomadic career took him even further afield and during World War One he served in the Army, the Royal Navy and the Royal Flying Corps.

Between 1919 and 1931, O'Brien played for Celtic, Alloa Athletic, Norwich City, South Shields, Queen's Park Rangers, Leicester City, Brooklyn Wanderers (USA), Derby County, Walsall, Norwich again and then Watford before being appointed Rangers' manager in May 1933.

He took over with the club in dire circumstances and was forced to sell prolific scorer George Goddard within weeks of becoming manager. O'Brien did wonders in lifting Rangers, a club with massive debts, to finish in fourth place in the Southern Section in 1933-34, but he left in April 1935 after another poor season. He later worked as assistant manager at Brentford and then managed Ipswich Town to the Southern League title in 1936-37.

Beset by personal problems, including the death of his wife, he died at Uxbridge in September 1940.

Billy Birrell (1935-1939)

Billy Birrell was Queen's Park Rangers' most successful manager since James Cowan and was unlucky not to take the club into the Second Division during his four seasons in charge at Loftus Road.

A former favourite with Middlesbrough, where he scored 63 goals in 235 League and Cup games, he came to Rangers after managing Raith Rovers and Bournemouth. Birrell, who was born in Fife in March 1897, had a tough time at Dean Court and Bournemouth had to seek re-election in 1934. But his fortunes changed after he took over from Mick O'Brien in April 1935.

Birrell was noted for the purchase of Tommy Cheetham, the linchpin of a free-scoring side, and he was in charge when Rangers registered a club record 8-1 FA Cup win against Bristol Rovers. In 1938 they just missed out on promotion to Division Two,

finishing only three points behind promoted Millwall.

Birrell left Loftus Road in May 1939, just after Cheetham had been sold to First Division Brentford, and took over at Chelsea, another First Division side. After working hard during the difficult war years, Birrell signed some fine players for the club, but although he took Chelsea to two FA Cup semi-finals in the early 1950s, much of his time was spent trying to keep them in the First Division. He retired in May 1952 and later worked as a clerk outside football. He died in November 1968.

Ted Vizard (1939-1944)

Welsh international winger Ted Vizard was one of the greatest players in Bolton Wanderers' history, but he was unlucky to be appointed manager of Queen's Park Rangers at the end of the 1938-39 season.

With the onset of war just around the corner, he never had an opportunity to build a side at Loftus Road.

Born in Cogan in June 1889, Vizard scored 70 goals in 512 games for the Trotters, gained two FA Cup winners' medals — including playing in the first Wembley Final — and won 22 international caps. After 21 years at Burnden Park, during which time he gained a BA degree, he managed Swindon Town from April 1933 to May 1939, when he took over from Billy Birrell at Loftus Road.

He contributed to Rangers' modest successes in wartime football before taking over from Major Frank Buckley at Wolverhampton Wanderers in April 1944. Despite taking Wolves to third place in Division One in the first peacetime season of 1946-47, he was replaced by Stan Cullis in June 1948. He later managed non-League Cradley Heath and ran a pub in the West Midlands. He died in Wolverhampton in December 1973.

Dave Mangnall (1944-1952)

Dave Mangnall, who was born in Wigan in September 1905, was a bustling centre-forward who scored plenty of goals for First Division Huddersfield Town and then helped Millwall, a Third Division South club at the time, to the 1937 FA Cup semi-finals and then into Division Two the following season.

He was 33 when he joined Queen's Park Rangers in May 1939 (see also *A-Z of Rangers Stars)* and was reluctant to take on the role of player-manager towards the end of the war. But in due course he built an excellent side and in 1948 took the club into the Second Division for first time.

Mangall was the first Rangers manager to spend £5,000 on one player — Fred Durrant — but four tough seasons in the higher division saw the break-up of his fine side — there was, for instance, the £10,000 transfer of goalkeeper Reg Allen to Manchester United — and after relegation in 1952, he left the club. He did not manage in the Football League again and died in Penzance in April 1962.

Jack Taylor (1952-1959)

Former Wolves, Norwich City and Hull City full-back Jack Taylor was manager of Queen's Park Rangers during a very bleak period in the club's history.

Born in Barnsley in February 1914, he played in the same Wolves side as his brother Frank before being transferred to Norwich in June 1938. After guesting for Barnsley and Watford during the war he joined Hull in July 1947 and when the Tigers won the Third Division North title under Raich Carter in 1948-49, Taylor appeared in 32 League games. From May 1950 to June 1952, he was player-manager of non-League Weymouth and then replaced Dave Mangnall at newly-relegated QPR.

At Loftus Road he did some solid work, picking up a few useful players from non-League football, but lack of success in the Third Division South meant that attendances dropped dramatically and QPR were also victims of two humiliating FA Cup defeats against non-League opposition, losing 4-0 to amateurs Walthamstow Avenue at Highbury in 1954-55 and then being hammered 6-1 by Southern League Hereford United in 1957-58.

Taylor left Rangers in May 1959, to take over at Leeds United, but within a year, Leeds were relegated to Division Two and he resigned in March 1961, even though he still had 12 months of his £2,000-per-annum contract to run. He left League football and died in his home-town in February 1978.

Alec Stock (1959-1968)

Desperate for a return to the relatively heady days of the late 1940s, Queen's Park Rangers looked to the inspirational Alec Stock, a former QPR inside-forward who had pulled off one of the great FA Cup upsets of all time when his Yeovil team beat star-studded Sunderland in the 1949 FA Cup.

Stock was born in Somerset in March 1917 and was on the books of both Tottenham and Charlton before making his League debut for QPR against Reading in February 1938. He made a handful of appearances before war was declared, during which he guested for a number of clubs before joining the Royal Armoured Corps, eventually reaching the rank of major.

At the age of 26, Stock became player-manager of Yeovil Town and their famous Cup victory over Sunderland pushed him into the limelight. As manager of Leyton Orient he guided them to some enjoyable Cup runs and into Division Two before spending a 53-day spell as Arsenal's assistant manager. After returning to Brisbane Road, Stock spent three months as manager of AS Roma before another spell at Orient, whom he finally left in February 1959.

Rangers appointed him in August that year and so began the most exciting period in the club's history. Stock soon began to rebuild the side, but with the arrival of chairman Jim Gregory in November 1964 he was able to transform the club. Stock developed a youth set-up which was the envy of many clubs and also he bought well, most notably the signing of Rodney Marsh. Indeed, the Rangers team was built around the enigmatic number-ten and in 1967, Stock achieved for Rangers a unique double of Third Division championship and Wembley victory in the League Cup Final against West Brom. It was the greatest season in the club's history.

The following season, Rangers won promotion to Division One, but with internal pressures mounting, Stock resigned without selecting a First Division team at Loftus Road and Bill Dodgin took over as caretaker boss until the arrival of Tommy Docherty in November. Stock later enjoyed success with Luton Town (who he helped out of Division Three) and Fulham (who he took to the 1975 FA Cup Final) and became a director at QPR in April 1977, was caretaker manager at Loftus Road in July 1978 after the departure of Frank Sibley, and manager and then a director of Bournemouth.

Tommy Docherty (1968 & 1979-80)

Tommy Docherty was one of the most colourful managers in the game but in his first spell at Loftus Road he spent only 28 days in charge of Queen's Park Rangers, who were just one of his many clubs. He returned some years later, but again found life difficult at the Bush.

Born in the Gorbals district of Glasgow in August 1928, Docherty played for Celtic, Preston and Arsenal as a hard-tackling wing-half who won international honours for Scotland. He became player-coach at Chelsea in 1961 and was appointed caretaker manager at Stamford Bridge in September that year, after Ted Drake had left.

He was given the job permanently in January 1962 and although he could not prevent Chelsea's relegation to Division Two, he got them straight back up the following year. They won the League Cup in 1965, were FA Cup runners-up in 1967, and four times Docherty broke the club's transfer record. However, after Joe Mears died, Docherty could not work with the new chairman and in November 1967 he went to manage Rotherham United.

Docherty could not prevent their eventual relegation to Division Three but he swept through Millmoor like a hurricane, clearing out all but two first teamers. In November 1968 he was tempted back to London and First Division football with QPR, following the departure of Alec Stock from Loftus Road. Docherty soon realised that he had made a mistake, however, and he resented what he saw as interference from Jim Gregory. He was soon off to manage Aston Villa and although proving a favourite with the fans in his early days at Villa Park, he was sacked in November 1970 with Villa bottom of Division Two.

There followed spells at Oporto, Hull City (as assistant manager) and as Scotland's national team manager before he took over at Manchester United, who were relegated to the Second Division in his first full season. He soon got them back, but even two FA Cup Final appearances — United were victorious in one — and third place in Division One could not protect him after an affair with the wife of the club's physiotherapist was made public.

In September 1977 he took over at Derby County but then there was the dramatic collapse of a libel case against Willie Morgan and Granada TV, when Docherty admitted that he had lied in court. His days at Derby were also controversial as players came and went with remarkable frequency.

In May 1979 he returned to QPR, was sacked almost immediately, reinstated after nine days and also arrested by the Derby police who were investigating allegations of financial corruption at the Baseball Ground. After being taken back to Derby he was released without charge and returned to Loftus Road.

Frank Sibley (for 12 months), then Alec Stock (as caretaker) and then Steve Burtenshaw had filled the manager's seat in a period of less than two years before Docherty — appointed with Rangers already doomed to the Second Division — returned. His reputation helped to keep many 'name' players at the club, but with the side struggling in the lower division and the sales of Clive Allen, for a club record fee of £1.25m, and Paul Goddard, his position became untenable.

Docherty left Rangers again in October 1980 and later worked in various capacities with Preston, Sydney Olympic, South Melbourne, Wolves and Altrincham before leaving soccer to concentrate on his work as an after-dinner speaker.

Les Allen (1968-1971)

Les Allen was a member of Spurs' great double-winning side before he joined QPR (see *A-Z of Rangers Stars*). He took over as player-manager in December 1968, after the shock departure of Alec Stock and the stormy month-long reign of Tommy Docherty.

Allen sold Roger Morgan to Tottenham Hotspur for a Rangers incoming record fee of £110,000, then bought Terry Venables from Spurs for another club record amount of £50,000, but could not keep Rangers in the First Division. It was a difficult time and with more behind-the-scenes problems and the indifferent form of some players, Allen resigned in January 1971.

Perhaps, like so many great players, he was not cut out to be a manager, for his time at Swindon Town ended in that club's relegation to the Third Division in 1974, after which Allen left League football. Les Allen is still a regular spectator at Loftus Road, watching Bradley, the latest of the Allen clan.

Gordon Jago (1971-1974)

Former Charlton Athletic centre-half Gordon Jago was Les Allen's assistant and took over in January 1971, when Allen quit. During his time in charge at Loftus Road, Jago sold Rodney Marsh to Manchester City for a profit of £90,000 and took Rangers back into the First Division in 1973, building a side with the right combination of experience and youth. But in October 1974, with the club in a lowly League position, he moved to manage Millwall.

Jago, who was born in Poplar in October 1932 and won England Youth honours, had made almost 150 appearances for Charlton before becoming player-manager of non-League Eastbourne United in July 1962. He was appointed assistant manager and coach at Fulham in August 1968 and then managed Baltimore Bays in the NASL and was director of coaching for the United States Soccer Federation before Rangers made him their coach in 1970.

After his days at Rangers, Millwall were relegated at the end of his first season in charge at The Den, but he took them back to the Second Division before quitting English soccer in December 1978 following an increase in violent behaviour by the fans. He moved back to the USA and was coach to Tampa Bay Rowdies, who he took to two NASL Soccer Bowl victories. He later coached California Surf and, after the collapse of the NASL, worked for Dallas Sidekicks in the Major Indoor Soccer League.

Dave Sexton (1974-1977)

When he took over from Gordon Jago in October 1974, Dave Sexton inherited a Queen's Park Rangers team with a great potential that was soon to be realised. And as if to underline Rangers' rising status, in the same month as Sexton's appointment, Gerry Francis became the first QPR player to skipper an international side when he captained England.

In his first season at Loftus Road, Sexton bought Don Masson for £300,000 and saw Rangers climb up the table to finish 11th. The following season of 1975-76 was even better as Rangers achieved their best-ever final placing in the Football League, when they finished runners-up to Liverpool and qualified for Europe for the first time. They reached the quarter-finals of the UEFA Cup the following season and won a place in the League Cup semi-finals in 1976-77.

In July 1977, however, Sexton was tempted away to manage Manchester United, following Tommy Docherty's controversial departure from Old Trafford. United had a poor first season under Sexton but then reached the 1979 FA Cup Final, where they lost 3-2 to a last-minute Arsenal goal; the following season they were runners-up to Liverpool in the First Division. Sexton had spent £1 million on Gordon McQueen and £825,000 on Ray Wilkins. Another £1 million was spent on Gary Birtles but he was disappointing and in April 1981, Sexton was sacked, despite United having won their previous seven games.

A relegation struggle as manager of Coventry City followed before Sexton was appointed to the England set-up, as assistant to Bobby Robson and having a leading role in the FA's School of Excellence. In 1992-93 he was chief coach at Aston Villa, the FA Premier League runners-up.

Indeed, it was as a coach, rather than a manager, that Sexton had made his name. He was born in Islington in April 1930, son of boxer Archie Sexton, and after non-League soccer with Newmarket and Chelmsford City, he had a few games for Luton Town before joining West Ham in April 1952. After scoring 26 goals in 77 appearances for the Hammers, he was transferred to Leyton Orient and then played for Brighton and Crystal Palace before his career was ended by a knee injury.

He worked as an assistant coach at Chelsea before his first managerial job with Leyton Orient in January 1965, but resigned at the end of that year with Orient bottom of the Second Division. There followed a spell coaching at Fulham and Arsenal before Sexton got his second chance in management, when he replaced Tommy Docherty at Chelsea in October 1967.

Chelsea lifted the FA Cup in 1970 and the European Cup-winners' Cup the following year. In 1972 they lost the League Cup Final to Stoke and then decided to build the three-tier stand at Stamford Bridge which almost bankrupted the club. Now financially shackled — earlier in his days at Chelsea he had been able to spend freely — Sexton also lost players like Osgood and Hudson and in October 1974 he was sacked. Thirteen days later he took over as manager of Queen's Park Rangers.

Frank Sibley (1977-1978)

After Dave Sexton's departure to Old Trafford, Rangers turned to coach and former player Frank Sibley (see *A-Z of Rangers Stars*) to manage the side. They struggled throughout 1977-78 and missed relegation by only one point. Sibley used many players and signed Leighton James from Derby County and Dave Needham from Notts County, as well as blooding Paul Goddard amongst others from the junior ranks.

However, he was given no time to rebuild and it had become obvious that the recent good times had come to an abrupt end. Sibley resigned in July 1978, to be replaced initially by Alec Stock and eventually Steve Burtenshaw. He had a brief and unhappy spell in charge at Walsall in the spring of 1979, where he was unable to prevent the Saddlers from relegation to Division Four and was dismissed.

In 1984, he returned to Loftus Road as reserve-team manager, acting as caretaker boss from December of that year until the end of 1984-85 when he became coach once more. After a year assisting Millwall, Sibley again drifted back across the capital to his Shepherd's Bush roots to act as assistant

coach to Gerry Francis, a position he still holds.

Steve Burtenshaw (1978-1979)

In August 1978, Steve Burtenshaw was appointed as Queen's Park Rangers new manager. He had been assistant to Gordon Lee at Everton and was also making a return to Loftus Road, having coached under Gordon Jago in 1973, although this was his second and last manager's position in League football.

Burtenshaw had played for Brighton for 14 years, making 237 League appearances for the Sussex club before a coaching position at Arsenal and a fleeting nine months as Sheffield Wednesday manager. For QPR he signed Glenn Roeder from Orient, and Rachid Harkouk from Crystal Palace with Don Givens leaving Loftus Road to sign for Birmingham.

The 1978-79 season started badly, however, and Rangers' highest place was 13th in October. One win in 20 matches, plus the departure of Phil Parkes for £565,000 to West Ham, sent QPR plummeting to the bottom three and relegation.

Perhaps the lasting memory of Burtenshaw's year in charge was his introduction of Clive Allen to League football, the youngster crowning his debut with a hat-trick against Coventry. Jim Gregory sacked Burtenshaw before the last match of the season to install a familiar and controversial figure as his successor. After leaving Loftus Road, Burtenhsaw scouted for Arsenal and, apart from a brief caretaker manager's role in March 1986, never pursued management again.

Terry Venables (1980-1984)

An England international at every level, former Queen's Park Rangers captain and a member of the great 1976 team, Terry Venables was popular with the fans and well-liked by chairman Jim Gregory (see also *A-Z of Rangers Stars*).

After a fine playing career with Chelsea, Spurs, QPR and Crystal Palace, Venables took his first steps in management with Palace in June 1976. He took over from Malcolm Allison and in his first season in charge guided the Selhurst Park club to promotion from Division Three. Further promotion to Division One followed and suddenly Palace were 'the Team of the Eighties'. But, despite some big signings, this potential was never realised and in October 1980, after a boardroom row and with Palace trying to shrug off a poor start, Venables resigned.

He immediately joined QPR as manager and soon made his mark. Always the innovator, he was instrumental, in the summer of 1981, in the club's change to a plastic playing surface. He then took Rangers to their first-ever FA Cup Final and then returned the club to the First Division in 1983.

With Jim Gregory looking to step down, Venables was offered a chance to take control of Queen's Park Rangers, but the man who was seen by many as a future England manager was lured away by Spanish giants Barcelona in 1984. Under Venables they won the Spanish League championship but lost a European Cup Final before he returned to England to manage Tottenham Hotspur, where his vision and energy led to the club being saved from the clutches of Robert Maxwell.

Alas, his 'dream ticket' with millionaire Alan Sugar turned sour at the end of the 1992-93 season, when Sugar had him removed from Tottenham, although Venables fought back with a High Court injunction. The matter, though, looked far from being resolved to his satisfaction.

Venables, incidentally, co-wrote the TV series *Hazell* and also a novel *They Used to Play on Grass*, well before QPR installed their artificial pitch at Loftus Road.

Alan Mullery MBE (1984)

Alan Mullery, who was born in Notting Hill in November 1941, was a fine wing-half who established himself in Fulham's

Second Division promotion team of 1958-59. Spurs signed him for £72,500 in March 1964 and after taking some time to win over the fans at White Hart Lane, he went on to make 374 senior appearances for Tottenham, scoring 30 goals. He played for Spurs in the 1967 FA Cup Final, when they beat Chelsea, scored the winner in the 1972 UEFA Cup Final, when he was skipper, and also led the side to victory in the 1971 League Cup Final.

Mullery won 35 full England caps, playing in the 1970 World Cup finals in Mexico. He re-signed for Fulham in the 1972 close season, playing in another all-London FA Cup Final when the Cottagers lost to West Ham in 1975. That year he was voted Footballer of the Year and awarded the MBE for his services to the game.

In his first managerial job he got Brighton into the First Division, but had little success as manager of Queen's Park Rangers or at his other clubs, Charlton, Crystal Palace and another spell with Brighton. He was Rangers' manager from June 1984, when he arrived from Palace, until December that year. He signed Garry Bannister, John Byrne and Robbie James during his brief spell in charge, and sold Clive Allen to Spurs.

Jim Smith (1985-1988)

After Alan Mullery's departure, Frank Sibley was appointed caretaker manager of Queen's Park Rangers before Jim Smith came from Oxford United, the club he had taken into the First Division for the first time in their history.

In Smith's first season with Rangers, the club beat Chelsea 6-0 and reached Wembley with an appearance in the Milk Cup Final. They beat Chelsea, Forest and Liverpool to get there, but in the Final they lost, ironically, to Oxford United, Smith's former club.

The 1987-88 season began with an impressive run which saw Rangers top of the table in the opening weeks before they eventually finished in fifth place. Early the following season, new chairman David Bulstrode died suddenly and, soon afterwards, Smith moved to struggling Newcastle United.

It was not a good move, however, for he found a hotbed of politics at St James' Park. The Magpies were relegated to Division Two at the end of the season and Smith, fed-up of behind-the-scenes bickering, resigned in March 1991. After a spell as coach under Colin Todd at Middlesbrough, he became manager of Portsmouth and took the club to the FA Cup semi-finals in his first season, when they missed a Wembley appearance after a penalty shoot-out with Liverpool. The following season, Smith took Pompey close to promotion into the Premier League, although they failed in the play-offs.

Born in Sheffield in October 1940, Jim Smith signed for Sheffield United but never played in their first team and made his living as a full-back in the lower divisions with Aldershot, Halifax and Lincoln City before becoming player-manager of non-League Boston United. He later managed Colchester United to promotion from Division Four, did good work at Blackburn Rovers without getting them into the First Division, and then saw Birmingham City relegated to Division Two before taking them straight back.

He moved to Oxford United in March 1982 and took them from the Third to the First Division in successive seasons. It was that sort of ability which attracted Queen's Park Rangers.

Trevor Francis (1988-1989)

Peter Shreeves was appointed caretaker manager when Jim Smith went to Newcastle, but he soon controversially moved aside when former England striker Trevor Francis was promoted to player-manager by chairman Richard Thompson.

A Devonian — he was born at Plymouth in April 1954 — Francis burst upon the League scene as a free-scoring teenager with Birmingham City in the early 1970s before Brian Clough made him Britain's first £1 million footballer when he was transferred to Nottingham Forest in February 1979.

Francis, holder of 52 full England caps, scored the winner for Forest in the 1979 European Cup Final before moving to Manchester City and then played for Sampdoria, Atalanta and Glasgow Rangers before Jim Smith signed him for QPR in March 1988 on a free transfer.

Francis bought Andy Sinton and David Bardsley as the club suffered an unprecedented injury crisis, but his management style was criticised — particularly over his disciplining of Martin Allen who missed training around the time his daughter was born — and, despite securing the services of Ray Wilkins, Francis was forced to leave. He moved to Sheffield Wednesday and although they were relegated in his first season, he took them straight back to Division One. In 1993 the Owls reached two Wembley Cup Finals under his management.

Don Howe (1989-1991)

Don Howe was a hugely experienced coach, particularly with Arsenal and England, when he was brought to Loftus Road by player-manager Trevor Francis. Howe took over when Francis left and his first major move was to buy Roy Wegerle, who became the first £1 million player in Queen's Park Rangers' history.

David Seaman and Paul Parker joined Rangers' list of internationals before Seaman was sold for £1.3m to Arsenal at end of the 1989-90 season. The highlight of the following year was a 3-1 win at Anfield before Howe was dismissed with Rangers in mid-table.

Howe, who was born in Wolverhampton in October 1935, skippered West Brom for many years and won his 23 full England caps all in a row. He was a skilful full-back who later in his career played at right-half and inside-right. For West Brom he made 379 first-team appearances before being transferred to Arsenal, where he clocked up another 74 games before retiring through injury in March 1966.

He was coach when Arsenal won the double in 1971 and coached them to another three Wembley Cup Finals and a European Cup-winners' Cup Final. He was not very successful as manager of West Brom and asked to be released as Arsenal's manager when he discovered that Terry Venables had been approached to replace him. Howe was coach at Plough Lane when Wimbledon won the FA Cup in 1988 and was reluctant to take over as QPR's manager, although he was officially chief coach.

He was equally reluctant to step up at Coventry City when Terry Butcher was sacked in January 1992 and after a two-month spell as joint manager with Bobby Gould (with whom he had enjoyed success at Wimbledon), he stepped down to become Ian Porterfield's assistant at Chelsea. Howe was suffering from a heart complaint and did not want to travel as he was expected to do with Coventry.

Howe was assistant manager of the England team in the early 1980s and also worked for Galatasaray of Turkey, in Saudi Arabia and with Bristol Rovers.

Gerry Francis (1991-)

Gerry Francis was a QPR hero of the 1970s (see also *A-Z of Rangers Stars*), who had enjoyed managerial success with Bristol Rovers before returning to Loftus Road as manager in June 1991.

He built a young side around the experience of Ray Wilkins and on New Year's Day 1992, in front of a nationwide TV audience, his side demolished Manchester United 4-1 at Old Trafford, thus severely damaging United's title hopes.

Francis managed to retain key players at the club and nurtured Les Ferdinand into an England centre-forward. Early in the 1992-93 season, Rangers headed the top section for first time in five years and the fans felt that, under Francis, the good times might be just around the corner once again. In the end he got them into fifth place, London's most successful club of the season.

Queen's Park Rangers on their lap of honour after the 1967 League Cup Final victory over West Bromwich Albion.

A-Z of Rangers Stars

Sam Abel

Signed in 1934 from Fulham for £400, Sam Abel made his League debut against Brighton on 15 September that year. He was originally a centre-forward, having scored 57 goals in 96 League games for the Cottagers, but QPR converted him into a defender. He proved a typical full-back of his day — 5ft 11in in height but solidly built, weighing in at around 13st 2lb. The majority of his football for Queen's Park Rangers was played during the war years when he became very popular with the crowds for his robust approach to the game. He occasionally played on the wing and would have been a much more significant personality in QPR history, had the war years not interrupted his career. He made 209 League and Cup appearances for QPR.

Bert Addinall

Albert Addinall began playing for Queen's Park Rangers during the latter years of the war and signed official forms in the 1946 close season. He broke into the first team regularly during the four seasons that Rangers spent in the Second Division, from 1948 to 1952. Leading scorer on a number of occasions, he was eventually transferred to Brighton in January 1953. Addinall was a typical centre-forward of the era, fairly aggressive and always committed to goalscoring. He netted 74 goals in 172 League and Cup games for Rangers. For Brighton he continued his scoring form with 31 goals in 60 League games before ending his League career with Crystal Palace, whom he joined in July 1954. He then moved into non-League soccer with Snowdon.

Clive Allen

Clive Allen is a member of the famous Allen footballing family and came to the club through his father Les' association with Queen's Park Rangers. He signed full-time professional forms in September 1978 and made his debut in November that year, as a substitute against Chelsea. Allen played only occasionally during that first season and became a first-team regular as an 18-year-old in 1979-80. His 30 goals during that campaign brought him to the attention of many clubs and in the close season of 1980 he signed for Arsenal for £1.2m. However, he never had the chance to prove his abilities to the Gunners as they in turn transferred him to Crystal Palace before the season started. Allen did not really achieve his potential at Selhurst Park and Terry Venables brought him back to the Bush. The following season, Allen scored a further 21 goals for the club and continued to be their leading scorer through to the end of 1983-84. In August 1984 he was transferred to Tottenham Hotspur for £750,000. For Spurs he played as a lone striker and responded with 49 goals in 1986-87 to break the club record set by Jimmy Greaves. That earned him the PFA Player of the Year and the FWA Footballer of the Year awards. Clive Allen earned three of his five England caps whilst with Queen's Park Rangers, but failed to score on any of those appearances, although many considered he got an excellent goal in the game against Turkey but the effort was disallowed. He subsequently played in the French League with Bordeaux (again a £1 million move) and for Manchester City, Chelsea and West Ham United. For QPR he scored 83 goals in 147 senior games.

Les Allen

A nomination for Queen's Park Rangers Hall of Fame, Les Allen was a key figure in the great side of the mid-1960s. He brought flair, experience and goalscoring to a side that was rapidly developing into the finest that the club had ever fielded up to that time. He joined QPR in July 1965 and in his four seasons with them he proved vital to their promotion, in successive seasons, from the Third Division to become members of the First for the first time in the club's history. He was also a member of the successful League Cup winning side in the competition's first Wembley Final. He began his career at Stamford Bridge in September 1954 but competition for places there was fierce and so in December 1959 he moved to Spurs with Johnny Brooks coming in the other direction. At White Hart Lane, Allen was a member of Spurs' finest side which won the League and FA Cup double in 1960-61. He played in every game that season, scoring 23 goals. He managed QPR from 1968 to 1971 before moving to Swindon Town as boss. His 146 senior appearances for Rangers yielded him 62 goals.

Martin Allen

Another member of the famous family, Martin Allen is a cousin of Clive. He played for the Queen's Park Rangers youth sides, signing professional forms in May 1983, and had the distinction of making his debut in a UEFA Cup match against Reykjavik in October 1984. He quickly developed into an aggressive midfield ball-winner with great drive and determination. Allen left the club in September 1989, following a disagreement with manager Trevor Francis, and signed for West Ham United for £550,000. He made 154/13 senior appearances for Rangers, scoring 19 goals.

Reg Allen

Reg Allen joined QPR from Corona, a local works team, and made his League debut in November 1938. He quickly established himself as first-choice goalkeeper and remained so up until the suspension of League fixtures upon the outbreak of war in September 1939. Allen joined the Army and was captured during the early part of the war, spending the next few years as a prisoner-of-war before returning to England in 1944. During the first four seasons after the war, he emerged as the best goalkeeper in the lower divisions and it was no surprise when he was subsequently transferred to Manchester United in June 1950 for £12,000. The fee was then a record for a goalkeeper, which truly reflected his ability. Alas, after 75 games for Manchester United, Allen had to retire from football through injury. In his career with Rangers he made 252 senior appearances.

Peter Angell

Consistency was the hallmark of Peter Angell during the 12 years that he was with QPR. He signed from non-League Slough Town in July 1953 and played the last of his 450 games for the club in the 1964-65 season. In today's terms he would be described as a midfield player with a tendency to get forward, hence his relatively good scoring record of 39 goals. He also played a number of games at outside-left.

Jimmy Armstrong

Born at Lemington-on-Tyne, Jimmy Armstrong played for Easington Colliery before signing as a professional for Clapton Orient in 1926. After only two League games for Orient, Armstrong was transferred to Queen's Park Rangers in July 1928 and after a quiet first season with the club he established himself as a first-team regular. He was 6ft tall, weighed 12st and had a reputation for being an old-fashioned, hard-working, left-half. In 1934, he joined Watford after 133 League and Cup games for Rangers.

Gary Bannister

Relatively small for a modern striker, Gary Bannister nevertheless scored 72 goals in 172 senior appearances during four seasons with Queen's Park Rangers, following his £100,000 move from Sheffield Wednesday in August 1984. A player appreciated by both his fellow professionals and supporters for his speed and neat play, he scored a famous hat-trick for Rangers, in 6-0 defeat of Chelsea in March 1986, and netted another the following year. Before being transferred to Wednesday he was with Coventry City, whom he joined as an apprentice, and later spent a second spell with Coventry. He later moved to West Brom and was on loan to Oxford United before signing for Nottingham Forest. An England Under-21 international, Bannister helped Wednesday to the FA Cup semi-finals in 1983 and into the First Division the following year. For the Owls he netted 66 goals (several from the penalty spot) in 142/1 senior games.

David Bardsley

Following spells at Blackpool, Watford and Oxford United, David Bardsley joined Queen's Park Rangers in September 1989 for £375,000. It proved an excellent move for both player and club as he settled at right-back and, through a series of outstanding club performances, ultimately went on to gain England honours. His full international debut came against Spain in September 1992, as a second-half substitute, but he was injured after only 18 minutes play. Since that time he has continued to be part of the England set-up, a situation endorsed by his quality play in the Premier League. He has so far made 177 appearances for Rangers, scoring six goals.

Simon Barker

Having played as an apprentice for Blackburn Rovers, Simon Barker signed professional forms for them in 1982 and by the following season had established himself as a first-team regular. In 182 League appearances for Blackburn he scored 35 goals and developed into a very useful midfield player. During that period he gained England Under-21 honours before being transferred to Queen's Park Rangers in July 1988 for £400,000. Now in his fifth season with the club, he continues to turn in good performances which have contributed to Rangers' satisfactory position in the First Division and subsequently the Premier League. By the end of 1992-93 he had made 187 appearances for Rangers, scoring 17 goals.

William Barnes

William Barnes played for Queen's Park Rangers for six seasons as a regular winger — normally on the left — and altogether made 234 League and Cup appearances for the club, scoring 37 goals. He was born in West Ham but played for Sheffield United, spending some three seasons with the Blades before returning to London to join his home team, West Ham United. He subsequently went to Luton Town for a spell before joining Rangers in 1907. Barnes was a member of the team that won the Southern League in 1907-08 and also in the side that repeated the feat in 1911-12. He played for QPR in all three of the FA Charity Shield matches in which the club appeared during the early part of the century. He was club captain and an important player during the early 1900s. In 1913 he moved to Southend United.

Walter Barrie

Walter Barrie was on West Ham United's books in 1931-32 but did not play in the Hammers' first team before joining Queen's Park Rangers in the close season. He made his League debut against Watford on 24 September that year and played for Rangers for six seasons — making 169 League and Cup appearances — before being transferred to Carlisle United in 1938. Barrie was born in Scotland, at Kirkcaldy, and initially joined Hibernian as a part-time professional. He was a regular first-teamer throughout his stay with QPR, normally filling the right-back position. He was a member of the QPR team which won the London Challenge Cup in 1938, but the highlight of his career was probably the goal he scored against Brighton in April 1937. It was the only one of his career.

Brian Bedford

This truly remarkable goalscorer was virtually ever-present in Rangers' side from

1959-60 to 1964-65. In that time he became probably the most feared centre-forward in the Third Division and his 180 goals are a testimony to that. His career had begun to improve after he joined Bournemouth in August 1956, after fairly lean spells at Reading and Southampton. In July 1959, after scoring 32 goals in 75 League games for Bournemouth, he was transferred to Queen's Park Rangers and from that moment his career really took off. Subsequent to his spell with Rangers he had spells with Scunthorpe United and finished his career at Brentford in 1966. For Rangers he made 283 senior appearances.

Jimmy Birch

Jimmy Birch came to the notice of Queen's Park Rangers whilst playing reserve-team football for Aston Villa, who he was with in 1910-11 and 1911-12. During that spell he scored some 49 goals for Villa in all matches and this form prompted Rangers to sign him in August 1912. He stood only 5ft 7in tall but was a stocky, bustling inside-forward with a consistently high scoring rate. He made his debut for Rangers against Plymouth Argyle on 5 September 1912 and scored in that game. Birch was a regular first-teamer throughout his period with Rangers which lasted from 1912 to 1926. Had World War One not intervened, he might well have approached 500 appearances for the club. As it was he made 363 in League and Cup, scoring 144 goals.

Jack Blackman

Following a successful amateur career during which he collected a number of inter-league and cup medals, Jack Blackman — real first name John — joined Queen's Park Rangers in 1932. Although only 5ft 9in high, he was a regular scorer during his five years with the club, averaging over a goal every other game with 69 in 116 senior appearances. He was transferred to Crystal Palace in October 1935. For Palace, Blackman scored 55 goals in 107 League games but the war took a big slice out of his career and in May 1946 he moved into non-League football with Guildford City.

Wilf Bott

Wilf Bott started his professional career with Doncaster Rovers, who transferred him to Huddersfield Town late in 1931. At Leeds Road he caught the eye as an inside-forward or a fast raiding winger. With Huddersfield he was their top scorer and made over 100 League appearances before being transferred to Newcastle United in December 1934. At St James' Park he proved his ability as an all-round attacking forward, scoring 15 goals in 44 League and Cup games, which encouraged Queen's Park Rangers to sign him in August 1936. He played regularly for the first team up until the war, scoring 42 goals in 102 senior appearances before joining non-League Lancaster Town.

Stan Bowles

When Stan Bowles signed for Queen's Park Rangers in September 1972, some commentators said that it was a high-risk expense at £112,000. How wrong they were, for Bowles was probably the finest player to appear for the club. He was a talent that did not fully blossom until he was in his mid-20s, by which time he had played for Manchester City, Bury, Crewe Alexandra and Carlisle United and had moved on from most of those clubs in controversial circumstances. As the great Rangers side of the mid-1970s, built around quality players like Parkes, McLintock, Webb, Francis, Thomas, etc., grew, so did the reputation of Stan Bowles, when his ability to improve his game and adapt his genius was a revelation. With his flair and ability, it was natural that he would eventually be selected by

England, although he was capped only five times. He never seemed to settle to the different environment of the international squad and preferred the more manageable atmosphere of club football. At the end of 1979, he moved to Nottingham Forest where he played for a short spell under Brian Clough, then went to Orient and ultimately Brentford, where he ended his Football League career. Both on and off the field he was a colourful character, to say the least, but he certainly lit up Loftus Road. His tangible contribution was 97 goals in 315 senior games.

John Bowman

John Bowman was the first individual to make a major all-round contribution to the early years of Queen's Park Rangers. He started his football career with Burslem Park, a prominent Staffordshire junior team, and later went to Burslem Port Vale and then to Stoke. In 1901 he journeyed south to join Queen's Park Rangers and never have they had a more enthusiastic, more loyal servant. Bowman played, as did many of that time, as an amateur and was almost lost to Queen's Park Rangers in his commitment to remain an amateur. The offer of the post as secretary to the club enabled him to alter his decision and continue his contribution to the formative years of QPR as a top side in the Southern League. As a player he would be described in today's terms as a brilliant midfielder who tackled effectively and fed his forwards with constructive passes. His subsequent years of service to the club as secretary were equally important in those early days of Rangers' development. In the summer of 1905 he joined Norwich City but later returned to Rangers and became a director of the club for whom he had made 110 senior appearances.

Harry Brown

Harry Brown was a goalkeeper who made his reputation at Rangers during the latter years of World War Two but who moved to Notts County following Reg Allen's return from a prisoner-of-war camp. He signed for Notts County and played for them through until October 1949 when he joined Derby County as part of a deal which took former England forward Frank Broome to Meadow Lane. This fine 'keeper returned to Queen's Park Rangers during 1951 and played for the club for a further five years before moving to the West Country to see his Football League career out with Plymouth Athletic and Torquay United. In his two spells with Rangers he totalled 285 League and Cup appearances.

Jack Burns

Signed as an amateur from Crypto, a local business side, Jack Burns played for Queen's Park Rangers for four seasons, scoring 34 goals in 125 League and Cup games. Throughout that time he retained his status as an amateur and finally left the club in 1931 to play for Brentford.

Martyn Busby

Following his apprenticeship with the club, midfielder Martyn Busby made his League debut against Leicester City in April 1970. He went on to play regular first-team football for Rangers over the next ten years, making 145/22 senior appearances and scoring 20 goals, without ever commanding an automatic selection for the first team. Loan spells with Portsmouth and a one-year transfer to Notts County interrupted this spell with the club before he was transferred to Burnley in February 1980. At Turf Moor he played only a few games before retiring from League football.

John Byrne

After impressive performances against Rangers in the League Cup, John Byrne was signed from York City in October 1984. He quickly became one of many talented number-tens to have played for Queen's Park Rangers. Good on the ball and attractive to watch, he played for the club for four seasons during which time he appeared at Wembley in the 1986 Milk Cup Final. In May 1988 he was transferred to the French club, Le Havre, for a fee of £175,000, after scoring 36 goals in 128/21 senior appearances for Rangers. He subsequently returned to England to play for Brighton and appeared in Sunderland's 1992 FA Cup Final team. He later moved to Millwall and then returned to Brighton on loan.

Bobby Cameron

A talented Scottish Schoolboy international inside-forward, signed by Queen's Park Rangers from Port Glasgow in June 1950, Bobby Cameron took a couple of seasons to establish himself as the automatic selection for the number-ten position, but for seven seasons he was a first-team regular and altogether he made 275 first-team appearances, scoring 62 goals for Rangers. His cultured displays drew recognition from Leeds United, who signed him in July 1959. But he found himself in a struggling Second Division side at Elland Road and went into non-League soccer with Gravesend & Northfleet before making a return with Southend United. He later emigrated to Australia.

Reg Chapman

Reg Chapman was a local lad from Shepherd's Bush who signed for the club he had followed as a boy. He was a 'stopper' centre-half and Queen's Park Rangers, for whom he made 108 senior appearances, was his only League club. He retired from League football in 1953.

Tommy Cheetham

Tommy Cheetham began his career as a quality schoolboy player, an inside-left who played for his native Byker side, near Newcastle upon Tyne. Cheetham joined the Royal Artillery and subsequently won prominence in Army football in India. He returned to Aldershot, subsequently signing as an amateur for Rangers in 1935 and became a professional later that year. A very consistent scorer who averaged over a goal a game in his first season, he ended his first League campaign with 36 goals from only 34 games and also took part in an international trial. Altogether he made 124 senior appearances, scoring 91 goals and in March 1939 signed for Brentford for £5,000. The war soon interrupted his career and by the time the League resumed, he was almost 36. Brentford transferred him to Lincoln City, but he showed that he still had his old scoring flair and netted 31 goals in 47 League games for the Imps before retiring.

Dave Clement

Dave Clement was a very talented full-back who developed with Queen's Park Rangers through the junior teams and on to the England Youth set-up. He made his League debut in April 1967 and quickly commanded a regular place at right-back in the great side of the 1970s. Clement progressed to win five full England caps and had made 476 senior appearances by the time he left Loftus Road in June 1979 to join Bolton Wanderers for £170,000. He subsequently went on to play for Fulham and Wimbledon before dying tragically in 1982, when he committed suicide, allegedly during a bout of severe depression following a broken leg.

Harry Collins

Harry Collins was Rangers' regular first-team goalkeeper from 1901 to 1904, having joined the club from Burnley, for whom he had made 33 League and FA Cup appearances in 1900-01, when the Clarets just failed to regain promotion to the First Division. He was born in the North-East, at Hebburn, in 1876 and developed his early football talents there, gaining a number of junior honours with Birtley and Hebburn Argyle. Collins, an extremely popular player, captained the QPR side during 1902-03 and was first-choice 'keeper throughout his time with QPR, making 121 senior appearances in all. In 1905 he moved north to join Everton but played only three League games for them.

John Collins

A local lad, John Collins signed from Queen's Park Rangers juniors as a professional in August 1959 and made his debut against Barnsley in April 1960. From 1961 onwards he was a fairly regular member of the first team and a useful scorer with 56 goals in 193 senior appearances. Oldham signed this talented inside-forward in October 1966 and he subsequently played for Reading and Luton Town before joining Cambridge United in February 1971. At the end of his playing days he rejoined Rangers as a member of the coaching staff.

Bill Coward

Bill Coward scored on his League debut in March 1928, against Torquay United, having been signed by Rangers from Windsor & Eton in January that year. Standing 5ft 6in tall and weighing only 10st 7lb, he was a neat, tricky outside-right who played regularly for the first team for some five seasons, scoring 26 goals in 138 League and Cup games.

Joe Cunningham

Signed from the Scottish junior club Lochie, Joe Cunningham kept goal for Rangers' first team for some five seasons. He had a reputation for being a serious character and was rated one of the top 'keepers in the Third Division. He was transferred to Walsall in 1932 after making 174 first-team appearances for Rangers.

Ian Dawes

One of the many quality players developed through the Queen's Park Rangers' youth policy, Ian Dawes came to prominence late in the 1981-82 season. He made his debut for the first team against Rotherham on 27 March 1982 and by the time the FA Cup Final against Tottenham came around in May 1982, he was firmly established as a member of the first-team squad and could have certainly covered for Ian Gillard. From the beginning of the following season he retained his first-team spot for four successive seasons and proved himself a most reliable and competent left-back. Apart from his defensive qualities, he liked to get forward wide on the left-hand side and was a competent crosser of the ball. In 1986 he finally made a Wembley appearance as a member of the Queen's Park Rangers side for the Milk Cup Final. He was to play for another two years before moving to Millwall in August 1988 for a fee of £150,000 after 270 senior appearances for Rangers. Millwall had just been promoted to Division One for the first time in their history and Dawes went on to make well over 150 League appearances for the Lions, who were eventually relegated again.

Sam Downing

Born in 1885 at Willesden Green, close to Queen's Park Rangers 'heartland', left-half Sam Downing — 5ft 10in tall, weighing 12st 10lb — gave fine service to the club. He developed through amateur clubs Willesden Green and Willesden Town and played for West Hampstead prior to re-signing for Queen's Park Rangers in April 1903. During his second period with the Rangers he rarely missed a game and although principally a defender, he scored 23 goals in his five seasons with the club. He was transferred to Chelsea in 1909, after making 190 senior appearances for Rangers, and later played for Croydon Common.

Ray Drinkwater

A Geordie who signed for Queen's Park Rangers from Portsmouth in February of 1958, Ray Drinkwater made his League debut for the club against Coventry City in March that year and was the regular first-team goalkeeper for the following five seasons, although his experience at Fratton Park had been limited to only eight League appearances. A tall, agile and reliable 'keeper, he made 214 senior appearances for Rangers, his only other League club. Although hailing from the North-East, he had joined Pompey from Guildford City.

Mark Falco

Mark Falco arrived at Queen's Park Rangers at the age of 28, having been with Tottenham, Chelsea, Watford and Glasgow

Rangers. A regular goalscorer with all those clubs, he had four seasons at Shepherd's Bush, during which time he scored 33 goals in 81/25 games, a fine striking rate. Falco moved to Millwall in August 1991 for a fee of £175,000 — having been purchased by Queen's Park Rangers for £400,000 in 1987. A former England Youth international, Falco suffered an injury with Spurs that ruled him out of their 1982 FA Cup Final against QPR, but he had recovered sufficiently to play his part in their UEFA Cup success of 1984.

Alec Farmer

A wing-half who had appeared for Kettering Town, Nottingham Forest (for whom he played in 16 League games) and Yeovil & Petters United before joining Queen's Park Rangers early in 1934, Alec Farmer was born at Lochgelly, Scotland, in 1909. Up until the outbreak of World War Two, his career with QPR saw him in and out of the first team. He had made 80 League appearances by the time the competition was suspended and had not played at all in 1938-39. During the war years, Farmer appeared in some 80 games and stayed on afterwards to become assistant trainer. He was still connected with the club well into the 1950s.

Des Farrow

A signing from Leicester City, where he was an amateur, towards the end of World War Two, Des Farrow played for Queen's Park Rangers in both the Second and Third Divisions up until the time he was transferred to Stoke City in October 1952. A relatively slightly-built wing-half, he made up for his lack of muscle with excellent distribution. For QPR he made 158 League and Cup appearances, but appeared in only eight League games for the Potters.

Terry Fenwick

One of the many fine players to come from the North-East, Terry Fenwick began his League career as a full-back with Crystal Palace. He was one of a number of players who joined Queen's Park Rangers in December 1980, shortly after Terry Venables was appointed manager of the club. Fenwick developed his game whilst at Shepherd's Bush and ultimately was selected for England, taking part in the World Cup finals in Mexico in 1986. He has the distinction of being the player most capped by England whilst with Rangers, collecting 19 of his 20 caps with the club. For QPR most of his appearances were made in the centre-back position and it was these performances that brought him international recognition. He was a key member of the side that won the Second Division title in 1982-83 and finished fifth in Division One the following season. In December 1987, after making 307/1 senior appearances and scoring 45 goals, he was transferred to Spurs for £550,000, again following Venables to a new club. Fenwick was to gain only one further international cap whilst at Spurs, the club against whom he had played for QPR in the 1982 FA Cup Final, and after suffering a broken leg in October 1989 he missed the rest of the season. He was loaned to Leicester City to regain match fitness but further injury followed and then he became the third First Division player in three years to be imprisoned following a motoring offence.

Les Ferdinand

Les Ferdinand was snapped up by QPR for £15,000 in April 1987 after they had spotted him playing for Hayes in the Vauxhall-Opel League. Although given an early debut, coming on as a substitute against Coventry in August that year, he found his chances few at Loftus Road and was loaned to Brentford before spending a year in the Turkish League with Besiktas. After his return to Loftus Road, he was kept out of the side by players like Trevor Francis, Colin Clarke, Mark Falco and Roy Wegerle, but when Rangers suffered a crop of injuries, Ferdinand responded with some vital goals in 1990-91 as QPR fought to get away from the bottom of the First Division. He began 1991-92 as first choice under new boss Gerry Francis but then lost out to newcomer Garry Thompson. Ferdinand fought his way back again and in 1992-93 was selected for the full England side. By the end of that season he had scored 46 goals in 99 senior appearances for Rangers, including two hat-tricks in three days over Easter 1993.

Wayne Fereday

Signed as a full-time professional by Tommy Docherty following an apprenticeship with QPR, Wayne Fereday made an impressive debut against Bristol Rovers in August 1980, scoring two goals. But he was still only 17 and made only 11 first-team appearances until the 1984-85 season, when he was a fairly regular member of the side. Outstandingly fast, Fereday was at his best playing wide on the left, but occasionally played at centre-forward and later in his career he played a number of games at full-back. He gained England Under-21 honours before leaving Rangers in July 1989, for a £300,000 fee when he was signed for Newcastle United by former QPR manager Jim Smith. He later played for Bournemouth and West Brom.

Joe Fidler

Joe Fidler came to Rangers via Sheffield United and Fulham, making his debut in September 1906 against Clapton Orient. He was a member of the side which won the Southern League championship in 1907-08 and he appeared for the club in both of their FA Charity Shield matches against Manchester United, in April and August 1908. He was a regular member of the first team until 1911 and made his last appearances for the club during 1912-13. A stocky, accomplished full-back, strong in the tackle, he appeared in 192 senior games for Rangers before being transferred to Woolwich Arsenal in February 1913. After the Gunners he played for Port Vale.

Mike Fillery

Signed by Chelsea as an apprentice in August 1978, Mike Fillery appeared for England at Schoolboy and Youth level. He was a fairly regular member of Chelsea's first team, although for most of his time at Stamford Bridge they were a Second Division club, before being transferred to Queen's Park Rangers in August 1983, for £200,000. A player of great talent, he perhaps never quite fulfilled his potential. Strong on the ball and with good vision, on his day he was a very accomplished player, but with his apparently relaxed approach to the game he never really endeared himself to Rangers' fans and after four seasons, in which he made 114/3 senior appearances, he moved to Portsmouth in July 1987 on a free transfer. He later appeared for Oldham and had a loan spell with Millwall.

Arthur Fitzgerald

A strong tackling left-half who joined Rangers as a young player from Reading in 1936, Arthur Fitzgerald was a regular member of QPR's Third Division South side in the seasons leading up World War Two. By the time the competition was suspended he had made 106 League appearances for QPR but never reappeared for the club, for by the time League football was resumed in 1946 he had moved to Aldershot, for whom he made 59 League appearances in the Third Division South.

Gerry Francis

A local lad, born at Chiswick, Gerry Francis was the product of the Queen's Park Rangers youth scheme which was so successful in the late 1960s. He made his League debut, as a substitute, against Liverpool in March 1969 and following occasional appearances the next season he established himself as a regular first-teamer in the 1970-71 programme. He won his first full England cap in October 1974, against

Czechoslovakia, and was made captain of the national side in 1975. He remains the only Queen's Park Rangers player to have achieved that honour. In 1976, Francis suffered an injury that was to finish his international career and restrict his League football opportunities for the following two seasons. He fought back to become a regular again in 1978-79, but never quite regained his form of earlier years. He then moved through a number of transfer deals, going to Crystal Palace in 1979, for £450,000, and returning to Shepherd's Bush in February 1980 for a £150,000 fee. He was transferred to Coventry City in February 1982 and finished his career with a few games for Exeter City. Francis moved into management and after a spell in charge of Exeter he moved to Bristol Rovers and took them to the old Second Division. Astute dealings in the transfer market had made Rovers financially secure during his period with the club. In May 1991 he was appointed chief coach at Queen's Park Rangers and his performance during his first two years in charge are showing all the signs of continuing his contributions to the success of the club. As a Rangers player he made over 350 senior appearances and scored 65 goals.

Ian Gillard

Ian Gillard joined Rangers from school and made his League debut as an 18-year-old in November 1968, against Nottingham Forest. He served the club magnificently over some 14 seasons and was virtually a permanent selection at left-back during the whole of his period at Loftus Road. Capped by England Under-23s, he subsequently won full international recognition in 1974, when he gained the first of three caps. A member of the 1982 FA Cup Final side, he made nearly 500 appearances for Rangers before moving to Aldershot in July 1982.

Don Givens

Signed by Gordon Jago from Luton Town in July 1972, Don Givens had six very successful seasons with Queen's Park Rangers, during which he made 293/1 senior appearances and scored 101 goals. He was outstanding as a central striker who played a little deeper in the team which almost won the First Division championship in 1976 and his performances were underlined by his regular selection for the Republic of Ireland. His 56 appearances for the Republic — scoring 19 goals which were a national record at one time — are testimony to his ability to play at the highest level. Whilst at Rangers he became their most capped player. His original entry into League football was with Manchester United and, indeed, he won his first two international caps before making his first-team debut for United in August 1969. He subsequently played for Luton Town and joined Queen's Park Rangers in July 1972 for £40,000 at the age of 23. He left the club in August 1978, signing for Birmingham City for £150,000. After a loan spell with Bournemouth, he ended his League career with Sheffield United.

George Goddard

George Goddard first came to the notice of Queen's Park Rangers whilst playing for Redhill and working in the local bus garage. Following his transfer to Rangers in June 1926, his contribution was both immediate and quite stunning. Over the next eight seasons he appeared in 259 League and Cup games, scoring a remarkable 189 goals. In 1929-30, he netted 37 League goals plus a couple in the FA Cup to make a total of 39 for the season — and from only 45 games. His career goals tally still stands as the record for any player whilst with Queen's Park Rangers. Goddard was transferred to Brentford in December 1933, at a time when the Bees were making their highly successful push towards Division One. He later played for Wolves, Sunderland and Southend United.

Ted Goodier

In November 1931 two half-backs, Les Adlam and Ted Goodier, joined Queen's

Park Rangers from Oldham Athletic for a combined fee of £1,500. Adlam went on to make 64 senior appearances in two seasons before being transferred to Cardiff, whilst Goodier was to play regular first-team football for Rangers the next four seasons, clocking up 152 League and Cup appearances. A tall rugged defender, Goodier was the most consistent of performers during those early years of the 1930s and when he left the club in 1935 to go to Watford — in exchange for Harry Lowe — he was sorely missed. His only League goal came against Norwich City in February 1933. After Watford, Goodier served Crewe and Rochdale (where he was player-manager) and managed Birmingham, Wigan and Oldham.

John Gregory

An outside-left who played for Rangers for ten years, Birmingham-born John Gregory's best football years were taken away from him through the advent World War One. He came to the notice of Queen's Park Rangers whilst playing for Willenhall Swifts in the Birmingham League, where apart from his clever wing play he scored 19 goals and was also selected to play in a Junior international match against Scotland. Rangers signed him in 1912 and he was a regular first-team player up until the end of 1922-23 season, when he was transferred to Yeovil Town.

John Gregory

Scunthorpe-born John Gregory was signed by Terry Venables to strengthen Rangers' midfield in the team he was building in the early 1980s. Gregory, whose father played for West Ham, Scunthorpe and Aldershot, was a cultured player who developed fairly late, being 27 when he signed for Rangers from Brighton in June 1981 for £275,000. He began his career with Northampton Town and played well over 200 first-team games for the Cobblers before moving to Aston Villa in 1977. Two years later, he signed for Brighton. Gregory developed his game substantially whilst with Rangers and gained the first of six full England caps against Australia. A first-team regular with Rangers for some five seasons, he had made 188/2 senior appearances and scored 43 goals for QPR by the time he was transferred to Derby County in December 1985 for a fee of £100,000. He helped Derby from the Third to the First Division and later held coaching and temporary manager's jobs at Portsmouth, Plymouth, Bolton and Leicester.

Cyril Hatton

An elegant player who joined the club from Notts County in exchange for goalkeeper Harry Brown in April 1946, Cyril Hatton formed a fine inside-forward partnership with Fred Ramscar in the first two seasons after World War Two and made a substantial contribution to Rangers' first-ever promotion to the Second Division in 1948. For a creative player he also collected a useful number of goals, particularly in those early seasons. In June 1953, after scoring 87 goals in 208 senior appearances, he was transferred to Chesterfield, where he ended his League career with ten goals in 36 games.

Tony Hazell

Signing professional forms in October 1964 after apprenticeship with the junior side, Tony Hazell played first-team football at Loftus Road for some 11 seasons. As a junior with the club he had played for the England Youth team and in his first full professional season, when he was still only 17, he played in 32 games. He was a member of the famous 1967 League Cup winning side which also gained promotion to Division Two that season. The 1967-68 season saw him gain further honours when Rangers were runners-up in the Second Division and were promoted to the First Division for the first time in the club's history. A tenacious wing-half, he subsequently switched to full-back prior to his transfer to Millwall in December 1974 for a fee of £40,000. In a magnificent career with QPR he had made 407/7 appearances in the first team. With the Lions he added 153 League games to his tally and then wound down his career with Crystal Palace and Charlton.

Bob Hazell

Jamaican-born Bob Hazell had four good seasons with Queen's Park Rangers following his transfer from Wolverhampton Wanderers in September 1979 for a fee of £240,000. At 6ft 1in and weighing over 15st, Hazell was a traditional centre-half but he was also an accomplished passer of the ball and used to enjoy getting forward. His most memorable performance came in an FA Cup semi-final against West Bromwich Albion, when he marked the dangerous Cyrille Regis out of the game. A member of Rangers' 1982 FA Cup Final side, he moved to Leicester City in September 1983, for a fee of £100,000 and ultimately had a three-season spell with Port Vale. For QPR he made 117/7 senior appearances.

Bill Heath

Signed from local football in the early years of World War Two and essentially a central defender, Bill Heath occasionally proved his versatility by playing at centre-forward and full-back. He was never quite an automatic choice for the first team but was always a strongly committed player for the club, for whom he made 130 senior appearances before switching to Southern League soccer with Dover in July 1953.

Len Hill

Born in February 1899, Len Hill spent his early days in the Southend area, where he gained a number of school representative honours. He played for Southend United Reserves in 1914-15 and upon the outbreak of World War One joined the 9th Lancers and served in France. Medically discharged in 1919 with a double fracture of the skull, his determination to succeed at football led to him rejoin Southend and subsequently he signed for Queen's Park Rangers in August 1920 and made his debut against Watford the following month. A competent goalkeeper, he quickly earned a reputation of being one of the best in the Third Division during the early 1920s. After four and a half seasons with Rangers, in which he appeared in 176 League and Cup games, he was transferred to Southampton in 1925. After ten League games for the Saints he moved to Rochdale.

Alfred Hitch

An early handbook describes centre-half Alfred Hitch as 'a wise, prominent figure on the field who does not, nevertheless, believe in superfluous embroidery'. As can be gathered from that statement, Hitch was a very solid defender and he played for QPR in the club's early days of professionalism. He started his career with Walsall Unity in 1895-6 and had spells with Grays United and Nottingham Forest. At 5ft 8in he was relatively short for centre-half — although those were the days when that man was not a stopper but a genuine half-back linking defence with attack — he nevertheless enjoyed a great ability for timing his headers. He played for the club from 1899 through to 1905, except for season 1901-02 when he was with Nottingham Forest, and his 183 senior appearances are a testimony to his contribution to the early years of Rangers' existence.

John Hollins

After 12 years with Chelsea, gaining England Youth, Under-23, 'B' and full honours, John Hollins joined Queen's Park Rangers in June 1975 for a fee of £80,000. Although some considered him to be at the end of his First Division career, he played four seasons with the superb Queen's Park Rangers side of the mid-1970s and after his move to Highbury in July 1979 he was to play another five seasons with Arsenal and then Chelsea again. A totally committed

player who earned a reputation for honest aggressive defending, be it as a midfield defensive player or at full-back, Hollins was one of the finest players of his era. He made 177/6 first-team appearances for QPR and was manager of Chelsea from June 1985 to March 1988.

Ernie Howe

Originally a defender with Hounslow Town, Ernie Howe joined Fulham in 1973 and played five seasons with the Cottagers before being transferred to Queen's Park Rangers in December 1977. In his first 18 months with Rangers he was a first choice in the centre of defence, but following the arrival of Bob Hazell he was in and out of the side in his remaining three years at Loftus Road. Portsmouth signed him for

£50,000 in August 1982, after he had made 106 League and Cup appearances for QPR. When he joined Rangers for £50,000 he was one of the first players to have his transfer fee set by an independent tribunal.

Peter Hucker

Goalkeeper Peter Hucker will be best remembered for his brilliant performance in the 1982 FA Cup Final against Spurs. He developed through the Queen's Park Rangers youth set-up and signed professional forms in July 1977, breaking into the first team during the 1981-82 season. Thereafter, he was the regular 'keeper before being transferred to Oxford United in February 1987 for a fee of £100,000. A goalkeeper not given to great showmanship, he was one who turned in excellent performances on a regular basis. After a loan spell with West Brom he left the Manor Ground to play for Millwall and Aldershot. For Rangers, Hucker appeared in 188 League and Cup games.

Ron Hunt

Another fine product of Rangers' youth team of the early 1960s, Ron Hunt matured to first-team football in 1964 and by the following season had become the permanent first-choice centre-half, perhaps best remembered for his foray into the West Brom penalty area towards the end of the 1967 League Cup Final. Following his collision with the Albion goalkeeper, the ball ran loose to Mark Lazarus who netted that famous winning goal. This sort of commitment was Ron Hunt's contribution to the club during the 1960s. An aggressive but talented central defender, his career was ended prematurely through a serious knee injury after he had made 249/6 senior appearances.

Tony Ingham

No historical record of Queen's Park Rangers would be complete without a testimony to Tony Ingham. As a young man playing football in the Harrogate area, he was spotted by Leeds United and played three first-team games for them prior to being signed by Queen's Park Rangers in June 1950. After two seasons of irregular first-team action, Ingham made the left-back spot his own for the next ten seasons, during which time he hardly missed a game, finishing with 548 appearances for the club, a record which is unlikely to be broken. Apart from his playing contribution, he subsequently served Rangers in the capacity of commercial manager and for a short period acted as club secretary, subsequently becoming a director of the club. He is a quiet man and would often remind people that 'it's only a game', a statement which belies his contribution to Queen's Park Rangers, both as a player and administrator.

Arthur Jefferson

Affectionately known as 'rubber legs' by those who stood behind the goal at the School End, Arthur Jefferson was one of the characters of Queen's Park Rangers between 1936 and 1949. Totally committed to winning the ball, with a great sliding tackle to assist his endeavours, he was not a player to venture forward very often. That is endorsed by the fact that during his 365 appearances for the club he scored only one goal, against Bury in March 1949. Jefferson was transferred to Aldershot in March 1950, but when his playing days were over he returned to Shepherd's Bush to run a local fish and chip shop in association with another former player 'Smudger' Smith. Arthur Jefferson is still a welcome regular visitor to Loftus Road.

Reg John

Reg John wore Rangers' colours from 1920 through to 1926, during which time he proved to be a strong, determined tackler with sound defensive qualities. He was a very mobile and committed individual who had a tremendous love for the game and for Queen's Park Rangers. Originally from Aberdare, John made his League debut for Rangers in November 1920, against Southampton, and went on to play in over 140 games for the club before joining Charlton Athletic in 1926. He made only eight League appearances for Charlton.

Mike Keen

Born in High Wycombe during the early months of World War Two, Mike Keen was taken on as a schoolboy by Queen's Park Rangers and after making his debut in the first team in September 1959, against York City, he was virtually a regular first-teamer until his transfer to Luton Town in January 1969 for a fee of £18,500, with 440 senior appearances and 45 goals to his name. As a tall, rangey and powerful wing-half, he made a valuable contribution to the club in the early days of Rangers' emergence from Third Division obscurity. His best years with QPR were towards the end of his time at Loftus Road, when he was captain of the 1967 League Cup winning side at Wembley as Rangers lifted their first major trophy. The following season he was ever-present for the fifth successive season, as Rangers won promotion to the First Division, and he appeared in early fixtures of the club's first-ever season in the top flight. After 145 League games for Luton, Keen moved to Watford and ended his career with them, where another 124 League games took his career tally to a remarkable 662.

Pat Kerrins

Although born in Fulham, Pat Kerrins developed with the Queen's Park Rangers' junior sides berfore making his first appearance in League football against Exeter City in February 1954. At 5ft 11in he was tall for a winger, and he was skilful and an excellent crosser of the ball. He played League football for some seven seasons at Rangers, prior to his transfer to Crystal Palace and subsequent move to Southend United, where he finished his career. For QPR he played in 155 League and Cup games, scoring 30 goals.

Jim Langley

Left-back Jim Langley joined Queen's Park Rangers apparently in the twilight of his career, being 36 when he was signed from neighbours Fulham, for £5,000 in July 1965. Yet he shared in one of Rangers' most glorious seasons. Langley was born in Kilburn in 1929 and after playing for Yiewsley, Hayes and Brentford as an amateur, had nine League games as an outside-left for Leeds United before moving to Brighton, where he was converted to full-back. With Third Division Brighton he made 174 appearances and won England 'B' and Football League representative honours. Langley was transferred to Fulham in February 1957 and made 356 League

and Cup appearances for them, won three full England caps, played in two FA Cup semi-finals and helped the Cottagers into Division One. He was ever-present in his first season with Rangers and in 1966-67, was a key member of the side which won the League Cup and the Third Division title. Shortly afterwards he went to manage Hillingdon Borough. Langley made almost 650 League appearances overall and was only the second full-back to score 50 League goals.

Mark Lazarus

One of the more difficult things to know as a Queen's Park Rangers' fan during the Mark Lazarus years was whether he was playing for the club or being transferred — or even returning to Loftus Road. Lazarus, who was born in Stepney in 1938, was signed by Leyton Orient from Barking in 1957. He first came to QPR in September 1960, moved to Wolves in September 1961, back to Rangers in February 1962, on to Brentford in April 1964, back again to Queen's Park Rangers in November 1965, on to Crystal Palace in November 1967 and finally back to his first club, Orient, in 1969. However, Queen's Park Rangers were to get the best from this fast, aggressive winger who in his overall total of 235 senior appearances for the club, scored 84 goals, a relatively high number for a winger in that era. Although he came from a large family who were renowned for their performances in the boxing ring, he chose to make his mark in football and certainly did that in April 1967, when he scored the winning goal in League Cup Final at Wembley. The same season he helped Rangers to the Third Division title. A tremendous character who retired from League football to join Folkestone Town in 1971, Mark Lazarus appeared in 442 League games overall. When he helped Orient into Division Two in 1970, it was the fourth successive season that he had played in a promotion side after going with QPR from the Third to the First Division and then playing in the Palace side that was promoted to Division One.

Mike Leach

London-born Mike Leach joined Queen's Park Rangers as an apprentice and quickly developed, gaining early recognition as an England Youth international. He signed as a full-time professional in February 1964 and played five games in the latter part of that season. Leach played first-team football for the next 13 seasons, becoming a regular in 1967-68 and making 337/24 appearances overall with 70 goals. He was respected by all the managers under whom he played for his total commitment to the team and his likeable personality. Essentially a team player who scored critical goals for the club in their rise through the Second Division to play in the top flight, Leach had the distinction of being part of both Second Division promotion sides, in 1968 and again in 1973. He spent the year following his departure from QPR playing for Detroit Express in the NASL, but returned in 1978 to play a few League games for Cambridge United. In 1992 he died from cancer at a tragically early age.

Stuart Leary

Born in South Africa, Stuart Leary was spotted by Charlton Athletic's well-developed scouting network there, playing centre-forward for the Clyde club. He travelled to England to sign for Charlton in February 1950 and played at The Valley for ten years, making over 370 League appearances for the club. After a dispute with Charlton, he was put on the transfer list and in December 1962, Rangers were fortunate to sign him for a relatively small fee of £17,000. In the three seasons he played for Rangers, he gave excellent service before retiring in 1966 to give more time to his professional cricket career which he continued to pursue with Kent for a number of years. For Rangers he made 104 senior appearances, scoring 32 goals. He died in 1988.

Arthur Longbottom

The Longbottom twin brothers' football developed strongly whilst they were serving with the RAF in the Middle East on National Service. After returning to the UK, Arthur signed for Methley United and was soon spotted by Queen's Park Rangers, for whom he signed in March 1954. A neat, competent inside-forward, he played from 1954 through to 1961, when he was transferred to Port Vale after scoring 67 goals in 212 senior appearances for QPR. He later had brief careers with Millwall, Oxford United and Colchester United.

Harry Lowe

A Scot who came south in 1930 to sign for Watford, Harry Lowe played for five years with that club until being transferred to Queen's Park Rangers in June 1935, in exchange for Ted Goodier. An inside-forward with considerable ball skills, he was a regular first-teamer up to the early war years. Also a good golfer, he finished his football career playing for Guildford. For Rangers he made 238 League and Cup appearances, scoring 51 goals.

Alan McDonald

A strong, dominant centre-back, Alan McDonald has been a regular first-teamer for QPR since 1985. Signed by the club following a recommendation from their scout in Belfast, he graduated through the junior sides and his commanding performances quickly drew him to the attention of the Northern Ireland selectors. Since winning his first cap in the 1985-86 season, he has continued to appear regularly for the national team, is currently the Northern Ireland captain and is now Rangers' most capped player. Before he made his Rangers' first-team debut, McDonald spent a period on loan at Charlton, where he gained valuable League experience. He has been a member of the first team for 12 years, all of which have been spent in the First Division/Premier League, which is a testimony to his consistently high performances for the club. By the end of the 1992-93 season he had made 348 senior appearances for Queen's Park Rangers, scoring 12 goals.

John McDonald

A native of Ayr, John McDonald had a varied career before joining Queen's Park Rangers from Grimsby Town in the close season of 1907, having also played for Blackburn Rovers and Leeds City. A very experienced right-back, in his first season with Rangers he played in the side which won the Southern League title and he went on to repeat that achievement in the 1911-12 campaign. He also played in Queen's Park Rangers' three FA Charity Shield games and was virtually ever-present during his spell with the club until his retirement in 1913.

Billy McEwan

Billy McEwan, whose best years were interrupted by World War Two, was yet another of the consistent players who came to the club from Scotland. He joined Rangers from Glasgow junior club, Petershill, in 1938 and won a first-team place in the League matches leading up to the war. During the hostilities, McEwan first became a policeman but subsequently joined the RAF and whilst stationed near Blackpool he played alongside many of the international players of the day. After the war he became a regular member of the Rangers' first team and was in the side that won the club's first Third Division championship in 1948. A player of some skill who normally turned out at inside-forward or as a winger, he was also a regular goalscorer and altogether netted 51 in 170 League and Cup games for Rangers before being transferred to Leyton Orient in February 1950. He moved into non-League soccer with Gravesend a year later.

Frank McLintock

Another very astute piece of business by manager Dave Sexton brought Frank McLintock from Arsenal to Queen's Park Rangers for a fee of £30,000 in June 1973. He was approaching 34 when signed and few expected him to play such a prominent role for the club. The Rangers side in which he was part of a secure central defence made a determined run for the League Championship in 1976, only to be pipped by Liverpool in the last game of the season by a single point. Initially a strong-tackling, highly mobile wing-half with Leicester City, McLintock eventually settled at centre-half in his latter seasons at Highbury and commanded that position whilst at Queen's Park Rangers. He played in four FA Cup Finals (once for Leicester) and two League Cup Finals, but finished on the winning side at Wembley only once. With Arsenal he also won a League championship medal, Fairs Cup winners' medal, six caps for Scotland and was voted Footballer of the Year in 1971, after he had helped the Gunners to the double. He had made 162/1 senior appearances for Rangers when he retired in 1971 and later managed Leicester and Brentford and was assistant manager at Millwall. He was awarded the MBE in 1972.

Joe Mallet

Joe Mallett was another of the players signed by Queen's Park Rangers before World War Two, whose career was never fully fulfilled due to the hostilities. A cultured wing-half who occasionally appeared at inside-forward, he approached 300 appearances for the club, the majority of which were wartime games. Mallett had two spells with Charlton Athletic, both of which culminated in a transfer to Queen's Park Rangers, and in February 1947 he moved to Southampton for £5,000. Although he was then 31, he served the Saints for the next six seasons, making 215 appearances. He ended his career with Leytion Orient and later coached at Nottingham Forest.

Terry Mancini

Terry Mancini, a footballer from a famous East London boxing family, had a career which did not really develop until he was over 30. He was signed as junior by Watford

in 1961 and then became a full-time professional, playing for the Vicarage Road club until 1967, when he went to South Africa to play for Port Elizabeth. He returned later that year to join Orient, with whom he spent four seasons, and at the age of 29, he was signed by Queen's Park Rangers, who were then a Second Division side. Mancini played for Rangers for three full seasons, including being in the side when QPR gained promotion to the First Division in 1973. Virtually ever-present the following season, his reliable performances at the centre of defence brought him to the attention of Arsenal, who bought him for £25,000 in October 1974. From Highbury he went to Aldershot on a free transfer in September 1976 and ended his League career with them. Despite being an Eastender, Mancini was qualified for the Republic of Ireland and gained one full cap. A distinctive figure with his cheerful smile and balding head, his competitive spirit made him a popular player with the Rangers' fans. For QPR he made 111 senior appearances

Dave Mangnall

Although he was one of the game's most prolific pre-war strikers, Dave Mangnall played in only three League games for QPR after signing for them in the 1939 close season. However, in wartime football he appeared 128 times, scoring 77 goals, and remained with the club until 1952. His career began as an amateur with Doncaster Rovers but he made his League debut whilst playing for Leeds United in September 1929. He moved to Huddersfield Town three months later, for £3,000, and was a member of their fine side in the early 1930s, scoring a club record 42 League and Cup goals in 1931-32. He was transferred to Birmingham in 1933 and then, following a spell with West Ham, he joined Millwall in 1936. Between the wars his total of 218 League appearances had brought him 141 goals. When his playing days were drawing to an end, he was appointed manager of QPR, taking over from Ted Vizard in 1944 and continuing in the job until 1952. He was in charge when Queen's Park Rangers on their first-ever promotion to the Second Division in 1948, but lost his job when they were relegated four years later.

Dickie March

A native of the North-East, Dickie March joined Rangers from the junior club, Crawcrook Albion, in 1932. A consistent and wholehearted player who appeared at wing-half for some eight seasons leading up to World War Two, he made almost 300 senior appearances which included a few during the war. He retired during the conflict and took a job on the administrative staff of the club in 1946.

Ben Marsden

Hanley-born Ben Marsden was signed from Port Vale in the late months of 1920 and made his debut against Brentford on 27 December of that year. He was Rangers' regular right-back for five seasons before being transferred to Reading in 1925, after 132 League and Cup appearances for QPR.

Rodney Marsh

'Rod-nee, Rod-nee, Rod-nee,' was the cry to be heard from the Loftus Road terraces when the man who was probably the most popular player in Queen's Park Rangers' history was on the field. A hugely talented individual with great skill and flair, Marsh was without question the most influential player in the success of the club during the late 1960s. Originally an apprentice with Fulham, he was signed by Alec Stock from that club for £15,000 in March 1966 and from the moment he joined Rangers he influenced the club's progress. He was a scorer of very special goals, including a spectacular effort in the 1967 League Cup Final win over West Brom. He led the attractive style played by the Rangers through 1966 up until their entry into the First Division in 1969; and following relegation the next season he continued to play for Queen's Park Rangers in the Second Division for three years. His talent, however, was in great demand as by this time he had won the first of nine England caps. After a number of offers for his services he signed for Manchester City, for £200,000, and played with them for three and a half seasons before going to play in the NASL for Tampa Bay Rowdies. His flamboyant style suited the American scene and apart from a short spell back in the UK with Fulham in 1977, he has made his home in the USA and is closely involved with soccer in Florida. For Rangers, Marsh made 242 senior appearances, scoring 134 goals.

Bill Mason

A goalkeeper who played in Surrey amateur football and made 43 appearances for Fulham before being transferred to Queen's Park Rangers in July 1933, Bill Mason established himself in the first team during 1934-35 and was the regular League 'keeper up to the war, remaining in the side during

the first three seasons of wartime football. He was one of the first in a long line of top quality goalkeepers at Queen's Park Rangers, being succeeded by such men as Harry Brown and Reg Allen. In all senior games for Rangers he appeared 251 times, 91 of them during the war, when he retired.

Don Masson

Approaching 29 years of age, Don Masson was another signing who underlined the quality of Dave Sexton's judgement. A dour, strong-tackling but highly creative midfield player, he began his career with Middlesbrough before joining Rangers from Notts County in December 1974 for £100,000. He had helped Notts climb from the Fourth to the Second Division and two years after moving to Loftus Road he earned the first of 17 caps for Scotland. After four good years with the Rangers, in which he made 144 League and Cup appearances and helped QPR finish First Division runners-up, he moved to Derby County in October 1977 in exchange for Leighton James. It was a bad deal for Derby. James was valued at £300,000 and after a bad season at the Baseball Ground, Masson returned to Notts County on a free transfer. He helped the Magpies into Division One in 1981.

Gary Micklewhite

Tommy Docherty had known Gary Micklewhite as a young player at Manchester United and he was to be one of his first signings as manager of Queen's Park Rangers. It was some time before Micklewhite established himself in the first team, but from 1981 through to 1985 he was a regular, usually playing wide on the right. Energetic, hard-working and competitive, he was at his best in highly competitive matches. He came on as substitute for Clive Allen in the 1982 FA Cup Final and performed admirably. His performance in the first match earned him selection in the starting line-up for the replay, when again he had another good match. After five seasons at the Bush, Micklewhite was transferred to Derby County in February 1985 and he left Rangers for a fee of £75,000, after 115/12 senior appearances. Micklewhite helped Derby from the Third to the First Division and then went down with them again to the Second and he was given a free transfer at the end of 1993.

Archie Mitchell

Born at Smethwick, Archie Mitchell spent two seasons with Aston Villa before joining Rangers in 1907. One of the best centre-halves in the country at that time, he played in three inter-League games in 1913-14, distinguishing himself when he captained the Southern League side against the Football League. He played for the Rangers until 1921, when he was transferred to Brentford after making 467 League and Cup appearances. Had World War One not intervened, he could well have made over 500 appearances for the club. He was captain of the side that met Blackburn Rovers in the FA Charity Shield in 1912 and was the most influential player at Rangers throughout his career.

Ian Morgan

Fast and skilful, Ian Morgan invariably played on the opposite wing to his twin brother, Roger. Both had developed through Essex schools football, reaching the professional ranks through Rangers' youth scheme. He was substitute in the League Cup Final but was ever-present in the promotion run to the First Division in 1968. In October 1973, he joined Watford for a fee of £10,000, after making 175/4 senior appearances and scoring 28 goals.

Roger Morgan

The elder of the Morgan twins, Roger was clearly the better player, having gained caps for England at Youth and Under-23 level. A product of the high-quality youth scheme set-up in the early 1960s, he signed professional forms in September 1964 and was to play regularly in the first team until 1969, when he was transferred to Tottenham Hotspur for £110,000. A confident player on the ball, he scored a rare headed goal in the 1967 League Cup Final, a goal which started the fine Rangers' comeback in that memorable match. He played some 70 games for Spurs prior to retiring from football through injury. For Rangers he made 206 senior appearances and scored 44 goals.

Andy Neil

Andy Neil hailed from Kilmarnock and played for his home-town club before spending a number of seasons with Brighton & Hove Albion. He joined Arsenal from Brighton in March 1924, for £3,000, and was transferred back to Brighton in March 1926. A slightly built but skilful inside-forward, he made his League debut for Rangers in August 1927 and played for the club for the following three seasons, making 112 League and Cup appearances. A pastry cook by trade, he scored ten goals in 54 League games for the Gunners but managed to find the net only once for QPR.

Warren Neill

Born in Acton, Warren Neill came to attention of Queen's Park Rangers in schools football and gained international recognition at that level. He was developed through the Rangers' youth scheme before making his League debut in September 1980 and became a regular in the first team in 1982. A reliable performer, he played in the 1986 Milk Cup Final at Wembley. Neill was transferred to Portsmouth in July 1988, for a fee of £110,000, and made over 150 appearances for Pompey to add to the 209/6 senior games he had clocked up with QPR.

George Newlands

At 5ft 8in and 13st, George Newlands typified the traditional full-back of his time. He was born in Glasgow in 1882 and began playing for Vale of Clyde and Oakhead Juniors. Later he assisted Norwich City for a spell. In the six years he was with Queen's Park Rangers, he played in 186 League and Cup games and was proud of his only goal, scored against Brentford in January 1902. A popular player with supporters, he was equally at home at left or right-back. He was a quiet and unassuming individual but one with a fearless reputation as a player who gave tremendous service to the club in its formative years. He returned to Norwich City in 1907.

Brian Nicholas

Brian Nicholas, who was born in Aberdare in 1933, joined Queen's Park Rangers as a 15-year-old junior player. Despite his Welsh birthplace he won England schoolboy honours before turning professional with Rangers in May 1950. Nicholas made his League debut the following season and matured into a fine wing-half. He played for Rangers for three full seasons, making 121 League and Cup appearances before being transferred to London rivals, Chelsea, in July 1955. Chelsea had just won the League Championship and had a large first-team squad, so Nicholas' opportunities were limited at Stamford Bridge. Early in 1958, he moved to Third Division South club, Coventry City, and made 121 senior appearances before Jimmy Hill let him go to Rugby Town in July 1962.

Gilbert Ovens

A native of Bristol, Gilbert Ovens began his playing career with Bristol Rovers before being transferred to Chelsea. He did not appear in the League side at Stamford Bridge and Rangers signed him 1911. Initially he played at full-back but subsequently gave consistent performances for the club as a half-back. A member of the 1912 Southern League championship winning team, he also played in the FA Charity Shield game against Blackburn Rovers that year. His League career was ended by the outbreak of World War One.

Paul Parker

Born in East London, Paul Parker signed for Fulham as an apprentice and moved up to their professional ranks in 1981. His outstanding performances at full-back for Fulham brought much attention from the bigger clubs, but surprisingly he remained with the Cottagers until June 1987, when he was transferred to Queen's Park Rangers for a bargain fee of £200,000. Parker played four seasons for Queen's Park Rangers and further enhanced his reputation. Whilst with the club he gained his first England caps and was a member of Bobby Robson's 1990 World Cup team in Italy. He was

transferred to Manchester United in August 1991 for a club record fee of £2 million. He has also gained caps at Youth, 'B' and England Under-21 level.

Phil Parkes

Birmingham-born Phil Parkes was a very formidable figure as a goalkeeper, standing 6ft 3in and weighing over 15st. He was signed as an amateur by Walsall in 1967 and in a career spanning 23 years of League football, he gained England Under-21, Under-23 and 'B' honours as well as one full cap. Parkes is in contention with Reg Allen and Peter Springett for recognition as the finest goalkeeper to have played for QPR. When he moved to West Ham in February 1979, after making 406 senior appearances for Rangers, the fee of £565,000 was a world record for a goalkeeper. He had done much to help Rangers into the

First Division and then into runners-up spot in the top flight; for the Hammers he continued his remarkable career with appearances in the 1980 and 1981 FA Cup Finals. He made 344 League appearances for West Ham — exactly the same number he had made for QPR — and ended his career with three League games for Ipswich Town. He is one of a select band of players to have appeared in over 700 League games.

Johnny Pattison

A prominent junior player in Scotland, Johnny Pattison signed for Motherwell but found himself in competition for a place in their first team. Spotted by Queen's Park Rangers whilst playing in the lower reaches, he signed for the club in 1937 and was establishing himself as a first-team regular when World War Two broke out. He played a number of times during the war and gained a permanent place at outside-left in the successful Third Division South side immediately after the war. Essentially one-footed, he was fast, tricky and a very good crosser of the ball. A member of the 1948 championship winning side, he was transferred to Leyton Orient in 1950 and then joined Dover a year later. For Rangers he made 165 League and Cup appearances, scoring 51 goals.

George Petchey

A stalwart figure of the Rangers side during the 1950s, Eastender George Petchey had a reputation for being one of the finest wing-halves in the lower divisions during that time. A tough-tackling, no-nonsense player, he joined Queen's Park Rangers in 1953, after two League games for West Ham, and played 271 senior games for the club prior to his transfer to Crystal Palace in June 1960. In his first season at Selhurst he was ever-present in the side promoted to Division Three and helped Palace into Division Two before his career was ended by an eye injury. He later managed Orient and Millwall and then coached the junior players at Brighton.

William Pierce

A Geordie from Ashington, that hotbed of football talent, William Pierce signed for Queen's Park Rangers from the junior side of Bedlington Colliery and made his League debut against Swansea Town in October 1923, when he was only 16 years old. A hard-tackling full-back, he was to be a regular first-team player for eight seasons before joining Carlisle United in 1931, after 193 League and Cup appearances for Rangers.

Johnny Poppitt

Born in West Sleekburn, County Durham, Johnny Poppitt signed for Queen's Park Rangers from Derby County in September 1950. A junior athletics champion, he was one of the fastest defenders in the game and made his Rangers debut against Birmingham City in September 1950 and was the right-back partner to Tony Ingham for the majority of games over the next four seasons. After the 1953-54 season he retired from League football and signed for Chelmsford City. He had made 111 League and Cup appearances for Rangers. Poppitt had joined the Rams during the war and although a reserve full-back at the Baseball Ground, he made his League debut as an emergency centre-forward. After Chelmsford he did the rounds of non-League clubs in the East Midlands.

George Powell

A local boy, George Powell was born at Fulham and moved across from that club to Loftus Road as an amateur in December 1946. He was persuaded to sign professional forms and quickly justified that by making his League debut against Reading in November 1947. He was a member of the promotion-winning side of 1948 and by the following season was turning in outstanding performances which brought him to the verge of international recognition. He played for Rangers up until 1953, when he retired from League football after 155 senior appearances.

Ivor Powell

Ivor Powell was born in the Rhonnda and became one of the few Third Division players to win an international cap. He was virtually a Queen's Park Rangers discovery. He came to Shepherd's Bush as an amateur in 1936 and signed as professional the following season. He made his debut in January 1939 and would obviously have played substantially more games for the club had the war not intervened. He served in India and played with the likes of Tommy Walker, Denis Compton and his Rangers club mate, Billy McEwan. A stocky, competitive wing-half who gained eight caps for Wales, Powell was transferred to Aston Villa in December 1948, after 157 League and Cup appearances for QPR. He later played for Port Vale, was player-manager of Bradford and manager of Carlisle United.

Mike Powell

Born at Slough, Buckinghamshire, and signed by Rangers from their youth side, Mike Powell originally appeared as an inside-forward. He was a tall, strong player and it was this attribute that ultimately converted him to a central defender, a position which he played fairly regularly from 1952 to 1959. When he was unable to command a regular first-team place he joined local non-League club Yiewsley in the summer of 1959, after 108 League and Cup games for QPR.

Henry Pullen

Discovered playing for his home-town team of Kettering, Henry Pullen signed for Queen's Park Rangers in 1910. It was in the 1911-12 season that he came through to command a regular first-team place in the side that won Southern League championship. He played in the FA Charity Shield match that season, against Blackburn Rovers. A regular first-team member for four years before World War One, he made 202 League and Cup appearances for Rangers before being transferred to Newport County after the first post-war season.

Alf Ridyard

A tall, commanding centre-half who was signed by Queen's Park Rangers from West Bromwich in March 1938, Alf Ridyard played in only 23 League games for the club prior to World War Two. But through the troubled years that followed he was virtually the only continuous link, week after week, and made just under 200 appearances in those seven wartime seasons. After the war, he was to make only 11 further first-team appearances, taking him to 232 senior games in all. His wartime service with the club was recognised with a benefit match. When he stepped down from playing, he became club coach for a while and later he was on the club's scouting staff.

Glenn Roeder

Queen's Park Rangers skipper in the first game of the 1982 FA Cup Final, Glenn Roeder was suspended for the replay, having been sent off in a League game at Luton Town two weeks earlier. He was a tall, stylish player with a deceptive change of pace which made him very effective when going forward from defensive positions. Originally signed from Orient in August 1978, for £250,000, he was with Rangers until late 1983, when he transferred to Newcastle United for a fee of £150,000, following a loan spell with Notts County. Whilst with QPR he gained England 'B' honours and altogether played in 181 senior games for the club. After Newcastle he played for Watford and then returned to Orient as a non-contract player.

Jack Rose

Jack Rose joined Queen's Park Rangers during the war years from non-League

Peterborough United and played in over 100 matches in wartime competition before making his League debut in 1946. He ultimately played in only 18 peacetime competitive games before retiring in 1948.

George Rounce

George Rounce played junior football for Tilbury in the Kent League and with Uxbridge. He signed for Queen's Park Rangers in February 1928 and made a scoring debut against Merthyr Town on 25th of that month. Lightly built and only 5ft 7in tall, he was a very constructive and skilful inside-forward who played regularly for the first team from the moment he joined the club up until he was transferred to Fulham in March 1933. For Rangers he made 188 League and Cup appearances and scored 71 goals. Unable to establish himself at Craven Cottage, he moved to Bristol Rovers but his career was cut short when he contracted tuberculosis, from which he died at the age of 31.

Keith Rutter

In the 1950s, Queen's Park Rangers made two significant signings from non-League club Methley United: Keith Rutter was the first, signed in July 1954, and he later recommended Arthur Longbottom, who joined Rangers in February 1955. Both were to give outstanding service to the Rangers but it was Rutter who was the backbone of the side from 1954 through to 1963, when he moved to Colchester United after 362 appearances for Rangers. He was without question the best centre-half in the Third Division for most of that time and his consistency and fitness enabled him to play in all except seven of the club's League matches between 1956-57 and 1961-62.

Keith Sanderson

An astute signing by Alec Stock from Plymouth Argyle in June 1965, Keith Sanderson, a former Cambridge soccer Blue, spent four years with Rangers and in that time he gained a League Cup winners' medal, Third Division championship medal, Second Division runners-up medal and played a few games for the club in their first-ever season in the First Division. One of the last amateurs to appear in a Football League game, he later became a part-time professional. He was a competent inside-forward whose consistency and hard-work balanced so well with Rodney Marsh and Les Allen in that fine team of the mid-1960s. In March 1970 he left League football when he moved to the east of England and played for Goole Town. For Rangers he had made 118/6 senior appearances and scored 12 goals. In 1989 he wrote a letter to *The Times,* criticising modern football.

David Seaman

When David Seaman signed for Queen's Park Rangers in August 1986, for a bargain fee of £225,000, he had already gained England Under-21 caps and had played for three League clubs — Leeds United,

Peterborough United and Birmingham City. It was at Queen's Park Rangers, however, that he was to gain recognition as a top-class goalkeeper and it was with QPR that he gained the first of nine full caps. After playing in 175 senior games for Rangers he was transferred to Arsenal in July 1990, for a fee of £1.3m. Another of the many quality goalkeepers to play for Rangers. In 1993 he helped the Gunners to two Wembley Finals.

Don Shanks

A Fulham apprentice and England Youth international, Don Shanks signed as a professional for Luton Town in 1970. He joined Queen's Park Rangers in November 1974, for a fee of £35,000, but it was some three years before he broke through to be a regular first-team player. From the

1977-78 season through to 1980-81 campaign he was a regular selection. He joined Brighton & Hove Albion on a free transfer in August 1981 and subsequently played in Hong Kong and made a single appearance for Wimbledon. For Rangers, full-back Shanks made 201/5 senior appearances.

Charlie Shaw

Relatively short for a goalkeeper at 5ft 9in, Charlie Shaw developed his football in Scottish junior soccer and first came to the notice of Queen's Park Rangers when playing for Port Glasgow. Having signed for the Scottish junior club in 1905, he joined QPR in the 1907 close season. In that first year he helped the club win the Southern League title and he played in both FA Charity Shield matches at Stamford Bridge. A regular choice for the next five seasons, he won another Southern League championship medal in 1912 and made his third Charity Shield appearance. By the end of his final season with the club, 1912-13, he had made over 250 appearances for the Rangers.

Ernie Shepherd

Ernie Shepherd joined Queen's Park Rangers at the age of 31, having had League experience with Fulham, West Bromwich Albion and Hull City. Indeed, in 1948-49 he played for all those clubs — and they all won promotion. He surprised many by the consistency of his performances for QPR as the regular outside-left, making 231 appearances in his six seasons and scoring 53 goals. He left the Bush in 1956, for Southern League Hastings United, and later was trainer at Bradford, managed Southend United and coached Orient and in Dubai. He had made his League debut in the last game before World War Two, during which he guested for Bradford City and Huddersfield Town in his native Yorkshire.

Frank Sibley

Frank Sibley was truly dedicated to Queen's Park Rangers. He joined the club as a junior and became its youngest-ever first-team debutant when he appeared against Aldershot in September 1963, before his 16th birthday. Sibley began his career as an inside-forward but successfully converted into a strong, attacking wing-half. He captained the England Youth side and was a member of the 1967 League Cup winning team. But he was unlucky with injuries throughout his career and retired in 1971 to take up a position on the coaching staff. A brief excursion into football management with Walsall, and a similar brief spell in 1984-85 as caretaker manager of Rangers, did not suit him and this knowledgeable, likeable man subsequently returned to the coaching staff. For Rangers he made 165/3 senior appearances.

Andy Sinton

Andy Sinton had seven seasons of League football under his belt before joining Queen's Park Rangers for a fee of £300,000 in March 1989. He began his career with Cambridge United before moving to Brentford but it was with Rangers that he developed his full potential which eventually led to international recognition with England. Sinton is very adaptable, for whilst playing most of his Queen's Park Rangers matches as a winger, he has also appeared in midfield and has even played at left-back for England. Fast, skilful and capable of some thunderous shooting, has still the potential to become a regular in the England team. By the end of the 1992-93 season he had made 190 senior appearances for QPR, scoring 25 goals.

Albert Smith

Born in Fenton, near Stoke-on-Trent, Albert Smith signed for Birmingham but never appeared in the Blues' first team and was one of those young men called up for military service in the early days of World War Two. Whilst in the Royal Artillery, he was awarded the BEM for bravery. He came to Loftus Road during the war and made 75 appearances in wartime competitions before League football resumed in 1946. A member of the promotion-winning side of 1947-48, he left the club in 1949 and played in non-League football with Ashford and Dover, but has always kept his contacts with the Rangers. For QPR he totalled 144 appearances in all games including wartime.

Conway Smith

An inside-forward with a powerful shot and a consistent record as a goalscorer, Con Smith was signed from Huddersfield Town in March 1951. A member of the fairly consistent and settled side that Rangers had during the early 1950s, he made 180 senior appearances and scored 84 goals before his transfer to Halifax Town in June 1956. For Halifax he scored 73 goals in 183 League games.

J.W.Smith

Although he played for Queen's Park Rangers during World War One, J.W.Smith was formally signed from Third Lanark in April 1919. He joined the club for its last season in the Southern League and played through the first two campaigns in the Football League. At 5ft 8in he was fairly short for the centre-forward role but he scored very consistently over his three League seasons, sharing the responsibility with Jimmy Birch. In 1922 he was transferred to Swansea Town after netting 66 goals in 159 senior games for Rangers.

Peter Springett

The younger of the two goalkeeping brothers, Peter Springett signed for QPR as a professional in May 1963 and in the following two seasons shared the goalkeeping responsibilities with Frank Smith. By the time the 1965-66 season came around, he had made the first-team spot his own and the following season he was ever-present in the side that won the Third Division title and took the League Cup in that memorable Wembley Final. At the end of that season he joined Sheffield Wednesday in a unique transfer which brought his brother, Ron, back from the Owls in exchange, with Rangers receiving £35,000 to balance the deal. An excellent 'keeper who was unlucky not to receive full recognition as an England player, Peter Springett was capped at Youth and Under-23 level. For Rangers he made 160 first-team appearances. After 180 League games for Wednesday, he appeared in 191 for Barnsley before retiring to become a policeman.

Ron Springett

Ron Springett made his debut for QPR in November 1955 and established himself as the permanent first-team goalkeeper the following season. His spectacular performances were soon recognised by the bigger clubs and in March 1958 he was transferred to Sheffield Wednesday, whom he was to serve with some distinction for around ten years. Whilst he had learnt his trade with the Rangers, he got his full recognition with the Owls and between 1959 and 1966 he won 33 England caps. Although he did not play in the 1966 World Cup, he was a member of Alf Ramsey's squad that won the trophy. After his return to Rangers, following the exchange deal involving his brother (mentioned above), Ron made a further 45 League appearances before his retirement in 1969. Altogther for Rangers he appeared in 103 League and Cup games, and for the Owls he made 384 senior appearances. For Wednesday he was a key member of their

Second Division championship side of 1958-59 and was on the losing side in the 1966 FA Cup Final. He and Peter played on opposite sides only twice and QPR lost both.

Simon Stainrod

Simon Stainrod wore Queen's Park Rangers' celebrated number-ten shirt with some distinction through the period from 1980 to 1985. His best season was the 1981-82 campaign when, apart from playing in all Rangers' FA Cup ties when they reached the Final, he also appeared 39 times in the League side, scoring 24 goals. He was a regular member of the side the following year, when they won the Second Division championship, and played in the First Division for some 60 games prior to his transfer to his home-town Sheffield Wednesday for a fee of £250,000. Stainrod played in only 15 games for the Owls before falling out with Harold Wilkinson. He subsequently played for Aston Villa and Stoke City before going to play for Strasbourg in the French League. Returning to the UK to play for Falkirk, he was ultimately appointed their player-manager. He is building a good managerial reputation in Scotland and in 1992 became manager of Dundee. For Rangers he scored 62 goals in 143/2 senior appearances.

Syd Sweetman

Right-back Syd Sweetman joined Queen's Park Rangers from Hampstead Town in February 1925 and spent his first four years with the club trying to establish a first-team place. He finally made it in 1928-29, when he was an ever-present. He was transferred to Millwall in the summer of 1929 after making 102 League and Cup appearances. Some 25 years later, his nephew, Stan, joined Rangers but never made a first-team appearance.

Reg Swinfen

Reg Swinfen, a stocky, bustling centre-forward who played occasional games for the first team up to World War Two, probably missed his best opportunity of starring for the club with the intervention of hostilities. He appeared fairly regularly through the war period, often turning out at full-back or alternatively on the wing. He played in only one League game for the club after the war, which took his overall tally to 31 League games and 86 wartime appearances. He scored 36 goals in the war and six in peacetime.

Dave Thomas

The signing of Dave Thomas from Burnley — then QPR's biggest rivals in Division Two — in October 1972, for a fee of £165,000, was one of the best purchases Gordon Jago ever made for Queen's Park Rangers. A tall rangey wing-forward who could play on either flank, in his first season Thomas was part of the team who were promoted to Division One and he was a regular choice in the fine side that finished runners-up in the First Division in 1976. Very fast and an excellent crosser of the ball, he earned eight caps for England whilst playing for Rangers. He returned to his native Lancashire in August 1977, when Everton signed him for a fee of £200,000, after he had made 219/1 senior appearances and scored 33 goals. He later had brief careers with Wolves, Middlesbrough and Portsmouth and also played for Vancouver Whitecaps in the NASL. When he made his debut for Burnley, he was their youngest-ever First Division player

Bill Thompson

Bill Thompson played for West Bromwich Albion for two seasons, but owing to a dispute over terms he spent the 1911-12 season turning out for non-League Haslington. Rangers stepped in to resurrect his career and he joined the club for the 1912-13 season. A small, light-framed, tricky outside-right, Thompson played for Rangers during the seasons from 1912 through to 1920, when he was transferred to Newport County. During World War One he returned to his native North-East and guested for South Shields. For Rangers he

made 139 League appearances, a total that would obviously have been a lot more, but for the war.

Terry Venables

A bright, inventive midfield player, Terry Venables' record is a testimony to his abilities. He was the first individual to be capped at every level from Schoolboy and even Amateur level through to the full England side, for whom he appeared twice in 1965. He joined Chelsea in 1958-59, as a 15-year-old, and was in their Second Division promotion side of 1962-63 and won a League Cup winners' medal in 1965 before being transferred to Spurs for £80,000 in May 1966. With Tottenham he gained an FA Cup winners' medal in 1967 (when they beat his former club, Chelsea, in the Final) and signed for Rangers in June 1969 for £70,000, following the club's relegation to the Second Division. Four years later he was the captain of the side that regained Rangers' First Division status. In September, he left Loftus Road in an exchange deal that bought Don Rogers of Crystal Palace to Rangers. After his glittering career as a player ended at Palace, Venables became manager of that club. However, his friendship with Jim Gregory, the chairman of Queen's Park Rangers, brought Venables back to Loftus Road in 1980 and he quickly made his mark by taking QPR to their first FA Cup Final, where they lost to Spurs in a replay in 1982. The following season he led them to the Second Division championship. In 1983, Gregory stood down from his chairmanship and offered to Venables a chance to buy the club. This was under consideration for some time but ultimately, he decided to take the post of chief coach at Barcelona and left at the end of 1983-84 season. Venables subsequently returned to English football and joined Tottenham Hotspur, initially as team manager, but during the boardroom upheavals he became managing director with Alan Sugar buying the majority of the shares. Alas, at the end of 1992-93 their 'dream ticket' had become a nightmare for both men.

Gary Waddock

Gary Waddock is probably the most popular player to have appeared for Rangers over the last 30 years. A bright-eyed, ginger-haired enthusiast for the game, Waddock made 100 per cent commitment to every tackle and to every game. A bad injury in 1986 looked likely to end of his career, but he refused to accept the medical diagnosis and fought his way back to fitness. This caused a problem for both player and club as the insurance money for his early retirement had been paid out, so whilst the problem was resolved he went to Belgium to play for Charleroi, until 1989-90 when he returned to the UK and signed for Millwall, where he proved his fitness by playing a schedule of 40 League games the following season. He gained caps for the Republic of Ireland at 'B', Under-21 and Under-23 level before becoming a member of the senior squad and gaining 20 full caps. In February 1992, he rejoined Rangers but he did not make a first-team appearance before being transferred to Bristol Rovers at the end of the year. Overall, his Rangers appearances in all senior games totalled 227/13.

William Wake

William Wake learnt his football in the Newcastle district, having been born at Barnbury Castle in 1887. He had a short spell with Newcastle United before coming south when he assisted both Plymouth Argyle and Exeter City. Wake joined Queen's Park Rangers in 1909 and played regular first-team football at left-half for over five seasons. A member of the side that won the Southern League in 1912, he played in the FA Charity Shield match against Blackburn Rovers that year. Wake made 240 senior appearances for Rangers.

Ian Watson

Ian Watson was signed from Chelsea by Alec Stock in July 1965, for £10,000, and was the regular right-back for the majority of the following season. He made only occasional first-team appearances in the following two years, but he was an essential part of the squad which won the Third Division title, along with the Football League Cup, in 1967. On Rangers' promotion to the First Division in 1968-69, he was the only ever-present in that first season in the top flight and he continued to give good service up to the mid-1970s, when he left League football after 226/6 League and Cup appearances.

David Webb

David Webb was another astute signing by Dave Sexton in his early years as manager of Queen's Park Rangers. Webb had previously served Orient, Southampton and Chelsea, for whom he scored the winning goal in the 1970 FA Cup Final replay against Leeds and then gained a European Cup-winners' Cup medal the following season. In May 1974, Rangers paid Chelsea £120,000 for Webb, who was a crucial part of the team which took the club to runners-up spot in the First Division in 1976. His total commitment and his enthusiastic style made him immensely popular with both the crowd and his fellow players. His worst moment for Rangers was probably his miss in the penalty competition against AEK Athens in the UEFA Cup. But he soon won the fans over again by placing the ball on the spot and 'scoring' during the kick-in before the next home match. He later played for Leicester City and Derby County before taking up managerial appointments at Bournemouth and Southend United. He was appointed caretaker manager of his first football love, Chelsea, in February 1993, but was dismissed at the end of the season and became manager of Brentford. For Rangers he made 146/1 senior appearances.

Roy Wegerle

Striker Roy Wegerle was discovered playing in South African soccer but after a brief trial with Manchester United, he joined Chelsea via USA club, Tampa Bay Rowdies, for £100,000. Wegerle struggled for a first-team place at Stamford Bridge and after a loan spell with Swindon, moved to Luton Town for £75,000 in July 1988. In December 1989, QPR paid an astonishing £1 million for a player of such limited experience but he repaid them with 31 goals in 89/4 League and Cup games, top-scoring in 1990-91 with 18 in the League including one which was voted ITV's Goal of the Season. In March 1992, ambitious Blackburn Rovers paid £1.2 million for him but he failed to make an impression and was eventually transferred to Coventry City. Wegerle made his international debut for the USA in 1992.

Jack White

Early handbooks claim that Jack White's outstanding features were his well-timed tackling and powerful kicking and his cool, resourceful temperament. His real first name was Jabez and he began his football career with Ollenshaw United and moved through Grays Anchor and Swanscombe before signing for Grays United as a professional. His play was brought to the attention of Rangers, who signed him in the close season of 1901. Capable of playing in a number of positions, he was, however, essentially a full-back and it was in that position that he played in most of his 140 League and Cup games for QPR. He was a member of the Southern League championship-winning team of 1908 and moved to Leeds City in May that year. After 60 Second Division games for them, he was transferred to Merthyr Town.

Alf Whyman

Alf Whyman first came to prominence in local football at Tottenham and was spotted by Queen's Park Rangers playing for New Brompton. He scored twice on his debut, against Watford in September 1909, and was generally used by Rangers as a utility man, having played both at half-back and in the forward line. His role as the general utility man meant that he played in some two-thirds of the first-team games over his first six seasons with the club and that role is reflected in his selection as 12th man for the FA Charity Shield game against Blackburn Rovers in 1912. In all he made 206 senior appearances for Rangers, scoring 25 goals, although his career was interrupted by World War One.

Steve Wicks

Steve Wicks began his career with Chelsea, for whom he played 118 games before moving to Derby County for a short spell in 1979, prior to signing for Queen's Park Rangers in September that year. He was ever-present for the remainder of that season and, apart from a brief spell with Crystal Palace in 1981, he played for Rangers for seven seasons. He appeared in a few games in the Second Division championship side of 1982-83 and was a regular central defender in Rangers' first three seasons back in the First Division. He returned to Chelsea in August 1986, for a fee of £400,000, but played in only a further 30-plus games for them before injury ended his career. Wicks gained Youth and Under-21 honours and came very close to playing for the full England team. For Rangers he made 220/1 senior appearances.

Ray Wilkins MBE

Ray Wilkins is a player of tremendous talent who has served, with great dignity, Chelsea, Manchester United, AC Milan, Paris St-Germain, Glasgow Rangers and, more recently, Queen's Park Rangers. A midfield controller in every sense of the word, Wilkins has matured with age and even at 36 he is still orchestrating with skill and vision in the FA Premier League, although he suffered a broken leg in a freak training accident during 1992-93. In his career spanning some 20 years at the top level, Wilkins has played at England Under-21 and Under-23 levels and gained 84 full caps. For Rangers he has so far made 138 senior appearances, scoring ten goals. He has been involved in some big money moves and in August 1979, Manchester United paid Chelsea some £875,000 for his magnificent ball-passing skills.

Pat Woods

Islington-born Pat Woods came up through the Queen's Park Rangers junior sides and signed professional forms in June 1950, making his first-team debut against Coventry City in January 1953. From the start of the next season he gradually made the right-back position his own and, along with Tony Ingham, formed an almost permanent full-back partnership for over five seasons. A chirpy character, he left the club in 1961 to emigrate to Australia but returned some two years later and joined Colchester United for a short spell. For QPR he made 326 appearances in League and Cup football.

Queen's Park Rangers' Records

Highest Attendances
Football League 35,353
(Leeds United • Division One • 27.4.74)
FA Cup 41,097
(Leeds United • Round Three • 9.1.32)
League Cup 28,739
(Aston Villa • Semi-final • 1.2.77)
Other 23,009
(AEK Athens • UEFA Round Four • 16.3.77)

Biggest Victory
Football League (h) 9-2
(Tranmere Rovers • Division Three • 3.12.60)
Football League (a) 7-1
(Mansfield Town • Division Three • 24.9.66)
FA Cup (h) 7-0
(Barry • Round One • 6.11.61)
FA Cup (a) 8-1
(Bristol Rovers • Round One • 27.11.37)
League Cup (h) 8-1
(Crewe Alexandra • Round Two • 4.10.83)
League Cup (a) 5-1
(Hull City • Round Two • 8.10.85)
Other (h) 6-2
(Partizan Belgrade • UEFA Round Two • 24.10.84)
Other (a) 7-0
(SK Brann • UEFA Round One • 29.9.76)

Biggest Defeat
Football League (h) 0-5
(Burnley • Division Two • 21.1.50)
Football League (a) 1-8
(Mansfield Town • Division Three • 15.3.63)
(Manchester United • Division One • 19.3.69)
FA Cup (h) 0-3
(Luton Town • Third Qualifying Round • 1.11.02)
(Charlton Athletic • Round Three • 16.1.30)
FA Cup (a) 1-6
(Burnley • Round Three • 6.1.62)
(Hereford United • Round Two • 7.12.57)
League Cup (h) 0-4
(Newcastle United • Round Three • 8.10.74)
League Cup (a) 0-4
(Reading • Round Two • 23.9.64)
Other (h) 1-3
(Reading • Simod Cup Round One • 21.12.87)
Other (a) 0-4
(Manchester United • FA Charity Shield • 29.8.08)
(Partizan Belgrade • UEFA Round Two • 7.11.84)
(Southampton • ZDS Round Two • 20.11.90)

Most Points
(2 for a win)
67 • Division Three • 1966-67
(3 for a win)
85 • Division Two • 1982-83

Least Points
(2 for a win)
18 • Division One • 1968-69
(3 for a win)
46 • Division One • 1990-91

Most League Goals in season
111 • Division Three • 1961-62

Least League goals in season
34 • Southern League • 1901-02, 1902-03
37 • Division Three South • 1923-24, 1925-26

Most Appearances (career)
Tony Ingham • (548) • (League 514, FAC 30, LC 4)

Most Goals (career)
George Goddard • 189 • (League 177, FAC 12)

Most Goals (season)
Rodney Marsh • 44 • (League 30, FAC3, LC11) • 1966-67

Oldest Player
Jimmy Langley • 38 years 96 days
(13.5.67 v Oxford United • Division Three)

Youngest Player
Frank Sibley • 15 years 275 days
(4.9.63 v Aldershot • League Cup Round One)

Record Transfer fee (Received)
£2,000,000 • Paul Parker(Manchester United) • August 1991

Record Transfer Fee (Paid)
£1,000,000 • Roy Wegerle (Luton Town) • December 1989

Most Capped Player
Alan McDonald (41 — Northern Ireland)

Ever-Presents (All games, League & Cup)

Season	Games	Player(s)
1899-1900	38 Games	H.CLUTTERBUCK Alex McCONNELL
1900-01	32 Games	H.CLUTTERBUCK Tom GRAY Alfred HITCH
1901-02	33 Games	Harry COLLINS
1902-03	31 Games	Harry COLLINS
1905-06	35 Games	W.YENSON
1907-08	41 Games	Charlie SHAW
1908-09	43 Games	Charlie SHAW
1909-10	49 Games	Charlie SHAW
1910-11	39 Games	Charlie SHAW
1911-12	41 Games	W.BARNES W.WAKE
1912-13	40 Games	Jimmy BIRCH Archie MITCHELL
1913-14	43 Games	H.PULLEN W.THOMPSON
1914-15	41 Games	R.McLEOD
1916-17	39 Games	Archie MITCHELL
1919-20	43 Games	J.SMITH
1920-21	44 Games	G.GRANT J.SMITH
1922-23	46 Games	Leonard HILL
1926-27	42 Games	J.LOFTHOUSE
1928-29	43 Games	George GODDARD Sidney SWEETMAN
1932-33	47 Games	E.BEECHAM
1933-34	46 Games	D.ASHMAN
1936-37	45 Games	William MASON
1938-39	46 Games	Harry LOWE
1942-43	35 Games	Harry BROWN
1944-45	36 Games	Joe MALLETT
1956-57	49 Games	Cecil ANDREWS Tony INGHAM Ron SPRINGETT
1957-58	49 Games	Tony INGHAM George PETCHEY Keith RUTTER
1958-59	48 Games	Tony INGHAM George PETCHEY
1959-60	49 Games	Jimmy ANDREWS Tony INGHAM Keith RUTTER Pat WOODS
1960-61	50 Games	Tony INGHAM Keith RUTTER
1961-62	52 Games	Mike KEEN
1963-64	50 Games	Mike KEEN
1964-65	51 Games	Mike KEEN
1965-66	53 Games	Mike KEEN Jimmy LANGLEY
1966-67	58 Games	Mike KEEN
1967-68	46 Games	Allan HARRIS Mike KEEN Ian MORGAN
1968-69	42 Games	Ian WATSON
1969-70	51 Games	Tony HAZELL
1970-71	45 Games	Dave CLEMENT
1971-72	48 Games	Dave CLEMENT Tony HAZELL Phil PARKES
1973-74	51 Games	Stan BOWLES Don GIVENS Phil PARKES
1974-75	49 Games	Ian GILLARD
1975-76	48 Games	Don MASSON Phil PARKES
1979-80	48 Games	David McCREERY
1982-83	45 Games	Ian DAWES
1983-84	46 Games	Ian DAWES Peter HUCKER
1984-85	55 Games	Gary BANNISTER Ian DAWES Peter HUCKER
1985-86	52 Games	Ian DAWES
1987-88	48 Games	Paul PARKER
1989-90	50 Games	Andy SINTON
1990-91	44 Games	David BARDSLEY Andy SINTON Ray WILKINS

Ever-Presents (League games only)

Season	Games	Player(s)
1919-20	42 Games	J.BALDOCK
1943-44	30 Games	Joe MALLETT
1945-46	20 Games	Jack ROSE
1960-61	46 Games	Peter ANGELL Ray DRINKWATER
1966-67	46 Games	Peter SPRINGETT
1967-68	42 Games	Tony HAZELL
1972-73	42 Games	Gerry FRANCIS
1980-81	42 Games	Ian GILLARD
1982-83	42 Games	John GREGORY Peter HUCKER
1985-86	42 Games	Alan McDONALD
1991-92	42 Games	Jan STĚJSKAL

QPR in the League

1920-1921 DIVISION 3

	P	W	D	L	F	A	W	D	L	F	A	Pts
Crystal P	42	15	4	2	45	17	9	7	5	25	17	59
Southampton	42	14	5	2	46	10	5	11	5	18	18	54
QPR	**42**	**14**	**4**	**3**	**38**	**11**	**8**	**5**	**8**	**23**	**21**	**53**
Swindon T	42	14	5	2	51	17	7	5	9	22	32	52
Swansea T	42	9	10	2	32	19	9	5	7	24	26	51
Watford	42	14	4	3	40	15	6	4	11	19	29	48
Millwall	42	11	5	5	25	8	7	6	8	17	22	47
Merthyr T	42	13	5	3	46	20	2	10	9	14	29	45
Luton T	42	14	6	1	51	15	2	6	13	10	41	44
Bristol R	42	15	3	3	51	22	3	4	14	17	35	43
Plymouth A	42	10	7	4	25	13	1	14	6	10	21	43
Portsmouth	42	10	8	3	28	14	2	7	12	18	34	39
Grimsby T	42	12	5	4	32	16	3	4	14	17	43	39
Northampton T	42	11	4	6	32	23	4	4	13	27	52	38
Newport Co	42	8	5	8	20	23	6	4	11	23	41	37
Norwich C	42	9	10	2	31	14	1	6	14	13	39	36
Southend U	42	13	2	6	32	20	1	6	14	12	41	36
Brighton & HA	42	11	6	4	28	20	3	2	16	14	41	36
Exeter C	42	9	7	5	27	15	1	8	12	12	39	35
Reading	42	8	4	9	26	22	4	3	14	16	37	31
Brentford	42	7	9	5	27	23	2	3	16	15	44	30
Gillingham	42	6	9	6	19	24	2	3	16	15	50	28

1921-1922 DIVISION 3 South

	P	W	D	L	F	A	W	D	L	F	A	Pts
Southampton	42	14	7	0	50	8	9	8	4	18	13	61
Plymouth A	42	17	4	0	43	4	8	7	6	20	20	61
Portsmouth	42	13	5	3	38	18	5	12	4	24	21	53
Luton T	42	16	2	3	47	9	6	6	9	17	26	52
QPR	**42**	**13**	**7**	**1**	**36**	**12**	**5**	**6**	**10**	**17**	**32**	**49**
Swindon T	42	10	7	4	40	21	6	6	9	32	39	45
Watford	42	9	9	3	34	21	4	9	8	20	27	44
Aberdare A	42	11	6	4	38	18	6	4	11	19	33	44
Brentford	42	15	2	4	41	17	1	9	11	11	26	43
Swansea T	42	11	8	2	40	19	2	7	12	10	28	41
Merthyr T	42	14	2	5	33	15	3	4	14	12	41	40
Millwall	42	6	13	2	22	10	4	5	12	16	32	38
Reading	42	10	5	6	28	15	4	5	12	12	32	38
Bristol R	42	8	8	5	32	24	6	2	13	20	43	38
Norwich C	42	8	10	3	29	17	4	3	14	21	45	37
Charlton A	42	10	6	5	28	19	3	5	13	15	37	37
Northampton T	42	13	3	5	30	17	0	8	13	17	54	37
Gillingham	42	11	4	6	36	20	3	4	14	11	40	36
Brighton & HA	42	9	6	6	33	19	4	3	14	12	32	35
Newport Co	42	8	7	6	22	18	3	5	13	22	43	34
Exeter C	42	7	5	9	22	29	4	7	10	16	30	34
Southend U	42	7	5	9	23	23	1	6	14	11	51	27

1922-1923 DIVISION 3 South

	P	W	D	L	F	A	W	D	L	F	A	Pts
Bristol C	42	16	4	1	43	13	8	7	6	23	27	59
Plymouth A	42	18	3	0	47	6	5	4	12	14	23	53
Swansea C	42	13	6	2	46	14	9	3	9	32	31	53
Brighton & HA	42	15	3	3	39	13	5	8	8	13	21	51
Luton T	42	14	4	3	47	18	7	3	11	21	31	49
Millwall	42	9	10	2	27	13	5	8	8	18	27	46
Portsmouth	42	10	5	6	34	20	9	3	9	24	32	46
Northampton T	42	13	6	2	40	17	4	5	12	14	27	45
Swindon T	42	14	4	3	41	17	3	7	11	21	39	45
Watford	42	10	6	5	35	23	7	4	10	22	31	44
QPR	**42**	**10**	**4**	**7**	**34**	**24**	**6**	**6**	**9**	**20**	**25**	**42**
Charlton A	42	11	6	4	33	14	3	8	10	22	37	42
Bristol R	42	7	9	5	25	19	6	7	8	10	17	42
Brentford	42	9	4	8	27	23	4	8	9	14	28	38
Southend U	42	10	6	5	35	18	2	7	12	14	36	37
Gillingham	42	13	4	4	38	18	2	3	16	13	41	37
Merthyr T	42	10	4	7	27	17	1	10	10	12	31	36
Norwich C	42	8	7	6	29	26	5	3	13	22	45	36
Reading	42	9	8	4	24	15	1	6	14	12	40	34
Exeter C	42	10	4	7	27	18	3	3	15	20	66	33
Aberdare A	42	6	8	7	25	23	3	3	15	17	47	29
Newport Co	42	8	6	7	28	21	0	5	16	12	49	27

1923-1924 DIVISION 3 South

	P	W	D	L	F	A	W	D	L	F	A	Pts
Portsmouth	42	15	3	3	57	11	9	8	4	30	19	59
Plymouth A	42	13	6	2	46	15	10	3	8	24	19	55
Millwall	42	17	3	1	45	11	5	7	9	19	27	54
Swansea T	42	18	2	1	39	10	4	6	11	21	38	52
Brighton & HA	42	16	4	1	56	12	5	5	11	12	25	51
Swindon T	42	14	5	2	38	11	3	8	10	20	33	47
Luton T	42	11	7	3	35	19	5	7	9	15	25	46
Northampton T	42	14	3	4	40	15	3	8	10	24	32	45
Bristol R	42	11	7	3	34	15	4	6	11	18	31	43
Newport Co	42	15	4	2	39	15	2	5	14	17	49	43
Norwich C	42	13	5	3	45	18	3	3	15	15	41	40
Aberdare A	42	9	9	3	35	18	3	5	13	10	40	38
Merthyr T	42	11	8	2	33	19	0	8	13	12	46	38
Charlton A	42	8	7	6	26	20	3	8	10	12	25	37
Gillingham	42	11	6	4	27	15	1	7	13	16	43	37
Exeter C	42	14	3	4	33	17	1	4	16	4	35	37
Brentford	42	9	8	4	33	21	5	0	16	21	50	36
Reading	42	12	2	7	35	20	1	7	13	16	37	35
Southend U	42	11	7	3	35	19	1	3	17	18	65	34
Watford	42	8	8	5	35	18	1	7	13	10	36	33
Bournemouth	42	6	8	7	19	19	5	3	13	21	46	33
QPR	**42**	**9**	**6**	**6**	**28**	**26**	**2**	**3**	**16**	**9**	**51**	**31**

1924-1925 DIVISION 3 South

	P	W	D	L	F	A	W	D	L	F	A	Pts
Swansea T	42	17	4	0	51	12	6	7	8	17	23	57
Plymouth A	42	17	3	1	55	12	6	7	8	22	26	56
Bristol C	42	14	5	2	40	10	8	4	9	20	31	53
Swindon T	42	17	2	2	51	13	3	9	9	15	25	51
Millwall	42	12	5	4	35	14	6	8	7	23	24	49
Newport Co	42	13	6	2	35	12	7	3	11	27	30	49
Exeter C	42	13	4	4	37	19	6	5	10	22	29	47
Brighton & HA	42	14	3	4	43	17	5	5	11	16	28	46
Northampton T	42	12	3	6	34	18	8	3	10	17	26	46
Southend U	42	14	1	6	34	18	5	4	12	17	43	43
Watford	42	12	3	6	22	20	5	6	10	16	27	43
Norwich C	42	10	8	3	39	18	4	5	12	14	33	41
Gillingham	42	11	8	2	25	11	2	6	13	10	33	40
Reading	42	9	6	6	28	15	5	4	12	9	23	38
Charlton A	42	12	6	3	31	13	1	6	14	15	35	38
Luton T	42	9	10	2	34	15	1	7	13	15	42	37
Bristol R	42	10	5	6	26	13	2	8	11	16	36	37
Aberdare A	42	13	4	4	40	21	1	5	15	14	46	37
QPR	**42**	**10**	**6**	**5**	**28**	**19**	**4**	**2**	**15**	**14**	**44**	**36**
Bournemouth	42	8	6	7	20	17	5	2	14	20	41	34
Brentford	42	8	7	6	28	26	1	0	20	10	65	25
Merthyr T	42	8	3	10	24	27	0	2	19	11	50	21

1925-1926 DIVISION 3 South

	P	W	D	L	F	A	W	D	L	F	A	Pts
Reading	42	16	5	0	49	16	7	6	8	28	36	57
Plymouth A	42	16	2	3	71	33	8	6	7	36	34	56
Millwall	42	14	6	1	52	12	7	5	9	21	27	53
Bristol C	42	14	3	4	42	15	7	6	8	30	36	51
Brighton & HA	42	12	4	5	47	33	7	5	9	37	40	47
Swindon T	42	16	2	3	48	22	4	4	13	21	42	46
Luton T	42	16	4	1	60	25	2	3	16	20	50	43
Bournemouth	42	10	5	6	44	30	7	4	10	31	61	43
Aberdare A	42	11	6	4	50	24	6	2	13	24	42	42
Gillingham	42	11	4	6	36	19	6	4	11	17	30	42
Southend U	42	13	2	6	50	20	6	2	13	28	53	42
Northampton T	42	13	3	5	47	26	4	4	13	35	54	41
Crystal P	42	16	1	4	50	21	3	2	16	25	58	41
Merthyr T	42	13	3	5	51	25	1	8	12	18	50	39
Watford	42	12	5	4	47	26	3	4	14	26	63	39
Norwich C	42	11	5	5	35	26	4	4	13	23	47	39
Newport Co	42	11	5	5	39	27	3	5	13	25	47	38
Brentford	42	12	4	5	44	32	4	2	15	25	62	38
Bristol R	42	9	4	8	44	28	6	2	13	22	41	36
Exeter C	42	13	2	6	54	25	2	3	16	18	45	35
Charlton A	42	9	7	5	32	23	2	6	13	16	45	35
QPR	**42**	**5**	**7**	**9**	**23**	**32**	**1**	**2**	**18**	**14**	**52**	**21**

1926-1927 DIVISION 3 South

	P	W	D	L	F	A	W	D	L	F	A	Pts
Bristol C	42	19	1	1	71	24	8	7	6	33	30	62
Plymouth A	42	17	4	0	52	14	8	6	7	43	47	60
Millwall	42	16	2	3	55	19	7	8	6	34	32	56
Brighton & HA	42	15	4	2	61	24	6	7	8	18	26	53
Swindon T	42	16	3	2	64	31	5	6	10	36	54	51
Crystal P	42	12	6	3	57	33	6	3	12	27	48	45
Bournemouth	42	13	2	6	49	24	5	6	10	29	42	44
Luton T	42	12	9	0	48	19	3	5	13	20	47	44
Newport Co	42	15	4	2	40	20	4	2	15	17	51	44
Bristol R	42	12	4	5	46	28	4	5	12	32	52	41
Brentford	42	10	9	2	46	20	3	5	13	24	41	40
Exeter C	42	14	4	3	46	18	1	6	14	30	55	40
Charlton A	42	13	5	3	44	22	3	3	15	16	39	40
QPR	**42**	**9**	**8**	**4**	**41**	**27**	**6**	**1**	**14**	**24**	**44**	**39**
Coventry C	42	11	4	6	44	33	4	3	14	27	53	37
Norwich C	42	10	5	6	41	25	2	6	13	18	46	35
Merthyr T	42	11	5	5	42	25	2	4	15	21	55	35
Northampton T	42	13	4	4	36	23	2	1	18	23	64	35
Southend U	42	12	3	6	44	25	2	3	16	20	52	34
Gillingham	42	10	5	6	36	26	1	5	15	18	46	32
Watford	42	9	6	6	36	27	3	2	16	21	60	32
Aberdare A	42	8	2	11	38	48	1	5	15	24	53	25

1927-1928 DIVISION 3 South

	P	W	D	L	F	A	W	D	L	F	A	Pts
Millwall	42	19	2	0	87	15	11	3	7	40	35	65
Northampton T	42	17	3	1	67	23	6	6	9	35	41	55
Plymouth A	42	17	2	2	60	19	6	5	10	25	35	53
Brighton & HA	42	14	4	3	51	24	5	6	10	30	45	48
Crystal P	42	15	3	3	46	23	3	9	9	33	49	48
Swindon T	42	12	6	3	60	26	7	3	11	30	43	47
Southend U	42	14	2	5	48	19	6	4	11	32	45	46
Exeter C	42	11	6	4	49	27	6	6	9	21	33	46
Newport Co	42	12	5	4	52	38	6	4	11	29	46	45
QPR	**42**	**8**	**5**	**8**	**37**	**35**	**9**	**4**	**8**	**35**	**36**	**43**
Charlton A	42	12	5	4	34	27	3	8	10	26	43	43
Brentford	42	12	4	5	49	30	4	4	13	27	44	40
Luton T	42	13	5	3	56	27	3	2	16	38	60	39
Bournemouth	42	12	6	3	44	24	1	6	14	28	55	38
Watford	42	10	5	6	42	34	4	5	12	26	44	38
Gillingham	42	10	3	8	33	26	3	8	10	29	55	37
Norwich C	42	9	8	4	41	26	1	8	12	25	44	36
Walsall	42	9	6	6	52	35	3	3	15	23	66	33
Bristol R	42	11	3	7	41	36	3	1	17	26	57	32
Coventry C	42	5	8	8	40	36	6	1	14	27	60	31
Merthyr T	42	7	6	8	38	40	2	7	12	15	51	31
Torquay U	42	4	10	7	27	36	4	4	13	26	67	30

1928-1929 DIVISION 3 South

	P	W	D	L	F	A	W	D	L	F	A	Pts
Charlton A	42	14	5	2	51	22	9	3	9	35	38	54
Crystal P	42	14	2	5	40	25	9	6	6	41	42	54
Northampton T	42	14	6	1	68	23	6	6	9	28	34	52
Plymouth A	42	14	6	1	51	13	6	6	9	32	38	52
Fulham	42	14	3	4	60	31	7	7	7	41	40	52
QPR	**42**	**13**	**7**	**1**	**50**	**22**	**6**	**7**	**8**	**32**	**39**	**52**
Luton T	42	16	3	2	64	28	3	8	10	25	45	49
Watford	42	15	3	3	55	31	4	7	10	24	43	48
Bournemouth	42	14	4	3	54	31	5	5	11	30	46	47
Swindon T	42	12	5	4	48	27	3	8	10	27	45	43
Coventry C	42	9	6	6	35	23	5	8	8	27	34	42
Southend U	42	10	7	4	44	27	5	4	12	36	48	41
Brentford	42	11	4	6	34	21	3	6	12	22	39	38
Walsall	42	11	7	3	47	25	2	5	14	26	54	38
Brighton & HA	42	14	2	5	39	28	2	4	15	19	48	38
Newport Co	42	8	6	7	37	28	5	3	13	32	58	35
Norwich C	42	12	3	6	49	29	2	3	16	20	52	34
Torquay U	42	10	3	8	46	36	4	3	14	20	48	34
Bristol R	42	9	6	6	39	28	4	1	16	21	51	33
Merthyr T	42	11	6	4	42	28	0	2	19	13	75	30
Exeter C	42	7	6	8	49	40	2	5	14	18	48	29
Gillingham	42	7	8	6	22	24	3	1	17	21	59	29

1929-1930 DIVISION 3 South

	P	W	D	L	F	A	W	D	L	F	A	Pts
Plymouth A	42	18	3	0	63	12	12	5	4	35	26	68
Brentford	42	21	0	0	66	12	7	5	9	28	32	61
QPR	**42**	**13**	**5**	**3**	**46**	**26**	**8**	**4**	**9**	**34**	**42**	**51**
Northampton T	42	14	6	1	53	20	7	2	12	29	38	50
Brighton & HA	42	16	2	3	54	20	5	6	10	33	43	50
Coventry C	42	14	3	4	54	25	5	6	10	34	48	47
Fulham	42	12	6	3	54	33	6	5	10	33	50	47
Norwich C	42	14	4	3	55	28	4	6	11	33	49	46
Crystal P	42	14	5	2	56	26	3	7	11	25	48	46
Bournemouth	42	11	6	4	47	24	4	7	10	25	37	43
Southend U	42	11	6	4	41	19	4	7	10	28	40	43
Clapton O	42	10	8	3	38	21	4	5	12	17	41	41
Luton T	42	13	4	4	42	25	1	8	12	22	53	40
Swindon T	42	10	7	4	42	25	3	5	13	31	58	38
Watford	42	10	4	7	37	30	5	4	12	23	43	38
Exeter C	42	10	6	5	45	29	2	5	14	22	44	35
Walsall	42	10	4	7	45	24	3	4	14	26	54	34
Newport Co	42	9	9	3	48	29	3	1	17	26	56	34
Torquay U	42	9	6	6	50	38	1	5	15	14	56	31
Bristol R	42	11	3	7	45	31	0	5	16	22	62	30
Gillingham	42	9	5	7	38	28	2	3	16	13	52	30
Merthyr T	42	5	6	10	39	49	1	3	17	21	86	21

1930-1931 DIVISION 3 South

	P	W	D	L	F	A	W	D	L	F	A	Pts
Notts Co	42	16	4	1	58	13	8	7	6	39	33	59
Crystal P	42	17	2	2	71	20	5	5	11	36	51	51
Brentford	42	14	3	4	62	30	8	3	10	28	34	50
Brighton & HA	42	13	5	3	45	20	4	10	7	23	33	49
Southend U	42	16	0	5	53	26	6	5	10	23	34	49
Northampton T	42	10	6	5	37	20	8	6	7	40	39	48
Luton T	42	15	3	3	61	17	4	5	12	15	34	46
QPR	**42**	**15**	**0**	**6**	**57**	**23**	**5**	**3**	**13**	**25**	**52**	**43**
Fulham	42	15	3	3	49	21	3	4	14	28	54	43
Bournemouth	42	11	7	3	39	22	4	6	11	33	51	43
Torquay U	42	13	5	3	56	26	4	4	13	24	58	43
Swindon T	42	15	5	1	68	29	3	1	17	21	65	42
Exeter C	42	12	6	3	55	35	5	2	14	29	55	42
Coventry C	42	11	4	6	55	28	5	5	11	20	37	41
Bristol R	42	12	3	6	49	36	4	5	12	26	56	40
Gillingham	42	10	6	5	40	29	4	4	13	21	47	38
Walsall	42	9	5	7	44	38	5	4	12	34	57	37
Watford	42	9	4	8	41	29	5	3	13	31	46	35
Clapton O	42	12	3	6	47	33	2	4	15	16	58	35
Thames	42	12	5	4	34	20	1	3	17	20	73	34
Newport Co	42	10	5	6	45	31	1	1	19	24	80	28
Norwich C	42	10	7	4	37	20	0	1	20	10	56	28

1931-1932 DIVISION 3 South

	P	W	D	L	F	A	W	D	L	F	A	Pts
Fulham	42	15	3	3	72	27	9	6	6	39	35	57
Reading	42	19	1	1	65	21	4	8	9	32	46	55
Southend U	42	12	5	4	41	18	9	6	6	36	35	53
Crystal P	42	14	7	0	48	12	6	4	11	26	51	51
Brentford	42	11	6	4	40	22	8	4	9	28	30	48
Luton T	42	16	1	4	62	25	4	6	11	33	45	47
Exeter C	42	16	3	2	53	16	4	4	13	24	46	47
Brighton & HA	42	12	4	5	42	21	5	8	8	31	37	46
Cardiff C	42	14	2	5	62	29	5	6	10	25	44	46
Norwich C	42	12	7	2	51	22	5	5	11	25	45	46
Watford	42	14	4	3	49	27	5	4	12	32	52	46
Coventry C	42	17	2	2	74	28	1	6	14	34	69	44
QPR	**42**	**11**	**6**	**4**	**50**	**30**	**4**	**6**	**11**	**29**	**43**	**42**
Northampton T	42	12	3	6	48	26	4	4	13	21	43	39
Bournemouth	42	8	8	5	42	32	5	4	12	28	46	38
Clapton O	42	7	8	6	41	35	5	3	13	36	55	35
Swindon T	42	12	2	7	47	31	2	4	15	23	53	34
Bristol R	42	11	6	4	46	30	2	2	17	19	62	34
Torquay U	42	9	6	6	49	39	3	3	15	23	67	33
Mansfield T	42	11	5	5	54	45	0	5	16	21	63	32
Gillingham	42	8	6	7	26	26	2	2	17	14	56	28
Thames	42	6	7	8	35	35	1	2	18	18	74	23

1932-1933 DIVISION 3 South

	P	W	D	L	F	A	W	D	L	F	A	Pts
Brentford	42	15	4	2	45	19	11	6	4	45	30	62
Exeter C	42	17	2	2	57	13	7	8	6	31	35	58
Norwich C	42	16	3	2	49	17	6	10	5	39	38	57
Reading	42	14	5	2	68	30	5	8	8	35	41	51
Crystal P	42	14	4	3	51	21	5	4	12	27	43	46
Coventry C	42	16	1	4	75	24	3	5	13	31	53	44
Gillingham	42	14	4	3	54	24	4	4	13	18	37	44
Northampton T	42	16	5	0	54	11	2	3	16	22	55	44
Bristol R	42	13	5	3	38	22	2	9	10	23	34	44
Torquay U	42	12	7	2	51	26	4	5	12	21	41	44
Watford	42	11	8	2	37	22	5	4	12	29	41	44
Brighton & HA	42	13	3	5	42	20	4	5	12	24	45	42
Southend U	42	11	5	5	39	27	4	6	11	26	55	41
Luton T	42	12	8	1	60	32	1	5	15	18	46	39
Bristol C	42	11	5	5	59	37	1	8	12	24	53	37
QPR	**42**	**9**	**8**	**4**	**48**	**32**	**4**	**3**	**14**	**24**	**55**	**37**
Aldershot	42	11	6	4	37	21	2	4	15	24	51	36
Bournemouth	42	10	7	4	44	27	2	5	14	16	54	36
Cardiff C	42	12	4	5	48	30	0	3	18	21	69	31
Clapton O	42	7	8	6	39	35	1	5	15	20	58	29
Newport Co	42	9	4	8	42	42	2	3	16	19	63	29
Swindon T	42	7	9	5	36	29	2	2	17	24	76	29

1933-1934 DIVISION 3 South

	P	W	D	L	F	A	W	D	L	F	A	Pts
Norwich C	42	16	4	1	55	19	9	7	5	33	30	61
Coventry C	42	16	3	2	70	22	5	9	7	30	32	54
Reading	42	17	4	0	60	13	4	8	9	22	37	54
QPR	**42**	**17**	**2**	**2**	**42**	**12**	**7**	**4**	**10**	**28**	**39**	**54**
Charlton A	42	14	5	2	53	27	8	3	10	30	29	52
Luton T	42	14	3	4	55	28	7	7	7	28	33	52
Bristol R	42	14	4	3	49	21	6	7	8	28	26	51
Swindon T	42	13	5	3	42	25	4	6	11	22	43	45
Exeter C	42	12	5	4	43	19	4	6	11	25	38	43
Brighton & HA	42	12	7	2	47	18	3	6	12	21	42	43
Clapton O	42	14	4	3	60	25	2	6	13	15	44	42
Crystal P	42	11	6	4	40	25	5	3	13	31	42	41
Northampton T	42	10	6	5	45	32	4	6	11	26	46	40
Aldershot	42	8	6	7	28	27	5	6	10	24	44	38
Watford	42	12	4	5	43	16	3	3	15	28	47	37
Southend U	42	9	6	6	32	27	3	4	14	19	47	34
Gillingham	42	8	8	5	49	41	3	3	15	26	55	33
Newport Co	42	6	9	6	25	23	2	8	11	24	47	33
Bristol C	42	7	8	6	33	22	3	5	13	25	63	33
Torquay U	42	10	4	7	32	28	3	3	15	21	65	33
Bournemouth	42	7	7	7	41	37	2	2	17	19	65	27
Cardiff C	42	6	4	11	32	43	3	2	16	25	62	24

1934-1935 DIVISION 3 South

	P	W	D	L	F	A	W	D	L	F	A	Pts
Charlton A	42	17	2	2	62	20	10	5	6	41	32	61
Reading	42	16	5	0	59	23	5	6	10	30	42	53
Coventry C	42	14	5	2	56	14	7	4	10	30	36	51
Luton T	42	12	7	2	60	23	7	5	9	32	37	50
Crystal P	42	15	3	3	51	14	4	7	10	35	50	48
Watford	42	14	2	5	53	19	5	7	9	23	30	47
Northampton T	42	14	4	3	40	21	5	4	12	25	46	46
Bristol R	42	14	6	1	54	27	3	4	14	19	50	44
Brighton & HA	42	15	4	2	51	16	2	5	14	18	46	43
Torquay U	42	15	2	4	60	22	3	4	14	21	53	42
Exeter C	42	11	5	5	48	29	5	4	12	22	46	41
Millwall	42	11	4	6	33	26	6	3	12	24	36	41
QPR	**42**	**14**	**6**	**1**	**49**	**22**	**2**	**3**	**16**	**14**	**50**	**41**
Clapton O	42	13	3	5	47	21	2	7	12	18	44	40
Bristol C	42	14	3	4	37	18	1	6	14	15	50	39
Swindon T	42	11	7	3	45	22	2	5	14	22	56	38
Bournemouth	42	10	5	6	36	26	5	2	14	18	45	37
Aldershot	42	12	6	3	35	20	1	4	16	15	55	36
Cardiff C	42	11	6	4	42	27	2	3	16	20	55	35
Gillingham	42	10	7	4	36	25	1	6	14	19	50	35
Southend U	42	10	4	7	40	29	1	5	15	25	49	31
Newport Co	42	7	4	10	36	40	3	1	17	18	72	25

1935-1936 DIVISION 3 South

	P	W	D	L	F	A	W	D	L	F	A	Pts
Coventry C	42	19	1	1	75	12	5	8	8	27	33	57
Luton T	42	13	6	2	56	20	9	6	6	25	25	56
Reading	42	18	0	3	52	20	8	2	11	35	42	54
QPR	**42**	**14**	**4**	**3**	**55**	**19**	**8**	**5**	**8**	**29**	**34**	**53**
Watford	42	12	3	6	47	29	8	6	7	33	25	49
Crystal P	42	15	4	2	64	20	7	1	13	32	54	49
Brighton & HA	42	13	4	4	48	25	5	4	12	22	38	44
Bournemouth	42	9	6	6	36	26	7	5	9	24	30	43
Notts Co	42	10	5	6	40	25	5	7	9	20	32	42
Torquay U	42	14	4	3	41	27	2	5	14	21	35	41
Aldershot	42	9	6	6	29	21	5	6	10	24	40	40
Millwall	42	9	8	4	33	21	5	4	12	25	50	40
Bristol C	42	11	5	5	32	21	4	5	12	16	38	40
Clapton O	42	13	2	6	34	15	3	4	14	21	46	38
Northampton T	42	12	5	4	38	24	3	3	15	24	66	38
Gillingham	42	9	5	7	34	25	5	4	12	32	52	37
Bristol R	42	11	6	4	48	31	3	3	15	21	64	37
Southend U	42	8	7	6	38	21	5	3	13	23	41	36
Swindon T	42	10	5	6	43	33	4	3	14	21	40	36
Cardiff C	42	11	5	5	37	23	2	5	14	23	50	36
Newport Co	42	8	4	9	36	44	3	5	13	24	67	31
Exeter C	42	7	5	9	38	41	1	6	14	21	52	27

1936-1937 DIVISION 3 South

	P	W	D	L	F	A	W	D	L	F	A	Pts
Luton T	42	19	1	1	69	16	8	3	10	34	37	58
Notts Co	42	15	3	3	44	23	8	7	6	30	29	56
Brighton & HA	42	15	5	1	49	16	9	0	12	25	27	53
Watford	42	14	4	3	53	21	5	7	9	32	39	49
Reading	42	14	5	2	53	23	5	6	10	23	37	49
Bournemouth	42	17	3	1	45	20	3	6	12	20	39	49
Northampton T	42	15	4	2	56	22	5	2	14	29	46	46
Millwall	42	12	4	5	43	24	6	6	9	21	30	46
QPR	**42**	**12**	**2**	**7**	**51**	**24**	**6**	**7**	**8**	**22**	**28**	**45**
Southend U	42	10	8	3	49	23	7	3	11	29	44	45
Gillingham	42	14	5	2	36	18	4	3	14	16	48	44
Clapton O	42	10	8	3	29	17	4	7	10	23	35	43
Swindon T	42	12	4	5	52	24	2	7	12	23	49	39
Crystal P	42	11	7	3	45	20	2	5	14	17	41	38
Bristol R	42	14	3	4	49	20	2	1	18	22	60	36
Bristol C	42	13	3	5	42	20	2	3	16	16	50	36
Walsall	42	11	3	7	38	34	2	7	12	25	51	36
Cardiff C	42	10	5	6	35	24	4	2	15	19	63	35
Newport Co	42	7	7	7	37	28	5	3	13	30	70	34
Torquay U	42	9	5	7	42	32	2	5	14	15	48	32
Exeter C	42	9	5	7	36	37	1	7	13	23	51	32
Aldershot	42	5	6	10	29	29	2	3	16	21	60	23

1937-1938 DIVISION 3 South

	P	W	D	L	F	A	W	D	L	F	A	Pts
Millwall	42	15	3	3	53	15	8	7	6	30	22	56
Bristol C	42	14	6	1	37	13	7	7	7	31	27	55
QPR	**42**	**15**	**3**	**3**	**44**	**17**	**7**	**6**	**8**	**36**	**30**	**53**
Watford	42	14	4	3	50	15	7	7	7	23	28	53
Brighton & HA	42	15	3	3	40	16	6	6	9	24	28	51
Reading	42	17	2	2	44	21	3	9	9	27	42	51
Crystal P	42	14	4	3	45	17	4	8	9	22	30	48
Swindon T	42	12	4	5	33	19	5	6	10	16	30	44
Northampton T	42	12	4	5	30	19	5	5	11	21	38	43
Cardiff C	42	13	7	1	57	22	2	5	14	10	32	42
Notts Co	42	10	6	5	29	17	6	3	12	21	33	41
Southend U	42	12	5	4	43	23	3	5	13	27	45	40
Bournemouth	42	8	10	3	36	20	6	2	13	20	37	40
Mansfield T	42	12	5	4	46	26	3	4	14	16	41	39
Bristol R	42	10	7	4	28	20	3	6	12	18	41	39
Newport Co	42	9	10	2	31	15	2	6	13	12	37	38
Exeter C	42	10	4	7	37	32	3	8	10	20	38	38
Aldershot	42	11	4	6	23	14	4	1	16	16	45	35
Clapton O	42	10	7	4	27	19	3	0	18	15	42	33
Torquay U	42	7	5	9	22	28	2	7	12	16	45	30
Walsall	42	10	4	7	34	37	1	3	17	18	51	29
Gillingham	42	9	5	7	25	25	1	1	19	11	52	26

1938-1939 DIVISION 3 South

	P	W	D	L	F	A	W	D	L	F	A	Pts
Newport Co	42	15	4	2	37	16	7	7	7	21	29	55
Crystal P	42	15	4	2	49	18	5	8	8	22	34	52
Brighton & HA	42	14	5	2	43	14	5	6	10	25	35	49
Watford	42	14	6	1	44	15	3	6	12	18	36	46
Reading	42	12	6	3	46	23	4	8	9	23	36	46
QPR	**42**	**10**	**8**	**3**	**44**	**15**	**5**	**6**	**10**	**24**	**34**	**44**
Ipswich T	42	14	3	4	46	21	2	9	10	16	31	44
Bristol C	42	14	5	2	42	19	2	7	12	19	44	44
Swindon T	42	15	4	2	53	25	3	4	14	19	52	44
Aldershot	42	13	6	2	31	15	3	6	12	22	51	44
Notts Co	42	12	6	3	36	16	5	3	13	23	38	43
Southend U	42	14	5	2	38	13	2	4	15	23	51	41
Cardiff C	42	12	1	8	40	28	3	10	8	21	37	41
Exeter C	42	9	9	3	40	32	4	5	12	25	50	40
Bournemouth	42	10	8	3	38	22	3	5	13	14	36	39
Mansfield T	42	10	8	3	33	19	2	7	12	11	43	39
Northampton T	42	13	5	3	41	20	2	3	16	10	38	38
Port Vale	42	10	5	6	36	23	4	4	13	16	35	37
Torquay U	42	7	5	9	27	28	7	4	10	27	42	37
Clapton O	42	10	9	2	40	16	1	4	16	13	39	35
Walsall	42	9	6	6	47	23	2	5	14	21	46	33
Bristol R	42	8	8	5	30	17	2	5	14	25	44	33

1939-1940 DIVISION 3 South

	P	W	D	L	F	A	W	D	L	F	A	Pts
Reading	3	2	0	0	6	0	0	1	0	2	2	5
Exeter C	3	0	1	0	2	2	2	0	0	3	1	5
Notts Co	2	1	0	0	2	1	1	0	0	4	2	4
Ipswich T	3	1	1	0	3	1	0	1	0	2	2	4
Brighton & HA	3	1	1	0	2	1	0	1	0	3	3	4
Cardiff C	3	0	0	1	2	4	2	0	0	3	1	4
Crystal P	3	1	0	0	3	0	1	0	1	5	9	4
Bournemouth	3	1	1	0	12	2	0	0	1	1	2	3
Bristol C	3	0	1	1	4	5	1	0	0	1	0	3
Mansfield T	3	0	0	0	4	5	1	1	0	4	3	3
Norwich C	3	0	0	1	1	2	1	1	0	3	2	3
Clapton O	3	0	2	0	2	2	0	1	0	1	1	3
Southend U	3	1	0	0	3	2	0	1	1	0	1	3
Torquay U	3	0	2	0	2	2	0	1	0	2	2	3
Walsall	3	1	0	0	1	0	0	1	1	2	3	3
QPR	**3**	**0**	**1**	**0**	**2**	**2**	**0**	**1**	**1**	**2**	**3**	**2**
Watford	3	0	1	1	2	3	0	1	0	2	2	2
Northampton T	3	1	0	1	2	2	0	0	1	0	10	2
Aldershot	3	0	0	1	0	1	0	1	1	3	4	1
Swindon T	3	0	1	1	2	3	0	0	1	0	1	1
Bristol R	3	0	1	0	2	2	0	0	2	0	5	1
Port Vale	2	0	0	1	0	1	0	1	0	0	0	1

1947-1948 DIVISION 3 South

	P	W	D	L	F	A	W	D	L	F	A	Pts
QPR	**42**	**16**	**3**	**2**	**44**	**17**	**10**	**6**	**5**	**30**	**20**	**61**
Bournemouth	42	13	5	3	42	13	11	4	6	34	22	57
Walsall	42	13	5	3	37	12	8	4	9	33	28	51
Ipswich T	42	16	1	4	42	18	7	2	12	25	43	49
Swansea T	42	14	6	1	48	14	4	6	11	22	38	48
Notts Co	42	12	4	5	44	27	7	4	10	24	32	46
Bristol C	42	11	4	6	47	26	7	3	11	30	39	43
Port Vale	42	14	4	3	48	18	2	7	12	15	36	43
Southend U	42	11	8	2	32	16	4	5	12	19	42	43
Reading	42	10	5	6	37	28	5	6	10	19	30	41
Exeter C	42	11	6	4	34	22	4	5	12	21	41	41
Newport Co	42	9	8	4	38	28	5	5	11	23	45	41
Crystal P	42	12	5	4	32	14	1	8	12	17	35	39
Northampton T	42	10	5	6	35	28	4	6	11	23	44	39
Watford	42	6	6	9	31	37	8	4	9	26	42	38
Swindon T	42	6	10	5	21	20	4	6	11	20	26	36
Leyton O	42	8	5	8	31	32	5	5	11	20	41	36
Torquay U	42	7	6	8	40	29	4	7	10	23	33	35
Aldershot	42	5	10	6	22	26	5	5	11	23	41	35
Bristol R	42	7	3	11	39	34	6	5	10	32	41	34
Norwich C	42	8	3	10	33	34	5	5	11	28	42	34
Brighton & HA	42	8	4	9	26	31	3	8	10	17	42	34

1948-1949 DIVISION 2

	P	W	D	L	F	A	W	D	L	F	A	Pts
Fulham	42	16	4	1	52	14	8	5	8	25	23	57
WBA	42	16	3	2	47	16	8	5	8	22	23	56
Southampton	42	16	4	1	48	10	7	5	9	21	26	55
Cardiff C	42	14	4	3	45	21	5	9	7	17	26	51
Tottenham H	42	14	4	3	50	18	3	12	6	22	26	50
Chesterfield	42	9	7	5	24	18	6	10	5	27	27	47
West Ham U	42	13	5	3	38	23	5	5	11	18	35	46
Sheffield W	42	12	6	3	36	17	3	7	11	27	39	43
Barnsley	42	10	7	4	40	18	4	5	12	22	43	40
Luton T	42	11	6	4	32	16	3	6	12	23	41	40
Grimsby T	42	10	5	6	44	28	5	5	11	28	48	40
Bury	42	12	5	4	41	23	5	1	15	26	53	40
QPR	**42**	**11**	**4**	**6**	**31**	**26**	**3**	**7**	**11**	**13**	**36**	**39**
Blackburn R	42	12	5	4	41	23	3	3	15	12	40	38
Leeds U	42	11	6	4	36	21	1	7	13	19	42	37
Coventry C	42	12	3	6	35	20	3	4	14	20	44	37
Bradford	42	8	8	5	37	26	5	3	13	28	52	37
Brentford	42	7	10	4	28	21	4	4	13	14	32	36
Leicester C	42	6	10	5	41	38	4	6	11	21	41	36
Plymouth A	42	11	4	6	33	25	1	8	12	16	39	36
Nottingham F	42	9	6	6	22	14	5	1	15	28	40	35
Lincoln C	42	6	7	8	31	35	2	5	14	22	56	28

1949-1950 DIVISION 2

	P	W	D	L	F	A	W	D	L	F	A	Pts
Tottenham H	42	15	3	3	51	15	12	4	5	30	20	61
Sheffield W	42	12	7	2	46	23	6	9	6	21	25	52
Sheffield U	42	9	10	2	36	19	10	4	7	32	30	52
Southampton	42	13	4	4	44	25	6	10	5	20	23	52
Leeds U	42	11	8	2	33	16	6	5	10	21	29	47
Preston NE	42	12	5	4	37	21	6	4	11	23	28	45
Hull C	42	11	8	2	39	25	6	3	12	25	47	45
Swansea T	42	11	3	7	34	18	6	6	9	19	31	43
Brentford	42	11	5	5	21	12	4	8	9	23	37	43
Cardiff C	42	13	3	5	28	14	3	7	11	13	30	42
Grimsby T	42	13	5	3	53	25	3	3	15	21	48	40
Coventry C	42	8	6	7	32	24	5	7	9	23	31	39
Barnsley	42	11	6	4	45	28	2	7	12	19	39	39
Chesterfield	42	12	3	6	28	16	3	6	12	15	31	39
Leicester C	42	8	9	4	30	25	4	6	11	25	40	39
Blackburn R	42	10	5	6	30	15	4	5	12	25	45	38
Luton T	42	8	9	4	28	22	2	9	10	13	29	38
Bury	42	10	8	3	37	19	4	1	16	23	46	37
West Ham U	42	8	7	6	30	25	4	5	12	23	36	36
QPR	**42**	**6**	**5**	**10**	**21**	**30**	**5**	**7**	**9**	**19**	**27**	**34**
Plymouth A	42	6	6	9	19	24	2	10	9	25	41	32
Bradford	42	7	6	8	34	34	3	5	13	17	43	31

1950-1951 DIVISION 2

	P	W	D	L	F	A	W	D	L	F	A	Pts
Preston NE	42	16	3	2	53	18	10	2	9	38	31	57
Manchester C	42	12	6	3	53	25	7	8	6	36	36	52
Cardiff C	42	13	7	1	36	20	4	9	8	17	25	50
Birmingham C	42	12	6	3	37	20	8	3	10	27	33	49
Leeds U	42	14	4	3	36	17	6	4	11	27	38	48
Blackburn R	42	13	3	5	39	27	6	5	10	26	39	46
Coventry C	42	15	3	3	51	25	4	4	13	24	34	45
Sheffield U	42	11	4	6	44	27	5	8	8	28	35	44
Brentford	42	13	3	5	44	25	5	5	11	31	49	44
Hull C	42	12	5	4	47	28	4	6	11	27	42	43
Doncaster R	42	9	6	6	37	32	6	7	8	27	36	43
Southampton	42	10	9	2	38	27	5	4	12	28	46	43
West Ham U	42	10	5	6	44	33	6	5	10	24	36	42
Leicester C	42	10	4	7	42	28	5	7	9	26	30	41
Barnsley	42	9	5	7	42	22	6	5	10	32	46	40
QPR	**42**	**13**	**5**	**3**	**47**	**25**	**2**	**5**	**14**	**24**	**57**	**40**
Notts Co	42	7	7	7	37	34	6	6	9	24	26	39
Swansea T	42	14	1	6	34	25	2	3	16	20	52	36
Luton T	42	7	9	5	34	23	2	5	14	23	47	32
Bury	42	9	4	8	33	27	3	4	14	27	59	32
Chesterfield	42	7	7	7	30	28	2	5	14	14	41	30
Grimsby T	42	6	8	7	37	38	2	4	15	24	57	28

1951-1952 DIVISION 2

	P	W	D	L	F	A	W	D	L	F	A	Pts
Sheffield W	42	14	4	3	54	23	7	7	7	46	43	53
Cardiff C	42	18	2	1	52	15	2	9	10	20	39	51
Birmingham C	42	11	6	4	36	21	10	3	8	31	35	51
Nottingham F	42	12	6	3	41	22	6	7	8	36	40	49
Leicester C	42	12	6	3	48	24	7	3	11	30	40	47
Leeds U	42	13	7	1	35	15	5	4	12	24	42	47
Everton	42	12	5	4	42	25	5	5	11	22	33	44
Luton T	42	9	7	5	46	35	7	5	9	31	43	44
Rotherham U	42	11	4	6	40	25	6	4	11	33	46	42
Brentford	42	11	7	3	34	20	4	5	12	20	35	42
Sheffield U	42	13	2	6	57	28	5	3	13	33	48	41
West Ham U	42	13	5	3	48	29	2	6	13	19	48	41
Southampton	42	11	6	4	40	25	4	5	12	21	48	41
Blackburn R	42	11	3	7	35	30	6	3	12	19	33	40
Notts Co	42	11	5	5	45	27	5	2	14	26	41	39
Doncaster R	42	9	4	8	29	28	4	8	9	26	32	38
Bury	42	13	2	6	43	22	2	5	14	24	47	37
Hull C	42	11	5	5	44	23	2	6	13	16	47	37
Swansea T	42	10	4	7	45	26	2	8	11	27	50	36
Barnsley	42	8	7	6	39	33	3	7	11	20	39	36
Coventry C	42	9	5	7	36	33	5	1	15	23	49	34
QPR	**42**	**8**	**8**	**5**	**35**	**35**	**3**	**4**	**14**	**17**	**46**	**34**

1952-1953 DIVISION 3 South

	P	W	D	L	F	A	W	D	L	F	A	Pts
Bristol R	46	17	4	2	55	19	9	8	6	37	27	64
Millwall	46	14	7	2	46	16	10	7	6	36	28	62
Northampton T	46	18	4	1	75	30	8	6	9	34	40	62
Norwich C	46	16	6	1	56	17	9	4	10	43	38	60
Bristol C	46	13	8	2	62	28	9	7	7	33	33	59
Coventry C	46	15	5	3	52	22	4	7	12	25	40	50
Brighton & HA	46	12	6	5	48	30	7	6	10	33	45	50
Southend U	46	15	5	3	41	21	3	8	12	28	53	49
Bournemouth	46	15	3	5	49	23	4	6	13	25	46	47
Watford	46	12	8	3	39	21	3	9	11	23	42	47
Reading	46	17	3	3	53	18	2	5	16	16	46	46
Torquay U	46	15	4	4	61	28	3	5	15	26	60	45
Crystal P	46	12	7	4	40	26	3	6	14	26	56	43
Leyton O	46	12	7	4	52	28	4	3	16	16	45	42
Newport Co	46	12	4	7	43	34	4	6	13	27	48	42
Ipswich T	46	10	7	6	34	28	3	8	12	26	41	41
Exeter C	46	11	8	4	40	24	2	6	15	21	47	40
Swindon T	46	9	5	9	38	33	5	7	11	26	46	40
Aldershot	46	8	8	7	36	29	4	7	12	25	48	39
QPR	**46**	**9**	**9**	**5**	**37**	**34**	**3**	**6**	**14**	**24**	**48**	**39**
Gillingham	46	10	7	6	30	26	2	8	13	25	48	39
Colchester U	46	9	9	5	40	29	3	5	15	19	47	38
Shrewsbury T	46	11	5	7	38	35	1	7	15	30	56	36
Walsall	46	5	9	9	35	46	2	1	20	21	72	24

1953-1954 DIVISION 3 South

	P	W	D	L	F	A	W	D	L	F	A	Pts
Ipswich T	46	15	5	3	47	19	12	5	6	35	32	64
Brighton & HA	46	17	3	3	57	31	9	6	8	29	30	61
Bristol C	46	18	3	2	59	18	7	3	13	29	48	56
Watford	46	16	3	4	52	23	5	7	11	33	46	52
Northampton T	46	18	4	1	63	18	2	7	14	19	37	51
Southampton	46	17	5	1	51	22	5	2	16	25	41	51
Norwich C	46	13	5	5	43	28	7	6	10	30	38	51
Reading	46	14	3	6	57	33	6	6	11	29	40	49
Exeter C	46	12	2	9	39	22	8	6	9	29	36	48
Gillingham	46	14	3	6	37	22	5	7	11	24	44	48
Leyton O	46	14	5	4	48	26	4	6	13	31	47	47
Millwall	46	15	3	5	44	24	4	6	13	30	53	47
Torquay U	46	10	10	3	48	33	7	2	14	33	55	46
Coventry C	46	14	5	4	36	15	4	4	15	25	41	45
Newport Co	46	14	4	5	42	28	5	2	16	19	53	44
Southend U	46	15	2	6	46	22	3	5	15	23	49	43
Aldershot	46	11	5	7	45	31	6	4	13	29	55	43
QPR	**46**	**10**	**5**	**8**	**32**	**25**	**6**	**5**	**12**	**28**	**43**	**42**
Bournemouth	46	12	5	6	47	27	4	3	16	20	43	40*
Swindon T	46	13	5	5	48	21	2	5	16	19	49	40*
Shrewsbury T	46	12	8	3	48	34	2	4	17	17	42	40
Crystal P	46	11	7	5	41	30	3	5	15	19	56	40
Colchester U	46	7	7	9	35	29	3	3	17	15	49	30
Walsall	46	8	5	10	22	27	1	3	19	18	60	26

1954-1955 DIVISION 3 South

	P	W	D	L	F	A	W	D	L	F	A	Pts
Bristol C	46	17	4	2	62	22	13	6	4	39	25	70
Leyton O	46	16	2	5	48	20	10	7	6	41	27	61
Southampton	46	16	6	1	49	19	8	5	10	26	32	59
Gillingham	46	12	8	3	41	28	8	7	8	36	38	55
Millwall	46	14	6	3	44	25	6	5	12	28	43	51
Brighton & HA	46	14	4	5	47	27	6	6	11	29	36	50
Watford	46	11	9	3	45	26	7	5	11	26	36	50
Torquay U	46	12	6	5	51	39	6	6	11	31	43	48
Coventry C	46	15	5	3	50	26	3	6	14	17	33	47
Southend U	46	13	5	5	48	28	4	7	12	35	52	46
Brentford	46	11	6	6	44	36	5	8	10	38	46	46*
Norwich C	46	13	5	5	40	23	5	5	13	20	37	46*
Northampton T	46	13	5	5	47	27	6	3	14	26	54	46
Aldershot	46	12	6	5	44	23	4	7	12	31	48	45
QPR	**46**	**13**	**7**	**3**	**46**	**25**	**2**	**7**	**14**	**23**	**50**	**44**
Shrewsbury T	46	14	5	4	49	24	2	5	16	21	54	42
Bournemouth	46	7	8	8	32	29	5	10	8	25	36	42
Reading	46	7	10	6	32	26	6	5	12	33	47	41
Newport Co	46	8	8	7	32	29	3	8	12	28	44	38
Crystal P	46	9	11	3	32	24	2	5	16	20	56	38
Swindon T	46	10	8	5	30	19	1	7	15	16	45	37
Exeter C	46	9	7	7	30	31	2	8	13	17	42	37
Walsall	46	9	6	8	49	36	1	8	14	26	50	34
Colchester U	46	7	6	10	33	40	2	7	14	20	51	31

1955-1956 DIVISION 3 South

	P	W	D	L	F	A	W	D	L	F	A	Pts
Leyton O	46	18	3	2	76	20	11	5	7	30	29	66
Brighton & HA	46	20	2	1	73	16	9	5	9	39	34	65
Ipswich T	46	16	6	1	59	28	9	8	6	47	32	64
Southend U	46	16	4	3	58	25	5	7	11	30	55	53
Torquay U	46	11	10	2	48	21	9	2	12	38	42	52
Brentford	46	11	8	4	40	30	8	6	9	29	36	52
Norwich C	46	15	4	4	56	31	4	9	10	30	51	51
Coventry C	46	16	4	3	54	20	4	5	14	19	40	49
Bournemouth	46	13	6	4	39	14	6	4	13	24	37	48
Gillingham	46	12	3	8	38	28	7	7	9	31	43	48
Northampton T	46	14	3	6	44	27	6	4	13	23	44	47
Colchester U	46	14	4	5	56	37	4	7	12	20	44	47
Shrewsbury T	46	12	9	2	47	21	5	3	15	22	45	46
Southampton	46	13	6	4	60	30	5	2	16	31	51	44
Aldershot	46	9	9	5	36	33	3	7	13	34	57	40
Exeter C	46	10	6	7	39	30	5	4	14	19	47	40
Reading	46	10	2	11	40	37	5	7	11	30	42	39
QPR	**46**	**10**	**7**	**6**	**44**	**32**	**4**	**4**	**15**	**20**	**54**	**39**
Newport Co	46	12	2	9	32	26	3	7	13	26	53	39
Walsall	46	13	5	5	43	28	2	3	18	25	56	38
Watford	46	8	5	10	31	39	5	6	12	21	46	37
Millwall	46	13	4	6	56	31	2	2	19	27	69	36
Crystal P	46	7	3	13	27	32	5	7	11	27	51	34
Swindon T	46	4	10	9	18	22	4	4	15	16	56	30

1956-1957 DIVISION 3 South

	P	W	D	L	F	A	W	D	L	F	A	Pts
Ipswich T	46	18	3	2	72	20	7	6	10	29	34	59
Torquay U	46	19	4	0	71	18	5	7	11	18	46	59
Colchester U	46	15	8	0	49	19	7	6	10	35	37	58
Southampton	46	15	4	4	48	20	7	6	10	28	32	54
Bournemouth	46	15	7	1	57	20	4	7	12	31	42	52
Brighton & HA	46	15	6	2	59	26	4	8	11	27	39	52
Southend U	46	14	3	6	42	20	4	9	10	31	45	48
Brentford	46	12	9	2	55	29	4	7	12	23	47	48
Shrewsbury T	46	11	9	3	45	24	4	9	10	27	55	48
QPR	**46**	**12**	**7**	**4**	**42**	**21**	**6**	**4**	**13**	**19**	**39**	**47**
Watford	46	11	6	6	44	32	7	4	12	28	43	46
Newport Co	46	15	6	2	51	18	1	7	15	14	44	45
Reading	46	13	4	6	44	30	5	5	13	36	51	45
Northampton T	46	15	5	3	49	22	3	4	16	17	51	45
Walsall	46	11	7	5	49	25	5	5	13	31	49	44
Coventry C	46	12	5	6	52	36	4	7	12	22	48	44
Millwall	46	13	7	3	46	29	3	5	15	18	55	44
Plymouth A	46	10	8	5	38	31	6	3	14	30	42	43
Aldershot	46	11	5	7	43	35	4	7	12	36	57	42
Crystal P	46	7	10	6	31	28	4	8	11	31	47	40
Exeter C	46	8	8	7	37	29	4	5	14	24	50	37
Gillingham	46	7	8	8	29	29	5	5	13	25	56	37
Swindon T	46	12	3	8	43	33	3	3	17	23	63	36
Norwich C	46	7	5	11	33	37	1	10	12	28	57	31

1957-1958 DIVISION 3 South

	P	W	D	L	F	A	W	D	L	F	A	Pts
Brighton & HA	46	13	6	4	52	30	11	6	6	36	34	60
Brentford	46	15	5	3	52	24	9	5	9	30	32	58
Plymouth A	46	17	4	2	43	17	8	4	11	24	31	58
Swindon T	46	14	7	2	47	16	7	8	8	32	34	57
Reading	46	14	5	4	52	23	7	8	8	27	28	55
Southampton	46	16	3	4	78	31	6	7	10	34	41	54
Southend U	46	14	5	4	56	26	7	7	9	34	32	54
Norwich C	46	11	9	3	41	28	8	6	9	34	42	53
Bournemouth	46	16	5	2	54	24	5	4	14	27	50	51
QPR	**46**	**15**	**6**	**2**	**40**	**14**	**3**	**8**	**12**	**24**	**51**	**50**
Newport Co	46	12	6	5	40	24	5	8	10	33	43	48
Colchester U	46	13	5	5	45	27	4	8	11	32	52	47
Northampton T	46	13	1	9	60	33	6	5	12	27	46	44
Crystal P	46	12	5	6	46	30	3	8	12	24	42	43
Port Vale	46	12	6	5	49	24	4	4	15	18	34	42
Watford	46	9	8	6	34	27	4	8	11	25	50	42
Shrewsbury T	46	10	6	7	29	25	5	4	14	20	46	40
Aldershot	46	7	9	7	31	34	5	7	11	28	55	40
Coventry C	46	10	9	4	41	24	3	4	16	20	57	39
Walsall	46	10	7	6	37	24	4	2	17	24	51	37
Torquay U	46	9	7	7	33	34	2	6	15	16	40	35
Gillingham	46	12	5	6	33	24	1	4	18	19	57	35
Millwall	46	6	6	11	37	36	5	3	15	26	55	31
Exeter C	46	10	4	9	37	35	1	5	17	20	64	31

1958-1959 DIVISION 3

	P	W	D	L	F	A	W	D	L	F	A	Pts
Plymouth A	46	14	7	2	55	27	9	9	5	34	32	62
Hull C	46	19	3	1	65	21	7	6	10	25	34	61
Brentford	46	15	5	3	49	22	6	10	7	27	27	57
Norwich C	46	13	6	4	51	29	9	7	7	38	33	57
Colchester U	46	15	2	6	46	31	6	8	9	25	36	52
Reading	46	16	4	3	15	21	5	4	14	27	42	50
Tranmere R	46	15	3	5	53	22	6	5	12	29	45	50
Southend U	46	14	6	3	52	26	7	2	14	33	54	50
Halifax T	46	14	5	4	48	25	7	3	13	32	52	50
Bury	46	12	9	2	51	24	5	5	13	18	34	48
Bradford C	46	13	4	6	47	25	5	7	11	37	51	47
Bournemouth	46	12	9	2	40	18	5	3	15	29	51	46
QPR	**46**	**14**	**6**	**3**	**49**	**28**	**5**	**2**	**16**	**25**	**49**	**46**
Southampton	46	12	7	4	57	33	5	4	14	31	47	45
Swindon T	46	13	4	6	39	25	3	9	11	20	32	45
Chesterfield	46	12	5	6	40	26	5	5	13	27	38	44
Newport Co	46	15	2	6	43	24	2	7	14	26	44	43
Wrexham	46	12	6	5	40	30	2	8	13	23	47	42
Accrington S	46	10	8	5	42	31	5	4	14	29	56	42
Mansfield T	46	11	5	7	38	42	3	8	12	35	56	41
Stockport Co	46	9	7	7	33	23	4	3	16	32	55	36
Doncaster R	46	13	2	8	40	32	1	3	19	10	58	33
Notts Co	46	5	9	9	33	39	3	4	16	22	57	29
Rochdale	46	8	7	8	21	26	0	5	18	16	53	28

1959-1960 DIVISION 3

	P	W	D	L	F	A	W	D	L	F	A	Pts
Southampton	46	19	3	1	68	30	7	6	10	38	45	61
Norwich C	46	16	4	3	53	24	8	7	8	29	30	59
Shrewsbury T	46	12	7	4	58	34	6	9	8	39	41	52
Grimsby T	46	12	7	4	48	27	6	9	8	39	43	52
Coventry C	46	14	6	3	44	22	7	4	12	34	41	52
Brentford	46	13	6	4	46	24	8	3	12	32	37	51
Bury	46	13	4	6	26	23	8	5	10	28	28	51
QPR	**46**	**14**	**7**	**2**	**45**	**16**	**4**	**6**	**13**	**28**	**38**	**49**
Colchester U	46	15	6	2	51	22	3	5	15	32	52	47
Bournemouth	46	12	8	3	47	27	5	5	13	25	45	47
Reading	46	13	3	7	49	34	5	7	11	35	43	46
Southend U	46	15	3	5	49	28	4	5	14	27	46	46
Newport Co	46	15	2	6	59	36	5	4	14	21	43	46*
Port Vale	46	16	4	3	51	19	3	4	16	29	60	46*
Halifax T	46	13	3	7	42	27	5	7	11	28	45	46
Swindon T	46	12	6	5	39	30	7	2	14	30	48	46
Barnsley	46	13	6	4	45	25	2	8	13	20	41	44
Chesterfield	46	13	3	7	41	31	5	4	14	30	53	43
Bradford C	46	10	7	6	39	28	5	5	13	27	46	42
Tranmere R	46	11	8	4	50	29	3	5	15	22	46	41
York C	46	11	5	7	38	26	2	7	14	19	47	38
Mansfield T	46	11	4	8	55	48	4	2	17	26	64	36
Wrexham	46	12	5	6	39	30	2	3	18	29	71	36
Accrington S	46	4	5	14	31	53	7	0	16	26	70	27

1960-1961 DIVISION 3

	P	W	D	L	F	A	W	D	L	F	A	Pts
Bury	46	18	3	2	62	17	12	5	6	46	28	68
Walsall	46	19	4	0	62	20	9	2	12	36	40	62
QPR	**46**	**18**	**4**	**1**	**58**	**23**	**7**	**6**	**10**	**35**	**37**	**60**
Watford	46	12	7	4	52	27	8	5	10	33	45	52
Notts Co	46	16	3	4	52	24	5	6	12	30	53	51
Grimsby T	46	14	4	5	48	32	6	6	11	29	37	50
Port Vale	46	15	3	5	63	30	2	12	9	33	49	49
Barnsley	46	15	5	3	56	30	6	2	15	27	50	49
Halifax T	46	14	7	2	42	22	2	10	11	29	56	49
Shrewsbury T	46	13	7	3	54	26	2	9	12	29	49	46
Hull C	46	13	6	4	51	28	4	6	13	22	45	46
Torquay U	46	8	12	3	37	26	6	5	12	38	57	45
Newport Co	46	12	7	4	51	30	5	4	14	30	60	45
Bristol C	46	15	4	4	50	19	2	6	15	20	49	44
Coventry C	46	14	6	3	54	25	2	6	15	26	58	44
Swindon T	46	13	6	4	41	16	1	9	13	21	39	43
Brentford	46	10	9	4	41	28	3	8	12	15	42	43
Reading	46	13	5	5	48	29	1	7	15	24	54	40
Bournemouth	46	8	7	8	34	39	7	3	13	24	37	40
Southend U	46	10	8	5	38	26	4	3	16	22	50	39
Tranmere R	46	11	5	7	53	50	4	3	16	26	65	38
Bradford C	46	8	8	7	37	36	3	6	14	28	51	36
Colchester U	46	8	5	10	40	44	3	6	14	28	57	33
Chesterfield	46	9	6	8	42	29	1	6	16	25	58	32

1961-1962 DIVISION 3

	P	W	D	L	F	A	W	D	L	F	A	Pts
Portsmouth	46	15	6	2	48	23	12	5	6	39	24	65
Grimsby T	46	18	3	2	49	18	10	3	10	31	38	62
Bournemouth	46	14	8	1	42	18	7	9	7	27	27	59
QPR	**46**	**15**	**3**	**5**	**65**	**31**	**9**	**8**	**6**	**46**	**42**	**59**
Peterboro' U	46	16	0	7	60	38	10	6	7	47	44	58
Bristol C	46	15	3	5	56	27	8	5	10	38	45	54
Reading	46	14	5	4	46	24	8	4	11	31	42	53
Northampton T	46	12	6	5	52	24	8	5	10	33	33	51
Swindon T	46	11	8	4	48	26	6	7	10	30	45	49
Hull C	46	15	2	6	43	20	5	6	12	24	34	48
Bradford	46	13	5	5	47	27	7	2	14	33	51	47
Port Vale	46	12	4	7	41	23	5	7	11	24	35	45
Notts Co	46	14	5	4	44	23	3	4	16	23	51	43
Coventry C	46	11	6	6	38	26	5	5	13	26	45	43
Crystal P	46	8	8	7	50	41	6	6	11	33	39	42
Southend U	46	10	7	6	31	26	3	9	11	26	43	42
Watford	46	10	9	4	37	26	4	4	15	26	48	41
Halifax T	46	9	5	9	34	35	6	5	12	28	49	40
Shrewsbury T	46	8	7	8	46	37	5	5	13	27	47	38
Barnsley	46	9	6	8	45	41	4	6	13	26	54	38
Torquay U	46	9	4	10	48	44	6	2	15	28	56	36
Lincoln C	46	4	10	9	31	43	5	7	11	26	44	35
Brentford	46	11	3	9	34	29	2	5	16	19	64	34
Newport Co	46	6	5	12	29	38	1	3	19	17	64	22

1962-1963 DIVISION 3

	P	W	D	L	F	A	W	D	L	F	A	Pts
Northampton T	46	16	6	1	64	19	10	4	9	45	41	62
Swindon T	46	18	2	3	60	22	4	12	7	27	34	58
Port Vale	46	16	4	3	47	25	7	4	12	25	33	54
Coventry C	46	14	6	3	54	28	4	11	8	29	41	53
Bournemouth	46	11	12	0	39	16	7	4	12	24	30	52
Peterboro' U	46	11	5	7	48	33	9	6	8	45	42	51
Notts Co	46	15	3	5	46	29	4	10	9	27	45	51
Southend U	46	11	7	5	38	24	8	5	10	37	53	50
Wrexham	46	14	6	3	54	27	6	3	14	30	56	49
Hull C	46	12	6	5	40	22	7	4	12	34	47	48
Crystal P	46	10	7	6	38	22	7	6	10	30	36	47
Colchester U	46	11	6	6	41	35	7	5	11	32	58	47
QPR	**46**	**9**	**6**	**8**	**44**	**36**	**8**	**5**	**10**	**41**	**40**	**45**
Bristol C	46	10	9	4	54	38	6	4	13	46	54	45
Shrewsbury T	46	13	4	6	57	41	3	8	12	26	40	44
Millwall	46	11	6	6	50	32	4	7	12	32	55	43
Watford	46	12	3	8	55	40	5	5	13	27	45	42
Barnsley	46	12	6	5	39	28	3	5	15	24	46	41
Bristol R	46	11	8	4	45	29	4	3	16	25	59	41
Reading	46	13	4	6	51	30	3	4	16	23	48	40
Bradford	46	10	9	4	43	36	4	3	16	36	61	40
Brighton & HA	46	7	6	10	28	38	5	6	12	30	46	36
Carlisle U	46	12	4	7	41	37	1	5	17	20	52	35
Halifax T	46	8	3	12	41	51	1	9	13	23	55	30

1963-1964 DIVISION 3

	P	W	D	L	F	A	W	D	L	F	A	Pts
Coventry C	46	14	7	2	62	32	8	9	6	36	29	60
Crystal P	46	17	4	2	38	14	6	10	7	35	37	60
Watford	46	16	6	1	57	28	7	6	10	22	31	58
Bournemouth	46	17	4	2	47	15	7	4	12	32	43	56
Bristol C	46	13	7	3	52	24	7	8	8	32	40	55
Reading	46	15	5	3	49	26	6	5	12	30	36	52
Mansfield T	46	15	8	0	51	20	5	3	15	25	42	51
Hull C	46	11	9	3	45	27	5	8	10	28	41	49
Oldham A	46	13	3	7	44	35	7	5	11	29	35	48
Peterboro' U	46	13	6	4	52	27	5	5	13	23	43	47
Shrewsbury T	46	13	6	4	43	19	5	5	13	30	61	47
Bristol R	46	9	6	8	52	34	10	2	11	39	45	46
Port Vale	46	13	6	4	35	13	3	8	12	18	36	46
Southend U	46	9	10	4	42	26	6	5	12	35	52	45
QPR	**46**	**13**	**4**	**6**	**47**	**34**	**5**	**5**	**13**	**29**	**44**	**45**
Brentford	46	11	4	8	54	36	4	10	9	33	44	44
Colchester U	46	10	8	5	45	26	2	11	10	25	42	43
Luton T	46	12	2	9	42	41	4	8	11	22	39	42
Walsall	46	7	9	7	34	35	6	5	12	25	41	40
Barnsley	46	9	9	5	34	29	3	6	14	34	65	39
Millwall	46	9	4	10	33	29	5	6	12	20	38	38
Crewe A	46	10	5	8	29	26	1	7	15	21	51	34
Wrexham	46	9	4	10	50	42	4	2	17	25	65	32
Notts Co	46	7	8	8	29	26	2	1	20	16	66	27

1964-1965 DIVISION 3

	P	W	D	L	F	A	W	D	L	F	A	Pts
Carlisle U	46	14	5	4	46	24	11	5	7	30	29	60
Bristol C	46	14	6	3	53	18	10	5	8	39	37	59
Mansfield T	46	17	4	2	61	23	7	7	9	34	38	59
Hull C	46	14	6	3	51	25	9	6	8	40	32	58
Brentford	46	18	4	1	55	18	6	5	12	28	37	57
Bristol R	46	14	7	2	52	21	6	8	9	30	37	55
Gillingham	46	16	5	2	45	13	7	4	12	25	37	55
Peterboro' U	46	16	3	4	61	33	6	4	13	24	41	51
Watford	46	13	8	2	45	21	4	8	11	26	43	50
Grimsby T	46	11	10	2	37	21	5	7	11	31	46	49
Bournemouth	46	12	4	7	40	24	6	7	10	32	39	47
Southend U	46	14	4	5	48	24	5	4	14	30	47	46
Reading	46	12	8	3	45	26	4	6	13	25	44	46
QPR	**46**	**15**	**5**	**3**	**48**	**23**	**2**	**7**	**14**	**24**	**57**	**46**
Workington	46	11	7	5	30	22	6	5	12	28	47	46
Shrewsbury T	46	10	6	7	42	38	5	6	12	34	46	42
Exeter C	46	8	7	8	33	27	4	10	9	18	25	41
Scunthorpe U	46	9	8	6	42	27	5	4	14	23	45	40
Walsall	46	9	4	10	34	36	6	3	14	21	44	37
Oldham A	46	10	3	10	40	39	3	7	13	21	44	36
Luton T	46	6	8	9	32	36	5	3	15	19	58	33
Port Vale	46	7	6	10	27	33	2	8	13	14	43	32
Colchester U	46	7	6	10	30	34	3	4	16	20	55	30
Barnsley	46	8	5	10	33	31	1	6	16	21	59	29

1965-1966 DIVISION 3

	P	W	D	L	F	A	W	D	L	F	A	Pts
Hull C	46	19	2	2	64	24	12	5	6	45	38	69
Millwall	46	19	4	0	47	13	8	7	8	29	30	65
QPR	**46**	**16**	**3**	**4**	**62**	**29**	**8**	**6**	**9**	**33**	**36**	**57**
Scunthorpe U	46	9	8	6	44	34	12	3	8	36	33	53
Workington	46	13	6	4	38	18	6	8	9	29	39	52
Gillingham	46	14	4	5	33	19	8	4	11	29	35	52
Swindon T	46	11	8	4	43	18	8	5	10	31	30	51
Reading	46	13	5	5	36	19	6	8	9	34	44	51
Walsall	46	13	7	3	48	21	7	3	13	29	43	50
Shrewsbury T	46	13	7	3	48	22	6	4	13	25	42	49
Grimsby T	46	15	6	2	47	25	2	7	14	21	37	47
Watford	46	12	4	7	33	19	5	9	9	22	32	47
Peterboro' U	46	13	6	4	50	26	4	6	13	30	40	46
Oxford U	46	11	3	9	38	33	8	5	10	32	41	46
Brighton & HA	46	13	4	6	48	28	3	7	13	19	37	43
Bristol R	46	11	10	2	38	15	3	4	16	26	49	42
Swansea T	46	14	4	5	61	37	1	7	15	20	59	41
Bournemouth	46	9	8	6	24	19	4	4	15	14	37	38
Mansfield T	46	10	5	8	31	36	5	3	15	28	53	38
Oldham A	46	8	7	8	34	33	4	6	13	21	48	37
Southend U	46	15	1	7	43	28	1	3	19	11	55	36
Exeter C	46	9	6	8	36	28	3	5	15	17	51	35
Brentford	46	9	4	10	34	30	1	8	14	14	39	32
York C	46	5	7	11	30	44	4	2	17	23	62	27

1966-1967 DIVISION 3

	P	W	D	L	F	A	W	D	L	F	A	Pts
QPR	**46**	**18**	**4**	**1**	**66**	**15**	**8**	**11**	**4**	**37**	**23**	**67**
Middlesbrough	46	16	3	4	51	20	7	6	10	36	44	55
Watford	46	15	5	3	39	17	5	9	9	22	29	54
Reading	46	13	7	3	45	20	9	2	12	31	37	53
Bristol R	46	13	8	2	47	28	7	5	11	29	39	53
Shrewsbury T	46	15	5	3	48	24	5	7	11	29	38	52
Torquay U	46	17	3	3	57	20	4	6	13	16	34	51
Swindon T	46	14	5	4	53	21	6	5	12	28	38	50
Mansfield T	46	12	4	7	48	37	8	5	10	36	42	49
Oldham A	46	15	4	4	51	16	4	6	13	29	47	48
Gillingham	46	11	9	3	36	18	4	7	12	22	44	46
Walsall	46	12	8	3	37	16	6	2	15	28	56	46
Colchester U	46	14	3	6	52	30	3	7	13	24	43	44
Leyton O	46	10	9	4	36	27	3	9	11	22	41	44
Peterboro' U	46	12	4	7	40	31	2	11	10	26	40	43
Oxford U	46	10	8	5	41	29	5	5	13	20	37	43
Grimsby T	46	13	5	5	46	23	4	4	15	15	45	43
Scunthorpe U	46	13	4	6	39	26	4	4	15	19	47	42
Brighton & HA	46	10	8	5	37	27	3	7	13	24	44	41
Bournemouth	46	8	10	5	24	24	4	7	12	15	33	41
Swansea T	46	9	9	5	50	30	3	6	14	35	59	39
Darlington	46	8	7	8	26	28	5	4	14	21	53	37
Doncaster R	46	11	6	6	40	40	1	2	20	18	77	32
Workington	46	9	3	11	35	35	3	4	16	20	54	31

1967-1968 DIVISION 2

	P	W	D	L	F	A	W	D	L	F	A	Pts
Ipswich T	42	12	7	2	45	20	10	8	3	34	24	59
QPR	**42**	**18**	**2**	**1**	**45**	**9**	**7**	**6**	**8**	**22**	**27**	**58**
Blackpool	42	12	6	3	33	16	12	4	5	38	27	58
Birmingham C	42	12	6	3	54	21	7	8	6	29	30	52
Portsmouth	42	13	6	2	43	18	5	7	9	25	37	49
Middlesbrough	42	10	7	4	39	19	7	5	9	21	35	46
Millwall	42	9	10	2	35	16	5	7	9	27	34	45
Blackburn R	42	13	5	3	34	16	3	6	12	22	33	43
Norwich C	42	12	4	5	40	30	4	7	10	20	35	43
Carlisle U	42	9	9	3	38	22	5	4	12	20	30	41
Crystal P	42	11	4	6	34	19	3	7	11	22	37	39
Bolton W	42	8	6	7	37	28	5	7	9	23	35	39
Cardiff C	42	9	6	6	35	29	4	6	11	25	37	38
Huddersfield T	42	10	6	5	29	23	3	6	12	17	38	38
Charlton A	42	10	6	5	43	25	2	7	12	20	43	37
Aston Villa	42	10	3	8	35	30	5	4	12	19	34	37
Hull C	42	6	8	7	25	23	6	5	10	33	50	37
Derby Co	42	8	5	8	40	35	5	5	11	31	43	36
Bristol C	42	7	7	7	26	25	6	3	12	22	37	36
Preston NE	42	8	7	6	29	24	4	4	13	14	41	35
Rotherham U	42	7	4	10	22	32	3	7	11	20	44	31
Plymouth A	42	5	4	12	26	36	4	5	12	12	36	27

1968-1969 DIVISION 1

	P	W	D	L	F	A	W	D	L	F	A	Pts
Leeds U	42	18	3	0	41	9	9	10	2	25	17	67
Liverpool	42	16	4	1	36	10	9	7	5	27	14	61
Everton	42	14	5	2	43	10	7	10	4	34	26	57
Arsenal	42	12	6	3	31	12	10	6	5	25	15	56
Chelsea	42	11	7	3	40	24	9	3	9	33	29	50
Tottenham H	42	10	8	3	39	22	4	9	8	22	29	45
Southampton	42	13	5	3	41	21	3	8	10	16	27	45
West Ham U	42	10	8	3	47	22	3	10	8	19	28	44
Newcastle U	42	12	7	2	40	20	3	7	11	21	35	44
WBA	42	11	7	3	43	26	5	4	12	21	41	43
Manchester U	42	13	5	3	38	18	2	7	12	19	35	42
Ipswich T	42	10	4	7	32	26	5	7	9	27	34	41
Manchester C	42	13	6	2	49	20	2	4	15	15	35	40
Burnley	42	11	6	4	36	25	4	3	14	19	57	39
Sheffield W	42	7	9	5	27	26	3	7	11	14	28	36
Wolves	42	7	10	4	26	22	3	5	13	15	36	35
Sunderland	42	10	6	5	28	18	1	6	14	15	49	34
Nottingham F	42	6	6	9	17	22	4	7	10	28	35	33
Stoke C	42	9	7	5	24	24	0	8	13	16	39	33
Coventry C	42	8	6	7	32	22	2	5	14	14	42	31
Leicester C	42	8	8	5	27	24	1	4	16	12	44	30
QPR	**42**	**4**	**7**	**10**	**20**	**33**	**0**	**3**	**18**	**19**	**62**	**18**

1969-1970 DIVISION 2

	P	W	D	L	F	A	W	D	L	F	A	Pts
Huddersfield T	42	14	6	1	36	10	10	6	5	32	27	60
Blackpool	42	10	9	2	25	16	10	4	7	31	29	53
Leicester C	42	12	6	3	37	22	7	7	7	27	28	51
Middlesbrough	42	15	4	2	36	14	5	6	10	19	31	50
Swindon T	42	13	7	1	35	17	4	9	8	22	30	50
Sheffield U	42	16	2	3	50	10	6	3	12	23	28	49
Cardiff C	42	12	7	2	38	14	6	6	9	23	27	49
Blackburn R	42	15	2	4	42	19	5	5	11	12	31	47
QPR	**42**	**13**	**5**	**3**	**47**	**24**	**4**	**6**	**11**	**19**	**33**	**45**
Millwall	42	14	4	3	38	18	1	10	10	18	38	44
Norwich C	42	13	5	3	37	14	3	6	12	12	32	43
Carlisle U	42	10	6	5	39	28	4	7	10	19	28	41
Hull C	42	11	6	4	43	28	4	5	12	29	42	41
Bristol C	42	11	7	3	37	13	2	6	13	17	37	39
Oxford U	42	9	9	3	23	13	3	6	12	12	29	39
Bolton W	42	9	6	6	31	23	3	6	12	23	38	36
Portsmouth	42	8	4	9	39	35	5	5	11	27	45	35
Birmingham C	42	9	7	5	33	22	2	4	15	18	56	33
Watford	42	6	8	7	26	21	3	5	13	18	36	31
Charlton A	42	7	8	6	23	28	0	9	12	12	48	31
Aston Villa	42	7	8	6	23	21	1	5	15	13	41	29
Preston NE	42	7	6	8	31	28	1	6	14	12	35	28

1970-1971 DIVISION 2

	P	W	D	L	F	A	W	D	L	F	A	Pts
Leicester C	42	12	7	2	30	14	11	6	4	27	16	59
Sheffield U	42	14	6	1	49	18	7	8	6	24	21	56
Cardiff C	42	12	7	2	39	16	8	6	7	25	25	53
Carlisle U	42	16	3	2	39	13	4	10	7	26	30	53
Hull C	42	11	5	5	31	16	8	8	5	23	25	51
Luton T	42	12	7	2	40	18	6	6	9	22	25	49
Middlesbrough	42	13	6	2	37	16	4	8	9	23	27	48
Millwall	42	13	5	3	36	12	6	4	11	23	30	47
Birmingham	42	12	7	2	30	12	5	5	11	28	36	46
Norwich C	42	11	8	2	34	20	4	6	11	20	32	44
QPR	**42**	**11**	**5**	**5**	**39**	**22**	**5**	**6**	**10**	**19**	**31**	**43**
Swindon T	42	12	7	2	38	14	3	5	13	23	37	42
Sunderland	42	11	6	4	34	21	4	6	11	18	33	42
Oxford U	42	8	8	5	23	23	6	6	9	18	25	42
Sheffield W	42	10	7	4	32	27	2	5	14	19	42	36
Portsmouth	42	9	4	8	32	28	1	10	10	14	33	34
Orient	42	5	11	5	16	15	4	5	12	13	36	34
Watford	42	6	7	8	18	22	4	6	11	20	38	33
Bristol C	42	9	6	6	30	28	1	5	15	16	36	31
Charlton A	42	7	6	8	28	30	1	8	12	13	35	30
Blackburn R	42	5	8	8	20	28	1	7	13	17	41	27
Bolton W	42	6	5	10	22	31	1	5	15	13	43	24

1971-1972 DIVISION 2

	P	W	D	L	F	A	W	D	L	F	A	Pts
Norwich C	42	13	8	0	40	16	8	7	6	20	20	57
Birmingham	42	15	6	0	46	14	4	12	5	14	17	56
Millwall	42	14	7	0	38	17	5	10	6	26	29	55
QPR	**42**	**16**	**4**	**1**	**39**	**9**	**4**	**10**	**7**	**18**	**19**	**54**
Sunderland	42	11	7	3	42	24	6	9	6	25	33	50
Blackpool	42	12	6	3	43	16	8	1	12	27	34	47
Burnley	42	13	4	4	43	22	7	2	12	27	33	46
Bristol C	42	14	3	4	43	22	4	7	10	18	27	46
Middlesbrough	42	16	4	1	31	11	3	4	14	19	37	46
Carlisle U	42	12	6	3	38	22	5	3	13	23	35	43
Swindon T	42	10	6	5	29	16	5	6	10	18	31	42
Hull C	42	10	6	5	33	21	4	4	13	16	32	38
Luton T	42	7	8	6	25	24	3	10	8	18	24	38
Sheffield W	42	11	7	3	33	22	2	5	14	18	36	38
Oxford U	42	10	8	3	28	17	2	6	13	15	38	38
Portsmouth	42	9	7	5	31	26	3	6	12	28	42	37
Orient	42	12	4	5	32	19	2	5	14	18	42	37
Preston NE	42	11	4	6	32	21	1	8	12	20	37	36
Cardiff C	42	9	7	5	37	25	1	7	13	19	44	34
Fulham	42	10	7	4	29	20	2	3	16	16	48	34
Charlton A	42	9	7	5	33	25	3	2	16	22	52	33
Watford	42	5	5	11	15	25	0	4	17	9	50	19

1972-1973 DIVISION 2

	P	W	D	L	F	A	W	D	L	F	A	Pts
Burnley	42	13	6	2	44	18	11	8	2	28	17	62
QPR	**42**	**16**	**4**	**1**	**54**	**13**	**8**	**9**	**4**	**27**	**24**	**61**
Aston Villa	42	12	5	4	27	17	6	9	6	24	30	50
Middlesbrough	42	12	6	3	29	15	5	7	9	17	28	47
Bristol C	42	10	7	4	34	18	7	5	9	29	33	46
Sunderland	42	12	6	3	35	17	5	6	10	24	32	46
Blackpool	42	12	6	3	37	17	6	4	11	19	34	46
Oxford U	42	14	2	5	36	18	5	5	11	16	25	45
Fulham	42	11	6	4	32	16	5	6	10	26	33	44
Sheffield W	42	14	4	3	40	20	3	6	12	19	35	44
Millwall	42	12	5	4	33	18	4	5	12	22	29	42
Luton T	42	6	9	6	24	23	9	2	10	20	30	41
Hull C	42	9	7	5	39	22	5	5	11	25	37	40
Nottingham F	42	12	5	4	32	18	2	7	12	15	34	40
Orient	42	11	6	4	33	18	1	6	14	16	35	36
Swindon T	42	8	9	4	28	23	2	7	12	18	37	36
Portsmouth	42	7	6	8	21	22	5	5	11	21	37	35
Carlisle U	42	10	5	6	30	24	1	7	13	10	28	34
Preston NE	42	6	8	7	19	25	5	4	12	18	39	34
Cardiff C	42	11	4	6	32	21	0	7	14	11	37	33
Huddersfield T	42	7	9	5	21	20	1	8	12	15	36	33
Brighton & HA	42	7	8	6	32	31	1	5	15	14	52	29

1973-1974 DIVISION 1

	P	W	D	L	F	A	W	D	L	F	A	Pts
Leeds U	42	12	8	1	38	18	12	6	3	28	13	62
Liverpool	42	18	2	1	34	11	4	11	6	18	20	57
Derby Co	42	13	7	1	40	16	4	7	10	12	26	48
Ipswich T	42	10	7	4	38	21	8	4	9	29	37	47
Stoke C	42	13	6	2	39	15	2	10	9	15	27	46
Burnley	42	10	9	2	29	16	6	5	10	27	37	46
Everton	42	12	7	2	29	14	4	5	12	21	34	44
QPR	**42**	**8**	**10**	**3**	**30**	**17**	**5**	**7**	**9**	**26**	**35**	**43**
Leicester C	42	10	7	4	35	17	3	9	9	16	24	42
Arsenal	42	9	7	5	23	16	5	7	9	26	35	42
Tottenham H	42	9	4	8	26	27	5	10	6	19	23	42
Wolves	42	11	6	4	30	18	2	9	10	19	31	41
Sheffield U	42	7	7	7	25	22	7	5	9	19	27	40
Manchester C	42	10	7	4	25	17	4	5	12	14	29	40
Newcastle U	42	9	6	6	28	21	4	6	11	21	27	38
Coventry C	42	10	5	6	25	18	4	5	12	18	36	38
Chelsea	42	9	4	8	36	29	3	9	9	20	31	37
West Ham U	42	7	7	7	36	32	4	8	9	19	28	37
Birmingham C	42	10	7	4	30	21	2	6	13	22	43	37
Southampton	42	8	10	3	30	20	3	4	14	17	48	36
Manchester U	42	7	7	7	23	20	3	5	13	15	28	32
Norwich C	42	6	9	6	25	27	1	6	14	12	35	29

1974-75 DIVISION 1

	P	W	D	L	F	A	W	D	L	F	A	Pts
Derby Co	42	14	4	3	41	18	7	7	7	26	31	53
Liverpool	42	14	5	2	44	17	6	6	9	16	22	51
Ipswich T	42	17	2	2	47	14	6	3	12	19	30	51
Everton	42	10	9	2	33	19	6	9	6	23	23	50
Stoke C	42	12	7	2	40	18	5	8	8	24	30	49
Sheffield U	42	12	7	2	35	20	6	6	9	23	31	49
Middlesbrough	42	11	7	3	33	14	7	5	9	21	26	48
Manchester C	42	16	3	2	40	15	2	7	12	14	39	46
Leeds U	42	10	8	3	34	20	6	5	10	23	29	45
Burnley	42	11	6	4	40	29	6	5	10	28	38	45
QPR	**42**	**10**	**4**	**7**	**25**	**17**	**6**	**6**	**9**	**29**	**37**	**42**
Wolves	42	12	5	4	43	21	2	6	13	14	33	39
West Ham U	42	10	6	5	38	22	3	7	11	20	37	39
Coventry C	42	8	9	4	31	27	4	6	11	20	35	39
Newcastle U	42	12	4	5	39	23	3	5	13	20	49	39
Arsenal	42	10	6	5	31	16	3	5	13	16	33	37
Birmingham C	42	10	4	7	34	28	4	5	12	19	33	37
Leicester C	42	8	7	6	25	17	4	5	12	21	43	36
Tottenham H	42	8	4	9	29	27	5	4	12	23	36	34
Luton T	42	8	6	7	27	26	3	5	13	20	39	33
Chelsea	42	4	9	8	22	31	5	6	10	20	41	33
Carlisle U	42	8	2	11	22	21	4	3	14	21	38	29

1975-1976 DIVISION 1

	P	W	D	L	F	A	W	D	L	F	A	Pts
Liverpool	42	14	5	2	41	21	9	9	3	25	10	60
QPR	**42**	**17**	**4**	**0**	**42**	**13**	**7**	**7**	**7**	**25**	**20**	**59**
Manchester U	42	16	4	1	40	13	7	6	8	28	29	56
Derby Co	42	15	3	3	45	30	6	8	7	30	28	53
Leeds U	42	13	3	5	37	19	8	6	7	28	27	51
Ipswich T	42	11	6	4	36	23	5	8	8	18	25	46
Leicester C	42	9	9	3	29	24	4	10	7	19	27	45
Manchester C	42	14	5	2	46	18	2	6	13	18	28	43
Tottenham H	42	6	10	5	33	32	8	5	8	30	31	43
Norwich C	42	10	5	6	33	26	6	5	10	25	32	42
Everton	42	10	7	4	37	24	5	5	11	23	42	42
Stoke C	42	8	5	8	25	24	7	6	8	23	26	41
Middlesbrough	42	9	7	5	23	11	6	3	12	23	34	40
Coventry C	42	6	9	6	22	22	7	5	9	25	35	40
Newcastle U	42	11	4	6	51	26	4	5	12	20	36	39
Aston Villa	42	11	8	2	32	17	0	9	12	19	42	39
Arsenal	42	11	4	6	33	19	2	6	13	14	34	36
West Ham U	42	10	5	6	26	23	3	5	13	22	48	36
Birmingham C	42	11	5	5	36	26	2	2	17	21	49	33
Wolves	42	7	6	8	27	25	3	4	14	24	43	30
Burnley	42	6	6	9	23	26	3	4	14	20	40	28
Sheffield U	42	4	7	10	19	32	2	3	16	14	50	22

1976-1977 DIVISION 1

	P	W	D	L	F	A	W	D	L	F	A	Pts
Liverpool	42	18	3	0	47	11	5	8	8	15	22	57
Manchester C	42	15	5	1	38	13	6	9	6	22	21	56
Ipswich T	42	15	4	2	41	11	7	4	10	25	28	52
Aston Villa	42	17	3	1	55	17	5	4	12	21	33	51
Newcastle U	42	14	6	1	40	15	4	7	10	24	34	49
Manchester U	42	12	6	3	41	22	6	5	10	30	40	47
WBA	42	10	6	5	38	22	6	7	8	24	34	45
Arsenal	42	11	6	4	37	20	5	5	11	27	39	43
Everton	42	9	7	5	35	24	5	7	9	27	40	42
Leeds U	42	8	8	5	28	26	7	4	10	20	25	42
Leicester C	42	8	9	4	30	28	4	9	8	17	32	42
Middlesbrough	42	11	6	4	25	14	3	7	11	15	31	41
Birmingham C	42	10	6	5	38	25	3	6	12	25	36	38
QPR	**42**	**10**	**7**	**4**	**31**	**21**	**3**	**5**	**13**	**16**	**31**	**38**
Derby Co	42	9	9	3	36	18	0	10	11	14	37	37
Norwich C	42	12	4	5	30	23	2	5	14	17	41	37
West Ham U	42	9	6	6	28	23	2	8	11	18	42	36
Bristol C	42	8	7	6	25	19	3	6	12	13	29	35
Coventry C	42	7	9	5	34	26	3	6	12	14	33	35
Sunderland	42	9	5	7	29	16	2	7	12	17	38	34
Stoke C	42	9	8	4	21	16	1	6	14	7	35	34
Tottenham H	42	9	7	5	26	20	3	2	16	22	52	33

1977-1978 DIVISION 1

	P	W	D	L	F	A	W	D	L	F	A	Pts
Nottingham F	42	15	6	0	37	8	10	8	3	32	16	64
Liverpool	42	15	4	2	37	11	9	5	7	28	23	57
Everton	42	14	4	3	47	22	8	7	6	29	23	55
Manchester C	42	14	4	3	46	21	6	8	7	28	30	52
Arsenal	42	14	5	2	38	12	7	5	9	22	25	52
WBA	42	13	5	3	35	18	5	9	7	27	35	50
Coventry C	42	13	5	3	48	23	5	7	9	27	39	48
Aston Villa	42	11	4	6	33	18	7	6	8	24	24	46
Leeds U	42	12	4	5	39	21	6	6	9	24	32	46
Manchester U	42	9	6	6	32	23	7	4	10	35	40	42
Birmingham C	42	8	5	8	32	30	8	4	9	23	30	41
Derby Co	42	10	7	4	37	24	4	6	11	17	35	41
Norwich C	42	10	8	3	28	20	1	10	10	24	46	40
Middlesbrough	42	8	8	5	25	19	4	7	10	17	35	39
Wolves	42	7	8	6	30	27	5	4	12	21	37	36
Chelsea	42	7	11	3	28	20	4	3	14	18	49	36
Bristol C	42	9	6	6	37	26	2	7	12	12	27	35
Ipswich T	42	10	5	6	32	24	1	8	12	15	37	35
QPR	**42**	**8**	**8**	**5**	**27**	**26**	**1**	**7**	**13**	**20**	**38**	**33**
West Ham U	42	8	6	7	31	28	4	2	15	21	41	32
Newcastle U	42	4	6	11	26	37	2	4	15	16	41	22
Leicester C	42	4	7	10	16	32	1	5	15	10	38	22

1978-1979 DIVISION 1

	P	W	D	L	F	A	W	D	L	F	A	Pts
Liverpool	42	19	2	0	51	4	11	6	4	34	12	68
Nottingham F	42	11	10	0	34	10	10	8	3	27	16	60
WBA	42	13	5	3	38	15	11	6	4	34	20	59
Everton	42	12	7	2	32	17	5	10	6	20	23	51
Leeds U	42	11	4	6	41	25	7	10	4	29	27	50
Ipswich T	42	11	4	6	34	21	9	5	7	29	28	49
Arsenal	42	11	8	2	37	18	6	6	9	24	30	48
Aston Villa	42	8	9	4	37	26	7	7	7	22	23	46
Manchester U	42	9	7	5	29	25	6	8	7	31	38	45
Coventry C	42	11	7	3	41	29	3	9	9	17	39	44
Tottenham H	42	7	8	6	19	25	6	7	8	29	36	41
Middlesbrough	42	10	5	6	33	21	5	5	11	24	29	40
Bristol C	42	11	6	4	34	19	4	4	13	13	32	40
Southampton	42	9	10	2	35	20	3	6	12	12	33	40
Manchester C	42	9	5	7	34	28	4	8	9	24	28	39
Norwich C	42	7	10	4	29	19	0	13	8	22	38	37
Bolton W	42	10	5	6	36	28	2	6	13	18	47	35
Wolves	42	10	4	7	26	26	3	4	14	18	42	34
Derby Co	42	8	5	8	25	25	2	6	13	19	46	31
QPR	**42**	**4**	**9**	**8**	**24**	**33**	**2**	**4**	**15**	**21**	**40**	**25**
Birmingham C	42	5	9	7	24	25	1	1	19	13	39	22
Chelsea	42	3	5	13	23	42	2	5	14	21	50	20

1979-1980 DIVISION 2

	P	W	D	L	F	A	W	D	L	F	A	Pts
Leicester C	42	12	5	4	32	19	9	8	4	26	19	55
Sunderland	42	16	5	0	47	13	5	7	9	22	29	54
Birmingham C	42	14	5	2	37	16	7	6	8	21	22	53
Chelsea	42	14	3	4	34	16	9	4	8	32	36	53
QPR	**42**	**10**	**9**	**2**	**46**	**25**	**8**	**4**	**9**	**29**	**28**	**49**
Luton T	42	9	10	2	36	17	7	7	7	30	28	49
West Ham U	42	13	2	6	37	21	7	5	9	17	22	47
Cambridge U	42	11	6	4	40	23	3	10	8	21	30	44
Newcastle U	42	13	6	2	35	19	2	8	11	18	30	44
Preston NE	42	8	10	3	30	23	4	9	8	26	29	43
Oldham A	42	12	5	4	30	21	4	6	11	19	32	43
Swansea C	42	13	1	7	31	20	4	8	9	17	33	43
Shrewsbury T	42	12	3	6	41	23	6	2	13	19	30	41
Orient	42	7	9	5	29	31	5	8	8	19	23	41
Cardiff C	42	11	4	6	21	16	5	4	12	20	32	40
Wrexham	42	13	2	6	26	15	3	4	14	14	34	38
Notts Co	42	4	11	6	24	22	7	4	10	27	30	37
Watford	42	9	6	6	27	18	3	7	11	12	28	37
Bristol R	42	9	8	4	33	23	2	5	14	17	41	35
Fulham	42	6	4	11	19	28	5	3	13	23	46	29
Burnley	42	5	9	7	19	23	1	6	14	20	50	27
Charlton A	42	6	6	9	25	31	0	4	17	14	47	22

1980-1981 DIVISION 2

	P	W	D	L	F	A	W	D	L	F	A	Pts
West Ham U	42	19	1	1	53	12	9	9	3	26	17	66
Notts Co	42	10	8	3	26	15	8	9	4	23	23	53
Swansea C	42	12	5	4	39	19	6	9	6	25	25	50
Blackburn R	42	12	8	1	28	7	4	10	7	14	22	50
Luton T	42	10	6	5	35	23	8	6	7	26	23	48
Derby Co	42	9	8	4	34	26	6	7	8	23	26	45
Grimsby T	42	10	8	3	21	10	5	7	9	23	32	45
QPR	**42**	**11**	**7**	**3**	**36**	**12**	**4**	**6**	**11**	**20**	**34**	**43**
Watford	42	13	5	3	34	18	3	6	12	16	27	43
Sheffield W	42	14	4	3	38	14	3	4	14	15	37	42
Newcastle U	42	11	7	3	22	13	3	7	11	8	32	42
Chelsea	42	8	6	7	27	15	6	6	9	19	26	40
Cambridge U	42	13	1	7	36	23	4	5	12	17	42	40
Shrewsbury T	42	9	7	5	33	22	2	10	9	13	25	39
Oldham A	42	7	9	5	19	16	5	6	10	20	32	39
Wrexham	42	5	8	8	22	24	7	6	8	21	21	38
Orient	42	9	8	4	34	20	4	4	13	18	36	38
Bolton W	42	10	5	6	40	27	4	5	12	21	39	38
Cardiff C	42	7	7	7	23	24	5	5	11	21	36	36
Preston NE	42	8	7	6	28	26	3	7	11	13	36	36
Bristol C	42	6	10	5	19	15	1	6	14	10	36	30
Bristol R	42	4	9	8	21	24	1	4	16	13	41	23

1981-1982 DIVISION 2

	P	W	D	L	F	A	W	D	L	F	A	Pts
Luton T	42	16	3	2	48	19	9	10	2	38	27	88
Watford	42	13	6	2	46	16	10	5	6	30	26	80
Norwich C	42	14	3	4	41	19	8	2	11	23	31	71
Sheffield W	42	10	8	3	31	23	10	2	9	24	28	70
QPR	**42**	**15**	**4**	**2**	**40**	**9**	**6**	**2**	**13**	**25**	**34**	**69**
Barnsley	42	13	4	4	33	14	6	6	9	26	27	67
Rotherham U	42	13	5	3	42	19	7	2	12	24	35	67
Leicester C	42	12	5	4	31	19	6	7	8	25	29	66
Newcastle U	42	14	4	3	30	14	4	4	13	22	36	62
Blackburn R	42	11	4	6	26	15	5	7	9	21	28	59
Oldham A	42	9	9	3	28	23	6	5	10	22	28	59
Chelsea	42	10	5	6	37	30	5	7	9	23	30	57
Charlton A	42	11	5	5	33	22	2	7	12	17	43	51
Cambridge U	42	11	4	6	31	19	2	5	14	17	34	48
Crystal P	42	9	2	10	25	26	4	7	10	9	19	48
Derby Co	42	9	8	4	32	23	3	4	14	21	45	48
Grimsby T	42	5	8	8	29	30	6	5	10	24	35	46
Shrewsbury T	42	10	6	5	26	19	1	7	13	11	38	46
Bolton W	42	10	4	7	28	24	3	3	15	11	37	46
Cardiff C	42	9	2	10	28	32	3	6	12	17	29	44
Wrexham	42	9	4	8	22	22	2	7	12	18	34	44
Orient	42	6	8	7	23	24	4	1	16	13	37	39

1982-1983 DIVISION 2

	P	W	D	L	F	A	W	D	L	F	A	Pts
QPR	**42**	**16**	**3**	**2**	**51**	**16**	**10**	**4**	**7**	**26**	**20**	**85**
Wolves	42	14	5	2	42	16	6	10	5	26	28	75
Leicester C	42	11	4	6	36	15	9	6	6	36	29	70
Fulham	42	13	5	3	36	20	7	4	10	28	27	69
Newcastle U	42	13	6	2	43	21	5	7	9	32	32	67
Sheffield W	42	9	8	4	33	23	7	7	7	27	24	63
Oldham A	42	8	10	3	38	24	6	9	6	26	23	61
Leeds U	42	7	11	3	28	22	6	10	5	23	24	60
Shrewsbury T	42	8	9	4	20	15	7	5	9	28	33	59
Barnsley	42	9	8	4	37	28	5	7	9	20	27	57
Blackburn R	42	11	7	3	38	21	4	5	12	20	37	57
Cambridge U	42	11	7	3	26	17	2	5	14	16	43	51
Derby Co	42	7	10	4	27	24	3	9	9	22	34	49
Carlisle U	42	10	6	5	44	28	2	6	13	24	42	48
Crystal P	42	11	7	3	31	17	1	5	15	12	35	48
Middlesbrough	42	8	7	6	27	29	3	8	10	19	38	48
Charlton A	42	11	3	7	40	31	2	6	13	23	55	48
Chelsea	42	8	8	5	31	22	3	6	12	20	39	47
Grimsby T	42	9	7	5	32	26	3	4	14	13	44	47
Rotherham	42	6	7	8	22	29	4	8	9	23	39	45
Burnley	42	10	4	7	38	24	2	4	15	18	42	44
Bolton W	42	10	2	9	30	26	1	9	11	12	35	44

1983-1984 DIVISION 1

	P	W	D	L	F	A	W	D	L	F	A	Pts
Liverpool	42	14	5	2	50	12	8	9	4	23	20	80
Southampton	42	15	4	2	44	17	7	7	7	22	21	77
Nottingham F	42	14	4	3	47	17	8	4	9	29	28	74
Manchester U	42	14	3	4	43	18	6	11	4	28	23	74
QPR	**42**	**14**	**4**	**3**	**37**	**12**	**8**	**3**	**10**	**30**	**25**	**73**
Arsenal	42	10	5	6	41	29	8	4	9	33	31	63
Everton	42	9	9	3	21	12	7	5	9	23	30	62
Tottenham H	42	11	4	6	31	24	6	6	9	33	41	61
West Ham U	42	10	4	7	39	24	7	5	9	21	31	60
Aston Villa	42	14	3	4	34	22	3	6	12	25	39	60
Watford	42	9	7	5	36	31	7	2	12	32	46	57
Ipswich T	42	11	4	6	34	23	4	4	13	21	34	53
Sunderland	42	8	9	4	26	18	5	4	12	16	35	52
Norwich C	42	9	8	4	34	20	3	7	11	14	29	51
Leicester C	42	11	5	5	40	30	2	7	12	25	38	51
Luton T	42	7	5	9	30	33	7	4	10	23	33	51
WBA	42	10	4	7	30	25	4	5	12	18	37	51
Stoke C	42	11	4	6	30	23	2	7	12	14	40	50
Coventry C	42	8	5	8	33	33	5	6	10	24	44	50
Birmingham C	42	7	7	7	19	18	5	5	11	20	32	48
Notts Co	42	6	7	8	31	36	4	4	13	19	36	41
Wolves	42	4	8	9	15	28	2	3	16	12	52	29

1984-1985 DIVISION 1

	P	W	D	L	F	A	W	D	L	F	A	Pts
Everton	42	16	3	2	58	17	12	3	6	30	26	90
Liverpool	42	12	4	5	36	19	10	7	4	32	16	77
Tottenham H	42	11	3	7	46	31	12	5	4	32	20	77
Manchester U	42	13	6	2	47	13	9	4	8	30	34	76
Southampton	42	13	4	4	29	18	6	7	8	27	29	68
Chelsea	42	13	3	5	38	20	5	9	7	25	28	66
Arsenal	42	14	5	2	37	14	5	4	12	24	35	66
Sheffield W	42	12	7	2	39	21	5	7	9	19	24	65
Nottingham F	42	13	4	4	35	18	6	3	12	21	30	64
Aston Villa	42	10	7	4	34	20	5	4	12	26	40	56
Watford	42	10	5	6	48	30	4	8	9	33	41	55
WBA	42	11	4	6	36	23	5	3	13	22	39	55
Luton T	42	12	5	4	40	22	3	4	14	17	39	54
Newcastle U	42	11	4	6	33	26	2	9	10	22	44	52
Leicester C	42	10	4	7	39	25	5	2	14	26	48	51
West Ham U	42	7	8	6	27	23	6	4	11	24	45	51
Ipswich T	42	8	7	6	27	20	5	4	12	19	37	50
Coventry C	42	11	3	7	29	22	4	2	15	18	42	50
QPR	**42**	**11**	**6**	**4**	**41**	**30**	**2**	**5**	**14**	**12**	**42**	**50**
Norwich C	42	9	6	6	28	24	4	4	13	18	40	49
Sunderland	42	7	6	8	20	26	3	4	14	20	36	40
Stoke C	42	3	3	15	18	41	0	5	16	6	50	17

1985-1986 DIVISION 1

	P	W	D	L	F	A	W	D	L	F	A	Pts
Liverpool	42	16	4	1	58	14	10	6	5	31	23	88
Everton	42	16	3	2	54	18	10	5	6	33	23	86
West Ham U	42	17	2	2	48	16	9	4	8	26	24	84
Manchester U	42	12	5	4	35	12	10	5	6	35	24	76
Sheffield W	42	13	6	2	36	23	8	4	9	27	31	73
Chelsea	42	12	4	5	32	27	8	7	6	25	29	71
Arsenal	42	13	5	3	29	15	7	4	10	20	32	69
Nottingham F	42	11	5	5	38	25	8	6	7	31	28	68
Luton T	42	12	6	3	37	15	6	6	9	24	29	66
Tottenham H	42	12	2	7	47	25	7	6	8	27	27	65
Newcastle U	42	12	5	4	46	31	5	7	9	21	41	63
Watford	42	11	6	4	40	22	5	5	11	29	40	59
QPR	**42**	**12**	**3**	**6**	**33**	**20**	**3**	**4**	**14**	**20**	**44**	**52**
Southampton	42	10	6	5	32	18	2	4	15	19	44	46
Manchester C	42	7	7	7	25	26	4	5	12	18	31	45
Aston Villa	42	7	6	8	27	28	3	8	10	24	39	44
Coventry C	42	6	5	10	31	35	5	5	11	17	36	43
Oxford U	42	7	7	7	34	27	3	5	13	28	53	42
Leicester C	42	7	8	6	35	35	3	4	14	19	41	42
Ipswich T	42	8	5	8	20	24	3	3	15	12	31	41
Birmingham C	42	5	2	14	13	25	3	3	15	17	48	29
WBA	42	3	8	10	21	36	1	4	16	14	53	24

1986-1987 DIVISION 1

	P	W	D	L	F	A	W	D	L	F	A	Pts
Everton	42	16	4	1	49	11	10	4	7	27	20	86
Liverpool	42	15	3	3	43	16	8	5	8	29	26	77
Tottenham H	42	14	3	4	40	14	7	5	9	28	29	71
Arsenal	42	12	5	4	31	12	8	5	8	27	23	70
Norwich C	42	9	10	2	27	20	8	7	6	26	31	68
Wimbledon	42	11	5	5	32	22	8	4	9	25	28	66
Luton T	42	14	5	2	29	13	4	7	10	18	32	66
Nottingham F	42	12	8	1	36	14	6	3	12	28	37	65
Watford	42	12	5	4	38	20	6	4	11	29	34	63
Coventry C	42	14	4	3	35	17	3	8	10	15	28	63
Manchester U	42	13	3	5	38	18	1	11	9	14	27	56
Southampton	42	11	5	5	44	24	3	5	13	25	44	52
Sheffield W	42	9	7	5	39	24	4	6	11	19	35	52
Chelsea	42	8	6	7	30	30	5	7	9	23	34	52
West Ham U	42	10	4	7	33	28	4	6	11	19	39	52
QPR	**42**	**9**	**7**	**5**	**31**	**27**	**4**	**4**	**13**	**17**	**37**	**50**
Newcastle U	42	10	4	7	33	29	2	7	12	14	36	47
Oxford U	42	8	8	5	30	25	3	5	13	14	44	46
Charlton A	42	7	7	7	26	22	4	4	13	19	33	44
Leicester C	42	9	7	5	39	24	2	2	17	15	52	42
Manchester C	42	8	6	7	28	24	0	9	12	8	33	39
Aston Villa	42	7	7	7	25	25	1	5	15	20	54	36

1987-1988 DIVISION 1

	P	W	D	L	F	A	W	D	L	F	A	Pts
Liverpool	40	15	5	0	49	9	11	7	2	38	15	90
Manchester U	40	14	5	1	41	17	9	7	4	30	21	81
Nottingham F	40	11	7	2	40	17	9	6	5	27	22	73
Everton	40	14	4	2	34	11	5	9	6	19	16	70
QPR	**40**	**12**	**4**	**4**	**30**	**14**	**7**	**6**	**7**	**18**	**24**	**67**
Arsenal	40	11	4	5	35	16	7	8	5	23	23	66
Wimbledon	40	8	9	3	32	20	6	6	8	26	27	57
Newcastle U	40	9	6	5	32	23	5	8	7	23	30	56
Luton T	40	11	6	3	40	21	3	5	12	17	37	53
Coventry C	40	6	8	6	23	25	7	6	7	23	28	53
Sheffield W	40	10	2	8	27	30	5	6	9	25	36	53
Southampton	40	6	8	6	27	26	6	6	8	22	27	50
Tottenham H	40	9	5	6	26	23	3	6	11	12	25	47
Norwich C	40	7	5	8	26	26	5	4	11	14	26	45
Derby Co	40	6	7	7	18	17	4	6	10	17	28	43
West Ham U	40	6	9	5	23	21	3	6	11	17	31	42
Charlton A	40	7	7	6	23	21	2	8	10	15	31	42
Chelsea	40	7	11	2	24	17	2	4	14	26	51	42
Portsmouth	40	4	8	8	21	27	3	6	11	15	39	35
Watford	40	4	5	11	15	24	3	6	11	12	27	32
Oxford U	40	5	7	8	24	34	1	6	13	20	46	31

1988-1989 DIVISION 1

	P	W	D	L	F	A	W	D	L	F	A	Pts
Arsenal	38	10	6	3	35	19	12	4	3	38	17	76
Liverpool	38	11	5	3	33	11	11	5	3	32	17	76
Nottingham F	38	8	7	4	31	16	9	6	4	33	27	64
Norwich C	38	8	7	4	23	20	9	4	6	25	25	62
Derby Co	38	9	3	7	23	18	8	4	7	17	20	58
Tottenham H	38	8	6	5	31	24	7	6	6	29	22	57
Coventry C	38	9	4	6	28	23	5	9	5	19	19	55
Everton	38	10	7	2	33	18	4	5	10	17	27	54
QPR	**38**	**9**	**5**	**5**	**23**	**16**	**5**	**6**	**8**	**20**	**21**	**53**
Millwall	38	10	3	6	27	21	4	8	7	20	31	53
Manchester U	38	10	5	4	27	13	3	7	9	18	22	51
Wimbledon	38	10	3	6	30	19	4	6	9	20	27	51
Southampton	38	6	7	6	25	26	4	8	7	27	40	45
Charlton A	38	6	7	6	25	24	4	5	10	19	34	42
Sheffield W	38	6	6	7	21	25	4	6	9	13	26	42
Luton T	38	8	6	5	32	21	2	5	12	10	31	41
Aston Villa	38	7	6	6	25	22	2	7	10	20	34	40
Middlesbrough	38	6	7	6	28	30	3	5	11	16	31	39
West Ham U	38	3	6	10	19	30	7	2	10	18	32	38
Newcastle U	38	3	6	10	19	28	4	4	11	13	35	31

1989-1990 DIVISION 1

	P	W	D	L	F	A	W	D	L	F	A	Pts
Liverpool	38	13	5	1	38	15	10	5	4	40	22	79
Aston Villa	38	13	3	3	36	20	8	4	7	21	18	70
Tottenham H	38	12	1	6	35	24	7	5	7	24	23	63
Arsenal	38	14	3	2	38	11	4	5	10	16	27	62
Chelsea	38	8	7	4	31	24	8	5	6	27	26	60
Everton	38	14	3	2	40	16	3	5	11	17	30	59
Southampton	38	10	5	4	40	27	5	5	9	31	36	55
Wimbledon	38	5	8	6	22	23	8	8	3	25	17	55
Nottingham F	38	9	4	6	31	21	6	5	8	24	26	54
Norwich C	38	7	10	2	24	14	6	4	9	20	28	53
QPR	**38**	**9**	**4**	**6**	**27**	**22**	**4**	**7**	**8**	**18**	**22**	**50**
Coventry C	38	11	2	6	24	25	3	5	11	15	34	49
Manchester U	38	8	6	5	26	14	5	3	11	20	33	48
Manchester C	38	9	4	6	26	21	3	8	8	17	31	48
Crystal P	38	8	7	4	27	23	5	2	12	15	43	48
Derby Co	38	9	1	9	29	21	4	6	9	14	19	46
Luton T	38	8	8	3	24	18	2	5	12	19	39	43
Sheffield W	38	8	6	5	21	17	3	4	12	14	34	43
Charlton A	38	4	6	9	18	25	3	3	13	13	32	30
Millwall	38	4	6	9	23	25	1	5	13	16	40	26

1990-1991 DIVISION 1

	P	W	D	L	F	A	W	D	L	F	A	Pts
Arsenal	38	15	4	0	51	10	9	9	1	23	8*	83
Liverpool	38	14	3	2	42	13	9	4	6	35	27	76
Crystal P	38	11	6	2	26	17	9	3	7	24	24	69
Leeds U	38	12	2	5	46	23	7	5	7	19	24	64
Manchester C	38	12	3	4	35	25	5	8	6	29	28	62
Manchester U	38	11	4	4	34	17	5	8	6	24	28†	59
Wimbledon	38	8	5	28	22	6	8	5	25	24	56	
Nottingham F	38	11	4	4	42	21	3	8	8	23	29	54
Everton	38	9	5	5	26	15	4	7	8	24	31	51
Topttenham H	38	8	9	2	35	22	3	7	9	16	28	49
Chelsea	38	10	6	3	33	25	3	4	12	25	44	49
QPR	**38**	**8**	**5**	**6**	**27**	**22**	**4**	**5**	**10**	**17**	**31**	**46**
Sheffield U	38	9	3	7	23	23	4	4	11	13	32	46
Southampton	38	9	6	4	33	22	3	3	13	25	47	45
Norwich C	38	9	3	7	27	32	4	3	12	14	32	45
Coventry C	38	10	6	3	30	16	1	5	13	12	33	44
Aston Villa	38	7	9	3	29	25	2	5	12	17	33	41
Luton T	38	7	5	7	22	18	3	2	14	20	43	37
Sunderland	38	6	6	7	15	16	2	4	13	23	44	34
Derby Co	38	3	8	8	25	36	2	1	16	12	39	24

1991-1992 DIVISION 1

	P	W	D	L	F	A	W	D	L	F	A	Pts
Leeds U	42	13	8	0	38	13	9	8	4	36	24	82
Manchester U	42	12	7	2	34	13	9	8	4	29	20	78
Sheffield W	42	13	5	3	39	24	8	7	6	23	25	75
Arsenal	42	12	7	2	51	22	7	8	6	30	24	72
Manchester C	42	13	4	4	32	14	7	6	8	29	34	70
Liverpool	42	13	5	3	34	17	3	11	7	13	23	64
Aston Villa	42	13	3	5	31	16	4	6	11	17	28	60
Nottingham F	42	10	7	4	36	27	6	4	11	24	31	59
Sheffield U	42	9	6	6	29	23	7	3	11	36	40	57
Crystal P	42	7	8	6	24	25	7	7	7	29	36	57
QPR	**42**	**6**	**10**	**5**	**25**	**21**	**6**	**8**	**7**	**23**	**26**	**54**
Everton	42	8	8	5	28	19	5	6	10	24	32	53
Wimbledon	42	10	5	6	32	20	3	9	9	21	33	53
Chelsea	42	7	8	6	31	30	6	6	9	19	30	53
Tottenham H	42	7	3	11	33	35	8	4	9	25	28	52
Southampton	42	7	5	9	17	28	7	5	9	22	27	52
Oldham A	42	11	5	5	46	36	3	4	14	17	31	51
Norwich C	42	8	6	7	29	28	3	6	12	18	35	45
Coventry C	42	6	7	8	18	15	5	4	12	17	29	44
Luton T	42	10	7	4	25	17	0	5	16	13	54	42
Notts Co	42	7	5	9	24	29	3	5	13	16	33	40
West Ham U	42	6	6	9	22	24	3	5	13	15	35	38

1992-1993 PREMIER LEAGUE

	P	W	D	L	F	A	W	D	L	F	A	Pts
Manchester U	42	14	5	2	39	14	10	7	4	28	17	84
Aston Villa	42	13	5	3	36	16	8	6	7	21	24	74
Norwich C	42	13	6	2	31	19	8	3	10	30	46	72
Blackburn R	42	13	4	4	38	18	7	7	7	30	28	71
QPR	**42**	**11**	**5**	**5**	**41**	**32**	**6**	**7**	**8**	**22**	**23**	**63**
Liverpool	42	13	4	4	41	18	3	7	11	21	37	59
Sheffield W	42	9	8	4	34	26	6	6	9	21	25	59
Tottenham H	42	11	5	5	40	25	5	6	10	20	41	59
Manchester C	42	7	8	6	30	25	8	4	9	26	26	57
Arsenal	42	8	6	7	25	20	7	5	9	15	18	56
Chelsea	42	9	7	5	29	22	5	7	9	22	32	56
Wimbledon	42	9	4	8	32	23	5	8	8	24	32	54
Everton	42	7	6	8	26	27	8	2	11	27	28	53
Sheffield U	42	10	6	5	33	19	4	4	13	21	34	52
Coventry C	42	7	4	10	29	28	6	9	6	23	29	52
Ipswich T	42	8	9	4	29	22	4	7	10	21	33	52
Leeds U	42	12	8	1	40	17	0	7	14	17	45	51
Southampton	42	10	6	5	30	21	3	5	13	24	40	50
Oldham A	42	10	6	5	43	30	3	4	14	20	44	49
Crystal P	42	6	9	6	27	25	5	7	9	21	36	49
Middlesbrough	42	8	5	8	33	27	3	6	12	21	48	44
Nottingham F	42	6	4	11	17	25	4	6	11	24	37	40

Bradley Allen, another member of the famous footballing family. Signed as a junior in 1988, he began to establish himself in the first season of the FA Premier League.

Darren Peacock, a £350,000 signing from Hereford United in December 1990. He has been a regular in Rangers' first team ever since.

QPR Against Other Clubs

KEY: FA = FA Cup; LC = League Cup; UE = UEFA Cup; CT = Centenary Trophy; ZD = Zenith Data Systems Cup; CS = FA Charity Shield; WC = War Cup; WF = War Fund; LonC = London Cup; Vic = Victory Cup.

Aberdare Athletic

Season	Div	Home	Away
Football League			
1921-22	3S	W 1-0	L 2-4
1922-23	3S	W 4-1	D 0-0
1923-24	3S	W 3-0	D 1-1
1924-25	3S	W 4-1	D 1-1
1925-26	3S	L 1-3	L 0-1
1926-27	3S	W 3-0	W 2-0

Accrington Stanley

Season	Div	Home	Away
Football League			
1958-59	3	W 3-1	W 4-2
1959-60	3	W 5-1	W 2-1

AEK Athens

Season	Div	Home	Away
1976-77	UE4	W 3-0	L 0-3

AFC Bournemouth

Season	Div	Home	Away
Football League			
1923-24	3S	L 0-1	L 1-3
1924-25	3S	L 0-2	W 2-0
1925-26	3S	D 2-2	L 1-4
1926-27	3S	D 1-1	L 2-6
1927-28	3S	W 2-0	W 2-1
1928-29	3S	D 0-0	W 3-2
1929-30	3S	W 3-1	D 0-0
1930-31	3S	W 3-0	L 0-2
1931-32	3S	L 0-3	D 2-2
1932-33	3S	W 3-1	L 0-3
1933-34	3S	W 1-0	L 2-3
1934-35	3S	W 2-1	W 2-0
1935-36	3S	W 2-0	W 1-0
1936-37	3S	L 1-2	L 1-3
1937-38	3S	L 1-2	D 1-1
1938-39	3S	W 2-0	L 2-4
1939-40	3S		D 2-2
Regional League			
	B	W 2-1	L 0-3
	D	W 5-0	L 0-1
1945-46	LC	L 0-1	D 1-1
Football League			
1946-47	3S	W 3-0	D 1-1
1947-48	3S	W 1-0	W 1-0
1952-53	3S	W 2-1	L 0-1
1953-54	3S	W 2-1	W 1-0
1954-55	3S	D 1-1	D 2-2
1955-56	3S	L 0-1	L 0-1
1956-57	3S	W 2-1	L 0-1
1957-58	3S	W 3-0	L 1-4
1958-59	3	L 0-4	L 0-2
1959-60	3	W 3-0	D 1-1
1960-61	3	W 3-1	L 0-1
1961-62	3	D 1-1	L 1-3
1962-63	3	W 1-0	L 1-2
1963-64	3	W 1-0	L 2-4
1964-65	3	D 1-1	L 0-2
1965-66	3	W 5-0	D 1-1
1966-67	3	W 4-0	W 3-1
	FA2	W 2-0	
1977-78	LC2	W 2-0	

Aldershot

Season	Div	Home	Away
1927-28	FA1	L 1-2	
Football League			
1932-33	3S	D 2-2	L 0-2
1933-34	3S	L 2-4	L 1-3
1934-35	3S	W 2-0	L 0-1
1935-36	3S	W 5-0	W 3-1
1936-37	3S	W 3-0	D 0-0
1937-38	3S	W 3-0	L 0-1
1938-39	3S	W 7-0	L 0-2
Regional League			
1939-40	B	W 4-1	W 3-1
	D	W 3-1	W 1-0
1940-41	Sth		L 1-5
	LonC	L 2-3	W 4-2
	WC	W 4-2	L 1-2
1941-42		L 0-2	L 1-4
	LonC	W 2-1	W 2-0
Football League			
1943-44	Sth	D 2-2	W 3-1
1944-45	Sth	W 3-0	D 1-1
	WC	W 2-1	W 2-0
1946-47	3S	W 4-1	W 2-1
1947-48	3S	D 0-0	W 4-1
1952-53	3S	D 2-2	L 1-4
1953-54	3S	L 0-2	W 4-1
1954-55	3S	W 5-0	L 0-2
1955-56	3S	D 2-2	W 2-1
1956-57	3S	L 0-1	L 2-4
1957-58	3S	L 0-1	D 1-1
1963-64	LC1		L 1-3
1964-65	LC2	W 5-2	
1966-67	LC2	W 2-0	D 1-1

Arsenal

Season	Div	Home	Away
London Combination			
1915-16	Pri	D 1-1	L 1-2
1916-17		L 2-3	D 0-0
1917-18		W 2-0	L 0-2
		L 0-3	L 0-3
1918-19		L 2-3	L 0-1
		L 0-2	W 3-1
1920-21	FA1	W 2-0	
1921-22	FA1	L 1-2	D 0-0
Football League			
1940-41	Sth	W 3-2	L 2-3
London War League			
1941-42		L 0-1	L 1-4
Football League			
1942-43	Sth	W 3-2	L 0-3
	WC		L 1-4
1943-44	Sth	D 1-1	L 0-5
	WC	D 1-1	W 4-1
Football League			
1944-45	Sth	W 3-2	L 0-2
1968-69	1	L 0-1	L 1-2
1973-74	1	W 2-0	D 1-1
1974-75	1	D 0-0	D 2-2
1975-76	1	W 2-1	L 0-2
1976-77	1	W 2-1	L 2-3
	LC5	W 2-1	
1977-78	1	W 2-1	L 0-1
1978-79	1	L 1-2	L 1-5
1983-84	1	W 2-0	W 2-0
1984-85	1	W 1-0	L 0-1
1985-86	1	L 0-1	L 1-3
1986-87	1	L 1-4	L 1-3
1987-88	1	W 2-0	D 0-0
1988-89	1	D 0-0	L 1-2
	CT1	L 0-2	
1989-90	1	W 2-0	L 0-3
	FA4	W 2-0	D 0-0
1990-91	1	L 1-3	L 0-2
1991-92	1	D 0-0	D 1-1
1992-93	P	D 0-0	D 0-0

Ashford Town

Season	Div	Home	Away
1961-62	FA2		W 3-0

Aston Villa

Season	Div	Home	Away
1919-20	FA		L 1-2
Football League			
1967-68	2	W 3-0	W 2-1
1968-69	FA3		L 1-2
1969-70	2	W 4-2	D 1-1
1972-73	2	W 1-0	W 1-0
1975-76	1	D 1-1	W 2-0
1976-77	1	W 2-1	D 1-1
	LCSF	D 0-0	D 2-2
Replay			L 0-3
1977-78	1	L 1-2	D 1-1
	LC3		L 0-1
1978-79	1	W 1-0	L 1-3
1983-84	1	W 2-1	L 1-2
1984-85	1	W 2-0	L 2-5
	LC3	W 1-0	
1985-86	1	L 0-1	W 2-1
1986-87	1	W 1-0	W 1-0
1988-89	1	W 1-0	L 1-2
1989-90	1	D 1-1	W 3-1
1990-91	1	W 2-1	D 2-2
1991-92	1	L 0-1	W 1-0
1992-93	P	W 2-1	L 0-2

Barnet

Season	Div	Home	Away
1931-32	FA1		W 7-3
1945-46	FA1	W 2-1	W 6-2
1972-73	FA3	D 0-0	W 3-0

Barnsley

Season	Div	Home	Away
1909-10	FA4		L 0-1
Football League			
1948-49	2	D 2-2	L 0-4
1949-50	2	L 0-5	L 1-3
1950-51	2	W 2-1	L 0-7
1951-52	2	D 1-1	L 1-3
1959-60	3	W 1-0	L 1-2
1960-61	3	W 4-2	D 3-3
1961-62	3	W 3-0	W 4-2
1962-63	3	W 2-1	D 0-0
1963-64	3	D 2-2	L 1-3
1964-65	3	W 3-2	D 0-0
1981-82	2	W 1-0	L 0-3
1982-83	2	W 3-0	W 1-0

Barry Town

Season	Div	Home	Away
1961-62	FA1	W 7-0	D 1-1

Bath City

Season	Div	Home	Away
1964-65	FA1		W 2-0

Bedminster

Season	Div	Home	Away
Southern League			
1899-90	1st	W 2-1	L 1-4

Birmingham City

Season	Div	Home	Away
1913-14	FA3		W 2-1
Football League			
1950-51	2	W 2-0	D 1-1
1951-52	2	L 0-2	L 0-1
1966-67	LCSF	W 3-1	W 4-1
1967-68	2	W 2-0	L 0-2
1969-70	2	W 2-1	L 0-3
1970-71	2	W 5-2	L 1-2
1971-72	2	W 1-0	D 0-0
	LC2	W 2-0	
1973-74	1	D 2-2	L 0-4
	FA4	W 2-0	
1974-75	1	L 0-1	L 1-4
1975-76	1	W 2-1	D 1-1
1976-77	1	D 2-2	L 1-2
1977-78	1	D 0-0	L 1-2
1978-79	1	L 1-3	L 1-3
1979-80	2	D 1-1	L 1-2
1983-84	1	W 2-1	W 2-0
1985-86	1	W 3-1	L 0-2

Blackburn Rovers

Season	Div	Home	Away
1911-12		CS	L 1-2
Football League			
1948-49	2	W 4-2	L 0-2
1949-50	2	L 2-3	D 0-0
1950-51	2	W 3-1	L 1-2
1951-52	2	W 2-1	L 2-4
1967-68	2	W 3-1	W 1-0
1969-70	2	L 2-3	W 1-0
1970-71	2	W 2-0	W 2-0
1980-81	2	D 1-1	L 1-2
1981-82	2	W 2-0	L 1-2
1982-83	2	D 2-2	W 3-1
1986-87	LC2	W 2-1	D 2-2
1990-91	LC3	W 2-1	
1992-93	P	L 0-3	L 0-1

Blackpool

Season	Div	Home	Away
Football League			
1967-68	2	W 2-0	W 1-0
1969-70	2	W 6-1	D 1-1
1971-72	2	L 0-1	D 1-1
1972-73	2	W 4-0	L 0-2
1981-82	FA4	W 5-1	D 0-0
1989-90	FA5	D 0-0	D 2-2
Replay		W 3-0	

Bolton Wanderers

Season	Div	Home	Away
Football League			
1967-68	2	W 2-0	D 2-2
1969-70	2	L 0-4	L 4-6
1970-71	2	W 4-0	D 2-2
1978-79	1	L 1-3	L 1-2
1980-81	2	W 3-1	W 2-1
1981-82	2	W 7-1	L 0-1
1982-83	2	W 1-0	L 2-3

Bradford

Season	Div	Home	Away
Southern League			
1907-08	1st	W 2-0	D 2-2
1910-11	FA1		L 3-5
Football League			
1948-49	2	W 1-0	D 0-0
1949-50	2	L 0-1	L 0-1
1961-62	3	L 1-2	D 3-3
1962-63	3	L 1-2	W 3-0

Bradford City

Season	Div	Home	Away
1911-12	FA1	D 0-0	L 0-4
Football League			
1958-59	3	W 3-0	L 0-1
1959-60	3	W 5-0	L 1-3
1960-61	3	W 1-0	D 1-1
1979-80	LC2	W 2-1	W 2-0

Brentford

Season	Div	Home	Away
Southern League			
1901-02	1st	W 3-2	D 1-1
1902-03	1st	W 3-0	W 2-0
1903-04	1st	W 1-0	W 4-1
1904-05	1st	W 3-2	D 0-0
	FAQ	L 1-2	
1905-06	1st	L 1-2	D 2-2
1906-07	1st	D 1-1	L 1-4
1907-08	1st	W 1-0	D 1-1
1908-09	1st	W 3-0	D 0-0
1909-10	1st	D 0-0	W 1-0
1910-11	1st	W 2-0	D 1-1
1911-12	1st	W 4-0	W 2-1
1912-13	1st	W 2-1	W 2-0
London Combination			
1915-16	Pr	L 1-2	L 0-4
	Sec	D 1-1	L 0-4
1916-17		W 2-0	W 4-1
		D 2-2	D 0-0
1917-18		L 0-4	D 1-1
		L 2-6	L 1-6
1918-19		W 2-1	L 1-5
		D 0-0	D 1-1
Southern League			
1919-20	1st	W 2-0	L 1-2
Football League			
1920-21	3	W 1-0	W 2-0
1921-22	3S	D 1-1	L 1-5
1922-23	3S	D 1-1	W 3-1
1923-24	3S	W 1-0	W 1-0
1924-25	3S	W 1-0	W 1-0
1925-26	3S	D 1-1	W 2-1
1926-27	3S	D 1-1	L 2-4
1927-28	3S	L 2-3	W 3-0
1928-29	3S	D 2-2	D 1-1
1929-30	3S	W 2-1	L 0-3
1930-31	3S	W 3-1	L 3-5
1931-32	3S	L 1-2	L 0-1
1932-33	3S	L 2-3	L 0-2
Regional League			
1939-40	B	W 1-0	W 7-0
Football League			
1940-41	Sth	L 1-2	
	LonC	D 0-0	L 2-4
London War League			
1941-42		L 3-4	L 3-4
	WC	L 1-2	L 0-1
Football League			
1942-42	Sth	W 4-1	L 0-2
	WC	W 2-0	W 2-1
1943-44	Sth	W 3-2	W 5-2
1944-45	Sth	D 1-1	L 1-3
1945-46	FA5	L 1-3	D 0-0
1948-49	2	W 2-0	W 3-0
1949-50	2	D 3-3	W 2-0
1950-51	2	D 1-1	L 1-2
1951-52	2	W 3-1	D 0-0
	FA3		L 1-3
1954-55	3S	D 1-1	D 1-1
1955-56	3S	D 1-1	L 0-2
1956-57	3S	D 2-2	L 0-2
1957-59	3S	W 1-0	D 1-1

Brentford continued...

Season	Div	Home	Away
1958-59	3	L 1-2	L 0-1
1959-60	3	L 2-4	D 1-1
1960-61	3	D 0-0	L 0-2
1961-62	3	W 3-0	W 4-1
1963-64	3	D 2-2	D 2-2
1964-65	3	L 1-3	L 2-5
1965-66	3	W 1-0	L 1-6

Brighton & Hove Albion

Southern League

Season	Div	Home	Away
1903-04	1st	D 1-1	W 3-1
1904-05	1st	L 1-2	L 0-3
1905-06	1st	D 0-0	L 2-3
1906-07	1st	L 0-2	L 0-2
1907-08	1st	W 1-0	W 3-2
1908-09	1st	L 1-2	D 1-1
1909-10	1st	W 1-0	L 0-2
1910-11	1st	D 0-0	L 1-2
1911-12	1st	W 2-0	L 1-3
1912-13	1st	D 0-0	L 1-4
1913-14	1st	W 3-0	L 0-1
1914-15	1st	L 0-1	L 0-1
1919-20	1st	W 3-1	W 3-2

Football League

Season	Div	Home	Away
1920-21	3	W 4-0	L 1-2
1921-22	3S	W 3-0	L 1-2
1922-23	3S	D 0-0	L 0-2
1923-24	3S	W 1-0	L 0-3
1924-25	3S	W 2-0	L 0-5
1925-26	3S	L 0-2	L 1-2
1926-27	3S	D 2-2	L 1-4
1927-28	3S	W 5-0	W 3-1
1928-29	3S	W 3-2	L 1-2
1929-30	3S	W 3-1	W 3-2
1930-31	3S	W 4-1	D 1-1
1931-32	3S	D 1-1	L 0-1
1932-33	3S	L 0-1	L 1-4
1933-34	3S	W 2-0	W 1-0
1934-35	3S	W 2-1	L 1-5
	FA2	L 1-2	
1935-36	3S	W 3-2	D 1-1
1936-37	3S	L 2-3	L 1-4
	FA1	W 5-1	
1937-38	3S	W 2-1	L 1-3
1938-39	3S	L 1-2	L 1-3

Regional League

Season	Div	Home	Away
1939-40	B	W 3-2	L 1-3
	D	W 5-4	W 2-1

London War League

Season	Div	Home	Away
1941-42		W 3-0	W 5-2

Football League

Season	Div	Home	Away
1942-43	Sth	L 3-4	W 3-2
1943-44	Sth	W 1-0	L 1-3
1944-45	Sth	W 4-0	D 1-1
1946.47	3S	W 2-0	W 2-0
1947-48	3S	W 2-0	W 5-0
1952-53	3S	D 3-3	L 0-2
1953-54	3S	L 1-2	L 1-3
1954-55	3S	W 3-2	L 1-4
1955-56	3S	W 2-1	D 1-1
1956-57	3S	D 0-0	L 0-1
1957-59	3S	L 0-1	D 1-1
1962-63	3	D 2-2	D 2-2
1965-66	3	W 4-1	W 2-0
1966-67	3	W 3-0	D 2-2
1972-73	2	W 2-0	W 2-1

Brighton United

Southern League

Season	Div	Home	Away
1899-1900	1st	W 6-0	L 1-2

(Brighton Utd withdrew from League, results expunged)

Bristol City

Southern League

Season	Div	Home	Away
1899-1900	1st	D 1-1	L 3-5
1900-01	1st	W 2-0	L 0-2
1913-14	FA1	D 2-2	W 2-0

Football League

Season	Div	Home	Away
1922-23	3S	L 1-2	L 2-3
1924-25	3S	W 3-0	L 0-5
1925-26	3S	L 0-2	L 1-3
1926-27	3S	L 1-2	L 0-1
1932-33	3S	D 1-1	W 3-2
1933-34	3S	W 1-0	W 2-0
1934-35	3S	W 4-1	L 1-5
1935-36	3S	W 4-1	D 0-0
1936-37	3S	W 5-0	L 2-3
1937-38	3S	L 0-2	L 0-2
1938-39	3S	W 3-1	D 2-2
1945-46	WC	W 4-2	L 0-2
1946-47	3S	W 1-0	D 1-1
1947-48	3S	W 2-0	L 1-2
1952-53	3S	W 2-1	D 4-4
1953-54	3S	L 0-1	W 2-1
1954-55	3S	D 1-1	D 1-1
1960-61	3	D 1-1	D 1-1
1961-62	3	W 4-1	L 0-2
1962-63	3	W 3-1	W 4-2
1963-64	3	L 0-2	L 1-2
1964-65	3	W 1-0	L 0-2
1967-68	2	W 3-1	W 2-0
1969-70	2	D 2-2	L 0-2
1970-71	2	W 2-1	D 0-0
1971-72	2	W 3-0	L 0-2
1972-73	2	D 1-1	W 2-1
1976-77	1	L 0-1	L 0-1
1977-78	1	D 2-2	D 1-1
1978-79	1	W 1-0	L 0-2
1980-81	2	W 4-0	W 1-0
1981-82	LC3	W 3-0	

Bristol Rovers

Southern League

Season	Div	Home	Away
1899-1900	1st	W 3-0	L 0-1
1900-01	1st	W 4-3	L 1-2
1901-02	1st	D 0-0	L 1-4
1902-03	1st	W 2-0	L 0-4
1903-04	1st	W 2-1	D 1-1
1904-05	1st	W 5-0	D 0-0
1905-06	1st	W 7-0	L 1-2
1906-07	1st	D 1-1	L 1-3
	FA1	L 0-1	D 0-0
1907-08	1st	W 5-3	W 1-0
1908-09	1st	W 4-2	D 0-0
1909-10	1st	W 2-1	L 0-2
1910-11	1st	L 1-2	D 0-0
1911-12	1st	W 4-2	W 2-0
1912-13	1st	W 2-0	L 0-3
1913-14	2st	W 1-0	L 1-2
1914-15	1st	W 2-1	W 3-1
1919-20	1st	W 7-1	W 2-0
1920-21	3	W 2-1	L 0-3
1921-22	3S	L 1-2	D 1-1
1922-23	3S	W 3-1	W 3-1
1923-24	3S	L 1-2	L 1-2
1924-25	3S	L 1-2	L 0-3
1925-26	3S	W 2-1	L 0-5
1926-27	3S	D 2-2	L 1-4
1927-28	3S	W 4-2	W 4-0
1928-29	3S	L 0-3	D 1-1
1929-30	3S	W 2-1	L 1-4
1930-31	3S	W 2-0	L 0-3
	FA3		L 1-3
1931-32	3S	W 2-1	D 1-1
1932-33	3S	D 1-1	L 1-4
1933-34	3S	W 1-0	L 1-4
1934-35	3S	W 2-0	L 0-2
1935-36	3S	W 4-0	W 1-0
1936-37	3S	W 2-1	D 1-1
1937-38	3S	W 4-0	D 1-1
	FA1		W 8-1
1938-39	3S	D 1-1	D 0-0
1946-47	3S	L 0-2	L 1-3
1947-48	3S	W 5-2	W 1-0
1952-53	3S	L 0-1	L 1-2
1962-63	3	L 3-5	D 0-0
1963-64	3	W 1-0	D 0-0
1964-65	3	W 3-1	L 1-3
1965-66	3	W 4-1	L 0-1
1966-67	3	W 3-0	L 1-2
1971-72	LC4	D 1-1	L 0-1
1979-80	2	W 2-0	W 3-1
1980-81	2	W 4-0	W 2-1

Burnley

Season	Div	Home	Away
1920-21	FA2		L 2-4
1961-62	FA3		L 1-6
1967-68	LC4	L 1-2	

Football League

Season	Div	Home	Away
1968-69	1	L 0-2	D 2-2
1971-72	2	W 3-1	L 0-1
1972-73	2	W 2-0	D 1-1
1973-74	1	W 2-1	L 1-2
1974-75	1	L 0-1	L 0-3
1975-76	1	W 1-0	L 0-1
1979-80	2	W 7-0	W 3-0
1982-83	2	W 3-2	L 1-2

Bury

Season	Div	Home	Away
1936-37	FA3		L 0-1

Football League

Season	Div	Home	Away
1948-49	2	W 3-1	D 0-0
1949-50	2	W 1-0	D 0-0
1950-51	2	W 3-2	W 1-0
1951-52	2	W 3-2	L 1-3
1958-59	3	W 2-1	L 1-3
1959-60	3	W 2-0	L 0-2
1960-61	3	W 3-1	L 0-1
1976-77	LC3	W 2-1	
1987-88	LC3		L 0-1
1992-93	LC3		W 2-0

1.FC Cologne

Season	Div	Home	Away
1976-77	UE3	W 3-0	L 1-4

Cambridge United

Football League

Season	Div	Home	Away
1979-80	2	D 2-2	L 1-2
1980-81	2	W 5-0	L 0-1
1981-82	2	W 2-1	L 0-1
1982-83	2	W 2-1	W 4-1

Cardiff City

Southern League

Season	Div	Home	Away
1913-14	1st	L 0-2	L 0-3
1914-15	1st	W 3-0	L 0-2
1919-20	1st	D 0-0	L 0-4

Football League

Season	Div	Home	Away
1931-32	3S	L 2-3	W 4-0
1932-33	3S	W 5-1	W 5-2
1933-34	3S	W 4-0	L 1-3
1934-35	3S	D 2-2	L 1-2
1935-36	3S	W 5-1	L 2-3
1936-37	3S	W 6-0	L 0-2
1937-38	3S	W 2-1	D 2-2
1938-39	3S	W 5-0	L 0-1
1946-47	3S	L 2-3	D 2-2
1948-49	2	D 0-0	L 0-3
1949-50	2	L 0-1	L 0-4
1950-51	2	W 3-2	L 2-4
1951-52	2	D 1-1	L 1-3
1967-68	2	W 1-0	L 0-1
1969-70	2	W 2-1	L 2-4
1970-71	2	L 0-1	L 0-1
	LC2	W 4-0	
1971-72	2	W 3-0	D 0-0
1972-73	2	W 3-0	D 0-0
1976-77	LC2		W 3-1
1979-80	2	W 3-0	L 0-1
1980-81	2	W 2-0	L 0-1
1981-82	2	W 2-0	W 2-1
1988-89	LC2	W 3-0	W 4-1
1989-90	FA3	W 2-0	D 0-0

Carlisle United

Football League

Season	Div	Home	Away
1962-63	3	D 2-2	W 5-2
1963-64	FA3		L 0-2
1964-65	3	L 1-2	L 0-2
1966-67	LC5	W 2-1	
1967-68	2	W 1-0	L 1-3
1969-70	2	D 0-0	L 2-3
1970-71	2	D 1-1	L 0-3
1971-72	2	W 3-0	W 4-1
1972-73	2	W 4-0	W 3-1
1974-75	1	W 2-1	W 2-1
1982-83	2	W 1-0	L 0-1
1985-86	FA3		L 0-1

Charlton Athletic

Football League

Season	Div	Home	Away
1921-22	3S	W 3-1	D 1-1
1922-23	3S	L 1-2	D 1-1
1923-24	3S	D 0-0	L 0-3
1924-25	3S	D 0-0	L 0-2
	FAQ	D 1-1	W 2-1
1925-26	3S	D 2-2	D 1-1
	FA2	D 1-1	L 0-1
1926-27	3S	W 2-1	L 0-2
1927-28	3S	D 3-3	L 0-1
1928-29	3S	D 2-2	D 2-2
1929-30	FA3	L 0-3	D 1-1
1933-34	3S	W 2-1	W 2-1
1934-35	3S	L 0-3	L 1-3
1940-41	Sth	W 2-0	L 2-6

London War League

Season	Div	Home	Away
1941-42		D 0-0	L 1-3

Football League

Season	Div	Home	Away
1942-43	Sth	W 2-0	L 2-3
1943-44	Sth	D 3-3	L 0-1
1944-45	Sth	L 2-3	W 2-1
1967-68	2	W 2-1	D 3-3
1969-70	2	D 1-1	D 1-1
	FA4		W 3-2
1970-71	2	L 1-4	W 3-0
1971-72	2	W 2-0	L 1-2
1975-76	LC3	D 1-1	W 3-0
1979-80	2	W 4-0	D 2-2
1981-82	2	W 4-0	W 2-1
1982-83	2	W 5-1	W 3-1
1986-87	1	D 0-0	L 1-2
	LC3		L 0-1
1987-88	1	W 2-0	W 1-0
1988-89	1	W 1-0	D 1-1
	LC3	W 2-1	
1989-90	1	L 0-1	L 0-1

Chatham

Southern League

Season	Div	Home	Away
1899-1900	1st	W 5-3	L 3-5
1900-01	1st	W 3-0	

(Chatham withdrew from League, results expunged)

Chelsea

London Combination

Season	Div	Home	Away
1915-16	Pri	W 1-0	L 1-5
	Sec	L 0-3	L 0-3
1916-17		L 1-2	L 0-3
		D 2-2	L 1-3
1917-18		L 0-1	W 2-1
		L 1-2	L 0-1
1918-19		D 2-2	L 0-2
		W 3-2	L 0-3
	Vic		L 0-2

Regional League

Season	Div	Home	Away
1939-40	B	W 3-2	D 0-0

Football League

Season	Div	Home	Away
1940-41	Sth	L 2-3	L 1-3
	LonC	W 5-2	W 3-2
	WC	W 2-0	W 4-2

London War League

Season	Div	Home	Away
1941-42		W 2-1	L 1-3

Football League

Season	Div	Home	Away
1942-43	Sth	W 4-1	D 1-1
1943-44	Sth	L 2-11	W 3-1
1968-69	1	L 0-4	L 1-2
1969-70	FA6	L 2-4	
1973-74	1	D 1-1	D 3-3
	FA3	W 1-0	D 0-0
1974-75	1	W 1-0	W 3-0
1977-78	1	D 1-1	L 1-3
1978-79	1	D 0-0	W 3-1
1979-80	2	D 2-2	W 2-0
1980-81	2	W 1-0	D 1-1
1981-82	2	L 0-2	L 1-2
1982-83	2	L 1-2	W 2-0
1984-85	1	D 2-2	L 0-1
1985-86	1	W 6-0	D 1-1
	LC5	D 1-1	W 2-0
1986-87	1	D 1-1	L 1-3
1987-88	1	W 3-1	D 1-1
1989-90	1	W 4-2	D 1-1
1990-91	1	W 1-0	L 0-2
1991-92	1	D 2-2	L 1-2
1992-93	P	D 1-1	L 0-1

Chesterfield

Football League

Season	Div	Home	Away
1948-49	2	D 1-1	L 1-2
1949-50	2	W 3-2	L 1-2
1950-51	2	D 1-1	L 1-3
1958-59	3	D 2-2	W 3-2
1959-60	3	D 3-3	W 4-0
1960-61	3	L 1-2	W 1-0

Civil Service

Season	Div	Home	Away
1899-1900	FAQ	W 3-0	

Clapton

Season	Div	Home	Away
1924-25	FAQ	D 4-4	W 2-0
1957-58	FA1	W 3-1	D 1-1

Colchester United

Football League

Season	Div	Home	Away
1952-53	3S	W 1-0	D 1-1
1953-54	3S	D 0-0	L 0-5
1954-55	3S	W 4-1	L 0-1
1955-56	3S	W 6-2	L 1-4
1956-57	3S	D 1-1	D 1-1
1957-58	3S	W 1-0	L 1-2
1958-59	3	W 4-2	L 0-3
1959-60	3	W 3-1	L 0-2
	FA1		W 3-2
1960-61	3	W 3-2	W 1-0
1962-63	3	L 1-2	L 1-2
1963-64	3	D 0-0	L 0-2
	FA2		W 1-0
1964-65	3	W 5-0	W 2-1
1965-66	FA1	W 4-0	D 3-3
1966-67	3	W 2-1	W 3-1
	LC1	W 5-0	

Coventry City

Southern League

Season	Div	Home	Away
1908-09	1st	W 4-2	L 1-2
1909-10	1st	W 4-0	L 0-4
1910-11	1st	W 5-0	L 2-3
1911-12	1st	D 0-0	D 0-0
1912-13	1st	W 4-0	D 1-1
1913-14	1st	W 3-0	W 1-0

Football League

Season	Div	Home	Away
1926-27	3S	D 1-1	L 0-1
1927-28	3S	L 1-5	D 0-0
1928-29	3S	W 3-1	D 0-0
1929-30	3S	W 3-1	W 3-2
1930-31	3S	W 2-0	L 0-2
1931-32	3S	D 1-1	L 0-1
1932-33	3S	D 3-3	L 0-7
1933-34	3S	L 0-1	W 1-0
1934-35	3S	L 1-1	L 1-4
1935-36	3S	D 0-0	L 1-6
1948-49	2	L 0-3	D 1-1
1949-50	2	W 2-0	D 0-0
1950-51	2	W 3-1	L 0-3
1951-52	2	L 1-4	D 0-0
1952-53	3S	L 0-4	L 0-2
1953-54	3S	L 0-3	L 1-3
1954-55	3S	W 3-2	L 1-5
1955-56	3S	L 1-2	L 1-4
1956-57	3S	D 1-1	L 1-5
1957-58	3S	W 3-0	D 1-1
1959-60	3	W 2-1	D 0-0
1960-61	3	W 2-1	D 4-4
	FA2	L 1-2	
1961-62	3	W 4-1	W 3-2
1962-63	3	L 1-3	L 1-4
1963-64	3	L 3-6	L 2-4
1968-69	1	L 0-1	L 0-5
1973-74	1	W 3-0	W 1-0
	FA5	W 3-2	D 0-0
1974-75	1	W 2-0	D 1-1
1975-76	1	W 4-1	D 1-1
1976-77	1	D 1-1	L 0-2
1977-78	1	W 2-1	L 1-4
1978-79	1	W 5-1	L 0-1
1983-84	1	W 2-1	L 0-1
1984-85	1	W 2-1	L 0-3
1985-86	1	L 0-2	L 1-2
1986-87	1	W 3-1	L 1-4
1987-88	1	L 1-2	D 0-0
1988-89	1	W 2-1	W 3-0
1989-90	1	D 1-1	D 1-1
	LC3	L 1-2	
1990-91	1	W 1-0	L 1-3
1991-92	1	D 1-1	D 2-2
1992-93	P	W 2-0	W 1-0

Crewe Alexandra

Season	Div	Home	Away
1930-31	FA2		W 4-2

Football League

Season	Div	Home	Away
1963-64	3	W 2-0	L 0-2
1983-84	LC2	W 8-1	L 0-3

Crouch End Vampires

Season	Div	Home	Away
1901-02	FAQ	W 2-0	

Croydon Common

Southern League

Season	Div	Home	Away
1909-10	1st	D 4-4	W 3-0
1914-15	1st	W 1-0	L 0-1

London Combination

Season	Div	Home	Away
1915-16	Pri	W 2-1	W 1-0

Crystal Palace

Southern League

Season	Div	Home	Away
1906-07	1st	W 1-0	L 1-5
1907-08	1st	L 1-2	W 3-2
1908-09	1st	D 1-1	L 0-3
1909-10	1st	L 1-2	W 1-0
1910-11	1st	D 0-0	L 1-2
1911-12	1st	W 3-2	L 0-3
1912-13	1st	W 2-0	W 2-1
1913-14	1st	W 3-0	L 1-2
1914-15	1st	W 3-2	D 2-2

London Combination

Season	Div	Home	Away
1915-16	Pri	W 5-1	L 0-1
1916-17		W 1-0	L 0-4
		W 3-2	L 0-3
1917-18		W 4-1	L 1-4
		W 2-1	W 2-0
	WF	W 2-1	L 1-3
1918-19		W 3-2	L 2-4
		W 3-2	W 2-0

Southern League

Season	Div	Home	Away
1919-20	1st	L 2-3	L 0-1

Football League

Season	Div	Home	Away
1920-21	3	W 3-0	D 0-0
1922-23	FA1	W 1-0	
1925-26	3S	L 1-3	L 0-1
1926-27	3S	L 0-2	L 1-2
1927-28	3S	W 2-0	D 1-1
1928-29	3S	D 1-1	W 4-1
1929-30	3S	W 4-1	D 1-1
1930-31	3S	W 4-0	L 0-4
1931-32	3S	D 2-2	D 1-1
1932-33	3S	W 2-1	W 1-0
1933-34	3S	W 2-1	L 1-4
1934-35	3S	D 3-3	W 3-2
1935-36	3S	W 3-0	W 2-0
1936-37	3S	L 1-3	D 0-0
1937-38	3S	W 1-0	L 0-4
1938-39	3S	L 1-2	W 1-0
	FA1	W 3-0	D 1-1

Regional League

Season	Div	Home	Away
1939-40	D	L 2-5	D 2-2
1940-41	WC	W 3-2	W 1-0
	LonC	W 2-1	W 2-1

London War League

Season	Div	Home	Away
1941-42		L 1-3	L 1-2

Football League

Season	Div	Home	Away
1942-43	Sth	W 3-0	W 1-0
1944-45	Sth	D 0-0	L 4-7
1945-46	FA	D 0-0	D 0-0
Replay			W 1-0
1946-47	3S	L 1-2	D 0-0
1947-48	3S	W 1-0	W 1-0
1952-53	3S	D 1-1	L 2-4
1953-54	3S	D 1-1	W 3-0
1954-55	3S	W 1-0	L 1-2
1955-56	3S	L 0-3	D 1-1
1956-57	3S	W 4-2	L 1-2
1957-58	3S	W 4-2	W 3-2
1961-62	3	W 1-0	D 2-2
	LC1	W 5-2	
1962-63	3	W 4-1	L 0-1
1963-64	3	L 3-4	L 0-1
1967-68	2	W 2-1	L 0-1
1981-82	2	W 1-0	D 0-0
	FA6	W 1-0	
1982-83	2	D 0-0	W 3-0
1989-90	1	W 2-0	W 3-0
1990-91	1	L 1-2	D 0-0
1991-92	1	W 1-0	D 2-2
	ZDQF	L 2-3	
1992-93	P	L 1-3	D 1-1

Darlington

Season	Div	Home	Away
1932-33	FA3		L 0-2

Football League

Season	Div	Home	Away
1966-67	3	W 4-0	D 0-0

Derby County

Season	Div	Home	Away
1947-48	FA6	D 1-1	L 0-5

Football League

Season	Div	Home	Away
1962-68	2	L 0-1	L 0-4
1969-70	FA5	W 1-0	
1972-73	FA5		L 2-4
1973-74	1	D 0-0	W 2-1
1974-75	1	W 4-1	L 2-5
1975-76	1	D 1-1	W 5-1
1976-77	1	D 1-1	L 0-2
1977-78	1	D 0-0	L 0-2
1978-79	1	D 2-2	L 1-2
1980-81	2	W 3-1	D 3-3
	LC2	D 0-0	D 0-0
1981-82	2	W 3-0	L 1-3
1982-83	2	W 4-1	L 0-2
1987-88	1	D 1-1	W 2-0
1988-89	1	L 0-1	W 1-0
1989-90	1	L 0-1	L 0-2
1990-91	1	D 1-1	D 1-1

Doncaster Rovers

Football League

Season	Div	Home	Away
1950-51	2	L 1-2	W 2-0
1951-52	2	L 0-2	L 0-4
1958-59	3	W 3-1	L 0-2
1966-67	3	W 6-0	D 1-1
1984-85	FA3		L 0-1

Dorchester Town

Season	Div	Home	Away
1956-57	FA1	W 4-0	

Everton

Season	Div	Home	Away
1914-15	FA3	L 1-2	
1949-50	FA3	L 0-2	

Football League

Season	Div	Home	Away
1951-52	2	D 4-4	L 0-3
1968-69	1	L 0-1	L 0-4
1973-74	1	W 1-0	L 0-1
1974-75	1	D 2-2	L 1-2
1975-76	1	W 5-0	W 2-0
1976-77	1	L 0-4	W 3-1
1977-78	1	L 1-5	D 3-3
1978-79	1	D 1-1	L 1-2
1983-84	1	W 2-0	L 1-3
1984-85	1	D 0-0	L 0-2
1985-86	1	W 3-0	L 3-4
1986-87	1	L 0-1	D 0-0
1987-88	1	W 1-0	L 0-2
1988-89	1	D 0-0	L 1-4
	SCSF		L 0-1
1989-90	1	W 1-0	L 0-1
1990-91	1	D 1-1	L 0-3
1991-92	1	W 3-1	D 0-0
1992-93	P	W 4-2	W 5-3

Exeter City

Southern League

Season	Div	Home	Away
1908-09	1st	D 1-1	L 0-1
1909-10	1st	W 2-0	D 0-0
1910-11	1st	W 1-0	D 2-2
1911-12	1st	D 0-0	D 1-1
1912-13	1st	W 2-1	L 1-3
1913-14	1st	L 2-3	D 0-0
1914-15	1st	L 0-2	W 1-0
1919-20	1st	D 0-0	W 1-0

Football League

Season	Div	Home	Away
1920-21	3	W 2-1	W 1-0
1921-22	3S	W 2-1	W 1-0
1922-23	3S	W 2-0	W 2-1
1923-24	3S	W 2-0	L 0-3
1924-25	3S	L 1-4	W 3-1
1925-26	3S	D 0-0	L 0-3
1926-27	3S	D 1-1	W 2-0
1927-28	3S	L 0-1	L 0-4
1928-29	3S	W 1-0	D 1-1
1929-30	3S	W 2-0	W 2-0
1930-31	3S	W 7-2	L 0-2
1931-32	3S	W 1-0	L 2-6
1932-33	3S	L 1-3	L 0-2
1933-34	3S	W 2-0	D 1-1
1934-35	3S	D 1-1	L 0-3
1935-36	3S	W 3-1	D 0-0
1936-37	3S	W 4-0	W 3-0
1937-38	3S	W 4-0	L 4-0
1938-39	3S	W 5-0	D 1-1
1946-47	3S	W 2-0	L 0-3
1947-48	3S	W 3-1	W 2-1
1952-53	3S	D 1-1	D 2-2
1953-54	3S	D 0-0	D 0-0
1954-55	3S	L 1-2	L 1-2
1955-56	3S	W 1-0	L 0-2
1956-57	3S	W 5-3	D 0-0
1957-58	3S	D 1-1	D 0-0
1964-65	3	D 0-0	D 2-2
1965-66	3	W 1-0	D 0-0

Fulham

Season	Div	Home	Away
1899-1900	FAQ	W 3-0	
1900-01	FAQ	W 7-0	

Southern League

Season	Div	Home	Away
1903-04	1st	D 1-1	D 2-2
	FAQ	D 1-1	L 1-3
1904-05	1st	W 2-0	W 2-1
1905-06	1st	L 1-3	L 0-1
	FA1		L 0-1
1906-07	1st	L 0-2	D 1-1

London Combination

Season	Div	Home	Away
1915-16	Pri	W 2-1	W 1-0
1916-17		L 1-7	L 0-2
		W 2-0	D 0-0
1917-18		L 2-3	L 1-2
		L 0-1	L 0-1
1918-19		L 0-3	D 3-3
		L 0-1	L 0-1

Football League

Season	Div	Home	Away
1928-29	3S	W 2-1	L 0-5
1929-30	3S	D 0-0	W 2-0
1930-31	3S	L 0-2	W 2-0
1931-32	3S	W 3-1	W 3-1

Regional League

Season	Div	Home	Away
1939-40	B	D 2-2	W 8-3

Football League

Season	Div	Home	Away
1940-41	Sth	L 2-5	L 1-3
		L 2-3	
	LonC	L 5-7	L 1-4

London War League

Season	Div	Home	Away
1941-42		L 2-5	W 3-0

Football League

Season	Div	Home	Away
1942-43	Sth	W 2-1	L 2-4
1943-44	Sth	D 3-3	D 2-2
1944-45	Sth	D 4-4	D 2-2
1948-49	2	W 1-0	L 0-5
1970-71	LC3		L 0-2
1971-72	2	D 0-0	W 3-0
	FA3	D 1-1	L 1-2
1972-73	2	W 2-0	W 2-0
1978-79	FA3		L 0-2
1979-80	2	W 3-0	W 2-0
1982-83	2	W 3-1	D 1-1

Gillingham

Southern League

Season	Div	Home	Away
1899-1900	1st	W 2-0	W 3-0
1900-01	1st	W 2-0	L 1-2
1901-02	1st	D 1-1	W 1-0
1902-03	1st	L 1-2	D 0-0
1903-04	1st	W 3-0	L 0-2
1904-05	1st	W 2-0	L 0-4
1905-06	1st	W 4-0	W 2-0
1906-07	1st	W 3-0	L 1-2
1907-08	1st	D 2-2	W 4-0
1908-09	1st	W 2-1	L 0-1
1909-10	1st	W 1-0	D 1-1
1910-11	1st	W 5-0	L 0-1
1911-12	1st	W 3-0	W 2-1
1912-13	1st	W 2-0	D 0-0
1913-14	1st	D 0-0	L 0-1
1914-15	1st	W 3-0	W 1-0
1919-20	1st	D 0-0	W 1-0

Football League

Season	Div	Home	Away
1920-21	3	L 0-1	W 2-1
1921-22	3S	W 1-0	W 2-1
1922-23	3S	W 2-1	W 1-0
1923-24	3S	D 1-1	D 0-0
1924-25	3S	D 1-1	L 0-1
1925-26	3S	L 0-1	L 0-3
1926-27	3S	D 1-1	D 2-2
1927-28	3S	D 3-3	W 2-1
1928-29	3S	W 1-0	D 0-0
1929-30	3S	W 2-1	L 1-3
1930-31	3S	W 1-0	D 2-2
1931-32	3S	W 7-0	L 0-1
1932-33	3S	D 1-1	L 1-4
1933-34	3S	W 5-0	W 4-1
1934-35	3S	W 2-0	D 0-0
1935-36	3S	W 5-2	D 2-2
1936-37	3S	L 0-1	D 0-0
1937-38	3S	W 2-0	W 5-1
1947-48	FA3	W 3-1	D 1-1
1952-53	3S	D 1-1	L 0-3
1953-54	3S	W 3-1	L 0-1
1954-55	3S	D 1-1	L 1-3
1955-56	3S	D 2-2	W 2-0
1956-57	3S	W 5-0	W 1-0
1957-58	3S	D 1-1	D 1-1
1963-64	FA1	W 4-1	
1964-65	3	W 3-1	D 2-2
1965-66	3	L 1-3	L 1-3
1966-67	3	W 2-0	D 2-2

Glossop

Southern League

Season	Div	Home	Away
1914-15	FA1	W 2-1	

Gravesend United

Southern League

Season	Div	Home	Away
1899-1900	1st	W 3-1	W 3-1
1900-01	1st	W 4-2	D 2-2

Gravesend & Northfleet

Season	Div	Home	Away
1925-26	FA1	W 2-0	D 2-2

Grimsby Town

Football League

Season	Div	Home	Away
1920-21	3	W 2-0	L 1-2
1948-49	2	L 1-2	L 1-4
1949-50	2	L 1-2	D 1-1
1950-51	2	W 7-1	D 2-2
1959-60	3	D 0-0	L 1-3
1960-61	3	W 2-0	L 1-3
1961-62	3	W 3-2	D 1-1
1964-65	3	D 1-1	D 0-0
1965-66	3	W 3-0	L 2-4
1966-67	3	W 5-1	D 1-1
1980-81	2	W 1-0	D 0-0
1981-82	2	W 1-0	L 1-2
	FA5	W 3-1	
1982-83	2	W 4-0	D 1-1
1992-93	LC2	W 2-1	L 1-2

Guildford City

Season	Div	Home	Away
1928-29	FA1		L 2-4
1965-66	FA2	W 3-0	

Halifax Town

Season	Div	Home	Away
1912-13	FA1	W 4-2	
Football League			
1958-59	3	W 3-1	L 1-2
1959-60	3	W 3-0	L 1-3
1960-61	3	W 5-1	D 1-1
1961-62	3	W 6-2	D 1-1
1962-63	3	W 5-0	W 4-1

Hartlepool United

Season	Div	Home	Away
1938-39	FA2		W 2-0

Hereford United

Season	Div	Home	Away
1957-58	FA2		L 1-6

Hinckley Athletic

Season	Div	Home	Away
1962-63	FA2	W 7-2	

Huddersfield Town

Season	Div	Home	Away
1931-32	FA4		L 0-5
1948-48	FA3	D 0-0	L 0-5
Football League			
1967-68	2	W 3-0	L 0-1
1969-70	2	W 4-2	L 0-2
1972-73	2	W 3-1	D 2-2
1983-84	FA3		L 1-2

Hull City

Football League

Season	Div	Home	Away
1949-50	2	L 1-4	D 1-1
1950-51	2	W 3-1	L 1-5
1951-52	2	D 1-1	L 1-4
1958-59	3	D 1-1	L 0-1
1960-61	3	W 2-1	L 1-3
1961-62	3	D 1-1	L 1-3
1962-63	3	W 4-1	L 1-4
1963-64	3	L 0-2	L 0-3
1964-65	3	W 2-1	L 1-3
1965-66	3	D 3-3	W 3-1
1967-68	2	D 1-1	L 0-2
	LC2	W 2-1	
1969-70	2	W 3-0	W 2-1
1970-71	2	D 1-1	D 1-1
1971-72	2	W 2-1	D 1-1
1972-73	2	D 1-1	L 1-4
1985-86	LC2	W 3-0	W 5-1
1991-92	LC2	W 5-1	W 3-0

Ipswich Town

Football League

Season	Div	Home	Away
1938-39	3S	D 0-0	L 0-1
1945-46	3SN	W 2-0	L 1-2
	WC	W 4-1	L 0-1
	FA2	W 4-0	W 2-0
1946-47	3S	L 1-3	D 1-1
1947-48	3S	W 2-0	L 0-1
1952-53	3S	D 2-2	W 1-0
1953-54	3S	W 3-1	L 1-2
1955-56	3S	D 1-1	L 1-4
1956-57	3S	L 0-2	L 0-4
1967-68	2	W 1-0	D 2-2
1968-69	1	W 2-1	L 0-3
1973-74	1	L 0-1	L 0-1
1974-75	1	W 1-0	L 1-2
1975-76	1	W 3-1	D 1-1
1976-77	1	W 1-0	D 2-2
1977-78	1	D 3-3	L 2-3
1978-79	1	L 0-4	L 1-2
1983-84	1	W 1-0	W 2-0
	LC3		L 2-3
1984-85	1	W 3-0	D 1-1
	LC5	L 1-2	D 0-0
1985-86	1	W 1-0	L 0-1
1992-93	P	D 0-0	D 1-1

Kettering Town

Southern League

Season	Div	Home	Away
1900-01	1st	W 2-0	L 1-2
1901-02	1st	W 2-1	L 0-3
1902-03	1st	W 4-2	W 1-0
1903-04	1st	W 2-0	L 1-2
1933-34	FA1	W 6-0	

KR Reykjavik

Season	Div	Home	Away
1984-85	UE1	W 4-0	W 3-0

Leeds City

Season	Div	Home	Away
1914-15	FA2	W 1-0	

Leeds United

Season	Div	Home	Away
1931-32	FA3	W 3-1	
Football League			
1948-49	2	W 2-0	W 2-1
1949-50	2	D 1-1	D 1-1
1950-51	2	W 3-0	D 2-2
1951-52	2	D 0-0	L 0-3
1968-69	1	L 0-1	L 1-4
1973-74	1	L 0-1	D 2-2
1974-75	1	D 1-1	W 1-0
1975-76	1	W 2-0	L 1-2
1976-77	1	D 0-0	W 1-0
1977-78	1	D 0-0	L 0-3
1978-79	1	L 1-4	L 3-4
	LC4	L 0-2	
1982-83	2	W 1-0	W 1-0
1986-87	FA5		L 1-2
1990-91	1	W 2-0	W 3-2
	LC4	L 0-3	
1991-92	1	W 4-1	L 0-2
1992-93	P	W 2-1	D 1-1

Leicester City

Season	Div	Home	Away
1940-41	WC	W 2-1	L 1-6
Football League			
1948-49	2	W 4-1	W 3-2
1949-50	2	W 2-0	L 2-3
1950-51	2	W 3-0	L 2-6
1951-52	2	W 1-0	L 0-4
1966-67	LC4	W 4-2	
1968-69	1	D 1-1	L 0-2
1969-70	2	D 1-1	L 1-2
1970-71	2	L 1-3	D 0-0
1973-74	1	D 0-0	L 0-2
	FA6	L 0-2	
1974-75	1	W 4-2	L 1-3
1975-76	2	W 1-0	W 1-0
1976-77	1	W 3-2	D 2-2
1977-78	1	W 3-0	D 0-0
1979-80	2	L 1-4	L 0-2
1981-82	2	W 2-0	L 2-3
1982-83	2	D 2-2	W 1-0
1983-84	1	W 2-0	L 1-2
1984-85	1	W 4-3	L 0-4
1985-86	1	W 2-0	W 4-1
1986-87	1	L 0-1	L 1-4
	FA3	W 5-2	

Leyton Orient

Southern League

Season	Div	Home	Away
1906-07	1st	W 2-0	L 0-3
1907-08	1st	W 5-2	W 5-2
1908-09	1st	L 0-3	L 0-1
1909-10	1st	W 2-1	W 1-0
1910-11	1st	W 5-3	L 1-2
1911-12	1st	W 1-0	W 1-0
London Combination			
1915-16	Pr	D 0-0	W 2-0
	Sec	D 1-1	D 1-1
1916-17		D 0-0	L 1-2
1917-18		W 2-0	W 2-1
		W 6-1	W 1-0
1918-19		W 3-1	W 5-1
		W 5-2	W 5-1
Football League			
1929-30	3S	D 1-1	W 4-2
1930-31	3S	W 4-2	W 3-2
1931-32	3S	W 3-2	L 0-3
1932-33	3S	W 2-1	D 2-2
1933-34	3S	W 2-0	D 2-2
1934-35	3S	W 6-3	L 1-3
1935-36	3S	W 4-0	L 0-1
1936-37	3S	W 2-1	D 0-0
1937-38	3S	W 3-2	D 1-1
1938-39	3S	D 1-1	L 1-2
Regional League			
1939-40	D	W 4-0	L 3-4
Football League			
1940-41	Sth	D 3-3	W 3-0
London War League			
1941-42		W 2-1	D 0-0
Football League			
1942-43	Sth	W 3-1	W 4-0
	WC	W 8-1	D 1-1
1943-44	Sth	W 6-2	W 3-2
	WC	W 6-0	W 5-2
1944-45	Sth	D 3-3	W 3-0
1945-46	3SN	W 3-0	W 2-0
	WC	W 6-0	D 0-0
1946-47	3S	W 2-0	D 1-1
1947-48	3S	L 1-2	W 3-1
1952-53	3S	W 1-0	L 0-5
1953-54	3S	W 2-1	D 2-2
1954-55	3S	W 2-0	L 0-3
1955-56	3S	L 0-1	L 1-7
1966-67	3S	W 4-1	D 0-0
1970-71	2	W 5-1	W 1-0
1971-72	2	W 1-0	L 0-2
1972-73	2	W 3-1	D 2-2
1974-75	LC2	D 1-1	W 3-0
1979-80	2	D 0-0	D 1-1
1980-81	2	D 0-0	L 0-4
1981-82	2	W 3-0	D 1-1

(until 1946 known as Clapton Orient, 1967 to 1987 known as Orient)

Lincoln City

Season	Div	Home	Away
1929-30	FA2	W 2-1	
Football League			
1948-49	2	W 2-0	D 0-0
1961-62	3	L 1-3	W 5-0
1971-72	LC3	W 4-2	

Liverpool

Season	Div	Home	Away
1913-14	FA4		L 1-2
Football League			
1968-69	1	L 1-2	L 0-2
1973-74	1	D 2-2	L 1-2
1974-75	1	L 0-1	L 1-3
1975-76	1	W 2-0	L 0-2
1976-77	1	D 1-1	L 1-3
1977-78	1	W 2-0	L 0-1
1978-79	1	L 1-3	L 1-2
1983-84	1	L 0-1	L 0-2
1984-85	1	L 0-2	D 1-1
1985-86	1	W 2-1	L 1-4
	LCSF	W 1-0	D 2-2
1986-87	1	L 1-3	L 1-2
1987-88	1	L 0-1	L 0-4
1988-89	1	L 0-1	L 0-2
1989-90	1	W 3-2	L 1-2
	FA6	D 2-2	L 0-1
1990-91	1	D 1-1	W 3-1
1991-92	1	D 0-0	L 0-1
1992-93	P	L 0-1	L 0-1

London Welsh

Season	Div	Home	Away
1899-1900	FAP	W 4-2	

Luton Town

Season	Div	Home	Away
1899-1900	FAQ	W 4-1	D 1-1
Southern League			
1900-01	1st	L 1-3	D 2-2
	FAQ		L 0-3
1901-02	1st	D 2-2	L 0-1
	FAQ		L 0-2
1902-03	1st	W 3-1	L 1-4
	FAQ	L 0-3	
1903-04	1st	W 2-1	L 0-1
1904-05	1st	L 1-2	D 1-1
1905-06	1st	L 2-3	L 2-3
1906-07	1st	W 2-0	D 1-1
1907-08	1st	W 3-1	D 0-0
1908-09	1st	W 4-0	L 0-1
1909-10	1st	W 4-0	D 1-1
1910-11	1st	D 3-3	W 1-0
1911-12	1st	W 2-0	W 3-1
1914-15	1st	L 0-3	W 4-2
London Combination			
1916-17	1st	L 1-4	L 0-6
		D 2-2	L 0-2
Southern League			
1919-20	1st	W 4-0	L 1-2
Football League			
1920-21	3	W 4-1	L 1-2
1921-22	3S	W 1-0	L 1-3
1922-23	3S	W 4-0	L 0-1
1923-24	3S	L 0-2	L 0-2
1924-25	3S	W 2-1	L 0-3
1925-26	3S	W 1-0	L 0-4
1926-27	3S	W 1-0	L 0-2
1927-28	3S	W 3-2	W 1-0
1928-29	3S	D 1-1	L 2-3
1929-30	3S	W 1-0	L 1-2
	FA1		W 3-2
1930-31	3S	W 3-1	L 1-5
1931-32	3S	W 3-1	L 1-4
1932-33	3S	W 3-1	L 1-3
1933-34	3S	W 2-1	L 2-4
1934-35	3S	W 3-0	D 1-1
1935-36	3S	D 0-0	L 0-2
1936-37	3S	W 2-1	W 1-0
1942-43	Sth	D 2-2	W 2-1
1943-44	WC	W 5-0	W 4-3
1944-45	Sth	W 7-1	L 1-2
1947-48	FA5	W 3-1	
1948-49	2	L 0-3	D 0-0
1949-50	2	W 3-0	W 2-1
1950-51	2	D 1-1	L 0-2
1951-52	2	D 0-0	W 1-0
1963-64	3	D 1-1	D 4-4
1964-65	3	W 7-1	L 0-2
1970-71	2	L 0-1	D 0-0
1971-72	2	W 1-0	D 1-1
1972-73	2	W 2-0	D 2-2
1974-75	1	W 2-1	D 1-1
1979-80	2	D 2-2	D 1-1
1980-81	2	W 3-2	L 0-3
1981-82	2	L 1-2	L 2-3
1983-84	1	L 0-1	D 0-0
1984-85	1	L 2-3	L 0-2
1985-86	1	D 1-1	L 0-2
1986-87	1	D 2-2	L 0-1
	FA4	W 2-1	D 1-1
1987-88	1	W 2-0	L 1-2
	FA5	D 1-1	L 0-1
1988-89	1	D 1-1	D 0-0
1989-90	1	D 0-0	D 1-1
1990-91	1	W 6-1	W 2-1
1991-92	1	W 2-1	W 1-0

Manchester City

Football League

Season	Div	Home	Away
1950-51	2	L 1-2	L 2-5
1968-69	1	D 1-1	L 1-3
1969-70	LC5		L 0-3
1973-74	1	W 3-0	L 0-1
1974-75	1	W 2-0	L 0-1
1975-76	1	W 1-0	D 0-0
1976-77	1	D 0-0	D 0-0
1977-78	1	D 1-1	L 1-2
1978-79	1	W 2-1	L 1-3
1985-86	1	D 0-0	L 0-2
1986-87	1	W 1-0	D 0-0
1989-90	1	L 1-3	L 0-1
1990-91	1	W 1-0	L 1-2
1991-92	1	W 4-0	D 2-2
	LC3	L 1-3	D 0-0
1992-93	P	D 1-1	D 1-1
	FA4	L 1-2	

Manchester United

Season	Div	Home	Away
1907-08	CS		D 1-1
1908-09	CS		L 0-4
Football League			
1968-69	1	L 2-3	L 1-8
1973-74	1	W 3-0	L 1-2
1975-76	1	W 1-0	L 1-2
1976-77	1	W 4-0	L 0-1
	FA4		L 0-1
1977-78	1	D 2-2	L 1-3
1978-79	1	D 1-1	L 0-2
1983-84	1	D 1-1	L 1-3
1984-85	1	L 1-3	L 0-3
1985-86	1	W 1-0	L 0-2
1986-87	1	D 1-1	L 0-1
1987-88	1	L 0-2	L 1-2
1988-89	1	W 3-2	D 0-0
	FA3	D 2-2	D 0-0
Replay			L 0-3
1989-90	1	L 1-2	D 0-0
1990-91	1	D 1-1	L 1-3
	FA3		L 1-2
1991-92	1	D 0-0	W 4-1
1992-93	P	L 1-3	D 0-0

Mansfield Town

Football League

Season	Div	Home	Away
1931-32	3S	D 1-1	D 2-2
1937-38	3S	D 1-1	L 2-3
1938-39	3S	W 3-0	D 2-2
1945-46	3SN	W 3-2	W 6-2
	WC	W 3-0	D 0-0
1946-47	3S	W 3-1	W 3-0
1958-59	3	D 1-1	W 4-3
1959-60	3	W 2-0	L 3-4
1963-64	3	W 2-0	L 0-1
1964-65	3	W 2-0	L 1-8
1965-66	3	L 1-2	L 1-2
1966-67	3	D 0-0	W 7-1
1969-70	LC2	W 4-0	D 2-2
1979-80	LC3		W 3-0

Margate

Season	Div	Home	Away
1935-36	FA1		L 1-3

Merthyr Town

Southern League

Season	Div	Home	Away
1912-13	1st	W 4-1	D 0-0
1913-14	1st	L 0-1	W 2-1
1919-20	1st	D 0-0	W 4-1
Football League			
1920-21	3	W 4-2	L 1-3

Merthyr Town continued...

Season	Div	Home	Away
1921-22	3S	D 0-0	L 0-2
1922-23	3S	D 1-1	W 1-0
1923-24	3S	W 3-0	L 0-2
1924-25	3S	D 1-1	W 3-2
1925-26	3S	D 1-1	L 0-1
1926-27	3S	W 5-1	L 0-4
1927-28	3S	D 0-0	W 4-0
1928-29	3S	W 8-0	W 2-1
1929-30	3S	W 2-0	W 4-1
1932-33	FA1	W 5-1	D 1-1

Middlesbrough

Season	Div	Home	Away
1912-13	FA2		L 2-3
1946-47	FA3	D 1-1	L 1-3
Football League			
1966-67	3	W 4-0	D 2-2
1967-68	2	D 1-1	L 1-3
1969-70	2	W 4-0	L 0-1
1970-71	2	D 1-1	L 2-6
1971-72	2	W 1-0	L 2-3
1972-73	2	D 2-2	D 0-0
1974-75	1	D 0-0	W 3-1
1975-76	1	W 4-2	D 0-0
1976-77	1	W 3-0	W 2-0
1977-78	1	D 1-1	W 1-0
1978-79	1	D 1-1	W 2-0
1981-82	FA3	D 1-1	W 3-2
1982-83	2	W 6-1	L 1-2
1988-89	1	D 0-0	L 0-1
1992-93	P	D 3-3	W 1-0

Millwall

Southern League

Season	Div	Home	Away
1899-1900	1st	W 2-0	W 3-1
	FA2	L 0-2	
1900-01	1st	L 0-2	W 1-0
1901-02	1st	L 0-2	L 1-6
1902-03	1st	L 0-1	L 0-6
1903-04	1st	W 2-1	L 0-4
1904-05	1st	D 1-1	D 0-0
1905-06	1st	W 2-1	L 0-2
1906-07	1st	W 2-1	L 0-7
1907-08	1st	L 2-3	D 0-0
1908-09	1st	D 2-2	W 1-0
1909-10	1st	L 1-2	L 0-1
1910-11	1st	W 2-1	D 1-1
1911-12	1st	D 1-1	D 1-1
1912-13	1st	D 1-1	L 1-2
1913-14	1st	W 1-0	L 0-2
1914-15	1st	L 0-1	L 1-3
London Combination			
1915-16	Pr	L 1-5	L 1-3
	Sec	W 2-0	L 2-6
1916-17		L 0-4	L 1-2
		D 0-0	L 0-1
1917-18		W 1-0	L 2-4
		W 4-1	W 1-0
	WF	W 4-3	L 1-3
1918-19		W 1-0	L 1-4
		W 3-0	D 1-1
Southern League			
1919-20	1st	L 1-2	D 0-0
Football League			
1920-21	3	D 0-0	D 0-0
1921-22	3S	W 6-1	D 0-0
1922-23	3S	L 2-3	D 0-0
1923-24	3S	D 1-1	L 0-3
1924-25	3S	D 0-0	L 0-3
1925-26	3S	W 3-0	L 0-3
1926-27	3S	D 1-1	L 1-2
1927-28	3S	L 0-1	L 1-6
1934-35	3S	W 1-0	L 0-2
1935-36	3S	L 2-3	L 0-2
1936-37	3S	L 0-1	L 0-2
1937-38	3S	L 0-2	W 4-1
1940-41	Sth	W 2-1	L 1-3
London War League			
1941-42		W 4-1	W 2-1
	WC	W 2-0	D 2-2
Football League			
1942-43	Sth	W 3-2	W 2-1
1943-44	Sth	W 2-0	W 4-3
1944-45	Sth	W 4-1	D 3-3
1950-51	FA3	L 3-4	
1952-53	3S	L 1-3	L 1-2
1953-54	3S	W 4-0	L 0-4
1954-55	3S	L 1-2	W 1-0
1955-56	3S	W 4-0	L 0-2
1956-57	3S	D 0-0	L 0-2
1957-58	3S	W 3-0	L 0-5
1962-63	3	L 2-3	D 0-0
1963-64	3	W 2-0	D 2-2
1965-66	3	W 6-1	L 1-2
1967-68	2	W 3-1	D 1-1
1969-70	2	W 3-2	L 0-2
1970-71	2	W 2-0	L 0-3
1971-72	2	D 1-1	D 0-0
1972-73	2	L 1-3	W 1-0
1987-88	LC2	W 2-1	D 0-0
1988-89	1	L 1-2	L 2-3
1989-90	1	D 0-0	W 2-1

New Brighton

Season	Div	Home	Away
1933-34	FA2	D 1-1	W 4-0

Newcastle United

Football League

Season	Div	Home	Away
1968-69	1	D 1-1	L 2-3
1973-74	1	W 3-2	W 3-2
1974-75	1	L 1-2	D 2-2
	LC3	L 0-4	
1975-76	1	W 1-0	W 2-1
	LC4	L 1-3	
	FA3	D 0-0	L 1-2
1976-77	1	L 1-2	L 0-2
1977-78	1	L 0-1	W 3-0
1979-80	2	W 2-1	L 2-4
1980-81	2	L 1-2	L 0-1
1981-82	2	W 3-0	W 4-0
1982-83	2	W 2-0	L 0-1
1984-85	1	D 5-5	L 0-1
1985-86	1	W 3-1	L 1-3
1986-87	1	W 2-1	W 2-0
1987-88	1	D 1-1	D 1-1
1988-89	1	W 3-0	W 2-1

Newport County

Southern League

Season	Div	Home	Away
1919-20	1st	W 1-0	L 0-3
Football League			
1920-21	3	W 2-0	W 3-1
1921-22	3S	W 2-1	W 1-0
1922-23	3S	D 1-1	L 0-1
1923-24	3S	L 0-3	L 1-2
1924-25	3S	W 4-3	D 0-0
1925-26	3S	L 0-2	L 1-4
1926-27	3S	W 2-0	W 2-0
1927-28	3S	W 4-2	W 6-1
1928-29	3S	D 0-0	D 0-0
1929-30	3S	W 4-1	W 5-4
1930-31	3S	W 7-1	W 3-2
1932-33	3S	W 6-1	L 1-5
1933-34	3S	W 2-1	W 2-1
1934-35	3S	W 4-1	L 1-2
1935-36	3S	D 1-1	W 4-3
1936-37	3S	W 6-2	W 2-1
1937-38	3S	D 0-0	D 1-1
1938-39	3S	D 0-0	L 0-2
1947-48	3S	W 1-0	D 0-0
1952-53	3S	W 4-2	L 0-2
1953-54	3S	W 5-1	L 1-2
1954-55	3S	W 2-0	L 0-4
1955-56	3S	D 0-0	L 1-2
1956-57	3S	D 1-1	D 1-1
1957-58	3S	D 1-1	L 2-4
1958-59	3	W 4-2	L 1-3
1959-60	3	W 3-0	W 3-2
1960-61	3	W 2-0	W 3-1
1961-62	3	W 4-0	W 4-2
1962-63	FA1	W 3-2	

Northampton Town

Southern League

Season	Div	Home	Away
1901-02	1st	L 5-1	L 1-4
1902-03	1st	D 0-0	D 1-1
1903-04	1st	W 4-1	L 1-2
1904-05	1st	L 1-2	D 1-1
1905-06	1st	W 6-1	D 1-1
1906-07	1st	W 5-0	W 2-1
1907-08	1st	L 2-3	W 2-1
1908-09	1st	D 1-1	D 0-0
1909-10	1st	W 2-0	D 0-0
1910-11	1st	D 1-1	D 0-0
1911-12	1st	W 2-1	L 1-5
1912-13	1st	W 3-2	D 0-0
1913-14	1st	D 0-0	D 2-2
1914-15	1st	D 0-0	D 1-1
1919-20	1st	W 5-1	L 0-2
Football League			
1920-21	3	L 1-2	W 3-0
1921-22	3S	W 4-0	L 0-1
1922-23	3S	W 3-2	L 2-4
1923-24	3S	W 3-2	L 0-3
1924-25	3S	W 2-0	L 0-1
1925-26	3S	W 3-2	L 2-3
1926-27	3S	W 4-2	L 0-1
1927-28	3S	L 0-4	L 0-1
1928-29	3S	W 4-1	L 2-4
1929-30	3S	L 0-2	L 1-2
1930-31	3S	L 0-2	L 0-6
1931-32	3S	W 3-2	L 1-6
1932-33	3S	D 1-1	L 1-2
1933-34	3S	W 2-1	L 1-2
1934-35	3S	W 3-1	L 0-1
1935-36	3S	L 0-1	W 4-1
1936-37	3S	W 3-2	W 1-0
1937-38	3S	D 1-1	W 2-0
1938-39	3S	W 3-0	L 0-1
1945-46	3SN	W 4-1	W 2-0
1946-47	3S	W 1-0	D 4-4
1947-48	3S	W 2-0	D 1-1
1952-53	3S	D 2-2	L 2-4
1953-54	3S	D 1-1	L 1-2
1954-55	3S	W 1-0	W 3-1
1955-56	3S	W 3-2	L 2-5
1956-57	3S	W 1-0	L 0-3
1957-58	3S	W 1-0	W 5-1
1961-62	3	W 2-0	D 1-1
1962-63	3	L 1-3	L 0-1

Norwich City

Southern League

Season	Div	Home	Away
1905-06	1st	D 0-0	L 0-4
1906-07	1st	D 1-1	L 0-1
1907-08	1st	W 3-1	W 1-0
1908-09	1st	D 2-2	L 2-3
1909-10	1st	W 1-0	D 0-0
	FA1	W 3-0	D 0-0
1910-11	1st	D 1-1	D 0-0
1911-12	1st	L 1-2	D 1-1
1912-13	1st	W 1-0	L 0-2
1913-14	1st	D 1-1	W 3-2
1914-15	1st	D 1-1	L 1-2
1919-20	1st	W 1-0	L 1-3
Football League			
1920-21	3	W 2-0	L 0-2
1921-22	3S	W 2-0	D 0-0
1922-23	3S	W 2-0	D 1-1
1923-24	3S	W 2-1	L 0-5
1924-25	3S	L 1-2	L 0-5
1925-26	3S	L 0-1	D 1-1
1926-27	3S	W 4-0	W 1-0
1927-28	3S	D 0-0	L 1-3
1928-29	3S	W 3-0	L 1-3
1929-30	3S	W 3-2	L 0-3
1930-31	3S	W 3-1	D 1-1
1931-32	3S	D 2-2	L 1-2
1932-33	3S	D 2-2	L 2-3
1933-34	3S	W 5-2	L 0-1
Regional League			
1939-40	D	D 0-0	L 1-3
Football League			
1945-46	3SN	L 1-2	D 1-1
1946-47	3S	D 1-1	W 1-0
	FA2	W 2-0	D 4-4
1947-48	3S	W 3-1	L 2-5
1952-53	3S	W 3-1	L 0-2
1953-54	3S	L 0-2	D 2-2
1954-55	3S	W 2-1	D 1-1
1955-56	3S	L 2-3	L 0-1
1956-57	3S	W 3-1	W 2-1
1957-58	3S	D 1-1	L 0-2
1958-59	3	W 2-1	L 1-5
1959-60	3	D 0-0	L 0-1
1967-68	2	W 2-0	D 0-0
1969-70	2	W 4-0	L 0-1
1970-71	2	L 0-1	L 0-3
1971-72	2	D 0-0	D 0-0
1973-74	1	L 1-2	D 0-0
1975-76	1	W 2-0	L 2-3
1976-77	1	L 2-3	L 0-2
1977-78	1	W 2-1	D 1-1
1978-79	1	D 0-0	D 1-1
1981-82	2	W 2-0	W 1-0
1983-84	1	W 2-0	W 3-0
1984-85	1	D 2-2	L 0-2
1986-87	1	D 1-1	L 0-1
1987-88	1	W 3-0	D 1-1
1988-89	1	D 1-1	L 0-1
1989-90	1	W 2-1	D 0-0
1990-91	1	L 1-3	L 0-1
1991-92	1	L 0-2	W 1-0
	ZD2		W 2-1
1992-93	P	W 3-1	L 1-2

Notts County

Season	Div	Home	Away
1923-24	FA1	L 1-2	
Football League			
1930-31	3S	W 4-1	L 0-2
1935-36	3S	D 2-2	L 0-3
1936-37	3S	L 0-2	W 2-1
1937-38	3S	W 2-1	D 2-2
1938-39	3S	L 0-1	D 0-0
1945-46	3SN	W 6-0	W 1-0
	WC	W 3-1	W 3-0
1946-47	3S	W 4-1	W 2-1
1947-48	3S	W 4-1	D 1-1
1950-51	2	W 1-0	D 3-3
1951-52	2	L 1-4	D 0-0
1958-59	3	W 2-1	W 1-0
1960-61	3	W 2-0	L 1-2
1961-62	3	W 2-0	D 0-0
1962-63	3	L 0-1	L 2-3
1963-64	3	W 3-2	D 2-2
1974-75	FA4	W 3-0	
1979-80	2	L 1-3	L 0-1
1980-81	2	D 1-1	L 1-2
	LC3		L 1-4
1983-84	1	W 1-0	W 3-0
1991-92	1	D 1-1	W 1-0

Nottingham Forest

Season	Div	Home	Away
1933-34	FA3		L 0-4
Football League			
1948-49	2	W 2-1	D 0-0
1951-52	2	W 4-3	L 1-3
1961-62	LC2	L 1-2	
1968-69	1	W 2-1	L 0-1
1972-73	2	W 3-0	D 0-0
1977-78	1	L 0-2	L 0-1
	FA5	D 1-1	D 1-1
Replay			L 1-3
1978-79	1	D 0-0	D 0-0
1983-84	1	L 0-1	L 2-3
1984-85	1	W 3-0	L 0-2
1985-86	1	W 2-1	L 0-4
	LC4	W 3-1	
1986-87	1	W 3-1	L 0-1
1987-88	1	W 2-1	L 0-4
1988-89	1	L 1-2	D 0-0
	LC5		L 2-5
1989-90	1	W 2-0	D 2-2
1990-91	1	L 1-2	D 1-1
1991-92	1	L 0-2	D 1-1
1992-93	P	W 4-3	L 0-1

Nuneaton Borough

Season	Div	Home	Away
1953-54	FA2	D 1-1	W 2-1

Oldham Athletic

Football League

Season	Div	Home	Away
1963-64	3	W 3-2	L 1-2
1964-65	3	D 1-1	L 3-5
1965-66	3	D 1-1	W 2-0
1966-67	3	L 0-1	W 1-0
1979-80	2	W 4-3	D 0-0
1980-81	2	W 2-0	L 0-1
1981-82	2	D 0-0	L 0-2
1982-83	2	W 1-0	W 1-0
1991-92	1	L 1-3	L 1-2
1992-93	P	W 3-2	D 2-2

Oxford United

Football League

Season	Div	Home	Away
1965-66	3	L 2-3	W 3-1
1966-67	3	W 3-1	L 1-2
1967-68	LC3	W 5-0	
1969-70	2	L 1-2	D 0-0
1970-71	2	W 2-0	W 3-1
1971-72	2	W 4-2	L 1-3
1972-73	2	D 0-0	L 0-2
	FA4		W 2-0
1985-86	1	W 3-1	D 3-3
	LCF		L 0-3
1986-87	1	D 1-1	W 1-0
1987-88	1	W 3-2	L 0-2

Partizan Belgrade

Season	Div	Home	Away
1984-85	UE2	W 6-2	L 0-4

Peterborough United

Football League

Season	Div	Home	Away
1961-62	3	D 3-3	L 1-5
1962-63	3	D 0-0	W 2-1
1963-64	3	W 3-0	L 1-2
1964-65	4	W 3-2	L 1-6
	FA2	D 3-3	L 1-2
1965-66	3	W 2-1	D 1-1
1966-67	3	D 0-0	W 2-0
1968-69	LC1		L 2-4
1990-91	LC2	W 3-1	D 1-1

Plymouth Argyle

Southern League

Season	Div	Home	Away
1903-04	1st	W 1-0	D 1-1
1904-05	1st	W 2-1	L 1-3
1905-06	1st	W 2-0	D 1-1
1906-07	1st	D 0-0	L 1-2

Plymouth continued...

Season	Div	Home	Away
1907-08	1st	D 0-0	D 1-1
1908-09	1st	W 1-0	L 0-2
1909-10	1st	W 2-1	W 2-0
1910-11	1st	W 1-0	D 1-1
1911-12	1st	W 2-0	W 1-0
1912-13	1st	W 2-1	L 0-2
1913-14	1st	D 0-0	L 0-2
1914-15	1st	D 1-1	D 1-1
1919-20	1st	W 1-0	D 0-0
Football League			
1920-21	3	W 4-0	L 0-1
1921-22	3S	W 2-0	L 0-4
1922-23	3S	L 2-3	L 0-2
1923-24	3S	W 3-2	L 0-2
1924-25	3S	L 0-1	L 0-1
1925-26	3S	L 0-4	L 1-3
1926-27	3S	W 4-2	L 0-2
1927-28	3S	L 0-1	L 0-3
1928-29	3S	W 2-0	W 2-1
1929-30	3S	L 1-2	L 0-4
1948-49	2	W 2-1	L 1-3
1949-50	2	L 0-2	W 2-0
1956-57	3S	W 3-0	W 2-1
1957-58	3S	W 1-0	L 1-3
1958-59	3	W 2-1	L 2-3
1967-68	2	W 4-1	W 1-0
1973-74	LC4	L 0-3	

Poole Town

Season	Div	Home	Away
1946-47	FA1	D 2-2	W 6-0
1966-67	FA1	W 3-2	

Portsmouth

Season	Div	Home	Away
Southern League			
1899-1900	1st	L 2-4	L 1-5
1900-01	1st	W 3-2	D 1-1
1901-02	1st	D 1-1	L 0-1
1902-03	1st	W 4-3	L 1-2
1903-04	1st	W 6-1	D 0-0
1904-05	1st	W 2-0	L 1-4
1905-06	1st	W 2-0	D 0-0
1906-07	1st	L 2-3	D 2-2
1907-08	1st	W 3-2	L 0-1
1908-09	1st	D 0-0	L 1-3
1909-10	1st	L 3-5	L 0-4
1910-11	1st	W 1-0	D 1-1
1912-13	1st	D 1-1	D 1-1
1913-14	1st	W 1-0	D 1-1
1914-15	1st	L 1-2	D 1-1
London Combination			
1916-17	1st	L 1-7	W 3-2
Southern League			
1919-20	1st	D 1-1	L 2-4
Football League			
1920-21	3	D 0-0	D 0-0
1921-22	3S	D 1-1	L 0-1
1922-23	3S	L 0-1	D 1-1
1923-24	3S	L 0-2	L 0-7
Regional League			
1939-40	B	W 5-2	L 1-2
London War League			
1941-42		L 0-2	L 1-3
Football League			
1943-44	Sth	D 1-1	D 1-1
1944-45	Sth	W 1-0	L 1-4
1961-62	3	L 0-1	L 1-4
1967-68	2	W 2-0	D 1-1
1969-70	2	W 2-0	W 3-1
1970-71	2	W 2-0	L 0-2
1971-72	2	D 1-1	L 0-1
1972-73	2	W 5-0	W 1-0
1981-82	LC2	W 5-0	D 2-2
1987-88	1	W 2-1	W 1-0

Port Vale

Season	Div	Home	Away
Football League			
1938-39	3S	D 2-2	W 2-1
1945-46	3SN	W 4-1	D 0-0
	WC	W 4-2	W 2-0
1946-47	3S	W 2-0	D 2-2
1947-48	3S	W 2-1	W 2-0
1953-54	FA3	L 0-1	
1957-58	3S	W 2-1	L 1-2
1959-60	3	D 2-2	D 0-0
	FA2	D 3-3	L 1-2
1960-61	3	W 1-0	W 1-0
	LC1	D 2-2	L 1-3
1961-62	3	W 2-1	W 3-2
1962-63	3	W 3-1	L 2-3
1963-64	3	W 3-0	L 0-2
1964-65	3	W 3-1	D 0-0

Preston North End

Season	Div	Home	Away
Football League			
1949-50	2	D 0-0	L 2-3
1950-51	2	L 1-4	L 0-1
1962-63	LC1	L 1-2	
1967-68	2	W 2-0	W 2-0
	FA3	L 1-3	
1969-70	2	D 0-0	D 0-0
1971-72	2	W 2-1	D 1-1
1972-73	2	W 3-0	D 1-1
1978-79	LC2		W 3-1
1979-80	2	D 1-1	W 3-0
1980-81	2	D 1-1	L 2-3

Reading

Season	Div	Home	Away
Southern League			
1899-1900	1st	L 1-2	L 0-2
1900-01	1st	D 0-0	L 0-3
1901-02	1st	W 1-0	L 1-7
1902-03	1st	L 1-3	L 0-1
1903-04	1st	D 1-1	D 1-1
1904-05	1st	W 4-2	L 0-3
1905-06	1st	W 3-0	L 0-1
1906-07	1st	L 0-1	D 0-0
1907-08	1st	W 1-0	W 3-0
	FA1	W 1-0	
1908-09	1st	L 2-3	L 0-2
1909-10	1st	W 1-0	D 0-0
1911-12	1st	W 3-0	W 1-0
1912-13	1st	D 1-1	L 0-1
1913-14	1st	W 1-0	W 1-0
1914-15	1st	L 0-1	D 2-2
London Combination			
1915-16	Sec	L 2-6	L 2-1
Southern League			
1919-20	1st	D 0-0	W 1-0
Football League			
1920-21	3	W 2-0	D 0-0
1921-22	3S	D 1-1	W 1-0
1922-23	3S	W 1-0	D 0-0
1923-24	3S	L 1-4	L 0-4
1924-25	3S	W 1-0	L 1-2
1925-26	3S	L 1-2	L 1-2
1931-32	3S	W 2-0	L 2-3
1932-33	3S	L 0-3	L 1-3
1933-34	3S	D 0-0	L 0-5
1934-35	3S	W 2-0	D 0-0
1935-36	3S	L 0-1	W 2-1
1936-37	3S	D 0-0	L 0-2
1937-38	3S	W 3-0	L 0-1
1938-39	3S	D 2-2	W 4-2
Regional League			
1939-40	B	W 3-0	L 0-2
	D	W 2-1	L 1-4
Football League			
1940-41	Sth	W 4-1	L 0-2
London War League			
1941-42		W 4-0	D 2-2
Football League			
1942-43	Sth	W 3-2	W 2-1
1943-44	Sth	W 2-0	D 0-0
1944-45	Sth	W 5-1	D 1-1
1946-47	3S	W 2-0	L 0-1
1947-48	3S	W 2-0	L 2-3
1952-53	3S	W 1-0	L 0-2
1953-54	3S	W 2-0	L 1-3
1954-55	3S	L 2-3	L 1-3
1955-56	3S	D 3-3	L 1-3
1956-57	3S	D 1-1	L 0-1
1957-58	3S	W 3-0	L 0-3
1958-59	3	W 2-0	D 2-2
1959-60	3	W 2-0	L 0-2
1960-61	3	W 5-2	L 1-3
1961-62	3	L 3-6	W 2-0
1962-63	3	W 3-2	D 1-1
1963-64	3	W 4-2	W 2-1
1964-65	3	L 0-1	L 3-5
	LC2		L 0-4
1965-66	3	L 0-2	L 1-2
1966-67	3	W 2-1	D 2-2
1987-88	SC1	L 1-3	

Rochdale

Season	Div	Home	Away
Football League			
1958-59	3	W 3-0	D 2-2

Rotherham United

Season	Div	Home	Away
Football League			
1951-52	2	L 2-3	L 0-1
1967-68	2	W 6-0	W 3-1
1981-82	2	D 1-1	L 0-1
1982-83	2	W 4-0	D 0-0
	LC2	D 0-0	L 1-2

Scunthorpe United

Season	Div	Home	Away
1931-32	FA2		W 4-1
Football League			
1964-65	3	W 2-1	L 1-2
1965-66	3	W 1-0	W 2-1
1966-67	3	W 5-1	W 2-0

Sheffield United

Season	Div	Home	Away
1922-23	FA4	L 0-1	
Football League			
1949-50	2	L 1-3	D 1-1
1950-51	2	W 2-1	L 0-2
1951-52	2	W 4-2	W 2-1
1969-70	2	W 2-1	L 0-2
1970-71	2	D 2-2	D 1-1
1973-74	1	D 0-0	D 1-1
1974-75	1	W 1-0	D 1-1
1975-76	1	W 1-0	D 0-0
1990-91	1	L 1-2	L 0-1
1991-92	1	W 1-0	D 0-0
1992-93	P	W 3-2	W 2-1

Sheffield Wednesday

Season	Div	Home	Away
Football League			
1948-49	2	L 1-3	L 0-2
1949-50	2	D 0-0	L 0-1
1951-52	2	D 2-2	L 1-2
1966-67	FA3		L 0-3
1968-69	1	W 3-2	L 0-4
1970-71	2	W 1-0	L 0-1
1971-72	2	W 3-0	D 0-0
1972-73	2	W 4-2	L 1-3
1973-74	LC3	W 8-2	
1980-81	2	L 1-2	L 0-1
1981-82	2	W 2-0	W 3-1
1982-83	2	L 0-2	W 1-0
1984-85	1	D 0-0	L 1-3
1985-86	1	D 1-1	D 0-0
1986-87	1	D 2-2	L 1-7
1987-88	1	D 1-1	L 1-3
1988-89	1	W 2-0	W 2-0
	SC3		W 1-0
1989-90	1	W 1-0	L 0-2
1991-92	1	D 1-1	L 1-4
1992-93	P	W 3-1	L 0-1
	LC4		L 0-4

Sheppey United

Season	Div	Home	Away
Southern League			
1899-1900	1st	L 2-3	L 1-3

Shrewsbury Town

Season	Div	Home	Away
Football League			
1952-53	3S	W 1-0	W 3-0
	FA1	D 2-2	D 2-2
Replay			L 1-4
1953-54	3S	D 0-0	D 1-1
	FA1	W 2-0	
1954-55	3S	W 2-0	L 0-1
1955-56	3S	D 1-1	D 1-1
1956-57	3S	W 2-1	D 0-0
1957-58	3S	W 3-0	L 1-2
1959-60	3	D 1-1	D 1-1
1960-61	3	D 1-1	L 1-4
1961-62	3	W 3-1	W 2-1
1962-63	3	D 0-0	W 3-0
1963-64	3	L 3-4	W 2-1
1964-65	3	W 2-1	L 2-3
1965-66	3	W 2-1	D 0-0
	FA3	D 0-0	L 0-1
1966-67	3	D 2-2	D 0-0
1975-76	LC2		W 4-1
1976-77	FA3	W 2-1	
1979-80	2	W 2-1	L 0-3
1980-81	2	D 0-0	D 3-3
1981-82	2	W 2-1	L 1-2
1982-83	2	W 4-0	D 0-0

SK Brann

Season	Div	Home	Away
1976-77	UE1	W 4-0	W 7-0

Slovan Bratislava

Season	Div	Home	Away
1976-77	UE2	W 5-2	D 3-3

Southampton

Season	Div	Home	Away
Southern League			
1899-1900	1st	W 1-0	L 1-5
1900-01	1st	L 0-1	L 1-5
1901-02	1st	L 0-1	L 2-4
1902-03	1st	D 0-0	L 0-2
1903-04	1st	L 0-3	L 1-2
1904-05	1st	D 1-1	W 1-0
1905-06	1st	L 0-3	L 1-2
1906-07	1st	L 1-2	W 3-0
1907-08	1st	W 3-0	L 2-5
1908-09	1st	L 1-2	W 4-1
1909-10	1st	D 1-1	D 1-1
1910-11	1st	W 3-1	L 0-1
1911-12	1st	D 1-1	D 0-0
1912-13	1st	W 1-0	W 1-0
1913-14	1st	W 3-1	W 2-0
1914-15	1st	W 4-3	L 0-3
London Combination			
1916-17	1st	W 4-0	L 1-2
Southern League			
1919-20	1st	W 2-1	L 1-2
Football League			
1920-21	3	D 0-0	D 2-2
1921-22	3S	D 2-2	D 1-1
Regional League			
1939-40	B	W 4-1	W 2-1
Football League			
1942-43	Sth	W 3-1	L 2-4
	WC	W 2-1	L 1-4
1943-44	Sth	W 7-0	D 2-2
1944-45	Sth	L 4-5	W 5-4
1945-46	FA4	W 4-3	W 1-0
1948-49	2	L 1-3	L 0-3
1949-50	2	W 1-0	W 2-1
1950-51	2	W 2-0	D 2-2
1951-52	2	W 2-1	D 1-1
1953-54	3S	L 0-1	L 1-3
1954-55	3S	D 2-2	D 2-2
1955-56	3S	W 4-0	L 0-4
1956-57	3S	L 1-2	W 2-1
1957-58	3S	W 3-2	L 0-5
1958-59	3	D 2-2	L 0-1
	FA2	L 0-1	
1959-60	3	L 0-1	L 1-2
1968-69	1	D 1-1	L 2-3
1973-74	1	D 1-1	D 2-2
1978-79	1	L 0-1	D 1-1
1983-84	1	W 4-0	D 0-0
1984-85	1	L 0-4	D 1-1
	LC4	D 0-0	D 1-1
Replay		W 4-0	
1985-86	1	L 0-2	L 0-3
1986-87	1	W 2-1	L 1-5
1987-88	1	W 3-0	W 1-0
1988-89	1	L 0-1	W 4-1
1989-90	1	L 1-4	W 2-0
1990-91	1	W 2-1	L 1-3
	ZD2		L 0-4
1991-92	1	D 2-2	L 1-2
	FA3		L 0-2
1992-93	P	W 3-1	W 2-1

Southend United

Season	Div	Home	Away
Southern League			
1908-09	1st	W 2-1	D 0-0
1909-10	1st	D 2-2	W 1-0
	FA2	W 3-2	D 0-0
1910-11	1st	D 1-1	W 2-1
1913-14	1st	D 0-0	W 2-1
1914-15	1st	W 4-2	D 1-1
1919-20	1st	D 2-2	D 2-2
Football League			
1920-21	3	W 2-0	L 0-1
1921-22	3S	W 1-0	W 2-1
1922-23	3S	W 1-0	L 0-2
1923-24	3S	D 0-0	L 2-4
1924-25	3S	W 3-1	L 0-1
1925-26	3S	D 2-2	L 1-2
1926-27	3S	W 3-2	W 3-0
1927-28	3S	W 3-2	L 0-7
1928-29		W 3-1	W 3-0
1929-30	3S	L 2-5	L 0-1
1930-31	3S	L 0-2	L 0-2
1931-32	3S	W 2-1	D 0-0
1932-33	3S	W 6-1	W 1-0
1933-34	3S	W 4-0	W 2-0
1934-35	3S	D 1-1	L 0-2
1935-36	3S	W 2-1	W 1-0
1936-37	3S	W 7-2	W 2-3
1937-38	3S	W 1-0	L 1-2
1938-39	3S	D 1-1	L 1-2
Regional League			
1939-40	D	W 3-1	W 1-0
	WC		L 0-1
Football League			
1945-46	3SN	W 4-1	W 2-1
	WC	W 4-0	D 0-0
1946-47	3S	W 1-0	W 3-1
1947-48	3S	W 3-2	D 0-0
1952-53	3S	W 3-2	L 0-2
1953-54	3S	W 1-0	L 1-4
1954-55	3S	D 1-1	D 2-2
1955-56	3S	L 1-2	L 1-5

Southend United continued...

Season	Div	Home	Away
1955-56	FA1		L 0-2
1956-57	3S	W 3-0	L 0-3
1957-58	3S	D 1-1	L 0-6
1958-59	3	L 1-3	L 0-4
1959-60	3	D 0-0	L 2-3
1960-61	3	W 2-1	D 0-0
1961-62	3	W 5-3	W 3-2
1962-63	3	W 1-0	W 3-1
1963-64	3	L 4-5	W 3-1
1964-65	3	W 2-0	D 0-0
1965-66	3	W 2-1	W 3-1
1974-75	FA3	W 2-0	D 2-2

South Liverpool

Season	Div	Home	Away
1936-37	FA2		W 1-0

South Shields

Season	Div	Home	Away
1922-23	FA3	W 3-0	
1969-70	FA3	W 4-1	

Stockport County

Season	Div	Home	Away
1924-25	FA1	L 1-3	

Football League

Season	Div	Home	Away
1958-59	3	D 0-0	W 3-2
1989-90	LC2	W 2-1	D 0-0

Stoke City

Southern League

Season	Div	Home	Away
1911-12	1st	W 1-0	W 2-0
1912-13	1st	W 1-0	D 0-0
1947-48	FA4	W 3-0	

Football League

Season	Div	Home	Away
1968-69	1	W 2-1	D 1-1
1973-74	1	D 3-3	L 1-4
1974-75	1	L 0-1	L 0-1
1975-76	1	W 3-2	W 1-0
1976-77	1	W 2-0	L 0-1
1983-84	1	W 6-0	W 2-1
1984-85	1	W 2-0	W 2-0

Sunderland

Season	Div	Home	Away
1956-57	FA3		L 0-4

Football League

Season	Div	Home	Away
1968-69	1	D 2-2	D 0-0
1970-71	2	W 2-0	L 1-3
1971-72	2	W 2-1	W 1-0
1972-73	2	W 3-2	W 3-0
1976-77	1	W 2-0	L 0-1
1979-80	2	D 0-0	L 0-3
1983-84	1	W 3-0	L 0-1
1984-85	1	W 1-0	L 0-3
1990-91	1	W 3-2	W 1-0

Swansea City

Season	Div	Home	Away
1913-14	FA2		W 2-1

Southern League

Season	Div	Home	Away
1919-20	1st	W 2-0	L 1-3

Football League

Season	Div	Home	Away
1920-21	3	D 1-1	W 3-1
1921-22	3S	W 1-0	L 0-1
1922-23	3S	W 2-1	L 0-3
1923-24	3S	D 2-2	L 0-2
1924-25	3S	D 0-0	L 0-2
1947-48	3S	D 0-0	L 1-3
1949-50	2	D 0-0	W 1-0
1950-51	2	D 1-1	L 0-1
1951-52	2	D 1-1	W 3-2
1962-63	FA3		L 0-2
1965-66	3	W 6-2	L 2-4
1966-67	3	W 4-2	W 3-1
	LC3	W 2-1	
1978-79	LC3	W 2-0	
1979-80	2	W 3-2	W 2-1
1980-81	2	D 0-0	W 2-1

(until 1970 known as Swansea Town)

Swindon Town

Southern League

Season	Div	Home	Away
1899-1900	1st	L 3-5	L 0-4
1900-01	1st	W 7-1	L 2-4
1901-02	1st	W 4-0	W 3-0
1902-03	1st	W 2-0	L 0-2
1903-04	1st	W 1-0	D 1-1
1904-05	1st	W 4-1	D 0-0
1905-06	1st	W 3-0	W 2-1
1906-07	1st	W 6-1	D 0-0
1907-08	1st	W 2-1	L 3-8
	FA2		L 1-2
1908-09	1st	W 5-1	L 1-3
1909-10	1st	L 0-3	L 0-1
1910-11	1st	W 1-0	L 1-2
1911-12	1st	L 1-3	D 1-1
1912-13	1st	W 2-0	L 1-4
1913-14	1st	W 4-2	L 0-3
1914-15	1st	W 4-2	W 2-1
1919-20	1st	W 2-1	L 2-5

Football League

Season	Div	Home	Away
1920-21	3	W 1-0	W 1-0
1921-22	3S	D 0-0	L 0-2
1922-23	3S	L 0-2	L 0-1
1923-24	3S	D 2-2	D 0-0
1924-25	3S	W 1-0	L 3-5
1925-26	3S	D 1-1	L 0-2
1926-27	3S	L 0-1	L 2-6
1927-28	3S	L 0-1	W 2-0
1928-29	3S	W 4-2	L 1-2
1929-30	3S	W 8-3	D 2-2
1930-31	3S	L 1-2	L 1-4
1931-32	3S	L 1-2	W 2-1
1932-33	3S	W 4-2	D 0-0
1933-34	3S	W 1-0	L 1-3
1934-35	3S	D 1-1	L 1-3
1935-36	3S	W 5-1	D 2-2
1936-37	3S	D 1-1	D 1-1
1937-38	3S	W 3-0	W 3-1
	FA2		L 1-2
1938-39	3S	W 2-1	D 2-2
1946-47	3S	W 7-0	L 2-3
1947-48	3S	L 0-2	D 0-0
1952-53	3S	D 1-1	W 3-1
1953-54	3S	L 0-2	W 1-0
1954-55	3S	W 3-1	L 0-2
1955-56	3S	W 1-0	W 1-0
1956-57	3S	W 3-0	L 0-1
1957-58	3S	W 2-1	D 1-1
1958-59	3	W 2-1	L 0-2
1959-60	3	W 2-0	L 1-2
1960-61	3	W 3-1	L 0-1
1961-62	3	W 6-1	D 0-0
1962-63	3	D 2-2	L 0-5
1965-66	3	W 3-2	L 1-2
1966-67	3	W 3-1	D 1-1
1969-70	2	W 2-0	D 0-0
1970-71	2	W 4-2	L 0-1
	FA3	L 1-2	
1971-72	2	W 3-0	D 0-0
1972-73	2	W 5-0	D 2-2
1992-93	FA3	W 3-0	

Thames

Football League

Season	Div	Home	Away
1930-31	3S	W 3-0	L 0-1
	FA1	W 5-0	
1931-32	3S	W 6-0	L 2-3

Tooting & Mitcham

Season	Div	Home	Away
1956-57	FA2		W 2-0

Torquay United

Football League

Season	Div	Home	Away
1927-28	3S	L 2-3	L 0-1
1928-29	3S	W 5-1	W 4-3
1929-30	3S	D 1-1	W 3-1
1930-31	3S	L 1-2	L 2-6
1931-32	3S	W 3-1	W 3-2
1932-33	3S	D 1-1	L 1-3
	FA2	W 3-1	D 1-1
1933-34	3S	W 2-0	D 1-1
1934-35	3S	W 5-1	L 0-7
1935-36	3S	W 2-1	L 2-4
1936-37	3S	W 3-0	D 1-1
1937-38	3S	W 6-3	W 2-0
1938-39	3S	D 1-1	W 3-2
1946-47	3S	D 0-0	D 0-0
1947-48	3S	D 3-3	D 1-1
1952-53	3S	L 0-1	D 1-1
1953-54	3S	W 5-1	D 2-2
1954-55	3S	W 4-2	L 2-3
1955-56	3S	W 3-1	L 0-2
1956-57	3S	L 0-1	L 0-3
1957-58	3S	D 1-1	L 1-3
1960-61	3	D 3-3	W 6-1
1961-62	3	W 6-0	D 2-2
1966-67	3	W 2-1	D 1-1

Tottenham Hotspur

Southern League

Season	Div	Home	Away
1899-1900	1st	D 0-0	L 0-1
1900-01	1st	W 2-1	L 1-4
1901-02	1st	L 0-3	L 0-2
1902-03	1st	L 0-4	D 0-0
1903-04	1st	W 2-0	D 2-2
1904-05	1st	L 1-2	L 1-5
1905-06	1st	D 0-0	L 1-2
1906-07	1st	W 3-1	L 0-2
1907-08	1st	D 3-3	L 2-3

London Combination

Season	Div	Home	Away
1915-16	Prim	L 0-4	L 1-2
	Sec	L 1-3	D 0-0
1916-17		D 1-1	W 5-4
1917-18		L 2-3	W 1-0
		L 2-7	W 2-1
1918-19		D 1-1	D 0-0
		W 7-1	W 3-2

Football League

Season	Div	Home	Away
1940-41	Sth	D 1-1	W 3-2

London War League

Season	Div	Home	Away
1941-42		W 1-0	L 1-3

Football League

Season	Div	Home	Away
1942-43	Sth	L 0-1	L 0-6
1943-44	Sth	W 1-0	D 2-2
1944-45	Sth	D 0-0	L 2-4
	LC(s)	W 1-0	D 1-1
1948-49	2	D 0-0	L 0-1
1949-50	2	L 0-2	L 0-3
1968-69	1	D 1-1	L 2-3
1973-74	1	W 3-1	D 0-0
	LC2	W 1-0	
1974-75	1	L 0-1	W 2-1
1975-76	1	D 0-0	W 3-0
1976-77	1	W 2-1	L 0-3
1978-79	1	D 2-2	D 1-1
1980-81	FA3	D 0-0	L 1-3
1981-82	FAF		D 1-1
Replay			L 0-1
1983-84	1	W 2-1	L 2-3
1984-85	1	D 2-2	L 0-5
1985-86	1	L 2-5	D 1-1
1986-87	1	W 2-0	L 0-1
1987-88	1	W 2-0	D 1-1
1988-89	1	W 1-0	D 2-2
1989-90	1	W 3-1	L 2-3
1990-91	1	D 0-0	D 0-0
1991-92	1	L 1-2	L 0-2
1992-93	P	W 4-1	L 2-3

Tranmere Rovers

Football League

Season	Div	Home	Away
1958-59	3	D 1-1	L 0-2
1959-60	3	W 2-1	W 3-0
1960-61	3	W 9-2	W 2-1
1969-70	LC3	W 6-0	

Walsall

Football League

Season	Div	Home	Away
1927-28	3S	D 1-1	D 2-2
1928-29	3S	D 2-2	L 1-3
1929-30	3S	D 2-2	L 0-4
1930-31	3S	W 3-0	W 2-0
1936-37	3S	W 2-0	W 4-2
1937-38	3S	W 3-1	W 3-0
1938-39	3S	W 3-0	W 1-0
1939-40	3S		L 0-1
1945-46	3SN	W 4-0	D 1-1
1946-47	3S	W 1-0	W 2-0
1947-48	3S	W 2-1	W 1-0
1952-53	3S	W 4-2	D 1-1
1953-54	3S	W 2-0	L 0-2
1954-55	3S	D 1-1	L 1-4
1955-56	3S	W 3-2	D 2-2
1956-57	3S	W 1-0	W 2-0
1957-58	3S	W 1-0	W 2-1
1958-59	FA1		W 1-0
1960-61	3S	W 1-0	L 3-4
1963-64	3S	W 3-0	W 2-0
1964-65	3S	W 1-0	L 1-4
1965-66	3S	W 2-1	W 1-0
	LC1	D 1-1	L 2-3
1966-67	3S	D 0-0	L 0-2

Walthamstow Avenue

Season	Div	Home	Away
1934-35	FA1	W 2-0	
1954-55	FA1	D 2-2	D 2-2
Replay			L 0-4
1960-61	FA1	W 3-2	

Wandsworth

Season	Div	Home	Away
1899-1900	FAQ		W 7-1

Watford

Southern League

Season	Div	Home	Away
1900-01	1st	W 1-0	W 1-0
	FAQ	W 4-1	D 1-1
1901-02	1st	L 0-1	D 1-1
1902-03	1st	W 3-0	W 2-0
1904-05	1st	L 4-1	L 0-1
1905-06	1st	W 6-0	W 4-3
1906-07	1st	D 0-0	L 0-1
1907-08	1st	D 3-3	W 3-0
1908-09	1st	W 2-0	D 0-0
1909-10	1st	W 4-3	D 1-1
1910-11	1st	W 4-1	L 0-2
1911-12	1st	D 1-1	W 3-0
1912-13	1st	W 2-0	W 2-1
1913-14	1st	W 3-2	L 0-2
1914-15	1st	L 2-5	D 2-2

London Combination

Season	Div	Home	Away
1915-16	Pri	W 3-1	L 1-5
	Sec	D 2-2	L 0-6
1916-17		P-P	L 0-2
		W 2-1	W 2-1

Southern League

Season	Div	Home	Away
1919-20	1st	W 3-0	L 0-1

Football League

Season	Div	Home	Away
1920-21	3	L 1-2	W 2-0
1921-22	3S	D 1-1	D 2-2
1922-23	3S	L 1-2	W 3-0
1923-24	3S	W 2-1	W 2-0
1924-25	3S	D 0-0	L 0-1
1925-26	3S	W 2-0	L 1-3
1926-27	3S	L 2-4	W 2-1
1927-28	3S	W 2-1	D 3-3
1928-29	3S	W 3-2	L 1-4
1929-30	3S	D 0-0	D 1-1
1930-31	3S	L 2-3	W 4-0
1931-32	3S	D 4-4	D 2-2
1932-33	3S	W 2-1	D 2-2
1933-34	3S	D 0-0	D 0-0
1934-35	3S	W 2-1	L 0-2
1935-36	3S	W 3-1	L 1-2
1936-37	3S	L 1-2	L 0-2
1937-38	3S	W 2-0	L 1-3
1938-39	3S	W 1-0	L 1-4
1939-40	3S	D 2-2	

Regional League

Season	Div	Home	Away
	D	W 2-0	D 1-1

Football League

Season	Div	Home	Away
1940-41	Sth	W 4-2	D 3-3

London War League

Season	Div	Home	Away
1941-42		L 1-5	W 5-0

Football League

Season	Div	Home	Away
1943-44	Sth	W 3-1	D 2-2
1945-46	3SN	D 1-1	W 2-0
	WC	W 2-1	W 3-1
1946-47	3S	W 2-1	W 2-0
1947-48	3S	W 5-1	W 1-0
1952-53	3S	D 2-2	D 1-1
1953-54	3S	L 0-4	W 2-0
1954-55	3S	W 2-1	D 1-1
1955-56	3S	W 3-2	W 1-0
1956-57	3S	W 3-1	W 4-2
1957-58	3S	W 3-0	D 0-0
1960-61	3	W 2-1	W 3-0
1961-62	3	L 1-2	L 2-3
1962-63	3	D 2-2	W 5-2
1963-64	3	W 1-0	L 1-3
1964-65	3	D 2-2	W 2-0
1965-66	3	D 1-1	W 2-1
1966-67	3	W 4-1	L 0-1
1969-70	2	W 2-1	W 1-0
1970-71	2	D 1-1	W 2-1
1971-72	2	W 3-0	W 2-0
1979-80	2	D 1-1	W 2-1
	FA3	L 1-2	
1980-81	2	D 0-0	D 1-1
1981-82	2	D 0-0	L 0-4
	LC4		L 1-4
1983-84	1	D 1-1	L 0-1
1984-85	1	W 2-0	D 1-1
1985-86	1	W 2-1	L 0-2
	LC3		W 1-0
1986-87	1	W 3-2	W 3-0
1987-88	1	D 0-0	W 1-0
1988-89	SC4		D 1-1

Wealdstone

Season	Div	Home	Away
1977-78	FA3	W 4-0	

Wellingborough

Southern League

Season	Div	Home	Away
1901-02	1st	W 1-0	L 0-1
1902-03	1st	W 2-0	L 1-2
1903-04	1st	W 3-0	D 1-1
1904-05	1st	L 1-2	W 4-0

West Bromwich Albion

Football League

Season	Div	Home	Away
1948-49	2	L 0-2	D 1-1
1966-67	LCF		W 3-2
1968-69	1	L 0-4	L 1-3
1972-73	LC2		L 1-2
1976-77	1	W 1-0	D 1-1
1977-78	1	W 2-1	L 0-2

Conway Smith scores for Rangers against Walthamstow Avenue in the FA Cup first round at Loftus Road in November 1954.

Above: Rangers on the defence against West Brom in the 1967 League Cup Final. *Below:* Rodney Marsh is in tears after the great Wembley victory. Veteran Jim Langley comforts him.

West Brom continued...

Season	Div	Home	Away
1978-79	1	L 0-1	L 1-2
1981-82	FASF		W 1-0
1982-83	FA3		L 2-3
1983-84	1	D 1-1	W 2-1
1984-85	1	W 3-1	D 0-0
1985-86	1	W 1-0	W 1-0

West Hamstead

Season	Div	Home	Away
1899-1900	FAQ	W 5-0	

West Ham United

Southern League

Season	Div	Home	Away
1899-1900	1st	W 2-0	W 2-1
1900-01	1st	L 0-2	L 1-2
1901-02	1st	W 2-1	L 0-4
1902-03	1st	D 0-0	L 0-2
1903-04	1st	W 2-1	L 0-1
1904-05	1st	W 1-0	W 3-1
1905-06	1st	L 0-1	L 0-2
1906-07	1st	W 2-0	L 1-2
1907-08	1st	W 4-0	L 0-3
1908-09	1st	W 3-0	L 0-2
	FA1	D 0-0	L 0-1
1909-10	1st	D 3-3	W 2-1
	FA3	W 1-0	D 1-1
1910-11	1st	L 0-2	L 0-3
1911-12	1st	W 4-1	L 0-3
1912-13	1st	L 0-1	L 0-1
1913-14	1st	D 2-2	L 1-4
1914-15	1st	D 1-1	D 2-2
London Combination			
1915-16	Pri	D 1-1	L 1-2
1916-17		L 0-4	L 3-5
1917-18		L 0-3	L 0-4
		D 1-1	L 0-4
1918-19		W 1-0	L 1-4
		L 1-3	W 4-0
1938-39	FA3	L 1-2	
Football League			
1940-41	Sth	L 1-5	W 3-2
London War League			
1941-42		W 2-1	L 0-2
Football League			
1942-43	Sth	W 5-2	W 3-1
1943-44	Sth	W 3-0	D 1-1
1944-45	Sth	L 0-1	L 2-4
	WC	D 1-1	L 0-5
1948-49	2	W 2-1	L 0-2
1949-50	2	L 0-1	L 0-1
1950-51	2	D 3-3	L 1-4
1951-52	2	W 2-0	L 2-4
1968-69	1	D 1-1	L 3-4
1973-74	1	D 0-0	W 3-2
1974-75	1	L 0-2	D 2-2
	FA5		L 1-2
1975-76	1	D 1-1	L 0-1
1976-77	1	D 1-1	L 0-1
	LC4		W 2-0
1977-78	1	W 1-0	D 2-2
	FA4	W 6-1	D 1-1
1979-80	2	W 3-0	L 1-2
1980-81	2	W 3-0	L 0-3
1983-84	1	D 1-1	D 2-2
1984-85	1	W 4-2	W 3-1
1985-86	1	L 0-1	L 1-3
1986-87	1	L 2-3	D 1-1
1987-88	1	L 0-1	W 3-0
	FA4	W 3-1	
1988-89	1	W 2-1	D 0-0
1991-92	1	D 0-0	D 2-2

(1899-1900 known as Thames Ironworks)

West Norwood

Season	Div	Home	Away
1901-02	FAQ	W 4-0	

Wigan Borough

Season	Div	Home	Away
1922-23	FA2		W 4-2

Wimbledon

Football League

Season	Div	Home	Away
1986-87	1	W 2-1	D 1-1
1987-88	1	W 1-0	W 2-1
1988-89	1	W 4-3	L 0-1
	LC4	D 0-0	W 1-0
1989-90	1	L 2-3	D 0-0
1990-91	1	L 0-1	L 0-3
1991-92	1	D 1-1	W 1-0
1992-93	P	L 1-2	W 2-0

Wolverhampton Wanderers

Season	Div	Home	Away
1899-1900	FA1	D 1-1	W 1-0
Football League			
1968-69	1	L 0-1	L 1-3
1969-70	LC4	W 3-1	
1973-74	1	D 0-0	W 4-2
1974-75	1	W 2-0	W 2-1
1975-76	1	W 4-2	D 2-2
1977-78	1	L 1-3	L 0-1
1978-79	1	D 3-3	L 0-1
1979-80	LC4	D 1-1	L 0-1
1982-83	2	W 2-1	L 0-4
1983-84	1	W 2-1	W 4-0

Workington

Football League

Season	Div	Home	Away
1964-65	3	W 2-1	D 0-0
1965-66	3	W 4-1	D 1-1
1966-67	3	W 4-1	W 2-0

Wrexham

Football League

Season	Div	Home	Away
1958-59	3	W 5-0	L 0-1
1959-60	3	W 2-1	D 1-1
1962-63	3	L 1-2	L 1-3
1963-64	3	W 1-0	W 1-0
1979-80	2	D 2-2	W 3-1
1980-81	2	L 0-1	D 1-1
1981-82	2	D 1-1	W 3-1

Yeovil Town

Season	Div	Home	Away
1987-88	FA3		W 3-0

York City

Football League

Season	Div	Home	Away
1959-60	3	D 0-0	L 1-2
1965-66	3	W 7-2	D 2-2
1984-85	LC2	W 4-1	W 4-2

1899-1900

Southern League Division 1

Date	Opponent	Result	Scorers	Att	Bedingfield	Clutterbuck	Cowie	Crawford	Evans	Gaylard	Hannah	Haywood	Hitch	Jordan	Keech	Knowles	McConnell	Misslewhite	Skinner	Smith	Tennant	Turnbull	White
Sep 9	(a) Tottenham H	L 0-1		16,000	9	1	11	4				8			6	2	3			7	5	10	
16	(h) New Brompton	W 2-0	Turnbull, Bedingfield	6,300	9	1	11	4				8			6		2		3	7	5	10	
Oct 7	(a) Bristol C	L 3-5	Tennant, Bedingfield, Evans	4,000	10	1		4	11			8	5	7	6	2	3				9		
11	(a) Gravesend U	W 3-1	Bedingfield 2, Haywood	4,000	10	1		4				8	5		6	2	3			7	9	11	
21	(a) Southampton	L 1-5	Crawford	5,000	9	1	11	4				8	5		6	2	3			7		10	
Nov 11	(a) Chatham	L 3-5	Hitch, Cowie, Turnbull	3,000		1	11	4	10			8	5		6	2	3					7	9
25	(a) Sheppey U	L 1-3	Keech	2,000		1	11		9		8		5		6	2	3			4		7	10
Dec 2	(h) Reading	L 1-2	Cowie	6,000		1	11	4	9			8	5			2	3			6		7	10
16	(h) Bristol R	W 3-0	Haywood 2, White	4,000	9	1	11	4		2		8	5				3		6	7			10
23	(a) Portsmouth	L 1-5	Bedingfield	5,000	9	1		4				8	5			2	3		6	7		10	11
25	(h) Thames Iron	W 2-0	Bedingfield 2	5,500	9	1	11	4				8	5			2	3		6			7	10
30	(a) Thames Iron	W 2-1	White, Turnbull	4,000	9	1					11	10	5		6	2	3				4	7	8
Jan 4	(h) Tottenham H	D 0-0		8,000	9	1	7	4			11	8	5		6	2	3						10
13	(a) New Brompton	W 3-0	White 2, Evans	3,000	9	1		4	7		11	8	5		6	2	3						10
20	(h) Gravesend U	W 3-1	White, Bedingfield, Smith	3,000	9	1					11	8	5		6	2	3			7	4		10
Feb 24	(h) Chatham	W 5-3	Tennant 2, Bedingfield 2, White	4,000	10	1		4	11	2			5		6		3			7	9		8
Mar 3	(a) Millwall	W 3-1	Tennant 2, Hannah	6,000	10	1		4		2	11		5		6		3			7	9		8
5	(h) Bristol C	D 1-1	White	4,000	9	1	10	4			11		5		6	2	3			7			8
10	(h) Sheppey U	L 2-3	Bedingfield 2 (1 pen)	3,000	9	1		4			11	8	5		6		2		3	7			10
24	(a) Reading	L 0-2		1,000		1	11	4		2	7	8	5		6		3					10	9
Apr 7	(h) Portsmouth	L 2-4	Bedingfield (pen), Turnbull	3,000	9	1					7	11	5		4	2	3		6			8	10
14	(h) Bedminster	W 2-1	Bedingfield, Turnbull	2,500	9	1		7			11				4	2	3	5	6			10	8
16	(h) Swindon T	L 3-5	Bedingfield 2, Turnbull	3,000	9	1		7			11		5		4	2	3		6			10	8
18	(a) Swindon T	L 0-4		2,000	9	1		7	8		11		5		4	2	3		6			10	
21	(a) Bristol R	L 0-1		2,000	9	1		7	8		11				4	2	3		6		5	10	
23	(h) Millwall	W 2-0	Evans, Hannah	6,000	9	1		7	8		11				4	2	3		6		5	10	
25	(a) Bedminster	L 1-4	Bedingfield	2,000	9	1		7			11				4	2	3		6		5	10	8
28	(h) Southampton	W 1-0	Keech	4,000	9	1		7			11				4	2	3		6		5	10	8
				App	24	28	11	24	9	4	17	17	21	1	24	22	28	1	13	13	12	19	20
				Goals	17		2	1	3		2	3	1		2					1	5	6	7

Brighton United & Cowes withdrew from League

FA Cup

Date	Opponent	Result	Scorers	Att	Bedingfield	Clutterbuck	Cowie	Crawford	Evans	Gaylard	Hannah	Haywood	Hitch	Jordan	Keech	Knowles	McConnell	Misslewhite	Skinner	Smith	Tennant	Turnbull	White	Round
Sep 23	(h) London Welsh	W 4-2	Bedingfield, Smith, Turnbull 2	4,987	9	1	11	4				8			6	2	3			7	5	10		Prel
30	(h) Fulham	W 3-0	Haywood, Bedingfield, Turnbull	5,000	9	1	11	4		2		8			6		3			7	5	10		Q1
Oct 14	(h) West Hampstead	W 5-0	Turnbull 3 (1 pen), Smith, Haywood	6,000	9	1	11	4				8	5		6	2	3			7		10		Q2
28	(a) Wandsworth	W 7-1	Keech 3, Evans 2, Hitch, Haywood	1,000		1	10	4	11			8	5		9	2	3			7	6			Q3
Nov 18	(h) Civil Service	W 3-0	Haywood, Hitch, Turnbull	3,000		1	11		9			8	5	7	6	2	3			4		10		Q4
Dec 9	(a) Luton T	D 1-1	Evans	3,000	9	1		4	11	2		8	5				3		6	7			10	Q5
13	(h) Luton T	W 4-1	Haywood, Bedingfield, White, Smith	2,000	9	1		4	11	2		8	5				3		6	7			10	Rep
Jan 27	(h) Wolves	D 1-1	Haywood	10,000	9	1		4			11	8	5		6	2	3					7	10	1
31	(a) Wolves	W 1-0	Bedingfield	7,000	9	1		4			11	8	5		6	2	3					7	10	Rep
Feb 17	(h) Millwall	L 0-2		12,000	9	1		4			11	8	5		6	2	3			7			10	2
				App	8	10	5	9	4	3	3	10	8	1	8	7	10		2	8	3	6	5	
				Goals	4				3			6	2		3					3		7	1	

Attendance Summary

	ATTENDANCES			AVERAGE		
	Home	Away	Total	Home	Away	Total
League	62,300	59,000	121,300	4,450	4,200	4,350
FA Cup	42,987	11,000	53,987	6,150	3,650	5,400
Total	105,287	70,000	175,287	5,000	4,100	4,600

1900-01

Southern League Division 1

Date		Opponent	Result	Scorers	Att	Bellingham	Christie	Clutterbuck	Cole	Downing	Foxall	Goldie	Gray	Hitch	Humphries	Keech	Lennox	McConnell	Newbigging	Newlands	Pointing	Ronaldson	Skinner	Turnbull
Sep	1	(a) Bristol R	L 1-2	Downing	3,000		9	1	2	8	11		7	5		4		3					6	10
	8	(h) Swindon T	W 7-1	Downing 3, Gray 2, Humphries, Hitch	4,000	2		1		8	11	9	7	5	10	4		3					6	
	15	(a) Reading	L 0-3		4,000	2		1		8	11	9	7	5	10	4		3					6	
	22	(h) Watford	W 1-0	Goldie	5,000	2		1		8	11	9	7	5	10	4					3		6	
	29	(a) Kettering T	L 1-2	Downing	3,000	2	9	1		8		11	7	5	10	4				3			6	
Oct	6	(h) Luton T	L 1-3	Humphries	4,000	2		1		8	11		7	5	10	4		3					6	9
	13	(a) Gravesend U	D 2-2	Gray, Downing	3,000	2		1		8	11		7	5	10	4		3					6	9
	20	(h) Tottenham H	W 2-1	Gray, Humphries	5,000	2		1		8	11		7	5	10	4			9	3			6	
	27	(h) Millwall	L 0-2		5,000	2		1		8	11		7	5	10	4			9	3			6	
Nov	10	(h) Southampton	L 0-1		9,000	2		1			11	9	7	5	10	4			8	3			6	
Dec	1	(a) New Brompton	L 1-2	Ronaldson	2,000	2		1			11		7	5	10			3	8	4		9	6	
	15	(h) Bristol R	W 4-3	Hitch (pen), Ronaldson, Humphries, Downing	8,000			1		8	11		7	5	10	4		3		2		9	6	
	22	(a) Swindon T	L 2-4	Humphries, Keech	4,000			1		8	11		7	5	10	4		3		2		9	6	
	29	(h) Reading	D 0-0		5,000		8	1			11		7	5	10		4	3		2		9	6	
Jan	5	(a) Watford	W 1-0	Skinner	2,000			1			11		7	5	10		4	3	8	2		9	6	
	12	(a) Luton T	D 2-2	Gray, Humphries	3,000			1			11		7	5	10	8	4	3		2		9	6	
	19	(h) Kettering T	W 2-0	Foxall, Humphries	4,000		8	1			11		7	5	10		4	3		2		9	6	
	26	(h) New Brompton	W 2-0	Christie, Humphries	3,000		8	1			11		7	5	10		4	3		2		9	6	
Feb	9	(a) Bristol C	L 0-2		5,000		8	1			11		7	5	10		4	3		2		9	6	
	16	(a) Millwall	W 1-0	Gray	7,000		8	1			11		7	5	10		4	3		2		9	6	
	23	(h) West Ham U	L 0-2		6,000		8	1			11		7	5	10	6	4	3		2		9		
Mar	2	(a) Southampton	L 1-5	Gray	4,000			1		8	11		7	5	10		4	3		2		9	6	
	9	(h) Portsmouth	W 3-2	Ronaldson 2, Gray	5,000	4		1		8	11		7	5	10			3		2		9	6	
	16	(h) Gravesend U	W 4-2	Foxall, Humphries, Hitch, Ronaldson	5,000	4		1		8	11		7	5	10			3		2		9	6	
	23	(h) Bristol C	W 2-0	Ronaldson 2	5,000	4		1		8	11		7	5	10			3		2		9	6	
	30	(a) Tottenham H	L 1-4	Downing	4,000	4		1		8	11		7	5	10			3		2		9	6	
Apr	5	(a) West Ham U	L 1-2	Downing	9,000			1		8	11		7	5	10		4	3		2		9	6	
	27	(a) Portsmouth	D 1-1	Ronaldson	3,000	4		1		8	11		7	5	10			3		2		9	6	
					App	15	8	28	1	18	27	5	28	28	27	14	10	23	5	22	1	18	27	3
					Goals		1			9	2	1	8	3	9	1						8	1	

Chatham withdrew from league

FA Cup

Date		Opponent	Result	Scorers	Att	Bellingham	Christie	Clutterbuck	Cole	Downing	Foxall	Goldie	Gray	Hitch	Humphries	Keech	Lennox	McConnell	Newbigging	Newlands	Pointing	Ronaldson	Skinner	Turnbull	Round
Nov	3	(h) Fulham	W 7-0	Goldie 2, Foxall 2, Downing, Gray, Hitch	4,000	2		1		8	11	9	7	5	10	4				3			6		Q3
	17	(a) Watford	D 1-1	Gray	4,000			1			11	9	7	5	10	4		3	8	2			6		Q4
	21	(h) Watford	W 4-1	Humphries 3, Newbigging	2,000	2		1			11	9	7	5	10			3	8	4			6		Rep
Dec	8	(a) Luton T	L 0-3		5,000			1		8	11	9	7	5	10	4		3		2			6		Q5
					App	2		4		2	4	4	4	4	4	3		3	2	4			4		
					Goals					1	2	2	2	1	3				1						

Attendance Summary

	ATTENDANCES			AVERAGE		
	Home	Away	Total	Home	Away	Total
League	73,000	56,000	129,000	5,200	4,000	4,600
FA Cup	6,000	9,000	15,000	3,000	4,500	3,750
Total	79,000	65,000	144,000	4,950	4,050	4,500

1901-02

Southern League Division 1

Date	Opponent	Res	Score	Scorers	Att	Aston	Bowman	Christie	Collins	Edwards	Evans	Freeman	Handforth	Jordan	Keech	King	Lennox	McKinlay	McQueen	Millar	Newlands	Pryce	Seeley	Stewart	Wheldon	White
Sep 7	(h) Watford	L	0-1		5,000	3	5		1	6		4				7			10	9	2	8	11			
14	(a) Tottenham H	L	0-2		10,000	3			1			5	11	7	4		6		10	9	2	8				
28	(a) Portsmouth	L	0-1		7,000	3	4	8	1	11					6	7			10	9	2					5
Oct 5	(h) Swindon T	W	4-0	Price, Millar, Stewart, McQueen	3,000	3			1			5			4				10	9	2	8	11	7		6
12	(a) Brentford	D	1-1	Millar	3,000	3			1			5	11		4				10	9	2	8		7		6
19	(h) Kettering T	W	2-1	McQueen, Seeley	5,000	3			1			5			4				10	9	2	8	11	7		6
26	(a) Luton T	L	0-1		5,000	3			1			5			4			10	11	9	2	8		7		6
Nov 9	(h) West Ham U	W	2-1	McQueen, Pryce	4,000	3	4		1			5			6				10	9	2	8	11	7		
16	(a) Reading	L	1-7	Millar	5,000	11	5		1			6				7		4	8	9	3				10	2
23	(h) Southampton	L	0-1		6,000		4		1			5			6				10	9	2	8	11	7		3
Dec 7	(h) New Brompton	D	1-1	McQueen	2,300	3			1			5			6	7				9	4	8	10	11		2
21	(a) Watford	D	1-1	Millar	2,300	3			1			5			6					9	4	8	7	11	10	2
28	(h) Tottenham H	L	0-3		12,000	3	4		1			5						6		9		8	7	11	10	2
Jan 4	(a) Wellingborough	L	0-1		1,500	3	4		1			5			6	9			8				7	11	10	2
11	(h) Portsmouth	D	1-1	Stewart	5,000	3	5		1			6				9			8		4		7	11	10	2
18	(a) Swindon T	W	3-0	Aston (pen), King, Wheldon	4,000	3	5		1			6				9			8		4		7	11	10	2
25	(h) Brentford	W	3-2	Newlands, Wheldon, Stewart	2,000	3	5		1			6				9			8		4		7	11	10	2
Feb 1	(a) Kettering T	L	0-3		4,000	3			1			5			6	9			8		4		7	11	10	2
8	(h) Luton T	D	2-2	King, Wheldon	3,000	3	5		1			6				7			8	9	4			11	10	2
15	(h) Millwall	L	0-2		4,000	3	5		1			6		7					8	9	4		11		10	2
22	(a) West Ham U	L	0-4		4,000	3			1			5			6				8	9	4		7	11	10	2
Mar 1	(h) Reading	W	1-0	McQueen	3,000	11			1	6		5			4				8	9	3		7		10	2
8	(a) Southampton	L	2-4	Wheldon, McQueen (pen)	2,000		5		1			6			4				8	9	3		7	11	10	2
15	(h) Bristol R	D	0-0		3,000		4		1	6	9	5	11		10	7					3	8				2
22	(a) Northampton T	L	1-4	Millar	3,000		4		1	6		5				7			10	9	3	8		11		2
27	(a) New Brompton	W	1-0	McQueen	3,000	3	4		1	6		5				7			10	9	2	8		11		
29	(h) Northampton T	W	5-1	McQueen 2, Wheldon 2, Millar	4,000		4		1	6		5				7			8	9	3			11	10	2
Apr 12	(a) Millwall	L	1-6	Millar	4,500	3	4		1	6		5			10	7			8	9				11		2
19	(h) Wellingborough	W	1-0	Seeley	4,000	3	5	8	1	6		4							10	9			7	11		2
30	(a) Bristol R	L	1-4	Edwards	3,000	3	5		1	6		4						8	10	9			7	11		2
					App	25	20	2	30	10	1	29	3	2	17	15	1	4	26	24	25	14	19	23	14	26
					Goals	1				1						2			9	7	1	2	2	3	6	

FA Cup

Date	Opponent	Res	Score	Scorers	Att	Aston	Bowman	Christie	Collins	Edwards	Evans	Freeman	Handforth	Jordan	Keech	King	Lennox	McKinlay	McQueen	Millar	Newlands	Pryce	Seeley	Stewart	Wheldon	White	Round
Nov 2	(h) Crouch End	W	2-0	Stewart, Millar	1,500	3	4		1			5			6				10	9	2	8	11	7			Q3
20	(h) West Norwood	W	4-0	Millar 4	3,000	3	4		1			5			6				10	9	2	8	11	7			Q4
30	(a) Luton T	L	0-2		5,000	3	4		1						6				10	9	2	8	11	7		5	Q5
					App	3	3		3			2			3				3	3	3	3	3	3		1	
					Goals															5				1			

Attendance Summary

	ATTENDANCES			AVERAGE		
	Home	Away	Total	Home	Away	Total
League	65,300	61,300	126,600	4,350	4,100	4,200
FA Cup	4,500	5,000	9,500	2,250	5,000	3,150
Total	69,800	66,300	136,100	4,100	4,150	4,100

1902-03

Southern League Division 1

Date	Opponent	Result	Scorers	Att	Abbott	Blackwood	Bowman	Brown	Busby	Clipsham	Collins	Colvin	Edwards A	Edwards J	Freeman	Hamilton	Hitch	King	Mayes	Musslewhite	Newlands	Pryce	Skinner	White	Wilson
Sep 3	(h) Wellingborough	W 2-0	Busby 2	5,000	9		4		10		1	7		3		8	5				2		6		11
6	(a) Tottenham H	D 0-0		13,000	9		4		10		1	7		3		8	5				2		6		11
13	(h) West Ham U	D 0-0		7,000			4		10		1	7		3		8	5	9			2		6		11
20	(a) Portsmouth	L 1-2	Hitch	10,000	9		4		10		1	7		3		8	5				2		6		11
27	(h) New Brompton	L 1-2	Wilson	6,000			4		10		1	7		3		8	5	9			2		6		11
Oct 4	(a) Swindon T	L 0-2		4,000	9		4		10		1	7		3		8	5				2		6		11
11	(h) Kettering T	W 4-2	Wilson, Hitch, Busby, Collins	5,000			4		11		1	7		3		8	5	9					6	2	10
18	(a) Luton T	L 1-4	Edwards	4,000	9				11		1	7		3		8	5				4		6	2	10
25	(h) Reading	L 1-3	Hamilton	7,000				9	11		1			3	4	8		7		5			6	2	10
Nov 8	(a) Southampton	L 0-2		4,000	10		5	9	11	4	1	7			6	8					3			2	
22	(a) Bristol R	L 0-4		5,000			4		11	6	1	7		3	5	9		8			2				10
29	(h) Northampton T	D 0-0		4,000		8		9	11		1	7	6	3	4		5				2				10
Dec 6	(a) Watford	W 2-0	Brown 2	4,000		10	4	9			1				6	7	5		8		2			3	11
20	(h) Tottenham H	L 0-4		7,000	8	10	4	9			1			3	6	7	5							2	11
27	(a) West Ham U	L 0-2		2,500	8	10	4				1			3	6	7	5	9						2	11
Jan 3	(h) Portsmouth	W 4-3	Blackwood 2, Hitch, Brown	6,000	8	10	4	9			1				6	7	5				3			2	11
10	(a) New Brompton	D 0-0		3,000	8		4	9			1			3	6	7	5				2	10			11
17	(h) Swindon T	W 2-0	Brown 2	4,000	8		4	9			1			3	6	7	5				2	10			11
24	(a) Kettering T	W 1-0	Brown	5,000	8		4		10		1		6			7	5				3	9		2	11
31	(h) Luton T	W 3-1	Abbott 2, Hamilton	5,000	8	10	4	9			1		6			7	5				3			2	11
Feb 14	(h) Millwall	L 0-1		7,000	8		4	9			1			3	6	7	5				2	10			11
21	(h) Southampton	D 0-0		10,000	8	10	4	9			1				6	7	5				3			2	11
Mar 4	(h) Brentford	W 3-0	Blackwood 2, Freeman	5,000	8	10	4	9			1			3	6	7	5				2				11
7	(h) Bristol R	W 2-0	Blackwood, Young (og)	4,000	8	10	4	9			1		6	3	5	7					2				11
21	(h) Watford	W 3-0	Blackwood 2, Brown	4,000	8	10	4	9			1				6	7	5				3			2	11
28	(a) Brentford	W 2-0	Blackwood 2	4,000	8	10	4	9			1				6	7	5				3			2	11
31	(a) Northampton T	D 1-1	Brown	3,000	8	10	4	9			1				6	7	5				3			2	11
Apr 4	(a) Millwall	L 0-6		2,000	8	9	4		7		1				6		5				3	10		2	11
14	(a) Wellingborough	L 1-2	Blackwood	2,000	8	9	4	10			1				6	7	5				3			2	11
18	(a) Reading	L 0-1		4,000	8	9	4	10			1				6	7	5				3			2	11
				App	23	15	27	18	14	2	30	11	4	18	20	28	26	6	1	1	26	5	9	17	29
				Goals	2	10		8	3			1		1	1	2	3								2

1 own-goal

FA Cup

Date	Opponent	Result	Att	Abbott	Blackwood	Bowman	Brown	Busby	Clipsham	Collins	Colvin	Edwards A	Edwards J	Freeman	Hamilton	Hitch	King	Mayes	Musslewhite	Newlands	Pryce	Skinner	White	Wilson	Round
Nov 1	(h) Luton T	L 0-3	8,000	9		4		11	5	1			3		7		8					6	2	10	Q3
			App	1		1		1	1	1			1		1		1					1	1	1	
			Goals																						

Attendance Summary

	ATTENDANCES Home	Away	Total	AVERAGE Home	Away	Total
League	86,000	69,500	155,500	5,750	4,650	5,200
FA Cup	8,000		8,000	8,000		8,000
Total	94,000	69,500	163,500	5,900	4,650	5,250

1903-04

Southern League Division 1

Date	Opponent	Res	Score	Scorers	Att	Abbott	Archer	Banner	Blackwood	Bowman	Brown	Bull	Collins	Cross	Downing	Edwards	Freeman	Hamilton	Hitch	Leather	Lyon	McCairns	McGowan	Mayes	Milward	Murphy	Newlands	Skilton	White	Wilson
Sep 5 (h)	Brentford	W	1-0	Brown	10,000		2		10	4	9		1	7			6		5						8		3			11
12 (a)	West Ham U	L	0-1		6,000		2		10	4	9		1				6	7	5						8		3			11
19 (h)	Tottenham H	W	2-0	McGowan, Abbott	6,000	8	2			4	9	6	1	11				7	5				10				3			
26 (a)	Luton T	L	0-1		6,000	8	2			4	9	6	1					7	5				10			11	3			
Oct 3 (h)	New Brompton	W	3-0	McGowan 2, Milward	7,000		2			4	9	6	1					7	5				10		8		3			11
10 (a)	Kettering T	L	1-2	Milward	2,000		2			4		6	1	7					5				10		8	9	3			11
17 (h)	Southampton	L	0-3		15,000	8	2		10	4	9	6	1					7	5								3			11
24 (a)	Fulham	D	2-2	Blackwood 2	16,000					4		6	1					7	5		2	8	10			9			3	11
Nov 7 (a)	Swindon T	D	1-1	Blackwood	8,000					4			1		6			7	5		2		10		8	9	3			11
14 (h)	Northampton T	W	4-1	Blackwood 3, Milward	5,000		2		10	4			1	7	6				5						8	9	3			11
21 (h)	Reading	D	1-1	Blackwood	10,000		2		10	4			1	11	6			7	5						8	9	3			
28 (a)	Wellingborough	D	1-1	Murphy	4,000		2		10	4			1		6	11		7	5						8	9	3			
Dec 5 (h)	Bristol R	W	2-1	Blackwood, Hamilton	5,000		2		10	4			1		6			7	5						8	9	3			11
12 (a)	Brighton & HA	W	3-1	Milward 2, Blackwood	5,000		2		10	4			1		6			7	5						8	9	3			11
19 (h)	Portsmouth	W	6-1	Blackwood 3, Murphy 2, Hitch	8,000		2		10	4			1		6			7	5						8	9	3			11
28 (a)	Northampton T	L	1-2	Wilson	3,000		2	5	10				1	7	4	6									8	9	3			11
Jan 2 (a)	Brentford	W	4-1	Milward 2, Blackwood, Murphy (pen)	5,000		2	6	10				1		4			7							8	9	3		5	11
9 (h)	West Ham U	W	2-1	Murphy, Milward	6,000		2	4	10				1		6			7	5						8	9	3			11
16 (a)	Tottenham H	D	2-2	Blackwood 2	12,000		2		10				1		6			7	5						8	9	3		4	11
30 (a)	New Brompton	L	0-2		1,000		2		10	4			1		6			7	5						8	9	3			11
Feb 6 (h)	Kettering T	W	2-0	Murphy, Blackwood	4,000		2		10	4			1		6			7	5						8	9	3			11
13 (a)	Southampton	L	1-2	Blackwood	7,000		2		10	4			1		6			7	5						8	9	3			11
20 (h)	Fulham	D	1-1	Cross	12,000		2		10	4			1	7	6				5						8	9	3			11
27 (a)	Millwall	L	0-4		8,000		2			4			1	7	6				5					8	10	9	3			11
Mar 5 (h)	Swindon T	W	1-0	Blackwood	5,000		2		10	4		6	1	7											8	9	3		5	11
12 (h)	Plymouth A	W	1-0	Abbott	6,000	8	2		10	4		6	1	7					5						9		3			11
13 (a)	Plymouth A	D	1-1	Brown	6,000		2			8	9	4	1						5				10		7		3		6	11
17 (h)	Luton T	W	2-1	Milward, Brown (pen)	4,000		2		10	4	9	6	1	7					5						8		3			11
19 (a)	Reading	D	1-1	Blackwood	5,000		2		10	4	9	6	1	7					5						8		3			11
26 (h)	Wellingborough	W	3-0	Bowman, Milward, Blackwood	10,000		2		10	5	9	4			6					1				7	8		3			11
Apr 2 (a)	Bristol R	D	1-1	Cross	7,000		2		10	4			1	7	6				5					9	8		3			11
9 (h)	Brighton & HA	D	1-1	Milward	3,500				10		9	4	1		6			7	5						8		3		2	11
16 (a)	Portsmouth	D	0-0		6,000		2			7	9		1			6			5						8	10	3		4	11
30 (h)	Millwall	W	2-1	Murphy, Skilton	7,000		2	7		4			1		6				5						8	10		9	3	11
					App	4	31	4	24	29	12	13	33	13	20	3	2	19	30	1	2	1	7	3	30	22	32	1	8	30
					Goals	2			20	1	3			2				1	1				3		11	7		1		1

FA Cup

Date	Opponent	Res	Score	Scorers	Att	Abbott	Archer	Banner	Blackwood	Bowman	Brown	Bull	Collins	Cross	Downing	Edwards	Freeman	Hamilton	Hitch	Leather	Lyon	McCairns	McGowan	Mayes	Milward	Murphy	Newlands	Skilton	White	Wilson	Round
Oct 31 (h)	Fulham	D	1-1	Murphy	12,000					4		6	1					7	5		2	8	10			9	3			11	Q3
Nov 4 (a)	Fulham	L	1-3	Brown	18,000					4	9	6	1					7	5		2	8	10				3			11	Rep
					App					2	1	2	2					2	2		2	2	2			1	2			2	
					Goals						1															1					

Attendance Summary

	ATTENDANCES			AVERAGE		
	Home	Away	Total	Home	Away	Total
League	123,500	107,000	230,500	7,250	6,300	6,800
FA Cup	12,000	18,000	30,000	12,000	18,000	15,000
Total	135,500	125,000	260,500	7,550	6,950	7,250

1904-05

Southern League Division 1

Date	Opponents	Result	Scorers	Att	Archer	Bevan	Blackwood	Bowman	Collins	Cross J	Cross W	Downing	Edwards	Evans	Hitch	Howes	Leather	Lyon	Milward	Murphy	Newlands	Ronaldson	Ryder	Shufflebottom	Singleton	Skilton	Stewart	White
Sep 3	(h) Plymouth A	W 2-1	Blackwood 2	12,000	2	9	10	4	1	6					5						3	8			11		7	
10	(a) West Ham U	W 3-1	Bevan 2 (1 pen), Hitch	14,000	2	9	10	4	1	6	7				5						3	8					11	
17	(h) Reading	W 4-2	Bevan 2 (1 pen), W.Cross, Hitch	16,000	2	9		4	1	6	7				5					10	3	8					11	
24	(a) Bristol R	D 0-0		6,000	2	9		4	1	6	7				5					10	3	8					11	
Oct 1	(h) Northampton T	L 1-2	Stewart	9,000	2	9		4	1	6	7				5							8	10				11	3
8	(a) Portsmouth	L 1-4	Ronaldson	12,000	2	9		4	1	6	7				5							8	10				11	3
15	(h) Brentford	W 3-2	Ronaldson, W.Cross, Blackwood	12,000	2	9	10	6	1	4	7				5						3	8			11			
22	(a) Brighton & HA	L 0-3		6,000	2	9	10		1	4	7	6									3	8			11			5
29	(a) Millwall	D 0-0		7,000	2	8	10	5	1	4	7	6									3				11	9		
Nov 5	(h) Tottenham H	L 1-2	Stewart	16,000	2	8	10	4	1	6					5					7	3					9	11	
12	(a) Luton T	D 1-1	Ronaldson	6,000	2	9		4		6	7				5	1				10	3	8					11	
19	(h) Swindon T	W 4-1	Bevan 3, Ronaldson	6,000	2	9		4					6		5	1		3		7		8	10				11	
26	(a) New Brompton	L 0-4		4,000	2	9		4			7		6		5	1		3				8	10		11			
Dec 3	(h) Wellingborough	L 1-2	Hitch	4,000	2	9	10	4		6	7				5	1		3				8			11			
17	(h) Fulham	W 2-0	Bowman, Bevan	14,000	2	10		4			7		6		5	1					3	8				9	11	
24	(a) Watford	L 0-1		6,000	2	10		4			7		6		5	1					3	8				9	11	
31	(a) Plymouth A	L 1-3	Milward	8,000	2	10		4		6	7				5	1			8	11	3	9						
Jan 7	(h) West Ham U	W 1-0	Hitch	7,000		10			1	4	7	6			5			2	8		3					9	11	
14	(a) Reading	L 0-3		8,000	2	9			1	4		6								7	3	8	10		11			5
21	(h) Bristol R	W 5-0	Milward, Hitch, Skilton, Edwards, Murphy	11,000				6	1	4	7		11		5			2	8	10	3					9		
28	(a) Northampton T	D 1-1	Ronaldson	4,000				6	1	4	7		11		5			2	8		3	10				9		
Feb 11	(a) Brentford	D 0-0		8,000		9		6	1	4	7		11		5			2	8	10	3							
18	(h) Brighton & HA	L 1-2	Ronaldson	3,000		9		6	1	4					5			2	8		3	10			11		7	
25	(h) Millwall	D 1-1	Bevan	9,000		9		4	1			6		7	5			2	8		3	10			11			
Mar 4	(a) Tottenham H	L 1-5	Bevan	7,000		10		4				6			5	1		2	8	7	3	9			11			
11	(h) Luton T	L 1-2	Bevan	4,000		9		4	1			10			5			2		7	3	8			11			6
18	(a) Swindon T	D 0-0		4,000	2	9		4	1			7			5				8				10	6	11			3
25	(h) New Brompton	W 2-0	Ryder 2	6,000		9		4	1			6			5			2	8	7	3		10		11			
Apr 1	(a) Wellingborough	W 4-0	Bevan 4	900	2	9		4	1			6			5				8	7	3		10		11			
8	(h) Southampton	D 1-1	Milward	12,000		9		4	1		7	6			5			2	8		3		10		11			
15	(a) Fulham	W 2-1	Hitch, Bevan	12,000	2	9				4		6			5	1		3	8	7			10		11			
22	(h) Watford	W 4-1	Bevan 3 (pen), Hitch	5,000		9				4		6			5	1		2	8	7	3		10		11			
25	(h) Portsmouth	W 2-0	Hitch (pen), Murphy	5,000		9				4		6			5	1		2	8	7	3		10		11			
29	(a) Southampton	W 1-0	Bevan	4,000		9				4		6			5		1		8	7	3		10		11			2
				App	21	32	7	27	22	23	19	15	7	1	31	11	1	16	16	17	27	21	13	1	19	7	13	7
				Goals		20	3	1			2		1		8				3	2		6	2			1	2	

FA Cup

Date	Opponents	Result	Scorers	Att	Archer	Bevan	Blackwood	Bowman	Collins	Cross J	Cross W	Downing	Edwards	Evans	Hitch	Howes	Leather	Lyon	Milward	Murphy	Newlands	Ronaldson	Ryder	Shufflebottom	Singleton	Skilton	Stewart	White	Round
Dec 10	(h) Brentford	L 1-2	Ryder	10,000	2	9		4		6	7				5	1		3				8	10				11		Q6
				App	1	1		1		1	1				1	1		1				1	1				1		
				Goals																			1						

Attendance Summary

	ATTENDANCES			AVERAGE		
	Home	Away	Total	Home	Away	Total
League	151,000	116,900	267,900	8,900	6,900	7,900
FA Cup	10,000		10,000	10,000		10,000
Total	161,000	116,900	277,900	8,950	6,900	7,950

1905-06

Southern League Division 1

Date	Opponent	Res	Score	Scorers	Att	Bevan	Brewis	Cowan	Downing	Edwards	Fletcher	Fox	Gardner	Guy-Watson	Hitch	Howes	Kingsley	Lyon	McCargill	McLarney	Moger	Murphy	Newlands	Roberts	Ryder	Sugden	Thompson	Wassel	White	Yenson
Sep 2	(h) New Brompton	W	4-0	Sugden 3, Bevan	10,000	9			5				11		4		1			2		7	3		10	8				6
9	(a) Portsmouth	D	0-0		3,000	9			6	11					5		1			2		7	3		10	8				4
16	(h) Swindon T	W	3-0	Ryder 2, Bevan	8,000	9			6				11		5		1			2		7	3		10	8				4
23	(a) Millwall	L	0-2		15,000	9			6				11		5		1			2		7	3		10	8				4
30	(h) Luton T	L	2-3	Sugden, Ryder	10,000	9			6				11		5		1	2				7	3		10	8				4
Oct 7	(a) Tottenham H	L	1-2	Sugden	18,000		9		6	11					5		1	3		2		7			10	8				4
14	(h) Brentford	L	1-2	Hitch	10,000	9			6	11					5		1	3		2		7			10	8				4
21	(a) Norwich C	L	0-4		5,000	9			6						5		1	3		2		7		11	10	8				4
28	(h) Plymouth A	W	2-0	Yenson, Ryder	10,000				6						5		1	2					3	11	10	8	7		4	9
Nov 4	(a) Southampton	L	1-2	Thompson	5,000				6						5		1	2					3	11	10	8	7		4	9
11	(h) Reading	W	3-0	Downing 2, Sugden	7,000				6						5		1	2					3	11	10	8	7		4	9
18	(a) Watford	W	4-3	Thompson 3, Bevan	7,000	9			6								1	2						11	10	8	7	3	5	4
25	(h) Brighton & HA	D	0-0		5,000	9			6								1	2						11	10	8	7	3	5	4
Dec 2	(a) West Ham U	L	0-2		12,000	9			6								1			2			3	11	10	8	7		5	4
9	(h) Fulham	L	1-3	Thompson	16,000	10			6						5		1	2					3	11		8	7		4	9
16	(h) Northampton T	W	6-1	Bevan 3 (1 pen), Ryder, Sugden, Cowan	8,000	9		11	6						5		1						3		10	8	7		2	4
23	(a) Bristol R	L	1-2	Ryder	6,000				6		8				5		1					7	3	11	10	9			2	4
30	(a) New Brompton	W	2-0	Ryder, Brewis	4,000		9		6		8				5	1							3	11	10	7			2	4
Jan 6	(h) Portsmouth	W	2-0	Ryder, Murphy	5,000				6		8				5	1		11				9	3		10		7		2	4
20	(a) Swindon T	W	2-1	Fletcher, Ryder	4,000	9			6		8				5	1		11					3		10		7		2	4
27	(h) Millwall	W	2-1	Yenson, Ryder	9,000	11			6		8				5	1						9	3		10		7		2	4
Feb 3	(a) Luton T	L	2-3	Ryder, Murphy	4,000	11			6		8				5	1						9	3		10	7			2	4
10	(h) Tottenham H	D	0-0		10,000	11			6						5	1							3	9	10	8	7		2	4
17	(a) Brentford	D	2-2	Fletcher 2	3,000	11					10				5	1							3	9	6	8	7		2	4
24	(h) Norwich C	D	0-0		12,000	9					10				5		1						3	11	6	8	7		2	4
Mar 3	(a) Plymouth A	D	1-1	Fletcher	5,000	9					10				5		1						3	11	6	8	7		2	4
14	(h) Southampton	L	0-3		7,000	9			6		8				5	1							3	11	10	7			2	4
17	(a) Reading	L	0-1		7,000	9			6		8				5	1							3	11	10	7			2	4
24	(h) Watford	W	6-0	Bevan 2, Fletcher, Ryder, Roberts, Brooks (og)	9,000	9			6		8				5	1							3	11	10		7		2	4
31	(a) Brighton & HA	L	2-3	Ryder, Sugden	4,000	9			6		8				5	1							3	11	10	7			2	4
Apr 7	(h) West Ham U	L	0-1		15,000	9			6		8				5	1							3	11	10	7			2	4
14	(a) Fulham	L	0-1		15,000	9					8	3			5		1		6					11	10	7			2	4
21	(a) Northampton T	D	1-1	Yenson	3,000						8		4		5			2	6		1		3	11	10	7				9
28	(h) Bristol R	W	7-0	Fletcher 2, Ryder 2, Bevan 2, Thompson	5,000	9					8			1	5				6					11	10		7	3	2	4
					App	26	2	1	28	3	17	1	5	1	31	12	20	13	3	8	1	12	27	22	33	29	17	3	25	34
					Goals	10	1	1	2		7				1							2		1	15	8	6			3

1 own-goal

FA Cup

Date	Opponent	Res	Score	Att	Bevan	Brewis	Cowan	Downing	Edwards	Fletcher	Fox	Gardner	Guy-Watson	Hitch	Howes	Kingsley	Lyon	McCargill	McLarney	Moger	Murphy	Newlands	Roberts	Ryder	Sugden	Thompson	Wassel	White	Yenson	Round
Jan 13	(a) Fulham	L	0-1	7,000				6		8				5	1		11				9	3		10		7		2	4	1
				App				1		1				1	1		1				1	1		1		1		1	1	
				Goals																										

Attendance Summary

	ATTENDANCES Home	Away	Total	AVERAGE Home	Away	Total
League	156,000	120,000	276,000	9,200	7,050	8,100
FA Cup		7,000	7,000		7,000	7,000
Total	156,000	127,000	283,000	9,200	7,050	8,100

1906-07

Southern League Division 1

Month	Match	Result	Scorers	Att	Anderson	Blake	Brewis	Downing	Fidler	Fletcher	Green	Howes	Lyon	McCargill	McLean	Moger	Newlands	O'Donnell	Ryder	Skilton	Sugden	Taylor	Thompson	Webb	White	Yenson
Sep	1 (a) Luton T	D 1-1	Anderson	6,000	9	11		6			7	1			5		3	8	10						2	4
	8 (h) Crystal P	W 1-0	Downing	6,000	9	11		6			7	1			5		3	8	10						2	4
	15 (a) Brentford	L 1-4	Ryder	12,000	9	11		6			7	1			5		3	8	10						2	4
	19 (a) Swindon T	D 0-0		6,000	9	11		6			7	1			5		3	8	10						2	4
	22 (h) Millwall	W 2-1	O'Donnell, Ryder	10,000		11		6			7	1			5		3	9	10		8				2	4
	29 (a) Clapton O	L 0-3		8,000		11		6	3		7	1			5			9	10		8				2	4
Oct	6 (h) Portsmouth	L 2-3	O'Donnell, Sugden (pen)	7,000		11	10				7	1	3		5			9	6		8				2	4
	13 (a) New Brompton	L 1-2	Brewis	6,000		11	9	6			7	1	3		5				10		8				2	4
	20 (h) Plymouth A	D 0-0		8,000		11	9	6		8	7	1	2				3		10						5	4
	27 (a) Brighton & HA	L 0-2		7,000		11	9	6		8	7	1	2				3		10						5	4
Nov	3 (h) Reading	L 0-1		7,000		11	9	6		8	7	1	2				3		10						5	4
	10 (a) Watford	L 0-1		5,000		11		6		8	7	1	2		5		3				10				4	9
	17 (h) Northampton T	W 5-0	Fletcher 3, Green, Sugden	5,000				6		8	9	1	2		5		3		11		10		7			4
	24 (h) Bristol R	D 1-1	Green	6,000				6		8	9	1	2		5		3		11		10		7			4
Dec	1 (a) Fulham	D 1-1	Thompson	20,000				6		8	9	1	2		5		3		11		10		7			4
	8 (h) Southampton	L 1-2	Green	15,000				6		8	9	1	2	4	5		3		11		10		7			
	22 (h) Tottenham H	W 3-1	Ryder, Green, O'Donnell	15,000				6		8	9	1			5		3	7	11		10				2	4
	26 (h) Norwich C	D 1-1	Fletcher	6,000				6		8	9	1	3		5			7	11		10				2	4
	29 (h) Luton T	W 2-0	Green 2	5,000				6		8	9	1	3		5			7	11		10				2	4
Jan	5 (a) Crystal P	L 1-5	Fletcher	7,000	10			6		8	9	1	2		5		3	7	11						4	
	26 (a) Millwall	L 0-7		5,000		11		6			9		3		5	1			10		8	4	7		2	
Feb	2 (h) Clapton O	W 2-0	Sugden 2	8,000	8			6	3				2		5	1			11	9	10		7			4
	9 (a) Portsmouth	D 2-2	Sugden, Skilton	7,000	8			6	3		7	1	2		5				11	9	10					4
	16 (h) New Brompton	W 3-0	Skilton 2, Sugden	5,000	8			6	3		7	1	2		5				11	9	10					4
	23 (a) Plymouth A	L 1-2	O'Donnell	5,000	8			6	3		7	1	2					11		9	10				5	4
	25 (a) West Ham U	L 1-2	Anderson	6,000	9			6	3	8	7	1	2					11			10				5	4
Mar	2 (h) Brighton & HA	L 0-2		8,000	9			6	3	8	7	1	2		5			11			10					4
	9 (a) Reading	D 0-0		5,000	8			6	3		7	1	2		5			11		9	10					4
	11 (h) Brentford	D 1-1	Sugden	16,000	8			6	3		7		2		5			11		9	10			1		4
	16 (h) Watford	D 0-0		8,000	8			6	3		7		2		5			11		9	10			1		4
	23 (a) Northampton T	W 2-1	Yenson (pen), O'Donnell	2,000	8			6	3		7		2		5			11		9	10			1		4
	29 (a) Norwich C	L 0-1		10,000				6	3	8	7		2		5			11		9	10			1		4
	30 (a) Bristol R	L 1-3	Skilton	7,000				6	3	8	7				5			11		9	10			1		4
Apr	1 (h) Swindon T	W 6-1	Skilton 2, O'Donnell 2, Sugden 2	5,000				6	3	8	7				5			11		9	10			1	2	4
	6 (h) Fulham	L 0-2		14,000				6	3	8	7				5			11		9	10			1	2	4
	13 (a) Southampton	W 3-0	Green 2, Anderson	3,000	10			6	3	8	7				5			11		9				1	2	4
	20 (h) West Ham U	W 2-0	Skilton, Fletcher	5,000	10			6	3	8	7				5			11		9				1	2	4
	27 (a) Tottenham H	L 0-2		7,000	9	11		6	3	8	7							10				5		1	2	4
				App	18	14	5	37	18	21	37	26	25	1	32	2	15	25	23	14	27	2	6	10	25	35
				Goals	3		1	1		6	8							7	3	7	9		1			1

FA Cup

Month	Match	Result	Att	Anderson	Blake	Brewis	Downing	Fidler	Fletcher	Green	Howes	Lyon	McCargill	McLean	Moger	Newlands	O'Donnell	Ryder	Skilton	Sugden	Taylor	Thompson	Webb	White	Yenson	Round
Jan	12 (a) Bristol R	D 0-0	6,000				6		8	9	1			5		3	7	11		10				2	4	1
	14 (h) Bristol R	L 0-1	8,000				6		8	9	1			5		3	7	11		10				2	4	Rep
			App				2		2	2	2			2		2	2	2		2				2	2	
			Goals																							

Attendance Summary

	ATTENDANCES			AVERAGE		
	Home	Away	Total	Home	Away	Total
League	159,000	134,000	293,000	8,350	7,050	7,700
FA Cup	8,000	6,000	14,000	8,000	6,000	7,000
Total	167,000	140,000	307,000	8,350	7,000	7,650

1907-08

Southern League Division 1

Date	Opponent	Res	Score	Scorers	Att	Ainsworth	Anderson	Barnes	Cannon	Corbett	Downing	Fidler	Gittens	Hitchcock	Lowe	Lintott	McDonald	McLean	Mitchell	Morris	Pentland	Rogers	Shaw	Skilton	Snelgrove	Sugden	Walker	White	Yenson
Sep 2	(h) Tottenham H	D	3-3	Gittens 2, Hitchcock	8,000		6	11				3	10	9				5	4		7	8	1					2	
7	(h) New Brompton	D	2-2	Rogers, Hitchcock	4,000			11		2		3	10	9		6		5			7	8	1						4
14	(a) Tottenham H	L	2-3	Walker, Barnes	12,000			11				3	10			6	2	5	4		7	8	1				9		
21	(h) Swindon T	W	2-1	Sugden 2	5,000			11				3	10			6	2	5			7		1			8	9		4
28	(a) Crystal P	W	3-2	Gittens 2, Walker	8,000			11				3	10			6	2	5			7	8	1				9		4
Oct 5	(h) Luton T	W	3-1	Barnes, Gittens, Pentland	10,000			11				3	10			6		5	4		7	8	1				9	2	
12	(a) Brighton & HA	W	3-2	White, Walker, Gittens	8,000			11				3	10			6		5	4		7		1	8			9	2	
19	(h) Portsmouth	W	3-2	Pentland, Skilton, Gittens	10,000			11				3	10			6		5	4		7		1	8			9	2	
26	(a) Bradford	D	2-2	Skilton, Walker	15,000			11			6	3	10					5	4				1	8			9	2	7
Nov 2	(h) Millwall	L	2-3	Gittens, Walker	16,000			11			6	3	10			5			4		7		1	8			9	2	
9	(a) Brentford	D	1-1	Downing	10,000			11			6	3	10			5			4		7		1	8			9	2	
16	(h) Bristol R	W	5-3	Pentland 2, Barnes, Walker, Skilton	10,000			11			6	3	10			5			4		7		1	8			9	2	
23	(a) Clapton O	W	5-2	Walker 2, Gittens 2, Pentland (pen)	5,000			11			6	3	10					5	4		7		1	8			9	2	
30	(h) Reading	W	1-0	Pentland (pen)	10,000			11			6	3	10			5					7		1	8			9	2	4
Dec 7	(a) Watford	W	3-0	Walker, Gittens, Skilton	6,000			11			6	3	10					5			7		1	8			9	2	4
14	(h) Norwich C	W	3-1	Pentland 2, Downing	6,000			11			6	3	10			5					7		1	8			9	2	4
21	(a) Northampton T	W	2-1	Pentland 2	6,000			11			6	3	10					5			7		1	8			9	2	4
25	(h) Plymouth A	D	0-0		29,786			11			6	3	10			5					7		1	8			9	2	4
26	(a) West Ham U	L	0-3		15,000			11			6		10			5	3				7		1	8			9	2	4
28	(h) Southampton	W	3-0	Walker 2, Sugden	7,000			11			6		10				3	5			7		1			8	9	2	4
Jan 4	(a) New Brompton	W	4-0	Barnes, Sugden, Downing, Gittens	6,000			11			6		10				3	5			7		1			8	9	2	4
25	(h) Crystal P	L	1-2	Ainsworth	6,000	11					6	3	10			5					7		1			8	9	2	4
Feb 8	(h) Brighton & HA	W	1-0	Barnes	8,000			11			6	3	10			4		5			7		1			8		2	9
15	(a) Portsmouth	L	0-1		4,000			11			6	3	10					5	4		7		1	8			9	2	
22	(h) Bradford	W	2-0	Barnes, Walker	7,000			11			6	3	10			4		5			7		1			8	9	2	
26	(a) Luton T	D	0-0		4,000			11			6	3	10					5			7		1			8	9	2	4
29	(a) Millwall	D	0-0		12,000			11	8		6	2	10			4	3	5			7		1				9		
Mar 7	(h) Brentford	W	1-0	Cannon	10,000			11	8		6	3	10			4	2	5			7		1				9		
14	(a) Bristol R	W	1-0	Downing	12,000			11	8		6	3	10				2	5			7		1	9					4
21	(h) Clapton O	W	5-2	Gittens, Pentland (pen), Skilton, Lintott, Barnes	6,000			11	8		6	3	10			4	2	5			7		1	9					
28	(a) Reading	W	3-0	Gittens 2, Cannon	5,000			11	8		6	3	10			4	2	5			7		1	9					
Apr 4	(h) Watford	D	3-3	Barnes, Cannon, Pentland	8,000			11	8		6	3	10				2	5			7		1	9					4
11	(a) Norwich C	W	1-0	Gittens	4,000			11	8		6	3	10			4	2	5			7		1	9					
17	(a) Plymouth A	D	1-1	Barnes	15,000			11	8		6	3	10				2	5			7		1	9					4
18	(h) Northampton T	L	2-3	Pentland, Barnes	14,000			11			6	3	10					5	4		7		1	9	8			2	
20	(h) West Ham U	W	4-0	Cannon 3, Pentland	10,000			11	8		6	3	10				2	5			7		1				9		4
25	(a) Southampton	L	2-5	Walker, Snelgrove	2,000			11			6				3					5	7		1		8	10	9	2	4
29	(a) Swindon T	L	3-8	Walker 2, Ainsworth	1,500	11					6				3					5	7		1		8	10	9	2	4
					App	2	1	36	9	1	30	33	36	2	2	22	15	28	12	2	37	5	38	21	3	9	28	25	21
					Goals	2		10	6		4		16	2		1					14	1		5	1	4	15	1	

FA Cup

Date	Opponent	Res	Score	Scorers	Att	Ainsworth	Anderson	Barnes	Cannon	Corbett	Downing	Fidler	Gittens	Hitchcock	Lowe	Lintott	McDonald	McLean	Mitchell	Morris	Pentland	Rogers	Shaw	Skilton	Snelgrove	Sugden	Walker	White	Yenson	Round
Jan 11	(h) Reading	W	1-0	Barnes	28,000			11			6		10			5	3				7		1			8	9	2	4	1
Feb 1	(a) Swindon T	L	1-2	Walker	9,771			11			6	3	10			4		5			7		1			8	9	2		2
					App			2			2	1	2			2	1	1			2		2			2	2	2	1	
					Goals			1																			1			

FA Charity Shield

Date	Opponent	Res	Score	Scorers	Att	Ainsworth	Anderson	Barnes	Cannon	Corbett	Downing	Fidler	Gittens	Hitchcock	Lowe	Lintott	McDonald	McLean	Mitchell	Morris	Pentland	Rogers	Shaw	Skilton	Snelgrove	Sugden	Walker	White	Yenson
Apr 27	(n*) Manchester U	D	1-1	Cannon	12,000			11	8		6	3	10			4	2	5			7		1	9					
					App			1	1		1	1	1			1	1	1			1		1	1					
					Goals								1																

*Played at Stamford Bridge, Chelsea.

Attendance Summary

	ATTENDANCES			AVERAGE		
	Home	Away	Total	Home	Away	Total
League	184,786	150,500	335,286	9,750	7,900	8,800
FA Cup	28,000	9,771	37,771	28,000	9,771	18,900
Charity Shield		12,000	12,000		12,000	12,000
Total	212,786	172,271	385,057	10,650	8,200	9,400

1908-09

Southern League Division 1

Date	Opponent	Result	Scorers	Att	Barnes	Cannon	Downing	Drake	Duff	Fidler	Gillespie	Gittens	Greer	King	Law	Lintott	MacDonald	McDonald	McEwan	McKenzie	McLean	McNaught	Mitchell	Morris	Rogers	Shaw	Skilton	Snelgrove
Sep 1	(a) West Ham U	L 0-2		7,000	11	8	6	10		3						4	7	2		9	5					1		
7	(h) Watford	W 2-0	McKenzie, Barnes	4,000	11	8	6	10	4	3						5	7	2		9						1		
10	(a) Northampton T	D 0-0		6,000	11	8	6	10		3								2		9	5	7	4			1		
14	(h) Portsmouth	D 0-0		5,000	11	8	6	10		3						5		2		9			4		7	1		
16	(a) Watford	D 0-0		3,000		8	6	10		3					11			2		9	5		4		7	1		
19	(h) Plymouth A	W 1-0	Cannon	10,000	11	8	6		4	3		10				5		2		9					7	1		
23	(a) Reading	L 0-2		4,000	11	8	6			3		10						2		9			4	5	7	1		
28	(a) Brentford	D 0-0		5,000	11	8	6			3		10						2					4	5	7	1	9	
Oct 3	(a) Portsmouth	L 1-3	Barnes	10,000	11	8	6			3		10				5	7	2					4			1	9	
12	(h) Coventry C	W 4-2	Downing 2, Barnes, Gittens	7,000	11		6			3		10					7	2		9	5		4		8	1		
17	(h) West Ham U	W 3-0	Skilton 2, Rogers	6,000	11		6		4	3		10				5	7	2							8	1	9	
21	(a) Crystal P	L 0-3		5,000	11		6	10		3							7	2			5		4		8	1	9	
26	(h) New Brompton	W 2-1	Rogers, Cannon	2,000	11	8	6	10		3						5	9	2					4		7	1		
Nov 2	(h) Southend U	W 2-1	Drake, Barnes	5,000	11	8	6	10		3							9	2			5		4		7	1		
7	(h) Brentford	W 3-0	Drake 2, Barnes	10,000	11		6	10		3							7	2			5		4		8	1	9	
11	(a) Brighton & HA	D 1-1	Barnes	5,000	11	8	6	10		3						5	7	2					4			1	9	
21	(a) Swindon T	L 1-3	Barnes	5,000	11			10		3				8		6	7	2			5		4			1	9	
23	(h) Clapton O	L 0-3		2,000	11			10		3				8			7	2		6	5		4			1	9	
Dec 5	(h) Millwall	D 2-2	Rogers 2	7,000	10		6	9	4	3	2				11		7							5	8	1		
25	(h) Norwich C	D 2-2	Rogers, Downing	20,000	11		6	10	4	3			9				7	2						5	8	1		
26	(a) Southampton	W 4-1	Skilton, Downing, Rogers, Law	14,000	10	7	6		4						11			2	3					5	8	1	9	
28	(a) Millwall	W 1-0	Greer	5,000	10		6		4	3			9		11		7	2					5			1	8	
Jan 25	(h) Bristol R	W 4-2	Rogers, Drake, Greer, Morris	5,000	11		6	10	4	3			9				7	2						5	8	1		
Feb 8	(a) Luton T	L 0-1		5,000	11		6	10	4	3			9				7	2						5	8	1		
20	(h) Exeter C	D 1-1	Skilton	7,000	11	7	6	10	4	3			9					2						5	8	1		
24	(a) Exeter C	L 0-1		4,000	11		6	10	4	3								2				7		5	9	1		8
Mar 1	(a) Coventry C	L 1-2	Drake	5,671	11		6	10	4	3								2				7		5	9	1		8
10	(a) New Brompton	L 0-1		3,000	11		6		4	3			10				7	2						5	9	1		8
15	(h) Luton T	W 4-0	Barnes 2, Downing (pen), Morris	2,000	11		6		4	3								2				7		5	10	1	9	8
22	(h) Brighton & HA	L 1-2	Downing	3,000	11		6		4	3								2				7		5	10	1	9	8
27	(h) Swindon T	W 5-1	Skilton 3, Rogers, Greer	8,000	11		6		4	3			10					2				7		5		1	9	8
29	(a) Bristol R	D 0-0		2,000	11		6			3			10					2				7	4	5		1	9	8
Apr 3	(h) Crystal P	D 1-1	Greer	6,000	11		6			3			10					2				7	4	5		1	9	8
9	(h) Southampton	L 1-2	Greer	12,000	11				4	3			10					2				7	6	5	8	1	9	
10	(a) Plymouth A	L 0-2		7,000	11				4	3			10					2				7	6	5	8	1	9	
12	(a) Norwich C	L 2-3	Greer, Rogers	10,000	11	9			4	3			10					2			6	7		5	8	1		
13	(h) Reading	L 2-3	Barnes, Cannon	2,000	11	9			6	3			10	8				2				7	4	5		1		
19	(h) Northampton T	D 1-1	Skilton	3,000	11					3			10					2			6	7	4	5	8	1	9	
26	(a) Clapton O	L 0-1		4,000	11	9				3			10					2			6	7	4	5		1	8	
28	(a) Southend U	D 0-0		2,000	11	9				3			10					2			6	7	4	5	8	1		
				App	39	18	31	19	20	39	1	6	16	3	4	9	18	39	1	9	13	15	23	23	27	40	19	8
				Goals	10	3	6	5				1	6		1					1				2	9		8	

FA Cup

Date	Opponent	Result	Scorers	Att	Barnes	Cannon	Downing	Drake	Duff	Fidler	Gillespie	Gittens	Greer	King	Law	Lintott	MacDonald	McDonald	McEwan	McKenzie	McLean	McNaught	Mitchell	Morris	Rogers	Shaw	Skilton	Snelgrove	Round
Jan 16	(h) West Ham U	D 0-0		17,000	11		6	10	4	3			9				7	2						5	8	1			1
20	(a) West Ham U	L 0-1		10,000	10		6		4	3			9		11		7	2					5		8	1			Rep
				App	2		2	1	2	2			2		1		2	2					1	1	2	2			
				Goals																									

FA Charity Shield

Date	Opponent	Result	Scorers	Att	Barnes	Cannon	Downing	Drake	Duff	Fidler	Gillespie	Gittens	Greer	King	Law	Lintott	MacDonald	McDonald	McEwan	McKenzie	McLean	McNaught	Mitchell	Morris	Rogers	Shaw	Skilton	Snelgrove
Aug 29	(n*) Manchester U	L 0-4		10,000	11	8	6			3		10				4		2			5	7				1	9	
				App	1	1	1			1		1				1		1			1	1				1	1	
				Goals																								

*Played at Stamford Bridge, Chelsea.

Attendance Summary

	ATTENDANCES			AVERAGE		
	Home	Away	Total	Home	Away	Total
League	126,000	111,671	237,671	6,300	5,600	5,950
FA Cup	17,000	10,000	27,000	17,000	10,000	13,500
Charity Shield		10,000	10,000		10,000	10,000
Total	143,000	131,671	274,671	6,800	6,000	6,400

1909-10

Southern League Division 1

Date		Opponents	Result	Scorers	Att	Barnes	Dine	Ferguson	Fidler	Greer	Hartwell	Logan	McDonald	McNaught	Mitchell	Morris	Radnage	Shaw	Steer	Swann	Travers	Wake	Wentworth	Whyman	Wilson	Wyatt
Sep	1	(h) Watford	W 4-3	Whyman 2, Hartwell, Travers (pen)	5,000	11			3		5	2		7	4			1	8		9	6		10		
	4	(a) Southend U	W 1-0	Barnes	5,000	11			3		5	2		7	4			1	8		9	6		10		
	8	(a) Watford	D 1-1	McNaught	3,000	11			3		5		2	7	4			1	8		9	6		10		
	11	(h) Clapton O	W 2-1	Steer, Whyman	7,000	11			3				2	7			5	1	8		9	6	4	10		
	18	(a) Plymouth A	W 2-0	Steer, McNaught	9,000	11			3				2	7	4	5		1	8		9	6		10		
	25	(h) Southampton	D 1-1	Steer	13,000	11			3				2	7	4	5		1	8		9	6		10		
Oct	2	(a) Croydon Comm	W 3-0	Travers 2, Steer	5,000	11			3	10	5		2	7	4			1	8		9	6				
	4	(h) Reading	W 1-0	Steer	4,000	11			3	10	5		2	7	4			1	8		9	6				
	9	(h) Millwall	L 1-2	McNaught	16,000	11			3		5		2	7	4			1		8	9	6		10		
	16	(a) New Brompton	D 1-1	Greer	7,000				3	11	5		2	7	4			1	8		9	6		10		
	18	(h) Coventry C	W 4-0	Steer 3, Travers	5,000				3	11	5		2	7	4			1	8		9	6		10		
	23	(h) Northampton T	W 2-0	Steer, Barnes	10,000	11			3	10	5		2	7	4			1	8		9	6				
	30	(h) Exeter C	W 2-0	Barnes, McNaught	10,000	11			3		5		2	7	4			1	8		9	6		10		
Nov	6	(a) Luton T	D 1-1	Steer	7,000	11			3		5		2	7	4			1	8		9	6		10		
	13	(h) Swindon T	L 0-3		12,000	11			3	10	5		2	7	4			1	8		9			6		
	20	(a) Crystal P	W 1-0	Steer	12,000	11			3	10	5		2	7	4			1	8			6		9		
	27	(h) Brighton & HA	W 1-0	Steer	8,000	11				10	5	3	2	7	4			1	8			6		9		
Dec	4	(a) West Ham U	W 2-1	Barnes, Hartwell	14,000	11				10	5	3	2	7	4			1	8			6		9		
	11	(h) Portsmouth	L 3-5	Whyman, Steer 2	8,000	11				10	5	3	2	7	4			1	8			6		9		
	25	(h) Norwich C	W 1-0	Wilson	20,000	11			3		5		2		4			1	8		7	6		9	10	
	28	(a) Coventry C	L 0-4		7,000	11			3			5	2	7	4			1	8		9	6		10		
Jan	1	(a) Brentford	W 1-0	Steer	12,000	11			3		5		2	7	4		6	1	9		8			10		
	8	(h) Southend U	D 2-2	Steer 2	6,000	11			3		5		2	7	4			1	9		8	6		10		
	22	(a) Clapton O	W 1-0	Steer	7,000	11			3		5		2	7	4			1	9		8	6		10		
	29	(h) Plymouth A	W 2-1	Whyman, Travers	7,000	11			3	10	5		2	7	4			1	8		9			6		
Feb	12	(h) Croydon Comm	D 4-4	Barnes 2, Whyman, Travers	6,000	11			3		5	2		7	4			1	9		8	6		10		
	26	(h) New Brompton	W 1-0	Steer	8,000	11			3		5		2	7	4			1	9		8	6		10		
Mar	12	(a) Exeter C	D 0-0		6,000	11			3		5		2			4		1	9		8	6		10		7
	14	(a) Bristol R	L 0-2		10,000	11			3		5		2			4		1	9		8	6		10		7
	19	(h) Luton T	W 4-0	Barnes 2, Steer 2	6,000	11			3		5		2			4		1	9		8	6		10		7
	25	(h) Brentford	D 0-0		25,000	11			3		5		2			4		1		8	9	6		10		7
	28	(a) Norwich C	D 0-0		10,000	11			3		5		2					1	9		8	6	4	10		7
	30	(a) Reading	D 0-0		2,000	11			3		5		2					1	9	7	8	6	4	10		
Apr	2	(h) Crystal P	L 1-2	Swann	10,000	11			3		5		2					1	9	8		6	4	10		7
	7	(a) Northampton T	D 0-0		3,000	11			3		5		2					1	9		8	6	4	10		7
	9	(a) Brighton & HA	L 0-2		10,000	11			3	10	5		2					1			8	6	4	9		7
	13	(a) Southampton	D 1-1	Steer	3,000	11			3		5		2	7				1	9		8	6	4	10		
	16	(h) West Ham U	D 3-3	Barnes, Travers, Whyman	7,000	11	4		3	8	5		2	7				1			9	6		10		
	18	(a) Millwall	L 0-1		9,000	11			3		5		2	7	4			1	9		8	6		10		
	23	(a) Portsmouth	L 0-4		6,000	11			3	8	5		2		4			1	9			6		10		7
	28	(a) Swindon T	L 0-1		3,000	11			3	8	5		2	7	4			1	9			6		10		
	30	(h) Bristol R	W 2-1	Wyman, Mitchell (pen)	6,000	11			3	8	5		2		4			1	9			6		10		7
					App	40	1		39	16	38	7	39	30	30	6	2	42	38	4	34	39	7	39	1	10
					Goals	9				1	2			4	1				22	1	7			8	1	

FA Cup

Date		Opponents	Result	Scorers	Att	Barnes	Dine	Ferguson	Fidler	Greer	Hartwell	Logan	McDonald	McNaught	Mitchell	Morris	Radnage	Shaw	Steer	Swann	Travers	Wake	Wentworth	Whyman	Wilson	Wyatt	Round
Jan	15	(a) Norwich C	D 0-0		10,000	11			3		5		2	7	4			1	9		8	6		10			1
	19	(h) Norwich C	W 3-0	Steer, McNaught, Whyman	5,000	11			3		5		2	7	4			1	9		8	6		10			Rep
Feb	5	(a) Southend U	D 0-0		5,000	11			3		5		2	7	4			1	9		8	6		10			2
	9	(h) Southend U	W 3-2	Steer 2, Travers	11,000	11			3		5		2	7	4			1	9		8	6		10			Rep
	19	(a) West Ham U	D 1-1	Steer	31,000	11		7	3		5		2		4			1	9		8	6		10			3
	24	(h) West Ham U	*W 1-0	Steer	18,500	11		7	3		5		2		4			1	9		8	6		10			Rep
Mar	5	(a) Barnsley	L 0-1		23,500	11			3		5		2	7	4			1	9		8	6		10			4
					App	7		2	7		7		7	5	7			7	7		7	7		7			
					Goals									1					5		1			1			

* After extra-time

Attendance Summary

	ATTENDANCES			AVERAGE		
	Home	Away	Total	Home	Away	Total
League	199,000	150,000	349,000	9,500	7,150	8,300
FA Cup	47,000	57,000	104,000	15,650	14,250	14,850
Total	246,000	207,000	453,000	10,250	8,300	9,250

1910-11

Southern League Division 1

Date		Opponent	Res	Score	Scorers	Att	Barnes	Bradshaw	Brindley	Brown	Browning	Butterworth	Fidler	Hartwell	Law	Lee	McDonald	McKie	McNaught	Mitchell	Morris	Pullen	Radnage	Shaw	Steer	Wake	Whyman	Wilson
Sep	3	(h) Coventry C	W	5-0	Whyman 2, Bradshaw 2, Hartwell	15,000	11	8	7				3	5			2			4				1	9	6	10	
	10	(a) New Brompton	L	0-1		10,000	11	8	7				3	5			2			4				1	9	6	10	
	12	(h) West Ham U	L	0-2		14,000	11		7				3	5			2	8		4				1	9	6	10	
	17	(h) Millwall	W	2-1	Barnes, McKie	15,000	11		7				3	5			2	8		4				1	9	6	10	
	24	(a) Norwich C	D	0-0		9,000	11						3	5			2		7	4				1	9	6	10	8
Oct	1	(a) West Ham U	L	0-3		15,000	11						3	5			2	8	7	4				1	9	6	10	
	8	(h) Luton T	D	3-3	Steer, Browning, McNaught	12,000	11				10		3	5			2		7	4				1	9	6		8
	15	(a) Portsmouth	D	1-1	Browning	9,000	11				10		3	5			2		7	4				1	9	6		8
	22	(h) Northampton T	D	1-1	Steer	10,000	11		7		10		3	5			2			4				1	9	6		8
	29	(a) Brighton & HA	L	1-2	Steer	12,000	11		7		10		3	5			2			4				1	9	6	8	
Nov	5	(h) Exeter C	W	1-0	Browning	8,000	11		7		10		3	5			2			4				1	9	6	8	
	12	(a) Swindon T	L	1-2	Browning	8,000	11				10		3				2		7	4	5			1	9	6	8	
	19	(h) Bristol R	L	1-2	Steer	9,000	11				10		3			2		9	7	4	5		6	1	8			
	26	(a) Crystal P	L	1-2	Browning	6,000	11				10	6	3			2		9	7	4	5			1			8	
Dec	3	(h) Brentford	W	2-0	Browning, Whyman	15,000	11				10	6				3	2	9	7	4	5			1			8	
	10	(a) Clapton O	L	1-2	Browning	4,000	11				10	6				3	2	9	7	4	5			1	8			
	17	(h) Watford	W	4-1	Browning 3, McKie	4,000			11		10	6	3				2	9		4	5			1	8		7	
	24	(a) Plymouth A	D	1-1	Steer	8,000			11		10	6	3				2	9		4	5			1	8		7	
	26	(a) Southampton	L	0-1		10,000			11		10	6	3	5			2	9		4				1	8		7	
	27	(h) Southampton	W	3-1	McKie 2, Whyman	12,000			11		10	6	3				2	9		4	5			1	8		7	
	31	(a) Coventry C	L	2-3	Browning, McKie	6,000			11		10	6	3	5			2	9		4				1	8		7	
Jan	7	(h) New Brompton	W	5-0	Browning 2, Steer 2, Whyman	5,000			11		10	6	3				2	9		4	5			1	8		7	
	21	(a) Millwall	D	1-1	Steer	6,000	11		7		10	4	3				2	9		5				1	8	6		
	28	(h) Norwich C	D	1-1	Browning	6,000			11		10	4	3				2	9		5				1	8	6	7	
Feb	11	(a) Luton T	W	1-0	McKie	6,000			11		10	4	3				2	9		5				1	8	6	7	
	18	(h) Portsmouth	W	1-0	McKie	7,000			11		10	4	3				2	9		5				1	8	6	7	
	25	(a) Northampton T	D	0-0		5,000	11				10	4	3				2	9		5				1	8	6	7	
Mar	4	(h) Brighton & HA	D	0-0		6,000	11			8	10	4	3				2	9		5				1		6	7	
	11	(a) Exeter C	D	2-2	McKie, Steer	8,000	11				10	4	3				2	9		5				1	8	6	7	
	18	(h) Swindon T	W	1-0	Browning	8,000	11				10	4	3				2	9		5				1	8	6	7	
	25	(a) Bristol R	D	0-0		6,000	11				10	4	3				2	9		5				1	8	6	7	
Apr	1	(h) Crystal P	D	0-0		8,000	11				10	4	3				2	9		5				1	8	6	7	
	8	(a) Brentford	D	1-1	Hartwell	8,000	11			8		4	3	5			2		7					1	9	6		10
	14	(h) Southend U	D	1-1	Browning	15,000	11			8	10	4	3	5			2	9						1		6	7	
	15	(h) Clapton O	W	5-3	McKie 2, Brown 2, Whyman	7,000	11			8	10	4	3	5			2	9						1		6	7	
	17	(a) Southend U	W	2-1	Barnes, Browning	6,000	11			8	10	4	3	5			2	9	7					1		6		
	22	(a) Watford	L	0-2		6,000	11			*	10	6	3	5			2	9	7	4				1				
	29	(h) Plymouth A	W	1-0	Browning	6,000	11			8	10	4	3	5	7			9				2		1		6		
						App	29	2	17	6	31	25	36	19	1	4	35	28	12	33	9	1	1	38	30	27	28	5
						Goals	2	2		2	18			2				10	1						9		6	

* Brown missed the train and did not play

FA Cup

Date		Opponent	Res	Score	Scorers	Att	Barnes	Bradshaw	Brindley	Brown	Browning	Butterworth	Fidler	Hartwell	Law	Lee	McDonald	McKie	McNaught	Mitchell	Morris	Pullen	Radnage	Shaw	Steer	Wake	Whyman	Wilson	Round
Jan	14	(a) Bradford	L	3-5	McKie 2, Steer	25,000			11		10	6	3				2	9		4	5			1	8		7		1
						App			1		1	1	1				1	1		1	1			1	1		1		
						Goals												2							1				

Attendance Summary

	ATTENDANCES			AVERAGE		
	Home	Away	Total	Home	Away	Total
League	182,000	148,000	330,000	8,650	7,050	7,850
FA Cup		25,000	25,000		25,000	25,000
Total	182,000	173,000	355,000	8,650	7,850	8,250

1911-12

Southern League Division 1

Date	Opponent	Result	Scorers	Att	Barnes	Browning	Butterworth	Fidler	King	McDonald	McKie	Mitchell	Nicholls	Ovens	Pullen	Revill	Shaw	Smith	Thornton	Tosswill	Wake	Whyman
Sep 2	(a) Plymouth A	W 1-0	Revill	10,000	11	10	4	3		2	9	5				8	1	7			6	
9	(h) Reading	W 3-0	McKie 2, Revill	10,000	11		4	3		2	9	5				8	1	7	10		6	
16	(a) Watford	W 3-0	McKie, Thornton, Revill	3,000	11		4	3		2	9	5				8	1	7	10		6	
23	(h) New Brompton	W 3-0	Revill 2, McKie	12,000	11		4	3		2	9	5				8	1	7	10		6	
30	(a) Exeter C	D 1-1	McKie (pen)	4,000	11		4			2	9	5		3		8	1	7	10		6	
Oct 7	(h) Brentford	W 4-0	McKie 2 (pen), Revill, Smith	15,000	11					2	9	5		3		8	1	7	10		6	4
14	(h) Luton T	W 2-0	Revill, McKie	14,000	11					2	9	5		3		8	1	7	10		6	4
21	(a) Millwall	D 1-1	Barnes	25,000	11					2	9	5			3	8	1	7	10		6	4
28	(h) West Ham U	W 4-1	McKie, Smith, Revill, Thornton	25,000	11		4			2	9	5			3	8	1	7	10		6	
Nov 4	(a) Bristol R	W 2-0	McKie, Revill	16,000	11		4			2	9	5			3	8	1	7	10		6	
11	(h) Swindon T	L 1-3	McKie	25,000	11		4	3		2	9	5				8	1	7	10		6	
18	(a) Northampton T	L 1-5	McKie	6,000	11		4	3		2	9	5				8	1	7	10		6	
25	(h) Brighton & HA	W 2-0	Thornton (pen), Mitchell	8,000	11		4			2	9	5			3	8	1	7	10		6	
Dec 2	(a) Stoke	W 2-0	Barnes, McKie	5,000	11		4			2	9	5			3	8	1		10		6	7
9	(h) Coventry C	D 0-0		6,000	11		4				9	5		2	3	8	1	7	10		6	
16	(a) Clapton O	W 1-0	Thornton	4,000	11						9	5		2	3	8	1	7	10		6	4
23	(h) Norwich C	L 1-2	Smith	8,000	11						9	5		2	3	8	1	7	10		6	4
25	(h) Crystal P	W 3-2	Thornton 2, Revill	8,000	11		4	3				5		2		8	1	7	10		6	9
26	(a) Crystal P	L 0-3		22,000	11	10			8		9	5		2	3		1	7			6	4
30	(h) Plymouth A	W 2-0	Revill 2	9,000	11	10						5		2	3	8	1	7	9		6	4
Jan 6	(a) Reading	W 1-0	Ovens	4,000	11	10				2		5		4	3	8	1	7	9		6	
20	(h) Watford	D 1-1	Browning	10,000	11	10				2		5	1	4	3			7	9		6	8
27	(a) New Brompton	W 2-1	Barnes, Thornton	6,000	11	10				2		5		4	3	8	1	7	9		6	
Feb 3	(h) Exeter C	D 0-0		5,000	11					2	9	5		4	3	8	1	7	10		6	
10	(a) Brentford	W 2-1	Revill, Barnes	8,000	11	10				2	9	5		4	3	8	1	7			6	
17	(a) Luton T	W 3-1	Smith 2, McKie	6,000	11					2	9	5		4	3	8	1	7	10		6	
24	(h) Millwall	D 1-1	Mitchell (pen)	5,000	11	10			9	2		5		4	3	8	1	7			6	
Mar 2	(a) West Ham U	L 0-3		10,000	11					2	9	5		4	3	8	1	7	10		6	
9	(h) Bristol R	W 4-2	Thornton 2, Revill, McKie	6,000	11		4			2	9	5			3	8	1	7	10		6	
16	(a) Swindon T	D 1-1	Smith	8,000	11		4			2	9	5			3	8	1	7	10		6	
23	(h) Northampton T	W 2-1	Smith, McKie	5,000	11					2	9	5		4	3	8	1	7	10		6	
30	(a) Brighton & HA	L 1-3	Revill	7,000	11					2	9			4	3	8	1	7	10		6	5
Apr 5	(h*) Southampton	D 1-1	Tosswill	26,000	11					2	9	5		4	3	7	1		10	8	6	
6	(h*) Stoke	W 1-0	Whyman	20,000	11					2	9	5		4	3	8	1	7	10		6	
8	(a) Southampton	D 0-0		12,000	11				7	2		5		4	3	8	1		10	9	6	
13	(a) Coventry C	D 0-0		8,000	11					2	9	5		4	3	8	1	7	10		6	
20	(h) Clapton O	W 1-0	Thornton	8,000	11					2		5		4	3	8	1	7	10	9	6	
27	(a) Norwich C	D 1-1	Smith	6,000	11					2	9	5		4	3	8	1	7	10		6	
				App	38	8	15	7	3	32	30	37	1	25	28	36	37	35	34	3	38	11
				Goals	4	1					16	2		1		15		8	10	1		1

*Played at the White City

FA Cup

Date	Opponent	Result	Scorers	Att	Barnes	Browning	Butterworth	Fidler	King	McDonald	McKie	Mitchell	Nicholls	Ovens	Pullen	Revill	Shaw	Smith	Thornton	Tosswill	Wake	Whyman	Round
Jan 13	(h) Bradford C	D 0-0		18,000	11	10				2		5		4	3	8	1	7	9		6		1
18	(a) Bradford C	L 0-4		10,000	11	10			9	2		5		4	3	8	1				6	7	Rep
				App	2	2			1	2		2		2	2	2	2	1	1		2	1	
				Goals																			

FA Charity Shield

Date	Opponent	Result	Scorers	Att	Barnes	Browning	Butterworth	Fidler	King	McDonald	McKie	Mitchell	Nicholls	Ovens	Pullen	Revill	Shaw	Smith	Thornton	Tosswill	Wake	Whyman
May 4	(n†) Blackburn R	L 1-2	Revill	7,111	11					2	9	5			3	8	1	7	10		6	4
				App	1					1	1	1			1	1	1	1	1		1	1
				Goals												1						

†Played at White Hart Lane, London.

Attendance Summary

	ATTENDANCES			AVERAGE		
	Home	Away	Total	Home	Away	Total
League	261,000	170,000	431,000	13,750	8,950	11,350
FA Cup	18,000	10,000	28,000	18,000	10,000	14,000
Charity Shield		7,111	7,111		7,111	7,111
Total	279,000	187,111	466,111	13,950	8,900	11,350

1912-13

Southern League Division 1

Date	Match	Result	Scorers	Att	Anderson	Barnes	Birch	Broster	Browning	Day	Fidler	Gaul	Gregory	Higgins	Ives	Jackman	McDonald	McKie	Mitchell	Nicholls	Ovens	Pullen	Revill	Sangster	Shaw	Thompson	Thornton	Wake	Weblin	Whyman	Wingrove
Sep 5	(h) Plymouth A	W 2-1	Birch 2	10,000		11	9										2		5		4	3	8		1	7		6		10	
7	(h) Norwich C	W 1-0	Birch	9,000	8	11	9										2		5		4	3			1	7	10	6			
14	(a) Gillingham	D 0-0		7,000	8	11	9		10								2		5		4	3			1	7		6			
21	(h) Northampton T	W 3-2	Birch, Anderson, Browning	12,000	8	11	9		10								2		5		4	3		7	1			6			
28	(a) Stoke	D 0-0		6,000		11	9		10								2		5		4	3	8		1	7		6			
Oct 5	(a) Brentford	W 2-0	Wake, Richards (og)	13,200		11	9		10								2		5		4	3	8		1	7		6			
12	(h) Millwall	D 1-1	Revill	16,000		11	9		10								2		5		4	3	8		1	7		6			
19	(a) Bristol R	L 0-3		5,000		11	9		10								2		5		4	3	8		1	7		6			
26	(h) Swindon T	W 2-0	Kay (og), Ovens	8,000		11	9		10								2		5		4	3	8		1	7		6			
Nov 2	(a) Portsmouth	D 1-1	Birch	12,000		11	9		10								2		5		4	3	8	7	1					6	
9	(h) Exeter C	W 2-1	Mitchell, Revill	8,000		11	9		10								2		5		4	3	8		1	7		6			
16	(a) West Ham U	L 0-1		10,000		11	9		10								2		5		4	3	8		1	7		6			
23	(h) Brighton & HA	D 0-0		11,000		11	9		10		3						2		5				8		1	7		6		4	
Dec 7	(h) Watford	W 2-0	Birch 2	8,000		11	8						9				2		5		4	3			1	7		6		10	
14	(a) Merthyr T	D 0-0		3,000		11	8		10				9						5			3			1	7		6	2	4	
21	(h) Crystal P	W 2-0	Revill 2	10,000		11	8					9							5			3	10		1	7		6	2	4	
25	(h) Southampton	W 1-0	Birch	20,000		11	8				2	9							5			3	10	7	1			6		4	
26	(a) Southampton	W 1-0	McKie	3,000		11	8	6			2							9	5			3	10	7	1					4	
28	(a) Norwich C	L 0-2		6,000		11	8											9	5		4	3	10		1	7		6	2		
30	(a) Coventry C	D 1-1	Thompson	5,000		11	8											9	5		4	3	10		1	7		6	2		
Jan 4	(h) Gillingham	W 2-0	Birch, Barnes	7,000		11	8				2							9	5		4	3	10		1	7		6			
25	(h) Stoke	W 1-0	Whyman	9,000		11	8				2								5		4	3	10		1	7		6		9	
Feb 8	(h) Brentford	W 2-1	Birch, Richards (og)	16,000		11	8					9					2		5		4	3	10		1	7		6			
15	(a) Millwall	L 1-2	Gaul	14,000		11	8					9					2	10	5		4	3			1	7		6			
22	(a) Northampton T	D 0-0		6,000		11	8										2	10	5		4	3			1	7		6		9	
Mar 1	(a) Swindon T	L 1-4	McKie	6,000		11	8										2	10	5		4	3			1	7		6		9	
8	(h) Portsmouth	D 1-1	Birch	8,000		11	8			9			10				2		5		4	3			1	7		6			
15	(a) Exeter C	L 1-3	Birch	6,000		11	8			9							2		5	1	4	3	10			7				6	
21	(a) Reading	L 0-1		15,000			8			9		10		2		11			5		4	3			1	7		6			
22	(h) West Ham U	L 0-1		15,000		11	8										2	9	5			3	10		1	7		4		6	
24	(h) Reading	D 1-1	Gaul	7,000			8					9		2		11		10	5		4	3			1	7				6	
29	(a) Brighton & HA	L 1-4	Birch	5,000			8					9				11	2	10	5		4	3			1	7				6	
Apr 5	(h) Coventry C	W 4-0	Whyman, Gaul, Birch, Revill	6,000		11	8					9							5		4	3	10		1	7			2	6	
10	(h) Bristol R	W 2-0	Gaul 2	4,000		11	8			9									5		4	3	10		1	7			2	6	
13	(a) Watford	W 2-1	Gaul, Ovens	4,000		11	8					9							5		4	3	10		1	7			2	6	
19	(h) Merthyr T	W 4-1	Ives 2, Gaul, Revill	7,000			8	11				9			7				5		4	3	10		1				2	6	
23	(a) Plymouth A	L 0-2		4,000		11	8					9							5		4	3	10		1	7				6	2
26	(a) Crystal P	W 2-1	Birch, Gaul	8,000		11	8	6				9							5		4	3	10		1	7			2		
				App	3	34	38	3	12	4	5	12	3	2	1	3	22	10	38	1	32	37	26	4	37	33	1	27	9	20	1
				Goals	1	1	15		1			8			2			2	1		2		6			1		1		2	

3 own-goals

FA Cup

Date	Match	Result	Scorers	Att	Anderson	Barnes	Birch	Broster	Browning	Day	Fidler	Gaul	Gregory	Higgins	Ives	Jackman	McDonald	McKie	Mitchell	Nicholls	Ovens	Pullen	Revill	Sangster	Shaw	Thompson	Thornton	Wake	Weblin	Whyman	Wingrove	Round
Jan 11	(h) Halifax T	W 4-2	Revill, Birch, Whyman, Ovens	11,000		11	8				2								5		4	3	10		1	7		6		9		1
Feb 1	(a) Middlesbrough	L 2-3	Birch 2	25,000		11	8				2								5		4	3	10		1	7		6		9		2
				App		2	2				2								2		2	2	2		2	2		2		2		
				Goals			3														1		1							1		

Attendance Summary

	ATTENDANCES Home	Away	Total	AVERAGE Home	Away	Total
League	191,000	138,200	329,200	10,050	7,250	8,650
FA Cup	11,000	25,000	36,000	11,000	25,000	18,000
Total	202,000	163,200	365,200	10,100	8,150	9,150

1913-14

Southern League Division 1

Date	Opponents	Result	Scorers	Att	Baldock	Birch	Blake	Broster	Fortune	Gaul	Gregory	Higgins	Ives	Jefferies	Matthews	Miller	Mitchell	Nicholls	Ovens	Pennifer	Pullen	Strugnell	Thompson	Wake	Weblin	Whyman	Wilde	Wingrove
Sep 1	(a) Swindon T	L 0-3		7,000		8							11			9	5	1	4		3	10	7			6		2
6	(a) Gillingham	L 0-1		6,000		8							11			9	5	1	4		3	10	7			6		2
13	(h) Merthyr T	L 0-1		10,000		8				9			11				5	1	4		3	10	7	6				2
20	(a) Northampton T	D 2-2	Birch, Gaul	5,000		8				9	10		11				5	1	4		3		7	6				2
27	(h) West Ham U	D 2-2	Miller, Birch	14,000		8					10		11	1		9	5				3		7	6		4		2
Oct 4	(a) Southend U	W 2-1	Gregory, Birch	6,000						8	10	2	11			9	5	1	4		3		7	6				
11	(h) Plymouth A	D 0-0		7,000		8			11		10	2				9		1	4		3		7	6		5		
18	(a) Brighton & HA	L 0-1		6,000		8					10	2	11			9	5	1	4		3		7	6				
25	(h) Southampton	W 3-1	Gregory, Ives, Miller	3,000							10	2	11			9	5	1	4		3	8	7	6				
Nov 1	(a) Portsmouth	D 1-1	Pullen	12,000							10	2	11			9	5	1	4		3	8	7	6				
8	(h) Reading	W 1-0	Miller	10,000		8					10	2	11			9		1	4		3		7	6		5		
15	(a) Millwall	L 0-2		10,000							10	2	11			9		1	4		3	8	7	6		5		
22	(h) Crystal P	W 3-0	Miller 2, Birch	10,000		8					10	2	11			9	5	1	4		3		7	6				
29	(a) Exeter C	D 0-0		6,300		8					10	2	11			9	5	1	4		3		7	6				
Dec 6	(h) Coventry C	W 3-0	Birch 2, Baldock	8,000	8	9					10	2	11				5	1	4		3		7	6				
13	(a) Cardiff C	L 0-3		12,000	10	8						2	11				5	1	4	9	3		7	6				
20	(h) Watford	W 3-2	Birch 2, Mitchell (pen)	6,000	8	9					10	2	11				5	1			3		7	6		4		
25	(h) Norwich C	D 1-1	Birch	15,000		8				9	10		11				5	1	4		3		7	6	2			
26	(a) Norwich C	W 3-2	Miller 3	7,000		8					10	2	11			9	5	1	4		3		7			6		
27	(h) Gillingham	D 0-0		8,000		8			11		10	2				9	5	1	4		3		7	6				
Jan 3	(a) Merthyr T	W 2-1	Birch, Gregory	7,000		8			11		10	2				9	5	1	4		3		7	6				
17	(h) Northampton T	D 0-0		10,000		8			11		10	2				9	5	1	4		3		7			6		
24	(a) West Ham U	L 1-4	Miller	11,000					11		10					9	5	1	4		3		7	6		8		2
Feb 7	(h) Southend U	D 0-0		3,000		8			11			2						1	4	9	3	10	7	6		5		
14	(a) Plymouth A	L 0-2		5,000					11		10						5	1		9	3	8	7	6		4		2
28	(a) Southampton	W 2-0	Birch, Gregory	8,000		8			11		10					9	5	1	2		3		7	6		4		
Mar 12	(h) Swindon T	W 4-2	Skiller (og), Miller 2, Birch	15,000		8		4			10		11			9	5	1	2		3		7			6		
21	(h) Millwall	W 1-0	Gregory	12,000		8		4			10		11			9	5	1	2		3		7			6		
26	(h) Portsmouth	W 1-0	Gregory	6,000		8	9	4			10		11				5	1	2		3		7			6		
28	(a) Crystal P	L 1-2	Whyman	7,000		8		4			10		11			9	5	1	2		3		7			6		
Apr 4	(h) Exeter C	L 2-3	Birch, Miller	5,000		8					10		11			9	5	1	2		3		7	6		4		
10	(h) Bristol R	W 1-0	Birch	8,000		8					10		11			9	5	1	2		3		7	6		4		
11	(a) Coventry C	W 1-0	Birch	8,500		8					10		11			9	5	1			3		7	6		4		2
13	(a) Bristol R	L 1-2	Thompson	12,000		8	9						11				5	1			3	10	7	6		4		2
18	(h) Cardiff C	L 0-2		8,000		8							11			9	5	1			3	10	7	6		4		2
23	(h) Brighton & HA	W 3-0	Miller 2, Birch	7,000		8					10		11		1	9	5		2		3		7	6		4		
25	(a) Watford	L 0-2		4,000							10		11			9	5	1	4		3	8	7	6		8		2
29	(a) Reading	W 1-0	Thompson	5,000							10		11		1	9			4		3		7		2	6	5	
				App	3	30	2	4	8	4	31	17	30	1	2	28	33	35	32	3	38	11	38	29	2	25	1	11
				Goals	1	16				1	6		1			14	1				1		2			1		

1 own-goals

FA Cup

Date	Opponents	Result	Scorers	Att	Baldock	Birch	Blake	Broster	Fortune	Gaul	Gregory	Higgins	Ives	Jefferies	Matthews	Miller	Mitchell	Nicholls	Ovens	Pennifer	Pullen	Strugnell	Thompson	Wake	Weblin	Whyman	Wilde	Wingrove	Round
Jan 10	(h) Bristol C	D 2-2	Miller, Birch	18,000		8			11		10	2				9	5	1	4		3		7	6					1
15	(a) Bristol C	*W 2-0	Birch, Gregory	14,000		8			11		10	2				9	5	1	4		3		7	6					Rep
31	(a) Swansea T	W 2-1	Birch 2	15,000		8			11		10	2				9	5	1	4		3		7	6					2
Feb 21	(a) Birmingham C	W 2-1	Gregory, Miller	33,000		8			11		10	2				9	5	1	4		3		7	6					3
Mar 7	(a) Liverpool	L 1-2	Mitchell (pen)	36,500		8			11		10					9	5	1	2		3		7	6		4			4
				App		5			5		5	4				5	5	5	5		5		5	5		1			
				Goals		4					2					2	1												

* After extra-time

Attendance Summary

	ATTENDANCES Home	Away	Total	AVERAGE Home	Away	Total
League	165,000	144,800	309,800	8,700	7,600	8,150
FA Cup	18,000	98,500	116,500	18,000	24,650	23,300
Total	183,000	243,300	426,300	9,150	10,600	9,900

1914-15

Southern League Division 1

Month	Date/Opponent	Result	Scorers	Att	Baldock	Birch	Broster	Donald	Gregory	Higgins	Ives	Loney	McKinney	McLeod	Miller	Millington	Mitchell	Ovens	Pullen	Simons	Thompson	Wake	Whyman	Wilde	Wingrove
Sep	1 (a) Millwall	L 1-3	Miller	6,000		8			10		11			1	9	2	5	4	3		7	6			
	5 (h) Reading	L 0-1		4,000		8			10		11			1	9	2	5	4	3		7	6			
	12 (a) Southampton	L 0-3		12,000		8		11	10					1	9	2	5	4	3		7		6		
	16 (a) Luton T	W 4-2	Birch 2, Donald, Whyman	4,000		8		11	10	2				1	9		5	4	3		7		6		
	19 (h) Northampton T	D 0-0		5,000		8		11	10	2				1	9		5	4	3		7		6		
	26 (a) Watford	D 2-2	Birch, Whyman	5,000		8		11	10	2				1	9		5	4	3		7		6		
Oct	3 (h) Plymouth A	D 1-1	Miller	6,000		8		11	10	2				1	9		5	4	3		7	6			
	10 (a) West Ham U	D 2-2	Baldock 2	7,000	10	8		11		2				1	9		5		3		7	6	4		
	17 (h) Norwich C	D 1-1	Baldock	6,000	10	8		11						1	9	2	5	4	3		7	6			
	24 (a) Gillingham	W 1-0	Thompson	7,000		8	10	11						1	9	2	5	4	3		7	6			
	31 (h) Brighton & HA	L 0-1		5,000	10	8	4	11		2				1	9	3					7	6		5	
Nov	7 (a) Cardiff C	L 0-2		10,000	9	8		7	10		11			1		2	5	4	3			6			
	14 (h) Exeter C	L 0-2		10,000		8		11	10					1		2	5	4	3	9	7	6			
	28 (h) Portsmouth	L 1-2	Thompson	4,000	10	8		11						1		2	5	4	3	9	7		6		
Dec	5 (a) Swindon T	W 2-1	Simons, Birch	1,000		8	4	11						1	9	2	5		3	10	7	6			
	12 (h) Southend U	W 4-2	Broster, Donald, Miller, Simons	4,000		8	4	11						1	9	2	5		3	10	7	6			
	19 (a) Crystal P	D 2-2	Simons, Gregory	3,000		8	4	11	10					1		2	5		3	9	7		6		
	25 (a) Bristol R	W 3-1	Birch 2, Miller	8,000		8	4	11						1	9	2	5		3	10	7		6		
	26 (h) Bristol R	W 2-1	Miller, Simons	3,000		8	4	11						1	9	2	5		3	10	7		6		
	28 (h) Millwall	L 0-1		12,000		8	4			2	11			1	9		5		3	10	7	6			
Jan	2 (a) Reading	D 2-2	Birch 2	5,000		8	4	7			11			1	9	2	5		3	10			6		
	16 (h) Southampton	W 4-3	Miller 2, Simons, Birch	4,000		8	4	11						1	9	2		5	3	10	7		6		
	23 (a) Northampton T	D 1-1	Miller	3,000	8		4	11						1	9	2		5	3	10	7		6		
Feb	6 (a) Plymouth A	D 1-1	Birch	3,000		8	4	11						1	9	2	5		3	10	7		6		
	13 (h) West Ham U	D 1-1	Birch	5,000		8	4	11						1	9	2	5		3	10	7		6		
	27 (h) Gillingham	W 3-0	Miller 2, Mitchell	5,000		8	4	11					7	1	9		5		3	10			6		2
Mar	6 (a) Brighton & HA	L 0-1		4,000		8	4	11					7	1	9		5		3	10			6		2
	13 (h) Cardiff C	W 3-0	Miller 2, Gregory	4,000		8	4	11	10					1	9				3		7		6	5	2
	18 (h) Watford	L 2-5	Miller, Birch	5,000		8	4	11	10					1	9		5		3		7		6		2
	20 (a) Exeter C	W 1-0	Birch	3,000		8	4	11						1	9	2			3	10	7		6	5	
	24 (a) Norwich C	L 1-2	Donald	3,000		8	4	11						1	9	2			3	10	7		6	5	
	27 (h) Luton T	L 0-3		3,000		8	4	11	10					1	9	2			3		7		6	5	
Apr	2 (h) Croydon Comm	W 1-0	Baldock	3,000	10	8	4	11						1	9	2	5		3		7		6		
	3 (a) Portsmouth	D 1-1	Birch	6,000	10	8	4	11						1	9	2	5		3		7	6			
	5 (a) Croydon Comm	L 0-1		6,000	10	8	4	11						1	9	2	5		3		7	6			
	10 (h) Swindon T	W 4-2	Birch, Baldock, Thompson, Miller	7,000	10	8	4	11						1	9	2	5		3		7	6			
	17 (a) Southend U	D 1-1	Whyman	2,000		8	4	11						1	9	2	5		3	10	7		6		
	24 (h) Crystal P	W 3-2	Simons 2, Donald	5,000	10	8	4	11				2		1		3				9	7		6	5	
				App	11	37	26	35	13	7	5	1	2	38	33	28	30	14	36	19	34	15	24	6	4
				Goals	5	15	1	4	2						14		1			7	3		3		

FA Cup

Month	Date/Opponent	Result	Scorers	Att	Baldock	Birch	Broster	Donald	Gregory	Higgins	Ives	Loney	McKinney	McLeod	Miller	Millington	Mitchell	Ovens	Pullen	Simons	Thompson	Wake	Whyman	Wilde	Wingrove	Round
Jan	9 (h) Glossop	W 2-1	Birch, Miller	7,000		8	4	11						1	9	2	5		3	10	7		6			1
	30 (h) Leeds C	W 1-0	Simons	10,000		8	4	11						1	9	2	5		3	10	7		6			2
Feb	20 (h*) Everton	L 1-2	Birch	33,000		8	4	11						1	9	2	5		3	10	7		6			3
				App		3	3	3						3	3	3	3		3	3	3		3			
				Goals		2									1					1						

*Played at Stamford Bridge, Chelsea, London.

Attendance Summary

	ATTENDANCES Home	Away	Total	AVERAGE Home	Away	Total
League	100,000	98,000	198,000	5,250	5,150	5,200
FA Cup	50,000		50,000	16,650		16,650
Total	150,000	98,000	248,000	6,800	5,150	6,050

1915-16

London Combination

Date	Opponents	Result	Scorers	Att	1	2	3	4	5	6	7	8	9	10	11
Sep 4 (a)	Millwall	L 1-3	Humphries	7,000	Matthews F	Loney	Draper	Smith A	Mitchell	Gregory	Nisbet	Smith B	Humphries	Baldock	Fox
11 (h)	Croydon Comm	W 2-1	Fox, Coleman	3,000	..	..	Linkson	Gregory	..	Wake	..	Coleman	..	..	..
18 (a)	Arsenal	L 1-2	Humphries	8,000	..	Linkson	Draper	..	..	..	..	..	..	..	..
25 (h)	Brentford	L 1-2	Humphries		Nixon	Loney	..	Smith A	..	..	..	..	..	..	..
Oct 2 (a)	West Ham U	L 1-2	Fox	4,000	..	Draper	Loney	Wake	Gregory	Baldock	Fox	Simons	Blake	Coleman	Humphries
9 (h)	Tottenham H	L 0-4		4,000	Matthews F	..	..	Gregory	Mitchell	Wake	Hunter	Coleman	Humphries	Simons	Fox
16 (a)	Crystal P	L 0-1			Jeffries	Wood	Draper	Smith A	..	..	Elliott	Nicholson	Simons	Baldock	..
23 (h)	Chelsea	W 1-0	Coleman	6,000	..	Loney	Wingrove	Wood	..	..	Hicks	Coleman	Humphries	Gregory	..
30 (h)	Fulham	W 2-1	Humphries 2	3,000	..	..	Linkson	Gregory	..	..	..	Dale	..	Baldock	..
Nov 6 (a)	Clapton O	W 2-0	Dale, Simons		..	..	..	Wood	..	..	..	..	Simons	..	..
13 (h)	Millwall	L 1-5	Baldock	3,000	..	..	..	Smith A	..	Wood	..	..	Humphries	..	..
20 (a)	Croydon Comm	W 1-0	Humphries	1,000	..	..	..	Wood	..	Wake	..	..	..	..	..
27 (h)	Arsenal	D 1-1	Hicks	2,000	..	..	Draper	Baldock	..	..	MatthewsA	Hicks	..	Dale	..
Dec 4 (a)	Brentford	L 0-4		1,200	..	..	Linkson	..	..	..	Hicks	Poulton	Simons	..	..
11 (h)	West Ham U	D 1-1	Dale	2,000	Nixon	..	..	Wood	..	..	Nisbet	Dale	..	Baldock	..
18 (a)	Tottenham H	L 1-2	Simons	3,000	..	..	..	..	..	..	..	..	..	..	..
25 (a)	Watford	L 1-5	Humphries	500	Jeffries	Bellamy	Mitchell	Baldock	Dale	..	..	Hicks	Humphries	Simons	..
27 (h)	Watford	W 3-1	Humphries, Nisbet 2	2,000	..	Loney	Linkson	Whyman	Mitchell	..	..	Dale	..	Baldock	Ives
Jan 1 (h)	Crystal P	W 5-1	Opp own-goal, Baldock, Fox, Nisbet, Humphreys	1,500	Nixon	..	..	Wood	..	..	..	..	..	..	Fox
8 (a)	Chelsea	L 1-5	Mitchell (pen)	10,000	..	Linkson	Loney	Wake	..	Wood	Fox	..	..	..	Nisbet
15 (a)	Fulham	W 1-0	Mitchell	5,000	..	..	Draper	Whyman	..	Baldock	Nisbet	..	..	Simons	Fox
22 (h)	Clapton O	D 0-0		2,000	..	Loney	Linkson	Baldock	..	Draper	..	..	..	Hicks	..
Feb 5 (h)	Chelsea	L 0-3		3,000	..	Linkson	Draper	Simons	..	Dale	MatthewsA	Hicks	..	Nisbet	..
12 (a)	Watford	L 0-6		1,000	Jeffries	Draper	Hooper	Dale	Wake	Somerville	..	Jackman	..	Walsh	..
19 (h)	Brentford	D 1-1	Simons	2,500	..	Hooper	Draper	Somerville	Mitchell	Wake	Hicks	Dale	Simons	Fox	Humphries
Mar 4 (h)	Clapton O	D 1-1	Wagstaffe		Nixon	Linkson	Pullen	Loney	Dale	..	Donald	Birch	Humphries	Wagstaffe	Fox
11 (a)	Tottenham H	D 0-0		3,000	..	..	..	..	Birch	..	..	Hicks	Simons	Hughes	..
18 (h)	Watford	D 2-2	Birch, Thompson		Jeffries	Draper	..	Somerville	Mitchell	..	..	Birch	Thompson	McRae	..
25 (a)	Brentford	L 0-4		2,000	Matthews F	Loney	..	Hooper	..	..	..	Hicks	Simons	Somerville	..
Apr 1 (h)	Reading	L 2-6	Mitchell, Hicks	3,000	Jeffries	Draper	..	Whyman	Loney	..	Hooper	..	Humphries	Mitchell	..
8 (a)	Clapton O	D 1-1	Hicks		..	Loney	..	..	Mitchell	..	Donald	Dale	Thompson	Hicks	..
15 (h)	Tottenham H	L 1-3	Dale	4,000	..	..	..	Hooper	Somerville	..	..	..	Simons	..	..
21 (a)	Millwall	L 2-6	Donald 2	5,000	..	Draper	..	Somerville	Mitchell	..	..	..	Hicks	Nisbet	..
22 (a)	Reading	W 2-1	Fox, Simons		..	..	..	Whyman	..	..	..	..	Simons	Hicks	..
24 (h)	Millwall	W 2-0	Broster, Simons	3,000	..	Loney	..	Broster	Somerville	..	..	..	..	..	..
29 (a)	Chelsea	L 0-3		12,000	..	..	..	Whyman	Mitchell	..	..	..	..	Baldock	..

Above the bold line results from the Principle Tournament, below the Subsidiary games.

London Combination (Principle)
Appearances: J.W.Baldock 20, Bellamy 1, Blake 1, Coleman 6, G.Dale 14, W.Draper 9, Elliott 1, G.F.Fox 21, John Gregory 7, A.Hicks 9, Humphries 17, Hunter 1, Ben Ives 1, H.Jefferies 10, Linkson 14, B.Loney 18, A.Matthews 1, F.Matthews 4, Archie Mitchell 21, Nicholson 1, D.Nisbet 12, Nixon 8, Poulton 1, H.T.Simons 9, A.Smith 4, B.Smith 1, W.Wake 18, A.Whyman 2, J.Wingrove 1, Wood 9.
Goalscorers: J.W.Baldock 2, Coleman 2, G.Dale 2, G.F.Fox 3, A.Hicks 1, Humphries 9, Archie Mitchell 2, D.Nisbet 3, H.T.Simons 2, Opponents own-goal 1.

London Combination (Subsidiary)
Appearances: J.W.Baldock 1; Jimmy Birch 3, J.Broster 1, G.Dale 10, D.Donald 10, W.Draper 7, G.F.Fox 14, A.Hicks 10, H.Hooper 5, Hughes 1, Humphries 5, Jackman 1, H.Jefferies 10, Linkson 3, B.Loney 8, McRae 1, A.Matthews 2, F.Matthews 1, Archie Mitchell 9, D.Nisbet 2, Nixon 3, H.Pullen 11, H.T.Simons 8, J.Somerville 7, W.Thompson 2, Wagstaffe 1, W.Wake 13, Walsh 1, A.Whyman 4.
Goalscorers: Jimmy Birch 1; J Broster 1, G.Dale 1, D.Donald 2, G.F.Fox 1, A.Hicks 2, Archie Mitchell 1, H.T.Simons 3, W.Thompson 1, Wagstaffe 1.

Appearances Total: J.W.Baldock 21, Bellamy 1, Jimmy Birch 3, Blake 1, J.Broster 1, Coleman 6, G.Dale 24, D.Donald 10, W.Draper 16, Elliott 1, G.F.Fox 35, John Gregory 7, A.Hicks 19, H.Hooper 5, Hughes 1, Humphries 22, Hunter 1, Ben Ives 1, Jackman 1, H.Jefferies 20, Linkson 17, B.Loney 26, McRae 1, A.Matthews 3, F.Matthews 5, Archie Mitchell 30, Nicholson 1, D.Nisbet 14, Nixon 11, Poulton 1, H.Pullen 11, H.T.Simons 17, A.Smith 4, B.Smith 1, J.Somerville 7, W.Thompson 2, Wagstaffe 1, W.Wake 31, Walsh 1, A.Whyman 6, J.Wingrove 1, Wood 9.
Goalscorers Total: J.W.Baldock 2, Jimmy Birch 1, J.Broster 1, Coleman 2, G.Dale 3, D.Donald 2, G.F.Fox 4, A.Hicks 3, Humphries 9, Archie Mitchell 3, D.Nisbet 3, H.T.Simons 5, W.Thompson 1, Wagstaffe 1, Opponents own-goal 1.

1916-17

London Combination

					1	2	3	4	5	6	7	8	9	10	11
Sep	2 (h) Luton T	L 1-4	Dale		Durston	Loney	Somerville	Dale	Mitchell	Green	Nisbet	Birch	Pennifer	Drysdale	Fox
	9 (a) Portsmouth	W 3-2	Pennifer, Matthews, Smith (og)	2,000	..	..	Hooper	Green	..	Dale	..	Matthews	..	Lewis	..
	16 (h) Millwall	L 0-4		4,000	..	..	Draper	Pennifer	..	..	..	..	Saxon	..	..
	23 (a) Watford	L 0-2		1,000	..	Draper	Hooper	Barrington	..	..	Fox	Lewis	Pennifer	Hicks	Donald
	30 (h) Clapton O	D 0-0		3,000	..	Loney	Draper	Hooper	..	Baldock	Hicks	..	..	Dale	Fox
Oct	7 (a) Fulham	L 0-2		5,000	..	Draper	Loney	Baldock	..	Lewis	Fox	Salmon	Teabay	Matthews	Dale
	14 (a) Southampton	L 1-2	Fox		Winyard	Hooper	Draper	Lewis	..	Baldock	Teabay	..	Thompson	Dale	Fox
	21 (h) West Ham U	L 0-4		3,000	..	Loney	..	..	..	Hooper	Donald	Dale	Pennifer	Thompson	..
	28 (a) Tottenham H	W 5-4	Dale, Salmon 2, Mitchell, Opp own-goal	4,000	..	..	..	Green	..	Baldock	..	Salmon	Dale	Lawrence	..
Nov	4 (h) Crystal P	W 1-0	Lawrence		Durston	..	..	..	..	Wright	..	Lewis	..	..	..
	11 (a) Brentford	W 4-1	Lawrence 3, Dale	2,000	..	..	..	..	..	..	..	Baldock	..	..	..
	18 (h) Chelsea	L 1-2	Dale		Wren	..	..	Richards	..	..	..	..	..	..	..
	25 (a) Luton T	L 0-6		3,000	Durston	Hooper	Toms	Green	..	..	Birkett	Wash	Beale	..	Lewis
Dec	2 (h) Portsmouth	L 1-7	Kinlin		..	Kirk	Shult	Wise	..	..	Brown	Hassan	Soffe	Kinlin	Goddard
	9 (a) Millwall	L 1-2	Hassan	5,000	Winyard	Virtue	Beckerley	Wake	..	Grendon	Lawrence	Howie	Needham	Hassan	Simons
	23 (a) Clapton O	L 1-2	Mitchell		..	Whyman	Draper	Grendon	..	Wake	Thompson	Hassan	..	Lawrence	Wright
	25 (h) Arsenal	L 2-3	Dale, Hassan	3,000	..	Hooper	..	..	..	..	Virtue	..	Dale	Baldock	Goddard
	26 (a) Arsenal	D 0-0		4,500	..	Whyman	..	..	..	Wright	Butler	..	Baldock	Lawrence	..
	30 (h) Fulham	L 1-7	Lawrence	3,000	..	Hooper	..	..	..	..	Wash	..	Dale	..	..
Jan	6 (h) Southampton	W 4-0	Hassan 2, Lawrence, Baldock	1,000	Durston	Loney	..	Whyman	..	..	Thompson	..	Baldock	..	..
	13 (a) West Ham U	L 3-5	Dale, Lawrence, Whyman	5,000	Denoon	..	..	Grendon	..	Whyman	Baldock	..	Dale	..	..
	20 (h) Tottenham H	D 1-1	Hassan	1,200	..	Whyman	..	..	Thwaites	Wright	..	..	Mitchell	..	..
	27 (a) Crystal P	L 0-4			..	Grendon	..	Thwaites	Mitchell	Howie	Goddard	Lawrence	Marshall	Hassan	Baldock
Feb	3 (h) Brentford	W 2-0	Whiting, Hassan	1,000	..	Loney	..	Grendon	..	Whyman	Baldock	Hassan	Whiting	Lawrence	Strickland
	10 (a) Chelsea	L 0-3		4,000	..	Whyman	..	..	..	Wright	..	..	Dale	..	Goddard
	17 (h) Watford	W 2-1	Lawrence, Hassan		..	Loney	..	..	..	..	..	..	Whiting	..	..
	24 (a) Luton T	L 0-2			..	Toms	..	Baldock	..	..	Butler	Dale	..	Lewis	..
Mar	3 (a) Fulham	D 0-0		3,000	..	Draper	Loney	Wright	..	Grendon	Whyman	Lawrence	..	Hassan	Dale
	10 (h) Crystal P	W 3-2	Lawrence, Hassan 2	700	..	Loney	Draper	Grendon	..	Wright	Whiting	Hassan	Fleming	Lawrence	..
	17 (a) Millwall	L 0-1		5,000	..	..	..	..	..	..	Baldock	..	Whiting	Dale	Goddard
	24 (h) Brentford	D 2-2	Dale, Barlow		..	Grendon	..	Langford	..	..	Butler	Barlow	..	..	Baldock
	31 (a) Watford	W 2-1	Goddard, Grimsdell (og)		..	Loney	..	Grendon	..	Whyman	Baldock	Lewis	Barlow	..	Goddard
Apr	6 (h) Chelsea	D 2-2	Hassan, Baldock	3,500	..	White	..	..	..	Wright	Lewis	Hassan	Baldock	Lawrence	Crossley
	7 (h) Luton T	D 2-2	Dale 2	3,000	..	Loney	..	..	..	Broster	..	..	Dale	Whyman	..
	9 (a) Chelsea	L 1-3	Lawrence	7,000	..	Draper	White	Wright	..	Grendon	Crossley	Lawrence	Baldock	Hassan	Butler
	14 (h) Fulham	W 2-0	Dale, Baldock	1,500	..	Loney	Draper	Grendon	..	Wright	Lewis	Hassan	..	Dale	James
	19 (a) Brentford	D 0-0		1,000	..	..	White	Langford	..	..	..	..	..	..	Draper
	21 (a) Crystal P	L 0-3			..	..	Draper	..	..	..	..	..	Barlow	..	Baldock
	28 (h) Millwall	D 0-0		6,000	..	Draper	White	Wright	..	Grendon	Whyman	Dale	Whiting	Hughes	Lewis

London Combination
Appearances: J.W.Baldock 24, Barlow 3, Barrington 1, Beale 1, Beckerley 1, Jimmy Birch 1, Birkett 1, J.Broster 1, J.Brown 1, Butler 4, Crossley 3, G.Dale 27, J.Denoon 19, D.Donald 6, W.Draper 34, Drysdale 1, J.Durston 11, Fleming 1, G.F.Fox 12, J.Goddard 13, H.Green 6, F.Grendon 21, V.Hassan 22, A.Hicks 2, H.Hooper 8, D.Howie 2, Hughes 1, James 1, Kinlin 1, Kirk 1, Langford 3, W.Lawrence 20, L.R.Lewis 17, B.Loney 22, Marshall 1, A.Matthews 3, Archie Mitchell 39, Needham 2, D.Nisbet 3, Pennifer 6, Richards 1, Salmon 3, Saxon 1, Shult 1, H.T.Simons 1, Soffe 1, J.Somerville 1, Strickland 1, Teabay 2, W.Thompson 4, Thwaites 2, Toms 2, Virtue 2, W.Wake 3, Wash 2, J.White 4, J.Whiting 8, A.Whyman 11, W.Winyard 8, Wise 1, Wren 1, A.Wright 23.

London Combination
Goalscorers: J.W.Baldock 3, Barlow 1, G.Dale 10, G.F.Fox 1, T.Goddard 1, V.Hassan 10, Kinlin 1, W.Lawrence 10, A.Matthews 1, Archie Mitchell 2, Pennifer 1, Salmon 2, J.Whiting 1, A.Whyman 1, Opponents own-goals 3.

1917-18

London Combination

				1	2	3	4	5	6	7	8	9	10	11
Sep 1 (a) Arsenal	L 0-2		6,000	Denoon	White	Draper	Grendon	Mitchell	Wright	Whyman	Smith	Gregory	Dale	Fox
8 (h) West Ham U	L 0-3		5,000	..	..	..	..	..	..	Lewis	Gregory	Baldock	..	..
15 (a) Fulham	L 1-2	Gregory	4,000	..	..	Loney	..	..	..	..	Over	Gregory	..	Walters
22 (h) Crystal P	W 4-1	Dale, Thurman, Fox 2		..	..	Draper	..	..	..	Over	Coleman	Dale	Thurman	Fox
29 (h) Clapton O	W 2-0	Dale, Thurman		..	Loney	White	..	..	..	Lewis	Gregory	..	..	..
Oct 6 (a) Millwall	L 2-4	Mitchell, Dale	3,500	..	White	Draper	..	..	..	..	..	..	..	..
13 (h) Tottenham H	L 2-3	Mitchell, Thompson	2,000	..	Loney	White	..	..	..	Draper	Griffen	Thompson	..	..
20 (a) Chelsea	W 2-1	Dale 2	7,500	..	..	..	..	..	..	Thompson	Gregory	Dale	..	..
27 (h) Arsenal	W 2-0	Mitchell (pen), Brown	5,000	..	..	Draper	..	..	..	..	Baldock	..	Brown	..
Nov 3 (a) West Ham U	L 0-4		4,500	..	..	White	..	..	..	Draper	..	..	Smith	..
10 (h) Fulham	L 2-3	Dale, Thurman	3,000	..	..	..	..	..	..	..	..	..	Thurman	..
17 (a) Crystal P	L 1-4	Dale		..	White	Draper	..	..	Griffin	Baldock	Cousins	..	Edwards	..
24 (a) Clapton O	W 2-1	Fox, Campbell		..	..	..	..	..	Wright	Griffin	Brown	Campbell	Thurman	..
Dec 1 (h) Millwall	W 1-0	Brown	3,000	..	..	Loney	..	..	Draper	Cousins	..	Dale	Campbell	..
8 (a) Tottenham H	W 1-0	Smith	3,000	..	..	Draper	..	Baldock	Wright	Jefferson	..	Smith	Thurman	..
15 (h) Chelsea	L 0-1		4,000	..	..	..	..	Mitchell	..	..	..	Hassan	Dale	..
22 (a) Arsenal	L 0-3		3,000	..	..	..	..	..	..	..	..	..	..	..
25 (a) Brentford	D 1-1	Walters		..	Loney	White	..	..	..	..	..	Walters	..	..
26 (h) Brentford	L 0-4			..	..	..	..	..	..	..	..	..	..	..
29 (h) West Ham U	D 1-1	Smith	2,500	..	..	..	..	..	..	..	Dale	Smith	Crossland	..
Jan 5 (a) Fulham	L 0-1		4,000	..	..	..	Draper	..	Grendon	..	Walters	..	Dale	..
12 (h) Crystal P	W 2-1	Walters, Smith	2,000	..	..	..	Wright	.,.	Draper	..	Brown	..	Walters	..
19 (h) Clapton O	W 6-1	Brown, Dale, Fox 3, Walters	2,000	..	..	Draper	Grendon	Smith	Baldock	..	..	Dale	..	..
26 (a) Millwall	W 1-0	Mitchell	4,000	..	..	..	..	Mitchell	..	..	..	..	..	..
Feb 2 (h) Tottenham H	L 2-7	Walters, Smith	3,000	Baldock	..	..	..	..	Wright	Cousins	Dale	Smith	..	..
9 (a) Brentford	L 1-6	Jones	3,000	Duffield	Hawkins	..	..	Jones	Baldock	Hales	Kellar	Handford	Thurman	..
16 (h) Arsenal	L 0-3		3,500	..	Steer	..	..	Mitchell	Wright	Jefferson	Brown	Smith	Walters	..
23 (a) West Ham U	L 0-4		6,500	Denoon	..	..	..	..	..	Trindale	Sanders	Thurman	Dale	..
Mar 2 (h) Fulham	L 0-1		3,500	..	..	..	..	Downing	Baldock	Hassan	MacLinton	Mitchell	Thurman	..
9 (a) Crystal P	W 2-0	MacLinton, Jones		..	..	Baldock	..	..	Wright	Dale	..	Jones	Walters	..
16 (a) Clapton O	W 1-0	Grendon		..	..	Draper	..	Mitchell	Downing	..	Brown	MacLinton	..	..
23 (h) Millwall	W 4-1	MacLinton, Walters 3	3,000	..	..	..	..	..	..	Jefferson	Walters	..	Dale	..
29 (a) Chelsea	L 0-1		3,000	..	Draper	Downing	Baldock	..	Grendon	..	..	Dale	Brown	..
30 (a) Tottenham H	W 2-1	Fox, Smith	5,000	..	Mitchell	Draper	..	Grendon	Downing	Dale	Smith	MacLinton	Thurman	..
Apr 1 (h) Chelsea	L 1-2	Fox	6,000	..	..	..	Read	..	Baldock	..	Munson	..	Walters	..
6 (h) Brentford	L 2-6	MacLinton 2	1,500	..	Steer	..	Grendon	Downing	..	..	MacLinton	Thurman	..	..

War Fund

				1	2	3	4	5	6	7	8	9	10	11
Apr 13 (h) Crystal P	W 2-1	Britton, Archibald	1,000	Denoon	Steer	Draper	Grendon	Downing	Wright	Britton	Baldock	MacLinton	Archibald	Fox
20 (a) Crystal P	L 1-3	Dale		..	..	..	..	Mitchell	Downing	Jefferson	..	Dale	..	..
27 (h) Millwall	W 4-3	Jefferson, Walters, MacLinton 2	2,000	Duffield	..	..	Green	Dale	Wright	..	Walters	MacLinton	..	..
May 4 (a) Millwall	L 1-3	Archibald		..	..	..	Downing	Mitchell	..	..	..	..	..	..

London Combination
Appearances: J.W.Baldock 16, J.Brown 14, Campbell 2, Coleman 1, Cousins 3, Crossland 1, G.Dale 29, J.Denoon 33, Downing 7, W.Draper 29, Duffield 2, Edwards 1, G.F.Fox 35, John Gregory 6, F.Grendon 35, Griffin 3, Hales 1, Handford 1, V.Hassan 3, Hawkins 1, Jefferson 13, Jones 2, Kellar 1, L.R.Lewis 4, B.Loney 16, MacLinton 7, Archie Mitchell 31, Munson 1, Over 2, Read 1, Sanders 1, J.W.Smith 10, Steer 7, W.Thompson 3, Thurman 13, Trindale 1, Walters 14, J.White 21, A.Whyman 1, A.Wright 24.
Goalscorers: J.Brown 3, Campbell 1, W.Draper 8, G.F.Fox 8, John Gregory 1, F.Grendon 1, Jones 2, MacLinton 4, Archie Mitchell 4, J.W.Smith 5, W.Thompson 1, Thurman 3, Walters 7.

War Fund
Appearances: Archibald 4, J.W.Baldock 2, Britton 1, G.Dale 2, J.Denoon 2, Downing 3, W.Draper 4, Duffield 2, G.F.Fox 4, H.Green 1, F.Grendon 2, Jefferson 3, MacLinton 3, Archie Mitchell 2, Steer 4, Walters 2, A.Wright 3.
Goalscorers: Archibald 2, Britton 1, G.Dale 1, Jefferson 1, MacLinton 2, Walters 1.

Appearances Total: Archibald 4, J.W.Baldock 18, Britton 1, J.Brown 14, Campbell 2, Coleman 1, Cousins 3, Crossland 1, G.Dale 31, J.Denoon 35, Downing 10, W.Draper 33, Duffield 4, Edwards 1, G.F.Fox 39, H.Green 1, John Gregory 6, F.Grendon 37, Griffin 3, Hales 1, Handford 1, V.Hassan 3, Hawkins 1, Jefferson 16, Jones 2, Kellar 1, L.R.Lewis 4, B.Loney 16, MacLinton 10, Archie Mitchell 33, Munson 1, Over 2, Read 1, Sanders 1, J.W.Smith 10, Steer 11, W.Thompson 3, Thurman 13, Trindale 1, Walters 16, J.White 21, A.Whyman 1, A.Wright 27.
Goalscorers Total: Archibald 2, J.Brown 3, Campbell 1, G.Dale 1, W.Draper 8, G.F.Fox 8, John Greogry 1, F.Grendon 1, Jefferson 1, Jones 2, MacLinton 6, Archie Mitchell 4, J.W.Smith 5, W.Thompson 1, Thurman 3, Walters 8.

1918-19

London Combination

Date	Opponents	Result	Scorers	Att	1	2	3	4	5	6	7	8	9	10	11
Sep 7	(h) Arsenal	L 2-3	Smith, Walters	7,000	Denoon	Steer	Draper	Wright	Mitchell	Baldock	Jefferson	Dale	Smith	Walters	Fox
14	(a) Crystal P	L 2-4	Jefferson, Walters	3,000	..	..	Downing	Smith	..	Congreve	..	Dodd	MacLinton	Brown	Walters
21	(a) Clapton O	W 5-1	Brown, Dale 4		..	..	Draper	Grendon	..	Baldock	Cope	Brown	Dale	Walters	Fox
28	(h) Millwall	W 1-0	Congreve	3,000	..	..	..	Wright	..	..	MacLinton	Congreve	Brown	..	..
Oct 5	(a) Fulham	D 3-3	Congreve, Smith 2	4,000	..	..	..	Grendon	..	..	Dale	..	Smith	..	Jefferson
12	(h) Brentford	W 2-1	Fox, Dale		..	..	..	..	..	Downing	Cope	Brown	Dale	..	Fox
19	(a) West Ham U	L 1-4	Dale	6,500	..	..	..	..	..	Baldock	MacLinton	..	..	..	..
26	(h) Chelsea	D 2-2	Dale 2	7,500	..	..	..	..	..	Downing	..	Dale	Smith	Congreve	..
Nov 2	(a) Arsenal	L 0-1		6,000	..	..	..	..	Downing	Wake	..	Brown	Mitchell	Walters	..
9	(h) Crystal P	W 3-2	Dale 2, Walters		..	..	..	..	Mitchell	..	..	..	Dale	..	..
16	(h) Clapton O	W 3-1	Fox, Dale, Brown		..	Jenkins	..	Downing	..	..	Cope	..	..	Baldock	..
23	(a) Millwall	L 1-4	Downing	5,000	..	Steer	..	Grendon	Downing	..	Dale	Congreve	Smith	Walters	..
30	(h) Fulham	L 0-3		5,500	..	..	..	..	Mitchell	..	..	..	..	..	..
Dec 7	(a) Brentford	L 1-5	Congreve	8,000	..	..	..	..	..	..	Jefferson	Smith	Dale	Congreve	..
14	(h) West Ham U	W 1-0	Smith	1,000	..	Whyman	..	..	..	..	..	Brown	Smith	Walters	..
21	(a) Chelsea	L 0-2		15,000	Durston	Wingrove	..	..	..	..	..	..	..	Congreve	..
25	(h) Tottenham H	D 1-1	Mitchell	7,500	..	..	Steer	..	..	..	Butler	Dale	Page	..	..
26	(a) Tottenham H	D 0-0		6,000	Denoon	..	Whyman	..	..	..	..	Brown	Dale	..	..
28	(h) Arsenal	L 0-2		4,000	..	..	..	..	..	..	..	..	..	..	..
Jan 4	(a) Crystal P	W 2-0	Smith, Congreve	5,000	..	..	..	..	..	Baldock	Jefferson	Smith	..	..	..
11	(a) Clapton O	W 5-1	Mitchell, Smith 2, Gregory, Dale		..	..	..	..	..	..	..	..	..	Gregory	..
18	(h) Millwall	W 3-0	Gregory, Jefferson, Dale	6,500	..	Mitchell	..	..	Wake	..	..	..	..	..	..
25	(a) Fulham	L 0-1		12,000	..	Wingrove	..	..	Mitchell	..	..	..	..	..	..
Feb 1	(h) Brentford	D 0-0		8,500	..	..	..	..	..	..	..	..	..	..	..
8	(a) West Ham U	W 4-0	Dale, Gregory, Smith, Jefferson	12,000	..	..	..	..	..	..	..	..	..	..	..
15	(h) Tottenham H	W 7-1	Smith, Gregory 3, Mitchell, Dale, Jefferson	9,000	..	..	..	..	..	..	..	..	..	..	..
22	(a) Arsenal	W 3-1	Gregory, Dale 2	13,000	..	Draper	..	..	..	..	..	..	..	..	..
Mar 1	(h) Crystal P	W 3-2	Smith 2, Dale		..	..	..	..	..	..	..	..	..	..	..
8	(h) Clapton O	W 5-2	Smith 3, Gregory, Mitchell	7,500	..	Pullen	..	..	..	..	..	..	..	..	..
15	(a) Millwall	D 1-1	Gregory	20,000	..	..	..	..	..	..	..	..	..	..	..
22	(h) Fulham	L 0-1		10,000	..	..	..	..	..	Wake	..	..	..	..	..
29	(a) Brentford	D 1-1	Brown	12,000	..	..	Wingrove	..	..	Baldock	MacLinton	..	Brown	..	..
Apr 5	(h) West Ham U	L 1-3	Brown	7,500	..	Millington	Pullen	..	Whyman	..	Jefferson	..	..	..	..
12	(a) Tottenham H	W 3-2	Gregory, Smith, Bay (og)	20,000	..	Draper	..	Wake	..	..	..	Dale	Smith	..	..
18	(h) Chelsea	W 3-2	Birch 2, Smith	15,000	..	Millington	..	Wright	Mitchell	..	..	Birch	..	..	Donald
21	(a) Chelsea	L 0-3		20,000	..	..	..	Whyman	..	..	Fox	..	..	..	..

London Victory Cup

Date	Opponents	Result	Scorers	Att	1	2	3	4	5	6	7	8	9	10	11
Mar 20	(a) Chelsea	L 0-2			Denoon	Pullen	Whyman	Grendon	Mitchell	Baldock	Jefferson	Smith	Dale	Gregory	Fox

London Combination
Appearances J.W.Baldock 22, Jimmy Birch 2, J.Brown 14, Butler 3, Congreve 12, Cope 3, G.Dale 27, J.Denoon 34, Dodd 1, D.Donald 2, Downing 6, W.Draper 18, J.Durston 2, G.F.Fox 33, John Gregory 16, F.Grendon 29, Jefferson 21, Jenkins 1, MacLinton 7, T.Millington 3, Archie Mitchell 33, Page 1, H.Pullen 8, J.W.Smith 26, Steer 14, W.Wake 14, Walters 12, A.Whyman 18, J.Wingrove 11, A.Wright 3.
Goalscorers: Jimmy Birch 2, J.Brown 4, Congreve 4, G.Dale 18, Downing 1, G.F.Fox 2, John Gregory 10, Jefferson 4, Archie Mitchell 4, J.W.Smith 16, Walters 3, Opponents own-goal 1.

Victory Cup
Appearances: J.W.Baldock 1, G.Dale 1, J.Denoon 1, G.F.Fox 1, John Gregory 1, F.Grendon 1, Jefferson 1, Archie Mitchell 1, H.Pullen 1, J.W.Smith 1, A.Whyman 1.

Appearances Total: J.W.Baldock 23, Jimmy Birch 2, J.Brown 14, Butler 3, Congreve 12, Cope 3, G.Dale 28, J.Denoon 35, Dodd 1, D.Donald 2, Downing 6, W.Draper 18, J.Durston 2, G.F.Fox 34, John Gregory 17, F.Grendon 30, Jefferson 22, Jenkins 1, MacLinton 7, T.Millington 3, Archie Mitchell 34, Page 1, H.Pullen 9, J.W.Smith 27, Steer 14, W.Wake 14, Walters 12, A.Whyman 19, J.Wingrove 11, A.Wright 3.
Goalscorers Total: Jimmy Birch 2, J.Brown 4, Congreve 4, G.Dale 18, Downing 1, G.F.Fox 2, John Gregory 10, Jefferson 4, Archie Mitchell 4, J.W.Smith 16, Walters 3, Opponents own-goal 1.

1919-20

Southern League Division 1

Date	Opponents	Res	Score	Scorers	Att	Baldock	Berry	Birch	Blackman	Broster	Cain	Chester	Donald	Fox	Gregory	Haggan	Lowe	Merrick	Miller	Mitchell	Olsen	Pidgeon	Pullen	Ramsey	Smith	Sutch	Thompson	Watts	Whyman	Wilde	Wingrove	Woodhouse
Aug 30	(a) Bristol R	W	2-0	Donald, Gregory	7,000	6		8	2	4			11		10			1		5			3		9		7					
Sep 1	(a) Plymouth A	D	0-0		7,000	6		8		4			11		10			1		5			3		9		7				2	
6	(h*) Reading	D	0-0		10,000	6		8	2	4			11		10			1		5			3		9		7					
8	(h) Plymouth A	W	1-0	Mitchell (pen)	6,000	6		8	2	4			11		10			1		5			3		9		7					
13	(a) Southampton	L	1-2	Donald	7,000	6		8	2	4			11		10			1		5			3		9		7					
20	(h) Luton T	W	4-0	Gregory 2, Birch, Smith	6,000	6		8		4			11		10			1		5			3		9		7		2			
25	(h) Southend U	D	2-2	Birch 2	6,000	6		8		4			11		10			1		5			3		9		7				2	
27	(a) Gillingham	W	1-0	Birch	8,000	6		8		4			7	11	10			1		5			3		9						2	
Oct 4	(h) Swansea T	W	2-0	Donald, Birch	12,000	6		8		4			7	11	10			1		5			3		9						2	
11	(a) Exeter C	W	1-0	Gregory	6,000	6		8		4			7	11	10			1					3		9					5	2	
16	(h) Newport C	W	1-0	Birch	6,000	6		8					7	11	10			1		5			3		9					4	2	
18	(h) Cardiff C	D	0-0		10,000	6		8					7	11	10			1		5			3		9					4	2	
25	(h) Watford	W	3-0	Donald, Whyman, Smith	14,000	6		8		4			11		10			1		5			3		9				7		2	
Nov 1	(a) Swindon T	L	2-5	Birch, Gregory	10,000	6		8		4			11		10			1		5			3		9				7		2	
8	(h) Millwall	L	1-2	Birch	10,000	6		8		4			11				10	1		5			3		9				7		2	
15	(a) Brighton & HA	W	3-2	Smith 2, Birch	13,000	6		8	2	4		7		11	10			1		5			3		9							
29	(a) Portsmouth	L	2-4	Baldock, Broster	17,000	6		8	2	4			7	11	10			1		5			3		9							
Dec 6	(h) Northampton T	W	5-1	Smith 3, Baldock, Birch	7,000	6		8		4			11		10			1		5			3	7	9						2	
13	(a) Crystal P	L	0-1		12,000	6		8		4			11		10			1		5			3	7	9						2	
25	(h) Brentford	W	2-0	Mitchell, Broster	15,000	6		8		4			11		10			1		5			3	7	9						2	
26	(a) Brentford	L	1-2	Smith	13,623	6		8		4			11		10			1		2				7	9					5	3	
27	(a) Norwich C	L	1-3	Birch	12,000	6		8					11		10			1		2				7	9				4	5	3	
Jan 3	(h) Bristol R	W	7-1	Smith 4, Sutch 2, Donald	10,000	6		8		4			11					1		2					9	10	7			5	3	
17	(a) Reading	W	1-0	Smith	10,000	6		8	3	4			11		10			1		5					9		7				2	
24	(h) Southampton	W	2-1	Donald, Gregory	14,000	6		8	3	4			11		10			1		5					9		7				2	
Feb 14	(a) Swansea T	L	1-3	Smith	20,000	6	1	8	3	4			11		10					5					9		7				2	
17	(h) Gillingham	D	0-0		10,000	6	1	8	3	4			11		10										9		7		5		2	
21	(h) Exeter C	D	0-0		7,000	6	1	8	3	4			11		10					5					9		7				2	
28	(a) Cardiff C	L	0-4		17,000	6	1	8	3	4			11		10					5					9		7				2	
Mar 6	(a) Watford	L	0-1		7,000	6		8		4			11		10			1		5			3	7	9						2	
13	(h) Swindon T	W	2-1	Birch, Gregory	8,000	6		8		4			11		10			1		5			3	7	9						2	
20	(a) Millwall	D	0-0		26,000	6		8		4			11		10			1		5			3	7	9						2	
22	(a) Luton T	L	1-2	Birch	4,000	6				4	5		11		10			1	8				3	7	9						2	
27	(h) Brighton & HA	W	3-1	Gregory 3	8,000	6		8		4			11		10			1		5			3	7	9						2	
Apr 2	(a) Merthyr T	W	4-1	Birch 2, Smith, Ramsey	8,000	6		8		4			11		10			1		5			3	7	9						2	
3	(a) Newport C	L	0-3		9,000	6		8						11	10			1			5		3	7	9						2	4
5	(h) Merthyr T	D	0-0		7,000	6			2	4	5		11		10			1	8			7			9						3	
10	(h) Portsmouth	D	1-1	Birch	10,000	6		8	2		4		11		10			1		5		7			9						3	
17	(a) Northampton T	L	0-2		7,000	6		8	2	4			11		10			1		5		7	3		9							
24	(h) Crystal P	L	2-3	Gregory 2	14,000	6		8	2	4	5		11		10			1				7			9						3	
26	(a) Southend U	D	2-2	Gregory 2	8,000	6		8	2		4		11		10	5		1				7			9						3	
30	(h) Norwich C	W	1-0	Gregory	12,000	6		8	2		4		11		10			1		5		7			9			3				
					App	42	4	40	18	35	6	1	40	8	40	1	1	38	2	35	1	6	28	12	42	1	14	1	6	6	33	1
					Goals	2		16		2			6		15					2				1	15	2			1			

*First match played at Loftus Road

FA Cup

Date	Opponents	Res	Score	Scorers	Att	Baldock	Berry	Birch	Blackman	Broster	Cain	Chester	Donald	Fox	Gregory	Haggan	Lowe	Merrick	Miller	Mitchell	Olsen	Pidgeon	Pullen	Ramsey	Smith	Sutch	Thompson	Watts	Whyman	Wilde	Wingrove	Woodhouse	Round
Jan 10	(a) Aston Villa	L	1-2	Birch	33,000			8	6	4			11		10			1		5			3		9		7				2		1
					App			1	1	1			1		1			1		1			1		1		1				1		
					Goals			1																									

Attendance Summary

	ATTENDANCES Home	Away	Total	AVERAGE Home	Away	Total
League	202,000	228,623	430,623	9,600	10,900	10,250
FA Cup		33,000	33,000		33,000	33,000
Total	202,000	261,623	463,623	9,600	11,900	10,800

1920-21

Football League Division 3

Date	Opponents	Result	Scorers	Att	Ashford	Baldock	Birch	Blackman	Chandler	Clayton	Donald	Faulkner	Gould	Grant	Gregory	Grimsdell	Hill	John	McGovern	Manning	Marsden	Middlemiss	Mitchell	O'Brien	Price	Smith	Watts	Wingrove
Aug 28	(h) Watford	L 1-2	Birch	20,000			8	2				7		5	10				4			11		6	1	9		3
Sep 2	(h) Northampton T	L 1-2	Birch	14,000			8	2				7		5	10				4			11		6	1	9		3
4	(a) Watford	W 2-0	Birch 2	9,000			8	2				7		4	10	3	1					11	5	6		9		
6	(a) Northampton T	W 3-0	Gregory, Smith, Middlemiss	6,000			8	2				7		4	10	3	1					11	5	6		9		
11	(h) Reading	W 2-0	Gregory, Smith	15,000			8	2				7		4	10	3	1					11	5	6		9		
18	(a) Reading	D 0-0		9,000			8	2				7		4	10	3	1					11	5	6		9		
25	(h) Luton T	W 4-1	Birch 2, Gregory (pen), Mitchell	20,000			8	2				7		4	10	3	1					11	5	6		9		
Oct 2	(a) Luton T	L 1-2	Birch	10,000			8	2				7		4	10	3	1					11	5	6		9		
9	(h) Southend U	W 2-0	Smith, Dorsett (og)	20,000			8	2				7		4	10	3	1					11	5	6		9		
16	(a) Southend U	L 0-1		8,000		6	8	2				7		4	10	3	1					11	5			9		
23	(a) Swansea T	W 3-1	Gregory, Birch, Manning	16,000			8	2			11	7		4	6	3	1			10			5			9		
30	(h) Swansea T	D 1-1	Manning	20,000			8	2			11	7		4	6	3	1			10			5			9		
Nov 6	(a) Southampton	D 2-2	Manning, Gregory	15,000			8	2			11	7		5	6	3		4		10			1			9		
13	(h) Southampton	D 0-0		20,000			8	2			11	7		4	6	3	1			10			5			9		
20	(a) Grimsby T	L 1-2	Smith	8,000				2			11	7		4	10	3	1			8			5	6		9		
27	(h) Grimsby T	W 2-0	Smith, Gregory	10,000			8	2				7		4	10	3	1					11	5	6		9		
Dec 4	(a) Brighton & HA	L 1-2	Gregory	9,000			8	2				7		4	10	3	1					11	5	6		9		
11	(h) Brighton & HA	W 4-0	Smith 3, Birch	7,000			8	2						4	10	3	1			7		11	5	6		9		
18	(h) Crystal P	W 3-0	Birch 2, Gregory	18,000			8							4	10	3	1			7		11	5	6		9		2
25	(a) Brentford	W 2-0	Smith 2	20,000			8							6	10	3	1			7		11	5	4		9		2
27	(h) Brentford	W 1-0	Birch	25,000			8							4	10		1			7	2	11	5	6		9		3
Jan 1	(a) Crystal P	D 0-0		20,000			8		10					4	11		1			7			5	6		9	3	2
15	(a) Merthyr T	L 1-3	Birch	15,000			8		9					4	11	3	1			7			5	6		10		2
22	(h) Merthyr T	W 4-2	Gregory, Manning, Birch (pen), Smith	9,000			8		9					5	11		1	4		7				6		10	3	2
Feb 5	(a) Norwich C	L 0-2		9,000				2	9			7		4	11	3	1			8			5	6		10		
12	(a) Plymouth A	L 0-1		14,000	6		8	2			11			4	10		1			7				5		9		3
17	(h) Norwich C	W 2-0	Gregory, Birch	4,000			8	3			11			4	10		1			7			5	6		9		2
26	(a) Exeter C	W 1-0	Smith	10,000	6						11	7		4	10		1			8	2		5			9		3
Mar 5	(h) Exeter C	W 2-1	Gregory 2	15,000							11	7		4	10		1			8	2		5	6		9		3
12	(a) Millwall	D 0-0		25,000	6						11	7		4	10		1			8	2			5		9		3
17	(h) Plymouth A	W 4-0	Smith 2, Clayton, Gregory	8,000	6					8	11	7		4	10		1				2			5		9		3
19	(h) Millwall	D 0-0		20,000	6					8	11	7		4	10		1				2			5		9		3
25	(a) Bristol R	L 0-3		15,000							11	7		4	10		1			8	2		5	6		9		3
26	(h) Newport C	W 2-0	Mitchell, Smith	10,000					10		11	7	1	4						8	2		5	6		9		3
28	(h) Bristol R	W 2-1	Mitchell, Smith	15,000						10	11	7	1	4						8	2		5	6		9		3
Apr 2	(a) Newport C	W 3-1	Smith, Chandler, Manning	15,000					8		11	7		4						10	2		5	6	1	9		3
9	(h) Gillingham	L 0-1		10,000					8		11	7		4	10						2		5	6	1	9		3
16	(a) Gillingham	W 2-1	Gregory, Smith	8,000					8		11	7		4	10						2		5	6	1	9		3
23	(h) Swindon T	W 1-0	Chandler	12,000				3	8		11	7		4	10						2		5	6	1	9		
30	(a) Swindon T	W 1-0	Gregory	7,000					8		11	7		4	10						2		5	6	1	9		3
May 2	(h) Portsmouth	D 0-0		5,000					8		11	7		4	10		1				2		5	6		9		3
7	(a) Portsmouth	D 0-0		13,000					8		11	7		4	10		1				2		5	6		9		3
				App	5	1	25	22	12	3	22	33	2	42	39	20	32	2	2	22	16	16	35	36	7	42	2	24
				Goals			15		2	1					15					5		1	3			18		

1 own-goal

FA Cup

Date	Opponents	Result	Scorers	Att	Ashford	Baldock	Birch	Blackman	Chandler	Clayton	Donald	Faulkner	Gould	Grant	Gregory	Grimsdell	Hill	John	McGovern	Manning	Marsden	Middlemiss	Mitchell	O'Brien	Price	Smith	Watts	Wingrove	Round
Jan 8	(h) Arsenal	W 2-0	Chandler, O'Brien	20,000			8		10					4	11	3	1			7			5	6		9		2	1
29	(a) Burnley	L 2-4	Smith, Birch	41,007			8	2	9					4	11		1			7			5	6		10		3	2
				App			2	1	2					2	2	1	2			2			2	2		2		2	
				Goals			1		1															1		1			

Attendance Summary

	ATTENDANCES			AVERAGE		
	Home	Away	Total	Home	Away	Total
League	297,000	261,000	558,000	14,150	12,400	13,300
FA Cup	20,000	41,007	61,007	20,000	41,007	30,500
Total	317,000	302,007	619,007	14,400	13,700	14,050

1921-22

Division 3 South

Date	Match	Result	Scorers	Att	Ashford	Bailey	Bain	Birch	Blackman	Bradshaw	Burnham	Chandler	Clayton	Edgley	Faulkner	Grant	Gregory	Hill	John	Knight	Lock	Marsden	O'Brien	Ramsey	Reed	Smith	Thompson	Vigrass
Aug 27	(h) Swindon T	D 0-0		18,000				8	3			9		7		4	10	1				2	6	11	5			
29	(a) Newport C	W 1-0	Birch	10,000				8	3			9		7			10	1	4			2	6	11	5			
Sep 3	(a) Swindon T	L 0-2		10,000				8	3			9		7			10	1	4			2	6	11	5			
5	(h) Newport C	W 2-1	Birch, Smith	7,000				8	3						7		10	1	4			2	6	11	5	9		
10	(a) Norwich C	D 0-0		9,000					3			8			7		10	1	4			2	6	11	5	9		
17	(h) Norwich C	W 2-0	Gregory, Smith (pen)	15,000					3				10	11	7	4	8	1				2	6		5	9		
24	(a) Reading	W 1-0	Gregory	12,000					3	7			10	11		4	8	1				2	6		5	9		
Oct 1	(h) Reading	D 1-1	Birch	16,000				8	3	7				11		4	10	1				2	6		5	9		
8	(a) Bristol R	D 1-1	Smith	16,000				8	3	7				11		4	10	1				2	6		5	9		
15	(h) Bristol R	L 1-2	O'Brien	10,000				8	3	7				11		4	10	1				2	6		5	9		
22	(a) Brentford	L 1-5	Birch	16,000				8	3			9	10	11	7	4		1				2	6		5			
29	(h) Brentford	D 1-1	Smith	15,000	6			8	3	7				11			10	1	4						5	9	2	
Nov 5	(a) Aberdare A	L 2-4	Birch, Gregory	12,000				8	3					11	7	4	10	1				2	5		6	9		
12	(h) Aberdare A	W 1-0	Knight	12,000			3	8	2					11	7	4	10			9	1		5		6			
19	(a) Brighton & HA	L 1-2	Faulkner	9,000			3	8	2					11	7	4	10			9	1		5		6			
26	(h) Brighton & HA	W 3-0	O'Brien, Birch 2	12,000			3	8			6	10			7	4	11				1	2	5			9		
Dec 3	(a) Watford	D 2-2	Gregory, Birch	8,000			3	8			6	10			7	4	11				1	2	5			9		
10	(h) Watford	D 1-1	Birch	8,000			3	8			6	10			7	4	11				1	2	5			9		
17	(a) Charlton A	D 1-1	Chandler	12,000			3	8			6	10			7	4	11				1	2	5			9		
24	(h) Charlton A	W 3-1	O'Brien, Smith, Chandler	12,000			3	8			6	10		7		4	11	1				2	5			9		
26	(h) Southampton	D 2-2	Birch, Chandler	18,000			3	8			6	10		7		4	11	1				2	5			9		
27	(a) Southampton	D 1-1	Birch	20,940				8	3		6	10		7			11	1				2	5		4	9		
31	(h) Northampton T	W 4-0	Birch 2, Smith 2	10,000			3	8	2		6	10		7			11	1					5		4	9		
Jan 14	(a) Northampton T	L 0-1		6,000			3	8	2		6	10		7		4		1					5	11		9		
21	(h) Gillingham	W 1-0	Chandler	5,000			3	8			6	10		7		4	11	1				2	5			9		
28	(a) Gillingham	W 2-1	Smith 2	10,000				8	3		6	10		7		4	11	1				2	5			9		
Feb 4	(h) Millwall	W 6-1	Edgley, Smith, Grant, Birch, Chandler 2	6,000				8	3		6	10		7		4	11	1				2	5			9		
11	(a) Millwall	D 0-0		22,000			3	8			6	10		7		4	11	1				2	5			9		
18	(h) Exeter C	W 2-1	Chandler, Gregory	10,000			3	8			6	10		7		4	11	1				2	5			9		
25	(a) Exeter C	W 1-0	Edgely	7,000			3	8			6	10		7		4	11	1				2	5			9		
Mar 4	(h) Swansea T	W 1-0	Birch	5,000			3	8			6	10		7		4	11	1				2			5	9		
11	(a) Swansea T	L 0-1		10,000			3	8			6	10		7		4	11	1				2	5			9		
18	(a) Southend U	W 2-1	Edgely, Birch	7,000			3	8			6	10		7		4	11	1				2			5	9		
25	(h) Southend U	W 1-0	Edgely	12,000			3	8			6	10		7			11	1	4			2			5	9		
Apr 1	(a) Portsmouth	L 0-1		8,000			3	8			6	10		7			11	1	4			2			5	9		
8	(h) Portsmouth	D 1-1	Chandler	10,000	6		3	8			5	10		7			11	1	4			2				9		
14	(h) Luton T	W 1-0	Gregory	11,000	6		3	8			5	9		11	7		10	1	4			2						
15	(a) Merthyr T	L 0-2		4,000	6		3	8			5			11	7		10	1	4			2				9		
17	(a) Luton T	L 1-3	Birch	16,000	6		3	8			5			11	7		10	1	4			2				9		
22	(h) Merthyr T	D 0-0		4,000		3		8			5	9		11	7		10	1	4			2						6
29	(a) Plymouth A	L 0-4		19,000			3				5	9		11	7	4	10	1				2				8		6
May 6	(h) Plymouth A	W 2-0	Eastwood (og), Edgely	18,000			3	8			5	9		11	7		10	1	4			2						6
				App	5	1	25	38	20	5	27	30	3	36	17	27	40	36	13	2	6	37	30	6	21	33	1	3
				Goals				17				8		5	1	1	6			1			3			10		

1 own-goal

FA Cup

Date	Match	Result	Scorers	Att	Ashford	Bailey	Bain	Birch	Blackman	Bradshaw	Burnham	Chandler	Clayton	Edgley	Faulkner	Grant	Gregory	Hill	John	Knight	Lock	Marsden	O'Brien	Ramsey	Reed	Smith	Thompson	Vigrass	Round
Jan 7	(a) Arsenal	D 0-0		31,000			3	9			6	11		8	7			1	4			2	5			10			1
11	(h) Arsenal	L 1-2	Smith	21,411			3	8			6	10		11	7	4		1				2	5			9			Rep
				App			2	2			2	2		2	2	1		2	1			2	2			2			
				Goals																						1			

Attendance Summary

	ATTENDANCES			AVERAGE		
	Home	Away	Total	Home	Away	Total
League	234,000	243,940	477,940	11,150	11,600	11,400
FA Cup	31,000	21,411	52,411	31,000	21,411	26,200
Total	265,00	265,351	530,351	12,050	12,050	12,050

1922-23

Division 3 South

Date	Opponent	Res	Score	Scorers	Att	Bain	Birch	Burnham	Butler	Chandler	Davis	Edgley	Gardner	Gregory C	Gregory J	Grimsdell	Hart	Hill	John	Lane	Leach	Marsden	Parker	Rance	Vigrass	Watson	Watts
Aug 26	(h) Watford	L	1-2	Birch	20,000	3	8	5		10		7		11	4			1			6	2	9				
28	(a) Norwich C	D	1-1	Davis	10,000	3	8			9	10	7		11	6			1	4			2			5		
Sep 2	(a) Watford	W	3-0	Chandler 2, Davis	10,000	3	8			9	10	7		11	6			1	4			2			5		
4	(h) Norwich C	W	2-0	C.Gregory, Birch	8,000	3	8			9	10	7		11	6			1	4			2			5		
9	(h) Gillingham	W	2-1	Birch 2	9,000	3	8			9	10	7		11	6			1	4			2			5		
11	(a) Brentford	W	3-1	Parker 2 (1 pen), Birch	15,000		8			10		7		11	6			1	4			3	9		5	2	
16	(a) Gillingham	W	1-0	Birch (pen)	8,000		8			10		7		11	6	3		1	4				9		5	2	
23	(h) Brighton & HA	D	0-0		12,000	3	8			10		7		11	6			1	4			2	9		5		
30	(a) Brighton & HA	L	0-2		11,000	3	8				10	7		11	6			1	4			2	9	5			
Oct 7	(h) Swindon T	L	0-2		12,000	3	8		7	9	10			11	6	2		1	4					5			
14	(a) Swindon T	L	0-1		8,000	3	8		7		10			11	6			1	4				9	5		2	
21	(h) Charlton A	L	1-2	Birch	11,000	3	8			10		7		11	6			1	4			2	9	5			
28	(a) Charlton A	D	1-1	Birch	10,000	3	8	6		10	9	7		11				1	4			2		5			
Nov 4	(a) Aberdare A	D	0-0		7,000	3	8				9	7		11			10	1	4	6		2		5			
11	(h) Aberdare A	W	4-1	Davis 3, Hart	8,000	3	8				9	7		11			10	1	4	6		2		5			
18	(a) Newport C	L	0-1		8,000	3	8				9	7		11			10	1	4			2		5	6		
25	(h) Newport C	D	1-1	Hart	9,000	3	8				9	7		11			10	1	4			2		5	6		
Dec 9	(h) Brentford	D	1-1	Marsden (pen)	19,000	3	8			6	9	7		11			10	1				2			5	4	
16	(h) Bristol C	L	1-2	Marsden (pen)	12,000	3			7	10	8			11	6			1	4			2	9		5		
23	(a) Bristol C	L	2-3	Davis 2	15,000	3			7	10	8			11	6			1				2	9	5	4		
25	(h) Luton T	W	4-0	Parker 2, Birch 2	16,000	3	8		7	10				11				1	4			2	9	5	6		
26	(a) Luton T	L	0-1		11,000	3	8		7	10	9	11			6			1		2				5	4		
30	(h) Portsmouth	L	0-1		9,000	3	8		7	10		11			6			1				2	9	5	4		
Jan 6	(a) Portsmouth	D	1-1	Parker	12,000	3	7			10	8	11			6			1	4			2	9		5		
20	(h) Millwall	L	2-3	Parker, Davis	10,000	3	7			10	8	11			6			1	4			2	9		5		
27	(a) Millwall	D	0-0		20,000	3		6	7	10	8	11			5			1	4				9			2	
Feb 10	(a) Plymouth A	L	0-2		11,000	3	7			10	8	11			6			1	4			2	9		5		
17	(h) Bristol R	W	3-1	Parker, Davis, Chandler	9,000	3	7		11	10	8				6			1	4			2	9		5		
Mar 3	(h) Reading	W	1-0	Davis	10,000	3	7			10	8	11			6			1	4			2	9		5		
15	(h) Plymouth A	L	2-3	Birch, Parker	4,000	3	7			10	8	11			6			1	4			2	9		5		
17	(a) Southend U	L	0-2		6,630		7		11	10	8			9	6			1	4	3					5	2	
21	(a) Reading	D	0-0		4,000	3	7		11	10	8				6			1	4			2	9		5		
24	(h) Southend U	W	1-0	Davis	8,000				7	10	8	11			6			1	4			2	9		5		3
26	(a) Bristol R	W	3-1	Parker, Chandler, Davis	18,000				7	10	8	11			6			1	4			2	9		5		3
30	(h) Swansea T	W	2-1	Davis, Chandler	18,000	3			7	10	8	11			6			1	4			2	9		5		
31	(a) Merthyr T	W	1-0	Parker	5,000	3			7	10	8			11	6			1	4			2	9		5		
Apr 2	(a) Swansea T	L	0-3		23,000				7	6	8	11		10	3			1	4			2	9		5		
7	(h) Merthyr T	D	1-1	Vigrass	8,000	3			7	4	8	11	10		6			1				2	9		5		
14	(a) Exeter C	W	2-1	Parker 2	6,000	3			7	4	8	11	10		6			1					9		5	2	
26	(h) Exeter C	W	2-0	Parker 2	6,000	3	10		7	4	8	11			6			1				2	9		5		
28	(a) Northampton T	L	2-4	Parker 2	7,000	3	8	6	7	4	10	11						1					9		5	2	
May 6	(h) Northampton T	W	3-2	Chandler, Edgley, Williams (og)	9,000	3	8		7	9	10	11						1	4	6		2			5		
					App	36	32	4	21	36	35	33	2	24	33	2	5	42	33	5	1	34	28	13	33	8	2
					Goals		11			6	13	1		1			2					2	16		1		

1 own-goal

FA Cup

Date	Opponent	Res	Score	Scorers	Att	Bain	Birch	Burnham	Butler	Chandler	Davis	Edgley	Gardner	Gregory C	Gregory J	Grimsdell	Hart	Hill	John	Lane	Leach	Marsden	Parker	Rance	Vigrass	Watson	Watts	Round
Jan 13	(h) Crystal P	W	1-0	Gregory	18,030	3	7			10	8	11			6			1	4			2	9		5			1
Feb 3	(a) Wigan B	W	4-2	Parker 2, Chandler, Birch	23,454	3	8			11	10	7			6			1	4			2	9		5			2
24	(h) South Shields	W	3-0	Parker 2, Gregory	15,099	3	7			10	8	11			6			1	4			2	9		5			3
Mar 10	(h) Sheffield U	L	0-1		20,000	3	7			10	8	11			6			1	4			2	9		5			4
					App	4	4			4	4	4			4			4	4			4	4		4			
					Goals		1			1					2								4					

Attendance Summary

	ATTENDANCES			AVERAGE		
	Home	Away	Total	Home	Away	Total
League	227,000	225,630	452,630	10,800	10,750	10,750
FA Cup	53,129	23,454	76,583	17,700	23,454	19,150
Total	280,129	249,084	529,213	11,650	11,300	11,500

1923-24

Division 3 South

Date	Opponent	Result	Scorers	Att	Abbott	Bain	Benson	Birch	Butler	Cameron	Davis	Dobinson	Drabble	Field	Goodman	Hart	Hill	Hurst	John	Johnson	Keen	Knowles	Marsden	Oxley	Parker	Pierce	Robinson	Vigrass	Waller	Waugh	Wood
Aug 25	(h) Brentford	W 1-0	Parker	18,000		3	11	8		6	10						1		4		7		2		9			5			
27	(h) Bristol R	L 1-2	Parker	8,000		3	11	8		6	10						1		4		7		2		9			5			
Sep 1	(a) Brentford	W 1-0	Birch	12,000		3	11	8		6	10						1		4		7		2		9			5			
5	(a) Bristol R	L 1-2	Davis	8,000		3	11	8		6	10						1		4		7		2		9			5			
8	(a) Swindon T	D 0-0		6,000		3	11			6	10						1		4		7		2	8	9			5			
12	(h) Newport C	L 0-3		5,000		3		8	11	6	9						1		4		7		2	10						5	
15	(h) Swindon T	D 2-2	Birch, Davis	6,000		3		8	11	6	9						1		4		7		2	10						5	
22	(a) Watford	W 2-0	Birch, Davis	8,218		3		8	11	6	9						1		4		7		2	10						5	
29	(h) Watford	W 2-1	Birch, Marsden (pen)	6,000		3		8	11	6	9						1		4		7		2	10						5	
Oct 6	(a) Swansea T	L 0-2		18,000	5		11	8		6	10						1		4		7		2	9		3					
13	(h) Swansea T	D 2-2	Davis, Marsden (pen)	12,000	5	3	11			6	10						1		4		7		2	8	9						
20	(a) Northampton T	L 0-3		8,994	5	3	11	8		6	10	9					1		4		7		2								
27	(h) Northampton T	W 3-2	Davis 2, Robinson	9,000				8		6	9					4	1				11		2	7		3	10	5			
Nov 3	(a) Gillingham	D 0-0		9,000	3			4		6	8						1				11		2	7	9		10	5			
10	(h) Gillingham	D 1-1	Davis	9,000	3		11	4			8					6	1				7		2		9		10	5			
Dec 1	(h) Plymouth A	W 3-2	Parker, Birch, Davis	8,000		3	11	4			8						1		6		7		2		9		10	5			
8	(a) Plymouth A	L 0-2		8,000	3		11	4			7						1		6		8		2		9		10	5			
15	(h) Merthyr T	W 3-0	Parker 2, Marsden (pen)	7,000			11	4			8						1		6		7		2		9	3		5			10
22	(a) Merthyr T	L 0-2		2,000			11	4			8						1		6		7		2		9	3		5			10
25	(h) Charlton A	D 0-0		15,000			11	4			8						1		6		7		2		9	3		5			10
26	(a) Charlton A	L 0-3		10,000			11	4			8						1		6		7		2		9	3		5			10
29	(h) Portsmouth	L 0-2		8,000		2	11	4			8						1		6		7				9	3				5	10
Jan 1	(a) Newport C	L 1-2	Parker	6,000	3	2	11	4			8						1		6		7				9			5			10
5	(a) Portsmouth	L 0-7		11,085	3	2		8		4	9						1		6		7				11			5			10
19	(h) Brighton & HA	W 1-0	Parker	4,000		2		8	11	6	10			1					4					7	9	3		5			
26	(a) Brighton & HA	L 0-3		8,000		2		8	11	6	9			1					4					7		3		5			10
Feb 2	(h) Luton T	L 0-2		9,000		2		4	11	6	10			1				8			7				9	3		5			
9	(a) Luton T	L 0-2		6,000		2			11	6		8					1		4		7				9	3		5			10
16	(h) Reading	L 1-4	Birch	6,000		2		8	11	6							1		4	10	7				9	3		5			
23	(a) Reading	L 0-4		10,000		2		7	11								1		4	10		5			9	3		6			8
Mar 1	(h) Bournemouth	L 0-1		8,000		3			11	6			1			4				8	7	5			9	2			10		
8	(a) Bournemouth	L 1-3	Johnson	5,000		3		8	7	6			1			4				9		5		11		2			10		
15	(a) Millwall	L 0-3		25,000	2	3		8	7								1		4	10		5		11	9			6			
22	(h) Millwall	D 1-1	Parker	15,000		3		8									1		4	10		5		11	9	2		6			7
29	(a) Aberdare A	D 1-1	Birch	5,000		3		8									1		4	10		5		11	9	2		6			7
Apr 5	(h) Aberdare A	W 3-0	Parker 2, Johnson	6,000		3		8									1		4	10		5		11	9	2		6			7
12	(a) Southend U	L 2-4	Parker, Birch	5,000		3		8									1		4	10		5		11	9	2		6			7
18	(h) Norwich C	W 2-1	Parker (pen), Johnson	10,000		3		8							11		1		4	10		5			9	2		6			7
19	(h) Southend U	D 0-0		8,000	3			8		6							1		4	10	11	5			9	2					7
21	(a) Norwich C	L 0-5		12,000	3			8									1		4	10	11	5			9	2		6			7
26	(a) Exeter C	L 0-3		5,000	3			8									1		4	10	11	5			9	2		6			7
May 3	(h) Exeter C	W 2-0	Parker 2	6,000		3				6							1	8	4	10		5		11	9	2					7
				App	12	30	17	37	13	24	27	2	2	3	1	4	37	2	36	14	31	13	21	18	33	24	5	30	2	5	19
				Goals				8			8									3			3		14		1				

FA Cup

Date	Opponent	Result	Scorers	Att	Abbott	Bain	Benson	Birch	Butler	Cameron	Davis	Dobinson	Drabble	Field	Goodman	Hart	Hill	Hurst	John	Johnson	Keen	Knowles	Marsden	Oxley	Parker	Pierce	Robinson	Vigrass	Waller	Waugh	Wood	Round
Jan 12	(h) Notts C	L 1-2	Davis	15,000		2		8	11	6	10						1		4		7				9	3		5				1
				App		1		1	1	1	1						1		1		1				1	1		1				
				Goals							1																					

Attendance Summary

	ATTENDANCES			AVERAGE		
	Home	Away	Total	Home	Away	Total
League	183,000	188,297	371,297	8,700	8,950	8,850
FA Cup	15,000		15,000	15,000		15,000
Total	198,000	188,297	386,297	9,000	9,950	9,000

1924-25

Division 3 South

Date	Opponent	Res	Scorers	Att	Birch	Bolam	Brown C	Brown H	Dand	Evans	Fenwick	Field	Ford	Harris	Hart	Hill	Hurst	John	Johnson	Knowles	Lillie	Marsden	Moore	Myers	Ogley	Pierce	Pigg	Sweetman	Symes	Thompson	Wicks	Wood	Young
Aug 30	(a) Newport C	D 0-0		10,000			7	9					11			1		4	10	5	3	2	8		6								
Sep 3	(h) Watford	D 0-0		9,000			7	9					11			1		4	10	5	3	2	8		6								
6	(h) Bristol R	L 1-2	H.Brown	12,000			7	9					11			1		4	10	5	3	2	8		6								
10	(a) Watford	L 0-1		6,000	8		7	9					11	6		1		4		5		2	10		3								
13	(a) Exeter C	W 3-1	H.Brown, Moore, Crompton (og)	6,000	8		7	9					11	6		1		4		5		2	10		3								
17	(a) Southend U	L 0-1		8,000	8		7	9					11	6		1		4		5		2	10		3								
20	(h) Swansea T	D 0-0		9,000	8		7	9		2		1	11	6				4		5			10		3								
24	(a) Plymouth A	L 0-1		5,000	8		7	9		2		1	11	6				4		5			10		3								
27	(a) Reading	L 1-2	Hart	1,000	8		7	9		2		1	11	6	10			4		5					3								
Oct 4	(h) Merthyr T	D 1-1	Birch	7,000	8		7	9		2	4		11	6	10	1				5					3								
11	(a) Brentford	W 1-0	H.Brown	8,000	8		7	9			4		11	6		1			10	5		2			3								
18	(a) Charlton A	L 0-2		5,000	8		7	9			4		11	6		1			10	5		2			3								
25	(h) Millwall	D 0-0		12,000	8		7	9			4		11	6		1				5		2		10	3								
Nov 1	(a) Luton T	L 0-3		4,000	8		7				4		11	6		1				5		2		10	3							9	
8	(h) Gillingham	D 1-1	Marsden (pen)	9,000			7						11	6				4	9			2	8	10	5				3		1		
15	(a) Swindon T	L 3-5	Myers 2, Johnson	7,000	8		7			3			11	6				4	9	5				10		2					1		
22	(h) Brighton & HA	W 2-0	Johnson 2	9,000	8		7						11	6		1		4	9	5				10	3	2							
Dec 6	(h) Bristol C	W 3-0	Moore 2, Johnson	6,000		11	7							6		1		4	9	5			8	10	3	2							
20	(h) Aberdare A	W 4-1	Birch 2, Johnson, Myers	9,000	8		7				5		11	6				4	9					10	3	2					1		
25	(h) Norwich C	L 1-2	Ogley	6,000	8		7		4		5		11	6					9				10		3	2					1		
26	(a) Norwich C	L 0-5		12,000	8		7				4		11	6					9			2	10		5	3					1		
27	(h) Newport C	W 4-3	Ford 2, Johnson, Moore	4,000	8		7				5	1	11						9			2	10		6	3				4			
Jan 17	(h) Exeter C	L 1-4	Moore	10,000	8		7						11	6		1				5			10	9	3	2				4			
24	(a) Swansea T	L 0-2		6,000	8		7			3		1	11					4	9	5		2		10	6								
31	(h) Reading	W 1-0	Johnson	6,000			7					1	11	4					9	5		2	8	10	6				3				
Feb 7	(a) Merthyr T	W 3-2	Johnson 2, Ford	5,000	8		7			3		1	11	4					9			2		10	6			5					
14	(h) Brentford	W 1-0	C.Brown	10,000	8		7			3		1	11	4					9					10	6	2		5					
21	(h) Charlton A	D 0-0		10,000	8		7			3		1	11	4					9					10	6	2		5					
28	(a) Millwall	L 0-3		16,000	8		7			3		1	11	4					9					10	6	2		5					
Mar 7	(h) Luton T	W 2-1	Hurst 2	7,000	8		7			3		1	11				9		10							2	6	5		4			
14	(a) Gillingham	L 0-1		6,000	8		7			3		1	11				9		10							2	6	5		4			
18	(a) Bristol R	L 0-3		5,000	8		7			3	6					1	9		10				11			2		5		4			
21	(h) Bournemouth	L 0-2		7,000	7					3		1	11						9	5		2	10		6					4			8
28	(a) Brighton & HA	L 0-5		7,000	8		7			3	6	1					9			5		2	11	10						4			
Apr 4	(h) Plymouth A	L 0-1		11,000	8	7				3	6	1					9						11	10		2		5		4			
11	(a) Bristol C	L 0-5		9,000	8		7			3	5	1							9				11	10	6	2				4			
13	(h) Northampton T	W 2-0	Johnson, Birch	8,000	8		7				5	1	11					4	9				10		6	2			3				
14	(a) Northampton T	L 0-1		8,000	8		7				5	1	11					4	9				10		6	2			3				
18	(h) Swindon T	W 1-0	Pierce (pen)	9,000	8		7				5	1	11					4	9				10		6	2			3				
22	(a) Bournemouth	W 2-0	Hurst, John	8,000	8		7				5	1	11				9	4					10		6	2			3				
25	(a) Aberdare A	D 1-1	Birch	4,000	8		7				5	1	11				9	4					10		6	2			3				
May 2	(h) Southend U	W 3-1	Birch, Ogley (pen), Hurst	7,000	8		7				5	1	11				9	4					10		6	2			3				
				App	36	2	40	13	1	17	19	22	37	24	2	15	8	21	27	22	3	18	26	17	36	22	2	8	8	9	5	1	1
				Goals	6		1	3					3		1		4	1	10			1	5	3	2	1							

1 own-goal

FA Cup

Date	Opponent	Res	Scorers	Att	Birch	Bolam	Brown C	Brown H	Dand	Evans	Fenwick	Field	Ford	Harris	Hart	Hill	Hurst	John	Johnson	Knowles	Lillie	Marsden	Moore	Myers	Ogley	Pierce	Pigg	Sweetman	Symes	Thompson	Wicks	Round
Nov 29	(h) Clapton	D 4-4	Myers 4	5,000	8		7						11	6		1		4	9	5				10	3	2						Q5
Dec 4	(a) Clapton	W 2-0	Birch 2	4,700	8		7						11	6		1		4	9	5				10	3	2						Rep
13	(h) Charlton A	D 1-1	Myers (pen)	13,000	8		7						11	6		1		4	9	5				10	3	2						Q6
18	(a) Charlton A	W 2-1	Myers, Birch	5,000	8		7						11	6		1		4	9	5				10	3	2						Rep
Jan 10	(h) Stockport C	L 1-3	Myers	19,640	8		7						11	6		1			9	5				10	3	2				4		1
				App	5		5						5	5		5		4	5	5				5	5	5				1		
				Goals	3																			7								

Attendance Summary

	ATTENDANCES			AVERAGE		
	Home	Away	Total	Home	Away	Total
League	177,000	146,000	323,000	8,450	6,950	7,700
FA Cup	42,640	11,135	53,775	14,200	5,550	10,750
Total	219,640	157,135	376,775	9,159	6,850	8,000

1925-26

Division 3 South

Date	Opponent	Res	Score	Scorers	Att	Barr	Birch	Brown	Burgess	Cable	Campbell	Edwards	Field	Ford	Harris	Hebden	Hirst	John	Johnson	Kerr	Middleton	Murdin	Paterson	Pierce	Pigg	Plunkett	Richmond	Rowe	Smith	Spotiswood	Sweetman	Symes	Thompson	Whitehead	Young
Aug 29	(a) Gillingham	L	0-3		8,000			7	10		9				6	1		4			8			2		3	5			11					
Sep 3	(h) Reading	L	1-2	Campbell	11,000			7	10		9				6	1		4			8			2		3	5			11					
5	(h) Merthyr T	D	1-1	Spotiswood	9,000	8		7			9				6	1	4				10					3	5			11	2				
9	(a) Reading	L	1-2	Burgess	6,000	5	8	7	9						6	1	4				10					3				11	2				
12	(a) Newport C	L	1-4	Burgess	11,000		8	7	9				1		6		4				10					3	5			11	2				
19	(h) Luton T	W	1-0	Johnson	5,000		8							7		1	4		9		10			2	6	3	5			11					
23	(a) Exeter C	L	0-3		5,000		10							11		1	4		9		8			2	6	3	5			7					
26	(a) Brentford	W	2-1	Johnson, Birch	10,700		8	7	10							1	4		9					2	6	3				11			5		
Oct 3	(a) Bristol R	L	0-5		5,000		8	7	10							1	4		9					2	6	3				11			5		
8	(h) Exeter C	D	0-0		4,000		8	7								1			10		4			2	6		9			11		3	5		
10	(h) Swindon T	D	1-1	Middleton	10,000			7			8			11		1	4		9		10			2	6							3	5		
17	(h) Watford	W	2-0	Whitehead, Middleton	9,000			7						11		1		4	10		8			2	6							3	5	9	
24	(a) Brighton & HA	L	1-2	Middleton	7,000			7						11		1		4	10		8			2	6							3	5	9	
31	(h) Bristol C	L	0-2		6,000			7	10					11		1		4			8			2	6							3	5	9	
Nov 7	(a) Crystal P	L	0-1		5,000			7	10					11		1	5	4						2	6							3	8	9	
21	(a) Norwich C	D	1-1	Whitehead	8,000		7		10					11		1	5	4						2	6							3	8	9	
Dec 5	(a) Plymouth A	L	1-3	Whitehead	12,000		7		10					11		1	5	4						2	6							3	8	9	
19	(a) Northampton T	L	2-3	Spotiswood, Burgess	5,219			7	10							1	5	4						2	6					11		3	8	9	
25	(h) Charlton A	D	2-2	Burgess, C.Brown	10,000			7	10	5					9	1		4						2	6					11		3	8		
26	(a) Charlton A	D	1-1	Burgess	13,000			7	10	5			1		9			4						2	6					11		3		8	
28	(h) Millwall	W	3-0	Cable 2, Whitehead	9,000			7	10	5			1	11	9			4						2	6							3		8	
Jan 2	(h) Gillingham	L	0-1		8,000			7	10				1	11	9		5	4						2	6							3		8	
16	(a) Merthyr T	L	0-1		5,000				10					11		1	5	4			7		8	2	6							3		9	
23	(h) Newport C	L	0-2		7,000			7	10							1	5	4					8	2	6					11		3		9	
30	(a) Luton T	L	0-4		8,000			7	10	5						1	6	4	9				8	2		3				11					
Feb 6	(h) Brentford	D	1-1	Burgess	15,000		7		10					11	6	1	5	4					8	2		3								9	
13	(h) Bristol R	W	2-1	Ford (pen), C.Brown	10,000			7	10					11	6	1	5	4					8	2		3								9	
20	(a) Swindon T	L	0-2		5,000			7	10					11	6	1	5	4					8	2		3								9	
25	(h) Aberdare A	L	1-3	Burgess	6,000			7	10					11	6	1	5	4				9	8	2		3									
27	(a) Watford	L	1-3	Young	6,000			7	10					11	6	1					5		9								2	3	4		8
Mar 4	(h) Southend U	D	2-2	Patterson, Young	4,000				10	5						1	4				6		9							11	2	3		7	8
6	(h) Brighton & HA	L	0-2		13,000				10	5						1	4				6		9	3						11	2			7	8
13	(a) Bristol C	L	1-3	Patterson	10,000			7	10	5						1		4			6		9	3						11	2				8
27	(a) Millwall	L	0-3		18,000			7	10							1	4			9	6		8	3			5			11	2				
30	(h) Crystal P	L	1-3	Burgess	7,000			7	10							1	4			9	6		8	3			5			11	2				
Apr 2	(h) Bournemouth	D	2-2	Whitehead, Patterson	8,000					5		7				1		4			6		10	3						11	2			9	8
3	(h) Norwich C	L	0-1		8,000					5		7				1		4			6		10	3						11	2			9	8
5	(a) Bournemouth	L	1-4	Rowe	6,000		10			5		7				1		4			6					3		11			2			9	8
10	(a) Southend U	L	1-2	Middleton	7,000		7		8	5						1	4				6		10	3				11			2			9	
17	(h) Plymouth A	L	0-4		8,000		7		8	5						1	4				6		10	3				11			2			9	
24	(a) Aberdare A	L	0-1		3,000		7		8	5								4			6		10					11	1		2	3		9	
May 1	(h) Northampton T	W	3-2	Birch 2, Middleton	5,000		7		8					11				4			6		10	3			5		1		2			9	
					App	2	15	27	32	13	4	3	4	18	14	36	26	26	9	2	26	1	19	35	19	15	10	4	2	22	16	18	13	24	7
					Goals		3	2	8	2	1			1					2		5		3					1		2				5	2

FA Cup

Date	Opponent	Res	Score	Scorers	Att	Barr	Birch	Brown	Burgess	Cable	Campbell	Edwards	Field	Ford	Harris	Hebden	Hirst	John	Johnson	Kerr	Middleton	Murdin	Paterson	Pierce	Pigg	Plunkett	Richmond	Rowe	Smith	Spotiswood	Sweetman	Symes	Thompson	Whitehead	Round
Nov 28	(a) Gravesend & N	D	2-2	Birch 2	5,165		7		10					11		1	5	4						2	6							3	8	9	1
Dec 2	(h) Gravesend & N	W	2-0	Birch 2	6,000		7		10					11		1	5	4						2	6							3	8	9	Rep
12	(h) Charlton A	D	1-1	Hirst	11,000		7		10					11		1	5	4						2	6							3	8	9	2
17	(a) Charlton A	L	0-1		7,246		8	7	10					11		1	5	4						2	6							3		9	Rep
					App		4	1	4					4		4	4	4						4	4							4	3	4	
					Goals		4										1																		

Attendance Summary

	ATTENDANCES			AVERAGE		
	Home	Away	Total	Home	Away	Total
League	172,000	163,919	335,919	8,200	7,800	8,000
FA cup	17,000	12,411	29,411	8,500	6,200	7,350
Total	189,000	176,330	365,330	8,200	7,650	7,950

1926-27

Division 3 South

Date	Opponent	Result	Scorers	Att	Bowers	Burgess	Cable	Charlesworth	Collier	Cunningham	Drew	Eggleton	Goddard	Gough	Hamilton	Hawley	Hebden	Hooper	Lofthouse	McAllister	Middleton	Mustard	Paterson	Pierce	Salt	Swan	Sweetman	Varco	Waterall	Wilcox	Young
Aug 28	(a) Crystal P	L 1-2	Vargo	15,000					4					6	7	5	1	2	11				10					8		9	3
Sep 1	(a) Gillingham	D 2-2	Lofthouse, Wilcox	6,000		8			4					6	7	5	1	2	11				10							9	3
4	(h) Coventry C	D 1-1	Lofthouse	14,000		8		7	4					6		5	1	2	11				10							9	3
11	(a) Brentford	L 2-4	Patterson, Goddard	15,000					4				9	6	7	5	1	2	11				10							8	3
18	(a) Charlton A	L 0-2		10,000							7		9	6			1	2	11		4		10						5	8	3
20	(a) Aberdare A	W 2-0	Goddard 2	2,000		8		7					9	6			1	2	11		4		10						5		3
25	(h) Bristol C	L 1-2	Middleton	10,000		8		7					9	6		5	1	2	11		4		10	3							
30	(h) Aberdare A	W 3-0	Goddard, Lofthouse, Brophy (og)	5,000		8		7					9	6		5	1	2	11		4		10								3
Oct 2	(a) Bournemouth	L 2-6	Young (pen), Goddard	6,000	4	8		7					9	6			1	2	11		10				5						3
9	(h) Plymouth A	W 4-2	Lofthouse 2, Middleton, Goddard	14,000		8							9	6	7	5	1	2	11		10				4						3
16	(h) Bristol R	D 2-2	Burgess, Goddard	7,000		8							9	6	7	5	1	2	11		10				4						3
23	(a) Millwall	L 1-2	Middleton	14,000			5						9	6	7		1	2	11	8	10				4						3
30	(h) Northampton T	W 4-2	Lofthouse 2, Goddard, McAllister	10,000		10				1			9	6	7	5		2	11	8	4										3
Nov 6	(a) Brighton & HA	L 1-4	Goddard	11,000		10	5			1			9		7	4		2	11	8	6			3							
13	(h) Norwich C	W 4-0	Goddard 2, Lofthouse, Vargo	8,000			5			1			9		7			2	11	4	6		10					8			3
20	(a) Luton T	L 0-2		5,000			5			1			9		7			2	11	4	6		10					8			3
Dec 4	(a) Merthyr T	L 0-4		2,000				7		1			9						11	4	6		10	2	5			8			3
11	(a) Plymouth A	L 0-2		10,000		10				1			9			5			11	4	6	7		2				8			3
18	(a) Swindon T	L 2-6	Goddard 2	10,000		10		8		1			9			5			11	4	6	7		2							3
25	(h) Watford	L 2-4	Young, Mustard	10,000			5	8					9				1		11	4	6	7		2				10			3
27	(a) Watford	W 2-1	Charlesworth, Lofthouse	13,000				7	4			5	9				1		11	8	6	10		2							3
Jan 1	(h) Gillingham	D 1-1	Goddard	8,000				7	4			5	9				1		11	8	6	10		2							3
8	(h) Southend U	W 3-2	Charlesworth, Middleton, Goddard	8,000				7				5	9	6			1		11	4	10	8		2							3
15	(h) Crystal P	L 0-2		10,000		8		7				5	9	6			1		11	4	10			2							3
22	(a) Coventry C	L 0-1		5,000				7				5	9	6			1		11	4	10	8		3			2				
Feb 5	(h) Charlton A	W 2-1	Goddard 2	19,000				7				5	9	6			1		11	4	10	8		3			2				
12	(a) Bristol C	L 0-1		14,000		10		7				5	9	6			1		11	4		8		3		10	2				
19	(h) Bournemouth	D 1-1	Lofthouse	6,000				7	4			5	9	6			1		11		10	8		3			2				
24	(h) Exeter C	D 1-1	Lofthouse	4,000				7	4							5	1		11	6	10			3			2	9		8	
Mar 5	(a) Bristol R	L 1-4	Wilcox	5,000					4			5	9				1		11		6	7		3		10	2			8	
12	(h) Millwall	D 1-1	Goddard	15,000				7	4	1		5	9						11		6			3		10	2			8	
19	(a) Northampton T	L 0-1		5,375				7	4	1		5	9						11		6			3		10	2			8	
26	(h) Brighton & HA	D 2-2	Mustard, Lofthouse	10,000					4	1		5	9						11	8	6	7		3		10	2				
Apr 2	(a) Norwich C	W 1-0	Lofthouse	13,000					4	1			9			5			11	6		7				10	2	8			3
9	(h) Luton T	W 1-0	Goddard	5,000				4		1			9			5			11		6	7				10	2	8			3
15	(a) Newport C	W 2-0	Goddard, Varco	9,000				7	4	1			9			5			11	6						10	2	8			3
16	(a) Southend U	W 3-0	Charlesworth, Swan, Goddard	8,000				7	4	1			9			5			11	6						10	2	8			3
18	(h) Newport C	W 2-0	Goddard, Young (pen)	12,000				7	4	1			9			5			11	6						10	2	8			3
23	(h) Merthyr T	W 5-1	Young 2 (2 pens), Varco, Patterson, Goddard	9,000					4	1			9			5			11	6			7			10	2	8			3
30	(a) Exeter C	W 2-0	Lofthouse, Patterson	5,000					4	1			9			5			11	6			7			10	2	8			3
May 5	(h) Brentford	D 1-1	Hawley	9,000					4	1			9			5			11	6			7			10	2	8			3
7	(h) Swindon T	L 0-1		10,000					4	1			9			5			11	6			7			10	2	8			3
				App	1	14	5	23	20	19	1	12	38	19	10	22	23	16	42	26	28	14	15	19	5	14	18	16	2	9	31
				Goals		1		3					23			1			14	1	4	2	3			1		4		2	5

1 own-goal

Queen's Park Rangers did not enter the FA Cup this season

Attendance Summary

	ATTENDANCES			AVERAGE		
	Home	Away	Total	Home	Away	Total
League	203,000	183,375	386,375	9,650	8,750	9,200
Total	203,000	183,375	386,375	9,650	8,750	9,200

1927-28

Division 3 South

Date	Opponent	Result	Scorers	Att	Beats	Burns	Collier	Coward	Crompton	Cunningham	Duthie	Eggleton	Gilhooley	Goddard	Hawley	Johnson	Kellard	Lofthouse	Mustard	Neil	Paterson	Pierce	Roberts	Rounce	Stephenson	Swan	Sweetman	Turner	Woodward	Young
Aug 27	(h) Newport C	W 4-2	Goddard 2 (1 pen), Lofthouse, Swan	15,489			4			1			5	9				11		8					7	10	2	6		3
Sep 1	(h) Gillingham	D 3-3	Goddard 2, Lofthouse	8,000			4			1			5	9				11		8					7	10	2	6		3
3	(a) Swindon T	W 2-0	Swan, Johnson	8,000			4			1			5			9		11		8		3			7	10	2	6		
7	(a) Gillingham	W 2-1	Johnson, Neil	5,000			4			1			5			9		11		8		3			7	10	2	6		
10	(h) Brentford	L 2-3	Lofthouse 2	20,000			4			1				9	5			11		8		3			7	10	2	6		
17	(h) Watford	W 2-1	Swan, Goddard	15,000			4			1				9	5			11		8		3			7	10	2	6		
19	(a) Bournemouth	W 2-1	Lofthouse, Goddard	5,000			4			1				9	5			11		8		3			7	10	2	6		
24	(a) Charlton A	L 0-1		18,000			4			1					5	9		11		8		3			7	10	2	6		
Oct 1	(h) Bristol R	W 4-2	Goddard 3, Collier	8,000			4			1				9	5			11		8		3			7	10	2	6		
8	(a) Plymouth A	L 0-3		14,000			4			1				9	5			11		8					7	10	2	6		3
15	(h) Merthyr T	D 0-0		14,000			4			1				9	5			11	7	8		3				10	2	6		
22	(a) Crystal P	D 1-1	Lofthouse	7,000			4			1	10	5		9				11	7	8		3					2	6		
29	(h) Millwall	L 0-1		19,000			4			1	10	5		9				11	7	8		3					2	6		
Nov 5	(a) Luton T	W 1-0	Goddard	6,000			4			1		5		9		10			7		8	3	11				2	6		
12	(h) Exeter C	L 0-1		8,000			4			1		5		9					7	10	8	3	11				2	6		
19	(a) Torquay U	L 0-1		3,000			4			1	10	5		9				11		8					7		2	6		3
Dec 3	(a) Northampton T	L 0-1		9,683						1	4	5		9		10		11	7	8		2						6		3
17	(a) Brighton & HA	W 3-1	Goddard 2, Lofthouse	8,000						1	4	5		9				11	8	10		2			7			6		3
24	(h) Bournemouth	W 2-0	Goddard, Mustard	8,000						1	4	5		9				11	8	10		2			7			6		3
27	(a) Coventry C	D 0-0		5,000						1	4	5		9				11	8	10		2			7			6		3
Jan 7	(h) Swindon T	L 0-1		12,000						1	4	5		9				11	8	10		2			7			6		3
14	(h) Southend U	W 3-2	Burns, Mustard, Young (pen)	8,000		8				1		5		9		10		11	7	4		2						6		3
21	(a) Brentford	W 3-0	Goddard 2, Burns	12,000		8				1		5		9		10		11	7	4		2						6		3
28	(a) Watford	D 3-3	Lofthouse 2, Goddard	5,000		8				1		5		9		10		11	7	4		2						6		3
Feb 4	(h) Charlton A	D 3-3	Goddard 2, Burns	12,000		8				1		5		9		10		11	7	4		2						6		3
11	(a) Bristol R	W 4-0	Goddard 2, Johnson, Lofthouse	7,000		8				1		5		9		10		11	7	4		2						6		3
18	(h) Plymouth A	L 0-1		19,000		8				1		5		9		10		11	7	4		2						6		3
25	(a) Merthyr T	W 4-0	Goddard 3, Rounce	3,000						1		5		9				11	7	4		2		8		10		6		3
Mar 3	(h) Crystal P	W 2-0	Swan, Goddard	17,000								5		9				11	7	4		2		8		10		6	1	3
10	(a) Millwall	L 1-6	Beats	20,000	9	8						5						11	7	4		2				10		6	1	3
17	(h) Luton T	W 3-2	Johnson, Burns, Lofthouse	11,000		8					6	5				9		11		4		2		10	7				1	3
24	(a) Exeter C	L 0-4		4,500		8						5		9				11		4		2		10	7			6	1	3
31	(h) Torquay U	L 2-3	Coward, Rounce	6,000		8		7		1			5	9				11		4		2		10				6		3
Apr 6	(a) Newport C	W 6-1	Goddard 2, Burns, Young (pen), Coward, Rounce	4,000		8		7		1			5	9				11		4		2		10				6		3
7	(a) Southend U	L 0-7		10,000		8		7		1			5	9				11		4		2		10				6		3
9	(h) Walsall	D 1-1	Young (pen)	10,000		8		7		1			5	9				11		4		2		10				6		3
10	(a) Walsall	D 2-2	Lofthouse, Rounce	5,000		8		7		1			5	9				11		4		2		10				6		3
14	(h) Northampton T	L 0-4		8,000		8		7		1		5		9		10				4		2	11					6		3
21	(a) Norwich C	L 1-3	Johnson	5,000						1	6	5				9			8	4		2	11	10	7					3
26	(h) Coventry C	L 1-5	Rounce	5,000				7		1	6	5				9		11	8	4		2		10						3
28	(h) Brighton & HA	W 5-0	Johnson 2, Rounce, Lothouse, Young (pen)	10,000		8						5				9		11	7	4		2		10				6	1	3
May 3	(h) Norwich C	D 0-0		4,000					5			6				9	10	11	7	4		2		8					1	3
				App	1	16	16	7	1	36	11	26	9	33	7	17	1	38	23	41	2	38	4	13	18	14	16	38	6	30
				Goals	1	5	1	2						26		7		13	2	1				6		4				4

FA Cup

Date	Opponent	Result	Scorers	Att	Beats	Burns	Collier	Coward	Crompton	Cunningham	Duthie	Eggleton	Gilhooley	Goddard	Hawley	Johnson	Kellard	Lofthouse	Mustard	Neil	Paterson	Pierce	Roberts	Rounce	Stephenson	Swan	Sweetman	Turner	Woodward	Young	Round
Nov 30	(h) Aldershot	L 1-2	Johnson	4,000			4			1		5		9		10		11	7	8							2	6		3	1
				App			1			1		1		1		1		1	1	1							1	1		1	
				Goals												1															

Attendance Summary

	ATTENDANCES Home	Away	Total	AVERAGE Home	Away	Total
League	237,489	164,183	401,672	11,300	7,800	9,550
FA Cup	4,000		4,000	4,000		4,000
Total	241,489	164,183	405,672	11,000	7,800	9,450

1928-29

Division 3 South

Date	Opponent	Result	Scorers	Att	Armstrong	Burns	Cockburn	Coward	Cunningham	Eggleton	Foster	Goddard	Johnson	Kellard	McNab	Neil	Nixon	Pierce	Price	Rogers	Rounce	Smith	Sweetman	Thompson	Vallence	Whatmore	Woodward	Young
Aug 25	(a) Torquay U	W 4-3	Goddard 3, Burns	12,000		8	5	7	1			9			4	6			11				2			10		3
30	(h) Newport C	D 0-0		8,000		8	5	7	1			9			4	6			11				2			10		3
Sep 1	(h) Gillingham	W 1-0	Coward	10,000		8	5	7	1			9			4				11		10		2	6				3
6	(a) Newport C	D 0-0		4,000			5	7	1			9	10		4						8	11	2	6				3
8	(a) Plymouth A	W 2-1	Goddard 2	12,000		8	5	7	1			9			4						10	11	2	6				3
15	(h) Fulham	W 2-1	Young (pen), Goddard	22,000		8	5	7	1			9			4						10	11	2	6				3
22	(a) Brentford	D 1-1	Smith	21,699		8	5	7	1			9			4						10	11	2	6				3
29	(a) Bristol R	D 1-1	Goddard	8,000		8	5	7	1			9			4	6					10	11	2					3
Oct 6	(h) Watford	W 3-2	Goddard, McNab, Coward	18,000		8	5	7	1			9			4	6					10	11	2					3
13	(a) Walsall	L 1-3	Rounce	9,000		8	5	7	1			9			4	6					10	11	2					3
20	(h) Bournemouth	D 0-0		10,000			5	7	1		8	9			4	6						11	2			10		3
27	(a) Merthyr T	W 2-1	Rounce (pen), Goddard	3,000		8	5	7	1			9			4						10	11	2	6				3
Nov 3	(h) Southend U	W 3-1	Burns, Rounce, Goddard	11,000		8	5	7	1			9			4	6					10	11	2					3
10	(a) Exeter C	D 1-1	Burns	4,000	4	8	5	7	1			9						3			10	11	2	6				
17	(h) Brighton & HA	W 3-2	Young, Rounce, Goddard	12,000		8	5	7				9			4	6					10	11	2				1	3
Dec 1	(h) Charlton A	D 2-2	Goddard 2	12,000		8	5	7				9			4						10	11	2	6			1	3
8	(a) Northampton T	L 2-4	Goddard 2	12,000		8	5	7	1			9				4					10	11	2	6				3
15	(h) Coventry C	W 3-1	Rogers 2, Goddard	10,000		8	5	7	1			9				4				10		11	2	6				3
22	(a) Luton T	L 2-3	Goddard 2	10,000		8	5	7	1			9				4				10		11	2	6				3
25	(h) Swindon T	W 4-2	Rogers, Burns, Goddard, Kellard	10,000		8	5		1			9		7		4				10		11	2			6		3
26	(a) Swindon T	L 1-2	Dickenson (og)	10,000		8			1	5		9		7		4				10		11	2	6				3
29	(h) Torquay U	W 5-1	Goddard 3, Burns, Oxley (og)	10,000		8		7	1	5		9				4				10		11	2	6				3
Jan 5	(a) Gillingham	D 0-0		10,000		8	5	7	1			9			4					10		11	2	6				3
19	(h) Plymouth A	W 2-0	Burns, McNab	20,000		8	5	7	1			9			4					10		11	2	6				3
26	(a) Fulham	L 0-5		30,000		8	5	7	1			9			4					10		11	2			6		3
Feb 2	(h) Brentford	D 2-2	Coward, Herod (og)	13,500		8	5	7	1			9			4					10			2	6		11		3
9	(h) Bristol R	L 0-3		12,000			5	7	1			9			4					10	8		2	6		11		3
16	(a) Watford	L 1-4	Rogers	8,000				7	1	5		9			4	6				10			2		8	11		3
23	(h) Walsall	D 2-2	Goddard, Young (pen)	12,000		8			1	5		9		7		4						11	2	6		10		3
Mar 2	(a) Bournemouth	W 3-2	Haywood (og), Rounce, Goddard	5,000		8	5	7	1			9			4	6		3			10		2			11		
9	(h) Merthyr T	W 8-0	Goddard 4, Burns 3, Rounce	12,000		8		7	1			9			4	6	5	3			10		2			11		
16	(a) Southend U	W 3-0	Burns 2, Goddard	6,000		8		7	1			9			4	6	5	3			10		2			11		
23	(h) Exeter C	W 1-0	Goddard	12,000		8		7	1			9			4	6	5	3			10		2			11		
29	(a) Crystal P	W 4-1	Goddard 3, Coward	3,400		8	5	7	1			9			4	6		3			10		2			11		
30	(a) Brighton & HA	L 1-2	Pierce	10,000		8	5	7	1			9			4	6		3			10		2			11		
Apr 1	(h) Crystal P	D 1-1	Goddard	25,000		8	5	7	1			9			4	6	3				10		2			11		
6	(h) Norwich C	W 3-0	Coward 2, Rounce	15,000			5	7	1			9		8	4	6	3				10		2			11		
13	(a) Charlton A	D 2-2	Coward, Rounce	12,000		8	5	7				9			4	6		3			10	11	2				1	
20	(h) Northampton T	W 4-1	Rounce, Goddard, Burns, Whatmore	21,909		8	5	7	1			9			4	6		3			10		2			11		
22	(a) Norwich C	L 1-3	Goddard	7,000		8	5	7			4	9				6		3			10		2			11	1	
27	(a) Coventry C	D 0-0		18,000		8	5	7	1			9			4	6		3			10		2			11		
May 4	(h) Luton T	D 1-1	Goddard	12,000		8	5	7	1		4	9				6		3			10		2			11		
				App	1	37	35	39	38	4	3	42	1	4	32	29	5	12	3	11	28	24	42	18	1	21	4	28
				Goals		12		7				37		1	2			1		4	9	1				1		3

4 own-goals

FA Cup

Date	Opponent	Result	Scorers	Att	Armstrong	Burns	Cockburn	Coward	Cunningham	Eggleton	Foster	Goddard	Johnson	Kellard	McNab	Neil	Nixon	Pierce	Price	Rogers	Rounce	Smith	Sweetman	Thompson	Vallence	Whatmore	Woodward	Young	Round
Nov 24	(a) Guildford C	L 2-4	Goddard, Burns	10,000		8	5	7				9			4	6					10	11	2				1	3	1
				App		1	1	1				1			1	1					1	1	1				1	1	
				Goals		1						1																	

Attendance Summary

	ATTENDANCES Home	Away	Total	AVERAGE Home	Away	Total
League	288,409	245,699	534,108	13,750	11,700	12,700
FA Cup		10,000	10,000		10,000	10,000
Total	288,409	255,699	544,108	13,750	11,600	12,650

1929-30

Division 3 South

Date	Opponents	Res	Scorers	Att	Armstrong	Burns	Cockburn	Coward	Cunningham	Evans	Foster	Goddard	Gretton	Harris	Hebden	Howe	McNab	Moffatt	Neil	Nixon	Pickett	Pierce	Pollard	Rogers	Rounce	Whatmore	Wiles G	Wiles H	Yates	Young
Aug 31 (a)	Crystal P	D 1-1	H.Wiles	20,000			5		1			9		3			4	7	6			2			10			8		11
Sep 5 (h)	Walsall	D 2-2	Goddard, Moffat	7,000			5		1			9					4	7	6			2			10		3	8		11
7 (h)	Gillingham	W 2-1	Goddard, Moffat	12,000		8			1			9					4	7	6	5		2			10		3			11
9 (a)	Walsall	L 0-4		5,000					1		4	9						7		5		2			10		3	8	6	11
14 (a)	Northampton T	L 1-2	Rounce	12,712			5		1			9					4	7	6			3	2		8	10				11
16 (h)	Fulham	D 0-0		10,000			5		1			9					4	7	6			3	2		8	10				11
21 (h)	Exeter C	W 2-0	Young, Rounce	13,000			5		1			9					4	7	6			3	2		8	10				11
28 (a)	Southend U	L 0-1		11,000			5		1			9					4	7	6			3	2		8	10				11
Oct 5 (h)	Luton T	W 1-0	Goddard	12,000		8	5		1			9					4	7	6			3	2		10					11
12 (a)	Bournemouth	D 0-0		7,000		8	5		1			9					4	7	6			3	2		10					11
19 (h)	Clapton O	D 1-1	Rounce	15,000		8	5	7	1			9				11	4		6			3	2		10					
26 (a)	Coventry C	W 3-2	Howe 2, Goddard	12,000		8	5	7	1			9				11	4		6			3	2		10					
Nov 2 (h)	Watford	D 0-0		12,000	6	8	5	7	1			9				11	4					3	2		10					
9 (a)	Newport C	W 5-4	H.Wiles 3, Goddard, Rounce	5,000			5	7	1			9				11	4					3	2		10	6		8		
16 (h)	Torquay U	D 1-1	Fowler (og)	4,000	6	8	5	7				9				11	4				1	3	2					10		
Dec 7 (a)	Swindon T	D 2-2	Coward, Howe	4,000		8	5	7					1			11	4		6			3	2		10			9		
21 (a)	Bristol R	L 1-4	Goddard	7,000		8	5	7	1			9				11			4			3	2	10		6				
25 (a)	Norwich C	L 0-3		11,000		8	5	7	1			9				11	4		6			3	2		10					
26 (h)	Norwich C	W 3-2	Goddard 3	12,000		8	5	7	1			9				11	4		6			3	2		10					
28 (h)	Crystal P	W 4-1	Rounce 2 (1 pen), Burns, Goddard	11,000		8	5	7	1			9				11	4		6			2	3		10					
Jan 4 (a)	Gillingham	L 1-3	Goddard	4,000		8	5	7	1			9				11	4		6			3	2		10					
18 (h)	Northampton T	L 0-2		10,000		8	5		1			9					4	7	6			3	2		10					11
25 (a)	Exeter C	W 2-0	Moffat, Goddard	5,000		8	5		1			9					4	7	6			3	2		10					11
Feb 1 (h)	Southend U	L 2-5	Rounce, Goddard	8,000			5			8		9			1		4	7	6			3	2		10					11
8 (a)	Luton T	L 1-2	Goddard	6,000	5	8						9	1	3				7	4	2					10				6	11
15 (h)	Bournemouth	W 3-1	Goddard 2 (1 pen), Coward	10,000	5			7				9	1	3		11			4	2					10			8	6	
22 (a)	Clapton O	W 4-2	Goddard 2, Rounce 2 (1 pen)	15,000	5	8		7				9	1	3		11			4	2					10				6	
Mar 1 (h*)	Coventry C	W 3-1	Howe 2, Armstrong	25,000	5	8		7	1			9		3		11			4	2					10				6	
3 (a)	Merthyr T	W 4-1	Goddard 3, H.Wiles	3,000	5			7	1			9		3		11			4	2					10			8	6	
8 (a)	Watford	D 1-1	Bresford (og)	10,000	5	8		7	1			9		3		11			4	2					10				6	
13 (h)	Plymouth A	L 1-2	Goddard (pen)	4,000	5	8		7	1			9		3		11			4	2					10				6	
15 (h)	Newport C	W 4-1	Goddard 3, Wheeler (og)	10,000	5	8		7	1			9		3		11			4				2		10	6				
22 (a)	Torquay U	W 3-1	Armstrong, Burns, Rounce	6,000	5	8		7	1			9		3		11			4				2		10	6				
27 (h)	Brighton & HA	W 3-1	Goddard 2, Marsden (og)	5,000	5	8			1			9		3		11		7	4				2		10	6				
29 (h)	Merthyr T	W 2-0	Goddard, Rounce	11,000	5	8		7	1			9		3		11			4				2		10	6				
Apr 5 (a)	Plymouth A	L 0-4		20,000	5	8		7	1		4	9		3		11							2		10	6				
12 (h)	Swindon T	W 8-3	Goddard 4, Rounce 3, Coward	6,000	5	8		7	1			9				11						3	2		10		4		6	
18 (h)	Brentford	W 2-1	Rounce, Goddard (pen)	22,179	5	8		7	1			9		3		11			4	2					10				6	
19 (a)	Brighton & HA	W 3-2	Goddard 3	6,000	5	8		7	1			9		3		11			4	2					10	6				
21 (a)	Brentford	L 0-3		20,000	5	8		7	1			9		3		11			4				2		10	6				
26 (h)	Bristol R	W 2-1	H.Wiles, Armstrong	8,000	5	8			1			9		3		11			4	2					10	6		7		
May 3 (a)	Fulham	W 2-0	Rounce, Goddard	20,000	5	8			1			9				11			4	2					10	6	3	7		
				App	20	31	22	25	36	1	2	41	4	17	1	28	22	15	36	13	1	25	27	1	40	15	5	10	10	14
				Goals	3	2		3				37				5		3							16			6		1

*Played at Highbury, London.

4 own-goals

FA Cup

Date	Opponents	Res	Scorers	Att	Armstrong	Burns	Cockburn	Coward	Cunningham	Evans	Foster	Goddard	Gretton	Harris	Hebden	Howe	McNab	Moffatt	Neil	Nixon	Pickett	Pierce	Pollard	Rogers	Rounce	Whatmore	Wiles G	Wiles H	Yates	Young	Round
Nov 30 (a)	Luton T	W 3-2	Goddard, Coward, Pierce (pen)	9,000		8	5	7				9				11	4		6		1	3	2		10						1
Dec 12 (h)	Lincoln C	W 2-1	Burns 2	13,097		8	5	7	1			9				11	4		6			2	3		10						2
Jan 11 (a)	Charlton A	D 1-1	Goddard	22,300		8	5	7	1			9				11	4		6			3	2		10						3
16 (h)	Charlton A	L 0-3		22,000		8	5	7	1			9					4		6			3	2		10					11	Rep
				App		4	4	4	3			4				3	4		4		1	4	4		4					1	
				Goals		2		1				2										1									

Attendance Summary

	ATTENDANCES Home	Away	Total	AVERAGE Home	Away	Total
League	227,179	209,712	436,891	10,800	10,000	10,000
FA Cup	35,097	31,300	66,397	17,548	15,650	16,599
Total	262,276	241,012	503,288	11,400	10,500	10,950

1930-31

Division 3 South

Date	Opponent	Result	Scorers	Att	Armstrong	Burns	Coward	Cunningham	Daniels	Embleton	Ferguson	Goddard	Harris	Hoten	Howe	Legge	Lewis	Nixon	Pickett	Pierce	Pollard	Rounce	Sales	Shepherd	Smith	Stephenson	Tutt	Vango	Whatmore	Wiles G	Wiles H
Aug 30	(h) Thames	W 3-0	Hoten 2, Goddard	12,000	5	8		1	11			9	3	10		7		2							4				6		
Sep 3	(a) Bournemouth	L 0-2		6,000	5			1	11			9	3	10		7					2	8			4				6		
6	(a) Norwich C	D 1-1	Goddard	11,000	5	8		1	11			9		10		7					2				4				6	3	
11	(h) Watford	L 2-3	Daniels, Goddard	5,000	5	8		1	11			9		10		7		2			3				4				6		
13	(h) Brighton & HA	W 4-1	Rounce 2, Burns, Coward	8,000	5	6	7	1	11		8							3			2	10			4						9
17	(a) Watford	W 4-0	Rounce, H.Wiles, Daniels, Goddard	6,000	5	6	7	1	11		8							2			3	10			4						9
20	(h) Walsall	W 3-0	Ferguson, H.Wiles, Burns	9,000	5	6	7	1	11		8							3			2	10			4						9
27	(a) Coventry C	L 0-2		15,000	5	6	7	1	11		8	9						2				10			4					3	
Oct 4	(h) Fulham	L 0-2		15,000	5	6	7	1	11		8							2				10			4					3	9
11	(a) Swindon T	L 1-4	Coward	6,000	5		7	1	11					10				2		3		8	4						6		9
18	(a) Torquay U	L 2-6	Burns, H.Wiles	5,000	5	8	7		11									2	1	3		10	4						6		9
23	(h) Northampton T	L 0-2		8,000	5	8	7		11									2	1		3		4	10					6		9
Nov 1	(a) Brentford	L 3-5	Coward, H.Wiles, Nixon	12,000	5	8	7								11			2	1		3	10	4						6		9
8	(h) Crystal P	W 4-0	Rounce 3 (1 pen), Goddard	15,000	5	8	7	1					3		11						2	10	4	9					6		
15	(a) Southend U	L 0-2		6,000	5		7	1					3		11						2	10	4	9		8			6		
22	(h) Luton T	W 3-1	Burns, Rounce, Shepherd	7,000	5	8	7	1					3		11						2	10	4	9					6		
Dec 6	(h) Newport C	W 7-1	Goddard 3, Burns 2, Armstrong, Rounce	8,000	5	8	7	1				9	3		11						2	10	4						6		
17	(a) Gillingham	D 2-2	Goddard, Howe	5,000	5		7	1			8	9	3		11						2		4	10					6		
20	(h) Exeter C	W 7-2	Goddard 4, Rounce 2, Coward	8,000		8	7	1				9	3		11						2	10	4		5				6		
25	(h) Notts C	W 4-1	Burns 3, Goddard	12,000		8	7	1				9	3		11						2	10	4		5				6		
26	(a) Notts C	L 0-2		14,000		8	7	1			11	9	3								2	10	4		5				6		
27	(a) Thames	L 0-1		8,000		8	7	1	11			9	3								2	10	4		5				6		
Jan 3	(h) Norwich C	W 3-1	Goddard 2, Rounce	8,000		8		1				9	3	11							2	10	4		5				6		7
14	(a) Bristol R	L 0-3		3,314				1				9	3	10		7					2	8	4				11	5	6		
17	(a) Brighton & HA	D 1-1	Rounce	10,000		8		1				9	3		11	7					2	10	4		5				6		
24	(a) Walsall	W 2-0	John, (og) Hoten	5,000		8		1			6	9	3	11		7				2		10	4		5						
31	(h) Coventry C	W 2-0	Howe, Rounce	8,000			7	1			6	9	3		11							8	4		5				10	2	
Feb 7	(a) Fulham	W 2-0	Coward, Goddard	22,000		8	7	1			6	9	3		11							10	4		5					2	
14	(h) Swindon T	L 1-2	Daniels	10,000			7	1	11		6	9	3									8	4		5				10	2	
21	(h) Torquay U	L 1-2	Burns	10,000	5	8	7	1				9	3		11							10	4						6	2	
28	(a) Northampton T	L 0-6		8,000	5	8		1				9	3		11	7					2	10			4				6		
Mar 7	(h) Brentford	W 3-1	Goddard 2, Howe	10,000	5	8		1		7	6	9			11						2	10			4					3	
14	(a) Crystal P	L 0-4		18,500	5	8		1		7	6	9			11						2	10			4					3	
21	(h) Southend U	L 0-2		7,000	5		7	1			6	9	2		11								4	10		8				3	
28	(a) Luton T	L 1-5	Shepherd	7,000	5	8	7				6	9							1		2	10	4	11						3	
Apr 3	(h) Clapton O	W 4-2	Goddard 2 (1 pen), Shepherd, Whatmore	7,000	5	8	7					9	3						1			10		11	4				6	2	
4	(h) Bristol R	W 2-0	Rounce, Goddard	7,000	5	8	7					9	3						1	2		10		11	4				6		
6	(a) Clapton O	W 3-2	H.Wiles, Rounce, Goddard	6,000	5	8						9	3						1		2	10	4	11					6		7
11	(a) Newport C	W 3-2	Goddard 2, Shepherd	5,000		8						9	3		11				1		2		4	10				5	6		7
18	(h) Gillingham	W 1-0	H.Wiles	7,000	5	8	7						3						1		2	10	4	11					6		9
25	(a) Exeter C	L 0-2		5,000	5	8	7						3			9			1		2	10	4	11					6		
May 2	(h) Bournemouth	W 3-0	Hoten, Lewis, Rounce	8,000	5		7						3	9	11		8		1		2	10	4						6		
				App	30	33	29	31	14	2	15	28	28	9	18	9	1	11	11	4	29	35	28	13	24	2	1	2	31	12	12
				Goals	1	10	5		3		1	25		4	3	1		1				16		4					1		6

1 own-goal

FA Cup

Date	Opponent	Result	Scorers	Att	Armstrong	Burns	Coward	Cunningham	Daniels	Embleton	Ferguson	Goddard	Harris	Hoten	Howe	Legge	Lewis	Nixon	Pickett	Pierce	Pollard	Rounce	Sales	Shepherd	Smith	Stephenson	Tutt	Vango	Whatmore	Wiles G	Wiles H	Round
Nov 29	(h) Thames	W 5-0	Goddard 2 (1 pen), Burns 2, Rounce	9,000	5	8	7					9	3		11				1		2	10	4						6			1
Dec 13	(a) Crewe A	W 4-2	Goddard 2, Howe, Rounce	8,200	5	8	7	1				9	3		11						2	10	4						6			2
Jan 10	(a) Bristol R	L 1-3	Coward	24,000		8	7	1				9	3		11						2	10	4		5				6			3
				App	2	3	3	2				3	3		3				1		3	3	3		1				3			
				Goals		2	1					4			1							2										

Attendance Summary

	ATTENDANCES			AVERAGE		
	Home	Away	Total	Home	Away	Total
League	189,000	183,814	372,814	9,000	8,753	8,877
FA Cup	9,000	32,200	41,200	9,000	16,100	13,733
Total	198,000	216,014	414,014	9,000	9,392	9,200

1931-32
Division 3 South

Date	Opponent	Result	Scorers	Att	Adlam	Armstrong	Blackman	Collins	Coward	Cribb	Cunningham	Goddard	Goodier	Haley	Hall	Harris	Howe	Lewis	Nixon	Pickett	Pollard	Rounce	Sales	Smith	Tutt	Vango	Whatmore	Wiles G	Wiles H	Wilson	Wyper
Aug 29 (a)	Brentford	L 0-1		25,000		5				11		9				3		8		1	2	10	4				6				7
31 (a)	Bristol R	D 1-1	Haley	15,000		5				11		9		8		3				1	2	10	4				6				7
Sep 5 (h)	Bournemouth	L 0-3		18,907		5				11		9				3		8		1	2	10	4				6				7
10 (h)	Swindon T	L 1-2	Lewis	7,615		5				11		9		10	3			8		1	2	4					6				7
12 (a)	Crystal P	D 1-1	Goddard	8,000		5				11		9		10	3			8		1	2		4			6					7
16 (a)	Swindon T	W 2-1	Goddard, Cribb	5,000		5				11		9		10	3			8		1	2		4			6					7
19 (h)	Watford	D 4-4	Goddard 4	16,456		5				11		9		8	3					1	2	10	4			6					7
26 (a)	Mansfield T	D 2-2	England (og), Lewis	3,000		5				11		9		4	3			8	2	1		10				6					7
Oct 3 (h)	Brighton & HA	D 1-1	Goddard	13,768		5				11	1	9		4	3			8	2			10				6					7
10 (a)	Norwich C	L 1-2	Lewis	15,000		5				11	1	9			3			8	2				4			6				10	7
17 (a)	Exeter C	L 2-6	Coward, Lewis	5,000		5			7	11		9		4	3			8	2	1		10				6					
24 (h)	Coventry C	D 1-1	Wilson	12,590		5			7	11		9			3			8		1						6	4	2		10	
31 (a)	Gillingham	L 0-1		6,000		5			7	11		9			3	2		8		1		10				6	4				
Nov 7 (h)	Luton T	W 3-1	Cribb 2, Goddard	10,949		5		8	7	11		9				3			2	1		10				6	4				
14 (a)	Cardiff C	W 4-0	Cribb 2, Goddard, Roberts (og)	4,000	4	5		8	7	11		9	6			3			2	1		10									
21 (h)	Northampton T	W 3-2	Cribb 2, Coward	12,073	4	5		8	7	11		9	6			3			2	1		10									
Dec 5 (h)	Southend U	W 2-1	Robinson (og), Goddard	17,853	4	5			7	11		9	6		3	2				1		10								8	
19 (h)	Thames	W 6-0	Goddard 3, Tutt 2, Wilson (pen)	7,352	4	5		10	7			9	6		3	2				1					11					8	
25 (a)	Torquay U	W 3-2	Collins 2, Cribb	7,000	4	5		10	7	11		9	6		3	2				1										8	
26 (h)	Torquay U	W 3-1	Wilson, Cribb, Goddard	24,083	4	5		10	7	11		9	6		3	2				1										8	
28 (a)	Fulham	W 3-1	Goddard 2, Cribb	23,157	4	5			7	11		9	6		3	2				1		10								8	
Jan 2 (h)	Brentford	L 1-2	Cribb (pen)	33,508	4	5			7	11		9	6		3	2				1		10								8	
13 (a)	Reading	L 2-3	Blackman 2	4,500	4	5	9	8	7	11			6		3	2				1		10									
16 (a)	Bournemouth	D 2-2	Armstrong, Coward	5,000	4	5	9	8	7	11			6		3	2				1		10									
28 (h)	Crystal P	D 2-2	Blackman, Rounce	8,324	4	5	9		7	11			6		3					1	2	10								8	
30 (a)	Watford	D 2-2	Howe, Blackman	11,838	4	5	9			11			6		3		7			1	2	10								8	
Feb 6 (h)	Mansfield T	D 1-1	Blackman	12,034	4	5	9			11			6		3		7			1	2	10								8	
13 (a)	Brighton & HA	L 0-1		7,000	4	5		8		11			6		3				2	1		10								9	7
20 (h)	Norwich C	D 2-2	Blackman, Cribb	9,587	4	5	9		7	11			6		3				2	1		10								8	
27 (h)	Exeter C	W 1-0	Blackman	14,373	4	5	9		7				6		3				2	1		10			11					8	
Mar 5 (a)	Coventry C	L 0-1		5,000	4	5	9		7				6		3				2	1		10			11					8	
10 (h)	Gillingham	W 7-0	H.Wiles 4, Haley 2, Coward	3,886	4	5		11	7				6	8	3				2	1									9	10	
19 (a)	Luton T	L 1-4	H.Wiles	8,000	4	5			7				6	8	3				2	1					11				9	10	
25 (a)	Clapton O	L 0-3		12,000	4		9		11		1		6		3				2			8		5					7	10	
26 (h)	Cardiff C	L 2-3	Rounce, Haley	8,279	4		9		11				6	8	3				2	1		10		5					7		
28 (h)	Clapton O	W 3-2	H.Wiles, Coward, Tutt	11,490	4	5			7				6		3				2	1		10			11				9	8	
Apr 2 (a)	Northampton T	L 1-6	H.Wiles	6,898	4	5			7				6	8	3				2	1					11				9	10	
9 (h)	Reading	W 2-0	H.Wiles 2	6,710	4	5			7		1		6	8	3		11		2			10							9		
16 (a)	Southend U	D 0-0		8,000	4	5		10	7		1		6	8	3				2								11		9		
23 (h)	Fulham	W 3-1	H.Wiles 2, Haley	21,527	4	5					1	7	6	8	3				2			10					11		9		
30 (a)	Thames	L 2-3	Rounce 2	3,000	4	5					1	7	6	8	3				2			10					11		9		
May 7 (h)	Bristol R	W 2-1	Goddard, Whatmore	7,141	4	5					1	9	6	8	3				2			10					11		7		
				App	28	40	10	11	26	28	8	25	28	17	36	15	3	11	22	34	10	31	7	2	6	10	11	1	11	20	11
				Goals		1	7	2	5	12		17		5			1	4				4			3		1		11	3	

3 own-goals

FA Cup

Date	Opponent	Result	Scorers	Att	Adlam	Armstrong	Blackman	Collins	Coward	Cribb	Cunningham	Goddard	Goodier	Haley	Hall	Harris	Howe	Lewis	Nixon	Pickett	Pollard	Rounce	Sales	Smith	Tutt	Vango	Whatmore	Wiles G	Wiles H	Wilson	Wyper	Round
Nov 28 (a)	Barnet	W 7-3	Cribb 3, Goddard 2, Coward 2	6,853	4	5			7	11		9	6		3	2				1		10								8		1
Dec 12 (a)	Scunthorpe U	W 4-1	Rounce 3, Cribb	7,943	4	5			7	11		9	6		3	2				1		10								8		2
Jan 9 (h)	Leeds U	W 3-1	Cribb 2, Rounce	41,097	4	5	9		7	11			6		3	2				1		10								8		3
23 (a)	Huddersfield T	L 0-5		31,394	4	5	9		7	11			6		3	2				1		8					10					4
				App	4	4	2		4	4		2	4		4	4				4		4					1			3		
				Goals					2	6		2										4										

Attendance Summary

	ATTENDANCES Home	Away	Total	AVERAGE Home	Away	Total
League	278,505	187,393	465,898	13,262	8,923	11,093
FA Cup	41,097	46,190	87,287	41,097	15,397	21,822
Total	319,602	233,583	553,185	14,527	9,733	12,026

1932-33

Division 3 South

Date	Opponents	Result	Scorers	Att	Adlam	Armstrong	Ashman	Barrie	Beecham	Blackman	Brown	Collins	Goddard	Gofton	Goodier	Hall	Hill	Howe	Jobson	Jones	March	Marcroft	Nixon	Rounce	Russell	Wiles
Aug 27	(h) Brentford	L 2-3	Goddard, Brown	24,347	4		2		1		11	10	9		6	3			5			7		8		
Sep 1	(h) Aldershot	D 2-2	Goddard, Rounce	5,963	4	5	2		1		11		9		6	3	8					7		10		
3	(a) Southend U	W 1-0	Rounce	8,000	4	5	3		1				9		6		8	11				7	2	10		
7	(a) Aldershot	L 0-2		5,000	4	5	3		1		11		9		6		8					7	2	10		
10	(h) Crystal P	W 2-1	Wiles, Blackman	15,920	4	5	3		1	8	11		9		6					10			2			7
17	(a) Gillingham	L 1-4	Brown	6,000	4	5	3		1	8	11		9		6					10			2			7
24	(h) Watford	W 2-1	Brown, Marcroft	10,617	4	5		2	1		11		9		6	3				8		7		10		
Oct 1	(a) Cardiff C	W 5-2	Marcroft 3, Goddard, Blackman	5,000	4	5		2	1	9	11				6	3				8		7		10		
8	(h) Reading	L 0-3		11,213	4	5		2	1	9	11				6	3				8		7		10		
15	(a) Norwich C	L 2-3	Marcroft, Goddard	6,000	4			2	1	9	10		8		6	3		11	5			7				
22	(h) Coventry C	D 3-3	Gofton, Collins, Brown	7,575	4	5		2	1		10	8		9	6	3		11				7				
29	(a) Bristol C	W 3-2	Brown 2, Gofton	6,000	4	5		2	1		10		8	9	6	3		11				7				
Nov 5	(h) Northampton T	D 1-1	Gofton	8,858	4	5		2	1		10		8	9	6	3		11				7				
12	(a) Clapton O	D 2-2	Howe, Gofton	8,000	4	5		2	1		10		8	9	6	3		11				7				
19	(h) Swindon T	W 4-2	Goddard 2, Gofton 2	5,765	4	5		2	1		11		8	9	6	3						7		10		
Dec 3	(h) Newport C	W 6-1	Brown 2, Gofton 2, Rounce, Marcroft	6,477	4	5		2	1		11		8	9	6	3						7		10		
17	(h) Exeter C	L 1-3	Rounce	7,448	4	5		2	1		11		8	9	6	3						7		10		
24	(a) Torquay U	L 1-3	Goddard	5,000			3	2	1	8	11		9		6			7	5		4			10		
26	(h) Brighton & HA	L 0-1		9,140		5	3	2	1	8	11		9		6			7			4			10		
27	(a) Brighton & HA	L 1-4	Brown	12,000	5			2	1	8	11		9		6						4	7	3	10		
31	(a) Brentford	L 0-2		20,000	8	5		2	1	7	11		9		6	3	4							10		
Jan 7	(h) Southend U	W 6-1	Goddard 2, Brown 2, Blackman, Wilson (og)	5,551		5		2	1	7	11		9		6	3	4							10		8
18	(a) Bournemouth	L 0-3		4,000		6		2	1		11	8	9			3	4		5			7		10		
21	(a) Crystal P	W 1-0	Rounce	12,000			6	2	1			8	9		5	3	4	11				7		10		
28	(h) Gillingham	D 1-1	Wiles	4,132			6	2	1			8			5	3	4	11				7		10		9
Feb 4	(a) Watford	D 2-2	Howe, Rounce	5,000			6	2	1	7		8	9		5		4	11						10	3	
11	(h) Cardiff C	W 5-1	Goddard 2, Rounce 2, Collins	5,130			6	2	1		7	8	9		5	3	4	11						10		
18	(a) Reading	L 1-3	Goddard	7,000			3	2	1		7	8	9		5		6	11			4			10		
25	(h) Norwich C	D 2-2	Goodier, Howe	4,549			6	2	1		11	8	9		5			7			4			10	3	
Mar 5	(a) Coventry C	L 0-7		11,000			6	2	1		11	8	9		5			7			4			10	3	
11	(h) Bristol C	D 1-1	Blackman	6,305		5		2	1	9	11		8		6	3		7			4			10		
18	(a) Northampton T	L 1-2	Brown	5,000		5		2	1	9	10		8		6	3		11			4					7
25	(h) Clapton O	W 2-1	Howe, Blackman	5,283		5		2	1	9					6		8	11		10	4	7			3	
Apr 1	(a) Swindon T	D 0-0		4,000	4	5		2	1	9	11				6		8			10		7			3	
8	(h) Bournemouth	W 3-1	Hill, Blackman, Jones	4,139	4	5		2	1	9	11				6		8			10		7			3	
14	(h) Bristol R	D 1-1	Blackman	6,646	4	5		2	1	9	11				6		8			10		7			3	
15	(a) Newport C	L 1-5	Marcroft	7,000	4	5		2	1	9	11	10	8		6							7			3	
17	(a) Bristol R	L 1-4	Brown	10,000	4	5		2	1	8	10				6	3		11				7				9
18	(a) Luton T	L 1-3	Blackman	3,000	4	5		2	1	8					6	3		11		10		7				9
22	(h) Luton T	W 3-1	Blackman 2, Marcroft	2,800	4	5		2	1	8	11				6	3				10		7				9
29	(a) Exeter C	L 0-2		5,000	4	5		2	1	8	11				6	3				10		7				9
May 6	(h) Torquay U	D 1-1	Blackman	3,042	4	5		2	1	9	11		8		6	3				10		7				
				App	28	31	15	36	42	23	36	11	30	7	41	26	15	20	4	13	9	29	5	24	8	9
				Goals						11	13	2	12	8	1		1	4		1		8		8		2

1 own-goal

FA Cup

Date	Opponents	Result	Scorers	Att	Adlam	Armstrong	Ashman	Barrie	Beecham	Blackman	Brown	Collins	Goddard	Gofton	Goodier	Hall	Hill	Howe	Jobson	Jones	March	Marcroft	Nixon	Rounce	Russell	Wiles	Round
Nov 26	(a) Merthyr T	D 1-1	Rounce	6,500	4	5		2	1		11		8	9	6	3						7		10			1
28	(h) Merthyr T	W 5-1	Goddard 3, Marcroft, Rounce	6,000	4	5		2	1		11		8	9	6	3						7		10			Rep
Dec 10	(a) Torquay U	D 1-1	Rounce	5,000	4	5		2	1		11		8	9	6	3						7		10			2
12	(h) Torquay U	W 3-1	Rounce 3	7,000	4	5		2	1		11		8	9	6	3						7		10			Rep
Jan 14	(a) Darlington	L 0-2		7,639		5		2	1	7	11		9			3	4				6			10		8	3
				App	4	5		5	5	1	5		5	4	4	5	1				1	4		5		1	
				Goals									3									1		6			

Attendance Summary

	ATTENDANCES			AVERAGE		
	Home	Away	Total	Home	Away	Total
League	160,900	154,000	314,900	7,662	7,333	7,498
FA Cup	13,000	19,139	32,139	6,500	6,380	6,428
Total	173,900	173,139	347,039	7,561	7,214	7,384

1933-34

Division 3 South

Date		Opponents	Result		Scorers	Att	Allen	Ashman	Barrie	Beecham	Blackman	Blake	Brown	Clarke	Devine	Eaton	Emmerson	Farmer	Goddard	Goodier	Hammond	Jones	Langford	March	Mason	Rivers	Russell
Aug	26	(h) Brighton & HA	W	2-0	Clarke 2	15,646		3	2	1		6		11	10	8	7		9	5						4	
	30	(a) Swindon T	L	1-3	Emmerson	10,000		3	2	1		6		11	10	8	7		9	5						4	
Sep	2	(a) Aldershot	L	1-3	Devine	5,000		3	2	1		6		11	10	8	7		9	5				4			
	7	(h) Swindon T	W	1-0	Eaton	7,000		3	2	1		6		11	10	8	7		9	5				4			
	9	(h) Luton T	W	2-1	Emmerson, Clarke	10,000		3	2	1		6		11		8	7		9	5			10	4			
	16	(a) Northampton T	L	1-2	Devine	7,000		3	2	1		6		11	10	8	7		9	5				4			
	23	(h) Torquay U	W	2-0	Blackman, Emmerson	8,000		3	2	1	9	6		11	10	8	7			5				4			
	30	(a) Exeter C	D	1-1	Blackman	15,000	8	3	2	1	9	6		11	10		7			5				4			
Oct	7	(a) Newport C	W	2-1	Jones (og), Blackman	8,000	8	3	2	1	9	6		11	10		7			5				4			
	14	(h) Norwich C	W	5-2	Emmerson 2, Blackman 2, Clarke	10,000	8	3	2	1	9	6		11	10		7			5				4			
	21	(h) Cardiff C	W	4-0	Blake 2, Emmerson, Blackman	9,000	8	3	2	1	9	6		11	10		7			5				4			
	28	(a) Bournemouth	L	2-3	Allen, Clarke	6,000	8	3		1	9	6		11	10		7			5				4			2
Nov	4	(h) Charlton A	W	2-1	Blackman, Clarke	11,000	8	3	2	1	9	6		11	10		7			5				4			
	11	(a) Watford	D	0-0		12,000	8	3	2	1	9	6		11	10		7			5				4			
	18	(h) Reading	D	0-0		12,000	8	3	2	1	9	6		11	10		7			5				4			
Dec	2	(h) Southend U	W	4-0	Brown, Devine, Emmerson, Blake	10,000	8	3	2	1	9	6	11		10		7			5				4			
	16	(h) Crystal P	W	2-1	Blackman, Blake	13,000		3	2	1	9	6	11		10	8	7			5				4			
	23	(a) Gillingham	W	4-1	Blackman 3, Eaton	7,000		3	2	1	9	6	11		10	8	7			5				4			
	25	(h) Clapton O	W	2-0	Blackman, Brown	20,000		3	2	1	9	6	11		10	8	7			5				4			
	26	(a) Clapton O	D	2-2	Blackman 2	12,000		3	2	1	9	6	11		10	8	7			5				4			
	30	(a) Brighton & HA	W	1-0	Blackman	6,000		3	2	1	9	6	11		10	8	7			5				4			
Jan	6	(h) Aldershot	L	2-4	Devine, Blake	16,000		3	2	1	9	6	11		10	8	7			5				4			
	18	(a) Coventry C	W	1-0	Emmerson	9,703		3	2		9	6	11			8	7			5			10	4	1		
	20	(a) Luton T	L	2-4	Kingham 2 (2 og's)	8,000		3	2		9	6	11			8	7			5			10	4	1		
	27	(h) Northampton T	W	2-1	Brown 2	5,000	8	3	2		9	6	11		10		7			5				4	1		
Feb	3	(a) Torquay U	D	1-1	Brown	3,000	8	3	2		9	6	11		10		7	5						4	1		
	10	(h) Exeter C	W	2-0	Emmerson, Blackman	8,000	8	3	2		9		11		10		7	5					6	4	1		
	17	(h) Newport C	W	2-1	Devine, Allen	11,000	8	3	2		9		11		10		7	5					6	4	1		
	24	(a) Norwich C	L	0-1		20,000	8	3	2		9		11		10		7			5			6	4	1		
Mar	3	(a) Cardiff C	L	1-3	Brown	6,000	8	3	2		9	6	11		10		7			5				4	1		
	10	(h) Bournemouth	W	1-0	Brown	10,000	8	3	2	1	9		11				7			5			10	4		6	
	17	(a) Charlton A	W	2-1	Emmerson, Blackman	16,000	8	3	2	1	9	6	11		10		7	5						4			
	24	(h) Watford	D	0-0		8,000	8	3	2	1	9	6	11		10		7	5						4			
	30	(h) Bristol C	W	1-0	Blackman	10,000	8	3	2	1	9	6	11		10		7			5				4			
	31	(a) Reading	L	0-5		12,000	8	3	2	1	9	6	11		10		7			5				4			
Apr	2	(a) Bristol C	W	2-0	Devine, Blackman	11,000	8	3	2	1	9	6	11		10		7	5						4			
	7	(h) Coventry C	L	0-1		10,000	8	3	2	1	9	6	11		10		7	5						4			
	14	(a) Southend U	W	2-0	Devine, Blackman	5,000	8	3	2	1	9	6	11		10			5			7			4			
	18	(a) Bristol R	L	1-4	Hammond	3,000	8	3	2	1	9	6	11		10			5			7			4			
	21	(h) Bristol R	W	1-0	March	7,000	8	3	2	1	9	6						5			7	11	10	4			
	28	(a) Crystal P	L	1-4	Blackman	8,000		3	2	1	9	6			8			5			7	11	10	4			
May	5	(h) Gillingham	W	5-0	Blackman 3, Hammond, Devine	5,000	8	3	2	1	9	6			10			5			7	11		4			
						App	26	42	41	34	36	38	24	15	37	15	37	12	6	30	5	3	9	40	8	3	1
						Goals	2				24	5	7	6	8	2	10				2			1			

3 own-goals

FA Cup

Date		Opponents	Result		Scorers	Att	Allen	Ashman	Barrie	Beecham	Blackman	Blake	Brown	Clarke	Devine	Eaton	Emmerson	Farmer	Goddard	Goodier	Hammond	Jones	Langford	March	Round
Nov	25	(h) Kettering T	W	6-0	Blackman 2, Emmerson 2, Allen, Brown	14,000	8	3	2	1	9	6	11		10		7			5				4	1
Dec	9	(h) New Brighton	D	1-1	Blackman	12,000	8	3	2	1	9	6	11		10		7			5				4	2
	11	(a) New Brighton	W	4-0	Blackman 4	5,062		3	2	1	9	6	11		10	8	7			5				4	Rep
Jan	13	(a) Nottingham F	L	0-4		21,170		3	2	1	9	6	11		10	8	7			5				4	3
						App	2	4	4	4	4	4	4		4	2	4			4				4	
						Goals	1				7		1				2								

Attendance Summary

	ATTENDANCES			AVERAGE		
	Home	Away	Total	Home	Away	Total
League	215,646	189,703	405,349	10,269	9,033	9,652
FA Cup	26,000	26,232	52,222	13,000	13,116	13,058
Total	241,646	215,935	457,581	10,506	9,388	9,947

1934-35
Division 3 South

Date		Opponent	Result	Scorers	Att	Abel	Allen	Ashman	Barrie	Bartlett	Beecham	Blackman	Blake	Connor	Crawford	Devine	Dutton	Emmerson	Farmer	Goodier	Hammond	Langford	March	Mason	Reed	Ridley	Russell	Trodd	Watson	Wright
Aug	25 (a)	Swindon T	L 1-3	Reed	12,000		8	3	2		1				11	10	6	7		5			4		9					
	30 (h)	Crystal P	D 3-3	Blake (pen), Crawford, Blackman	9,415			3	2		1	8	6		11	10		7	4	5					9					
Sep	1 (h)	Aldershot	W 2-0	Reed 2	13,000			3	2		1	8	6		11	10			4	5	7				9					
	5 (a)	Crystal P	W 3-2	Hammond, Blackman, Reed	15,843			3	2		1	8	6		11	10			4	5	7				9					
	8 (a)	Cardiff C	L 1-2	Farquarson (og)	13,000			3	2		1	8	6		11	10			4	5	7				9					
	15 (h)	Brighton & HA	W 2-1	Blackman, Abel	9,000	8			2		1	9	6		7	10				5			4				3		11	
	22 (a)	Luton T	D 1-1	Crawford	8,000	8			2		1	9	6		7	10				5			4				3		11	
	29 (h)	Southend U	D 1-1	Abel	9,000	8			2		1	9	6		7	10				5			4				3		11	
Oct	6 (a)	Bristol R	L 0-2		8,000	8			2		1	9	6		11	10				5			4				3		7	
	13 (h)	Charlton A	L 0-3		18,000		8		2		1		6		11	10		7		5			4		9		3			
	20 (a)	Gillingham	D 0-0		6,000			3	2			8			7	10	6		4	5				1	9				11	
	27 (h)	Reading	W 2-0	Dutton, Watson	10,000			3	2			8	4				10		6	5	7			1	9				11	
Nov	3 (a)	Millwall	L 0-2		14,000			3	2	5		7	4			8	10		6					1	9				11	
	10 (h)	Coventry C	D 1-1	Crawford	6,000	9		3	2				4		11	8	10	7	6	5				1						
	17 (a)	Watford	L 0-2		8,000	9		3	2				4		11	8	10	7	6	5				1						
Dec	1 (a)	Exeter C	L 0-3		4,000			3	2			9			11	8	10	7	5			6	4	1						
	15 (a)	Northampton T	L 0-1		6,000		8			5		9			11	10				6	7		4	1		2	3			
	22 (h)	Bournemouth	W 2-1	Crawford, Blackman	5,000		8			5		9			11	10		7		6			4	1		2	3			
	25 (h)	Clapton O	W 6-3	Blackman 2, Emmerson, Crawford, Devine, Allen	9,244		8		2			9	6		11	10		7		5			4	1			3			
	26 (a)	Clapton O	L 1-3	Crawford	11,446		8		2			9	6		11		10	7		5			4	1			3			
	29 (h)	Swindon T	D 1-1	Blake	8,000		8	3	2			9	6		11	10		7		5			4	1						
Jan	1 (h)	Bristol C	W 4-1	Blackman, Crawford, Allen, Emmerson	3,000		8	3	2			9	6		11	10		7		5			4	1						
	5 (a)	Aldershot	L 0-1		4,000		8	3	2			9	6		11			7		5		10	4	1						
	12 (h)	Newport C	W 4-1	Blackman 2, Dutton, Emmerson	6,000		8					9	6		11		10	7		5			4	1		2	3			
	19 (h)	Cardiff C	D 2-2	Blackman, Dutton	5,000		8		2			9	6				10	7		5			4	1			3		11	
	26 (a)	Brighton & HA	L 1-5	Allen	4,000		8	3				9	6	11						5	7		4	1		2				10
Feb	2 (h)	Luton T	W 3-0	Blackman 2, Crawford	6,000	7	8					9	6		11				10	5			4	1		2	3			
	9 (a)	Southend U	L 0-2		5,000	7	8	3				9	6		11				10	5			4	1		2				
	16 (h)	Bristol R	W 2-0	Abel, Dutton	7,000	7	8	3				9	6				11		10	5			4	1		2				
	23 (a)	Charlton A	L 1-3	Allen	17,964	7	8	3				9	6				11		10	5			4	1		2				
Mar	2 (h)	Gillingham	W 2-0	Farmer, Blackman	10,000	9						8	6		11				10	5	7		4	1		2	3			
	9 (a)	Reading	D 0-0		6,000	7						9	6		11		8		10	5			4	1		2	3			
	16 (h)	Millwall	W 1-0	Farmer	11,000							9	6	11			8	7	10	5			4	1		2	3			
	23 (a)	Coventry C	L 1-4	Blackman	8,000	7	4					9	6	11			8		10	5				1		2	3			
	30 (h)	Watford	W 2-1	Blackman, Blake (pen)	8,000	7	4					9	6	11			8		10	5				1		2	3			
Apr	6 (a)	Newport C	L 1-2	Blackman	3,000	7	4					9	6	11			8		10	5				1		2	3			
	13 (h)	Exeter C	D 1-1	Farmer	6,000	7	8					9	6				11		10	5				1		2	3	4		
	19 (h)	Torquay U	W 5-1	Blackman 2, Blake, Farmer, Dutton	6,000	7	8					9	6				11		10	5				1		2	3	4		
	20 (a)	Bristol C	L 1-5	Bridge (og)	7,000	7	8					9	6				11		10	5				1		2	3	4		
	22 (a)	Torquay U	L 0-7		5,000	7	8	3	2			9	6				11		10	5				1				4		
	27 (h)	Northampton T	W 3-1	Farmer 2, Blackman	5,000	7	8	3	2			9	6				11		10	5				1				4		
May	4 (a)	Bournemouth	W 2-0	Farmer, Dutton	5,000		8	3	2			9	6				11		10	5	7			1				4		
					App	20	25	21	25	3	10	38	37	5	26	20	23	15	26	40	8	2	24	32	9	17	21	6	8	1
					Goals	3	4					19	4		8	1	6	3	7		1				4				1	

2 own-goals

FA Cup

Date		Opponent	Result	Scorers	Att	Abel	Allen	Ashman	Barrie	Bartlett	Beecham	Blackman	Blake	Connor	Crawford	Devine	Dutton	Emmerson	Farmer	Goodier	Hammond	Langford	March	Mason	Reed	Ridley	Russell	Trodd	Watson	Wright	Round
Nov	24 (h)	Walthamstow A	W 2-0	Emmerson, Devine	9,000	9		3	2				4		11	8	10	7	5			6		1							1
Dec	8 (h)	Brighton & HA	L 1-2	Crawford	14,000		8		4	5		9			11	10				6	7			1		2	3				2
					App	1	1	1	2	1		1	1		2	2	1	1	1	1	1	1		2		1	1				
					Goals										1	1		1													

Attendance Summary

	ATTENDANCES Home	Away	Total	AVERAGE Home	Away	Total
League	169,659	171,253	340,912	8,079	8,155	8,117
FA Cup	23,000		23,000	11,500		11,500
Total	192,659	171,253	363,912	8,376	8,155	8,271

1935-36

Division 3 South

Date	Opponents	Result	Scorers	Att	Abel	Allen	Ballentyne	Banks	Barrie	Bartlett	Blackman	Blake	Carr	Cheetham	Clarke	Coggins	Crawford	Farmer	Fletcher	Hammond	Lowe	Lumsden	March	Masson	Molloy	Ovenstone	Rowe	Russell	Samuel	Vincent
Aug 31	(h) Millwall	L 2-3	Blackman, Lowe	15,000	7			11			9	6	2								8		4	1			3		10	5
Sep 4	(a) Brighton & HA	D 1-1	Hammond	8,000								6	2	9			11		8	7	10		4	1			3			5
7	(a) Torquay U	L 2-4	Hammond, Samuel	6,000	9							6	2				11			7	8		4	1			3		10	5
12	(h) Brighton & HA	W 3-2	Cheetham 2, Lowe	5,000	9							6	2				11			7	8		4	1			3		10	5
14	(h) Aldershot	W 5-0	Cheetham 4, Hammond	11,000		4				5			2	9			11		8	7	10			1	6		3			
16	(a) Luton T	L 0-2		8,000		4				5			2	9			11		8	7	10			1	6		3			
21	(a) Swindon T	D 2-2	Crawford, Lowe	11,000		4				5			2	9			11		8		10	7		1	6		3			
28	(h) Coventry C	D 0-0		16,000		4				5			2	9			11		8		10	7	6	1				3		
Oct 5	(a) Newport C	W 4-3	Cheetham 3, Lowe	5,000		4				5			2	9			11		8		10	7	6	1				3		
12	(h) Exeter C	W 3-1	Cheetham 2, Abel	12,000		4				5			2	9			11		8		10	7	6	1				3		
19	(a) Notts C	L 0-3		9,000		4				5			2	9			11		8		10	7	6	1				3		
26	(h) Bristol R	W 4-0	Cheetham (pen), Lumsden 2, Farmer	9,000		4			2	5				9			11	6	8		10	7		1				3		
Nov 2	(a) Clapton O	L 0-1		15,000		4		11	2	5		6		9					8		10	7		1				3		
9	(h) Bournemouth	W 2-0	Cheetham, Ovenstone	12,000		4			2	5				9					8		10	7	6	1		11		3		
16	(a) Northampton T	W 4-1	Ballantyne, Cheetham 2, Ovenstone	5,000		4	10		2	5				9							8	7	6	1		11		3		
23	(h) Crystal P	W 3-0	Cheetham 3	10,000		4	10		2	5				9							8	7	6	1		11		3		
Dec 7	(h) Cardiff C	W 5-1	Lumsden 3, Cheetham 2	3,000		4	10		2	5				9							8	7	6	1		11	3			
21	(h) Southend U	W 2-1	Ballentyne, Cheetham	10,000			10		2	5		6		9							8	7	4	1		11	3			
25	(h) Watford	W 3-1	Cheetham 2, Ballentyne	18,000		4	10		2	5				9							8	7	6	1		11	3			
26	(a) Watford	L 1-2	Lowe	14,000		4			2	5				9					10		8	7	6	1		11	3			
28	(a) Millwall	L 0-2		13,000					2	5			3	9		1			10		8	7	6			11				4
Jan 4	(h) Torquay U	W 2-1	Cheetham, Samuel	9,000	7				2	5				9		1					8		6			11	3		10	4
15	(a) Reading	W 2-1	Cheetham 2	7,000	7	4				5				9		1					8		6			11	3	2	10	
18	(a) Aldershot	W 3-1	Lowe 2, Abel	3,000	7	4				5				9		1					8		6			11	3	2	10	
25	(h) Swindon T	W 5-1	Cheetham 2, Lowe 2, Abel	11,000	7	4				5				9		1					8		6			11	3	2	10	
Feb 1	(a) Coventry C	L 1-6	Samuel	19,000	7	4		11	2	5				9		1					8		6				3		10	
8	(h) Newport C	D 1-1	Crawford	12,000		4		11	2	5				9			7				8		6	1			3		10	
15	(a) Exeter C	D 0-0		5,000		4			2	5				9							8	7	6	1		11	3		10	
22	(h) Notts C	D 2-2	Cheetham, Ovenstone	7,000		4			2	5				9				10	8			7	6	1		11	3			
29	(a) Bournemouth	W 1-0	Cheetham	6,000		4	10		2	5				9					8			7	6	1		11	3			
Mar 7	(h) Gillingham	W 5-2	Cheetham 3, Lowe, Crawford	12,000		4	10		2	5				9			11		8			7	6	1			3			
14	(a) Bristol R	W 1-0	Cheetham	10,000		4	10		2	5				9			11		8			7	6	1			3			
21	(h) Northampton T	L 0-1		13,000		4	10		2	5				9			11		8			7	6	1			3			
28	(a) Crystal P	W 2-0	Cheetham, Crawford	22,389		4	10		2	5				9			11		8			7	6	1			3			
Apr 4	(h) Reading	L 0-1		12,000		4	10		2	5				9			11		8			7	6	1			3			
10	(h) Bristol C	W 4-1	Lowe 3, Crawford	14,000		4	10		2	5							11	8			9	7	6	1			3			
11	(a) Cardiff C	L 2-3	Crawford, Lowe	10,000		4	10		2	5							11	8			9	7	6	1			3			
13	(a) Bristol C	D 0-0		10,000		4	10	7	2	5							11	8			9		6	1			3			
18	(h) Clapton O	W 4-0	Lowe, Banks, Crawford, Farmer	15,000		4	10	7	2	5							11	8			9		6	1			3			
22	(a) Gillingham	D 2-2	Banks, Cheetham	2,000				11	2	5				9			7	10			8		6	1			3			4
25	(a) Southend U	W 1-0	Farmer	5,000	9			11		5			2		8		7	10					6	1			3			4
May 2	(h) Luton T	D 0-0		24,000		4		11		5			2	9			7	10			8		6	1			3			
				App	9	33	15	9	26	38	1	6	14	34	1	6	24	9	20	5	34	25	37	36	3	15	32	12	10	8
				Goals	3		3	2			1			36			7	3		3	15	5				3			3	

FA Cup

Date	Opponents	Result	Scorers	Att	Abel	Allen	Ballentyne	Banks	Barrie	Bartlett	Blackman	Blake	Carr	Cheetham	Clarke	Coggins	Crawford	Farmer	Fletcher	Hammond	Lowe	Lumsden	March	Masson	Molloy	Ovenstone	Rowe	Russell	Samuel	Vincent	Round
Nov 30	(a) Margate	L 1-3	Cheetham	7,000		4	10		2	5				9							8	7	6	1		11	3				1
				App		1	1		1	1				1							1	1	1	1		1	1				
				Goals										1																	

Attendance Summary

	ATTENDANCES			AVERAGE		
	Home	Away	Total	Home	Away	Total
League	250,000	193,389	443,389	11,905	9,209	10,557
FA Cup		7,000	7,000		7,000	7,000
Total	250,000	200,389	450,389	11,905	9,109	10,474

1936-37

Division 3 South

Date		Opponents	Result	Scorers	Att	Abel	Allen	Ballentyne	Banks	Barrie	Bartlett	Bott	Cameron	Carr	Charlton	Cheetham	Clarke	Crawford	Farmer	Fitzgerald	James	Jefferson	Lowe	Lumsden	McMahon	March	Mason	Moralee	Rowe	Swinfen	Vincent
Aug	29	(a) Bristol C	L 2-3	Cheetham, Lowe	15,000		4			2	5	11	10	3		9		7					8			6	1				
	31	(a) Millwall	L 0-2		16,200		4			2	5	11	10			9		7				3	8			6	1				
Sep	5	(h) Torquay U	W 3-0	Bott 2 (1 pen), Lowe	12,000		4	10		2	5	11				9		7				3	8			6	1				
	12	(a) Notts C	W 2-1	Bott 2 (1 pen)	6,000		4	10		2	5	11				9						3	8		7	6	1				
	17	(h) Millwall	L 0-1		12,000		4	10		2	5	11				9						3	8		7	6	1				
	19	(h) Clapton O	W 2-1	Banks, Lowe	12,000		4		11	2	5					9						3	10		7	6	1			8	
	23	(a) Crystal P	D 0-0		9,467		4					11				9						2	8		7	6	1		3	10	5
	26	(a) Walsall	W 4-2	Cheetham 2, Allen, Lowe	8,000		4	8				11				9						2	10		7	6	1		3		5
Oct	3	(h) LutonT	W 2-1	Bott, Lowe (pen)	22,000	7	4	8				11				9						2	10			6	1		3		5
	10	(a) Cardiff C	L 0-2		28,000	7	4	8				11				9						2	10			6	1		3		5
	17	(h) Swindon T	D 1-1	Lowe	12,000	7		8			5	11				9						2	10			6	1		3		4
	24	(a) Aldershot	D 0-0		4,000			8				11				9			5			2	10	7		6	1		3		4
	31	(h) Gillingham	L 0-1		5,000			8				11				9					5	2	10	7		6	1		3		4
Nov	7	(a) Newport C	W 2-1	Lowe 2	10,000							11				9				10	5	2	8	7		6	1		3		4
	14	(h) Southend U	W 7-2	Fitzgerald 2, Lowe 2, Lumsden, March, Cheetham	12,000											9				10	5	2	8	7	11	6	1		3		4
	21	(a) Watford	L 0-2		13,000											9				10	5	2	8	7	11	6	1		3		4
Dec	5	(a) Bournemouth	L 1-3	Fitzgerald	7,000							7				9				10	5	2	8		11	6	1		3		4
	19	(a) Bristol R	D 1-1	Cheetham	8,000							7			8	9			5	10		2			11	6	1		3		4
	25	(h) Exeter C	W 4-0	Bott, Fitzgerald, Cheetham, Charlton	14,000							7			8	9			5	10		2	4		11	6	1		3		
	26	(h) Bristol C	W 5-0	Cheetham 2, Fitzgerald, Charlton, Bott	12,000							7			8	9			5	10		2	4		11	6	1		3		
	28	(a) Exeter C	W 3-0	Bott, Cheetham, Charlton	5,000							7			8	9			5	10		2	4		11	6	1		3		
Jan	2	(a) Torquay U	D 1-1	Fitzgerald	4,000			8				7				9			5	10		2	4		11	6	1		3		
	9	(h) Notts C	L 0-2		20,000							7			8	9			5	10		2	4		11	6	1		3		
	21	(h) Brighton & HA	L 2-3	Bott, Lowe	4,000							7				9	8		5	10		2	4		11	6	1		3		
	23	(a) Clapton O	D 0-0		8,000		4			2		7							5	10		3	8		11		1	6		9	
Feb	4	(h) Walsall	W 2-0	Lowe 2	4,000					2		7			9				5	10		3	8		11	4	1	6			
	6	(a) Luton T	W 1-0	Charlton	12,000					2					9				5	10			8	7	11	4	1	6	3		
	13	(h) Cardiff C	W 6-0	Charlton 3, Fitzgerald 3	11,000					2				3	9				5	10			8	7	11	4	1	6			
	18	(h) Northampton T	W 3-2	Fitzgerald 2, Charlton	4,000					2				3	8	9			5	10			4	7	11	6	1				
	20	(a) Swindon T	D 1-1	Fitzgerald	6,000					2				3	9				5	10			8	7	11	6	1				4
	27	(h) Aldershot	W 3-0	Fitzgerald 2, Lumsden	7,000					2				3	9				5	10			8	7	11	6	1				4
Mar	6	(a) Gillingham	D 0-0		6,000					2				3	9				5	10			8	7	11	6	1				4
	13	(h) Newport C	W 6-2	Swinden 3, Fitzgerald, Lowe, Lumsden	4,000					2				3					5	10			8	7	11	4	1	6		9	
	20	(a) Southend U	L 2-3	Fitzgerald 2	9,000					2				3	9				5	10			8	7	11	4	1	6			
	26	(h) Reading	D 0-0		17,000									3		7			5	10			8		11	4	1	6		9	2
	27	(h) Watford	L 1-2	McMahon	9,000					2				3		7			5	10			8		11	6	1			9	4
	29	(a) Reading	L 0-2		12,000					2			8	3	9				5	10			7		11	6	1				4
Apr	3	(a) Brighton & HA	L 1-4	Barrie	8,000					2			10	3	9		8		5				7		11	6	1				4
	10	(h) Bournemouth	L 1-2	Cameron	7,000				7	2			8	3					5	10			9		11	4	1	6			
	17	(a) Northampton T	W 1-0	Lowe	3,000				7	2			8	3					5	10			9		11	4	1	6			
	24	(h) Bristol R	W 2-1	Lowe 2	8,000					2			8			9			5	10			7		11	4	1	6			3
May	1	(h) Crystal P	L 1-3	McMahon	6,000					2			8		7				5	10			9		11	4	1	6	3		
					App	3	11	10	3	23	7	23	8	14	16	28	2	3	26	28	5	25	41	13	33	41	42	11	20	6	20
					Goals		1		1	1		9	1		8	9				17			17	3	2	1				3	

FA Cup

Date		Opponents	Result	Scorers	Att	Abel	Allen	Ballentyne	Banks	Barrie	Bartlett	Bott	Cameron	Carr	Charlton	Cheetham	Clarke	Crawford	Farmer	Fitzgerald	James	Jefferson	Lowe	Lumsden	McMahon	March	Mason	Moralee	Rowe	Swinfen	Vincent	Round
Nov	28	(h) Brighton & HA	W 5-1	Fitzgerald 3, Cheetham, McMahon	16,000							7				9				10	5	2	8		11	6	1		3		4	1
Dec	12	(a) South Liverpool	W 1-0	Fitzgerald	6,000							7				9			5	10		2	8		11	6	1		3		4	2
Jan	16	(a) Bury	L 0-1		13,638							7			8	9			5	10		2	4		11	6	1		3			3
					App							3			1	3			2	3	1	3	3		3	3	3		3		2	
					Goals											1				4					1							

Attendance Summary

	ATTENDANCES			AVERAGE		
	Home	Away	Total	Home	Away	Total
League	214,000	197,667	411,667	10,190	9,413	9,802
FA Cup	16,000	19,638	35,638	16,000	9,819	11,879
Total	230,000	217,305	447,305	10,445	9,448	9,940

1937-38
Division 3 South

Date		Opponents	Res	Score	Scorers	Att	Barrie	Bott	Cape	Charlton	Cheetham	Clarke	Farmer	Fitzgerald	Gilfillan	James	Jefferson	Lowe	McCarthy	McMahon	Mallett	March	Mason	Moralee	Pattison	Prior	Reay	Ridyard	Smith	Stock	Swinfen
Aug	28	(h) Brighton & HA	W	2-1	Cheetham, Fitzgerald	14,000			7		9		5	10			3	8		11		4	1	6					2		
	30	(a) Millwall	W	4-1	Lowe, Cape, Cheetham, Fitzgerald	18,000			7		9		5	10			3	8		11		4	1	6					2		
Sep	4	(a) Bournemouth	D	1-1	Cape	8,000			7		9		5	10			3	8		11		4	1	6					2		
	9	(h) Millwall	L	0-2		7,000			7		9		5	10			3	8		11		4	1	6					2		
	11	(h) Cardiff C	W	2-1	Cape, Lowe	12,000			7		9			10		5	3	8		11		4	1	6					2		
	15	(a) Torquay U	W	2-0	Fitzgerald, Lowe	5,000		11	7					10		5	3	8				4	1	6		9			2		
	18	(a) Walsall	W	3-0	Prior 2, Bott	8,000		11	7					10		5	3	8				4	1	6		9			2		
	25	(h) Northampton T	D	1-1	Cape	12,000		11	7				5	10			3	8				4	1	6		9			2		
Oct	2	(a) Bristol R	D	1-1	Prior	12,000		11	7			8				5	3	10				4	1	6		9			2		
	9	(h) Mansfield T	D	1-1	Bott	15,000		11	7			8				5	3	10				4	1	6		9			2		
	16	(a) Reading	L	0-1		5,000		11	7			8		10	1	5	3					4		6		9			2		
	23	(h) Crystal P	W	1-0	McMahon	12,000			7		9			10	1	5	3	4		11	8	6							2		
	30	(a) Notts C	D	2-2	Cape, Cheetham	10,000			7		9				1	5	3	4	10	11	8	6							2		
Nov	6	(h) Newport C	D	0-0		12,000			7		9				1	5	3	4	10	11	8	6							2		
	13	(a) Bristol C	L	0-2		15,000		11	9					10	1	5	3	7			8	6							2		4
	20	(h) Watford	W	2-0	Bott (pen), Cheetham	13,000		11	7		9			10	1	5	3	4			8	6							2		
Dec	4	(h) Exeter C	W	4-0	Bott 2, Fitzgerald, Cheetham	10,000		11	7		9			10	1	5	3	4			8	6							2		
	18	(h) Aldershot	W	3-0	Fitzgerald, Cheetham, Mallett	9,000		11	7		9			10	1	5	3	4			8	6							2		
	25	(h) Southend U	W	1-0	Fitzgerald	18,000		11	7		9			10	1	5	3	4			8	6							2		
	27	(a) Southend U	L	1-2	Fitzgerald	6,000		11	7		9			10	1	5	3	4			8	6							2		
	28	(a) Swindon T	W	3-1	Cheetham 2, Bott	7,000		11	7		9			10	1	5	3	4			8	6							2		
Jan	1	(a) Brighton & HA	L	1-3	Bott	10,000		11	7		9			10	1	5	3	4			8	6							2		
	8	(a) Gillingham	W	5-1	Fitzgerald, Mallett, Bott 2, Hartley (og)	7,000		11	7		9			10	1	5	3	4			8	6							2		
	15	(h) Bournemouth	L	1-2	Bott	13,000		11	7		9			10	1	5	3	4			8	6							2		
	22	(a) Cardiff C	D	2-2	Fitzgerald	25,000		11	7		9			10	1	5	3	4			8	6							2		
	29	(h) Walsall	W	3-1	Charlton, Fitzgerald, Shelton (og)	12,000		11	7	9				10	1	5	3	4			8	6							2		
Feb	5	(a) Northampton T	W	2-0	Cape, Fitzgerald	7,000		11	7	9				10	1	5	3	4			8	6							2		
	12	(h) Bristol R	W	4-0	Bott 2, Mallett, Fitzgerald	12,000		11	7	9				10	1	5	3	4			8	6							2		
	19	(a) Mansfield T	L	2-3	Cape, Charlton	8,000		11	7	9				10	1	5	3	4			8	6							2		
	26	(h) Reading	W	3-0	Fitzgerald 2, Stock	15,000		11	7					10	1	5	3	4			8	6							2	9	
Mar	5	(a) Crystal P	L	0-4		25,000		11	7		9			10	1	5	3	4			8	6							2		
	12	(h) Notts C	W	2-1	Fitzgerald, Smith	19,000			7				6	9		5	3	4	10		8		1		11				2		
	19	(a) Newport C	D	1-1	Cape	9,000		11	7					10		5	3	4			8	6	1						2	9	
	26	(h) Bristol C	L	0-2		22,958		11	7					10		5	3	4			8	6	1						2	9	
Apr	2	(a) Watford	L	1-3	Bott	18,000		11	7					10		5		4			8	6	1				3		2	9	
	9	(h) Gillingham	W	2-0	Cheetham, Mallett	10,000	2		7		9		6					4	10		8		1		11		3	5			
	15	(a) Clapton O	D	1-1	Pattison	13,000	2		7		9							4	10		8	6	1		11		3	5			
	16	(a) Exeter C	W	4-0	Cheetham 2, Bott, McCarthy	4,000	2	11			9			10				4	8		7	6	1					5	3		
	18	(h) Clapton O	W	3-2	Bott, Fitzgerald, McCarthy	18,000	2	11			9			10				4	8		7	6	1					5	3		
	23	(h) Swindon T	W	3-0	Bott, Cheetham, McCarthy	15,000	2	11	7		9			10				4	8			6	1					5	3		
	30	(a) Aldershot	L	0-1		5,000	2	11	7		9			10				4	8			6	1				3	5			
May	7	(h) Torquay U	W	6-3	Cheetham 2, McCarthy 2, Fitzgerald, Bott	6,000		11	7		9			6				4	10		8		1				3	5	2		
						App	6	31	40	4	26	3	7	36	21	30	34	41	10	8	29	39	21	11	3	6	5	7	39	4	1
						Goals		17	9	2	14			17				3	5	1	4				1	3			1	1	

2 own-goals

FA Cup

Date		Opponents	Res	Score	Scorers	Att	Barrie	Bott	Cape	Charlton	Cheetham	Clarke	Farmer	Fitzgerald	Gilfillan	James	Jefferson	Lowe	McCarthy	McMahon	Mallett	March	Mason	Moralee	Pattison	Prior	Reay	Ridyard	Smith	Stock	Swinfen	Round
Nov	27	(a) Bristol R	W	8-1	Fitzgerald 3, Cheetham 3, Bott 2	7,000		11	7		9			10	1	5	3	4			8	6							2			1
Dec	11	(a) Swindon T	L	1-2	Cape	9,000		11	7		9			10	1	5	3	4			8	6							2			2
						App		2	2		2			2	2	2	2	2			2	2							2			
						Goals		2	1		3			3																		

Attendance Summary

	ATTENDANCES			AVERAGE		
	Home	Away	Total	Home	Away	Total
League	276,958	225,000	501,958	13,188	10,714	11,951
FA Cup		16,000	16,000		8,000	8,000
Total	276,958	241,000	517,958	13,188	10,478	11,772

1938-39

Division 3 South

Date	Opponent	Result	Scorers	Att	Abel	Allen	Black	Bott	Cape	Cheetham	Devine	Fitzgerald	Gilmore	James	Jefferson	Lowe	McCarthy	McEwan	Mallett	March	Mason	Pattison	Pearson	Powell	Reay	Ridyard	Smith	Stock	Swinfen	Warburton
Aug 27	(a) Reading	W 4-2	Fitzgerald 2, Bott, Fulwood (og)	14,000	3			11	7	9	8	10		5		4				6	1								2	
Sep 1	(h) Exeter C	W 5-0	Cheetham 2, Bott 2, Fitzgerald	7,000	3			11	7	9	8	10		5		4				6	1								2	
3	(h) Bristol R	D 1-1	Devine	16,000	3			11	7	9	8	10		5		4				6	1								2	
7	(a) Southend U	L 1-2	McCarthy	7,000	3			11	7	9		10		5		4	8			6	1						2			
10	(a) Brighton & HA	L 1-3	Bott	10,000	3			11	7	9				5		4	8			6	1						2			10
17	(h) Bournemouth	W 2-0	Cheetham, James	12,000					7	9		10		5		4				6	1	11			3		2			8
24	(a) Walsall	W 1-0	Cheetham	8,000					7	9		10		5		4				6	1	11			3		2			8
Oct 1	(h) Mansfield T	W 3-0	Bott, Cape, Cheetham	12,519				11	7	9		10		5		4				6	1				3		2			8
8	(a) Swindon T	D 2-2	Bott, Lowe	11,000				11		9		10		5		4				6	1		7		3				2	8
15	(h) Port Vale	D 2-2	Cheetham 2	14,000				11		9		10		5		4				6	1		7		3				2	8
22	(a) Torquay U	W 3-2	Cheetham 2, Fitzgerald	6,000				11		9		10		5		4				6	1		7				3		2	8
29	(h) Crystal P	L 1-2	Fitzgerald	17,500					11	9		10		5		4				6	1		7				3		2	8
Nov 5	(a) Bristol C	D 2-2	Cheetham 2	10,000					11	9				5	3	4	10			6	1		7						2	8
12	(h) Aldershot	W 7-0	Cheetham 4, McCarthy, March, Swinfen	15,000						9				5	3	4	10			6	1	11	7						2	8
19	(a) Notts C	D 0-0		13,500				11		9				5	3	4	10			6	1		7						2	8
Dec 3	(a) Newport C	L 0-2		11,000		1		11		9				5	3	4	10			6			7						2	8
17	(a) Watford	L 1-4	Pearson	9,000		1		11		9				5	3	4	10			6			7						2	8
24	(h) Reading	D 2-2	Bott, Devine	5,000		1		11		9	8	10	6	5	3	4							7						2	
26	(a) Cardiff C	L 0-1		35,000		1		11	7	9	8	10	6	5	3	4													2	
27	(h) Cardiff C	W 5-0	Cheetham 2, Devine, McCarthy, Cape	14,000		1		11	7	9	8				3	4	10			6						5	2			
31	(a) Bristol R	D 0-0		8,000		1	11		7	9	8		6		3	4	10									5	2			
Jan 9	(h) Northampton T	W 3-0	Cheetham 3	5,000		1	11		7	9					3	4	10			6						5	2			
14	(h) Brighton & H	L 1-2	Cheetham	15,000		1	11		7	9					3	4	10			6						5	2			8
21	(a) Bournemouth	L 2-4	Cape, Lowe	6,000		1	11		7	9		10	6	5	3	4											2			8
28	(h) Walsall	W 3-0	Cheetham, Lowe, Fitzgerald	10,500		1	11		7	9		10		5	3	8				6				4			2			
Feb 4	(a) Mansfield T	D 2-2	Stimpson (og), Lowe	5,523		1			7	9		10		5	3	8				6		11		4			2			
11	(h) Swindon T	W 2-1	Bott, Mallett	15,000		1		11	7					5	3	4			8	6							2	9		10
18	(a) Port Vale	W 2-1	Fitzgerald 2	7,000		1		11	7			10		5	3	4			8	6							2	9		
25	(h) Torquay U	D 1-1	Lowe	8,000		1		11	7			10		5	3	4			8	6							2	9		
Mar 4	(a) Crystal P	W 1-0	McEwan	13,328		1						10			3	4		7	8	6		11				5	2	9		
11	(h) Bristol C	W 3-1	Fitzgerald, McEwan, Stock	10,000		1						10		5	3	4		7	8	6		11					2	9		
18	(a) Aldershot	L 0-2		6,000		1						10		5	3	4		7	8	6		11					2	9		
25	(h) Notts C	L 0-1		9,000		1						10	6	5	3	4		7	8			11					2	9		
Apr 1	(a) Northampton T	L 0-1		6,000		1						10		5	3	4		7	8	6		11					2	9		
7	(h) Ipswich T	D 0-0		15,161		1						6			3	10		7	8			11		4		5	2		9	
8	(h) Newport C	D 0-0		18,000		1						6			3	10		9	8			11		4		5	2	7		
10	(a) Ipswich T	L 0-1		18,963		1						10		5	3	6		7	8			11		4			2	9		
15	(a) Clapton O	L 1-2	Smith (pen)	9,000		1						10		5	3	6		7	8			11		4			2	9		
22	(h) Watford	W 1-0	Mallett	8,000		1		11				10		5	3	4		7	8	6							2		9	
24	(h) Clapton O	D 1-1	Swinfen	3,000		1		11				10			3	6		7	8					4		5	2		9	
29	(a) Exeter C	D 1-1	Stock	8,000		1		10							3	6		7	8				11	4		5	2	9		
May 6	(h) Southend U	D 1-1	McCarthy	6,000		1						8	6		3	4	10	7				11			2	5			9	
				App	5	27	5	21	21	26	7	30	6	32	30	42	12	13	15	30	15	14	11	8	6	10	29	12	18	17
				Goals				8	3	22	3	9		1		5	4	2	2	1			1				1	2	2	

2 own-goals

FA Cup

Date	Opponent	Result	Scorers	Att	Abel	Allen	Black	Bott	Cape	Cheetham	Devine	Fitzgerald	Gilmore	James	Jefferson	Lowe	McCarthy	McEwan	Mallett	March	Mason	Pattison	Pearson	Powell	Reay	Ridyard	Smith	Stock	Swinfen	Warburton	Round
Nov 26	(a) Crystal P	D 1-1	Cheetham	33,276		1		11		9				5	3	4	10			6			7						2	8	1
28	(h) Crystal P	W 3-0	Cheetham 2, Bott (pen)	16,000		1		11		9				5	3	4	10			6			7						2	8	Rep
Dec 10	(a) Hartlepools U	W 2-0	Cheetham, McCarthy	11,094		1		11		9				5	3	4	10			6			7						2	8	2
Jan 7	(h) West Ham U	L 1-2	Cheetham	22,408		1		11	7	9			6		3	4	10									5	2			8	3
				App		4		4	1	4			1	3	4	4	4			3			3			1	1		3	4	
				Goals				1		5							1														

Attendance Summary

	ATTENDANCES Home	Away	Total	AVERAGE Home	Away	Total
League	235,680	222,314	457,994	11,223	10,586	10,905
FA Cup	38,408	44,370	82,778	19,204	22,185	20,694
Total	274,088	266,684	540,772	11,917	11,595	11,756

1939-40

Division 3 South

Date	Opponent	Result	Scorers	Att	Allen	Bonass	Farmer	Fitzgerald	Jefferson	Lowe	Mallett	Mangnall	March	McEwan	Reay	Ridyard	Stock	Swinfen
Aug 26	(h) Watford	D 2-2	Mangnall 2	8,000	1	11		10	3	4	8	9	6	7	2	5		
30	(a) Bournemouth	D 2-2	Mangnall, Swinfen	4,000	1	11		10	3	4		9	6		2	5	7	8
Sep 2	(a) Walsall	L 0-1		5,000	1	11	6	10	3	4		9			2	5	7	8
				App	3	3	1	3	3	3	1	3	2	1	3	3	2	2
				Goals								3						1

Season halted due to World War Two

League South B

Date	Opponent	Result	Scorers	Att
Oct 21	(a) Reading	L 0-2		5,000
28	(h) Fulham	D 2-2	Mangnall, McCarthy	5,000
Nov 4	(a) Portsmouth	L 1-2	Mangnall	3,000
11	(h) Brentford	W 1-0	McCarthy	8,000
18	(h) Aldershot	W 4-1	Mangnall 2, Mallett, McEwan	5,200
25	(a) Bournemouth	L 0-3		4,000
Dec 2	(h) Chelsea	W 3-2	Mallett, Mangnall 2	8,010
9	(a) Southampton	W 2-1	March, McEwan	1,500
16	(h) Brighton & HA	W 3-2	Mangnall, March, McEwan	2,000
25	(a) Fulham	W 8-3	Mangnall 3, Mallett 3, McCarthy, Bonass	6,000
26	(h) Portsmouth	W 5-2	Mangnall 4, Mallett	5,188
30	(a) Brentford	W 7-0	Mallett, McCarthy, McEwan, Bonass 2, Mangnall, Opp own-goal	4,000
Jan 1	(h) Reading	W 3-0	Mallett, Mangnall 2	1,500
6	(a) Aldershot	W 3-1	Mangnall 2, McEwan	2,000
13	(h) Bournemouth	W 2-1	Mangnall, McEwan	8,136
20	(a) Chelsea	D 0-0		8,819
Feb 8	(h) Southampton	W 4-1	Bonass, McEwan 3	2,000
May 4	(a) Brighton & HA	L 1-3	Martin (og)	1,500

League Cup Preliminary

Date	Opponent	Result	Scorers	Att
Apr 13	(a) Southend U	L 0-1		4,000

League South D

Date	Opponent	Result	Scorers	Att
Feb 10	(h) Southend U	W 3-1	McEwan, March, Bonass	3,908
24	(h) Crystal P	L 2-5	McCarthy 2	6,500
Mar 2	(a) Reading	L 1-4	Mangnall	2,000
9	(a) Brighton & HA	W 2-1	McEwan, Mallett	1,500
16	(h) Norwich C	D 0-0		4,205
22	(a) Watford	D 1-1	Mangnall	7,500
23	(h) Aldershot	W 3-1	Mangnall 2, McEwan	5,196
25	(h) Watford	W 2-0	McCarthy, McEwan	6,258
30	(a) Clapton O	l 3-4	McEwan, Mangnall 2	3,000
Apr 3	(a) Bournemouth	L 0-1		
6	(a) Southend U	W 1-0	McEwan	2,500
10	(a) Aldershot	W 1-0	Mangnall	2,000
20	(h) Brighton & HA	W 5-4	Mangnall 3, Mallett, McEwan	3,000
May 13	(a) Crystal P	D 2-2	Mangnall 2	3,954
18	(h) Clapton O	W 4-0	McCarthy, Mallett, McEwan, Mangnall	2,000
23	(h) Reading	W 2-1	Mangnall, McEwan	
25	(a) Norwich C	L 1-3	Mangnall	1,500
Jun 1	(h) Bournemouth	W 5-0	Mangnall 2, McCarthy 2, McEwan	1,000

1940-41

League South

Aug	31 (a) Fulham	L 1-3	Swinfen	3,000
Sep	7 (h) Clapton O	D 3-3	Bott 2, Ridyard	1,000
	21 (h) Charlton A	W 2-0	Bott, Swinfen	2,000
	28 (h) Arsenal	W 3-2	Swinfen 2, Lowe	2,500
Oct	5 (h) Tottenham H	D 1-1	Lowe	1,500
	12 (h) Chelsea	L 2-3	Daniels, Bott	1,500
	19 (a) Chelsea	L 1-3	Swinfen	1,500
	26 (a) Charlton A	L 2-6	Mangnall, Opp own-goal	500
Nov	2 (a) Clapton O	W 3-0	McCarthy 2, Mangnall	200
	16 (h) Fulham	L 2-5	Mangnall, Daniels	1,000
	23 (a) Millwall	L 1-3	Lowe	500
	30 (h) Millwall	W 2-1	Mangnall, Lowe	400
Dec	7 (a) Tottenham H	W 3-2	Mangnall 2, Mallett	1,367
	14 (a) Arsenal	L 2-3	Butt, Ridyard	1,300
	21 (h) Reading	W 4-1	Mangnall 2, Lowe, Mallett	500
	25 (a) Brentford	L 1-2	Mangnall	1,200
	28 (a) Reading	L 0-2		2,000
May	10 (a) Aldershot	L 1-5	Ling	2,000
	17 (h) Watford	W 4-2	Ling 2, Mangnall 2	1,500
	24 (a) Watford	D 3-3	Ling, Davie, Mangnall	2,000
	31 (h) West Ham U	L 1-5	Mangnall	2,000
Jun	2 (h) Fulham	L 2-3	Bonass, Halford	2,500
	7 (a) West Ham U	W 3-2	L.Compton 2, Mills	2,100

London Cup

Jan	4 (a) Fulham	L 1-4	Mangnall	1,000
	11 (h) Fulham	L 5-7	Lowe, Mallett, Bonass, Bott, Mangnall	2,256
	25 (h) Aldershot	L 2-3	Mallett 2	1,000
Feb	1 (h) Chelsea	W 5-2	Lowe, Mangnall, McEwan 2, Bott	1,900
	8 (a) Aldershot	W 4-2	Mangnall, Daniels, Adam, Mallett	2,000
Apr	12 (a) Crystal P	W 2-1	Mangnall, Fitzgerald	5,000
	14 (a) Brentford	L 2-4	Mangnall, Daniels	
	19 (h) Crystal P	W 2-1	A.Dawes 2	2,000
	26 (h) Brentford	D 0-0		6,000
May	3 (a) Chelsea	W 3-2	Mangnall 2, Davie	4,000

War Cup

Feb	15 (a) Crystal P	W 1-0	Mallett	3,700
	22 (h) Crystal P	W 3-2	Opp own-goal, Daniels, Lowe	3,500
Mar	3 (a) Aldershot	L 1-2	Mangnall	2,500
	8 (h) Aldershot	W 4-2	Adam, Lowe, Mangnall 2	2,733
	15 (h) Chelsea	W 2-0	Mangnall 2	5,575
	22 (a) Chelsea	W 4-2	Mangnall 2, Webb, Mallett	7,232
	29 (h) Leicester C	W 2-1	Mangnall 2	5,700
Apr	5 (a) Leicester C	L 1-6	Mallett	10,000

1941-42

London League

Aug	30 (a) Brighton & HA	W 5-2	Mahon, Davie 3, Patterson	3,000
Sep	6 (h) Brentford	L 3-4	Mallett, Halford, Mahon	8,000
	13 (a) Crystal P	L 1-2	Halford	4,500
	20 (h) Fulham	L 2-5	Eastham 2	5,500
	27 (a) Tottenham H	L 1-3	Mangnall	5,955
Oct	4 (h) Portsmouth	L 0-2		4,000
	11 (h) Chelsea	W 2-1	Mahon, Mallett	6,000
	18 (h) Charlton A	D 0-0		5,000
	25 (a) West Ham U	L 0-2		5,300
Nov	1 (h) Watford	L 1-5	Patterson	3,000
	8 (a) Aldershot	L 1-4	Patterson	4,000
	15 (h) Millwall	W 4-1	Stock 2, Mahon, Patterson	3,500
	22 (a) Arsenal	L 1-4	Patterson	7,377
	29 (a) Clapton O	D 0-0		2,000
Dec	6 (a) Reading	D 2-2	Armstrong, Kirkham	4,000
	13 (h) Brighton & HA	W 3-0	Mangnall 2, Armstrong	3,000
	20 (a) Brentford	L 3-4	Mangnall 2, Abel	3,500
	25 (h) Crystal P	L 1-3	Harris	
	27 (a) Fulham	W 3-0	J.Moore, Opp own-goal, Mangnall	3,771
Jan	3 (h) Tottenham H	W 1-0	Mallett	4,500
	10 (a) Portsmouth	L 1-3	Mangnall	5,000
	17 (a) Chelsea	L 1-3	Mangnall	1,829
	24 (a) Charlton A	L 1-3	Mangnall	2,500
	31 (h) West Ham U	W 2-1	Armstrong, Farmer	5,000
Feb	14 (h) Aldershot	L 0-2		3,086
	21 (a) Millwall	W 2-1	Hatton 2	1,000
	28 (h) Arsenal	L 0-1		8,932
Mar	7 (h) Clapton O	W 2-1	Hatton, Mangnall	2,000
	14 (h) Reading	W 4-0	Hatton 2, Mangnall 2	4,000
May	2 (a) Watford	W 5-0	W.Heath 2, McEwan 2, Lowe	1,721

London War Cup

Mar	21 (a) Millwall	D 2-2	Hatton 2	5,000
	28 (a) Aldershot	W 2-0	Kirkham, Hatton	3,000
Apr	4 (h) Brentford	L 1-2	Kirkham	3,000
	6 (h) Aldershot	L 1-2	Lowe	
	11 (a) Brentford	L 0-1		7,310
	18 (h) Millwall	W 2-0	Hatton 2	4,500

1942-43

League South

Aug	29(a) Chelsea	D 1-1	Mallett	6,787
Sep	5(h) Tottenham H	L 0-1		4,300
	12(a) Clapton O	W 4-0	Mangnall, Sibley, Stock 2	1,000
	19(a) Crystal P	W 1-0	Stock	5,600
	26(h) Brentford	W 4-1	Swinfen 3, Mallett	8,000
Oct	3(h) Millwall	W 3-2	Hatton, Swinfen 2	4,479
	10(a) Reading	W 2-1	Hatton, Ridyard	4,000
	17(h) Luton T	D 2-2	Hatton, Burley	4,700
	24(a) Brighton & HA	W 3-2	Burley, Swinfen, Sibley	3,000
	31(h) Southampton	W 3-1	Swinfen, Hatton, Reay	4,826
Nov	7(h) West Ham U	W 5-2	Hatton, Swinfen 4	6,852
	14(a) Arsenal	L 0-3		14,646
	21(a) Charlton A	L 2-3	Hatton, Burley	3,019
	28(h) Chelsea	W 4-1	Burley, Swinfen, Sibley, Hatton	8,900
Dec	5(a) Tottenham H	L 0-6		8,295
	12(h) Clapton O	W 3-1	Mangnall 3	4,493
	19(h) Crystal P	W 3-0	Hatton 2, Burley	3,900
	25(h) Fulham	W 2-1	Mangnall, Sibley	4,000
	26(a) Fulham	L 2-4	Ridyard, Burley	7,919
Jan	2(a) Brentford	L 0-2		7,500
	9(a) Millwall	W 2-1	Mangnall, Smith	4,000
	16(h) Reading	W 3-2	Swinfen, Mangnall 2	4,800
	23(a) Luton T	W 2-1	Burley, Abel	3,000
	30(h) Brighton & HA	L 3-4	Sibley, Mangnall 2	3,900
Feb	6(a) Southampton	L 2-4	Burley, Parkinson	9,000
	13(a) West Ham U	W 3-1	Mangnall, Swinfen 2	6,000
	20(h) Arsenal	W 3-2	Heathcote, Burley 2	13,465
	27(h) Charlton A	W 2-0	Pattison, Heathcote	4,800

League Cup South (Group 2)

Mar	6(a) Brentford	W 2-1	McEwan, Burley	10,520
	13(h) Southampton	W 2-1	Mallett, McEwan	8,025
	20(a) Clapton O	D 1-1	Heathcote	3,000
	27(h) Brentford	W 2-0	Burley, Heathcote	9,954
Apr	3(a) Southampton	L 1-4	Mallett	13,000
	10(h) Clapton O	W 8-1	Heathcote 4, Pattison 2, Swinfen, Burley	5,000
	24(n*) Arsenal	L 1-4	Pattison	54,008

*Semi-final played at Stamford Bridge, London.

1943-44

League South

Aug	28(a) Chelsea	W 3-1	Heathcote 2, De Busser	9,469
Sep	4(h) Tottenham H	W 1-0	Heathcote	10,700
	11(a) Clapton O	W 3-2	Heathcote 2, Swinfen	3,000
	18(h) Watford	W 3-1	Heathcote 2, Pattison	
	25(a) Portsmouth	D 1-1	McEwan	10,000
Oct	2(a) Reading	D 0-0		9,000
	9(h) Millwall	W 2-0	Mangnall, Burley	9,901
	16(h) Aldershot	D 2-2	Mangnall, Heathcote	9,391
	23(a) Brighton & HA	L 1-3	Heathcote	3,500
	30(h) Southampton	W 7-0	Heathcote 3, McEwan, Pattison 2, Griffiths	7,060
Nov	6(a) West Ham U	D 1-1	Heathcote	16,100
	13(a) Arsenal	L 0-5		20,014
	20(a) Charlton A	L 0-1		3,896
	27(h) Chelsea	L 2-11	Swinfen, Pearson	6,000
Dec	4(a) Tottenham H	D 2-2	Heathcote 2	12,485
	11(h) Clapton O	W 6-2	Swinfen 2, Burley, Heathcote 2, Opp own-goal	4,000
	18(a) Fulham	D 2-2	Sibley, Ramscar	6,000
	25(a) Brentford	W 5-2	Somerfield 2, Heathcote 2, Lowes	11,200
	26(h) Brentford	W 3-2	Swinfen, Heathcote, Somerfield	
Jan	1(a) Watford	D 2-2	Somerfield, Heathcote	4,483
	8(h) West Ham U	W 3-0	Heathcote 2, Little	11,944
	22(h) Reading	W 2-0	Heathcote 2	4,500
	29(a*) Millwall	W 4-3	Lowes, Somerfield, Burley, Heathcote	5,000
Feb	5(a) Aldershot	W 3-1	Sheen, Burley, Lowes	5,000
	12(h) Brighton & HA	W 1-0	Sheen	7,200
Apr	1(a) Southampton	D 2-2	De Lisle, Heathcote	4,000
	10(h) Portsmouth	D 1-1	Mangnall	
	22(h) Fulham	D 3-3	Heathcote, Mallett, Jones	4,000
	29(h) Arsenal	D 1-1	Jones	10,000
May	6(h) Charlton A	D 3-3	Heathcote, Lowes 2	6,000

*Played at the Boleyn Ground, West Ham, London.

League Cup South (Group 2)

Feb	19(a) Clapton O	W 5-2	Swinfen 2, Burley 2, Sibley	2,000
	26(h) Arsenal	D 1-1	Swinfen	15,000
Mar	4(a) Luton T	W 4-3	Heathcote 3, Ramscar	3,000
	11(h) Clapton O	W 6-0	Dean 2, Swinfen 3, Sheen	7,000
	18(a) Arsenal	W 4-1	Heathcote, Jones, Sheen, Swinfen	17,367
	25(h) Luton T	W 5-0	Heathcote 3, Swinfen, Jones	6,000

1944-45

League South

Month	Date	Opponent	Result	Scorers	Att
Aug	26 (a)	Crystal P	L 4-7	Heathcote 3, Fitzgerald	7,000
Sep	2 (h)	Southampton	L 4-5	Sibley, Fitzgerald, Heathcote, Jones	5,000
	9 (a)	Fulham	D 2-2	Fitzgerald 2	8,000
	16 (h)	West Ham U	L 0-1		8,000
	23 (a)	Arsenal	L 0-2		15,336
	30 (a)	Reading	D 1-1	Mallett	6,510
Oct	7 (h)	Millwall	W 4-1	Bain, Ridyard, Sibley, Cheetham	6,000
	14 (a)	Clapton O	W 3-0	Heathcote, Mallett, Burley	3,000
	21 (a)	Brentford	L 1-3	Jones	16,000
	28 (h)	Brighton & HA	W 4-0	Jones 2, Attwell, Smith	6,000
Nov	4 (a)	Portsmouth	L 1-4	Burley	10,000
	11 (a)	Aldershot	D 1-1	Heathcote	3,000
	18 (a)	Charlton A	W 2-1	Heathcote 2	6,500
	25 (h)	Luton T	W 7-1	Abel, Heathcote 3, Mallett, Daniels 2	5,000
Dec	2 (h)	Crystal P	D 0-0		8,661
	9 (a)	Southampton	W 5-4	Heathcote, Daniels 2, Mallett, Abel	9,300
	16 (h)	Fulham	D 4-4	Heathcote 3, Darragon	10,000
	23 (h)	Tottenham H	D 0-0		13,011
	25 (a)	Tottenham H	L 2-4	Abel, Lowes	16,958
	30 (a)	West Ham U	L 2-4	Daniels, Shaw	9,000
Jan	6 (h)	Arsenal	W 3-2	Heathcote 2, Sibley	10,000
	13 (h)	Reading	W 5-1	Sibley, Somerfield, Daniels, Mallett 2	6,272
	20 (a)	Millwall	D 3-3	Heathcote 2, Daniels	3,000
	27 (h)	Clapton O	D 3-3	Shaw 2, Mallett	2,000
Mar	17 (h)	Brentford	D 1-1	Darragon	5,000
	24 (a)	Brighton & HA	D 1-1	Shaw	4,000
	31 (h)	Portsmouth	W 1-0	Heathcote	5,000
Apr	14 (h)	Aldershot	W 3-0	Addinall 2, Gillies	5,000
	21 (h)	Charlton A	L 2-3	Addinall, Shaw	7,000
	28 (a)	Luton T	L 1-2	Addinall	2,500

League Cup South (Group 3)

Month	Date	Opponent	Result	Scorers	Att
Feb	3 (a)	Tottenham H	D 1-1	Heathcote	20,331
	10 (h)	Aldershot	W 2-1	Daniels, Ridyard	7,700
	17 (h)	West Ham U	D 1-1	Heathcote	17,000
	24 (h)	Tottenham H	W 1-0	Heathcote	30,000
Mar	3 (a)	Aldershot	W 2-0	Gillies, Opp own-goal	4,000
	10 (a)	West Ham U	L 0-5		20,000

1945-46

Division 3 South (North Region)

Month	Date	Opponent	Result	Scorers	Att
Aug	25 (a)	Southend U	W 2-1	Crack 2	8,000
Sep	1 (h)	Southend U	W 4-1	Mallett, Hatton 2, Neary	8,360
	5 (a)	Clapton O	W 2-0	Crack, Heathcote	4,000
	8 (h)	Walsall	W 4-0	Neary 3, Heathcote	8,000
	12 (a)	Mansfield T	W 6-2	Neary 2, Mallett 2, Heathcote, Somerfield	7,000
	15 (a)	Walsall	D 1-1	Salmon	7,000
	19 (h)	Clapton O	W 3-0	Heathcote 2, Mallett	6,485
	22 (a)	Port Vale	D 0-0		8,000
	29 (h)	Port Vale	W 4-1	Mallett, Heathcote, Neary, Abel	13,750
Oct	6 (h)	Ipswich T	W 2-0	Heathcote, Mallett	18,000
	13 (a)	Ipswich T	L 1-2	Mallett	16,000
	20 (a)	Northampton T	W 2-0	Neary, Heathcote	9,000
	27 (h)	Northampton T	W 4-1	Heathcote 3, Addinall	9,000
Nov	3 (h)	Notts C	W 6-0	Neary 2, Heathcote 4	15,000
	10 (a)	Notts C	W 1-0	Heathcote	23,186
Dec	1 (a)	Watford	W 2-0	Whitehead, Neary	11,215
	25 (a)	Norwich C	D 1-1	Ridyard	20,082
	26 (h)	Norwich C	L 1-2	Neary	19,000
	29 (h)	Mansfield T	W 3-2	Ridyard, Heathcote 2	9,965
Jan	1 (h)	Watford	D 1-1	Ridyard	4,000

Division 3 South (North) Cup

Month	Date	Opponent	Result	Scorers	Att
Jan	12 (h)	Ipswich T	W 4-1	Stock 2, Heathcote, Mallett	12,000
	19 (a)	Ipswich T	L 0-1		9,508
Feb	2 (a)	Bristol C	L 0-2		10,800
	16 (h)	Southend U	W 4-0	Mallett, Stock 2, Heath	7,000
	23 (a)	Mansfield T	D 0-0		5,000
Mar	2 (h)	Mansfield T	W 3-0	Heath 2, Boxshall	5,000
	9 (a)	Watford	W 3-1	Pattison, Heath 2	5,000
	16 (h)	Watford	W 2-1	Heath, McEwan	8,838
	23 (h)	Port Vale	W 4-2	Heath 2, McEwan, Neary	10,000
	30 (a)	Port Vale	W 2-0	Opp own-goal, Neary	10,000
Apr	6 (h)	Notts C	W 3-1	Mallett, Neary, Chapman	15,000
	13 (a)	Notts C	W 3-0	Pattison 2, McEwan	9,000
	17 (a)	Southend U	D 0-0		
	19 (h)	Bristol C	W 4-2	Hatton, Pattison, McEwan, Neary	17,500
	20 (a)	Clapton O	D 0-0		14,000
	22 (h)	Clapton O	W 6-0	Heathcote, Pattison 2, Neary 2, Opp own-goal	17,000
	27 (a)	(SF) Bournemouth	D 1-1	Heathcote	13,000
May	1 (h)	Bournemouth	L 0-1		15,000

1945-46 FA Cup

Month	Date	Opponent	Result	Scorers	Att	Addinall	Allen	Blizzard	Brown	Daniels	Farrow	Heath	Heathcote	Jefferson	Mallett	Neary	Pattison	Reay	Ridyard	Rose	Stock	Swinfen	Whitehead	Round
Nov	17 (a)	Barnet	W 6-2	Heathcote, Mallett 2, Neary 3	6,800		1	10		4	6		9		8	7			5	2		3	11	1/1
	24 (h)	Barnet	W 2-1	Swinfen, Neary	11,600		1			4	6		9	3	8	7			5	2		10	11	1/2
Dec	8 (h)	Ipswich T	W 4-0	Neary, Stock, Addinall 2	12,000	9	1			4	6			3	8	7			5	2	10		11	2/1
	15 (a)	Ipswich T	W 2-0	Daniels, Addinall	12,000	9	1	7		4	6			3	8				5	2	10		11	2/2
Jan	5 (h)	Crystal P	D 0-0		20,080		1			4		6	9	3	8	7	11		5	2	10			3/1
	9 (a)	Crystal P *	D 0-0		26,400		1			4		6		3	8	9	11		5	2	10		7	3/2
	14 (n†)	Crystal P	W 1-0	Addinall	23,000	9		7	1	4	6			3	8		11		5	2	10			Rep
	26 (a)	Southampton	W 1-0	Addinall	19,000	9	1			4	6			3	8	7			5	2	10		11	4/1
	30 (h)	Southampton	W 4-3	Addinall 3, Stock	16,000	9	1			4	6			3	8	7	11		5	2	10			4/2
Feb	9 (h)	Brentford	L 1-3	Pattison	19,885	9	1			4	6			3	8		11		5	2	10	7		5/1
	14 (a)	Brentford	D 0-0		20,000	9	1			4	6	10		3	8		11	2	5			7		5/2
					App	7	10	3	1	11	9	3	3	10	11	7	6	1	11	10	8	4	6	
					Goals	8				1			1		2	5	1				2	1		

*Abandoned after 117 minutes. †Played at Craven Cottage, Fulham.

1946-47

Division 3 South

Date	Opponent	Res	Scorers	Att	Addinall	Allen	Armitage	Barr	Buzzard	Boxshall	Chapman	Daniels	Dudley	Durrant	Harris	Hatton	Heath	Heathcote	Jefferson	McEwan	Mallett	Mills	Neary	Parkinson	Pattison	Powell	Reay	Ridyard	Rose	Saphin	Smith	Swinfen
Aug 31	(h) Watford	W 2-1	Mallett 2	23,000		1						4				8		9	3	7	10				11	6		5	2			
Sep 4	(a) Bournemouth	D 1-1	Neary	5,000		1						4				10			3	9	8		7		11	6		5	2			
7	(a) Walsall	W 2-0	Neary 2	11,000		1						4							3	7	8		9		11	6		5	2		10	
11	(h) Leyton O	W 2-0	Pattison, Neary	15,163		1						4							3	7	8		9		11	6		5	2		10	
14	(h) Reading	W 2-0	Heath, McEwan	19,862		1	10				5						9		3	7	8				11	6			2		4	
21	(a) Crystal P	D 0-0		27,517		1	10				5						9		3	7	8				11	6			2		4	
25	(h) Bournemouth	W 3-0	Pattison 2, Mallett	19,000	9	1					5								3	7	8	10			11	6			2		4	
28	(h) Torquay U	D 0-0		22,000		1					5			9					3	7	8	10			11	6			2		4	
Oct 5	(a) Mansfield T	W 3-0	Neary, Durrant, Pattison	13,459		1					5			9					3		8	10	7		11	6			2		4	
12	(h) Bristol R	L 0-2		18,000		1					5			9		10					8		7		11	6			2		4	3
19	(a) Cardiff C	D 2-2	Durrant, Hatton	50,000		1					5			9		10			3		8		7		11	6			2		4	
26	(h) Norwich C	D 1-1	Hatton	15,000		1					5			9		10			3		8		7		11	6	2				4	
Nov 2	(a) Notts C	W 2-1	Neary, Heathcote	25,000		1		5								10		9	3		8		7		11	6			2		4	
9	(h) Northampton T	W 1-0	McEwan	20,000		1		5								10		9	3	7	8				11	6			2		4	
16	(a) Aldershot	W 2-1	Shepperd (og), Pattison	8,000		1		5								10		9	3	7	8				11	6			2		4	
23	(h) Brighton & HA	W 2-0	Hatton 2	15,000		1		5				4				10	6	9	3		8		7		11				2			
Dec 7	(h) Port Vale	W 2-0	Harris, Mills	13,000		1							2		9				3	7	8	10			11	6		5			4	
21	(h) Swindon T	W 7-0	Pattison 2, McEwan 2, Hatton, Mills, Powell	10,000		1							2			9			3	7	8	10			11	6		5			4	
25	(h) Ipswich T	L 1-3	Hatton	14,595		1							2			9			3	7	8	10			11	6		5			4	
26	(a) Ipswich T	D 1-1	Hatton	20,227		1					5		2			9			3	7	8	10			11	6					4	
28	(a) Watford	W 2-0	Mallett 2	18,553		1				7	5		2			10			3	9	8				11	6					4	
Jan 4	(h) Walsall	W 1-0	Boxshall	16,000		1				7	5		2			10			3	9	8				11	6					4	
18	(a) Reading	L 0-1		19,185	9	1				11	5		2						3	7	8	10				6					4	
25	(h) Crystal P	L 1-2	Pattison	13,022	9	1				10	5	4	2						3	7	8				11	6						
Feb 8	(h) Mansfield T	W 3-1	Boxshall, Durrant, Pattison	7,776		1				10	5		2	9						7	8				11	6	3				4	
15	(a) Bristol R	L 1-3	Durrant	18,781		1				7	6		2	9					3	8	10				11	5					4	
Mar 1	(a) Norwich C	W 1-0	Mills	14,436		1			4		6		2	9					3	7		10		8	11	5						
5	(a) Exeter C	L 0-3		4,000		1			4	7	6		2						3	9		10		8	11	5						
8	(h) Notts C	W 4-1	Pattison, Durrant 2, Chapman	10,000		1			4		6		2	9					3	7		10		8	11	5						
15	(a) Northampton T	D 4-4	Parkinson 2, Mills, Durrant	10,000		1			4		6		2	9					3	7		10		8	11	5						
22	(h) Aldershot	W 4-1	Hatton 3, Durrant	15,000		1			4	7	6		2	9		10			3					8	11	5						
29	(a) Brighton & HA	W 2-0	McEwan 2	8,000							6		2	9		10			3	7				8	11	5				1	4	
Apr 4	(h) Southend U	W 1-0	Durrant	20,000		1					6		2	9		10			3	7				8	11	5					4	
5	(h) Exeter C	W 2-0	Durrant, Pattison	16,000		1					6		2	9		10			3	7		8			11	5					4	
7	(a) Southend U	W 3-1	Durrant, McEwan, Mills	23,000		1				11	6		2	9		8			3	7		10				5					4	
12	(a) Port Vale	D 2-2	Durrant, Boxshall	17,000		1				11	6		2	9		10			3	7				8		5					4	
19	(h) Bristol C	W 1-0	McEwan	22,000		1					6		2	9		10			3	7				8	11	5						
26	(a) Swindon T	L 2-3	Durrant, Hatton	23,000		1				11	6		2	9		10			3	7				8		5					4	
May 3	(a) Leyton O	D 1-1	Hatton	20,000		1				11		6	2	9		8			3	7		10				5					4	
10	(a) Bristol C	D 1-1	Durrant	25,000		1							2	9		8	6		3	7		10			11	5					4	
17	(a) Torquay U	D 0-0		7,500		1							2	9		8	6		3	7		10			11	5					4	
24	(h) Cardiff C	L 2-3	Wardle (og), Pattison	25,000		1							2	9		8	6		3	7		10			11	5					4	
				App	3	41	2	4	5	12	27	7	26	22	1	26	6	5	40	35	26	18	9	10	37	41	2	7	15	1	33	1
				Goals						3	1			14	1	12	1	1		8	5	5	6	2	12	1						

FA Cup

Date	Opponent	Res	Scorers	Att	Addinall	Allen	Armitage	Barr	Buzzard	Boxshall	Chapman	Daniels	Dudley	Durrant	Harris	Hatton	Heath	Heathcote	Jefferson	McEwan	Mallett	Mills	Neary	Parkinson	Pattison	Powell	Reay	Ridyard	Rose	Saphin	Smith	Swinfen	Round
Nov 30	(h) Poole T	D 2-2	Pattison, Hatton	15,000	9	1						4				10	6		3	7					11	8		5	2				1
Dec 4	(a) Poole T	W 6-0	Mallett 2, Hatton, Harris, Pattison 2	9,000											9	10			3	7	8				11	6	2	5		1	4		Rep
12	(a) Norwich C	D 4-4	Pattison, McEwan, Mills 2	26,307		1					5		2			9			3	7	8	10			11	6					4		2
18	(h) Norwich C	W 2-0	Hatton, Mills	13,900		1							2			9			3	7	8	10			11	6		5			4		Rep
Jan 11	(h) Middlesbrough	D 1-1	Pattison	24,549		1				7	5		2			10			3	9	8				11	6					4		3
15	(a) Middlesbrough	L 1-3	Boxshall	31,270		1				7	5		2			10			3	9	8				11	6					4		Rep
				App	1	5				2	3	1	4		1	6	1		6	6	5	2			6	6	1	3	1	1	5		
				Goals						1					1	3				1	2	3			5								

Attendance Summary

	ATTENDANCES			AVERAGE		
	Home	Away	Total	Home	Away	Total
League	349,418	368,658	718,076	16,639	17,555	17,097
FA Cup	53,449	66,577	120,026	17,816	22,192	20,004
Total	402,867	435,235	838,102	16,786	18,135	7,460

1947-48

Division 3 South

	Date	Opponent	Result	Scorers	Att	Adams	Addinall	Allen	Boxshall	Chapman	Daniels	Dudley	Durrant	Hartburn	Hatton	Heath	Jefferson	McEwan	Mills	Parkinson	Pattison	Powell G	Powell I	Ramscar	Reay	Ridyard	Rose	Saphin	Smith A	Smith G	Stewart
Aug	23(h)	Norwich C	W 3-1	Hatton, McEwan, Pattison	20,000			1				2	9	7	10	6	3	8			11		4							5	
	25(a)	Brighton & HA	W 5-0	Hatton 3, Durrant 2	17,000			1				2	9	7	10	6		8			11		4		3					5	
	30(a)	Bristol R	W 1-0	Durrant	15,000			1				2	9	7	10	6		8			11		4		3					5	
Sep	4(h)	Brighton & HA	W 2-0	McEwan, Hatton	17,600			1				2	9	7	10	6		8			11		4		3					5	
	6(h)	Northampton T	W 2-0	McEwan, Pattison	21,000			1				2	9	7	10	6		8			11		4		3					5	
	11(a)	Notts C	D 1-1	Durrant	19,315			1		6		2	9	7	10			8			11		4		3					5	
	13(a)	Aldershot	W 4-1	Durrant 2, Pattison, Hatton	8,837			1		6		2	9		10			7	8		11		4		3					5	
	18(h)	Notts C	W 4-1	Pattison 2, Hatton, McEwan	14,500			1		6		2	9		10			7	8		11		4		3					5	
	20(h)	Crystal P	W 1-0	Chapman	24,736			1		10		2	9		8			7			11		4		3				6	5	
	25(h)	Exeter C	W 3-1	Hatton 2, Durrant	17,500			1		6		2	9	7	10			8			11		4		3					5	
	27(a)	Torquay U	D 1-1	G.Smith	10,350			1		6		2	9	7	10			8			11		4		3					5	
Oct	2(h)	Southend U	W 3-2	Hatton 2, Pattison	17,000			1		6		2	9		10			7		8	11		4		3					5	
	4(h)	Swindon T	L 0-2		24,500			1		6		2	9	7	10				8		11		4		3					5	
	11(a)	Swansea T	L 1-3	Durrant	28,000			1		6		2	9		10			7	8		11		4		3					5	
	18(h)	Bournemouth	W 1-0	Durrant	25,000			1	7	6		2	9		10			8			11				3				4	5	
	25(a)	Ipswich T	L 0-1		24,161			1		6		2	9		10			7			11		4	8	3					5	
Nov	1(h)	Bristol C	W 2-0	Boxshall, Pattison	28,205			1	7	6		2	9				3	8			11		4	10						5	
	8(a)	Reading	L 2-3	Durrant, Boxshall	23,256			1	8	6			9					7			11	2	4	10	3					5	
	15(h)	Walsall	W 2-1	Hatton, Hartburn	26,100			1		6			9	11	10		3	7				2	4	8						5	
	22(a)	Leyton O	W 3-1	Durrant, Hatton 2	16,915			1			6		9	11	10		3	7				2	4	8		5					
Dec	6(a)	Newport C	D 0-0		15,000			1			6		9	11	10		3	7				2	4	8						5	
	26(a)	Watford	W 1-0	Jones (og)	18,000			1			6		9	11	10		3	7				2	4	8						5	
	27(h)	Watford	W 5-1	Pattison, Boxshall 2, Hatton, McEwan	18,005			1	7		6				10		3	9			11	2	4	8						5	
Jan	3(h)	Bristol R	W 5-2	McEwan, Hatton, Boxshall 2, Hartburn	22,000			1	7		6			11	10		3	9				2	4	8						5	
	31(h)	Aldershot	D 0-0		21,000			1	9		6			11	10		3	7				2	4	8						5	
Feb	14(h)	Torquay U	D 3-3	Ramscar, Boxshall, Hatton	21,000			1	9		6			11	10		3	7				2	4	8						5	
	21(a)	Swindon T	D 0-0		13,000			1	9					11	10		3	7				2	4	8					6	5	
Mar	13(h)	Ipswich T	W 2-0	Hatton, Boxhall	16,204				7					11	9		3					2	4	10				1	6	5	8
	15(a)	Crystal P	W 1-0	Hartburn	22,086				7					11	9		3					2	4	10				1	6	5	8
	20(a)	Bristol C	L 1-2	Hatton	20,699								9	11	10		3					2	4	8				1	6	5	7
	26(a)	Port Vale	W 2-0	Boxshall 2	18,000		9		7					11			3		10			2	4					1	6	5	8
	27(h)	Reading	W 2-0	Boxshall, Hatton	25,000				7					11	9		3		10			2	4					1	6	5	8
	29(h)	Port Vale	W 2-1	Addinall, A.Smith	23,350		9		7					11			3		10			2	4					1	6	5	8
Apr	3(a)	Walsall	W 1-0	Addinall	17,872		9		7					11			3		10			2	4					1	6	5	8
	8(a)	Northampton T	D 1-1	Hartburn	11,000				7					11		9	3		10			2	4					1	6	5	8
	10(h)	Leyton O	L 1-2	Stewart	27,480			1	7					11			3		10			2	4	8					6	5	9
	14(a)	Bournemouth	W 1-0	Durrant	25,495			1					9	7	8		3		10		11	2	4						6	5	
	17(a)	Exeter C	W 2-1	Hartburn 2	13,000			1					9	11	8		3		10			2	4						6	5	7
	21(a)	Norwich C	L 2-5	Hatton, A.Smith	30,086			1					9	11	8		3		10			2	4						6	5	7
	24(h)	Newport C	W 1-0	I.Powell	22,000	7		1						11	9		3		10				4			5	2		6		8
	26(h)	Swansea T	D 0-0		27,500	7		1						11	9		3		10				4			5	2		6		8
May	1(a)	Southend U	D 0-0		16,500			1	7				9		10		3		11			2	4			5			6		8
					App	2	3	34	17	14	7	17	27	31	35	6	26	26	16	1	20	23	41	16	16	4	2	8	18	38	14
					Goals		2		11	1			12	6	21			6			8		1	1					2	1	1

1 own-goal

FA Cup

	Date	Opponent	Result	Scorers	Att	Adams	Addinall	Allen	Boxshall	Chapman	Daniels	Dudley	Durrant	Hartburn	Hatton	Heath	Jefferson	McEwan	Mills	Parkinson	Pattison	Powell G	Powell I	Ramscar	Reay	Ridyard	Rose	Saphin	Smith A	Smith G	Stewart	Round
Jan	10(a)	Gillingham	D 1-1	Boxshall	23,002			1	9		6				10		3	7			11	2	4	8						5		3
	17(h)	Gillingham	W 3-1	Hatton, Hartburn, McEwan	28,000			1	9		6			11	10		3	7				2	4	8						5		Rep
	24(h)	Stoke C	W 3-0	Hatton 2, Ramscar	24,100			1	9		6			11	10		3	7				2	4	8						5		4
Feb	7(h)	Luton T	W 3-1	Boxshall, Hatton, McEwan	30,564			1	7		6			11	10		3	9				2	4	8						5		5
	28(h)	Derby C	D 1-1	Hartburn	28,358			1	7					11	10	9	3					2	4	8					6	5		6
Mar	6(a)	Derby C	L 0-5		31,588			1	9					11	10		3	7				2	4	8					6	5		Rep
					App			6	6		4			5	6	1	6	5			1	6	6	6					2	6		
					Goals				2					2	4			2						1								

Attendance Summary

	ATTENDANCES Home	Away	Total	AVERAGE Home	Away	Total
League	459,680	383,572	843,252	21,889	18,265	20,077
FA Cup	111,022	54,590	165,612	27,755	27,295	27,602
Total	570,702	438,162	1,008,864	22,828	19,050	21,018

1948-49

Division 2

Date	Opponent	Res	Scorers	Att	Adams	Addinall	Allen	Bennett	Dudley	Duggan	Durrant	Farrow	Gibbons	Hartburn	Hatton	Heath	Hill	Hudson	Jefferson	Lennon	McEwan	Millbank	Mills	Nicholas	Parkinson	Pattison	Pointon	Powell G	Powell I	Ramscar	Reay	Smith A	Smith G	Stewart	Wardle
Aug 21	(a) Luton T	D 0-0		22,764		9	1							11	10				3		7		8					2	4			6	5		
26	(h) Leicester C	W 4-1	Addinall 3, Hartburn	24,200		9	1							11	10				3		7		8					2	4			6	5		
28	(h) Bradford	W 1-0	Addinall	26,000		9	1							11	10				3		7		8					2	4			6	5		
30	(a) Leicester C	W 3-2	Hatton 2, Mills	36,961		9	1							11	10				3		7		8					2	4			6	5		
Sep 4	(a) Southampton	L 0-3		27,600		9	1							11	10				3		7		8					2	4			6	5		
9	(h) Cardiff C	D 0-0		20,700		9	1							11	10				3		7		8					2	4			6	5		
11	(h) Barnsley	D 2-2	Addinall 2	21,000		9	1							11	10				3		7	4	8					2				6	5		
13	(a) Cardiff C	L 0-3		40,000		9	1								10						7		6			11		2	5	8		4			
18	(a) Grimsby T	L 1-4	Pattison	15,141		9	1		2					7									10			11		3	4	8		6	5		
25	(h) Nottingham F	W 2-1	Hartburn, Pattison	19,361		9	1		3					7	10											11		2	4	8		6	5		
Oct 2	(a) Fulham	L 0-5		30,000		9	1							7	10				3							11		2	4	8		6	5		
9	(h) Brentford	W 2-0	Hartburn, Hudson	25,500		9	1					6		7	10			11	3									2	4	8			5		
16	(a) Tottenham H	L 0-1		69,718		9	1					6		7	10	5		11	3									2	4	8					
23	(h) West Ham U	W 2-1	Hatton, Hudson	27,000			1					6	9	7	10	5		11	3									2	4	8					
30	(a) Bury	D 0-0		19,238	11		1					6	9		10	5			3		7							2	4	8					
Nov 6	(h) West Brom A	L 0-2		24,200	7		1					6		11	10				3									2	4	8			5	9	
13	(a) Chesterfield	L 1-2	Hartburn	12,000			1					6	9	11	10				3		7							2	4	8			5		
20	(h) Lincoln C	W 2-0	Hatton, Gibbons	19,000			1					6	9	11	10				3		7							2	4	8			5		
27	(a) Sheffield W	L 0-2		34,346			1					10		11		6	9		3		7							2	4	8			5		
Dec 4	(h) Coventry C	L 0-3		16,500			1					6	9	11	10				3	8	7							2	4				5		
11	(a) Leeds U	W 2-1	Gibbons, Pattison	26,420			1					6	9	7	10				3						4	11		2					5	8	
18	(h) Luton T	L 0-3		16,500			1					6	9	7	10				3						4	11		2					5	8	
25	(a) Blackburn R	L 0-2		31,526			1							7		6			3				10		4	11		2	9				5	8	
27	(h) Blackburn R	W 4-2	Parkinson 2, Hatton, Hartburn	17,091			1				9	6		7	10				3						4	11		2					5	8	
Jan 1	(a) Bradford	D 0-0		15,178			1				9	6		7	10				3						4	11		2					5	8	
22	(a) Barnsley	L 0-4		20,357			1					6	7						3				10		4	11	9	2		8			5		
29	(h) Southampton	L 1-3	Pointon	20,000			1					6				5		11	3						4	10	9	2						8	7
Feb 5	(h) Grimsby T	L 1-2	Hudson	19,813		10	1			8						6		11	3						4		9	2					5		7
12	(a) Nottingham F	D 0-0		26,115		10	1			8		6						11	3						4		9	2					5		7
26	(h) Fulham	W 1-0	Ramscar	28,000			1			8		6						11	3						4		9	2		10			5		7
Mar 5	(a) Brentford	W 3-0	Hudson, Pointon, Duggan	29,411		10	1			7						6		11	3						4		9	2		8			5		
12	(h) Tottenham H	D 0-0		25,371		10	1			7						6		11	3						4		9	2		8			5		
19	(a) West Ham U	L 0-2		26,000				1		10						6		11	3						4		9	2		8			5		7
26	(h) Bury	W 3-1	Duggan, Jefferson, Ramscar	20,000			1			10				11		6			3						4		9	2		8			5		7
Apr 2	(a) West Brom A	D 1-1	Pointon	35,093			1			7						6	10		3						4		9	2		8			5		11
9	(h) Chesterfield	D 1-1	Hill	25,000			1			7						6	10		3						4		9	2		8			5		11
15	(h) Plymouth A	W 2-1	Stewart, Pointon	22,000			1			7				11		6	10		3						4		9	2					5	8	
16	(a) Lincoln C	D 0-0		11,500		10	1			7				11		6			3						4		9	2					5	8	
18	(a) Plymouth A	L 1-3	Addinall	20,140		10	1			7				11		6			3						4		9	2					5	8	
23	(h) Sheffield W	L 1-3	Heath	25,000		10		1		7						6			3						4		9				2		5	8	11
30	(a) Coventry C	D 1-1	Stewart	14,519		10	1			7						6			3						4		9				2		5	8	11
May 7	(h) Leeds U	W 2-0	Addinall 2	16,730		10	1			7							6		3					4			9			8	2		5		11
				App	2	22	40	2	2	15	2	17	8	27	22	18	5	10	39	1	13	1	11	1	21	11	17	39	20	21	3	11	37	12	11
				Goals		9				2			2	5	5	1	1	4	1				1		2	3	4			2				2	

Muir played number-3 against Cardiff City (a)

FA Cup

Date	Opponent	Res	Scorers	Att	Adams	Addinall	Allen	Bennett	Dudley	Duggan	Durrant	Farrow	Gibbons	Hartburn	Hatton	Heath	Hill	Hudson	Jefferson	Lennon	McEwan	Millbank	Mills	Nicholas	Parkinson	Pattison	Pointon	Powell G	Powell I	Ramscar	Reay	Smith A	Smith G	Round
Jan 8	(h) Huddersfield T	D 0-0		26,000			1				9	6		7	10				3						4	11		2					5	3
15	(a) Huddersfield T	L 0-5		31,075			1				9	6							3				10		4	11		2					5	Rep
				App			2				2	2		1	1				2				1		2	2		2					2	
				Goals																														

Stewart played number-8 in both FA Cup rounds, Campbell played number-7 in replay.

Attendance Summary

	ATTENDANCES			AVERAGE		
	Home	Away	Total	Home	Away	Total
League	458,966	564,027	1,022,993	21,855	26,858	24,356
FA Cup	26,000	31,075	57,075	26,000	31,075	28,538
Total	484,966	595,102	1,080,068	22,044	27,050	24,547

1949-50

Division 2

Date	Opponents	Result	Scorers	Att	Adams	Addinall	Allen	Best	Chapman	Dudley	Duggan	Farrow	Hatton	Heath	Hill	Hudson	Jefferson	McEwan	McKay	Mills	Neary	Nelson	Parkinson	Pattison	Pointon	Powell	Ramscar	Reay	Saphin	Wardle	Woodward
Aug 20	(a) Leeds U	D 1-1	Pointon	30,000			1				7		10		6		3						4	11	9		8	2			5
24	(h) Brentford	D 3-3	Pattison 2 (2 pens), Pointon	28,000			1				7		10		6		3						4	11	9		8	2			5
27	(h) Southampton	W 1-0	Hudson	23,000			1			2	7		10		6	11	3						4		9		8				5
31	(a) Brentford	W 2-0	Hatton, Wardle	29,411			1			2	7		10		6	11	3						4		9		8				5
Sep 3	(a) Coventry C	D 0-0		22,610		9	1			2	7		10	3	6	11							4				8				5
7	(h) Preston NE	D 0-0		20,000		9	1			2	7		10		6	11	3						4				8				5
10	(h) Luton T	W 3-0	Addinall, Duggan, Hatton	20,500		9	1			2	7		10		6	11	3						4				8				5
14	(a) Preston NE	L 2-3	Addinall, Robertson (og)	27,000		9	1			2	7		10		6	11	3						4				8				5
17	(a) Barnsley	L 1-3	Addinall	19,700		9	1			2	7		10		6	11	3						4				8				5
24	(h) West Ham U	L 0-1		24,000		9	1			2	7		10		6		3						4	11			8				5
Oct 1	(a) Sheffield U	D 1-1	Ramscar	32,000		9	1		5	2	7		10		6		3						4		11		8				
8	(h) Hull C	L 1-4	Duggan	28,000		9	1			3	10		4		6										11	2	8			7	5
15	(a) Sheffield W	L 0-1		31,748		9	1			2	7	6	10	3									4				8			11	5
22	(h) Plymouth A	L 0-2		17,000			1			2	7	6	10				3						4		9		8			11	5
29	(a) Chesterfield	L 1-2	Neary	12,231		10	1				7	6	8				3				9		4	11		2					5
Nov 5	(h) Bradford	L 0-1		8,000	7	10	1					6	8				3				9		4	11		2					5
12	(a) Leicester C	L 2-3	Addinall, Parkinson	26,045		7	1					10		5	6		3				9		8	11		2					4
19	(h) Bury	W 1-0	Neary	15,110		8	1		5			10			6		3		11		9					2				7	4
26	(a) Tottenham H	L 0-3		62,873			1		5			6	8		10		3		11		9					2				7	4
Dec 3	(h) Cardiff C	L 0-1		12,000			1		5			6	10				3				7		4		9	2				11	8
10	(a) Blackburn R	D 0-0		17,000		10	1	8	5			6	4	3				7			9					2				11	
17	(h) Leeds U	D 1-1	Best	13,385		10	1	8	5			6	4	3				7			9					2				11	
24	(a) Southampton	W 2-1	Neary 2	22,000		10	1	8	5			6	4	3				7			9					2				11	
26	(a) Grimsby T	D 1-1	Hudson	22,336		10	1		5			6	4	3		11		8			9					2				7	
27	(h) Grimsby T	L 1-2	Addinall	22,884		10	1		5			6	4	3		11		7			9					2				8	
31	(h) Coventry C	W 2-0	McEwan, Best	16,768			1	10	5			6	4	3				8			9			11		2				7	
Jan 14	(a) Luton T	W 2-1	Neary, Mills	16,291			1	9	5			6	4	3				8		10	7					2				11	
21	(h) Barnsley	L 0-5		16,795				9	5			6	4	3				8			7				10	2			1	11	
Feb 4	(a) West Ham U	L 0-1		26,000			1		5		10		4	3	6			8	11		9					2				7	
18	(h) Sheffield U	L 1-3	McKay	20,170			1				8		6	3					11	10	9	4				2				7	5
25	(a) Hull C	D 1-1	Mills	25,000			1				8		6	3					11	10	9	4				2				7	5
Mar 4	(h) Sheffield W	D 0-0		23,177			1				8		6	3					11	10	9	4				2				7	5
11	(a) Plymouth A	W 2-0	Addinall, Best	23,380		8	1	9					6	3					11	10		4				2				7	5
18	(h) Chesterfield	W 3-2	Addinall 2, Wardle	18,406		8	1	9					6	3					11	10		4				2				7	5
25	(a) Bradford	L 0-1		17,898		8	1	9			10	6		3					11			4				2				7	5
Apr 1	(h) Tottenham H	L 0-2		29,644		8	1	9				6		3					11	10		4				2				7	5
7	(h) Swansea T	D 0-0		23,092		8	1	9					6	3					11	10		4				2				7	5
8	(a) Cardiff C	L 0-4		18,000		8	1	9		2		6		3					11	10		4								7	5
10	(a) Swansea T	W 1-0	Hudson	23,094		8	1	9					6	3					11	10		4				2				7	5
15	(h) Leicester C	W 2-0	Addinall 2	15,000		9	1					6	8	3		11				10		4				2				7	5
22	(a) Bury	D 0-0		11,383		9	1					6	8	3		11				10		4				2				7	5
29	(h) Blackburn R	L 2-3	Addinall, Hatton	10,257		9	1					6	8	3		11				10		4				2				7	5
				App	1	28	41	13	13	13	20	22	37	25	16	12	17	9	13	13	18	13	17	7	9	28	14	2	1	28	32
				Goals		11		3			2		3			3		1	1	2	5		1	2	2		1			2	

1 own-goal

FA Cup

Date	Opponents	Result		Att	Adams	Addinall	Allen	Best	Chapman	Dudley	Duggan	Farrow	Hatton	Heath	Hill	Hudson	Jefferson	McEwan	McKay	Mills	Neary	Nelson	Parkinson	Pattison	Pointon	Powell	Ramscar	Reay	Saphin	Wardle	Woodward	Round
Jan 7	(h) Everton	L 0-2		22,433			1	10	5			6	4	3		11		8			9					2				7		3
				App			1	1	1			1	1	1		1		1			1					1				1		
				Goals																												

Attendance Summary

	ATTENDANCES			AVERAGE		
	Home	Away	Total	Home	Away	Total
League	405,188	516,000	921,188	19,295	24,571	21,933
FA Cup	22,433		22,433	22,433		22,433
Total	427,621	516,000	943,621	19,437	24,571	21,945

1950-51

Division 2

Date	Opponent	Res	Score	Scorers	Att	Addinall	Cameron	Chapman	Clayton	Davies	Duggan	Farrow	Gullan	Hatton	Heath	Ingham	McKay	Mills	Muir	Nelson	Nicholas	Parkinson	Poppitt	Powell	Saphin	Shepherd	Smith	Stewart	Wardle	Waugh	Woodward
Aug 19	(h) Chesterfield	D	1-1	Hatton	25,000	9								8	3			10		4		6		2	1	11				7	5
24	(h) Notts C	W	1-0	Hatton	16,000	9								10	3			8		4		6		2	1	11				7	5
26	(a) Leicester C	L	2-6	Addinall, Shepherd	28,600	9						6		10	3			8		4		5		2	1	11			7		
31	(a) Notts C	D	3-3	Addinall 2, Wardle	33,404	9		5				6		10	3			8			4			2	1	11			7		
Sep 2	(h) Manchester C	L	1-2	Hatton	21,593	9		5				6		10	3			8			4			2	1	11			7		
6	(a) Bury	W	1-0	Addinall	8,888	9		5				6	1	10	3			8			4			2				11	7		
9	(a) Coventry C	L	0-3		22,298	9		5	4		10	6	1		3			8						2		11			7		
16	(h) Cardiff C	W	3-2	Hatton (pen), Heath, Wardle	19,143	9		5				6	1	10	3			8		4				2		11			7		
23	(a) Birmingham C	D	1-1	Addinall	27,000	9		5				6	1	10	3			8		4			2			11			7		
30	(h) Grimsby T	W	7-1	Shepherd 3, Addinall 2, Hatton 2	16,241	9		5				6	1	10	3			8		4			2			11			7		
Oct 7	(a) West Ham U	L	1-4	Addinall	26,300	9		5				6	1	10	3			8		4			2			11			7		
14	(h) Swansea T	D	1-1	Addinall	19,161	9		5			7	6	1	10	3			8		4			2			11					
21	(a) Luton T	L	0-2		15,691	9		5			7	6	1		3		8	10		4			2			11					
28	(h) Leeds U	W	3-0	Shepherd, Hatton (pen), Mills	15,835	9		5				6	1	10	3			8		4			2			11			7		
Nov 4	(a) Barnsley	L	0-7		20,000	9		5				6	1	10	3			8		4			2			11			7		
11	(h) Sheffield U	W	2-1	Hatton, Addinall	16,194	9		5				6	1	10	3			8		4			2			11			7		
18	(a) Hull C	L	1-5	Hatton	33,866	9		5				6	1	10	3			8		4			2			11			7		
25	(h) Doncaster R	L	1-2	Hatton	16,752	9		5				6	1	10	3	2		8		4			7			11					
Dec 2	(a) Brentford	L	1-2	Addinall	23,010	9		5				6	1	10	3	2				4		8				11			7		
9	(h) Blackburn R	W	3-1	Addinall 2, Hatton (pen)	13,490	9						6	1	10		3				4		8	2			11				7	5
16	(a) Chesterfield	L	1-3	Addinall	7,407	9						6	1	10		3				4		8	2			11				7	5
23	(h) Leicester C	W	3-0	Addinall, Hatton, Shepherd	11,017	9						6	1	10		3				4		8	2			11				7	5
25	(h) Preston NE	L	1-4	Waugh	16,790	9						6	1	10		3					4	8	2			11				7	5
26	(a) Preston NE	L	0-1		36,000	9					10	6			3						4	8	2		1	11				7	5
Jan 13	(h) Coventry C	W	3-1	Addinall, Hatton (pen), Shepherd	17,279	9	8				10	6				3						4	2		1	11				7	5
20	(a) Cardiff C	L	2-4	Shepherd 2	20,000	9	8				10	6				3						4	2		1	11				7	5
27	(h) Brentford	D	1-1	Davies	26,171	10			6	9	8					3						4	2		1	11				7	5
Feb 3	(h) Birmingham C	W	2-0	Farrow (pen), Shepherd	12,071	9			6			10				3			8			4	2		1	11				7	5
17	(a) Grimsby T	D	2-2	Farrow, Shepherd	14,005	9			6		8	10				3						4	2		1	11				7	5
24	(h) West Ham U	D	3-3	Clayton, Farrow, Duggan	21,336	9			6		8	10				3						4	2		1	11				7	5
Mar 3	(a) Swansea T	L	0-1		20,000	9			6		8	10				3						4	2		1	11				7	5
10	(h) Luton T	D	1-1	Shepherd	13,592	9			6		8	10				3						4	2		1	11				7	5
17	(a) Leeds U	D	2-2	Shepherd, Smith	18,094	9			6			10				3						4	2		1	11	8			7	5
23	(h) Southampton	W	2-0	Farrow, Smith	19,711	9			6			10				3						4	2		1	11	8			7	5
24	(h) Barnsley	W	2-1	Waugh, Smith	15,774	9			6			10				3						4	2		1	11	8			7	5
26	(a) Southampton	D	2-2	Addinall 2	20,875	9			6		8	10				3						4	2		1	11				7	5
31	(a) Sheffield U	L	0-2		16,000	9			6			10				3						4	2		1	11	8			7	5
Apr 4	(a) Manchester C	L	2-5	Hatton, Smith	21,474	9						6		10	3							4	2		1	11	8			7	5
7	(h) Hull C	W	3-1	Farrow 2, Smith	14,628				6			10	1	9		3						4	2			11	8			7	5
14	(a) Doncaster R	W	2-0	Clayton, Smith	17,000				6			10	1	9		3						4	2			11	8			7	5
25	(a) Blackburn R	L	1-2	Hatton	9,700				6			10	1	9		3						4	2			11	8			7	5
May 5	(h) Bury	W	3-2	Hatton, Shepherd, Smith	11,116				6			10	1	9		3						4	2			11	8			7	5
					App	38	2	16	16	1	12	39	22	26	21	23	1	18	1	18	5	27	33	8	20	41	9	1	14	25	25
					Goals	18			2	1	1	6		16	1			1								14	7		2	2	

1 own-goal

FA Cup

Date	Opponent	Res	Score	Scorers	Att	Addinall	Cameron	Chapman	Clayton	Davies	Duggan	Farrow	Gullan	Hatton	Heath	Ingham	McKay	Mills	Muir	Nelson	Nicholas	Parkinson	Poppitt	Powell	Saphin	Shepherd	Smith	Stewart	Wardle	Waugh	Woodward	Round
Jan 6	(h) Millwall	L	3-4	Parkinson 2, Addinall	25,777	9					10			4	3						6	8	2		1	11				7	5	3
					App	1					1			1	1						1	1	1		1	1				1	1	
					Goals	1																2										

Attendance Summary

	ATTENDANCES			AVERAGE		
	Home	Away	Total	Home	Away	Total
League	358,802	436,772	795,574	17,086	20,799	18,942
FA Cup	25,777		25,777	25,777		25,777
Total	384,579	436,772	821,351	17,481	20,799	19,101

1951-52

Division 2

Date	Opponent	Result	Scorers	Att	Addinall	Brown	Cameron	Chapman	Clayton	Farrow	Gilberg	Gullan	Hatton	Heath	Hill	Hold	Ingham	McKay	Muir	Nicholas	Poppitt	Powell	Richardson	Shepherd	Smith	Spence	Stewart	Tomkys	Underwood	Waugh
Aug 18 (h)	West Ham U	W 2-0	Addinall, Shepherd	19,443	9	1		5	4		6		10	3							2			11	8					7
20 (h)	Hull C	D 1-1	Smith	16,726	9	1		5	4		6			3					7		2			11	8		10			
25 (a)	Coventry C	D 0-0		22,649	9	1		5	4		6			3				11	7		2				8		10			
30 (a)	Hull C	L 1-4	Smith	19,661	9	1		5	4		6			3				11	7		2				8		10			
Sep 1 (h)	Swansea T	D 1-1	Smith	18,262	9	1		5	4		6			3					7		2			11	8		10			
3 (h)	Blackburn R	W 2-1	Addinall 2	13,291	9	1	10		4		6			5							2	3		11	8					7
8 (a)	Bury	L 1-3	Clayton	13,115	9	1	10	5	4		6			3								2		11	8					7
15 (h)	Luton T	D 0-0		17,271	9	1	10	5		6	4			3							2			11	8					7
22 (a)	Notts C	D 0-0		23,185	9			5	4	6	10	1									2	3		11	8					7
29 (h)	Brentford	W 3-1	Gilberg, Shepherd, Smith	25,221		1	8	5	4	6	10										2	3		11	9					7
Oct 6 (a)	Doncaster R	L 0-4		20,000		1	8	5	4	6	10										2	3		11	9					7
13 (h)	Everton	D 4-4	Shepherd 2, Waugh, Gilberg	17,148	9	1		5	4	6	10										2	3		11	8					7
20 (a)	Southampton	D 1-1	Smith	19,200	9	1		5	4	6	10										2	3		11	8					7
27 (h)	Sheffield W	D 2-2	Addinall, Smith	18,439	9	1		5	4	6	10										2	3		11	8					7
Nov 3 (a)	Leeds U	L 0-3		22,875	9	1		5	4	6	10										2	3		11	8					7
10 (h)	Rotherham U	L 2-3	Gilberg, Smith	18,693	9	1			4	6	10			5							2	3		11	8					7
17 (a)	Cardiff C	L 1-3	Gilberg	25,000	9	1				6	4			5							2	3		11	8		10			7
24 (h)	Birmingham C	L 0-2		14,836	9	1				6	4			5			3					2		11	8		10	7		
Dec 1 (a)	Leicester C	L 0-4		23,193	9	1				6	4			5	8		3					2		11			10			7
8 (h)	Nottingham F	W 4-3	Smith, Hatton (pen), Shepherd, Gilberg	12,005	9	1				6	10		4	5							2	3		11	8					7
15 (a)	West Ham U	L 2-4	Gilberg, Hatton (pen)	17,500	9	1				6	10		4	5							2	3		11	8					7
24 (h)	Coventry C	L 1-4	Smith	12,783		1		5		6	8		10							4	2	3		11	9					7
25 (a)	Barnsley	L 1-3	Hatton	15,004		1				6	8		10		7					4	2	3			9	5				11
26 (h)	Barnsley	D 1-1	Smith	13,758		1				6	8		10		7					4	2	3			9	5				11
29 (a)	Swansea T	W 3-2	Gilberg, Hill, Addinall	18,000	9	1					8			6	7		3			4		2			10	5				11
Jan 1 (a)	Blackburn R	L 2-4	Nicholas, Addinall	28,700	9	1					8			6	7		3			4		2			10	5				11
5 (h)	Bury	W 3-2	Addinall, Gilberg, Smith	14,000	9	1					8			6	7		3			4		2			10	5				11
19 (a)	Luton T	W 1-0	Addinall	15,242	9					6	4	1			10							3	2	11	8	5				7
26 (h)	Notts C	L 1-4	Gilberg	18,782	9					6	4				10							3	2	11	8	5			1	7
Feb 9 (a)	Brentford	D 0-0		26,000	9					6	4				10		3					2		11	8	5			1	7
16 (h)	Doncaster R	L 0-2		14,676						6	8	1		4	7		3					2			9	5	10			11
Mar 1 (a)	Everton	L 0-3		38,172	9					6	8	1		4			3	11				2			10	5				7
8 (h)	Southampton	W 2-1	Addinall, Hold	18,936	9	1				6	4					8	3		7			2			10	5				11
15 (a)	Sheffield W	L 1-2	Muir	41,706	9	1				6	4					8	3		7			2			10	5				11
22 (h)	Leeds U	D 0-0		15,099	9	1				6	4					8	3		7			2			10	5				11
29 (a)	Rotherham U	L 0-1		9,000	9	1			4	6	10						3					2		11	8	5				7
Apr 5 (h)	Cardiff C	D 1-1	Smith	17,827	9	1			4	6	10						3					2		11	8	5				7
12 (a)	Birmingham C	L 0-1		28,000	9	1			4	6	10						3					2		11	8	5				7
14 (h)	Sheffield U	W 4-2	Addinall 2, Farrow, Muir	12,662	9	1			4	6	10								7		3	2			8	5				11
19 (h)	Leicester C	W 1-0	Addinall	16,731	9	1			4	6							3		8		2			11	10	5				7
26 (a)	Nottingham F	L 1-3	Muir	19,011	9	1			4	6	8						3		7		2			11	10	5				
May 3 (a)	Sheffield U	W 2-1	Stewart, Smith	9,000	9	1			4	6							3				2			11	8	5	10			7
				App	36	36	5	15	22	32	40	4	6	19	10	3	17	3	10	6	25	33	2	29	41	20	9	1	2	36
				Goals	12				1	1	9		3		1	1			3	1				5	13		1			1

FA Cup

Date	Opponent	Result	Scorers	Att	Addinall	Brown	Cameron	Chapman	Clayton	Farrow	Gilberg	Gullan	Hatton	Heath	Hill	Hold	Ingham	McKay	Muir	Nicholas	Poppitt	Powell	Richardson	Shepherd	Smith	Spence	Stewart	Tomkys	Underwood	Waugh	Round
Jan 12 (a)	Brentford	L 1-3	Shepherd	35,000	9	1					4			6	10		3					2		11	8	5				7	3
				App	1	1					1			1	1		1					1		1	1	1				1	
				Goals																				1							

Attendance Summary

	ATTENDANCES			AVERAGE		
	Home	Away	Total	Home	Away	Total
League	346,589	454,677	801,266	16,504	21,651	19,078
FA Cup		35,000	35,000		35,000	35,000
Total	346,589	489,677	836,266	16,504	22,258	19,448

1952-53

Division 3 South

Date	Opponent	Res	Score	Scorers	Att	Addinall	Brown	Cameron	Chapman	Clayton	Crickson	Farrow	Gilberg	Gullan	Harrison	Hatton	Heath	Higgis	Hold	Ingham	Muir	Mountford	Nicholas	Parsons	Poppitt	Powell G	Powell M	Quinn	Shepherd	Smith	Spence	Stewart	Tomkys	Waugh	Woods
Aug 23	(a) Exeter C	D	2-2	Smith 2	15,078	9	1			4			6							3					2				11	8	5	10		7	
25	(h) Watford	D	2-2	Stewart, Smith	23,005	9	1			4			6							3					2				11	8	5	10		7	
30	(h) Coventry C	L	0-4		14,238	9	1			4			6						10	3					2				11	8	5			7	
Sep 4	(a) Watford	D	1-1	Shepherd	22,068	9	1			4			6						10	3					2				11	8	5			7	
6	(a) Norwich C	L	0-2		26,642		1	10					8										4		2	3	5		11	7	6		9		
8	(h) Walsall	W	4-2	Tomkys 2, Gilberg, Smith	9,269		1	10					8										4		2	3	5		11	7	6		9		
13	(h) Colchester U	W	1-0	Muir	13,837		1	10					8							3	7		4		2		5		11		6		9		
18	(a) Walsall	D	1-1	Cameron	7,023		1	10				6	8							3	7		4		2		5		11				9		
20	(a) Aldershot	L	1-4	Shepherd	8,316		1	10				6	8							3	7		4		2		5		11				9		
25	(a) Leyton O	L	0-5		8,000	9	1	10				6	8				5			3	11		4		2								7		
27	(h) Swindon T	D	1-1	Addinall	10,664	9	1	10				6	11							3	7		4		2		5			8					
Oct 2	(a) Shrewsbury T	W	3-0	Shepherd 2, Smith	5,088	9	1	10		4		6	7							3					2				11	8	5				
4	(h) Southend U	W	3-2	Smith 2, Addinall	14,675	9	1	10		4		6	7							3					2				11	8	5				
11	(a) Brighton & HA	L	0-2		18,000	9	1	10		4		6	7							3					2				11	8	5				
18	(h) Newport C	W	4-2	Quinn, Shepherd 2, Addinall	14,800	9	1			4		6	7							3					2			10	11	8	5				
25	(a) Crystal P	L	2-4	Addinall, Ingham	19,050	9	1			4			6							3		7			2			10	11	8	5				
Nov 1	(h) Bristol C	W	2-1	Mountford, Addinall	14,661	9	1						6							3		7	4		2			10	11	8	5				
8	(a) Torquay U	D	1-1	Parsons	6,770	9	1	10					8							3		7	4	6	2				11		5				
15	(h) Northampton T	D	2-2	Shepherd, Gilberg	14,839	9	1	10					8							3		7	4	6	2				11		5				
29	(h) Ipswich T	D	2-2	Addinall 2	8,857	9	1	10					6							3		7	4		2				11	8	5				
Dec 13	(h) Bournemouth	W	2-1	Nicholas, Cameron	7,931	9	1	10		6			8							3		7	4		2				11		5				
20	(h) Exeter C	D	1-1	Clayton	6,219	9	1	10		6			8							3		7	4		2				11		5				
26	(h) Bristol R	L	0-1		13,850	9	1	10		6			8							3		7	4		2				11		5				
27	(a) Bristol R	L	1-2	Gilberg	30,892		1	10		6			8							3		7	4		2		5		11				9		
Jan 3	(a) Coventry C	L	0-2		15,063	9	1	8					10		6					3		7	4				5		11						2
10	(a) Gillingham	L	0-3		11,907	9	1	8					10		6					3			4			2			11		5			7	
17	(h) Norwich C	W	3-1	Tomkys, Waugh 2	12,971		1	10	5											3		8	4			2			11		6		9	7	
24	(a) Colchester U	D	1-1	Harrison (og)	7,959			10	5					1						3		8	4			2			11		6		9	7	
31	(h) Gillingham	D	1-1	Tomkys	10,444			10	5					1						3		8	4			2			11		6		9	7	
Feb 7	(h) Aldershot	D	2-2	Smith, Waugh	10,589				5					1		10				3			4			2			11	8	6		9	7	
14	(a) Swindon T	W	3-1	Hatton 2, Smith	6,972		1		5	6						10				3			4			2			11	8			9	7	
21	(a) Southend U	L	0-2		12,000		1		5	6						10				3			4			2			11	8			9	7	
28	(h) Brighton & HA	D	3-3	Higgins, Hatton, Jennings (og)	15,128		1		5							10		9		3		8	4			2			11		6			7	
Mar 7	(a) Newport C	L	0-2		8,500		1		5									9		3		8	4			2			11	10	6			7	
14	(h) Crystal P	D	1-1	Cameron	12,846		1	10	5											3		7	4			2			11	8	6		9		
21	(a) Bristol C	D	4-4	Mountford, Cameron, Smith 2	19,898		1	10	5	6										3		7	4		2				11	8			9		
28	(h) Torquay U	L	0-1		8,059		1	10	5	6										3		7	4		2				11	8			9		
Apr 3	(a) Millwall	L	1-2	Smith	23,905		1	10		6								9		3			4		2		5		11	8				7	
4	(a) Northampton T	L	2-4	Tomkys, Cameron	12,642		1	10	6											3		7	4			2	5		11	8			9		
6	(h) Millwall	L	1-3	Smith	12,411		1	8		6	4					10				3					2		5		11				9	7	
11	(h) Leyton O	L	0-1		10,880		1	10		6	4									3		7			2		5			8			9	11	
18	(a) Ipswich T	W	1-0	Hatton	8,372		1	8		4					9	10				3		7			2		5		11		6				
20	(h) Shrewsbury T	W	1-0	Shepherd	7,126		1	8		4					9	10				3		7			2		5		11		6				
25	(h) Reading	W	1-0	Harrison	10,325		1	8		4					9	10				3		7			2		5		11		6				
29	(a) Reading	L	0-2		8,000		1	8		4					9	10				3		7			2		5		11		6				
May 2	(a) Bournemouth	L	0-1		8,269		1	10		6						9						7	4		3	2	5		11	8					
					App	20	43	34	12	25	2	8	26	3	6	10	1	3	2	43	5	25	31	2	34	14	17	3	43	25	31	2	19	16	1
					Goals	7		5		1			3		1	4		1		1	1	2	1	1				1	8	13		1	5	3	

2 own-goals

FA Cup

Date	Opponent	Res	Score	Scorers	Att	Addinall	Brown	Cameron	Chapman	Clayton	Crickson	Farrow	Gilberg	Gullan	Harrison	Hatton	Heath	Higgis	Hold	Ingham	Muir	Mountford	Nicholas	Parsons	Poppitt	Powell G	Powell M	Quinn	Shepherd	Smith	Spence	Stewart	Tomkys	Waugh	Round
Nov 22	(h) Shrewsbury T	D	2-2	Cameron 2	11,475	9	1	10					8							3		7	4	6	2				11		5				1
27	(a) Shrewsbury T	D	2-2	Addinall, Smith	5,000	9	1	10					8							3		7	4		2				11	6	5				Rep
Dec 2	(n*) Shrewsbury T	L	1-4	Smith	3,799	9	1	10		4			8							3		7			2				11	6	5				Rep
					App	3	3	3		1			3							3		3	2	1	3				3	2	3				
					Goals	1		2																						2					

*Played at Villa Park, Birmingham.

Attendance Summary

	ATTENDANCES Home	Away	Total	AVERAGE Home	Away	Total
League	277,574	307,336	584,910	12,068	13,362	12,715
FA Cup	11,475	8,799	20,274	11,475	4,400	6,758
Total	289,049	316,135	605,184	12,044	12,645	12,351

1953-54

Division 3 South

Date	Opponent	Result	Scorers	Att.	Allen	Angell	Barley	Brown	Cameron	Clark	Clayton	Fallon	Gullan	Hawkins	Hurrel	Ingham	Kerrins	Mountford	Nicholas	Petchey	Poppitt	Pounder	Powell	Quinn	Shepherd	Smith	Spence	Taylor G	Taylor J	Tomkys	Woods
Aug 19	(h) Brighton & HA	L 1-2	Shepherd	16,546				1	8		6			9		3		7		10	2				11		4		5		
22	(a) Bristol C	W 2-1	Petchey, Cameron	20,602				1	8		6			9		3		7		10	2				11		4		5		
26	(a) Norwich C	D 2-2	Clayton, Hawkins	23,448				1	8		6			9		3		7		10	2				11		4		5		
29	(h) Aldershot	L 0-2		12,008			9	1	8		6					3		7		10	2				11		4		5		
31	(h) Norwich C	L 0-2		11,633			9	1	8		6					3		7	4		2				11	10			5		
Sep 5	(a) Swindon T	W 1-0	Cameron	15,409			9	1	8		6					3		7	4	10	2				11				5		
7	(h) Southampton	L 0-1		11,207			9	1	8		6					3		7	4	10	2				11				5		
12	(h) Walsall	W 2-0	Petchey, Hawkins	12,197		11		1	8		6			9		3		7	4	10									5		2
16	(a) Southampton	L 1-3	Hawkins	16,246				1						9	8	3		7	4						11	10	6		5		2
19	(a) Shrewsbury T	D 1-1	Smith	11,000				1	8		4	6		9		3		7							11	10			5		2
21	(h) Crystal P	D 1-1	Shepherd	7,346				1	8		6			9		3			4						11	10			5	7	2
26	(h) Exeter C	D 0-0		12,946							6		1	9		3			4					8	11	10			5	7	2
30	(a) Crystal P	W 3-0	Smith 2, Shepherd	9,080		6					9		1			3			4					8	11	10			5	7	2
Oct 3	(a) Newport C	L 1-2	Hurrell	6,817		6					9		1		10	3			4						11	8			5	7	2
10	(h) Northampton T	D 1-1	Shepherd	13,207		6					9		1			3			4				5	8	11	10				7	2
17	(a) Torquay U	D 2-2	Smith 2	8,184		9					6		1			3			4				5	8	11	10				7	2
24	(h) Watford	L 0-4		15,442		9		1	8		6					3			4						11	10			5	7	2
Nov 7	(h) Southend U	W 1-0	Tomkys	9,886				1	8		6					3			4	9					11	10			5	7	2
14	(a) Reading	L 1-3	Shepherd	14,786		6		1	8						10	3			4	9					11				5	7	2
28	(a) Millwall	L 0-4		17,452		6		1	8						10	3			4	9					11				5	7	2
Dec 5	(h) Ipswich T	W 3-1	Petchey, Woods, Shepherd	13,720		6		1	10						8				4	9	3				11				5	7	2
19	(h) Bristol C	L 0-1		8,033		6		1	8						10	3			4	9					11				5	7	2
25	(a) Colchester U	L 0-5		6,155		6		1	8							3			4	9	2				11	10		7	5		
26	(h) Colchester U	D 0-0		10,650		6		1	10							3			4	9	2			8	11				5	7	
Jan 2	(a) Aldershot	W 4-1	Petchey 3, Cameron	5,543		6		1	10							3			4	9	2			8				11	5	7	
16	(h) Swindon T	L 0-2		9,032		6		1	10							3			4	9	2			8	11				5	7	
23	(a) Walsall	L 0-2		8,734		6		1	10										4	8	3		9		11				5	7	2
30	(h) Coventry C	L 0-3		5,224		6		1	10		4									9	3			8	11				5	7	2
Feb 6	(h) Shrewsbury T	D 0-0		7,755		6		1	10	9						3			4				5		11	8			2	7	
13	(a) Exeter C	D 0-0		8,000		6		1	8	9						3	11		4			7	5			10			2		
20	(h) Newport C	W 5-1	Cameron 3, Kerrins, Smith	10,433		6		1	10	9						3	11		4			7	5			8			2		
27	(a) Northampton T	L 1-2	Clark	8,259		6		1	8	9						3	11		4			7	5			10			2		
Mar 6	(h) Torquay U	W 5-1	Clark, Smith 2, Kerrins, Cameron	11,137		6		1	8	9						3	11		4			7	5			10			2		
13	(a) Leyton O	D 2-2	Clark, Angell	4,100		6			8	9			1			3	11		4			7	5			10			2		
20	(h) Millwall	W 4-0	Kerrins, Clark, Pounder, Smith	13,402		6		1	8	9						3	11		4			7	5			10			2		
27	(a) Southend U	L 1-4	Angell	10,000		6		1	8	9						3	11		4			7	5			10			2		
Apr 3	(h) Reading	W 2-0	Smith, Tomkys	9,871		6			8	9	4		1			3	11						5			10			2	7	
7	(a) Bournemouth	W 1-0	Clark	5,722	7	6			8	9	4		1			3							5		11	10			2		
10	(a) Ipswich T	L 1-2	Cameron	15,309		6			8	9	4		1			3						7	5		11	10			2		
12	(a) Coventry C	L 1-3	Clark	4,785		6		1	8	9	4					3				10		7	5		11				2		
16	(a) Gillingham	L 0-1		10,169				1	8	9	4					3							5		11	10			2	7	6
17	(h) Bournemouth	W 2-1	Shepherd, Smith	10,811				1		9	4						7			6			5	8	11	10			2		3
19	(h) Gillingham	W 3-1	Smith, Kerrins, Lewin (og)	9,475						9	4		1				7			6			5	8	11	10			2		3
24	(a) Watford	W 2-0	Angell, Cameron	10,711		6			8	9	4		1			3	7						5		11	10					2
26	(h) Leyton O	W 2-1	Cameron, Aldous (og)	9,311		6			8	9	4		1			3	11					7	5			10					2
30	(a) Brighton & HA	L 1-3	Pounder	10,645		6			8	9	4		1			3	11					7	5			10					2
				App	1	31	4	33	38	18	28	1	13	8	6	41	13	10	30	21	14	11	21	10	34	29	5	2	41	20	23
				Goals		3			10	6	1			3	1		4			6		2			7	2				2	1

2 own-goals

FA Cup

Date	Opponent	Result	Scorers	Att.	Allen	Angell	Barley	Brown	Cameron	Clark	Clayton	Fallon	Gullan	Hawkins	Hurrel	Ingham	Kerrins	Mountford	Nicholas	Petchey	Poppitt	Pounder	Powell	Quinn	Shepherd	Smith	Spence	Taylor G	Taylor J	Tomkys	Woods	Round
Nov 21	(h) Shrewsbury T	W 2-0	Hurrell 2	13,076		6		1	8						10	3			4	9					11				5	7	2	1
Dec 12	(h) Nuneaton B	D 1-1	Tomkys	18,316		6		1	8		5				10	3			4	9					11					7	2	2
17	(a) Nuneaton B	W 2-1	Petchey, Shepherd	13,083		6		1	8						10	3			4	9					11				5	7	2	Rep
Jan 9	(h) Port Vale	L 0-1		17,474		6		1	10							3			4	9	2			8	11				5	7		3
				App		4		4	4		1				3	4			4	4	1			1	4				3	4	3	
				Goals											2					1					1					1		

Attendance Summary

	ATTENDANCES Home	Away	Total	AVERAGE Home	Away	Total
League	251,272	251,156	502,428	10,925	10,920	10,922
FA Cup	48,866	13,083	61,949	16,289	13,083	15,487
Total	300,138	264,239	564,377	11,544	11,098	11,288

1954-55

Division 3 South

	Match	Result	Scorers	Att	Angell	Brown	Cameron	Clark	Fidler	Gullan	Ingham	Kerrins	Longbottom	Nicholas	Petchey	Pounder	Powell	Rutter	Shepherd	Silver	Smith	Tomkys	Woods
Aug	21 (h) Watford	W 2-1	Cameron, Clark	19,606	6	1	8	9			3			4		7	5		11		10		2
	24 (a) Southend U	D 2-2	Cameron, Smith	8,505	6	1	8		9					4		7	5	3	11		10		2
	28 (a) Bournemouth	D 2-2	Smith 2	13,665	6	1	8		9					4		7	5	3	11		10		2
	30 (h) Southend U	D 1-1	Shepherd	11,819	6		8		9	1				4		7	5	3	11		10		2
Sep	4 (a) Brentford	D 1-1	Clark	9,783			8		9	1				4	6	7	5	3	11		10		2
	7 (h) Aldershot	W 5-0	Smith 2 (2 pens), Fidler 2, Petchey	10,946			8		9	1				4	6	7	5	3	11		10		2
	11 (h) Newport C	W 2-0	Shepherd, Rutter	13,089			8	9		1				4	6	7	5	3	11		10		2
	15 (a) Aldershot	L 0-2		5,169			8	9		1				4	6	7	5	3	11		10		2
	18 (a) Exeter C	L 1-2	Cameron	8,911			8	9		1	3			4	6	7	5	2	11		10		
	22 (a) Swindon T	L 0-2		6,423	6	1	8	9			3	7		4	10		5	2	11				
	25 (h) Colchester U	W 4-1	Pounder, Clark, Cameron, Elder (og)	11,828	6	1	8	9			3			4	10	7	5	2	11				
	27 (h) Swindon T	W 3-1	Smith 2 (1 pen), Pounder	8,148	6	1	8	9			3			4		7	5	2	11		10		
Oct	2 (a) Norwich C	D 1-1	Smith	20,353	6	1	8	9			3				4	7	5	2	11		10		
	9 (h) Southampton	D 2-2	Smith, Wilkins (og)	16,800	6	1		9			3			4	8	7	5	2	11		10		
	16 (a) Millwall	W 1-0	Clark	21,062	6	1	8	9			3				4	7	5	2	11		10		
	23 (h) Leyton O	W 2-0	Smith, Clark	22,022	6	1	8	9			3				4	7	5	2	11		10		
	30 (a) Brighton & HA	L 1-4	Shepherd	14,825	6	1	8	9			3				4	7	5	2	11		10		
Nov	6 (h) Reading	L 2-3	Shepherd, Smith	13,307	6	1	8	9			3				4	7	5	2	11		10		
	13 (a) Shrewsbury T	L 0-1		7,372	11	1	8		9		3			4	6		5				10	7	2
	27 (a) Bristol C	D 1-1	Tomkys	17,657	6	1	8		9		3	11		4			5				10	7	2
Dec	4 (h) Torquay U	W 4-2	Smith 2 (1 pen), Cameron 2	8,257	6		8	9	7		3	11		1	4			5			10		2
	18 (a) Watford	D 1-1	Cameron	11,427	6	1	8	9	7		3			4				5	11		10		2
	25 (h) Northampton T	W 1-0	Clark	8,666	6	1	8	9	7		3			4				5	11		10		2
	27 (a) Northampton T	W 3-1	Clark 2, Angell	12,623	6	1	8	9	7		3			4			5	2	11		10		
Jan	1 (h) Bournemouth	D 1-1	Angell	8,969	6	1	8	9			3			4			5	2	11		10	7	
	15 (h) Brentford	D 1-1	Clark	9,783	6	1	8	9				11		4			5	3			10	7	2
	22 (a) Newport C	L 0-4		5,457	6	1		9			3	11		4	8		5	2			10	7	
	29 (h) Coventry C	W 3-2	Smith, Cameron, Kerrins	12,471	6	1	8	9			3	7		4			5		11		10		2
Feb	5 (h) Exeter C	L 1-2	Smith	9,574	6	1	8	9			3	7		4			5		11		10		2
	12 (a) Colchester U	L 0-1		4,903	6	1	10	9	7		3			4			5		11		8		2
	19 (h) Norwich C	W 2-1	Angell, Cameron	6,478	6	1	10	9			3	7		4			5		11		8		2
	26 (a) Southampton	D 2-2	Clark, Shepherd	12,396	6	1	10	9			3	7		4			5		11		8		2
Mar	5 (h) Millwall	L 1-2	Shepherd	11,984	6	1	10	9			3	7		4			5		11		8		2
	12 (a) Leyton O	L 0-3		17,513	6	1	10	9			3		8	4			5		11			7	2
	19 (h) Brighton & HA	W 3-2	Clark 2, Shepherd	9,149	6	1	10	9			3	7	8	4			5		11				2
	26 (a) Reading	L 1-3	Kerrins	6,066	6	1	10	9			3	7	8	4			5	2	11				
Apr	2 (h) Shrewsbury T	W 2-0	Clark, Cameron	8,409	6	1	10	9			3	7	8	4			5		11				2
	8 (a) Crystal P	L 1-2	Clark	17,238	6	1	10	9			3			4		7	5		11		8		2
	9 (a) Walsall	L 1-4	Smith	13,018	6	1	10	9			3	11		4		7	5				8		2
	11 (h) Crystal P	W 1-0	Clark	8,922	6	1	10	9			3	7	8	4				5	11				2
	16 (h) Bristol C	D 1-1	Shepherd	12,456	6	1	10	9			3		8	4		7		5	11				2
	20 (a) Gillingham	L 1-3	Pounder	9,528	6	1	10	9			3		8	4		7		5	11				2
	23 (a) Torquay U	L 2-3	Longbottom, Cameron	6,146	6	1	10	9			3		8		4	7		5	11				2
	25 (h) Walsall	D 1-1	Cameron	6,201	6	1	10	9			3		8	4		7		5	11				2
	30 (h) Gillingham	D 1-1	Cameron	9,052	6	1	10	9			3		8	4				5	11			7	2
May	2 (a) Coventry C	L 1-5	Smith	7,381	6	1	10	9			3		8	4				5	11			7	2
				App	41	39	44	39	12	6	38	15	11	40	17	23	36	32	40		33	8	32
				Goals	3		13	15	2			2	1		1	3		1	8		17	1	

2 own-goals

FA Cup

	Match	Result	Scorers	Att	Angell	Brown	Cameron	Clark	Fidler	Gullan	Ingham	Kerrins	Longbottom	Nicholas	Petchey	Pounder	Powell	Rutter	Shepherd	Silver	Smith	Tomkys	Woods	Round
Nov	20 (h) Walthamstow A	D 2-2	Fidler, Smith	16,299	6	1	8		9		3				4	7	5		11		10		2	1
	23 (a) Walthamstow A	D 2-2	Fidler, Tomkys	10,500	6	1	8		9		3				4		5		11		10	7	2	Rep
	29 (n*) Walthamstow A	L 0-4		11,939	6		8	9			3	11		4			5			1	10	7	2	Rep
				App	3	2	3	1	2		3	1		1	2	1	3		2	1	3	2	3	
				Goals					2												1	1		

*Played at Highbury, London.

Attendance Summary

	ATTENDANCES			AVERAGE		
	Home	Away	Total	Home	Away	Total
League	257,936	257,421	515,357	11,215	11,192	11,203
FA Cup	16,299	22,439	38,738	16,299	11,220	12,913
Total	274,235	279,860	554,095	11,426	11,194	11,308

1955-56

Division 3 South

					Angell	Brown	Cameron	Clark	Crickson	Dawson	Dean	Hellawell	Ingham	Kerrins	Longbottom	McKay	Nelson	Petchey	Pounder	Powell	Quinn	Rhodes	Rutter	Shepherd	Smith	Springett	Temby	Tomkys	Woods
Aug	20 (a) Brighton & HA	D 1-1	Clark	14,510	6	1	10	9					3	7	8			4		5				11					2
	22 (h) Brentford	D 1-1	Cameron	11,491	6	1	10	9	4				3	7	8					5				11					2
	27 (h) Southampton	W 4-0	Shepherd 2, Smith, Angell	10,588	6	1	10	9					3	7				4		5				11	8				2
	30 (a) Brentford	L 0-2		12,947	6	1	10				9		3			7		4		5				11	8				2
Sep	3 (a) Shrewsbury T	D 1-1	Shepherd	11,223	6	1	10	9					3	7				4		5	8			11					2
	5 (h) Crystal P	L 0-3		9,009	6	1	10	9					3	7				4		5	8			11					2
	10 (h) Ipswich T	D 1-1	Clark	11,689	6	1	8	9					3	7				4		5	10			11					2
	14 (a) Crystal P	D 1-1	Shepherd	10,543	6	1	10	9					3			7		4		5				11	8				2
	17 (a) Walsall	D 2-2	Smith, Clark	12,427	6	1	10	9					3			7		4		5				11	8				2
	19 (a) Northampton T	L 2-5	Smith 2	9,735	6	1	10	9					3					4	7	5				11	8				2
	24 (h) Torquay U	W 3-1	Cameron 2, Smith	10,462	6	1	10	9					3			7	2	4		5				11	8				
	26 (h) Swindon T	W 1-0	Cameron	5,107	6	1	10	9					3	7				4		5				11	8				2
Oct	1 (a) Newport C	L 1-2	Smith	7,375	4	1	10	9					3	7				6		5				11	8				2
	8 (h) Southend U	L 1-2	Shepherd	11,822	6	1	10	9					3			7		4		5				11	8				2
	15 (a) Exeter C	L 0-2		8,741	6	1	10	9					3		7			4					5	11	8				2
	22 (h) Leyton O	L 0-1		11,782	6	1	10	9					3	11	8			4	7				5						2
	29 (a) Colchester U	L 1-4	Clark	7,339	6	1	10	9									3	4					5	11	8			7	2
Nov	5 (h) Norwich C	L 2-3	Petchey, Smith	10,108	6		10						3					9					5	11	8	1	4	7	2
	12 (a) Bournemouth	L 0-1		6,934	6		10						3		7			9					5	11	8	1	4		2
	26 (a) Millwall	L 0-2		7,602	6	1	10		4		8		3					9	7	5				11					2
Dec	3 (h) Reading	D 3-3	Smith 2, Angell	7,044	6	1	4						3				2	9	7	5	10			11	8				
	17 (h) Brighton & HA	W 2-1	Cameron, Clark	7,604	6	1	10	9					3				2	4	7				5	11	8				
	24 (a) Southampton	L 0-4		9,502	6	1	10	9					3				2	4	7				5	11	8				
	26 (a) Aldershot	W 2-1	Smith 2	6,366	6	1	10						3					4	7				5	11	8			9	2
	27 (h) Aldershot	D 2-2	Cameron 2	8,334	6	1	10	9					3	11				4	7				5		8				2
	31 (h) Shrewsbury T	D 1-1	Smith	7,730	6		10	9					3					4	7				5	11	8	1			2
Jan	7 (h) Gillingham	D 2-2	Smith 2	7,306	11	1	10	9			6		3					4	7				5		8				2
	14 (a) Ipswich T	L 1-4	Clark	12,169	11	1	10	9			6		3					4	7				5		8				2
	21 (h) Walsall	W 3-2	Petchey 2, Pounder	6,527	6	1	8	9					3					4	7				5	11	10				2
	28 (a) Watford	W 1-0	Angell	5,784	6	1		9							8		3	4	7				5		10			11	2
Feb	4 (a) Torquay U	L 0-2		5,176	6	1		9							8		3	4	7				5		10			11	2
	11 (h) Newport C	D 0-0		3,871	6	1		9							8		3	4	7				5		10			11	2
	18 (a) Southend U	L 1-5	Smith	6,951	6	1	8	9									3	4	7				5		10			11	2
	25 (h) Exeter C	W 1-0	Cameron	6,859	6	1	9					11	3		8			4	7				5		10				2
Mar	3 (a) Leyton O	L 1-7	Shepherd	12,614	6	1	9						3		8			4	7				5	11	10				2
	10 (h) Colchester U	W 6-2	Shepherd 2, Kerrins, Cameron, Smith, Petchey	7,905		1	10	9		6			3	7				4		5				11	8				2
	17 (a) Norwich C	L 0-1		13,335	6	1	10	9					3	7				4		5				11	8				2
	24 (h) Bournemouth	L 0-1		5,779	6	1	10	9	4				3	7						5				11	8				2
	30 (h) Coventry C	L 1-2	Cameron	10,898	6	1	10	9			4		3	11	8	7				5									2
	31 (a) Gillingham	W 2-0	Clark, Cameron	5,462	6	1	10	9			4		3	11	8				7	5									2
Apr	3 (a) Coventry C	L 1-4	Clark	16,714	6	1	10	9			4		3							5				11	8			7	2
	7 (h) Millwall	W 4-0	Clark, Shepherd, Ingham, Smith (pen)	13,402			10	9			6		3	7				4		5				11	8	1			2
	14 (a) Reading	L 1-3	Cameron	4,697			10	9			6		3	7				4		5		2		11	8	1			
	21 (h) Watford	W 3-2	Kerrins, Cameron, Angell	7,564	11		10	9			6		3	7				4		5		2			8	1			
	25 (a) Swindon T	W 1-0	Smith	4,617	11		10	9			6		3	7				4				2	5		8	1			
	28 (h) Northampton T	W 3-2	Clark 2, Smith	7,113	11		10	9			6		3	7				4				2	5		8	1			
				App	43	38	43	38	3	1	12	1	41	20	12	6	9	41	19	25	4	4	21	32	37	8	2	8	38
				Goals	4		13	11					1	2				4	1					9	19				

FA Cup

					Angell	Brown	Cameron	Clark	Crickson	Dawson	Dean	Hellawell	Ingham	Kerrins	Longbottom	McKay	Nelson	Petchey	Pounder	Powell	Quinn	Rhodes	Rutter	Shepherd	Smith	Springett	Temby	Tomkys	Woods	Round
Nov	19 (a) Southend U	L 0-2		15,000	6	1	10		4		8		3					9	7				5	11					2	1
				App	1	1	1		1		1		1					1	1				1	1					1	
				Goals																										

Attendance Summary

	ATTENDANCES			AVERAGE		
	Home	Away	Total	Home	Away	Total
League	199,994	212,763	412,757	8,695	9,251	8,973
FA Cup		15,000	15,000		15,000	15,000
Total	199,994	227,763	427,757	8,695	9,490	9,101

1956-57

Division 3 South

Date	Opponent	Result	Scorers	Att	Andrews	Angell	Balogun	Cameron	Dawson	Dean	Hellawell	Ingham	Kerrins	Lay	Locke	Longbottom	Peacock	Petchey	Powell	Quigley	Quinn	Rhodes	Rutter	Springett	Temby	Woods
Aug 18	(a) Reading	L 0-1		11,417	6	11		10			7	3						4	5	9	8			1		2
20	(a) Plymouth A	W 2-1	Angell, Longbottom	15,718	6	11					7	3				8		4		9	10		5	1		2
25	(h) Newport C	D 1-1	Hellawell	7,863	6	11					7	3				8		4		9	10		5	1		2
27	(h) Plymouth A	W 3-0	Quigley 2, Hellawell	8,450	6	11					7	3			10	8		4		9			5	1		2
Sep 1	(a) Colchester U	D 1-1	Quigley	8,179	6	11					7	3			10	8		4		9			5	1		2
6	(a) Northampton T	L 0-3		7,591	6	11					7	3			10	8		4		9			5	1		2
8	(h) Norwich C	W 3-1	Angell, Locke, Quigley	12,631	6	11					7	3			10	8		4		9			5	1		2
10	(h) Northampton T	W 1-0	Longbottom	10,785	6	11					7	3			10	8		4		9			5	1		2
15	(a) Coventry C	L 1-5	Quigley	18,160	6	11					7	3			10	8		4		9			5	1		2
19	(a) Swindon T	L 0-1		8,705	6						7	3	11					4		9	10		5	1	8	2
22	(h) Southampton	L 1-2	Hellawell	12,792	6						7	3	11		10	8		4		9			5	1		2
24	(h) Swindon T	W 3-0	Quigley 2, Temby	9,526	6						7	3	11					4		9	10		5	1	8	2
29	(a) Exeter C	D 0-0		7,312	6	11					7	3			10			4		9			5	1	8	2
Oct 6	(a) Aldershot	L 2-4	Cameron, Hellawell	5,609	6	11		8			7	3			10			4		9			5	1		2
13	(h) Watford	W 3-1	Hellawell, Balogun, Brown (og)	14,211	6		9	8			7	3	11		10			4					5	1		2
20	(a) Shrewsbury T	D 0-0		8,463	6		9	8			7	3	11		10			4					5	1		2
27	(h) Walsall	W 1-0	Kerrins	9,461	6		9	8			7	3	11		10			4					5	1		2
Nov 3	(a) Ipswich T	L 0-4		12,778	6		9	8			7	3	11		10			4					5	1		2
10	(h) Bournemouth	W 2-1	Petchey, Locke	8,554	6		9	8			7	3	11		10			4					5	1		2
24	(h) Millwall	D 0-0		10,427	6	11	9				7	3			10	8		4					5	1		2
Dec 1	(a) Brighton & HA	L 0-1		9,770	6	11					7	3			10	8		4		9			5	1		2
15	(h) Reading	D 1-1	Peacock	5,472	6			10			7	3	11			8	9	4					5	1		2
22	(a) Newport C	D 1-1	Peacock	7,638	6			10			7	3	11			8	9	4					5	1		2
25	(a) Crystal P	L 1-2	Peacock	9,988	6			10			7	3	11			8	9	4					5	1		2
26	(h) Crystal P	W 4-2	Cameron 2, Kerrins 2	5,307	6			9			7	3	11	5	10	8		4						1		2
29	(h) Colchester U	D 1-1	Kerrins	8,801	6			9			7	3	11		10	8		4					5	1		2
Jan 12	(a) Norwich C	W 2-1	Longbottom, Pointer (og)	11,722	6			10			7	3	11			8	9	4					5	1		2
19	(h) Coventry C	D 1-1	Petchey	7,863	6			10			7	3	11			8	9	4					5	1		2
Feb 2	(a) Southampton	W 2-1	Hellawell, Longbottom	17,074	6			10			7	3	11			8	9	4					5	1		2
9	(h) Exeter C	W 5-3	Longbottom 3, Kerrins, Andrews	8,639	6			10			7	3	11			8	9	4					5	1		2
16	(h) Aldershot	L 0-1		10,525	6			10			7	3	11			8	9	4					5	1		2
23	(a) Watford	W 4-2	Temby, Cameron, Balogun, Shipwright (og)	4,428	6		9	10			7	3	11					4					5	1	8	2
Mar 2	(h) Shrewsbury T	W 2-1	Balogun, Temby	9,984	6		9	10			7	3	11					4					5	1	8	2
9	(a) Gillingham	W 1-0	Kerrins	7,581	6		9	10			7	3	11			8		4					5	1		2
16	(h) Ipswich T	L 0-2		12,303	6		9	10			7	3	11			8		4					5	1		2
23	(a) Bournemouth	L 0-1		12,552	6		9	10			7	3	11			8		4					5	1		2
25	(h) Southend U	W 3-0	Peacock, Longbottom, Hellawell	6,412	6			10		4	7	3	11			8	9						5	1		2
20	(h) Torquay U	L 0-1		9,605	6			10		4	7	3	11			8	9						5	1		2
Apr 6	(a) Millwall	L 0-2		10,834	6			10		4	7	3	11			8				9			5	1		2
13	(h) Brighton & HA	D 0-0		6,957	6		9	10	7			3	11			8		4					5	1		2
15	(a) Southend U	L 0-3		6,052	6		9	10			7	3	11			8		4				2	5	1		
19	(a) Brentford	L 0-2		13,841	6			9		10	7	3	11			8		4					5	1		2
20	(a) Walsall	W 2-0	Longbottom 2	7,560	6	11		10				3	7			8	9	4					5	1		2
22	(h) Brentford	D 2-2	Longbottom, Dargie (og)	9,661	6	11					7	3			10	8	9	4					5	1		2
27	(a) Torquay U	L 0-3		8,564	6	11		10			7	3				8	9	4					5	1		2
29	(h) Gillingham	W 5-0	Longbottom 3, Kerrins, Cameron	6,237	6			10			7	3	11			8	9	4					5	1		2
				App	46	16	13	31	1	4	44	46	31	1	19	34	14	43	1	16	5	1	44	46	5	45
				Goals	1	2	3	5			7		7		2	14	4	2		7					3	

4 own-goals

FA Cup

Date	Opponent	Result	Scorers	Att	Andrews	Angell	Balogun	Cameron	Dawson	Dean	Hellawell	Ingham	Kerrins	Lay	Locke	Longbottom	Peacock	Petchey	Powell	Quigley	Quinn	Rhodes	Rutter	Springett	Temby	Woods	Round
Nov 17	(h) Dorchester	W 4-0	Hellawell, Balogun, Locke, Cameron	9,764	6		9	8			7	3	11		10			4					5	1		2	1
Dec 8	(a) Tooting & Mitch	W 2-0	Balogun, Longbottom	11,450	6		9	10			7	3	11			8		4					5	1		2	2
Jan 5	(a) Sunderland	L 0-4		30,577	6			10			7	3	11			8	9	4					5	1		2	3
				App	3		2	3			3	3	3		1	2	1	3					3	3		3	
				Goals			2	1			1				1	1											

Attendance Summary

	ATTENDANCES Home	Away	Total	AVERAGE Home	Away	Total
League	212,466	231,536	444,002	9,238	10,067	9,652
FA Cup	9,764	42,027	51,791	9,764	21,014	17,264
Total	222,230	273,563	495,793	9,260	10,942	10,118

1957-58

Division 3 South

Date	Opponents	Result	Scorers	Att	Allum	Andrews	Angell	Cameron	Colgan	Dawson	Drinkwater	Finney	Fry	Ingham	Kerrins	Locke	Longbottom	Orr	Peacock	Petchey	Powell	Rutter	Smith	Springett	Standley	Tomkys	Woods
Aug 24	(h) Brentford	W 1-0	Petchey	15,734		6	11	8				9		3			7			4		5	10	1			2
26	(h) Colchester U	W 1-0	Cameron	12,328		6	11	8				9		3			7			4		5	10	1			2
31	(a) Southend U	L 0-6		15,883		6	11	8				9		3			7			4		5	10	1			2
Sep 2	(a) Colchester U	L 1-2	Finney	8,992	7	6	11					9		3			8			4		5	10	1			2
7	(h) Brighton & HA	L 0-1		11,139		6	11					9		3	7		8			4		5	10	1			2
11	(a) Swindon T	D 1-1	Angell	10,730		6	11					10		3	7		8		9	4		5		1			2
14	(a) Southampton	L 0-5		15,965		6	11					10		3	7		8		9	4		5		1			2
16	(h) Swindon T	W 2-1	Locke 2	8,413			6	9				8		3	7	10		11		4		5		1			2
21	(h) Newport C	D 1-1	Woods	9,183			6	8				9		3	7	10		11		4		5		1			2
23	(h) Millwall	W 3-0	Locke 3	11,327		6	11	8						3		10	7			4		5	9	1			2
28	(a) Port Vale	L 1-2	Locke	12,816		6	11	8						3		10	7			4		5	9	1			2
30	(a) Millwall	L 0-5		12,784		6	11	8						3		10	7			4		5	9	1			2
Oct 5	(h) Plymouth A	W 1-0	Locke	11,354			6	8		7				3	11	10				4		5	9	1			2
12	(a) Norwich C	L 0-2		19,460			6	8		7				3	11	10				4		5	9	1			2
19	(h) Bournemouth	W 3-0	Angell, Woods, Woollard (og)	9,007			6	8		7				3	11	10				4		5	9	1			2
26	(a) Walsall	W 2-1	Longbottom 2	7,560			6			7				3	11	10	8			4		5	9	1			2
Nov 2	(h) Coventry C	W 3-0	Kerrins 2, Locke	9,246			6			7				3	11	10	8			4		5	9	1			2
9	(a) Shrewsbury T	L 1-2	Longbottom	6,514			6			7				3	11	10	8			4		5	9	1			2
23	(a) Northampton T	W 5-1	Longbottom 4, E.Smith	7,525			6	9		7				3	11		8			4		5	10	1			2
30	(h) Watford	W 3-0	Ingham, Longbottom, Petchey	10,236			6	9		7				3	11		8			4		5	10	1			2
Dec 14	(h) Torquay U	D 1-1	Woods	6,093			6	9		7			1	3	11		8			4		5	10				2
21	(a) Brentford	D 1-1	Cameron	12,804			6	10		7				3	11		8			4		5		1	9		2
25	(a) Gillingham	D 1-1	Standley	7,233			6	10		7				3	11		8			4		5		1	9		2
26	(h) Gillingham	D 1-1	Woods	8,658		6		10		7				3	11		8			4		5		1	9		2
28	(h) Southend U	D 1-1	Standley	10,072			6	10	2	7				3	11		8			4		5		1	9		
Jan 11	(a) Brighton & HA	D 1-1	Longbottom	13,322			6	10		7				3	11		8			4		5		1	9		2
18	(h) Southampton	W 3-2	Longbottom 2, Woods (pen)	8,611			6	10		7				3	11		8			4		5		1	9		2
25	(a) Reading	L 0-3		11,455			6	10		7				3	11		8			4		5		1	9		2
Feb 1	(a) Newport C	L 2-4	Dawson, Longbottom	7,543			6	10		7				3	11		8			4		5		1	9		2
8	(h) Port Vale	W 2-1	Cameron, Longbottom	7,594			6	10		7				3	11		8			4		5		1	9		2
15	(a) Plymouth A	L 1-3	Cameron	17,068			6	10		7				3	11		8			4		5		1	9		2
22	(h) Norwich C	D 1-1	Cameron	7,935			6	10		7		8		3	11					4		5		1	9		2
Mar 1	(a) Bournemouth	L 1-4	Dawson	12,711			6	10	2	7				3	11		8			4		5		1	9		
3	(h) Aldershot	L 0-1		7,744			6	10		7				3	11		8			4		5		1	9		2
8	(h) Walsall	W 1-0	Cameron	6,548			6	9		7				3		10	8			4		5		1		11	2
15	(a) Coventry C	D 1-1	Locke	7,673		11	6			7	1			3		10	8			4		5				9	2
17	(h) Reading	W 3-0	Woods, Longbottom, Petchey	8,838			6			7	1			3		10	8			4	9	5				11	2
22	(h) Northampton T	W 1-0	Longbottom	7,531			6	9		7	1			3		10	8			4		5				11	2
29	(a) Torquay U	L 1-3	Locke	5,172			6	9		7	1			3		10	8			4		5				11	2
Apr 4	(h) Exeter C	D 1-1	Cameron	10,223			6	9		7	1			3		10	8	11		4		5					2
7	(a) Exeter C	D 0-0		7,078			6	10			1			3		11	8	7		4		5			9		2
12	(a) Watford	D 0-0		8,022			6	10		7	1			3		11	8			4		5			9		2
16	(a) Crystal P	W 3-2	Longbottom, Kerrins, Locke	18,712			6	10		7	1			3	9	11	8			4		5					2
19	(h) Crystal P	W 4-2	Kerrins, Longbottom, Cameron, Locke	11,868			6	10		7	1			3	9	11	8			4		5					2
24	(a) Aldershot	D 1-1	Kerrins	4,050			6	10		7	1			3	9		8	11		4		5					2
28	(h) Shrewsbury T	W 3-0	Kerrins 2, Locke	6,193			6	10		7	1			3	9	11	8			4		5					2
				App	1	12	45	37	2	33	11	10	1	46	31	22	40	5	2	46	1	46	17	34	15	5	44
				Goals			2	8		2		1		1	7	13	17			3			1		2		6

1 own-goal

FA Cup

Date	Opponents	Result	Scorers	Att	Allum	Andrews	Angell	Cameron	Colgan	Dawson	Drinkwater	Finney	Fry	Ingham	Kerrins	Locke	Longbottom	Orr	Peacock	Petchey	Powell	Rutter	Smith	Springett	Standley	Tomkys	Woods			Round
Nov 16	(a) Clapton	D 1-1	Dawson	8,000			6	9		7				3	11	10	8			4		5		1			2			1
18	(h) Clapton	W 3-1	Longbottom, Locke, Walsh (og)	12,786			6	9		7				3	11	10	8			4		5		1			2			Rep
Dec 7	(a) Hereford U	L 1-6	E.Smith	14,000		6		9		7				3	11		8			4		5	10	1			2			2
				App		1	2	3		3				3	3	2	3			3		3	1	3			3			
				Goals						1						1	1						1						1	

Attendance Summary

	ATTENDANCES Home	Away	Total	AVERAGE Home	Away	Total
League	215,875	251,072	466,947	9,386	10,916	10,151
FA Cup	12,786	22,000	34,786	12,786	11,000	11,595
Total	228,661	273,072	501,733	9,528	10,923	10,239

1958-59

Division 3

Date	Opponents	Result	Scorers	Att	Anderson	Angell	Cameron	Clark	Colgan	Dawson	Drinkwater	Ingham	Kelly	Kerrins	Locke	Longbottom	Pearson	Petchey	Powell	Richardson	Rutter	Tomkys	Welton	Whitelaw	Woods
Aug 23	(a) Reading	D 2-2	Longbottom 2	16,931		6	10			7	1	3		9	11	8		4			5				2
25	(h) Tranmere R	D 1-1	Cameron	12,393		6	10			7	1	3		9	11	8		4			5				2
30	(h) Colchester U	W 4-2	Kerrins 2, Longbottom, Locke	9,852		6	10			7	1	3		9	11	8		4			5				2
Sep 1	(a) Tranmere R	L 0-2		13,959		6	10			7	1	3		9		8	11	4			5				2
6	(a) Bournemouth	L 0-2		11,890		6	10	11		7	1	3		9		8		4			5				2
9	(a) Doncaster R	L 0-2		10,725		6	10			7	1	3		9	11	8		4			5				2
13	(h) Norwich C	W 2-1	Longbottom, Kerrins	10,498		6	10				1	3		9	11	8		4			5	7			2
15	(h) Doncaster R	W 3-1	Longbottom, Cameron, Kerrins	10,118		6	10			7	1	3		9	11	8		4			5				2
20	(a) Southend U	L 0-4		13,534		6	10			7	1	3		9	11	8		4			5				2
22	(a) Stockport C	W 3-2	Longbottom 3	7,458		6	10			7	1	3		9		8		4			5	11			2
27	(h) Bury	W 2-1	Tomkys 2	9,680		6				7	1	3		9	10	8		4			5	11			2
29	(h) Stockport C	D 0-0		7,458		6	10			7	1	3		9	11	8		4			5				2
Oct 4	(a) Mansfield T	W 4-3	Longbottom, Dawson, Cameron, Angell	10,033		6	10			7	1	3		9	11	8		4			5				2
7	(a) Rochdale	D 2-2	Cameron, Tomkys	4,276		6	10			7	1	3		9		8		4			5	11			2
11	(h) Chesterfield	D 2-2	Kerrins, Tomkys	9,452		6	10			7	1	3		9		8		4			5	11			2
20	(a) Newport C	L 1-3	Cameron	8,410		6	10			7	1	3		9		8		4			5	11			2
25	(h) Halifax T	W 3-1	Longbottom 3	9,607		6	10			7	1	3		9		8		4			5	11			2
Nov 1	(a) Accrington S	W 4-2	Dawson 2, Tomkys, Longbottom	6,498		6	10			7	1	3		9		8		4			5	11			2
8	(h) Southampton	D 2-2	Longbottom, Petchey	11,287		6	10			7	1	3		9		8		4			5	11			2
22	(h) Brentford	L 1-2	Kerrins	13,784		6	10			7	1	3		9		8		4			5	11			2
29	(a) Hull C	L 0-1		11,705	7	6	10				1	3		9		8		4			5	11			2
Dec 13	(a) Swindon T	L 0-2		8,037		6	10				1	3	9	11		8		4			5	7			2
20	(h) Reading	W 2-0	Kerrins, Pearson	6,909		6					1	3	9	11		8	10	4			5	7			2
26	(a) Plymouth A	L 2-3	Angell, Tomkys	30,665		6					1	3	9	11		8	10	4			5	7			2
27	(h) Plymouth A	W 2-1	Pearson, Longbottom	15,768		6					1	3	9	11		8	10	4			5	7			2
Jan 3	(a) Colchester U	L 0-3		8,719							1	3	9	11		8	10	4		6	5	7			2
17	(h) Bournemouth	L 0-4		6,041		6					1	3	9	11		8	10	4	5		2	7			
31	(a) Norwich C	L 1-5	Longbottom	16,781		6	9	11			1	3		7	10	8		4			5				2
Feb 7	(h) Southend U	L 1-3	Petchey	6,361		6		11		7		3		9		8	10	4			5		1		2
14	(a) Bury	L 1-3	Clark	5,072		6		11		7		3			10		8	4	5			9	1		2
21	(h) Mansfield T	D 1-1	Locke	5,007		6		11		7		3			10	8		4	5			9	1		2
28	(a) Chesterfield	W 3-2	Locke 2, Tomkys	8,711		6		11		7	1	3			10	8		4			5	9			2
Mar 7	(h) Newport C	W 4-2	Longbottom 2, Locke, Angell	5,707		6		11		7	1	3			10	8		4			5	9			2
14	(a) Halifax T	L 1-2	Locke	5,586		6		11		7	1	3			10	8		4			5	9			2
16	(h) Bradford C	W 3-0	Pearson 2, Whitelaw	7,578	7	6		11			1	3			10		8	4			5			9	2
21	(h) Accrington S	W 3-1	Anderson, Pearson, Tigue (og)	8,005	7	6		11			1	3			10		8	4			5			9	2
27	(h) Notts C	W 2-1	Whitelaw, Pearson	12,044	7	6		11			1	3			10		8	4			5			9	2
28	(a) Southampton	L 0-1		9,808		6		11			1	3			10		8	4			5	7		9	2
30	(a) Notts C	W 1-0	Angell	6,956	7	6			2		1	3			11	8	10	4			5			9	
Apr 4	(h) Wrexham	W 5-0	Anderson 2, Whitelaw, Angell, Longbottom	8,670	7	6		11			1	3				8	10	4			5			9	2
8	(a) Wrexham	L 0-1		5,738	7	6		11			1	3				8	10	4			5			9	2
11	(a) Brentford	L 0-1		15,905	7	6		11			1	3				8	10	4			5			9	2
18	(h) Hull C	D 1-1	Whitelaw	9,325	7	6		11			1	3			10	8		4			5			9	2
20	(h) Rochdale	W 3-0	Angell, Longbottom, Whitelaw	7,290	7	6		11			1	3			10	8		4			5			9	2
25	(a) Bradford C	L 0-1		6,895		6		11			1	3			10	8		4	9		5	7			2
27	(h) Swindon T	W 2-1	Angell, Tomkys	7,628		6		11			1	3			10	8		4			5	7		9	2
				App	10	45	22	19	1	25	43	46	6	29	25	41	16	46	4	1	44	25	3	11	44
				Goals	3	7	5	1		3				7	6	20	6	2				8		5	

1 own-goal

FA Cup

Date	Opponents	Result	Scorers	Att	Anderson	Angell	Cameron	Clark	Colgan	Dawson	Drinkwater	Ingham	Kelly	Kerrins	Locke	Longbottom	Pearson	Petchey	Powell	Richardson	Rutter	Tomkys	Welton	Whitelaw	Woods	Round
Nov 15	(a) Walsall	W 1-0	Dawson	15,123		6	10			7	1	3		9		8		4			5	11			2	1
Dec 6	(h) Southampton	L 0-1		13,166		6	10			7	1	3		11		8		4			5	9			2	2
				App		2	2			2	2	2		2		2		2			2	2			2	
				Goals						1																

Attendance Summary

	ATTENDANCES Home	Away	Total	AVERAGE Home	Away	Total
League	210,462	244,292	454,754	9,151	10,621	9,886
FA Cup	13,166	15,123	28,289	13,166	15,123	14,144
Total	223,628	259,415	483,043	9,318	10,809	10,063

1959-60

Division 3

Month	Date	Opponents	Result	Scorers	Att	Andrews	Angell	Bedford	Cini	Clark	Collins	Drinkwater	Golding	Hasty	Ingham	Keen	Kerrins	Locke	Longbottom	Pearson	Petchey	Pinner	Rutter	Whitelaw	Whitfield	Woods
Aug	22 (h)	Swindon T	W 2-0	Longbottom, Whitelaw	12,206	11	6	10	7						3				8		4	1	5	9		2
	24 (a)	Southend U	L 2-3	Whitelaw 2	12,197	11	6	10	7						3				8		4	1	5	9		2
	29 (a)	Chesterfield	W 4-0	Pearson 2, Bedford, Whitelaw	8,890	11	6	8							3				7	10	4	1	5	9		2
	31 (h)	Southend U	D 0-0		13,488	10	6	8		11					3				7		4	1	5	9		2
Sep	5 (h)	Newport C	W 3-0	Bedford 2, Longbottom	10,774	11	6	8							3				7	10	4	1	5	9		2
	7 (a)	York C	L 1-2	Pearson	10,593	11		8							3	6			7	10	4	1	5	9		2
	12 (a)	Accrington S	W 2-1	Andrews, Longbottom	5,336	11	6	8							3				7	10	4	1	5	9		2
	14 (h)	York C	D 0-0		11,257	11	6	8					7		3					10	4	1	5	9		2
	19 (h)	Bournemouth	W 3-0	Bedford, Golding, Nelson (og)	11,410	11	6	10					7		3				8		4	1	5	9		2
	21 (a)	Coventry C	D 0-0		16,759	11	6	10					7		3				8		4	1	5	9		2
	26 (a)	Tranmere R	W 3-0	Golding 2, Bedford	11,252	11	6	9				1	7		3				8		4		5		10	2
	28 (h)	Coventry C	W 2-1	Golding 2	16,154	11	6	9					7		3				8		4	1	5		10	2
Oct	3 (h)	Wrexham	W 2-1	Angell 2	12,732	11	6	9					7		3				8		4	1	5		10	2
	5 (h)	Grimsby T	D 0-0		15,257	11	6						7		3	10			8		4	1	5	9		2
	10 (a)	Mansfield T	L 3-4	Locke 2, Petchey	7,526	11	6					1	7		3	10		9	8		4		5			2
	13 (a)	Grimsby T	L 1-3	Angell	6,024	11	6	10							3			7	8		4	1	5	9		2
	17 (h)	Halifax T	W 3-0	Longbottom, Whitelaw, Petchey	13,787	11	6	10					7		3				8		4	1	5	9		2
	24 (a)	Bury	L 0-2		10,079	11	6	10					7		3				8		4	1	5	9		2
	31 (h)	Brentford	L 2-4	Bedford 2	16,532	11	6	10					7		3				8		4	1	5	9		2
Nov	7 (a)	Southampton	L 1-2	Bedford	18,619	11	6	10				1	7		3	9			8		4		5			2
	21 (a)	Shrewsbury T	D 1-1	Bedford	10,084	11	6	10				1	7		3	4					9		5		8	2
	28 (h)	Port Vale	D 2-2	Bedford 2	8,775	11	6	10		7					3	4					9	1	5		8	2
Dec	12 (a)	Barnsley	L 1-2	Bedford	4,450	11	6	10		7		1			3	4			8		9		5			2
	19 (a)	Swindon T	L 1-2	Andrews	5,798	11		9		7		1			3	6			8		4		5		10	2
	26 (h)	Colchester U	W 3-1	Bedford 2, Angell	6,480	10	6	9	7			1			3			11	8		4		5			2
	28 (a)	Colchester U	L 0-2		9,025	10	6	9	7			1			3			11	8		4		5			2
Jan	16 (a)	Newport C	W 3-2	Bedford 3	4,194	10		9				1			3	4	7	11	8		6		5			2
	23 (h)	Accrington S	W 5-1	Andrews 2, Kerrins, Locke, Bedford	4,721	10		9				1			3	4	7	11	8		6		5			2
	30 (a)	Norwich C	L 0-1		17,053	10		9				1			3	4	7	11	8				5		6	2
Feb	6 (a)	Bournemouth	D 1-1	Bedford	9,865	10		9				1			3	4	7	11	8		6		5			2
	20 (h)	Tranmere R	W 2-1	Andrews, Keen	5,019	10		9		11		1			3	4	7		8		6		5			2
	27 (h)	Mansfield T	W 2-0	Woods (pen), Longbottom	7,834	10	6	9		11		1			3	4	7		8				5			2
Mar	5 (a)	Halifax T	L 1-3	Woods (pen)	6,731	11	10	9				1	7		3	4			8		6		5			2
	7 (h)	Reading	W 2-0	Andrews, Bedford	6,715	10	6	9	8	11		1			3	4			7				5			2
	12 (h)	Bury	W 2-0	Cini, Andrews	9,088	10	6	9	8	11		1			3	4			7				5			2
	19 (a)	Port Vale	D 0-0		7,049	10	6	8	7	11		1			3	4					9		5			2
	26 (h)	Southampton	L 0-1		11,734	10	6	9		11		1			3	4	7	8					5			2
	28 (h)	Chesterfield	D 3-3	Bedford 2, Petchey	14,346	10	6	8		11		1			3	4		7			9		5			2
Apr	2 (a)	Reading	L 0-2		8,975	10	6	9		11		1	7		3	4					8		5			2
	9 (h)	Shrewsbury T	D 1-1	Bedford	6,831	10	6	9		11		1	7		3				8		4		5			2
	15 (h)	Bradford C	W 5-0	Bedford 2, Longbottom, Petchey, Andrews	6,798	10		9		11		1	7		3	4			8		6		5			2
	16 (a)	Brentford	D 1-1	Golding	16,025	10		9		11		1	7		3	4			8		6		5			2
	18 (a)	Bradford C	L 1-3	Andrews	6,265	10		9		11		1	7		3	4			8		6		5			2
	23 (h)	Norwich C	D 0-0		15,319	10		9		11		1	7		3	4			8		6		5			2
	30 (h)	Barnsley	W 1-0	Andrews	5,700	10		9		11	8	1	7		3	4					6		5			2
May	4 (a)	Wrexham	D 1-1	Woods	2,819	10		9			8		7	11	3	4					6	1	5			2
					App	46	33	44	7	18	2	27	22	1	46	27	7	10	37	5	41	19	46	15	7	46
					Goals	10	4	25	1				6			1	1	3	6	3	4			5		3

1 own-goal

FA Cup

Month	Date	Opponents	Result	Scorers	Att	Andrews	Angell	Bedford	Cini	Clark	Collins	Drinkwater	Golding	Hasty	Ingham	Keen	Kerrins	Locke	Longbottom	Pearson	Petchey	Pinner	Rutter	Whitelaw	Whitfield	Woods	Round
Nov	14 (a)	Colchester U	W 3-2	Petchey, Bedford, Angell	8,866	11	6	10					7		3	4			8		9	1	5			2	1
Dec	5 (h)	Port Vale	D 3-3	Longbottom 2, Bedford	11,143	11	6	9		7					3	4			8			1	5		10	2	2
	7 (a)	Port Vale	L 1-2	Andrews	9,513	11	6	9		7		1			3	4			8				5		10	2	Rep
					App	3	3	3		2		1	1		3	3			3		1	2	3		2	3	
					Goals	1	1	2											2		1						

Attendance Summary

	ATTENDANCES			AVERAGE		
	Home	Away	Total	Home	Away	Total
League	242,957	215,608	458,565	10,563	9,374	9,969
FA Cup	11,143	18,379	29,522	11,143	9,190	9,841
Total	254,100	233,987	488,087	10,588	9,359	9,961

1960-61

Division 3

					Andrews	Angell	Baker	Barber	Bedford	Bottoms	Carey	Clark	Cockell	Drinkwater	Evans	Golding	Ingham	Keen	Lazarus	Longbottom	Pinner	Rutter	Whitaker	Whitfield	Woods
Aug	20(a) Bournemouth	L 0-1		12,222	10	6			9		2	11		1		7	3	4		8		5			
	25(a) Notts C	L 1-2	Andrews	15,174	10	6			9		2	11		1		7	3	4		8		5			
	27(h) Bradford C	W 1-0	Bedford	7,075		6			10		4	11		1		7	3			8		5		9	2
	29(h) Notts C	W 2-0	Clark 2	8,307	10	6			9		4	11		1		7	3			8		5			2
Sep	3(a) Barnsley	D 3-3	Whitfield 2, Bedford	6,162	10	6			8		4	11		1		7	3					5		9	2
	5(a) Coventry C	D 4-4	Bedford 2, Andrews, Clark	15,804	10	6		7	8		4	11		1			3					5		9	2
	10(h) Newport C	W 2-0	Whitfield, Barber	7,353	10	6		7	8		4	11		1			3					5		9	2
	12(h) Coventry C	W 2-1	Bedford, Woods	9,199	10	6		7	8		4	11		1			3					5		9	2
	17(a) Colchester U	W 1-0	Lazarus	5,750	10	6			8		4	11		1			3		7			5		9	2
	19(h) Brentford	D 0-0		12,863	11	6			8		4			1			3		7	10		5		9	2
	24(h) Grimsby T	W 2-0	Andrews, Longbottom	10,977	10	6					4	11		1			3		7	8		5		9	2
	27(a) Brentford	L 0-2		15,282	10	6					4	11		1			3		7	8		5		9	2
Oct	1(a) Hull C	L 1-3	Bedford	9,333	10	6			8		4	11		1		7	3					5		9	2
	3(h) Reading	W 5-2	Bedford 2, Lazarus 2, Barber	8,402	10	6		7	9			11		1			3	4	8			5			2
	8(h) Torquay U	D 3-3	Lazarus 2, Bedford	7,795	10	6		7	9			11		1			3	4	8			5			2
	15(a) Port Vale	W 1-0	Bedford	8,802		6		7	9	10		11		1			3	4	8			5			2
	22(h) Southend U	W 2-1	Woods, Bedford	6,006		6		7	9			11		1			3	4	8	10		5			2
	29(a) Chesterfield	W 1-0	Carey	4,474		6		11	10		8			1			3	4	7			5		9	2
Nov	12(a) Walsall	L 3-4	Bedford 2, Lazarus	10,044		6			10		8			1			3	4	7	11		5		9	2
	19(h) Shrewsbury T	D 1-1	Bedford	7,680		6			10				4	1	9		3	8	7	11		5			2
Dec	3(h) Tranmere R	W 9-2	Bedford 2, Clark 2, Lazarus 2, Evans 2, Andrews	4,805	10	6			8			11		1	9		3	4	7			5			2
	10(a) Watford	W 3-0	Lazarus, Woods, Clark	15,546	10	6			8			11		1	9		3	4	7			5			2
	17(h) Bournemouth	W 3-1	Bedford 2, Evans	6,952	10	6			8			11		1	9		3	4	7			5			2
	26(a) Bristol C	D 1-1	Bedford	10,484	10	6			8					1	9		3	4	7	11		5			2
	27(h) Bristol C	D 1-1	Woods	15,391	10	6			8			11		1	9		3	4	7			5			2
	31(a) Bradford C	D 1-1	Evans	8,405	10	6			8			11	4	1	9		3		7			5			2
Jan	14(h) Barnsley	W 4-2	Bedford, Andrews, Evans, Keen	8,859	11	6			8				4	1	9		3	10	7			5			2
	23(a) Newport C	W 3-1	Evans 2, Bedford	6,610	11	6			8				4	1	9		3	10	7			5			2
	28(h) Bury	W 3-1	Bedford 3	14,672	11	6			8				4	1	9		3	10		7		5			2
Feb	4(h) Colchester U	W 3-2	Evans, Bedford, Lazarus	10,348	11	6			8				4	1	9		3	10	7			5			2
	11(a) Grimsby T	L 1-3	Bedford	10,599		6		7	8	10				1	9		3	4		11		5			2
	18(h) Hull C	W 2-1	Keen, Bedford	12,725		6			8					1	9		3	4	7	10		5	11		2
	25(a) Tranmere R	W 2-1	Evans, Woods	9,226		6			8					1	9	7	3	4		10		5	11		2
Mar	4(h) Port Vale	W 1-0	Evans	12,711		6	2		8					1	9	7	3	4		10		5	11		
	11(a) Southend U	D 0-0		10,987		6	2		8					1	9		3	4	7	10		5	11		
	18(h) Chesterfield	L 1-2	Bedford	8,858	10	6	2		8					1	9		3	4	7			5	11		
	25(a) Bury	L 0-1		14,701	11	6	2		8				4	1	9		3	10		7		5			
	31(h) Swindon T	W 3-1	Angell, Barber, Evans	14,436	10	11	2	7	8				6	1	9		3	4				5			
Apr	1(h) Walsall	W 1-0	Longbottom	14,288	10	6	2		8					1	9		3	4		7		5	11		
	3(a) Swindon T	L 0-1		11,568	10	6	2		8					1	9		3	4		7		5	11		
	8(a) Shrewsbury T	L 1-4	Evans	8,386		6	2		8					1	9		3	4	7	11		5	10		
	15(h) Halifax T	W 5-1	Bedford 4, Lazarus	9,069	11	6	2		10					1	9		3	4	7	8		5			
	17(a) Halifax T	D 1-1	Andrews	4,194	11	6	2		10					1	9		3	4	7	8		5			
	22(a) Torquay U	W 6-1	Evans 3, Lazarus, Bedford, Opp own-goal	5,436	11	6	2		10					1	9		3	4	7	8		5			
	26(a) Reading	L 1-3	Longbottom	15,058		6	2	11	10					1	9		3	4	7	8		5			
	29(h) Watford	W 2-1	Evans, Longbottom	10,328		6	2	11	10					1	9		3	4	7	8		5			
				App	32	46	13	12	44	2	15	21	8	46	27	8	46	34	29	26		46	8	12	31
				Goals	6	1		3	33		1	6			16			2	12	4				3	5

1 own-goal

FA Cup

					Andrews	Angell	Baker	Barber	Bedford	Bottoms	Carey	Clark	Cockell	Drinkwater	Evans	Golding	Ingham	Keen	Lazarus	Longbottom	Pinner	Rutter	Whitaker	Whitfield	Woods	Round
Nov	5(h) Walthamstow A	W 3-2	Bedford 3	5,373	11	6			10		8			1			3	4	7			5		9	2	1
	26(h) Coventry C	L 1-2	Longbottom	8,927					10			11	6	1			3	4	7	8		5		9	2	2
				App	1	1			2		1	1	1	2			2	2	2	1		2		2	2	
				Goals					3											1						

League Cup

					Andrews	Angell	Baker	Barber	Bedford	Bottoms	Carey	Clark	Cockell	Drinkwater	Evans	Golding	Ingham	Keen	Lazarus	Longbottom	Pinner	Rutter	Whitaker	Whitfield	Woods	Round
Oct	17(h) Port Vale	D 2-2	Lazarus, Rutter	6,600				7	9	10	4	11	6				3		8		1	5			2	1
	19(a) Port Vale	L 1-3	Bedford	6,800	10	6		7	9			11		1			3	4	8			5			2	Rep
				App	1	1		2	2	1	1	2	1	1			2	1	2		1	2			2	
				Goals					1										1			1				

Attendance Summary

	ATTENDANCES			AVERAGE		
	Home	Away	Total	Home	Away	Total
League	229,099	230,200	459,299	9,961	10,009	9,985
League Cup	6,600	6,800	13,400	6,600	6,800	6,700
FA Cup	14,300		14,300	7,150		7,150
Total	249,999	237,000	486,999	9,615	9,875	9,740

1961-62

Division 3

Date	Opponent	Res	Scorers	Att	Anderton	Andrews	Angell	Baker	Barber	Bedford	Bentley	Cockell	Collins	Drinkwater	Evans	Francis	Ingham	Keen	Lazarus	McCelland	Rutter	Slack	Towers	Williams
Aug 19	(h) Brentford	W 3-0	Towers, Bedford, Evans	16,796			6	2	11	8	5			1	9		3	4	7				10	
21	(h) Reading	L 3-6	Lazarus 2, Angell	12,847		11	6	2		8	5			1	9		3	4	7				10	
28	(a) Barnsley	W 4-2	Bedford, Angell (pen), Towers, Evans	7,605		11	6			8	2			1	9		3	4	7		5		10	
30	(a) Reading	W 2-0	Towers 2	19,509		11	6			8	2			1	9		3	4	7		5		10	
Sep 2	(h) Portsmouth	L 0-1		12,856		11	6			8	2			1	9		3	4	7		5		10	
4	(h) Swindon T	W 6-1	Lazarus 2, Towers 2, Barber, Evans	10,112			6		11	8	2			1	9		3	4	7		5		10	
9	(a) Crystal P	D 2-2	Lazarus 2	27,179			6		11	8	2			1	9		3	4	7		5		10	
16	(h) Bournemouth	D 1-1	Lazarus	12,946			6	2	11	8				1		9		4	7		5		10	3
23	(a) Watford	L 2-3	Towers, McCelland	16,426			6	2	11	8				1	9		3	4		7	5		10	
25	(h) Halifax T	W 6-2	Bedford 3, Evans 2, McCelland	11,775			6	2	11	8				1	9		3	4		7	5		10	
30	(h) Hull C	D 1-1	Francis	9,950			6	2	11	8				1		9	3	4		7	5		10	
Oct 7	(a) Newport C	W 4-2	McCelland, Bedford, Barber, Evans	5,440			6	2	11	8				1	9		3	4		7	5		10	
9	(h) Lincoln C	L 1-3	Evans	9,995			6	2	11	8				1	9		3	4		7	5		10	
14	(h) Southend U	W 5-3	Bedford 4, Angell	10,519			6		11	8	2		10	1	9		3	4		7	5			
17	(a) Swindon T	D 0-0		11,314			6		11	8	2		10	1	9			4		7	5			3
21	(a) Grimsby T	D 1-1	Collins	6,420			6		11	8	2		10	1	9			4		7	5			3
28	(h) Coventry C	W 4-1	Barber 2, Bedford, Evans	9,881			6		11	8	2		10	1	9			4		7	5			3
Nov 11	(h) Port Vale	W 2-1	Bedford, Angell (pen)	6,971			6			8	2		10	1	9			4		7	5		11	3
18	(a) Bristol C	L 0-2		10,624			6		11	8	2		10	1	9			4		7	5			3
Dec 2	(a) Notts C	D 0-0		7,980			6			8	2		10	1	9		3	4		7	5		11	
9	(h) Shrewsbury T	W 3-1	Bedford 3	7,326			6		11	8	2			1	9		3	4		7	5		10	
16	(a) Brentford	W 4-1	Bedford 2, McCelland, Reeves (og)	11,800			6		11	8	2			1	9		3	4		7	5		10	
26	(a) Torquay U	D 2-2	McCelland, Keen	4,459			6		11	8	2			1	9		3	4		7	5		10	
30	(h) Torquay U	W 6-0	Evans 3, Towers 2, Collins	9,067			6		11		2		8	1	9		3	4		7	5		10	
Jan 13	(a) Portsmouth	L 1-4	Towers	17,727			6		11	8	2			1	9		3	4		7	5		10	
20	(h) Crystal P	W 1-0	Evans	17,786	6					8	2		11	1	9		3	4		7	5		10	
Feb 3	(a) Bournemouth	L 1-3	Towers	11,645	6				11		2		10	1	9		3	4		7	5		8	
10	(h) Watford	L 1-2	McCelland	11,142	6				11		2		10	1	9		3	4		7	5		8	
16	(a) Hull C	L 1-3	Bedford	3,237	6				11	8			10	1	9		3	4		7	5			2
18	(a) Peterborough U	L 1-5	Collins	11,922					11	8		6	10	1	9		3	4		7	5			2
24	(h) Newport C	W 4-0	Bedford, McCelland, Lazarus 2	7,813			6			8			10	1	9		3	4	11	7	5			2
Mar 3	(a) Southend U	W 3-2	Bedford, Collins, Shields (og)	8,234			6			8			10	1	9		3	4	11	7	5			2
10	(h) Grimsby T	W 3-2	Bedford 2, Angell	8,374			6			8			10	1	9		3	4	11	7	5			2
14	(a) Coventry C	W 3-2	Bedford 3	8,626			6			8			10	1	9		3	4	11	7	5			2
19	(h) Barnsley	W 3-0	Keen, Bedford, Evans	10,150			6			8			10	1	9		3	4	11	7	5			2
24	(h) Peterborough U	D 3-3	Evans, McCelland, Bedford	13,430			6			8			10	1	9		3	4	11	7	5			2
31	(a) Port Vale	W 3-2	Collins, Bedford, Angell	4,936			6			8			10	1	9		3	4	11	7	5			2
Apr 7	(h) Bristol C	W 4-1	Evans 2, Bedford 2	11,364			6			8			10	1	9		3	4	11	7	5			2
11	(h) Bradford	L 1-2	Lazarus	11,291			6			8			10	1	9		3	4	11	7	5			2
14	(a) Bradford	D 3-3	Bedford 3	8,744			6			8	2			1	9		3	4	11	7	5		10	
21	(h) Notts C	W 2-0	Bedford, McCelland	9,911			6			8	2			1	9		3	4	11	7	5		10	
23	(h) Northampton T	W 2-0	Evans, Towers	10,381			6			8	2			1	9		3	4	11	7	5		10	
24	(a) Northampton T	D 1-1	McCelland	12,533						8	2		10	1	9		3	4	11	7	5			6
28	(a) Shrewsbury T	W 2-1	Towers, McCelland	5,823						8	2			1	9		3	4	11	7	5		10	6
30	(a) Lincoln C	W 5-0	Lazarus 2, Towers 2, Collins	6,635			6			8	2		10	1			3	4	11	7			9	5
May 3	(a) Halifax T	D 1-1	Evans	2,060			6			8	2		10		9		3	4	11	7	5	1		
				App	4	4	39	8	23	43	29	1	25	45	43	2	40	46	24	38	43	1	28	20
				Goals			6		4	34			6		18	1		2	12	11			15	

2 own-goals

FA Cup

Date	Opponent	Res	Scorers	Att	Anderton	Andrews	Angell	Baker	Barber	Bedford	Bentley	Cockell	Collins	Drinkwater	Evans	Francis	Ingham	Keen	Lazarus	McCelland	Rutter	Slack	Towers	Williams	Round
Nov 4	(a) Barry T	D 1-1	McLellan (og)	5,500			6			8	2		10	1	9			4		7	5		11	3	1
6	(h) Barry T	W 7-0	Bedford 3, Collins 2, Evans 2	11,328			6		11	8	2		10	1	9			4		7	5			3	Rep
25	(a) Ashford T	W 3-0	Collins, McCelland, Evans	5,000			6			8	2		10	1	9		3	4		7	5		11		2
Jan 6	(a) Burnley	L 1-6	Evans	28,352			6			8	2		11	1	9		3	4		7	5		10		3
				App			4		1	4	4		4	4	4		2	4		4	4		3	2	
				Goals						3			3		4										

1 own-goal

League Cup

Date	Opponent	Res	Scorers	Att	Anderton	Andrews	Angell	Baker	Barber	Bedford	Bentley	Cockell	Collins	Drinkwater	Evans	Francis	Ingham	Keen	Lazarus	McCelland	Rutter	Slack	Towers	Williams	Round
Sep 13	(h) Crystal P	W 5-2	Bedford 2, Francis 2, Angell	10,565			6	2	11	8				1		9	3	4	7		5		10		1
Oct 11	(h) Nottingham F	L 1-2	Towers	11,198			6		11	8	2		7	1	9		3	4			5		10		2
				App			2	1	2	2	1		1	2	1	1	2	2	1		2		2		
				Goals			1			2						2							1		

Attendance Summary

	ATTENDANCES Home	Away	Total	AVERAGE Home	Away	Total
League	252,683	230,878	483,561	10,986	10,038	10,512
League Cup	21,763		21,763	10,882		10,882
FA Cup	11,328	38,852	50,180	11,328	12,951	12,545
Total	285,774	269,730	555,504	10,991	10,374	10,683

1962-63

Division 3

Date	Opponent	Result	Scorers	Att	Angell	Baker	Barber	Bedford	Bentley	Collins	Drinkwater	Dugdale	Evans	Ingham	Keen	Large	Lazarus	Leary	Malcolm	McCelland	Rutter	Smith	Springett	Taylor	Williams
Aug 18	(h) Brighton & HA	D 2-2	Lazarus, Bedford	11,056	6			8	2		1		9	3	4	10	11			7	5				
20	(h) Halifax T	W 5-0	Bedford 2, McCelland, Keen, Lazarus	10,623				8	2	10	1		9	3	4	6	11			7	5				
24	(a) Carlisle U	W 5-2	Lazarus 2 (1 pen), Bedford 2, Evans	8,116				8	2	10	1		9	3	4	6	11			7	5				
27	(a) Halifax T	W 4-1	McCelland, Angell (pen), Bedford, Lazarus	7,070	6			8	2	10	1			3	4	9	11			7	5				
Sep 1	(h) Swindon T	D 2-2	McCelland, Large	12,573	6			8	2	10	1			3	4	9	11			7	5				
3	(h) Crystal P	W 4-1	Bedford 2, Angell (pen), Large	16,853	6			8	2	10	1			3	4	9	11			7	5				
8	(a) Peterborough U	W 2-1	McCelland, Bedford	14,481	6			8	2	10	1			3	4	9	11			7	5				
12	(a) Crystal P	L 0-1		21,958	6			8	2	10	1			3	4	9	11			7	5				
15	(h) Barnsley	W 2-1	Large 2	11,246	6			8	2	10	1				4	9	11			7	5				3
17	(h) Wrexxham	L 1-2	Lazarus	13,175	6			8	2	10	1				4	9	11			7	5				3
22	(a) Northampton T	L 0-1		15,469	3		11	8			1		9		4	6	10			7	5				2
29	(a) Southend U	W 3-1	Barber, Lazarus, McCelland	12,564	6		11		2	10	1				4	9	8			7	5				3
Oct 6	(h) Notts C	L 0-1		15,594	6		11		2	10	1				4	9	8			7	5				3
10	(a) Wrexham	L 1-3	Lazarus	15,417	6		11	10			1		9	3	4		8			7	5				2
13	(a) Bournemouth	L 1-2	Bedford	11,678	6		11	10		8	1		9	3	4		7				5				2
22	(h) Hull C	W 4-1	Bedford 3, Lazarus	18,281	6			8	2		1	5	9	3	10		11		4	7					
27	(a) Bradford	W 3-0	McCelland 3	8,552	6			8	2	10	1	5	9	3			11		4	7					
Nov 10	(a) Bristol C	W 4-2	Bedford 2, Barber, McCelland	13,262	6		11	8	2	10	1	5		3		9			4	7					
17	(h) Reading	W 3-2	Large, Collins, Malcolm	10,238	6			8	2	10	1	5		3		9	11		4	7					
Dec 1	(h) Shrewsbury T	D 0-0		10,360	6	2		8			1	5		3	10	9	11		4	7					
8	(a) Millwall	D 0-0		13,743	6	2		8		10	1	5		3		9	11		4	7					
15	(a) Brighton & HA	D 2-2	Bedford, Lazarus	11,282	6	2		8			1	5		3	10		11	9	4	7					
22	(h) Carlisle U	D 2-2	Lazarus 2	9,733	6	2		8			1	5		3	10		11	9	4	7					
Jan 12	(a) Swindon T	L 0-5		7,450	2		10	8			1			3	5	6	11	9	4	7					
Feb 9	(h) Northampton T	L 1-3	Bedford	14,238	2			8		10	1			3	6		11	9	4	7	5				
23	(a) Notts C	L 2-3	Lazarus, Bedford	8,208	2		11	10			1			3	6		8	9	4	7	5				
Mar 2	(h) Bournemouth	W 1-0	Bedford	8,387	2		11	10			1	5		3	6		8	9	4	7					
9	(a) Coventry C	L 1-4	Leary	15,029	6		11	10				5		3			8	9	4	7		1			2
16	(h) Bradford	L 1-2	Malcolm	7,555	2		11	8						3	6		10	9	4	7		1			5
23	(a) Watford	W 5-2	Bedford 2, Lazarus 2, Malcolm	10,618			11	8						3	4		10	9	6	7		1		2	5
30	(h) Bristol C	W 3-1	Collins, Leary, Barber	5,683			11	8		7				3	4		10	9	6			1		2	5
Apr 1	(h) Colchester U	L 1-2	Malcolm	7,688			11	8		7				3	4		10	9	6			1		2	5
5	(a) Reading	D 1-1	Bedford	7,836			11	8		7				3	4		10	9	6			1		2	5
8	(h) Southend U	W 1-0	Lazarus	7,540			11	8		7				3	4		10	9	6			1		2	5
12	(h) Bristol R	L 3-5	Bedford, Leary, Lazarus	10,169			11	6		10				3	5		8	9	4	7		1		2	
13	(h) Port Vale	W 3-1	Leary 2, Collins	5,690			11	8		10				3	6		7	9	4			1		2	5
15	(a) Bristol R	D 0-0		12,299			11	8		10				3	6		7	9	4			1		2	5
20	(h) Shrewsbury T	W 3-0	Lazarus, Malcolm, Leary	3,890			11	8		10				3	6		7	9	4			1		2	5
22	(a) Colchester U	L 1-2	McCelland	6,556			11	8		10				3	6			9	4	7		1		2	5
25	(a) Hull C	L 1-4	Leary	5,894			11	8		10				3	6			9	4	7		1		2	5
27	(h) Millwall	L 2-3	Leary, McCelland	8,583			11	8		10				3	6			9	4	7		1		2	5
29	(a) Port Vale	L 2-3	Leary, Sproson (og)	5,974	2		11	8		10				3	6		7	9	4			1			5
May 10	(a) Barnsley	D 0-0		4,847		2	11	8		10				3	6		7	9	4			1			5
13	(h) Watford	D 2-2	Barber, Collins	5,040		2	11	8		10				3	6		7	9	4			1			5
18	(h) Peterborough U	D 0-0		5,959	2		11			10				3	4		7	9	8				1	6	5
22	(h) Coventry C	L 1-3	Collins	3,245	2		11	9		10				3	8		7		4				1	6	5
				App	30	6	28	43	16	33	27	10	8	41	41	18	42	24	31	33	17	17	2	14	25
				Goals	2		4	23		5			1		1	5	18	9	5	11					

1 own-goal

FA Cup

Date	Opponent	Result	Scorers	Att	Angell	Baker	Barber	Bedford	Bentley	Collins	Drinkwater	Dugdale	Evans	Ingham	Keen	Large	Lazarus	Leary	Malcolm	McCelland	Rutter	Smith	Springett	Taylor	Williams	Round
Nov 3	(h) Newport C	W 3-2	Barber 2, Large	12,252	6		11		2	10	1	5		3		9	7		4	8						1
24	(h) Hinkley A	W 7-2	Bedford 3, McCelland, Collins, Lazarus, Large	13,008	6			8	2	10	1	5		3		9	11		4	7						2
Jan 26	(a) Swansea T	L 0-2		12,500	2			10			1	5		3	8	6	11	9	4	7						3
				App	3		1	2	2	2	3	3		3	1	3	3	1	3	3						
				Goals			2	3		1						2	1			1						

League Cup

Date	Opponent	Result	Scorers	Att	Angell	Baker	Barber	Bedford	Bentley	Collins	Drinkwater	Dugdale	Evans	Ingham	Keen	Large	Lazarus	Leary	Malcolm	McCelland	Rutter	Smith	Springett	Taylor	Williams	Round
Sep 24	(h) Preston NE	L 1-2	Collins	11,005	3			8		10			9		4	6	11			7	5	1			2	1
				App	1			1		1			1		1	1	1			1	1	1			1	
				Goals						1																

Attendance Summary

	ATTENDANCES			AVERAGE		
	Home	Away	Total	Home	Away	Total
League	229,509	242,193	471,702	9,979	10,530	10,254
League Cup	11,005		11,005	11,005		11,005
FA cup	25,260	12,500	37,760	12,630	12,500	12,587
Total	265,774	254,693	520,467	10,222	10,612	10,409

1963-64

Division 3

Date	Opponents	Result	Scorers	Att	Angell	Bedford	Brady P	Brady R	Collins	Gibbs	Graham	Keen	Lazarus	Leary	McLeod	McQuade	Malcolm	Sibley	Smith	Springett	Taylor	Vafiadis	Whittaker
Aug 24 (a)	Oldham A	L 1-2	Graham	12,969	3	8		5	11	6	10	4	7	9						1			2
26 (a)	Shrewsbury T	W 2-1	Bedford 2	7,951	3	8		5	11	6	10	4	7	9						1			2
31 (h)	Peterborough U	W 3-0	Leary 2, Angell	10,971	3	8		5	10	4	11	6	7	9						1			2
Sep 7 (a)	Southend U	W 3-1	Lazarus 2, Leary	13,145	3	8		5	10	4	11	6	7	9						1			2
9 (h)	Shrewsbury T	L 3-4	Graham 2, Bedford	11,090	3	8		5	10	4	11	6	7	9						1			2
14 (h)	Watford	W 1-0	Bedford	10,829	3	8		5	10	4	11	6	7	9						1			2
17 (a)	Bristol R	D 0-0		12,293	3	8		5	10			6	7	9		11	4			1			2
21 (a)	Colchester U	L 0-2		5,418	3	8		5	10			6	7	9		11	4			1			2
28 (h)	Millwall	W 2-0	Bedford, McQuade	9,788	3	8		5	10	6		4		9		11				1		7	2
30 (h)	Bristol R	W 1-0	Lazarus	8,713	3	8		5	10	6		4	7	9						1		11	2
Oct 4 (a)	Barnsley	L 1-3	Bedford	5,647	3	8		5	10	6		4	7	9		11				1			2
7 (h)	Bournemouth	W 1-0	Angell	10,035	3	8		5	10	6		4	7	9						1		11	2
12 (a)	Mansfield T	L 0-1		10,869	3	8			10	4	11	6		9						1	5	7	2
16 (a)	Bournemouth	L 2-4	Collins, Vafiadis	9,244	3	8		5	10	6		4	7	9						1		11	2
19 (h)	Notts C	W 3-2	Collins, Lazarus, Birkinshaw (og)	7,175	3	8		5	10	6		4	7	9						1		11	2
21 (h)	Hull C	L 0-2		9,836	3			5	10	8		6	7	9		11	4			1			2
26 (a)	Crewe A	L 0-2		5,114	3	8		5	11		10	4	7	9			6			1			2
30 (a)	Hull C	L 0-3		7,932	3	8	2	5	10	9		4	7				6		1			11	
Nov 2 (h)	Crystal P	L 3-4	Collins 2, Bedford	12,241	3	10	2	5	11	6		8	7	9			4			1			
9 (a)	Walsall	W 2-0	Lazarus, Graham	7,961	3	8	2	5			10	6	7	9		11	4			1			
23 (a)	Luton T	D 4-4	Leary 2, Graham, McQuade	6,598	3	9	2	5		4	10	6	7	8		11				1			
30 (h)	Coventry C	L 3-6	Bedford 2, Keen	10,997	3	9	2	5	10			6	7	8		11	4			1			
Dec 14 (h)	Oldham A	W 3-2	Bedford 2, Leary	5,265	2	10	3	5		9		6	7	8		11	4			1			
21 (a)	Peterborough U	L 1-2	Angell	6,418	2	8	3	5		9		6	7	10		11	4			1			
28 (h)	Bristol C	L 0-2		6,917	2	8	3	5		9		6	7	10		11	4			1			
Jan 11 (h)	Southend U	L 4-5	Leary 2, Vafiadis, Bedford	4,694		8	3	5			10	6		9	11		4			1	2	7	
18 (a)	Watford	L 1-3	Graham	11,550		8	3	5			10	6		9	11		4			1	2	7	
Feb 1 (h)	Colchester U	D 0-0		5,225			3	5	8	9	10	6			11	7	4		1		2		
8 (a)	Millwall	D 2-2	McLeod, Leary	11,154	3	8	2	5	7		10	6		9	11		4		1				
22 (h)	Mansfield T	W 2-0	Humble (og), Bedford	4,780	3	8	2	5			10	6		9	11	7	4		1				
29 (a)	Brentford	D 2-2	Bedford 2	12,200	3	8	2	5			10	6		9	11	7	4		1				
Mar 7 (h)	Crewe A	W 2-0	Graham, Riggs (og)	3,676	3	8	2	5		6	10	4		9	11	7			1				
10 (a)	Bristol C	L 1-2	McLeod	8,869	3	8	2			6	10	5		9	11		4	7	1				
14 (a)	Crystal P	L 0-1		15,307	3	8	2	5	7		10	6		9	11		4		1				
20 (h)	Brentford	D 2-2	Bedford 2	9,351	3	8	2	5	11		10	6		9		7	4		1				
27 (h)	Wrexham	W 1-0	Collins	7,867	3	8	2	5	10			6		9	11	7	4		1				
28 (a)	Reading	W 2-1	McLeod 2	7,886		8	3	5	10			6		9	11		4	7	1		2		
30 (a)	Wrexham	W 1-0	Collins	7,790		8	3	5	10			6		9	11		4	7	1		2		
Apr 6 (a)	Port Vale	L 0-2		7,167		8	3	5	10			6		9	11	7	4		1		2		
11 (a)	Coventry C	L 2-4	Collins 2	27,384	2	8	3	5	7	6		10		9	11		4		1				
14 (h)	Reading	W 4-2	Bedford, Keen, Vafiadis, Leary	6,264	3	8	2	5	10			6		9	11		4		1			7	
18 (h)	Port Vale	W 3-0	Bedford 2, Leary	4,955	3	8	2	5	10			6		9	11		4		1			7	
25 (a)	Notts C	D 2-2	Vafiadis, Leary	2,861	3	8	2	5	10			6		9	11		4		1			7	
27 (h)	Barnsley	D 2-2	Bedford 2	8,434	3	8	2	5	11		10	6		9			4		1			7	
29 (h)	Luton T	D 1-1	Bedford	5,025	3	8	2		10			6		9		11	4		1		5	7	
May 1 (h)	Walsall	W 3-0	Keen 2, Collins	5,539		8	3	5	10	6		9				11	4		1		2	7	
				App	39	44	29	43	35	25	21	46	23	43	17	20	31	3	20	26	9	15	17
				Goals	3	23			9		7	4	5	12	4	2						4	

3 own-goals

FA Cup

Date	Opponents	Result	Scorers	Att	Angell	Bedford	Brady P	Brady R	Collins	Gibbs	Graham	Keen	Lazarus	Leary	McLeod	McQuade	Malcolm	Sibley	Smith	Springett	Taylor	Vafiadis	Whittaker	Round
Nov 16 (h)	Gillingham	W 4-1	Bedford, Leary, Malcolm, Graham	12,141	3	9	2	5			10	6	7	8		11	4			1				1
Dec 7 (a)	Colchester U	W 1-0	Leary	6,841	2	8	3	5		9		6	7	10		11	4			1				2
Jan 4 (a)	Carlisle U	L 0-2		15,359	2		3	5	10	9		6	7	8		11	4			1				3
				App	3	2	3	3	1	2	1	3	3	3		3	3			3				
				Goals		1					1			2			1							

League Cup

Date	Opponents	Result	Scorers	Att	Angell	Bedford	Brady P	Brady R	Collins	Gibbs	Graham	Keen	Lazarus	Leary	McLeod	McQuade	Malcolm	Sibley	Smith	Springett	Taylor	Vafiadis	Whittaker	Round
Sep 4 (a)	Aldershot	L 1-3	Bedford	6,800		8	3	5			10	6		9		11	4	7		1			2	1
				App		1	1	1			1	1		1		1	1	1		1			1	
				Goals		1																		

Attendance Summary

	ATTENDANCES Home	Away	Total	AVERAGE Home	Away	Total
League	179,667	223,727	403,394	7,812	9,727	8,769
League Cup		6,800	6,800		6,800	6,800
FA Cup	12,141	22,200	34,341	12,141	11,100	11,443
Total	191,808	252,727	444,535	7,992	9,720	8,891

1964-65

Division 3

Date		Opponent	Result	Scorers	Att	Angell	Bedford	Brady P	Brady R	Collins	Gibbs	Hazell	Hunt	Jacks	Keen	Leach	Leary	McAdams	McLeod	McQuade	Malcolm	Morgan I	Morgan R	Nash	Sibley	Smith	Springett	Taylor
Aug	22	(a) Barnsley	D 0-0		5,544	6	8	2	5	7					10		9		11		4					1		3
	24	(h) Southend U	W 2-0	Bedford, Leary	6,709	6	8	2	5	7					10		9		11		4					1		3
	28	(h) Scunthorpe U	W 2-1	Keen 2	7,674	6	8	2	5	7					10		9		11		4					1		3
	31	(a) Southend U	D 0-0		10,764	6	8	2	5	7					10		9		11		4					1		3
Sep	5	(a) Walsall	L 1-4	Collins	4,190	6	8	2	5	7					10		9		11		4					1		3
	7	(h) Reading	L 0-1		7,233	6	8	2	5	7	4				10		9		11							1		3
	11	(h) Watford	D 2-2	Bedford, Leary	8,833	6	8	2	5	7					10		9		11		4					1		3
	16	(a) Reading	L 3-5	Keen 2, Bedford	10,258	6	8	2	5	7	4				10		9		11							1		3
	18	(a) Workington	D 0-0		7,400	6	8	2	5	10					4		9		11						7		1	3
	25	(h) Hull C	W 2-1	Keen, McAdams	6,639		10	2	5	8					6			9	11		4	7		3			1	
Oct	3	(a) Gillingham	D 2-2	Keen, Bedford	12,561		10	2	5	8		4			6			9				7	11	3			1	
	5	(h) Shrewsbury T	W 2-1	Bedford, R.Morgan	5,722		10	2	5	8		4			6			9				7	11	3			1	
	9	(h) Brentford	L 1-3	Keen	11,063		10	2	5	8					6			9			4	7	11	3			1	
	13	(a) Bristol C	L 0-2		11,133		10	2	5	8		4			6			9				7	11	3			1	
	17	(a) Colchester U	W 2-1	Collins, Jones (og)	3,529		10	2	5	8		4			6			9				7	11	3			1	
	19	(h) Bristol C	W 1-0	Bedford	5,578		10	2	5	8		4			6		9					7	11	3			1	
	23	(h) Port Vale	W 3-1	Bedford, I.Morgan, R.Morgan	4,489		10	2	5	8		4			6		9					7	11	3			1	
	30	(a) Carlisle U	L 0-2		9,483		10	2	5	8		4			6		9					7	11	3			1	
Nov	6	(h) Luton T	W 7-1	Bedford 3, Keen 3 (2 pens), R.Morgan	5,175		10	2	5	8		4			6		9					7	11	3			1	
	21	(h) Grimsby T	D 1-1	R.Morgan	6,213		10		5	8		4			6		9					7	11	3		1		2
	28	(a) Peterborough U	L 1-6	Collins	8,337		10		5	8		4			6		9		7				11	3		1		2
Dec	11	(h) Barnsley	W 3-2	Bedford 3	3,364		10	2	5			6			8			9	11		4	7		3		1		
	18	(a) Scunthorpe U	L 1-2	McAdams	5,187		10	2	5	8		3			6			9	11		4	7				1		
	26	(a) Bristol R	L 1-3	R.Morgan	17,698		10	2	5	8		3			6			9			4	7	11			1		
	28	(h) Bristol R	W 3-1	Bedford 2, Keen	5,220		10		3	8		2	5		6			9			4	7	11			1		
Jan	1	(h) Walsall	W 1-0	Bedford	4,841		10		3	8		2	5		6			9			4	7	11			1		
	16	(a) Watford	W 2-0	Leary, I.Morgan	7,526				3	10		2	5		6		8	9			4	7	11			1		
	29	(h) Bournemouth	D 1-1	Bedford	3,520		8		3	10		2	5		6			9			4	7	11			1		
Feb	6	(a) Hull C	L 1-3	McAdams	23,574		10		3			2	5		6		8	9	11		4	7				1		
	13	(h) Gillingham	W 3-1	Bedford, Collins, McAdams	6,633		10		3	8		2	5		6			9			4	7	11			1		
	20	(a) Brentford	L 2-5	I.Morgan, Keen	12,400		10		3	8		2	5		6			9			4	7	11			1		
	26	(h) Colchester U	W 5-0	McAdams 3, Bedford, Leach	4,220		10		6			2	5		4	8		9				7	11	3		1		
Mar	6	(a) Bournemouth	L 0-2		6,315					8		2	5		6	10		9	11		4	7		3		1		
	12	(h) Carlisle U	L 1-2	Bedford	5,934		8			10		2	5		6			9			4	7	11	3		1		
	15	(a) Mansfield T	L 1-8	Bedford	9,180		8		5	10		2			6			9			4	7	11			1		3
	20	(a) Luton T	L 0-2		3,998		8	2	5	10		4			6			9				7	11				1	3
	26	(h) Mansfield T	W 2-0	Bedford, Collins	5,400		8	2	5	10		4			6		9		11				7			1		3
	31	(a) Exeter C	D 2-2	Leary 2	5,615			2	5						6	10	9	8	11				7		4		1	3
Apr	3	(a) Grimsby T	D 0-0		3,974			2	5			4			6	10	9	8	11				7				1	3
	5	(h) Workington	W 2-1	Hazell, Leary	4,642		10	2	5			4			6	8	9		11				7				1	3
	10	(h) Peterborough U	W 3-2	Bedford, Leary, Collins	4,971		8	2	5	10		4			6		9		11				7				1	3
	12	(a) Shrewsbury T	L 2-3	McAdams, I.Morgan	3,415			2	5	8					6		10	9	11			7			4		1	3
	16	(a) Oldham A	L 3-5	Collins 2, Keen	7,951			2	5	8					6		9	10	11			7			4		1	3
	17	(a) Port Vale	D 0-0		4,816		8	2	5	7					6		9	10	11						4		1	3
	19	(h) Oldham A	D 1-1	Leary	3,260		10	2	5	8					6		9		11			7		3	4		1	
	23	(h) Exeter C	D 0-0		4,062		8	2	5	7				10	6			9			4	11				1		3
					App	9	40	33	44	40	2	29	10	1	46	5	26	27	24		22	30	27	17	6	26	20	22
					Goals		23			8		1			13	1	8	8				4	5					

1 own-goal

FA Cup

Date		Opponent	Result	Scorers	Att	Angell	Bedford	Brady P	Brady R	Collins	Gibbs	Hazell	Hunt	Jacks	Keen	Leach	Leary	McAdams	McLeod	McQuade	Malcolm	Morgan I	Morgan R	Nash	Sibley	Smith	Springett	Taylor	Round
Nov	14	(h) Bath C	W 2-0	Collins, Leary	7,398		10	2	5	8		4			6		9					7	11	3		1			1
Dec	5	(h) Peterborough U	D 3-3	R.Brady, Keen (pen), Bedford	6,502	3	9		5	8		2			6		10				4	7	11			1			2
	9	(a) Peterborough U	L 1-2	McAdams	15,000		10	2	5	7		3			6		9	8			4		11			1			Rep
					App	1	3	2	3	3		3			3		3	1			2	2	3	1		3			
					Goals		1		1	1					1		1	1											

League Cup

Date		Opponent	Result	Scorers	Att	Angell	Bedford	Brady P	Brady R	Collins	Gibbs	Hazell	Hunt	Jacks	Keen	Leach	Leary	McAdams	McLeod	McQuade	Malcolm	Morgan I	Morgan R	Nash	Sibley	Smith	Springett	Taylor	Round
Sep	2	(h) Aldershot	W 5-2	Bedford 2, Collins 2, Angell	3,528	6	8	2	5	7					10		9			11	4					1		3	1
	23	(a) Reading	L 0-4		7,271	6	10	2	5	7					4		8		11						9		1	3	2
					App	2	2	2	2	2					2		2		1	1	1				1	1	1	2	
					Goals	1	2			2																			

Attendance Summary

	ATTENDANCES			AVERAGE		
	Home	Away	Total	Home	Away	Total
League	131,395	194,848	326,243	5,713	8,472	7,092
League Cup	3,528	7,271	10,799	3,528	7,271	5,400
FA Cup	13,900	15,000	28,900	6,950	15,000	9,633
Total	148,823	217,119	365,942	5,724	8,685	7,175

1965-66

Division 3

Date		Opponent	Result	Scorers	Att	Allen	Bedford	Brady	Collins	Hazell	Hunt	Keen	Langley	Lazarus	Leach	Leary	McAdams	Marsh	Morgan I	Morgan R	Mortimore	Moughton	Sanderson	Sibley	Smith	Springett	Taylor	Watson
Aug	21 (a)	Brentford	L 1-6	R.Morgan	15,209	8		5	7	4		6	3				9			11			10		1			2
	23 (h)	Brighton & HA	W 4-1	Keen (pen), Collins, Allen, McAdams	10,480	8			7	6	5	4	3				9			11			10			1		2
	28 (h)	Mansfield T	L 1-2	McAdams	6,405	8			7	4	5	6	3				9			11			10			1		2
Sep	4 (a)	Hull C	W 3-1	Allen 2, R.Morgan	20,478	8			7	6	5	4	3				9			11			10			1		2
	11 (h)	Reading	L 0-2		6,800	8			7	6		4	3				9			11	5		10			1		2
	14 (a)	Scunthorpe U	W 2-1	Allen, Collins	5,362	8			7	6		4	3		9					11	5		10			1		2
	18 (a)	Exeter C	D 0-0		6,223	8			7	6		4	3		9					11	5		10			1		2
	25 (h)	Peterborough U	W 2-1	Collins, Langley (pen)	5,094	8			7	4		6	3			9				11	5		10			1		2
Oct	2 (a)	Millwall	L 1-2	Leach	14,465	8			7	4*		6	3		9				11		5		10	12	1			2
	4 (h)	Scunthorpe U	W 1-0	Keen	6,726	8				4		6	3		9				7	11	5		10	12		1		2*
	9 (a)	York C	D 2-2	Allen, I.Morgan	6,553	8				4		6	3		9				7	11	5		10			1	2	
	16 (h)	Oxford U	L 2-3	Sanderson, Allen	8,448	8				4		6	3		9				7	11	5		10			1		2
	23 (a)	Swansea T	L 2-4	Collins, Allen	7,949	8			7*	6		10	3		9					11	5		12	4		1	2	
	30 (h)	Walsall	W 2-1	Sibley, Langley (pen)	5,228	8			7	12		4	3		9					11	5*		10	6	1		2	
Nov	5 (a)	Workington	D 1-1	McAdams	4,464	8			11		5	4	3	7			9						10	6		1		2
	20 (a)	Southend U	W 3-1	Allen 2, Lazarus	6,690	9			8		5	4	3	7						11			10	6		1		2
	23 (a)	Brighton & HA	W 2-0	Allen 2	10,689	9			8		5	4	3	7						11			10	6		1		2
	27 (h)	Swindon T	W 3-2	Allen 3	6,872	9			8		5	4	3	7						11			10	6		1		2
Dec	11 (h)	Grimsby T	W 3-0	Collins, R.Morgan, Thompson (og)	6,671	9			8		5	4	3	7						11			10	6		1		2
	18 (a)	Oxford U	W 3-1	Allen 2, R.Morgan	8,786	9			8		5	4	3	7						11			10	6		1		2
Jan	1 (h)	York C	W 7-2	Allen 3, Collins 2, Lazarus, R.Morgan	7,811	9			8		5	4	3	7						11			10	6		1		2
	8 (a)	Bournemouth	D 1-1	R.Morgan	7,616	9			8		5	4	3	7						11			10	6		1		2
	15 (h)	Swansea T	W 6-2	R.Morgan 3, Collins 2, Lazarus	7,042	9			8		5	4	3	7						11			10	6		1		2
	29 (h)	Brentford	W 1-0	R.Morgan	14,506	9			8		5	4	3	7						11			10	6		1		2
Feb	5 (a)	Mansfield T	L 1-2	Collins	4,166				8		5	4	3	7	9					11			10	6		1		2
	15 (h)	Watford	D 1-1	Langley (pen)	8,191	9			8		5	4	3	7						11			10	6		1		2
	19 (h)	Hull C	D 3-3	Collins 3	12,327	9*			8	12	5	4	3	7						11			10	6		1		2
Mar	5 (a)	Watford	W 2-1	Keen, R.Morgan	11,600	9			8		5	4	3	7						11			10	6		1		2
	12 (h)	Exeter C	W 1-0	Allen	7,542	9			8		5	4	3	7	10					11				6		1		2
	19 (a)	Peterborough U	D 1-1	Collins	7,487	9			8		5	4	3	7				10		11				6		1		2
	26 (h)	Millwall	W 6-1	Marsh 2, Collins, Allen, Lazarus, R.Morgan	16,610	9			8*		5	4	3	7				10		11			12	6		1		2
Apr	2 (h)	Workington	W 4-1	Allen 2, Marsh, Lazarus	8,016	9					5	4	3	7				10		11			8	6		1		2
	8 (h)	Bristol R	W 4-1	Allen, Collins, Marsh, Lazarus	13,372	9			8		5	4	3	7				10		11				6		1		2
	9 (a)	Shrewsbury T	D 0-0		4,791	9					5	4	3	7				10		11			8	6		1		2
	12 (a)	Bristol R	L 0-1		9,203	12			10		5	4	3	7				9*		11			8	6		1		2
	16 (h)	Southend U	W 2-1	Lazarus 2	7,028				7		5	4	3	9				10		11			8	6		1		2
	23 (a)	Swindon T	L 1-2	Keen	13,802	9					5	4	3	7				10		11			8	6		1		2
	25 (h)	Gillingham	L 1-3	Marsh	7,582	9			8	6	5	4	3	7*				10		11			12			1		2
	30 (h)	Shrewsbury T	W 2-1	Allen, Marsh	5,713	9			7		5	4	3					10		11			8	6		1		2
May	2 (h)	Oldham A	D 1-1	Allen	6,850	9			8		5	4	3					10	7	11			6			1		2
	7 (a)	Grimsby T	L 2-4	R.Morgan, Marsh	5,586	9				2	5	4	3	7				10		11			8	6		1		
	13 (a)	Reading	L 1-2	Collins	6,554	9			8	6	5	4	3						7	11			10			1	2	
	18 (a)	Gillingham	L 1-3	Collins	7,147	9			8		5*	4	3	12				10	7	11			6			1		2
	21 (h)	Bournemouth	W 5-0	Lazarus 3, Allen 2	4,732	9						5	3	7				10	8	11		6	4			1		2
	25 (a)	Oldham A	W 2-0	Allen, Marsh	7,969	9						5	3	7				10	8	11		6				1	4	2
	28 (a)	Walsall	W 1-0	Allen	8,103	9				2		5	3	7				10	11	8		6	4			1		
					App	43		1	36	17	32	46	46	28	10	1	6	16	10	44	10	3	39	27	3	43	5	40
					Sub	1				2				1									3	2				
					Goals	30			18			4	3	11	1		3	8	1	13			1	1				

1 own-goal

FA Cup

Date		Opponent	Result	Scorers	Att	Allen	Bedford	Brady	Collins	Hazell	Hunt	Keen	Langley	Lazarus	Leach	Leary	McAdams	Marsh	Morgan I	Morgan R	Mortimore	Moughton	Sanderson	Sibley	Smith	Springett	Taylor	Watson	Round
Nov	13 (a)	Colchester U	D 3-3	Collins, Allen, Sanderson	6,693	8			7		5	4	3				9			11			10	6		1		2	1
	17 (h)	Colchester U	W 4-0	Allen 2, R.Morgan, Sanderson	6,166	8			7		5	4	3				9			11			10	6		1		2	Rep
Dec	4 (h)	Guildford C	W 3-0	Hunt (og), Sibley, Lazarus	8,343	9			8		5	4	3	7						11			10	6		1		2	2
Jan	22 (h)	Shrewsbury T	D 0-0		15,738	9			8		5	4	3	7						11			10	6		1		2	3
	26 (a)	Shrewsbury T	L 0-1		14,779	9			8		5	4	3	7						11			10	6		1		2	Rep
					App	5			5		5	5	5	3			2			5			5	5		5		5	
					Goals	3			1					1						1			2	1					

1 own-goal

League Cup

Date		Opponent	Result	Scorers	Att	Allen	Bedford	Brady	Collins	Hazell	Hunt	Keen	Langley	Lazarus	Leach	Leary	McAdams	Marsh	Morgan I	Morgan R	Mortimore	Moughton	Sanderson	Sibley	Smith	Springett	Taylor	Watson	Round
Sep	1 (h)	Walsall	D 1-1	Sissons (og)	3,529	8	10		11	6	5	4	3				9						7			1		2	1
	7 (a)	Walsall	L 2-3	R.Morgan, Collins	12,236	8			7	6	5	4	3				9			11			10			1		2	Rep
					App	2	1		2	2	2	2	2				2			1			2			2		2	
					Goals				1											1									

1 own-goal

Substitutions are denoted by including these symbols:
Number 12 = *; 13 = †; 14 = ‡; 15 = §; 16 = °.

Attendance Summary

	ATTENDANCES			AVERAGE		
	Home	Away	Total	Home	Away	Total
League	190,046	200,892	390,938	8,263	8,734	8,499
League Cup	3,529	12,236	15,765	3,529	12,236	7,883
FA Cup	30,247	21,472	51,719	10,082	10,736	10,344
Total	223,822	234,600	458,422	8,290	9,023	8,649

1966-67

Division 3

Date	Opponent	Result	Scorers	Att	Allen	Clement	Collins	Hazell	Hunt	Keen	Keetch	Kelly	Langley	Lazarus	Leach	Marsh	Morgan I	Morgan R	Moughton	Sanderson	Sibley	Springett	Watson	Wilks
Aug 20(h)	Shrewsbury T	D 2-2	Allen, Marsh	6,343	9		8	3	5	4				7		10		11			6	1	2	
27(a)	Watford	L 0-1		9,957	9			2	5	4			3	7		10		11		8	6	1		
Sep 3(h)	Swindon T	W 3-1	Lazarus 2, R.Morgan	7,900	9			3	5	4				7		10		11		8	6	1	2	
6(h)	Middlesbrough	W 4-0	Marsh 3, Allen	8,807	9			3	5	4				7		10		11		8	6	1	2	
10(a)	Reading	D 2-2	Langley (pen), I.Morgan	7,792	9			3		5			12	7		10	8	11		4	6	1	2*	
17(h)	Doncaster R	W 6-0	R.Morgan 2, Keen 2, Sanderson, Marsh	8,090	9			2	5	4			3	7		10		11		8	6	1		
24(a)	Mansfield T	W 7-1	Marsh 3, Allen 2, Langley (pen), Sanderson	6,262	9			2	5	4			3			10	7	11		8	6	1		
26(a)	Middlesbrough	D 2-2	Marsh, Lazarus	13,091	9			2	5	4			3	7		10		11		8	6	1		
Oct 1(h)	Grimsby T	W 5-1	Allen 2, Marsh, Lazarus, R.Morgan	9,097	9			2	5	4			3	7		10	8	11			6	1		
8(h)	Swansea T	W 4-2	Allen 2, Sanderson, Marsh	11,047	9			2	5	4			3	7		10		11		8	6	1		
15(a)	Bournemouth	W 3-1	R.Morgan 2, Marsh	12,402	9			2	5	4			3	7		10		11		8	6	1		
19(a)	Torquay U	D 1-1	Langley (pen)	7,698					5	4			3	7	9	10		11		8	6	1	2	
22(h)	Leyton O	W 4-1	Allen 2, Lazarus, Marsh	16,719	9			2	5	4			3	7		10		11		8	6	1		
29(a)	Gillingham	D 2-2	Keen, Marsh	11,801	9			2	5	4			3	7		10		11		8	6	1		
Nov 5(h)	Workington	W 4-1	Marsh 2, Langley (pen), Allen	9,094	9			2	5	4			3	7		10		11		8	6	1		
12(a)	Scunthorpe U	W 2-0	Marsh 2	4,912	9			2	5	4			3	7		10		11		8	6	1		
15(h)	Torquay U	W 2-1	R.Morgan, Allen	10,385	9			2	5	4			3	7		10		11		8	6	1		
19(h)	Oldham A	L 0-1		14,413	9			2	5	4			3	7		10		11		8	6	1		
Dec 3(h)	Bristol R	W 3-0	Allen, Sanderson, Lazarus	13,312	9				5	4			3	7		10		11		8	6	1	2	
10(a)	Colchester U	W 3-1	R.Morgan 2, Marsh	8,195	9				5	4			3	7		10		11		8	6	1	2	
17(a)	Shrewsbury T	D 0-0		6,520	9*				5	4			3	7		10	12	11		8	6	1	2	
26(h)	Brighton & HA	W 3-0	Sanderson, Lazarus, Marsh	17,875	9				5	4			3	7		10		11		8	6	1	2	
27(a)	Brighton & HA	D 2-2	R.Morgan, Wilks	22,947					5	4			3	7		10		11		8	6	1	2	9
31(h)	Watford	W 4-1	Marsh 2, Sibley, Lazarus	17,703	9				5	4			3	7		10		11		8	6	1	2	
Jan 14(h)	Reading	W 2-1	Marsh, R.Morgan	14,341	9				5	4			3	7		10		11		8	6	1	2	
21(a)	Doncaster R	D 1-1	Keen	12,062	9				5	4			3	7		10		11		8	6	1	2	
Feb 4(h)	Mansfield T	D 0-0		14,721	9			2	5	4			3	7		10		11		8	6	1		
11(a)	Grimsby T	D 1-1	I.Morgan	7,012	9			2	5	4			3	7		10	8	11			6	1		
20(a)	Peterborough U	W 2-0	Crawford (og), Lazarus	6,410	9			2	5	4			3	7		10		11		8	6	1		
25(a)	Swansea T	W 3-1	Lazarus 3	11,000				2	5	4			3	7		10*	12	11		8	6	1		9
Mar 7(h)	Bournemouth	W 4-0	Marsh 2, Allen, Keen	21,558	9			2	5	4			3	7		10	12	11		8*	6	1		
11(h)	Peterborough U	D 0-0		16,716	9			2	5	4	3			7		10	8	11			6	1		
18(a)	Leyton O	D 0-0		14,607	9			2	5	4			3	7		10		11		8	6	1		
24(h)	Darlington	W 4-0	Marsh, Langley (pen), Lazarus, Allen	18,601	9			2	5	4			3	7		10	11			8	6	1		
25(h)	Gillingham	W 2-0	I.Morgan, Marsh	14,712	9			2	5	4			3	7		10	11			8	6	1		
27(a)	Darlington	D 0-0		9,914	9			2	5	4			3	7		10		11		8	6	1		
Apr 1(a)	Workington	W 2-0	I.Morgan, Langley (pen)	4,010	9			2	5	4			3	7*		10	12	11	6	8		1		
8(h)	Scunthorpe U	W 5-1	Marsh 2, Lazarus 2, Keen	13,113	9	5		2		4			3	7		10		11	6	8		1		
11(a)	Walsall	L 0-2		11,881	9			2	5	4	12		3	7		10*		11		8	6	1		
15(a)	Oldham A	W 1-0	Wilks	14,359	9			2	5	4			3				7	11		8	6	1	12	10*
22(h)	Oxford U	W 3-1	Wilks 2, Lazarus	15,365	9			2	5	4			3	7				11		8	6	1		10
25(h)	Walsall	D 0-0		11,860	9			2	5	4			3	7				11		8	6	1		10
29(a)	Bristol R	L 1-2	Leach	17,600				3	5	4				7	9		8	11	6			1	2	10
May 2(a)	Swindon T	D 1-1	Wilks	21,210	9			6	5	4			3	7			8	11				1	2	10
6(h)	Colchester U	W 2-1	Sanderson, Allen	10,935	9			2	5	4			3	7		10		11		8	6	1		
13(a)	Oxford U	L 1-2	Marsh	10,141	9			2	5	4			3	7		10		11		8	6	1		
				App	42	1	1	37	44	46	1		40	44	2	41	10	44	3	40	42	46	15	7
				Sub app							1		1				4						1	
				Goals	16					6			5	16	1	30	4	11		6	1			5

1 own-goal

FA Cup

Date	Opponent	Result	Scorers	Att	Allen	Clement	Collins	Hazell	Hunt	Keen	Keetch	Kelly	Langley	Lazarus	Leach	Marsh	Morgan I	Morgan R	Moughton	Sanderson	Sibley	Springett	Watson	Wilks	Round
Nov 26(h)	Poole T	W 3-2	Marsh 3	9,534	9			2*	5	4		1	3	7		10	12	11		8	6				1
Jan 7(h)	Bournemouth	W 2-0	Langley (pen), Lazarus	12,102	9				5	4			3	7		10		11		8	6	1	2		2
28(a)	Sheffield W	L 0-3		40,038	9				5	4			3	7		10	12	11		8	6	1	2*		3
				App	3			1	3	3		1	3	3		3		3		3	3	2	2		
				Sub app													2								
				Goals									1	1		3									

League Cup

Date	Opponent	Result	Scorers	Att	Allen	Clement	Collins	Hazell	Hunt	Keen	Keetch	Kelly	Langley	Lazarus	Leach	Marsh	Morgan I	Morgan R	Moughton	Sanderson	Sibley	Springett	Watson	Wilks	Round
Aug 23(h)	Colchester U	W 5-0	Marsh 4, Lazarus	5,497	9				5	4			3	7		10		11		8	6	1	2		1
Sep 14(a)	Aldershot	D 1-1	Allen	5,349	9			2	5	4			3	7		10	8	11		6		1			2
20(h)	Aldershot	W 2-0	Langley (pen), Marsh	7,848	9			2	5	4			3	7		10		11		8	6	1			Rep
Oct 12(h)	Swansea T	W 2-1	Hazell, Keen	12,988	9			3	5	4				7		10		11		8	6	1	2		3
25(h)	Leicester C	W 4-2	Allen 2, R.Morgan, Lazarus	20,735	9			2	5	4			3	7		10		11		8	6	1			4
Dec 7(h)	Carlisle U	W 2-1	Marsh 2	19,146	9				5	4			3	7		10		11		8	6	1	2		5
Jan 17(a)	Birmingham C	W 4-1	Marsh, R.Morgan, Lazarus, Allen	34,295	9				5	4			3	7		10		11		8	6	1	2		SF/1
Feb 7(h)	Birmingham C	W 3-1	Marsh 2, Keen	24,604	9			2	5	4			3	7		10		11		8	6	1			SF/2
Mar 4(☆)	West Brom A	W 3-2	R.Morgan, Marsh, Lazarus	97,952	9			2	5	4			3	7		10		11		8	6	1			F
				App	9			6	9	9			8	9		9	1	9		9	8	9	4		
				Sub app																					
				Goals	4			1		2			1	4		11		3							

☆Played at Wembley Stadium

Substitutions are denoted by including these symbols:
Number 12 = *; 13 = †; 14 = ‡; 15 = §; 16 = °.

1967-68

Division 2

Date	Opponent	Result	Scorers	Att	Allen	Clarke	Clement	Finch	Harris	Hazell	Hunt	Keen	Keetch	Kelly	Lazarus	Leach	McGovern	Marsh	Morgan I	Morgan R	Sanderson	Sibley	Springett	Watson	Wilks
Aug 19	(a) Portsmouth	D 1-1	R.Morgan	23,261	9		2		3	6		4	5		7	10			8	11			1		
22	(a) Bristol C	W 2-0	Leach 2	20,228	9		2		3	6		4	5		7	10			8	11			1		
26	(h) Norwich C	W 2-0	Keen, I.Morgan	14,526	9		2*		3	6	5	4			7	10			8	11			1	12	
29	(h) Bristol C	W 3-1	I.Morgan, Allen, R.Morgan	15,448	9		2*		3	6	5	4		1	7	10			8	11				12	
Sep 2	(a) Rotherham U	W 3-1	Leach, Allen, Lazarus	7,811	9*				3	6	5	4			7	10			8	11	12		1	2	
5	(h) Aston Villa	W 3-0	Sanderson 2, Lazarus	21,438			2		3	6	5	4			7	10			8	11	9		1		
9	(h) Derby C	L 0-1		18,431	12		2		3	6	5	4			7	9			8*	11	10		1		
16	(a) Preston NE	W 2-0	R.Morgan, Leach	15,791	9		2		3	6	5	4			12	10			7*	11	8		1		
23	(h) Charlton A	W 2-1	I.Morgan, Allen	18,953	9		2		3	6	5	4			7	10			8	11			1		
30	(a) Crystal P	L 0-1		38,006	9		2*		3	6	5	4	12		7	10			8	11			1		
Oct 7	(h) Bolton W	W 1-0	Wilks	16,848			2		3	6	12	4	5			9			7	11	8*		1		10
14	(a) Hull C	L 0-2		14,240	8		2		3	6		4	5			9			7	11			1		10
21	(h) Millwall	W 3-1	R.Morgan, Keen, Allen	23,887	9				3	2		4	5		7				8	11		6	1		10
28	(a) Blackpool	W 1-0	Allen	21,635	9*		2		3	6		4	5		7	12			8	11		10	1		
Nov 11	(a) Carlisle U	L 1-3	Sibley	12,454	9		2		3	6		4	5		7				8	11		10	1		
18	(h) Middlesbrough	D 1-1	Marsh	17,557	9				3	2		4	5		7			10	8	11		6	1		
25	(a) Huddersfield T	L 0-1		14,615	9				3	2		4	5		7*			10	8	11	12	6	1		
Dec 2	(h) Ipswich T	W 1-0	Marsh	16,266	9		2		3	6		4	5					10	8	11			1		7
9	(a) Birmingham C	L 0-2		25,281	9*		2		3	6		4	5					10	7	11	8		1		12
12	(h) Blackburn R	W 3-1	Marsh, Wilks, Sanderson	12,917			2		3	6		4	5					10	7	11	8		1		9
16	(h) Portsmouth	W 2-0	I.Morgan, Keen	20,195			2		3	6		4	5					10	7	11	8		1		9
23	(a) Norwich C	D 0-0		24,043			2		3	6		4	5					10	7	11	8		1	12	9*
26	(a) Plymouth A	W 1-0	Keen (pen)	21,003			2		3	6		4	5				9	10	7	11	8		1		
30	(h) Plymouth A	W 4-1	Marsh 2, Keen 2	15,889			2		3	6		4	5					10	7	11	8		1		9
Jan 6	(h) Rotherham U	W 6-0	I.Morgan 2, Leach 2, R.Morgan, Marsh	16,782			2		3	6		4	5			9		10	7	11	8		1		
20	(h) Preston NE	W 2-0	Marsh 2	16,633			2		3	6		4	5			9		10	7	11	8		1		
Feb 3	(a) Charlton A	D 3-3	R.Morgan 2, Marsh	21,507			2		3	6		4	5			9		10	7	11	8		1		
10	(h) Crystal P	W 2-1	Wilks, I.Morgan	18,954			2		3	6		4	5					10	7	11	8		1		9
17	(a) Derby C	L 0-4		22,836			2		3	6		4	5			9		10	7	11	8		1		
24	(a) Bolton W	D 1-1	R.Morgan	14,733		9	2		3	6		4	5					10	7	11	8		1		
Mar 9	(h) Hull C	D 1-1	Marsh (pen)	17,705		9			3	6		4	5					10	8	11			1	2	7
16	(a) Millwall	D 1-1	Marsh	21,396	8	9	2		3	6		4	5					10	7	11			1		
23	(h) Blackpool	W 2-0	I.Morgan, Clarke	18,498	8	9	2		3	6		4	5					10	7	11			1		
30	(a) Blackburn R	W 1-0	Clarke	16,141	8	9	2		3	6		4	5					10	7	11			1		
Apr 6	(h) Carlisle U	W 1-0	Clarke	18,103	8	9	2*		3	6		4	5					10	7	11			1	12	
12	(h) Cardiff C	W 1-0	I.Morgan	23,043	8	9			3	6		4	5						7	11			1	2	10
13	(a) Middlesbrough	L 1-3	Allen	20,849	8	9			3	6	5	4				12			7	11*			1	2	10
16	(a) Cardiff C	L 0-1		20,045		9		2	3	6	5	4		1		8		10	7	11					
20	(h) Huddersfield T	W 3-0	Marsh 2, Legg (og)	19,646		9		2	3	6		4	5	1		8		10	7	11					
27	(a) Ipswich T	D 2-2	Marsh (pen), Leach	28,000	12	9		2	3	6		4	5	1		8		10	7	11*					
May 4	(h) Birmingham C	W 2-0	Leach, I.Morgan	25,985	11	9*			3	6		4	5	1		8		10	7					2	12
11	(a) Aston Villa	W 2-1	Leach, Bradley (og)	33,785	11	9			3	6		4	5	1		8		10	7					2	
				App	24	13	30	3	42	42	10	42	32	6	14	21	1	25	42	40	16	5	36	6	12
				Sub app	2						1		1		1	2					2			4	2
				Goals	6	3						6			2	9		14	10	8	3	1			3

2 own-goals

FA Cup

Date	Opponent	Result	Scorers	Att	Allen	Clarke	Clement	Finch	Harris	Hazell	Hunt	Keen	Keetch	Kelly	Lazarus	Leach	McGovern	Marsh	Morgan I	Morgan R	Sanderson	Sibley	Springett	Watson	Wilks	Round
Jan 27	(h) Preston NE	L 1-3	Keen	18,425			2*		3	6		4	5			9		10	7	11	8		1		12	3
				App			1		1	1		1	1			1		1	1	1	1		1			
				Sub app																					1	
				Goals								1														

League Cup

Date	Opponent	Result	Scorers	Att	Allen	Clarke	Clement	Finch	Harris	Hazell	Hunt	Keen	Keetch	Kelly	Lazarus	Leach	McGovern	Marsh	Morgan I	Morgan R	Sanderson	Sibley	Springett	Watson	Wilks	Round
Sep 12	(h) Hull C	W 2-1	Leach, Keen	16,609	9		2		3	6	5	4			7	10			8	11			1			2
Oct 10	(h) Oxford U	W 5-1	Wilks 5	16,989	8		2		3		5	4	6			9			7	11			1		10	3
31	(h) Burnley	L 1-2	Sibley	24,213	9		2		3	6		4	5		7				8	11		10	1			4
				App	3		3		3	2	2	3	2		2	2			3	3		1	3		1	
				Sub app																						
				Goals								1				1						1			5	

Substitutions are denoted by including these symbols:
Number 12 = *; 13 = †; 14 = ‡; 15 = §; 16 = °.

Attendance Summary 1966-1967

	ATTENDANCES			AVERAGE		
	Home	Away	Total	Home	Away	Total
League	302,707	251,783	554,490	13,161	10,947	12,054
League Cup	90,818	137,596	228,414	15,136	45,865	25,379
FA Cup	21,636	40,038	61,674	10,818	40,038	20,558
Total	415,161	429,417	844,578	13,392	15,904	14,562

Attendance Summary 1967-1968

	ATTENDANCES			AVERAGE		
	Home	Away	Total	Home	Away	Total
League	387,704	437,660	825,364	18,462	20,841	19,652
League Cup	57,811		57,811	19,270		19,270
FA Cup	18,425		18,425	18,425		18,425
Total	463,940	437,660	901,600	18,558	20,841	19,600

1968-69

Division 1

Date	Match	Result	Scorers	Att	Allen	Bridges	Clarke	Clement	Finch	Francis	Gillard	Glover	Harris	Hazell	Hunt	Keen	Keetch	Kelly	Leach	McGovern	Marsh	Metchick	Morgan I	Morgan R	Sanderson	Sibley	Spratley	Springett	Watson	Wilks
Aug 10	(h) Leicester C	D 1-1	Allen	21,494	12		9*		2				3	6		4							7	11		8		1	5	10
14	(a) Leeds U	L 1-4	Wilks	31,612	9				2				3	6		4							7	11		8		1	5	10
17	(a) Wolves	L 1-3	I.Morgan	30,854									3	6		4	5	1	9				7	11		8			2	10
20	(h) Sunderland	D 2-2	Allen, Clarke	20,500	8		9						3	2		4		1	10*				7	11	12	6			5	
24	(h) Manchester C	D 1-1	Bridges	19,716	8	9							3	2		4		1					7	11	10	6			5	
27	(a) Ipswich T	L 0-3		24,049		9	10						3	2		4		1	8				7			6			5	11
31	(a) Arsenal	L 1-2	Wilks	44,507	11	9		2					3	8		4		1	10*				7			6			5	12
Sep 7	(a) Liverpool	L 0-2		46,025		11	9*						3	8	12	4	5						7		10	6		1	2	
14	(h) Chelsea	L 0-4		26,358		9							3	8	12	4	5		11*				7		10	6		1	2	
21	(a) Stoke C	D 1-1	R.Morgan	15,543	10	9							3	4			5	1	8*				7	11		6			2	12
28	(h) Southampton	D 1-1	Allen	20,765	10	9							3	4	5			1	8				7	11		6			2	
Oct 5	(a) West Brom A	L 1-3	Clarke	23,027		10	9						3	4	5			1	8			12	7*	11		6			2	
8	(h) Ipswich T	W 2-1	Bridges, R.Morgan	17,992	9	7							3	6		4	5	1	8					11					2	10
12	(h) Sheffield W	W 3-2	Wilks, Bridges, Leach	19,044	9	7							3	6	5	4		1	8*			12		11					2	10
19	(a) Newcastle U	L 2-3	Wilks, Moncur (og)	34,840	9	7							3	6	5	4		1	8					11					2	10
26	(h) Manchester U	L 2-3	Leach, Wilks	31,138	9	7							3	6	5	4		1	8					11					2	10
Nov 2	(a) West Ham U	L 3-4	Leach 2, Bridges	36,008	9	7							3	6	5	4			8					11				1	2	10
9	(h) Burnley	L 0-2		22,572	9	7							3	6	5	4*		1	8				12	11					2	10
16	(a) Everton	L 0-4		42,958	9	7		3						6	8	5		1			10			11		4			2	
23	(h) Nottingham F	W 2-1	Marsh, Hazell	18,857		9		2			3			6				1		8	10		7	11		4			5	
Dec 7	(h) Coventry C	L 0-1		17,921				2					3	6					9		10		7	11		4		1	5	8
14	(a) Sheffield W	L 0-4		22,004		7							3	6	5	4			9		10		8	11				1	2	
21	(h) Newcastle U	D 1-1	Bridges	16,444		7	9						3	6	5	8	4				10			11				1	2	
26	(h) West Brom A	L 0-4		18,649	12	7*	9						3	6	5	8	4				10			11				1	2	
Jan 11	(h) West Ham U	D 1-1	Clarke	28,645			9	3				12			5		6		8		10*		7	11		4	1		2	
18	(a) Burnley	D 2-2	Marsh, Leach	12,674			9	3			12				5		6		8		10		7	11		4	1*		2	
24	(h) Leeds U	L 0-1		26,163			9	3			12				5		6	1	8*		10		7	11		4			2	
29	(a) Tottenham H	L 2-3	Clement, Clarke (pen)	38,766			9	3						12	5		6*	1			10		7	11		4			2	8
Feb 1	(h) Everton	L 0-1		26,476			9	3						4	5			1			10		7	11		6			2	8
15	(h) Tottenham H	D 1-1	Clarke	30,013	8	11	9	3						4	5			1			10		7			6			2	
22	(a) Coventry C	L 0-5		26,399		11	9	3					6	4	5			1	8		10		7						2	
Mar 4	(a) Nottingham F	L 0-1		21,055			9	12			3			4	5		6		8*		10		7				1		2	11
8	(h) Wolves	L 0-1		17,901			9	12			3	8		4	5		6				10		7				1		2	11*
12	(a) Leicester C	L 0-2		24,554			9					11	3	4	5		6		8		10		7				1		2	
15	(a) Manchester C	L 1-3	Leach	28,859			9				3	11		4	5		6		8		10		7				1		2	
19	(a) Manchester U	L 1-8	Marsh	37,053			9*	3				11		4	5		12		8		10		7			6	1		2	
22	(h) Arsenal	L 0-1		23,076		8		3				11		4	5				9		10		7			6	1		2	
29	(h) Liverpool	L 1-2	Bridges	16,792		11	9			12			3	4	5*		6		8		10						1		2	7
Apr 5	(a) Southampton	L 2-3	Marsh, Bridges	22,103		11	9	2					3	6	5				8		10		7				1		4	
7	(a) Sunderland	D 0-0		18,928		11		2					3	6	5				9				7			8	1		4	10
12	(h) Stoke C	W 2-1	Leach 2	12,489		11	9	2					3	6	5				10				7			8*	1		4	12
19	(a) Chelsea	L 1-2	Bridges	41,263		11	9	2					3	6	5				8		10		7				1		4	
				App	14	27	23	17	2		4	5	29	38	29	19	16	20	30	1	22		32	25	3	25	13	9	42	17
				Sub app	2			2		1	2	1		1	2		1					2	1		1					3
				Goals	3	8	5	1						1					8		4		1	2						5

1 own-goal

FA Cup

Date	Match	Result	Scorers	Att	Allen	Bridges	Clarke	Clement	Finch	Francis	Gillard	Glover	Harris	Hazell	Hunt	Keen	Keetch	Kelly	Leach	McGovern	Marsh	Metchick	Morgan I	Morgan R	Sanderson	Sibley	Spratley	Springett	Watson	Wilks	Round
Jan 4	(a) Aston Villa	L 1-2	I.Morgan	39,854			9	3				10			5		4		8				7	11		6	1		2		3
				App			1	1				1			1		1		1				1	1		1	1		1		
				Sub app																											
				Goals																			1								

League Cup

Date	Match	Result	Scorers	Att	Allen	Bridges	Clarke	Clement	Finch	Francis	Gillard	Glover	Harris	Hazell	Hunt	Keen	Keetch	Kelly	Leach	McGovern	Marsh	Metchick	Morgan I	Morgan R	Sanderson	Sibley	Spratley	Springett	Watson	Wilks	Round
Sep 3	(a) Peterborough U	L 2-4	Keen, Clarke	11,408	11	9	12	2	3					8		4		1					7*			6			5	10	2
				App	1	1		1	1					1		1		1					1			1			1	1	
				Sub app			1																								
				Goals			1									1															

Substitutions are denoted by including these symbols:
Number 12 = *; 13 = †; 14 = ‡; 15 = §; 16 = °.

Attendance Summary

	ATTENDANCES			AVERAGE		
	Home	Away	Total	Home	Away	Total
League	453,005	623,081	1,076,086	21,572	29,671	25,621
League Cup		11,408	11,408		11,408	11,408
FA Cup		39,854	39,854		39,854	39,854
Total	453,005	674,343	1,127,348	21,572	29,391	25,622

1969-70

Division 2

Date	Opponent	Result	Scorers	Att	Bridges	Busby	Clark	Clarke	Clement	Ferguson	Francis	Gillard	Harris	Hazell	Hunt	Kelly	Leach	McGovern	Marsh	Metchick	Mobley	Morgan	Sibley	Spratley	Turpie	Venables	Watson	Wilks
Aug 9	(h) Hull C	W 3-0	Clark, Clarke, Leach	15,781	7		11	9	3					6	5	1	12		10			8				4*	2	
16	(a) Preston NE	D 0-0		11,179	7		11	9	3					6	5	1			10			8				4	2	
20	(a) Watford	W 1-0	Bridges	26,698	7			9	3				12	6	5	1	11		10				8*			4	2	
23	(h) Millwall	W 3-2	Bridges 2, Clement	19,735	7			9*	3				12	6	5	1	11		10				8			4	2	
26	(h) Blackpool	W 6-1	Marsh 3, Bridges 2, Venables (pen)	19,227	7		11		3					6	5	1	9		10				8			4	2	
30	(a) Birmingham C	L 0-3		32,660	7		11		3					6	5	1	9		10				8			4	2	
Sep 6	(h) Huddersfield T	W 4-2	Marsh, I.Morgan, Bridges, Venables (pen)	18,746	7				3					6	5	1	9		10			11	8			4	2	
13	(a) Portsmouth	W 3-1	Clement, Francis, Bridges	21,969	7			9	3		11			6	5	1*			10				4		12		2	8
17	(a) Blackburn R	W 1-0	Leach	15,945				9	2					6	5	1	7		10			11	4		3			8
20	(h) Swindon T	W 2-0	Wilks, Clarke	22,799				9	3					6	5		7		10			11	4	1			2	8
27	(a) Cardiff C	L 2-4	Venables (pen), Bridges	30,083	7			9	3					6	5		8		10			11		1		4	2	
Oct 4	(h) Middlesbrough	W 4-0	Bridges 2, Clarke, Clement	21,421	7			9	3					6			8		10		5	11		1		4	2	
7	(h) Preston NE	D 0-0		21,127	7			9	2			3		6		1	8		10		5	11*	12			4		
11	(a) Norwich C	L 0-1		20,399	7			9	3					6	12	1	11		10		5		8*			4	2	
18	(a) Carlisle U	L 2-3	Clement, Clarke	11,900	7			9	3					6	8	1	11		10		5					4	2	
25	(h) Charlton A	D 1-1	Metchick	20,577	7		11*	9	3					6		1	8		10	12	5					4	2	
Nov 1	(a) Aston Villa	D 1-1	Marsh	31,428	7			9				12	3	6	8	1	11*		10		5					4	2	
8	(h) Sheffield U	W 2-1	Bridges, Clarke	19,852	7		12	9					3	6	8	1	11		10		5					4*	2	
11	(h) Watford	W 2-1	Clarke, Hazell	19,719	7		11	9					3	6	4	1	8		10		5						2	
15	(a) Bristol C	L 0-2		18,893	7		11	9	12				3	6	4	1	8		10		5*						2	
22	(h) Leicester C	D 1-1	Bridges	21,027	11			9	2	8	7		3	6	5		4		10					1				
29	(a) Bolton W	L 4-6	Leach, Bridges, Clement, Marsh	6,957	11			9	2	8			3	6	5		7		10					1		4		
Dec 6	(h) Oxford U	L 1-2	Bridges	12,018	7			9	2	10	11		3	6	5		8							1		4		
13	(h) Portsmouth	W 2-0	Clarke, Bridges	11,831	7			9	2	11		3		6		1	10						4			8	5	
26	(a) Millwall	L 0-2		13,982	7			9	2	10		3		6		1	11				5					8	4	
27	(h) Birmingham C	W 2-1	Bridges 2	15,688	7			9	2	10	11	3		6	4	1										8	5	
Jan 10	(a) Swindon T	D 0-0		18,219	7			9	2	11		3		6		1			10				4			8	5	
17	(h) Cardiff C	W 2-1	Gillard, Marsh	22,033	7			9	2	11		3		6					10				4	1		8	5	
20	(a) Huddersfield T	L 0-2		21,432	7			9	2	11		3		6		1			10		12		4*			8	5	
31	(a) Middlesbrough	L 0-1		25,811				9	2	11*		3		6		1	12		10		5					8	4	7
Feb 14	(a) Hull C	W 2-1	Marsh, Clarke	12,698	7			9	2	11		3		6		1			10		5					8	4	
17	(h) Norwich C	W 4-0	Venables (pen), Clarke, Bridges, Marsh	17,270	7			9*	2	11		3		6		1	12		10		5					8	4	
24	(a) Sheffield U	L 0-2		25,724	7				2	11		3		6		1	9		10		5*	12				8	4	
28	(h) Aston Villa	W 4-2	Bridges 2, Marsh 2	17,057	7			9	2	11		3		6		1			10			8				4	5	
Mar 14	(h) Bolton W	L 0-4		13,596	7			9	2	11		3*	12	6	5	1			10			8				4		
21	(a) Oxford U	D 0-0		13,760	7								3	6			9	4	10		5			1		8	2	11
27	(h) Carlisle U	D 0-0		16,343	7						12		3	6			9	4	10		5			1		8*	2	11
28	(h) Bristol C	D 2-2	Bridges, Francis	11,017	7					11	8		3	6			9	4	10		5			1			2	
31	(a) Charlton A	D 1-1	Watson	13,738	7					11	8		3	6			9		10		5			1		4	2	
Apr 4	(a) Blackpool	D 1-1	Leach	19,516	7					11	8		3	6			9		10		5			1		4	2	
14	(h) Blackburn R	L 2-3	Venables (pen), Hazell	11,161	7*					11	8		3	6			9		10		5	12		1		4	2	
18	(a) Leicester C	L 1-2	Marsh (pen)	20,391		4			2	11	8	3		6			9		10		5	7		1				
				App	38	1	7	31	32	20	9	14	13	42	21	28	30	3	38		21	11	13	14	1	34	35	6
				Sub app			1		1		1	1	3		1		3			1	1	2	1		1			
				Goals	21		1	9	5		2	1		2			4		12	1		1				5	1	1

FA Cup

Date	Opponent	Result	Scorers	Att	Bridges	Busby	Clark	Clarke	Clement	Ferguson	Francis	Gillard	Harris	Hazell	Hunt	Kelly	Leach	McGovern	Marsh	Metchick	Mobley	Morgan	Sibley	Spratley	Turpie	Venables	Watson	Wilks	Round
Jan 3	(h) South Shields	W 4-1	Marsh 2, Clarke, Ferguson	16,811	7			9	2	8	11	3		6		1			10							4	5		3
24	(a) Charlton A	W 3-2	Marsh 2, Clarke	30,262	7			9	2	11		3		6		1			10		5					8	4		4
Feb 7	(h) Derby C	W 1-0	Mackay (og)	27,685	7			9	2	11		3		6		1			10		5					8	4		5
21	(h) Chelsea	L 2-4	Venables (pen), Bridges	33,572	7				2	11		3		6		1	9		10		5					8	4		6
				App	4			3	4	4	1	4		4		4	1		4		3					4	4		
				Sub app																									
				Goals	1			2		1									4							1			

1 own-goal

League Cup

Date	Opponent	Result	Scorers	Att	Bridges	Busby	Clark	Clarke	Clement	Ferguson	Francis	Gillard	Harris	Hazell	Hunt	Kelly	Leach	McGovern	Marsh	Metchick	Mobley	Morgan	Sibley	Spratley	Turpie	Venables	Watson	Wilks	Round
Sep 3	(a) Mansfield T	D 2-2	Bridges, Watson	9,759	7		11		3					6	5	1	9		10				8			4	2		2
9	(h) Mansfield T	W 4-0	Venables (pen), Clement, Marsh, Clarke	17,315	7			12	3					6	5	1	9*		10			11	8			4	2		Rep
23	(h) Tranmere R	W 6-0	Marsh 4, Leach, Clarke	17,477				9	4			3		6	5		7		10			11		1			2	8	3
Oct 15	(h) Wolves	W 3-1	Clarke 2, Bridges	29,971	7		11	9	3					6		1	8		10		5					4	2		4
29	(a) Manchester C	L 0-3		42,058	7			9	3					6		1	8		10	11	5					4	2		5
				App	4		2	3	5			1		5	3	4	5		5	1	2	2	2	1		4	5	1	
				Sub app					1																				
				Goals	2			4	1								1		5							1	1		

Substitutions are denoted by including these symbols:
Number 12 = *; 13 = †; 14 = ‡; 15 = §; 16 = °.

Attendance Summary

	ATTENDANCES Home	Away	Total	AVERAGE Home	Away	Total
League	368,025	413,382	781,407	17,525	19,685	18,605
League Cup	64,763	51,817	116,580	21,588	25,908	23,316
FA Cup	78,068	30,262	108,330	26,023	30,262	27,082
Total	510,856	495,461	1,006,317	18,921	20,644	19,732

1970-71
Division 2

Date	Opponent	Result	Scorers	Att	Bridges	Busby	Clement	Evans	Ferguson	Francis	Gillard	Harris	Hazell	Hunt	Leach	McCulloch	McGovern	Marsh	Mobley	Morgan	Parkes	Salvage	Saul	Sibley	Spratley	Venables	Watson	Wilks
Aug 15	(a) Birmingham C	L 1-2	Bridges	30,785	7		2			11	3		6	5	10								9	8	1	4		
22	(h) Leicester C	L 1-3	Venables (pen)	17,090	7*		2			12	3		6	5	11			10			1		9	8		4		
29	(h) Bolton W	D 2-2	Venables 2 (1 pen)	10,940	7		3		8				2	5	11			10			1		9	6		4		
Sep 2	(a) Blackburn R	W 2-0	Leach, Saul	7,783	7		3		11	12			2	5	8*			10			1		9	6		4		
5	(h) Watford	D 1-1	Venables (pen)	18,656	7		3		11	8			2	5				10			1		9	6		4		
12	(a) Sheffield W	L 0-1		14,920	7	12	3		11*	8			2	5				10			1		9	6		4		
19	(h) Bristol C	W 2-1	Marsh, Bridges	13,367	7		3		11	8			2	5				10			1		9	6		4		
26	(a) Middlesbrough	L 2-6	Clement, Marsh	16,788			3*		11	8			2	5				10		7	1		9	6		4	12	
29	(h) Luton T	L 0-1		19,273		4	3			7								10	5	11	1		9	6		8	2	
Oct 3	(h) Orient	W 5-1	Marsh 2, I.Morgan 2, Venables (pen)	14,500		9	3		7				6	4				10	5	11	1					8	2	
10	(a) Swindon T	L 0-1		17,465			2		7		3		6	4				10		11	1		9			8	5	
17	(h) Birmingham C	W 5-2	Marsh 3, Venables, McCulloch	13,074			2		11		3		6	4		9		10		7	1					8	5	
21	(a) Oxford U	W 3-1	Venables, Ferguson, Francis	15,058		9*	2		11	12	3		6	5				10		7	1					8	4	
24	(h) Portsmouth	W 2-0	Clement, I.Morgan	14,709			2		11	9	3*		6	4		12		10	5	7	1					8		
31	(a) Millwall	L 0-3		15,909			4			8	3	12	6	5		9		10		7	1		11				2*	
Nov 7	(h) Cardiff C	L 0-1		11,267		6	4			11		3	2	5	7			10			1		9			8		
14	(a) Sheffield U	D 1-1	Hunt	19,672		6	4		11	7		3	2	5	9			10			1					8		
21	(a) Hull C	D 1-1	Leach	15,606		6	4		11	7		3	2	5	9	12		10*			1					8		
28	(h) Charlton A	L 1-4	Leach	14,027		4	2		11	7		3	6	5	9	8					1					10		
Dec 5	(a) Sunderland	L 1-3	Leach	14,721		6	2		11	7		3	4	5	10						1		9			8		
12	(h) Carlisle U	D 1-1	Marsh	8,880		6	2		11	7		3	4	5	9			10		12	1					8*		
19	(a) Leicester C	D 0-0		23,865		4	3			11				5	9		7	10			1		8	6			2	
Jan 9	(a) Luton T	D 0-0		22,234			3		11	8				5	9*	12		10		7	1			6		4	2	
16	(h) Oxford U	W 2-0	Francis, Marsh	10,900			3		11	8			6	5	9			10		7	1					4	2	
Feb 6	(h) Sunderland	W 2-0	Venables, Leach	11,707			3		11	8				5	9			10		7*	1			6		4	2	12
13	(a) Carlisle U	L 0-3		9,074			3		11	8*			12	5	9			10		7	1			6		4	2	
20	(h) Hull C	D 1-1	Marsh	13,418			3		11	8				5	9	12		10		7*	1			6		4	2	
27	(h) Millwall	W 2-0	Francis, Marsh	15,698			3		11	8				5	9		12	10			1			6		4*	2	7
Mar 6	(a) Portsmouth	L 0-2		10,402			3		11	8				5	9		4	10			1			6			2	7
13	(h) Sheffield U	D 2-2	Marsh 2	12,317			3		11	8			2	5	9		7	10			1			6		4		
20	(a) Cardiff C	L 0-1		23,133		12	3			8			2	5	9		11*	10		7	1			6		4		
23	(h) Norwich C	L 0-1		9,927			3		11	8			2	5	9			10		7	1			6		4		
27	(a) Watford	W 2-1	Marsh 2	16,825			2			8	3		6	5	7*		4	10		12	1	11	9					
Apr 3	(h) Bolton W	W 4-0	Marsh 3, Leach	8,613			2		7	8	3		6	5	9			10			1	11				4		
6	(h) Sheffield W	W 1-0	Marsh	11,371			2	5	7	8	3		6		9	12		10			1	11*				4		
10	(a) Norwich C	L 0-3		15,651			2	5	11	8	3		6		7			10			1		9			4		
12	(a) Oreint	W 1-0	McCulloch	11,949		4*	2	5	7	8	3		6			9		10			1		11			12		
17	(h) Swindon T	W 4-2	Clement, Venables 2, McCulloch	11,571		4*	2	5		8	3		6			9		10		12	1		11			7		
20	(a) Charlton A	W 3-0	McCulloch 2, Marsh	16,117			2	5		7	3		6	4		9*		10		12	1		11			8		
24	(a) Bristol C	D 0-0		12,522			9	5		7	3		6	4				10			1		11			8	2	
27	(h) Blackburn R	W 2-0	Marsh, Francis	9,343			2	5	7*	8	3		12	6		9		10			1		11			4		
May 1	(h) Middlesbrough	D 1-1	Francis	10,390			2	5		7	3		6	4		9		10			1		11			8		
				App	7	12	42	8	30	35	17	6	33	37	25	8	5	39	3	15	41	3	22	19	1	37	15	2
				Sub app		2				3		1	2			5	1			4						1	1	1
				Goals	2		3		1	5				1	6	5		21		3			1			10		

FA Cup

Date	Opponent	Result	Scorers	Att	Bridges	Busby	Clement	Evans	Ferguson	Francis	Gillard	Harris	Hazell	Hunt	Leach	McCulloch	McGovern	Marsh	Mobley	Morgan	Parkes	Salvage	Saul	Sibley	Spratley	Venables	Watson	Wilks	Round
Jan 2	(h) Swindon T	L 1-2	Marsh (pen)	14,840		4	3			11				5	9		7	10			1			6		8	2		3
				App		1	1			1				1	1		1	1			1			1		1	1		
				Sub app																									
				Goals														1											

League Cup

Date	Opponent	Result	Scorers	Att	Bridges	Busby	Clement	Evans	Ferguson	Francis	Gillard	Harris	Hazell	Hunt	Leach	McCulloch	McGovern	Marsh	Mobley	Morgan	Parkes	Salvage	Saul	Sibley	Spratley	Venables	Watson	Wilks	Round
Sep 8	(h) Cardiff C	W 4-0	Bridges, Saul, Marsh, Venables (pen)	15,025	7	12	3*		11	8			2	5				10			1		9	6		4			2
Oct 6	(a) Fulham	L 0-2		31,729		9	3		7				6	4				10	5	11	1					8	2		3
				App	1	1	2		2	1			2	2				2	1	1	2		1	1		2	1		
				Sub app		1																							
				Goals	1													1					1			1			

Substitutions are denoted by including these symbols:
Number 12 = *; 13 = †; 14 = ‡; 15 = §; 16 = °.

Attendance Summary

	ATTENDANCES Home	Away	Total	AVERAGE Home	Away	Total
League	270,098	341,419	611,517	12,862	16,258	14,560
League Cup	15,025	31,729	46,754	15,025	31,729	23,377
FA Cup	14,840		14,840	14,840		14,840
Total	299,963	373,148	673,111	13,042	16,961	14,958

1971-72

Division 2

Date	Opponent	Result	Scorers	Att	Busby	Clement	Evans	Ferguson	Francis	Gillard	Hazell	Hunt	Leach	McCulloch	McGovern	Mancini	Marsh	Morgan	O'Rourke	Parkes	Salvage	Saul	Seary	Venables	Watson
Aug 14 (h)	Sheffield W	W 3-0	Marsh 2 (1 pen), Francis	13,270	7	2			8	3	6	5	11	9			10			1				4	
21 (a)	Middlesbrough	L 2-3	McCulloch, Marsh	20,574	7*	2			8	3	6	5	11	9			10			1	12			4	
28 (h)	Millwall	D 1-1	Marsh	16,730	7	2			8	3	6	5	11	9			10			1				4	
31 (a)	Fulham	W 3-0	Saul, Matthewson (og), McCulloch	21,187	7	2			8	3	6	5		9			10			1		11		4	
Sep 4 (a)	Swindon T	D 0-0		15,915	7	2				3	6	5*		9			10			1	8	11	12	4	
11 (h)	Preston NE	W 2-1	McCulloch, Saul	13,578	7	2			8	3	6	5*		9	12		10			1		11		4	
18 (a)	Burnley	L 0-1		13,770	7	2			8	3	6	5		9			10			1		11		4	
25 (h)	Watford	W 3-0	Marsh 2, McCulloch	15,698	7	2			8	3	6	5		9			10			1		11		4	
29 (a)	Oxford U	L 1-3	Busby	11,670	7	2			8	3	6	5		9			10			1		11		4	
Oct 2 (a)	Norwich C	D 0-0		22,950		2			8	3	6	5		9			10	7		1		11		4	
9 (h)	Birmingham C	W 1-0	Marsh	16,039	7	2			8*	3	6	5		9			10			1	12	11		4	
16 (a)	Sheffield W	D 0-0		16,716	7	2				3	4	5	12	9*		6	10			1		11		8	
19 (h)	Luton T	W 1-0	Leach	15,858	7	2				3	6	12	8			5	10		9*	1		11		4	
23 (a)	Blackpool	D 1-1	Marsh	16,417	7	3					2	5	8	9		6	10			1		11		4	
30 (h)	Portsmouth	D 1-1	I.Morgan	15,934	7*	3			8		2	5				6	10	12	9	1		11		4	
Nov 6 (a)	Cardiff C	D 0-0		16,914		2			8*		3	6		11		5	10	7	9	1		12		4	
13 (h)	Bristol C	W 3-0	O'Rourke, Merrick (og), Marsh	14,898		2			8		3	6	9			5	10	7	11	1		4			
20 (h)	Hull C	W 2-1	O'Rourke, I.Morgan	16,627		2			8		3	6*	9			5	10	7	11	1		12		4	
27 (a)	Charlton A	L 1-2	Clement	16,223		2			8*		3	5	9			6	10	7	11	1		12		4	
Dec 4 (h)	Sunderland	W 2-1	Marsh, O'Rourke	13,576		2			8		3	5	9			6	10	7	11	1				4	
11 (a)	Carlisle U	W 4-1	Leach, O'Rourke, Marsh 2	9,243		2			8		3	5	9	12		6	10	7	11	1				4*	
18 (h)	Swindon T	W 3-0	Marsh 2, Venables	13,517		2			8		3	5	9			6	10	7	11	1				4	
27 (a)	Orient	L 0-2		19,081		2			8		3	5	9	12		6	10	7*	11	1				4	
Jan 1 (h)	Burnley	W 3-1	Leach 2, Marsh	14,614		2			8		3	5	9			6	10		11	1		7		4	
8 (a)	Millwall	D 0-0		24,266		2			8		3	5	9			6	10		11	1		7		4	
22 (h)	Oxford U	W 4-2	Marsh 2, Saul, Leach	13,288		2		11	8		3	5	9			6	10			1		7		4	
29 (a)	Luton T	D 1-1	Francis	17,280		2		11	8		3	5	9			6	10			1		7		4	
Feb 12 (h)	Blackpool	L 0-1		13,690	12	2		11	8*		3	5	9			6	10			1		7		4	
19 (a)	Portsmouth	L 0-1		15,563	4	2		11	8		3	5	9			6	10		7	1					
Mar 4 (a)	Bristol C	L 0-2		11,105	8	2			7	3	5	4	12	9		6	10*		11	1					
11 (a)	Birmingham C	D 0-0		35,557	4	2	5	10	7	3	6		12	8					9*	1	11				
18 (h)	Middlesbrough	W 1-0	Clement	11,467	4	2	5	10	8	3	6			9					7	1	11				
25 (a)	Preston NE	D 1-1	O'Rourke	12,304	4*	2	5	10	8	3	6		9	12					7	1	11				
31 (a)	Watford	W 2-0	Evans, Salvage	13,719	4	2	5	10	8	3	6		9						7	1	11				
Apr 1 (h)	Orient	W 1-0	O'Rourke	12,042	4	2	5	10	8	3	6		9						7	1	11				
3 (h)	Norwich C	D 0-0		25,227	4	2	5	10	8	3	6		9						7	1	11				
8 (a)	Hull C	D 1-1	O'Rourke	12,830	4	2	5	10	8	3	6		9	12					7	1	11*				
15 (h)	Charlton A	W 2-0	Francis, Leach	12,976	4	2	5*	10	8	3	6		9	12					7	1	11				
22 (a)	Sunderland	W 1-0	Busby	13,751	4	2		10	8	3	6		9			5			7	1	11				
25 (h)	Fulham	D 0-0		20,605	4	2		10	8	3	6		9	12		5			7	1	11*				
29 (h)	Carlisle U	W 3-0	Clement, Leach, O'Rouke	7,616	4	2		10	8		6		9			5			7	1	11				3
May 2 (h)	Cardiff C	W 3-0	Ferguson, O'Rourke, Leach	8,430	4	2		10	8		6		9			5			7	1	11				3
				App	28	42	8	16	38	24	42	29	28	17		23	30	9	26	42	13	18		27	2
				Sub app	1							1	3	6	1			1			2	3	1		
				Goals	2	3	1	1	3				8	4			17	2	9		1	3		1	

2 own-goals

FA Cup

Date	Opponent	Result	Scorers	Att	Busby	Clement	Evans	Ferguson	Francis	Gillard	Hazell	Hunt	Leach	McCulloch	McGovern	Mancini	Marsh	Morgan	O'Rourke	Parkes	Salvage	Saul	Seary	Venables	Watson	Round
Jan 15 (h)	Fulham	D 1-1	Mancini	23,707		2			8		3	5	9	12		6	10		11	1		7*		4		3
18 (a)	Fulham	L 1-2	Clement	24,181		2			8		3	5	9			6	10		11	1		7		4		Rep
				App		2			2		2	2	2			2	2		2	2		2		2		
				Sub app										1												
				Goals		1										1										

League Cup

Date	Opponent	Result	Scorers	Att	Busby	Clement	Evans	Ferguson	Francis	Gillard	Hazell	Hunt	Leach	McCulloch	McGovern	Mancini	Marsh	Morgan	O'Rourke	Parkes	Salvage	Saul	Seary	Venables	Watson	Round
Sep 7 (h)	Birmingham C	W 2-0	Francis, Marsh	15,032	7	2			8	3	6	5		9			10			1		11		4		2
Oct 5 (h)	Lincoln C	W 4-2	I.Morgan, McCulloch, Marsh, Saul	12,723		2			8	3	6	5		9			10	7		1		11		4		3
26 (h)	Bristol R	D 1-1	Marsh	17,045	7	3	6		8		2	5		9*			10	12		1		11		4		4
Nov 2 (a)	Bristol R	L 0-1		24,373		2	5	11	8		3	6					10	7		1	12	9*		4		Rep
				App	2	4	2	1	4	2	4	4		3			4	2		4		4		4		
				Sub app														1			1					
				Goals					1					1			3	1				1				

Substitutions are denoted by including these symbols:
Number 12 = *; 13 = †; 14 = ‡; 15 = §; 16 = °.

Attendance Summary

	ATTENDANCES			AVERAGE		
	Home	Away	Total	Home	Away	Total
League	305,608	357,035	662,715	14,556	17,002	15,779
League Cup	44,800	24,373	69,173	14,933	24,373	17,293
FA Cup	23,707	24,181	47,888	23,707	24,181	23,944
Total	374,187	405,589	779,776	14,967	17,634	16,245

1972-73

Division 2

Date		Opponent	Res	Score	Scorers	Att	Beck	Bowles	Busby	Clement	Delve	Evans	Ferguson	Francis	Gillard	Givens	Hazell	Hunt	Leach	McCulloch	Mancini	Morgan	O'Rourke	Parkes	Salvage	Spratley	Thomas	Venables	Watson
Aug	12	(a) Swindon T	D	2-2	Busby, Leach	14,170			7	2		5		8		11	6		10				9	1				4	3
	19	(h) Sheffield W	W	4-2	Francis, O'Rourke, Givens, Leach	12,977			7	2		5		8		11	6		10				9	1				4	3
	26	(a) Preston NE	D	1-1	O'Rourke	9,242			7	2		5		8		11	6		10				9	1				4	3
Sep	2	(h) Middlesbrough	D	2-2	Givens, O'Rourke	10,601			7	2		5		8		11	6		10				9	1				4	3
	9	(a) Burnley	D	1-1	Busby	10,798			7	2		5		8		11	6			9			10*	1	12			4	3
	16	(h) Nottingham F	W	3-0	Givens, Bowles, McCulloch	12,528		10	7	2		5		8		11*	6			9				1	12			4	3
	19	(h) Bristol C	D	1-1	Francis	11,586		10	7	2		5		8		11	6			9				1				4	3
	23	(a) Orient	D	2-2	Leach, Bowles	9,942		10	7	2		5		8			6		11	9				1				4	3
	26	(a) Hull C	L	1-4	Givens	8,289		10	7	2		5		8		11	6			9				1				4	3
	30	(h) Cardiff C	W	3-0	Givens 2, Bowles	11,182		10	7	2		5	12	8	3*	11	6		9					1				4	
Oct	7	(h) Carlisle U	W	4-0	Leach, Busby, Evans, Francis	11,755		10	7	2		5		8		11	6		9					1				4	3
	14	(a) Aston Villa	W	1-0	Francis	34,045		10	7	2		5		8		11	6		9					1				4	3
	17	(a) Fulham	W	2-0	Bowles, Givens	17,000		10	7*	2		5		8		11	6		9	12				1				4	3
	21	(h) Sunderland	W	3-2	Bowles 2, Givens	17,356		10		2		5		8		11	6		9					1			7	4	3
	28	(a) Blackpool	L	0-2		14,160		10		2		5		8		11	6		9					1			7	4	3
Nov	4	(h) Hull C	D	1-1	Bowles	13,619		10		2		5		8		11	6		9					1			7	4	3
	11	(a) Bristol C	W	2-1	Givens 2	12,570		10		2		5		8		11	6		9					1			7	4	3
	18	(h) Millwall	L	1-3	Bowles	15,837		10		2		5*		8	3	11	6		9				12	1			7	4	
	25	(a) Portsmouth	W	1-0	Givens	8,460		10		2				8	3	11	6		12		5	7	9*	1				4	
Dec	2	(h) Oxford U	D	0-0		9,790		10		2				8	3	11	6				5	7	9	1			4		
	9	(a) Luton T	D	2-2	Givens, Clement	13,670		10		2	9			8	3	11	6				5			1			7	4	
	23	(a) Brighton & HA	W	2-1	Givens 2	13,735		10		2				8	3	11	6		9		5			1			7	4	
	26	(h) Orient	W	3-1	Leach, Givens, Thomas	15,062	12	10		2*				8	3	11	6		9		5			1			7	4	
	30	(a) Sheffield W	L	1-3	Leach	20,185		10			12			8	3	11	6		9		5			1			7	4*	2
Jan	6	(h) Preston NE	W	3-0	Givens 2, Francis	10,519		10					7	8		11	2	6	4*		5			1	12		9		3
	20	(a) Middlesbrough	D	0-0		8,398		10*		3	12			8		11	6		4		5			1			9	7	2
	27	(h) Burnley	W	2-0	Leach, Givens	22,518		10		2	4			8		11	6		9		5					1	7		3
Feb	6	(h) Huddersfield T	W	3-1	Givens 2, Thomas	13,539		10		2	4			8		11		6	9		5			1			7		3
	10	(a) Nottingham F	D	0-0		11,617		10		2	4			8		11	6		9		5			1			7		3
	17	(h) Swindon T	W	5-0	Bowles 3, Francis, Givens	13,472		10		2				8		11	6		9		5			1			7	4	3
Mar	3	(a) Carlisle U	W	3-1	Thomas, Bowles, Clement	8,729		10		2				8		11	6		9		5			1			7	4	3
	6	(a) Huddersfield T	D	2-2	Francis, Leach	8,627				2	10			8		11	6		9		5			1			7	4	3
	10	(h) Aston Villa	W	1-0	Leach	21,578				2	10			8		11	6		9		5			1			7	4	3
	24	(h) Blackpool	W	4-0	Bowles, Francis, Thomas, Hatton (og)	15,714		10		2				8		11	6		9		5			1			7	4	3
	31	(h) Portsmouth	W	5-0	Thomas, Lewis (og), Venables, Leach, Mancini	14,086		10		2				8		11	6		9		5			1			7	4	3
Apr	7	(a) Oxford U	L	0-2		12,144		10		2				8		11	6		9		5			1			7	4	3
	14	(h) Luton T	W	2-0	Mancini, Givens	16,471		10		2*	12			8		11	6		9		5			1			7	4	3
	18	(a) Cardiff C	D	0-0		11,958		10		2				8		11	6		9		5			1			7	4	3
	21	(a) Millwall	W	1-0	Givens	16,212		10		2				8		11	6		9		5			1			7	4	3
	24	(h) Brighton & HA	W	2-0	Francis, Bowles	16,625		10		2				8		11	6		9		5			1			7	4	3
	28	(h) Fulham	W	2-0	Clement, Bowles	22,187		10		2				8		11	6		9		5			1			7	4	3
May	9	(a) Sunderland	W	3-0	Bowles 2, Thomas	43,265		10		2				8		11	6		9		5			1			7	4	3
						App		35	13	40	6	18	1	42	8	41	41	2	35	5	24	2	7	41		1	28	37	35
						Sub app	1				3		1						1	1			1		3				
						Goals		17	3	3		1		9		23			10	1	2		3				6	1	

2 own-goals

FA Cup

Date		Opponent	Res	Score	Scorers	Att	Beck	Bowles	Busby	Clement	Delve	Evans	Ferguson	Francis	Gillard	Givens	Hazell	Hunt	Leach	McCulloch	Mancini	Morgan	O'Rourke	Parkes	Salvage	Spratley	Thomas	Venables	Watson	Round
Jan	13	(h) Barnet	D	0-0		13,626		10		3			7			11	2	6	4		5			1	8		9			3
	16	(a) Barnet	W	3-0	Leach, Bowles, Mancini	10,919		10		3			7	8		11	4		6		5			1			9		2	Rep
Feb	3	(a) Oxford U	W	2-0	Clement, Givens	16,057		10		2	4			8		11	6*	12	9		5					1	7		3	4
	24	(a) Derby C	L	2-4	Leach, Givens	38,100		10		2				8		11	6		9		5			1			7	4	3	5
						App		4		4	1		2	3		4	4	1	4		4			3	1	1	4	1	3	
						Sub app												1												
						Goals		1		1						2			2		1									

League Cup

Date		Opponent	Res	Score	Scorers	Att	Beck	Bowles	Busby	Clement	Delve	Evans	Ferguson	Francis	Gillard	Givens	Hazell	Hunt	Leach	McCulloch	Mancini	Morgan	O'Rourke	Parkes	Salvage	Spratley	Thomas	Venables	Watson	Round
Sep	6	(a) West Brom A	L	1-2	Givens	8,282			7	2		5		8		11	6		10	12			9*	1				4	3	2
						App			1	1		1		1		1	1		1				1	1				1	1	
						Sub app														1										
						Goals										1														

Substitutions are denoted by including these symbols:
Number 12 = *; 13 = †; 14 = ‡; 15 = §; 16 = °.

Attendance Summary

	ATTENDANCES Home	Away	Total	AVERAGE Home	Away	Total
League	309,002	307,216	616,218	14,714	14,629	14,672
League Cup		8,282	8,282		8,282	8,282
FA cup	13,626	65,076	78,702	13,626	21,690	19,676
Total	322,628	380,574	703,202	14,665	15,223	14,962

1973-74

Division 1

Date	Opponent	Res	Scorers	Att	Abbott	Beck	Bowles	Busby	Clement	Delve	Evans	Francis	Gillard	Givens	Hazell	Leach	McLintock	Mancini	Parkes	Thomas	Venables	Watson
Aug 25 (h)	Southampton	D 1-1	Givens	18,602			10		2	8				11	6	9		5	1	7	4	3
29 (a)	Norwich C	D 0-0		24,860			10		2	8				11	6	9		5	1	7	4	3
Sep 1 (a)	Manchester U	L 1-2	Francis	44,156			10		2			8		11	6	9		5	1	7	4	3
4 (h)	West Ham U	D 0-0		28,360			10		2			8		11	6	9		5	1	7	4	3
8 (h)	Stoke C	D 3-3	Leach, Venables (pen), Mancini	18,118			10		2			8		11	6	9		5	1	7	4	3
10 (a)	West Ham U	W 3-2	Givens 2, Abbott	26,000	7		10		2			8		11	6	9		5	1		4	3
15 (a)	Everton	L 0-1		30,795			10				6	8	3	11	2	9		5	1	7	4	
22 (h)	Birmingham C	D 2-2	Hynd (og), Bowles	18,701	12		10		2			8		11	3	9*	6	5	1	7	4	
29 (a)	Newcastle U	W 3-2	Thomas, Francis, Leach	26,173			10		2			8		11	3	9	6	5	1	7	4	
Oct 6 (h)	Chelsea	D 1-1	Bowles	31,009			10		2			8		11	3	9	6	5	1	7	4	
13 (a)	Burnley	L 1-2	Thomas	18,297			10		2		5	8		11	3	9	6		1	7	4	
20 (a)	Wolves	W 4-2	Bowles 2, Leach, Francis (pen)	19,350			10		2	12		8		11*	3	9	6	5	1	7	4	
27 (h)	Arsenal	W 2-0	Givens, Bowles	29,115			10		2			8		11	3	9	6	5	1	7	4	
Nov 3 (a)	Derby C	W 2-1	Francis, Bowles	30,647			10		2			8		11	3	9	6	5	1	7	4	
10 (h)	Coventry C	W 3-0	Bowles, Francis, Venables	20,416			10		2	12		8		11	3	9*	6	5	1	7	4	
17 (a)	Manchester C	L 0-1		30,486			10	9*	2	12		8		11	3		6	5	1	7	4	
24 (h)	Liverpool	D 2-2	Bowles, McLintock	26,254			10		2			8		11	3	9	6	5	1	7	4	
Dec 1 (a)	Leeds U	D 2-2	Thomas, Bowles	32,194			10		2			8		11	3	9	6	5	1	7	4	
8 (h)	Sheffield U	D 0-0		15,843		12	10		2	4*		8		11	3	9	6	5	1	7		
15 (a)	LeicesterC	L 0-2		17,614			10		2			8		11	3	9	6	5	1	7	4	
22 (h)	Newcastle U	W 3-2	Clement, Givens, Bowles	15,757			10		2			8	3	11		9	6	5	1	7	4	
26 (a)	Tottenham H	D 0-0		30,762			10		2			8	3	11		9	6	5	1	7	4	
29 (a)	Stoke C	L 1-4	Leach	18,910		12	10		2		5	8	3	11		9	6		1	7	4*	
Jan 1 (h)	Manchester U	W 3-0	Bowles 2, Givens	32,339			10		2			8	3	11		9	6	5	1	7	4	
12 (h)	Everton	W 1-0	Givens	19,051			10		2			8	3	11		9	6	5	1	7	4	
19 (a)	Southampton	D 2-2	Bowles, Francis (pen)	22,689			10		2			8	3	11	6	9		5	1	7	4	
Feb 2 (h)	Leicester C	D 0-0		22,646			10		2			8	3	11		9	6	5	1	7	4	
5 (h)	Norwich C	L 1-2	Bowles	12,427			10		2			8	3	11		9	6	5	1	7	4	
23 (a)	Chelsea	D 3-3	Bowles 2, Givens	34,264	12		10		2			8	3	11		9	6	5	1	7*	4	
27 (h)	Burnley	W 2-1	Thomas, Bowles (pen)	21,306	4		10		2			8	3	11		9	6	5	1	7		
Mar 2 (h)	Tottenham H	W 3-1	Givens, Bowles, Francis	25,775	4*		10		2			8	3	11	12	9	6	5	1	7		
16 (h)	Wolves	D 0-0		21,209			10		2			8	3	11	12	9	6	5	1	7	4*	
23 (a)	Coventry C	W 1-0	Francis	18,804	12		10	4	2			8	3	11*		9	6	5	1	7		
30 (h)	Derby C	D 0-0		19,795			10	12	2			8	3	11		9	6	5	1	7	4*	
Apr 6 (a)	Liverpool	L 1-2	Thomas	54,027			10		2			8	3	11	6	9		5	1	7	4	
9 (h)	Manchester C	W 3-0	Leach 2, Bowles	20,461		4	10		2			8	3	11	6	9		5	1	7		
12 (h)	Ipswich T	L 0-1		27,567		4	10		2			8	3	11	6	9		5	1	7		
15 (a)	Ipswich T	L 0-1		26,100	12		10		2*			8	3	11	6	9		5	1	7	4	
20 (a)	Sheffield U	D 1-1	Givens	17,933			10	9*			6	8	3	11	2	12		5	1	7	4	
23 (a)	Birmingham C	L 0-4		39,160			10	9			6	8	3	11	2			5	1	7	4	
27 (h)	Leeds U	L 0-1		35,353			10	2				8	3	11	6	9		5	1	7	4	
30 (a)	Arsenal	D 1-1	Bowles	40,396		12	10		2*			8	3	11	6	9		5	1	7	4	
				App	3	2	42	5	38	3	5	40	23	42	29	39	26	40	42	41	36	6
				Sub app	4	3		1		3					2	1						
				Goals	1		20		1			8		10		6	1	1		5	2	

1 own-goal

FA Cup

Date	Opponent	Res	Scorers	Att	Abbott	Beck	Bowles	Busby	Clement	Delve	Evans	Francis	Gillard	Givens	Hazell	Leach	McLintock	Mancini	Parkes	Thomas	Venables	Watson	Round
Jan 5 (a)	Chelsea	D 0-0		31,540			10		2			8	3	11		9	6	5	1	7	4		3
15 (h)	Chelsea	W 1-0	Bowles	28,573			10*		2			8	3	11	12	9	6	5	1	7	4		Rep
26 (h)	Birmingham C	W 2-0	Leach, Givens	23,367			10		2			8	3	11		9	6	5	1	7	4		4
Feb 16 (a)	Coventry C	D 0-0		30,081			10					8	3	11	2	9	6	5	1	7	4		5
19 (h)	Coventry C	W 3-2	Givens, Thomas, Bowles	28,010			10					8	3	11	2	9	6	5	1	7	4		Rep
Mar 9 (h)	Leicester C	L 0-2		34,078			10		2			8	3	11		9	6	5	1	7	4		6
				App			6		4			6	6	6	2	6	6	6	6	6	6		
				Sub app											1								
				Goals			2							2		1				1			

League Cup

Date	Opponent	Res	Scorers	Att	Abbott	Beck	Bowles	Busby	Clement	Delve	Evans	Francis	Gillard	Givens	Hazell	Leach	McLintock	Mancini	Parkes	Thomas	Venables	Watson	Round
Oct 8 (h)	Tottenham H	W 1-0	Givens	23,353			10*	12	2			8		11	3	9	6	5	1	7	4		2
Nov 6 (h)	Sheffield W	W 8-2	Cameron (og), Mullen (og), Francis, Bowles, Givens 2, Leach 2	16,043			10	12	2			8		11	3	9	6*	5	1	7	4		3
20 (h)	Plymouth A	L 0-3		19,072			10	9*	2	12		8		11	3		6	5	1	7	4		4
				App			3	1	3			3		3	3	2	3	3	3	3	3		
				Sub app				2		1													
				Goals			1					1		3		2							

2 own-goals

Substitutions are denoted by including these symbols:
Number 12 = *; 13 = †; 14 = ‡; 15 = §; 16 = °.

Attendance Summary

	ATTENDANCES			AVERAGE		
	Home	Away	Total	Home	Away	Total
League	480,104	603,617	1,083,724	22,862	28,744	25,803
League Cup	58,468		58,468	19,489		19,489
FA Cup	114,028	61,621	175,649	28,507	30,810	29,275
Total	652,600	665,238	1,317,838	23,307	28,923	25,840

1974-75

Division 1

Date	Opponents	Result	Scorers	Att	Abbott	Beck	Bowles	Busby	Clement	Francis	Gillard	Givens	Hazell	Leach	McLintock	Mancini	Masson	Parkes	Pritchett	Rogers	Shanks	Teale	Thomas	Venables	Webb	Westwood
Aug 16	(a) Sheffield U	D 1-1	Francis	16,082	9	10			2	8	3	11				5		1					7	4	6	
21	(a) Leeds U	W 1-0	Francis	31,497	9	10		12	2	8	3	11				5*		1					7	4	6	
24	(h) Stoke C	L 0-1		21,117		9	10*	4	2	8	3	11		12		5		1					7		6	
27	(h) Leeds U	D 1-1	Givens	24,965		9	10	12	2*	8	3	11				5		1					7	4	6	
31	(a) Luton T	D 1-1	Bowles (pen)	18,835		9	10	2		8	3	11				5		1					7	4	6	
Sep 7	(h) Birmingham C	L 0-1		16,058		9	10	2		8*	3	11		12		5						1	7	4	6	
14	(a) Leicester C	L 1-3	Francis	19,763			10	9	2	8	3	11	6	4				1					7		5	
21	(h) Newcastle U	L 1-2	Keeley (og)	18,594			10	9	2	8	3	11	6	4				1					7		5	
24	(h) Everton	D 2-2	Givens, Busby	16,638	10*			9	2	8	3	11	6	4				1		12			7		5	
28	(a) Manchester C	L 0-1		30,647	10	4		9	2	8	3	11*	6					1		12			7		5	
Oct 5	(h) Ipswich T	W 1-0	Francis	19,494		4	10		2	8	3	11	6	9*		5		1		12			7			
12	(a) Arsenal	D 2-2	Bowles (pen) 2	26,690			10		2	8	3	11		4	5			1		9			7		6	
19	(h) Liverpool	L 0-1		27,392		4	10		2	8	3	11			5			1		9			7		6	
26	(a) Wolves	W 2-1	Givens 2	20,320			10		2	8	3	11	4		5			1		9			7		6	
Nov 2	(h) Coventry C	W 2-0	Bowles, Givens	17,256			10		2		3	11	4	9	5			1		8			7		6	
9	(a) Derby C	L 2-5	Leach, Bowles	23,339		12	10		2	8	3	11	4	9*	5			1					7		6	
16	(h) Carlisle U	W 2-1	Thomas, Bowles	15,700			10		6	8	3	11	2	4	5			1		9			7			
23	(a) Middlesbrough	W 3-1	Bowles, Givens, Rogers	27,330			10		2	8	3	11	6	4	5			1		9			7			
27	(a) Stoke C	L 0-1		22,403			10		2	8	3	11	6	4	5			1		9			7			
30	(h) West Ham U	L 0-2		28,356			10		2	8	3	11	4		5			1		9			7		6	
Dec 7	(a) Burnley	L 0-3		16,487			10		2	8	3	11		9	5			1			4		7		6	
14	(h) Sheffield U	W 1-0	Rogers	13,244		10			2	8	3	11		9	5		4	1		7					6	
21	(a) Tottenham H	W 2-1	Bowles 2 (1 pen)	21,150		8	10		2		3	11		9	5		4	1					7		6	
26	(h) Leicester C	W 4-2	Beck, Thomas, Givens, Westwood	17,311		8			6		3	11		9*	5		4	1			2		7		10	12
28	(a) Chelsea	W 3-0	Givens 2, Francis	38,917		9	10		2	8	3	11			5		4	1					7		6	
Jan 11	(h) Burnley	L 0-1		19,359		9	10		2	8	3	11			5		4	1					7		6	
18	(a) West Ham U	D 2-2	Masson, Bowles (pen)	28,772		9	10		2	8	3	11			5		4	1					7		6	
Feb 1	(h) Derby C	W 4-1	Givens 3, Thomas	20,686		9	10		2	8	3	11			5		4	1					7		6	
8	(a) Coventry C	D 1-1	Leach	18,807		9	10		2	8*	3	11		12	5		4	1					7		6	
22	(a) Carlisle U	W 2-1	Givens 2	13,176		9	10	12	6		3	11			5		4*	1		8	2		7			
25	(h) Middlesbrough	D 0-0		18,487		9	10		2	8	3	11			5		4	1					7		6	
Mar 1	(h) Luton T	W 2-1	Givens, Rogers	19,583		9	10	8	2		3	11			5		4	1		12			7*		6	
8	(a) Everton	L 1-2	Givens	39,567		9	10	8	2		3	11			5		4	1					7		6	
15	(h) Manchester C	W 2-0	Rogers 2	22,102			10	9		8	3				5		4	1		11	2		7		6	
18	(h) Chelsea	W 1-0	Thomas	25,324		12	10	9		8	3				5		4	1		11	2		7		6*	
22	(a) Birmingham C	L 1-4	Thomas	32,853			10*	9		8	3	11			5		4	1		12	2		7		6	
29	(h) Tottenham H	L 0-1		25,461		9				8	3	11			5		4	1		10	2		7		6	
31	(a) Newcastle U	D 2-2	Francis (pen), Gillard	28,490	12	9				8	6	11*		10	5		4	1	3		2		7			
Apr 5	(h) Wolves	W 2-0	Givens, Thomas	16,596	12	9	10			8	6	11			5*		4	1	3		2		7			
12	(a) Ipswich T	L 1-2	Gillard	28,709	12	9	10			8	6	11			5*		4	1	3		2		7			
19	(h) Arsenal	D 0-0		24,362	5	9	10				6	11		8			4	1	3		2		7			
26	(a) Liverpool	L 1-3	Francis (pen)	42,546	10	9				8	3	11		12	5*		4	1			2		7		6	
				App	6	27	33	12	31	35	42	40	12	16	30	7	21	41	4	13	12	1	41	5	33	
				Sub app	3	2		3						4						5						1
				Goals		1	10	1		7	2	17		2			1			5			6			1

1 own-goal

FA Cup

Date	Opponents	Result	Scorers	Att	Abbott	Beck	Bowles	Busby	Clement	Francis	Gillard	Givens	Hazell	Leach	McLintock	Mancini	Masson	Parkes	Pritchett	Rogers	Shanks	Teale	Thomas	Venables	Webb	Westwood	Round
Jan 4	(a) Southend U	D 2-2	Gillard, Francis	18,100		7	10		2	8	3	11		9	5		4	1							6		3
7	(h) Southend U	W 2-0	Givens 2	21,484		9	10		2	8	3	11			5		4	1					7		6		Rep
24	(h) Notts C	W 3-0	Thomas, Bowles (pen), Givens	23,428		9	10		2	8	3	11			5		4	1					7		6		4
Feb 15	(a) West Ham U	L 1-2	Clement	39,193		9	10*		2		3	11		8	5		4	1		12			7		6		5
				App		4	4		4	3	4	4		2	4		4	4					3		4		
				Sub app																1							
				Goals			1		1	1	1	3											1				

League Cup

Date	Opponents	Result	Scorers	Att	Abbott	Beck	Bowles	Busby	Clement	Francis	Gillard	Givens	Hazell	Leach	McLintock	Mancini	Masson	Parkes	Pritchett	Rogers	Shanks	Teale	Thomas	Venables	Webb	Westwood	Round
Sep 10	(h) Orient	D 1-1	Francis	14,304			10	9	2	8	3	11				5						1	7	4	6		2
17	(a) Orient	W 3-0	Francis, Givens, Bowles	11,750		2	10	6		8	3	11	4	9				1					7		5		Rep
Oct 8	(h) Newcastle U	L 0-4		15,815		4	10		2	8	3	11	6			5		1					7		12	9*	3
				App		2	3	2	2	3	3	3	2	1		2		2				1	3	1	2	1	
				Sub app																					1		
				Goals			1			2		1															

Substitutions are denoted by including these symbols:
Number 12 = *; 13 = †; 14 = ‡; 15 = §; 16 = °.

Attendance Summary

	ATTENDANCES Home	Away	Total	AVERAGE Home	Away	Total
League	428,085	546,380	974,465	20,385	26,018	23,202
League Cup	30,119	11,750	41,869	15,060	11,750	13,956
FA Cup	44,912	57,293	102,205	22,456	28,646	25,551
Total	503,116	615,423	1,118,539	20,125	25,643	22,827

1975-76

Division 1

Date	Opponent	Result	Scorers	Att	Abbott	Beck	Bowles	Busby	Clement	Francis	Gillard	Givens	Hollins	Leach	McLintock	Masson	Nutt	Parkes	Shanks	Tagg	Thomas	Webb
Aug 16	(h) Liverpool	W 2-0	Francis, Leach	27,113			10		2	8	3	11	4*	12	5	9		1			7	6
19	(h) Aston Villa	D 1-1	Francis	21,986	6	12	10		2	8	3	11		4	5*	9		1			7	
23	(a) Derby C	W 5-1	Bowles 3 (1 pen), Thomas, Clement	27,590	5	12	10		2	8	3	11		4		9		1		6	7*	
26	(a) Wolves	D 2-2	Givens 2	19,380	5		10		2	8	3	11		4		9		1		6	7	
30	(h) West Ham U	D 1-1	Givens	28,408	5		10		2	8*	3	11	12	4		9		1		6	7	
Sep 6	(a) Birmingham C	D 1-1	Thomas	27,305	5		10		2			11	8	4		9		1		6	7	3
13	(h) Manchester U	W 1-0	Webb	29,237			10		2	8	3	11		4	5	9		1			7	6
20	(a) Middlesbrough	D 0-0		24,867			10		2	8	3	11*	12	4	5	9		1			7	6
23	(h) Leicester C	W 1-0	Leach	19,292			10		2	8	3	11		4	5	9		1			7	6
27	(h) Newcastle U	W 1-0	Leach	22,981			10		2	8	3	11		4	5	9		1			7	6
Oct 4	(a) Leeds U	L 1-2	Bowles (pen)	30,943			10		2	8	3	11	4		5	9		1			7	6
11	(h) Everton	W 5-0	Francis 2, Givens, Masson, Thomas	23,022			10		2	8	3	11		4	5	9		1			7	6
18	(a) Burnley	L 0-1		20,409			10		2	8	3	11	5	4		9		1			7	6
25	(h) Sheffield U	W 1-0	Givens	21,161			10		2	8	3	11		4	5	9		1			7	6
Nov 1	(a) Coventry C	D 1-1	Givens	17,845			10		2	8	3	11		4	5	9		1			7	6
8	(h) Tottenham H	D 0-0		28,454			10		2	8	3	11		4	5	9		1			7	6
15	(a) Ipswich T	D 1-1	Givens	25,546					2	8	3	11	10	4	5	9		1			7	6
22	(h) Burnley	W 1-0	Bowles	17,390			10		2	8	3	11		4	5	9		1			7	6
29	(h) Stoke C	W 3-2	Masson, Clement, Webb	22,328		8	10		2		3		4	11*	5	9	12	1			7	6
Dec 6	(a) Manchester C	D 0-0		36,066					2	8	3	11	4	10	5	9		1			7	6
13	(h) Derby C	D 1-1	Nutt	25,465					2	8	3	11	4	10	5	9*	12	1			7	6
20	(a) Liverpool	L 0-2		39,182			10		2	8	3	11	4		5	9		1			7	6
26	(h) Norwich C	W 2-0	Masson, Bowles	21,774			10		2	8	3	11		4	5	9		1			7	6
27	(a) Arsenal	L 0-2		39,021			10		2	8	3	11	4		5	9		1			7	6
Jan 10	(a) Manchester U	L 1-2	Givens	58,312	12		10*		2	8	3	11	4	7	5	9		1				6
17	(h) Birmingham C	W 2-1	Masson 2	16,759		8	10		2		3	11	4		5	9		1			7	6
24	(a) West Ham U	L 0-1		26,677		8			2		3	11	4	10	5*	9	12	1			7	6
31	(a) Aston Villa	W 2-0	Hollins, Francis	32,223					2	8	3	11	4	10	5	9		1			7	6
Feb 7	(h) Wolves	W 4-2	Givens 2, Thomas, Francis (pen)	17,153			10		2	8	3	11	5	4		9		1			7	6
14	(a) Tottenham H	W 3-0	Francis 2, Givens	28,200			10		2	8	3	11	5	4		9		1			7	6
21	(h) Ipswich T	W 3-1	Wark (og), Webb, Thomas	22,593			10		2	8	3	11	5	4*	12	9		1			7	6
25	(a) Leicester C	W 1-0	Thomas	24,340			10		2	8	3	11	4		5	9		1			7	6
28	(a) Sheffield U	D 0-0		21,949			10		2		3	11	4	8	5	9		1			7	6
Mar 6	(h) Coventry C	W 4-1	Thomas, Francis, Givens, Masson	19,731			10		2	8	3	11	4		5	9		1			7	6
13	(a) Everton	W 2-0	Bowles, Leach	25,186			10		2	8*	3	11	4	12	5	9		1			7	6
20	(a) Stoke C	W 1-0	Webb	22,848			10		2		3	11	4	8	5	9		1			7	6
27	(h) Manchester C	W 1-0	Webb	29,883			10			8	3	11	4	12	5*	9		1	2		7	6
Apr 3	(a) Newcastle U	W 2-1	McLintock, Bowles	30,134			10			8	3	11	4		5	9		1	2		7	6
10	(h) Middlesbrough	W 4-2	Francis 2 (1 pen), Givens, Bowles	24,342			10		2	8	3	11	4		5	9		1			7	6
17	(a) Norwich C	L 2-3	Thomas, Powell (og)	31,231			10		2	8	3	11	4		5	9		1			7	6
19	(h) Arsenal	W 2-1	McLintock, Francis (pen)	30,362			10		2	8	3	11	4		5	9		1			7	6
24	(h) Leeds U	W 2-0	Thomas, Bowles	31,002			10		2	8	3	11	4		5	9		1			7	6
				App	5	3	37		40	36	41	41	28	28	34	42		42	2	4	41	38
				Sub app	1	2							2	3	1		3					
				Goals			10		2	12		13	1	4	2	6	1				9	5

2 own-goals

FA Cup

Date	Opponent	Result	Scorers	Att	Abbott	Beck	Bowles	Busby	Clement	Francis	Gillard	Givens	Hollins	Leach	McLintock	Masson	Nutt	Parkes	Shanks	Tagg	Thomas	Webb	Round
Jan 3	(h) Newcastle U	D 0-0		20,102			10		2	8	3	11*	12	4	5	9		1			7	6	3
7	(a) Newcastle U	L 1-2	Masson	37,225			10*	12	2	8	3	11	4	7	5	9		1				6	Rep
				App			2		2	2	2	2	1	2	2	2		2			1	2	
				Sub app				1					1										
				Goals												1							

League Cup

Date	Opponent	Result	Scorers	Att	Abbott	Beck	Bowles	Busby	Clement	Francis	Gillard	Givens	Hollins	Leach	McLintock	Masson	Nutt	Parkes	Shanks	Tagg	Thomas	Webb	Round
Sep 9	(a) Shrewsbury T	W 4-1	Webb, Masson, Thomas, Leach	11,250	6		10		2	8		11		4	5	9		1			7	3	2
Oct 7	(h) Charlton A	D 1-1	Bowles	20,434			10		2	8	3	11		4	5	9		1			7	6	3
14	(a) Charlton A	W 3-0	Thomas, Masson, Bowles	31,583			10		2	8	3	11	12	4	5*	9		1			7	6	Rep
Nov 11	(h) Newcastle U	L 1-3	Leach	21,162			10*		2	8	3	11	12	4	5	9		1			7	6	4
				App	1		4		4	4	3	4		4	4	4		4			4	4	
				Sub app									2										
				Goals			2							2		2					2	1	

Substitutions are denoted by including these symbols:
Number 12 = *; 13 = †; 14 = ‡; 15 = §; 16 = °.

Attendance Summary

	ATTENDANCES			AVERAGE		
	Home	Away	Total	Home	Away	Total
League	500,436	609,254	1,109,690	23,830	29,012	26,421
League Cup	41,596	42,833	84,429	20,798	21,416	21,107
FA Cup	20,102	37,225	57,327	20,102	37,225	28,664
Total	562,134	689,312	1,251,446	23,422	28,721	26,072

1976-77

Division 1

Date	Opponents	Result	Scorers	Att	Abbott	Bowles	Busby	Clement	Cunningham	Eastoe	Francis	Gillard	Givens	Hollins	Kelly	Leach	McLintock	Masson	Nutt	Parkes	Richardson	Shanks	Thomas	Webb
Aug 21	(h) Everton	L 0-4		24,449		10	8*	2				3	11	4		6	5	9		1		12	7	
23	(a) West Ham U	L 0-1		31,668	6	10		2				3	11	4		8	5	9		1			7	
28	(a) Ipswich T	D 2-2	Givens, Masson	24,491	6	10		2				3	11	4		8	5	9		1			7	
4	(h) West Brom A	W 1-0	Gillard	18,876		10		2				3	11	4		8	5	9		1			7	6
11	(h) Aston Villa	W 2-1	Masson, Clement	23,602		10		2				3	11	4	8*	12	5	9		1			7	6
18	(a) Leicester C	D 2-2	Givens, Hollins	18,439		10		2				3	11	4	8*	12	5	9		1			7	6
25	(h) Stoke C	W 2-0	Bowles, Givens	21,621		10		2				3	11	4	8		5	9		1			7	6
Oct 2	(a) Arsenal	L 2-3	Thomas, McLintock	39,442		10		2	8			3	11	4			5	9	12	1*			7	6
5	(h) Norwich C	L 2-3	Masson (pen), Webb	16,086		10		2				3	11	4	8		5	9		1			7	6
16	(a) Manchester C	D 0-0		40,751		10		2		12		3	11*	4	8		5	9		1			7	6
23	(h) Sunderland	W 2-0	McLintock, Bowles	22,408		10		2				3	11	4	8		5	9		1			7	6
30	(a) Birmingham C	L 1-2	Eastoe	31,471		10		2		7		3	11	4		8	5	9		1				6
Nov 6	(h) Derby C	D 1-1	Givens	22,527		10		2				3	11	4	8		5	9		1			7	6
9	(a) Coventry C	L 0-2		16,190		10		2				3	11	4		8	5	9		1			7	6
20	(h) Middlesbrough	W 3-0	Givens (pen), Masson, Bowles	16,037		10							11	3	8	4	5	9		1		2	7	6
27	(a) Newcastle U	L 0-2		39,013				2		10		3	11	4	8		5	9		1			7	6
Dec 11	(a) Liverpool	L 1-3	Eastoe	37,154		10		2		7		3	11	5	4	8		9		1				6
27	(a) Norwich C	L 0-2		27,343		10		2		12		3	11	5	4	8		9		1			7	6*
Jan 11	(h) Tottenham H	W 2-1	Bowles, Clement	24,266		10		2		7		3	11	4		8	5	9		1				6
22	(a) Everton	W 3-1	Leach, Masson, Bowles	26,875		10		2*	12	7		3	11	4		8	5	9		1				6
Feb 12	(a) West Brom A	D 1-1	Francis	18,364		10		2			8	3	11	4			5	9		1			7	6
26	(h) Leicester C	W 3-2	Givens, Hollins, Francis (pen)	20,386				2		9	8	3	11	4	10	12	5*			1			7	6
Mar 5	(a) Stoke C	L 0-1		15,454		10		12			8	3	11*	2	4		5	9		1			7	6
8	(h) Leeds U	D 0-0		20,386				2		11	8	3		4	10		5	9			1		7	6
12	(h) Arsenal	W 2-1	Francis, Hollins	26,191				2		12	8	3	11	4	10		5	9			1		7*	6
19	(a) Bristol C	L 0-1		22,441		10*		2	8	7		3	11	4			5	9		1		12		6
22	(h) Manchester C	D 0-0		17,619	5			2		8		3	11	4	10			9		1		12	7*	6
Apr 2	(a) Sunderland	L 0-1		27,850	5				10	7		3	11	4		8		9		1		2		6
4	(h) West Ham U	D 1-1	Eastoe	24,930	6					7		3	11	4		8	5	9		1		2		10
9	(a) Tottenham H	L 0-3		32,680	5					10		3	11		4	8		9		1		2	7	6
14	(h) Coventry C	D 1-1	Masson (pen)	15,445	5				12	10		3	11		4	8		9		1		2	7*	6
16	(a) Middlesbrough	W 2-0	Abbott, Masson	14,500	10			2		7		3	11	4	8		5	9		1				6
19	(h) Manchester U	W 4-0	Eastoe 2, Givens, Kelly	28,848	12			2*		7	8	3	11	4	10		5	9		1				6
23	(h) Newcastle U	L 1-2	Givens	20,544	10					7		3	11	4	8		5	9		1		2		6
26	(h) Bristol C	L 0-1		14,576				2		7	8	3	11	4	10		5	9*		1			12	6
30	(a) Manchester U	L 0-1		50,788				2		7	8	3	11	4	10		5	9		1				6
May 7	(h) Liverpool	D 1-1	Givens	29,832				2		10	8	3	11	4			5	9		1			7	6
11	(a) Derby C	L 0-2		21,312				2*		10		3	11	4	8		5	9		1		12	7	6
14	(a) Leeds U	W 1-0	Eastoe	22,226						10	8	3	11	2	4		5	9		1			7	6
16	(h) Ipswich T	W 1-0	Givens	19,171						10	8*	3	11	2	4	12	5	9		1			7	6
20	(a) Aston Villa	D 1-1	Abbott	28,056	6			2		10		3	11	4	8		5	9		1			7	
23	(h) Birmingham C	D 2-2	Masson, Webb	14,976	12					10		3	11	2	4*	8	5	9		1			7	6
				App	10	22	1	32	3	24	11	41	41	40	28	16	36	41		40	2	6	30	38
				Sub app	2			1	2	3						4			1			4	1	
				Goals	2	5		2		6	3	1	10	3	1	1	2	8					1	2

FA Cup

Date	Opponents	Result	Scorers	Att	Abbott	Bowles	Busby	Clement	Cunningham	Eastoe	Francis	Gillard	Givens	Hollins	Kelly	Leach	McLintock	Masson	Nutt	Parkes	Richardson	Shanks	Thomas	Webb	Round
Jan 8	(h) Shrewsbury T	W 2-1	Bowles, Givens	18,285		10		2		7		3	11	4		8	5	9		1				6	3
29	(a) Manchester U	L 0-1		57,422		10				7		3	11	4		8	5	9		1		2		6	4
				App		2		1		2		2	2	2		2	2	2		2		1		2	
				Sub app																					
				Goals		1							1												

League Cup

Date	Opponents	Result	Scorers	Att	Abbott	Bowles	Busby	Clement	Cunningham	Eastoe	Francis	Gillard	Givens	Hollins	Kelly	Leach	McLintock	Masson	Nutt	Parkes	Richardson	Shanks	Thomas	Webb	Round
Sep 1	(a) Cardiff C	W 3-1	Bowles, Thomas, Clement	23,618		10		2				3	11*	4		8	5	9		1		12	7	6	2
21	(h) Bury	W 2-1	McLintock, Givens	13,069		10		2				3	11	4	8		5	9		1			7	6	3
Oct 27	(a) West Ham U	W 2-0	Bowles, Clement	24,565		10		2				3	11	4	8	12	5	9		1			7*	6	4
Dec 1	(h) Arsenal	W 2-1	Masson, Webb	27,621		10		2				3	11	4	8	12	5*	9		1			7	6	5
Feb 1	(h) Aston Villa	D 0-0		28,739		10				9		3	12	4*		8	5	9		1		2	7	6	SF/1
16	(a) Aston Villa	D 2-2	Francis, Eastoe	48,439		10		2		12	8	3	11	4*			5	9		1			7	6	SF/2
22	(n*) Aston Villa	L 0-3		40,438		10		2		9	8	3	11				5	4		1			7	6	Rep
				App		7		6		2	2	7	6	6	3	2	7	7		7		1	7	7	
				Sub app						1			1			2						1			
				Goals		2		2		1	1		1				1	1					1	1	

*Played at Highbury, London.

UEFA Cup

Date	Opponents	Result	Scorers	Att	Abbott	Bowles	Busby	Clement	Cunningham	Eastoe	Francis	Gillard	Givens	Hollins	Kelly	Leach	McLintock	Masson	Nutt	Parkes	Richardson	Shanks	Thomas	Webb	Round
Sep 15	(h) SK Brann	W 4-0	Bowles 3, Masson	14,698		10		2				3	11	4		8	5	9		1			7	6	1/1
29	(a) SK Brann	W 7-0	Bowles 3, Givens 2, Thomas, Webb	11,000		10	14	2				3	11	4		8‡	5	9		1			7	6	1/2
Oct 20	(a) Slovan Bratislava	D 3-3	Bowles 2, Givens	40,000		10		2				3	11	4		8	5	9		1			7	6	2/1
Nov 3	(h) Slovan Bratislava	W 5-2	Givens 3 (1 pen), Bowles, Clement	22,001		10		2				3	11	4		8	5	9		1			7	6	2/2
24	(h) 1.FC Cologne	W 3-0	Givens, Webb, Bowles	21,143		10		2				3	11	4		8	5	9		1			7	6	3/1
Dec 7	(a) 1.FC Cologne	L 1-4#	Masson	50,000		10		2		14		3	11	4		8‡	5	9		1			7	6	3/2
Mar 2	(h) AEK Athens	W 3-0	Francis 2 (2 pens), Bowles	23,009		10					8	3	11	2	4		5	9		1			7	6	QF/1
16	(a) AEK Athens	L 0-3☆		35,000		10				7		3	11	4	8		5	9		1		2		6	QF/2
				App		8		6		1	1	8	8	8	2	6	8	8		8		1	7	8	
				Sub app			1			1															
				Goals		11		1			2		7					2					1	2	

#Won on away-goals rule. ☆Lost on penalties.

Substitutions are denoted by including these symbols:
Number 12 = *; 13 = †; 14 = ‡; 15 = §; 16 = °.

1977-78

Division 1

Date	Opponent	Result	Scorers	Att	Abbott	Bowles	Busby	Clement	Cunningham	Eastoe	Francis	Gillard	Givens	Goddard	Hollins	Howe	James	Leach	McGee	Masson	Needham	Parkes	Perkins	Richardson	Shanks	Wallace	Webb	Williams
Aug 20(h)	Aston Villa	L 1-2	Eastoe	25,431		10		2		7	8*	3	11		4					9	5	1					6	12
23(a)	Wolves	L 0-1		22,278	8*	10		2		7		3	11		4			12		9	5	1					6	
27(a)	Norwich C	D 1-1	Needham	17,914		10		2		7		3	11*		4			8		9	5	1					6	12
Sep 3(h)	Leicester C	W 3-0	Givens, Francis, Needham	14,516		10		2		7	8		11		4					9	5	1			3		6	
10(a)	West Ham U	D 2-2	Eastoe, Lock (og)	26,922		10		2		7	8		11*		4					9	5	1			3		6	12
17(h)	Manchester C	D 1-1	Francis	24,668	12	10		2		7*	8	3	11							9	5	1					6	4
24(h)	Chelsea	D 1-1	Masson	26,267		10		2		7	8*	3	11		4					9	5	1					6	12
Oct 1(a)	Bristol C	D 2-2	Masson, Eastoe	20,947	6	10	8	2		7		3*	11		4					9	5	1						12
4(a)	Birmingham C	L 1-2	Masson	21,304	6	10	8	2		7*			11					4		9	5	1			3			12
8(h)	Everton	L 1-5	Eastoe	20,495	6	10	8	2		7			11		12			4*		9	5	1			3			
15(a)	Arsenal	L 0-1		36,172		10	8	2		7		3	11		4					9	5	1			6			
22(h)	Nottingham F	L 0-2		24,248		10	8	2		7		3	11*		4					9	5	1			6			12
29(h)	West Brom A	W 2-1	Eastoe, Bowles	18,800	5	10		2*		7		3	9		4		8					1			6	12		11
Nov 5(a)	Middlesbrough	D 1-1	Busby	18,329	6	10	7					3	9		4		8				5			1	2	12		11*
12(h)	Liverpool	W 2-0	James, Bowles	25,625		10	6		12	7*		3	9		4		8				5			1	2			11
19(a)	Coventry C	L 1-4	Givens	20,411	12	10	6					3	9		4		8		7*		5			1	2			11
26(h)	Manchester U	D 2-2	Needham, Givens	25,367		10			6			3	9		4		8	7			5			1	2	11		
Dec 3(a)	Leeds U	L 0-3		26,597		10			6			3	9		4		8	7			5			1	2	11		
10(h)	Newcastle U	L 0-1		15,251		10			6		8	3	9		4		7				5			1	2	11		
17(a)	Liverpool	L 0-1		38,249			12		6		8	3	9		4	5		10						1	2	11*		7
26(h)	Derby C	D 0-0		18,197		10			6	11	8	3	9		4	5	7							1	2			
27(a)	Ipswich T	L 2-3	Bowles (pen), McGee	22,317		10			6	11*	8	3	9		4	5	7		12					1	2			
31(h)	Wolves	L 1-3	Shanks	16,067		10			6	9*	8	3	11		4	5	7		12					1	2			
Jan 2(a)	Aston Villa	D 1-1	Smith (og)	34,750		10	12		6	9*	8	3	11		4	5	7					1			2			
14(h)	Norwich C	W 2-1	Eastoe, Cunningham	14,247		10			6	7	8	3	11		4	5	9*					1			2	12		
21(a)	Leicester C	D 0-0		16,288		10			6		8*	3	11		4	5	9					1			2	7		12
Feb 11(a)	Manchester C	L 1-2	Abbott	39,860	6	10	8	2				3	11		4	5	9					1			7			
25(h)	Bristol C	D 2-2	Bowles (pen), Busby	17,051	6	10	8	2				3	11		4	5	9					1			7			
Mar 4(a)	Everton	D 3-3	Shanks, Hollins, Howe	33,861		10	8*	2	6			3	11		4	5			9			1			7	12		
14(h)	West Ham U	W 1-0	Cunningham	20,394		10	8	2	6			3	11		4	5	9*		12			1			7			
22(a)	West Brom A	L 0-2		21,000			8	2	6			3	11		4	5	9		10			1			7			
25(h)	Ipswich T	D 3-3	McGee 2, James	15,563		10	8	2	6			3	11*		4	5	9		12			1			7			
27(a)	Derby C	L 0-2		20,155		10	8	2	6			3			4	5	9		11*			1			7	12		
Apr 1(h)	Middlesbrough	W 1-0	Busby	12,925		10	8	2				3			4	5			11			1	6		7	9		
8(a)	Manchester U	L 1-3	Bowles (pen)	42,677		10	8	2				3			4	5	12		11*			1	6		7	9		
11(h)	Arsenal	W 2-1	Shanks, Bowles	25,683		10	8	2				3	11*	12	4	5	9		7			1			6			
15(h)	Coventry C	W 2-1	Goddard, James	17,062		10	8*	2				3		11	4	5	9		7			1			6			12
18(a)	Nottingham F	L 0-1		30,339		10		2				3		11	4	5	9		7			1			6			8
22(a)	Newcastle U	W 3-0	Givens, McGee, Hollins	13,000		10		2				3	11	12	4	5	9		7*			1			6			8
25(h)	Birmingham C	D 0-0		16,049		10		2				3	11	12	4	5	9		8			1			6			7*
29(h)	Leeds U	D 0-0		23,993		10		2				3	11	12	4	5	9		7			1			6	8*		
May 2(a)	Chelsea	L 1-3	James	21,201		10		2				3	11	7	4	5	9		8*					1	6			12
				App	8	40	19	29	15	19	13	38	37	3	39	23	26	6	13	12	18	31	2	11	36	8	7	9
				Sub app	2		2		1					4	1		1	1	4							5		10
				Goals	1	6	3		2	6	2		4	1	2	1	4		4	3	3				3			

2 own-goals

FA Cup

Date	Opponent	Result	Scorers	Att	Abbott	Bowles	Busby	Clement	Cunningham	Eastoe	Francis	Gillard	Givens	Goddard	Hollins	Howe	James	Leach	McGee	Masson	Needham	Parkes	Perkins	Richardson	Shanks	Wallace	Webb	Williams	Round
Jan 7(h)	Wealdstone	W 4-0	Givens, James, Bowles (pen), Howe	16,158		10			6			3	11		4	5	9	7*				1			2	8		12	3
28(a)	West Ham U	D 1-1	Howe	35,556	6	10	8	2				3	11		4	5	9					1			7				4
31(h)	West Ham U	W 6-1	Givens, Hollins, Busby 2, Bowles (pen), James	24,057	6	10	8	2				3	11		4	5	9					1			7				Rep
Feb 18(h)	Nottingham F	D 1-1	Busby	26,803	6	10	8	2				3	11		4	5	9					1			7				5
27(a)	Nottingham F	D 1-1	Shanks	40,097	6	10	8	2				3	11		4	5	9*		12			1			7				Rep
Mar 2(a)	Nottingham F	L 1-3	Bowles	32,000	6	10	9		8			3	11*		4	5			7			1			2			12	Rep
				App	5	6	5	4	2			6	6		6	6	5	1	1			6			6	1			
				Sub app															1									2	
				Goals		3	3						2		1	2	2								1				

League Cup

Date	Opponent	Result	Scorers	Att	Abbott	Bowles	Busby	Clement	Cunningham	Eastoe	Francis	Gillard	Givens	Goddard	Hollins	Howe	James	Leach	McGee	Masson	Needham	Parkes	Perkins	Richardson	Shanks	Wallace	Webb	Williams	Round
Aug 31(h)	Bournemouth	W 2-0	Givens, Eastoe	10,006		10		2		7	8	3*	11		4					9	5	1					6	12	2
Oct 26(a)	Aston Villa	L 0-1		34,481	12	10		2		7		3	9		4						5*	1			6	11		8	3
				App		2		2		2	1	2	2		2					1	2	2			1	1	1	1	
				Sub app	1																							1	
				Goals						1			1																

Substitutions are denoted by including these symbols:
Number 12 = *; 13 = †; 14 = ‡; 15 = §; 16 = °.

Attendance Summary 1976-1977

	ATTENDANCES			AVERAGE		
	Home	Away	Total	Home	Away	Total
League	442,776	586,508	1,029,284	21,085	27,929	24,507
League Cup	69,429	137,060	206,489	23,143	34,265	29,498
UEFA Cup	80,851	136,000	216,851	20,213	34,000	27,106
FA Cup	18,285	57,422	75,707	18,285	57,422	37,854
Total	611,341	916,990	1,528,331	21,081	30,566	25,904

Attendance Summary 1977-1978

	ATTENDANCES			AVERAGE		
	Home	Away	Total	Home	Away	Total
League	417,899	544,571	962,470	19,900	25,932	22,916
League Cup	10,006	34,481	44,487	10,006	34,481	22,244
FA Cup	67,018	107,653	174,671	22,339	35,884	29,112
Total	494,923	686,705	1,181,628	19,797	27,468	23,633

1978-79

Division 1

Date	Opponents	Result	Scorers	Att	Abbott	Allen	Bowles	Busby	Clement	Cunningham	Eastoe	Elsey	Francis	Gillard	Goddard	Hamilton	Harkouk	Hollins	Howe	James	McGee	Parkes	Richardson	Roeder	Shanks	Wallace	Walsh
Aug 19	(a) Liverpool	L 1-2	McGee	50,793			10	7	2		9		8	3				4	5		11	1			6		
22	(h) West Brom A	L 0-1		15,481			10	9*	2		7		8	3				4	5	11	12	1			6		
26	(h) Nottingham F	D 0-0		17,971			10	9			7		8	3			12	4*	5		11	1		2	6		
Sep 2	(a) Arsenal	L 1-5	McGee	33,474			10	9			7		8	3				4	5		11	1		6	2		
9	(h) Manchester U	D 1-1	Gillard	23,477			10	6			7		8	3	12		9*	4	5		11	1			2		
16	(a) Middlesbrough	W 2-0	Harkouk, Eastoe	12,822	12		10	9		6	7			3			8	4	5		11*	1			2		
23	(h) Aston Villa	W 1-0	Harkouk	16,410			10	9		6	7			3			8	4	5		11	1			2		
30	(a) Wolves	L 0-1		14,250	12		10			6*	7		8	3			9	4	5		11		1		2		
Oct 7	(h) Bristol C	W 1-0	Busby	15,707			10	12		6	7		8	3			9*	4	5		11	1			2		
14	(a) Southampton	D 1-1	Goddard	22,803			10	6		7	9			3*	12		11	4	5		8	1			2		
21	(h) Everton	D 1-1	Gillard	21,171			10	6			7		8	3			9	4	5		11	1			2		
28	(a) Ipswich T	L 1-2	Francis	20,428			10	6		11	7		8*	3			9	4	5		12	1			2		
Nov 4	(h) Chelsea	D 0-0		22,876		12	10	6		11	7*			3			9	4	5		8	1			2		
11	(h) Liverpool	L 1-3	Eastoe	26,626			10	8	2		7			3			9	4	5		11	1			6		
18	(a) Nottingham F	D 0-0		28,036			10	9	2	11	7		8	3				4	5			1			6		
25	(a) Derby C	L 1-2	Howe	19,702				9	2	11	7		8	3				4	5		12	1			6	10*	
Dec 2	(h) Bolton W	L 1-3	Harkouk	11,635				9	2		7		8	3		12	11	4	5		10*	1			6		
9	(a) Coventry C	L 0-1		18,717				10	2		7			3*	12	9	11	4	5			1		8	6		
16	(h) Manchester C	W 2-1	Hamilton 2	12,902			10		2		9		8*	3		12	11	4	5			1		6	7		
26	(h) Tottenham H	D 2-2	Bowles (pen), Shanks	24,845			10		2		8			3		9	11*	4	5		12	1		6	7		
30	(h) Leeds U	L 1-4	Eastoe	17,435		12	10		2		8			3	11	9		6	5*			1		4	7		
Jan 20	(h) Middlesbrough	D 1-1	Goddard	9,899			10		2				8	3	11	9		6	5			1		4	7		
31	(a) Norwich C	D 1-1	Francis	14,203			10	12	2				8	3	11	9		4	5			1		6	7*		
Feb 10	(h) Wolves	D 3-3	Roeder, Busby, Gillard	11,814			10	12	2				8	3	11	9		4	5*			1		6	7		
13	(h) Arsenal	L 1-2	Shanks	21,125			10	6	2				8	3	11	9		4				1		5	7		
24	(h) Southampton	L 0-1		13,636		12	10	6	2				8	3	11	9*		4					1	5	7		
28	(a) Manchester U	L 0-2		36,085			10	6	2		9		8	3	11			4					1	5	7		
Mar 3	(a) Everton	L 1-2	Goddard	24,809			10		2		9*		8	3	11	12		4	5				1	6	7		
6	(a) Birmingham C	L 1-3	Busby	12,650			10	12	2*		9		8	3	11			4	5				1	6	7		
17	(a) Chelsea	W 3-1	Goddard, Roeder, Busby	25,871			10	12	2		9		8	3	11*			4	5				1	6	7		
20	(a) Aston Villa	L 1-3	Allen	24,310		12	10	11	2		9*		8	3				4	5				1	6	7		
24	(a) West Brom A	L 1-2	McGee	23,678				9	2			11	8	3				4	5		10		1	6	7		
31	(h) Derby C	D 2-2	Goddard, Walsh	13,988			10	12	2				8	3*	11			4	5				1	6	7		9
Apr 3	(a) Bristol C	L 0-2		15,687		12		8	2						11			4	5		10		1	6	3*	7	9
7	(a) Bolton W	L 1-2	Goddard	21,119				10	2				8		11			4	5		7		1	6		3	9
13	(h) Norwich C	D 0-0		14,654		12		10	2						11			4	5		7		1	6	8	3*	9
14	(a) Tottenham H	D 1-1	Clement	28,853			10	7	2				8		11			4	5				1	6	3		9
21	(a) Manchester C	L 1-3	Busby	30,694				4	2				8	3	11				5		10		1	6	7		9
28	(h) Coventry C	W 5-1	Allen 3, Shanks, Walsh (pen)	10,950		11		7	2					3	10			4	5				1	6	8		9
May 4	(a) Leeds U	L 3-4	Walsh, Roeder, Busby	20,121		11		7				12	8	3	10*			4	5				1	6	2		9
7	(h) Birmingham C	L 1-3	Roeder	9,600		11						7*	8	3	10			4	5				1	6	2	12	9
11	(h) Ipswich T	L 0-4		9,819		11		7	2				8	3	10			4					1	5	6		9
				App		4	30	29	29	9	26	2	31	38	20	8	14	41	38	1	18	24	18	27	41	4	10
				Sub app	2	6		6				1			3	3	1				4					1	
				Goals		4	1	6	1		3		2	3	6	2	3		1		3			4	3		3

FA Cup

Date	Opponents	Result	Scorers	Att	Abbott	Allen	Bowles	Busby	Clement	Cunningham	Eastoe	Elsey	Francis	Gillard	Goddard	Hamilton	Harkouk	Hollins	Howe	James	McGee	Parkes	Richardson	Roeder	Shanks	Wallace	Walsh	Round
Jan 9	(a) Fulham	L 0-2		21,119			10	11*	2	4	8			3		9	12	6	5			1			7			3
				App			1	1	1	1	1			1		1		1	1			1			1			
				Sub app													1											
				Goals																								

League Cup

Date	Opponents	Result	Scorers	Att	Abbott	Allen	Bowles	Busby	Clement	Cunningham	Eastoe	Elsey	Francis	Gillard	Goddard	Hamilton	Harkouk	Hollins	Howe	James	McGee	Parkes	Richardson	Roeder	Shanks	Wallace	Walsh	Round
Aug 29	(a) Preston NE	W 3-1	Baxter (og), Eastoe 2	14,913			10	9			7		8	3				4	5		11	1		6	2			2
Oct 3	(h) Swansea C	W 2-0	McGee, Eastoe	18,513	12		10*			6	7		8	3			9	4	5		11		1		2			3
Nov 11	(h) Leeds U	L 0-2		22,769			10	8	2	12	7			3			9*	4	5		11	1			6			4
				App			3	2	1	1	3		2	3			2	3	3		3	2	1	1	3			
				Sub app	1					1																		
				Goals							3										1							

1 own-goal

Substitutions are denoted by including these symbols:
Number 12 = *; 13 = †; 14 = ‡; 15 = §; 16 = °.

Attendance Summary

	ATTENDANCES			AVERAGE		
	Home	Away	Total	Home	Away	Total
League	342,021	499,105	841,126	16,287	23,767	20,027
League Cup	41,282	14,913	56,195	20,641	14,913	18,732
FA Cup		21,119	21,119		21,119	21,119
Total	383,303	535,137	918,440	16,665	23,267	19,966

1979-80

Division 2

Date	Opponent	Result	Scorers	Att	Allen	Bowles	Burke	Busby	Currie	Davidson	Elsey	Gillard	Goddard	Hamilton	Harkouk	Hazell	Hill	Howe	McCreery	Neal	Pape	Roeder	Rogers	Shanks	Waddock	Wallace	Walsh	Wicks	Woods
Aug 18	(h) Bristol R	W 2-0	Allen, Goddard	12,652	9						2	3	11	10				5	4	7		6		8					1
22	(a) Cardiff C	L 0-1		11,656	9			4			2	3	7					5	8	11		6		10					1
25	(h) Leicester C	L 1-4	Allen (pen)	13,091	9			11		12	2*	3	10					5	4	7		6		8					1
Sep 1	(a) Notts C	L 0-1		8,745	9	11					2	3	10		12			5*	4	7		6		8					1
8	(h) Fulham	W 3-0	Goddard, Allen, Currie	17,105	9	7	11		10			3	8		12	5*			4			6		2					1
15	(a) Swansea C	W 2-1	Burke, Stephenson (og)	16,000	9	7	11					3	8		10*	5			4			6		2	12				1
22	(h) West Ham U	W 3-0	Allen 2, Goddard	24,692	9	7	11		8			3	10			5			4			6		2					1
29	(a) Oldham A	D 0-0		8,974	9	7			8*			3	10		12	5			4			6		2				11	1
Oct 6	(a) Watford	W 2-1	Allen, Roeder	22,341	9	7	11					3	10			5			4			8		2				6	1
9	(h) Cardiff C	W 3-0	Allen 2, Roeder	12,225	9	7	11					3	10*			5			4			8		2			12	6	1
13	(h) Preston NE	D 1-1	Goddard	14,316	9	7	11*					3	10			5			4			8		2			12	6	1
20	(a) Sunderland	L 0-3		25,201	9*	7	11					3	10			5			4			8		2			12	6	1
27	(h) Burnley	W 7-0	Goddard 2, Allen 2, Roeder, Shanks, McCreery	11,261	9	7	11*					3	10						4			5		2		8	12	6	1
Nov 3	(a) Bristol R	W 3-1	Thomas (og), Roeder, Allen	8,531	9	7			10			3	11			5*			4			8		2			12	6	1
10	(a) Luton T	D 1-1	Allen	19,619	9	7	12		10*			3	11			5			4			8		2				6	1
17	(h) Shrewsbury T	W 2-1	McCreery, Roeder	12,048	9	7			10			3*	11			5			4			8		2	12			6	1
24	(h) Charlton A	W 4-0	Allen 2 (1 pen), Roeder, Bowles	13,003	9	7	12						11*			5			4			8		2	10	3		6	1
Dec 1	(a) Cambridge U	L 1-2	Bowles	8,083	9	7							10			5	11*		4			8		2	12	3		6	1
8	(h) Wrexham	D 2-2	Goddard 2	11,652	9	7			12			3	10			5	11		4			8*		2				6	1
15	(a) Newcastle U	L 2-4	Goddard, Roeder	24,986	9			12	10*			3	7			5	11		4			8		2				6	1
18	(h) Chelsea	D 2-2	Allen 2	26,598	9		11*	12				3	7			5			4			8		2	10			6	1
27	(a) Leicester C	L 0-2		20,743	9				10			3	7*			5	11		4			8		2	12			6	1
Jan 1	(a) Birmingham C	L 1-2	Allen	25,963	9		12	6	8*								11		4					2	10	3	7	5	1
12	(h) Notts C	L 1-3	Allen	9,613	9		11						8						4	12		6		2	10	3	7*	5	1
19	(a) Fulham	W 2-0	Waddock, Burke	11,579	9		11		10			3*	7						4			6		2	8	12		5	1
Feb 2	(h) Swansea C	W 3-2	Allen (pen), Goddard 2	11,153	9		11		10			3*	7						4			6		2	8	12		5	1
9	(a) West Ham U	L 1-2	Goddard	26,037	9		11*		10			3	7			8			4			6		2	12			5	1
12	(h) Orient	D 0-0		11,361	9		11		8			3	10			6			4					2	7			5	1
16	(h) Oldham A	W 4-3	Allen 2 (1 pen), McCreery, Goddard	8,372	9		11		8*			3	10			5			4			7		2	12			6	1
23	(a) Preston NE	W 3-0	Allen, Roeder, Goddard	10,350	9		11		10			3	7			5			4			8		2				6	1
Mar 1	(h) Sunderland	D 0-0		15,613	9		11		10			3	7			5			4			8		2				6	1
8	(a) Burnley	W 3-0	Gillard, Allen, Shanks	7,490	9		11		10*			3	7			5	12		4			8		2				6	1
14	(h) Watford	D 1-1	Currie	16,504	9		11*		10			3	7			5	12		4			8		2				6	1
22	(h) Luton T	D 2-2	Goddard 2	15,054	9		11		10			3	7		12	5			4			8*		2				6	1
29	(a) Shrewsbury T	L 0-3		9,050			11		10			3	7			5			4	9*		8		2	12			6	1
Apr 2	(a) Chelsea	W 2-0	Busby, Burke	31,035			11	9	10			3	7						4			6		2	8			5	1
5	(h) Birmingham C	D 1-1	Burke	16,609	9		11	8	10			3	7						4			6		2				5	1
8	(a) Orient	D 1-1	Allen	12,000	9		11	8	10			3	7						4			6		2				5	1
12	(h) Cambridge U	D 2-2	Allen, Busby	11,643	9		11	8	10			3*	7			12			4			6		2				5	1
19	(a) Charlton A	D 2-2	Allen 2	6,975	9		11	7*	10			3	8						4		1	6		2	12			5	
26	(h) Newcastle U	W 2-1	Roeder, McCreery	11,245			11		10			3	7*			12	8		9			6	2	4				5	1
May 3	(a) Wrexham	W 3-1	Currie, Hazell, Allen	6,268	9		11		10			3				7	8		4			6	2					5	1
				App	39	16	28	8	27		4	38	40	1	1	27	7	4	42	5	1	40	2	41	8	5	2	35	41
				Sub app			3	2	1	1					4	2	2			1					8	2	5		
				Goals	28	2	4	2	3			1	16			1			4			9		2	1				

2 own-goals

FA Cup

Date	Opponent	Result	Scorers	Att	Allen	Bowles	Burke	Busby	Currie	Davidson	Elsey	Gillard	Goddard	Hamilton	Harkouk	Hazell	Hill	Howe	McCreery	Neal	Pape	Roeder	Rogers	Shanks	Waddock	Wallace	Walsh	Wicks	Woods	Round
Jan 5	(h) Watford	L 1-2	Hazell	19,398	9		12		10							6	11		4					2	8	3	7*	5	1	3
				App	1				1							1	1		1					1	1	1	1	1	1	
				Sub app			1																							
				Goals												1														

League Cup

Date	Opponent	Result	Scorers	Att	Allen	Bowles	Burke	Busby	Currie	Davidson	Elsey	Gillard	Goddard	Hamilton	Harkouk	Hazell	Hill	Howe	McCreery	Neal	Pape	Roeder	Rogers	Shanks	Waddock	Wallace	Walsh	Wicks	Woods	Round
Aug 28	(h) Bradford C	W 2-1	McCreery, Neal	8,560	9	11		4				3	10*					5	8	7		6		2	12				1	2/1
Sep 5	(a) Bradford C	W 2-0	Gillard, Roeder	11,372	9	7			10			3	8		11	5			4			6		2					1	2/2
25	(a) Mansfield T	W 3-0	Bowles, Allen, Currie	9,485	9	7	11*		8			3	10			5			4			6		2				12	1	3
Oct 30	(h) Wolves	D 1-1	Allen	20,984	9	7			10*			3	12			5			4			8		2			11	6	1	4
Nov 6	(a) Wolves	L 0-1		26,014	9	7*	12		10			3	11			5			4			8		2				6	1	Rep
				App	5	5	1	1	4			5	4		1	4		1	5	1		5		5			1	2	5	
				Sub app			1						1												1			1		
				Goals	2	1			1			1							1	1		1								

Substitutions are denoted by including these symbols:
Number 12 = *; 13 = †; 14 = ‡; 15 = §; 16 = °.

Attendance Summary

	ATTENDANCES			AVERAGE		
	Home	Away	Total	Home	Away	Total
League	295,810	321,626	617,436	14,087	15,316	14,701
League Cup	29,544	46,871	76,415	14,772	15,624	15,283
FA Cup	19,398		19,398	19,398		19,398
Total	344,752	368,497	713,249	14,365	15,354	14,860

1980-81

Division 2

Date	Opponents	Result	Scorers	Att	Burke	Burridge	Currie	Fenwick	Fereday	Flanagan	Francis	Gillard	Hazell	Howe	Hill	Hucker	King	Langley	McCreery	Micklewhite	Muir	Neal	Neill	Roeder	Sealy	Shanks	Silkman	Stainrod	Stewart	Waddock	Walsh	Wicks	Wilkins	Woods
Aug 16	(a) Oldham A	L 0-1		6,986	11		10					3			7				2			12		6		8				4	9*	5		1
19	(h) Bristol R	W 4-0	Fereday 2, Hazell, Shanks	9,731	11		10		7			3	9*		12				2					6		8				4		5		1
23	(h) Swansea C	D 0-0		10,854	11		10		7*			3	12					9	2					6		8				4		5		1
30	(a) Chelsea	D 1-1	Langley	23,381	11*		10		7			3						9	2				12	6		8				4		5		1
Sep 6	(a) Notts C	L 1-2	Hill (pen)	7,197					7*			3	12		11			9	2				10	6		8				4		5		1
13	(h) Newcastle U	L 1-2	Hazell	10,865	11		10		7*			3	5		12			9	2					6		8				4				1
20	(a) Sheffield W	L 0-1		15,195	12		10					3*			11		8	9	7					6		2				4		5		1
27	(h) Bristol C	W 4-0	Neal 2, Langley, Shanks	8,551	11		10					3						9	2			7		6		8				4		5		1
Oct 4	(a) Blackburn R	L 1-2	Neal	12,209			10					3					7	9*	2			11		6		8			12	4		5		1
7	(h) Orient	D 0-0		9,627			10					3					7	8	11			9		6		2				4		5		1
11	(h) Bolton W	W 3-1	Langley, Burke (pen), Neal	8,641	11		10					3	6				7	8*	4			9				2				12		5		1
18	(a) Derby C	D 3-3	King 2, Langley	16,021	11							3					8	10	7			9		6		2				4		5		1
22	(a) Cardiff C	L 0-1		4,489	11*							3	12				8	10	7			9		6		2				4		5		1
25	(h) Wrexham	L 0-1		9,050	11*				12			3					8	10	7			9		6		2				4		5		1
Nov 1	(a) Grimsby T	D 0-0		10,015								3		7			8	10				9		6*		2	11			4		5	12	1
8	(h) Luton T	W 3-2	Neal 2, King	10,082								3		6			8	10	12			9*		7		2	11			4		5		1
11	(a) Bristol R	W 2-1	King, Langley	6,636								3		6			8	10				9		7		2	11			4		5		1
15	(h) Oldham A	W 2-0	Silkman (pen), Neal	8,223								3		6			8	10		12		9		7		2*	11			4		5		1
22	(a) Preston NE	L 2-3	Roeder, Neal	6,725								3		6			8					9		7		2	11	10		4		5		1
29	(h) Shrewsbury T	D 0-0		7,982								3					8	6				9		7		2	11	10		4		5		1
Dec 6	(a) Cambridge U	L 0-1		6,349			6					3					8					9		7		2	11	10		4		5		1
19	(a) Bolton W	W 2-1	Stainrod, Flanagan	6,315			10	4		7		3					8							6		2	11	9				5		1
26	(h) West Ham U	W 3-0	Silkman, Currie, Stainrod	23,811		1	10*	4		7		3					8							6		2	11	9		12		5		
27	(a) Watford	D 1-1	King	22,911		1		4		7		3					8							6		2	11	9		10		5		
Jan 10	(h) Preston NE	D 1-1	Stainrod	8,415		1	10	4				3					8					7		6		2	11	9				5		
17	(h) Chelsea	W 1-0	Langley	22,873		1	10	4				3					8	7						6		2	11	9				5		
31	(a) Swansea C	W 2-1	Langley, King	12,518		1	10	4				3					8	7						6		2	11*	9		12		5		
Feb 3	(h) Cardiff C	W 2-0	Fenwick, Langley	9,834		1	10	4				3					8	7						6		2	11	9				5		
7	(a) Newcastle U	L 0-1		20,442		1	10	4				3					8	7						6		2	11	9				5		
14	(h) Notts C	D 1-1	Howe	11,457		1	10	4				3	5	6			8	7								2	11	9						
21	(a) Bristol C	W 1-0	Waddock	10,988		1	10	4				3	6*				8	7								2	11	9		12		5		
28	(h) Sheffield W	L 1-2	Stainrod	15,104		1	10	4		12	8	3						7						6		2	11*	9				5		
Mar 7	(h) Blackburn R	D 1-1	Francis	9,513		1	10*	4		7	8	3						12						6		2	11	9				5		
21	(h) Derby C	W 3-1	Francis 2, Flanagan	8,905		1	10	4		7	8	3					12							6	9	2	11*					5		
28	(a) Wrexham	D 1-1	Waddock	5,887		1	10	4		9	8	3					12							6	7	2				11*		5		
31	(a) Orient	L 0-4		6,724		1	10	4		7	8	3*												6	9	2	12			11		5		
Apr 4	(h) Grimsby T	W 1-0	Francis (pen)	8,906		1	10			7	8	3												6	9	2	4			11		5		
11	(a) Luton T	L 0-3		12,112	12	1	10			7	8	3*												6	9	2	4			11		5		
18	(h) Watford	D 0-0		10,571	11	1	10	4		9	8	3											2	6						7		5		
21	(a) West Ham U	L 0-3		24,599	12	1	10	4		9	8	3											2	6	11					7		5*		
25	(h) Cambridge U	W 5-0	Sealy 2, Muir 2, Roeder	6,648		1	10	2		9	8	3		5							11			6	7					4				
May 2	(a) Shrewsbury T	D 3-3	Fenwick, Waddock, Flanagan	5,714			10	2		9		3		5		1					11			6	8					7			4	
				App	11	19	31	19	5	13	10	42	5	8	3	1	24	24	14		2	15	3	39	8	38	22	15		29	1	38	1	22
				Sub app	3				1	1			3		2		2	1	1	1		1	1				1		1	4			1	
				Goals	1		1	2	2	3	4		2	1	1		6	8			2	8		2	2	2	2	4		3				

FA Cup

Date	Opponents	Result	Scorers	Att	Burke	Burridge	Currie	Fenwick	Fereday	Flanagan	Francis	Gillard	Hazell	Howe	Hill	Hucker	King	Langley	McCreery	Micklewhite	Muir	Neal	Neill	Roeder	Sealy	Shanks	Silkman	Stainrod	Stewart	Waddock	Walsh	Wicks	Wilkins	Woods	Round
Jan 3	(h) Tottenham H	D 0-0		28,829		1		4		7		3					8							6		2	11	9		10		5			3
7	(a) Tottenham H	L 1-3	Stainrod	36,294		1	10	4		7*		3					8		12					6		2	11	9				5			Rep
				App		2	1	2		2		2					2							2		2	2	2		1		2			
				Sub app															1																
				Goals																								1							

League Cup

Date	Opponents	Result	Scorers	Att	Burke	Burridge	Currie	Fenwick	Fereday	Flanagan	Francis	Gillard	Hazell	Howe	Hill	Hucker	King	Langley	McCreery	Micklewhite	Muir	Neal	Neill	Roeder	Sealy	Shanks	Silkman	Stainrod	Stewart	Waddock	Walsh	Wicks	Wilkins	Woods	Round
Aug 26	(h) Derby C	D 0-0		11,244	11		10					3	7					9	2					6		8				4		5			2/1
Sep 3	(a) Derby C	D 0-0[1]		16,728			10*		7			3			11			9	2				12	6		8				4		5			2/2
23	(a) Notts C	L 1-4	Langley	6,644	3		10*						12				7	9	2			11		6		8				4		5			3
				App	2		3		1			2	1		1		1	3	3			1		3		3				3		3			
				Sub app									1										1												
				Goals														1																	

[1] Queen's Park Rangers won 5-3 on penalties

Woods played number-one in all three matches

Substitutions are denoted by including these symbols:
Number 12 = *; 13 = †; 14 = ‡; 15 = §; 16 = °.

Attendance Summary 1980-1981

	ATTENDANCES Home	Away	Total	AVERAGE Home	Away	Total
League	229,643	243,413	473,056	10,938	11,591	11,263
League Cup	11,244	23,372	34,616	11,244	11,686	11,539
FA cup	28,829	36,294	65,123	28,829	36,294	35,562
Total	269,716	303,079	572,795	11,727	12,628	12,187

Attendance Summary 1981-1982

	ATTENDANCES Home	Away	Total	AVERAGE Home	Away	Total
League	264,103	229,206	493,309	12,576	10,915	11,745
League Cup	22,717	25,953	48,670	11,358	12,976	12,168
FA Cup	61,797	262,061	323,858	15,449	52,412	35,984
Total	348,617	517,220	865,837	12,912	18,472	15,742

1981-82

Division 2

Date	Opponent	Result	Scorers	Att	Allen	Burke	Burridge	Currie	Dawes	Fenwick	Fereday	Flanagan	Francis	Gillard	Gregory	Hazell	Howe	Hucker	King	Micklewhite	Neill	O'Connor	Roeder	Sealy	Stainrod	Stewart	Waddock	Wicks	Wilkins
Aug 29	(a) Wrexham	W 3-1	King, Allen 2	4,665	9		1			3		7	8		2	5			10				6		11		4		
Sep 1	(h) Luton T	L 1-2	King	18,703	9		1			3		7	8		2	5			10				6		11		4		
5	(h) Newcastle U	W 3-0	King, Roeder, Stainrod	14,176	9*		1	4		3		7	8	12	2	5			10				6		11				
12	(a) Grimsby T	L 1-2	Gregory	9,587	9		1	4		3		7	8	12	2		5		10*				6		11				
19	(h) Crystal P	W 1-0	Stainrod	17,039	9		1	10		3		7		11	2	5							6		8		4		
22	(a) Oldham A	L 0-2		6,421	9		1	10		3		7		11	2	5							6		8		4		
26	(a) Derby C	L 1-3	Gregory	11,246	9		1	10		3		7*		11	2	5							6	12	8		4		
Oct 3	(h) Blackburn R	W 2-0	Gregory, Allen	9,541	9		1	10		3				11	2	5				7			6		8		4		
10	(h) Norwich C	W 2-0	Gregory, Stainrod	11,806	9	12	1	10		3				11	2	5				7*			6		8		4		
18	(a) Orient	D 1-1	Gillard	8,192	9*	12	1			3		8		11	2	5				7			6		10		4		
24	(h) Leicester C	W 2-0	Stainrod, Gregory	12,419	9	12	1			3		8	7*	11	2	5							6		10		4		
31	(a) Charlton A	W 2-1	Stainrod, Allen	11,133	9		1			3		8	7	11	2	5							6		10		4		
Nov 7	(h) Rotherham U	D 1-1	Flanagan	10,949		9	1			3		8	7*	11	2	5							6	12	10		4		
14	(a) Sheffield W	W 3-1	Stainrod 3	17,024	9*		1			3		8		11	2	12	5			7			6		10		4		
21	(a) Shrewsbury T	L 1-2	Flanagan	4,765	9		1			3		8		11	2		5			7			6		10		4		
24	(h) Oldham A	D 0-0		9,477	9*		1			3		8		11	2		5			7			6	12	10		4		
28	(h) Cardiff C	W 2-0	Stainrod 2	10,225			1			3		8		11	2		5			7			6	9	10		4		
Dec 5	(a) Bolton W	L 0-1		6,076		12	1			3*		8		11	2		5			7			6	9	10		4		
12	(h) Barnsley	W 1-0	Flanagan	10,972			1			3	12	8		11	2		5			7			6	9*		10	4		
26	(h) Chelsea	L 0-2		22,022	12		1			3		8		11			5			7		2	6	9*		10	4		
Jan 16	(h) Wrexham	D 1-1	Stainrod	10,066	7			9		3		12		11	8		5	1			2*		6		10		4		
30	(a) Crystal P	D 0-0		15,267	7			8		2				3	11		5	1		9			6		10		4		
Feb 6	(h) Grimsby T	W 1-0	Gregory	8,753	7			8		2	9			3	11		5	1					6		10		4		
9	(a) Cambridge U	L 0-1		4,822	7			8*		2	9			3	11		5	1		12			6		10		4		
16	(a) Blackburn R	L 1-2	Allen	6,884	9					2		8		3	11		5	1		7	4		6		10				
20	(h) Derby C	W 3-0	Hazell, Fenwick, Flanagan	8,890	9					2		8		3	11*	5		1		7	4		6		10				12
27	(a) Norwich C	W 1-0	Roeder	15,928	9			7				8		3	11	5	2	1			4		6		10				
Mar 9	(a) Watford	L 0-4		16,862				7				8		3	11	5	9	1			2		6		10		4		
13	(a) Leicester C	L 2-3	Currie, Stainrod	17,812	9	12		7				8		3	11*	5	2	1					6		10		4		
20	(h) Charlton A	W 4-0	Allen 3, Fenwick	13,116	9	12		7		4		8		3*		5		1		11	2		6		10				
27	(a) Rotherham U	L 0-1		10,472	9	12			11	3		8				5		1*		7	2				10		4	6	
29	(h) Sheffield W	W 2-0	Flanagan, Stainrod	11,710	9			7	3			8			11			1		4	2		6		10			5	
Apr 6	(h) Orient	W 3-0	Hazell, Flanagan, Stainrod	10,531	9			7		2		8		3		5		1		11			6		10*	12	4		
10	(a) Chelsea	L 1-2	Gregory	18,365	9			7				8		3	11	5		1			2		6		10		4		
12	(h) Watford	D 0-0		22,091	9				3			8				5		1		11	2		7		10		4	6	
17	(h) Shrewsbury T	W 2-1	Flanagan, Allen	11,148	9	10		7*	3	2	12	8						1		11			6				4	5	
24	(a) Cardiff C	W 2-1	Allen, Micklewhite	5,979	9					2		8		3	11			1		7			6		10		4	5	
May 1	(h) Bolton W	W 7-1	Gregory, Micklewhite, Flanagan 2, Fenwick (pen), Allen, Stainrod	10,002	9	12				2*		8		3	11			1		7			6		10		4	5	
5	(a) Newcastle U	W 4-0	Gregory, Allen, Flanagan, Stainrod	10,670	9	12				2		7		3	11			1		8*			6		10		4	5	
8	(a) Barnsley	L 0-3		10,579	9	12				2		8		3		5		1		7			11		10*		4	6	
11	(a) Luton T	L 2-3	Fenwick, Stainrod	16,457	9				3	11		8						1		7	2		6		10		4	5	
15	(h) Cambridge U	W 2-1	Allen, Fenwick (pen)	10,467	9			7		2		8		3	11	5		1		12			6		10		4*		
				App	36	2	20	20	5	36	2	36	7	33	34	23	16	22	4	24	11	1	41	4	39	2	35	9	
				Sub app	1	10					2	1		2		1				2				3		1			1
				Goals	13			1		5		10		1	9	2			3	2			2		17				

FA Cup

Date	Opponent	Result	Scorers	Att	Allen	Burke	Burridge	Currie	Dawes	Fenwick	Fereday	Flanagan	Francis	Gillard	Gregory	Hazell	Howe	Hucker	King	Micklewhite	Neill	O'Connor	Roeder	Sealy	Stainrod	Stewart	Waddock	Wicks	Wilkins	Round
Jan 2	(h) Middlesbrough	D 1-1	Stainrod	12,100						3		8		11			5	1		7	2		6		10	9	4			3
18	(a) Middlesbrough	W 3-2	Stainrod 2, Neill	14,819	7			8*		2		9		3	11		5	1			12		6		10		4			Rep
23	(a) Blackpool	D 0-0		10,227	7			8		2		9		3	11		5	1					6		10		4			4
26	(h) Blackpool	W 5-1	Allen 4, Stainrod (pen)	11,700	7			8		2		9*		3	11		5	1					6		10	12	4			Rep
Feb 13	(h) Grimsby T	W 3-1	Stainrod, Allen, Howe	13,344	9					2	12	8		3	11		5	1		7			6		10		4*			5
Mar 6	(h) Crystal P	W 1-0	Allen	24,653	9			7				8		3	11	5		1			2		6		10		4			6
Apr 3	(n*) West Brom A	W 1-0	Allen	45,015	9			7		2		8		3		5		1		11			6		10		4			SF
May 22	(n‡) Tottenham H	D 1-1	Fenwick	100,000	9*			7		2		8		3	11	5		1		12			6		10		4			F
27	(n‡) Tottenham H	L 0-1		92,000		12		7		2		8		3	11	5		1		9*	6				10		4			Rep
				App	7			7		8		9		9	7	4	5	9		4	3		8		9	1	9			
				Sub app		1					1									1	1					1				
				Goals	7					1							1				1				5					

*Played at Highbury, London. ‡Played at Wembley Stadium.

League Cup

Date	Opponent	Result	Scorers	Att	Allen	Burke	Burridge	Currie	Dawes	Fenwick	Fereday	Flanagan	Francis	Gillard	Gregory	Hazell	Howe	Hucker	King	Micklewhite	Neill	O'Connor	Roeder	Sealy	Stainrod	Stewart	Waddock	Wicks	Wilkins	Round
Oct 6	(h) Portsmouth	W 5-0	Ellis (og), Gregory 2, Micklewhite 2	13,502	9	12	1	10*		3				11	2	5				7			6		8		4			2/1
Oct 27	(a) Portsmouth	D 2-2	Flanagan, Micklewhite	7,677		9	1			3		8		11	2	5*				7			6		10	12	4			2/2
Nov 10	(h) Bristol C	W 3-0	Flanagan, Stainrod, Allen	9,215	9		1			3		8*		11	2	5				7			6		10	12			4	3
Dec 1	(a) Watford	L 1-4	Stainrod (pen)	18,276			1			3		8		11	2	7*	5			12			6	9	10		4			4
				App	2	1	4	1		4		3		4	4	4	1			3			4	1	4		3		1	
				Sub app		1														1						2				
				Goals	1							2			2					3					2					

1 own-goal

Substitutions are denoted by including these symbols:
Number 12 = *; 13 = †; 14 = ‡; 15 = §; 16 = °.

1982-83

Division 2

Month	Date	Opponent	Result	Scorers	Att	Allen	Benstead	Burke	Currie	Dawes	Duffield	Fenwick	Fereday	Flanagan	Gregory	Hazell	Hucker	Micklewhite	Neill	O'Connor	Roeder	Sealy	Stainrod	Stewart	Waddock	Wicks	Wilkins
Aug	28 (a)	Newcastle U	L 0-1		36,185			12		3		6			11	5	1	7*	2			9	10	8	4		
	31 (h)	Cambridge U	W 2-1	Sealy 2	9,686					3		6			11	5	1	7	2			9	10	8	4		
Sep	4 (h)	Derby C	W 4-1	Gregory, Fenwick (pen), Stainrod 2	10,217					3		6			11	5	1	7	2			9	10	8*	4		12
	7 (a)	Fulham	D 1-1	Stainrod	15,004					3		6			11	5	1	7	2			9	10	8	4		
	11 (a)	Oldham A	W 1-0	Gregory	4,266					3		6			11	5	1	7	2			9	10	8*	4		12
	18 (h)	Sheffield W	L 0-2		13,733			12		3		6			11	5	1	7*	2			9	10	8	4		
	25 (a)	Leicester C	W 1-0	O'Neill (og)	10,647					3		6	12		11	5	1	7	2			9	10	8*	4		
	28 (h)	Crystal P	D 0-0		12,194					3		6	12		11	5	1	7*	2			9	10	8	4		
Oct	2 (h)	Burnley	W 3-2	Neill, Allen, Micklewhite	9,145	10				3		6			11	5	1	7	2			9		8	4		
	9 (a)	Barnsley	W 1-0	Allen	13,270	9*				3		6			11	5	1	7	2				10	8	4		12
	16 (h)	Shrewsbury T	W 4-0	Allen, Flanagan, Micklewhite, Gregory	9,275	9				3		6	12	8*	11	5	1	7	2			10			4		
	23 (a)	Middlesbrough	L 1-2	Allen	7,892	9				3		6	12		11	5	1	7	2			10		8*	4		
	30 (h)	Bolton W	W 1-0	Stainrod	9,363	9			12	3		6			11	5	1	7	2				10	8*	4		
Nov	6 (a)	Rotherham U	D 0-0		7,402	9				3		6			11	5	1	7	2			12	10	8*	4		
	13 (h)	Blackburn R	D 2-2	Allen, Fenwick (pen)	9,149	9			10	3		6			11	5	1	7*	2	12		4		8			
	20 (a)	Cambridge U	W 4-1	Wicks, Sealy, Allen 2	5,685	9				3		6			11	5	1	7	2			8	10	12		4*	
	27 (h)	Carlisle U	W 1-0	Fenwick	9,398	9				3		6			11	5	1	7	2		4	8	10				
Dec	4 (a)	Leeds U	W 1-0	Allen	11,528	9				3		6			11	5	1	7	2		4	8	10				
	11 (h)	Grimsby T	W 4-0	Neill, Sealy, Gregory, Micklewhite	9,811	9				3		6		12	11	5	1	7	2		4	8	10*				
	18 (a)	Wolves	L 0-4		15,423	9*				3		6			11	5	1	7	2		4	8	10	12			
	27 (h)	Chelsea	L 1-2	Sealy	23,744	9		12		3		6			11	5	1	7*		2	4	8		10			
	29 (a)	Charlton A	W 3-1	Micklewhite 2, Sealy	13,306	9				3		6		10*	11	5	1	7	2		4	8		12			
Jan	3 (a)	Derby C	L 0-2		14,007	9				3		6		8	11*	5	1	7	2		4	10		12			
	15 (h)	Newcastle U	W 2-0	Gregory 2	13,972	9				3		6		10	11	5	1	7	2			8			4		
	22 (a)	Crystal P	W 3-0	Allen 2, Hazell	14,621	9				3		6		10	11	5	1	7	2			8			4		
Feb	5 (h)	Oldham A	W 1-0	Sealy	8,903	9				3		6		10	11		1	7	2			8			4	5	
	19 (h)	Barnsley	W 3-0	Gregory, Sealy, Flanagan	10,271	9*				3		6		10	11		1	7	2			8	12		4	5	
	26 (a)	Shrewsbury T	D 0-0		4,378	9*				3		6		10	11		1	7	2			8	12		4	5	
Mar	5 (h)	Middlesbrough	W 6-1	Allen 3, Micklewhite, Flanagan, Gregory	9,596	9				3				10	11	5	1	7			2	8			4	6	
	12 (a)	Bolton W	L 2-3	Gregory (pen), Sealy	6,373	9				3*			12	10	11	5	1				2	8	7		4	6	
	19 (h)	Rotherham U	W 4-0	Sealy, Flanagan, Gregory 2	9,541					3		6		10	11	5	1	7	2			8	9		4		
	22 (h)	Charlton A	W 5-1	Sealy 2, Hazell, Gregory, Stainrod	10,776	12				3		6		10	11	5	1	7*	2			8	9		4		
	26 (a)	Blackburn R	W 3-1	Stainrod 2, Flanagan	5,317					3		6		10	11	5	1	7	2			8	9		4		
Apr	4 (a)	Chelsea	W 2-0	Gregory, Sealy	20,821	12				3		6		10	11	5	1		2			8*	9		4	7	
	9 (h)	Leicester C	D 2-2	Gregory, Sealy	16,301					3		6		10	11	5	1	7	2			8	9		4		
	19 (a)	Sheffield W	W 1-0	Flanagan	11,713					3		6		10	11	5	1		2			8	9		4	7	
	23 (h)	Leeds U	W 1-0	Hart (og)	19,573					3		6		10	11	5	1		2			8	9		4	7	
	30 (a)	Carlisle U	L 0-1		5,724			12		3		6		10*	11	5	1		2			8	9		4	7	
May	2 (h)	Fulham	W 3-1	Gregory, Sealy, Stainrod	24,431					3		6		10	11	5	1		2			8	9		4	7	
	7 (h)	Wolves	W 2-1	Flanagan, Hazell	19,854					3		6		10*	11	5	1	12	2			8	9		4	7	
	10 (a)	Burnley	L 1-2	Sealy	7,191	10				3		6			11	5	1		2			8	9		4	7	
	14 (a)	Grimsby T	D 1-1	Stainrod	9,598			6		3	12			10*	11	5	1		2			8	9		4	7	
					App	23		1	1	42		39		21	42	39	42	33	39	1	9	39	29	15	33	14	
					Sub app	2		4	1		1		5	1				1		1		1	2	4			3
					Goals	13						3		7	15	3		6	2			16	9			1	

2 own-goals

FA Cup

Month	Date	Opponent	Result	Scorers	Att	Allen	Benstead	Burke	Currie	Dawes	Duffield	Fenwick	Fereday	Flanagan	Gregory	Hazell	Hucker	Micklewhite	Neill	O'Connor	Roeder	Sealy	Stainrod	Stewart	Waddock	Round
Jan	8 (a)	West Brom A	L 2-3	Fenwick (pen), Micklewhite	16,528	10	1	12		3		4		9		5*		7	2		6	11			8	3
					App	1	1			1		1		1		1		1	1		1	1			1	
					Sub app			1																		
					Goals							1						1								

League Cup

Month	Date	Opponent	Result	Scorers	Att	Allen	Benstead	Burke	Currie	Dawes	Duffield	Fenwick	Fereday	Flanagan	Gregory	Hazell	Hucker	Micklewhite	Neill	O'Connor	Roeder	Sealy	Stainrod	Stewart	Waddock	Round
Oct	5 (a)	Rotherham U	L 1-2	Gregory	5,603	8				3		6			11	5	1	7	2			9	10		4	2/1
	26 (h)	Rotherham U	D 0-0		9,653	9				3		6			11	5	1	7	2			8*	10	12	4	2/2
					App	2				2		2			2	2	2	2	2			2	2		2	
					Sub app																			1		
					Goals										1											

Substitutions are denoted by including these symbols:
Number 12 = *; 13 = †; 14 = ‡; 15 = §; 16 = °.

Attendance Summary

	ATTENDANCES			AVERAGE		
	Home	Away	Total	Home	Away	Total
League	268,933	240,351	509,284	12,806	11,445	12,126
League Cup	9,653	5,603	15,256	9,653	5,603	7,628
FA Cup		16,528	16,528		16,528	16,528
Total	278,586	262,482	541,068	12,663	11,412	12,024

1983-84

Division 1

Date	Opponents	Result	Scorers	Att	Allen	Burke	Charles	Dawes	Fenwick	Fereday	Fillery	Flanagan	Gregory	Hazell	Hucker	McDonald	Micklewhite	Neill	Roeder	Sealy	Stainrod	Stewart	Waddock	Wicks
Aug 27	(a) Manchester U	L 1-3	Allen	48,742	9			3			12	8*	11	5	1		7	2	6		10		4	
29	(a) Southampton	D 0-0		19,522	9			3	6		8*	12	11	5	1		7	2			10		4	
Sep 3	(h) Aston Villa	W 2-1	Stainrod, Withe (og)	16,922	9			3	6		8		11*	5	1		7	2			10	12	4	
6	(h) Watford	D 1-1	Stainrod	17,111	9			3	6			12	11	5	1		7	2			10	8*	4	
10	(a) Nottingham F	L 2-3	Dawes, Stainrod	14,607				3	6				11	5	1		7	2		9	10	8	4	
17	(h) Sunderland	W 3-0	Fenwick (pen), Stainrod, Allen	12,929	9			3	6				11	5*	1		7	2		12	10	8	4	
24	(a) Wolves	W 4-0	Allen 2, Gregory, Stainrod	11,511	9			3	6				11*		1	5	7	2		12	10	8	4	
Oct 1	(h) Arsenal	W 2-0	Gregory, Neill	26,293	9			3	6				11		1	5	7	2			10	8	4	
15	(a) Ipswich T	W 2-0	Stainrod, Gregory	17,959	9			3	6	12			11		1	5	7	2*			10	8	4	
22	(h) Liverpool	L 0-1		27,140	9			3	6	2			11		1	5	7				10	8	4	
29	(a) Norwich C	W 3-0	Fenwick 2 (1 pen), Stainrod	16,532	9*			3	6	12			11		1		7	2			10	8	4	5
Nov 5	(h) Luton T	L 0-1		15,853	9			3	6				11		1		7	2			10	8	4	5
12	(a) Coventry C	L 0-1		11,755				3	6			12	11		1	5	7	2		9	10	8	4*	
19	(h) Birmingham C	W 2-1	Stainrod, Fenwick	10,824				3	6		11				1		7	2		9	10	8	4	5
26	(a) Tottenham H	L 2-3	Stainrod, Fenwick (pen)	38,789				3	6		11	12			1		7	2		9	10*	8	4	5
Dec 3	(h) Notts C	W 1-0	Waddock	10,217				3	6		7		11		1			2		9	10	8	4	5
10	(a) West Brom A	W 2-1	Fenwick, Stainrod	11,717			12	3	6		7		11		1			2		9*	10	8	4	5
17	(h) Everton	W 2-0	Charles 2	11,608			9	3	6		7		11		1			2			10	8	4	5
24	(a) Leicester C	L 1-2	Fenwick (pen)	17,440			9	3	6		7		11		1			2			10	8	4	5
31	(a) Aston Villa	L 1-2	Charles	19,978			9	3	6		7		11		1			2			10	8	4	5
Jan 2	(h) Wolves	W 2-1	Wicks, Gregory	12,875			9	3	6	12	7		11		1			2			10	8	4*	5
13	(h) Manchester U	D 1-1	Fenwick	16,309			9	3	6		7		11		1			2			10	8	4	5
17	(h) Stoke C	W 6-0	Charles 2, Stainrod, Gregory, Stewart, Fillery	9,320			9*	3	6		7		11		1		12	2			10	8	4	5
Feb 4	(a) Arsenal	W 2-0	Stewart, Fenwick	31,014			9*	3	6	12	7		11		1			2			10	8	4	5
7	(h) West Ham U	D 1-1	Stainrod	20,102				3	6	9	7*		11		1		12	2			10	8	4	5
11	(h) Nottingham F	L 0-1		16,692			9*	3	6	12	7		11		1			2			10	8	4	5
14	(h) Norwich C	W 2-0	Dawes, Waddock	12,901		9		3	6		7		11		1			2			10	8	4	5
25	(a) Liverpool	L 0-2		32,206		12	9	3	6		7*		11		1			2			10	8	4	5
Mar 3	(a) Luton T	D 0-0		11,922	12		9*	3	6		7		11		1			2			10	8	4	5
7	(a) Sunderland	L 0-1		13,538	9			3	6		7*		11		1		12	2			10	8	4	5
10	(h) Coventry C	W 2-1	Stainrod, Allen	10,284	9			3	6				11		1		7	2			10	8	4	5
17	(a) Watford	L 0-1		18,645	9			3	6				11		1		7	2			10	8	4	5
24	(h) Southampton	W 4-0	Wicks, Micklewhite, Allen, Waddock	15,407	9			3	6	11	8				1		7	2			10		4	5
31	(a) West Ham U	D 2-2	Allen 2	21,099	9	12		3	6	11*	8				1		7	2			10		4	5
Apr 7	(h) Ipswich T	W 1-0	Allen	12,251	9			3	6	11	8				1		7	2			10		4	5
14	(a) Birmingham C	W 2-0	Gregory, Fenwick	10,255	9			3	6	12	8		11		1		7	2			10		4*	5
21	(h) Leicester C	W 2-0	Allen, Fereday	12,360	9	12		3	6	4	8		11*		1		7	2			10			5
23	(a) Stoke C	W 2-1	Allen, Fereday	15,735	9			3	6	4	8		11		1		7	2			10			5
28	(h) Tottenham H	W 2-1	Fereday, Gregory	24,937	9	12		3	6	4	8*		11		1		7	2			10			5
May 5	(a) Notts C	W 3-0	Allen 3	7,309	9			3	6	4	8		11		1		7	2			10			5
7	(h) West Brom A	D 1-1	Fereday	14,418	9			3	6	4	8		11		1		7	2			10			5
12	(a) Everton	L 1-3	Micklewhite	20,679	9		12	3	6	4	8		11*		1		7	2				10		5
				App	24	1	10	42	41	11	29	1	37	6	42	5	27	41	1	6	41	30	36	31
				Sub app	1	4	2			6	1	4					3			2		1		
				Goals	14		5	2	10	4	1		7				2	1			13	2	3	2

1 own-goal

FA Cup

Date	Opponents	Result	Scorers	Att	Allen	Burke	Charles	Dawes	Fenwick	Fereday	Fillery	Flanagan	Gregory	Hazell	Hucker	McDonald	Micklewhite	Neill	Roeder	Sealy	Stainrod	Stewart	Waddock	Wicks	Round
Jan 7	(a) Huddersfield T	L 1-2	Gregory	11,924			9	3	6	12	7		11		1			2			10	8*	4	5	3
				App			1	1	1		1		1		1			1			1	1	1	1	
				Sub app						1															
				Goals									1												

League Cup

Date	Opponents	Result	Scorers	Att	Allen	Burke	Charles	Dawes	Fenwick	Fereday	Fillery	Flanagan	Gregory	Hazell	Hucker	McDonald	Micklewhite	Neill	Roeder	Sealy	Stainrod	Stewart	Waddock	Wicks	Round
Oct 4	(h) Crewe A	W 8-1	Stainrod 3, Waddock, Allen, Stewart, Micklewhite, McDonald	8,911	9			3	6	12			11		1	5	7*	2			10	8	4		2/1
25	(a) Crewe A	L 0-3		3,662	9			3	6	2	11				1	5	7*			12	10	8	4		2/2
Nov 9	(a) Ipswich T	L 2-3	Stewart, Gregory	12,341	9*			3	6		12		11		1	5	7	2			10	8	4		3
				App	3			3	3	1	1		2		3	3	3	2			3	3	3		
				Sub app						1	1									1					
				Goals	1								1			1	1				3	2	1		

Substitutions are denoted by including these symbols:
Number 12 = *; 13 = †; 14 = ‡; 15 = §; 16 = °.

Attendance Summary

	ATTENDANCES Home	Away	Total	AVERAGE Home	Away	Total
League	326,753	410,954	737,707	15,560	19,569	17,564
League Cup	8,911	16,003	24,914	8,911	8,002	8,305
FA Cup		11,924	11,924		11,924	11,924
Total	335,664	438,881	774,545	15,257	18,287	16,838

1984-85

Division 1

Date	Opponent	Result	Scorers	Att	Allen	Bannister	Burke	Byrne	Charles	Chivers	Cooper	Dawes	Fenwick	Fereday	Fillery	Gregory	Hucker	James	Kerslake	McDonald	Micklewhite	Neill	Robinson	Stainrod	Stewart	Waddock	Wicks
Aug 25	(h) West Brom A	W 3-1	Stainrod 2, Fenwick	12,802		9*						3	6	12	8	11	1				7	2		10	4		5
28	(a) Watford	D 1-1	Bannister	23,615		9						3	6	12	8	11	1				7	2		10	4*		5
Sep 1	(a) Liverpool	D 1-1	Fereday	33,982		9						3	6	4	8	11	1				7	2		10			5
8	(h) Nottingham F	W 3-0	Fereday 2, Bannister	13,507		9						3	6	4	8	11	1				7	2		10			5
15	(a) Tottenham H	L 0-5		31,655		9						3	6	4	8	11	1				7	2		10			5
22	(h) Newcastle U	D 5-5	Bannister, Stainrod, Gregory, Wicks, Micklewhite	14,234		9						3	6	4	8*	11	1				7	2		10	12		5
29	(a) Southampton	D 1-1	Fereday	18,497		9						3	6	4	8	11	1				7	2		10*	12		5
Oct 6	(h) Luton T	L 2-3	Fillery, Bannister	12,051		9						3	6	4	8	11	1				7	2		10			5
13	(a) Ipswich T	D 1-1	Gregory	15,733		9						3	6	4	8	11	1			5	7	2		10			
20	(h) Coventry C	W 2-1	Stainrod 2	10,427		9						3	6	4	8	11	1				7*	2		10	12		5
27	(a) Norwich C	L 0-2		14,731		9		12				3	6	4	8	11	1				7*	2		10			5
Nov 3	(a) Sunderland	L 0-3		16,408		9		12				3	6		8*	11	1				7	2		10		4	5
10	(h) Sheffield W	D 0-0		13,390		9		10*		2		3	6	7		11	1				12				8	4	5
17	(a) Arsenal	L 0-1		34,953		9		8		2		3	6	7*		11	1	12						10		4	5
24	(h) Aston Villa	W 2-0	Gregory, Bannister	11,689		9						3	6	7		11	1					2		10	8	4	5
Dec 1	(a) Leicester C	L 0-4		10,218		9						3	6	7		11	1					2		10	8	4	5
4	(h) Stoke C	W 2-0	Bannister, Gregory	8,403		9		7*				3	6			11	1	8				2		10	12	4	5
8	(h) Everton	D 0-0		14,338		9						3	6			11	1	12		7		2*		10	8	4	5
15	(a) Manchester U	L 0-3		36,134		9						3	6			11	1			7		2		10	8	4	5
21	(h) Liverpool	L 0-2		11,007		9		12		5		3	6			11	1			7		2*		10	8	4	
26	(h) Chelsea	D 2-2	Bannister, McDonald	26,610		9		10		5		3	6		8	11	1	2		7						4	
29	(a) Stoke C	W 2-0	James, Fillery	10,811		9		10*		5		3	6		8	11	1	2		7			12			4	
Jan 1	(a) West Ham U	W 3-1	Byrne, Bannister, Waddock	20,857		9		10		5		3	6		8	11	1	2*		7			12			4	
12	(h) Tottenham H	D 2-2	Bannister 2	27,404		9		10		5		3	6		8	11	1	2		7						4	
26	(a) West Brom A	D 0-0		9,200		9		10*		5		3	6		8		1	2			11		12			4	7
Feb 2	(h) Southampton	L 0-4		10,664		9		10		5		3	6		8	11	1	2								4	7
9	(a) Nottingham F	L 0-2		12,001		9		10		5		3	6		8	11	1	2*			12					4	7
23	(h) Sunderland	W 1-0	Byrne	10,063		9		10				3	6	2	8	11	1						7			4	5
Mar 2	(h) Norwich C	D 2-2	Fereday, Wicks	12,975		9		10			8*	3	6	2		11	1	12					7			4	5
9	(a) Coventry C	L 0-3		8,988		9		10		12		3	6	2	8	11	1						7*			4	5
16	(h) Ipswich T	W 3-0	Fereday 2, Bannister	9,158		9		12		2		3	6	10	8	11	1						7*			4	5
23	(a) Luton T	L 0-2		9,373	12	9		7*		2		3		10	8	11	1	6		5						4	
30	(h) Watford	W 2-0	Fillery 2	12,771		9		10		2		3	6	11*	8		1			7					12	4	5
Apr 6	(a) Chelsea	L 0-1		20,320		9		10		2		3	6	11	8		1			7						4	5
8	(h) West Ham U	W 4-2	Byrne, Bannister 2, Fenwick (pen)	16,085		9		10		2		3	6	11*	8		1	12		7						4	5
13	(a) Newcastle U	L 0-1		20,711	11*	9		10		2		3	6		8		1	7	12							4	5
20	(h) Arsenal	W 1-0	James	20,189	11	9		10*		2		3	6		8	12	1	5		7						4	
23	(a) Sheffield W	L 1-3	Fillery	22,394	11	9				2		3	6	12	8	10*	1	5		7						4	
27	(a) Aston Villa	L 2-5	Bannister 2	12,023		9				2		3	6		8	12	1	10		7*			11			4	5
May 4	(h) Leicester C	W 4-3	Fillery, Gregory, Bannister, Robinson	9,071		9				2		3	6	12	8*	11	1	10					7			4	5
6	(a) Everton	L 0-2		50,514		9				2		3	6		8	11*	1	10		12			7			4	5
11	(h) Manchester U	L 1-3	Bannister	20,483	8*	9				2		3	6	12		11	1	10					7			4	5
				App	4	42		19		22	1	42	41	21	32	35	42	16		15	13	18	8	19	8	31	33
				Sub app	1			4		1				5		2		4	1	1	2		3		5		
				Goals		17		3					2	7	6	5		2		1	1		1	5		1	2

FA Cup

Date	Opponent	Result	Scorers	Att	Allen	Bannister	Burke	Byrne	Charles	Chivers	Cooper	Dawes	Fenwick	Fereday	Fillery	Gregory	Hucker	James	Kerslake	McDonald	Micklewhite	Neill	Robinson	Stainrod	Stewart	Waddock	Wicks	Round
Jan 5	(a) Doncaster R	L 0-1		10,583		9		10*		5		3	6	12	8	11	1			7			2			4		3
				App		1		1		1		1	1		1	1	1			1			1			1		
				Sub app										1														
				Goals																								

League Cup

Date	Opponent	Result	Scorers	Att	Allen	Bannister	Burke	Byrne	Charles	Chivers	Cooper	Dawes	Fenwick	Fereday	Fillery	Gregory	Hucker	James	Kerslake	McDonald	Micklewhite	Neill	Robinson	Stainrod	Stewart	Waddock	Wicks	Round
Sep 25	(a) York C	W 4-2	Bannister 2, Fenwick (pen), Fereday	10,012		9						3	6	4	8	11	1				7	2		10			5	2/1
Oct 9	(h) York C	W 4-1	Bannister 2, Fereday, Micklewhite	7,544		9					12	3	6	4	8*	11	1				7	2		10			5	2/2
30	(h) Aston Villa	W 1-0	Gregory	12,574		9		12			7*	3	6	4		11	1					2		10		8	5	3
Nov 20	(a) Southampton	D 1-1	Fenwick (pen)	14,830		9						3	6	7		11	1					2		10	8	4	5	4
27	(h) Southampton	D 0-0		13,754	12	9						3	6	7*		11	1					2		10	8	4	5	Rep
Dec 12	(h) Southampton	W 4-0	Waddock, Neill, Fenwick 2 (1 pen)	12,702		9						3	6	12		11	1			7		2		10	8*	4	5	Rep
Jan 23	(a) Ipswich T	D 0-0		16,143		9				5		3	6		8		1				11	2		10		4	7	5
28	(h) Ipswich T	L 1-2	Bannister	14,653		9				5		3	6	12	8*	11	1				2			10		4	7	Rep
				App		8				2	1	8	8	5	4	7	8			1	4	7		8	3	6	8	
				Sub app	1			1			1			2														
				Goals		5							4	2		1					1	1				1		

UEFA Cup

Date	Opponent	Result	Scorers	Att	Allen	Bannister	Burke	Byrne	Charles	Chivers	Cooper	Dawes	Fenwick	Fereday	Fillery	Gregory	Hucker	James	Kerslake	McDonald	Micklewhite	Neill	Robinson	Stainrod	Stewart	Waddock	Wicks	Round
Sep 18	(a) Vikingur	W 3-0	Stainrod 2, Bannister	1,600		9§			15			3	6	4°	8	11	1				7	2		10	16		5	1/1
Oct 2	(h) Vikingur	W 4-0	Bannister 3, Charles	6,196	16	9			10		14	3	6	4	8‡	11	1					2°			7		5	1/2
24	(h) Partizan Belgrade	W 6-2	Gregory, Fereday, Neill, Stainrod, Bannister 2	7,836		9	16					3	6	4	8	11	1					2		10	7°		5	2/1
Nov 7	(a) Partizan Belgrade	L 0-4		45,000		9				2		3	6	4	8	11	1				14			10		7‡	5	2/2
				App		4			1	1		4	4	4	4	4	4				1	3		3	2	1	4	
				Sub app	1		1		1		1										1				1			
				Goals		6			1					1		1						1		3				

Home games played at Highbury, London.

Substitutions are denoted by including these symbols:
Number 12 = *; 13 = †; 14 = ‡; 15 = §; 16 = °.

1985-86

Division 1

Match	Result	Scorers	Att	Allen	Bakholt	Bannister	Barron	Byrne	Chivers	Dawes	Fenwick	Fereday	Fillery	Gregory	Hucker	James	Kerslake	McDonald	Neill	Robinson	Rosenior	Waddock	Walker	Wicks
Aug 17(h) Ipswich T	W 1-0	Byrne	12,755			9		12	2	3	6	10		11	1	7*		5		8		4		
20(a) West Ham U	L 1-3	Byrne	15,530			9		7	2	3	6	10		11	1	12		5		8*		4		
24(a) Aston Villa	W 2-1	Bannister 2	11,896	7		9		10*	2	3	6	12		11	1	8		5				4		
27(h) Nottingham F	W 2-1	Bannister, Fenwick (pen)	10,748	7		9		10	2	3	6			11	1	8		5				4		
31(a) Newcastle U	L 1-3	Fenwick	25,026	7		9		10*	2	3	6	12		11	1	8		5				4		
Sep 3(h) Arsenal	L 0-1		15,993	7		9		10	2*	3	6	8		11	1			5			12	4		
7(h) Everton	W 3-0	Bannister 2, Byrne	16,544	7		9		10	2	3	6	8		11	1			5				4		
14(a) Watford	L 0-2		15,771	7		9		10	2	3	6	8		11	1			5			12	4*		
21(a) Luton T	L 0-2		9,508	7		9		10	2	3	6	8		11	1			5				4		
28(h) Birmingham C	W 3-1	Rosenior, Bannister, Dawes	10,911			9	1			3	6	8		11			7	2			10	4		5
Oct 5(h) Liverpool	W 2-1	Fenwick, Bannister	24,621			9	1			3	6	8	11				7	2			10	4		5
12(a) Manchester U	L 0-2		48,865	12		9	1			3	6	8	11				7*	2			10	4		5
19(h) Manchester C	D 0-0		13,471			9	1	12		3	6		8*	11			7	2			10	4		5
26(a) Southampton	L 0-3		15,615			9	1	12		3	6	11				8	7*	2			10	4		5
Nov 2(h) Sheffield W	D 1-1	James	12,123	7		9	1	10		3		11	8			12		2		6		4*		5
9(a) West Brom A	W 1-0	Robinson	9,016	12		9	1	10*		3	6	11	8			7		2		4				5
16(h) Leicester C	W 2-0	Wicks, Fereday	11,085	12		9	1	10		3	6	11	8			7*		2		4				5
23(a) Tottenham H	D 1-1	Byrne	20,335	12		9	1	10		3	6	11*	8			7		2		4				5
30(h) Coventry C	L 0-2		11,101	11*		9	1	10		3	6		8			7	12	2		4				5
Dec 7(h) West Ham U	L 0-1		23,836	7		9*	1	10		3	6	11	8					2		4	12			5
14(a) Ipswich T	L 0-1		12,032	9			1	10	6	3		11	8			7		2		4				5
17(h) Aston Villa	L 0-1		11,237				1	10	2	3		11	8			9		6		4			7	5
28(a) Arsenal	L 1-3	Bannister	25,770			9	1	10		3	6	12	8					4	2	7			11*	5
Jan 1(h) Oxford U	W 3-1	Allen, Fereday, Byrne	16,348	8		9	1	10		3	6	11						2	4	7				5
11(a) Everton	L 3-4	Bannister 2, Byrne	26,015	8		9	1	10		3	6	11				12		2	4	7*				5
18(h) Newcastle U	W 3-1	Fenwick 2 (1 pen), Robinson	13,159			9	1	10		3	6	11				8		2	4	7				5
Feb 1(a) Nottingham F	L 0-4		11,558	12		9	1	10		3		11	6			8		2	4	7*				5
8(a) Manchester C	L 0-2		20,414	5	12	9		10		3	6				1	7		2	4		8		11*	
22(h) Luton T	D 1-1	Byrne	16,252	8		9	1	10		3	6	11	7					2	4					5
Mar 1(a) Birmingham C	L 0-2		7,093	8			1	10*		3	6	11	7				12	2	4		9			5
8(a) Liverpool	L 1-4	Rosenior	26,219	10*			1			3	6		11			8	12	2	4	7	9			5
11(h) Southampton	L 0-2		14,174				1	12		3	6					8	10	2	4	7	9*		11	5
15(h) Manchester U	W 1-0	Byrne	23,407	7		9	1	10		3	6					8	11*	2	4	12				5
19(a) Chelsea	D 1-1	Kerslake	17,871	7		9*	1			3	6		10			8	12	2	4	11				5
22(h) Watford	W 2-1	Fenwick (pen), Robinson	14,069	7		9	1			3	6	10*				8	12	2	4	11				5
29(a) Oxford U	D 3-3	Walker, Allen, Fenwick (pen)	11,910	8		9	1	12		3	5					6		2*	4	7	11		10	
31(h) Chelsea	W 6-0	Bannister 3, Byrne 2, Rosenior	18,584	7		9	1	10		3	6*	4				8		2		11	12			5
Apr 8(a) Sheffield W	D 0-0		13,157	7		9	1	10		3	6	4				8		2		11				5
12(h) West Brom A	W 1-0	Bannister	11,866	7*		9	1	10		3	6	4				8		2		11	12			5
14(a) Leicester C	W 4-1	Allen, Bannister, Robinson, Byrne	7,724	7		9	1	12	5	3	6	4*						2	8	11	10			
26(h) Tottenham H	L 2-5	Rosenior, Bannister	17,768	7		9	1	10	5	3		4				8	6	2		11*	12			
May 3(a) Coventry C	L 1-2	Byrne	14,084					10	12	3	6*	11			1	8	7	2	4		9			5
			App	26		36	31	30	13	42	37	30	17	11	11	25	9	42	16	25	12	15	5	29
			Sub app	5	1			6	1			3				3	5			1	6			
			Goals	3		16		12		1	7	2				1	1			4	4		1	1

FA Cup

Match	Result	Scorers	Att	Allen	Bakholt	Bannister	Barron	Byrne	Chivers	Dawes	Fenwick	Fereday	Fillery	Gregory	Hucker	James	Kerslake	McDonald	Neill	Robinson	Rosenior	Waddock	Walker	Wicks	Round
Jan 13(a) Carlisle U	L 0-1		5,080	8		9	1	10		3	6					7		2	4*	11	12			5	3
			App	1		1	1	1		1	1					1		1	1	1				1	
			Sub app																		1				
			Goals																						

League Cup

Match	Result	Scorers	Att	Allen	Bakholt	Bannister	Barron	Byrne	Chivers	Dawes	Fenwick	Fereday	Fillery	Gregory	Hucker	James	Kerslake	McDonald	Neill	Robinson	Rosenior	Waddock	Walker	Wicks	Round
Sep 24(h) Hull C	W 3-0	Kerslake, Dawes, Bannister	7,021			9	1	10	2*	3	6	8		11			7				12	4		5	2/1
Oct 8(a) Hull C	W 5-1	Kerslake 2, Rosenior 2, Fillery	4,287	8		9	1	12		3	6		11*				7	2			10	4		5	2/2
29(a) Watford	W 1-0	Byrne	16,826	7		9	1	10		3	6*	11	8					2		12		4		5	3
Nov 25(h) Nottingham F	W 3-1	Fenwick (pen), Bannister, Byrne	13,052	12		9	1	10		3	6		8			7	11*	2		4				5	4
Jan 22(h) Chelsea	D 1-1	Byrne	27,000			9	1	10		3	6	11				8		2	4	7				5	5
29(a) Chelsea	W 2-0	McDonald, Robinson	27,937	12		9	1	10*		3		11	6			8		2	4	7				5	Rep
Feb 12(h) Liverpool	W 1-0	Fenwick	15,051	7		9	1	10		3	6	11				8		2	4					5	SF/1
Mar 5(a) Liverpool	D 2-2	Whelan (og), Gillespie (og)	23,863	10		9*	1			3	6	12	11			8		2	4	7				5	SF/2
Apr 20(☆)Oxford U	L 0-3		90,396	7*		9	1	10		3	6					8		2	4	11	12			5	F
☆Played at Wembley Stadium.			App	5		9	9	7	1	9	8	5	5	1		6	3	8	5	5	1	3		9	
			Sub app	2				1				1								1	2				
			Goals			2		3		1	2		1				3	1		1	2				

2 own-goals

Substitutions are denoted by including these symbols:
Number 12 = *; 13 = †; 14 = ‡; 15 = §; 16 = °.

Attendance Summary 1984-1985

	ATTENDANCES			AVERAGE		
	Home	Away	Total	Home	Away	Total
League	297,321	433,118	730,439	14,158	20,625	17,391
League Cup	61,227	40,985	102,212	12,245	13,662	12,776
UEFA Cup	14,032	46,600	60,632	7,016	23,300	15,158
FA Cup		10,583	10,583		10,583	10,583
Total	372,580	531,286	903,866	13,306	19,677	16,434

Attendance Summary 1985-1986

	ATTENDANCES			AVERAGE		
	Home	Away	Total	Home	Away	Total
League	320,062	365,409	685,471	15,241	17,400	16,321
League Cup	62,124	163,309	225,433	15,531	32,662	25,048
FA Cup		5,080	5,080		5,080	5,080
Total	382,186	533,798	915,984	15,287	19,770	17,615

1986-87

Division 1

Date	Opponents	Result	Scorers	Att	Allen	Bannister	Barron	Brazil	Byrne	Channing	Chivers	Dawes	Fenwick	Ferdinand	Fereday	Fillery	James	Kerslake	Lee	McDonald	Maguire	Neill	Peacock	Robinson	Rosenior	Seaman	Waddock	Walker
Aug 23 (a)	Southampton	L 1-5	Allen	14,711	8	9*		12	10		6	3			11		4			5		2		7		1		
26 (h)	Watford	W 3-2	Allen, Fereday, Bannister	14,021	4	9			12		6	3			11		8	7*		5		2			10	1		
30 (h)	Aston Villa	W 1-0	Bannister	13,003	4	9			10		6	3			11		8		7	5		2				1		
Sep 3 (a)	Newcastle U	W 2-0	Byrne, Bannister (pen)	23,080	4	9			10		6	3			11		8		7	5		2				1		
6 (a)	Everton	D 0-0		30,173	4				10		6	3			11		8		7	5		2			9	1		
13 (h)	West Ham U	L 2-3	James, Byrne	19,257	4				10		6	3			11*		8		7	5		2		12	9	1		
20 (a)	Manchester C	D 0-0		17,744	4	9		12	10*		6	3			11		8		7	5				2		1		
27 (h)	Leicester C	L 0-1		10,021	4	9		12	10		6	3	5*		2		8		7							1		11
Oct 4 (a)	Norwich C	L 0-1		15,894	4	9		10*			6	3			2		8			5				12		1	7	11
11 (h)	Wimbledon	W 2-1	Bannister, McDonald	14,112	4*	9			10		6	3			2		8		7	5				12		1		11
18 (a)	Nottingham F	L 0-1		17,199	4	9			10		6	3			2		8		7	5						1	11*	12
25 (h)	Tottenham H	W 2-0	Allen, Byrne	21,579	4	9			10		6	3			2		8			5						1	7	11
Nov 1 (a)	Luton T	L 0-1		9,085	4	9*			10	11	6	3	5		2		8					7				1		12
8 (h)	Liverpool	L 1-3	Bannister	24,045	4*	9			10		6	3	7		2		8			5					12	1		11
15 (h)	Oxford U	D 1-1	Byrne	12,369	4	9			10		6	3	7		2*		8			5				11		1		12
22 (a)	Manchester U	L 0-1		42,235	4	9			10		6	3	7		2*		12		8	5					11	1		
29 (h)	Sheffield W	D 2-2	Bannister, McDonald	10,241	4	9			10		6	3	7						8	5		2	11*		12	1		
Dec 6 (a)	Arsenal	L 1-3	Bannister	34,048	4	9			10		6	3	7		11				8*	5		2	12			1		
13 (h)	Charlton A	D 0-0		10,299	4	9			10		6*	3	8		11		12		7	5		2				1		
20 (a)	West Ham U	D 1-1	Fenwick (pen)	17,290	4	9			10*				6			12	3		7	5		2	11	8		1		
27 (h)	Coventry C	W 3-1	Byrne, Bannister, Allen	10,053	4	9			10			3	6				2		7	5			11*	8	12	1		
28 (a)	Oxford U	W 1-0	James	11,082	4	9			12		6	3					2		7	5	11			8	10*	1		
Jan 1 (a)	Chelsea	L 1-3	Byrne	20,982	4				10		6	3			9		2		7	5	11*			8		1		12
3 (h)	Everton	L 0-1		19,287	4				10		6		9		12		3		7	5		2		8		1		11*
24 (h)	Southampton	W 2-1	Byrne, Bannister	10,200		9			10				6		11	8*	3		7	5		2			12	1		4
Feb 7 (a)	Aston Villa	W 1-0	Keown (og)	13,109	7				10				6		11	8	3			5	2				9	1		4
14 (h)	Newcastle U	W 2-1	Byrne, Fillery	10,731	7	9			10				6		11	8	3			5		2				1		4
28 (h)	Manchester C	W 1-0	Allen	12,739	7	9			10				6		11	8	3				5	2	12			1		4*
Mar 7 (a)	Tottenham H	L 0-1		21,071	7	9			10				6		11	8	3		12	5	4*	2				1		
14 (h)	Nottingham F	W 3-1	Bannister, Fereday, McDonald	11,896	7	9			10				6		11	8	3		4	5		2				1		
18 (a)	Liverpool	L 1-2	Fillery	28,988	7	9			10				6		11	8	3		4	5		2				1		
21 (a)	Wimbledon	D 1-1	Rosenior	6,938	7	9			10				6			8	3		4	5		2			12	1		11*
25 (h)	Leicester C	L 1-4	Rosenior	7,384		9			10*				6		11	8	3		4	5	12	2			7	1		
28 (h)	Norwich C	D 1-1	Rosenior	9,834		9			10				6		11	8	3		4	5		2			7	1		
Apr 6 (a)	Watford	W 3-0	Bannister 3	13,839		9			12						11	8	3		4	5	6	2	10*		7	1		
11 (h)	Luton T	D 2-2	Byrne 2	11,164		9			10						11	8	3		4	5	6	2			7	1		
18 (h)	Chelsea	D 1-1	Bannister	18,081		9			10						11	8	3		4	5	6	2	12		7*	1		
20 (a)	Coventry C	L 1-4	Bannister	20,925		9				3				12	11	8*			4	5	6	2	10		7	1		
25 (h)	Manchester U	D 1-1	Byrne	17,414	7	9			10						11	8*	3		4	5	6	2	12			1		
May 2 (a)	Sheffield W	L 1-7	Peacock	16,501			1		9			3*		12	11	8	6			5	4	2	7		10			
4 (h)	Arsenal	L 1-4	McDonald	13,387					10						11	8	3	7*		5	6	2	12		9	1	4	
9 (a)	Charlton A	L 1-2	Rosenior	7,769					10		4				11		3	12	7	5	6	2	8*		9	1		
				App	32	34	1	1	37	2	23	23	21		36	17	37	2	29	39	13	29	7	8	15	41	4	11
				Sub app				3	3					2	1	1	2	1	1		1		5	3	5			4
				Goals	5	15			11				1		2	2	2			4			1		4			

1 own-goal

FA Cup

Date	Opponents	Result	Scorers	Att	Allen	Bannister	Barron	Brazil	Byrne	Channing	Chivers	Dawes	Fenwick	Ferdinand	Fereday	Fillery	James	Kerslake	Lee	McDonald	Maguire	Neill	Peacock	Robinson	Rosenior	Seaman	Waddock	Walker	Round
Jan 10 (h)	Leicester C	W 5-2	Fenwick 2 (1 pen), Lee, James, Byrne	9,684		9‡			10				6		11*	8	3		7	5		2	12		14	1		4	3
31 (a)	Luton T	D 1-1	Fenwick (pen)	12,707	8	9			10				6		11		3		7	5		2			12	1		4*	4
Feb 4 (h)	Luton T	W 2-1	Fenwick, Byrne	15,848	7	9*			10				6		11	8	3			5	2				12	1		4	Rep
21 (a)	Leeds U	L 1-2	Rennie (og)	31,324	7	9			10		5		6		11	8‡	3		12		14	2				1		4*	5
				App	3	4			4		1		4		4	3	4		2	3	1	3				4		4	
				Sub app															1		1		1		3				
				Goals					2				4				1		1										

1 own-goal

League Cup

Date	Opponents	Result	Scorers	Att	Allen	Bannister	Barron	Brazil	Byrne	Channing	Chivers	Dawes	Fenwick	Ferdinand	Fereday	Fillery	James	Kerslake	Lee	McDonald	Maguire	Neill	Peacock	Robinson	Rosenior	Seaman	Waddock	Walker	Round
Sep 23 (h)	Blackburn R	W 2-1	Byrne, Brazil	6,510	4	9‡		12	10		6	3			11*		8		7					2	5	1		14	2/1
Oct 7 (a)	Blackburn R	D 2-2	Bannister, Walker	5,100	4	9		10*			6	3			2		8		7	5				12		1		11	2/2
28 (a)	Charlton A	L 0-1		6,926	4	9			10		6	3	12		2		8			5					14	1	7*	11‡	3
				App	3	3		1	2		3	3			3		3		2	2				1	1	3	1	2	
				Sub app				1					1											1	1			1	
				Goals		1		1	1																			1	

Substitutions are denoted by including these symbols:
Number 12 = *; 13 = †; 14 = ‡; 15 = §; 16 = °.

Attendance Summary

	ATTENDANCES			AVERAGE		
	Home	Away	Total	Home	Away	Total
League	293,733	390,047	683,780	13,987	18,573	16,280
League Cup	6,510	12,026	18,536	6,510	6,013	6,179
FA Cup	25,532	44,031	69,563	12,766	22,016	17,391
Total	325,775	446,104	771,879	13,574	17,844	15,753

1987-88

Division 1

Date	Opponent	Result	Scorers	Att	Allen	Bannister	Brock	Byrne	Channing	Coney	Dawes	Dennis	Falco	Fenwick	Ferdinand	Fereday	Fleming	Francis	Johns	Kerslake	Law	McDonald	Maddix	Maguire	Neill	O'Neill	Parker	Peacock	Pizanti	Roberts	Seaman
Aug 15	(a) West Ham U	W 3-0	Stewart (og), Bannister, Brock	22,881	7	9	11	10		8		3		6		2						5					4				1
19	(h) Derby C	D 1-1	Bannister	11,561	7	9	11	10		8		3		6		2						5					4				1
22	(h) Arsenal	W 2-0	Byrne, McDonald	15,981	7	9	11	10‡		8		3		6		2						5					4	14			1
29	(a) Southampton	W 1-0	Brock	15,532	7	9	11	10		8	3			6		2						5					4				1
Sep 2	(h) Everton	W 1-0	Allen	15,380	7	9	11	10		8	3			6		2						5					4				1
5	(a) Charlton A	W 1-0	Coney	7,726	7	9	11	10‡		8	3			6		2						5					4				1
12	(h) Chelsea	W 3-1	Bannister 3	22,583	7	9	11	10		8	3			6		2						5					4	14			1
19	(a) Oxford U	L 0-2		9,800	7	9	11	10‡		8	3*			6		2						5			12		4	14			1
26	(h) Luton T	W 2-0	Coney, Fenwick (pen)	11,175	7	9	11	10		8	3			6		2*						5			12		4				1
Oct 3	(a) Wimbledon	W 2-1	Bannister, Fenwick (pen)	8,552	7	9	11	10		8	3			6								5			2		4				1
17	(a) Liverpool	L 0-4		43,735	7	9	11	10		8*	3			6								5		14	2‡		4		12		1
24	(h) Portsmouth	W 2-1	Byrne, Fenwick	13,170	7	9	11	10‡		8	3			6		14						5		12	2*		4				1
31	(a) Norwich C	D 1-1	Allen	14,522	7			10‡	11	8	3			6		9									2	5	4		14		1
Nov 7	(h) Watford	D 0-0		12,101	7		11	10	9*	8	3			6		14						5		12	2‡		4				1
14	(a) Tottenham H	D 1-1	Coney	28,113	7		11	10‡	9	8		3		6		2						5					4	14			1
21	(h) Newcastle U	D 1-1	Wharton (og)	11,794	7	9	11	10‡	12	8		3		6		2						5*					4	14			1
28	(a) Sheffield W	L 1-3	Bannister	16,933	7	9	11*	14	10	8	3			6		2‡							12			5	4				1
Dec 5	(h) Manchester U	L 0-2		20,632	7	9	11	10		14	3		8‡	6		2								5			4				1
13	(a) Nottingham F	L 0-4		18,130	7	9	11*	10		8‡		3	14	6		2						5		12			4				1
18	(h) Coventry C	L 1-2	Falco	7,229	7	9‡	11	10		14		3	8	6		2						5					4			1	
26	(a) Chelsea	D 1-1	Kerslake	18,020	7	9	11				3		8	6					1	10‡		5		14	2		4				
28	(h) Oxford U	W 3-2	Falco 2, Allen	9,125	7	9‡	11				3		8	6		14			1	10		5			2		4				
Jan 1	(h) Southampton	W 3-0	Bannister, Falco, Fereday	8,631	7	9	11			12	2	3	8*			14			1	10‡		5		6			4				
2	(a) Arsenal	D 0-0		28,271	7	9	11*		12		2	3	8			10			1			5		6			4				
16	(h) West Ham U	L 0-1		14,909	7	9	11*	14			2	3	8			10‡			1	12		5		6			4				
Feb 6	(h) Charlton A	W 2-0	Falco, Byrne	11,512	7	9	11*	14			2		8			10			1	12		5		6			4		3‡		
13	(a) Everton	L 0-2		24,724	7	9	11	14			2*				8	10			1			5		6	12		4		3‡		
27	(h) Wimbledon	W 1-0	Byrne	9,080	7‡			9			2		8			10	14			11			5	6	3		4				1
Mar 5	(h) Liverpool	L 0-1		23,171				9*		12	2		8			10	14			11		5	7‡	6	3		4				1
16	(h) Nottingham F	W 2-1	Coney, Fereday	8,316				8*	12	9	2					10				7		5	11	6	3		4				1
19	(h) Norwich C	W 3-0	Channing, Coney, Fereday	9,032	7*			14	11	9‡	3	12				10				8		5	6		2		4				1
26	(a) Portsmouth	W 1-0	Coney	13,041	7				11‡	9	3		14			10		12		8*		5	6		2		4				1
Apr 1	(a) Watford	W 1-0	McDonald	16,083	7				14	9	3					10		11		8‡		5		6	2		4				1
4	(h) Tottenham H	W 2-0	Kerslake 2	14,783	7‡				14	12	3		9			10		11*		8		5		6	2		4				1
9	(a) Newcastle U	D 1-1	Kerslake (pen)	18,403	7					12	3		9			10		11‡		8*		5	14	6	2		4				1
13	(a) Derby C	W 2-0	Allen, Fereday	14,214	7						3		9			10		11		8‡		5	14	6	2		4				1
19	(a) Luton T	L 1-2	Kerslake (pen)	6,735	7				6	12	3		9			10		11‡		8*		5			2		4		14		1
23	(h) Sheffield W	D 1-1	Coney	12,541	7					9	3		12			10		11‡		8	14	5	6*		2		4				1
30	(a) Manchester U	L 1-2	McDonald	37,733	7				12	9	3		6			10*		11		8		5			2		4				1
May 7	(a) Coventry C	D 0-0		16,089	7				12	9	3		14			10		11		8		5			2‡		4		6*		1
				App	38	24	26	22	7	25	33	10	15	22	1	33		8	7	16		36	6	13	20	2	40		3	1	32
				Sub app				5	7	7		1	4			4	2	1		2	1		3	5	3			5	3		
				Goals	4	8	2	4	1	7			5	3		4				5		3									

2 own-goals

FA Cup

Date	Opponent	Result	Scorers	Att	Allen	Bannister	Brock	Byrne	Channing	Coney	Dawes	Dennis	Falco	Fenwick	Ferdinand	Fereday	Fleming	Francis	Johns	Kerslake	Law	McDonald	Maddix	Maguire	Neill	O'Neill	Parker	Peacock	Pizanti	Roberts	Seaman	Round
Jan 9	(a) Yeovil T	W 3-0	Falco 2, Brock	9,717	7	9*	11			12	2	3	8			10‡			1	14		5		6			4					3
30	(h) West Ham U	W 3-1	Pizanti, Bannister, Allen	23,651	7	9	11	14			2		8			10‡			1			5		6			4		3			4
Feb 20	(h) Luton T	D 1-1	Neill	15,356	7	9‡	11	14			2		8			10			1			5		6	3		4					5
24	(a) Luton T	L 0-1		10,854	7		11	9		12	2		8*			10				14		5		6	3‡		4				1	Rep
				App	4	3	4	1			4	1	4			4			3			4		4	2		4		1		1	
				Sub app				2		2										2												
				Goals	1	1	1						2												1				1			

League Cup

Date	Opponent	Result	Scorers	Att	Allen	Bannister	Brock	Byrne	Channing	Coney	Dawes	Dennis	Falco	Fenwick	Ferdinand	Fereday	Fleming	Francis	Johns	Kerslake	Law	McDonald	Maddix	Maguire	Neill	O'Neill	Parker	Peacock	Pizanti	Roberts	Seaman	Round
Sep 23	(h) Millwall	W 2-1	Bannister, McDonald	11,865	7	9	11	10		8	3			6		2						5					4				1	2/1
Oct 6	(a) Millwall	D 0-0		11,225	7	9	11	10		8	3			6								5			2		4				1	2/2
27	(a) Bury	L 0-1		5,384	7	9*		10	12		3			6	14	8‡						5			2		4		11		1	3
				App	3	3	2	3		2	3			3		2						3			2		3		1		3	
				Sub app					1						1																	
				Goals		1																1										

Simod Cup

Date	Opponent	Result	Scorers	Att	Allen	Bannister	Brock	Byrne	Channing	Coney	Dawes	Dennis	Falco	Fenwick	Ferdinand	Fereday	Fleming	Francis	Johns	Kerslake	Law	McDonald	Maddix	Maguire	Neill	O'Neill	Parker	Peacock	Pizanti	Roberts	Seaman	Round
Dec 21	(h) Reading	L 1-3	Allen	4,004	7		11	10*	2		8	3	9	6					1	12		5					4					1
				App	1		1	1	1		1	1	1	1					1			1					1					
				Sub app																1												
				Goals	1																											

Substitutions are denoted by including these symbols:
Number 12 = *; 13 = †; 14 = ‡; 15 = §; 16 = °.

Attendance Summary

	ATTENDANCES			AVERAGE		
	Home	Away	Total	Home	Away	Total
League	262,706	379,237	641,943	13,135	18,962	16,049
League Cup	11,865	16,609	28,474	11,865	8,304	9,491
Simod Cup	4,004		4,004	4,004		4,004
FA Cup	39,007	20,571	59,578	19,504	10,286	14,894
Total	317,582	416,417	733,999	13,233	17,351	15,292

1988-89

Division 1

Date	Opponent	Result	Scorers	Att	Allen B	Allen M	Ardíles	Barker	Brock	Channing	Clarke	Coney	Dennis	Falco	Fereday	Fleming	Francis	Gray	Herrera	Johns	Kerslake	Law	McCarthy	McDonald	Maddix	Maguire	Parker	Pizanti	Reid	Seaman	Sinton	Spackman	Stein
Aug 27	(a) Manchester U	D 0-0		46,377		7	6	11	8				3	9	2		10*							5			4			1			12
Sep 3	(h) Southampton	L 0-1		9,454		7	6	11	8*				3	9	2		10‡							5	12		4			1			14
10	(a) Norwich C	L 0-1		11,174		7	12	8*	11‡			9	3	14	2									5	6		4			1			10
17	(h) Sheffield W	W 2-0	Francis 2 (1 pen)	8,011		7			11				3		9		8					2		5	6		4			1			10
24	(a) Derby C	W 1-0	Stein	14,008		7		11				12	3		9		8				2			5	6		4			1			10*
Oct 1	(a) Millwall	L 2-3	Allen, Francis	14,103		7		12	11*				3‡	14	9		8			1	2			5		6	4						10
8	(h) Nottingham F	L 1-2	Stein	11,295		7			11			10	3*		9		8			1				5	2	6	4						12
15	(h) West Ham U	W 2-1	Maddix, Stein	14,566		3		2	11‡			12		7	9		8			1	14			5	6		4						10*
22	(a) Arsenal	L 1-2	Falco	33,202		3		2	11					7	9		8‡				14			5	6		4			1			10
29	(a) Luton T	D 0-0		8,453		3		2*	11			12		7	9		8‡				14			5	6		4			1			10
Nov 5	(h) Newcastle U	W 3-0	Maddix, Allen, Falco	11,013		3		2*	12					7	9		8				14			5	6	11	4			1			10‡
12	(a) Middlesbrough	L 0-1		20,565		3	14	2	12					7	9		8							5	6	11*	4			1			10‡
19	(h) Liverpool	L 0-1		20,065		3	12	2‡	11					7	9		8*				14			5	6		4	10		1			
26	(a) Tottenham H	D 2-2	Falco, Francis	26,698		3	5‡	2*	11					7	9		8				12				6	14	4	10		1			
Dec 3	(h) Coventry C	W 2-1	Francis, Falco	9,853		3			11			2	14	7	9		8								6	5	4‡	10		1			
10	(a) Charlton A	D 1-1	Francis	6,012		3								7	9		8				11			2	6	5	4	10		1			
17	(h) Everton	D 0-0		10,067				11*				10	3‡	7	9		8				12			2	6		4	5		1			14
26	(a) Aston Villa	L 1-2	Francis	25,106				11				10		7	9‡		8				6			2	12	3*	4	5		1			14
31	(a) Southampton	W 4-1	Allen, Barker, Falco 2	15,086		11	14	12				10		7			8					3		2	6		4	5*		1			9‡
Jan 2	(h) Norwich C	D 1-1	Falco	12,461		11		10						7			8				12	5		2	6		4	3		1			9*
14	(a) Wimbledon	L 0-1		7,118	12		2	8				10			9				14		11*	5			6		4	3‡		1			7
21	(h) Derby C	L 0-1		9,516				8				10			9*	2			12		11	5			6		4	3		1			7
Feb 4	(h) Millwall	L 1-2	Falco (pen)	10,881				12				10		9	11*			8				3‡		5	2		4	14		1		6	7
11	(a) Nottingham F	D 0-0		19,692				9		2		10						8*			12				5		4	3	11	1		6	7
18	(h) Arsenal	D 0-0		20,543				7‡		2		10	3*	9				8			14				5			11	4	1		6	12
25	(a) West Ham U	D 0-0		17,371				7		2		14	3*	9‡				8						5	10			12	4	1		6	11
Mar 11	(a) Newcastle U	W 2-1	Stein, Clarke	21,555							9	14	3		2			7*						5	12		4	11‡	10	1		6	8
21	(h) Luton T	D 1-1	Clarke	9,072		11		12			9				3			7*						5	2		4		10	1		6	8
25	(a) Sheffield W	W 2-0	Falco, Allen	18,804		11					9‡		3	12	2									5	14		4		10	1	7	6	8*
27	(h) Aston Villa	W 1-0	Sinton	11,378		7‡					9		3	8*	2									5	14		4		10	1	11	6	12
Apr 1	(a) Everton	L 1-4	Falco (pen)	23,028		7*					9		3	8	2									5			4		10	1	11	6	12
8	(h) Wimbledon	W 4-3	Clarke, Spackman, Falco, Reid	9,569		7				2‡	9		3	8*	14									5			4		10	1	11	6	12
15	(h) Middlesbrough	D 0-0		10,347		7				2	9		3	8*	14									5‡			4		10	1	11	6	12
22	(a) Coventry C	W 3-0	Clarke 2, Channing	11,319		12				2	9				3			7*			8				5		4		10	1	11	6	
29	(h) Charlton A	W 1-0	Sinton	13,452		12				2	9				3			7*			8				5		4		10‡	1	11	6	14
May 8	(h) Manchester U	W 3-2	Sinton, Gray 2	10,017						2	9				3‡			7			8			14	5		4		10*	1	11	6	12
13	(h) Tottenham H	W 1-0	Falco	21,873		3		10		2‡	9			14				7			8*			12	5		4			1	11	6	
16	(a) Liverpool	L 0-2		38,368		3		2			9			14				7‡			8			12	5		4		10*	1	11	6	
				App		26	4	21	12	9	12	11	16	22	29	1	19	11		3	11	6		27	28	7	36	13	14	35	10	16	19
				Sub app	1	2	4	4	2			5	1	5	2				2		10			3	5	1		2					12
				Goals		4		1		1	5			12			7	2							2				1		3	1	4

FA Cup

Date	Opponent	Result	Scorers	Att	Allen B	Allen M	Ardíles	Barker	Brock	Channing	Clarke	Coney	Dennis	Falco	Fereday	Fleming	Francis	Gray	Herrera	Johns	Kerslake	Law	McCarthy	McDonald	Maddix	Maguire	Parker	Pizanti	Reid	Seaman	Sinton	Spackman	Stein	Round
Jan 7	(a) Manchester U	D 0-0		36,222		11		12				10		7‡	9		8*					5		2	6		4	3		1			14	3
11	(h) Manchester U	D 2-2	Stein, McDonald	22,236			14	8				10	12		9						11	5*		2	6		4	3‡		1			7	Rep
23	(a) Manchester U	L 0-3		47,257	14			8		11		10				12					9*	5		2	6‡		4	3		1			7	Rep
				App		1		2		1		3		1	2		1				2	3		3	3		3	3		3			2	
				Sub app	1		1	1					1			1																	1	
				Goals																				1									1	

League Cup

Date	Opponent	Result	Scorers	Att	Allen B	Allen M	Ardíles	Barker	Brock	Channing	Clarke	Coney	Dennis	Falco	Fereday	Fleming	Francis	Gray	Herrera	Johns	Kerslake	Law	McCarthy	McDonald	Maddix	Maguire	Parker	Pizanti	Reid	Seaman	Sinton	Spackman	Stein	Round
Sep 28	(h) Cardiff C	W 3-0	Francis, Fereday, Allen	6,078		7		12	11				3		9‡		8			1	2			5	6	14	4						10*	2/1
Oct 12	(a) Cardiff C	W 4-1	Falco 2, Maddix, Stein	2,692				2	11‡			12		7	9		8*			1	14			5	6	3	4						10	2/2
Nov 2	(h) Charlton A	W 2-1	Francis 2	8,701		3		2	11					7‡	9		8				14			5	6		4			1			10	3
30	(h) Wimbledon	D 0-0		10,504		3	5‡		11			2		7	9		8								6	14	4	10		1				4
Dec 14	(a) Wimbledon	W 1-0	Falco	6,585		3						10	5	7	9		8				11‡			2	6		4	14		1				Rep
Jan 18	(a) Nottingham F	L 2-5	Stein, Kerslake	24,065	12		2*	8				10			9				14		11	5‡			6		4	3		1			7	5
				App		4	2	3	4			3	2	4	6		5			2	3	1		4	6	1	6	2		4			4	
				Sub app	1			1				1							1		2					2		1						
				Goals		1								3	1		3				1				1								2	

Simod Cup

Date	Opponent	Result	Scorers	Att	Allen B	Allen M	Ardíles	Barker	Brock	Channing	Clarke	Coney	Dennis	Falco	Fereday	Fleming	Francis	Gray	Herrera	Johns	Kerslake	Law	McCarthy	McDonald	Maddix	Maguire	Parker	Pizanti	Reid	Seaman	Sinton	Spackman	Stein	Round
Feb 1	(a) Sheffield W	W 1-0	Coney	3,957				8		2		10	11‡	9*	6						12			5	14		4	3		1			7	3
14	(a) Watford	D 1-1 #	Coney	8,103				9		2		10				12			11		8		4*		5			3		1		6	7	4
27	(a) Everton	L 0-1		7,472				7		2*		10	3						14		8			5	12		4	11‡		1		6	9	SF
			#Won on penalties	App				3		3		3	2	1	1				1		2		1	2	1		2	3		3		2	3	
				Sub app												1			1		1				2									
				Goals								2																						

Mercantile Centenary Credit Trophy

Date	Opponent	Result	Scorers	Att	Allen B	Allen M	Ardíles	Barker	Brock	Channing	Clarke	Coney	Dennis	Falco	Fereday	Fleming	Francis	Gray	Herrera	Johns	Kerslake	Law	McCarthy	McDonald	Maddix	Maguire	Parker	Pizanti	Reid	Seaman	Sinton	Spackman	Stein
Aug 31	(h) Arsenal	L 0-2		10,019		7	6‡	11*	8				3	9	2		10							5	12		4			1			14
				App		1	1	1	1				1	1	1		1							1			1			1			
				Sub app																					1								1
				Goals																													

Substitutions are denoted by including these symbols:
Number 12 = *; 13 = †; 14 = ‡; 15 = §; 16 = °.

1989-90

Division 1

Date	Match	Result	Scorers	Att	Allen	Bardsley	Barker	Channing	Clarke	Falco	Ferdinald	Francis	Herrera	Iorfa	Kerslake	Law	McDonald	Maddix	Parker	Reid	Roberts	Rutherford	Sansom	Seaman	Sinton	Spackman	Stein	Wegerle	Wilkins	Wright
Aug	19 (h) Crystal P	W 2-0	Wright 2 (1 pen)	16,161	7			2	9*	12							5	14	4	8‡			3	1	11	6				10
	22 (a) Chelsea	D 1-1	Clarke	24,354	7			2	9	12							5	14	4	8			3	1	11‡	6				10*
	26 (a) Norwich C	D 0-0		14,021			7	2	9‡	12					14		5		4	8			3	1	11	6				10*
	30 (h) Luton T	D 0-0		10,565			14	2	9	12							5		4	8‡			3	1	11	6	7*			10
Sep	9 (a) Manchester C	L 0-1		23,420			7*	2	9								5	14	4	8			3	1	11	6	12			10‡
	16 (h) Derby C	L 0-1		10,697		7	14	2	9			12					5		4	8‡			3	1	11	6				10*
	23 (a) Aston Villa	W 3-1	Francis 3	14,170		7		2	9			10‡					5	12	4	8*			3	1	11	6				14
	30 (a) Tottenham H	L 2-3	Bardsley, Francis	23,781		7	8	2	9	12		10*					5		4				3	1	11	6				
Oct	14 (h) Southampton	L 1-4	Francis	10,022		7	14	2	9			10					5	3	4*	8‡				1	11	6				12
	21 (h) Charlton A	L 0-1		10,608		7	8	2	9								5	4				14	3	1	11	6‡				10
	28 (a) Nottingham F	D 2-2	Sinton, Wright	9,442		7	6	2	9								5		4	8		10‡	3	1	11					14
Nov	4 (a) Wimbledon	D 0-0		5,912		7		2	9		14						5	10	4	8			3	1	11‡	6				
	11 (h) Liverpool	W 3-2	Wright 2 (1 pen), Falco	18,804			7	2	14	9							5	6	4	8			3	1	11					10‡
	18 (a) Arsenal	L 0-3		38,236			7	2‡	12	9*						6	5		4	8	1		3		11	14				10
	25 (h) Millwall	D 0-0		9,141		2	7		9		10*						5	6	4	8‡	1		3		11	14				12
Dec	2 (a) Crystal P	W 3-0	Maddix, Sinton 2	12,784		2			14	9	10‡						5	6	4	8	1		3		11				7	
	9 (h) Chelsea	W 4-2	Ferdinand 2, Falco, Clarke	17,935		2	12		14	9	10‡						5	6	4	8*	1		3		11				7	
	16 (a) Sheffield W	L 0-2		14,569		2*	8	12		9	10‡						5	6	4		1		3		11			14	7	
	26 (h) Coventry C	D 1-1	Falco	9,889		2	8			9							5	6	4				3	1	11			10	7	
	30 (h) Everton	W 1-0	Sinton	11,683		2	8			9						4	5	6					3	1	11			10	7	
Jan	1 (a) Manchester U	D 0-0		34,824		2	8			9						4	5	6					3	1	11			10‡	7	14
	13 (h) Norwich C	W 2-1	Falco, Clarke	11,439		2	8		14	9‡							5	6	4				3	1	11			10	7	
	20 (a) Luton T	D 1-1	Falco	9,703		2	8		14	9‡							5	6	4				3	1	11			10	7	
Feb	10 (a) Derby C	L 0-2		14,445		2	8	12	9								5	6*	4				3	1	11			10‡	7	14
	24 (a) Millwall	W 2-1	Barker, Wegerle	11,505		2	8		9							4	5	6					3	1	11			10	7	
Mar	3 (h) Arsenal	W 2-0	Wilkins, Wegerle	18,693		2	8		9								5	6	4				3	1	11			10	7	
	17 (h) Tottenham H	W 3-1	Wilkins, Sinton, Barker	16,691		2	8		9*	12							5	6	4				3	1	11			10	7	
	20 (h) Aston Villa	D 1-1	Clarke	15,856		2	8		9‡	14							5	6	4				3	1	11			10	7	
	24 (h) Nottingham F	W 2-0	Sinton, Barker	14,653		2	8		9‡	14							5	6	4				3	1	11			10	7	
	31 (a) Charlton A	L 0-1		8,768		2	8		9	14							5	6	4				3	1	11			10‡	7	
Apr	3 (a) Southampton	W 2-0	Maddix, Wegerle	14,757		2	8		9							5		6	4				3	1	11			10	7	
	7 (a) Everton	L 0-1		19,887		2	8	12	9							5*		6	4				3	1	11			10	7	
	11 (h) Manchester C	L 1-3	Wegerle	8,437		2	8*	12	9							5		6	4				3	1	11			10	7	
	14 (h) Manchester U	L 1-2	Channing	19,887		2		8	14	9‡	10						5	6	4				3	1	11				7	
	16 (a) Coventry C	D 1-1	Maddix	10,039		2		8	9	14	10						5	6	4				3‡	1	11				7	
	21 (h) Sheffield W	W 1-0	Clarke	10,448		2		8	9								5	6	4				3	1	11			10	7	
	28 (a) Liverpool	L 1-2	Wegerle	37,758		2		8	9				3			4	5	6						1	11			10	7	
May	5 (h) Wimbledon	L 2-3	Wegerle, Channing	9,676		2		8	9*		12			14		4	5	6					3	1	11			10‡	7	
				App	2	31	24	19	27	11	6	3	1			9	35	28	32	15	5	1	36	33	38	11	1	18	23	9
				Sub app			4	4	7	10	2	1		1	1			4				1				2	1	1		6
				Goals		1	3	2	5	5	2	5						3							6			6	2	5

FA Cup

Date	Match	Result	Scorers	Att	Allen	Bardsley	Barker	Channing	Clarke	Falco	Ferdinald	Francis	Herrera	Iorfa	Kerslake	Law	McDonald	Maddix	Parker	Reid	Roberts	Rutherford	Sansom	Seaman	Sinton	Spackman	Stein	Wegerle	Wilkins	Wright	Round
Jan	6 (a) Cardiff C	D 0-0		13,834		2	8			9							5	6	4				3	1	11			10	7		3
	10 (h) Cardiff C	W 2-0	Wilkins, Wegerle	12,226		2	8			9							5	6	4				3	1	11			10	7		Rep
	27 (a) Arsenal	D 0-0		43,483		2	8		9								5	6	4				3	1	11			10‡	7	14	4
	31 (h) Arsenal	W 2-0	Sansom, Sinton	21,547		2	8		9								5	6	4				3	1	11			10	7		Rep
Feb	18 (a) Blackpool	D 2-2	Clarke 2	9,641		2	8		9								5	6	4				3	1	11			10	7		5
	21 (h) Blackpool	D 0-0		15,323		2	8		9								5	6	4				3	1	11			10‡	7	14	Rep
	26 (h) Blackpool	W 3-0	Sinton, Sansom, Barker	12,775		2	8		9								5	6	4				3	1	11			10	7		Rep
Mar	11 (h) Liverpool	D 2-2	Wilkins, Barker	21,057		2	8		9	14							5	6	4				3	1	11			10‡	7		6
	14 (a) Liverpool	L 0-1		30,090		2	8		9	14							5	6	4				3	1	11			10‡	7		Rep
				App		9	9		7	2							9	9	9				9	9	9			9	9		
				Sub app						2																				2	
				Goals			2		2														2		2			1	2		

League Cup

Date	Match	Result	Scorers	Att	Allen	Bardsley	Barker	Channing	Clarke	Falco	Ferdinald	Francis	Herrera	Iorfa	Kerslake	Law	McDonald	Maddix	Parker	Reid	Roberts	Rutherford	Sansom	Seaman	Sinton	Spackman	Stein	Wegerle	Wilkins	Wright	Round
Sep	20 (h) Stockport C	W 2-1	Spackman, Clarke	6,745			8	2	9*	12		7‡					5		4	14			3	1	11	6				10	2/1
Oct	2 (a) Stockport C	D 0-0		5,997			7	2	9			10					5		4	8			3	1	11	6					2/2
	25 (h) Coventry C	L 1-2	Wright (pen)	9,277			6	2	9			10‡					5	4		7		14	3	1	11					8	3
				App			3	3	3			3					3	1	2	2			3	3	3	2				2	
				Sub app						1										1		1									
				Goals					1																	1				1	

Substitutions are denoted by including these symbols:
Number 12 = *; 13 = †; 14 = ‡; 15 = §; 16 = °.

Attendance Summary 1988-1989

	ATTENDANCES Home	Away	Total	AVERAGE Home	Away	Total
League	233,433	378,039	611,472	12,286	19,897	16,091
League Cup	25,283	33,615	58,898	8,428	11,205	9,816
Cent Trophy	11,872		11,872	11,872		11,872
Simod Cup		19,532	19,532		6,511	6,511
FA Cup	22,236	83,479	105,715	22,236	41,739	35,238
Total	292,824	514,665	807,489	12,201	19,062	15,833

Attendance Summary 1989-1990

	ATTENDANCES Home	Away	Total	AVERAGE Home	Away	Total
League	251,285	342,375	593,660	13,226	18,020	15,623
League Cup	16,022	5,997	22,019	8,011	5,997	7,340
FA Cup	82,928	97,048	179,976	16,586	24,262	19,997
Total	350,235	445,420	795,655	13,471	18,559	15,913

1990-91

Division 1

Date	Opponent	Result	Scorers	Att	Allen	Bardsley	Barker	Brevett	Caeser	Channing	Falco	Ferdinand	Herrera	Iorfa	Law	McCarthy	McDonald	Maddix	Meaker	Parker	Peacock	Roberts	Sansom	Sinton	Stéjskal	Tilson	Wegerle	Wilkins	Wilson
Aug 25	(a) Nottingham F	D 1-1	Wegerle	21,619		2	12			4	9‡	14					5	6				1	3	11			10	7*	8
29	(h) Wimbledon	L 0-1		9,762		2	12			4*	9	14					5	6				1	3	11			10‡	7	8
Sep 1	(h) Chelsea	W 1-0	Wegerle (pen)	19,813		2				6	9						5			4		1	3	11			10	7	8
8	(a) Manchester U	L 1-3	Wegerle (pen)	43,427		2	12				9						5	6*		4		1	3	11			10	7	8
15	(h) Luton T	W 6-1	Wegerle 2, Sinton, Wilkins, Falco, Parker	10,198		2					9‡	14					5	6		4		1	3	11			10	7	8
22	(a) Aston Villa	D 2-2	Wegerle (pen), Sinton	23,301		2						9					5	6		4		1	3	11			10	7	8
29	(a) Coventry C	L 1-3	Ferdinand	9,890		2*	14			12		9					5	6		4		1	3‡	11			10	7	8
Oct 6	(h) Tottenham H	D 0-0		21,405		2	8				14	9‡					5	6		4		1	3	11			10	7	
20	(a) Leeds U	W 3-2	Wegerle 2, Wilkins	27,443		2	8				14	9‡					5	6		4			3	11	1		10	7	
27	(h) Norwich C	L 1-3	Wegerle (pen)	11,103		2	8			12	14	9‡					5*	6		4			3	11	1		10	7	
Nov 3	(a) Everton	L 0-3		22,352		2	8				9						5	6‡		4			3	11	1		10	7	14
10	(a) Southampton	L 1-3	Falco	15,957	14	2‡	8				9						5	6		4			3	11	1		10	7	
17	(h) Crystal P	L 1-2	Wegerle	14,360		2	8				9				6		5			4		1	3	11			10	7	
24	(h) Arsenal	L 1-3	Wegerle (pen)	18,555		2	8						4	14	6	5						1	3	11			10	7	9‡
Dec 1	(a) Manchester C	L 1-2	Sinton	25,080		2	8		5				4	9*	6				12			1	3	11			10	7	
8	(a) Wimbledon	L 0-3		5,358		2	8		5		9		4*			12						1	3	11			10	7	6
15	(h) Nottingham F	L 1-2	Wegerle (pen)	10,156		2‡	8		5		9							6	14				3	11	1		10	7	4
23	(a) Derby C	D 1-1	Wegerle	16,429		2	8				9							6			5		3	11	1	4	10	7	
26	(h) Liverpool	D 1-1	Falco	17,848		2	8		5		9							6	14				3	11	1	4	10‡	7	
29	(h) Sunderland	W 3-2	Maddix, Wegerle (pen), Falco	11,072		2	8		5		9							6	14				3	11	1	4	10‡	7	
Jan 1	(a) Sheffield U	L 0-1		21,158		2	8				9							6	14		5		3	11‡	1	4	10	7	
12	(a) Chelsea	L 0-2		19,255		2	8				9							6	14		5		3	11	1	12	10‡	7	4*
19	(h) Manchester U	D 1-1	Falco	18,544		2	8				9							6	14		5		3	11	1	4	10‡	7	
Feb 2	(a) Luton T	W 2-1	Ferdinand 2	8,479	9	2	8					10						6	14		5		3	11‡	1	4		7	
16	(a) Crystal P	D 0-0		15,676	12	2	8				9*	10						6			5		3	11	1	4		7	
23	(h) Southampton	W 2-1	Ferdinand 2	11,009		2	8					9						6			5		3	11	1	4	10	7	
Mar 2	(h) Manchester C	W 1-0	Ferdinand	12,746		2	8					9		14				6			5		3	11	1	4	10‡	7	
16	(h) Coventry C	W 1-0	Ferdinand	9,510		2	8					9‡		14				6			5		3	11	1	4	10	7	
23	(a) Tottenham H	D 0-0		30,860		2	8	3				9						6			5			11	1	4	10	7	
30	(a) Liverpool	W 3-1	Ferdinand, Wegerle, Wilson	37,251	12	2	8	3				9						6			5			11‡	1	4	10*	7	14
Apr 1	(h) Derby C	D 1-1	Wegerle (pen)	12,036	9‡	2*	8	3						14				6		12	5			11	1	4	10	7	
6	(a) Sunderland	W 1-0	Tilson	17,899		2	8	3				9						6			5			11	1	4	10	7	
10	(h) Aston Villa	W 2-1	Allen, Tilson	11,539	14	2	8*	3				9‡						6		12	5			11	1	4	10	7	
13	(h) Sheffield U	L 1-2	Allen	13,801	9	2*	8	3										6	14	12	5			11	1	4	10‡	7	
17	(h) Leeds U	W 2-0	Wegerle, Barker	10,998		2	8	3									9	6			5			11	1	4	10	7	
23	(a) Arsenal	L 0-2		42,395	14*	2	8	3									9	6‡		12	5			11	1	4	10	7	
May 4	(a) Norwich C	L 0-1		13,469	9	2	8	3						12			6*			4	5			11	1		10	7	
11	(h) Everton	D 1-1	Wegerle	12,508	14	2	8	3									9	6‡		4	5			11	1		10	7	
				App	4	38	31	10	5	3	17	14	3	1	3	1	17	32		13	19	12	28	38	26	18	36	38	11
				Sub app	6		4			2	3	3		5		1			9	4						1			2
				Goals	2		1				5	8						1		1				3		2	18	2	1

FA Cup

Date	Opponent	Result	Scorers	Att	Allen	Bardsley	Barker	Brevett	Caeser	Channing	Falco	Ferdinand	Herrera	Iorfa	Law	McCarthy	McDonald	Maddix	Meaker	Parker	Peacock	Roberts	Sansom	Sinton	Stéjskal	Tilson	Wegerle	Wilkins	Wilson	Round
Jan 7	(a) Manchester U	L 1-2	Maddix	35,065		2	8			5*	9	14				12		6					3‡	11	1		10	7	4	3
				App		1	1			1	1							1					1	1	1		1	1	1	
				Sub app								1				1														
				Goals														1												

League Cup

Date	Opponent	Result	Scorers	Att	Allen	Bardsley	Barker	Brevett	Caeser	Channing	Falco	Ferdinand	Herrera	Iorfa	Law	McCarthy	McDonald	Maddix	Meaker	Parker	Peacock	Roberts	Sansom	Sinton	Stéjskal	Tilson	Wegerle	Wilkins	Wilson	Round
Sep 26	(h) Peterborough U	W 3-1	Ferdinand, Maddix, Wegerle	8,714		2	12					9					5	6		4		1	3	11			10	7	8*	2/1
Oct 9	(a) Peterborough U	D 1-1	Ferdinand	7,545		2	8					9					5	6		4		1	3	11			10	7		2/2
31	(h) Blackburn R	W 2-1	Falco, Barker	8,398		2	8				9				12		5*	6		4			3	11	1		10	7		3
Nov 27	(h) Leeds U	L 0-3		15,832		2	8						4	9	6							1	3	11			10	7	5	4
				App		4	3				1	2	1	1	1		3	3		3		3	4	4	1		4	4	2	
				Sub app			1								1															
				Goals			1				1	2						1									1			

Zenith Data Systems Cup

Date	Opponent	Result	Scorers	Att	Allen	Bardsley	Barker	Brevett	Caeser	Channing	Falco	Ferdinand	Herrera	Iorfa	Law	McCarthy	McDonald	Maddix	Meaker	Parker	Peacock	Roberts	Sansom	Sinton	Stéjskal	Tilson	Wegerle	Wilkins	Wilson	Round
Nov 20	(a) Southampton	L 0-4		5,071	9	2	8								5	6			14	4		1	3	11*			10‡	7	12	2
				App	1	1	1								1	1				1		1	1	1			1	1		
				Sub app															1										1	
				Goals																										

Substitutions are denoted by including these symbols:
Number 12 = *; 13 = †; 14 = ‡; 15 = §; 16 = °.

Attendance Summary

	ATTENDANCES			AVERAGE		
	Home	Away	Total	Home	Away	Total
League	256,963	417,298	674,261	13,524	21,963	17,744
League Cup	32,944	7,545	40,489	10,981	7,545	10,122
ZDS Cup		5,071	5,071		5,071	5,071
FA Cup		35,065	35,065		35,065	35,065
Total	289,907	464,979	754,886	13,178	21,135	17,157

1991-92

Division 1

Date	Opponent	Result	Scorers	Att	Allen	Bailey	Bardsley	Barker	Brevett	Channing	Ferdinand	Herrera	Holloway	Impey	Iorfa	McCarthy	McDonald	Maddix	Meaker	Peacock	Penrice	Ready	Roberts	Sinton	Stéjskal	Thompson	Tilson	Walsh	Wegerle	Wilkins	Wilson
Aug 17	(a) Arsenal	D 1-1	Bailey	38,099		7	2	8	3		9		12					6		5				11	1				10	4*	
21	(h) Norwich C	L 0-2		10,626		7‡	2	8	3		9		4					6		5				11	1	14			10		
24	(h) Coventry C	D 1-1	Wegerle	9,393		7	2	8	12		9‡		4					6		5				11	1	14			10		3*
28	(a) Liverpool	L 0-1		32,700		7	2	8			9‡		4					6		5				11	1	14			10		3
31	(a) Sheffield W	L 1-4	Bailey	25,022	11‡	7	2	8			9		4					6		5					1	14			10		3
Sep 4	(h) West Ham U	D 0-0		16,616		7	2	8	3		14		4‡					6		5					1	9			10		11
7	(h) Southampton	D 2-2	Barker, Thompson	9,237		7	2	8	3								12	6*		5				4	1	9			10		11
14	(a) Tottenham H	L 0-2		30,059			2*	8	3				12		14		5	6						11	1	9	4		10‡		7
17	(a) Luton T	W 1-0	Barker	9,985		14	2	8	3*				12				5	6						11	1	10	4	9‡			7
21	(h) Chelsea	D 2-2	Wilson, Peacock	19,579			2	8					4				5	6		3				11	1	9		10			7
28	(a) Crystal P	D 2-2	Barker, Wegerle	15,372		14	2	8					4				5	6		3				11	1	9			10‡		7
Oct 5	(h) Nottingham F	L 0-2		13,508		12	2	8			9		7					6		5*				11	1		4		10		3
19	(a) Wimbledon	W 1-0	Bailey	4,630		10	2	8					7					6		5				11	1	9	4				3
26	(h) Everton	W 3-1	Bailey, Barker 2	10,002		10	2	8					7					6		5				11	1	9	4				3
Nov 2	(h) Aston Villa	L 0-1		10,642		10	2	8					7					6		5	12			11	1	9	4*				3
16	(a) Leeds U	L 0-2		27,087			2	8			12		7					6		5	10			11	1	9*	4‡			14	3
23	(h) Oldham A	L 1-3	Ferdinand	8,947		7‡	2	8			9		14					6		5	10			11	1					4	3
30	(a) Notts C	W 1-0	Ferdinand	7,901			2	8			9					7	6			5	10			11	1					4	3
Dec 7	(h) Sheffield U	W 1-0	Wegerle	10,106			2	8					12			7	6			5	9*			11	1				10	4	3
14	(a) Manchester C	D 2-2	Wegerle, Bailey	21,437		14	2	8					12			7‡	6			5	9			11	1				10	4	3*
21	(a) Norwich C	W 1-0	Bailey	11,436		9	2	8					7				6			5				11	1				10	4	3
26	(h) Liverpool	D 0-0		21,693		9	2	8					7				6			5				11	1				10	4	3
28	(h) Sheffield W	D 1-1	Wilkins	12,990		9*	2	8					7				6			5				11	1	12			10	4	3
Jan 1	(a) Manchester U	W 4-1	Sinton, Bailey 3	38,554		9	2	8					7				6			5				11	1				10	4	3
11	(a) Coventry C	D 2-2	Penrice 2	11,999		9	2	8					7	11			6			5	12				1				10*	4	3
18	(h) Arsenal	D 0-0		20,497		9*	2	8					7				6			5	10			11	1				12	4	3
Feb 1	(h) Wimbledon	D 1-1	Penrice	9,194		9		8‡					7				6			5	10	2		11	1				14	4	3
8	(a) Everton	D 0-0		18,212		9*	2‡	8					7				6			5	10			11	1		14		12	4	3
15	(a) Oldham A	L 1-2	Wegerle	13,092			2	8*					7				6		12	5	9			11	1				10	4	3
22	(h) Notts C	D 1-1	Ferdinand	8,300			2				9		8	7			6			5	10			11	1					4	3
29	(a) Sheffield U	D 0-0		17,958			2				9		8				6			5	10			11	1		4			7	3
Mar 7	(h) Manchester C	W 4-0	Ferdinand 2, Wilson (pen), Barker	10,779			2	14			9		8	4			6			5	10‡			11	1					7	3
11	(h) Leeds U	W 4-1	Ferdinand, Allen, Sinton, Wilson (pen)	14,641	10		2	14			9		8	4			6			5				11‡	1					7	3
14	(a) Aston Villa	W 1-0	Ferdinand	19,630	10		2				9		8	4			6			5				11	1					7	3
21	(a) West Ham U	D 2-2	Allen 2	20,401	10‡		2	14			9		8	4			6			5				11	1					7	3
28	(h) Manchester U	D 0-0		22,603	10		2				9		8	4			6			5				11	1					7	3
Apr 4	(a) Southampton	L 1-2	Ferdinand	15,205	10		2	7			9		8	4			6	5			14			11‡	1						3
11	(h) Tottenham H	L 1-2	Sinton	20,678	10		2				9‡		8	4			6			5	14			11	1					7	3
18	(a) Chelsea	L 1-2	Allen	18,952	12		2				9		8	4*			6			5	10			11	1					7	3
20	(h) Luton T	W 2-1	Ferdinand 2	10,749	10*		2				9		8	4			6			5	12			11	1					7	3
25	(a) Nottingham F	D 1-1	Allen	22,228	10		2				9‡		8	4				6		5	14			11	1					7	3
May 2	(h) Crystal P	W 1-0	Humphrey (og)	14,903	10	14	2	11			9‡		8	4			6			5					1					7	3
				App	10	19	41	31	6		21		34	13		3	28	19		39	13	1		38	42	10	8	2	18	26	40
				Sub app	1	5		3	1		2		6		1		1		1		6					5	1		3	1	
				Goals	5	9		6			10									1	3			3		1			5	1	3

1 own-goal

FA Cup

Date	Opponent	Result	Scorers	Att	Allen	Bailey	Bardsley	Barker	Brevett	Channing	Ferdinand	Herrera	Holloway	Impey	Iorfa	McCarthy	McDonald	Maddix	Meaker	Peacock	Penrice	Ready	Roberts	Sinton	Stéjskal	Thompson	Tilson	Walsh	Wegerle	Wilkins	Wilson	Round
Jan 4	(a) Southampton	L 0-2		13,710		9	2	8					7				6*			5	12			11	1				10	4	3	3
				App		1	1	1					1				1			1				1	1				1	1	1	
				Sub app																	1											
				Goals																												

League Cup

Date	Opponent	Result	Scorers	Att	Allen	Bailey	Bardsley	Barker	Brevett	Channing	Ferdinand	Herrera	Holloway	Impey	Iorfa	McCarthy	McDonald	Maddix	Meaker	Peacock	Penrice	Ready	Roberts	Sinton	Stéjskal	Thompson	Tilson	Walsh	Wegerle	Wilkins	Wilson	Round
Sep 24	(a) Hull C	W 3-0	Thompson, Barker 2	4,979			2	8			12	14	4				5	6		3				11‡	1	9			10*		7	2/1
Oct 9	(h) Hull C	W 5-1	Bardsley, Thompson 2, Bailey 2	5,251		10	2	8					7	14				6*		5		12		11‡	1	9	4				3	2/2
29	(a) Manchester C	D 0-0		15,512		10	2	8					7					6		5				11	1	9	4				3	3
Nov 20	(h) Manchester C	L 1-3	Penrice	11,033		7	2	8	3		9							6		5	10				1					4	11	Rep
				App		3	4	4	1		1		3				1	4		4	1			3	4	3	2		1	1	4	
				Sub app							1	1		1								1										
				Goals		2	1	2													1					3						

Zenith Data Systems Cup

Date	Opponent	Result	Scorers	Att	Allen	Bailey	Bardsley	Barker	Brevett	Channing	Ferdinand	Herrera	Holloway	Impey	Iorfa	McCarthy	McDonald	Maddix	Meaker	Peacock	Penrice	Ready	Roberts	Sinton	Stéjskal	Thompson	Tilson	Walsh	Wegerle	Wilkins	Wilson	Round
Oct 23	(a) Norwich C	W 2-1	Sinton, Impey	4,436		10	2	8					7	12				6		5				11*	1	9	4				3	2
Nov 26	(h) Crystal P	L 2-3	Bardsley, Wilkins	4,492			2	8*		7‡	9		12	14			6			5	10		1	11						4	3	QF
				App		1	2	2		1	1		1				1	1		2	1		1	2	1	1	1			1	2	
				Sub app									1	2																		
				Goals			1							1										1						1		

Substitutions are denoted by including these symbols:
Number 12 = *; 13 = †; 14 = ‡; 15 = §; 16 = °.

Attendance Summary

	ATTENDANCES Home	Away	Total	AVERAGE Home	Away	Total
League	281,683	419,856	707,539	13,699	19,993	16,846
League Cup	16,284	20,491	36,775	8,142	10,246	9,194
ZDS Cup	4,492	4,436	8,928	4,492	4,436	4,464
FA Cup		13,710	13,710		13,710	13,710
Total	308,459	458,493	766,952	12,852	18,340	15,652

1992-93

FA Premier League

	Match	Res	Scorers	Att	Allen	Bailey	Bardsley	Barker	Brevett	Channing	Doyle	Ferdinand	Holloway	Impey	McDonald	Maddix	Meaker	Peacock	Penrice	Ready	Roberts	Sinton	Stéjskal	Thompson	White	Wilkins	Wilson
Aug	17 (a) Manchester C	D 1-1	Sinton	24,471		10	2					9*	8	7	6			5				11	1	12		4	3
	19 (h) Southampton	W 3-1	Ferdinand 2, Bardsley	10,925		10	2					9*	8	7	6			5			1	11		12		4	3
	22 (h) Sheffield U	W 3-2	Barker, Ferdinand, Bailey	10,932		10	2	7				9	8*		6			5				11	1	12		4	3
	26 (a) Coventry C	W 1-0	Impey	13,563		10	2	8				9*		7	6			5	12			11	1			4	3
	29 (a) Chelsea	L 0-1		22,910		10*	2	8				9		7	6			5	12			11	1			4	3
Sep	2 (h) Arsenal	D 0-0		20,861		10*	2	8				9		7	6			5	12		1	11				4	3
	5 (h) Ipswich T	D 0-0		12,806		10*	2	8				9		7	6			5	12			11	1			4	3
	12 (a) Southampton	W 2-1	Sinton, Channing	14,125				8		2*		9		7	6	12		5	10			11	1			4	3
	19 (h) Middlesbrough	D 3-3	Ferdinand, Penrice, Sinton (pen)	12,272				8		2		9	14	7	6	12		5‡	10			11	1			4	3*
	26 (a) Manchester U	D 0-0		33,287			2	12	3			9*	8	7		6		5	10			11	1			4	
Oct	3 (h) Tottenham H	W 4-1	Holloway, Wilkins, Penrice 2	19,845		9	2						8	7	6			5	10			11	1			4	3
	17 (a) Norwich C	L 1-2	Allen	16,009	12	9	2						8	7	6	14		5	10*			11‡	1			4	3
	24 (h) Leeds U	W 2-1	Bardsley, Ferdinand	19,326	10*		2	12				9	8	7	6			5				11	1			4	3
Nov	1 (a) Aston Villa	L 0-2		20,140	10	12	2	11				9	8	7*	6			5			1					4	3
	7 (a) Wimbledon	W 2-0	Wilkins, Allen	6,771	10		2					9	8	7	6			5			1	11				4	3
	23 (h) Liverpool	L 0-1		21,056	10		2					9	8	7	6			5			1	11				4	3
	28 (a) Blackburn R	L 0-1		15,850		10*	2					9	8	7	6			5	12			11	1			4	3
Dec	5 (h) Oldham A	W 3-2	Ferdinand 2, Penrice	11,804	12		2					9‡	8	7	6	14		5	10			11*	1			4	3
	12 (h) Crystal P	L 1-3	Penrice	14,571			2					9	8	7	6			5	10			11	1			4	3
	19 (a) Sheffield W	L 0-1		23,164			2	12				9	8	7*	6			5	10		1	11				4	3
	28 (h) Everton	W 4-2	Sinton 3, Penrice	14,802			2	7				9	8		6			5	10		1	11				4	3
Jan	9 (a) Middlesbrough	W 1-0	Ferdinand	15,616	12		2	8	3			9		7	6	14		5	10*		1	11‡					4
	18 (h) Manchester U	L 1-3	Allen	20,142	10	9	2	4					8	7	6			5*			1	11		12			3
	27 (h) Chelsea	D 1-1	Allen	15,806	10		2	4	3			9	8	11	6	5					1				14		7‡
	30 (a) Sheffield U	W 2-1	Allen, Holloway	16,366	10		2	4	3			9	8	7*	6	5		12			1						11
Feb	6 (h) Manchester C	D 1-1	Wilson (pen)	13,003	10		2	4	3			9		8	6	5					1	11					7
	9 (a) Ipswich T	D 1-1	White	17,354	10		2		3		4‡	9		8*	6	5		12			1	11			14		7
	20 (h) Coventry C	W 2-0	Pearce (og), Peacock	12,453	10		2	4	3			9		8				5		6	1	11					7
	24 (a) Nottingham F	L 0-1		22,436	10*	12	2	4	3			9		8		6		5			1	11					7
	27 (a) Tottenham H	L 2-3	Peacock, White	32,341			2	4‡	3			9		14	6	8		5			1	11			10		7
Nov	6 (h) Norwich C	W 3-1	Ferdinand 2, Wilson	13,892	12		2		3		4	9		7	6	5	11				1				10*		8
	10 (a) Liverpool	L 0-1		30,370			2		3		4	9		7	6	5‡	11	14			1				10		8
	13 (h) Wimbledon	L 1-2	Ferdinand	12,270	10		2		3		4	9*		7	6		11	5			1†		13		12		8
	20 (a) Oldham A	D 2-2	Allen, Sinton	10,946	10		2				4	9	8	7	6			5		14	1	11‡					3
	24 (h) Blackburn R	L 0-3		10,677	10	9	2		3				8	7	6					5	1	11					4
Apr	3 (a) Crystal P	D 1-1	Allen	14,705	10	9	2		3				8	7	6			5			1	11‡			14		4
	10 (h) Nottingham F	W 4-3	Ferdinand 3, Wilson (pen)	15,815	10		2					9	8	7	6			5			1	11				4	3
	12 (a) Everton	W 5-3	Impey, Ferdinand 3, Bardsley	19,057	10		2	12				9	8	7	6			5			1	11*				4	3
May	1 (a) Leeds U	D 1-1	Ferdinand	31,408	10		2	8				9		7	6			5			1	11				4	3
	4 (a) Arsenal	D 0-0		18,817	10		2	8‡	14			9		7	6			5			1	11				4	3
	9 (h) Aston Villa	W 2-1	Ferdinand, Allen	18,904	10		2	8				9		7	6			5			1	11				4	3
	11 (h) Sheffield W	W 3-1	Allen 2, Ferdinand	12,177	10		2	8				9		7	6			5			1	11				4	3
				App	21	13	40	21	14	2	5	37	23	39	39	9	3	35	10	2	28	36	14		3	27	41
				Sub app	4	2		4	1				1	1		5		3	5	1			1	4	4		
				Goals	10	1	3	1		1		20	2	2				2	6			7			2	2	3

1 own-goal

FA Cup

	Match	Res	Scorers	Att	Allen	Bailey	Bardsley	Barker	Brevett	Channing	Doyle	Ferdinand	Holloway	Impey	McDonald	Maddix	Meaker	Peacock	Penrice	Ready	Roberts	Sinton	Stéjskal	Thompson	White	Wilkins	Wilson	Round
Jan	4 (h) Swindon T	W 3-0	Ferdinand 2, Penrice	12,106			2	7				9	8	12	6			5	10*		1	11				4	3	3
	23 (h) Manchester C	L 1-2	Holloway	18,652	10	14	2	4	3			9	8		6	5					1	11‡					7	4
				App	1		2	2	1			2	2		2	1		1	1		2	2				1	2	
				Sub app		1								1														
				Goals								2	1						1									

League Cup

	Match	Res	Scorers	Att	Allen	Bailey	Bardsley	Barker	Brevett	Channing	Doyle	Ferdinand	Holloway	Impey	McDonald	Maddix	Meaker	Peacock	Penrice	Ready	Roberts	Sinton	Stéjskal	Thompson	White	Wilkins	Wilson	Round
Sep	23 (h) Grimsby T	W 2-1	Ferdinand 2	7,275		10*			3	2		9	8	7		6		5	12		1	11				4		2/1
Oct	6 (a) Grimsby T	L 1-2*	Bailey	8,443		9	2						8	7	6			5	10*			11	1	12		4	3	2/2
	27 (a) Bury	W 2-0	Allen, Peacock	4,680	10*		2	7				9	8		6			5			1	11		12		4	3	3
Dec	2 (a) Sheffield W	L 0-4		17,161			2	12				9	8	7*	6			5	10			11	1			4	3	4
				App	1	2	3	1	1	1		3	4	3	3	1		4	2		2	4	2			4	3	
				Sub app				1											1					2				
				Goals	1	1						2						1										

*Queen's Park Rangers won 6-5 on penalties

Substitutions are denoted by including these symbols:
Number 12 = *; 13 = †; 14 = ‡; 15 = §; 16 = °.

Attendance Summary

	ATTENDANCES			AVERAGE		
	Home	Away	Total	Home	Away	Total
League	314,339	419,706	734,045	14,969	19,986	17,477
League Cup	7,275	30,284	37,559	7,275	10,095	9,390
FA Cup	30,758		30,758	15,379		15,379
Total	352,372	449,990	802,362	14,682	18,750	16,716

Rangers in Other Competitions

London Midweek League

	P	W	D	L	F	A	Pts	Pos
1949-50	26	-	-	-	-	-	-	1st
1950-51	30	-	-	-	-	-	-	-
1951-52	20	7	4	9	28	49	18	8th
1952-53	18	4	2	12	19	51	10	
1953-54	22	14	5	3	61	33	33	1st
1954-55	20	-	-	-	-	-	-	
1955-56	14	1	3	10	12	38	5	8th
1966-67	32	21	7	4	83	30	49	2nd
1967-68	28	10	7	11	55	51	27	5th

Football Combination

	P	W	D	L	F	A	Pts	Pos
DIVISION 'B'								
1946-47	30	17	3	10	71	41	37	4th
DIVISION 'A'								
1947-48	30	11	10	9	53	50	32	6th
1948-49	30	13	6	11	51	51	32	6th
1949-50	30	8	6	16	42	52	22	15th
1950-51	30	13	6	11	55	53	32	5th
1951-52	30	10	2	18	33	70	22	13th
DIVISION TWO								
1952-53	30	11	7	12	30	38	29	9th
1953-54	30	9	5	16	40	58	23	15th
1954-55	30	6	6	18	41	75	18	15th
DIVISION ONE								
1955-56	42	18	4	20	62	86	40	18th
1956-57	42	9	8	25	69	116	26	31st
1957-58	42	12	2	28	75	125	26	31st
DIVISION TWO								
1958-59	32	14	6	12	65	69	34	9th
1959-60	38	14	4	20	66	90	32	15th
1960-61	38	13	9	16	75	87	35	14th
MIDWEEK								
1961-62	34	6	5	23	40	90	17	18th
1962-63	34	10	5	19	51	76	25	17th
DIVISION TWO								
1963-64	34	10	2	22	49	73	22	16th
1964-65	36	14	9	13	54	48	37	9th
1965-66	38	23	4	11	85	60	50	3rd
DIVISION ONE								
1968-69	25	8	7	10	39	45	23	14th
1969-70	25	7	5	13	38	47	19	21st
1970-71	42	21	7	14	72	60	49	7th
1971-72	40	15	15	10	72	46	45	6th
1972-73	40	19	8	13	54	46	46	6th
1973-74	42	18	11	13	74	51	47	8th
1974-75	40	13	13	14	58	69	39	12th
1975-76	42	15	11	16	60	62	41	12th
1976-77	42	19	8	15	60	41	46	9th
1977-78	42	16	15	11	71	53	47	9th
1978-79	42	27	8	7	103	57	62	3rd
1979-80	42	20	7	15	87	70	47	8th
1980-81	42	19	9	14	80	64	47	9th
1981-82	38	27	5	6	90	40	59	1st
1982-83	42	29	8	5	113	47	66	1st
1983-84	42	23	9	10	80	37	55	4th
1984-85	42	25	10	7	102	51	60	3rd
1985-86	42	21	7	14	91	69	49	10th
1986-87	38	19	8	11	78	69	46	7th
1987-88	38	18	8	12	68	54	44	7th
1988-89	38	6	5	27	36	79	17	19th
1989-90	38	14	5	19	65	93	47	13th
1990-91	38	14	8	16	60	62	50	10th
1991-92	38	22	5	11	76	44	71	4th
1992-93	38	19	11	8	70	46	68	3rd

South East Counties League

	P	W	D	L	F	A	Pts	Pos
1956-57	-	-	-	-	-	-	-	
1957-58	-	-	-	-	-	-	-	
1958-59	-	-	-	-	-	-	-	
1959-60	-	-	-	-	-	-	-	
1960-61	-	-	-	-	-	-	-	
1961-62	-	-	-	-	-	-	-	
1962-63	30	21	4	5	84	36	46	2nd
1963-64	30	23	6	1	106	30	52	1st
1964-65	30	21	2	7	94	40	44	2nd
1965-66	30	21	2	7	102	45	44	1st
1966-67	30	12	7	11	60	43	31	8th
1967-68	30	23	2	5	92	43	48	1st
1968-69	32	16	5	11	72	53	37	5th
1969-70	30	12	9	9	49	38	33	6th
1970-71	30	10	3	17	40	62	23	12th
1971-72	30	10	9	11	34	35	29	10th
1972-73	32	11	9	12	44	52	31	8th
1973-74	32	7	4	21	31	69	18	14th
1974-75	30	13	2	15	45	57	28	11th
1975-76	30	11	7	12	52	50	29	9th
1976-77	30	17	7	6	59	35	41	3rd
1977-78	30	21	4	5	72	35	46	1st
1978-79	30	9	3	18	44	68	21	15th
1979-80	30	15	8	7	75	38	38	2nd
1980-81	30	13	8	9	47	46	34	6th
1981-82	30	22	7	1	80	23	51	1st
1982-83	28	15	6	7	88	36	36	3rd
1983-84	30	10	11	9	52	55	31	7th
1984-85	30	6	6	18	45	71	18	15th
1985-86	30	6	8	16	35	65	20	14th
1986-87	30	8	4	18	32	60	20	14th
1987-88	30	18	6	6	48	25	42	3rd
1988-89	30	14	8	8	67	36	36	5th
1989-90	30	12	7	11	44	45	31	7th
1990-91	30	10	6	14	39	53	26	11th
1991-92	30	18	3	9	80	51	39	3rd
1992-93	30	18	1	11	81	55	37	4th

Football Combination Cup

	P	W	D	L	F	A	Pts	Pos
1946-47	14	-	-	-	-	-	-	-
SECTION FOUR								
1947-48	14	8	5	1	26	23	17	3rd
SECTION TWO								
1948-49	14	5	7	2	22	29	12	5th
1949-50	14	3	3	8	20	31	9	7th
1950-51	14	4	5	5	22	26	13	5th
1951-52	14	4	1	9	19	33	9	6th
1952-53	14	6	0	8	18	25	12	5th
1953-54	14	4	4	6	18	15	12	5th
1954-55	14	3	2	9	18	34	8	7th
GROUP D								
1968-69	10	6	2	2	24	16	14	-
GROUP B								
1969-70	10	-	-	-	-	-	-	-

Western League

	P	W	D	L	F	A	Pts	Pos
DIVISION ONE								
1900-01	16	7	4	5	39	25	18	4th
1901-02	16	5	1	10	17	43	11	8th
1902-03	16	6	2	8	18	31	14	7th
1903-04	16	5	5	6	15	21	15	6th
1904-05	20	6	3	11	27	45	15	11th
1905-06	20	11	4	5	33	27	26	1st
DIVISION ONE A								
1906-07	10	5	1	4	17	11	11	2nd
1907-08	12	5	1	6	20	23	11	5th
1908-09	12	6	1	5	28	24	13	2nd

FA Youth Cup

	Rnd	Date	Opponents		
1952-53	2nd	25.10.52	Twickenham	h	3-2
	3rd	29.11.52	Chelsea	h	3-1
	4th	27.12.52	Tottenham H	h	2-1
	5th	28.2.53	Brentford	a	0-3
1953-54	2nd	24.10.53	Chelsea	a	0-3
1954-55	1st	9.10.54	Chelsea	a	0-8
1955-56	1st	1.9.55	Luton Town	h	(scr)
1956-57	1st	17.9.56	Barnet	h	3-5
1957-58	Pre	25.9.57	Fulham	h	1-0
	1st	15.10.57	Leyton Orient	h	4-3
	2nd	29.10.57	Chelsea	a	0-4
1958-59	2nd	4.10.58	Millwall	h	4-1
1958-59	3rd	22.12.58	Arsenal	a	0-5
1959-60	Did not enter				
1960-61	Pre	10.9.60	West Thurrock	h	1-0
	1st		Tottenham H	a	0-7
1961-62	Pre	29.8.61	Hounslow W	h	12-2
	1st	24.10.61	Arsenal	a	1-4
1962-63	1st	8.11.62	Brentford	h	4-0
	2nd	26.12.62	Southampton	a	1-2
1963-64	1st	13.11.63	Southend U	a	4-2
	2nd	7.1.64	Watford	a	2-2
	(rep)	13.1.64	Watford	h	1-0
	3rd	20.1.64	Tottenham H	h	0-0
	(rep)	5.2.64	Tottenham H	a	2-1
	4th	17.2.64	Norwich City	h	2-1
	SF1	8.4.64	Swindon Town	h	0-2
	SF2	14.4.64	Swindon Town	a	1-4
1964-65	2nd	21.12.64	Chelsea	h	1-4
1965-66	2nd		Luton Town	a	3-0
	3rd	10.1.66	Leyton Orient	a	2-2
	(rep)	17.1.66	Leyton Orient	h	6-1
	4th	2.2.66	Norwich City	a	3-0
	5th	21.2.66	West Ham U	a	1-0
	SF1	4.4.66	Arsenal	h	1-1
	SF2	19.4.66	Arsenal	a	2-3
1966-67	2nd	13.12.66	Chelsea	h	3-4
1967-68	2nd	4.12.67	Watford	a	1-1
	(rep)	23.12.67	Watford	h	1-2
1968-69	1st	31.10.68	Friern Barnet	h	8-1
	2nd	27.11.68	Crystal Palace	h	3-1
	3rd	8.1.69	Chelsea	h	0-1
1969-70	2nd	2.12.69	Charlton Athletic	h	1-4
1970-71	1st	3.11.70	Oxford United	h	2-0
	2nd	1.12.70	Arsenal	h	0-6
1971-72	1st	3.11.71	Friern Barnet	a	1-1
	(rep)	8.11.71	Friern Barnet	h	5-0
	2nd	29.11.71	Brighton & HA	a	1-1
	(rep)	7.12.71	Brighton & HA	h	4-2
	3rd	28.12.71	West Ham U	h	3-1
	4th	25.1.72	Arsenal	a	0-2
1972-73	1st	4.11.72	Chingford	h	4-0
	2nd	21.11.72	Stevenage A	h	6-2
	3rd	4.1.73	Chelsea	a	0-4
1973-74	1st	29.9.73	Gillingham	a	5-2
	2nd	21.11.73	Portsmouth	a	2-0
	3rd	18.12.73	West Brom A	h	0-2
1974-75	1st	22.10.74	Viking Sports	a	0-1
1975-76	1st	27.10.75	Watford	h	1-0
	2nd	24.11.75	Southend U	h	1-1
	(rep)		Southend U	a	2-1
	3rd	22.12.75	Nottingham F	h	2-0
	4th		Huddersfield T	a	2-1
	5th	18.2.76	Wolves	h	0-1
1976-77	2nd	8.12.76	Chelsea	h	3-3
	(rep)		Chelsea	a	0-1
1977-78	2nd	12.12.77	Chelsea	a	1-5
1978-79	2nd	8.11.78	Hounslow	a	4-0
	3rd		Charlton Athletic	a	2-3
1979-80	1st	8.11.79	Swindon Town	h	2-1
	2nd	4.12.79	Luton Town	h	2-2
	(rep)	10.12.79	Luton Town	a	1-2
1980-81	1st		Addlestone & Weybridge	h	3-0
	2nd		Luton Town	a	4-3
	3rd	16.12.80	Arsenal	a	1-1
	(rep)	6.1.81	Arsenal	h	2-2
	(rep)	12.1.81	Arsenal	a	1-0
	4th	29.1.81	Coventry City	h	2-2
	(rep)	9.2.81	Coventry City	a	5-1
	5th	24.2.81	West Ham U	a	1-3
1981-82	1st	5.11.81	Barking	h	2-0
	2nd	21.12.81	Windsor & Eton	h	4-2
	3rd	5.1.82	Portsmouth	h	10-0
	4th	8.2.82	Burnley	h	3-0
	5th	1.3.82	Wolves	h	3-3
	(rep)	10.3.82	Wolves	a	1-2
1982-83	2nd	1.12.82	Ipswich Town	h	4-0
	3rd	3.1.83	Orient	a	1-1
	(rep)	8.1.83	Orient	h	1-1
	(rep)	19.1.83	Orient	a	2-1
1982-83	4th	3.2.83	Manchester U	h	0-4
1983-84	2nd	5.12.83	Woking	a	6-1
	3rd	5.1.84	Brentford	h	0-3
1984-85	2nd	6.12.84	Brentford	h	1-1
	(rep)	13.12.84	Brentford	a	2-0
	3rd	26.1.85	Norwich City	a	2-2
	(rep)	31.1.85	Norwich City	h	2-1
	4th	27.2.85	Millwall	h	0-2
1985-86	2nd	9.12.85	Charlton Athletic	a	1-3
1986-87	2nd	18.12.86	Fulham	a	1-2
1987-88	1st	2.11.87	Erith & Belvedere	a	2-0
	2nd	7.12.87	Dulwich Hamlet	a	0-0

	Rnd	Date	Opponents		
	(rep)	10.12.87	Dulwich Hamlet	h	6-0
	3rd	5.1.88	Southampton	a	0-3
1988-89	1st	10.11.88	Horley	a	5-0
	2nd	12.12.88	Fulham	h	3-1
	3rd	16.1.89	Watford	a	2-2
	(rep)	30.1.89	Watford	h	0-2
1989-90	1st	30.10.89	West Ham U	a	1-1
	(rep)	13.11.89	West Ham U	h	3-0
	2nd	27.11.89	Reading	h	3-1
	3rd	3.1.90	Portsmouth	a	1-1
	(rep)	15.1.90	Portsmouth	h	2-3
1990-91	2nd	19.11.90	Crystal Palace	a	3-3
	(rep)	29.11.90	Crystal Palace	h	0-1
1991-92	2nd	26.11.91	Cardiff City	a	1-0
	3rd	16.12.91	Plymouth Argyle	a	3-1
	4th	27.1.92	Brentford	h	5-1
	5th	26.2.92	Wimbledon	a	0-2
1992-93	2nd	7.12.92	Borehamwood	a	7-1
	3rd	19.1.93	Coventry City	h	5-3
	4th	26.1.93	Leeds United	a	1-5

London Challenge Cup

	Rnd	Date	Opponents		
1946-47	1st	21.10.46	Fulham	a	5-0
	2nd	28.10.46	Tottenham H	a	0-1
1947-48	1st	13.10.47	Enfield	h	3-1
	2nd	27.10.47	Chelsea	a	1-2
1948-49	1st	11.10.48	Leytonstone	h	4-1
	2nd	25.10.48	West Ham U	h	1-2
1949-50	1st	10.10.49	Barnet	h	
	2nd	24.10.49	Fulham	a	1-3
1950-51	1st	9.10.50	Dulwich Hamlet	a	2-2
	(rep)	16.10.50	Dulwich Hamlet	h	2-0
	2nd	23.10.50	Brentford	a	
1951-52	1st	10.51	Charlton Athletic	a	1-5
1952-53	1st	6.10.52	Charlton Athletic	h	1-1
	(rep)	13.10.52	Charlton Athletic	a	0-4
1953-54	1st	8.10.53	West Ham U	h	
1954-55	1st	4.10.54	Fulham	a	1-2
1955-56	1st	3.10.55	Barnet	h	3-1
	2nd	17.10.55	Millwall	a	1-1
	(rep)	24.10.55	Millwall	h	4-0
	SF	1.11.55	Arsenal	a	2-1
	F	15.11.55	Brentford	a	2-0
1956-57	1st	1.10.56	Walthamstow A	h	7-0
	2nd	15.10.56	Arsenal	a	2-2
	(rep)	22.10.56	Arsenal	h	1-3
1957-58	1st	7.10.57	Leyton Orient	h	3-4
1958-59	1st	6.10.58	Walthamstow A	h	
	2nd	20.10.58	Fulham	h	4-2
	SF	3.11.58	Tottenham H	a	
1959-60	1st	30.9.59	Millwall	h	
	2nd	19.10.59	Tottenham H	a	1-2
1960-61	1st	28.9.60	Fulham	h	2-0
	2nd	18.10.60	Chelsea	a	0-4
1961-62	1st	2.10.61	Bexleyheath	h	4-0
	2nd	16.10.61	Tottenham H	a	0-5
1962-63	1st	26.9.62	West Ham U	h	3-3
	(rep)	2.10.62	West Ham U	a	1-7
1963-64	1st	9.10.63	Fulham	h	0-1
1964-65	1st	5.10.64	Tooting & M	a	2-1
	2nd	19.11.64	Leyton Orient	a	0-2
1965-66	1st	6.10.65	Chelsea	h	1-0
	2nd	11.10.65	Bexley	h	3-1
	SF	1.11.65	Brentford	h	2-1
	F	10.5.66	Arsenal	a	4-0
1966-67	1st	28.9.66	Wembley	h	5-0
	2nd	18.10.66	Barnet	h	1-3
1967-68	1st	2.10.67	Barnet	a	
	2nd	16.10.67	Tottenham H	h	1-4
1968-69	1st	30.9.68	Fulham	a	5-2
	2nd	23.10.68	Crystal Palace	a	3-0
	SF	4.11.68	West Ham U	h	1-2
1969-70	1st	29.9.69	Chelsea	a	1-0
	2nd	13.10.69	Arsenal	h	1-3
1970-71	1st	30.9.70	Arsenal	a	0-0
	(rep)	7.10.70	Arsenal	h	0-1
1971-72	1st	28.9.71	Wimbledon	h	1-1
	(rep)	4.10.71	Wimbledon	a	4-1
	2nd	11.10.71	West Ham U	a	1-0
	SF	25.10.71	Orient	a	2-3
1972-73	1st	27.9.72	Crystal Palace	a	1-0
	2nd	4.10.72	Tottenham H	a	0-2
1973-74	1st	24.9.73	Millwall	a	1-0
	2nd	15.10.73	Brentford	a	0-0
	(rep)	31.10.73	Brentford	h	2-1
	SF	13.11.73	Hayes	h	0-0
	(rep)	8.4.74	Hayes	a	

London Minor Cup

	Rnd	Date	Opponents		
1958-59	2nd	11.58	Bexleyheath	a	
	SF	3.59	Dulwich Hamlet	a	
	F	23.4.59	Chelsea	h	
1960-61	1st	27.9.60	Chelsea	a	0-5
1962-63	1st	23.10.62	Tottenham H	h	3-4

London Youth Cup

	Rnd	Date	Opponents		
1963-64	1st	30.10.63	Chelsea	h	2-4
1964-65	2nd	17.2.65	Chelsea	a	2-1
	SF	16.4.65	Tottenham H	h	1-0
	F		Arsenal		
1965-66	1st		Bexley	h	4-2
	2nd	7.3.66	West Ham U	h	4-1
	SF	29.3.66	Charlton Athletic	a	
1966-67	1st	2.1.67	Brentford	h	1-0
	2nd	6.2.67	Chelsea	a	1-3

Southern Floodlight Cup

	Rnd	Date	Opponents		
1955-56	1st	31.10.55	Leyton Orient	h	0-1
1956-57	1st	8.10.56	Millwall	h	5-2
	2nd	26.11.56	Reading	h	1-2
1957-58	1st	14.10.57	Reading	h	0-0
	(rep)	6.11.57	Reading	a	2-5
1958-59	1st	13.10.58	Fulham	h	0-4
1959-60	1st	26.10.59	Leyton Orient	h	1-2

Division Three South Cup

	Rnd	Date	Opponents		
1933-34	2nd	28.2.34	Reading	h	2-0
	3rd	8.3.34	Brighton & HA	h	1-2
1934-35	2nd	18.10.34	Luton Town	h	2-1
	3rd	13.2.35	Watford	a	1-1
	(rep)	28.2.35	Watford	h	1-1
	(rep)	14.3.35	Watford	h	0-2
1935-36	2nd	23.10.35	Brighton & HA	a	1-2
1936-37	1st	7.10.36	Reading	a	1-2
1937-38	2nd	11.11.37	Clapton Orient	h	2-0
	3rd	1.3.38	Watford	h	2-3
1938-39	2nd	30.1.39	Aldershot	h	1-0
	3rd	20.2.39	Bournemouth	h	3-2
	SF	4.5.39	Port Vale	h	0-0
	(rep)		Port Vale	a	

(Last game not played)

Football League Jubilee

	Rnd	Date	Opponents		
1938-39		20.8.38	Northampton T	h	2-2
		22.8.38	Northampton T	a	0-0

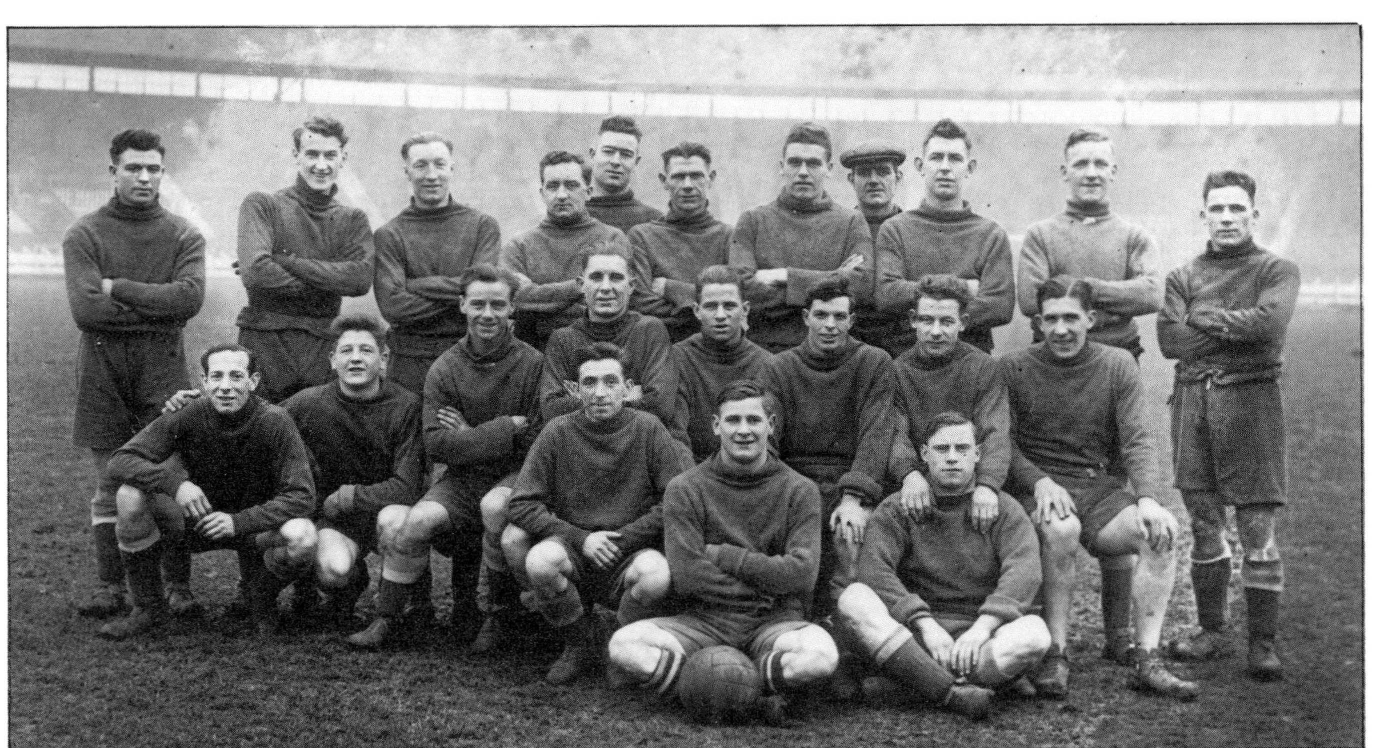

Rangers before their FA Cup game against Leeds United at the White City in January 1932. Standing (left to right:) G.Wiles, Pickett, Sales, Smith, Hall, Whatmore, Armstrong, Eggleton, Cunningham, Goodier, Pollard. Seated: Harris, March, Coward, Crabtree, Rounce, H.Wiles, Howe, Lews. On ground: Tutt, Blackman, Collins.

Hat-tricks (or better)

Season	Date	Gls	Player	Opponents	Comp
1899-1900	14 Oct 1899	3	P.Turnbull	v West Hampstead	FA Cup
	28 Oct 1899	3	W.Keech	v Wandsworth	FA Cup
1900-01	8 Sep 1900	3	S.Downing	v Swindon T	Sthn League
	21 Nov 1900	3	P.Humphries	v Watford	FA Cup
1901-02	20 Nov 01	4	H.Millar	v West Norwood	FA Cup
1903-04	14 Nov 03	3	J.Blackwood	v Northampton T	Sthn League
	19 Dec 03	3	J.Blackwood	v Portsmouth	Sthn League
1904-05	19 Nov 04	3	F.Bevan	v Swindon T	Sthn League
	1 Apr 05	4	F.Bevan	v Wellingborough	Sthn League
	22 Apr 05	3	F.Bevan	v Watford	Sthn League
1905-06	2 Sep 05	3	S Sugden	v New Brompton	Sthn League
	18 Nov 05	3	A.Thompson	v Watford	Sthn League
	16 Dec 05	3	F.Bevan	v Northampton T	Sthn League
1906-07	17 Nov 06	3	J.Fletcher	v Northampton T	Sthn League
1907-08	20 Apr 08	3	F.Cannon	v West Ham U	Sthn League
1908-09	27 Mar 09	3	P.Skilton	v Swindon T	Sthn League
1909-10	18 Oct 09	3	W.Steer	v Coventry C	Sthn League
1910-11	17 Dec 10	3	R.Browning	v Watford	Sthn League
1913-14	26 Dec 13	3	J.Miller	v Norwich C	Sthn League
1916-17	11 Nov 16	3	W.Lawrence	v Brentford	London Comb
1917-18	19 Jan 18	3	G.Fox	v Clapton Orient	London Comb
	23 Mar 18	3	Walters	v Millwall	London Comb
1918-19	21 Sep 18	4	G.Dale	v Clapton Orient	London Comb
	15 Feb 19	3	J.Gregory	v Tottenham H	London Comb
	8 Mar 19	3	J.Smith	v Clapton Orient	London Comb
1919-20	6 Dec 19	3	J.Smith	v Northampton T	Sthn League
	3 Jan 20	4	J.Smith	v Bristol R	Sthn League
	27 Mar 20	3	J.Gregory	v Brighton & HA	Sthn League
1920-21	11 Dec 20	3	J.Smith	v Brighton & HA	Division 3
1922-23	11 Nov 22	3	A.Davis	v Aberdare A	Division 3S
1924-25	29 Nov 24	4	C.Myers	v Clapton	FA Cup
1927-28	1 Oct 27	3	G.Goddard	v Bristol R	Division 3S
	25 Feb 28	3	G.Goddard	v Merthyr T	Division 3S
1928-29	25 Aug 28	3	G.Goddard	v Torquay U	Division 3S
	29 Dec 28	3	G.Goddard	v Torquay U	Division 3S
	9 Mar 29	4	G.Goddard	v Merthyr T	Division 3S
	9 Mar 29	3	Jack Burns	v Merthyr T	Division 3S
	29 Mar 29	3	G.Goddard	v Crystal P	Division 3S
1929-30	9 Nov 29	3	H.Wiles	v Newport Co	Division 3S
	26 Dec 29	3	G.Goddard	v Norwich C	Division 3S
	3 Mar 30	3	G.Goddard	v Merthyr T	Division 3S
	15 Mar 30	3	G.Goddard	v Newport Co	Division 3S
	12 Apr 30	4	G.Goddard	v Swindon T	Division 3S
	12 Apr 30	3	G.Rounce	v Swindon T	Division 3S
	19 Apr 30	3	G.Goddard	v Brighton & HA	Division 3S
1930-31	8 Nov 30	3	G.Rounce	v Crystal P	Division 3S
	6 Dec 30	3	G.Goddard	v Newport Co	Division 3S
	20 Dec 30	4	G.Goddard	v Exeter C	Division 3S
	25 Dec 30	3	Jack Burns	v Notts Co	Division 3S
1931-32	19 Sep 31	4	G.Goddard	v Watford	Division 3S
	28 Nov 31	3	S.Cribb	v Barnet	FA Cup
	12 Dec 31	3	G.Rounce	v Scunthorpe U	FA Cup
	19 Dec 31	3	G.Goddard	v Thames	Division 3S
	10 Mar 32	4	H.Wiles	v Gillingham	Division 3S
1932-33	1 Oct 32	3	E. Marcroft	v Cardiff C	Division 3S
	28 Nov 32	3	G.Goddard	v Merthyr T	FA Cup
	12 Dec 32	3	G.Rounce	v Torquay U	FA Cup
1933-34	11 Dec 33	4	J.Blackman	v New Brighton	FA Cup
	23 Dec 33	3	J.Blackman	v Gillingham	Division 3S
	5 May 34	3	J.Blackman	v Gillingham	Division 3S
1935-36	14 Sep 35	4	T.Cheetham	v Aldershot	Division 3S
	5 Oct 35	3	T.Cheetham	v Newport Co	Division 3S
	23 Nov 35	3	T.Cheetham	v Crystal P	Division 3S
	7 Dec 35	3	F.Lumsden	v Cardiff C	Division 3S
	7 Mar 36	3	T.Cheetham	v Gillingham	Division 3S
	10 Apr 36	3	H.Lowe	v Bristol C	Division 3S
1936-37	28 Nov 36	3	A.Fitzgerald	v Brighton & HA	FA Cup
	13 Feb 37	3	W.Charlton	v Cardiff C	Division 3S
	13 Feb 37	3	A.Fitzgerald	v Cardiff C	Division 3S
	13 Mar 37	3	R.Swinfen	v Newport Co	Division 3S
1937-38	27 Nov 37	3	A.Fitzgerald	v Bristol R	FA Cup
	27 Nov 37	3	T.Cheetham	v Bristol R	FA Cup
1938-39	12 Nov 38	4	T.Cheetham	v Aldershot	Division 3S
	9 Jan 39	3	T.Cheetham	v Northampton T	Division 3S
1939-40	25 Dec 39	3	D. Mangnall	v Fulham	League South
	25 Dec 39	3	J.Mallett	v Fulham	League South
	26 Dec 39	4	D. Mangnall	v Portsmouth	League South
	8 Feb 40	3	W. McEwan	v Southampton	League South
	20 Apr 40	3	D. Mangnall	v Brighton & HA	League South
1941-42	30 Aug 41	3	Davie	v Brighton & HA	London League
1942-43	26 Sep 42	3	R.Swinfen	v Brentford	League South
	7 Nov 42	4	R.Swinfen	v West Ham U	League South
1942-43	12 Dec 42	3	D. Mangnall	v Clapton Orient	League South
	10 Apr 43	4	W.Heathcote	v Clapton Orient	League Cup
1943-44	30 Oct 43	3	W.Heathcote	v Southampton	League South
	4 Mar 44	3	W.Heathcote	v Luton T	League Cup
	11 Mar 44	3	R.Swinfen	v Clapton Orient	League Cup
	25 Mar 44	3	W.Heathcote	v Luton T	League Cup
1944-45	26 Aug 44	3	W.Heathcote	v Crystal P	League South
	25 Nov 44	3	W.Heathcote	v Luton T	League South
	16 Dec 44	3	W.Heathcote	v Fulham	League South
1945-46	8 Sep 45	3	F.Neary	v Walsall	League South N
	27 Oct 45	3	W.Heathcote	v Northampton T	League South N
	3 Nov 45	4	W.Heathcote	v Notts Co	League South N
	17 Nov 45	3	F.Neary	v Barnet	FA Cup
	30 Jan 46	3	A.Addinall	v Southampton	FA Cup
1946-47	22 Mar 47	3	C.Hatton	v Aldershot	Division 3S
1947-48	22 Aug 47	3	C.Hatton	v Brighton & HA	Division 3S
1948-49	26 Aug 48	3	A.Addinall	v Leicester C	Division 2
1950-51	30 Sep 50	3	E.Shepherd	v Grimsby T	Division 2
1953-54	2 Jan 54	3	G.Petchey	v Aldershot	Division 3S
	20 Feb 54	3	R.Cameron	v Newport Co	Division 3S
1956-57	9 Feb 57	3	A.Longbottom	v Exeter C	Division 3S
	29 Apr 57	3	A.Longbottom	v Gillingham	Division 3S
1957-58	23 Sep 57	3	L.Locke	v Millwall	Division 3S
	23 Nov 57	4	A.Longbottom	v Northampton T	Division 3S
1958-59	22 Sep 58	3	A.Longbottom	v Stockport Co	Division 3
	25 Oct 58	3	A.Longbottom	v Halifax T	Division 3
1959-60	16 Jan 60	3	B.Bedford	v Newport Co	Division 3
1960-61	5 Nov 60	3	B.Bedford	v Walthamstow A	FA Cup
	28 Jan 61	3	B.Bedford	v Bury	Division 3
	15 Apr 61	4	B.Bedford	v Halifax T	Division 3
	22 Apr 61	3	B.Evans	v Torquay U	Division 3
1961-62	25 Sep 61	3	B.Bedford	v Halifax T	Division 3
	14 Oct 61	4	B.Bedford	v Southend U	Division 3
	6 Nov 61	3	B.Bedford	v Barry T	FA Cup
	9 Dec 61	3	B.Bedford	v Shrewsbury T	Division 3
	30 Dec 61	3	B.Evans	v Torquay U	Division 3
	14 Mar 62	3	B.Bedford	v Coventry C	Division 3
	14 Apr 62	3	B.Bedford	v Bradford	Division 3
1962-63	22 Oct 62	3	B.Bedford	v Hull C	Division 3
	27 Oct 62	3	J.McCelland	v Bradford	Division 3
	24 Nov 62	3	B.Bedford	v Hinckley A	FA Cup
1964-65	6 Nov 64	3	B.Bedford	v Luton T	Division 3
	6 Nov 64	3	M.Keen	v Luton T	Division 3
	11 Dec 64	3	B.Bedford	v Barnsley	Division 3
	26 Feb 65	3	W.McAdams	v Colchester U	Division 3
1965-66	27 Nov 65	3	L.Allen	v Swindon T	Division 3
	1 Jan 66	3	L.Allen	v York C	Division 3
	15 Jan 66	3	R.Morgan	v Swansea T	Division 3
	19 Feb 66	3	J.Collins	v Hull C	Division 3
	21 May 66	3	M.Lazarus	v Bournemouth	Division 3
1966-67	23 Aug 66	4	R.Marsh	v Colchester U	League Cup
	6 Sep 66	3	R.Marsh	v Middlesbrough	Division 3
	24 Sep 66	3	R.Marsh	v Mansfield T	Division 3
	26 Nov 66	3	R.Marsh	v Poole T	FA Cup
	25 Feb 67	3	M.Lazarus	v Swansea T	Division 3
1967-68	10 Oct 67	5	A.Wilks	v Oxford U	League Cup
1969-70	26 Aug 69	3	R.Marsh	v Blackpool	Division 2
	23 Sep 69	4	R.Marsh	v Tranmere R	League Cup
1970-71	17 Oct 70	3	R.Marsh	v Birmingham C	Division 2
	3 Apr 71	3	R.Marsh	v Bolton W	Division 2
1972-73	17 Feb 73	3	S.Bowles	v Swindon T	Division 2
1974-75	1 Feb 75	3	D.Givens	v Derby Co	Division 1
1975-76	23 Aug 75	3	S.Bowles	v Derby Co	Division 1
1976-77	15 Sep 76	3	S.Bowles	v Brann Bergen	UEFA Cup
	29 Sep 76	3	S.Bowles	v Brann Bergen	UEFA Cup
	3 Nov 76	3	D.Givens	v Slovan Bratislava	UEFA Cup
1978-79	28 Apr 79	3	C.Allen	v Coventry C	Division 1
1981-82	14 Nov 81	3	S.Stainrod	v Sheffield Wed	Division 2
	26 Jan 82	4	C.Allen	v Blackpool	FA Cup
	20 Mar 82	3	C.Allen	v Charlton A	Division 2
1982-83	5 Mar 83	3	C.Allen	v Middlesbrough	Division 2
1983-84	4 Oct 83	3	S.Stainrod	v Crewe Alex	League Cup
	5 May 84	3	C.Allen	v Notts Co	Division 1
1984-85	2 Oct 84	3	G.Bannister	v Reykjavik	UEFA Cup
1985-86	31 Mar 86	3	G.Bannister	v Chelsea	Division 1
1886-87	6 Apr 87	3	G.Bannister	v Watford	Division 1
1987-88	12 Sep 87	3	G.Bannister	v Chelsea	Division 1
1989-90	23 Sep 89	3	T.Francis	v Aston Villa	Division 1
1991-92	1 Jan 92	3	D.Bailey	v Manchester U	Division 1
1992-93	28 Dec 92	3	A.Sinton	v Everton	Premier
	10 Apr 93	3	L.Ferdinand	v Nottingham F	Premier
	12 Apr 93	3	L.Ferdinand	v Everton	Premier

Rangers Internationals

Bradley ALLEN — ENGLAND

Youth	Rep of Ireland	20.09.88	Rio de Janerio	2-0 (sub)
Youth	Greece	26 Oct 88	Birkenhead	5-0 (sub)
Youth	France	15 Nov 88	Bradford	1-1 (sub)
Youth	Spain	15 Jun 90	Faro	0-1
Youth	Syria	18 Jun 90	Faro	3-3
Youth	Uruguay	20 Jun 90	Faro	0-0
Youth	Belgium	24 Jul 90	Nyinegyháza	1-1(1 gl, sub)
Youth	USSR	26 Jul 90	Debrecen	1-3
Under-21	Hungary	12 May 92	Vac	2-2 (1 goal)
Under-21	Mexico	24 May 92	Toulon	1-1 (1 goal)
Under-21	Czechoslovakia	26 May 92	La Sage	1-2
Under-21	France	28 May 92	Aubagne	0-0
Under-21	Norway	12 Oct 92	Peterborough	0-2 (sub)
Under-21	Turkey	17 Nov 92	Brisbane Road	0-1
Under-21	Portugal	6 Jun 93	Miramas	2-0
Under-21	RCS	9 Jun 93	Saint Cyr	1-1 (sub)

Clive ALLEN — ENGLAND

Youth	Turkey	5 May 78	Wodzislaw	1-1 (sub)
Youth	Spain	7 May 78	Bukowas	1-0(1 gl, sub)
Youth	Poland	9 May 78	Chorzów	0-2
Youth	Las Palmas	8 Oct 78	Las Palmas	4-2 (3 goals)
Youth	USSR	10 Oct 78	Las Palmas	1-0
Youth	Las Palmas	12 Oct 78	Las Palmas	3-0 (1 goal)
Youth	Portugal	13 Nov 78	Monte Carlo	2-0 (1 goal)
Youth	Yugoslavia	15 Nov 78	Monte Carlo	1-1
Youth	Spain	17 Nov 78	Monte Carlo	1-1
Youth	Belgium	17 Jan 79	Brussels	4-0
Youth	Italy	28 Feb 79	Rome	1-0
Youth	Malta	26 May 79	Salzburg	3-0 (1 goal)
Youth	West Germany	28 May 79	Salzburg	2-0 (sub)
Youth	Bulgaria	31 May 79	Vienna	0-1
Youth	France	2 Jun 79	Vienna	0-0 (sub)
Under-21	East Germany	23 Apr 80	Jena	0-1 (sub)
Under-21	Norway	9 Sep 80	Southampton	3-0
Under-21	Romania	14 Oct 80	Ploieşti	0-4
Full	Brazil	10 Jun 84	Río de Janerio	2-0 (sub)
Full	Uruguay	13 Jun 84	Montevideo	0-2
Full	Chile	17 Jun 84	Santiago	0-0

Martin ALLEN — ENGLAND

Youth	USSR	3 Jun 85	Toulon	0-2
Youth	Mexico	5 Jun 85	Toulon	2-0 (sub)
Youth	France	7 Jun 85	Toulon	1-3
Under-21	Sweden	9 Sep 86	Östersund	1-1 (sub)
Under-21	Yugoslavia	10 Nov 87	Zemun	5-1 (sub)

BARNES — SOUTHERN LEAGUE

	Scottish League	24 Oct 10	Millwall	1-0

David BARDSLEY — ENGLAND

Full	Spain	9 Sep 92	Santander	0-1 (sub)
Full	Poland	19 May 93	Katowice	1-1

Graham BENSTEAD — ENGLAND

Youth	Austria	3 Sep 81	Umag	3-0 (sub)

Stan BOWLES — FOOTBALL LEAGUE

	Scottish League	27 Mar 74	Maine Road	5-0 (1 goal)

ENGLAND

Full	Portugal	3 Apr 74	Lisbon	0-0
Full	Wales	11 May 75	Cardiff	2-0 (1 goal)
Full	Northern Ireland	15 May 75	Wembley	1-0
Full	Italy	17 Nov 76	Rome	0-2
Full	Holland	9 Feb 77	Wembley	0-2

Ray BRADY — REPUBLIC OF IRELAND

Full	Austria	25 Sep 63	Vienna	0-0
Full	Austria	13 Oct 63	Dublin	3-2
Full	Spain	11 Mar 64	Seville	1-5
Full	Spain	8 Apr 64	Dublin	0-2
Full	Poland	10 May 64	Kraków	1-3
Full	Norway	13 May 64	Oslo	4-1

Kevin BROCK — ENGLAND

'B'	Malta	14 Oct 87	Ta'Qali	2-0

Martyn BUSBY — ENGLAND

Youth	Spain	31 Mar 71	Pamplona	2-3
Youth	Yugoslavia	22 May 71	Bardejov	1-0
Youth	Sweden	24 May 71	Poprad	1-0
Youth	Poland	26 May 71	Prešov	0-0
Youth	USSR	28 May 71	Prague	1-1
Youth	Portugal	30 May 71	Prague	3-0

John BYRNE — REPUBLIC OF IRELAND

Full	Italy	5 Feb 85	Dublin	1-2
Full	England	26 Mar 85	Wembley	1-2 (sub)
Full	Spain	26 May 85	Cork	0-0 (sub)
Full	Scotland	18 Feb 87	Glasgow	0-1 (sub)
Full	Belgium	29 Apr 87	Dublin	0-0 (sub)
Full	Brazil	23 May 87	Dublin	1-0
Full	Luxembourg	28 May 87	Luxembourg	2-0 (sub)
Full	Luxembourg	9 Sep 87	Dublin	2-1
Full	Bulgaria	14 Oct 87	Dublin	2-0 (sub)
Full	Israel	10 Nov 87	Dublin	5-0 (1 goal)
Full	Romania	23 Mar 88	Dublin	2-0
Full	Yugoslavia	27 Apr 88	Dublin	2-0 (sub)
Full	Poland	22 May 88	Dublin	3-0 (sub)

Justin CHANNING — ENGLAND

Youth	Brazil	29 Mar 86	Cannes	0-0 (sub)
Youth	Hungary	30 Mar 86	Cannes	2-0

Jeremy CHARLES — WALES

Full	Yugoslavia	14 Dec 83	Cardiff	1-1 (sub)
Full	Scotland	28 Feb 84	Glasgow	1-2

Colin CLARKE — NORTHERN IRELAND

Full	Malta	26 Apr 89	Valletta	2-0 (1 goal)
Full	Chile	26 May 89	Belfast	0-1
Full	Hungary	6 Sep 89	Belfast	1-2
Full	Rep of Ireland	11 Oct 89	Dublin	0-3
Full	Norway	27 Mar 90	Belfast	2-3

Dave CLEMENT — ENGLAND

Youth	France	23 May 66	Rijeka	1-2
Youth	Italy	25 May 66	Rijeka	1-1
Full	Wales	24 Mar 76	Wrexham	2-1 (sub)
Full	Wales	8 May 76	Cardiff	1-0
Full	Italy	28 May 76	New York	3-2
Full	Italy	17 Nov 76	Rome	0-2
Full	Holland	9 Feb 77	Wembley	0-2

Alan COMFORT — ENGLAND

Youth	Portugal	7 Apr 82	Cannes	3-0
Youth	Holland	9 Apr 82	Cannes	1-0
Youth	Czechoslovakia	11 Apr 82	Cannes	0-1
Youth	France	12 Apr 82	Cannes	0-1
Youth	Norway	13 Jul 82	Levanger	1-4

Dean CONEY — ENGLAND

Under-21	Turkey	13 Oct 87	Sheffield	1-1

Gary COOPER — ENGLAND

Youth	Qatar	4 Apr 83	Cannes	1-1
Youth	Switzerland	1 Sep 83	Porec	4-2 (1 goal)
Youth	Hungary	3 Sep 83	Umag	3-2
Youth	Yugoslavia	8 Sep 83	Pula	2-2
Youth	Iceland	1 Nov 83	Selhurst Park	3-0
Youth	East Germany	25 May 84	Moscow	1-1
Youth	USSR	27 May 84	Moscow	1-1
Youth	Luxembourg	29 May 84	Moscow	2-0
Youth	USSR	3 Jun 85	Toulon	0-2
Youth	France	7 Jun 85	Toulon	1-3
Under-17	Poland	12 Jul 83	Slagelse	1-0
Under-17	Norway	14 Jul 83	Slagelse	1-0
Under-17	Denmark	16 Jul 83	Slagelse	0-1

DONALD — LONDON COMBINATION

London	League	7 Apr 21	West Ham	1-2

Martin DUFFIELD — ENGLAND

Youth	Scotland	23 Mar 82	Coventry	2-2

Ian EVANS — WALES

Under-23	England	29 Nov 72	Wrexham	0-3
Under-23	Scotland	27 Feb 74	Aberdeen	0-3

Terry FENWICK — ENGLAND

Under-21	Norway	9 Sep 80	Southampton	3-0
Under-21	Romania	14 Oct 80	Ploieşti	0-4
Under-21*	Switzerland	18 Nov 80	Ipswich	5-0
Under-21	Rep of Ireland	25 Feb 81	Liverpool	1-0
Under-21	Romania	28 Apr 81	Swindon	3-0
Under-21	Norway	8 Sep 81	Dramen	0-0
Under-21	Hungary	17 Nov 81	Nottingham	2-0
Under-21	Scotland	19 Apr 82	Glasgow	1-0
Under-21	Scotland	28 Apr 82	Manchester	1-1
Under-21	West Germany	21 Sep 82	Sheffield	3-1
Under-21	West Germany	12 Oct 82	Bremen	2-3
(*As captain)				
Full	Wales	2 May 84	Wrexham	0-1 (sub)
Full	Scotland	26 May 84	Glasgow	1-1
Full	USSR	2 Jun 84	Wembley	0-2
Full	Brazil	10 Jun 84	Río de Janerio	2-0
Full	Uruguay	13 Jun 84	Montevideo	0-2
Full	Chile	17 Jun 84	Santiago	0-0
Full	Finland	22 May 85	Helsinki	1-1
Full	Scotland	25 May 85	Glasgow	0-1
Full	Mexico	9 Jun 85	Mexico City	0-1
Full	USA	16 Jun 85	Los Angeles	5-0
Full	Romania	11 Sep 85	Wembley	1-1
Full	Turkey	16 Oct 85	Wembley	5-0
Full	Northern Ireland	13 Nov 85	Wembley	0-0
Full	Egypt	29 Jan 86	Cairo	4-0
Full	Mexico	17 May 86	Los Angeles	3-0
Full	Portugal	3 Jun 86	Monterrey	0-1
Full	Morocco	6 Jun 86	Monterrey	0-0
Full	Poland	11 Jun 86	Monterrey	3-0
Full	Argentina	22 Jun 86	Mexico City	1-2

Wayne FEREDAY — ENGLAND

Under-21	Turkey	13 Nov 84	Bursa	0-0
Under-21	Rep of Ireland	25 Mar 85	Portsmouth	3-2 (sub)
Under-21	Finland	21 May 85	Mikkeli	1-3
Under-21	Turkey	15 Oct 85	Ashton Gate	3-0 (sub)
Under-21	Italy	23 Apr 86	Swindon	1-1

Les FERDINAND — ENGLAND

Full	San Marino	17 Feb 93	Wembley	6-0 (1 gl)
Full	Holland	28 Apr 93	Wembley	2-2
Full	Norway	2 Jun 93	Oslo	0-2
Full	USA	9 Jun 93	Boston	0-2

FIDLER — LONDON

	Birmingham	25 Oct 09	Fulham	1-3

SOUTHERN LEAGUE

	Scottish League	2 Oct 11	Glasgow	2-3

Gerry FRANCIS — ENGLAND

Under-23	Denmark	13 Nov 73	Portsmouth	1-1
Under-23	Scotland	13 Mar 74	Newcastle	2-0
Under-23	Turkey	11 May 74	Ankara	0-0
	(Abandoned at half-time)			
Under-23	Yugoslavia	15 May 74	Zrenjanin	0-1 (sub)
Under-23	France	19 May 74	Valence	2-2
Under-23*	Hungary	10 Mar 76	Budapest	0-3
Full	Czechoslovakia	30 Oct 74	Wembley	3-0
Full	Portugal	20 Nov 74	Wembley	0-0
Full	Wales	21 May 75	Wembley	2-2
Full	Scotland	24 May 75	Wembley	5-1 (2 goals)
Full*	Switzerland	3 Sep 75	Basle	2-1
Full*	Czechoslovakia	30 Oct 75	Bratislava	1-2
Full*	Portugal	19 Nov 75	Lisbon	1-1
Full*	Wales	8 May 76	Cardiff	1-0
Full*	Northern Ireland	11 May 76	Wembley	4-0 (1 goal)
Full*	Scotland	15 May 76	Glasgow	1-2
Full*	Brazil	23 May 76	Los Angeles	0-1
Other*	Team America	31 May 76	Philadelphia	3-1 (1 goal)
Full*	Finland	13 Jun 76	Helsinki	4-1

(*As captain)

Kevin GALLEN — ENGLAND

Under-18	Denmark	30 Mar 93	Stoke	4-2(1 gl, sub)

Steve GALLEN — REPUBLIC OF IRELAND

Under-21	Germany	9 Mar 93	Dublin	0-1

Ian GILLARD — ENGLAND

Under-23	Scotland	13 Mar 74	Newcastle	2-0
Under-23	Turkey	11 May 74	Ankara	0-0
	(Abandoned at half-time)			
Under-23	Yugoslavia	15 May 74	Zrenjanin	0-1
Under-23	France	19 May 74	Valence	2-2 (1 goal)
Under-23	Scotland	18 Dec 74	Aberdeen	3-0
Full	West Germany	12 Mar 75	Wembley	2-0
Full	Wales	21 May 75	Wembley	2-2
Full	Czechoslovakia	30 Oct 75	Bratislava	1-2

Don GIVENS — REPUBLIC OF IRELAND

Full	France	15 Nov 72	Dublin	2-1 (1 goal)
Full	USSR	13 May 73	Moscow	0-1
Full	Poland	16 May 73	Warsaw	0-2
Full	France	19 May 73	Paris	1-1
Full	Norway	6 Jun 73	Oslo	1-1
Full	Poland	21 Oct 73	Dublin	1-0
Full	Brazil	5 May 74	Río de Janerio	1-2
Full	Uruguay	8 May 74	Montevideo	0-2
Full	Chile	12 May 74	Santiago	2-1
Full	USSR	30 Oct 74	Dublin	3-0 (3 goals)
Full	Turkey	20 Nov 74	Izmir	1-1 (1 goal)
Full	West Germany	11 Mar 75	Dublin	1-0
Full	Switzerland	11 May 75	Dublin	2-1
Full	USSR	18 May 75	Moscow	1-2
Full	Switzerland	21 May 75	Basle	0-1
Full	Turkey	29 Oct 75	Dublin	4-0 (4 goals)
Full	Norway	24 Mar 76	Dublin	3-0
Full	Poland	26 May 76	Warsaw	2-0 (2 goals
Full	England	8 Sep 76	Wembley	1-1
Full	Turkey	13 Oct 76	Ankara	3-3 (1 goal)
Full	France	17 Nov 76	Paris	0-2
Full	Spain	9 Feb 77	Dublin	0-1
Full	France	30 Mar 77	Dublin	1-0
Full	Bulgaria	1 Jun 77	Sofia	1-2 (1 goal)
Full	Bulgaria	12 Oct 77	Dublin	0-0
Full	Norway	21 May 78	Oslo	0-0
Full	Denmark	24 May 78	Copenhagen	3-3

GREER — IRELAND

Full	England	13 Feb 09	Bradford	0-4
Full	Scotland	15 Mar 09	Glasgow	0-5
Full	Wales	20 Mar 09	Belfast	2-3

John GREGORY — ENGLAND

Full	Australia	12 Jun 83	Sydney	0-0
Full	Australia	15 Jun 83	Brisbane	1-0
Full	Australia	19 Jun 83	Melbourne	1-1
Full	Denmark	21 Sep 83	Wembley	0-1
Full	Hungary	12 Oct 83	Budapest	3-0
Full	Wales	2 May 84	Wrexham	0-1

E.F.GRIMSDELL — FA XI

	Cambridge University	18 Nov 20	Cambridge	0-1

Billy HAMILTON — NORTHERN IRELAND

Full	Scotland	13 May 78	Glasgow	1-1 (sub)

HARTWELL — SOUTHERN LEAGUE

	The League	11 Apr 10	Chelsea	2-2
	The League	14 Nov 10	Tottenham	3-2

Tony HAZELL — ENGLAND

Youth	Spain	17 Apr 64	Heilbronn	0-0
Youth	Spain	30 Mar 66	Swindon	3-0
Youth	Czechoslovakia	21 May 66	Rijeka	2-3
Youth	France	23 May 66	Rijeka	1-2
Youth	Italy	25 May 66	Rijeka	1-1

D.HIGGINS — THE SOUTH

	The North	24 Jan 14	Oxford	2-3

HILL — FOOTBALL LEAGUE

	The Army	10 Nov 21	Leyton	4-1

John HOLLINS — ENGLAND

'B'	Malaysia	30 May 78	Kuala Lumpur	1-1
'B'	New Zealand	7 Jun 78	Christchurch	4-0 (1 goal)
'B'	New Zealand	11 Jun 78	Wellington	3-1
'B'	New Zealand	14 Jun 78	Auckland	4-0
'B'	Singapore	18 Jun 78	Singapore	8-0

Peter HUCKER — ENGLAND

Under-21	Italy	18 Apr 84	Manchester	3-1
Under-21	Spain	17 May 84	Seville	1-0

Andrew IMPEY — ENGLAND

Under-21	Turkey	17 Nov 92	Brisbane Road	0-1

Leighton JAMES — WALES

Full	West Germany	14 Dec 77	Dortmund	1-1

Robbie JAMES — WALES

Full	Norway	26 Feb 85	Wrexham	1-1
Full	Scotland	27 Mar 85	Glasgow	1-0
Full	Spain	30 Apr 85	Wrexham	3-0
Full	Norway	5 Jun 85	Bergen	2-4
Full	Scotland	10 Sep 85	Cardiff	1-1
Full	Saudi Arabia	25 Feb 86	Dhahran	2-1
Full	Rep of Ireland	26 Mar 86	Dublin	1-0
Full	Uruguay	21 Apr 86	Cardiff	0-0
Full	Canada	20 Jun 86	Vancouver	3-0
Full	Canada	10 May 86	Toronto	0-2
Full	Finland	10 Sep 86	Helsinki	1-1
Full	USSR	18 Feb 87	Swansea	0-0
Full	Finland	1 Apr 87	Wrexham	4-0
Full	Czechoslovakia	29 Apr 87	Wrexham	1-1

Ivean JONES — WALES

Youth	Northern Ireland	23 Jan 80	Wrexham	0-0
Youth	Northern Ireland	13 Feb 80	Bangor	0-2

W.KEECH — SOUTHERN LEAGUE

	Amateurs of the South	26 Feb 1900	Queens Club	7-2

David KERSLAKE — ENGLAND

Youth	Portugal	7 Apr 82	Cannes	3-0 (1 goal)
Youth	Holland	9 Apr 82	Cannes	1-0
Youth	Czechoslovakia	11 Apr 82	Cannes	0-1
Youth	France	12 Apr 82	Cannes	0-1
Youth	Norway	13 Jul 82	Levanger	1-4
Youth	Denmark	15 Jul 82	Stjördal	5-2
Youth	Poland	17 Jul 82	Steinkjer	3-2 (1 goal)
Youth	R.I.Istra	2 Sep 82	Istra	3-1
Youth	USSR	4 Sep 82	Umag	1-0
Youth	Switzerland	6 Sep 82	Porec	2-0 (1 goal)
Youth	Yugoslavia	9 Sep 82	Pala	1-0
Youth	Israel Under-21	21 Feb 83	Tel Aviv	4-0
Youth	Israel Olympic	23 Feb 83	Tel Aviv	4-2 (2 goals)
Youth	Belgium	13 Apr 83	Birmingham	1-1
Youth	Spain	13 May 83	Stoke	1-0
Youth	Scotland	15 May 83	Birmingham	3-0
Youth	USSR	17 May 83	Villa Park	0-2
Youth	Czechoslovakia	20 May 83	Highbury	1-1
Youth	Italy	22 May 83	Watford	1-1
Youth	Switzerland	1 Sep 83	Porec	4-2
Youth	Hungary	3 Sep 83	Umag	3-2
Youth	West Germany	5 Sep 83	Pazin	2-0 (1 goal)
Youth	Yugoslavia	8 Sep 83	Pula	2-2
Youth	Iceland	12 Oct 83	Reykjavik	3-0
Youth	Iceland	1 Nov 83	Selhurst Park	3-0
Youth	Cameroon	1 Jun 85	Toulon	1-0
Youth	USSR	3 Jun 85	Toulon	0-2
Youth	Mexico	5 Jun 85	Toulon	2-0 (1 goal)
Youth	France	7 Jun 85	Toulon	1-3
Under-17	Poland	12 Jul 83	Slagelse	1-0
Under-17	Norway	14 Jul 83	Slagelse	1-0 (1 goal)
Under-17	Denmark	16 Jul 83	Slagelse	0-1
Under-21	Turkey	15 Oct 85	Ashton Gate	3-0

Brian LAW — WALES

Under-21	Poland	19 May 90	(h)	2-0
Under-21	England	15 Dec 90	Tranmere	0-0
Full	Sweden	25 Apr 90	Stockholm	2-4

Mick LEACH — ENGLAND

Youth	Northern Ireland	11 May 63	Oldham	1-1
Youth	Scotland	18 May 63	Dumfries	3-1 (1 goal)
Youth	Spain	17 Apr 64	Heilbronn	0-0

Evelyn LINTOTT — ENGLAND

Amateur	Ireland	7 Dec 07	Tottenham	6-1
Amateur	Holland	21 Dec 07	Darlington	12-2
Amateur	France	23 Mar 08	Park Royal	12-0
Amateur	Belgium	18 Apr 08	Brussels	8-2
Amateur	Germany	20 Apr 08	Berlin	5-1
Full	Ireland	15 Feb 08	Cliftonville	3-1
Full	Wales	16 Mar 08	Wrexham	7-1
Full	Scotland	4 Apr 08	Glasgow	1-1

Alan McCARTHY — ENGLAND

Youth	Rep of Ireland	20 Sep 88	Dublin	2-0

Doug McCLURE — ENGLAND

Youth	Portugal	7 Apr 82	Cannes	3-0
Youth	Holland	9 Apr 82	Cannes	1-0
Youth	Czechoslovakia	11 Apr 82	Cannes	0-1
Youth	France	12 Apr 82	Cannes	0-1
Youth	Norway	13 Jul 82	Levanger	1-4
Youth	Denmark	15 Jul 82	Stjördal	5-2
Youth	Poland	17 Jul 82	Steinkjer	3-2
Youth	R.I.Istra	2 Sep 82	Istra	3-1
Youth	USSR	4 Sep 82	Umag	1-0
Youth	Switzerland	6 Sep 82	Porec	2-0
Youth	Yugoslavia	9 Sep 82	Pala	1-0

David McCREERY — NORTHERN IRELAND

Full	England	17 Oct 79	Belfast	1-5
Full	Rep of Ireland	21 Nov 79	Belfast	1-0
Full	Scotland	16 May 80	Belfast	1-0 (sub)
Full	England	20 May 80	Wembley	1-1 (sub)
Full	Wales	23 May 80	Cardiff	1-0 (sub)
Full	Australia	11 Jun 80	Sydney	2-1 (sub)
Full	Australia	15 Jun 80	Melbourne	1-1
Full	Sweden	15 Oct 80	Belfast	3-0 (sub)
Full	Portugal	19 Nov 80	Lisbon	0-1 (sub)

Alan McDONALD — NORTHERN IRELAND

§ = Victory Shield (British Championship). ‡ = Friendly. † = English Schools 75th Anniversary (1978 or 79)

Schoolboy	England	§	Carlisle	0-0
	Scotland	§	(a) 0-1	
	Wales	§	Ballymena	4-0
	Rep of Ireland	‡	Dublin	3-1 (1 goal)
	W.Germany	†	Stoke	4-3
	Rep of Ireland	†	Merseyside	4-1 (1 goal)
	Scotland	†	Crewe	1-0
	Wales	†	Maine Road	2-1
Full	Romania	16 Oct 85	Bucharest	1-0
Full	England	13 Nov 85	Wembley	0-0
Full	France	26 Feb 86	Paris	0-0
Full	Denmark	26 Mar 86	Belfast	1-1 (1 goal)
Full	Morocco	23 Apr 86	Belfast	2-1
Full	Algeria	3 Jun 86	Guadalajara	1-1
Full	Spain	7 Jun 86	Guadalajara	1-2
Full	Brazil	12 Jun 86	Guadalajara	0-3
Full	England	15 Oct 86	Wembley	0-3
Full	Turkey	12 Nov 86	Izmir	0-0
Full	Israel	18 Feb 87	Tel Aviv	1-1
Full	England	1 Apr 87	Belfast	0-2
Full	Yugoslavia	29 Apr 87	Belfast	1-2
Full	Yugoslavia	14 Oct 87	Sarajevo	0-3
Full	Turkey	11 Nov 87	Belfast	1-0
Full	Poland	23 Mar 88	Belfast	1-1
Full	France	27 Apr 88	Belfast	0-0
Full	Malta	21 May 88	Belfast	3-0
Full	Rep of Ireland	14 Sep 88	Belfast	0-0
Full	Hungary	19 Oct 88	Budapest	0-1
Full	Spain	21 Dec 88	Seville	0-4
Full*	Chile	26 May 89	Belfast	0-1
Full	Hungary	6 Sep 89	Belfast	1-2
Full	Rep of Ireland	11 Oct 89	Dublin	0-3
Full*	Uruguay	18 May 90	Belfast	1-0
Full*	Yugoslavia	12 Sep 90	Belfast	0-2
Full*	Denmark	17 Oct 90	Belfast	1-1
Full*	Austria	14 Nov 90	Vienna	0-0
Full*	Faroe Islands	1 May 91	Belfast	1-1
Full*	Faroe Islands	11 Sep 91	Landskrona	5-0 (1 goal)
Full*	Scotland	19 Feb 92	Glasgow	0-1
Full*	Lithuania	28 Apr 92	Belfast	2-2
Full*	Germany	2 Jun 92	Bremen	1-1
Full*	Albania	9 Sep 92	Belfast	3-0
Full*	Spain	14 Oct 92	Belfast	0-0
Full*	Denmark	18 Nov 92	Belfast	0-1
Full*	Albania	17 Feb 93	Tiranë	2-1 (1 goal)
Full*	Rep of Ireland	31 Mar 93	Dublin	0-3
Full*	Spain	28 Apr 93	Seville	1-3
Full*	Lithuania	25 May 93	Vilnius	1-0
Full*	Latvia	2 Jun 93	Riga	2-1

(*As captain)

Paul McGEE — REPUBLIC OF IRELAND

Full	Turkey	5 Apr 78	Dublin	4-2 (1 goal)
Full	Norway	21 May 78	Oslo	0-0 (sub)
Full	Denmark	24 May 78	Copenhagen	3-3 (sub)
Full	Northern Ireland	20 Sep 78	Dublin	0-0
Full	England	25 Oct 78	Dublin	1-1
Full	Denmark	2 May 79	Dublin	2-0 (sub)
Full	Bulgaria	19 May 79	Sofia	0-1 (sub)
Full	Bulgaria	17 Oct 79	Dublin	3-0

Terry MANCINI — REPUBLIC OF IRELAND

Full	Poland	21 Oct 73	Dublin	1-0
Full	Brazil	5 May 74	Río de Janerio	1-2 (1 goal)
Full	Uruguay	9 May 74	Montevideo	0-2
Full	Chile	12 May 74	Santiago	2-1

Rodney MARSH — ENGLAND

Under-23	Scotland	7 Feb 68	Glasgow	2-1 (1 goal)
Under-23	Hungary	1 May 68	Everton	4-0 (1 goal)
Full	Switzerland	10 Nov 71	Wembley	1-1 (sub)

Don MASSON — SCOTLAND

Full	Wales	6 May 76	Glasgow	3-1
Full	Northern Ireland	8 May 76	Glasgow	3-0 (1 goal)
Full	England	15 May 76	Glasgow	2-1 (1 goal)
Full	Finland	8 Sep 76	Glasgow	6-0 (1 goal)
Full	Czechoslovakia	13 Oct 76	Prague	0-2
Full	Wales	28 May 77	Wrexham	0-0
Full	Northern Ireland	1 Jun 77	Glasgow	3-0
Full	England	4 Jun 77	Wembley	2-1
Full	Chile	15 Jun 77	Santiago	4-2
Full	Argentina	19 Jun 77	Buenos Aires	1-1 (1 goal)
Full	Brazil	23 Jun 77	São Paulo	0-2
Full	East Germany	7 Sep 77	Berlin	0-1
Full	Czechoslovakia	21 Sep 77	Glasgow	3-1
Full*	Wales	12 Oct 77	Liverpool	2-0 (1 goal)

(*As captain)

MITCHELL — SOUTHERN LEAGUE

	Irish League	11 Oct 13	Dublin	4-1
	Scottish League	13 Oct 13	Glasgow	0-5
	English League	9 Feb 14	Millwall	1-3
	Scottish League	13 Oct 14	Millwall	1-1
	English League	26 Oct 14	Highbury	1-2
	Irish League	31 Oct 14	Swansea	1-1

FA XI

	Cambridge University	18 Nov 20	Cambridge	0-1

Roger MORGAN — ENGLAND

Youth	Belgium	15 Apr 64	Ludwigshafen	3-0 (2 goals)
Youth	Spain	17 Apr 64	Heilbronn	0-0
Youth	Hungary	21 Apr 64	Wuppertal	5-0 (1 goal)
Youth	Italy	23 Apr 64	Marl-Huels	3-1
Youth	East Germany	25 Apr 64	Essen	2-3

Ian MUIR — ENGLAND

Youth	Romania	17 Oct 81	Adelaide	0-1

N.MURPHY — IRELAND

Full	England	25 Feb 05	Middlesbrough	1-1
Full	Scotland	18 Mar 05	Glasgow	0-4
Full	Wales	8 Apr 05	Cliftonville	2-2 (1 goal)

Mick O'BRIEN — FOOTBALL LEAGUE

	The Army	10 Nov 21	Leyton	4-1 (1 goal)

IRELAND

Full	Scotland	26 Feb 21	Belfast	0-2
Full	Scotland	4 Mar 22	Glasgow	1-2

Paul PARKER — ENGLAND

'B'	Malta	14 Oct 87	Ta'Qali	2-0
'B'	Italy	14 Nov 89	Brighton	1-1
'B'	Iceland	19 May 89	Reykjavik	2-0
Full	Albania	26 Apr 89	Wembley	1-1 (sub)
Full	Chile	23 May 89	Wembley	5-0
Full	Denmark	7 Jun 89	Copenhagen	0-0
Full	Yugoslavia	13 Dec 89	Wembley	2-1
Full	Uruguay	22 May 90	Wembley	1-2
Full	Holland	16 Jun 90	Cagliari	0-0
Full	Egypt	21 Jun 90	Cagliari	1-0
Full	Belgium	26 Jun 90	Bologna	1-0
Full	Cameroon	1 Jul 90	Naples	3-2
Full	West Germany	4 Jul 90	Turin	1-1
Full	Italy	7 Jul 90	Bari	1-2
Full	Hungary	12 Sep 90	Wembley	1-0
Full	Poland	17 Oct 90	Wembley	2-0
Full	USSR	21 May 91	Wembley	3-1
Full	Australia	1 Jun 91	Sydney	1-0
Full	New Zealand	3 Jun 91	Auckland	1-0

Phil PARKES — ENGLAND

Under-23	Wales	5 Jan 72	Swindon	2-0
Under-23	Scotland	16 Feb 72	Derby	2-2
Under-23	East Germany	22 Mar 72	Bristol	0-1
Under-23	Denmark	24 May 72	Naestved	1-1
Under-23	Czechoslovakia	1 Jun 73	Bratislava	0-3
Under-23	Czechoslovakia	28 Oct 75	Trnava	1-1
Under-21	Denmark	19 Sep 78	Hvidovre	2-1
Full	Portugal	3 Apr 74	Lisbon	0-0

Gavin PEACOCK — ENGLAND

Youth	USSR	3 Apr 85	Cannes	1-3 (sub)
Youth	Scotland	8 Apr 85	Cannes	2-1
Youth	Iceland	11 Sep 85	Reykjavík	5-0 (sub)
Youth	Brazil	2 Jun 87	Niterói	0-2 (sub)
Youth	Uruguay	10 Jun 87	Montevideo	2-2 (1 gl, sub)

Ivor POWELL — WALES

Full	England	13 Nov 46	Manchester	0-3
Full	England	18 Oct 47	Cardiff	0-3
Full	Scotland	12 Nov 47	Glasgow	2-1
Full	Northern Ireland	10 Mar 48	Wrexham	2-0
Full	Belgium	23 May 49	Liège	1-3

Karl READY — WALES

'B'	Canada	18 Mar 92	Wrexham	1-1
Under-21	Romania	19 May 92	Bucharest	3-2
Under-21	Belgium	17 Nov 92	Kortrijk	1-3
Under-21	Belgium	30 Mar 93	Cardiff	0-0
Under-21	RCS	27 Apr 93	Frýdek Mistek	1-1

Tony ROBERTS — WALES

Under-21	England	15 Dec 90	Tranmere	0-0
Under-21	Poland	30 May 91	(a)	2-1
'B'	Canada	18 Mar 92	Wrexham	1-1
Full	Rep of Ireland	17 Feb 93	Dublin	1-2 (sub)

Michael ROBINSON — REPUBLIC OF IRELAND

Full	Norway	1 May 85	Dublin	0-0
Full	Spain	26 May 85	Cork	0-0
Full	Switzerland	2 Jun 85	Dublin	3-0
Full	Denmark	13 Nov 85	Dublin	1-4 (sub)
Full	Wales	26 Mar 86	Dublin	0-1
Full	Czechoslovakia	27 May 86	Reykjavík	1-0

Glenn ROEDER — ENGLAND

'B'	New Zealand	15 Oct 79	Leyton	4-1

David SEAMAN — ENGLAND

'B'	Malta	14 Oct 87	Ta'Qali	2-0
'B'	Rep of Ireland	27 Mar 90	Cork	1-4
'B'	Czechoslovakia	24 Apr 90	Sunderland	2-0
Full	Saudi Arabia	16 Nov 88	Riyadh	1-1
Full	Denmark	7 Jun 89	Copenhagen	1-1 (sub)
Full	Czechoslovakia	25 Apr 90	Wembley	4-2 (sub)

Steve SCOTT — ENGLAND

Youth	Paraguay	24 Aug 85	Baku	2-2 (sub)
Youth	Mexico	29 Aug 85	Baku	0-1

SHAW — SOUTHERN LEAGUE

	English League	9 Oct 11	Stoke	1-2
	English League	30 Sep 12	Manchester	1-2
	Scottish League	14 Oct 12	Millwall	1-0
	Irish League	15 Mar 13	Millwall	1-1

Frank SIBLEY — ENGLAND

Youth	Spain	30 Mar 66	Swindon	3-0
Youth	Czechoslovakia	21 May 66	Rijeka	2-3
Youth	France	23 May 66	Rijeka	1-2
Youth	Italy	25 May 66	Rijeka	1-1

Andy SINTON — ENGLAND

'B'	Rep of Ireland	27 Mar 90	Cork	1-4
'B'	France	18 Feb 92	QPR	3-0
'B'	Czechoslovakia	24 Mar 92	Budějovice	1-0
Full	Poland	13 Nov 91	Poznań	1-1
Full	CIS	29 Apr 92	Moscow	2-2
Full	Hungary	12 May 92	Budapest	1-0 (sub)
Full	Brazil	17 May 92	Wembley	1-1
Full	France	14 Jun 92	Malmö	0-0
Full	Sweden	17 Jun 92	Stockholm	1-2
Full	Spain	9 Sep 92	Santander	0-1
Full	Turkey	31 Mar 93	İzmir	2-0
Full	Brazil	16 Jun 93	Washington	1-1
Full	Germany	19 Jun 93	Detroit	1-2

Peter SPRINGETT — ENGLAND

Youth	Spain	27 Feb 64	Murcia	2-1
Youth	Poland	26 Mar 64	Breda	1-1
Youth	Rep of Ireland	30 Mar 64	Middelburg	6-0
Youth	Austria	1 Apr 64	Rotterdam	2-1
Youth	Portugal	3 Apr 64	The Hague	4-0
Youth	Spain	5 Apr 64	Amsterdam	4-0

W.H.O.STEER — SOUTHERN LEAGUE

	The League	11 Apr 10	Chelsea	2-2

ENGLAND

Amateur	Belgium	26 Mar 10	Brussels	2-2 (1 goal)
Amateur	Switzerland	9 Apr 10	Park Royal	6-1 (2 goals)
Amateur	France	16 Apr 10	Brighton	10-1 (4 goals)
Amateur	Denmark	5 May 10	Copenhagen	1-2 (1 goal)
Amateur	France	23 Mar 11	Paris	3-0
Amateur	Germany	14 Apr 11	Berlin	2-2

LONDON

	Birmingham	3 Oct 10	Villa Park	3-0

Jan STEJSKAL — CZECHOSLOVAKIA

Full	Austria	19 Aug 92	Bratislava	2-2
Full	Belgium	2 Sep 92	Prague	1-2
Full	Faroe Islands	23 Sep 92	Košice	4-0

Ian STEWART — NORTHERN IRELAND

Full	France	24 Mar 82	Paris	0-4 (sub)
Full	France	4 Jul 82	Madrid	1-4
Full	West Germany	17 Nov 82	Belfast	1-0 (1 goal)
Full	Albania	15 Dec 82	Tiranë	0-0
Full	Turkey	30 Mar 83	Belfast	2-1
Full	Albania	27 Apr 83	Belfast	1-0 (1 goal)
Full	Scotland	24 May 83	Glasgow	0-0
Full	England	28 May 83	Belfast	0-0
Full	Wales	31 May 83	Belfast	0-1
Full	Austria	21 Sep 83	Belfast	3-1
Full	Turkey	12 Oct 83	Ankara	0-1
Full	West Germany	16 Nov 83	Hamburg	1-0
Full	Scotland	13 Dec 83	Glasgow	2-0
Full	England	4 Apr 84	Wembley	0-1
Full	Wales	22 May 84	Swansea	1-1
Full	Finland	27 May 84	Pori	0-1
Full	Romania	12 Sep 84	Belfast	3-2
Full	Finland	14 Nov 84	Belfast	2-1
Full	Israel	16 Oct 84	Belfast	3-0
Full	England	27 Feb 85	Belfast	0-1
Full	Spain	27 Mar 85	Palma	0-0
Full	Turkey	1 May 85	Belfast	2-0

Dave THOMAS — ENGLAND

Under-23	Denmark	13 Nov 73	Portsmouth	1-1 (sub)
Under-23	Turkey	11 May 74	Ankara	0-0
		(Abandoned at half-time)		
Under-23	France	19 May 74	Valence	2-2
Full	Czechoslovakia	30 Oct 74	Wembley	3-0 (sub)
Full	Portugal	2 Nov 74	Wembley	0-0
Full	Cyprus	16 Apr 75	Wembley	5-0 (sub)
Full	Cyprus	11 May 75	Limassol	1-0
Full	Wales	21 May 75	Wembley	2-2
Full	Scotland	24 May 75	Wembley	5-1 (sub)
Full	Czechoslovakia	30 Oct 75	Bratislava	1-2 (sub)
Full	Portugal	19 Nov 75	Lisbon	1-1 (sub)

THOMPSON — SOUTHERN LEAGUE

	English League	26 Oct 14	Highbury	1-2

Gary WADDOCK — REPUBLIC OF IRELAND

Full	Switzerland	30 Apr 80	Dublin	2-0
Full	Argentina	6 May 80	Dublin	0-1
Full	Wales	24 Feb 81	Dublin	1-3
Full	Poland	23 May 81	Bydgoszcz	0-3 (sub)
Full	Algeria	28 Apr 82	Algiers	0-2
Full	Iceland	13 Oct 82	Dublin	2-0
Full	Malta	30 Mar 83	Valletta	1-0
Full	Spain	27 Apr 83	Zaragoza	0-2
Full	Holland	22 Sep 82	Rotterdam	1-2 (sub)
Full	Iceland	21 Sep 83	Reykjavík	3-0 (1 goal)
Full	Holland	12 Oct 83	Dublin	2-3 (1 goal)
Full	Israel	4 Apr 84	Tel Aviv	0-3
Full	Italy	5 Feb 85	Dublin	1-2 (1 goal)
Full	Israel	27 May 85	Tel Aviv	0-0
Full	England	26 Mar 85	Wembley	1-2
Full	Norway	1 May 85	Dublin	0-0
Full	Spain	26 May 85	Cork	0-0
Full	USSR	16 Oct 85	Moscow	0-2

WAKE — LONDON

	Birmingham	25 Oct 09	Fulham	1-3
	Birmingham	2 Oct 11	Tottenham	2-3

SOUTHERN LEAGUE

	Scottish League	14 Oct 12	Millwall	1-0

Mick WALSH — REPUBLIC OF IRELAND

Full	Denmark	2 May 79	Dublin	2-0 (sub)
Full	Bulgaria	19 May 79	Sofia	0-1
Full	West Germany	22 May 79	Dublin	1-3 (sub)
Full	Argentina	29 May 79	Dublin	0-0

Gary WESTLEY — ENGLAND

Youth	Scotland	8 Apr 85	Cannes	1-0 (sub)
Youth	Iceland	11 Sep 85	Reykjavík	5-0 (sub)

Steve WICKS — ENGLAND

Under-21	Scotland	19 Apr 82	Glasgow	1-0

Chris WOODS — ENGLAND

Under-21	Bulgaria	20 Nov 79	Leicester	5-0
Under-21	East Germany	23 Apr 80	Jena	0-1
Under-21	Switzerland	18 Nov 80	Ipswich	5-0

Paul WRIGHT — SCOTLAND

Under-21	Yugoslavia	5 Sep 89	Slavonski Brod	1-4 (sub)

Rangers' Career Records

* = FA Charity Shield games. † = UEFA Cup games. Debut is Football League unless stated otherwise.

ABEL, Sam
Born: Neston, Cheshire, 30 Dec 1910.
Signed from: Fulham.
Debut v Brighton & Hove Albion, 15 Sep 1934 (1 goal).
Retired 1945.

		APPEARANCES					GOALS				
Season	Div	Lge	FA	LC	Oth	Total	Lge	FA	LC	Oth	Total
1934-35	3S	20	1			21	3				3
1935-36	3S	9				9	3				3
1936-37	3S	3				3					
1937-38	3S										
1938-39	3S	5				5					
1939-40	3S										
2nd WW		151			20	172	6				6
Total		188	1		20	209	12				12

ABBOTT, Harry
Born: Blackburn, 1883.
Signed from: Blackburn Rovers, 1902.
Debut v Wellingborough, 3 Sep 1902, Southern League.
Transferred to Bolton Wanderers 1904.

		APPEARANCES					GOALS				
Season	Div	Lge	FA	LC	Oth	Total	Lge	FA	LC	Oth	Total
1902-03	SL	23	1			24	2				2
1903-04	SL	4				4	2				2
Total		27	1			28	4				4

ABBOTT, Ron
Born: London, 2 Aug 1953.
Signed from: (apprentice), Jul 1971.
Debut v West Ham United, 10 Sep 1973 (1 goal).

		APPEARANCES					GOALS				
Season	Div	Lge	FA	LC	Oth	Total	Lge	FA	LC	Oth	Total
1973-74	1	3/4				3/4	1				1
1974-75	1	6/3				6/3					
1975-76	1	5/1		1		6/1					
1976-77	1	10/2				10/2	2				2
1977-78	1	8/2	5	0/1		13/3	1				1
1978-79	1	0/2		0/1		0/3					
Total		32/14	5	1/2		38/16	4				4

ABBOTT, Shirley
Born: Alfreton, 19 Feb 1899.
Signed from: Portsmouth.
Debut v Swansea Town, 6 Oct 1923.
Transferred to: Chesterfield.

		APPEARANCES					GOALS				
Season	Div	Lge	FA	LC	Oth	Total	Lge	FA	LC	Oth	Total
1923-24	3S	12				12					
Total		12				12					

ADAMS, Ernie
Born: Willesden, 3 Apr 1922.
Signed from: Preston North End, Sep 1947.
Debut v Newport County, 24 Apr 1948.

		APPEARANCES					GOALS				
Season	Div	Lge	FA	LC	Oth	Total	Lge	FA	LC	Oth	Total
1947-48	3S	2				2					
1948-49	2	2				2					
1949-50	2	1				1					
Total		5				5					

ADDINALL, Albert
Born: Paddington, 30 Jan 1921.
Signed from: R.A.F.
Debut Brentford, 17 Nov 1945.
Transferred to: Brighton & Hove Albion, Jan 1953.

		APPEARANCES					GOALS				
Season	Div	Lge	FA	LC	Oth	Total	Lge	FA	LC	Oth	Total
2nd WW		8	7		1	16	5	8			13
1946-47	3S	3	1			4					
1947-48	3S	3				3	2				2
1948-49	2	22				22	9				9
1949-50	2	28				28	11				11
1950-51	2	38	1			39	18	1			19
1951-52	2	36	1			37	12				12
1952-53	3S	20	3			23	7	1			8
Total		158	13		1	172	64	10			74

ADLAM, Leslie
Born: Guildford, 24 Jan 1906.
Signed from: Oldham Athletic, Nov 1931.
Debut v Cardiff City, 14 Nov 1931.
Transferred to: Cardiff City, Dec 1933.

		APPEARANCES					GOALS				
Season	Div	Lge	FA	LC	Oth	Total	Lge	FA	LC	Oth	Total
1931-32	3S	28	4			32					
1932-33	3S	28	4			32					
Total		56	8			64					

AINSWORTH
Debut v Crystal Palace, 25 Jan 1908 (1 goal), Southern League.

		APPEARANCES					GOALS				
Season	Div	Lge	FA	LC	Oth	Total	Lge	FA	LC	Oth	Total
1907-08	SL	2				2	2				2
Total		2				2	2				2

ALEXANDER, F.
Debut v Portsmouth, 10 Apr 1944.

		APPEARANCES					GOALS				
Season	Div	Lge	FA	LC	Oth	Total	Lge	FA	LC	Oth	Total
2nd WW		3			1	4					
Total		3			1	4					

ALLEN, Bradley
Born: Romford, 13 Sep 1971.
Signed from: (Juniors), Sep 1988.
Debut v Wimbledon, 14 Jan 1989 (sub).

		APPEARANCES					GOALS				
Season	Div	Lge	FA	LC	Oth	Total	Lge	FA	LC	Oth	Total
1988-89	1	0/1		0/1	0/1	0/3					
1989-90	1										
1990-91	1	4/6			1	5/6	2				2
1991-92	1	10/1				10/1	5				5
1992-93	Pr	21/4	1	1		23/4	10		1		11
Total		35/12	1	1/1	1/1	38/14	17		1		18

ALLEN, Clive
Born: Stepney, 20 May 1961.
Signed from: (apprentice), Sep 1978.
Debut v Chelsea, 4 Nov 1978 (sub).
Transferred to: Arsenal, Jun 1980 (£1,200,000); From: Crystal Palace, Jun 1981, (£450,000); To: Tottenham, Aug 1984 (£750,000).

		APPEARANCES					GOALS				
Season	Div	Lge	FA	LC	Oth	Total	Lge	FA	LC	Oth	Total
1978-79	1	4/6				4/6	4				4
1979-80	2	39	1	5		45	28		2		30
1981-82	2	36/1	7	2		45/1	13	7	1		21
1982-83	2	23/2	1	2		26/2	13				13
1983-84	1	24/1		3		27/1	14		1		15
Total		126/10	9	12		147/10	72	7	4		83

ALLEN, James
Born: Amble, Nottingham, 1913.
Signed from: Huddersfield Town.
Debut v Exeter City, 30 Sep 1933.
Transferred to: Mansfield Town Jun 1936; From: Huddersfield Town(1935-36); To: Clapton Orient, Jul 1937 (free).

		APPEARANCES					GOALS				
Season	Div	Lge	FA	LC	Oth	Total	Lge	FA	LC	Oth	Total
1933-34	3S	26	2			28	2	1			3
1934-35	3S	25	1			26	4				4
1935-36	3S	33	1			34					
1936-37	3S	11				11	1				1
Total		95	4			99	7	1			8

ALLEN, John
Born: Elderslie, 27 Jan 1932.
Signed from: Beith Juniors, Sep 1952.
Debut v Bournemouth, 7 Apr 1954.
Transferred to: Bournemouth, Jul 1954.

		APPEARANCES					GOALS				
Season	Div	Lge	FA	LC	Oth	Total	Lge	FA	LC	Oth	Total
1953-54	3S	1				1					
Total		1				1					

ALLEN, Les
Born: Dagenham, 4 Sep 1937.
Signed from: Tottenham Hotspur, Jul 1965 (£20,000).
Debut v Brentford, 21 Aug 1965.

		APPEARANCES					GOALS				
Season	Div	Lge	FA	LC	Oth	Total	Lge	FA	LC	Oth	Total
1965-66	3	43/1	5	2		50/1	30	3			33
1966-67	3	42	3	9		54	16		4		20
1967-68	2	24/2		3		27/2	6				6
1968-69	1	14/2		1		15/2	3				3
Total		123/5	8	15		146/5	55	3	4		62

ALLEN, Martin
Born: Reading, 14 Aug 1965.
Signed from: (apprentice), May 1983.
Debut v KR Reykjavic, 2 Oct 1984, UEFA Cup (sub).
Transferred to: West Ham United, Sep 1989 (£550,000).

		APPEARANCES					GOALS				
Season	Div	Lge	FA	LC	Oth	Total	Lge	FA	LC	Oth	Total
1984-85	1	4/1		0/1	0/1	4/3					
1985-86	1	26/5	1	5/2		32/7	3				3
1986-87	1	32	3	3		38	5				5
1987-88	1	38	4	3	1	46	4	1		1	6
1988-89	1	26/2	1/1	4	1	32/3	4		1		5
1989-90	1	2				2					
Total		128/8	9/1	15/3	2/1	154/13	16	1	1	1	19

ALLEN, Reg
Born: Marylebone, London, 3 May 1919.
Signed from: Corona.
Debut v Crystal Palace, 26 Nov 1938 FA Cup.
Transferred to: Manchester United, Jun 1950.

		APPEARANCES					GOALS				
Season	Div	Lge	FA	LC	Oth	Total	Lge	FA	LC	Oth	Total
1938-39	3S	27	4			31					
1939-40	3S	3				3					
2nd WW		21	9		17	47					
1946-47	3S	41	5			46					
1947-48	3S	34	6			40					
1948-49	2	40	2			42					
1949-50	2	41	1			42					
Total		207	27		17	251					

ALLUM, Albert
Born: Notting Hill, 15 Oct 1930.
Signed from: Brentford, Jun 1957.
Debut v Colchester United, 2 Sep 1957.

		APPEARANCES					GOALS				
Season	Div	Lge	FA	LC	Oth	Total	Lge	FA	LC	Oth	Total
1957-58	3S	1				1					
Total		1				1					

ANGELL, Peter
Born: Chalvey, 11 Jan 1932.
Signed from: Slough Town, Jul 1953.
Debut v Walsall, 12 Sep 1953.
Retired Jul 1965.

		APPEARANCES					GOALS				
Season	Div	Lge	FA	LC	Oth	Total	Lge	FA	LC	Oth	Total
1953-54	3S	31	4			35	3				3
1954-55	3S	41	3			44	3				3
1955-56	3S	43	1			44	4				4
1956-57	3S	16				16	2				2
1957-58	3S	45	2			47	2				2
1958-59	3	45	2			47	7				7
1959-60	3	33	3			36	4	1			5
1960-61	3	46	1	1		48	1				1
1961-62	3	39	4	2		45	6		1		7
1962-63	3	30	3	1		34	2				2
1963-64	3	39	3			42	3				3
1964-65	3	9	1	2		12					
Total		417	27	6		450	37	1	1		39

ANDERSON, George.
Born: Sunderland, 1881.
Signed from: Preston North End, 1912.
Debut v Norwich City, 7 Sep 1912, Southern League.

		APPEARANCES					GOALS				
Season	Div	Lge	FA	LC	Oth	Total	Lge	FA	LC	Oth	Total
1912-13	SL	3				3	1				1
Total		3				3	1				1

ANDERSON, Edward
Born: 1881.
Signed from: Sheffield United, 1906.
Debut v Luton Town, 1 Sep 1906 (1 goal), Southern League.

		APPEARANCES					GOALS				
Season	Div	Lge	FA	LC	Oth	Total	Lge	FA	LC	Oth	Total
1906-07	SL	18				18	3				3
1907-08	SL	1				1					
Total		19				19	3				3

ANDERSON, Tommy
Born: Edinburgh, 24 Sep 1934.
Signed from: Bournemouth, Nov 1958.
Debut v Hull City, 29 Nov 1958.
Transferred to: Torquay United, Jul 1959.

		APPEARANCES					GOALS				
Season	Div	Lge	FA	LC	Oth	Total	Lge	FA	LC	Oth	Total
1958-59	3	10				10	3				3
Total		10				10	3				3

ANDERTON, Sylvan
Born: Reading, 23 Nov 1934.
Signed from: Chelsea, Jan 1962.
Debut v Crystal Palace, 20 Jan 1962.

		APPEARANCES					GOALS				
Season	Div	Lge	FA	LC	Oth	Total	Lge	FA	LC	Oth	Total
1961-62	3	4				4					
Total		4				4					

ANDREWS, Cecil
Born: Alton, 1 Nov 1930.
Signed from: Crystal Palace, Jun 1956.
Debut v Reading, 18 Aug 1956.
Transferred to: Sittingbourne, Jul 1958.

		APPEARANCES					GOALS				
Season	Div	Lge	FA	LC	Oth	Total	Lge	FA	LC	Oth	Total
1956-57	3S	46	3			49	1				1
1957-58	3S	12	1			13					
Total		58	4			62	1				1

ANDREWS, Jimmy
Born: Angus, 1 Feb 1927.
Signed from: Leyton Orient, Jun 1959.
Debut v Swindon Town, 22 Aug 1959.

		APPEARANCES					GOALS				
Season	Div	Lge	FA	LC	Oth	Total	Lge	FA	LC	Oth	Total
1959-60	3	46	3			49	10	1			11
1960-61	3	32	1	1		34	6				6
1961-62	3	4				4					
Total		82	4	1		87	16	1			17

ARCHER, Arthur
Born: Derby, Apr 1877.
Signed from: New Brompton, 1903.
Debut v Brentford, 5 Sep 1903, Southern League.
Transferred to: Norwich City, 1905.

		APPEARANCES					GOALS				
Season	Div	Lge	FA	LC	Oth	Total	Lge	FA	LC	Oth	Total
1903-04	SL	31				31					
1904-05	SL	21	1			22					
Total		52	1			53					

ARCHIBALD
Debut v Crystal Palace, 13 Apr 1918, War Fund (1 goal).

		APPEARANCES					GOALS				
Season	Div	Lge	FA	LC	Oth	Total	Lge	FA	LC	Oth	Total
WW1					4	4				2	2
Total											

ARDILES, Ossie
Born: Córdoba, Argentina, 3 Aug 1952.
Signed from: Tottenham Hotspur, Aug 1988 (free).
Debut v Manchester United, 27 Aug 1988.
Transferred to: Swindon Town, Jul 89 (free).

		APPEARANCES					GOALS				
Season	Div	Lge	FA	LC	Oth	Total	Lge	FA	LC	Oth	Total
1988-89	1	4/4	0/1	2	1	7/5					
Total		4/4	0/1	2	1	7/5					

ARMITAGE, Stan
Born: Woolwich, 5 Jun 1919.
Debut v Reading, 14 Sep 1946.

		APPEARANCES					GOALS				
Season	Div	Lge	FA	LC	Oth	Total	Lge	FA	LC	Oth	Total
1946-47	3S	2				2					
Total		2				2					

ARMSTRONG, Jimmy
Born: Lymington.
Signed from: Clapton Orient.
Debut v Exeter City, 10 Nov 1928.
Transferred to: Watford, 1934.

		APPEARANCES					GOALS				
Season	Div	Lge	FA	LC	Oth	Total	Lge	FA	LC	Oth	Total
1928-29	3S	1				1					
1929-30	3S	20				20	3				3
1930-31	3S	30	2			32	1				1
1931-32	3S	40	4			44	1				1
1932-33	3S	31	5			36					
Total		122	11			133	5				5

ARMSTRONG, R.
Debut v Brighton & Hove Albion, 30 Aug 1941.

		APPEARANCES					GOALS				
Season	Div	Lge	FA	LC	Oth	Total	Lge	FA	LC	Oth	Total
2nd WW		11			1	12	3				3
Total		11			1	12	3				3

ASHFORD, H.
Signed from: Brentford, 1920.
Debut v Plymouth Argyle, 12 Feb 1921.

		APPEARANCES					GOALS				
Season	Div	Lge	FA	LC	Oth	Total	Lge	FA	LC	Oth	Total
1920-21	3	5				5					
1921-22	3S	5				5					
Total		10				10					

ASHMAN, Donald
Born: Staindrop, Durham, 9 Oct 1902.
Signed from: Middlesbrough, Jul 1932.
Debut v Brentford, 27 Aug 1932.
Transferred to: Darlington, 1935.

		APPEARANCES					GOALS				
Season	Div	Lge	FA	LC	Oth	Total	Lge	FA	LC	Oth	Total
1932-33	3S	15				15					
1933-34	3S	42	4			46					
1934-35	3S	21	1			22					
Total		78	5			83					

ASTON, Charles
Born: 1870.
Signed from: Aston Villa, 1901.
Debut v Watford, 7 Sep 1901, Southern League.
Transferred to: Burton United, 1902.

		APPEARANCES					GOALS				
Season	Div	Lge	FA	LC	Oth	Total	Lge	FA	LC	Oth	Total
1901-02	SL	25	3			28	1				1
Total		25	3			28	1				1

BACON, S.

		APPEARANCES					GOALS				
Season	Div	Lge	FA	LC	Oth	Total	Lge	FA	LC	Oth	Total
2nd WW		3				3					
Total		3				3					

BAILEY, Dennis
Born: Lambeth, 13 Nov 1965.
Signed from: Birmingham City, Jul 1991 (£175,000).
Debut v Arsenal, 17 Aug 1991 (1 goal).

		APPEARANCES					GOALS				
Season	Div	Lge	FA	LC	Oth	Total	Lge	FA	LC	Oth	Total
1991-92	1	19/5	1	3	2	25/5	9		2		11
1992-93	Pr	13/2	0/1	2		15/3	1		1		2
Total		32/7	1/1	5	2	40/8	10		3		13

BAILEY, S.
Debut v Merthyr Town, 22 Apr 1922.

		APPEARANCES					GOALS				
Season	Div	Lge	FA	LC	Oth	Total	Lge	FA	LC	Oth	Total
1921-22	3S	1				1					
Total		1				1					

BAIN, Ken
Signed from: Mid Rhondda.
Debut v Aberdare Athletic, 12 Nov 1921.

		APPEARANCES					GOALS				
Season	Div	Lge	FA	LC	Oth	Total	Lge	FA	LC	Oth	Total
1921-22	3S	25	2			27					
1922-23	3S	36	4			40					
1923-24	3S	30	1			31					
Total		91	7			98					

BAKER, Peter
Born: Walthamstow, 24 Aug 1934.
Signed from: Sheffield Wednesday, Mar 1961.
Debut v Port Vale, 4 Mar 1961.

		APPEARANCES					GOALS				
Season	Div	Lge	FA	LC	Oth	Total	Lge	FA	LC	Oth	Total
1960-61	3	13				13					
1961-62	3	8		1		9					
1962-63	3	6				6					
Total		27		1		28					

BAKHOLT, Kurt
Born: Odense, Denmark.
Debut v Manchester City, 8 Feb 1986 (sub).

		APPEARANCES					GOALS				
Season	Div	Lge	FA	LC	Oth	Total	Lge	FA	LC	Oth	Total
1985-86	1	0/1				0/1					
Total		0/1				0/1					

BALDOCK, J.W.
Signed from: (junior club).
Debut v Coventry City, 6 Dec 1913 (1 goal), Southern League.

		APPEARANCES					GOALS				
Season	Div	Lge	FA	LC	Oth	Total	Lge	FA	LC	Oth	Total
1913-14	SL	3				3	1				1
1914-15	SL	11				11	5				5
1st WW		83			3	86	5				5
1919-20	SL	42				42	2				2
1920-21	3	1				1					
Total		140			3	143	13				13

BALLENTYNE, Johnny
Born: Glasgow.
Signed from: Partick Thistle.
Debut v Northampton Town, 16 Nov 1935.
Transferred to: (not re-registered Jul 1937).

		APPEARANCES					GOALS				
Season	Div	Lge	FA	LC	Oth	Total	Lge	FA	LC	Oth	Total
1935-36	3S	15	1			16	3				3
1936-37	3S	10				10					
Total		25	1			26	3				3

BALOGAN, Jesilimi
Born: Nigeria, 27 Mar 1931.
Signed from: Skegness Town, Sep 1956.
Debut v Watford, 13 Oct 1956 (1 goal).
Transferred to: Holbeach United, Jul 1957.

		APPEARANCES					GOALS				
Season	Div	Lge	FA	LC	Oth	Total	Lge	FA	LC	Oth	Total
1956-57	3SD	13	2			15	3	2			5
Total		13	2			15	3	2			5

BANKS, Reg
Signed from: West Bromwich Albion.
Debut v Millwall, 31 Aug 1935.
Transferred to: Tunbridge Wells Rangers, Jul 1937 (free).

		APPEARANCES					GOALS				
Season	Div	Lge	FA	LC	Oth	Total	Lge	FA	LC	Oth	Total
1935-36	3S	9				9	2				2
1936-37	3S	3				3	1				1
Total		12				12	3				3

BANNER, William
Signed from: Chesterfield, 1903.
Debut v Northampton Town, 28 Dec 1903, Southern League.
Transferred to: Chesterfield, 1904.

		APPEARANCES					GOALS				
Season	Div	Lge	FA	LC	Oth	Total	Lge	FA	LC	Oth	Total
1903-04	SL	4				4					
Total		4				4					

BANNISTER, Gary
Born: Warrington, 22 Jul 1960.
Signed from: Sheffield Wednesday, Aug 1984 (£150,000).
Debut v West Bromwich Albion, 25 Aug 1984.
Transferred to: Coventry City, Mar 1988 (£300,000).

		APPEARANCES					GOALS				
Season	Div	Lge	FA	LC	Oth	Total	Lge	FA	LC	Oth	Total
1984-85	1	42	1	8	4	55	17		5	6	28
1985-86	1	36	1	9		46	16		2		18
1986-87	1	34	4	3		41	15		1		16
1987-88	1	24	3	3		30	8	1	1		10
Total		136	9	23	4	172	56	1	9	6	72

BARBER, Michael
Born: Kensington, 24 Aug 1941.
Signed from: Arsenal, Dec 1959.
Debut v Coventry City, 5 Sep 1960.
Transferred to: Notts County, Jul 1963.

		APPEARANCES					GOALS				
Season	Div	Lge	FA	LC	Oth	Total	Lge	FA	LC	Oth	Total
1960-61	3	12		2		14	3				3
1961-62	3	23	1	2		26	4				4
1962-63	3	28	1			29	4	2			6
Total		63	2	4		69	11	2			13

BARDSLEY, David
Born: Manchester, 11 Sep 1964.
Signed from: Oxford United, Sep 1989 (£375,000).
Debut v Derby County, 16 Sep 1989.

		APPEARANCES					GOALS				
Season	Div	Lge	FA	LC	Oth	Total	Lge	FA	LC	Oth	Total
1989-90	1	31	9			40	1				1
1990-91	1	38	1	4	1	44					
1991-92	1	42	1	4	2	48			1	1	2
1992-93	Pr	40	2	3		45	3				3
Total		151	13	11	3	177	4		1	1	6

BARKER, Simon
Born: Farnworth, 4 Nov 1964.
Signed from: Blackburn Rovers, Jul 1988 (£400,000).
Debut v Manchester United, 27 Aug 1988.

		APPEARANCES					GOALS				
Season	Div	Lge	FA	LC	Oth	Total	Lge	FA	LC	Oth	Total
1988-89	1	21/4	2/1	3/1	4	30/6	1				1
1989-90	1	24/4	9	3		36/4	3	2			5
1990-91	1	31/4	1	3/1	1	36/5	1		1		2
1991-92	1	31/3	1	4	2	38/3	6		2		8
1992-93	Pr	21/4	2	1/1		24/5	1				1
Total		128/19	15/1	14/3	7	164/23	12	2	3		17

BARLEY, Derek
Born: Highbury, 20 Mar 1932.
Signed from: Arsenal, May 1953.
Debut v Aldershot, 29 Aug 1953.
Transferred to: Aldershot, Jul 1954.

		APPEARANCES					GOALS				
Season	Div	Lge	FA	LC	Oth	Total	Lge	FA	LC	Oth	Total
1953-54	3S	4				4					
Total		4				4					

BARNES, William
Born: West Ham, 1885.
Signed from: Luton Town, 1907.
Debut v Tottenham Hotspur, 2 Sep 1907, Southern League.
Transferred to: Southend United, 1913.

		APPEARANCES					GOALS				
Season	Div	Lge	FA	LC	Oth	Total	Lge	FA	LC	Oth	Total
1907-08	SL	36	2		*1	39	10	1			11
1908-09	SL	39	2		*1	42	10				10
1909-10	SL	40	7			47	9				9
1910-11	SL	29				29	2				2
1911-12	SL	38	2		*1	41	4				4
1912-13	SL	34	2			36	1				1
Total		216	15		3	234	36	1			37

BARR, John
Born: Bridge of Weir, 9 Sep 1917.
Signed from: Third Lanark.

		APPEARANCES					GOALS				
Season	Div	Lge	FA	LC	Oth	Total	Lge	FA	LC	Oth	Total
2nd WW		8				8					
1946-47	3S	4				4					
Total		12				12					

BARR, W.
Debut v Merthyr Town, 5 Sep 1925.

		APPEARANCES					GOALS				
Season	Div	Lge	FA	LC	Oth	Total	Lge	FA	LC	Oth	Total
1925-26	3S	2				2					
Total		2				2					

BARRIE, Walter
Born: Kirkcaldy, 1911.
Signed from: West Ham United, 1932.
Debut v Watford, 24 Sep 1932.
Transferred to: Carlisle United, 1938.

		APPEARANCES					GOALS				
Season	Div	Lge	FA	LC	Oth	Total	Lge	FA	LC	Oth	Total
1932-33	3S	36	5			41					
1933-34	3S	41	4			45					
1934-35	3S	25	2			27					
1935-36	3S	26	1			27					
1936-37	3S	23				23	1				1
1937-38	3S	6				6					
Total		157	12			169	1				1

BARRON, Paul
Born: London, 16 Sep 1953.
Debut v Hull City, 24 Sep 1985, League Cup.

		APPEARANCES					GOALS				
Season	Div	Lge	FA	LC	Oth	Total	Lge	FA	LC	Oth	Total
1985-86	1	31	1	9		41					
1986-87	1	1				1					
Total		32	1	9		42					

BARTLETT, Frederick
Born: Reading, 5 Mar 1913.
Debut v Millwall, 3 Nov 1934.
Transferred to: Clapton Orient, Jul 1937 (free).

		APPEARANCES					GOALS				
Season	Div	Lge	FA	LC	Oth	Total	Lge	FA	LC	Oth	Total
1934-35	3S	3	1			4					
1935-36	3S	38	1			39					
1936-37	3S	7				7					
Total		48	2			50					

BEADELL, R.
Debut v Chelsea, 29 Aug 1942.

		APPEARANCES					GOALS				
Season	Div	Lge	FA	LC	Oth	Total	Lge	FA	LC	Oth	Total
2nd WW		1				1					
Total		1				1					

BEATS, E.
Signed from: Aston Villa.
Debut v Millwall, 10 Mar 1928 (1 goal).

		APPEARANCES					GOALS				
Season	Div	Lge	FA	LC	Oth	Total	Lge	FA	LC	Oth	Total
1927-28	3S	1				1	1				1
Total		1				1	1				1

BECK, John
Born: Edmonton, 25 May 1954.
Signed from: (apprentice), May 1972.
Debut v Orient, 26 Dec 1972 (sub).
Transferred to: Coventry City, Jun 1976 (£70,000).

		APPEARANCES					GOALS				
Season	Div	Lge	FA	LC	Oth	Total	Lge	FA	LC	Oth	Total
1972-73	2	0/1				0/1					
1973-74	1	2/3				2/3					
1974-75	1	27/2	4/1	2		33/3	1				1
1975-76	1	3/2				3/2					
Total		32/8	4/1	2		38/9	1				1

BEDFORD, Brian
Born: Ferndale, 24 Dec 1933.
Signed from: Bournemouth, Jul 1959.
Debut v Swindon Town, 22 Aug 1959.
Transferred to: Scunthorpe United, Sep 1965.

		APPEARANCES					GOALS				
Season	Div	Lge	FA	LC	Oth	Total	Lge	FA	LC	Oth	Total
1959-60	3	44	3			47	25	2			27
1960-61	3	44	2	2		48	33	3	1		37
1961-62	3	43	4	2		49	34	3	2		39
1962-63	3	43	2	1		46	23	3			26
1963-64	3	44	2	1		47	23	1	1		25
1964-65	3	40	3	2		45	23	1	2		26
1965-66	3			1		1					
Total		258	16	9		283	161	13	6		180

BEDINGFIELD, Frank
Born: Sunderland, 1877.
Signed from: Aston Villa, Aug 1899.
Debut v Tottenham Hotspur, 9 Sep 1899, Southerrn League.
Transferred to: Portsmouth, 1900.

		APPEARANCES					GOALS				
Season	Div	Lge	FA	LC	Oth	Total	Lge	FA	LC	Oth	Total
1899-1900	SL	24	8			32	17	4			21
Total		24	8			32	17	4			21

BEECHEM, Ernest.
Born: Hertford, 23 Aug 1896.
Signed from: Fulham, 1932.
Debut v Brentford, 27 Aug 1932.
Transferred to: Brighton & Hove Albion, Sep 1935.

		APPEARANCES					GOALS				
Season	Div	Lge	FA	LC	Oth	Total	Lge	FA	LC	Oth	Total
1932-33	3S	42	5			47					
1933-34	3S	34	4			38					
1934-35	3S	10				10					
Total		86	9			95					

BELLINGHAM, F.James
Born: Scotland, 1878.
Signed from: Falkirk, 1900.
Debut v Swindon Town, 8 Sep 1900, Southern League.
Transferred to: Grimsby Town, 1901.

		APPEARANCES					GOALS				
Season	Div	Lge	FA	LC	Oth	Total	Lge	FA	LC	Oth	Total
1900-01	SL	15	2			17					
Total		15	2			17					

BENNETT, Edward
Born: Kilburn, 22 Aug 1925.
Signed from: Southall, 1948.
Debut v West Ham United, 19 Mar 1949.

		APPEARANCES					GOALS				
Season	Div	Lge	FA	LC	Oth	Total	Lge	FA	LC	Oth	Total
1948-49	2	2				2					
Total		2				2					

BENSON, G.
Born: Burnley.
Signed from: Stalybridge Celtic.
Debut v Brentford, 25 Aug 1923.

		APPEARANCES					GOALS				
Season	Div	Lge	FA	LC	Oth	Total	Lge	FA	LC	Oth	Total
1923-24	3S	17				17					
Total		17				17					

BENSTEAD, Graham
Born: Aldershot, 20 Aug 1963.
Signed from: (apprentice), Jul 1981.
Debut v West Bromwich Albion, 8 Jan 1983, FA Cup.
Transferred to: Norwich City, Mar 1985.

		APPEARANCES					GOALS				
Season	Div	Lge	FA	LC	Oth	Total	Lge	FA	LC	Oth	Total
1982-83	2		1			1					
Total			1			1					

BENTLEY, Roy
Born: Bristol, 17 May 1924.
Signed from: Fulham, Jun 1961.
Debut v Brentford, 14 Aug 1961.

		APPEARANCES					GOALS				
Season	Div	Lge	FA	LC	Oth	Total	Lge	FA	LC	Oth	Total
1961-62	3	29	4	1		34					
1962-63	3	16	2			18					
Total		45	6	1		52					

BERRY, P.
Debut v Swansea Town, 14 Feb 1920, Southern League.

		APPEARANCES					GOALS				
Season	Div	Lge	FA	LC	Oth	Total	Lge	FA	LC	Oth	Total
1919-20	SL	4				4					
Total		4				4					

BEST, Tom
Born: Milford Haven.
Signed from: Cardiff City, Dec 1949.
Debut v Blackburn Rovers, 10 Dec 1949.

		APPEARANCES					GOALS				
Season	Div	Lge	FA	LC	Oth	Total	Lge	FA	LC	Oth	Total
1949-50	2	13	1			14	3				3
Total		13	1			14	3				3

BEVAN, Fred
Born: Hackney, 1880.
Signed from: Reading, 1904.
Debut v Plymouth Argyle, 3 Sep 1904, Southern League.
Transferred to: Bury, Jul 1906 (£340).

		APPEARANCES					GOALS				
Season	Div	Lge	FA	LC	Oth	Total	Lge	FA	LC	Oth	Total
1904-05	SL	32	1			33	20				20
1905-06	SL	26				26	10				10
Total		58	1			59	30				30

BIRCH, Jimmy
Born: Blackwell.
Signed from: Aston Villa, 1912.
Debut v Plymouth Argyle, 5 Sep 1912 (1 goal), Southern League.
Transferred to: Brentford, 1926.

		APPEARANCES					GOALS				
Season	Div	Lge	FA	LC	Oth	Total	Lge	FA	LC	Oth	Total
1912-13	SL	38	2			40	15	3			18
1913-14	SL	30	5			35	16	4			20
1914-15	SL	37	3			40	15	2			17
1st WW		6				6	3				3
1919-20	SL	40	1			41	16	1			17
1920-21	3	25	2			27	15	1			16
1921-22	3S	38	2			40	17				17
1922-23	3S	32	4			36	11	1			12
1923-24	3S	37	1			38	8				8
1924-25	3S	36	5			41	6	3			9
1925-26	3S	15	4			19	3	4			7
Total		334	29			363	125	19			144

BLACK, Sam
Born: Motherwell, 18 Nov 1905.
Signed from: Plymouth Argyle, Nov 1938.
Debut v Bristol Rovers, 31 Dec 1938.

		APPEARANCES					GOALS				
Season	Div	Lge	FA	LC	Oth	Total	Lge	FA	LC	Oth	Total
1938-39	3S	5				5					
Total		5				5					

BLACKMAN, Fred
Born: Brixton, 1889.
Signed from: Leeds City, 1919.
Debut v Bristol Rovers, 30 Aug 1919, Southern League.

		APPEARANCES					GOALS				
Season	Div	Lge	FA	LC	Oth	Total	Lge	FA	LC	Oth	Total
1919-20	SL	18	1			19					
1920-21	3	22	1			23					
1921-22	3S	20				20					
Total		60	2			62					

BLACKMAN, Jack
Born: Bermondsey, London, Jan 1912.
Signed from: (minor football), 1932.
Debut v Leeds United, 9 Jan 1932, FA Cup.
Transferred to: Crystal Palace, Oct 1935.

		APPEARANCES					GOALS				
Season	Div	Lge	FA	LC	Oth	Total	Lge	FA	LC	Oth	Total
1931-32	3S	10	2			12	7				7
1932-33	3S	23	1			24	11				11
1933-34	3S	36	4			40	24	7			31
1934-35	3S	38	1			39	19				19
1935-36	3S	1				1	1				1
Total		108	8			116	62	7			69

BLACKWOOD, John
Born: Glasgow, 1877.
Signed from: Reading, Nov 1902.
Debut v Northampton Town, 29 Nov 1902, Southern League.
Transferred to: West Ham United, 1904.

		APPEARANCES					GOALS				
Season	Div	Lge	FA	LC	Oth	Total	Lge	FA	LC	Oth	Total
1902-03	SL	15				15	10				10
1903-04	SL	24				24	20				20
1904-05	SL	7				7	3				3
Total		46				46	33				33

BLAKE, Albert
Born: Fulham.
Signed from: Watford, 1933.
Debut v Brighton & Hove Albion, 26 Aug 1933.
Transferred: 1936.

		APPEARANCES					GOALS				
Season	Div	Lge	FA	LC	Oth	Total	Lge	FA	LC	Oth	Total
1933-34	3S	38	4			42	5				5
1934-35	3S	37	1			38	4				4
1935-36	3S	6				6					
Total		81	5			86	9				9

BLAKE, F.J.C.
Debut v Portsmouth, 26 Nov 1914, Southern League.

		APPEARANCES					GOALS				
Season	Div	Lge	FA	LC	Oth	Total	Lge	FA	LC	Oth	Total
1913-14	SL	2				2					
Total		2				2					

BLAKE, Sid
Born: Whitley Bay.
Signed from: Newcastle United, 1906.
Debut v Luton Town, 1 Sep 1906, Southern League.
Transferred to: North Shields, 1908.

		APPEARANCES					GOALS				
Season	Div	Lge	FA	LC	Oth	Total	Lge	FA	LC	Oth	Total
1906-07	SL	14				14					
Total		14				14					

BLIZZARD, Les
Born: Acton, 13 Mar 1923.
Signed from: (local club).
Debut v Aldershot, 8 Nov 1941.
Transferred to: Bournemouth, May 1947.

		APPEARANCES					GOALS				
Season	Div	Lge	FA	LC	Oth	Total	Lge	FA	LC	Oth	Total
2nd WW		18	2		2	22					
1946-47	3S	5				5					
Total		23	2		2	27					

BOLAM, Robert.
Born: Birtley.
Signed from: South Shields.
Debut v Bristol City, 6 Dec 1924.

		APPEARANCES					GOALS				
Season	Div	Lge	FA	LC	Oth	Total	Lge	FA	LC	Oth	Total
1924-25	3S	2				2					
Total		2				2					

BONASS, Albert
Born: Yorkshire, 1912.
Signed from: Chesterfield.
Debut v Watford, 26 Aug 1939.

		APPEARANCES					GOALS				
Season	Div	Lge	FA	LC	Oth	Total	Lge	FA	LC	Oth	Total
1939-40	3S	3				3					
2nd WW		53			2	55	6			1	7
Total		56			2	58	6			1	7

BOTT, Wilfred
Born: Featherstone, Yorkshire, 25 Apr 1907.
Signed from: Newcastle United.
Debut v Bristol City, 29 Aug 1935.
Transferred to: Lancaster.

		APPEARANCES					GOALS				
Season	Div	Lge	FA	LC	Oth	Total	Lge	FA	LC	Oth	Total
1936-37	3S	23	3			26	9				9
1937-38	3S	31	2			33	17	2			19
1938-39	3S	21	4			25	8	1			9
2nd WW		18				18	5				5
Total		93	9			102	39	3			42

BOTTOMS, Michael
Born: Harrow, 11 Jan 1939.
Signed from: Harrow Town, Jul 1960.
Debut v Port Vale, 15 Oct 1960.
Transferred to: Oxford United, Jul 1962.

		APPEARANCES					GOALS				
Season	Div	Lge	FA	LC	Oth	Total	Lge	FA	LC	Oth	Total
1960-61	3	2		1		3					
Total		2		1		3					

BOWERS, Alfred
Born: Canning Town, 1899.
Signed from: Bristol Rovers.
Debut v Bournemouth, 2 Oct 1926.

		APPEARANCES					GOALS				
Season	Div	Lge	FA	LC	Oth	Total	Lge	FA	LC	Oth	Total
1926-27	3S	1				1					
Total		1				1					

BOWLES, Stan
Born: Manchester, 24 Dec 1948.
Signed from: Carlisle United, Sep 1972 (£112,000).
Debut v Nottingham Forest, 16 Sep 1972 (1 goal).
Transferred to: Nottingham Forest, Dec 1979 (£250,000).

		APPEARANCES					GOALS				
Season	Div	Lge	FA	LC	Oth	Total	Lge	FA	LC	Oth	Total
1972-73	2	35	4			39	17	1			18
1973-74	1	42	6	3		51	20	2	1		23
1974-75	1	33	4	3		40	10	1	1		12
1975-76	1	37	2	4		43	10		2		12
1976-77	1	22	2	7	†8	39	5	1	2	11	19
1977-78	1	40	6	2		48	6	3			9
1978-79	1	30	1	3		34	1				1
1979-80	2	16		5		21	2		1		3
Total		255	25	27	8	315	71	8	7	11	97

BOWMAN, John
Born: Middlesbrough, 23 Apr 1879.
Signed from: Stoke, 1901.
Debut v Watford, 7 Sep 1901, Southern League.
Transferred to: Norwich City, 1905.

		APPEARANCES					GOALS				
Season	Div	Lge	FA	LC	Oth	Total	Lge	FA	LC	Oth	Total
1901-02	SL	20	3			23					
1902-03	SL	27	1			28					
1903-04	SL	29	2			31	1				1
1904-05	SL	27	1			28	1				1
Total		103	7			110	2				2

BOXSHALL, Danny
Born: Bradford, 2 Apr 1920.
Signed from: The Army.
Debut v Watford, 1 Jan 1946.
Transferred to: Bristol City, May 1948.

		APPEARANCES					GOALS				
Season	Div	Lge	FA	LC	Oth	Total	Lge	FA	LC	Oth	Total
2nd WW		1			2	3				1	1
1946-47	3S	12	2			14	3	1			4
1947-48	3S	17	6			23	11	2			13
Total		30	8		2	40	14	3		1	18

BRADSHAW, J.
Signed from: Aberdare Athletic.
Debut v Reading, 24 Sep 1921.

		APPEARANCES					GOALS				
Season	Div	Lge	FA	LC	Oth	Total	Lge	FA	LC	Oth	Total
1921-22	3S	5				5					
Total		5				5					

BRADSHAW, J.
Born: Burnley.
Signed from: Chelsea.
Debut v Coventry City, 3 Sep 1910 (2 goals), Southern League.
Transferred to: Southend United.

		APPEARANCES					GOALS				
Season	Div	Lge	FA	LC	Oth	Total	Lge	FA	LC	Oth	Total
1910-11	SL	2				2	2				2
Total		2				2	2				2

BRADY, Pat
Born: Dublin, 11 Mar 1936.
Signed from: Millwall, Jul 1963.
Debut v Aldershot, 4 Sep 1963, League Cup.

		APPEARANCES					GOALS				
Season	Div	Lge	FA	LC	Oth	Total	Lge	FA	LC	Oth	Total
1963-63	3	29	3	1		33					
1964-65	3	33	2	2		37					
Total		62	5	3		70					

BRADY, Ray
Born: Dublin, 3 Jun 1937.
Signed from: Millwall, Jul 1963.
Debut v Oldham Athletic, 24 Aug 1963.

		APPEARANCES					GOALS				
Season	Div	Lge	FA	LC	Oth	Total	Lge	FA	LC	Oth	Total
1963-64	3	43	3	1		47					
1964-65	3	44	3	2		49	1				1
1965-66	3	1				1					
Total		88	6	3		97	1				1

BRAZIL, Alan
Born: Glasgow, 15 Jun 1959.
Signed from: Coventry City, Jul 1986 (£130,000).
Debut v Southampton, 23 Aug 1986 (sub).

		APPEARANCES					GOALS				
Season	Div	Lge	FA	LC	Oth	Total	Lge	FA	LC	Oth	Total
1986-87	1	1/3		1/1		2/4			1		1
Total		1/3		1/1		2/4			1		1

BREVETT, Rufus
Born: Derby, 24 Sep 1969.
Signed from: Doncaster Rovers, Feb 1991 (£150,000).
Debut v Tottenham Hotspur, 23 Mar 1991.

		APPEARANCES					GOALS				
Season	Div	Lge	FA	LC	Oth	Total	Lge	FA	LC	Oth	Total
1990-91	1	10				10					
1991-92	1	6/1		1		7/1					
1992-93	Pr	14/1	1	1		16/1					
Total		30/2	1	2		33/2					

BREWIS, Robert
Debut v Tottenham Hotspur, 7 Oct 1905, Southern League.
Transferred to: Lincoln City, 1907.

		APPEARANCES					GOALS				
Season	Div	Lge	FA	LC	Oth	Total	Lge	FA	LC	Oth	Total
1905-06	SL	2				2	1				1
1906-07	SL	5				5	1				1
Total		7				7	2				2

BRIDGES, Barry
Born: Norwich, 29 Apr 1941.
Signed from: Birmingham City, Aug 1968 (£50,000).
Debut v Manchester City, 24 Aug 1968 (1 goal).
Transferred to: Millwall, Sep 1970 (£40,000).

		APPEARANCES					GOALS				
Season	Div	Lge	FA	LC	Oth	Total	Lge	FA	LC	Oth	Total
1968-69	1	27		1		28	8				8
1969-70	2	38	4	4		46	21	1	2		24
1970-71	1	7		1		8	2		1		3
Total		72	4	6		82	31	1	3		35

BRINDLEY, Horace.
Signed from: Norwich City, 1910.
Debut v Coventry City, 3 Sep 1910, Southern League.
Transferred to: Lincoln City, 1913.

		APPEARANCES					GOALS				
Season	Div	Lge	FA	LC	Oth	Total	Lge	FA	LC	Oth	Total
1910-11	SL	17	1			18					
Total		17	1			18					

BROCK, Kevin
Born: Bicester, 9 Sep 1962.
Signed from: Oxford United, Aug 1987 (£100,000).
Debut v West Ham United, 15 Aug 1987 (1 goal).
Transferred to: Newcastle United, Dec 1988 (£300,000).

		APPEARANCES					GOALS				
Season	Div	Lge	FA	LC	Oth	Total	Lge	FA	LC	Oth	Total
1987-88	1	26	4	2	1	33	2	1			3
1988-89	1	12/2	1	4	1	18/2					
Total		38/2	5	6	2	51/2	2	1			3

BROSTER, John.
Born: Earlstown, Lancashire.
Signed from: Chorley.
Debut v Southampton, 26 Dec 1912, Southern League.
Transferred to: Rochdale, 1920.

		APPEARANCES					GOALS				
Season	Div	Lge	FA	LC	Oth	Total	Lge	FA	LC	Oth	Total
1912-13	SL	3				3					
1913-14	SL	4				4					
1914-15	SL	26	3			29	1				1
1st WW		2				2	1				1
1919-20	SL	35	1			36	2				2
Total		70	4			74	4				4

BROWN, Albert
Born: Tamworth, Warwickshire, 1879.
Signed from: Southampton, 1902.
Debut v Reading, 25 Oct 1902, Southern League.
Transferred to: Preston North End, 1905.

		APPEARANCES					GOALS				
Season	Div	Lge	FA	LC	Oth	Total	Lge	FA	LC	Oth	Total
1902-03	SL	18				18	8				8
1903-04	SL	12	1			13	3	1			4
Total		30	1			31	11	1			12

BROWN, A.Richard
Born: Pegswood, Northumberland.
Signed from: Blyth Spartans, Jul 1932.
Debut v Brentford, 27 Aug 1932 (1 goal).
Transferred to: Northampton Town.

		APPEARANCES					GOALS				
Season	Div	Lge	FA	LC	Oth	Total	Lge	FA	LC	Oth	Total
1932-33	3S	36	5			41	13				13
1933-34	3S	24	4			28	7	1			8
Total		60	9			69	20	1			21

BROWN, B.
Debut v Aldershot, 6 April 1942 (War Cup).

		APPEARANCES					GOALS				
Season	Div	Lge	FA	LC	Oth	Total	Lge	FA	LC	Oth	Total
2nd WW					1	1					
Total					1	1					

BROWN, Charles.
Born: Stakesford, 13 Jan.
Signed from: Southampton, 1924.
Debut v Newport County, 30 Aug 1924.

		APPEARANCES					GOALS				
Season	Div	Lge	FA	LC	Oth	Total	Lge	FA	LC	Oth	Total
1924-25	3S	40	5			45	1				1
1925-26	3S	27	1			28	2				2
Total		67	6			73	3				3

BROWN, Harry
Born: Kingsbury, 9 Apr 1924.
Debut v Millwall, 15 Nov 1941.
Transferred to: Notts County (exchange C.Halton); From: Derby County, Aug 1951; Transferred to: Plymouth Argyle, Aug 1956.

		APPEARANCES					GOALS				
Season	Div	Lge	FA	LC	Oth	Total	Lge	FA	LC	Oth	Total
2nd WW		67	1		17	85					
1951-52	2	36	1			37					
1952-53	3S	43	3			46					
1953-54	3S	33	4			37					
1954-55	3S	39	2			41					
1955-56	3S	38	1			39					
Total		256	12		17	285					

BROWN, H.
Signed from: Shildon United.
Debut v Newport County, 30 Aug 1924.

		APPEARANCES					GOALS				
Season	Div	Lge	FA	LC	Oth	Total	Lge	FA	LC	Oth	Total
1924-25	3S	13				13	3				3
Total		13				13	3				3

BROWN, J.
Debut v Portsmouth, 2 Dec 1916.

		APPEARANCES					GOALS				
Season	Div	Lge	FA	LC	Oth	Total	Lge	FA	LC	Oth	Total
WW1		29			29	7					7
Total		29			29	7				7	

BROWN, William
Born: Wellingborough.
Signed from: Kettering Town, 1910.
Debut v Brighton, 4 Mar 1911, Southern League.
Transferred to: Chelsea, 1912.

		APPEARANCES					GOALS				
Season	Div	Lge	FA	LC	Oth	Total	Lge	FA	LC	Oth	Total
1910-11	SL	7				7	2				2
Total		7				7	2				2

BROWNING, Robert
Debut v Luton Town, 8 Oct 1910 (1 goal), Southern League.
Transferred to: Southampton, 1913.

		APPEARANCES					GOALS				
Season	Div	Lge	FA	LC	Oth	Total	Lge	FA	LC	Oth	Total
1910-11	SL	31	1			32	18				18
1911-12	SL	8	2			10	1				1
1912-13	SL	12				12	1				1
Total		51	3			54	20				20

BULL, Albert
Born: Derby, 1875.
Signed from: Reading, 1903.
Debut v Tottenham Hotspur, 19 Sep 1903, Southern League.
Transferred to: New Brompton, 1905.

		APPEARANCES					GOALS				
Season	Div	Lge	FA	LC	Oth	Total	Lge	FA	LC	Oth	Total
1903-04	SL	13	2			15					
Total		13	2			15					

BURGESS, Dick.
Born: Stoke-on-Trent.
Signed from: Aberdare Athletic.
Debut v Gillingham, 29 Aug 1925.

		APPEARANCES					GOALS				
Season	Div	Lge	FA	LC	Oth	Total	Lge	FA	LC	Oth	Total
1925-26	3S	32	4			36	8				8
1926-27	3S	14				14	1				1
Total		46	4			50	9				9

BURKE, Steve
Born: Nottingham, 29 Sep 1960.
Signed from: Nottingham Forest, Sep 1979 (£150,000).
Debut v Fulham, 8 Sep 1979.
Transferred to: Doncaster Rovers, Sep 1986 (free).

		APPEARANCES					GOALS				
Season	Div	Lge	FA	LC	Oth	Total	Lge	FA	LC	Oth	Total
1979-80	2	28/3	0/1	1/1		29/5	4				4
1980-81	2	11/3		2		13/3	1				1
1981-82	2	2/10	0/1	1/1		3/12					
1982-83	2	1/4	0/1			1/5					
1983-84	1	1/4				1/4					
1984-85	1				†0/1	0/1					
Total		43/24	0/3	4/2	0/1	47/30	5				5

BURLEY, B.
Debut v Tottenham, 5 Sep 1942.

		APPEARANCES					GOALS				
Season	Div	Lge	FA	LC	Oth	Total	Lge	FA	LC	Oth	Total
2nd WW		61			17	78	16			5	21
Total		61			17	78	16			5	21

BURNHAM, G.
Born: Sunderland.
Signed from: Brighton & Hove Albion, 1921.
Debut v Brighton & Hove Albion, 26 Nov 1921.
Transferred to: Durham City, 1923.

		APPEARANCES					GOALS				
Season	Div	Lge	FA	LC	Oth	Total	Lge	FA	LC	Oth	Total
1921-22	3S	27	2			29					
1922-23	3S	4				4					
Total		31	2			33					

BURNS, Jack
Born: Fulham.
Signed from: Crypto.
Debut v Southend United, 14 Jan 1928.
Transferred to: Brentford, 1931.

		APPEARANCES					GOALS				
Season	Div	Lge	FA	LC	Oth	Total	Lge	FA	LC	Oth	Total
1927-28	3S	16				16	5				5
1928-29	3S	37	1			38	12	1			13
1929-30	3S	31	4			35	2	2			4
1930-31	3S	33	3			36	10	2			12
Total		117	8			125	29	5			34

BURRIDGE, John
Born: Workington, 3 Dec 1951.
Signed from: Crystal Palace, Dec 1980 (£150,000).
Debut v West Ham United, 26 Dec 1980.
Transferred to: Wolverhampton Wanderers, Aug 1982 (£75,000).

		APPEARANCES					GOALS				
Season	Div	Lge	FA	LC	Oth	Total	Lge	FA	LC	Oth	Total
1980-81	2	19	2			21					
1981-82	2	20		4		24					
Total		39	2	4		45					

BUSBY, Martyn
Born: Slough, 24 May 1953.
Signed from: (apprentice), Jul 1970.
Debut v Leicester City, 18 Apr 1970.
Transferred to: Notts County Oct 1976 (£35,000); From: Notts County Sep 1977 (£80,000).

		APPEARANCES					GOALS				
Season	Div	Lge	FA	LC	Oth	Total	Lge	FA	LC	Oth	Total
1969-70	2	1				1					
1970-71	2	12/2	1	1/1		14/3					
1971-72	2	28/1		2		30/1	2				2
1972-73	2	13		1		14	3				3
1973-74	1	5/1		1/2		6/3					
1974-75	1	12/3		2		14/3	1				1
1975-76	1		0/1			0/1					
1976-77	1	1			†0/1	1/1					
1977-78	1	19/2	5			24/2	3	3			6
1978-79	1	29/6	1	2		32/6	6				6
1979-80	2	8/2		1		9/2	2				2
Total		128/17	7/1	10/3	0/1	145/22	17	3			20

BUSBY, Walter
Born: Wellingborough, 1882.
Signed from: Wellingborough, 1902.
Debut v Wellingborough, 3 Sep 1902, Southern League.
Transferred to: Woolwich Arsenal, 1903.

		APPEARANCES					GOALS				
Season	Div	Lge	FA	LC	Oth	Total	Lge	FA	LC	Oth	Total
1902-03	SL	14	1			15	3				3
Total		14	1			15	3				3

BUTLER
Debut v Arsenal, 26 Dec 1916.

		APPEARANCES					GOALS				
Season	Div	Lge	FA	LC	Oth	Total	Lge	FA	LC	Oth	Total
WW1		7				7					
Total		7				7					

BUTLER, E.
Signed from: Ebbw Vale, 1922.
Debut v Swindon Town, 7 Oct 1922.
Transferred to: Hartlepools United.

		APPEARANCES					GOALS				
Season	Div	Lge	FA	LC	Oth	Total	Lge	FA	LC	Oth	Total
1922-23	3S	21				21					
1923-24	3S	13	1			14					
Total		34	1			35					

BUTTERWORTH, Herbert.
Born: Unsworth, 1885.
Signed from: Oldham Athletic, 1910.
Debut v Crystal Palace, 26 Nov 1910, Southern League.
Transferred to: Millwall, 1912.

		APPEARANCES					GOALS				
Season	Div	Lge	FA	LC	Oth	Total	Lge	FA	LC	Oth	Total
1910-11	SL	25	1			26					
1911-12	SL	15				15					
Total		40	1			41					

BYRNE, John
Born: Manchester, 1 Feb 1961.
Signed from: York City, Oct 1984 (£100,000).
Debut v Norwich City, 27 Oct 1984 (sub).
Transferred to: Le Havre, May 1988 (£175,000).

		APPEARANCES					GOALS				
Season	Div	Lge	FA	LC	Oth	Total	Lge	FA	LC	Oth	Total
1984-85	1	19/4	1			20/4	3				3
1985-86	1	30/6	1	7/1		38/7	12		3		15
1986-87	1	37/3	4	2		43/3	11	2	1		14
1987-88	1	22/5	1/2	3	1	27/7	4				4
Total		108/18	7/2	12/1	1	128/21	30	2	4		36

BYROM, William
Born: Blackburn.
Signed from: Burnley.

		APPEARANCES					GOALS				
Season	Div	Lge	FA	LC	Oth	Total	Lge	FA	LC	Oth	Total
2nd WW		1				1					
Total		1				1					

CABLE, Tommy
Born: 26 May, 1900.
Signed from: Leyton.
Debut v Charlton Athletic, 25 Dec 1925.
Transferred to: Tottenham, 1928.

		APPEARANCES					GOALS				
Season	Div	Lge	FA	LC	Oth	Total	Lge	FA	LC	Oth	Total
1925-26	3S	13				13	2				2
1926-27	3S	5				5					
Total		18				18	2				2

CAESER, GUS
Born: Harringey, 5 Mar 1966.
Signed from: Arsenal, Nov 1990 (loan).
Debut v Manchester City, 1 Dec 1990.

		APPEARANCES					GOALS				
Season	Div	Lge	FA	LC	Oth	Total	Lge	FA	LC	Oth	Total
1990-91	1	5				5					
Total		5				5					

CAIN, T.
Born: Earling.
Debut v Luton Town, 22 Mar 1920, Southern League.
Transferred to: Brentford, 1924.

		APPEARANCES					GOALS				
Season	Div	Lge	FA	LC	Oth	Total	Lge	FA	LC	Oth	Total
1919-20	SL	6				6					
Total		6				6					

CAMPBELL
Debut v Chelsea, 11 Oct 1941, League South.

		APPEARANCES					GOALS				
Season	Div	Lge	FA	LC	Oth	Total	Lge	FA	LC	Oth	Total
2nd WW		5				5					
Total		5				5					

CAMPBELL, Dougall
Born: Kirkintilloch, 14 Dec 1922.
Signed: Mar 1948.
Debut v Huddersfield Town, 15 Jan 1949, FA Cup.
Transferred to: Crewe Alexandra, Jul 1949.

		APPEARANCES					GOALS				
Season	Div	Lge	FA	LC	Oth	Total	Lge	FA	LC	Oth	Total
1948-49	2		1			1					
Total			1			1					

CAMPBELL, J.
Signed from: Pembroke Dock.
Debut v Gillingham, 29 Aug 1925.

		APPEARANCES					GOALS				
Season	Div	Lge	FA	LC	Oth	Total	Lge	FA	LC	Oth	Total
1925-26	3S	4				4	1				1
Total		4				4	1				1

CAMERON, J.
Born: Inverness.
Signed from: Heart of Midlothian.
Debut v Brentford, 25 Aug 1923.

		APPEARANCES					GOALS				
Season	Div	Lge	FA	LC	Oth	Total	Lge	FA	LC	Oth	Total
1923-24	3S	24	1			25					
Total		24	1			25					

CAMERON, Ken.
Born: Glasgow, 1905.
Signed from: Hull City.
Debut v Bristol City, 29 Aug 1936.
Transferred to: Rotherham United, Jul 1937 (free).

		APPEARANCES					GOALS				
Season	Div	Lge	FA	LC	Oth	Total	Lge	FA	LC	Oth	Total
1936-37	3S	8				8	1				1
Total		8				8	1				1

CAMERON, Robert
Born: Greenock, 23 Nov 1932.
Signed from: Port Glasgow, Jun 1950.
Debut v Coventry City, 13 Jan 1951.
Transferred to: Leeds United, Jul 1959.

		APPEARANCES					GOALS				
Season	Div	Lge	FA	LC	Oth	Total	Lge	FA	LC	Oth	Total
1950-51	2	2				2					
1951-52	2	5				5					
1952-53	3S	34	3			37	5	2			7
1953-54	3S	38	4			42	10				10
1954-55	3S	44	3			47	13				13
1955-56	3S	43	1			44	13				13
1956-57	3S	31	3			34	5	1			6
1957-58	3S	37	3			40	8				8
1958-59	3	22	2			24	5				5
Total		256	19			275	59	3			62

CANNON, Fred
Born: 8 Nov 1886.
Signed from: Hitchin, 1906.
Debut v Millwall, 29 Feb 1908, Southern League.
Transferred to: West Ham United, 1910.

		APPEARANCES					GOALS				
Season	Div	Lge	FA	LC	Oth	Total	Lge	FA	LC	Oth	Total
1907-08	SL	9			*1	10	6			1	7
1908-09	SL	18			*1	19	3				3
Total		29			2	29	9			1	10

CAPE, Jack
Born: Carlisle, 16 Nov 1911.
Signed from: Manchester United.
Debut v Brighton & Hove Albion, 28 Aug 1937.
Transferred to: Carlisle United, 1939.

		APPEARANCES					GOALS				
Season	Div	Lge	FA	LC	Oth	Total	Lge	FA	LC	Oth	Total
1937-38	3S	40	2			42	9	1			10
1938-39	3S	21	1			22	3				3
Total		61	3			64	12	1			13

CAREY, Peter
Born: Barking, 14 Apr 1933.
Signed from: Leyton Orient, Jul 1960.
Debut v Bournemouth, 20 Aug 1960.
Transferred to: Colchester United, Nov 1960.

		APPEARANCES					GOALS				
Season	Div	Lge	FA	LC	Oth	Total	Lge	FA	LC	Oth	Total
1960-61		15	1	1		17	1				1
Total		15	1	1		17	1				1

CARR, Bill
Born: Cambois.
Signed from: Derby County, Jul 1935.
Debut v Millwall, 31 Aug 1935.
Transferred to: Barrow, Jul 1937 (free).

		APPEARANCES					GOALS				
Season	Div	Lge	FA	LC	Oth	Total	Lge	FA	LC	Oth	Total
1935-36	3S	14				14					
1936-37	3S	14				14					
Total		28				28					

CHANDLER, Arthur
Born: London, 27 Nov 1895.
Signed from: Hampstead, 1920.
Debut v Crystal Palace, 1 Jan 1921.
Transferred to: Leicester City, 1923 (£3,000).

		APPEARANCES					GOALS				
Season	Div	Lge	FA	LC	Oth	Total	Lge	FA	LC	Oth	Total
1920-21	3	12	2			14	2	1			3
1921-22	3S	30	2			32	8				8
1922-23	3S	36	4			40	6	1			7
Total		78	8			86	16	2			18

CHANNING, Justin
Born: Reading, 19 Nov 1968.
Signed from: (apprentice), Aug 1986.
Debut v Luton Town, 1 Nov 1986.
Transferred to: Bristol Rovers, Jan 1993 (£275,000).

		APPEARANCES					GOALS				
Season	Div	Lge	FA	LC	Oth	Total	Lge	FA	LC	Oth	Total
1986-87	1	2				2					
1987-88	1	7/7		0/1	1	8/8	1				1
1988-89	1	9	1		3	13	1				1
1989-90	1	19/4		3		22/4	2				2
1990-91	1	3/2	1			4/2					
1991-92	1				1	1					
1992-93	Pr	2		1		3	1				1
Total		42/13	2	4/1	5	53/14	5				5

CHARLES, Jeremy
Born: Swansea, 26 Sep 1959.
Signed from: Swansea City, Nov 1983 (£80,000).
Debut v West Bromwich Albion, 10 Dec 1983 (sub).
Transferred to: Oxford United, Feb 1985 (£80,000).

		APPEARANCES					GOALS				
Season	Div	Lge	FA	LC	Oth	Total	Lge	FA	LC	Oth	Total
1983-84	1	10/2	1			11/2	5				5
1984-85	1			0/1	†1	0/2				1	1
Total		10/2	1	0/1	1	12	5			1	6

CHARLESWORTH, George
Born: Bristol, 29 Nov.
Signed from: Bristol Rovers.
Debut v Coventry City, 4 Sep 1926.
Transferred to: Crystal Palace, 1929.

		APPEARANCES					GOALS				
Season	Div	Lge	FA	LC	Oth	Total	Lge	FA	LC	Oth	Total
1926-27	3S	23				23	3				3
Total		23				23	3				3

CHARLTON, Bill
Born: South Stoneham, 1912.
Signed from: Wimbledon.
Debut v Bristol Rovers, 19 Nov 1936.
Transferred to: Barnet, 1938.

		APPEARANCES					GOALS				
Season	Div	Lge	FA	LC	Oth	Total	Lge	FA	LC	Oth	Total
1936-37	3S	16	1			17	8				8
1937-38	3S	4				4	2				2
Total		30	1			21	10				10

CHAPMAN, Reg
Born: Shepherd's Bush, 7 Sep 1921.
Debut v Ipswich Town, 12 Jan 1946 (League Cup).

		APPEARANCES					GOALS				
Season	Div	Lge	FA	LC	Oth	Total	Lge	FA	LC	Oth	Total
2nd WW					7	7				1	1
1946-47	3S	27	3			30	1				1
1947-48	3S	14				14	1				1
1949-50	2	13	1			14					
1950-51	2	16				16					
1951-52	2	15				15					
1952-53	3S	12				12					
Total		97	4		7	108	2			1	3

CHEETHAM, Tommy
Born: Newcastle upon Tyne, 11 Oct 1910.
Signed from: The Army (India).
Debut v Brighton & Hove Albion, 4 Sep 1935.
Transferred to: Brentford, Mar 1939 (£5,000).

		APPEARANCES					GOALS				
Season	Div	Lge	FA	LC	Oth	Total	Lge	FA	LC	Oth	Total
1935-36	3S	34	1			35	36	1			37
1936-37	3S	28	3			31	9	1			10
1937-38	3S	26	2			28	14	3			17
1938-39	3S	26	4			30	22	5			27
2nd WW			3		1	4	1				1
Total		117	10		1	128	82	10			92

CHESTER, A.
Signed from: Croydon Common.
Debut v Brighton & Hove Albion, 15 Nov 1919, Southern League.
Transferred to: Brentford.

		APPEARANCES					GOALS				
Season	Div	Lge	FA	LC	Oth	Total	Lge	FA	LC	Oth	Total
1919-20	SL	1				1					
Total		1				1					

CHIVERS, Gary
Born: Stockwell, 15 May 1960.
Signed from: Swansea City, Feb 1984 (free).
Debut v Partizan Belgrade, 7 Nov 1984, UEFA Cup.
Transferred to: Watford, Sep 1987 (free).

		APPEARANCES					GOALS				
Season	Div	Lge	FA	LC	Oth	Total	Lge	FA	LC	Oth	Total
1984-85	1	22/1	1	2	†1	26/1					
1985-86	1	13/1		1		14/1					
1986-87	1	23	1	3		27					
Total		58/2	2	6	1	67/2					

CHRISTIE, David
Born: Scotland.
Debut v Bristol Rovers, 1 Sep 1900, Southern League.

		APPEARANCES					GOALS				
Season	Div	Lge	FA	LC	Oth	Total	Lge	FA	LC	Oth	Total
1900-01	SL	8				8	1				1
1901-02	SL	2				2					
Total		10				10	1				1

CINI, Joe
Born: Malta.
Signed from: Floriana.
Debut v Swindon Town, 22 Aug 1959.
Transferred: Jul 1960.

		APPEARANCES					GOALS				
Season	Div	Lge	FA	LC	Oth	Total	Lge	FA	LC	Oth	Total
1959-60	3	7				7	1				1
Total		7				7	1				1

CLARKE, Charlie
Debut v Southend United, 25 Apr 1936.
Transferred to: Luton Town, 1938.

		APPEARANCES					GOALS				
Season	Div	Lge	FA	LC	Oth	Total	Lge	FA	LC	Oth	Total
1935-36	3S	1				1					
1936-37	3S	2				2					
1937-38	3S	3				3					
Total		6				6					

CLARK, Clive
Born: Leeds, 19 Dec 1940.
Signed from: Leeds United, Aug 1958.
Debut v Bournemouth, 6 Sep 1958.
Transferred to: West Bromwich Albion, Jan 1961. From: West Bromwich Albion, Jun 1969 (£30,000) To: Preston, Jun 1970 (£18,000).

		APPEARANCES					GOALS				
Season	Div	Lge	FA	LC	Oth	Total	Lge	FA	LC	Oth	Total
1958-59	3	19				19	1				1
1959-60	3	18	2			20					
1960-61	3	21	1	2		24	6				6
1969-70	2	7/1		2		9/1	1				1
Total		65/1	3	4		72/1	8				8

CLARK, Willie
Born: Larkhall, 25 Feb 1932.
Signed from: Petershill, Feb 1954.
Debut v Shrewsbury Town, 6 Feb 1954.

		APPEARANCES					GOALS				
Season	Div	Lge	FA	LC	Oth	Total	Lge	FA	LC	Oth	Total
1953-54	3S	18				18	6				6
1954-55	3S	39	1			40	15				15
1955-56	3S	38				38	11				11
Total		95	1			96	32				32

CLARKE, Colin
Born: Newry, 30 Oct 1962.
Signed from: Southampton, Mar 1989 (£750,000).
Debut v Newcastle United, 11 Mar 1989 (1 goal).
Transferred to: Portsmouth, Aug 1990 (£350,000).

		APPEARANCES					GOALS				
Season	Div	Lge	FA	LC	Oth	Total	Lge	FA	LC	Oth	Total
1988-89	1	12				12	5				5
1989-90	1	27/7	7	3		37/7	5	2	1		8
Total		39/7	7	3		49/7	10	2	1		13

CLARKE, George
Born: Bolsover, 24 Jul 1900.
Signed from: Crystal Palace, Jul 1933.
Debut v Brighton & Hove Albion, 26 Aug 1933 (2 goals).
Transferred to: Folkestone, 1934.

		APPEARANCES					GOALS				
Season	Div	Lge	FA	LC	Oth	Total	Lge	FA	LC	Oth	Total
1933-34	3S	15				15	6				6
Total		15				15	6				6

CLARKE, Frank
Born: Willenhall, 15 Jul 1942.
Signed from: Shrewsbury Town, Feb 1968 (£35,000).
Debut v Derby County, 17 Feb 1968.
Transferred to: Ipswich Town, Mar 1970 (£38,000).

		APPEARANCES					GOALS				
Season	Div	Lge	FA	LC	Oth	Total	Lge	FA	LC	Oth	Total
1967-68	2	13				13	3				3
1968-69	1	23	1	0/1		24/1	5		1		6
1969-70	2	31	3	3/1		37/1	9	2	4		15
Total		67	4	3/2		74/2	17	2	5		24

CLAYTON, H.
Debut v Plymouth Argyle, 17 Mar 1921.

		APPEARANCES					GOALS				
Season	Div	Lge	FA	LC	Oth	Total	Lge	FA	LC	Oth	Total
1920-21	3	3				3	1				1
1921-22	3S	3				3					
Total		6				6	1				1

CLAYTON, Lewis
Born: Barnsley, 7 Jun 1924.
Signed from: Barnsley, Aug 1950.
Debut v Coventry City, 9 Sep 1950.
Transferred to: Bournemouth, May 1955.

		APPEARANCES					GOALS				
Season	Div	Lge	FA	LC	Oth	Total	Lge	FA	LC	Oth	Total
1950-51	2	16				16	2				2
1951-52	2	22				22	1				1
1952-53	3S	25	1			26	1				1
1953-54	3S	28	1			29	1				1
Total		91	2			93	5				5

CLEMENT, Dave
Born: Battersea, 2 Feb 1948.
Signed from: (juniors), Jul 1965.
Debut v Scunthorpe United, 8 Apr 1967.
Transferred to: Bolton Wanderers, Jun 1979 (£170,000).

		APPEARANCES					GOALS				
Season	Div	Lge	FA	LC	Oth	Total	Lge	FA	LC	Oth	Total
1966-67	3	1				1					
1967-68	2	30	1	3		34					
1968-69	1	17/2	1	1		19/2	1				1
1969-70	2	32/1	4	5		41/1	5		1		6
1970-71	2	42	1	2		45	3				3
1971-72	2	42	2	4		48	3	1			4
1972-73	2	40	4	1		45	3	1			4
1973-74	1	38	4	3		45	1				1
1974-75	1	31	4	2		37		1			1
1975-76	1	40	2	4		46	2				2
1976-77	1	32/1	1	6	†6	45/1	2		2	1	5
1977-78	1	29	4	2		35					
1978-79	1	29	1	1		31	1				1
Total		403/4	29	34	6	472/4	21	3	3	1	28

CLIPSHAM
Signed from: Wandsworth, 1902.
Debut v Luton Town, 1 Nov 1902, FA Cup.

		APPEARANCES					GOALS				
Season	Div	Lge	FA	LC	Oth	Total	Lge	FA	LC	Oth	Total
1902-03	SL	2	1			3					
Total		2	1			3					

CLUTTERBUCK, H.J.
Born: Gloucester, Jun 1874.
Signed from: Small Heath, Aug 1899.
Debut v Tottenham Hotspur, 9 Sep 1899, Southern League.
Transferred to: Grimsby Town, 1901.

		APPEARANCES					GOALS				
Season	Div	Lge	FA	LC	Oth	Total	Lge	FA	LC	Oth	Total
1899-1900	SL	28	10			38					
1900-01	SL	28	4			32					
Total		56	14			70					

COCKBURN, William
Born: Willington.
Signed from: Liverpool.
Debut v Torquay United, 25 Aug 1928.
Transferred to: Swindon Town, 1930.

		APPEARANCES					GOALS				
Season	Div	Lge	FA	LC	Oth	Total	Lge	FA	LC	Oth	Total
1928-29	3S	35	1			36					
1929-30	3S	22	4			26					
Total		57	5			62					

COCKELL, David
Born: Ashford, Middlesex, 1 Feb 1939.
Signed from: Hounslow Town, Aug 1960.
Debut v Port Vale, 17 Oct 1960, League Cup.
Transferred to: Jul 1962.

		APPEARANCES					GOALS				
Season	Div	Lge	FA	LC	Oth	Total	Lge	FA	LC	Oth	Total
1960-61	3	8	1	1		10					
1961-62	3	1				1					
Total		9	1	1		11					

COGGINS, William
Born: Bristol, 16 Sep 1901.
Signed from: Leverton.
Debut v Millwall, 28 Dec 1935.
Transferred to: Bath City, 1936.

		APPEARANCES					GOALS				
Season	Div	Lge	FA	LC	Oth	Total	Lge	FA	LC	Oth	Total
1935-36	3S	6				6					
Total		6				6					

COLE, Jack
Born: Wales.
Debut v Bristol Rovers, 1 Sep 1900, Southern League.

		APPEARANCES					GOALS				
Season	Div	Lge	FA	LC	Oth	Total	Lge	FA	LC	Oth	Total
1900-01	SL	1				1					
Total		1				1					

COLEMAN
Debut v Croydon Common, 11 Sep 1915 (1 goal), London Combination.

		APPEARANCES					GOALS				
Season	Div	Lge	FA	LC	Oth	Total	Lge	FA	LC	Oth	Total
WW1		7				72				2	
Total		7				72				2	

COLGAN, Walter
Born: Castleford, 3 Apr 1937.
Signed from: Ashley Road FC, Jul 1954.
Debut v Southend United, 28 Dec 1957.
Transferred: Jul 1960.

		APPEARANCES					GOALS				
Season	Div	Lge	FA	LC	Oth	Total	Lge	FA	LC	Oth	Total
1957-58	3S	2				2					
1958-59	3	1				1					
Total		3				3					

COLLIER, John
Born: Dysart, 1 Feb 1897.
Signed from: Hull City.
Debut v Crystal Palace, 28 Aug 1926.
Transferred to: York City, 1928.

		APPEARANCES					GOALS				
Season	Div	Lge	FA	LC	Oth	Total	Lge	FA	LC	Oth	Total
1926-27	3S	20				20					
1927-28	3S	16	1			17	1				1
Total		36	1			37	1				1

COLLINS, John
Born: Chiswick, 10 Aug 1942.
Signed from: (juniors), Aug 1959.
Debut v Barnsley, 30 Apr 1960.
Transferred to: Oldham Athletic, Oct 1966.

		APPEARANCES					GOALS				
Season	Div	Lge	FA	LC	Oth	Total	Lge	FA	LC	Oth	Total
1959-60	3	2				2					
1960-61	3										
1961-62	3	25	4	1		30	6	3			9
1962-63	3	33	2	1		36	5	1	1		7
1963-64	3	35	1			36	9				9
1964-65	3	40	3	2		45	8	1	2		11
1965-66	3	36	5	2		43	18	1	1		20
1966-67	3	1				1					
Total		172	15	6		193	46	6	4		56

COLLINS, James
Born: London, 30 Jan 1911.
Signed from: Tooting & Mitcham.
Debut v Luton Town, 7 Nov 1931.
Transferred to: Tunbridge Wells Rangers, 1933.

		APPEARANCES					GOALS				
Season	Div	Lge	FA	LC	Oth	Total	Lge	FA	LC	Oth	Total
1931-32	3S	11				11	2				2
1932-33	3S	11				11	2				2
Total		22				22	4				4

COLLINS, Harry
Born: Wynlaton, County Durham, 1876.
Signed from: Burnley, 1900.
Debut v Watford, 7 Sep 1901, Southern League.
Transferred to: Everton, 1905.

		APPEARANCES					GOALS				
Season	Div	Lge	FA	LC	Oth	Total	Lge	FA	LC	Oth	Total
1901-02	SL	30	3			33					
1902-03	SL	30	1			31					
1903-04	SL	33	2			35					
1904-05	SL	22				22					
Total		115	6			121					

COLVIN, Robert
Born: Dumfries, 5 Dec 1878.
Signed from: Luton Town, 1901.
Debut v Wellingborough, 3 Sep 1902, Southern League.
Transferred to: Swindon Town, 1903.

		APPEARANCES					GOALS				
Season	Div	Lge	FA	LC	Oth	Total	Lge	FA	LC	Oth	Total
1902-03	SL	11				11	1				1
Total		11				11	1				1

CONEY, Dean
Born: Dagenham, 18 Sep 1963.
Signed from: Fulham, Jun 1987 (£50,000).
Debut v West Ham United, 15 Aug 1987.
Transferred to: Norwich City, Mar 1989.

		APPEARANCES					GOALS				
Season	Div	Lge	FA	LC	Oth	Total	Lge	FA	LC	Oth	Total
1987-88	1	25/7	0/2	2		27/9	7				7
1988-89	1	11/5	3	3/1	3	20/6				2	2
Total		36/12	3/2	5/1	3	47/15	7			2	9

CONGREAVE
Debut v Crystal Palace, 14 Sep 1918, London Combination.

		APPEARANCES					GOALS				
Season	Div	Lge	FA	LC	Oth	Total	Lge	FA	LC	Oth	Total
WW1		12				12	4				4
Total		12				12	4				4

CONNOR, Robert
Born: Newcastle upon Tyne, 1913.
Debut v Brighton & Hove Albion, 26 Jan 1935.

		APPEARANCES					GOALS				
Season	Div	Lge	FA	LC	Oth	Total	Lge	FA	LC	Oth	Total
1934-35	3S	5				5					
Total		5				5					

COOPER, Gary
Born: London, 20 Nov 1965.
Signed from: (apprentice).
Debut v KR Reykjavik, 2 Oct 1984, UEFA Cup (sub).
Transferred to: Torquay United.

		APPEARANCES					GOALS				
Season	Div	Lge	FA	LC	Oth	Total	Lge	FA	LC	Oth	Total
1984-85	1	1		1/1	†0/1	2/2					
Total		1		1/1	0/1	2/2					

CORBETT, Walter
Born: Wellington, 26 Nov 1880.
Signed from: Small Heath, Sep 1907 (loan)
Debut v New Brompton, 7 Sep 1907.

		APPEARANCES					GOALS				
Season	Div	Lge	FA	LC	Oth	Total	Lge	FA	LC	Oth	Total
1907-08	SL	1				1					
Total		1				1					

CORE
Debut v Clapton Orient, 21 Sep 1918, London Combination.

		APPEARANCES					GOALS				
Season	Div	Lge	FA	LC	Oth	Total	Lge	FA	LC	Oth	Total
WW1		3				3					
Total		3				3					

COTTAM
Debut v Crystal Palace, 25 Dec 1941, League South.

		APPEARANCES					GOALS				
Season	Div	Lge	FA	LC	Oth	Total	Lge	FA	LC	Oth	Total
2nd WW		1				1					
Total		1				1					

COUSINS
Debut v Crystal Palace, 17 Nov 1917, London Combination.

		APPEARANCES					GOALS				
Season	Div	Lge	FA	LC	Oth	Total	Lge	FA	LC	Oth	Total
WW1		3				3					
Total		3				3					

COWAN, James
Born: Jamestown, 17 Oct 1868.
Signed from: Aston Villa, 1906.
Debut v Northampton Town, 16 Dec 1905 (1 goal), Southern League.

		APPEARANCES					GOALS				
Season	Div	Lge	FA	LC	Oth	Total	Lge	FA	LC	Oth	Total
1905-06	SL	1				1	1				1
Total		1				1	1				1

COWARD, William
Born: Windsor.
Signed from: Windsor & Eton.
Debut v Torquay United, 31 Mar 1928 (1 goal).

		APPEARANCES					GOALS				
Season	Div	Lge	FA	LC	Oth	Total	Lge	FA	LC	Oth	Total
1927-28	3S	7				7	2				2
1928-29	3S	39	1			40	7				7
1929-30	3S	25	4			29	3	1			4
1930-31	3S	29	3			32	5	1			6
1931-32	3S	26	4			30	5	2			7
Total		126	12			138	22	4			26

COWIE, Andrew
Born: Lochee, Fifeshire, 1879.
Signed from: Manchester City, Aug 1899.
Debut v Tottenham Hotspur, 9 Sep 1899, Southern League.
Transferred to: Woolwich Arsenal, 1900.

		APPEARANCES					GOALS				
Season	Div	Lge	FA	LC	Oth	Total	Lge	FA	LC	Oth	Total
1899-1900	SL	11	5			16	2				2
Total		11	5			16	2				2

CRAWFORD, Gavan
Born: Kilmarnock, 1872.
Signed from: Millwall, Aug 1899.
Debut v Tottenham Hotspur, 9 Sep 1899, Southern League.

		APPEARANCES					GOALS				
Season	Div	Lge	FA	LC	Oth	Total	Lge	FA	LC	Oth	Total
1899-1900	SL	24	9			33	1				1
Total		24	9			33	1				1

CRAWFORD, John Forsyth
Born: Jarrow, 26 Sep 1896.
Signed from: Chelsea, May 1934.
Debut v Swindon Town, 25 Aug 1934.
Retired 1937.

		APPEARANCES					GOALS				
Season	Div	Lge	FA	LC	Oth	Total	Lge	FA	LC	Oth	Total
1934-35	3S	26	2			28	8	1			9
1935-36	3S	24				24	7				7
1936-37	3S	3				3					
Total		53	2			55	15	1			16

CRIBB, Stanley
Born: Gosport, 26 Sep 1896.
Signed from: West Ham United.
Debut v Brentford, 29 Aug 1931.
Transferred to: Cardiff City.

		APPEARANCES					GOALS				
Season	Div	Lge	FA	LC	Oth	Total	Lge	FA	LC	Oth	Total
1931-32	3S	28	4			32	12	6			18
Total		28	4			32	12	6			18

CRICKSON, Gerry
Born: Dover, 21 Sep 1934.
Signed from: (juniors), Sep 1951.
Debut v Millwall, 6 Apr 1953.

		APPEARANCES					GOALS				
Season	Div	Lge	FA	LC	Oth	Total	Lge	FA	LC	Oth	Total
1952-53	3S	2				2					
1953-54	3S										
1954-55	3S										
1955-56	3S	3	1			4					
Total		5	1			6					

CROMPTON, Norman
Born: Farnworth, 1905.
Signed from: Oldham Athletic.
Debut v Norwich City, 3 May 1928.
Transferred to: Horwich RMI.

		APPEARANCES					GOALS				
Season	Div	Lge	FA	LC	Oth	Total	Lge	FA	LC	Oth	Total
1927-28	3S	1				1					
Total		1				1					

CROSS, John
Born: 1879.
Signed from: Third Lanark, 1904.
Debut v Plymouth Argyle, 3 Sep 1904.

		APPEARANCES					GOALS				
Season	Div	Lge	FA	LC	Oth	Total	Lge	FA	LC	Oth	Total
1904-05	SL	23	1			24					
Total		23	1			24					

CROSS, William
Signed from: Third Lanark, 1903.
Debut v Brentford, 5 Sep 1903, Southern League.
Transferred to: Brentford, 1905.

		APPEARANCES					GOALS				
Season	Div	Lge	FA	LC	Oth	Total	Lge	FA	LC	Oth	Total
1903-04	SL	13				13	2				2
1904-05	SL	19	1			20	2				2
Total		32	1			33	4				4

CUNNINGHAM, Joseph
Born: Lochie.
Signed from: Newport County, 1926.
Debut v Northampton Town, 30 Oct 1926.
Transferred to: Walsall, 1932.

		APPEARANCES					GOALS				
Season	Div	Lge	FA	LC	Oth	Total	Lge	FA	LC	Oth	Total
1926-27	3S	19				19	3				3
1927-28	3S	36	1			37					
1928-29	3S	38				38					
1929-30	3S	36	3			39					
1930-31	3S	31	2			33					
1931-32	3S	8				8					
Total		168	6			174	3				3

CUNNINGHAM, Tommy
Born: London, 7 Dec 1955.
Signed from: Chelsea, May 1975 (free).
Debut v Arsenal, 2 Oct 1976.
Transferred to: Wimbledon, Mar 1979 (£50,000).

		APPEARANCES					GOALS				
Season	Div	Lge	FA	LC	Oth	Total	Lge	FA	LC	Oth	Total
1976-77	1	3/2				3/2					
1977-78	1	15/1	2			17/1	2				2
1978-79	1	9	1	1/1		11/1					
Total		27/3	3	1/1		31/4	2				2

CURRIE, Tony
Born: Edgware, 1 Jan 1950.
Signed from: Leeds United, Aug 1979 (£400,000).
Debut v Bradford City, 5 Sep 1979, League Cup.
Transferred to: Vancouver Whitecaps, May 1983 (£40,000).

		APPEARANCES					GOALS				
Season	Div	Lge	FA	LC	Oth	Total	Lge	FA	LC	Oth	Total
1979-80	2	27/1	1	4		32/1	3		1		4
1980-81	2	31	1	3		35	1				1
1981-82	2	20	7	1		28	1				1
1982-83	2	1/1				1/1					
Total		79/2	9	8		96/2	5		1		6

DALE, G.
Debut v Fulham, 30 Oct 1915, London Combination.

		APPEARANCES					GOALS				
Season	Div	Lge	FA	LC	Oth	Total	Lge	FA	LC	Oth	Total
WW1		107			3	110	21			1	22
Total		107			3	110	21			1	22

DAND, Robert
Born: Ilford.
Signed from: Reading.
Debut v Norwich City, 25 Dec 1924.

		APPEARANCES					GOALS				
Season	Div	Lge	FA	LC	Oth	Total	Lge	FA	LC	Oth	Total
1924-25	3S	1				1					
Total		1				1					

DANIELS, Arthur
Born: Manchester.
Signed from: Watford.
Debut v Thames, 30 Aug 1930.

		APPEARANCES					GOALS				
Season	Div	Lge	FA	LC	Oth	Total	Lge	FA	LC	Oth	Total
1930-31	3S	14				14	3				3
Total		14				14	3				3

DANIELS, Harry
Born: Kensington, 25 Jun 1920.
Signed from: (local club).
Debut v Leyton Orient, 22 Nov 1947, League South.
Transferred to: Brighton & Hove Albion, Aug 1948.

		APPEARANCES					GOALS				
Season	Div	Lge	FA	LC	Oth	Total	Lge	FA	LC	Oth	Total
2nd WW		48	10		22	80	9	1		4	14
1946-47	3S	7	1			8					
1947-48	3S	7	4			11					
Total		62	15		22	99	9	1		4	14

DARRAGON, W.
Debut v Southampton, 9 Dec 1944, League South.

		APPEARANCES					GOALS				
Season	Div	Lge	FA	LC	Oth	Total	Lge	FA	LC	Oth	Total
2nd WW		12			1	13	2				2
Total		12			1	13	2				2

DAVIDSON, Peter
Born: Newcastle upon Tyne, 31 Oct 1956.
Signed from: Berwick Rangers, Jul 1979 (£40,000).
Debut v Leicester City, 25 Aug 1979 (sub).
Transferred to: Berwick Rangers, Dec 1979 (£35,000).

		APPEARANCES					GOALS				
Season	Div	Lge	FA	LC	Oth	Total	Lge	FA	LC	Oth	Total
1979-80	2	0/1				0/1					
Total		0/1				0/1					

DAVIES, Edmund
Born: Oswestry, 5 Jun 1927.
Signed from: Arsenal, Apr 1950.
Debut v Brentford, 27 Jan 1951 (1 goal).
Transferred to: Crewe Alexandra, Jul 1951.

		APPEARANCES					GOALS				
Season	Div	Lge	FA	LC	Oth	Total	Lge	FA	LC	Oth	Total
1950-51		1				1	1				1
Total		1				1	1				1

DAVIS, A.
Born: Birmingham.
Signed from: Aston Villa, 1922.
Debut v Norwich City, 28 Aug 1922 (1 goal).
Transferred to: Notts County, 1924.

		APPEARANCES					GOALS				
Season	Div	Lge	FA	LC	Oth	Total	Lge	FA	LC	Oth	Total
1922-23	3S	35	4			39	13				13
1923-24	3S	27	1			28	8	1			9
Total		62	5			67	21	1			22

DAWES, Ian
Born: Croydon, 22 Feb 1963.
Signed from: (apprentice), Dec 1980.
Debut v Rotherham United, 27 Mar 1982..
Transferred to: Millwall, Aug 1988 (£150,000).

		APPEARANCES					GOALS				
Season	Div	Lge	FA	LC	Oth	Total	Lge	FA	LC	Oth	Total
1981-82	2	5				5					
1982-83	2	42	1	2		45					
1983-84	1	42	1	3		46	2				2
1984-85	1	42	1	8	4 (a)	55					
1985-86	1	42	1	9		52	1		1		2
1986-87	1	23		3		26					
1987-88	1	33	4	3	1	41					
Total		229	8	28	5	270	3		1		4

DAWSON, Alex
Born: Glasgow, 21 Oct 1933.
Signed from: Gourock Juniors, Feb 1957.
Debut v Brighton & Hove Albion, 13 Apr 1957.
Transferred to: Sittingbourne, Jul 1959.

		APPEARANCES					GOALS				
Season	Div	Lge	FA	LC	Oth	Total	Lge	FA	LC	Oth	Total
1956-57	3S	1				1					
1957-58	3S	33	3			36	2	1			3
1958-59	3	25	2			27	3	1			4
Total		59	5			64	5	2			7

DAWSON, George
Born: Glasgow, 13 Sep 1930.
Signed from: Motherwell, May 1955.
Debut v Colchester United, 10 Mar 1956.

		APPEARANCES					GOALS				
Season	Div	Lge	FA	LC	Oth	Total	Lge	FA	LC	Oth	Total
1955-56	3S	1				1					
Total		1				1					

DAY
Debut v Portsmouth, 8 Mar 1913, Southern League.

		APPEARANCES					GOALS				
Season	Div	Lge	FA	LC	Oth	Total	Lge	FA	LC	Oth	Total
1912-13	SL	4				4					
Total		4				4					

DE BUSSER, E.
Signed from: Belgian Army, Aug 1943.
Debut v Chelsea, 28 Aug 1943 (1 goal), League South.

		APPEARANCES					GOALS				
Season	Div	Lge	FA	LC	Oth	Total	Lge	FA	LC	Oth	Total
2nd WW		3				3	1				1
Total		3				3	1				1

DE LISLE.
Signed from: Southampton, Apr 1944 (loan).
Debut v Southampton, 1 Apr 1944 (1 goal), League South.

		APPEARANCES					GOALS				
Season	Div	Lge	FA	LC	Oth	Total	Lge	FA	LC	Oth	Total
2nd WW		1				1	1				1
Total		1				1	1				1

DEAN, Jobey
Born: Chesterfield, 25 Nov 1934.
Signed from: Thoresby Colliery, Nov 1952.
Debut v Brentford, 30 Aug 1955.
Transferred to: Bradford, Dec 1957.

		APPEARANCES					GOALS				
Season	Div	Lge	FA	LC	Oth	Total	Lge	FA	LC	Oth	Total
1955-56	3S	12	1			13					
1956-57	3S	4				4					
Total		16	1			17					

DELANEY, L.
Debut v Aldershot, 6 Apr 1942, War Cup.

		APPEARANCES					GOALS				
Season	Div	Lge	FA	LC	Oth	Total	Lge	FA	LC	Oth	Total
2nd WW					1	1					
Total					1	1					

DELVE, John
Born: London, 27 Sep 1953.
Signed from: (apprentice), Jul 1971.
Debut v Luton Town, 9 Dec 1972.
Transferred to: Plymouth Argyle, Jul 1974 (£25,000).

		APPEARANCES					GOALS				
Season	Div	Lge	FA	LC	Oth	Total	Lge	FA	LC	Oth	Total
1972-73	2	6/3	1			7/3					
1973-74	1	3/3		0/1		3/4					
Total		9/6	1	0/1		10/7					

DENNIS, Mark
Born: Streatham, 2 May 1961.
Signed from: Southampton, May 1987 (£50,000).
Debut v West Ham United, 15 Aug 1987.
Transferred to: Crystal Palace, Aug 1989 (£50,000).

		APPEARANCES					GOALS				
Season	Div	Lge	FA	LC	Oth	Total	Lge	FA	LC	Oth	Total
1987-88	1	10/1	1		1	12/1					
1988-89	1	16/1		2	3	21/1					
Total		26/2	1	2	4	33/2					

DENOON, J.
Debut v West Ham United, 13 Jan 1917, London Combination.

		APPEARANCES					GOALS				
Season	Div	Lge	FA	LC	Oth	Total	Lge	FA	LC	Oth	Total
WW1		86			3	89					
Total		86			3	89					

DEVINE, Joe
Born: Motherwell, 8 Aug 1905.
Signed from: Sunderland.
Debut v Brighton & Hove Albion, 26 Aug 1933.
Transferred to: Birmingham, Jan 1935.

		APPEARANCES					GOALS				
Season	Div	Lge	FA	LC	Oth	Total	Lge	FA	LC	Oth	Total
1933-34	3S	37	4			41	8				8
1934-35	3S	20	2			22	1	1			2
Total		57	6			63	9	1			10

DEVINE, John
Signed from: Aberdeen.
Debut v Reading, 27 Aug 1938.

		APPEARANCES					GOALS				
Season	Div	Lge	FA	LC	Oth	Total	Lge	FA	LC	Oth	Total
1938-39	3S	7				7	3				3
2nd WW		2				2					
Total		9				9	3				3

DINE, Joseph.
Born: King's Lynn, 12 Apr 1886.
Signed from: King's Lynn.
Debut v West Ham United, 16 Apr 1910, Southern League.
Transferred to: Ilford.

		APPEARANCES					GOALS				
Season	Div	Lge	FA	LC	Oth	Total	Lge	FA	LC	Oth	Total
1909-10	SL	1				1					
Total		1				1					

DOBINSON, Harold
Born: Darlington, 2 Mar 1898.
Signed from: Burnley.
Debut v Northampton Town, 20 Oct 1923.

		APPEARANCES					GOALS				
Season	Div	Lge	FA	LC	Oth	Total	Lge	FA	LC	Oth	Total
1923-24	3S	2				2					
Total		2				2					

DODD
Debut v Crystal Palace, 14 Sep 1918, London Combination.

		APPEARANCES					GOALS				
Season	Div	Lge	FA	LC	Oth	Total	Lge	FA	LC	Oth	Total
WW1		1				1					
Total		1				1					

DOLDING, D.
Debut v Clapton Orient, 11 Sep 1943, League South.

		APPEARANCES					GOALS				
Season	Div	Lge	FA	LC	Oth	Total	Lge	FA	LC	Oth	Total
2nd WW		1				1					
Total		1				1					

DONALD, David
Born: Coatbridge, 29 Dec 1878.
Signed from: Watford, 1914.
Debut v Southampton, 12 Sep 1914, Southern League.
Transferred to: Hamilton, 1920.

		APPEARANCES					GOALS				
Season	Div	Lge	FA	LC	Oth	Total	Lge	FA	LC	Oth	Total
1914-15	SL	35	3			38	4				4
1stWW		18				18	2				2
1919-20	SL	40	1			41	6				6
1920-21	3	22				22					
Total		115	4			119	12				12

DOWNING
Debut v Fulham, 2 March 1918, London Combination.

		APPEARANCES					GOALS				
Season	Div	Lge	FA	LC	Oth	Total	Lge	FA	LC	Oth	Total
WW1		13			3	16	1				1
Total		13			3	16	1				1

DOWNING, Sam
Born: Willesden Green, 19 Jan 1885.
Signed from: West Hampstead, 4 Apr 1903
Debut v Swindon Town, 7 Nov 1903 (1 goal), Southern League.

		APPEARANCES					GOALS				
Season	Div	Lge	FA	LC	Oth	Total	Lge	FA	LC	Oth	Total
1900-01	SL	18	2			20	9	1			10
1903-04	SL	20				20					
1904-05	SL	15				15					
1905-06	SL	28	1			29	2				2
1906-07	SL	37	2			39	1				1
1907-08	SL	30	2		*1	33	4				4
1908-09	SL	31	2		*1	34	6				6
Total		179	9		2	190	22	1			23

DOYLE, Maurice
Born: Ellesmere Port, 17 Oct 1969.
Signed from: Crewe Alexandra, April 1989 (£40,000).
Debut v Ipswich Town, 9 Feb 1993.

		APPEARANCES					GOALS				
Season	Div	Lge	FA	LC	Oth	Total	Lge	FA	LC	Oth	Total
1992-93	Pr	5				5					
Total		5				5					

DRABBLE, F.
Debut v Bournemouth, 1 Mar 1924.

		APPEARANCES					GOALS				
Season	Div	Lge	FA	LC	Oth	Total	Lge	FA	LC	Oth	Total
1923-24	3S	2				2					
Total		2				2					

DRAKE, Alonzo
Born: Rotherham, 16 Apr 1884.
Signed from: Small Heath, 1908.
Debut v West Ham United, 1 Sep 1908, Southern League.
Transferred to: Huddersfield Town, 1910.

		APPEARANCES					GOALS				
Season	Div	Lge	FA	LC	Oth	Total	Lge	FA	LC	Oth	Total
1908-09	SL	19	1			20	5				5
Total		19	1			20	5				5

DRAPER, W.
Debut v Millwall, 4 Sep 1915, London Combination.

		APPEARANCES					GOALS				
Season	Div	Lge	FA	LC	Oth	Total	Lge	FA	LC	Oth	Total
WW1		97			4	101	8				8
Total		97			4	101	8				8

DREW, W.
Debut v Charlton Athletic, 18 Sep 1926.

		APPEARANCES					GOALS				
Season	Div	Lge	FA	LC	Oth	Total	Lge	FA	LC	Oth	Total
1926-27	3S	1				1					
Total		1				1					

DRINKWATER, Ray
Born: Jarrow, 18 May 1931.
Signed from: Portsmouth, February 1958.
Debut v Coventry City, 15 Mar 1938.

		APPEARANCES					GOALS				
Season	Div	Lge	FA	LC	Oth	Total	Lge	FA	LC	Oth	Total
1957-58	3S	11				11					
1958-59	3	43	2			45					
1959-60	3	27	1			28					
1960-61	3	46	2	1		49					
1961-62	3	45	4	2		51					
1962-63	3	27	3			30					
Total		199	12	3		214					

DUDLEY, Reg
Born: Hemel Hempstead, 3 Feb 1915.
Signed from: Millwall, Dec 1946.
Debut v Port Vale, 7 Dec 1946.
Transferred to: Watford, Jul 1950.

		APPEARANCES					GOALS				
Season	Div	Lge	FA	LC	Oth	Total	Lge	FA	LC	Oth	Total
1946-47	3S	26	4			30					
1947-48	3S	17				17					
1948-49	2	2				2					
1949-50	2	13				13					
Total		58	4			62					

DUFF, Harry
Signed from: Manchester City.
Debut v Watford, 7 Sep 1908, Southern League.

		APPEARANCES					GOALS				
Season	Div	Lge	FA	LC	Oth	Total	Lge	FA	LC	Oth	Total
1908-09	SL	20	2			22					
Total		20	2			22					

DUFFIELD
Debut v Brentford, 9 Feb 1918, London Combination.

		APPEARANCES					GOALS				
Season	Div	Lge	FA	LC	Oth	Total	Lge	FA	LC	Oth	Total
WW1		2			2	4					
Total		2			2	4					

DUFFIELD, Martin
Born: Park Royal, 28 Feb 1964.
Signed from: (apprentice), Jan 1982.
Debut v Grimsby Town, 14 May 1983 (sub).

		APPEARANCES					GOALS				
Season	Div	Lge	FA	LC	Oth	Total	Lge	FA	LC	Oth	Total
1882-83	2	0/1				0/1					
Total		0/1				0/1					

DUGDALE, Jimmy
Born: Liverpool, 15 Jan 1932.
Signed from: Aston Villa, Oct 1962.
Debut v Hull City, 27 Oct 1962.

		APPEARANCES					GOALS				
Season	Div	Lge	FA	LC	Oth	Total	Lge	FA	LC	Oth	Total
1962-63	3	10	3			13					
Total		10	3			13					

DUGGAN, Ted
Born: London, 27 Jul 1922.
Signed from: Luton Town, Feb 1949.
Debut v Grimsby Town, 5 Feb 1949.

		APPEARANCES					GOALS				
Season	Div	Lge	FA	LC	Oth	Total	Lge	FA	LC	Oth	Total
1948-49	2	15				15	2				2
1949-50	2	20				20	2				2
1950-51	2	12	1			13	1				1
Total		47	1			48	5				5

DUMSDAY, J.

		APPEARANCES					GOALS				
Season	Div	Lge	FA	LC	Oth	Total	Lge	FA	LC	Oth	Total
2nd WW		1				1					
Total		1				1					

DURRANT, Fred
Born: Dover, 19 Jun 1921.
Signed from: Brentford, Sep 1946.
Debut v Torquay United, 28 Sep 1946.
Transferred to: Exeter City, Feb 1949.

		APPEARANCES					GOALS				
Season	Div	Lge	FA	LC	Oth	Total	Lge	FA	LC	Oth	Total
1946-47	3S	22				22	14				14
1947-48	3S	27				27	12				12
1948-49	2	2	2			4					
Total		51	2			53	26				26

DURSTON, J.
Debut v Luton Town, 2 Sept 1916, London Combination.

		APPEARANCES					GOALS				
Season	Div	Lge	FA	LC	Oth	Total	Lge	FA	LC	Oth	Total
WW1		13				13					
Total		13				13					

DUTHIE, John
Born: Aberdeen, 7 Jan 1903.
Signed from: Norwich City.
Debut v Crystal Palace, 22 Oct 1927.
Transferred to: York City, 1928.

		APPEARANCES					GOALS				
Season	Div	Lge	FA	LC	Oth	Total	Lge	FA	LC	Oth	Total
1927-28	3S	11				11					
Total		11				11					

DUTTON, Tom
Born: Southport, 7 Dec 1906.
Signed from: Leicester City.
Debut v Swindon Town, 25 Aug 1934.
Transferred to: Doncaster Rovers, Jun 1935.

		APPEARANCES					GOALS				
Season	Div	Lge	FA	LC	Oth	Total	Lge	FA	LC	Oth	Total
1934-35	3S	23	1			24	6				6
Total		23	1			24	6				6

EASTOE, Peter
Born: Tamworth, 2 Aug 1953.
Signed from: Swindon Town, Mar 1976 (£90,000).
Debut v Manchester City, 16 Oct 1976 (sub).
Transferred to: Everton, Mar 1979, (Exchange M.Walsh).

		APPEARANCES					GOALS				
Season	Div	Lge	FA	LC	Oth	Total	Lge	FA	LC	Oth	Total
1976-77	1	24/3	2	2/1	†1/1	29/5	6		1		7
1977-78	1	19		2		21	6		1		7
1978-79	1	26	1	3		30	3		3		6
Total		69/3	3	7/1	1/1	80/5	15		5		20

EATON, Frank
Born: Stockport.
Signed from: Reading, Jul 1933.
Debut v Brighton & Hove Albion, 26 Aug 1933.

		APPEARANCES					GOALS				
Season	Div	Lge	FA	LC	Oth	Total	Lge	FA	LC	Oth	Total
1933-34	3S	15	2			17	2				2
Total		15	2			17	2				2

EDGLEY, Harold
Born: Crewe, 1890.
Signed from: Aston Villa, 1921.
Debut v Swindon Town, 27 Aug 1921.
Transferred to: Stockport County, 1923.

		APPEARANCES					GOALS				
Season	Div	Lge	FA	LC	Oth	Total	Lge	FA	LC	Oth	Total
1921-22	3S	36	2			38	5				5
1922-23	3S	33	4			37	1				1
Total		69	6			75	6				6

EDWARDS, Albert
Signed from: Swindon Town, 1902.
Debut v Northampton Town, 29 Nov 1902, Southern League.

		APPEARANCES					GOALS				
Season	Div	Lge	FA	LC	Oth	Total	Lge	FA	LC	Oth	Total
1902-03	SL	4				4					
1903-04	SL	3				3					
1904-05	SL	7				7	1				1
1905-06	SL	3				3					
Total		17				17	1				1

EDWARDS, E.

		APPEARANCES					GOALS				
Season	Div	Lge	FA	LC	Oth	Total	Lge	FA	LC	Oth	Total
2nd WW		3				3					
Total		3				3					

EDWARDS, John
Born: 1875.
Signed from: Grays United, 1901, Southern League.
Debut v Watford, 7 Sep 1901.

		APPEARANCES					GOALS				
Season	Div	Lge	FA	LC	Oth	Total	Lge	FA	LC	Oth	Total
1901-02	SL	10				10	1				1
1902-03	SL	18	1			19	1				1
Total		28	1			29	2				2

EDWARDS, J.
Debut v Bournemouth, 2 Apr 1926.

		APPEARANCES					GOALS				
Season	Div	Lge	FA	LC	Oth	Total	Lge	FA	LC	Oth	Total
1925-26	3S	3				3					
Total		3				3					

EDWARDS, R.
Debut v Brentford, 11 Apr 1942, War Cup.

		APPEARANCES					GOALS				
Season	Div	Lge	FA	LC	Oth	Total	Lge	FA	LC	Oth	Total
2nd WW					1	1					
Total					1	1					

EGGLETON, Jimmy
Born: Southall, 1897.
Signed from: Watford, Oct 1926.
Debut v Watford, 27 Dec 1926. (Became club trainer)

		APPEARANCES					GOALS				
Season	Div	Lge	FA	LC	Oth	Total	Lge	FA	LC	Oth	Total
1926-27	3S	12				12					
1927-28	3S	26	1			27					
1928-29	3S	4				4					
Total		42	1			43					

ELSEY, Karl
Born: Swansea, 20 Nov 1958.
Signed from: Pembroke Borough, Jan 1979.
Debut v West Bromwich Albion, 24 Mar 1979.
Transferred to: Newport County, Jul 1980.

		APPEARANCES					GOALS				
Season	Div	Lge	FA	LC	Oth	Total	Lge	FA	LC	Oth	Total
1978-79	1	2/1				2/1					
1979-80	2	4				4					
Total		6/1				6/1					

EMBLETON, S.
Debut v Brentford, 7 Mar 1931.

		APPEARANCES					GOALS				
Season	Div	Lge	FA	LC	Oth	Total	Lge	FA	LC	Oth	Total
1930-31	3S	2				2					
Total		2				2					

EMMERSON, George
Born: Bishop Auckland, 15 May 1906.
Signed from: Cardiff City, Jul 1933 (exchange E.Marcroft).
Debut v Brighton & Hove Albion, 26 Aug 1933.
Transferred to: Rochdale, 1935.

		APPEARANCES					GOALS				
Season	Div	Lge	FA	LC	Oth	Total	Lge	FA	LC	Oth	Total
1933-34	3S	37	4			41	10	2			12
1934-35	3S	15	1			16	3	1			4
Total		52	5			57	13	3			16

EVANS, Bernard
Born: Chester, 4 Jan 1937.
Signed from: Wrexham, Oct 1960.
Debut v Shrewsbury Town, 19 Nov 1960.
Transferred to: Oxford United, Dec 1962.

		APPEARANCES					GOALS				
Season	Div	Lge	FA	LC	Oth	Total	Lge	FA	LC	Oth	Total
1960-61	3	27				27	16				16
1961-62	3	43	4	1		48	18	4			22
1962-63	3	8		1		9	1				1
Total		78	4	2		84	35	4			39

EVANS, C.
Born: Luton.
Signed: Jan 1929.
Debut v Southend United, 1 Feb 1930.

		APPEARANCES					GOALS				
Season	Div	Lge	FA	LC	Oth	Total	Lge	FA	LC	Oth	Total
1929-30	3S	1				1					
Total		1				1					

EVANS, Ian
Born: Egham, 30 Jan 1952.
Signed from: (apprentice), Jan 1970.
Debut v Sheffield Wednesday, 6 Apr 1971.
Transferred to: Crystal Palace, Sep 1974 (£30,000).

		APPEARANCES					GOALS				
Season	Div	Lge	FA	LC	Oth	Total	Lge	FA	LC	Oth	Total
1970-71	2	8				8					
1971-72	2	8		2		10	1				1
1972-73	2	18		1		19	1				1
1973-74	1	5				5					
Total		39		3		42	2				2

EVANS, J.Lloyd
Debut v Millwall, 25 Feb 1905, Southern League.
Transferred to: Brentford, 1907.

		APPEARANCES					GOALS				
Season	Div	Lge	FA	LC	Oth	Total	Lge	FA	LC	Oth	Total
1904-05	SL	1				1					
Total		1				1					

EVANS, Roger
Born: Bangor, 17 Nov 1879.
Signed from: Ilford, 1901.
Debut v Bristol Rovers, 15 Mar 1902, Southern League.
Transferred to: Clapton Orient, 1902.

		APPEARANCES					GOALS				
Season	Div	Lge	FA	LC	Oth	Total	Lge	FA	LC	Oth	Total
1901-02	SL	1				1					
Total		1				1					

EVANS, W.
Born: Llanglos.
Signed from: Southend United.
Debut v Swansea Town, 20 Sep 1924.

		APPEARANCES					GOALS				
Season	Div	Lge	FA	LC	Oth	Total	Lge	FA	LC	Oth	Total
1924-25	3S	17				17					
Total		17				17					

EVANS, William
Born: Llansaintffraid.
Signed from: London Welsh, 1889.
Debut v Bristol City, 7 Oct 1899, Southern League.

		APPEARANCES					GOALS				
Season	Div	Lge	FA	LC	Oth	Total	Lge	FA	LC	Oth	Total
1899-1900	SL	9	4			13	3	3			6
Total		9	4			13	3	3			6

FALCO, Mark
Born: Hackney, 22 Oct 1960.
Signed from: Glasgow Rangers, Dec 1987 (£400,000).
Debut v Manchester United, 5 Dec 1987.
Transferred to: Millwall, Aug 1991 (£175,000).

		APPEARANCES					GOALS				
Season	Div	Lge	FA	LC	Oth	Total	Lge	FA	LC	Oth	Total
1987-88	1	15/4	4		1	20/4	5	2			7
1988-89	1	22/5	1	4	2	29/5	12		3		15
1989-90	1	11/10	2/2	0/1		13/13	5				5
1990-91	1	17/3	1	1		19/3	5		1		6
Total		65/22	8/2	5/1	3	81/25	27	2	4		33

FALLON, Peter
Born: Dublin, 19 Oct 1922.
Signed from: Exeter City, Aug 1953.
Debut v Shrewsbury Town, 19 Sep 1953.
Retired injury, Jul 1954.

		APPEARANCES					GOALS				
Season	Div	Lge	FA	LC	Oth	Total	Lge	FA	LC	Oth	Total
1953-54	3S	1				1					
Total		1				1					

FARNER, Alec
Born: Lochgelly, 1909.
Signed from: Nottingham Forest.
Debut v Torquay United, 3 Feb 1934.

		APPEARANCES					GOALS				
Season	Div	Lge	FA	LC	Oth	Total	Lge	FA	LC	Oth	Total
1933-34	3S	12				12					
1934-35	3S	26	1			27	7				7
1935-36	3S	9				9	3				3
1936-37	3S	26	2			28					
1937-38	3S	7				7					
1938-39	3S										
1939-40	3S	1				1					
2nd WW		75			5	80	1				1
Total		156	3		5	164	11				11

FARROW, Desmond
Born: Peterborough, 11 Feb 1926.
Signed from: Leicester City.
Debut v Luton Town, 25 Nov 1944, League South.
Transferred to: Stoke City, Oct 1952.

		APPEARANCES					GOALS				
Season	Div	Lge	FA	LC	Oth	Total	Lge	FA	LC	Oth	Total
2nd WW		17	9		11	37					
1948-49	2	17	2			19					
1949-50	2	22	1			23					
1950-51	2	39				39	6				6
1951-52	2	32				32	1				1
1952-53	3S	8				8					
Total		135	12		11	158	7				7

FAULKNER, R.
Signed from: Blackburn Rovers.
Debut v Watford, 28 Aug 1920.
Transferred to: South Shields, 1923.

		APPEARANCES					GOALS				
Season	Div	Lge	FA	LC	Oth	Total	Lge	FA	LC	Oth	Total
1920-21	3	33				33					
1921-22	3S	17	2			19	1				1
Total		50	2			52	1				1

FERDINAND, Les
Born: Paddington, 18 Dec 1966.
Signed from: Hayes, Apr 1987 (£15,000).
Debut v Coventry City, 20 Apr 1987 (sub).

		APPEARANCES					GOALS				
Season	Div	Lge	FA	LC	Oth	Total	Lge	FA	LC	Oth	Total
1986-87	1	0/2				0/2					
1987-88	1	1		0/1		1/1					
1989-90	1	6/2				6/2	2				2
1990-91	1	14/3	0/1	2		16/4	8		2		10
1991-92	1	21/2		1/1		22/3	10				10
1992-93	Pr	37	2	3		42	20	2	2		24
Total		79/9	2/1	6/2		87/12	40	2	4		46

FEREDAY, Wayne
Born: Warley, 16 Jun 1963.
Signed from: (apprentice), Sep 1980.
Debut v Bristol Rovers, 19 Aug 1980 (2 goals).
Transferred to: Newcastle United, Jul 1989 (£300,000).

		APPEARANCES					GOALS				
Season	Div	Lge	FA	LC	Oth	Total	Lge	FA	LC	Oth	Total
1980-81	2	5/1		1		6/1	2				2
1981-82	2	2/2	0/1			2/3					
1982-83	2	0/5				0/5					
1983-84	1	11/6	0/1	1/1		12/8	4				4
1984-85	1	21/5	0/1	5/2	†4	30/8	7		2	1	10
1985-86	1	30/3		5/1		35/4	2				2
1986-87	1	36/1	4	3		43/1	2				2
1987-88	1	33/4	4	2		39/4	4				4
1988-89	1	29/2	2	6	2	39/2			1		1
Total		167/29	10/3	23/4	6	206/36	21		3	1	25

FERGUSON, Chris
Born: Kirkconnell.
Signed from: Chelsea.
Debut v Brighton & Hove Albion, 13 Sep 1930.
Transferred to: Wrexham, 1931.

		APPEARANCES					GOALS				
Season	Div	Lge	FA	LC	Oth	Total	Lge	FA	LC	Oth	Total
1930-31	3S	15				15	1				1
Total		15				15	1				1

FERGUSON, J.
Debut v West Ham United, 19 Feb 1910, FA Cup.

		APPEARANCES					GOALS				
Season	Div	Lge	FA	LC	Oth	Total	Lge	FA	LC	Oth	Total
1909-10	SL		2			2					
Total			2			2					

FERGUSON, Mike
Born: Burnley, 9 Mar 1943.
Signed from: Aston Villa, Nov 1969 (£20,000).
Debut v Leicester City, 22 Nov 1969.
Transferred to: Cambridge United, Jul 1973 (free).

		APPEARANCES					GOALS				
Season	Div	Lge	FA	LC	Oth	Total	Lge	FA	LC	Oth	Total
1969-70	2	20	4			24			1		1
1970-71	2	30		2		32	1				1
1971-72	2	16		1		17	1				1
1972-73	2	1/1	2			3/1					
Total		67/1	6	3		76/1	2	1			3

FENWICK, H.
Signed from: Shildon United.
Debut v Merthyr Town, 4 Oct 1924.

		APPEARANCES					GOALS				
Season	Div	Lge	FA	LC	Oth	Total	Lge	FA	LC	Oth	Total
1924-25	3S	19				19					
Total		19				19					

FENWICK, Terry
Born: Seaham, 17 Nov 1959.
Signed from: Crystal Palace, Dec 1980 (£100,000).
Debut v Bolton Wanderers, 19 Dec 1980.
Transferred to: Tottenham Hotspur, Dec 1987 (£550,000).

		APPEARANCES					GOALS				
Season	Div	Lge	FA	LC	Oth	Total	Lge	FA	LC	Oth	Total
1980-81	2	19	2			21	2				2
1981-82	2	36	8	4		48	5	1			6
1982-83	2	39	1	2		42	3	1			4
1983-84	1	41	1	3		45	10				10
1984-85	1	41	1	8	†4	54	2		4		6
1985-86	1	37	1	8		46	7		2		9
1986-87	1	21	4	0/1		25/1	1	4			5
1987-88	1	22		3	1	26	3				3
Total		256	18	28/1	5	307/1	33	6	6		45

FIDLER, Joseph
Born: 1885.
Signed from: Fulham, 1906.
Debut v Clapton Orient, 29 Sep 1906, Southern League.
Transferred to: Arsenal, 1913.

		APPEARANCES					GOALS				
Season	Div	Lge	FA	LC	Oth	Total	Lge	FA	LC	Oth	Total
1906-07	SL	18				18					
1907-08	SL	33	1		*1	35					
1908-09	SL	39	2		*1	40	42				
1909-10	SL	39	7			46					
1910-11	SL	36	1			37					
1911-12	SL	7				7					
1912-13	SL	5	2			7					
Total		177	13		2	192					

FIDLER, Tom
Born: Hounslow, 4 Sep 1953.
Signed from: Hounslow, May 1954.
Debut v Southend United, 24 Aug 1954.

		APPEARANCES					GOALS				
Season	Div	Lge	FA	LC	Oth	Total	Lge	FA	LC	Oth	Total
1954-55	3S	12	2			14	2	2			4
Total		12	2			14	2	2			4

FIELD, W.
Born: Oxford.
Signed from: Oxford City.
Debut v Brighton & Hove Albion, 19 Jan 1924.

		APPEARANCES					GOALS				
Season	Div	Lge	FA	LC	Oth	Total	Lge	FA	LC	Oth	Total
1922-23	3S	3				3					
1923-24	3S	22				22					
1924-25	3S	4				4					
Total		29				29					

FILLERY, Mike
Born: Mitcham, 17 Sep 1960.
Signed from: Chelsea, Aug 1983 (£175,000).
Debut v Manchester United, 27 Aug 1983 (sub).
Transferred to: Portsmouth, Jul 1987 (free).

		APPEARANCES					GOALS				
Season	Div	Lge	FA	LC	Oth	Total	Lge	FA	LC	Oth	Total
1983-84	1	29/1	1	1/1		31/2	1				1
1984-85	1	32	1	4	†4	41	6				6
1985-86	1	17		5		22			1		1
1986-87	1	17/1	3			20/1	2				2
Total		95/2	5	10/1	4	114/3	9		1		10

FINCH, Bobby
Born: London, 24 Aug 1948.
Signed from: (apprentice), Aug 1966.
Debut v Cardiff City, 16 Apr 1968.

		APPEARANCES					GOALS				
Season	Div	Lge	FA	LC	Oth	Total	Lge	FA	LC	Oth	Total
1967-68	2	3				3					
1968-69	1	2		1		3					
Total		5		1		6					

FINNEY, William
Born: Stoke-on-Trent, 5 Sep 1931.
Signed from: Birmingham City, May 1957.
Debut v Brentford, 24 Aug 1957.
Transferred to: Crewe Alexandra, Jul 1958.

		APPEARANCES					GOALS				
Season	Div	Lge	FA	LC	Oth	Total	Lge	FA	LC	Oth	Total
1957-58	3S	10				10	1				1
Total		10				10	1				1

FITZGERALD, Arthur
Born: Consborough, Yorkshire.
Signed from: Reading.
Debut v Newport County, 7 Nov 1936.
Transferred to: Aldershot.

		APPEARANCES					GOALS				
Season	Div	Lge	FA	LC	Oth	Total	Lge	FA	LC	Oth	Total
1936-37	3S	28	3			31	17	4			21
1937-38	3S	36	2			38	17	3			20
1938-39	3S	30				30	9				9
1939-40	3S	3				3					
2nd WW		9			5	14	4				4
Total		106	5		5	116	47	7			54

FLANAGAN, Mike
Born: Ilford, 9 Nov 1952.
Signed from: Crystal Palace, Dec 1980 (£150,000).
Debut v Bolton Wanderers, 19 Dec 1980 (1 goal).
Transferred to: Charlton Athletic, Jan 1984 (£50,000).

		APPEARANCES					GOALS				
Season	Div	Lge	FA	LC	Oth	Total	Lge	FA	LC	Oth	Total
1980-81	2	13/1	2			15/1	3				3
1981-82	2	36/1	9	3		48/1	10		2		12
1982-83	2	21/1	1			22/1	7				7
1983-84	1	1/4				1/4					
Total		71/7	12	3		86/7	20		2		22

FLEMING, Mark
Born: Hammersmith, 11 Aug 1969.
Signed from: Youth Training Scheme, Jan 1988.
Debut v Wimbledon, 27 Feb 1988 (sub).
Transferred to: Brentford, Jul 1989 (free).

		APPEARANCES					GOALS				
Season	Div	Lge	FA	LC	Oth	Total	Lge	FA	LC	Oth	Total
1987-88	1	0/2				0/2					
1988-89	1	1	0/1		0/1	1/2					
Total		1/2	0/1		0/1	1/4					

FLETCHER, Jack
Born: South Shields, 1910.
Signed from: Bournemouth.
Debut v Brighton & Hove Albion, 4 Sep 1935.
Transferred to: Clapton Orient.

		APPEARANCES					GOALS				
Season	Div	Lge	FA	LC	Oth	Total	Lge	FA	LC	Oth	Total
1935-36	3S	20				20					
Total		20				20					

FLETCHER, Jack
Signed from: West Ham United, 1905.
Debut v Bristol Rovers, 23 Dec 1905, Southern League.

		APPEARANCES					GOALS				
Season	Div	Lge	FA	LC	Oth	Total	Lge	FA	LC	Oth	Total
1905-06	SL	17	1			18	7				7
1906-07	SL	21	2			23	6				6
Total		38	3			41	13				13

FORD, E.
Born: 1910.
Signed from: Hinkley United.
Debut v Newport County, 30 Aug 1924.
Transferred to: Merthyr Town.

		APPEARANCES					GOALS				
Season	Div	Lge	FA	LC	Oth	Total	Lge	FA	LC	Oth	Total
1924-25	3S	37	5			42	3				3
1925-26	3S	18	4			22	1				1
Total		55	9			64	4				4

FORTUNE, James
Born: Dublin.
Signed from: Leeds City, 1912.
Debut v Plymouth Argyle, 11 Oct 1913, Southern League.

		APPEARANCES					GOALS				
Season	Div	Lge	FA	LC	Oth	Total	Lge	FA	LC	Oth	Total
1913-14	SL	8	5			13					
Total		8	5			13					

FOSTER, C.
Born: Aylesbury, 1910.
Signed from: Watford.
Debut v Bournemouth, 20 Oct 1928.

		APPEARANCES					GOALS				
Season	Div	Lge	FA	LC	Oth	Total	Lge	FA	LC	Oth	Total
1928-29	3S	3				3					
1929-30	3S	2				2					
Total		5				5					

FOX, G.F.
Debut v Gillingham, 27 Sep 1919, London Combination.

		APPEARANCES					GOALS				
Season	Div	Lge	FA	LC	Oth	Total	Lge	FA	LC	Oth	Total
1st WW		15			5	120	15				15
1919-20	SL	8				8					
Total		123				128	15				15

FOX, T.S.
Debut v Fulham, 14 Apr 1906, Southern League.

		APPEARANCES					GOALS				
Season	Div	Lge	FA	LC	Oth	Total	Lge	FA	LC	Oth	Total
1905-06	SL	1				1					
Total		1				1					

FOXALL, Abraham
Born: Sheffield, 1874.
Signed from: Liverpool, 1900.
Debut v Bristol Rovers, 1 Sep 1900, Southern League.
Transferred to: Gainsborough Trinity, 1903.

		APPEARANCES					GOALS				
Season	Div	Lge	FA	LC	Oth	Total	Lge	FA	LC	Oth	Total
1900-01	SL	27	4			31	2	2			4
Total		27	4			31	2	2			4

FRANCIS, E.

		APPEARANCES					GOALS				
Season	Div	Lge	FA	LC	Oth	Total	Lge	FA	LC	Oth	Total
2nd WW		1				1					
Total		1				1					

FRANCIS, George
Born: Acton, 4 Feb 1934.
Signed from: Brentford, May 1961.
Debut v Crystal Palace, 13 Sep 1961 (2 goals), League Cup.
Transferred to: Brentford, Nov 1961.

		APPEARANCES					GOALS				
Season	Div	Lge	FA	LC	Oth	Total	Lge	FA	LC	Oth	Total
1961-62	3	2		1		3	1		2		3
Total		2		1		3	1		2		3

FRANCIS, Gerry
Born: Chiswick, 6 Dec 1951.
Signed from: (apprentice), Jun 1969.
Debut v Liverpool, 29 Mar 1969 (sub).
Transferred to: Crystal Palace, Jul 1979 (£450,000), From: Crystal Palace, Feb 1980 (£150,000), To: Coventry City, Feb 1982 (£150,000).

		APPEARANCES					GOALS				
Season	Div	Lge	FA	LC	Oth	Total	Lge	FA	LC	Oth	Total
1968-69	1	0/1				0/1					
1969-70	2	9/1	1			10/1	2				2
1970-71	2	35/3	1/2	41		37	5				5
1971-72	2	38	2	4		41	3		1		4
1972-73	2	42	3	1		46	9				9
1973-74	1	40	6	3		49	8		1		9
1974-75	1	35	3	3		41	7	1	2		10
1975-76	1	36	2	4		42	12				12
1976-77	1	11		2	†1	14	3		1	2	6
1977-78	1	13		1		14	2				2
1978-79	1	31		2		33	2				2
1980-81	2	10				10	4				4
1981-82	2	7				7					
Total		307/5	18/2	21	1	347/7	57	1	5	2	65

FRANCIS, Trevor
Born: Plymouth, 19 Apr 1954.
Signed from: Glasgow Rangers, Mar 1988 (free).
Debut v Portsmouth, 26 Mar 1988 (sub).
Transferred to: Sheffield Wednesday, Jan 1990 (free).

		APPEARANCES					GOALS				
Season	Div	Lge	FA	LC	Oth	Total	Lge	FA	LC	Oth	Total
1987-88	1	8/1				8/1					
1988-89	1	19		5	2	26	7		3		10
1989-90	1	3/1		3		6/1	5				5
Total		30/2		8	2	40/2	12		3		15

FREEMAN, Ben
Born: Birmingham, 1878.
Signed from: Grays United, 1901.
Debut v Watford, 7 Sep 1901, Southern League.

		APPEARANCES					GOALS				
Season	Div	Lge	FA	LC	Oth	Total	Lge	FA	LC	Oth	Total
1901-02	SL	29	2			31					
1902-03	SL	20				20	1				1
1903-04	SL	2				2					
Total		51	2			53	1				1

FRY, Bob
Born: Pontypridd, 29 Jun 1935.
Signed from: Bath City, Aug 1957.
Debut v Torquay United, 14 Dec 1957.

		APPEARANCES					GOALS				
Season	Div	Lge	FA	LC	Oth	Total	Lge	FA	LC	Oth	Total
1957-58	3S	1				1					
Total		1				1					

GADSDEN, R.
Debut v Fulham, 25 Dec 1942, League South.

		APPEARANCES					GOALS				
Season	Div	Lge	FA	LC	Oth	Total	Lge	FA	LC	Oth	Total
2nd WW		10				10					
Total		10				10					

GARDNER, Andrew
Born: Leith, 26 Sep 1877.
Signed from: Brighton, 1905.
Debut v New Brompton, 2 Sep 1905, Southern League.
Retired, 1906.

		APPEARANCES					GOALS				
Season	Div	Lge	FA	LC	Oth	Total	Lge	FA	LC	Oth	Total
1905-06	SL	5				5					
Total		5				5					

GARDNER, William
Born: Durham, 1893.
Signed from: Spennymoor, 1922.
Debut v Merthyr Town, 7 Apr 1923.
Transferred to: Ashington, 1923.

		APPEARANCES					GOALS				
Season	Div	Lge	FA	LC	Oth	Total	Lge	FA	LC	Oth	Total
1922-23	3S	2				2					
Total		2				2					

GAUL, W.
Debut v Crystal Palace, 21 Dec 1912, Southern League.

		APPEARANCES					GOALS				
Season	Div	Lge	FA	LC	Oth	Total	Lge	FA	LC	Oth	Total
1912-13	SL	12				12	8				8
1913-14	SL	4				4	1				1
Total		16				16	9				9

GAYLARD, Hugh
Debut v Fulham, 30 Sep 1899, FA Cup.

		APPEARANCES					GOALS				
Season	Div	Lge	FA	LC	Oth	Total	Lge	FA	LC	Oth	Total
1899-1900	SL	4	3			7					
Total		4	3			7					

GIBBONS, John
Born: Charlton, 8 Apr 1925.
Signed from: Dartford, Dec 1947.
Debut v West Ham United, 23 Oct 1948.
Transferred to: Ipswich Town, Nov 1949.

		APPEARANCES					GOALS				
Season	Div	Lge	FA	LC	Oth	Total	Lge	FA	LC	Oth	Total
1948-49	2	8				8	2				2
Total		8				8	2				2

GIBBS, Derek
Born: Fulham, 22 Dec 1934.
Signed from: Leyton Orient, Aug 1963.
Debut v Oldham Athletic, 24 Aug 1963.

		APPEARANCES					GOALS				
Season	Div	Lge	FA	LC	Oth	Total	Lge	FA	LC	Oth	Total
1963-64	3	25	2			27					
1964-65	3	2				2					
Total		27	2			29					

GIBBS-KENNETT, R.
Debut v Aldershot, 6 Apr 1942, War Cup.

		APPEARANCES					GOALS				
Season	Div	Lge	FA	LC	Oth	Total	Lge	FA	LC	Oth	Total
2nd WW					1	1					
Total					1	1					

GILBERG, Harry
Born: Tottenham, 27 Jun 1923.
Signed from: Tottenham Hotspur, Aug 1951.
Debut v West Ham United, 18 Aug 1951.
Transferred to: Brighton & Hove Albion, Dec 1952.

		APPEARANCES					GOALS				
Season	Div	Lge	FA	LC	Oth	Total	Lge	FA	LC	Oth	Total
1951-52	2	40	1			41	9				9
1952-53	3S	26	3			29	3				3
Total		66	4			70	12				12

GILFILLAN, John
Born: Townhill, 1898.
Signed from: Portsmouth.
Debut v Reading, 16 Oct 1937.

		APPEARANCES					GOALS				
Season	Div	Lge	FA	LC	Oth	Total	Lge	FA	LC	Oth	Total
1937-38	3S	21	2			23					
Total		21	2			23					

GILHOOLEY, Michael
Born: Edinburgh, 26 Nov 1895.
Signed from: Bradford City.
Debut v Newport County, 27 Aug 1927.
Transferred to: 1928.

		APPEARANCES					GOALS				
Season	Div	Lge	FA	LC	Oth	Total	Lge	FA	LC	Oth	Total
1927-28	3S	9				9					
Total		9				9					

GILLARD, Ian
Born: Hammersmith, 9 Oct 1950.
Signed from: (apprentice), Oct 1968.
Debut v Nottingham Forest, 23 Nov 1968.
Transferred to: Aldershot, Jul 1982.

		APPEARANCES					GOALS				
Season	Div	Lge	FA	LC	Oth	Total	Lge	FA	LC	Oth	Total
1968-69	1	4/2				4/2					
1969-70	2	14/1	4	1		19/1	1				1
1970-71	2	17				17					
1971-72	2	24		2		26					
1972-73	2	8				8					
1973-74	1	23	6			29					
1974-75	1	42	4	3		49	2	1			3
1975-76	1	41	2	3		46					
1976-77	1	41	2	7	†8	58	1				1
1977-78	1	38	6	2		46					
1978-79	1	38	1	3		42	3				3
1979-80	2	38		5		43	1		1		2
1980-81	2	42	2	2		46					
1981-82	2	33/2	9	4		46/2	1				1
Total		403/5	36	32	8	479/5	9	1	1		11

GILLESPIE, J.
Born: 1886.
Signed from: Third Lanark.
Debut v Millwall, 5 Dec 1908, Southern League.

		APPEARANCES					GOALS				
Season	Div	Lge	FA	LC	Oth	Total	Lge	FA	LC	Oth	Total
1908-09	SL	1				1					
Total		1				1					

GILMORE, Henry (Mike)
Signed from: Bournemouth.
Debut v Reading, 24 Dec 1938.

		APPEARANCES					GOALS				
Season	Div	Lge	FA	LC	Oth	Total	Lge	FA	LC	Oth	Total
1938-39	3S	6	1			7					
Total		6	1			7					

GITTENS, Alfred
Born: Manchester, 1880.
Signed from: Luton Town, 1907.
Debut v Tottenham Hotspur, 2 Sep 1907 (2 goals).
Transferred to: Croydon Common, 1908, From: Croydon Common, 1908, To: Aston Villa, 1908.

		APPEARANCES					GOALS				
Season	Div	Lge	FA	LC	Oth	Total	Lge	FA	LC	Oth	Total
1907-08	SL	36	2		*1	39	16				16
1908-09	SL	6			*1	7	1				1
Total		42	2		2	46	17				17

GIVENS, Don
Born: Limerick, 9 Aug 1949.
Signed from: Luton Town, Jul 1972 (£40,000).
Debut v Swindon Town, 12 Aug 1972.
Transferred to: Birmingham City, Aug 1978 (£150,000).

		APPEARANCES					GOALS				
Season	Div	Lge	FA	LC	Oth	Total	Lge	FA	LC	Oth	Total
1972-73	2	41	4	1		46	23	2	1		26
1973-74	1	42	6	3		51	10	2	3		15
1974-75	1	40	4	3		47	17	3	1		21
1975-76	1	41	2	4		47	13				13
1976-77	1	41	2	6/1	†8	57/1	10	1	1	7	19
1977-78	1	37	6	2		45	4	2	1		7
Total		242	24	19/1	8	293/1	77	10	7	7	101

GLOVER, Alan
Born: Windsor, 21 Oct 1950.
Signed from: (apprentice), Mar 1968.
Debut v Aston Villa, 4 Jan 1969, FA Cup.
Transferred to: West Bromwich Albion, Jun 1969 (£70,000).

		APPEARANCES					GOALS				
Season	Div	Lge	FA	LC	Oth	Total	Lge	FA	LC	Oth	Total
1968-69	1	5/1	1			6/1					
Total		5/1	1			6/1					

GODDARD, George
Born: Gomshall, 1903.
Signed from: Redhill, Jun 1926.
Debut v Brentford, 11 Sep 1926 (1 goal).
Transferred to: Brentford, Dec 1933.

		APPEARANCES					GOALS				
Season	Div	Lge	FA	LC	Oth	Total	Lge	FA	LC	Oth	Total
1926-27	3S	38				38	23				23
1927-28	3S	33	1			34	26				26
1928-29	3S	42	1			43	37	1			38
1929-30	3S	41	4			45	37	2			39
1930-31	3S	28	3			31	25	4			29
1931-32	3S	25	2			27	17	2			19
1932-33	3S	30	5			35	12	3			15
1933-34	3S	6				6					
Total		243	16			259	177	12			189

GODDARD, Paul
Born: Harlington, 12 Oct 1959.
Signed from: (apprentice), Jul 1977.
Debut v Arsenal, 11 Apr 1978 (sub).
Transferred to: West Ham United, Aug 1980 (£1,000,000).

		APPEARANCES					GOALS				
Season	Div	Lge	FA	LC	Oth	Total	Lge	FA	LC	Oth	Total
1977-78	1	3/4				3/4	1				1
1978-79	1	20/3				20/3	6				6
1979-80	2	40		4/1		44/1	16				16
Total		63/7		4/1		67/8	23				23

GODDARD, T
Debut v Portsmouth, 2 Dec 1916, London Combination.

		APPEARANCES					GOALS				
Season	Div	Lge	FA	LC	Oth	Total	Lge	FA	LC	Oth	Total
WW1		13				13	1				1
Total		13				13	1				1

GOFTON, G
Signed from: Newcastle United.
Debut v Coventry City, 22 Oct 1932 (1 goal).

		APPEARANCES					GOALS				
Season	Div	Lge	FA	LC	Oth	Total	Lge	FA	LC	Oth	Total
1932-33	3S	7	4			11	8				8
Total		7	4			11	8				8

GOLDIE, William
Born: Scotland.
Debut v Swindon Town, 8 Sep 1900, Southern League.

		APPEARANCES					GOALS				
Season	Div	Lge	FA	LC	Oth	Total	Lge	FA	LC	Oth	Total
1900-01	SL	5	4			9	1	2			3
Total		5	4			9	1	2			3

GOLDING, Jimmy
Born: London, 23 Jan 1937.
Signed from: Tonbridge, Aug 1959.
Debut v York City, 14 Sep 1959.

		APPEARANCES					GOALS				
Season	Div	Lge	FA	LC	Oth	Total	Lge	FA	LC	Oth	Total
1959-60	3	22	1			23	6				6
1960-61	3	8				8					
Total		30	1			31	6				6

GOODIER, Ted
Born: Farnworth, Lancashire, 15 Oct 1902.
Signed from: Oldham Athletic, Nov 1931.
Debut v Cardiff City, 14 Nov 1931.
Transferred to: Watford (exchanged for H.Lowe).

		APPEARANCES					GOALS				
Season	Div	Lge	FA	LC	Oth	Total	Lge	FA	LC	Oth	Total
1931-32	3S	28	4			32					
1932-33	3S	41	4			45	1				1
1933-34	3S	30	4			34					
1934-35	3S	40	1			41					
Total		139	13			152	1				1

GOODMAN, W.
Debut v Norwich City, 18 Apr 1924.

		APPEARANCES					GOALS				
Season	Div	Lge	FA	LC	Oth	Total	Lge	FA	LC	Oth	Total
1923-24	3S	1				1					
Total		1				1					

GOUGH, C.
Born: South Cerney.
Signed from: Clapton Orient.
Debut v Crystal Palace, 28 Aug 1926.
Transferred to: Torquay United.

		APPEARANCES					GOALS				
Season	Div	Lge	FA	LC	Oth	Total	Lge	FA	LC	Oth	Total
1926-27	3S	19				19					
Total		19				19					

GOULD, H.L.
Signed from: X Division Metropolitan Police, 1920.
Debut v Newport County, 26 Mar 1921.

		APPEARANCES					GOALS				
Season	Div	Lge	FA	LC	Oth	Total	Lge	FA	LC	Oth	Total
1920-21	3	2				2					
Total		2				2					

GRAHAM, Malcolm
Born: Hall Green, 26 Jan 1934.
Signed from: Leyton Orient, Jul 1963.
Debut v Oldham Athletic, 24 Aug 1963 (1 goal).
Transferred to: Barnsley, Jul 1964.

		APPEARANCES					GOALS				
Season	Div	Lge	FA	LC	Oth	Total	Lge	FA	LC	Oth	Total
1963-64	3	21	1	1		23	7	1			8
Total		21	1	1		23	7	1			8

GRANT, G.
Born: London.
Signed from: Millwall, 1920.
Debut v Watford, 28 Aug 1920.

		APPEARANCES					GOALS				
Season	Div	Lge	FA	LC	Oth	Total	Lge	FA	LC	Oth	Total
1920-21	3	42	2			44					
1921-22	3S	27	1			28	1				1
Total		69	3			72	1				1

GRAY, Andy
Born: Lambeth, 22 Feb 1964.
Signed from: Aston Villa, Feb 1989 (£450,000).
Debut v Millwall, 4 Feb 1989.
Transferred to: Crystal Palace, Aug 1989 (£500,000).

		APPEARANCES					GOALS				
Season	Div	Lge	FA	LC	Oth	Total	Lge	FA	LC	Oth	Total
1988-89	1	11				11	2				2
Total		11				11	2				2

GRAY, Tom
Born: Grimsby, 1876.
Signed from: New Brompton.
Debut v Bristol Rovers, 1 Sep 1900, Southern League.
Transferred to: Bury, 1901.

		APPEARANCES					GOALS				
Season	Div	Lge	FA	LC	Oth	Total	Lge	FA	LC	Oth	Total
1900-01	SL	28	4			32	8	2			10
Total		28	4			32	8	2			10

GREEN, H.
Debut v Luton Town, 2 Sep 1916, London Combination.

		APPEARANCES					GOALS				
Season	Div	Lge	FA	LC	Oth	Total	Lge	FA	LC	Oth	Total
WW1		7			1	8					
Total		7			1	8					

GREEN, Tom
Born: Rock Ferry, 1882.
Signed from: Middlesbrough, 1906.
Debut v Luton Town, 1 Sep 1906, Southern League.
Transferred to: Stockport County, 1907.

		APPEARANCES					GOALS				
Season	Div	Lge	FA	LC	Oth	Total	Lge	FA	LC	Oth	Total
1906-07	SL	37	2			39	2				2
Total		37	2			39	2				2

GREER, W.
Debut v Norwich City, 25 Dec 1908, Southern League.

		APPEARANCES					GOALS				
Season	Div	Lge	FA	LC	Oth	Total	Lge	FA	LC	Oth	Total
1908-09	SL	16	2			18	6				6
1909-10	SL	16				16	1				1
Total		32	2			34	7				7

GREGORY, C.
Born: Birmingham.
Signed from: Sunderland, 1922.
Debut v Watford, 26 Aug 1922.
Transferred to: Yeovil Town.

		APPEARANCES					GOALS				
Season	Div	Lge	FA	LC	Oth	Total	Lge	FA	LC	Oth	Total
1922-23	3S	24				24	1				1
Total		24				24	1				1

GREGORY, John
Born: Birmingham.
Signed from: Willenhall Swifts, 1912.
Debut v Watford, 7 Dec 1912, Southern League.
Transferred to: Yeovil Town, 1923.

		APPEARANCES					GOALS				
Season	Div	Lge	FA	LC	Oth	Total	Lge	FA	LC	Oth	Total
1912-13	SL	3				3					
1913-14	SL	31	5			36	6	2			8
1914-15	SL	13				13	2				2
1st WW		29			1	30	11				11
1919-20	SL	40	1			41	15				15
1920-21	3	39	2			41	15				15
1921-22	3S	40				40	6				6
1922-23	3S	33	4			37		2			2
Total		228	12		1	241	55	4			59

GREGORY, John
Born: Scunthorpe, 11 May 1954.
Signed from: Brighton & Hove Albion, Jun 1981 (£275,000).
Debut v Wrexham, 29 Aug 1981.
Transferred to: Derby County, Nov 1985 (£100,000).

		APPEARANCES					GOALS				
Season	Div	Lge	FA	LC	Oth	Total	Lge	FA	LC	Oth	Total
1981-82	2	34	7	4		45	9		2		11
1982-83	2	42		2		44	15		1		16
1983-84	1	37	1	2		40	7	1	1		9
1984-85	1	35/2	1	7	†4	47/2	5		1	1	7
1985-86	1	11		1		12					
Total		159/2	9	16	4	188/2	36	1	5	1	43

GRENDON, F.

		APPEARANCES					GOALS				
Season	Div	Lge	FA	LC	Oth	Total	Lge	FA	LC	Oth	Total
WW1		84			3	87	1				1
Total		84			3	87	1				1

GRETTON, T.
Born: Walsall.
Signed from: Wolverhampton United.
Debut v Swindon Town, 7 Dec 1929.
Transferred to: Walsall, 1930.

		APPEARANCES					GOALS				
Season	Div	Lge	FA	LC	Oth	Total	Lge	FA	LC	Oth	Total
1929-30	3S	4				4					
Total		4				4					

GRIFFEN
Debut v Tottenham Hotspur, 13 Oct 1917, London Combination.

		APPEARANCES					GOALS				
Season	Div	Lge	FA	LC	Oth	Total	Lge	FA	LC	Oth	Total
WW1		3				3					
Total		3				3					

GRIFFITHS, J.
Debut v Southampton, 30 Oct 1943 (1 goal), League South.

		APPEARANCES					GOALS				
Season	Div	Lge	FA	LC	Oth	Total	Lge	FA	LC	Oth	Total
2nd WW		3				3	1				1
Total		3				3	1				1

GRIMSDELL, E.
Born: Watford.
Debut v Watford, 4 Sep 1920.
Transferred: 1921, From: Guildford United, 1922, To: Dartford, 1923.

		APPEARANCES					GOALS				
Season	Div	Lge	FA	LC	Oth	Total	Lge	FA	LC	Oth	Total
1920-21	3	20	1			21					
1922-23	3S	2				2					
Total		22	1			23					

GULLAN, Stanley
Born: Edinburgh, 26 Jan 1926.
Signed from: Clyde, Jul 1949.
Debut v Bury, 6 Sep 1950.

		APPEARANCES					GOALS				
Season	Div	Lge	FA	LC	Oth	Total	Lge	FA	LC	Oth	Total
1950-51	2	22				22					
1951-52	2	4				4					
1952-53	3S	3				3					
1953-54	3S	13				13					
1954-55	3S	6				6					
Total		48				48					

GUNNER, R.
Debut v Millwall, 21 March 1942, War Cup.

		APPEARANCES					GOALS				
Season	Div	Lge	FA	LC	Oth	Total	Lge	FA	LC	Oth	Total
2nd WW		9			4	13					
Total		9				4					

GUY-WATSON, H.
Debut v Bristol Rovers, 28 Apr 1906, Southern League.

		APPEARANCES					GOALS				
Season	Div	Lge	FA	LC	Oth	Total	Lge	FA	LC	Oth	Total
1905-06	SL	1				1					
Total		1				1					

HAGGAN, I.
Debut v Southend United, 26 Apr 1920.

		APPEARANCES					GOALS				
Season	Div	Lge	FA	LC	Oth	Total	Lge	FA	LC	Oth	Total
1919-20	SL	1				1					
Total		1				1					

HALEY, William
Born: Bexleyheath, 16 Feb 1904.
Signed from: Fulham.
Debut v Bristol Rovers, 31 Aug 1931 (1 goal).
Transferred to: Dartford, 1932.

		APPEARANCES					GOALS				
Season	Div	Lge	FA	LC	Oth	Total	Lge	FA	LC	Oth	Total
1931-32	3S	17				17	5				5
Total		17				17	5				5

HALL, Ernest
Born: Barndale, Coventry.
Signed from: Bedworth Town, 1930.
Debut v Swindon Town, 5 Sep 1931.
Transferred to: Chester.

		APPEARANCES					GOALS				
Season	Div	Lge	FA	LC	Oth	Total	Lge	FA	LC	Oth	Total
1931-32	3S	36	4			40					
1932-33	3S	26	5			31					
Total		62	9			71					

HAMILTON, Billy
Born: Belfast, 9 May 1957.
Signed from: Linfield, Apr 1978 (£25,000).
Debut v Bolton Wanderers, 2 Dec 1978 (sub).
Transferred to: Burnley, Nov 1979 (£60,000).

		APPEARANCES					GOALS				
Season	Div	Lge	FA	LC	Oth	Total	Lge	FA	LC	Oth	Total
1978-79	1	8/3	1			9/3	2				2
1979-80	2	1				1					
Total		9/3	1			10/3	2				2

HAMILTON, J.
Born: Nottingham.
Signed from: Blackpool, Jul 1926.
Debut v Crystal Palace, 28 Aug 1926.

		APPEARANCES					GOALS				
Season	Div	Lge	FA	LC	Oth	Total	Lge	FA	LC	Oth	Total
1926-27	3S	10				10					
Total		10				10					

HAMILTON, John
Born: Glasgow, 1880.
Signed from: Millwall Athletic.
Debut v Wellingborough, 3 Sep 1902, Souuthern League.

		APPEARANCES					GOALS				
Season	Div	Lge	FA	LC	Oth	Total	Lge	FA	LC	Oth	Total
1902-03	SL	28	1			29	2				2
1903-04	SL	19	2			21	1				1
Total		47	3			50	3				3

HAMMOND, Joseph
Born: West Ham, London, 1911.
Signed from: London Paper Mills.
Debut v Southend United, 14 Apr 1934.

		APPEARANCES					GOALS				
Season	Div	Lge	FA	LC	Oth	Total	Lge	FA	LC	Oth	Total
1933-34	3S	5				5	2				2
1934-35	3S	8	1			9	1				1
1935-36	3S	5				5	3				3
Total		18	1			19	6				6

HANDFORTH, Ernest
Debut v Tottenham Hotspur, 14 Sep 1901, Southern League.

		APPEARANCES					GOALS				
Season	Div	Lge	FA	LC	Oth	Total	Lge	FA	LC	Oth	Total
1901-02	SL	3				3					
Total		3				3					

HANNAH, James
Born: Glasgow.
Signed from: Sunderland, 1899.
Debut v Sheppey United, 25 Nov 1899, Southern League.

		APPEARANCES					GOALS				
Season	Div	Lge	FA	LC	Oth	Total	Lge	FA	LC	Oth	Total
1899-1900	SL	17	3			20	2				2
Total		17	3			20	2				2

HARKOUK, Rachid
Born: Chelsea, 19 May 1956.
Signed from: Crystal Palace, Jun 1978 (£100,000).
Debut v Nottingham Forest, 26 Aug 1978 (sub).
Transferred to: Notts County, Jun 1980 (£50,000).

		APPEARANCES					GOALS				
Season	Div	Lge	FA	LC	Oth	Total	Lge	FA	LC	Oth	Total
1978-79	1	14/1	0/1	2		16/2	3				3
1979-80	2	1/4		1		2/4					
Total		15/5	0/1	3		18/6	3				3

HARRIS, Allan
Born: Hackney, 28 Dec 1942.
Signed from: Chelsea, Jul 1967 (£30,000).
Debut v Portsmouth, 19 Aug 1967.
Transferred to: Plymouth Argyle, Mar 1971 (£9,500).

		APPEARANCES					GOALS				
Season	Div	Lge	FA	LC	Oth	Total	Lge	FA	LC	Oth	Total
1967-68	2	42	1	3		46					
1968-69	1	29				29					
1969-70	2	13/3				13/3					
1970-71	2	6/1				6/1					
Total		90/4	1	3		94/4					

HARRIS, Bernard
Born: Sheffield.
Signed from: Luton Town.
Debut v Crystal Palace, 31 Aug 1929.
Transferred to: Swindon Town, Jul 1933.

		APPEARANCES					GOALS				
Season	Div	Lge	FA	LC	Oth	Total	Lge	FA	LC	Oth	Total
1929-30	3S	17				17					
1930-31	3S	28	3			31					
1931-32	3S	15	4			19					
Total		60	7			67					

HARRIS, George
Born: High Wycombe.
Signed from: Notts County.
Debut v Watford, 10 Sep 1924.
Transferred to: Fulham, 1926.

		APPEARANCES					GOALS				
Season	Div	Lge	FA	LC	Oth	Total	Lge	FA	LC	Oth	Total
1924-25	3S	24	5			29					
1925-26		14				14					
Total		38	5			43					

HARRIS, Neil
Born: Glasgow, 9 Feb 1920.
Signed from: Swansea Town, Sep 1946.
Debut v Crystal Palace, 25 Dec 1941, League South.

		APPEARANCES					GOALS				
Season	Div	Lge	FA	LC	Oth	Total	Lge	FA	LC	Oth	Total
2nd WW		1				1	1				1
1946-47	3S	1	1			2	1	1			2
Total		2	1			3	2	1			3

HARRISON, James
Born: Hammersmith, 31 Jul 1928.
Signed from: Feb 1952.
Debut v Coventry City, 3 Jan 1953.

		APPEARANCES					GOALS				
Season	Div	Lge	FA	LC	Oth	Total	Lge	FA	LC	Oth	Total
1952-53	3S	6				6	1				1
Total		6				6	1				1

HART, Ernest
Born: Huddersfield.
Signed from: Folkestone.
Debut v Aberdare Athletic, 4 Nov 1922.

		APPEARANCES					GOALS				
Season	Div	Lge	FA	LC	Oth	Total	Lge	FA	LC	Oth	Total
1922-23	3S	5				5	2				2
Total		5				5	2				2

HART, G.
Signed from: Bedlington Colliery.
Debut v Northampton Town, 27 Oct 1923.

		APPEARANCES					GOALS				
Season	Div	Lge	FA	LC	Oth	Total	Lge	FA	LC	Oth	Total
1923-24	3S	4				4					
1924-25	3S	2				2	1				1
Total		6				6	1				1

HARTBURN, John
Born: Durham, 20 Dec 1920.
Signed from: Yeovil Town, Mar 1947.
Debut v Norwich City, 23 Aug 1947.
Transferred to: Watford, Sep 1949.

		APPEARANCES					GOALS				
Season	Div	Lge	FA	LC	Oth	Total	Lge	FA	LC	Oth	Total
1947-48	3S	31	5			36	6	2			8
1948-49	2	27	1			28	5				5
Total		58	6			64	11	2			13

HARTWELL, Ambrose
Born: Exeter, 28 Jun 1883.
Signed from: Bradford, 1909.
Debut v Watford, 1 Sep 1909 (1 goal).
Transferred to: Kidderminster, 1911.

		APPEARANCES					GOALS				
Season	Div	Lge	FA	LC	Oth	Total	Lge	FA	LC	Oth	Total
1909-10	SL	38	7			45	2				2
1910-11	SL	19				19	2				2
Total		57	7			64	4				4

HASSAN, V.
Debut v Portsmouth, 2 Dec 1916, London Combination.

		APPEARANCES					GOALS				
Season	Div	Lge	FA	LC	Oth	Total	Lge	FA	LC	Oth	Total
WW1		25				25	10				10
Total		25				25	10				10

HASTY, Paddy
Born: Belfast, 17 Mar 1932.
Signed from: Leyton Orient.
Debut v Wrexham, 4 May 1960.
Transferred to: Tooting & Mitcham.

		APPEARANCES					GOALS				
Season	Div	Lge	FA	LC	Oth	Total	Lge	FA	LC	Oth	Total
1959-60	3	1				1					
Total		1				1					

HATTON, Cyril
Born: Grantham, 14 Sep 1918.
Signed from: Notts County (exchange H.Brown).
Debut v Southend United, 1 Sep 1945 (2 goals), League South.
Transferred to: Chesterfield, Jun 1953.

		APPEARANCES					GOALS				
Season	Div	Lge	FA	LC	Oth	Total	Lge	FA	LC	Oth	Total
2nd WW		23			8	31	11			5	16
1946-47	3S	26	6			32	12	3			15
1947-48	3S	35	6			41	21	4			25
1948-49	2	22	1			23	5				5
1949-50	2	37	1			38	3				3
1950-51	2	26	1			27	16				16
1951-52	2	6				6	3				3
1952-53	3S	10				10	4				4
Total		185	15		8	208	75	7		5	87

HAWKINS, Bert
Born: Bristol, 29 Sep 1923.
Signed from: West Ham United, Jun 1953.
Debut v Brighton & Hove Albion, 19 Aug 1953.
Transferred to: Cheltenham, Jul 1954.

		APPEARANCES					GOALS				
Season	Div	Lge	FA	LC	Oth	Total	Lge	FA	LC	Oth	Total
1953-54	3S	8				8	3				3
Total		8				8	3				3

HAWLEY, Fred
Born: Derby, 28 Feb 1890.
Signed from: Brighton.
Debut v Crystal Palace, 28 Aug 1926.
Transferred to: Loughborough, 1928.

		APPEARANCES					GOALS				
Season	Div	Lge	FA	LC	Oth	Total	Lge	FA	LC	Oth	Total
1926-27	3S	22				22	1				1
1927-28	3S	7				7					
Total		29				29	1				1

HAYWOOD, Adam
Born: Horninglow, 1875.
Signed from: Woolwich Arsenal, Aug 1899.
Debut v Tottenham Hotspur, 9 Sep 1899, Southern League.
Transferred to: New Brompton, 1900.

		APPEARANCES					GOALS				
Season	Div	Lge	FA	LC	Oth	Total	Lge	FA	LC	Oth	Total
1899-1900	SL	17	10			27	3	6			9
Total		17	10			27	3	6			9

HAZELL, Bob
Born: Jamaica, 14 Jun 1959.
Signed from: Wolverhampton Wanderers, Sep 1979 (£240,000).
Debut v Bradford City, 5 Sep 1979, League Cup.
Transferred to: Leicester City, Sep 1983 (£100,000).

		APPEARANCES					GOALS				
Season	Div	Lge	FA	LC	Oth	Total	Lge	FA	LC	Oth	Total
1979-80	2	27/2	1	4		32/2	1	1			2
1980-81	2	5/3		1/1		6/4	2				2
1981-82	2	23/1	4	4		31/1	2				2
1982-83	2	39	1	2		42	3				3
1983-84	1	6				6					
Total		100/6	6	11/1		117/7	8	1			9

HAZELL, Tony
Born: High Wycombe, 19 Sep 1947.
Signed from: (juniors), Oct 1964.
Debut v Gillingham, 3 Oct 1964.
Transferred to: Millwall, Dec 1974 (£40,000).

		APPEARANCES					GOALS				
Season	Div	Lge	FA	LC	Oth	Total	Lge	FA	LC	Oth	Total
1964-65	3	29	3			32	1				1
1965-66	3	17/2		2		19/2					
1966-67	3	37	1	6		44				1	1
1967-68	2	42	1	2		45					
1968-69	1	38/1		1		39/1	1				1
1969-70	2	42	4	5		51	2				2
1970-71	2	33/2		2	35	/2					
1971-72	2	42	2	4		48					
1972-73	2	41	4	1		46					
1973-74	1	29/2	2	3		34/2					
1974-75	1	12		2		14					
Total		362/7	17	28		407/7	4			1	5

HEATH, Bill
Born: Stepney, 26 Jun 1920.
Debut v Clapton Orient, 7 Mar 1942, League South.
Transferred to: Dover, Jul 1953.

		APPEARANCES					GOALS				
Season	Div	Lge	FA	LC	Oth	Total	Lge	FA	LC	Oth	Total
2nd WW		5	9		14	28	2			8	10
1946-47	3S	6	1			7	1				1
1947-48	3S	6	1			7					
1948-49	2	18				18	1				1
1949-50	2	25	1			26					
1950-51	2	21	1			22	1				1
1951-52	2	19	1			20					
1952-53	3S	1				1					
Total		101	14		14	129	5			8	13

HEATHCOTE, W.
Born: Hemsworth, 29 Jun 1911.
Debut v Chelsea, 28 Aug 1943 (2 goals), League South.
Transferred to: Millwall, Dec 1946.

		APPEARANCES					GOALS				
Season	Div	Lge	FA	LC	Oth	Total	Lge	FA	LC	Oth	Total
2nd WW		74	3		23	100	69	1		19	89
1946-47	3S	5				5	1				1
Total		79	3		23	105	70	1		19	90

HEBDEN, George
Born: West Ham, 2 Jun 1900.
Signed from: Leicester City.
Debut v Gillingham, 29 Aug 1925.
Transferred to: Gillingham, 1927.

		APPEARANCES					GOALS				
Season	Div	Lge	FA	LC	Oth	Total	Lge	FA	LC	Oth	Total
1925-26	3S	36	4			40					
1926-27	3S	23				23					
1927-28	3S	1				1					
Total		60	4			64					

HELLAWELL, Michael
Born: Keighley, 30 Jun 1938.
Signed from: Salts, Aug 1955.
Debut v Exeter City, 25 Feb 1956.
Transferred to: Birmingham City, May 1957.

		APPEARANCES					GOALS				
Season	Div	Lge	FA	LC	Oth	Total	Lge	FA	LC	Oth	Total
1955-56	3S	1				1					
1956-57	3S	44	3			47	7	1			8
Total		45	3			48	7	1			8

HERRERA, Robert
Born: Torquay, 12 Jun 1970.
Signed from: Youth Training Scheme, Feb 1988.
Debut v Wimbledon, 14 Jan 1989 (sub).

		APPEARANCES					GOALS				
Season	Div	Lge	FA	LC	Oth	Total	Lge	FA	LC	Oth	Total
1988-89	1	0/2		0/1	1/1	1/4					
1989-90	1	1				1					
1990-91	1	3		1		4					
1991-92	1			0/1		0/1					
Total		4/2		1/2	1/1	6/5					

HIBBS, R.
Debut v Watford, 1 Jan 1946, League South.

		APPEARANCES					GOALS				
Season	Div	Lge	FA	LC	Oth	Total	Lge	FA	LC	Oth	Total
2nd WW		1				1					
Total		1				1					

HICKS, A.
Debut v Chelsea, 23 Oct 1915, London Combination.

		APPEARANCES					GOALS				
Season	Div	Lge	FA	LC	Oth	Total	Lge	FA	LC	Oth	Total
WW1		21				21	3				3
Total		21				21	3				3

HIGGINS, D.
Debut v Reading, 21 Mar 1913, Southern League.

		APPEARANCES					GOALS				
Season	Div	Lge	FA	LC	Oth	Total	Lge	FA	LC	Oth	Total
1912-13	SL	2				2					
1913-14	SL	17	4			21					
1914-15	SL	7				7					
Total		26	4			30					

HIGGINS, Ronald
Born: Silvertown, 14 Feb 1923.
Signed from: Brighton & Hove Albion, Jan 1953.
Debut v Brighton & Hove Albion, 28 Feb 1953 (1 goal).

		APPEARANCES					GOALS				
Season	Div	Lge	FA	LC	Oth	Total	Lge	FA	LC	Oth	Total
1952-53	3S	3				3	1				1
Total		3				3	1				1

HILL, Charles
Born: Cardiff, 6 Sep 1918.
Signed from: Torquay United, Mar 1949.
Debut v Sheffield Wednesday, 27 Nov 1948.
Transferred to: Swindon Town, Sep 1950.

		APPEARANCES					GOALS				
Season	Div	Lge	FA	LC	Oth	Total	Lge	FA	LC	Oth	Total
1948-49	2	5				5	1				1
1949-50	2	16				16					
Total		21				21	1				1

HILL, Gordon
Born: Sunbury, 1 Apr 1954.
Signed from: Derby County, Nov 1979 (£175,000).
Debut v Cambridge United, 1 Dec 1979.

		APPEARANCES					GOALS				
Season	Div	Lge	FA	LC	Oth	Total	Lge	FA	LC	Oth	Total
1979-80	2	7/2	1			8/2					
1980-81	2	3/2		1		4/2	1				1
Total		10/4	1	1		12/4	1				1

HILL, J.
Signed from: Barnsley.
Debut v Southend United, 3 Sep 1932.

		APPEARANCES					GOALS				
Season	Div	Lge	FA	LC	Oth	Total	Lge	FA	LC	Oth	Total
1932-33	3S	15	1			16	1				1
Total		15	1			16	1				1

HILL, Leonard
Born: Islington, Feb 1899.
Signed from: Southend United, 1920.
Debut v Watford, 4 Sep 1920.
Transferred to: Southampton, 1925.

		APPEARANCES					GOALS				
Season	Div	Lge	FA	LC	Oth	Total	Lge	FA	LC	Oth	Total
1920-21	3	32	2			34					
1921-22	3S	36	2			38					
1922-23	3S	42	4			46					
1923-24	3S	37	1			38					
1924-25	3S	15	5			20					
Total		162	14			176					

HILL, William
Born: Uxbridge, 9 Jun 1930.
Signed from: Uxbridge Town, Apr 1951.
Debut v Leicester City, 1 Dec 1951.

		APPEARANCES					GOALS				
Season	Div	Lge	FA	LC	Oth	Total	Lge	FA	LC	Oth	Total
1951-52	2	10	1			11	1				1
Total		10	1			11	1				1

HIRST, Henry
Born: Sheffield, 24 Oct 1899.
Signed from: Preston North End, May 1925.
Debut v Merthyr Town, 5 Sep 1925.
Transferred to: Charlton Athletic, Jan 1926.

		APPEARANCES					GOALS				
Season	Div	Lge	FA	LC	Oth	Total	Lge	FA	LC	Oth	Total
1925-26	3S	26	4			30		1			1
Total		26	4			30		1			1

HITCH, Alfred
Born: Walsall, 1878.
Signed from: Grays, 1899.
Debut v Bristol City, 7 Oct 1899, Southern League.
Transferred to: Nottingham Forest, Jul 1901, From: Nottingham Forest, Jul 1902.

		APPEARANCES					GOALS				
Season	Div	Lge	FA	LC	Oth	Total	Lge	FA	LC	Oth	Total
1899-1900	SL	21	8			29	1	2			3
1900-01	SL	28	4			32	3	1			4
1902-03	SL	26				26	3				3
1903-04	SL	30	2			32	1				1
1904-05	SL	31	1			32	8				8
1905-06	SL	31	1			32	1				1
Total		167	16			183	17	3			20

HITCHCOCK, E.
Debut v Tottenham Hotspur, 2 Sep 1907 (1 goal), Southern League.

		APPEARANCES					GOALS				
Season	Div	Lge	FA	LC	Oth	Total	Lge	FA	LC	Oth	Total
1907-08	SL	2				2	2				2
Total		2				2	2				2

HOLD, Oscar
Born: Barnsley, 19 Oct 1918.
Signed from: Everton, Feb 1952.
Debut v Southampton, 8 Mar 1952 (1 goal).
Transferred to: March Town, Jul 1953.

		APPEARANCES					GOALS				
Season	Div	Lge	FA	LC	Oth	Total	Lge	FA	LC	Oth	Total
1951-52	2	3				3	1				1
1952-53	3S	2				2					
Total		5				5	1				1

HOLLINS, John
Born: Guildford, 16 Jul 1946.
Signed from: Chelsea, Jun 1975 (£80,000).
Debut v Liverpool, 16 Aug 1975.
Transferred to: Arsenal, Jul 1979 (£75,000).

		APPEARANCES					GOALS				
Season	Div	Lge	FA	LC	Oth	Total	Lge	FA	LC	Oth	Total
1975-76	1	28/2	1/1	0/2		29/5	1				1
1976-77	1	40	2	6	8	56	3				3
1977-78	1	39/1	6	2		47/1	2	1			3
1978-79	1	41	1	3		45					
Total		148/3	10/1	11/2	8	177/6	6	1			7

HOLLOWAY, Ian
Born: Kingswood, 12 Mar 1963.
Signed from: Bristol Rovers, Aug 1991 (£225,000).
Debut v Arsenal, 17 Aug 1991 (sub).

		APPEARANCES					GOALS				
Season	Div	Lge	FA	LC	Oth	Total	Lge	FA	LC	Oth	Total
1991-92	1	34/6	1	3	1/1	39/7					
1992-93	Pr	23/1	2	4		29/1	2	1			3
Total		57/7	3	7	1/1	68/8	2	1			3

HOOPER, H.
Debut v Watford, 12 Feb 1916, London Combination.

		APPEARANCES					GOALS				
Season	Div	Lge	FA	LC	Oth	Total	Lge	FA	LC	Oth	Total
WW1		13				13					
Total		13				13					

HOOPER, Harold
Born: Brierley Hill, 1900.
Signed from: Leicester City.
Debut v Crystal Palace, 28 Aug 1926.

		APPEARANCES					GOALS				
Season	Div	Lge	FA	LC	Oth	Total	Lge	FA	LC	Oth	Total
1926-27	3S	16				16					
Total		16				16					

HOTEN, Ralph
Born: Pinxton, 27 Dec 1896.
Signed from: Northampton Town.
Debut v Thames, 30 Aug 1930 (2 goals).

		APPEARANCES					GOALS				
Season	Div	Lge	FA	LC	Oth	Total	Lge	FA	LC	Oth	Total
1930-31	3S	9				9	4				4
Total		9				9	4				4

HOWES, Arthur
Signed from: Brighton, 1904.
Debut v Luton Town, 12 Nov 1904, Southern League.

		APPEARANCES					GOALS				
Season	Div	Lge	FA	LC	Oth	Total	Lge	FA	LC	Oth	Total
1904-05	SL	11	1			12					
1905-06	SL	12	1			13					
1906-07	SL	26	2			28					
Total		49	4			53					

HOWE, Ernie
Born: Chiswick, 15 Feb 1953.
Signed from: Fulham, Dec 1977 (£50,000).
Debut v Liverpool, 17 Dec 1977.
Transferred to: Portsmouth, Aug 1982, (£50,000).

		APPEARANCES					GOALS				
Season	Div	Lge	FA	LC	Oth	Total	Lge	FA	LC	Oth	Total
1977-78	1	23	6			29	1	2			3
1978-79	1	38	1	3		42	1				1
1979-80	2	4		1		5					
1980-81	2	8				8	1				1
1981-82	2	16	5	1		22		1			1
Total		89	12	5		106	3	3			6

HOWE, H.
Born: Hemel Hempstead.
Signed from: Watford.
Debut v Clapton Orient, 19 Oct 1929.
Transferred to: Crystal Palace, 1933.

		APPEARANCES					GOALS				
Season	Div	Lge	FA	LC	Oth	Total	Lge	FA	LC	Oth	Total
1929-30	3S	28	3			31	5				5
1930-31	3S	18	3			21	3	1			4
1931-32	3S	3				3	1				1
1932-33	3S	20				20	4				4
Total		69	6			75	13	1			14

HOWE, D.
Debut v Millwall, 9 Dec 1916, London Combination.

		APPEARANCES					GOALS				
Season	Div	Lge	FA	LC	Oth	Total	Lge	FA	LC	Oth	Total
WW1		2				2					
Total		2				2					

HUCKER, Peter
Born: Hampstead, 28 Oct 1959.
Signed from: (apprentice), Jul 1977.
Debut v Shrewsbury Town, 2 May 1981.
Transferred to: Oxford United, Feb 1987 (£100,000).

		APPEARANCES					GOALS				
Season	Div	Lge	FA	LC	Oth	Total	Lge	FA	LC	Oth	Total
1980-81	2	1				1					
1981-82	2	22	9			31					
1982-83	2	42		2		44					
1983-84	1	42	1	3		46					
1984-85	1	42	1	8	†4	55					
1985-86	1	11				11					
Total		160	11	13	4	188					

HUDSON, Stan
Born: Fulham.
Signed from: Sep 1948.
Debut v Brentford, 9 Oct 1948 (1 goal).

		APPEARANCES					GOALS				
Season	Div	Lge	FA	LC	Oth	Total	Lge	FA	LC	Oth	Total
1948-49	2	10				10	4				4
1949-50	2	12	1			13	3				3
Total		22	1			23	7				7

HUGHES
Debut v Tottenham Hotspur, 11 Mar 1916, London Combination.

		APPEARANCES					GOALS				
Season	Div	Lge	FA	LC	Oth	Total	Lge	FA	LC	Oth	Total
WW1		2				2					
Total		2				2					

HUMPHRIES
Debut v Millwall, 4 Sep 1915 (1 goal), London Combination.

		APPEARANCES					GOALS				
Season	Div	Lge	FA	LC	Oth	Total	Lge	FA	LC	Oth	Total
WW1		22				22	9				9
Total		22				22	9				9

HUMPHREYS, Percy
Born: Cambridge, 3 Dec 1881.
Signed from: Cambridge St Mary's, 1900.
Debut v Swindon Town, 8 Sep 1900 (1 goal), Southern League.
Transferred to: Notts County, 1901.

		APPEARANCES					GOALS				
Season	Div	Lge	FA	LC	Oth	Total	Lge	FA	LC	Oth	Total
1900-01	SL	27	4			31	9	3			12
Total		27	4		31	9	3			12	

HUNT, Ron
Born: Paddington, 19 Dec 1945.
Signed from: (apprentice), Mar 1963.
Debut v Bristol Rovers, 28 Dec 1964.
Retired knee injury.

		APPEARANCES					GOALS				
Season	Div	Lge	FA	LC	Oth	Total	Lge	FA	LC	Oth	Total
1964-65	3	10				10					
1965-66	3	32	5	2		39					
1966-67	3	44	3	9		56					
1967-68	2	10/1		2		12/1					
1968-69	1	29/2	1			30/2					
1969-70	2	21/1		3		24/1					
1970-71	2	37	1	2		40	1				1
1971-72	2	29/1	2	4		35/1					
1972-73	2	2	1/1			3/1					
Total		214/5	13/1	22		249/6	1				1

HURREL, Willie
Born: Dundee, 28 Jan 1920.
Signed from: Millwall, Jul 1953.
Debut v Southampton, 16 Sep 1953.

		APPEARANCES					GOALS				
Season	Div	Lge	FA	LC	Oth	Total	Lge	FA	LC	Oth	Total
1953-54	3S	6	3			9	1	2			3
Total		6	3			9	1	2			3

HURST, W
Signed from: Derby County.
Debut v Luton Town, 2 Feb 1924.

		APPEARANCES					GOALS				
Season	Div	Lge	FA	LC	Oth	Total	Lge	FA	LC	Oth	Total
1923-24	3S	2				2					
1924-25	3S	8				8	4				4
Total		10				10	4				4

IMPEY, Andrew
Born: Hammersmith, 13 Sep 1971.
Signed from: Yeading, Aug 1990 (free).
Debut v Hull City, 9 Oct 1991, League Cup (sub).

		APPEARANCES					GOALS				
Season	Div	Lge	FA	LC	Oth	Total	Lge	FA	LC	Oth	Total
1991-92	1	13		0/1	0/2	13/3				1	1
1992-93	Pr	39/1	0/1	3		42/2	2				2
Total		52/1	0/1	3/1	0/2	55/5	2			1	3

INGHAM, Tony
Born: Harrogate, 18 Feb 1925.
Signed from: Leeds United, Jun 1950.
Debut v Doncaster Rovers, 25 Nov 1950.

		APPEARANCES					GOALS				
Season	Div	Lge	FA	LC	Oth	Total	Lge	FA	LC	Oth	Total
1950-51	2	23				23					
1951-52	2	17	1			18					
1952-53	3S	43	3			46	1				1
1953-54	3S	41	4			45					
1954-55	3S	38	3			41					
1955-56	3S	41	1			42	1				1
1956-57	3S	46	3			49					
1957-58	3S	46	3			49	1				1
1958-59	3	46	2			48					
1959-60	3	46	3			49					
1960-61	3	46	2	2		50					
1961-62	3	40	2	2		44					
1962-63	3	41	3			44					
Total		514	30	4		548	3				3

IORFA, Dononre
Born: Lagos, Nigeria, 1 Oct 1968.
Signed from: Standard Liège, Mar 1990 (£175,000).
Debut v Wimbledon, 5 May 1990 (sub).
Transferred to: Galatasaray, Dec 1991 (£100,000).

		APPEARANCES					GOALS				
Season	Div	Lge	FA	LC	Oth	Total	Lge	FA	LC	Oth	Total
1989-90	1	0/1				0/1					
1990-91	1	1/5		1		2/5					
1991-92	1	0/1				0/1					
Total		1/7		1		2/7					

IVES, C.Ben
Born: Hackney, 1889.
Signed from: Exeter City, 1912.
Debut v Merthyr Town, 19 Apr 1913 (2 goals), Southern League.
Transferred to: Clapton Orient, 1919.

		APPEARANCES					GOALS				
Season	Div	Lge	FA	LC	Oth	Total	Lge	FA	LC	Oth	Total
1912-13	SL	1				1	2				2
1913-14	SL	30				30	1				1
1914-15	SL	5				5					
1st WW		1				37					
Total		37				37	3				3

JACKMAN, V.
Debut v Reading, 21 Mar 1913, Southern League.

		APPEARANCES					GOALS				
Season	Div	Lge	FA	LC	Oth	Total	Lge	FA	LC	Oth	Total
1912-13	SL	3				3					
Total		3				3					

JACKS, George
Born: London, 14 Mar 1946.
Signed from: (apprentice), Jan 1964.
Debut v Exeter City, 23 Apr 1965.
Transferred to: Millwall, Jul 1965.

		APPEARANCES					GOALS				
Season	Div	Lge	FA	LC	Oth	Total	Lge	FA	LC	Oth	Total
1964-65	3	1				1					
Total		1				1					

JAMES, Leighton
Born: Llwchwyr, 16 Feb 1953.
Signed from: Derby County, Oct 1977 (exchange D.Masson).
Debut v West Bromwich Albion, 29 Oct 1977.
Transferred to: Burnley, Sep 1978 (£165,000).

		APPEARANCES					GOALS				
Season	Div	Lge	FA	LC	Oth	Total	Lge	FA	LC	Oth	Total
1977-78	1	26/1	5			31/1	4	2			6
1978-79	1	1				1					
Total		27/1	5			32/1	4	2			6

JAMES, Norman
Born: Bootle.
Signed from: Bradford City, Oct 1936.
Debut v Gillingham, 31 Oct 1936.
Transferred: 1939.

		APPEARANCES					GOALS				
Season	Div	Lge	FA	LC	Oth	Total	Lge	FA	LC	Oth	Total
1936-37	3S	5	1			6					
1937-38	3S	30	2			32					
1938-39	3S	32	3			35	1				1
Total		67	6			73	1				1

JAMES, Robbie
Born: Swansea, 23 Mar 1957.
Signed from: Stoke City, Oct 1984 (£100,000).
Debut v Arsenal, 17 Nov 1984 (sub).
Transferred to: Leicester City, Jun 1987 (£70,000).

		APPEARANCES					GOALS				
Season	Div	Lge	FA	LC	Oth	Total	Lge	FA	LC	Oth	Total
1984-85	1	16/4				16/4	2				2
1985-86	1	25/3	1	6		32/3	1				1
1986-87	1	37/2	4	3		44/2	2	1			3
Total		78/9	5	9		92/9	5	1			6

JEFFERIES, H.
Born: Bristol.
Signed from: Aberdare Athletic.
Debut v West Ham United, 27 Sep 1913, Southern League.

		APPEARANCES					GOALS				
Season	Div	Lge	FA	LC	Oth	Total	Lge	FA	LC	Oth	Total
1913-14	SL	1				1					
1st WW		20				20					
Total		21				21					

JEFFERSON
Debut v Tottenham, 8 Dec 1917, London Combination.

		APPEARANCES					GOALS				
Season	Div	Lge	FA	LC	Oth	Total	Lge	FA	LC	Oth	Total
WW1		34			4	38	4			1	5
Total		34			4	38	4			1	5

JEFFERSON, Arthur
Born: Rotherham, 14 Dec 1916.
Signed from: Peterborough United.
Debut v Millwall, 31 Aug 1936.
Transferred to: Aldershot, Mar 1950.

		APPEARANCES					GOALS				
Season	Div	Lge	FA	LC	Oth	Total	Lge	FA	LC	Oth	Total
1936-37	3S	25	3			28					
1937-38	3S	34	2			36					
1938-39	3S	30	4			34					
1939-40	3S	3				3					
2nd WW		102	9		16	127					
1946-47	3S	40	6			46					
1947-48	3S	26	6			32					
1948-49	2	39	2			41	1				1
1949-50	2	17				17					
Total		333	32		16	364	1				1

JENKINS
Debut v Clapton Orient, 16 Nov 1918, London Combination.

		APPEARANCES					GOALS				
Season	Div	Lge	FA	LC	Oth	Total	Lge	FA	LC	Oth	Total
WW1		1				1					
Total		1				1					

JOBSON, John
Debut v Brentford, 27 Aug 1932.

		APPEARANCES					GOALS				
Season	Div	Lge	FA	LC	Oth	Total	Lge	FA	LC	Oth	Total
1932-33	3S	4				4					
Total		4				4					

JOHN, Reg
Born: Llanelly, 22 Aug 1899.
Signed from: Aberdare Athletic, 1920.
Debut v Southampton, 6 Nov 1920.
Transferred to: Charlton Athletic, 1926.

		APPEARANCES					GOALS				
Season	Div	Lge	FA	LC	Oth	Total	Lge	FA	LC	Oth	Total
1920-21	3	2				2					
1921-22	3S	13	1			14					
1922-23	3S	33	4			37					
1923-24	3S	36	1			37					
1924-25	3S	21	4			25	1				1
1925-26	3S	26	4			30					
Total		131	14			145	1				1

JOHNS, Nicky
Born: Bristol, 8 Jun 1957.
Signed from: Charlton Athletic, Dec 1987 (£40,000).
Debut v Reading, 21 Dec 1987, Simod Cup.
Transferred to: Maidstone United.

		APPEARANCES					GOALS				
Season	Div	Lge	FA	LC	Oth	Total	Lge	FA	LC	Oth	Total
1987-88	1	7	3		1	11					
1988-89	1	3		2		5					
Total		10	3	2	1	16					

JOHNSON, H.
Born: Birmingham.
Debut v Reading, 16 Feb 1924.

		APPEARANCES					GOALS				
Season	Div	Lge	FA	LC	Oth	Total	Lge	FA	LC	Oth	Total
1923-24	3S	14				14	3				3
1924-25	3S	27	5			32	10				10
1925-26	3S	9				9	2				2
1926-27	3S										
1927-28	3S	17	1			18	7	1			8
1928-29	3S	1				1					
Total		68	6			74	22	1			23

JONES, Charlie
Born: Swansea, 1911.
Debut v Crystal Palace, 10 Sep 1932.

		APPEARANCES					GOALS				
Season	Div	Lge	FA	LC	Oth	Total	Lge	FA	LC	Oth	Total
1932-33	3S	13				13	1				1
1933-34	3S	3				3					
Total		16				16	1				1

JONES, G.
Debut v Southend United, 17 Apr 1946, South (North) Cup.

		APPEARANCES					GOALS				
Season	Div	Lge	FA	LC	Oth	Total	Lge	FA	LC	Oth	Total
2nd WW					1	1					
Total					1	1					

JORDAN, F.
Debut v Tottenham Hotspur, 14 Sep 1901, Southern League.

		APPEARANCES					GOALS				
Season	Div	Lge	FA	LC	Oth	Total	Lge	FA	LC	Oth	Total
1901-02	SL	2				2					
Total		2				2					

JORDAN, H.
Debut v Bristol City, 7 Oct 1899, Southern League.

		APPEARANCES					GOALS				
Season	Div	Lge	FA	LC	Oth	Total	Lge	FA	LC	Oth	Total
1899-1900	SL	1	1			2					
Total		1	1			2					

KEECH, William
Born: Irthlingburgh, 1876.
Signed from: Leicester Fosse, Aug 1899.
Debut v Tottenham Hotspur, 9 Sep 1899, Southern League.
Transferred to: Brentford, 1902.

		APPEARANCES					GOALS				
Season	Div	Lge	FA	LC	Oth	Total	Lge	FA	LC	Oth	Total
1899-1900	SL	24	8			32	2	3			5
1900-01	SL	14	3			17	1				1
1901-02	SL	17	3			20					
Total		55	14			69	3	3			6

KEEN, Mike
Born: Wycombe, 19 Mar 1940.
Debut v York City, 7 Sep 1959.
Transferred to: Luton Town, Jan 1969 (£18,500).

		APPEARANCES					GOALS				
Season	Div	Lge	FA	LC	Oth	Total	Lge	FA	LC	Oth	Total
1959-60	3	27	3			30	1				1
1960-61	3	34	2	1		37	2				2
1961-62	3	46	4	2		52	2				2
1962-63	3	41	1	1		43	1				1
1963-64	3	46	3	1		50	4				4
1964-65	3	46	3	2		51	13	1			14
1965-66	3	46	5	2		53	4				4
1966-67	3	46	3	9		58	6		2		8
1967-68	2	42	1	3		46	6	1	1		8
1968-69	1	19		1		20			1		1
Total		393	25	22		440	39	2	4		45

KEEN, James
Born: Newcastle upon Tyne, 25 Nov 1897.
Signed from: Newcastle United.
Debut v Brentford, 25 Aug 1923.
Transferred to: Hull City, 1924.

		APPEARANCES					GOALS				
Season	Div	Lge	FA	LC	Oth	Total	Lge	FA	LC	Oth	Total
1923-24	3S	31	1			32					
Total		31	1			32					

KEETCH, Bobby
Born: Tottenham, 25 Oct 1941.
Signed from: Fulham, Nov 1966 (free).
Debut v Peterborough United, 11 Mar 1967.
Transferred to: Durban City, May 1969 (£5,000).

		APPEARANCES					GOALS				
Season	Div	Lge	FA	LC	Oth	Total	Lge	FA	LC	Oth	Total
1966-67	3	1/1				1/1					
1967-68	2	32/1	1	2		35/1					
1968-69	1	16/1	1			17/1					
Total		49/3	2	2		53/3					

KELLARD, Thomas
Born: Oldham, 1905.
Signed from: Oldham Athletic.
Debut v Norwich City, 3 Feb 1928.
Transferred to: Burton Town, 1929.

		APPEARANCES					GOALS				
Season	Div	Lge	FA	LC	Oth	Total	Lge	FA	LC	Oth	Total
1927-28	3S	1				1					
1928-29	3S	4				4	1				1
Total		5				5	1				1

KELLY, (William) Brian
Born: Isleworth, 25 Sep 1937.
Signed: Nov 1958.
Debut v Swindon Town, 13 Dec 1958.

		APPEARANCES					GOALS				
Season	Div	Lge	FA	LC	Oth	Total	Lge	FA	LC	Oth	Total
1958-59	3	6				6					
Total		6				6					

KELLY, Eddie
Born: Glasgow, 7 Feb 1951.
Signed from: Arsenal, Sep 1976 (£60,000).
Debut v Aston Villa, 11 Sep 1976.
Transferred to: Leicester City, Jul 1977 (£50,000).

		APPEARANCES					GOALS				
Season	Div	Lge	FA	LC	Oth	Total	Lge	FA	LC	Oth	Total
1976-77	1	28		3	2	33	1				1
Total		28		3	2	33	1				1

KELLY, James
Signed from: Cambuslang Rangers.

		APPEARANCES					GOALS				
Season	Div	Lge	FA	LC	Oth	Total	Lge	FA	LC	Oth	Total
2nd WW		7				7					
Total		7				7					

KELLY, Mike
Born: London, 18 Oct 1942.
Signed from: Wimbledon, Mar 1966 (£1,000 & E.Wicks).
Debut v Poole Town, 26 Nov 1966, FA Cup.
Transferred to: Birmingham City, Aug 1970 (£16,000).

		APPEARANCES					GOALS				
Season	Div	Lge	FA	LC	Oth	Total	Lge	FA	LC	Oth	Total
1966-67	3		1			1					
1967-68	2	6				6					
1968-69	1	20		1		21					
1969-70	2	28	4	4		36					
Total		54	5	5		64					

KERR, A.
Born: Falkirk.
Debut v Millwall, 27 Nov 1926.

		APPEARANCES					GOALS				
Season	Div	Lge	FA	LC	Oth	Total	Lge	FA	LC	Oth	Total
1925-26	3S	2				2					
Total		2				2					

KERRINS, Pat
Born: Fulham.
Signed from: (juniors), Dec 1953.
Debut v Exeter City, 13 Feb 1954.
Transferred to: Crystal Palace, Jun 1960.

		APPEARANCES					GOALS				
Season	Div	Lge	FA	LC	Oth	Total	Lge	FA	LC	Oth	Total
1953-54	3S	13				13	4				4
1954-55	3S	15	1			16	2				2
1953-54	3S	20				20	2				2
1956-57	3S	31	3			34	7				7
1957-58	3S	31	3			34	7				7
1958-59	3	29	2			31	7				7
1959-60	3	7				7	1				1
Total		146	9			155	30				30

KERSLAKE, David
Born: Stepney, 19 Jun 1966.
Signed from: (apprentice), Jun 1983.
Debut v Newcastle United, 13 Apr 1985 (sub).
Transferred to: Swindon Town, Dec 1989 (£110,000).

		APPEARANCES					GOALS				
Season	Div	Lge	FA	LC	Oth	Total	Lge	FA	LC	Oth	Total
1984-85	1	0/1				0/1					
1985-86	1	9/5		3		12/5	1		3		4
1986-87	1	2/1				2/1					
1987-88	1	16/2	0/2		0/1	16/5	5				5
1988-89	1	11/10	2	3/2	2/1	18/13			1		1
1989-90	1	0/1				0/1					
Total		38/20	2/2	6/2	2/2	48/26	6		4		10

KING, A.
Debut v Bradford City, 18 Jan 1912, FA Cup.

		APPEARANCES					GOALS				
Season	Div	Lge	FA	LC	Oth	Total	Lge	FA	LC	Oth	Total
1911-12	SL	3	1			4					
Total		3	1			4					

KING, Andy
Born: Luton, 14 Aug 1956.
Signed from: Everton, Aug 1980 (£425,000)
Debut v Sheffield Wednesday, 20 Sep 1980.
Transferred to: West Bromwich Albion, Sep 1981 (£400,000).

		APPEARANCES					GOALS				
Season	Div	Lge	FA	LC	Oth	Total	Lge	FA	LC	Oth	Total
1980-81	2	24/2	2	1		27/2	6				6
1981-82	2	4				4	3				3
Total		28/2	2	1		31/2	9				9

KING, Arthur
Debut v Watford, 7 Sep 1901, Southern League.

		APPEARANCES					GOALS				
Season	Div	Lge	FA	LC	Oth	Total	Lge	FA	LC	Oth	Total
1901-02	SL	15				15	2				2
1902-03	SL	6	1			7					
Total		21	1			22	2				2

KING, P.
Debut v Aldershot, 14 Apr 1945, League South.

		APPEARANCES					GOALS				
Season	Div	Lge	FA	LC	Oth	Total	Lge	FA	LC	Oth	Total
2nd WW		2				2					
Total		2				2					

KING, R.
Debut v Swindon Town, 21 Nov 1908, Southern League.

		APPEARANCES					GOALS				
Season	Div	Lge	FA	LC	Oth	Total	Lge	FA	LC	Oth	Total
1908-09	SL	3				3					
Total		3				3					

KINGSLEY, Matthew
Born: Turton, 1876.
Signed from: West Ham United, 1905.
Debut v New Brompton, 2 Sep 1905, Southern League.
Transferred to: Rochdale, 1907.

		APPEARANCES					GOALS				
Season	Div	Lge	FA	LC	Oth	Total	Lge	FA	LC	Oth	Total
1905-06	SL	20				20					
Total		20				20					

KNIGHT, E.
Debut v Aberdare Athletic, 12 Nov 1921 (1 goal).

		APPEARANCES					GOALS				
Season	Div	Lge	FA	LC	Oth	Total	Lge	FA	LC	Oth	Total
1921-22	3S	2				2	1				1
Total		2				2	1				1

KNOWLES, Frank
Born: Hyde.
Signed from: Newport County.
Debut v Reading, 23 Feb 1924.

		APPEARANCES					GOALS				
Season	Div	Lge	FA	LC	Oth	Total	Lge	FA	LC	Oth	Total
1923-24	3S	13				13					
1924-25	3S	22	5			27					
Total		35	5			40					

KNOWLES, Joe
Born: Monkwearmouth, 1874.
Signed from: Sunderland, Aug 1899.
Debut v Tottenham Hospur, 9 Sep 1899.

		APPEARANCES					GOALS				
Season	Div	Lge	FA	LC	Oth	Total	Lge	FA	LC	Oth	Total
1899-1900	SL	22	7			29					
Total		22	7			29					

LANE, Harry
Born: Stoney Stratton, 23 Oct 1894.
Signed from: Charlton Athletic, 1922.
Debut v Aberdare Athletic, 4 Nov 1922.

		APPEARANCES					GOALS				
Season	Div	Lge	FA	LC	Oth	Total	Lge	FA	LC	Oth	Total
1922-23	3S	5				5					
Total		5				5					

LANGFORD, Walter
Born: Wolverhampton.
Signed from: Leicester City.
Debut v Luton Town, 9 Sep 1933.

		APPEARANCES					GOALS				
Season	Div	Lge	FA	LC	Oth	Total	Lge	FA	LC	Oth	Total
1933-34	3S	9				9					
1934-35	3S	2	1			3					
Total		11	1			12					

LANGLEY, Jim
Born: Kilburn, 7 Feb 1929.
Signed from: Fulham, Jul 1965 (£5,000).
Debut v Brentford, 21 Aug 1965.
Transferred to: Hillingdon, Nov 1967.

		APPEARANCES					GOALS				
Season	Div	Lge	FA	LC	Oth	Total	Lge	FA	LC	Oth	Total
1965-66	3	46	5	2		53	3				3
1966-67	3	40/1	3	8		51/1	5	1	1		7
Total		86/1	8	10		104/1	8	1	1		10

LANGLEY, Tommy
Born: Lambeth, 8 Feb 1958.
Signed from: Chelsea, Aug 1980 (£475,000).
Debut v Swansea City, 23 Aug 1980.
Transferred to: Crystal Palace, Mar 1981 (£200,000).

		APPEARANCES					GOALS				
Season	Div	Lge	FA	LC	Oth	Total	Lge	FA	LC	Oth	Total
1980-81	2	24/1		3		27/1	8		1		9
Total		24/1		3		27/1	8		1		9

LARGE, Frank
Born: Leeds, 26 Jan 1940.
Signed from: Halifax Town, Jun 1962.
Debut v Brighton & Hove Albion, 18 Aug 1962.
Transferred to: Northampton Town, Mar 1963.

		APPEARANCES					GOALS				
Season	Div	Lge	FA	LC	Oth	Total	Lge	FA	LC	Oth	Total
1962-63	3	18	3	1		22	5	2			7
Total		18	3	1		22	5	2			7

LAW, R.
Debut v Plymouth Argyle, 29 Apr 1911, Southern League.

		APPEARANCES					GOALS				
Season	Div	Lge	FA	LC	Oth	Total	Lge	FA	LC	Oth	Total
1910-11	SL	1				1					
Total		1				1					

LAW, Brian
Born: Merthyr Tydfil, 1 Jan 1970.
Signed from: (apprentice), Aug 1987.
Debut v Sheffield Wednesday, 23 Apr 1988 (sub).
Retired through injury.

		APPEARANCES					GOALS				
Season	Div	Lge	FA	LC	Oth	Total	Lge	FA	LC	Oth	Total
1987-88	1	0/1				0/1					
1988-89	1	6	3	1		10					
1989-90	1	9				9					
1990-91	1	3		1/1	1	5/1					
Total		18/1	3	2/1	1	2/2					

LAW, William
Born: Walsall, Nov 1882.
Signed from: Watford, 1908.
Debut v Watford, 16 Sep 1908, Southern League.
Transferred to: Glossop, 1910.

		APPEARANCES					GOALS				
Season	Div	Lge	FA	LC	Oth	Total	Lge	FA	LC	Oth	Total
1908-09	SL	4	1			5	1				1
Total		4	1			5	1				1

LAWRENCE, W.
Debut v Tottenham Hotspur, 25 Oct 1916, London Combination.

		APPEARANCES					GOALS				
Season	Div	Lge	FA	LC	Oth	Total	Lge	FA	LC	Oth	Total
WW1		20				20	10				10
Total		20				20	10				10

LAY, Peter
Born: Stratford, 4 Dec 1931.
Signed from: Nottingham Forest, Jul 1956.
Debut v Crystal Palace, 26 Dec 1956 (1 goal).

		APPEARANCES					GOALS				
Season	Div	Lge	FA	LC	Oth	Total	Lge	FA	LC	Oth	Total
1956-57	3S	1				1					
Total		1				1					

LAZARUS, Mark
Born: Stepney, 5 Dec 1938.
Signed from: Leyton Orient, Sep 1960.
Debut v Colchester United, 17 Sep 1960 (1 goal).
Transferred to: Wolverhampton Wanderers, Sep 1961; From: Wolverhampton Wanderers, Feb 1962; To: Brentford, Apr 1964 (£8,000); From: Brentford, Nov 1965 (£10,000); To: Crystal Palace, Nov 1967 (£10,000).

		APPEARANCES					GOALS				
Season	Div	Lge	FA	LC	Oth	Total	Lge	FA	LC	Oth	Total
1960-61	3	29	2	2		33	12		1		13
1961-62	3	24		1		25	12				12
1962-63	3	42	3	1		46	18	1			19
1963-64	3	23	3			26	5				5
1965-66	3	28/1	3			31/1	11	1			12
1966-67	3	44	3	9		56	16	1	4		21
1967-68	2	14/1		2		16/1	2				2
Total		204/2	14	15		233/2	76	3	5		84

LEACH, J.
Signed from: Aston Villa.
Debut v Watford, 26 Aug 1922.

		APPEARANCES					GOALS				
Season	Div	Lge	FA	LC	Oth	Total	Lge	FA	LC	Oth	Total
1922-23	3S	1				1					
Total		1				1					

LEACH, Mick
Born: London, 16 Jan 1947.
Signed from: (apprentice), Feb 1964.
Debut v Colchester United, 26 Feb 1965 (1 goal).
Transferred to: Detroit Express, Mar 1978 (£30,000).

		APPEARANCES					GOALS				
Season	Div	Lge	FA	LC	Oth	Total	Lge	FA	LC	Oth	Total
1964-65	3	5				5	1				1
1965-66	3	10				10	1				1
1966-67	3	2				2	1				1
1967-68	2	21/2	1	2		24/2	9		1		10
1968-69	1	30	1			31	8				8
1969-70	2	30/3	1	5		36/3	4		1		5
1970-71	2	25	1			26	6				6
1971-72	2	28/3	2			30/3	8				8
1972-73	2	35/1	4	1		40/1	10	2			12
1973-74	1	39/1	6	2		47/1	6	1	2		9
1974-75	1	16/4	2	1		19/4	2				2
1975-76	1	28/3	2	4		34/3	4		2		6
1976-77	1	16/4	2	2/2	†6	26/6	1				1
1977-78	1	6/1	1			7/1					
Total		291/22	23	17/2	6	337/24	61	3	6		70

LEARY, Stuart
Born: South Africa, 30 Apr 1933.
Signed from: Charlton Athletic, Dec 1962.
Debut v Brighton & Hove Albion, 15 Dec 1962.

		APPEARANCES					GOALS				
Season	Div	Lge	FA	LC	Oth	Total	Lge	FA	LC	Oth	Total
1962-63	3	24	1			25	9				9
1963-64	3	43	3	1		47	12	2			14
1964-65	3	26	3	2		31	8	1			9
1965-66	3	1				1					
Total		94	7	3		104	29	3			32

LEATHER, Jack
Born: 1875.
Signed from: Woolwich Arsenal.
Debut v Wellingborough, 26 Mar 1904, Southern League.

		APPEARANCES					GOALS				
Season	Div	Lge	FA	LC	Oth	Total	Lge	FA	LC	Oth	Total
1903-04	SL	1				1					
1904-05	SL	1				1					
Total		2				2					

LEE, Sammy
Born: Liverpool, 7 Feb 1959.
Signed from: Liverpool, Aug 1986 (£175,000).
Debut v Aston Villa, 30 Aug 1986.
Transferred to: CA Osasuna, Jul 1987 (£200,000).

		APPEARANCES					GOALS				
Season	Div	Lge	FA	LC	Oth	Total	Lge	FA	LC	Oth	Total
1986-87	1	29/1	2	2		33/2		1			1
Total		29/1	2	2		33/2		1			1

LEGGE, Albert
Born: Wednesford, 19 Jan 1901.
Signed from: Charlton Athletic.
Debut v Thames, 30 Aug 1930.

		APPEARANCES					GOALS				
Season	Div	Lge	FA	LC	Oth	Total	Lge	FA	LC	Oth	Total
1930-31	3S	9				9					
Total		9				9					

LEE, Thomas
Born: Bury, 1887.
Signed from: Fulham, 1910.
Debut v Bristol Rovers, 19 Nov 1910, Southern League.

		APPEARANCES					GOALS				
Season	Div	Lge	FA	LC	Oth	Total	Lge	FA	LC	Oth	Total
1910-11	SL	4				4					
Total		4				4					

LENNON, ALec
Born: Glasgow, 23 Jan 1925.
Signed from: Rotherham, Jan 1947.
Debut v Norwich City, 25 Dec 1945, League South.
Transferred to: Mansfield Town, Feb 1949.

		APPEARANCES					GOALS				
Season	Div	Lge	FA	LC	Oth	Total	Lge	FA	LC	Oth	Total
2nd WW		2				2					
1948-49	2	1				1					
Total		3				3					

LENNOX, Stuart
Debut v Reading, 29 Dec 1900, Southern League.

		APPEARANCES					GOALS				
Season	Div	Lge	FA	LC	Oth	Total	Lge	FA	LC	Oth	Total
1900-01	SL	10				10					
1901-02	SL	1				1					
Total		11				11					

LEWIS, Jim
Born: Hammersmith.
Signed from: Walthamstow Avenue.
Debut v Bournemouth, 2 May 1931 (1 goal).

		APPEARANCES					GOALS				
Season	Div	Lge	FA	LC	Oth	Total	Lge	FA	LC	Oth	Total
1930-31	3S	1				1	1				1
1931-32	3S	11				11	4				4
Total		12				12	5				5

LEWIS, L.
Debut v Portsmouth, 9 Sep 1916, London Combination.

		APPEARANCES					GOALS				
Season	Div	Lge	FA	LC	Oth	Total	Lge	FA	LC	Oth	Total
WW1		21				21					
Total		21				21					

LILLIE, J.
Born: Newcastle upon Tyne.
Signed from: Liverpool.
Debut v Newport County, 30 Aug 1924.
Transferred to: Clapton Orient.

		APPEARANCES					GOALS				
Season	Div	Lge	FA	LC	Oth	Total	Lge	FA	LC	Oth	Total
1924-25	3S	3				3					
Total		3				3					

LIBBY, J.
Debut v Brentford, 11 Apr 1942, War Cup.

		APPEARANCES					GOALS				
Season	Div	Lge	FA	LC	Oth	Total	Lge	FA	LC	Oth	Total
2nd WW					1	1					
Total					1	1					

LING, L.

		APPEARANCES					GOALS				
Season	Div	Lge	FA	LC	Oth	Total	Lge	FA	LC	Oth	Total
2nd WW		6				6	4				4
Total		6				6	4				4

LINKSON
Debut v Croydon Common, 11 Sep 1915, London Combination.

		APPEARANCES					GOALS				
Season	Div	Lge	FA	LC	Oth	Total	Lge	FA	LC	Oth	Total
WW1		17				17					
Total		17				17					

LINTON, Mac
Debut v Fulham, 2 Mar 1918, London Combination.

		APPEARANCES					GOALS				
Season	Div	Lge	FA	LC	Oth	Total	Lge	FA	LC	Oth	Total
WW1		14			3	17	4			2	6
Total		14			3	17	4			2	6

LINTOTT, Evelyn
Born: Godalming, 2 Nov 1883.
Signed from: Plymouth Argyle, 1907.
Debut v New Brompton, 7 Sep 1907, Southern League.
Transferred to: Bradford, 1908.

		APPEARANCES					GOALS				
Season	Div	Lge	FA	LC	Oth	Total	Lge	FA	LC	Oth	Total
1907-08	SL	22	2		*1	25	1				1
1908-09	SL	9			*1	10					
Total		31	2		2	35	1				1

LOCK, H.
Signed from: Glasgow Rangers, 1921.
Debut v Aberdare Athletic, 12 Nov 1921.
Transferred to: Bournemouth, 1922.

		APPEARANCES					GOALS				
Season	Div	Lge	FA	LC	Oth	Total	Lge	FA	LC	Oth	Total
1921-22	3S	6				6					
Total		6				6					

LOCKE, Leslie
Born: Perth, 24 Jan 1934.
Signed from: Bromley, May 1958.
Debut v Plymouth Argyle, 27 Aug 1956.
Transferred to: Guildford City, Jul 1960.

		APPEARANCES					GOALS				
Season	Div	Lge	FA	LC	Oth	Total	Lge	FA	LC	Oth	Total
1956-57	3S	19	1			20	2	1			3
1957-58	3S	22	2			24	13	1			14
1958-59	3	25				25	6				6
1959-60	3	10				10	3				3
Total		76	3			79	24	2			26

LOFTHOUSE, James
Born: St Helens.
Signed from: Bristol Rovers.
Debut v Crystal Palace, 28 Aug 1926.

		APPEARANCES					GOALS				
Season	Div	Lge	FA	LC	Oth	Total	Lge	FA	LC	Oth	Total
1926-27	3S	42				42	14				14
1927-28	3S	38	1			39	13				13
Total		80	1			81	27				27

LOGAN, W.
Born: Govanhill, Glasgow, 1887.
Signed from: Vale of Leven.
Debut v Watford, 1 Sep 1909, Southern League.

		APPEARANCES					GOALS				
Season	Div	Lge	FA	LC	Oth	Total	Lge	FA	LC	Oth	Total
1909-10	SL	7				7					
Total		7				7					

LONEY, B.
Debut v Crystal Palace, 24 Jan 1915, Southern League.

		APPEARANCES					GOALS				
Season	Div	Lge	FA	LC	Oth	Total	Lge	FA	LC	Oth	Total
1914-15	SL	1				1					
1st WW		64				64					
Total		65				65					

LONGBOTTOM, Arthur
Born: Leeds, 30 Jan 1933.
Signed from: Methley United, Mar 1954.
Debut v Leyton Orient, 12 Mar 1955.
Transferred to: Port Vale, May 1961.

		APPEARANCES					GOALS				
Season	Div	Lge	FA	LC	Oth	Total	Lge	FA	LC	Oth	Total
1954-55	3S	11				11	1				1
1955-56	3S	12				12					
1956-57	3S	34	2			36	14	1			15
1957-58	3S	40	3			43	17	1			18
1958-59	3	41	2			43	20				20
1959-60	3	37	3			40	6	2			8
1960-61	3	26	1			27	4	1			5
Total		201	11			212	62	5			67

LOWE, Harry
Born: Kingskettle, Fifeshire.
Signed from: Watford, Jun 1935 (exchange E.Goodier).
Debut v Millwall, 31 Aug 1935 (1 goal).
Transferred to: Guildford, 1939.

		APPEARANCES					GOALS				
Season	Div	Lge	FA	LC	Oth	Total	Lge	FA	LC	Oth	Total
1935-36	3S	34	1			35	15				15
1936-37	3S	41	3			44	17				17
1937-38	3S	41	2			43	3				3
1938-39	3S	42	4			46	5				5
1939-40	3S	3				3					
2nd WW		66			1	67	6			5	11
Total		227	10		1	238	46			5	51

LOWE, O.
Debut v Southampton, 25 Apr 1908, Southern League.

		APPEARANCES					GOALS				
Season	Div	Lge	FA	LC	Oth	Total	Lge	FA	LC	Oth	Total
1907-08	SL	2				2					
Total		2				2					

LOWE, W.
Debut v Millwall, 8 Nov 1919, Southern League.

		APPEARANCES					GOALS				
Season	Div	Lge	FA	LC	Oth	Total	Lge	FA	LC	Oth	Total
1919-20	SL	1				1					
Total		1				1					

LUMSDEN, Frank
Born: Sunderland.
Signed from: Huddersfield Town.
Debut v Swindon Town, 21 Sep 1935.
Transferred to: Burnley, Jul 1937 (free).

		APPEARANCES					GOALS				
Season	Div	Lge	FA	LC	Oth	Total	Lge	FA	LC	Oth	Total
1935-36	3S	25	1			26	5				5
1936-37	3S	13				13	3				3
Total		38	1			39	8				8

LYON, Frank
Born: Crewe, 23 Sep 1879.
Signed from: Watford, 1903.
Debut v Fulham, 24 Oct 1903, Southern League.
Transferred to: Chelsea, Apr 1906.

		APPEARANCES					GOALS				
Season	Div	Lge	FA	LC	Oth	Total	Lge	FA	LC	Oth	Total
1903-04	SL	2	2			4					
1904-05	SL	16	1			17					
1905-06	SL	13	1			14					
1906-07	SL	25				25					
Total		56	4			60					

McADAMS, Billy
Born: Belfast, 20 Jan 1934.
Signed from: Brentford, Sep 1964.
Debut v Hull City, 25 Sep 1964 (1 goal).
Transferred to: Barrow, Jul 1966.

		APPEARANCES					GOALS				
Season	Div	Lge	FA	LC	Oth	Total	Lge	FA	LC	Oth	Total
1964-65	3	27	1			28	8	1			9
1965-66	3	6	2	2		10	3				3
Total		33	3	2		38	11	1			12

McALLISTER, W.
Born: Glasgow.
Signed from: Middlesbrough.
Debut v Millwall, 23 Oct 1926.

		APPEARANCES					GOALS				
Season	Div	Lge	FA	LC	Oth	Total	Lge	FA	LC	Oth	Total
1926-27	3S	26				26	1				1
Total		26				26	1				1

McCAIRNS, Thomas
Born: Dinsdale, 22 Dec 1873.
Signed from: Wellingborough, 1903.
Debut v Fulham, 24 Oct 1903, Southern League.
Transferred to: Brighton & Hove Albion, 1903.

		APPEARANCES					GOALS				
Season	Div	Lge	FA	LC	Oth	Total	Lge	FA	LC	Oth	Total
1903-04	SL	1	2			3					
Total		1	2			3					

McCARGILL, H.
Signed from: Gateshead.
Debut v Fulham, 14 Apr 1906, Southern League.

		APPEARANCES					GOALS				
Season	Div	Lge	FA	LC	Oth	Total	Lge	FA	LC	Oth	Total
1905-06	SL	3				3					
1906-07	SL	1				1					
Total		4				4					

McCARTHY, Alan
Born: London, 11 Jan 1972.
Debut v Watford, 14 Feb 1989, Simod Cup.

		APPEARANCES					GOALS				
Season	Div	Lge	FA	LC	Oth	Total	Lge	FA	LC	Oth	Total
1988-89	1				1	1					
1990-91	1	1/1		0/1	1	2/2					
1991-92	1	3				3					
Total		4/1		0/1	2	6/2					

McCARTHY, Len
Born: Caeran.
Signed from: Portsmouth.
Debut v Notts County, 30 Oct 1937.

		APPEARANCES					GOALS				
Season	Div	Lge	FA	LC	Oth	Total	Lge	FA	LC	Oth	Total
1937-38	3S	10				10	5				5
1938-39	3S	12	4			16	4	1			5
2nd WW		41				41	11				11
Total		63	4			67	20	1			21

McCELLAND, John
Born: Bradford, 5 Mar 1935.
Signed from: Lincoln City, Sep 1961.
Debut v Watford, 23 Sep 1961 (1 goal).
Transferred to: Portsmouth, May 1963.

		APPEARANCES					GOALS				
Season	Div	Lge	FA	LC	Oth	Total	Lge	FA	LC	Oth	Total
1961-62	3	38	4			42	11	1			12
1962-63	3	33	2	1		36	11	1			12
Total		71	6	1		78	22	2			24

McCOLGAN, John
Born: Lanarkshire.
Signed from: Plymouth Argyle.

		APPEARANCES					GOALS				
Season	Div	Lge	FA	LC	Oth	Total	Lge	FA	LC	Oth	Total
2nd WW		2				2					
Total		2				2					

McCONNELL, Alex
Born: Mossend, Glasgow, 1878.
Signed from: Woolwich Arsenal, Aug 1899.
Debut v Tottenham Hotspur, 9 Sep 1899, Southern League.
Transferred to: Grimsby Town, 1901.

		APPEARANCES					GOALS				
Season	Div	Lge	FA	LC	Oth	Total	Lge	FA	LC	Oth	Total
1899-1900	SL	28	10			38					
1900-01	SL	23	3			26					
Total		51	13			64					

McCREERY, David
Born: Belfast, 16 Sep 1957.
Signed from: Manchester United, Aug 1979 (£200,000).
Debut v Bristol Rovers, 18 Aug 1979.
Transferred to: Tulsa Roughnecks, Jun 1981 (with D.Neal £225,000).

		APPEARANCES					GOALS				
Season	Div	Lge	FA	LC	Oth	Total	Lge	FA	LC	Oth	Total
1979-80	2	42	1	5		48	4		1		5
1980-81	2	14/1	0/1	3		17/2					
Total		56/1	1/1	8		65/2	4		1		5

McCULLOCH, Andy
Born: Northampton, 3 Jan 1950.
Signed from: Walton & Hersham, Oct 1970.
Debut v Birmingham City, 17 Oct 1970 (1 goal).
Transferred to: Cardiff City, Oct 1972 (£45,000).

		APPEARANCES					GOALS				
Season	Div	Lge	FA	LC	Oth	Total	Lge	FA	LC	Oth	Total
1970-71	2	8/5				8/5	5				5
1971-72	2	17/6	0/1	3		20/7	4		1		5
1972-73	2	5/1		0/1		5/2	1				1
Total		30/12	0/1	3/1		33/14	10		1		11

McDONALD, Alan
Born: Belfast, 12 Oct 1963.
Signed from: (apprentice), Aug 1981.
Debut v Wolverhampton Wanderers, 24 Sep 1983.

		APPEARANCES					GOALS				
Season	Div	Lge	FA	LC	Oth	Total	Lge	FA	LC	Oth	Total
1983-84	1	5		3		8			1		1
1984-85	1	15/1	1	1		17/1	1				1
1985-86	1	42	1	8		51			1		1
1986-87	1	39	3	2		44	4				4
1987-88	1	36	4	3	1	44	3		1		4
1988-89	1	27/3	3	4	3	37/3		1			1
1989-90	1	35	9	3		47					
1990-91	1	17		3		20					
1991-92	1	28/1	1	1	1	31/1					
1992-83	Pr	39	2	3		44					
Total		283/5	24	31	5	343/5	8	1	3		12

MacDONALD, J.
Signed from: Lincoln, 1908.
Debut v West Ham United, 1 Sep 1908, Southern League.

		APPEARANCES					GOALS				
Season	Div	Lge	FA	LC	Oth	Total	Lge	FA	LC	Oth	Total
1908-09	SL	18	2			20					
Total		18	2			20					

McDONALD, J.
Born: Ayr, 1882.
Signed from: Grimsby Town, 1907.
Debut v Tottenham Hotspur, 14 Sep 1907, Southern League.
Retired 1913.

		APPEARANCES					GOALS				
Season	Div	Lge	FA	LC	Oth	Total	Lge	FA	LC	Oth	Total
1907-08	SL	15	1		*1	17					
1908-09	SL	39	2		*1	42					
1909-10	SL	39	7			46					
1910-11	SL	35	1			36					
1911-12	SL	32	2		1	35					
1912-13	SL	22				22					
Total		182	13		3	198					

McEWAN, Billy
Born: Glasgow, 29 Aug 1914.
Signed from: Petershill (Glasgow).
Debut v Crystal Palace, 4 Mar 1939 (1 goal).
Transferred to: Leyton Orient, Feb 1950.

		APPEARANCES					GOALS				
Season	Div	Lge	FA	LC	Oth	Total	Lge	FA	LC	Oth	Total
1938-39	3S	13				13	2				2
1939-40	3S	1				1					
2nd WW		47			14	61	23			8	31
1946-47	3S	35	6			41	8	1			9
1947-48	3S	26	5			31	6	2			8
1948-49	2	13				13					
1949-50	2	9	1			10	1				1
Total		144	12		14	170	40	3		8	51

McEWAN, Robert
Born: 1881.
Signed from: Glossop, 1908.
Debut v Southampton, 26 Dec 1908.

		APPEARANCES					GOALS				
Season	Div	Lge	FA	LC	Oth	Total	Lge	FA	LC	Oth	Total
1908-09	SL	1				1					
Total		1				1					

McGEE, Paul
Born: Dublin, 19 Jun 1954.
Signed from: Toronto, Nov 1977 (£15,000).
Debut v Coventry City, 19 Nov 1977.
Transferred to: Preston North End, Oct 1979 (£100,000).

		APPEARANCES					GOALS				
Season	Div	Lge	FA	LC	Oth	Total	Lge	FA	LC	Oth	Total
1977-78	1	13/4	1/1			14/5	4				4
1978-79	1	18/4		3		21/4	3		1		4
Total		31/8	1/1	3		35/9	7		1		8

McGOVERN, Mick
Born: Hayes, 15 Feb 1951.
Signed from: (apprentice), Nov 1968.
Debut v Plymouth Argyle, 26 Dec 1967.
Transferred to: Swindon Town, Feb 1973 (£10,000).

		APPEARANCES					GOALS				
Season	Div	Lge	FA	LC	Oth	Total	Lge	FA	LC	Oth	Total
1967-68	2	1				1					
1968-69	1	1				1					
1969-70	2	3				3					
1970-71	2	5/1	1			6/1					
1971-72	2	0/1				0/1					
Total		10/2	1			11/2					

McGOVERN, T.
Born: Glasgow.
Signed from: Brentford.
Debut v Watford, 28 Aug 1920.

		APPEARANCES					GOALS				
Season	Div	Lge	FA	LC	Oth	Total	Lge	FA	LC	Oth	Total
1920-21	3	2				2					
Total		2				2					

McGOWAN, Frank
Debut v Tottenham Hotspur, 19 Sep 1903 (1 goal), Southern League.

		APPEARANCES					GOALS				
Season	Div	Lge	FA	LC	Oth	Total	Lge	FA	LC	Oth	Total
1903-04	SL	7	2			9	3				3
Total		7	2			9	3				3

McKAY, Johnny
Born: Port Glasgow, 27 Jun 1927.
Signed from: Irvine, Mar 1949.
Debut v Bury, 19 Nov 1949.

		APPEARANCES					GOALS				
Season	Div	Lge	FA	LC	Oth	Total	Lge	FA	LC	Oth	Total
1949-50	2	13				13	1				1
1950-51	2	1				1					
1951-52	2	3				3					
Total		17				17	1				1

McKAY, William
Born: Rothesay, 10 Mar 1927.
Signed from: Deal Town, Jul 1955.
Debut v Brentford, 30 Aug 1955.

		APPEARANCES					GOALS				
Season	Div	Lge	FA	LC	Oth	Total	Lge	FA	LC	Oth	Total
1955-56	3S	6				6					
Total		6				6					

McKENZIE, T.
Born: Inverness.
Signed from: Glossop.
Debut v West Ham United, 1 Sep 1908, Southern League.

		APPEARANCES					GOALS				
Season	Div	Lge	FA	LC	Oth	Total	Lge	FA	LC	Oth	Total
1908-09	SL	9				9	1				1
Total		9				9	1				1

McKIE, D.
Signed from: Chorley.
Debut v West Ham United, 12 Sep 1910, Southern League.

		APPEARANCES					GOALS				
Season	Div	Lge	FA	LC	Oth	Total	Lge	FA	LC	Oth	Total
1910-11	SL	28	1			29	10	2			12
1911-12	SL	30		1	*1	31	16				16
1912-13	SL	10				10	2				2
Total		68	1		1	70	28	2			30

McKINLEY
Debut v Luton Town, 26 Oct 1901, Southern League.

		APPEARANCES					GOALS				
Season	Div	Lge	FA	LC	Oth	Total	Lge	FA	LC	Oth	Total
1901-02	SL	4				4					
Total		4				4					

McKINNEY, E.
Signed from: Bloom Athletic, 1914.
Debut v Gillingham, 27 Feb 1915, Southern League.

		APPEARANCES					GOALS				
Season	Div	Lge	FA	LC	Oth	Total	Lge	FA	LC	Oth	Total
1914-15	SL	2				2					
Total		2				2					

McLARNEY, P.
Debut v New Brompton, 2 Sep 1905.

		APPEARANCES					GOALS				
Season	Div	Lge	FA	LC	Oth	Total	Lge	FA	LC	Oth	Total
1905-06	SL	8				8					
Total		8				8					

McLEAN, John
Born: Greenock, 1875.
Signed from: Millwall, 1906.
Debut v Luton Town, 1 Sep 1906.
Retired 1908.

		APPEARANCES					GOALS				
Season	Div	Lge	FA	LC	Oth	Total	Lge	FA	LC	Oth	Total
1906-07	SL	32	2			34					
1907-08	SL	28	1		*1	30					
1908-09	SL	13			*1	14					
Total		73	3		2	78					

McLEOD, George
Born: Inverness, 30 Nov 1932.
Signed from: Brentford, Jan 1964.
Debut v Southend United, 11 Jan 1964.

		APPEARANCES					GOALS				
Season	Div	Lge	FA	LC	Oth	Total	Lge	FA	LC	Oth	Total
1963-64	3	17				17	4				4
1964-65	3	24		1		25					
Total		41		1		42	4				4

McLEOD, R.
Signed from: Newport County.
Debut v Millwall, 1 Sep 1914, Southern League.

		APPEARANCES					GOALS				
Season	Div	Lge	FA	LC	Oth	Total	Lge	FA	LC	Oth	Total
1914-15	SL	38	3			41					
Total		38	3			41					

McLINTOCK, Frank
Born: Glasgow, 28 Dec 1939.
Signed from: Arsenal, Jun 1973 (£30,000).
Debut v Birmingham City, 22 Sep 1973.

		APPEARANCES					GOALS				
Season	Div	Lge	FA	LC	Oth	Total	Lge	FA	LC	Oth	Total
1973-74	1	26	6	3		35	1				1
1974-75	1	30	4			34					
1975-76	1	34/1	2	4		40/1	2				2
1976-77	1	36	2	7	†8	53	2		1		3
Total		126/1	14	14	8	162/1	5		1		6

McMAHON, Hugh
Born: Grangetown, Teesside.
Signed from: Reading.
Debut v Notts County, 12 Sep 1936.
Transferred to: Sunderland, Nov 1937.

		APPEARANCES					GOALS				
Season	Div	Lge	FA	LC	Oth	Total	Lge	FA	LC	Oth	Total
1936-37	3S	33	3			36	2	1			3
1937-38	3S	8				8	1				1
Total		41	3			44	3	1			4

McNAB, John
Born: Clelland.
Signed from: Liverpool.
Debut v Torquay United, 25 Aug 1928.
Retired 1930.

		APPEARANCES					GOALS				
Season	Div	Lge	FA	LC	Oth	Total	Lge	FA	LC	Oth	Total
1928-29	3S	32	1			33	2				2
1929-30	3S	22	4			26					
Total		54	5			59	2				2

McNAUGHT, J.W.
Debut v Manchester United, 29 Aug 1908, FA Charity Shield.

		APPEARANCES					GOALS				
Season	Div	Lge	FA	LC	Oth	Total	Lge	FA	LC	Oth	Total
1908-09	SL	15			*1	16					
1909-10	SL	30	5			35	4	1			5
1910-11	SL	12				12	1				1
Total		57	5		1	63	5	1			6

McNICKLE
Debut v Brighton, 13 Dec 1941, League South.

		APPEARANCES					GOALS				
Season	Div	Lge	FA	LC	Oth	Total	Lge	FA	LC	Oth	Total
2nd WW		1				1					
Total		1				1					

McQUADE, Terry
Born: Woodberry Down, 24 Feb 1941.
Signed from: Millwall, Jul 1963.
Debut v Aldershot, 4 Sep 1963, League Cup.
Transferred to: Dover Town.

		APPEARANCES					GOALS				
Season	Div	Lge	FA	LC	Oth	Total	Lge	FA	LC	Oth	Total
1963-64	3	20	3	1		24	2				2
1964-65	3			1		1					
Total		20	3	2		25	2				2

McQUEEN, Hugh
Born: Hart Hill, Scotland, 1 Oct 1867.
Signed from: Derby County, 1901.
Debut v Watford, 7 Sep 1901, Southern League.
Transferred to: Gainsborough Trinity, 1902.

		APPEARANCES					GOALS				
Season	Div	Lge	FA	LC	Oth	Total	Lge	FA	LC	Oth	Total
1901-02	SL	26	3			29	9				9
Total		26	3			29	9				9

MADDIX, Danny
Born: Ashford, 11 Oct 1967.
Signed from: Tottenham Hotspur, Jul 1987 (free).
Debut v Sheffield Wednesday, 28 Nov 1987 (sub).

		APPEARANCES					GOALS				
Season	Div	Lge	FA	LC	Oth	Total	Lge	FA	LC	Oth	Total
1987-88	1	6/3				6/3					
1988-89	1	28/5	3	6	1/3	38/8	2		1		3
1989-90	1	28/4	9	1		38/4	3				3
1990-91	1	32	1	3		36	1	1	1		3
1991-92	1	19		4	1	24					
1992-93	Pr	9/5	1	1		11/5					
Total		124/17	14	15	2/3	155/20	6	1	2		9

MAGUIRE, Gavin
Born: Hammersmith, 24 Nov 1967.
Signed from: (apprentice), Oct 1985.
Debut v Oxford United, 28 Dec 1986.
Transferred to: Portsmouth, Dec 1988 (£175,000).

		APPEARANCES					GOALS				
Season	Div	Lge	FA	LC	Oth	Total	Lge	FA	LC	Oth	Total
1986-87	1	13/1	1/1			14/2					
1987-88	1	13/5	4			17/5					
1988-89	1	7/1		1/2		8/3					
Total		33/7	5/1	1/2		39/10					

MALCOLM, Andy
Born: West Ham, 4 May 1933.
Signed from: Chelsea, Oct 1962.
Debut v Hull City, 22 Oct 1962.

		APPEARANCES					GOALS				
Season	Div	Lge	FA	LC	Oth	Total	Lge	FA	LC	Oth	Total
1962-63	3	31	3			34	5				5
1963-64	3	31	3	1		35		1			1
1964-65	3	22	2	1		25					
Total		84	8	2		94	5	1			6

MALLETT, Joe
Born: Gateshead, 8 Jan 1916.
Signed from: Charlton Athletic.
Debut v Crystal Palace, 23 Oct 1937.
Transferred to: Charlton Athletic, Jul 1938; From: Charlton Athletic, Feb 1939; To: Southampton, Feb 1947.

		APPEARANCES					GOALS				
Season	Div	Lge	FA	LC	Oth	Total	Lge	FA	LC	Oth	Total
1937-38	3S	29	2			31	4				4
1938-39	3S	15				15	2				2
1939-40	3S	1				1	3				3
2nd WW		167	10		37	214	59	1	11		71
1946-47	3S	26	5			31	5	2			7
Total		238	17		37	292	73	3	11		87

MANCINI, Terry
Born: Camden Town, 4 Oct 1942.
Signed from: Orient, Oct 1971 (£25,000).
Debut v Sheffield Wednesday, 16 Oct 1971.
Transferred to: Arsenal, Oct 1974 (£25,000).

		APPEARANCES					GOALS				
Season	Div	Lge	FA	LC	Oth	Total	Lge	FA	LC	Oth	Total
1971-72	2	23	2			25		1			1
1972-73	2	24	4			28	2	1			3
1973-74	1	40	6	3		49	1				1
1974-75	1	7		2		9					
Total		94	12	5		111	3	2			5

MANGNALL, Dave
Born: Wigan, 21 Sep 1908.
Signed from: Millwall.
Debut v Watford, 26 Aug 1939 (2 goals).

		APPEARANCES					GOALS				
Season	Div	Lge	FA	LC	Oth	Total	Lge	FA	LC	Oth	Total
1939-40	3S	3				3	3				3
2nd WW		117			11	128	77			19	96
Total		120			11	131	80			19	99

MANNING, J.
Signed from: Rotherham County.
Debut v Swansea Town, 23 Oct 1920 (1 goal).

		APPEARANCES					GOALS				
Season	Div	Lge	FA	LC	Oth	Total	Lge	FA	LC	Oth	Total
1920-21	3	22	2			24	5				5
Total		22	2			24	5				5

MARCH, Dicky
Born: Washington, County Durham.
Signed from: Crawcrook Albion.
Debut v Torquay United, 24 Dec 1932.

		APPEARANCES					GOALS				
Season	Div	Lge	FA	LC	Oth	Total	Lge	FA	LC	Oth	Total
1932-33	3S	9	1			10					
1933-34	3S	40	4			44					
1934-35	3S	24				24					
1935-36	3S	37	1			38					
1936-37	3S	41	3			44	1				1
1937-38	3S	39	2			41					
1938-39	3S	30	3			33	1				1
1939-40	3S	2				2					
2nd WW		57			2	59	3				3
Total		279	14		2	295	5				5

MARCROFT, Edward
Born: Rochdale, Apr 1910.
Signed from: Middlesbrough.
Debut v Brentford, 22 Aug 1932.
Transferred to: Cardiff City, Jul 1933 (exchange G.Emmerson).

		APPEARANCES					GOALS				
Season	Div	Lge	FA	LC	Oth	Total	Lge	FA	LC	Oth	Total
1932-33	3S	29	4			33	8	1			9
Total		29	4			33	8	1			9

MARSDEN, Ben
Born: Hanley.
Signed from: Port Vale, 1920.
Debut v Brentford, 27 Dec 1920.
Transferred to: Reading, 1925.

		APPEARANCES					GOALS				
Season	Div	Lge	FA	LC	Oth	Total	Lge	FA	LC	Oth	Total
1920-21	3	16				16					
1921-22	3S	37	2			39					
1922-23	3S	34	4			38	2				2
1923-24	3S	21				21	3				3
1924-25	3S	18				18	1				1
Total		126	6			132	6				6

MARSH, Rodney
Born: Hatfield, 11 Oct 1944.
Signed from: Fulham, Mar 1966 (£15,000).
Debut v Peterborough United, 19 Mar 1966.
Transferred to: Manchester City, Mar 1972 (£200,000).

		APPEARANCES					GOALS				
Season	Div	Lge	FA	LC	Oth	Total	Lge	FA	LC	Oth	Total
1965-66	3	16				16	8				8
1966-67	3	41	3	9		53	30	3	11		44
1967-68	2	25	1			26	14				14
1968-69	1	22				22	4				4
1969-70	2	38	4	5		47	12	4	5		21
1970-71	2	39	1	2		42	21	1	1		23
1971-72	2	30	2	4		36	17		3		20
Total		211	11	20		242	106	8	20		134

MASON, Bill
Born: Earlsfield, 1908.
Signed from: Fulham, Jul 1933.
Debut v Coventry City, 18 Jan 1934.
Retired during World War Two.

		APPEARANCES					GOALS				
Season	Div	Lge	FA	LC	Oth	Total	Lge	FA	LC	Oth	Total
1933-34	3S	8				8					
1934-35	3S	32	2			34					
1935-36	3S	36	1			37					
1936-37	3S	42	3			45					
1937-38	3S	21				21					
1938-39	3S	15				15					
2nd WW		86			5	91					
Total		240	6		5	251					

MASSON, Don
Born: Banchory, 26 Aug 1946.
Signed from: Notts County, Dec 1974 (£100,000).
Debut v Sheffield United, 14 Dec 1974.
Transferred to: Derby County, Oct 1977 (exchange L.James).

		APPEARANCES					GOALS				
Season	Div	Lge	FA	LC	Oth	Total	Lge	FA	LC	Oth	Total
1974-75	1	21	4			25	1				1
1975-76	1	42	2	4		48	6	1	2		9
1976-77	1	41	2	7	†8	58	8		1	2	11
1977-78	1	12		1		13	3				3
Total		116	8	12	8	144	18	1	3	2	24

MATTHEWS, A.
Debut v Arsenal, 27 Nov 1915, London Combination.

		APPEARANCES					GOALS				
Season	Div	Lge	FA	LC	Oth	Total	Lge	FA	LC	Oth	Total
WW1		6				6	1				1
Total		6				6	1				1

MATTHEWS, F.W.
Signed from: Hampstead Town.
Debut v Brighton & Hove Albion, 23 Apr 1914, Southern League.

		APPEARANCES					GOALS				
Season	Div	Lge	FA	LC	Oth	Total	Lge	FA	LC	Oth	Total
1913-14	SL	2				2					
1st WW		5				5					
Total		7				7					

MAYES, Tom
Signed from: Grays United.
Debut v Watford, 6 Dec 1902, Southern League.

		APPEARANCES					GOALS				
Season	Div	Lge	FA	LC	Oth	Total	Lge	FA	LC	Oth	Total
1902-03	SL	1				1					
1903-04	SL	3				3					
Total		4				4					

MEAKER, Michael
Born: Greenford, 18 Aug 1971.
Signed from: (trainee).
Debut v Southampton, 20 Nov 1990, ZDS Cup (sub).

		APPEARANCES					GOALS				
Season	Div	Lge	FA	LC	Oth	Total	Lge	FA	LC	Oth	Total
1990-91	1	0/9			0/1	0/10					
1991-92	1	0/1				0/1					
1992-93	Pr	3				3					
Total		3/10			0/1	3/11					

MERRICK, J.
Signed from: Aston Villa.
Debut v Bristol Rovers, 30 Aug 1919, Southern League.
Transferred to: Birmingham City.

		APPEARANCES					GOALS				
Season	Div	Lge	FA	LC	Oth	Total	Lge	FA	LC	Oth	Total
1919-20	SL	38	1			39					
Total		38	1			39					

METCHICK, Dave
Born: Derby, 14 Aug 1963.
Signed from: Peterborough United, Mar 1968 (£5,000).
Debut v West Bromwich Albion, 5 Oct 1968 (sub).
Transferred to: Arsenal, Sep 1970.

		APPEARANCES					GOALS				
Season	Div	Lge	FA	LC	Oth	Total	Lge	FA	LC	Oth	Total
1968-69	1	0/2				0/2					
1969-70	2	0/1		1		1/1	1				1
Total		0/3		1		1/3	1				1

MICKLEWHITE, Gary
Born: Southwark, 21 Mar 1961.
Signed from: Manchester United, Jul 1979.
Debut v Oldham Athletic, 5 Nov 1980 (sub).
Transferred to: Derby County, Feb 1985 (£75,000).

		APPEARANCES					GOALS				
Season	Div	Lge	FA	LC	Oth	Total	Lge	FA	LC	Oth	Total
1980-81	2	0/1				0/1					
1981-82	2	24/2	4/1	3/1		31/4	2		3		5
1982-83	2	33/1	1	2		36/1	6	1			7
1983-84	1	27/3		3		30/3	2		1		3
1984-85	1	13/2		4	†1/1	18/3	1		1		2
Total		97/9	5/1	12/1	1/1	115/12	11	1	5		17

MIDDLEMISS, Herbert
Born: 19 Dec 1888.
Signed from: Tottenham Hotspur, 1920.
Debut v Watford, 28 Aug 1920.
Retired 1921.

		APPEARANCES					GOALS				
Season	Div	Lge	FA	LC	Oth	Total	Lge	FA	LC	Oth	Total
1920-21	3	16				16	1				1
Total		16				16	1				1

MIDDLETON, Jack
Born: Sunderland.
Signed from: Leicester City, 1925.
Debut v Gillingham, 29 Aug 1925.
Transferred to: Aldershot, 1928.

		APPEARANCES					GOALS				
Season	Div	Lge	FA	LC	Oth	Total	Lge	FA	LC	Oth	Total
1925-26	3S	26				26	5				5
1926-27	3S	28				28	4				4
Total		54				54	9				9

MILLAR, Harry
Born: Paisley.
Signed from: Sheffield Wednesday, 1901.
Debut v Watford, 7 Sep 1901.

		APPEARANCES					GOALS				
Season	Div	Lge	FA	LC	Oth	Total	Lge	FA	LC	Oth	Total
1901-02	SL	24	3			27	7	5			12
Total		24	3			27	7	5			12

MILLBANK, Joe
Born: Edmonton, 30 Sep 1919.
Signed from: Crystal Palace, Jul 1948.
Debut v Barnsley, 11 Sep 1948.

		APPEARANCES					GOALS				
Season	Div	Lge	FA	LC	Oth	Total	Lge	FA	LC	Oth	Total
1948-49	2	1				1					
Total		1				1					

MILLER, J.
Born: Glasgow.
Signed from: Vale of Leven.
Debut v Swindon Town, 1 Sep 1913, Southern League.
Transferred to: Hartlepools United, 1921.

		APPEARANCES					GOALS				
Season	Div	Lge	FA	LC	Oth	Total	Lge	FA	LC	Oth	Total
1913-14	SL	28	5			33	14	2			16
1914-15	SL	33	3			36	14	1			15
1919-20	SL	2				2					
Total		63	8			71	28	3			31

MILLINGTON, T.
Born: Lancashire.
Signed from: Bury.
Debut v Millwall, 1 Sep 1914.

		APPEARANCES					GOALS				
Season	Div	Lge	FA	LC	Oth	Total	Lge	FA	LC	Oth	Total
1914-15	SL	28	3			31					
1st WW		3				3					
Total		31	3			34					

MILLS, Don
Born: Rotherham, 17 Aug 1926.
Signed from: Aug 1946.
Debut v Bournemouth, 25 Sep 1946.
Transferred to: Torquay United, Mar 1949; From: Torquay United, Jan 1950; To: Cardiff City, Feb 1951.

		APPEARANCES					GOALS				
Season	Div	Lge	FA	LC	Oth	Total	Lge	FA	LC	Oth	Total
1946-47	3S	18	2			20	5	3			8
1947-48	3S	16				16					
1948-49	2	11	1			12	1				1
1949-50	2	13				13	2				2
1950-51	2	18				18	1				1
Total		76	3			79	9	3			12

MILWARD, George
Signed from: Chesterfield, 1903.
Debut v Brentford, 5 Sep 1903, Southern League.

		APPEARANCES					GOALS				
Season	Div	Lge	FA	LC	Oth	Total	Lge	FA	LC	Oth	Total
1903-04	SL	30				30	11				11
1904-05	SL	16				16	3				3
Total		46				46	14				14

MISSLEWHITE, J.
Signed from: West Hampstead, 1899.
Debut v Bedminster, 14 Apr 1900, Southern League.

		APPEARANCES					GOALS				
Season	Div	Lge	FA	LC	Oth	Total	Lge	FA	LC	Oth	Total
1899-1900	SL	1				1					
1902-03	SL	1				1					
Total		2				2					

MITCHELL, Archie
Born: Smethwick.
Signed from: Aston Villa, 1907.
Debut v Tottenham Hotspur, 2 Sep 1907, Southern League.
Transferred to: Brentford, 1921.

		APPEARANCES					GOALS				
Season	Div	Lge	FA	LC	Oth	Total	Lge	FA	LC	Oth	Total
1907-08	SL	12				12					
1908-09	SL	23	1			24					
1909-10	SL	30	7			37	1				1
1910-11	SL	33	1			34					
1911-12	SL	37	2		*1	40	2				2
1912-13	SL	38	2			40	1				1
1913-14	SL	33	5			38	1	1			2
1914-15	SL	30	3			33	1				1
1st WW		133			3	136	13				13
1919-20	SL	35	1			36	2				2
1920-21	3	35	2			37					
Total		439	24		4	467	21	1			22

MOBLEY, Vic
Born: Oxford, 11 Oct 1943.
Signed from: Sheffield Wednesday, Oct 1969 (£55,000).
Debut v Middlesbrough, 4 Oct 1969.
Retired through injury.

		APPEARANCES					GOALS				
Season	Div	Lge	FA	LC	Oth	Total	Lge	FA	LC	Oth	Total
1969-70	2	21/1	3	2		26/1					
1970-71	2	3		1		4					
Total		24/1	3	3		30/1					

MOFFATT, H.
Born: Camerton.
Signed from: Walsall.
Debut v Crystal Palace, 31 Aug 1929.

		APPEARANCES					GOALS				
Season	Div	Lge	FA	LC	Oth	Total	Lge	FA	LC	Oth	Total
1929-30	3S	15				15	3				3
Total		15				15	3				3

MOGER, Harry
Born: Southampton, 1880.
Signed from: Manchester United.
Debut v Northampton Town, 21 Apr 1906, Southern League.

		APPEARANCES					GOALS				
Season	Div	Lge	FA	LC	Oth	Total	Lge	FA	LC	Oth	Total
1905-06	SL	1				1					
1906-07	SL	2				2					
Total		3				3					

MOLLOY, Pat
Born: Rosendale, 1911.
Signed from: Cardiff City.
Debut v Aldershot, 14 Sep 1935.
Transferred to: Stockport County.

		APPEARANCES					GOALS				
Season	Div	Lge	FA	LC	Oth	Total	Lge	FA	LC	Oth	Total
1935-36	3S	3				3					
Total		3				3					

MOORE
Debut v Fulham, 27 Dec 1941 (1 goal).

		APPEARANCES					GOALS				
Season	Div	Lge	FA	LC	Oth	Total	Lge	FA	LC	Oth	Total
2nd WW		1				1	1				1
Total		1				1	1				1

MOORE, James
Born: Barnsley.
Signed from: Halifax Town.
Debut v Newport County, 30 Aug 1924.
Transferred to: Crewe Alexandra.

		APPEARANCES					GOALS				
Season	Div	Lge	FA	LC	Oth	Total	Lge	FA	LC	Oth	Total
1924-25	3S	26				26	5				5
Total		26				26	5				5

MORALEE, Bill
Born: Crook.
Signed from: Bournemouth.
Debut v Clapton Orient, 23 Jan 1937.

		APPEARANCES					GOALS				
Season	Div	Lge	FA	LC	Oth	Total	Lge	FA	LC	Oth	Total
1936-37	3S	11				11					
1937-38	3S	11				11					
Total		22				22					

MORGAN, Roger
Born: Walthamstow, 14 Nov 1946.
Signed from: (apprentice), Sep 1964.
Debut v Gillingham, 3 Oct 1964.
Transferred to: Tottenham Hotspur, Feb 1969 (£110,000).

		APPEARANCES					GOALS				
Season	Div	Lge	FA	LC	Oth	Total	Lge	FA	LC	Oth	Total
1964-65	3	27	3			30	5				5
1965-66	3	44	5	1		50	13	1	1		15
1966-67	3	44	3	9		56	11		3		14
1967-68	2	40	1	3		44	8				8
1968-69	1	25	1			26	2				2
Total		180	13	13		206	39	1	4		44

MORGAN, Ian
Born: Walthamstow, 14 Nov 1946.
Signed from: (apprentice), Sep 1964.
Debut v Hull City, 25 Sep 1964.
Transferred to: Watford, Oct 1973 (£10,000).

		APPEARANCES					GOALS				
Season	Div	Lge	FA	LC	Oth	Total	Lge	FA	LC	Oth	Total
1964-65	3	30	2			32	4				4
1965-66	3	10				10	1				1
1966-67	3	10/4	0/2	1		11/6	4				4
1967-68	2	42	1	3		46	10				10
1968-69	1	32/1	1	1		34/1	1	1			2
1969-70	2	11/1		2		13/1	1				1
1970-71	2	15/4		1		16/4	3				3
1971-72	2	9/1		2/1		11/2	2		1		3
1972-73	2	2				2					
Total		161/11	4/2	10/1		175/14	26	1	1		28

MORRIS, S.
Born: 1888.
Signed from: Aston Villa, 1907.
Debut v Southampton, 25 Apr 1908, Southern League.
Transferred: 1911.

		APPEARANCES					GOALS				
Season	Div	Lge	FA	LC	Oth	Total	Lge	FA	LC	Oth	Total
1907-08	SL	2				2					
1908-09	SL	23	1			24	2				2
1909-10	SL	6				6					
1910-11	SL	9	1			10					
Total		40	2			42	2				2

MORTIMORE, John
Born: Farnborough.
Signed from: Chelsea, Sep 1965.
Debut v Reading, 11 Sep 1965.
Transferred to: Sunderland, Nov 1966.

		APPEARANCES					GOALS				
Season	Div	Lge	FA	LC	Oth	Total	Lge	FA	LC	Oth	Total
1965-66	3	10				10					
Total		10				10					

MOUGHTON, Colin
Born: London, 30 Dec 1947.
Signed from: (apprentice), Dec 1965.
Debut v Bournemouth, 21 May 1965.
Transferred to: Colchester United, Jul 1968.

		APPEARANCES					GOALS				
Season	Div	Lge	FA	LC	Oth	Total	Lge	FA	LC	Oth	Total
1965-66	3	3				3					
1966-67	3	3				3					
Total		6				6					

MOUNTFORD, George
Born: Stoke-on-Trent, 30 Mar 1921.
Signed from: Stoke City, Oct 1952.
Debut v Crystal Palace, 25 Oct 1952.

		APPEARANCES					GOALS				
Season	Div	Lge	FA	LC	Oth	Total	Lge	FA	LC	Oth	Total
1952-53	3S	25	3			28	2				2
1953-54	3S	10				10					
Total		35	3			38	2				2

MUIR, Ian
Born: Coventry, 5 May 1963.
Signed from: (apprentice), Sep 1980.
Debut v Cambridge United, 25 Apr 1981 (2 goals).
Transferred to: Birmingham City, Aug 1983.

		APPEARANCES					GOALS				
Season	Div	Lge	FA	LC	Oth	Total	Lge	FA	LC	Oth	Total
1980-81	2	2				2	2				2
Total		2				2	2				2

MUIR, William
Born: Ayr, 27 Aug 1925.
Signed from: Irvine, Feb 1948.
Debut v Cardiff City, 13 Sep 1948.
Transferred to: Torquay United, Oct 1952.

		APPEARANCES					GOALS				
Season	Div	Lge	FA	LC	Oth	Total	Lge	FA	LC	Oth	Total
1948-49	2	1				1					
1949-50	2										
1950-51	2	1				1					
1951-52	2	10				10	3				3
1952-53	3S	5				5	1				1
Total		17				17	4				4

MURDIN, S.
Debut v Aberdare Athletic, 25 Feb 1926.

		APPEARANCES					GOALS				
Season	Div	Lge	FA	LC	Oth	Total	Lge	FA	LC	Oth	Total
1925-26	3S	1				1					
Total		1				1					

MURPHY, Neil
Signed from: Sheffield United, 1903.
Debut v Luton Town, 26 Sep 1903, Southern League.
Transferred to: Luton Town, 1907.

		APPEARANCES					GOALS				
Season	Div	Lge	FA	LC	Oth	Total	Lge	FA	LC	Oth	Total
1903-04	SL	22	1			23	7	1			8
1904-05	SL	17				17	2				2
1905-06	SL	12	1			13	2				2
Total		51	2			53	11	1			12

MUSTARD, John
Born: Bold-on-Tyne, 1905.
Signed from: South Shields, Crawcrook Albion.
Debut v Plymouth Argyle, 11 Dec 1926.
Transferred to: South Shields, 1929.

		APPEARANCES					GOALS				
Season	Div	Lge	FA	LC	Oth	Total	Lge	FA	LC	Oth	Total
1926-27	3S	14				14	2				2
1927-28	3S	23	1			24	2				2
Total		37	1			38	4				4

MYERS, Colin
Born: Chapel Town.
Signed from: Northampton Town.
Debut v Millwall, 25 Oct 1924.
Transferred to: Exeter City.

		APPEARANCES					GOALS				
Season	Div	Lge	FA	LC	Oth	Total	Lge	FA	LC	Oth	Total
1924-25	3S	17	5			22	3	7			10
Total		17	5			22	3	7			10

NASH, Bobby
Born: London, 8 Feb 1946.
Signed from: (juniors), Feb 1964.
Debut v Hull City, 25 Sep 1964.
Transferred to: Exeter City, Jun 1966.

		APPEARANCES					GOALS				
Season	Div	Lge	FA	LC	Oth	Total	Lge	FA	LC	Oth	Total
1964-65	3	17	1			18					
Total		17	1			18					

NEAL, Dean
Born: Edmonton, 5 Jan 1961.
Signed from: (apprentice), Aug 1979.
Debut v Bristol Rovers, 18 Aug 1979.
Transferred to: Tulsa Roughnecks, Jun 1981 (with D.McCreery £225,000).

		APPEARANCES					GOALS				
Season	Div	Lge	FA	LC	Oth	Total	Lge	FA	LC	Oth	Total
1979-80	2	5/1		1		6/1			1		1
1980-81	2	15/1		1		16/1	8				8
Total		20/2		2		22/2	8		1		9

NEARY, Frank
Born: Aldershot, 6 Mar 1921.
Signed from: Finchley.
Debut v Southend United, 25 Aug 1945, Leaggue South.
Transfered to: West Ham United, Jan 1947; From: Leyton Orient, Oct 1949; To: Millwall, Aug 1950.

		APPEARANCES					GOALS				
Season	Div	Lge	FA	LC	Oth	Total	Lge	FA	LC	Oth	Total
2nd WW		15	6		8	29	12	5		6	23
1946-47	3S	9				9	6				6
1949-50	2	18	1			19	5				5
Total		42	7		8	57	23	5		6	34

NEEDHAM, Dave
Born: Leicester, 21 May 1949.
Signed from: Notts County, Jun 1977 (£90,000).
Debut v Aston Villa, 20 Aug 1977.
Transferred to: Nottingham Forest, Dec 1977 (£140,000).

		APPEARANCES					GOALS				
Season	Div	Lge	FA	LC	Oth	Total	Lge	FA	LC	Oth	Total
1977-78	1	18		2		20	3				3
Total		18		2		20	3				3

NEIL, Andy
Born: Kilmarnock.
Signed from: Brighton & Hove Albion.
Debut v Newport County, 27 Aug 1927.
Transferred: 1930.

		APPEARANCES					GOALS				
Season	Div	Lge	FA	LC	Oth	Total	Lge	FA	LC	Oth	Total
1927-28	3S	41	1			42	1				1
1928-29	3S	29	1			30					
1929-30	3S	36	4			40					
Total		106	6			112	1				1

NEILL, Warren
Born: Acton, 21 Nov 1962.
Signed from: (apprentice), Sep 1980.
Debut v Chelea, 30 Aug 1980 (sub).
Transferred to: Portsmouth, Jul 1988 (£110,000).

		APPEARANCES					GOALS				
Season	Div	Lge	FA	LC	Oth	Total	Lge	FA	LC	Oth	Total
1980-81	2	3/1		0/1		3/2					
1981-82	2	11	3/1			14/1		1			1
1982-83	2	39	1	2		42	2				2
1983-84	1	41	1	2		44	1				1
1984-85	1	18		7	3	28			1	1	2
1985-86	1	16	1	5		22					
1986-87	1	29	3			32					
1987-88	1	20/3	2	2		24/3		1			1
Total		177/4	11/1	18/1	3	209/6	3	2	1	1	7

NELSON, Dave
Born: Douglas Water, 3 Feb 1918.
Signed from: Brentford, Feb 1950.
Debut v Sheffield United, 18 Feb 1950.
Transferred to: Crystal Palace, Mar 1952.

		APPEARANCES					GOALS				
Season	Div	Lge	FA	LC	Oth	Total	Lge	FA	LC	Oth	Total
1949-50	2	13				13					
1950-51	2	18				18					
Total		31				31					

NELSON, William
Born: Silverton, 20 Sep 1929.
Signed from: West Ham United, Jul 1955.
Debut v Torquay United, 24 Sep 1955.

		APPEARANCES					GOALS				
Season	Div	Lge	FA	LC	Oth	Total	Lge	FA	LC	Oth	Total
1955-56	3S	9				9					
Total		9				9					

NEWBIGGING, Alex
Born: Scotland, 27 Dec 1879.
Signed from: Paisley Abercorn, 1900.
Debut v Tottenham Hotspur, 20 Oct 1900, Southern League.
Transferred to: Nottingham Forest.

		APPEARANCES					GOALS				
Season	Div	Lge	FA	LC	Oth	Total	Lge	FA	LC	Oth	Total
1900-01	SL	5	2			7		1			1
Total		5	2			7		1			1

NEWLANDS, George
Born: Glasgow, 1882.
Signed from: Parkhead Juniors, 1900.
Debut v Kettering Town, 29 Sep 1900, Southern League.
Transferred to: Norwich City, 1907.

		APPEARANCES					GOALS				
Season	Div	Lge	FA	LC	Oth	Total	Lge	FA	LC	Oth	Total
1900-01	SL	22	4			26					
1901-02	SL	25	3			28	1				1
1902-03	SL	26				26					
1903-04	SL	32	2			34					
1904-05	SL	27				27					
1905-06	SL	27	1			28					
1906-07	SL	15	2			17					
Total		174	12			186	1				1

NICHOLAS, Brian
Born: Aberdare, 20 Apr 1933.
Signed from: (juniors), May 1950.
Debut v Leeds United, 7 May 1949.
Transferred to: Chelsea, Jul 1955.

		APPEARANCES					GOALS				
Season	Div	Lge	FA	LC	Oth	Total	Lge	FA	LC	Oth	Total
1948-49	2	1				1					
1949-50	2										
1950-51	2	5	1			6					
1951-52	2	6				6	1				1
1952-53	3S	31	2			33	1				1
1953-54	3S	30	4			34					
1954-55	3S	40	1			41					
Total		113	8			121	2				2

NICHOLLS, A.
Debut v Watford, 20 Jan 1912, Southern League.

		APPEARANCES					GOALS				
Season	Div	Lge	FA	LC	Oth	Total	Lge	FA	LC	Oth	Total
1911-12	SL	1				1					
1912-13	SL	1				1					
1913-14	SL	35	5			40					
Total		37	5			42					

NISBET, D.
Debut v Millwall, 4 Sep 1915, London Combination.

		APPEARANCES					GOALS				
Season	Div	Lge	FA	LC	Oth	Total	Lge	FA	LC	Oth	Total
WW1		17				17	3				3
Total		17				17	3				3

NIXON
Debut v Brentford, 25 Sep 1915, London Combination.

		APPEARANCES					GOALS				
Season	Div	Lge	FA	LC	Oth	Total	Lge	FA	LC	Oth	Total
WW1		11				11					
Total		11				11					

NIXON, Tom
Born: Newcastle upon Tyne.
Signed from: Crawcrook Albion.
Debut v Merthyr Town, 9 Mar 1929.
Transferred to: Crystal Palace, Oct 1933.

		APPEARANCES					GOALS				
Season	Div	Lge	FA	LC	Oth	Total	Lge	FA	LC	Oth	Total
1928-29	3S	5				5					
1929-30	3S	13				13					
1930-31	3S	11				11	1				1
1931-32	3S	22				22					
1932-33	3S	5				5					
Total		56				56	1				1

NUTT, Phil
Born: London, 18 May 1958.
Signed from: (apprentice), Jul 1975.
Debut v Stoke City, 29 Nov 1975.

		APPEARANCES					GOALS				
Season	Div	Lge	FA	LC	Oth	Total	Lge	FA	LC	Oth	Total
1975-76	1	0/3				0/3	1				1
1976-77	1	0/1				0/1					
Total		0/4				0/4	1				1

O'BRIEN, Mick
Born: Dublin, 1893.
Signed from: South Shields, 1920.
Debut v Watford, 28 Aug 1920.
Transferred to: Leicester City, 1922.

		APPEARANCES					GOALS				
Season	Div	Lge	FA	LC	Oth	Total	Lge	FA	LC	Oth	Total
1920-21	3	36	2			38		1			1
1921-22	3S	30	2			32	3				3
Total		66	4			70	3	1			4

O'CONNOR, Mark
Born: Rochford, 10 Mar 1963.
Signed from: (apprentice), Jun 1980.
Debut v Chelsea, 26 Dec 1981.
Transferred to: Bristol Rovers, Aug 1984 (£30,000).

		APPEARANCES					GOALS				
Season	Div	Lge	FA	LC	Oth	Total	Lge	FA	LC	Oth	Total
1981-82	2	1				1					
1982-83	2	1/1				1/1					
Total		2/1				2/1					

O'DONNELL, Dennis
Signed from: Sunderland, 1906.
Debut v Luton Town, 1 Sep 1906.
Transferred to: Notts C, 1907.

		APPEARANCES					GOALS				
Season	Div	Lge	FA	LC	Oth	Total	Lge	FA	LC	Oth	Total
1906-07	SL	25	2			27	7				7
Total		25	2			27	7				7

OGLEY, William
Born: Rotherham, 1896.
Signed from: Newport County.
Debut v Newport County, 30 Aug 1924.
Transferred to: Castleford, 1925.

		APPEARANCES					GOALS				
Season	Div	Lge	FA	LC	Oth	Total	Lge	FA	LC	Oth	Total
1924-25	3S	36	5		41	2				2	
Total		36	5			41	2				2

OLSEN, C.
Debut v Newport County, 3 Apr 1920, Southern League.

		APPEARANCES					GOALS				
Season	Div	Lge	FA	LC	Oth	Total	Lge	FA	LC	Oth	Total
1919-20	SL	1				1					
Total		1				1					

O'NEILL, John
Born: Derry, 11 Mar 1958.
Signed from: Leicester City, Jul 1987 (£90,000).
Debut v Norwich City, 31 Oct 1987.
Transferred to: Norwich City, Dec 1987 £100,000.

		APPEARANCES					GOALS				
Season	Div	Lge	FA	LC	Oth	Total	Lge	FA	LC	Oth	Total
1987-88	1	2				2					
Total		2				2					

O'ROURKE, John
Born: Northampton, 11 Feb 1945.
Signed from: Coventry City, Oct 1971 (£60,000).
Debut v Luton Town, 19 Oct 1971.
Transferred to: Bournemouth, Jan 1974 (£40,000).

		APPEARANCES					GOALS				
Season	Div	Lge	FA	LC	Oth	Total	Lge	FA	LC	Oth	Total
1971-72	2	26	2			28	9				9
1972-73	2	7/1		1		8/1	3				3
Total		33/1	2	1		36/1	12				12

ORR, Douglas
Born: Glasgow, 8 Nov 1937.
Signed from: Hendon, 1957.
Debut v Swindon Town, 16 Sep 1957.

		APPEARANCES					GOALS				
Season	Div	Lge	FA	LC	Oth	Total	Lge	FA	LC	Oth	Total
1957-58	3S	5				5					
Total		5				5					

OVENS, Gilbert
Born: Bristol.
Signed from: Bristol Rovers, 1911.
Debut v Exeter City, 30 Sep 1911, Southern League.
Transferred to: 1915.

		APPEARANCES					GOALS				
Season	Div	Lge	FA	LC	Oth	Total	Lge	FA	LC	Oth	Total
1911-12	SL	25	2			27	1				1
1912-13	SL	32	2			34	2	1			3
1913-14	SL	32	5			37					
1914-15	SL	14				14					
Total		103	9			112	3	1			4

OVENSTONE, David
Born: St Monance.
Signed from: Raith Rovers.
Debut v Bournemouth, 9 Nov 1935 (1 goal).
Transferred to: Cardiff City, 1936.

		APPEARANCES					GOALS				
Season	Div	Lge	FA	LC	Oth	Total	Lge	FA	LC	Oth	Total
1935-36	3S	15	1			16	3				3
Total		15	1			16	3				3

OXLEY, Richard
Born: Wallsend, Jan 1895.
Signed from: Southport.
Debut v: Swindon Town, 8 Sep 1923.
Transferred to: Northampton Town, 1925.

		APPEARANCES					GOALS				
Season	Div	Lge	FA	LC	Oth	Total	Lge	FA	LC	Oth	Total
1923-24	3S	18				18					
Total		18				18					

PAGE
Debut v Tottenham Hotspur, 25 Dec 1918, London Combination.

		APPEARANCES					GOALS				
Season	Div	Lge	FA	LC	Oth	Total	Lge	FA	LC	Oth	Total
WW1		1				1					
Total		1				1					

PAINTER
Debut v Tottenham Hotspur, 27 Sep 1941, League South.

		APPEARANCES					GOALS				
Season	Div	Lge	FA	LC	Oth	Total	Lge	FA	LC	Oth	Total
2nd WW		2				2					
Total		2				2					

PAPE, Andy
Born: Hammersmith, 22 Mar 1962.
Signed from: (juniors), Jul 1980.
Debut v Charlton Athletic, 19 Apr 1980.

		APPEARANCES					GOALS				
Season	Div	Lge	FA	LC	Oth	Total	Lge	FA	LC	Oth	Total
1979-80	2	1				1					
Total		1				1					

PARKER, Paul
Born: West Ham, 4 Apr 1964.
Signed from: Fulham, Jun 1987 (£200,000).
Debut v West Ham United, 15 Aug 1987.
Transferred to: Manchester United, Aug 1991 (£2,000,000).

		APPEARANCES					GOALS				
Season	Div	Lge	FA	LC	Oth	Total	Lge	FA	LC	Oth	Total
1987-88	1	40	4	3	1	48					
1988-89	1	36	3	6	3	48					
1989-90	1	32	9	2		43					
1990-91	1	13/4		3	1	17/4	1				1
Total		121/4	16	14	5	156/4	1				1

PARKER, R.
Born: Stockton-on-Tees.
Signed from: South Shields, 1922.
Debut v Watford, 26 Aug 1922.
Transferred to: Millwall Athletic.

		APPEARANCES					GOALS				
Season	Div	Lge	FA	LC	Oth	Total	Lge	FA	LC	Oth	Total
1922-23	3S	28	4			32	16	4			20
1923-24	3S	33				33	14				14
Total		61	4			65	30	4			34

PARKES, Phil
Born: Sedgley, 8 Aug 1950.
Signed from: Walsall, Jun 1970 (£15,000).
Debut v Leicester City, 22 Aug 1970.
Transferred to: West Ham United, Feb 1979 (£565,000).

		APPEARANCES					GOALS				
Season	Div	Lge	FA	LC	Oth	Total	Lge	FA	LC	Oth	Total
1970-71	2	41	1	2		44					
1971-72	2	42	2	4		48					
1972-73	2	41	3	1		45					
1973-74	1	42	6	3		51					
1974-75	1	41	4	2		47					
1975-76	1	42	2	4		48					
1976-77	1	40	2	7	†8	57					
1977-78	1	31	6	2		39					
1978-79	1	24	1	2		27					
Total		344	27	27	8	406					

PARKINSON, Albert
Born: Camden Town, 30 Apr 1922.
Signed from: (local club).
Debut v Brentford, 2 Jan 1943, League South.

		APPEARANCES					GOALS				
Season	Div	Lge	FA	LC	Oth	Total	Lge	FA	LC	Oth	Total
2nd WW		4			4	8	1				1
1946-47	3S	10				10	2				2
1947-48	3S	1				1					
1948-49	2	21	2			23	2				2
1949-50	2	17				17	1				1
1950-51	2	27	1			28		2			2
Total		80	3		4	87	6	2			8

PARSONS, Derek
Born: Hammersmith, 24 Jan 1929.
Signed: Feb 1950.
Debut v Torquay United, 8 Nov 1952 (1 goal).

		APPEARANCES					GOALS				
Season	Div	Lge	FA	LC	Oth	Total	Lge	FA	LC	Oth	Total
1952-53	3S	2	1			3	1				1
Total		2	1			3	1				1

PATERSON, Jock
Signed from: Mid Rhondda, Jan 1926.
Debut v Merthyr Town, 16 Jan 1926.
Transferred to: Bristol Rovers, 1927.

		APPEARANCES					GOALS				
Season	Div	Lge	FA	LC	Oth	Total	Lge	FA	LC	Oth	Total
1925-26	3S	19				19	3				3
1926-27	3S	15				15	3				3
1927-28	3S	2				2					
Total		36				36	6				6

PATTISON, Johnny
Born: Glasgow, 19 Dec 1918.
Signed from: Motherwell.
Debut v Notts County, 12 Mar 1938.
Transferred to: Leyton Orient, Feb 1950.

		APPEARANCES					GOALS				
Season	Div	Lge	FA	LC	Oth	Total	Lge	FA	LC	Oth	Total
1937-38	3S	3				3	1				1
1938-39	3S	14				14		1			1
2nd WW		36	5		22	63	9	1		9	19
1946-47	3S	37	6			43	12	5			17
1947-48	3S	20	1			21	8				8
1948-49	2	11	2			13	3				3
1949-50	2	7				7	2				2
Total		128	14		22	164	35	7		9	51

PEACOCK, Darren
Born: Bristol, 3 Feb 1968.
Signed from: Hereford United, Dec 1990 (£350,000).
Debut v Derby County, 23 Dec 1990.

		APPEARANCES					GOALS				
Season	Div	Lge	FA	LC	Oth	Total	Lge	FA	LC	Oth	Total
1990-91	1	19				19					
1991-92	1	39	1	4	2	46	1				1
1992-93	Pr	35/3	1	4		40/3	2		1		3
Total		93/3	2	8	2	105/3	3		1		4

PEACOCK, Gavin
Born: Eltham, 18 Nov 1967.
Signed from: (apprentice), Nov 1984.
Debut v Sheffield Wednesday, 29 Nov 1986.
Transferred to: Gillingham, Dec 1987 (£40,000).

		APPEARANCES					GOALS				
Season	Div	Lge	FA	LC	Oth	Total	Lge	FA	LC	Oth	Total
1986-87	1	7/5	0/1			7/6	1				1
1987-88	1	0/5				0/5					
Total		7/10	0/1			7/11	1				1

PEACOCK, Terence
Born: Hull, 18 Apr 1935.
Signed from: Hull City, Aug 1956.
Debut v Reading, 15 Dec 1956 (1 goal).
Transferred to: Sittingbourne, Jul 1958.

		APPEARANCES					GOALS				
Season	Div	Lge	FA	LC	Oth	Total	Lge	FA	LC	Oth	Total
1956-57	3S	14	1			15	4				4
1957-58	3S	2				2					
Total		16	1			17	4				4

PEARSON, Harry
Born: Tamworth.
Signed from: Coventry City.
Debut v Swindon Town, 8 Oct 1938.

		APPEARANCES					GOALS				
Season	Div	Lge	FA	LC	Oth	Total	Lge	FA	LC	Oth	Total
1938-39	3S	11	3			14	1				1
Total		11	3			14	1				1

PEARSON, John
Born: Isleworth, 23 Apr 1935.
Signed from: Brentford, Jun 1958.
Debut v Tranmere Rovers, 1 Sep 1958.

		APPEARANCES					GOALS				
Season	Div	Lge	FA	LC	Oth	Total	Lge	FA	LC	Oth	Total
1958-59	3	16				16	6				6
1959-60	3	5				5	3				3
Total		21				21	9				9

PENNIFER, H.J.
Debut v Cardiff City, 13 Dec 1913.
Died in World War One.

		APPEARANCES					GOALS				
Season	Div	Lge	FA	LC	Oth	Total	Lge	FA	LC	Oth	Total
1913-14	SL	3				3					
1st WW		6				6	1				1
Total		9				9	1				1

PENRICE, Gary
Born: Bristol, 23 Mar 1964.
Signed from: Aston Villa, Oct 1991 (£650,000).
Debut v Aston Villa, 2 Nov 1991 (sub).

		APPEARANCES					GOALS				
Season	Div	Lge	FA	LC	Oth	Total	Lge	FA	LC	Oth	Total
1991-92	1	13/6	0/1	1	1	15/7	3		1		4
1992-93	Pr	10/5	1	2/1		13/6	6	1			7
Total		23/11	1/1	3/1	1	28/13	9	1	1		11

PENTLAND, Fred
Born: Wolverhampton, 18 Sep 1883.
Signed from: Brentford, 1907.
Debut v Tottenham Hotspur, 2 Sep 1907, Southern League.
Transferred to: Middlesbrough, Jul 1908, (£350).

		APPEARANCES					GOALS				
Season	Div	Lge	FA	LC	Oth	Total	Lge	FA	LC	Oth	Total
1907-08	SL	37	2		*1	40	14				14
Total		37	2		1	40	14				14

PERKINS, Steve
Born: London, 3 Oct 1954.
Signed from: Chelsea, Jun 1977.
Debut v Middlesbrough, 1 Apr 1978.
Transferred to: Wimbledon, Oct 1978.

		APPEARANCES					GOALS				
Season	Div	Lge	FA	LC	Oth	Total	Lge	FA	LC	Oth	Total
1977-78	1	2				2					
Total		2				2					

PETCHEY, George
Born: London, 24 Jun 1931.
Signed from: West Ham United, Jul 1953.
Debut v Brighton & Hove Albion, 19 Aug 1953.
Transferred to: Crystal Palace, Jun 1960.

		APPEARANCES					GOALS				
Season	Div	Lge	FA	LC	Oth	Total	Lge	FA	LC	Oth	Total
1953-54	3S	21	4			25	6	1			7
1954-55	3S	17	2			19	1				1
1955-56	3S	41	1			42	4				4
1956-57	3S	43	3			46	2				2
1957-58	3S	46	3			49	3				3
1958-59	3	46	2			48	2				2
1959-60	3	41	1			42	4	1			5
Total		255	16			271	22	2			24

PICKETT, Thomas
Born: Merthyr.
Debut v Torquay United, 16 Nov 1929.
Transferred to: Bristol Rovers, 1932.

		APPEARANCES					GOALS				
Season	Div	Lge	FA	LC	Oth	Total	Lge	FA	LC	Oth	Total
1929-30	3S	1	1			2					
1930-31	3S	11	1			12					
1931-32	3S	34	4			38					
Total		46	6			52					

PIDGEON, H.T.
Debut v Merthyr Town, 5 Apr 1920, Southern League.

		APPEARANCES					GOALS				
Season	Div	Lge	FA	LC	Oth	Total	Lge	FA	LC	Oth	Total
1919-20	SL	6				6					
Total		6				6					

PIERCE, William
Born: Ashington, 29 Oct 1907.
Signed from: Bedlington Colliery.
Debut v Swansea Town, 6 Oct 1923.
Transferred to: Carlisle United, 1931.

		APPEARANCES					GOALS				
Season	Div	Lge	FA	LC	Oth	Total	Lge	FA	LC	Oth	Total
1923-24	3S	24	1			25					
1924-25	3S	22	5			27	1				1
1925-26	3S	35	4			39					
1926-27	3S	19				19					
1927-28	3S	38				38					
1928-29	3S	12				12	1				1
1929-30	3S	25	4			29		1			1
1930-31	3S	4				4					
Total		179	14			193	2	1			3

PIGG, William
Born: Durham.
Signed from: Ashington.
Debut v Luton Town, 7 Mar 1925.
Transferred to: Carlisle United, 1926.

		APPEARANCES					GOALS				
Season	Div	Lge	FA	LC	Oth	Total	Lge	FA	LC	Oth	Total
1924-25	3S	2				2					
1925-26	3S	19	4			23					
Total		21	4			25					

PINNER, Mike
Born: Boston, 16 Feb 1934.
Signed from: Sheffield Wednesday, Jul 1959.
Debut v Swindon Town, 22 Aug 1959.
Transferred to: Manchester United, Feb 1961.

		APPEARANCES					GOALS				
Season	Div	Lge	FA	LC	Oth	Total	Lge	FA	LC	Oth	Total
1959-60	3	19	2			21					
1960-61	3			1		1					
Total		19	2	1		22					

PIZANTI, David
Born: Israel, 27 May 1962.
Signed from: 1.FC Cologne, Sep 1987 (£150,000).
Debut v Liverpool, 17 Oct 1987 (sub).

		APPEARANCES					GOALS				
Season	Div	Lge	FA	LC	Oth	Total	Lge	FA	LC	Oth	Total
1987-88	1	3/3	1	1		5/3		1			1
1988-89	1	13/2	3	2/1	3	21/3					
Total		16/5	4	3/1	3	26/6		1			1

PLUNKETT, A.
Born: Glasgow.
Signed from: Bury, Jul 1925.
Debut v Gillingham, 29 Aug 1925.

		APPEARANCES					GOALS				
Season	Div	Lge	FA	LC	Oth	Total	Lge	FA	LC	Oth	Total
1925-26	3S	15				15					
Total		15				15					

POINTING, William
Born: Andover, 1872.
Signed from: Southampton, 1900.
Debut v Watford, 22 Sep 1900, Southern League.

		APPEARANCES					GOALS				
Season	Div	Lge	FA	LC	Oth	Total	Lge	FA	LC	Oth	Total
1900-01	SL	1				1					
Total		1				1					

POINTON, William
Born: Hanley, 25 Nov 1920.
Signed from: Port Vale, Jan 1949.
Debut v Barnsley, 22 Jan 1949.
Transferred to: Brentford, Feb 1950.

		APPEARANCES					GOALS				
Season	Div	Lge	FA	LC	Oth	Total	Lge	FA	LC	Oth	Total
1948-49	2	17				17	4				4
1949-50	2	9				9	2				2
Total		26				26	6				6

POLLARD, Robert
Born: Wigan, 25 Jul 1901.
Signed from: Exeter City.
Debut v Northampton Town, 14 Sep 1929.
Transferred to: Cardiff City, 1932.

		APPEARANCES					GOALS				
Season	Div	Lge	FA	LC	Oth	Total	Lge	FA	LC	Oth	Total
1929-30	3S	27	4			31					
1930-31	3S	29	3			32					
1931-32	3S	10				10					
Total		66	7			73					

POPPITT, John
Born: West Sleekburn, 20 Jan 1923.
Signed from: Derby County, Sep 1950.
Debut v Birmingham City, 23 Sep 1950.
Transferred to: Chelmsford City, Jul 1954.

		APPEARANCES					GOALS				
Season	Div	Lge	FA	LC	Oth	Total	Lge	FA	LC	Oth	Total
1950-51	2	33	1			34					
1951-52	2	25				25					
1952-53	3S	34	3			37					
1953-54	3S	14	1			15					
Total		106	5			111					

POUNDER, Albert
Born: Charlton, 27 Jul 1931.
Signed from: Charlton Athletic, Feb 1954.
Debut v Exeter City, 13 Feb 1954.
Transferred to: Sittingbourne, Jul 1957.

		APPEARANCES					GOALS				
Season	Div	Lge	FA	LC	Oth	Total	Lge	FA	LC	Oth	Total
1953-54	3S	11				11	2				2
1954-55	3S	23	1			24	3				3
1955-56	3S	19	1			20	1				1
Total		53	2			55	6				6

POWELL, George
Born: Fulham, 11 Oct 1924.
Signed from: Fulham, Dec 1946.
Debut v Reading, 8 Nov 1947.

		APPEARANCES					GOALS				
Season	Div	Lge	FA	LC	Oth	Total	Lge	FA	LC	Oth	Total
1947-48	3S	23	6			29					
1948-49	2	39	2			41					
1949-50	2	28	1			29					
1950-51	2	8				8					
1951-52	2	33	1			34					
1952-53	3S	14				14					
Total		145	10			155					

POWELL, Ivor
Born: Bargoed, 5 Jul 1916.
Signed from: Bargoed.
Debut v Walsall, 28 Jan 1939.
Transferred to: Aston Villa, Dec 1948.

		APPEARANCES					GOALS				
Season	Div	Lge	FA	LC	Oth	Total	Lge	FA	LC	Oth	Total
1938-39	3S	8				8					
2nd WW		26			9	35					
1946-47	3S	41	6			47	1				1
1947-48	3S	41	6			47	1				1
1948-49	2	20				20					
Total		136	12		9	157	2				2

POWELL, Michael
Born: Slough, 18 Apr 1933.
Signed from: (juniors), Jan 1951.
Debut v Norwich City, 6 Sep 1952.
Transferred to: Yiewsley, Jul 1959.

		APPEARANCES					GOALS				
Season	Div	Lge	FA	LC	Oth	Total	Lge	FA	LC	Oth	Total
1952-53	3S	17				17					
1953-54	3S	21				21					
1954-55	3S	36	3			39					
1955-56	3S	25				25					
1956-57	3S	1				1					
1957-58	3S	1				1					
1958-59	3	4				4					
Total		105	3			108					

PRICE, E.
Signed from: Brentford.
Debut v Watford, 28 Aug 1920.

		APPEARANCES					GOALS				
Season	Div	Lge	FA	LC	Oth	Total	Lge	FA	LC	Oth	Total
1920-21	3	7				7					
Total		7				7					

PRICE, L.
Born: Carswys.
Signed from: Notts County.
Debut v Torquay United, 25 Aug 1928.

		APPEARANCES					GOALS				
Season	Div	Lge	FA	LC	Oth	Total	Lge	FA	LC	Oth	Total
1928-29	3S	3				3					
Total		3				3					

PRIOR, Stanley
Born: Swindon, 20 Dec, 1910.
Signed from: Charlton Athletic.
Debut v Torquay United, 15 Sep 1937.
Transferred to: Cheltenham Town, 1938.

		APPEARANCES					GOALS				
Season	Div	Lge	FA	LC	Oth	Total	Lge	FA	LC	Oth	Total
1937-38	3S	6				6	3				3
Total		6				6	3				3

PRITCHETT, Keith

Born: Glasgow, 8 Nov 1953.
Signed from: Doncaster Rovers, Jan 1975.
Debut v Newcastle United, 31 Mar 1975.
Transferred to: Brentford, Jul 1976.

		APPEARANCES					GOALS				
Season	Div	Lge	FA	LC	Oth	Total	Lge	FA	LC	Oth	Total
1974-75	1	4				4					
Total		4				4					

PRYCE, John

Born: Renton, 25 Jan 1874.
Signed from: Sheffield Wednesday, 1901.
Debut v Watford, 7 Sep 1901, Southern League.
Transferred to: Brighton & Hove Albion, 1903.

		APPEARANCES					GOALS				
Season	Div	Lge	FA	LC	Oth	Total	Lge	FA	LC	Oth	Total
1901-02	SL	14	3			17	2				2
1902-03	SL	5				5					
Total		19	3			22	2				2

PULLEN, Henry

Born: Kettering.
Signed from: Kettering Town, 1910.
Debut v Plymouth Argyle, 29 Apr 1911, Southern League.
Transferred to: Newport County, 1920.

		APPEARANCES					GOALS				
Season	Div	Lge	FA	LC	Oth	Total	Lge	FA	LC	Oth	Total
1910-11	SL	1				1					
1911-12	SL	28	2		1	31					
1912-13	SL	37	2			39					
1913-14	SL	38	5			43	1				1
1914-15	SL	36	3			39					
1st WW		19			1	20					
1919-20	SL	28	1			29					
Total		187	13		2	202	1				1

QUIGLEY, Thomas

Born: Mid Calder, 26 Mar 1932.
Signed from: Portsmouth, Jun 1956.
Debut v Reading, 18 Aug 1956.
Transferred to: Worcester City, Aug 1957.

		APPEARANCES					GOALS				
Season	Div	Lge	FA	LC	Oth	Total	Lge	FA	LC	Oth	Total
1956-57	3S	16				16	7				7
Total		16				16	7				7

QUINN, Gordon

Born: London, 11 May 1932.
Signed from: Eastcote BC, Aug 1952.
Debut v Newport County, 18 Oct 1952 (1 goal).
Transferred to: Plymouth Argyle, Sep 1956.

		APPEARANCES					GOALS				
Season	Div	Lge	FA	LC	Oth	Total	Lge	FA	LC	Oth	Total
1952-53	3S	3				3	1				1
1953-54	3S	10	1			11					
1954-55	3S										
1955-56	3S	4				4					
1956-57	3S	5				5					
Total		22	1			23	1				1

RADNAGE, J.J.

Signed from: Reading.
Debut v Clapton Orient, 11 Sep 1909, Southern League.

		APPEARANCES					GOALS				
Season	Div	Lge	FA	LC	Oth	Total	Lge	FA	LC	Oth	Total
1909-10	SL	2				2					
1910-11	SL	1				1					
Total		3				3					

RAMSCAR, Fred

Born: Salford, 24 Jan 1919.
Signed from: Wolverhampton Wanderers, Oct 1947.
Debut v Ipswich Town, 25 Oct 1947, League South.
Transferred to: Preston North End, Nov 1949.

		APPEARANCES					GOALS				
Season	Div	Lge	FA	LC	Oth	Total	Lge	FA	LC	Oth	Total
2nd WW		2			1	3	1			1	2
1947-48	3S	16	6			22	1	1			2
1948-49	3S	21				21	2				2
1949-50	2	14				14	1				1
Total		53	6		1	60	5	1		1	7

RAMSEY, Alex

Born: Gateshead.
Signed from: Newcastle United, 1921.
Debut v Swindon Town, 27 Aug 1921.

		APPEARANCES					GOALS				
Season	Div	Lge	FA	LC	Oth	Total	Lge	FA	LC	Oth	Total
1921-22	3S	6				6					
Total		6				6					

RAMSEY, C.B.

Debut v Northampton Town, 6 Dec 1919, Southern League.

		APPEARANCES					GOALS				
Season	Div	Lge	FA	LC	Oth	Total	Lge	FA	LC	Oth	Total
1919-20	SL	12				12	1				1
Total		12				12	1				1

RANCE, Charles

Born: 28 Feb 1899.
Signed from: Tottenham, 1922.
Debut v Brighton & Hove Albion, 30 Sep 1922.

		APPEARANCES					GOALS				
Season	Div	Lge	FA	LC	Oth	Total	Lge	FA	LC	Oth	Total
1922-23	3S	13				13					
Total		13				13					

READY, Karl

Born: Neath, 14 Aug 1972.
Signed from: (juniors).
Debut v Hull City, 9 Oct 1991, League Cup (sub).

		APPEARANCES					GOALS				
Season	Div	Lge	FA	LC	Oth	Total	Lge	FA	LC	Oth	Total
1991-92	1	1		0/1		1/1					
1992-93	Pr	2/1				2/1					
Total		3/1		0/1		3/2					

REAY, Ted

Born: Tynemouth, 5 Aug 1914.
Signed from: Sheffield United, Nov 1937.
Debut v Watford, 2 Apr 1938.

		APPEARANCES					GOALS				
Season	Div	Lge	FA	LC	Oth	Total	Lge	FA	LC	Oth	Total
1937-38	3S	5				5					
1938-39	3S	6				6					
1939-40	3S	3				3					
2nd WW		33	1		9	43	1				1
1946-47	3S	2	1			3					
1947-48	3S	16				16					
1948-49	2	3				3					
1949-50	2	2				2					
Total		70	2		9	81	1				1

REED, Arthur

Born: London.
Signed from: Tufnell Park, 1921.
Debut v Swindon Town, 27 Aug 1921.
Transferred to: Reading, 1922.

		APPEARANCES					GOALS				
Season	Div	Lge	FA	LC	Oth	Total	Lge	FA	LC	Oth	Total
1921-22	3S	21				21					
Total		21				21					

REED, Gordon

Born: Spennymoor, May 1913.
Signed from: Newport County.
Debut v Swindon Town, 25 Aug 1934 (1 goal).
Transferred to: Darlington, 1937.

		APPEARANCES					GOALS				
Season	Div	Lge	FA	LC	Oth	Total	Lge	FA	LC	Oth	Total
1934-35	3S	9				9	4				4
Total		9				9	4				4

REID, Barney (Johnny)

Signed from: Wilshaw Juniors, Jan 1938.

		APPEARANCES					GOALS				
Season	Div	Lge	FA	LC	Oth	Total	Lge	FA	LC	Oth	Total
2nd WW		2				2					
Total		2				2					

REID, Peter

Born: Huyton, 20 Jun 1956.
Signed from: Everton, Feb 1989 (free).
Debut v Nottingham Forest, 11 Feb 1989.
Transferred to: Manchester City, Dec 1989 (free).

		APPEARANCES					GOALS				
Season	Div	Lge	FA	LC	Oth	Total	Lge	FA	LC	Oth	Total
1988-89	1	14				14	1				1
1989-90	1	15		2/1		17/1					
Total		29		2/1		31/1	1				1

REVILL, E.J.

Signed from: Chesterfield, Jul 1911.
Debut v Plymouth Argyle, 2 Sep 1911 (1 goal), Southern League.

		APPEARANCES					GOALS				
Season	Div	Lge	FA	LC	Oth	Total	Lge	FA	LC	Oth	Total
1911-12	SL	36	2		*1	39	15			1	16
1912-13	SL	26	2			28	6	1			7
Total		62	4		1	67	21	1		1	23

RHODES, Albert

Born: Dinnington, 29 Apr 1936.
Signed from: Worksop Town, Dec 1954.
Debut v Reading, 14 Apr 1956.

		APPEARANCES					GOALS				
Season	Div	Lge	FA	LC	Oth	Total	Lge	FA	LC	Oth	Total
1955-56	3S	4				4					
1956-57	3S	1				1					
Total		5				5					

RICHARD, Hugh

Born: Kilmarnock.
Signed from: Coventry City, May 1925.
Debut v Gillingham, 29 Aug 1925.
Transferred to: Blyth Spartans, 1926.

		APPEARANCES					GOALS				
Season	Div	Lge	FA	LC	Oth	Total	Lge	FA	LC	Oth	Total
1925-26	3S	10				10					
Total		10				10					

RICHARDSON, Anthony

Born: Southwark, 7 Jan 1932.
Signed from: Slough SC, Apr 1951.
Debut v Luton Town, 19 Jan 1952.

		APPEARANCES					GOALS				
Season	Div	Lge	FA	LC	Oth	Total	Lge	FA	LC	Oth	Total
1951-52	2	2				2					
Total		2				2					

RICHARDSON, Derek

Born: London, 13 Jul 1956.
Signed from: Chelsea, Apr 1976 (free).
Debut v Leeds United, 8 Mar 1977.
Transferred to: Sheffield United, Dec 1979 (£50,000).

		APPEARANCES					GOALS				
Season	Div	Lge	FA	LC	Oth	Total	Lge	FA	LC	Oth	Total
1976-77	1	2				2					
1977-78	1	11				11					
1978-79	1	18		1		19					
Total		31		1		32					

RICHARDSON, Stuart

Born: Leeds, 12 Jun 1938.
Signed from: Methley United, Nov 1956.
Debut v Colchester United, 3 Jan 1959.
Transferred to: Oldham Athletic, Jul 1959.

		APPEARANCES					GOALS				
Season	Div	Lge	FA	LC	Oth	Total	Lge	FA	LC	Oth	Total
1958-59	3	1				1					
Total		1				1					

RIDLEY, J.Michael

Born: Burdon Hill.
Signed from: Reading.
Debut v Brighton & Hove Albion, 8 Dec 1934, FA Cup.

		APPEARANCES					GOALS				
Season	Div	Lge	FA	LC	Oth	Total	Lge	FA	LC	Oth	Total
1934-35	3S	17	1			18					
Total		17	1			18					

RIDYARD, Alfred

Born: Cudworth, Yorkshire, 5 Mar 1908.
Signed from: West Bromwich Albion, Mar 1938.
Debut v Gillingham, 9 Apr 1938.
Retired 1948.

		APPEARANCES					GOALS				
Season	Div	Lge	FA	LC	Oth	Total	Lge	FA	LC	Oth	Total
1937-38	3S	7				7					
1938-39	3S	10	1			11					
1939-40	3S	3				3					
2nd WW		153	10		33	196	8			1	9
1946-47	3S	7	3			10					
1947-48	3S	4				4					
Total		184	14		33	231	8			1	9

RIVERS, Walter

Born: Throckle, Northumberland, 8 Jan.
Signed from: Crystal Palace, Jul 1933.
Debut v Brighton & Hove Albion, 26 Aug 1933.
Transferred to: Gateshead.

		APPEARANCES					GOALS				
Season	Div	Lge	FA	LC	Oth	Total	Lge	FA	LC	Oth	Total
1933-34	3S	3				3					
Total		3				3					

ROBERTS, J.

Signed from: Watford.
Debut v Luton Town, 5 Nov 1927.

		APPEARANCES					GOALS				
Season	Div	Lge	FA	LC	Oth	Total	Lge	FA	LC	Oth	Total
1927-28	3S	4				4					
Total		4				4					

ROBERTS, Tony

Born: Bangor, 4 Aug 1969.
Signed from: Youth Training Scheme, Jul 1987.
Debut v Coventry City, 18 Dec 1987.

		APPEARANCES					GOALS				
Season	Div	Lge	FA	LC	Oth	Total	Lge	FA	LC	Oth	Total
1987-88	1	1				1					
1989-90	1	5				5					
1990-91	1	12		3	1	16					
1991-92	1				1	1					
1992-93	Pr	28	2	2		32					
Total		46	2	5	2	55					

ROBERTS, W.

Debut v Norwich City, 21 Oct 1905, Southern League.

		APPEARANCES					GOALS				
Season	Div	Lge	FA	LC	Oth	Total	Lge	FA	LC	Oth	Total
1905-06	SL	22				22	1				1
Total		22				22	1				1

ROBINSON, John

Signed from: Portsmouth.
Debut v Northampton Town, 27 Oct 1923.
Transferred to: 1924.

		APPEARANCES					GOALS				
Season	Div	Lge	FA	LC	Oth	Total	Lge	FA	LC	Oth	Total
1923-24	3S	5				5	1				1
Total		5				5	1				1

ROBINSON, Michael

Born: Leicester, 12 Jul 1958.
Signed from: Liverpool, Dec 1984 (£100,000).
Debut v Stoke City, 29 Dec 1984 (sub).
Transferred to: CA Osasuna, Jan 1987 (£150,000).

		APPEARANCES					GOALS				
Season	Div	Lge	FA	LC	Oth	Total	Lge	FA	LC	Oth	Total
1984-85	1	8/3	1			9/3	1				1
1985-86	1	25/1	1	5/1		31/2	4		1		5
1986-87	1	8/3		1/1		9/4					
Total		41/7	2	6/2		49/9	5		1		6

ROEDER, Glenn

Born: Woodford, 13 Dec 1955.
Signed from: Orient, Aug 1978 (£250,000).
Debut v Nottingham Forest, 26 Aug 1978.
Transferred to: Newcastle United, Dec 1983 (£150,000).

		APPEARANCES					GOALS				
Season	Div	Lge	FA	LC	Oth	Total	Lge	FA	LC	Oth	Total
1978-79	1	27		1		28	4				4
1979-80	2	40		5		45	9		1		10
1980-81	2	39	2	3		44	2				2
1981-82	2	41	8	4		53	2				2
1982-83	2	9	1			10					
1983-84	1	1				1					
Total		157	11	13		181	17		1		18

ROGERS, A.

Debut v Tottenham Hotspur, 2 Sep 1907, Southern League.
Transferred to: Bristol Rovers, 1910.

		APPEARANCES					GOALS				
Season	Div	Lge	FA	LC	Oth	Total	Lge	FA	LC	Oth	Total
1907-08	SL	5				5	1				1
1908-09	SL	27	2			29	9				9
Total		32	2			34	10				10

ROGERS, Albert

Born: Manchester.
Signed from: Southall.
Debut v Coventry City, 15 Dec 1928 (2 goals).

		APPEARANCES					GOALS				
Season	Div	Lge	FA	LC	Oth	Total	Lge	FA	LC	Oth	Total
1928-29	3S	11				11	4				4
1929-30	3S	1				1					
Total		12				12	4				4

ROGERS, Don

Born: Paulton, 25 Oct 1945.
Signed from: Crystal Palace, Sep 1974 (exchange T.Venables).
Debut v Everton, 24 Sep 1974 (sub).
Transferred to: Swindon Town, Mar 1976 (£33,000).

		APPEARANCES					GOALS				
Season	Div	Lge	FA	LC	Oth	Total	Lge	FA	LC	Oth	Total
1974-75	1	13/5	0/1			13/6	5				5
Total		13/5	0/1			13/6	5				5

ROGERS, Martyn

Born: Nottingham, 26 Jan 1960.
Signed from: Manchester United, Jul 1979.
Debut v Newcastle United, 26 Apr 1980.

		APPEARANCES					GOALS				
Season	Div	Lge	FA	LC	Oth	Total	Lge	FA	LC	Oth	Total
1974-75	2	2				2					
Total		2				2					

RONALDSON, Duncan
Born: Scotland, 1879.
Signed from: Vale of Clyde, 1900.
Debut v New Brompton, 1 Dec 1900 (1 goal).
Transferred to: Grimsby Town, Jul 1901; From: Bury.

		APPEARANCES					GOALS				
Season	Div	Lge	FA	LC	Oth	Total	Lge	FA	LC	Oth	Total
1900-01	SL	18				18	8				8
1904-05	SL	21	1			22	6				6
Total		39	1			40	14				14

ROSE, Jack
Born: Sheffield, 26 Oct 1921.
Signed from: Peterborough United.
Debut v Reading, 16 Jan 1943.

		APPEARANCES					GOALS				
Season	Div	Lge	FA	LC	Oth	Total	Lge	FA	LC	Oth	Total
2nd WW		76	9		33	118					
1946-47	3S	15	1			16					
1947-48	3S	2				2					
Total		93	10		33	136					

ROSENOIR, Leroy
Born: Clapton, 24 Mar 1964.
Signed from: Fulham, Aug 1982 (£100,000).
Debut v Arsenal, 3 Sep 1985 (sub).
Transferred to: Fulham, Jun 1987 (£100,000).

		APPEARANCES					GOALS				
Season	Div	Lge	FA	LC	Oth	Total	Lge	FA	LC	Oth	Total
1985-86	1	12/6	0/1	1/2		13/9	4		2		6
1986-87	1	15/5	0/3	1/1		16/9	4			4	
Total		27/11	0/4	2/3		29/18	8		2		10

ROUNCE, George
Born: Grays, 1905.
Signed from: Uxbridge.
Debut v Merthyr Town, 25 Feb 1928 (1 goal).
Transferred to: Fulham, Mar 1933.

		APPEARANCES					GOALS				
Season	Div	Lge	FA	LC	Oth	Total	Lge	FA	LC	Oth	Total
1927-28	3S	13				13	6				6
1928-29	3S	28	1			29	9				9
1929-30	3S	40	4			44	16				16
1930-31	3S	35	3			38	16	2			18
1931-32	3S	31	4			35	4	4			8
1932-33	3S	24	5			29	8	6			14
Total		171	17			188	59	12			71

ROWE, Alfred
Born: Poplar.
Signed from: Plymouth Argyle.
Debut v Bournemouth, 5 Apr 1926.

		APPEARANCES					GOALS				
Season	Div	Lge	FA	LC	Oth	Total	Lge	FA	LC	Oth	Total
1925-26	3S	4				4	1				1
Total		4				4	1				1

ROWE, Jonty
Born: Packmoor, Staffordshire.
Signed from: Reading, Jul 1935.
Debut v Millwall, 31 Aug 1935.
Transferred to: Port Vale, Jul 1937 (free).

		APPEARANCES					GOALS				
Season	Div	Lge	FA	LC	Oth	Total	Lge	FA	LC	Oth	Total
1935-36	3S	32	1			33					
1936-37	3S	20	3			23					
Total		52	4			56					

RUSSELL, Sidney
Born: Feltham, Oct 1911.
Signed from: Tunbridge Wells Rangers.
Debut v Watford, 4 Feb 1933.
Transferred to: Northampton Town.

		APPEARANCES					GOALS				
Season	Div	Lge	FA	LC	Oth	Total	Lge	FA	LC	Oth	Total
1932-33	3S	8				8					
1933-34	3S	1				1					
1934-35	3S	21	1			22					
1935-36	3S	12				12					
Total		42	1			43					

RUTHERFORD, Michael
Born: Sidcup, 6 Jun 1972.
Signed from: Trainee.
Debut v Charlton Athletic, 21 Oct 1989 (sub).

		APPEARANCES					GOALS				
Season	Div	Lge	FA	LC	Oth	Total	Lge	FA	LC	Oth	Total
1989-90	1	1/1		0/1		1/2					
Total		1/1		0/1		1/2					

RUTTER, Keith
Born: Leeds, 10 Sep 1931.
Signed from: Methley United, Jul 1954.
Debut v Southend United, 24 Aug 1954.
Transferred to: Colchester United, Feb 1963.

		APPEARANCES					GOALS				
Season	Div	Lge	FA	LC	Oth	Total	Lge	FA	LC	Oth	Total
1954-55	3S	32				32	1				1
1955-56	3S	21	1			22					
1956-57	3S	44	3			47					
1957-58	3S	46	3			49					
1958-59	3	44	2			46					
1959-60	3	46	3			49					
1960-61	3	46	2	2		50			1		1
1961-62	3	43	4	2		49					
1962-63	3	17		1		18					
Total		339	18	5		362	1		1		2

RYDER, Fred
Debut v Northampton Town, 1 Oct 1904.
Transferred to: Bolton Wanderers, 1907.

		APPEARANCES					GOALS				
Season	Div	Lge	FA	LC	Oth	Total	Lge	FA	LC	Oth	Total
1904-05	SL	13	1			14	2	1			3
1905-06	SL	33	1			34	15				15
1906-07	SL	23	2			25	3				3
Total		69	4			73	20	1			21

SALES, Arthur
Born: Lewes, 4 Mar 1900.
Signed from: Chelsea.
Debut v Swindon Town, 11 Oct 1930.
Transferred to: Bournemouth, 1933.

		APPEARANCES					GOALS				
Season	Div	Lge	FA	LC	Oth	Total	Lge	FA	LC	Oth	Total
1920-21	3S	28	3			31					
1931-32	3S	7				7					
Total		35	3			38					

SALT, Harold
Born: Sheffield.
Signed from: Peterborough United.
Debut v Bournemouth, 2 Oct 1926.
Transferred to: Grays United, 1928.

		APPEARANCES					GOALS				
Season	Div	Lge	FA	LC	Oth	Total	Lge	FA	LC	Oth	Total
1926-27	3S	5				5					
Total		5				5					

SALVAGE, Barry
Born: Bristol, 21 Dec 1947.
Signed from: Millwall, Mar 1971 (free).
Debut v Watford, 27 Mar 1971.
Transferred to: Brentford, Feb 1973 (£9,000).

		APPEARANCES					GOALS				
Season	Div	Lge	FA	LC	Oth	Total	Lge	FA	LC	Oth	Total
1970-71	2	3				3					
1971-72	2	13/2		0/1		13/3	1				1
1972-73	2	0/3	1			1/3					
Total		16/5	1	0/1		17/6	1				1

SAMUEL, David
Born: Swansea, 1911.
Signed from: Reading, Jun 1935.
Debut v Millwall, 31 Aug 1935.
Transferred to: Barrow.

		APPEARANCES					GOALS				
Season	Div	Lge	FA	LC	Oth	Total	Lge	FA	LC	Oth	Total
1935-36	3S	10				10	3				3
Total		10				10	3				3

SANDERSON, Keith
Born: Hull, 9 Oct 1940.
Signed from: Plymouth Argyle, Jun 1965 (£4,000).
Debut v Brentford, 21 Aug 1965.
Transferred to: Goole Town, Mar 1970.

		APPEARANCES					GOALS				
Season	Div	Lge	FA	LC	Oth	Total	Lge	FA	LC	Oth	Total
1965-66	3	39/3	5	2		46/2	1	2			3
1966-67	3	40	3	9		52	6				6
1967-68	2	16/2	1			17/2	3				3
1968-69	1	3/1				3/1					
Total		98/6	9	11		118/5	10	2			12

SANGSTER, J.
Signed from: Southall.
Debut v Northampton Town, 21 Sep 1912, Southern League.

		APPEARANCES					GOALS				
Season	Div	Lge	FA	LC	Oth	Total	Lge	FA	LC	Oth	Total
1912-13	SL	4				4					
Total		4				4					

SANSOM, Kenny
Born: Camberwell, 26 Sep 1958.
Signed from: Newcastle United, Jul 1989 (£300,000).
Debut v Crystal Palace, 19 Aug 1989.
Transferred to: Coventry City, Mar 1991 (£150,000).

		APPEARANCES					GOALS				
Season	Div	Lge	FA	LC	Oth	Total	Lge	FA	LC	Oth	Total
1989-90	1	36	9	3		48		2			2
1990-91	1	28	1	4	1	34					
Total		64	10	7	1	82		2			2

SAPHIN, Reg
Born: Kilburn, 8 Aug 1916.
Signed from: Ipswich Town, Jun 1946.
Debut v Poole Town, 4 Dec 1946, FA Cup.
Transferred to: Watford, Jul 1951.

		APPEARANCES					GOALS				
Season	Div	Lge	FA	LC	Oth	Total	Lge	FA	LC	Oth	Total
1946-47	3S	1	1			2					
1947-48	3S	8				8					
1948-49	2										
1949-50	2	1				1					
1950-51	2	20	1			21					
Total		30	2			32					

SAUL, Frank
Born: Canvey Island, 23 Aug 1943.
Signed from: Southampton, May 1943 (£40,000).
Debut v Birmingham City, 15 Aug 1970.
Transferred to: Millwall, Mar 1972 (£20,000).

		APPEARANCES					GOALS				
Season	Div	Lge	FA	LC	Oth	Total	Lge	FA	LC	Oth	Total
1970-71	2	22		1		23	1		1		2
1971-72	2	18/3	2	4		24/3	3		1		4
Total		40/3	2	5		47/3	4		2		6

SEALY, Tony
Born: Hackney, 7 May 1959.
Signed from: Crystal Palace, Mar 1981 (£80,000).
Debut v Derby County, 21 Mar 1981.
Transferred to: Fulham, Jan 1985 (£80,000).

		APPEARANCES					GOALS				
Season	Div	Lge	FA	LC	Oth	Total	Lge	FA	LC	Oth	Total
1980-81	2	8				8	2				2
1981-82	2	4/3		1		5/3					
1982-83	2	39/1	1	2		42/1	16				16
1983-84	1	6/2		0/1		6/3					
Total		57/6	1	3/1		61/7	18				18

SEAMAN, David
Born: Rotherham, 19 Sep 1963.
Signed from: Birmingham City, Aug 1986 (£225,000).
Debut v Southampton, 23 Aug 1986.
Transferred to: Arsenal, Jul 1990 (£1,300,000).

		APPEARANCES					GOALS				
Season	Div	Lge	FA	LC	Oth	Total	Lge	FA	LC	Oth	Total
1986-87	1	41	4	3		48					
1987-88	1	32	1	3		36					
1988-89	1	35	3	4	4	46					
1989-90	1	33	9	3		45					
Total		141	17	13	4	175					

SEARY, Ray
Born: Slough, 18 Sep 1952.
Signed from: (apprentice), Sep 1970.
Debut v Swindon Town, 4 Sep 1971 (sub).
Transferred to: Cambridge United, Mar 1974 (£3,000).

		APPEARANCES					GOALS				
Season	Div	Lge	FA	LC	Oth	Total	Lge	FA	LC	Oth	Total
1971-72	2	0/1				0/1					
Total		0/1				0/1					

SEELEY, George
Born: Southampton, 1879.
Signed from: Southampton, 1901.
Debut v Watford, 7 Sep 1901.
Transferred to: New Brighton, 1902.

		APPEARANCES					GOALS				
Season	Div	Lge	FA	LC	Oth	Total	Lge	FA	LC	Oth	Total
1901-02	SL	19	3			22	2				2
Total		19	3			22	2				2

SHANKS, Don
Born: London, 2 Oct 1952.
Signed from: Luton Town, Nov 1974 (£35,000).
Debut v Burnley, 7 Dec 1974.
Transferred to: Brighton & Hove Albion, Aug 1981 (free).

		APPEARANCES					GOALS				
Season	Div	Lge	FA	LC	Oth	Total	Lge	FA	LC	Oth	Total
1974-75	1	12				12					
1975-76	1	2				2					
1976-77	1	6/4	1	1/1	†1	9/5					
1977-78	1	36	6	1		43	3	1			4
1978-79	1	41	1	3		45	3				3
1979-80	2	41	1	5		47	2				2
1980-81	2	38	2	3		43	2				2
Total		176/4	11	13/1	1	201/5	10	1			11

SHAW, A.
Debut v Portsmouth, 10 Apr 1944, League South.

		APPEARANCES					GOALS				
Season	Div	Lge	FA	LC	Oth	Total	Lge	FA	LC	Oth	Total
2nd WW		12				12	5				5
Total		12				12	5				5

SHAW, Charlie
Born: Twechor, Dumbarton, 21 Sep 1885.
Signed from: Port Glasgow, 1907.
Debut v Tottenham Hotspur, 2 Sep 1907.
Transferred to: Glasgow Celtic, 1913.

		APPEARANCES					GOALS				
Season	Div	Lge	FA	LC	Oth	Total	Lge	FA	LC	Oth	Total
1907-08	SL	38	2		*1	41					
1908-09	SL	40	2		*1	43					
1909-10	SL	42	7			49					
1910-11	SL	38	1			39					
1911-12	SL	37	2		*1	40					
1912-13	SL	37	2			39					
Total		232	16		3	251					

SHEPHERD, Bill
Born: Ferryhill, County Durham.
Signed from: Watford, Jun 1930.
Debut v Northampton Town, 27 Oct 1930.
Transferred to: Coventry City, Jul 1931.

		APPEARANCES					GOALS				
Season	Div	Lge	FA	LC	Oth	Total	Lge	FA	LC	Oth	Total
1930-31	3S	13				13	4				4
Total		13				13	4				4

SHEPHERD, Ernest
Born: Wombwell, 14 Aug 1919.
Signed from: Hull City, Aug 1950.
Debut v Chesterfield, 19 Aug 1950.

		APPEARANCES					GOALS				
Season	Div	Lge	FA	LC	Oth	Total	Lge	FA	LC	Oth	Total
1950-51	2	41	1			42	14				14
1951-52	2	29	1			30	5	1			6
1952-53	3S	43	3			46	8				8
1953-54	3S	34	4			38	7	1			8
1954-55	3S	40	2			42	8				8
1955-56	3S	32	1			33	9				9
Total		219	12			231	51	2			53

SHUFFLEBOTTOM, G.
Born: 1881.
Signed from: Brentford, 1904.
Debut v Swindon Town, 18 Mar 1905, Southern League.

		APPEARANCES					GOALS				
Season	Div	Lge	FA	LC	Oth	Total	Lge	FA	LC	Oth	Total
1904-05	SL	1				1					
Total		1				1					

SIBLEY, Frank
Born: London, 4 Dec 1947.
Signed from: (apprentice), Feb 1965.
Debut v Aldershot, 4 Sep 1963, League Cup.

		APPEARANCES					GOALS				
Season	Div	Lge	FA	LC	Oth	Total	Lge	FA	LC	Oth	Total
1963-64	3	3		1		4					
1964-65	3	6		1		7					
1965-66	3	27/2	5			32/2	1	1			2
1966-67	3	42	3	8		53	1				1
1967-68	2	5		1		6	1		1		2
1968-69	1	25	1	1		27					
1969-70	2	13/1		2		15/1					
1970-71	2	19	1	1		21					
Total		140/3	10	15		165/3	3	1	1		5

SILKMAN, Barry
Born: London, 29 Jun 1952.
Signed from: Brentford, Oct 1980 (£20,000).
Debut v Grimsby Town, 1 Nov 1980.
Transferred to: Orient, Sep 1981 (£15,000).

		APPEARANCES					GOALS				
Season	Div	Lge	FA	LC	Oth	Total	Lge	FA	LC	Oth	Total
1980-81	2	22/1	2			24/1	2				2
Total		22/1	2			24/1	2				2

SILVER, Alan
Debut v Walthamstow Avenue, 29 Nov 1954, FA Cup.

		APPEARANCES					GOALS				
Season	Div	Lge	FA	LC	Oth	Total	Lge	FA	LC	Oth	Total
1954-55	3S		1			1					
Total			1			1					

SIMONS, H.T.
Born: Clapton, 1890.
Signed from: Fulham, 1914.
Debut v Exeter City, 14 Nov 1914, Southern League.

		APPEARANCES					GOALS				
Season	Div	Lge	FA	LC	Oth	Total	Lge	FA	LC	Oth	Total
1914-15	SL	19	3			22	7	1			8
1st WW		18				18	5				5
Total		37	3			40	12	1			13

SINGLETON, Harry
Born: Prescott, 1880.
Signed from: New Brompton, 1904.
Debut v Plymouth Argyle, 3 Sep 1904, Southern League.
Transferred to: Leeds City, 1905.

		APPEARANCES					GOALS				
Season	Div	Lge	FA	LC	Oth	Total	Lge	FA	LC	Oth	Total
1904-05	SL	19				19					
Total		19				19					

SINTON, Andy
Born: Newcastle upon Tyne, 19 Mar 1966.
Signed from: Brentford, May 1989 (£300,000).
Debut v Sheffield Wednesday, 25 Mar 1989.

		APPEARANCES					GOALS				
Season	Div	Lge	FA	LC	Oth	Total	Lge	FA	LC	Oth	Total
1988-89	1	10				10	3				3
1989-90	1	38	9	3		50	6	2			8
1990-91	1	38	1	4	1	44	3				3
1991-92	1	38	1	3	2	44	3			1	4
1992-93	Pr	36	2	4		42	7				7
Total		160	13	14	3	190	22	2		1	25

SKILTON, Percy
Signed from: Harrow.
Debut v Millwall, 30 Apr 1904 (1 goal), Southern League.

		APPEARANCES					GOALS				
Season	Div	Lge	FA	LC	Oth	Total	Lge	FA	LC	Oth	Total
1903-04	SL	1				1	1				1
1904-05	SL	7				7	1				1
1906-07	SL	14				14	7				7
1907-08	SL	21			*1	22	5				5
1908-09	SL	19			*1	20	8				8
Total		62			2	64	22				22

SKINNER, Harry
Born: Middlesex, 1875.
Signed from: Uxbridge Town, Aug 1899.
Debut v New Brompton, 16 Sep 1899, Southern League.
Transferred to: Grimsby Town, Jul 1901; From: Grimsby Town, 1902.

		APPEARANCES					GOALS				
Season	Div	Lge	FA	LC	Oth	Total	Lge	FA	LC	Oth	Total
1899-1900	SL	13	2			15					
1900-01	SL	27	4			31	1				1
1902-03	SL	9	1			10					
Total		49	7			56	1				1

SLACK, Rodney
Born: Farcet, 11 Apr 1940.
Signed from: Leicester City, Mar 1961.
Debut v Halifax Town, 3 May 1962.
Transferred to: Cambridge United, Jul 1962.

		APPEARANCES					GOALS				
Season	Div	Lge	FA	LC	Oth	Total	Lge	FA	LC	Oth	Total
1961-62	3	1				1					
Total		1				1					

SMITH, A.
Debut v Millwall, 4 Sep 1915, London Combination.

		APPEARANCES					GOALS				
Season	Div	Lge	FA	LC	Oth	Total	Lge	FA	LC	Oth	Total
WW1		4				4					
Total		4				4					

SMITH, Arthur
Born: Stourbridge, 1887.
Signed from: Brierley Athletic, 1911.
Debut v Plymouth Argyle, 2 Sep 1911, Southern League.
Transferred to: Birmingham, 1912.

		APPEARANCES					GOALS				
Season	Div	Lge	FA	LC	Oth	Total	Lge	FA	LC	Oth	Total
1911-12	SL	35	1		*1	37	8				8
Total		35	1		1	37	8				8

SMITH, Albert
Born: Fenton, Stoke-on-Trent, 27 Aug 1918.
Signed from: Birmingham City.
Debut v Portsmouth, 10 Jan 1942, League South.

		APPEARANCES					GOALS				
Season	Div	Lge	FA	LC	Oth	Total	Lge	FA	LC	Oth	Total
2nd WW		59			16	75	2				2
1946-47	3S	33	5			38					
1947-48	3S	18	2			20	2				2
1948-49	2	11				11					
Total		121	7		16	144	4				4

SMITH, Conway
Born: Huddersfield, 13 Jul 1926.
Signed from: Huddersfield Town, Mar 1951.
Debut v Leeds United, 17 Mar 1951 (1 goal).
Transferred to: Halifax Town, Jun 1956.

		APPEARANCES					GOALS				
Season	Div	Lge	FA	LC	Oth	Total	Lge	FA	LC	Oth	Total
1950-51	2	9				9	7				7
1951-52	2	41	1			42	13				13
1952-53	3S	25	2			27	13	2			15
1953-54	3S	29				29	12				12
1954-55	3S	33	3			36	17	1			18
1955-56	3S	37				37	19				19
Total		174	6			180	81	3			84

SMITH, E.
Debut v Brighton, 28 Oct 1944 (1 goal), League South.

		APPEARANCES					GOALS				
Season	Div	Lge	FA	LC	Oth	Total	Lge	FA	LC	Oth	Total
2nd WW		3				3	1				1
Total		3				3	1				1

SMITH, Edward
Born: London, 23 Mar 1929.
Signed from: Colchester United, Jul 1957.
Debut v Brentford, 24 Aug 1957.
Transferred to: Chelmsford, Jul 1958.

		APPEARANCES					GOALS				
Season	Div	Lge	FA	LC	Oth	Total	Lge	FA	LC	Oth	Total
1957-58	3S	17	1			18	1	1			2
Total		17	1			18	1	1			2

SMITH, Frank
Born: Colchester, 30 Apr 1936.
Signed from: Tottenham Hotspur, May 1962.
Debut v Preston North End, 24 Sep 1962, League Cup.

		APPEARANCES					GOALS				
Season	Div	Lge	FA	LC	Oth	Total	Lge	FA	LC	Oth	Total
1962-63	3	17		1		18					
1963-64	3	20				20					
1964-65	3	26	3	1		30					
1965-66	3	3				3					
Total		66	3	2		71					

SMITH, George
Born: Bromley, 23 Apr 1915.
Signed from: Brentford, Jun 1947.
Debut v Norwich City, 23 Aug 1947.
Transferred to: Ipswich Town, Sep 1949.

		APPEARANCES					GOALS				
Season	Div	Lge	FA	LC	Oth	Total	Lge	FA	LC	Oth	Total
1947-48	3S	38	6			44	1				1
1948-49	2	37	2			39					
Total		75	8			83	1				1

SMITH, J.W.
Signed from: Third Lanark, Apr 1919.
Debut v Arsenal, 1 Aug 1917, London Combination.
Transferred to: Swansea Town.

		APPEARANCES					GOALS				
Season	Div	Lge	FA	LC	Oth	Total	Lge	FA	LC	Oth	Total
1st WW		36			1	37	21				21
1919-20	SL	42	1			43	15				15
1920-21	3	42	2			44	18	1			19
1921-22	3S	33	2			35	10	1			11
Total		153	5		1	159	64	2			66

SMITH, Norman
Born: Newburn, 1897.
Signed from: Sheffield Wednesday, Aug 1930.
Debut v Thames, 30 Aug 1930.
Retired 1932.

		APPEARANCES					GOALS				
Season	Div	Lge	FA	LC	Oth	Total	Lge	FA	LC	Oth	Total
1930-31	3S	24	1			25					
1931-32	3S	2				2					
Total		26	1			27					

SMITH, Norman
Signed from: Charlton Athletic.
Debut v Brighton & Hove Albion, 28 Aug 1937.
Transferred to: Chelsea, 1939.

		APPEARANCES					GOALS				
Season	Div	Lge	FA	LC	Oth	Total	Lge	FA	LC	Oth	Total
1937-38	3S	39	2			41	1				1
1938-39	3S	29	1			30	1				1
Total		68	3			71	2				2

SMITH, Stephen
Signed from: Guildford United, May 1928.
Debut v Newport County, 6 Sep 1928.
Transferred to: Mansfield Town, 1929.

		APPEARANCES					GOALS				
Season	Div	Lge	FA	LC	Oth	Total	Lge	FA	LC	Oth	Total
1928-29	3S	24	1			25	1				1
Total		24	1			25	1				1

SMITH, Stephen R.
Born: Hednesford.
Signed from: Clapton Orient.
Debut v Aberdare Athletic, 24 Apr 1926.

		APPEARANCES					GOALS				
Season	Div	Lge	FA	LC	Oth	Total	Lge	FA	LC	Oth	Total
1925-26	3S	2				2					
Total		2				2					

SMITH, Tom
Born: Ashton-in-Makerfield, 1876.
Signed from: Southampton, Aug 1899.
Debut v Tottenham Hotspur, 9 Sep 1899, Southern League.
Transferred to: Preston North End.

		APPEARANCES					GOALS				
Season	Div	Lge	FA	LC	Oth	Total	Lge	FA	LC	Oth	Total
1899-1900	SL	13	8			21	1	3			4
Total		13	8			21	1	3			4

SNELGROVE, E.
Born: 1886.
Signed from: Sittingbourne, 1907.
Debut v Northampton Town, 18 Apr 1908.
Transferred to: 1909

		APPEARANCES					GOALS				
Season	Div	Lge	FA	LC	Oth	Total	Lge	FA	LC	Oth	Total
1907-08	SL	3				3	1				1
1908-09	SL	8				8					
Total		11				11	1				1

SOMERVILLE, J.
Debut v Watford, 12 Feb 1916, London Combination.

		APPEARANCES					GOALS				
Season	Div	Lge	FA	LC	Oth	Total	Lge	FA	LC	Oth	Total
WW1		8				8					
Total		8				8					

SPACKMAN, Nigel
Born: Romsey, 2 Dec 1960.
Signed from: Liverpool, Feb 1989 (£500,000).
Debut v Millwall, 4 Feb 1989.
Transferred to: Glasgow Rangers, Dec 1989 (£500,000).

		APPEARANCES					GOALS				
Season	Div	Lge	FA	LC	Oth	Total	Lge	FA	LC	Oth	Total
1988-89	1	16			2	18	1				1
1989-90	1	11/2		2		13/2			1		1
Total		27/2		2	2	31/2	1		1		2

SPENCE, Joseph
Born: Hartlepool, 10 Jan 1926.
Signed from: Portsmouth, Dec 1951.
Debut v Burnley, 25 Dec 1951.
Retired (injury) Jul 1955.

		APPEARANCES					GOALS				
Season	Div	Lge	FA	LC	Oth	Total	Lge	FA	LC	Oth	Total
1951-52	2	20	1			21					
1952-53	3S	31	3			34					
1953-54	3S	5				5					
Total		56	4			60					

SPOTISWOOD, Joe
Born: Carlisle.
Signed from: Swansea Town.
Debut v Gillingham, 29 Aug 1925.

		APPEARANCES					GOALS				
Season	Div	Lge	FA	LC	Oth	Total	Lge	FA	LC	Oth	Total
1925-26	3S	22				22	2				2
Total		22				22	2				2

SPRATLEY, Alan
Born: Maidenhead, 5 Jun 1949.
Signed from: (apprentice), Sep 1968.
Debut v Aston Villa, 4 Jan 1969, FA Cup.
Transferred to: Swindon Town, Jul 1973 (£10,000).

		APPEARANCES					GOALS				
Season	Div	Lge	FA	LC	Oth	Total	Lge	FA	LC	Oth	Total
1968-69	1	13	1			14					
1969-70	2	14		1		15					
1970-71	2	1				1					
1971-72	2										
1972-73	2	1	1			2					
Total		29	2	1		32					

SPRINGETT, Peter
Born: Fulham, 8 May 1946.
Signed from: (apprentice), May 1963.
Debut v Peterborough United, 18 May 1963.
Transferred to: Sheffield Wednesday, May 1967 (exchange R.Springett plus £35,000).

		APPEARANCES					GOALS				
Season	Div	Lge	FA	LC	Oth	Total	Lge	FA	LC	Oth	Total
1962-63	3	2				2					
1963-64	3	26	3	1		30					
1964-65	3	20		1		21					
1965-66	3	43	5	2		50					
1966-67	3	46	2	9		57					
Total		137	10	13		160					

SPRINGETT, Ron
Born: Fulham, 22 Jul 1937.
Signed from: Victoria United, Feb 1953.
Debut v Norwich City, 5 Nov 1955.
Transferred to: Sheffield Wednesday Mar 1958; From: Sheffield Wednesday, May 1967 (exchange P.Springett).

		APPEARANCES					GOALS				
Season	Div	Lge	FA	LC	Oth	Total	Lge	FA	LC	Oth	Total
1955-56	3S	8				8					
1956-57	3S	46	3			49					
1957-58	3S	34	3			37					
1967-68	3	36	1	3		40					
1968-69	1	9				9					
Total		133	7	3		143					

STAINROD, Simon
Born: Sheffield, 1 Feb 1959.
Signed from: Oldham Athletic, Nov 1980 (£270,000).
Debut v Preston North End, 22 Nov 1980.
Transferred to: Sheffield Wednesday, Feb 1985 (£250,000).

		APPEARANCES					GOALS				
Season	Div	Lge	FA	LC	Oth	Total	Lge	FA	LC	Oth	Total
1980-81	2	15	2			17	4	1			5
1981-82	2	39	9	4		52	17	5	2		24
1982-83	2	29/2		2		31/2	9				9
1983-84	1	41	1	3		45	13		3		16
1984-85	1	19		8	†3	30	5			3	8
Total		143/2	12	17	3	175/2	48	6	5	3	62

STANDLEY, Thomas
Born: Poplar, London, 23 Dec 1932.
Signed from: Basildon, May 1957.
Debut v Brentford, 21 Nov 1957.
Transferred to: Bournemouth, Nov 1958.

		APPEARANCES					GOALS				
Season	Div	Lge	FA	LC	Oth	Total	Lge	FA	LC	Oth	Total
1957-58	3S	15				15	2				2
Total		15				15	2				2

STEER
Debut v Arsenal, 16 Feb 1918, London Combination.

		APPEARANCES					GOALS				
Season	Div	Lge	FA	LC	Oth	Total	Lge	FA	LC	Oth	Total
WW1		21			4	25					
Total		21			4	25					

STEER, William
Born: Kingston upon Thames.
Signed from: Kingston Town, 1909.
Debut v Watford, 1 Sep 1909, Southern League.
Transferred to: Chelsea, 1912.

		APPEARANCES					GOALS				
Season	Div	Lge	FA	LC	Oth	Total	Lge	FA	LC	Oth	Total
1909-10	SL	38	7			45	22	5			27
1910-11	SL	30	1			31	9	1			10
Total		68	8			76	31	6			37

STEIN, Mark
Born: South Africa, 28 Jan 1966.
Signed from: Luton Town, Aug 1988 (£300,000).
Debut v Manchester United, 27 Aug 1988 (sub).
Transferred to: Oxford United, Sep 1989 (£200,000).

		APPEARANCES					GOALS				
Season	Div	Lge	FA	LC	Oth	Total	Lge	FA	LC	Oth	Total
1988-89	1	19/12	2/1	4	3/1	28/14	4	1	2		7
1989-90	1	1/1				1/1					
Total		20/13	2/1	4	3/1	29/15	4	1	2		7

STÉJSKAL, Jan
Born: Czechoslovakia, 15 Jan 1962.
Signed from: Sparta Prague, Oct 1990 (£600,000).
Debut v Leeds United, 20 Oct 1990.

		APPEARANCES					GOALS				
Season	Div	Lge	FA	LC	Oth	Total	Lge	FA	LC	Oth	Total
1990-91	1	26	1	1		28					
1991-92	1	42	1	4	1	48					
1992-83	Pr	14/1		2		16/1					
Total		82/1	2	7	1	92/1					

STEPHENSON, H.
Born: London.
Debut v Southend United, 15 Nov 1930.

		APPEARANCES					GOALS				
Season	Div	Lge	FA	LC	Oth	Total	Lge	FA	LC	Oth	Total
1930-31	3S	2				2					
Total		2				2					

STEPHENSON, J.
Born: Durham.
Signed from: Watford.
Debut v Newport County, 27 Aug 1927.
Transferred to: Norwich City.

		APPEARANCES					GOALS				
Season	Div	Lge	FA	LC	Oth	Total	Lge	FA	LC	Oth	Total
1927-28	3S	18				18					
Total		18				18					

STEWART, George
Born: Chimside, 18 Oct 1920.
Signed from: Brentford, Mar 1948.
Debut v Ipswich Town, 13 Apr 1948.
Transferred to: Shrewsbury Town, Jan 1953.

		APPEARANCES					GOALS				
Season	Div	Lge	FA	LC	Oth	Total	Lge	FA	LC	Oth	Total
1947-48	3S	14				14	1				1
1948-49	2	12	2			14	2				2
1950-51	2	1				1					
1951-52	2	9				9	1				1
1952-53	3S	2				2	1				1
Total		38	2			40	5				5

STEWART, Ian
Born: Belfast, 10 Sep 1961.
Signed from: (juniors), May 1980.
Debut v Blackburn Rovers, 4 Oct 1980 (sub).
Transferred to: Newcastle United, Aug 1985 (£100,000).

		APPEARANCES					GOALS				
Season	Div	Lge	FA	LC	Oth	Total	Lge	FA	LC	Oth	Total
1980-81	2	0/1				0/1					
1981-82	2	2/1	1/1	0/2		3/4					
1982-83	2	15/4		0/1		15/5					
1983-84	1	30/1	1	3		34/1	2		2		4
1984-85	1	8/5		3	†2/1	13/6					
Total		55/12	1/1	6/3	2/1	65/17	2		2		4

STEWART, John
Debut v Swindon Town, 5 Oct 1901, Southern League.
Transferred: Jul 1902; From: Hibernian.

		APPEARANCES					GOALS				
Season	Div	Lge	FA	LC	Oth	Total	Lge	FA	LC	Oth	Total
1901-02	SL	23	3			26	3	1			4
1904-05	SL	13	1			14	2				2
Total		36	4			40	5	1			6

STOCK, Alec
Born: Bath, 1917.
Signed from: Charlton Athletic, Feb 1938.
Debut v Reading, 26 Feb 1938 (1 goal).
Transferred to: Yeovil Town.

		APPEARANCES					GOALS				
Season	Div	Lge	FA	LC	Oth	Total	Lge	FA	LC	Oth	Total
1937-38	3S	14				14	1				1
1938-39	3S	12				12	2				2
1939-40	3S	2				2					
2nd WW		16	7		5	28	5	2		4	11
Total		44	7		5	56	8	2		4	14

STRUGNELL, H.H.
Signed from: Aston Villa.
Debut v Southampton, 25 Oct 1913, Southern League.

		APPEARANCES					GOALS				
Season	Div	Lge	FA	LC	Oth	Total	Lge	FA	LC	Oth	Total
1913-14	SL	11				11					
Total		11				11					

SUGDEN, Sidney
Born: Battersea, 1880.
Signed from: Nottingham Forest, 1905.
Debut v New Brompton, 2 Sep 1905, Southern League.
Transferred to: Brentford, 1909.

		APPEARANCES					GOALS				
Season	Div	Lge	FA	LC	Oth	Total	Lge	FA	LC	Oth	Total
1905-06	SL	29				29	8				8
1906-07	SL	27	2			29	9				9
1907-08	SL	9	2			11	4				4
Total		65	4			69	21				21

SUTCH, W.H.
Debut v Bristol Rovers, 3 Jan 1920 (2 goals), Southern League.

		APPEARANCES					GOALS				
Season	Div	Lge	FA	LC	Oth	Total	Lge	FA	LC	Oth	Total
1919-20	SL	1				1	2				2
Total		1				1	2				2

SWAN, Jack
Born: Easlington.
Signed from: Watford.
Debut v Bristol City, 12 Dec 1927.
Transferred: 1928.

		APPEARANCES					GOALS				
Season	Div	Lge	FA	LC	Oth	Total	Lge	FA	LC	Oth	Total
1926-27	3S	14				14	1				1
1927-28	3S	14				14	4				4
Total		28				28	5				5

SWANN, Hubert
Born: Lytham, 28 Mar 1882.
Signed from: Crystal Palace, 1909.
Debut v Millwall, 9 Oct 1909, Southern League.

		APPEARANCES					GOALS				
Season	Div	Lge	FA	LC	Oth	Total	Lge	FA	LC	Oth	Total
1909-10	SL	4				4	1				1
Total		4				4	1				1

SWEETMAN, Sidney
Born: London.
Signed from: Hampstead Town, Feb 1925.
Debut v Merthyr Town, 7 Feb 1925.
Transferred to: Millwall, 1929.

		APPEARANCES					GOALS				
Season	Div	Lge	FA	LC	Oth	Total	Lge	FA	LC	Oth	Total
1924-25	3S	8				8					
1925-26	3S	16				16					
1926-27	3S	18				18					
1927-28	3S	16	1			17					
1928-29	3S	42	1			43					
Total		100	2			102					

SWINFEN, Reg
Born: Battersea, 4 May 1915.
Debut v Clapton Orient, 19 Sep 1936.

		APPEARANCES					GOALS				
Season	Div	Lge	FA	LC	Oth	Total	Lge	FA	LC	Oth	Total
1936-37	3S	6				6	3				3
1937-38	3S	1				1					
1938-39	3S	18	3			21	2				2
1939-40	3S	2				2	1				1
2nd WW		66	4		16	86	26	1		9	36
1946-47	3S	1				1					
Total		94	7		16	117	32	1		9	42

SYMES, H.
Born: Acton.
Signed from: Aberdare Athletic.
Debut v Gillingham, 8 Nov 1924.

		APPEARANCES					GOALS				
Season	Div	Lge	FA	LC	Oth	Total	Lge	FA	LC	Oth	Total
1924-25	3S	8				8					
1925-26	3S	18	4			22					
Total		26	4			30					

TAGG, Tony
Born: Epsom, 10 Apr 1957.
Signed from: (apprentice), Mar 1975.
Debut v Derby County, 23 Aug 1975.
Transferred to: Millwall, Jul 1977 (free).

		APPEARANCES					GOALS				
Season	Div	Lge	FA	LC	Oth	Total	Lge	FA	LC	Oth	Total
1975-76	1	4				4					
Total		4				4					

TAYLOR
Debut v Millwall, 26 Jan 1907, Southern League.

		APPEARANCES					GOALS				
Season	Div	Lge	FA	LC	Oth	Total	Lge	FA	LC	Oth	Total
1906-07	SL	2				2					
Total		2				2					

TAYLOR, Brian
Born: London, 2 Jul 1944.
Signed from: (juniors), Mar 1962.
Debut v Watford, 23 Mar 1963.

		APPEARANCES					GOALS				
Season	Div	Lge	FA	LC	Oth	Total	Lge	FA	LC	Oth	Total
1962-63	3	14				14					
1963-64	3	9				9					
1964-65	3	22		2		24					
1965-66	3	5				5					
Total		50		2		52					

TAYLOR, Geoff
Born: Henstead, 22 Jan 1923.
Signed from: Bristol Rovers, Nov 1953.
Debut v Colchester United, 25 Dec 1953.

		APPEARANCES					GOALS				
Season	Div	Lge	FA	LC	Oth	Total	Lge	FA	LC	Oth	Total
1953-54	3S	2				2					
Total		2				2					

TAYLOR, Jim
Born: Hillingdon, 5 Nov 1917.
Signed from: Fulham, Apr 1953.
Debut v Brighton & Hove Albion, 19 Aug 1953.
Transferred to: Tunbridge Wells, Jul 1954.

		APPEARANCES					GOALS				
Season	Div	Lge	FA	LC	Oth	Total	Lge	FA	LC	Oth	Total
1953-54	3S	41	3			44					
Total		41	3			44					

TEALE, Richard
Born: Millom, 27 Feb 1952.
Signed from: Walton & Hersham, Jul 1973.
Debut v Birmingham City, 7 Sep 1974.
Transferred to: Fulham, Aug 1976.

		APPEARANCES					GOALS				
Season	Div	Lge	FA	LC	Oth	Total	Lge	FA	LC	Oth	Total
1974-75	1	1		1		2					
Total		1		1		2					

TEMBY, William
Born: Dover, 16 Sep 1934.
Signed from: Rhyl, Feb 1955.
Debut v Norwich City, 5 Nov 1955.

		APPEARANCES					GOALS				
Season	Div	Lge	FA	LC	Oth	Total	Lge	FA	LC	Oth	Total
1955-56	3S	2				2					
1956-57	3S	5				5	3				3
Total		7				7	3				3

TENNANT, William
Born: Coatbridge, Glasgow, 1875.
Signed from: Arthurlie, Aug 1899.
Debut v Tottenham Hotspur, 9 Sep 1899, Southern League.

		APPEARANCES					GOALS				
Season	Div	Lge	FA	LC	Oth	Total	Lge	FA	LC	Oth	Total
1899-1900	SL	12	3			15	5				5
Total		12	3			15	5				5

THOMAS, Dave
Born: Kirkby, 5 Oct 1950.
Signed from: Burnley, Oct 1972 (£165,000).
Debut v Sunderland, 21 Oct 1972.
Transferred to: Everton, Aug 1977 (£200,000).

		APPEARANCES					GOALS				
Season	Div	Lge	FA	LC	Oth	Total	Lge	FA	LC	Oth	Total
1972-73	2	28	4			32	6				6
1973-74	1	41	6	3		50	5	1			6
1974-75	1	41	3	3		47	6	1			7
1975-76	1	41	1	4		46	9		2		11
1976-77	1	30/1		7	†7	44/1	1		1	1	3
Total		181/1	14	17	7	219/1	27	2	3	1	33

THOMPSON, A.
Debut v Plymouth Argyle, 28 Oct 1905, Southern League.

		APPEARANCES					GOALS				
Season	Div	Lge	FA	LC	Oth	Total	Lge	FA	LC	Oth	Total
1905-06	SL	17	1			18	6				6
1906-07	SL	6				6	1				1
Total		23	1			24	7				7

THOMPSON, C.
Signed from: Newcastle United.
Debut v Brentford, 29 Oct 1921.

		APPEARANCES					GOALS				
Season	Div	Lge	FA	LC	Oth	Total	Lge	FA	LC	Oth	Total
1921-22	3S	1				1					
Total		1				1					

THOMPSON, Garry
Born: Birmingham, 7 Oct 1959.
Signed from: Crystal Palace, Aug 1991 (£100,000).
Debut v Norwich City, 21 Aug 1991 (sub).

		APPEARANCES					GOALS				
Season	Div	Lge	FA	LC	Oth	Total	Lge	FA	LC	Oth	Total
1991-92	1	10/5		3	1	14/5	1		3		4
1992-93	Pr	0/4		0/2		0/6					
Total		10/9		3/2	1	14/11	1		3		4

THOMPSON, J.
Signed from: Yeovil Town.
Debut v Newport County, 27 Dec 1924.

		APPEARANCES					GOALS				
Season	Div	Lge	FA	LC	Oth	Total	Lge	FA	LC	Oth	Total
1924-25	3S	9	1			10					
1925-26	3S	13	3			16					
Total		22	4			26					

THOMPSON, Oliver
Born: Gateshead, 1902.
Signed from: Chesterfield.
Debut v Gillingham, 1 Sep 1928.
Transferred to: York City, 1930.

		APPEARANCES					GOALS				
Season	Div	Lge	FA	LC	Oth	Total	Lge	FA	LC	Oth	Total
1928-29	3S	18				18					
Total		18				18					

THOMPSON, William
Born: Morpeth, Aug 1886.
Signed from: Plymouth Argyle, 1912.
Debut v Plymouth Argyle, 5 Sep 1912, Southern League.
Transferred to: South Shields, 1914; From: West Bromwich Albion; To: Newport County, 1920.

		APPEARANCES					GOALS				
Season	Div	Lge	FA	LC	Oth	Total	Lge	FA	LC	Oth	Total
1912-13	SL	33	2			35	1				1
1913-14	SL	38	5			43	2				2
1914-15	SL	34	3			37	3				3
1st WW		9				9	2				2
1919-20	SL	14	1			15					
Total		128	11			139	8				8

THORNTON, H.V.
Signed from: Sep 1911.
Debut v Reading, 9 Sep 1911, Southern League.
Died in World War One.

		APPEARANCES					GOALS				
Season	Div	Lge	FA	LC	Oth	Total	Lge	FA	LC	Oth	Total
1911-12	SL	34	1		•1	36	10				10
1912-13	SL	1				1					
Total		35	1		1	37	10				10

THURMAN
Debut v Crystal Palace, 22 Sep 1917 (1 goal), London Combination.

		APPEARANCES					GOALS				
Season	Div	Lge	FA	LC	Oth	Total	Lge	FA	LC	Oth	Total
WW1		13				13	3				3
Total		13				13	3				3

TILSON, Andy
Born: Huntington, 30 Jun 1966.
Signed from: Grimsby Town, Dec 1990 (£400,000).
Debut v Derby County, 23 Dec 1990.
Transferred to: Bristol Rovers, Nov 1992 (£375,000).

		APPEARANCES					GOALS				
Season	Div	Lge	FA	LC	Oth	Total	Lge	FA	LC	Oth	Total
1990-91	1	18/1				18/1	2				2
1991-92	1	8/1		2	1	11/1					
1992-93	Pr										
Total											

TOMKYS, Michael
Born: Kensington, 14 Dec 1932.
Signed from: Fulham, Nov 1951.
Debut v Birmingham City, 24 Nov 1951.

		APPEARANCES					GOALS				
Season	Div	Lge	FA	LC	Oth	Total	Lge	FA	LC	Oth	Total
1951-52	2	1				1					
1952-53	3S	19				19	5				5
1953-54	3S	20	4			24	2	1			3
1954-55	3S	8	2			10	1	1			2
1955-56	3S	8				8					
1957-58	3S	5				5					
1958-59	3	25	2			27	8				8
Total		86	8			94	16	2			18

TOSSWILL, John
Born: Eastbourne, 1890.
Signed from: 1911.
Debut v Southampton, 5 Apr 1912 (1 goal), Southern League.
Transferred to: Liverpool, 1912.

		APPEARANCES					GOALS				
Season	Div	Lge	FA	LC	Oth	Total	Lge	FA	LC	Oth	Total
1911-12	SL	3				3	1				1
Total		3				3					

TOWERS, (Edwin) Jim
Born: Shepherd's Bush, 15 Apr 1933.
Signed from: Brentford, May 1961.
Debut v Brentford, 19 Aug 1961 (1 goal).
Transferred to: Millwall, Aug 1962.

		APPEARANCES					GOALS				
Season	Div	Lge	FA	LC	Oth	Total	Lge	FA	LC	Oth	Total
1961-62	3	28	3	2		33	15		1		16
Total		28	3	2		33	15		1		16

TRAVERS, James
Born: Birmingham, Nov 1888.
Signed from: Aston Villa, 1909.
Debut v Watford, 1 Sep 1909 (1 goal), Southern League.
Transferred to: Leicester Fosse, 1910.

		APPEARANCES					GOALS				
Season	Div	Lge	FA	LC	Oth	Total	Lge	FA	LC	Oth	Total
1909-10	SL	34	7			41	7	1			8
Total		34	7			41	7	1			8

TRODD, W.
Signed from: Leyton.
Debut v Exeter City, 13 Apr 1935.

		APPEARANCES					GOALS				
Season	Div	Lge	FA	LC	Oth	Total	Lge	FA	LC	Oth	Total
1934-35	3S	6				6					
Total		6				6					

TURNBULL, Peter
Born: Lanquhar, 1875.
Signed from: Millwall Athletic, Aug 1899.
Debut v Tottenham Hotspur, 9 Sep 1899, Southern League.
Transferred to: Brentford, 1901.

		APPEARANCES					GOALS				
Season	Div	Lge	FA	LC	Oth	Total	Lge	FA	LC	Oth	Total
1899-1900	SL	19	6			25	6	7			13
1900-01	SL	3				3					
Total		22	6			28	6	7			13

TURNER, W.
Born: South Moor.
Signed from: Bury
Debut v Newport County, 27 Aug 1927.

		APPEARANCES					GOALS				
Season	Div	Lge	FA	LC	Oth	Total	Lge	FA	LC	Oth	Total
1927-28	3S	38	1			39					
Total		38	1			39					

TURPIE, Bobby
Born: London, 13 Nov 1949.
Signed from: (apprentice), Nov 1967.
Debut v Portsmouth, 13 Sep 1969 (sub).
Transferred to: Peterborough United, Jul 1970.

		APPEARANCES					GOALS				
Season	Div	Lge	FA	LC	Oth	Total	Lge	FA	LC	Oth	Total
1969-70	2	1/1				1/1					
Total		1/1				1/1					

TUTT, W.
Signed from: Canterbury Waverley.
Debut v Bristol Rovers, 14 Jan 1931.

		APPEARANCES					GOALS				
Season	Div	Lge	FA	LC	Oth	Total	Lge	FA	LC	Oth	Total
1930-31	3S	1				1					
1931-32	3S	6				6	3				3
Total		7				7	3				3

UNDERWOOD, Dave
Born: London, 15 Mar 1928.
Signed from: Edgware Town, Dec 1949.
Debut v Notts County, 26 Jan 1952.
Transferred to: Watford, Feb 1952.

		APPEARANCES					GOALS				
Season	Div	Lge	FA	LC	Oth	Total	Lge	FA	LC	Oth	Total
1951-52	2	2				2					
Total		2				2					

VAFIADIS, Seth
Born: London, 8 Sep 1945.
Signed from: Chelsea, Nov 1962.
Debut v Millwall, 28 Sep 1963.
Transferred to: Millwall, Sep 1964.

		APPEARANCES					GOALS				
Season	Div	Lge	FA	LC	Oth	Total	Lge	FA	LC	Oth	Total
1963-64	3	15				15	4				4
Total		15				15	4				4

VALLENCE, H.
Born: Edgbaston.
Signed from: Aston Villa.
Debut v Watford, 16 Feb 1929.
Transferred to: Brighton & Hove Albion.

		APPEARANCES					GOALS				
Season	Div	Lge	FA	LC	Oth	Total	Lge	FA	LC	Oth	Total
1928-29	3S	1				1					
Total		1				1					

VANGO, Alfred
Born: London.
Signed from: Walthamstow Avenue.
Debut v Bristol Rovers, 14 Jan 1931.
Transferred to: Clapton Orient.

		APPEARANCES					GOALS				
Season	Div	Lge	FA	LC	Oth	Total	Lge	FA	LC	Oth	Total
1930-31	3S	2				2					
1931-32	3S	10				10					
Total		12				12					

VARCO, Percy
Born: Cornwall.
Signed from: Aston Villa.
Debut v Crystal Palace, 28 Aug 1926 (1 goal).
Transferred to: Norwich City, 1927.

		APPEARANCES					GOALS				
Season	Div	Lge	FA	LC	Oth	Total	Lge	FA	LC	Oth	Total
1926-27	3S	16				16	4				4
Total		16				16	4				4

VENABLES, Terry
Born: Bethnal Green, 6 Jan 1943.
Signed from: Tottenham Hotspur, Jun 1969 (£70,000).
Debut v Hull City, 9 Aug 1969.
Transferred to: Crystal Palace, Sep 1974 (exchange D.Rogers).

		APPEARANCES					GOALS				
Season	Div	Lge	FA	LC	Oth	Total	Lge	FA	LC	Oth	Total
1969-70	2	34	4	4		42	5	1	1		7
1970-71	2	37/1	1	2		40/1	10		1		11
1971-72	2	27	2	4		33	1				1
1972-73	2	37	1	1		39	1				1
1973-74	1	36	6	3		45	2				2
1974-75	1	5		1		6					
Total		176/1	14	15		205/1	19	1	2		22

VIGRASS, J.
Signed from: Leek Alexandra.
Debut v Merthyr Town, 22 Apr 1922.

		APPEARANCES					GOALS				
Season	Div	Lge	FA	LC	Oth	Total	Lge	FA	LC	Oth	Total
1921-22	3S	3				3					
1922-23	3S	33	4			37	1				1
1923-24	3S	30	1			31					
Total		66	5			71	1				1

VINCENT, Ernie
Born: Spennymoor.
Signed from: Manchester United.
Debut v Millwall, 31 Aug 1935.
Transferred to: Doncaster Rovers, Jul 1937 (free).

		APPEARANCES					GOALS				
Season	Div	Lge	FA	LC	Oth	Total	Lge	FA	LC	Oth	Total
1935-36	3S	8				8					
1936-37	3S	20	2			22					
Total		28	2			30					

WADDOCK, Gary P.
Born: Kingsbury, 17 Mar 1962.
Signed from: (apprentice), Jul 1979.
Debut v Bradford City, 28 Aug 1979, League Cup (sub).
Retired through injury; From: Millwall, Feb 1992; To: Bristol Rovers, Nov 1992 (£100,000).

		APPEARANCES					GOALS				
Season	Div	Lge	FA	LC	Oth	Total	Lge	FA	LC	Oth	Total
1979-80	2	8/8	1	0/1		9/9	1				1
1980-81	2	29/4	1	3		33/4	3				3
1981-82	2	35	9	3		47					
1982-83	2	33	1	2		36					
1983-84	1	36	1	3		40	3		1		4
1984-85	1	31	1	†6	1	39	1		1		2
1985-86	1	15		3		18					
1986-87	1	4		1		5					
Total		191/12	14	21/1	1	227/13	8		2		10

WAKE, William
Born: Banbury Castle, 1887.
Signed from: Exeter City, 1909.
Debut v Watford, 1 Sep 1909, Southern League.

		APPEARANCES					GOALS				
Season	Div	Lge	FA	LC	Oth	Total	Lge	FA	LC	Oth	Total
1909-10	SL	39	7			46					
1910-11	SL	27				27					
1911-12	SL	38	2		*1	41					
1912-13	SL	27	2			29	1				1
1913-14	SL	29	5			34					
1914-15	SL	15				15					
1st WW		48				48					
Total		223	16		1	240	1				1

WALKER, Alfred
Born: Ripley, Aug 1888.
Signed from: Nottingham Forest, 1907.
Debut v Tottenham Hotspur, 14 Sep 1907 (1 goal), Southern League.

		APPEARANCES					GOALS				
Season	Div	Lge	FA	LC	Oth	Total	Lge	FA	LC	Oth	Total
1907-08	SL	28	2			30	15	1			16
Total		28	2			30	15	1			16

WALKER, Clive
Born: Oxford, 26 May 1957.
Signed from: Sunderland, Dec 1985 (£70,000).
Debut v Aston Villa, 17 Dec 1985.
Transferred to: Fulham, Oct 1987 (free).

		APPEARANCES					GOALS				
Season	Div	Lge	FA	LC	Oth	Total	Lge	FA	LC	Oth	Total
1985-86	1	5				5	1				1
1986-87	1	11/4	4	2/1		17/5			1		1
Total		16/4	4	2/1		22/5	1		1		2

WALLACE, Barry
Born: Plaistow, 17 Apr 1959.
Signed from: Aug 1977.
Debut v Aston Villa, 26 Oct 1977, League Cup.

		APPEARANCES					GOALS				
Season	Div	Lge	FA	LC	Oth	Total	Lge	FA	LC	Oth	Total
1977-78	1	8/5	1	1		10/5					
1978-79	1	4/1				4/1					
1979-80	2	5/2	1			6/2					
Total		17/8	2	1		20/8					

WALLER, William
Debut v Bournemouth, 1 Mar 1924.

		APPEARANCES					GOALS				
Season	Div	Lge	FA	LC	Oth	Total	Lge	FA	LC	Oth	Total
1923-24	3S	2				2					
Total		2				2					

WALSH, Mickey
Born: Chorley, 13 Aug 1954.
Signed from: Everton, Mar 1979 (exchange P.Eastoe).
Debut v Derby County, 31 Mar 1979 (1 goal).
Transferred to: FC Porto, Aug 1980 (£175,000).

		APPEARANCES					GOALS				
Season	Div	Lge	FA	LC	Oth	Total	Lge	FA	LC	Oth	Total
1978-79	1	10				10	3				3
1979-80	2	2/5	1	1		4/5					
1980-81	2	1				1					
Total		13/5	1	1		15/5	3				3

WALSH, Paul
Born: Plumstead, 1 Oct 1962.
Signed from: Tottenham Hotspur, Sep 1991 (loan).
Debut v Luton Town, 17 Sep 1991.

		APPEARANCES					GOALS				
Season	Div	Lge	FA	LC	Oth	Total	Lge	FA	LC	Oth	Total
1991-92	1	2				2					
Total		2				2					

WALTERS
Debut v Fulham, 15 Sep 1917, London Combination.

		APPEARANCES					GOALS				
Season	Div	Lge	FA	LC	Oth	Total	Lge	FA	LC	Oth	Total
WW1		26			2	28	10			1	11
Total		26			2	28	10			1	11

WARBURTON, Arthur
Born: Bury, 10 Sep 1908.
Signed from: Fulham.
Debut v Brighton & Hove Albion, 10 Sep 1938.

		APPEARANCES					GOALS				
Season	Div	Lge	FA	LC	Oth	Total	Lge	FA	LC	Oth	Total
1938-39	3S	17	4			21					
Total		17	4			21					

WARDLE, George
Born: Kimblesworth, 24 Sep 1919.
Signed from: Cardiff City, Jan 1949.
Debut v Southampton, 29 Jan 1949.
Transferred to: Darlington, Aug 1951.

		APPEARANCES					GOALS				
Season	Div	Lge	FA	LC	Oth	Total	Lge	FA	LC	Oth	Total
1948-49	2	11				11					
1949-50	2	28	1			29	2				2
1950-51	2	14				14	2				2
Total		53	1			54	5				4

WASSELL, Harold
Born: Stourbridge, 1879.
Signed from: Bristol Rovers, 1905.
Debut v Watford, 18 Nov 1905.

		APPEARANCES					GOALS				
Season	Div	Lge	FA	LC	Oth	Total	Lge	FA	LC	Oth	Total
1905-06	SL	3				3					
Total		3				3					

WATERALL, A.
Born: Nottingham.
Debut v Charlton Athletic, 18 Sep 1926.

		APPEARANCES					GOALS				
Season	Div	Lge	FA	LC	Oth	Total	Lge	FA	LC	Oth	Total
1926-27	3S	2				2					
Total		2				2					

WATSON, Edward
Born: Sholton, 1894.
Signed from: Sunderland.
Debut v Brentford, 11 Sep 1922.

		APPEARANCES					GOALS				
Season	Div	Lge	FA	LC	Oth	Total	Lge	FA	LC	Oth	Total
1922-23	3S	8				8					
Total		8				8					

WATSON, George
Born: Shotton Colliery, 1914.
Signed from: Durham City, 1934.
Debut v Bristol Rovers, 6 Oct 1934.

		APPEARANCES					GOALS				
Season	Div	Lge	FA	LC	Oth	Total	Lge	FA	LC	Oth	Total
1934-35	3S	8				8	1				1
Total		8				8	1				1

WATSON, Ian
Born: Hammersmith, 7 Jan 1944.
Signed from: Chelsea, Jul 1965 (£5,000).
Debut v Brentford, 21 Aug 1965.

		APPEARANCES					GOALS				
Season	Div	Lge	FA	LC	Oth	Total	Lge	FA	LC	Oth	Total
1965-66	3	40	5	2		47					
1966-67	3	15/1	2	4		21/1					
1967-68	2	6/4				6/4					
1968-69	1	42	1	1		44					
1969-70	2	35	4	5		44	1		1		2
1970-71	2	15/1	1	1		17/1					
1971-72	2	2				2					
1972-73	2	35	3	1		39					
1973-74	1	6				6					
Total		196/6	16	14		226/6	1		1		2

WATTS, T.F.
Debut v Norwich City, 30 Apr 1920, Southern League.

		APPEARANCES					GOALS				
Season	Div	Lge	FA	LC	Oth	Total	Lge	FA	LC	Oth	Total
1919-20	SL	1				1					
1920-21	3	2				2					
1921-22	3S	2				2					
Total		5				5					

WAUGH, L.
Debut v Newport County, 12 Sep 1923.

		APPEARANCES					GOALS				
Season	Div	Lge	FA	LC	Oth	Total	Lge	FA	LC	Oth	Total
1923-24	3S	5				5					
Total		5				5					

WAUGH, William
Born: Edinburgh, 27 Nov 1921.
Signed from: Luton Town, Jul 1950.
Debut v Chesterfield, 19 Aug 1950.
Transferred to: Bournemouth, Jul 1953.

		APPEARANCES					GOALS				
Season	Div	Lge	FA	LC	Oth	Total	Lge	FA	LC	Oth	Total
1950-51	2	25	1			26	2				2
1951-52	2	36	1			37	1				1
1952-53	3S	16				16	3				3
Total		77	2			79	6				6

WEBB, David
Born: East Ham, 9 Apr 1946.
Signed from: Chelsea, Jul 1974 (£120,000).
Debut v Sheffield United, 16 Aug 1974.
Transferred to: Leicester City, Sep 1977 (£50,000).

		APPEARANCES					GOALS				
Season	Div	Lge	FA	LC	Oth	Total	Lge	FA	LC	Oth	Total
1974-75	1	33	4	2/1		39/1					
1975-76	1	38	2	4		44	5			1	6
1976-77	1	38	2	7	†8	55	2		1	2	5
1977-78	1	7		1		8					
Total		116	8	14/1	8	146/1	7		2	2	11

WEBB, Issac
Born: Worcester, Oct 1874.
Signed from: Sunderland, 1906.
Debut v Brentford, 11 Mar 1907, Southern League.
Transferred to: West Bromwich Albion, 1910.

		APPEARANCES					GOALS				
Season	Div	Lge	FA	LC	Oth	Total	Lge	FA	LC	Oth	Total
1906-07	SL	10				10					
Total		10				10					

WEBB, J.

		APPEARANCES					GOALS				
Season	Div	Lge	FA	LC	Oth	Total	Lge	FA	LC	Oth	Total
2nd WW		13				13				1	1
Total		13				13					

WEBB, Ron
Born: Brentford, 13 Mar 1925.
Debut v Clapton Orient, 11 Sep 1943, League South.
Transferred to: Crystal Palace, Sep 1946.

		APPEARANCES					GOALS				
Season	Div	Lge	FA	LC	Oth	Total	Lge	FA	LC	Oth	Total
2nd WW		6				6					
Total		6				6					

WEBLIN, F.T.
Signed from: West Norwood.
Debut v Merthyr Town, 14 Dec 1912, Southern League.

		APPEARANCES					GOALS				
Season	Div	Lge	FA	LC	Oth	Total	Lge	FA	LC	Oth	Total
1912-13	SL	9				9					
1913-14	SL	2				2					
Total		11				11					

WEGERLE, Roy
Born: Johannesburg, South Africa, 19 Mar 1964.
Signed from: Luton Town, Dec 1989 (£1,000,000).
Debut v Sheffield Wednesday, 16 Dec 1989 (sub).
Transferred to: Blackburn Rovers, Mar 1992 (£1,000,000).

		APPEARANCES					GOALS				
Season	Div	Lge	FA	LC	Oth	Total	Lge	FA	LC	Oth	Total
1989-90	1	18/1	9			27/1	6	1			7
1990-91	1	36	1	4	1	42	18		1		19
1991-92	1	18/3	1	1		20/3	5				5
Total		72/4	11	5	1	89/4	29	1	1		31

WELTON, Pat
Born: Eltham, 3 May 1928.
Signed from: Leyton Orient, Mar 1958.
Debut v Southend United, 7 Feb 1959.

		APPEARANCES					GOALS				
Season	Div	Lge	FA	LC	Oth	Total	Lge	FA	LC	Oth	Total
1958-59	3	3				3					
Total		3				3					

WENTWORTH, F.
Debut v Watford, 1 Sep 1909, Southern League.

		APPEARANCES					GOALS				
Season	Div	Lge	FA	LC	Oth	Total	Lge	FA	LC	Oth	Total
1909-10	SL	7				7					
Total		7				7					

WESTWOOD, Danny
Born: Dagenham, 25 Jul 1953.
Signed from: Billericay, Jul 1974.
Debut v Newcastle United, 8 Oct 1974, League Cup.
Transferred to: Gillingham, Nov 1975 (£5,000).

		APPEARANCES					GOALS				
Season	Div	Lge	FA	LC	Oth	Total	Lge	FA	LC	Oth	Total
1974-75	1	0/1		1		1/1	1				1
Total		0/1		1		1/1	1				1

WHATMORE, Ernest
Born: Kidderminster.
Signed from: Bristol Rovers.
Debut v Torquay United, 25 Aug 1928.

		APPEARANCES					GOALS				
Season	Div	Lge	FA	LC	Oth	Total	Lge	FA	LC	Oth	Total
1928-29	3S	21				21	1				1
1929-30	3S	15				15					
1930-31	3S	31	3			34	1				1
1931-32	3S	11	1			12	1				1
Total		78	4			82	3				3

WHELDON, George
Born: Birmingham, 1 Nov 1871.
Signed from: West Bromwich Albion, 1901.
Debut v Reading, 16 Nov 1901, Southern League.
Transferred to: Portsmouth, 1902.

		APPEARANCES					GOALS				
Season	Div	Lge	FA	LC	Oth	Total	Lge	FA	LC	Oth	Total
1901-02	SL	14				14	6				6
Total		14				14	6				6

WHITAKER, Colin
Born: Leeds, 14 Jun 1932.
Signed from: Shrewsbury Town, Feb 1961.
Debut v Hull City, 18 Feb 1961.
Transferred to: Rochdale, May 1961.

		APPEARANCES					GOALS				
Season	Div	Lge	FA	LC	Oth	Total	Lge	FA	LC	Oth	Total
1960-61	3	8				8					
Total		8				8					

WHITE, Devon
Born: Nottingham, 2 Feb 1964.
Signed from: Cambridge United, Jan 1993 (£100,000).
Debut v Chelsea, 27 Jan 1993 (sub).

		APPEARANCES					GOALS				
Season	Div	Lge	FA	LC	Oth	Total	Lge	FA	LC	Oth	Total
1992-93	Pr	3/4				3/4	2				2
Total		3/4				3/4	2				2

WHITE, J.
Debut v Chelsea, 6 Apr 1917, London Combination.

		APPEARANCES					GOALS				
Season	Div	Lge	FA	LC	Oth	Total	Lge	FA	LC	Oth	Total
WW1		25				25					
Total		25				25					

WHITE, Jabez
Born: Droylesden, 1879.
Signed from: Grays United, 1901.
Debut v Portsmouth, 28 Sep 1901, Southern League.
Transferred to: Leeds City, 1908.

		APPEARANCES					GOALS				
Season	Div	Lge	FA	LC	Oth	Total	Lge	FA	LC	Oth	Total
1901-02	SL	26	1			27					
1902-03	SL	17	1			18					
1903-04	SL	8				8					
1904-05	SL	7				7					
1905-06	SL	25	1			26					
1906-07	SL	25	2			27					
1907-08	SL	25	2			27	1				1
Total		133	7			140	1				1

WHITE, W.
Debut v Chatham, 11 Nov 1899, Southern League.
Transferred to: Liverpool, 1901.

		APPEARANCES					GOALS				
Season	Div	Lge	FA	LC	Oth	Total	Lge	FA	LC	Oth	Total
1899-1900	SL	20	5			25	7	1			8
Total		20	5			25	7	1			8

WHITEHEAD, W.
Signed from: Swansea Town.
Debut v Watford, 17 Oct 1925 (1 goal).

		APPEARANCES					GOALS				
Season	Div	Lge	FA	LC	Oth	Total	Lge	FA	LC	Oth	Total
1925-26	3S	24	4			28	5				5
Total		24	4			28	5				5

WHITEHEAD, William
Born: Maltby, 6 Feb 1920.
Signed from: Maltby MCW.
Debut v Port Vale, 22 Sep 1945, League South.
Transferred to: Aldershot, Aug 1947.

		APPEARANCES					GOALS				
Season	Div	Lge	FA	LC	Oth	Total	Lge	FA	LC	Oth	Total
2nd WW		4	5			9	1	1			2
Total		4	5			9	1	1			2

WHITELAW, George
Born: Paisley, 1 Jan 1937.
Signed from: Sunderland, Mar 1959.
Debut v Bradford City, 16 Mar 1959 (1 goal).
Transferred to: Halifax Town, Oct 1959.

		APPEARANCES					GOALS				
Season	Div	Lge	FA	LC	Oth	Total	Lge	FA	LC	Oth	Total
1958-59	3	11				11	5				5
1959-60	3	15				15	5				5
Total		26				26	10				10

WHITFIELD, Ken
Born: Durham, 24 Mar 1930.
Signed from: Brighton & Hove Albion, Jul 1959.
Debut v Tranmere Rovers, 26 Sep 1959.

		APPEARANCES					GOALS				
Season	Div	Lge	FA	LC	Oth	Total	Lge	FA	LC	Oth	Total
1959-60	3	7	2			9					
1960-61	3	12	2			14	3				3
Total		19	4			23	3				3

WHITING, J
Debut v Brentford, 3 Feb 1917 (1 goal), London Combination.

		APPEARANCES					GOALS				
Season	Div	Lge	FA	LC	Oth	Total	Lge	FA	LC	Oth	Total
WW1		8				8	1				1
Total		8				8	1				1

WHITTAKER, Dick
Born: Dublin, 10 Oct 1934.
Signed from: Peterborough United, Jul 1963.
Debut v Oldham Athletic, 24 Aug 1963.

		APPEARANCES					GOALS				
Season	Div	Lge	FA	LC	Oth	Total	Lge	FA	LC	Oth	Total
1963-64	3	17		1		18					
Total		17		1		18					

WHYMAN, Alfred.
Born: 1887.
Signed from: New Brompton, 1909.
Debut v Watford, 1 Sep 1909 (2 goals), Southern League.
Transferred to: 1920.

		APPEARANCES					GOALS				
Season	Div	Lge	FA	LC	Oth	Total	Lge	FA	LC	Oth	Total
1909-10	SL	39	7			46	8	1			9
1910-11	SL	28	1			29	6				6
1911-12	SL	11	1		*1	13	1				1
1912-13	SL	20	2			22	2	1			3
1913-14	SL	25	1			26	1				1
1914-15	SL	24	3			27	3				3
1st WW		36			1	37	1				1
1919-20	SL	6				6	1				1
Total		189	15		2	206	23	2			25

WICKS, J.
Signed from: Reading.
Debut v Gillingham, 8 Nov 1924.

		APPEARANCES					GOALS				
Season	Div	Lge	FA	LC	Oth	Total	Lge	FA	LC	Oth	Total
1924-25	3S	5				5					
Total		5				5					

WICKS, Steve
Born: Reading, 3 Oct 1956.
Signed from: Derby County, Sep 1979 (£275,000).
Debut v Mansfield Town, 25 Sep 1979, League Cup (sub).
Transferred to: Crystal Palace, Jun 1981 (£250,000 & C.Allen); From: Crystal Palace, Mar 1982 (£325,000); To: Chelsea, Aug 1986 (£400,000).

		APPEARANCES					GOALS				
Season	Div	Lge	FA	LC	Oth	Total	Lge	FA	LC	Oth	Total
1979-80	2	35	1	2/1		38/1					
1980-81	2	38	2	3		43					
1981-82	2	9				9					
1982-83	2	14				14	1				1
1983-84	1	31	1			32	2				2
1984-85	1	33		8	†4	45	2				2
1985-85	1	29	1	9		39	1				1
Total		189	5	22/1	4	220/1	6				6

WILCOX, Jonah
Born: Devon.
Signed from: Bristol Rovers.
Debut v Crystal Palace, 28 Aug 1926.
Transferred to: Gillingham, 1927.

		APPEARANCES					GOALS				
Season	Div	Lge	FA	LC	Oth	Total	Lge	FA	LC	Oth	Total
1926-27	3S	9				9	2				2
Total		9				9	2				2

WILDE, J.
Debut v Reading, 29 Apr 1914, Southern League.

		APPEARANCES					GOALS				
Season	Div	Lge	FA	LC	Oth	Total	Lge	FA	LC	Oth	Total
1913-14	SL	1				1					
1914-15	SL	6				6					
1919-20	SL	6				6					
Total		13				13					

WILES, George
Born: East Ham, London.
Signed from: Sittingbourne, 1929.
Debut v Walsall, 5 Sep 1929.
Transferred to: Walsall, Jul 1933.

		APPEARANCES					GOALS				
Season	Div	Lge	FA	LC	Oth	Total	Lge	FA	LC	Oth	Total
1929-30	3S	5				5					
1930-31	3S	12				12					
1931-32	3S	1				1					
Total		18				18					

WILES, Harry
Born: East Ham, London.
Signed from: Sittingbourne, 1929.
Debut v Crystal Palace, 31 Aug 1929 (1 goal).
Transferred to: Walsall, Jul 1933.

		APPEARANCES					GOALS				
Season	Div	Lge	FA	LC	Oth	Total	Lge	FA	LC	Oth	Total
1929-30	3S	10				10	6				6
1930-31	3S	12				12	6				6
1931-32	3S	11				11	11				11
1932-33	3S	9	1			10	2				2
Total		42	1			43	25				25

WILKS, Alan
Born: London, 5 Oct 1946.
Signed from: Chelsea, May 1965 (free).
Debut v Brighton & Hove Albion, 27 Dec 1966 (1 goal).
Transferred to: Gillingham, Jul 1971 (£5,000).

		APPEARANCES					GOALS				
Season	Div	Lge	FA	LC	Oth	Total	Lge	FA	LC	Oth	Total
1966-67	3	7				7	5				5
1967-68	2	12/2	0/1	1		13/3	3		5		8
1968-69	1	17/3		1		18/3	5				5
1969-70	2	6		1		7	1				1
1970-71	2	2/1				2/1					
Total		44/6	0/1	3		47/7	14		5		19

WILKINS, Dean
Born: Hillingdon, 12 Jul 1962.
Signed from: (apprentice), May 1980.
Debut v Grimsby Town, 1 Nov 1980 (sub).
Transferred to: Brighton & Hove Albion, Aug 1983 (free).

		APPEARANCES					GOALS				
Season	Div	Lge	FA	LC	Oth	Total	Lge	FA	LC	Oth	Total
1980-81	2	1/1				1/1					
1981-82	2	0/1		1		1/1					
1982-83	2	0/3				0/3					
Total		1/5		1		2/5					

WILKINS, Ray
Born: Hillingdon, 14 Sep 1956.
Signed from: Glasgow Rangers, Dec 1989 (free).
Debut v Crystal Palace, 2 Dec 1989.

		APPEARANCES					GOALS				
Season	Div	Lge	FA	LC	Oth	Total	Lge	FA	LC	Oth	Total
1989-90	1	23	9			32	2	2			4
1990-91	1	38	1	4	1	44	2				2
1991-92	1	26/1	1	1	1	29/1	1			1	2
1992-93	Pr	27	1	4		32	2				2
Total		114/1	12	9	2	137/1	7	2		1	10

WILLIAMS, Bill
Born: Esher, 23 Aug 1942.
Signed from: Portsmouth, Jul 1961.
Debut v Bournemouth, 16 Sep 1961.
Transferred to: West Bromwich Albion, Jun 1963.

		APPEARANCES					GOALS				
Season	Div	Lge	FA	LC	Oth	Total	Lge	FA	LC	Oth	Total
1961-62	3	20	2			22					
1962-63	3	25		1		26					
Total		45	2	1		48					

WILLIAMS, Brian
Born: Salford, 5 Nov 1955.
Signed from: Bury, Jul 1977 (£70,000).
Debut v Aston Villa, 20 Aug 1977 (sub).
Transferred to: Swindon Town, Jun 1978 (£50,000).

		APPEARANCES					GOALS				
Season	Div	Lge	FA	LC	Oth	Total	Lge	FA	LC	Oth	Total
1977-78	1	9/10	0/2	1/1		10/13					
Total		9/10	0/2	1/1		10/13					

WILSON, Andy
Born: Newmans, 14 Feb 1896.
Signed from: Chelsea, Oct 1931.
Debut v Norwich City, 10 Oct 1931.
Transferred to: Nimes.

		APPEARANCES					GOALS				
Season	Div	Lge	FA	LC	Oth	Total	Lge	FA	LC	Oth	Total
1931-32	3S	20	3			23	3				3
Total		20	3			23	3				3

WILSON, Clive
Born: Manchester, 13 Nov 1961.
Signed from: Chelsea, Aug 1990 (£450,000).
Debut v Nottingham Forest, 25 Aug 1990.

		APPEARANCES					GOALS				
Season	Div	Lge	FA	LC	Oth	Total	Lge	FA	LC	Oth	Total
1990-91	1	11/2	1	2	0/1	14/3	1				1
1991-92	1	40	1	4	2	47	3				3
1992-93	Pr	41	2	3		46	3				3
Total		92/2	4	9	2/1	107/3	7				7

WILSON, K.

		APPEARANCES					GOALS				
Season	Div	Lge	FA	LC	Oth	Total	Lge	FA	LC	Oth	Total
2nd WW		1				1					
Total		1				1					

WILSON, Tom
Born: Preston, 20 Oct 1877.
Signed from: Manchester United, 1909.
Debut v Norwich City, 25 Dec 1909 (1 goal), Southern League.
Retired 1910.

		APPEARANCES					GOALS				
Season	Div	Lge	FA	LC	Oth	Total	Lge	FA	LC	Oth	Total
1909-10	SL	1				1	1				1
1910-11	SL	5				5					
Total		6				6	1				1

WILSON, Tom
Born: Preston, 20 Oct 1877.
Signed from: London Caledonia, 1902.
Debut v Wellingborough, 3 Sep 1902, Southern League.
Transferred to: Bolton Wanderers, 1904.

		APPEARANCES					GOALS				
Season	Div	Lge	FA	LC	Oth	Total	Lge	FA	LC	Oth	Total
1902-03	SL	29	1			30	2				2
1903-04	SL	30	2			32	1				1
Total		59	3			62	3				3

WINGROVE, J.
Signed from: Uxbridge.
Debut: Plymouth Argyle, 23 Apr 1913, Southern League.

		APPEARANCES					GOALS				
Season	Div	Lge	FA	LC	Oth	Total	Lge	FA	LC	Oth	Total
1912-13	SL	1				1					
1913-14	SL	11				11					
1914-15	SL	4				4					
1st WW		12				12					
1919-20	SL	33	1			34					
1920-21	3	24	2			26					
Total		85	3			88					

WINYARD, W.
Signed from: Millwall.
Debut v: Southampton, 14 Oct 1916, London Combination.

Season	Div	Lge	FA	LC	Oth	Total	Goals Lge	FA	LC	Oth	Total
WW1		8				8					
Total		8				8					

WOOD
Debut v: Crystal Palace, 16 Oct 1915, London Combination.

Season	Div	Lge	FA	LC	Oth	Total	Goals Lge	FA	LC	Oth	Total
WW1		9				9					
Total		9				9					

WOOD, Arthur
Born: Southampton, 8 May 1890.
Signed from: Newport County.
Debut v Merthyr Town, 15 Dec 1923.
Retired: (Knee-injury), 1929.

Season	Div	Lge	FA	LC	Oth	Total	Goals Lge	FA	LC	Oth	Total
1923-24	3S	19				19					
1924-25	3S	1				1					
Total		20				20					

WOODHOUSE, G.F.
Debut v: Newport County, 3 Apr 1920, Southern League.

Season	Div	Lge	FA	LC	Oth	Total	Goals Lge	FA	LC	Oth	Total
1919-20	SL	1				1					
Total		1				1					

WOODS, Chris
Born: Boston, 14 Nov 1959.
Signed from: Nottingham Forest, Jul 1979 (£250,000).
Debut v Bristol Rovers, 18 Aug 1979.
Transferred to: Norwich City, Mar 1981 (£250,000).

Season	Div	Lge	FA	LC	Oth	Total	Goals Lge	FA	LC	Oth	Total
1979-80	2	41	1	5		47					
1980-81	2	22		3		25					
Total		63	1	8		72					

WOODS, Pat
Born: Islington, 29 Apr 1933.
Signed from: (juniors), Jun 1950.
Debut v Coventry City, 3 Jan 1953.
Transferred to: Colchester United, Aug 1963.

Season	Div	Lge	FA	LC	Oth	Total	Goals Lge	FA	LC	Oth	Total
1952-53	3S	1				1					
1953-54	3S	23	3			26	1				1
1954-55	3S	32	3			35					
1955-56	3S	38	1			39					
1956-57	3S	45	3			48					
1957-58	3S	44	3			47	6				6
1958-59	3	44	2			46					
1959-60	3	46	3			49	3				3
1960-61	3	31	2	2		35	5				5
Total		304	20	2		326	15				15

WOODWARD, Horace
Born: London, 16 Jan 1924.
Signed from: Tottenham Hotspur, Jun 1949.
Debut v Leeds United, 20 Aug 1949.
Transferred to: Walsall, Jul 1953.

Season	Div	Lge	FA	LC	Oth	Total	Goals Lge	FA	LC	Oth	Total
1949-50	2	32				32					
1950-51	2	25	1			26					
Total		57	1			58					

WOODWARD, J.
Born: London.
Signed from: Watford.
Debut v Crystal Palace, 3 Mar 1928.
Transferred to: Merthyr Town, 1929.

Season	Div	Lge	FA	LC	Oth	Total	Goals Lge	FA	LC	Oth	Total
1927-28	3S	6				6					
1928-29	3S	4	1			5					
Total		10	1			11					

WRIGHT, A.
Debut v Crystal Palace, 4 Nov 1916, London Combination.

Season	Div	Lge	FA	LC	Oth	Total	Goals Lge	FA	LC	Oth	Total
WW1		50			3	53					
Total		50			3	53					

WRIGHT, E.
Debut v Brighton & Hove Albion, 26 Jan 1935.
Transferred to: Crewe Alexandra, 1935.

Season	Div	Lge	FA	LC	Oth	Total	Goals Lge	FA	LC	Oth	Total
1934-35	3S	1				1					
Total		1				1					

WRIGHT, Paul
Born: East Kilbride, 17 Aug 1967.
Signed from: Aberdeen, Jul 1989 (£275,000).
Debut v Crystal Palace, 19 Aug 1989 (2 goals).
Transferred to: Hibernian, Jan 1990 (£300,000).

Season	Div	Lge	FA	LC	Oth	Total	Goals Lge	FA	LC	Oth	Total
1989-90	1	9/6	0/2	2		11/8	5		1		6
Total		9/6	0/2	2		11/8	5		1		6

WYATT, A.
Debut v Exeter City, 12 Mar 1910, Southern League.

Season	Div	Lge	FA	LC	Oth	Total	Goals Lge	FA	LC	Oth	Total
1909-10	SL	10				10					
Total		10				10					

WYPER, W.Thomas
Born: Glasgow, 8 Oct 1900.
Signed from: Charlton Athletic.
Debut v Brentford, 29 Aug 1931.
Transferred to: Chester, 1932.

Season	Div	Lge	FA	LC	Oth	Total	Goals Lge	FA	LC	Oth	Total
1931-32	3S	11				11					
Total		11				11					

YATES, John
Born: Manchester.
Signed from: Aston Villa.
Debut v Walsall, 9 Sep 1929.

Season	Div	Lge	FA	LC	Oth	Total	Goals Lge	FA	LC	Oth	Total
1929-30	3S	10				10					
Total		10				10					

YENSON, William
Born: 1884.
Signed from: Bolton Wanderers, 1905.
Debut v New Brompton, 2 Sep 1905.
Transferred to: West Ham United, 1908.

Season	Div	Lge	FA	LC	Oth	Total	Goals Lge	FA	LC	Oth	Total
1905-06	SL	34	1			35	3				3
1906-07	SL	35	2			37	1				1
1907-08	SL	21	1			22					
Total		90	4			94	4				4

YIELLEYOYE, H.
Signed From: Belgian Army, Dec 1943.
Debut v: Tottenham Hotspur, 4 Dec 1943, League South.

Season	Div	Lge	FA	LC	Oth	Total	Goals Lge	FA	LC	Oth	Total
2nd WW		1				1					
Total		1				1					

YOUNG, Jack
Born: Whitburn.
Signed from: West Ham United.
Debut v Crystal Palace, 28 Aug 1926.

Season	Div	Lge	FA	LC	Oth	Total	Goals Lge	FA	LC	Oth	Total
1926-27	3S	31				31	5				5
1927-28	3S	30	1			31	4				4
1928-29	3S	28	1			29	3				3
Total		89	2			91	12				12

YOUNG, Herbert
Born: Liverpool, 4 Sep 1899.
Signed from: Newport County.
Debut v Crystal Palace, 31 Aug 1929.
Transferred to: Bristol Rovers, 1930.

Season	Div	Lge	FA	LC	Oth	Total	Goals Lge	FA	LC	Oth	Total
1929-30	3S	14	1			15	1				1
Total		14	1			15	1				1

YOUNG, William
Born: South Shields.
Signed from: Tyneside District, Feb 1925.
Debut v Bournemouth, 21 Mar 1925.
Transferred to: Gillingham, 1927.

Season	Div	Lge	FA	LC	Oth	Total	Goals Lge	FA	LC	Oth	Total
1924-25	3S	1				1					
1925-26	3S	7				7	2				2
Total		8				8	2				2

Paul Wright, a brief spell at QPR between Scottish clubs Aberdeen and Hibs.

Chris Woods, 72 games after a £250,000 move from Nottingham Forest.

Horace Woodward, joined QPR from Tottenham Hotspur in June 1949 and moved to Walsall four years later.